F V

THE
POE LOG

American Authors Log Series

Joel Myerson
GENERAL EDITOR

THE
POE LOG

A Documentary Life
of Edgar Allan Poe
1809–1849

DWIGHT THOMAS

AND

DAVID K. JACKSON

G.K. Hall & Co.
Boston
1987

The Poe Log

First Printing

Excerpts from *The Letters of Edgar Allan Poe*, John Ward Ostrom, editor (Cambridge, Mass.: Harvard University Press), Copyright 1948 by the President and Fellows of Harvard College; (c) 1976 by John Ward Ostrom, are reprinted by permission of the publishers.

Excerpts from *The Complete Works of Thomas Holley Chivers*, edited by Emma Lester Chase and Lois Ferry Parks, Copyright 1957 by Brown University, are reprinted by permission of the University Press of New England.

Library of Congress Cataloging-in-Publication Data

Thomas, Dwight.
    The Poe log.

    Bibliography: p. 855.
    Includes index.
    1. Poe, Edgar Allan, 1809–1849—Chronology.
2. Authors, American—19th century—Biography.
I. Jackson, David Kelly. II. Title.
PS2631.T47   1987   818'.309   86-19319
ISBN 0-8161-8734-7 (alk. paper)

Printed on permanent/durable acid-free paper and bound in the United States of America

Contents

Illustrations

ILLUSTRATIONS

Introduction

In 1951 the publication of Jay Leyda's *Melville Log* provided American literary scholars with a detailed chronological record of Herman Melville's life. The present compilation offers such a record for Edgar Allan Poe, another author whose career has been similarly obscured by the clouds of controversy and misunderstanding. Although Poe may not have possessed an altogether balanced and serene intellect, the designation *genius* has often been applied to him. He continues to evoke a divergent response from critics, with some vehemently proclaiming his merits and others just as loudly denying them. Apart from any critical considerations, it can be plausibly argued that Poe has been, and remains, the best known and most widely read American writer, both in the United States and abroad. No American has approached the level of achievement represented by Shakespeare and Dante; but what Poe accomplished in his short and tragic life leads one to wonder whether he might not have done so, given less adverse circumstances. His historical importance is clear. From 1835, when he assumed the editorship of the *Southern Literary Messenger*, until his death in 1849, he was the main protagonist in American letters, being simultaneously the leading critic, the most original poet, and the most versatile storyteller.

Poe has attracted more than his share of biographers, drawn no doubt by the pathos inherent in his constant struggles with poverty and alcoholism, and by the drama inherent in his ill-fated romances with women and his verbal battles with literary contemporaries. The resulting biographies have generally been works of journalism based on a derivative and superficial knowledge of his life and his milieu. Speculations abound: one commentator suggests that Poe was impotent while another tries to prove that he impregnated someone else's wife. Instructors of English casually refer to Poe's "drug addiction" as if this were an established fact, but there is no evidence to support any of these accusations. Poe and his associates almost always maintained a discreet silence on sexual matters, both in their private correspondence and in their public statements. Although Poe did describe the effects of opium in his stories, he is known to have read Thomas De Quincey's *Confessions of an English Opium Eater* (1822), a probable source for these allusions.

It is still popularly believed that Poe passed his life in obscurity and seclusion: this impression also proves mistaken. However unwilling Poe's contemporaries were to reward him financially, they amply supplied him with fame. The early stories and criticisms he contributed to the *Messenger* brought him to the attention of the American intelligentsia; his later fictions, most notably "The Murders in the Rue Morgue" and "The Gold-Bug," endeared him to a broad class of readers. With the appearance of "The Raven" in 1845, he became a celebrity, recognized everywhere as "Poe the poet." At some periods in his career he did indeed seek seclusion, but more often he sought to play an active and influential role in literary affairs. As a prominent editor and critic in the nation's largest cities, he was a highly visible figure; and he had occasion to meet, or correspond with, many other writers of his day, ranging from major authors like Charles Dickens or James Russell Lowell to provincial scribblers. Few who met Poe ever forgot him, so unique were his intellect and physiognomy. Some of his associates responded to him with devotion; others, with animosity. The man, like his writings, evoked divergent reactions; but this is hardly surprising. Poe both embodied and embraced contradictions. He possessed polished manners, enormous erudition, formidable conversational abilities, and an indescribable personal magnetism; in his better moments he was genial, kind, and entirely appealing. At other times he yielded to melancholy and self-pity; when drinking he could be abrasive and combative; when confronted with what he felt to be mediocrity or pretension, he rarely refrained from expressing contempt, either in his book reviews or his conversation.

The present compilation has nothing to do with such problematic tasks as aesthetic evaluation or psychoanalytic interpretation. It simply gives the verifiable facts of Poe's life as revealed in excerpts from contemporary documents: the letters he wrote or received, newspaper reports, magazine articles, reminiscences, and legal records. Some of these documents have long been known to scholars; many others have previously remained undiscovered or inaccessible. The compilers have attempted to include as much relevant material as possible; and while they could not exhaust all the potential sources of information, they may justly claim to have prepared a more comprehensive and reliable account than has hitherto been available. The documents excerpted in this compilation are arranged in chronological order; editorial commentary is minimal, allowing Poe and his associates to narrate events in their own words. The text has been divided into chapters corresponding to significant periods in Poe's life, each chapter being prefaced with a summary of events. Chapters I through IV, covering the years 1809–1837, were prepared by David K. Jackson; Chapters V through XI (1838–1849), by Dwight Thomas. With the exception of newspapers and magazines, each entry in the text concludes with an abbreviated source citation in parentheses. Books and articles are cited with the author's surname and (where appropriate) the year of publication; the only exceptions are the use of the letter *W* to indicate James A. Harrison's 1902 edition of Poe's *Works* and the letter *L* for John Ward Ostrom's 1948 edition of his *Letters*. Libraries holding manuscripts are represented by the standard abbreviations for these institutions used in the *National Union Catalog*. The "LIST OF SOURCES" following the text identifies all sources, both printed and manuscript. Persons frequently mentioned in the text are identified in the "BIOGRAPHICAL NOTES" preceding it. The compilers have wished that their chronicle of Poe's life would serve to some extent as the much-needed new bibliography of his writings. Although a complete list of the unsigned fillers and reviews that Poe ground out for newspapers and magazines is probably not possible, this compilation contains a more accurate and extensive register of his articles than such antiquated bibliographies as those by John W. Robertson (1934) and Charles F. Heartman and James R. Canny (1943). The index entries for the periodicals in question have a subheading for "Poe's contributions," enabling the reader to retrieve this data.

During their long years of research the compilers have become indebted to more individuals and institutions than can be acknowledged here. The initial inspiration for this project came from the late Jay B. Hubbell, Professor of English at Duke University and founding editor of *American Literature*; its completion would have been difficult without the meticulous edition of Poe's *Letters* and "Checklist" of his correspondence prepared by Professor Ostrom, who kindly answered requests for additional information. Both compilers received frequent advice and encouragement from Professors Burton R. Pollin and Benjamin Franklin Fisher, IV, as well as from Mrs. Maureen C. Mabbott. David K. Jackson first became interested in Poe in 1929, while an undergraduate at Duke University; his 1931 master's essay there, directed by Professor Hubbell, was published as *Poe and "The Southern Literary Messenger"* (1934; reprinted 1970). He wishes to express his indebtedness to, and honor the memory of, the distinguished Poe scholars who were his counsellors and friends in decades past: Lewis Chase, Thomas Ollive Mabbott, James Southall Wilson, and John Cook Wyllie. During his work on this project Mr. Jackson has been aided by Professors Clarence L. F. Gohdes (Duke University), Joseph V. Ridgely (Columbia University), and Martin S. Shockley (North Texas State University), as well as by Mrs. J. Elliott Irvine of Durham, North Carolina, Mrs. D. M. Skinner, Jr., of Princeton, New Jersey, Mrs. Agnes Bondurant Marcuson of Richmond, Virginia, and Edward G. Kidd of Richmond, Clerk for Division I of the Henrico County Circuit Court. Dwight Thomas first became interested in Poe in 1972, while a graduate student at the University of Pennsylvania; he wishes to express his indebtedness to Professor Robert Regan, who directed his doctoral dissertation "Poe in Philadelphia, 1838–1844" (Pennsylvania, 1978), and to Professors Hennig Cohen and Daniel Hoffman, who read the preliminary draft of that study and suggested improvements. His greatest debt has been to his parents, Mr. and Mrs. Huguenin Thomas, Jr., of Savannah, Georgia, who provided financial support for his research. Both compilers owe a unique and inexpressible debt to Joel Myerson, Professor of English at the University of South Carolina and editor of *Studies in the American Renaissance*, who guided them in preparing their book for publication. Without Professor Myerson's sympathy and understanding, and his sage editorial decisions, the project would have been abandoned like so many other ambitious and arduous enterprises.

Librarians throughout the country have performed herculean labors in Poe's behalf, responding to queries, photocopying manuscripts, lugging the unwieldy, dust-covered files of early nineteenth-century newspapers, producing scarce microfilms and out-of-print books by Interlibrary Loan. Although the compilers cannot possibly mention all these dedicated co-workers, they wish to express their deep appreciation to some of them: Edmund Berkeley, Jr., and Gregory A. Johnson (University of Virginia); Samuel M. Boone, Emerson Ford, Dr. Mattie Russell, and other staff members at the Perkins Library (Duke University); Janet Buda and James Lawton (Boston Public Library); Herbert Cahoon (Pierpont Morgan Library); Marie T. Capps (United States Military Academy at West Point); Margaret Cook and Clifford Currie (College of William and Mary); Bernard R. Crystal and Kenneth A. Lohf (Columbia University); Rodney G. Dennis (Houghton Library of Harvard University); Ellen S. Dunlap and David Farmer (Humanities Research Center, University of Texas at Austin); David Mike Hamilton (Huntington Library); Donald Haynes, Timothy Heigh, and Rebecca Johnson (Virginia State Library); Howell J. Heaney (Philadelphia Free Library); Shirley Jenkins (George Peabody Library of Johns Hopkins University); William H. Loos (Buffalo and Erie County Public Library, Buffalo, New York); Faye Lowry (Enoch Pratt Free Library of Baltimore); Frank Paluka (University of Iowa); Peter J. Parker, John Platt, and Timothy Bratton (Historical Society of Pennsylvania); Louis A. Rachow (Hampden-Booth Theatre Library of the Players Club); Hester Rich (Maryland Historical Society); E. Lee Shepard (Virginia Historical Society); Sarah Shields (Valentine Museum); Saundra Taylor (Lilly Library of Indiana University); Lillian Tonkin (Library Company of Philadelphia); Joyce Ann Tracy (American Antiquarian Society); and Marilyn Wheaton (Archives of American Art). Without naming particular individuals, the compilers also need to thank the efficient staffs of the Abernethy Library of American Literature at Middlebury College, the American Philosophical Society, the Beinecke Library of Yale University, the Brown

University Library, the Bucks County Historical Society, the Charleston Library Society, the Daughters of the American Revolution Library, the Davidson College Library, the Delaware Historical Society, the Durham County Public Library, the Georgia Historical Society, the Library of Congress, the Long Island Historical Society, the Newberry Library, the New York Historical Society, the New York Public Library, the Ohio Historical Society, the Pennsylvania State Library, the Providence Athenaeum, the Rhode Island Historical Society, the Savannah Public Library, the University of North Carolina Library at Chapel Hill, and the Van Pelt Library of the University of Pennsylvania. While the Poe Museum in Richmond cannot properly be classified as a library, it preserves books, manuscripts, and other materials relevant to its subject. For access to the Museum's collections, the compilers acknowledge the gracious assistance of Denise Bethel, Dr. Bruce V. English, Alan Golden, and Agnes Bondurant Marcuson.

To some extent the present compilation has been constructed on a foundation of previous books, especially the serious biographies of George E. Woodberry (1909) and Arthur Hobson Quinn (1941), and the numerous publications of Killis Campbell and Thomas Ollive Mabbott. The compilers are grateful to the respective presses for permission to quote short passages from the following indispensable titles: *The Correspondence of Thomas Holley Chivers* (Brown University Press), John Carl Miller's *Building Poe Biography* (Louisiana State University Press) and his *Poe's Helen Remembers* (University Press of Virginia), Sidney P. Moss's *Poe's Major Crisis* (Duke University Press), and the Ostrom edition of Poe's *Letters* (Harvard University Press for 1948 text, Gordian Press for 1966 supplement). For permission to quote unpublished manuscripts, the compilers wish to thank the Abernethy Library of American Literature at Middlebury College, the Archives of American Art, the Brown University Library, the College of William and Mary Library, the Columbia University Library, the Duke University Library, the Historical Society of Pennsylvania, the Houghton Library of Harvard University, the Humanities Research Center of the University of Texas at Austin, the Library of Congress, the Lilly Library of Indiana University, the National Archives, the New York Historical Society, the New York Public Library, the Philadelphia Free Library, the Pierpont Morgan Library, the Poe Museum of the Poe Foundation, the Trustees of the Boston Public Library, the United States Military Academy at West Point, the University of Virginia Library, the Valentine Museum, and the Virginia Historical Society.

Dwight Thomas
David K. Jackson

Biographical Notes
on Persons Mentioned in the Text

JOHN ADAMS (1773–1825), physician, was the Mayor of Richmond from 1819 until his death in 1825; he officially welcomed Lafayette to the city in late October 1824. Poe and his fellow Junior Volunteers obtained arms from Dr. Adams to serve as Lafayette's bodyguard. Adams was succeeded by Joseph Tate (1795–1839), one of John Allan's neighbors.

JAMES ALDRICH (1810–1856), poet and editor in New York City, had the misfortune to write "A Death-Bed," a brief poem which Poe believed plagiarized from Thomas Hood's earlier verses "The Death-Bed." Poe first made the accusation when reviewing Longfellow's *The Waif* for the New York *Evening Mirror* of 13–14 January 1845; he repeated it in the 17 February *Mirror* and the 8 March *Broadway Journal*, offering additional evidence of Aldrich's guilt.

CHARLES W. ALEXANDER (1796–1866) published several Philadelphia newspapers and magazines, including *Burton's Gentleman's Magazine*, *Alexander's Weekly Messenger*, and the *Daily Chronicle*.

JOHN ALLAN (1779–1834), Poe's foster father, was born on 10 September 1779 in Irvine, Ayrshire, Scotland. Shortly before 29 January 1795 he emigrated to Richmond, where he found employment with his uncle, the wealthy merchant William Galt. In 1800 Allan joined with Charles Ellis, another of Galt's employees, to establish the mercantile firm of Ellis & Allan; the partners sold Virginia tobacco to Europe and used the proceeds to purchase a wide variety of European manufactured goods, which they offered for sale in Richmond. On 4 June 1804 Allan became a naturalized American citizen. His first wife was FRANCES KEELING VALENTINE (1785–1829), whom he married on 5 February 1803. The union being childless, the couple took custody of Edgar Poe after his mother's death on 8 December 1811; at this time they were living over the Ellis & Allan store at the northeast corner of Main and Thirteenth Streets. In 1815 Allan returned to Great Britain to open a London office of Ellis & Allan, under the inverted name "Allan & Ellis"; he was accompanied by his foster son, his wife, and her unmarried sister Ann Moore Valentine. Allan's English venture proved unsuccessful; in 1820 he returned to Richmond. In 1824 the firm of Ellis & Allan was dissolved by mutual consent of the partners. With the death of William Galt on 26 March 1825, Allan's financial problems came to an end: he inherited a substantial portion of his bachelor uncle's estate. On 28 June he purchased "Moldavia," the imposing house at the southeast corner of Main and Fifth Streets formerly owned by the flour miller Joseph Gallego. Although Allan had initially been fond of his foster son Edgar and had taken pains to send him to good schools both in Richmond and in England, differences in temperament between the two became apparent as the boy entered adolescence; their relations were subsequently characterized by friction and misunderstanding. When Poe attended the University of Virginia in 1826, Allan neglected to provide him with sufficient funds to cover his expenses. Poe recklessly attempted to obtain more money by gambling, incurring large debts which Allan then refused to pay. After they quarrelled angrily on 18 and 19 March 1827, Poe stalked out of the Allan household and went to Boston, enlisting in the United States Army on 26 May. They were temporarily reconciled when Poe returned to Richmond following the 28 February 1829 death of his foster mother. Allan grudgingly helped the young man win an appointment to West Point; for the next several years he sent him sporadic financial assistance as well as occasional letters containing more censure than affection. On 5 October 1830 Allan married LOUISA GABRIELLA PATTERSON (1800–1881) of Elizabethtown, New Jersey; by this second wife he had three sons: John, Jr. (born 1831), William Galt (born 1832), and Patterson (born 1834). Allan died on 27 March 1834, after a lingering illness. In his will he did not mention Poe, but he provided for his illegitimate twin sons born around 1 July 1830 to Mrs. Elizabeth Wills (1780?–1863?) of Richmond. In his youth he had fathered another illegitimate son named Edwin Collier; from 1812 until 1817 he paid the tuition bills sent him by several Richmond schoolmasters for educating the boy.

MARY ALLAN (died 1850), the oldest of John Allan's sisters in Scotland, lived in the family's Bridgegate House in Irvine. The other sisters were AGNES NANCY, who married Allan Fowlds of Kilmarnock in 1799; JANE, who married first a Captain Johnston and later a Mr. Ferguson; and ELIZABETH, who married John Miller of Irvine.

ROBERT T. P. ALLEN (1813–1888) entered West Point with Poe in June 1830. In the autumn of 1834, not long after his graduation, Allen visited Baltimore, where an acquaintance told him that Poe was working in a brickyard. The reminiscence is not altogether implausible: Poe's cousin Henry Clemm seems to have been employed as a Baltimore stonecutter in the mid-1830's.

RICHARD CAREY AMBLER (1810–1877), one of Joseph H. Clarke's students,

recalled swimming with Poe in Shockoe Creek and hearing him recite verses satirizing the members of a Richmond debating society. According to Ambler, Thomas Willis White approached him in 1835 or 1836, urging him to persuade Poe to furnish overdue copy for the *Southern Literary Messenger*. In later life Ambler became a physician and farmer in Fauquier County, Virginia.

CHARLES ANTHON (1797–1867), Professor of Greek and Latin at Columbia, was an early supporter of the *Southern Literary Messenger*; in the July 1836 number Poe listed him among those authors who had written the magazine to express approval of its book reviews. Poe accorded Anthon an extensive notice in "Autography" (*Graham's* for November 1841).

ROBERT ARCHER (1794–1877), surgeon in the Army Medical Corps, met Poe at Fortress Monroe early in 1829. Dr. Archer subsequently became president of the Armory Iron Works in Richmond. In 1849, on seeing Poe after church services, he remarked to his niece Susan Archer Talley that the poet's appearance had changed little over the years.

NEIL ARNOTT (1788–1874), Scotch inventor and physician, met John Allan and his family in London. In a 15 May 1821 letter to Allan, then back in Richmond, Dr. Arnott observed that he still had "Master Edgar" (presumably a portrait of Poe) in one of his rooms.

JOHN STRODE BARBOUR (1790–1855), Virginia legislator and congressman, saw Poe as a small child during the summer of 1812, when the Allans were visiting White Sulphur Springs. In 1829 Barbour apparently recommended Poe for West Point.

ELIZABETH BARRETT BARRETT (1806–1861), English poetess, enjoyed considerable popularity in the United States. Poe contributed a long critique of her poetry to the *Broadway Journal* (4 and 12 January 1845 issues); he subsequently dedicated *The Raven and Other Poems* (1845) to her. Miss Barrett often discussed Poe in her letters to ROBERT BROWNING (1812–1889), whom she married in 1846.

CHARLES BAUDELAIRE (1821–1867), French poet, encountered several Poe stories in the Paris periodicals around 1847. He devoted much of his later life to translating Poe's writings.

PARK BENJAMIN (1809–1864) edited the *New World*, a New York weekly, from October 1839 until March 1844. Thomas Ollive Mabbott and other scholars have attributed to Poe an article headed "Our Magazine Literature" and signed with the initial "L.," which appeared in the *New World* on 11 March 1843. It was almost certainly written by Benjamin's cousin Charles Lanman (1819–1895), as reported in William W. Snowden's *Ladies' Companion* for April 1843.

NICHOLAS BIDDLE (1786–1844), eminent Philadelphian, was President of the United States Bank. In late 1840 Poe solicited his aid for the proposed *Penn Magazine*.

ROBERT MONTGOMERY BIRD (1806–1854), Philadelphia novelist and playwright, contributed to the *Southern Literary Messenger* during Poe's editorship.

JOHN BISCO published the *Broadway Journal* from 4 January until 24 October 1845.

ANNA BLACKWELL, English authoress, was the sister of Dr. Elizabeth Blackwell (1821–1910), the first woman physician in the United States. Anna boarded at Poe's Fordham cottage around October 1847. In the spring of 1848 she moved to Providence, Rhode Island, where she discussed Poe with Sarah Helen Whitman.

ELAM BLISS, New York publisher, brought out Poe's *Poems* (1831), as well as an edition of William Cullen Bryant's poetry and Edward V. Sparhawk's *Report of the Trial of John Jacob Astor's Claims to Lands in Putnam County* (1827).

ELI BOWEN (1824–1868) edited the *Columbia Spy*, a weekly newspaper in Columbia, Pennsylvania, from 30 November 1843 until 2 December 1844. He engaged Poe as his New York correspondent, publishing the resulting seven dispatches between 18 May and 6 July 1844. On 1 January 1848 Bowen became an editor of the Pottsville, Pennsylvania, *Miner's Journal*.

MATHEW B. BRADY (ca. 1823–1896), the famous photographer, seems to have been introduced to Poe in Washington in March 1843. He later made a daguerreotype of Poe at his New York studio, possibly in April 1849.

JOHN BRANSBY (1784–1857) was master of the Manor House School at Stoke Newington, near London, which Poe attended in 1818, 1819, and 1820.

CHARLES FREDERICK BRIGGS (1804–1877) was born on Nantucket Island, Massachusetts. After an early career as a seaman, he become an author and editor in New York City. A satiric first novel, *The Adventures of Harry Franco* (1839), established his reputation; he was hereafter known as "Harry Franco." In December 1844 he reached an agreement with the publisher John Bisco to issue his own weekly magazine, the *Broadway Journal*. Poe was engaged as a contributor from the opening number of 4 January 1845; on 21 February he became Briggs's co-editor. While Briggs was initially impressed with Poe's ability, he was soon disillusioned because of his partner's drinking and his attacks on Longfellow. In early July Briggs withdrew from the *Journal*, after having unsuccessfully attempted to purchase Bisco's interest. He subsequently displayed only animosity toward Poe, whom he ridiculed in an unsigned article in the *Evening Mirror* of 26 May 1846 and in his novel *The Trippings of Tom Pepper* (1847). Briggs had two notable friends and correspondents, the poet James Russell Lowell and the painter William Page. In later life he edited *Putnam's Monthly Magazine.*

CHARLES ASTOR BRISTED (1820–1874), well-to-do New Yorker, graduated from Trinity College, Cambridge, England, in 1845. After returning home he wrote for the *American Review* and other periodicals, simply for his own pleasure.

COTESWORTH P. BRONSON, authority on elocution, commissioned Poe to write a poem he could recite in his lectures; the result was "Ulalume," completed around October 1847. Bronson's daughter MARY ELIZABETH contributed a valuable reminiscence of Poe to the New York *Home Journal* of 21 July 1860 (reprinted in *American Literature,* May 1948).

JAMES BROOKS (1810–1873) edited the New York *Morning Express* from its commencement on 20 June 1836; the paper subsequently added evening, semiweekly, and weekly editions.

NATHAN COVINGTON BROOKS (1809–1898), Baltimore clergyman, editor, educator, and poet, was intimate with Poe during his residence in that city in the early 1830's. In the summer of 1838 Brooks solicited Poe's contributions for the *American Museum,* a Baltimore monthly which he edited with Joseph Evans Snodgrass.

DANIEL BRYAN (ca. 1790?–1866), minor poet, served as postmaster of Alexandria, Virginia, from 1820 to 1853. He corresponded with Poe during the summer of 1842.

WILLIAM CULLEN BRYANT (1794–1878) edited the New York *Evening Post.* Poe favorably noticed his poetry in the *Southern Literary Messenger* for January 1837, in *Burton's Gentleman's Magazine* for May 1840, and in *Godey's Lady's Book* for April 1846. The two men are known to have conversed at a soiree given by Caroline M. Kirkland, probably in 1845.

JOSEPH TINKER BUCKINGHAM (1779–1861) edited various Boston periodicals, including two monthlies, *Polyanthos* (1805–1807, 1812–1814) and the *New-England Magazine* (1831–1834), as well as a newspaper, the *Daily Courier* (1824–1848).

WILLIAM BURKE and his wife CHRISTIANA were Richmond schoolteachers. Poe entered Burke's "Seminary" for boys on 1 April 1823, during the session which had begun on 2 January. In June 1824 (or 1825) Burke was one of the bystanders who witnessed Poe's swimming feat in the James River. Along with John Hartwell Cocke, at whose Bremo Academy he had formerly taught, Burke may have persuaded John Allan to send Poe to the University of Virginia. Burke wrote two books, *The Rudiments of Latin Grammar* (1832) and *The Mineral Springs of Western Virginia* (1842); he translated parts of Virgil's *Aeneid* for the *Southern Literary Messenger.*

EBENEZER BURLING (died 1832) probably met Poe at the Richmond school of Joseph H. Clarke in the autumn of 1820; the two boys became intimate companions, as Elmira Shelton recalled in the 19 November 1875 interview she granted Edward V. Valentine. Burling's mother was the widow MARTHA BURLING (died 1846); she operated a Richmond boardinghouse after her husband's death, at the corner of Bank and Ninth Streets in 1819, and in 1821 at Main and Tenth, on Bank Square. His father THOMAS BURLING, a printer, had issued the Virginia Senate Journal.

CHARLES CHAUNCEY BURR (1815–1883), editor and clergyman, provided Poe with financial assistance during his July 1849 visit to Philadelphia. In the *Nineteenth Century* for February 1852, Burr defended Poe's character and published excerpts from his last letters to Maria Clemm, written between July and September 1849.

WILLIAM EVANS BURTON (1802–1860), English-born comic actor, emigrated to the United States in 1834, settling in Philadelphia. In July 1837 he issued the first number of *Burton's Gentleman's Magazine*, with Charles W. Alexander as publisher; in December 1838 he became its sole proprietor. In early May 1839 Burton accepted the offer of Poe's services, hiring him as assistant editor. He regarded Poe simply as an employee, never allowed him any control over the magazine, and refused to publish several of his blistering reviews. Poe was expected to perform proofreading and other trivial chores; Burton had acting engagements which kept him away from Philadelphia for weeks at a time. This unhappy relationship came to an end in late May 1840: Burton advertised his magazine for sale, intending to devote his energies to his new National Theatre, then under construction; Poe assumed that his employment would soon be terminated and consequently made preparations to circulate a prospectus announcing his own proposed journal, the *Penn Magazine*. When Burton learned of Poe's plan, he promptly fired him.

WILLIAM McCREERY BURWELL (1809–1888) became an editor of *DeBow's Review*. His recollections of Poe at the University of Virginia, originally published in the *New Orleans Times-Democrat* of 18 May 1884, were reprinted in the University's *Alumni Bulletin* for April 1923.

GEORGE BUSH (1796–1859), clergyman and scholar, was Professor of Hebrew at the New York University from 1831 to 1847. Around 1845 he became an enthusiastic Swedenborgian.

ELIZA JANE BUTTERFIELD (1828–1892) was a teacher at the Franklin Grammar School in Lowell, Massachusetts. Poe apparently conducted a brief flirtation with Miss Butterfield during his last visit to Annie Richmond and her family, in late May and early June 1849.

JULIA MAYO CABELL (1800–1860), Richmond matron, was the youngest daughter of Colonel John Mayo and Abigail DeHart Mayo, the uncle and aunt of Louisa G. Patterson (John Allan's second wife). In 1823 Julia married DR. ROBERT HENRY CABELL (1799–1876). Her sister Maria married GENERAL WINFIELD SCOTT (1786–1866). Julia, her husband, and her brother-in-law were friends of Poe.

EDWARD L. CAREY (1806–1845) and ABRAHAM HART (1810–1885) were the principals in Carey & Hart, Philadelphia publishers located at the southeast corner of Chestnut and Fourth Streets. The firm issued the *Gift*, a popular annual which contained the first printings of Poe's tales "William Wilson" (1840 ed.), "Eleonora" (1842 ed.), "The Pit and the Pendulum" (1843 ed.), and "The Purloined Letter" (1845 ed.).

MATHEW CAREY (1760–1839), printer and bookseller, emigrated to Philadelphia from Ireland in 1784; he soon became the leading American publisher. After his retirement in 1822, his son HENRY CHARLES CAREY (1793–1879) and son-in-law ISAAC LEA (1792–1886) continued his firm under the name Carey & Lea; they published original works by James Fenimore Cooper, Washington Irving, John P. Kennedy, John Neal, and Robert Montgomery Bird. After Henry C. Carey retired in 1838, the business was conducted by Isaac Lea and WILLIAM A. BLANCHARD under the name Lea & Blanchard; around 4 December 1839 they issued Poe's *Tales of the Grotesque and Arabesque*. The firm shared the same building at Chestnut and Fourth with Carey & Hart, an independent but allied concern begun by Henry's brother Edward L. Carey in 1829.

ROBERT CARTER (1819–1879), Boston journalist and abolitionist, served as the co-editor of James Russell Lowell's short-lived monthly, the *Pioneer* (January–March 1843).

JOSEPH RIPLEY CHANDLER (1792–

1880) edited the Philadelphia *United States Gazette*, a daily newspaper.

WILLIAM ELLERY CHANNING (1818–1901), Massachusetts poet and Transcendentalist, was the nephew of the eminent Unitarian clergyman who bore the same name. Although the younger Channing numbered Emerson, Hawthorne, and Thoreau among his friends, his poetry left much to be desired. Poe satirized his first volume of verse in *Graham's* for August 1843.

THOMAS HOLLEY CHIVERS (1809–1858), grandiloquent Georgia poet, was one of Poe's most devoted admirers. The two men frequently corresponded, with Poe constantly but unsuccessfully urging Chivers (the scion of a wealthy plantation family) to provide financial backing for his magazine projects. Chivers left a detailed reminiscence of several meetings he had with Poe when he visited New York in the summer of 1845.

LEWIS JACOB CIST (1818–1885), Cincinnati poet, contributed a poem entitled "Bachelor Philosophy" to Poe's proposed *Penn Magazine*.

LEWIS GAYLORD CLARK (1808–1873), editor of New York's *Knickerbocker Magazine*, often attacked Poe in his "Editor's Table." His twin brother **WILLIS GAYLORD CLARK** (1808–1841), a talented poet, edited the *Philadelphia Gazette* until his untimely death from tuberculosis, on 12 June 1841.

COLIN CLARKE (1792–1881), a graduate of William and Mary, abandoned the practice of law in 1834 and became a farmer in Gloucester County, Virginia. On 11 February 1836 Poe wrote John P. Kennedy that Clarke was "a gentleman of high respectability."

JOSEPH HANSON CLARKE (1790–1885), a Marylander, conducted a boys' school in Richmond from 1818 to 1823; he emphasized instruction in English, French, Latin, and Greek. Poe entered Clarke's school soon after his return from England in 1820. The two, master and student, later renewed their friendship in Baltimore, where Clarke spent the rest of his long teaching career.

THOMAS COTTRELL CLARKE (1801–1874), veteran Philadelphia publisher, issued the first number of his *Saturday Museum*, a weekly newspaper of folio size, on 10 December 1842. Shortly afterwards he agreed to publish Poe's long-planned literary journal, now retitled the *Stylus*, beginning in July 1843. While Clarke may have felt uncomfortable with Poe's drinking, his motive for withdrawing from the *Stylus* in May 1843 had more to do with the financial difficulties his own *Museum* was encountering. His daughter **ANNE E. C. CLARKE** left an informative account of Poe, which is quoted in John Sartain's *Reminiscences of a Very Old Man* (1899).

MARIA CLEMM (1790–1871) was born Maria Poe on 17 March 1790, the sister of Edgar's father David Poe, Jr. On 13 July 1817 she married **WILLIAM CLEMM, JR.** (1779–1826), a Baltimore widower of some social prominence. William's first wife, whom he married on 1 May 1804, had been **HARRIET POE** (1785–1815), the daughter of George Poe, Sr., and thus Maria's first cousin. William and Harriet had five children: William Eichelberger (born 1806), Josephine Emily (1808–1889), Georgianna Maria (born 1810), Catherine, and Harriet. William and Maria had three children: Henry (born 1818), Virginia Sarah or Maria (1820–1822), and Virginia Eliza (1822–1847). William Clemm, Jr., died on 8 February 1826, leaving his widow with only a negligible estate. Around this time Maria began to provide lodging and nursing for her invalid mother Elizabeth Cairnes Poe, who received an annuity of $240. Shortly after Edgar Poe arrived in Baltimore early in May 1829, he called on his aunt and grandmother; in the spring of 1831 he joined their household, then located on Wilks Street (later Eastern Avenue) between Exeter and High. Edgar served as companion and tutor to Mrs. Clemm's young daughter VIRGINIA ELIZA; his affection for both his aunt and his cousin increased, as did his emotional dependence on them. The death of Elizabeth Cairnes Poe on 7 July 1835 brought an end to the annuity which had been Mrs. Clemm's most reliable means of support. Early in October Edgar took his aunt and her daughter to Richmond, where he had secured employment on the *Southern Literary Messenger*. On 16 May 1836 Edgar and Virginia were married there; the union proved unusually happy, the partners being bound by a blood relationship as well as by a mutual love which had developed over several years of shared intimacy. Around 20 January 1842, during Poe's residence in Philadelphia, Virginia first suffered the pulmonary hemorrhaging symptomatic of tuberculosis. She died from this relentless disease at Fordham, outside New York City, on 30 January 1847. Mrs. Clemm now devoted herself to caring for Poe, who was prostrated by his wife's death and by his own struggles with ill health, poverty, and alcoholism. His death on 7 October 1849 left the elderly woman without immediate family and without financial resources; in the years following she had no permanent residence, but stayed with a succession of friends who were able to give her free room and board. In the spring of 1863 she gained admission to the Episcopal Church Home in Baltimore; she died in this charitable institution on 16 February 1871.

JOHN HARTWELL COCKE (1780–1866), Virginia scholar and soldier, resided at Bremo Plantation, on the James River north of Richmond. Cocke aided Thomas Jefferson in establishing the University of Virginia; he was a friend and correspondent of John Allan. At the plantation of his brother BOWLER COCKE, the Allans and Poe spent the Christmas holidays in 1811.

GEORGE HOOKER COLTON (1818–1847), Yale graduate, edited the *American Review* in New York. He purchased "The Raven" for his February 1845 number, paying Poe "not *over* $20."

ROBERT TAYLOR CONRAD (1810–1858) was a Philadelphia judge, playwright, and poet. Poe favorably noticed Conrad's writings in his lecture on "American Poetry" (21 November 1843 and subsequent dates) and in an unsigned sketch published in *Graham's* for June 1844.

PHILIP PENDLETON COOKE (1816–1850), Virginia poet, wrote Thomas Willis White in 1835, praising Poe's earliest contributions to the *Southern Literary Messenger* (letter quoted in September number). Cooke was one of the few American critics whose opinions Poe respected; the two men corresponded occasionally during Poe's Philadelphia and New York periods. In the January 1848 *Messenger* Cooke published an appreciative essay on Poe's later writings. His brother JOHN ESTEN COOKE (1830–1886), the novelist, attended Poe's 17 August 1849 lecture in Richmond.

ALEXANDER T. CRANE (born ca. 1829), office boy of the *Broadway Journal*, left a reminiscence of Poe in the Omaha, Nebraska, *Sunday World-Herald* of 13 July 1902 (reprinted in *Poe Studies*, December 1973).

CALEB CUSHING (1800–1879), Massachusetts politician and diplomat, delivered a lecture on Great Britain to the Boston Lyceum on 16 October 1845, immediately before Poe read his poem "Al Aaraaf" to the same audience. Cushing's address, reportedly long and tedious, was hardly a suitable prelude to a poetry reading; it almost certainly contributed to the lukewarm reception accorded Poe.

JOHN MONCURE DANIEL (1825–1865), acerbic editor of the Richmond *Semi-Weekly Examiner*, was challenged to a duel by Poe around August 1848. A reconciliation occurred in 1849: Daniel objectively reviewed Poe's 17 August and 24 September lectures and printed a revised copy of "The Raven." After Poe's death Daniel contributed several frank reminiscences of him to the *Examiner* (9, 12, 19 October 1849); these provided much of the substance for his longer article in the March 1850 *Southern Literary Messenger*.

PETER VIVIAN DANIEL (1784–1860) was one of the three members of the Virginia State Council whose aid Poe and the Junior Volunteers solicited in retaining arms issued to them for Lafayette's October 1824 visit to Richmond. Daniel later became an Associate Justice of the United States Supreme Court.

FELIX O. C. DARLEY (1822–1888), Philadelphia artist, furnished illustrations for the first printings of "The Gold-Bug" and Thomas Dunn English's *The Doom of the Drinker*.

RUFUS DAWES (1803–1859), Baltimore poetaster, was the subject of a devastating Poe critique in the October 1842 *Graham's*.

THOMAS RODERICK DEW (1802–1846), Professor of Economics at William and Mary, became its President in 1836. A frequent contributor to the *Southern Literary Messenger*, Dew corresponded with Poe about one of his submissions, an "Address" he delivered at the College on 10 October 1836; it appeared in the November *Messenger*, accompanied by Poe's note.

CHARLES DICKENS (1812–1870), English novelist, received a tumultuous welcome and much fatuous adulation during his first visit to the United States, 22 January to 7 June 1842. In the following autumn he annoyed his former hosts by issuing *American Notes for General Circulation*, a record of his trip which touched upon many national shortcomings, including slavery, prisons, railroads, and tobacco-chewing. Dickens granted Poe two interviews when he stopped in Philadelphia (5–9 March); after he returned to England he sought unsuccessfully to find a London publisher for Poe's stories.

JOHN DIXON, JR. (1768–1805), Richmond printer, was the son of John Dixon, Sr. (died 1791), and Rosanna Hunter Dixon (died 1790). Like his father, the younger Dixon printed the *Virginia Gazette*. He married SARAH VALENTINE (died 1807), the half sister of Ann Moore Valentine and Frances Keeling Valentine (John Allan's first wife). On 12 January 1795 Dixon assumed the legal guardianship of these two Valentine girls, who had been left orphans. MARY DIXON, his sister, married the merchant John Richard (1762–1824). In 1822 Richard purchased "Moldavia" from the estate of the flour miller Joseph Gallego; in 1825 John Allan purchased the house from Richard's estate. As the Richards were childless, they adopted Caroline Homasett, their niece as well as Gallego's; she married Philip Thornton, who had rescued her from the Richmond Theatre fire on 26 December 1811. Perhaps he was the son of the Dr. Philip Thornton who treated Poe in 1812. ROSANNA DIXON (1801?–1828), daughter of John Dixon, Jr., became the first wife of William Galt, Jr. GEORGE DIXON, JR. (1810?–1840), the son of John's brother George, married Mary I. Poitiaux, one of Michael B. Poitiaux's daughters, in 1833.

JESSE ERSKINE DOW (1809–1850), journalist and poet, was born in Thompson, Connecticut; he joined the United States Navy at an early age. In 1835 and 1836 Dow served on the frigate *Constitution* ("Old Ironsides") as private secretary to its controversial commander, Commodore Jesse Duncan Elliott (1782–1845). From 1837 until 1841 Dow held a clerkship in the Post Office Department in Washington. His popular "Sketches from the Log of Old Ironsides," based on his nautical experiences, appeared in *Burton's* from July 1839 until April 1840, during Poe's association with the magazine. In May 1840 Dow came to Philadelphia as a witness in the court martial of Commodore Elliott; at this time he often saw Poe, who seems to have introduced him to the novelist Frederick William Thomas. Dow spent the rest of his career in Washington, where he held minor political offices and edited several newspapers (the *Index, Daily Madisonian,* and *United States Journal*).

WILLIAM DRAYTON (1776–1846), jurist, preferred the title "Colonel" to that of judge; he earned the former during the War of 1812. From 1825 to 1833 he served in the United States Congress as a representative from South Carolina; there is no truth in the tradition that he was Poe's commanding officer at Fort Moultrie in 1827 and 1828. In the summer of 1833 Drayton settled in Philadelphia; he subsequently assisted Poe, who moved there in early 1838. Poe dedicated his *Tales of the Grotesque and Arabesque* to Drayton.

WILLIAM DUANE, JR. (1808–1882), Philadelphia scholar, was the son of William John Duane (1780–1865), Secretary of the Treasury under President Andrew Jackson. The younger Duane contributed to the *Southern Literary Messenger* during Poe's editorship; around March 1844 he lent Poe an early volume of the *Messenger*, which Maria Clemm inadvertently sold to a Philadelphia bookseller. Duane and Poe exchanged several angry letters before the missing volume was recovered.

FRANCIS HAROLD DUFFEE, Philadelphia stockbroker, dabbled in authorship. He gained some notoriety by unjustly accusing Poe of collusion with the committee which selected "The Gold-Bug" for a $100 prize.

JOHN STEPHENSON DU SOLLE (1810?–1876) edited the *Spirit of the Times*, a Philadelphia daily newspaper which has sometimes been confused with a New York sporting journal of the same name. A friend of Poe, Du Solle was a colorful and pugnacious figure; he later settled in New York City, where he became private secretary to the showman P. T. Barnum.

EVERT AUGUSTUS DUYCKINCK (1816–1878), New York bibliophile and scholar, conducted the monthly *Arcturus* (1840–1842) with his friend Cornelius

Mathews. In 1845 Duyckinck became editor of Wiley and Putnam's "Library of American Books," a position which kept him in frequent communication with Poe, Hawthorne, Melville, and many other authors. His younger brother GEORGE LONG DUYCKINCK (1823–1863) worked with him in editing the *Literary World* (1847, 1848–1853) and in compiling their *Cyclopaedia of American Literature* (2 vols., 1855).

CHARLES EAMES (1812–1867) edited the last volume of the *New World* (4 January until 10 May 1845); in this New York weekly he reprinted Poe's revised tale "Ligeia" as well as his poems "The Haunted Palace" and "The Raven." In the summer of 1845 Eames received a Navy Department appointment in Washington; here he became acquainted with Poe's friend Frederick William Thomas.

PLINY EARLE (1809–1892), a minor poet, was better known as an innovative physician who devoted his life to the treatment of mental illness. In 1840 he contributed a poem to Poe's proposed *Penn Magazine*.

JOHN HENRY EATON (1790–1856), Secretary of War under President Andrew Jackson, granted Poe an interview in Washington in July 1829. His nephew JOHN EATON HENDERSON (died 1836), from Tennessee, was one of Poe's tentmates at West Point.

ELIZABETH FRIES ELLET (1818–1877), poetess and translator, was the wife of Dr. William H. Ellet, a professor at the South Carolina College in Columbia; but she resided in New York City, where she belonged to the circle of bluestockings surrounding Poe. She became Poe's implacable enemy after he spurned her attempts at social intimacy.

CHARLES ELLIS (1771 or 1772–1840), business partner of John Allan, married Frances Allan's cousin MARGARET KEEL-

ING NIMMO (1790–1877) of Norfolk, Virginia. The couple had nine children: Thomas Harding (1814–1898), James Nimmo (1815?–1839), Charles Jr. (1817–1900), Elizabeth Thorowgood (1818–1900), Jane Shelton (1820–1901), John (1822–1823), Richard Shelton (1825–1867), Frances (1827–1886), and Powhatan (1829–1906). According to CHARLES ELLIS, JR., his father and John Allan opposed Frances Allan's adoption of Edgar Poe. Whether this is true or not, the senior Ellis opened his home to the Allan family when they returned from England in 1820. Poe became an older playmate of THOMAS H. ELLIS, who recorded his recollections in a letter published in the *Richmond Standard*, 7 May 1881, and in manuscripts now held by the Valentine Museum. POWHATAN ELLIS (1790–1863), a brother of the senior Ellis, became a United States Senator from Mississippi; on 13 March 1830 he wrote a letter recommending Poe for West Point.

THOMAS DUNN ENGLISH (1819–1902), the son of a Philadelphia carpenter, was a poet, physician, politician, editor, novelist, and lawyer; he did not achieve prominence in any field, and he has been remembered largely for his turbulent relationship with Poe. As early as 1837 English began to contribute crude, sententious verses to *Burton's Gentleman's Magazine* and other Philadelphia journals; in 1839 he met Poe, the new assistant editor of *Burton's*. Their subsequent intimacy soon bred mutual contempt, which neither could successfully conceal. In March 1843 an intoxicated Poe made fun of English at a social gathering in Fuller's Hotel, Washington. English retaliated by depicting Poe as a drunken literary critic in his temperance novel *The Doom of the Drinker* (1843). By 1845 the two men were superficially reconciled, with English lengthily reviewing Poe's *Tales* and *The Raven and Other Poems* in his New York monthly the *Aristidean*. The veneer of civility evaporated in early 1846, when English refused to assist Poe in an imbroglio involving Elizabeth F. Ellet. To *Godey's Lady's Book* for July Poe contributed a maliciously patronizing sketch of English, who then inserted a more abusive and somewhat libelous "Reply" in the New York *Evening Mirror*. Poe sued the *Mirror* for printing it, winning a substantial judgment on 17 February 1847. English played no further role in Poe's career, though he attacked him repeatedly in the *John-Donkey* (1848), a satiric weekly issued in Philadelphia.

GEORGE W. EVELETH, a young medical student in Maine, conducted a lengthy correspondence with Poe, beginning on 21 December 1845. Eveleth later provided transcripts of the letters he received to John H. Ingram, Poe's English biographer.

THEODORE SEDGWICK FAY (1807–1898), author and diplomat, was an associate editor of the *New-York Mirror*, which repeatedly lauded his two-volume novel *Norman Leslie* (1835). Poe condemned both the book and the "puffing" of it in the December 1835 *Southern Literary Messenger*, creating a sensation but antagonizing many of Fay's friends.

JOHN W. FERGUSSON (1821?–1909) was an apprentice printer and delivery boy employed on the *Messenger* during Poe's editorship.

JOSEPH M. FIELD (1810–1856), actor and journalist, edited the Saint Louis *Daily Reveille*; he often defended Poe in his paper, most notably in the 30 June 1846 issue.

MAUNSELL BRADHURST FIELD (1822–1875), lawyer and author, left a reminiscence of Poe's 3 February 1848 lecture on "The Universe."

JAMES THOMAS FIELDS (1817–1881), Boston publisher, was the junior partner in Ticknor & Company.

E. BURKE FISHER (1799?–1859?), minor author, contributed to the *Southern Literary Messenger* during Poe's editorship. Fisher engaged Poe as a contributor to his *Literary Examiner* (1839–1840), a Pittsburgh monthly, but alienated him by making unauthorized revisions to his articles.

OSCAR PENN FITZGERALD (1829–1911), Methodist bishop, recalled seeing Poe in the streets of Richmond in 1849.

EMILE DAURAND FORGUES (1813–1889), Paris journalist and critic, wrote under the pseudonym "Old Nick"; he translated Poe's "A Descent into the Maelström" (*Revue britannique*, September 1846) and "The Murders in the Rue Morgue" (*Le Commerce*, 12 October 1846). When a Paris newspaper wrongly accused Forgues of plagiarizing the latter story, he sued for libel; the resulting controversy did much to popularize Poe in France.

JANE FRANCES FOSTER (1823–1911), later the wife of J. C. Stocking, was an out-of-town friend of Mrs. James Yarrington. In the spring of 1836 Miss Foster, then only thirteen, stopped briefly at the Yarrington boardinghouse in Richmond; she thus happened to attend the 16 May wedding of Edgar Poe and Virginia Clemm.

JOHN WAKEFIELD FRANCIS (1789–1861) seems to have been the Poe family's physician during their residence in New York City (1844–1846). After they moved to Fordham around May 1846, they were treated by a Dr. Freeman.

JOHN FROST (1800–1859), Professor of Literature in the Philadelphia High School, also edited *Alexander's Weekly Messenger*. He favorably noticed Poe's "The Fall of the House of Usher," "William Wilson," and *Tales of the Grotesque and Arabesque* (*Messenger* for 4 September, 16 October, and 19 December 1839).

HIRAM FULLER (1814–1880) began his career as a schoolteacher and bookseller in Providence, Rhode Island; he moved to New York City in 1843. On 7 October 1844 George P. Morris and Nathaniel P. Willis engaged him as the business manager of their new enterprise, the *Evening Mirror* and *Weekly Mirror*. Fuller soon played an editorial role, signing his contributions with an asterisk; on 27 December 1845 he became the *Mirror*'s sole editor,

Morris and Willis withdrawing from the concern. Although Fuller admired Poe's stories and some of his criticisms, he objected to his sketches of "The Literati of New York City." In the *Evening Mirror* of 26 May 1846 he published Charles F. Briggs's unsigned attack on the series and its author; on 23 June he reprinted Thomas Dunn English's virulent "Reply" to Poe from the *Morning Telegraph*. Fuller himself then hammered Poe in a long string of editorials.

MARGARET FULLER (1810–1850) edited the *Dial*, the Transcendentalist quarterly, from July 1840 to April 1842. In late 1844 she accepted Horace Greeley's invitation to write for his *Daily Tribune*; she settled in New York City, where she made Poe's acquaintance, probably at one of Anne C. Lynch's soirees. She favorably reviewed James Russell Lowell's sketch of Poe, as well as the Wiley and Putnam editions of Poe's stories and poems (*Tribune* for 24 January, 11 July, 26 November 1845).

WILLIAM DAVIS GALLAGHER (1808–1894), Cincinnati editor and poet, sent Poe a copy of his anthology *Selections from the Poetical Literature of the West* (1841).

WILLIAM GALT (1755–1825) fled from his native Scotland after being implicated in smuggling; he entered the mercantile business in Richmond and became very wealthy. A bachelor, he adopted WILLIAM GALT, JR. (1801–1851) and JAMES GALT (1804–1876), two brothers who were not related to him. At his death in 1825 the brothers and his nephew John Allan were the chief beneficiaries of his estate.

JAMES MERCER GARNETT (1770–1843), Virginia educator and agriculturist, contributed to the *Southern Literary Messenger* under the pen name "Oliver Oldschool"; he was one of Poe's earliest and severest critics. Garnett's nephew ROBERT MERCER TALIAFERRO HUNTER (1809–1887), Virginia legislator and Confederate statesman, knew Poe at the University of Virginia. On 20 May 1875 Hunter wrote his friend HENRY TUTWILER (1807–

1884), then headmaster of a boys' school in Alabama, that he had helped Thomas Willis White put the *Messenger* to press during Poe's drinking bouts.

MILES GEORGE (born 1807), Richmond physician, entered the University of Virginia with Poe in February 1826. In an 18 May 1880 letter to Edward V. Valentine, Dr. George recalled that Poe covered the walls of his dormitory room with charcoal sketches, displaying great artistic talent. Two other students also described these drawings: THOMAS BOLLING of Nelson County, Virginia, who wrote Valentine on 10 July 1875, and JOHN WILLIS (1809–1885) of Orange County, Virginia, grandnephew of President James Madison and member of the state legislature, who wrote Sarah Helen Whitman sometime prior to 1874. The letters from George and Bolling are held by the Valentine Museum; William F. Gill excerpted Willis' letter in his 1877 biography (pp. 36–37).

JAMES GIBBON (1758–1835), a neighbor of John Allan, had distinguished himself as "the hero of Stony Point" during the Revolutionary War. From 1800 to 1835 Major Gibbon was Richmond's Collector of Customs. His daughter Mrs. Mary Gibbon Carter criticized the Poes in Baltimore for neglecting Edgar and Rosalie after their mother's death.

THOMAS WARE GIBSON of Indiana roomed with Poe at West Point and later subscribed to his *Poems* (1831). Gibson published his reminiscences of Poe in *Harper's* for November 1867.

BASIL LANNEAU GILDERSLEEVE (1831–1924), noted classicist, recalled seeing Poe on Broad Street, Richmond, in 1849.

WILLIAM MITCHELL GILLESPIE (1816–1868), New York author and civil engineer, attended Poe's 28 February 1845 lecture on the "Poets and Poetry of America."

WILLIAM J. GLENN (1822–1902), Richmond tailor, initiated Poe into the Sons of Temperance on 27 August 1849.

LOUIS ANTOINE GODEY (1804–1878) published *Godey's Lady's Book* from 1830 to 1877. Poe liked this rotund, affable Philadelphian as a man; he had scant respect for his magazine, which catered to the feminine hunger for fashion plates, sentimental fiction, and exemplary morality. The *Book* had a very large circulation and paid competitive prices to authors; Poe frequently contributed to it during his New York period.

MARY NEAL GOVE (1810–1884), health reformer, lecturer, and novelist, visited Poe's Fordham cottage on several occasions in 1846 and 1847; she described these visits in the *Six Penny Magazine* for February 1863. Mrs. Gove also left a shorter reminiscence of Poe in her novel *Mary Lyndon* (1855). Her marriage to Hiram Gove ended in divorce in 1848; she then married the physician Thomas Low Nichols (1815–1901), who recalled the publication of Poe's "Balloon-Hoax" in his *Forty Years of American Life* (1864).

GEORGE REX GRAHAM (1813–1894) acquired a proprietary interest in two Philadelphia journals in 1839, the *Saturday Evening Post* and the *Casket*. On 20 October 1840, having become sole proprietor of the *Casket*, he purchased *Burton's Gentleman's Magazine* for $3500; he combined these two monthlies to issue his *Graham's Magazine*, the first number being dated December 1840. In February 1841 he engaged Poe as the book review editor of *Graham's*, paying him a salary of $800 a year. Poe's relations with Graham were outwardly cordial; privately he was mildly contemptuous of this commercial publisher and his "namby-pamby" magazine, disgruntled with his employee status, and desirous of starting his own journal. Around 1 April 1842 Poe resigned; Graham hired Rufus W. Griswold to replace him. Although *Graham's* achieved a large circulation, Graham himself went bankrupt because of unwise stock speculations; in July 1848 he was forced to dispose of the magazine's controlling interest to Samuel D. Patterson, who had acquired the *Saturday Evening Post* in March 1843. Graham never regained his former prosperity.

HORACE GREELEY (1811–1872) edited the New York *Daily Tribune* from 1841 until 1872. The paper became influential throughout the United States; Greeley himself was almost a national institution.

RUFUS WILMOT GRISWOLD (1815–1857), Vermont-born anthologist and journalist, met Poe in the spring of 1841, when he was collecting materials for his most popular compilation, *The Poets and Poetry of America* (1842). Poe pointed out the book's shortcomings in his lecture on "American Poetry," delivered in Philadelphia on 21 November 1843 and repeated in other cities. Griswold never forgave him, although they subsequently maintained a facade of civility. In *The Prose Writers of America* (1847) Griswold favorably evaluated Poe's stories, commenting more briefly on his poetry and literary criticism. In 1849 he penned a vindictive obituary of Poe for the New York *Daily Tribune*, which was quoted or reprinted by many other papers. Three of Poe's friends (Nathaniel P. Willis, George R. Graham, and John Neal) published protests against this distorted characterization; Griswold responded by inserting a much longer, often malicious and false "Memoir" in his edition of Poe's works (1850). For several decades this "Memoir" served as the standard biography of Poe; it has had a lasting influence on the popular conception of his personality.

HIRAM H. HAINES (1802–1841), one of Poe's earliest admirers, edited three newspapers in Petersburg, Virginia: the *American Constellation* (1834–1838), *Th' Time o' Day* (1839), and the *Virginia Star* (1840–1841).

SARAH JOSEPHA HALE (1788–1879) became a professional writer to support herself and five children after the death of her husband in 1822. Mrs. Hale edited first the *Ladies' Magazine* (1828–1836); when Louis A. Godey united this Boston monthly to his more successful *Lady's Book* in 1837, he engaged her as his literary editor. In the autumn of 1840 she settled in Philadelphia, where she played an active role on *Godey's* and where she almost certainly made Poe's acquaintance. Her son DAVID EMERSON HALE (1814?–1839) attended West Point with Poe in 1830 and 1831.

FITZ-GREENE HALLECK (1790–1867), New York poet, reputedly lent Poe $100 for the *Broadway Journal* in December 1845.

SAMUEL HARKER (died 1850) edited the *Baltimore Republican*, a daily newspaper to which Poe contributed three notices of Thomas Willis White's *Southern Literary Messenger* (14 May, 13 June, and 10 July 1835).

GABRIEL HARRISON (1818–1902), actor, author, and painter, made Poe's acquaintance in the fall of 1844, at a tea and tobacco store he operated in lower Manhattan; they became occasional companions. After Poe's death Harrison often corresponded with his mother-in-law Mrs. Clemm.

WILLIAM HENRY HARRISON (1773–1841), military hero and public official, headed the Whig ticket in the 1840 Presidential election. He defeated the Democratic incumbent Martin Van Buren, but died after only one month in office, on 4 April 1841, apparently exhausted from trying to cope with hordes of office-seekers.

FRANCIS LISTER HAWKS (1798–1866), Episcopalian clergyman, was one of the editors of the *New York Review*, a theological quarterly to which Poe contributed a long critique of John L. Stephens' *Incidents of Travel in Egypt, Arabia Petraea, and the Holy Land* (October 1837).

NATHANIEL HAWTHORNE (1804–1864) was the only American author whom Poe deeply admired and consistently praised. He evaluated Hawthorne's stories in two long critiques (*Graham's* for April and May 1842, *Godey's* for November

1847); elsewhere he complained that the reading public had not given Hawthorne adequate financial compensation (New York *Evening Mirror* for 6 February 1845, *Broadway Journal* for 23 August 1845).

JOEL TYLER HEADLEY (1813–1897), author and historian, was prolific, popular, and mediocre. His *Letters from Italy* (1845) appeared as the third volume in Wiley and Putnam's "Library of American Books," following Poe's *Tales*.

JAMES EWELL HEATH (1792–1862), Richmond author, edited the first seven numbers of the *Southern Literary Messenger* (August 1834–March 1835); he was succeeded by Edward V. Sparhawk and then by Poe. After Poe's departure in January 1837, Heath again assisted its proprietor Thomas Willis White, although he never actually resumed the editorship. Heath was a perceptive critic hampered by the Victorian notion that literature must be morally instructive; the limitations of his sensibility are apparent in his reviews of Poe's fiction (*Messenger* for October 1839 and January 1840).

HENRY HERRING (1791?–1868), Baltimore lumber dealer, married Poe's aunt ELIZABETH ("ELIZA") POE (1792–1822) on 17 November 1814. Poe wrote several acrostic poems in the album of their daughter ELIZABETH REBECCA HERRING (1815–1889). On 2 December 1834 she married Arthur Turner Tutt of Woodville, Rappahannock County, Virginia, who died not long after. Her second husband was Edmund Morton Smith, headmaster of a Baltimore boys' school. Elizabeth's half sister MARY ESTELLE HERRING married James Warden. Around 1840 Henry Herring and Mary, then a widow, settled temporarily in Philadelphia, where they frequently saw Poe and his family.

JAMES HERRON, Virginia-born civil engineer, invented the trellis railway track. In June 1842 he sent Poe a gift of $20.

JOHN HILL HEWITT (1801–1890), jour-

nalist, musician, and poet, edited the *Baltimore Minerva and Emerald* (1829–1832), a literary weekly; around January 1830 he unfavorably reviewed Poe's *Al Aaraaf, Tamerlane, and Minor Poems*. In August 1832 Hewitt succeeded Lambert A. Wilmer as editor of the *Baltimore Saturday Visiter*. Concealing his identity under the pseudonym "Henry Wilton," he submitted a poem in the premium contest announced by the *Visiter's* proprietors on 15 June 1833. Poe won the larger award ($50) with his tale "MS. Found in a Bottle"; but Hewitt received the prize for poetry ($25) with "The Song of the Winds," which the judges selected instead of Poe's entry in this genre, "The Coliseum." Poe believed himself entitled to both prizes, regarding Hewitt's participation in the contest as unfair; they engaged in a brief street brawl a few days after their compositions were published in the 19 October *Visiter*. In September 1839 Hewitt became editor of the *Baltimore Clipper*, a new daily; he soon moved to Washington, where he again saw Poe in March 1843.

MARY ELIZABETH HEWITT (born 1818?), poetess, was the wife of James L. Hewitt, brother of John Hill Hewitt. A frequent contributor to periodicals, she became one of Poe's closest associates among the New York bluestockings.

BARDWELL HEYWOOD (1824?–1899), schoolteacher, was the brother of Annie Richmond of Lowell, Massachusetts, with whom Poe fell in love in 1848. Bardwell described Poe's visits to Lowell in several letters to another teacher, Miss Annie Sawyer (published in the *New England Quarterly*, September 1943). Bardwell's sister SARAH H. HEYWOOD (1829?–1913) left a reminiscence of Poe which was printed by two early biographers, William F. Gill and John H. Ingram.

THOMAS WENTWORTH HIGGINSON (1823–1911), Massachusetts author and soldier, attended Poe's poetry reading before the Boston Lyceum on 16 October 1845.

HENRY BECK HIRST (1817–1874), eccentric Philadelphia poet, was one of Poe's frequent companions during his residence in that city. Following Poe's instructions, Hirst prepared the biographical sketch of him published in the *Saturday Museum* for 25 February and 4 March 1843. In later life Hirst became addicted to absinthe; his last years were spent as an inmate of the insane department of the Blockley Almshouse, Philadelphia.

CHARLES FENNO HOFFMAN (1806–1884), New York litterateur, edited the *Literary World* from 8 May 1847 to 30 September 1848. He was a close friend of the anthologist Rufus W. Griswold, who selected a disproportionate number of his verses for *The Poets and Poetry of America* (1842).

EZRA HOLDEN (1803–1846) was co-editor of the Philadelphia *Saturday Courier*, in which he reviewed Poe's *Tales of the Grotesque and Arabesque* (2 November, 14 December 1839). Holden died in Washington on 20 March 1846; his partner Andrew McMakin then became the *Courier's* sole editor.

JOHN HENRY HOPKINS, JR. (1820–1891) was the eldest son of the first Protestant Episcopal bishop of Vermont, who bore the same name. The younger Hopkins graduated from the University of Vermont in 1839; in 1848, while a student at the General Theological Seminary in New York City, he published a laudatory synopsis of Poe's 3 February lecture on "The Universe" (*Morning Express*, 4 February). Hopkins' religious beliefs were conservative; and although he initially admired Poe, he ended their acquaintance after discovering traces of pantheism in the manuscript of the forthcoming *Eureka*. Hopkins reviewed Poe's book in the *Literary World* of 29 July 1848, vigorously denouncing its theological ambiguities. In later life he became a bishop.

JOSEPH HOPKINSON (1770–1842), Philadelphia jurist, wrote the patriotic song "Hail Columbia."

RICHARD HENRY HORNE (1803–1884), versatile British author, wrote *Orion* (1843), an epic poem admired by his contemporaries. Poe's enthusiastic review of it in the March 1844 *Graham's* led to a correspondence between the two men, which was cordial but not especially productive. Horne could not find a London periodical to purchase Poe's tale "The Spectacles"; Poe in turn failed to discover a New York publisher willing to reprint *Orion*.

CHARLES WILLIAM HUBNER (1835–1929), poet, editor, and librarian, left a reminiscence of Poe's funeral (8 October 1849).

HENRY NORMAN HUDSON (1814–1886), New England scholar and clergyman, delivered many lectures on Shakespeare.

FREEMAN HUNT (1804–1858) edited and published the *Merchants' Magazine* in New York; he favorably reviewed Poe's *Tales, The Raven and Other Poems*, and *Eureka* (August 1845, January 1846, and August 1848 issues).

JEDEDIAH HUNT, JR. (1815–1860), editor and poet, published a protest against the severity of Poe's criticism in the final issue of his Ithaca, New York, *National Archives*, dated 13 March 1845. On 17 March Poe wrote him a long letter defending his conduct; Hunt printed it on 29 April in the opening issue of his new weekly, the *Bainbridge Eagle* (Chenango County, New York).

ABIJAH METCALF IDE, JR. (1825–1873), a young farmer in South Attleborough, Massachusetts, initiated a correspondence with Poe on 1 October 1843, sending him specimens of unpublished poetry and soliciting his opinion. In 1845 Ide became a contributor to Poe's *Broadway Journal*.

JOHN HENRY INGRAM (1842–1916), Poe's English biographer, collected important information about him by corresponding with Sarah Helen Whitman, Annie Richmond, Marie Louise Shew, and George W. Eveleth.

WASHINGTON IRVING (1783–1859) held a revered place as the first American man of letters. While Poe felt that Irving's abilities were overrated, he recognized the value of his reputation. In the fall of 1839 he sent Irving "The Fall of the House of Usher" and "William Wilson," simply to elicit a word of praise which could be used to promote the forthcoming *Tales of the Grotesque and Arabesque*.

EDWARD WILLIAM JOHNSTON, journalist and librarian, was the son of a distinguished Virginia jurist and the older brother of the Confederate General Joseph Eggleston Johnston. An ardent Anglophile, Johnston wrote a controversial article for the Charleston, South Carolina, *Southern Review* of August 1831, condemning the idea that American authors needed to free themselves from British models. Many of his articles were signed with the pen name "Il Secretario," including the memoir of Hugh Swinton Legaré which appeared in New York's *American Review* for October 1845. Johnston became an early contributor to the *Southern Literary Messenger*; in 1836 he unsuccessfully sought to interest the New York branch of Saunders and Otley, an English firm, in publishing Poe's "Tales of the Folio Club."

JOHN BEAUCHAMP JONES (1810–1866), Baltimore journalist, contributed to *Burton's* during Poe's association with it. Jones edited the *Saturday Visiter* from 9 May 1840 until 8 November 1841, being succeeded by Joseph Evans Snodgrass.

WILLIAM ALFRED JONES (1817–1900), literary critic, was a friend of Evert A. Duyckinck, Cornelius Mathews, and other New York writers. Poe expressed his contempt for Jones's essays in the *Broadway Journal* of 20 September 1845.

JOHN KEESE (1805–1856), author and bookseller in New York City, edited an anthology *The Poets of America* (1839), *The Poetical Writings of Mrs. Elizabeth Oakes Smith* (1845), and the *Opal* for 1846 and 1847.

JOHN PENDLETON KENNEDY (1795–1870), Baltimore novelist and congressman, was one of the three judges who selected Poe's "MS. Found in a Bottle" as the prize story of the *Saturday Visiter* in October 1833. Poe immediately introduced himself to Kennedy, who befriended him and gave him material assistance to alleviate his poverty. In 1834 Kennedy unsuccessfully attempted to convince his publishers, Carey & Lea of Philadelphia, to issue Poe's "Tales of the Folio Club"; in 1835 he encouraged Thomas Willis White to employ the young author on the *Southern Literary Messenger*. Poe occasionally corresponded with Kennedy during his subsequent residences in Richmond, Philadelphia, and New York.

CAROLINE MATILDA KIRKLAND (1801–1864) was best known for her stories of Western frontier life. During 1845 she entertained Poe at one or more social gatherings in her New York home. In July 1847 she became the first editor of the *Union Magazine*; she printed Poe's sonnet to Sarah Anna Lewis ("An Enigma"), but rejected a more significant poem, "Ulalume." Poe favorably noticed both Mrs. Kirkland and her husband WILLIAM KIRKLAND (1800–1846) in his "Literati" sketches.

MARQUIS DE LAFAYETTE (1757–1834), French nobleman and soldier, was the most illustrious foreigner to fight for the American cause during the Revolutionary War. In 1824 Lafayette made a triumphal tour of the United States; when he visited Baltimore in early October, he inquired after Poe's grandfather David Poe, Sr.

ELIZA LAMBERT (1793?–1891) of Richmond was a friend of Edgar and Rosalie Poe. GENERAL WILLIAM LAMBERT, her brother, served as the city's mayor from 1840 until his death in 1853; his wife Marian Pickett Lambert was, like Rosalie, a beneficiary of Joseph Gallego's estate.

THOMAS HENRY LANE (1815–1900) began his career as a portrait painter in Philadelphia during the early 1840's; he later became a magazine publisher in New York City, issuing the *Aristidean* (1845) for his friend Thomas Dunn English. By late November 1845 Lane reached an understanding with Poe to publish the financially floundering *Broadway Journal*; they signed a contract on 3 December. According to English, Lane quickly discovered the extent of his partner's drinking problem and consequently made the decision to cease publication with the 3 January 1846 number.

JOHN HAZELHURST BONEVAL LATROBE (1803–1891), Baltimore lawyer and inventor, was one of the three judges who selected Poe's "MS. Found in a Bottle" as the prize story of the *Saturday Visiter* in October 1833.

ISAAC LEA (1792–1886), Philadelphia publisher and naturalist, was a partner in Carey & Lea, later Lea & Blanchard. In his maturity he devoted an increasing amount of time to his scientific studies and writings, which brought him his greatest renown; Poe acknowledged Lea's "private assistance" in the preface to *The Conchologist's First Book* (1839).

ZACCHEUS COLLINS LEE (1805–1859), a classmate of Poe at the University of Virginia, studied law under William Wirt and became an attorney in Baltimore. He attended Poe's funeral.

SARAH ANNA LEWIS (1824–1880), an ambitious but mediocre poetess, resided at 125 Dean Street, Brooklyn, with her husband, the attorney SYLVANUS D. LEWIS (died 1882). The couple probably made Poe's acquaintance sometime in 1846; around January 1847 they became frequent visitors to his cottage at Fordham. Although Poe lauded Mrs. Lewis' verses in several reviews published in 1848 and 1849, his remarks may be attributed to his gratitude for the favors and financial assistance he had received from her and her husband, rather than to any deep belief in her genius. After Poe's death his mother-in-law Mrs. Clemm occasionally stayed at the Lewis home; the couple were divorced in 1858. Mrs. Lewis spent her last years in London, where she attempted to convince the biographer John Henry Ingram of her importance in Poe's life.

GEORGE LIPPARD (1822–1854), Philadelphia novelist, editor, and social reformer, was Poe's constant admirer. They probably became acquainted in early 1842, when Lippard was an apprentice journalist on John S. Du Solle's paper, the *Spirit of the Times*. In 1843 and 1844 Lippard edited the *Citizen Soldier*; to this weekly he contributed "The Spermaceti Papers," satires aimed at the publisher George R. Graham and his associates. When Poe stopped in Philadelphia in July 1849, Lippard collected the money which enabled him to continue his trip to Richmond. He wrote a compassionate obituary of Poe for the *Quaker City*, 20 October 1849.

JANE ERMINA LOCKE (1805–1859), poetess, was born Ermina Starkweather in Worthington, Massachusetts, on 25 April 1805. In 1829 she married John G. Locke, a Boston attorney; the couple settled in Lowell, Massachusetts. In late December 1846 Mrs. Locke composed "An Invocation for Suffering Genius," a poem inspired by newspaper reports of Poe's illness and poverty; on 21 February 1847 she initiated a correspondence by sending him an expression of admiration and sympathy. Poe, who hoped to remarry after his wife's death, wishfully assumed that Mrs. Locke was a young widow. When she visited him at Fordham in June 1848, he finally learned that his correspondent was a middle-aged housewife with five children. Mrs. Locke arranged for Poe to lecture in Lowell on 10 July; while there he stayed at her residence, "Wamesit Cottage." When he returned to Lowell in late October, he permanently alienated her by the attentions he paid to her young neighbor, Annie Richmond.

JOSEPH LORENZO LOCKE (1808–1864), soldier, engineer, and journalist, was a major in the Confederate Army when he died on 5 October 1864. From 1829 to 1831 Locke, then a lieutenant, had been an assistant instructor of infantry tactics at West Point; Poe lampooned him in "Lines on Joe Locke."

RICHARD ADAMS LOCKE (1800–1871), British-born journalist in New York City, wrote a famous "Moon-Hoax" serialized in the *Sun* in August 1835: it announced the telescopic discovery of men and animals living on the moon. Poe discussed Locke and his hoax in "The Literati" (*Godey's* for October 1846).

JOHN LOFLAND, M.D. (1798–1849), eccentric poetaster, was born in Milford, Delaware, which he commemorated with his pseudonym "The Milford Bard." In the early 1830's Lofland lived in Baltimore, where he reputedly made Poe's acquaintance.

HENRY WADSWORTH LONGFELLOW (1807–1882) was the most popular American poet of the 1840's; Poe frequently commented on his writings, criticizing him for didacticism, a lack of constructive ability, and an imitativeness bordering on plagiarism. While Poe's censures were often unwarranted, his severity paradoxically grew out of a tendency to overrate Longfellow—to regard him as a creative genius who neglected to achieve his potential. Margaret Fuller may have been closer to the truth when she characterized Longfellow as a learned but derivative writer of intermediate powers, naturally indebted to previous literature (New York *Daily Tribune*, 10 December 1845).

WILLIAM WILBERFORCE LORD (1819–1907), clergyman and poet, published a volume of verse which Poe savagely reviewed in the *Broadway Journal* for 24 May 1845.

JOHN LOUD, Philadelphia piano manufacturer, called on Poe in Richmond in August 1849, offering him $100 to edit a volume of poems by his wife MARGUERITE ST. LEON LOUD (ca. 1800–1889).

Poe had previously praised Mrs. Loud in his "Autography" (*Graham's* for December 1841).

JAMES RUSSELL LOWELL (1819–1891), Massachusetts poet, editor, and critic, engaged Poe as a regular contributor to his short-lived Boston monthly, the *Pioneer* (January–March 1843). They conducted a cordial correspondence from 16 November 1842 until 12 December 1844. Although Lowell wrote a laudatory sketch of Poe for the February 1845 *Graham's*, their friendship ended soon after its publication. Poe's critical onslaughts on Longfellow, appearing in the *Broadway Journal* from 8 March until 5 April, struck Lowell as excessive and unfair. In late May he called on Poe in New York; their first and only meeting proved mutually disappointing, Poe having a hangover. In *A Fable for Critics* (1848) Lowell again evaluated Poe: "Three-fifths of him genius and two-fifths sheer fudge." Poe condemned the book in the March 1849 *Southern Literary Messenger*.

ANNE CHARLOTTE LYNCH (1815–1891), schoolteacher and poetess, entertained the New York literati at her celebrated soirees, held on Saturdays at her residence, 116 Waverley Place. A strict adherent to social propriety, she removed Poe's name from her guest list early in 1846, after the controversy over his handling of Elizabeth F. Ellet's letters. Miss Lynch frequently corresponded with Sarah Helen Whitman, to whom she provided unfavorable reports on Poe's character. In 1855 she married Vincenzo Botta (1818–1894), Professor of Italian in the New York University.

JOHN COLLINS McCABE (1810–1875), Richmond clergyman, collected his early verse and fiction in a volume entitled *Scraps* (1835); he frequently contributed to the *Southern Literary Messenger*. Although Poe diplomatically declined "The Consumptive Girl" in a 3 March 1836 letter, he admitted two other McCabe poems during his editorship (*Messenger* for July and September 1836).

BIOGRAPHICAL NOTES

MARIA JANE McINTOSH (1803–1878), Georgia-born authoress, settled in New York City in 1835; she wrote stories for children under the pseudonym "Aunt Kitty." In late May 1848 she made Poe's acquaintance at a social gathering in Fordham; in June she visited Providence, Rhode Island, where she casually informed Mrs. Whitman of Poe's interest in her. On 15 September Miss McIntosh gave him a letter of introduction to the Providence poetess, thus facilitating their first meeting.

JOHN NELSON McJILTON (1805–1875), Baltimore author and clergyman, contributed to the *Southern Literary Messenger* during Poe's editorship.

MORTON McMICHAEL (1807–1879), Philadelphia journalist and politician, favorably reviewed Poe's *Tales of the Grotesque and Arabesque* in the January 1840 *Godey's*.

WILLIAM MACKENZIE (1775–1829), Secretary of the Marine Insurance Company of Richmond, and his wife JANE SCOTT MACKENZIE (1783–1865) adopted Poe's sister Rosalie. The couple had ten children of their own, four of whom died in early childhood: John (born and died 1803), John Hamilton (born 1806), Mary Gallego (1811–1844), William Leslie (1813–1834), Jane Hancock (1815–1821), Joseph Gallego (1816–1821), Elizabeth Gray (1818–1821), Thomas Gilliat (1821–1867), Richard Neil or Neal (1823–1896), and Martha H. Gilliat (1826–1890). Poe and Rosalie were especially close to JOHN HAMILTON MACKENZIE, who married Louisa Lanier of Petersburg, Virginia, on 9 October 1827. John became Rosalie's chief guardian after the death of William Mackenzie; in later life he related his memories of Poe to Mrs. Susan Archer Weiss (formerly Miss Talley), who incorporated them in her *Home Life of Poe* (1907). MISS JANE MACKENZIE, William's unmarried sister, operated a Richmond girls' school which Rosalie attended, as did Elizabeth and Jane Ellis, the daughters of Charles Ellis. Michael B. Poitiaux taught music at this fashionable and expensive boarding institution.

When Poe visited Richmond in 1848 and 1849, he frequently called at "Duncan Lodge," the large house on the city's outskirts that Jane Scott Mackenzie built for her family in 1843.

CORNELIUS MATHEWS (1817–1889), New York City author, was best known as an advocate: he vigorously pleaded for an international copyright and unceasingly expounded the concept of an indigenous American literature freed from subservience to European models. His contemporaries often regarded him with amusement, because his own literary performances fell far short of his pronouncements. Mathews' close friend Evert A. Duyckinck, with whom he edited the monthly *Arcturus* (1840–1842), seems to have been alone in accepting him as a genius. In the February 1842 *Graham's* Poe scoffed at Mathews' pretentious epic *Wakondah*; during his subsequent residence in New York he found it expedient to praise Mathews, being indebted both to him and to Duyckinck.

JAMES HENRY MILLER (1788–1853), physician, founded the Washington Medical College in Baltimore. In October 1833 Dr. Miller served as one of the three judges who selected "MS. Found in a Bottle" as the prize story of the *Saturday Visiter*; he subsequently corresponded with Poe.

BENJAMIN BLAKE MINOR (1818–1905) edited and published the *Southern Literary Messenger* from August 1843 until October 1847. In 1845 Poe sent him a revised copy of "The Raven" (March number) as well as two short reviews (May number). Minor's history of the magazine appeared in 1905.

LUCIAN MINOR (1802–1858), lawyer, teacher, and temperance advocate, was the commonwealth attorney for Louisa County, Virginia. In February and March 1835 his friend Thomas Willis White urged him to become editor of the *Southern Literary Messenger*; Minor declined, but he remained one of White's faithful contributors and supporters.

JOHN KEARSLEY MITCHELL (1793–1858), Virginia-born doctor of medicine, was both friend and physician to the Poe family when they lived in Philadelphia. SILAS WEIR MITCHELL (1829–1914), the novelist, recalled seeing Poe in his father's office.

GEORGE POPE MORRIS (1802–1864), editor and poet, conducted the *New-York Mirror*, an influential literary weekly which ran from 1823 until 1842. On 8 April 1843 he revived the magazine as the *New Mirror*, with his friend Nathaniel P. Willis as co-editor. On 7 October 1844 the *Mirror* became a daily paper (*Evening Mirror*) with a weekly edition, thus obtaining the lower postage rates charged for newspapers. Poe was employed as a staff writer from October 1844 until February 1845. Morris and Willis withdrew from the *Mirror* on 27 December 1845, leaving it in the hands of Hiram Fuller. On 14 February 1846 Morris began a new weekly, the *National Press: A Journal for Home*; Willis joined him as co-editor on 21 November, the paper's name being changed to *Home Journal* at this time. Morris bore the title "General" by virtue of his association with the New York state militia; he was one of Poe's constant friends and admirers.

ROBERT MORRIS (ca. 1809–1874), Philadelphia journalist, poet, and banker, edited the *Pennsylvania Inquirer*, a daily newspaper. Poe praised Morris in "Autography" (*Graham's* for December 1841) and in his lecture on "American Poetry" (21 November 1843 and subsequent dates).

VALENTINE MOTT (1785–1865), Professor of Surgery at the New York University, examined Poe around March 1847. He reputedly confirmed the diagnosis of "brain lesion" made by Marie Louise Shew.

ANNA CORA MOWATT (1819–1870), actress and author, wrote the popular comedy *Fashion*, which opened at New York's Park Theatre on 26 March 1845. Poe reviewed the play at length in the *Broadway Journal* for 29 March and 5 April.

WILLIAM AUGUSTUS MUHLENBERG (1796–1877), Episcopal clergyman, was rector of New York's Church of the Holy Communion, Sixth Avenue and Twentieth Street. Poe attended a midnight service there on Christmas Eve 1847.

JAMES EDWARD MURDOCH (1811–1893), actor and elocutionist, recited "The Raven" from Poe's manuscript in the *Broadway Journal* office, early in February 1845.

JOHN NEAL (1793–1876), lawyer, novelist, and editor, spent most of his long career in his native city, Portland, Maine. Neal was the first American critic to recognize Poe's merits; in the September and December 1829 numbers of the *Yankee*, he printed excerpts from "Fairyland," "Al Aaraaf," and "Tamerlane," predicting a brilliant future for the young poet.

JOSEPH CLAY NEAL (1807–1847), Philadelphia journalist, won popularity with his humorous *Charcoal Sketches* (1838). He edited first the *Pennsylvanian*, a daily newspaper, and later the *Saturday Gazette*, a weekly.

MORDECAI MANUEL NOAH (1785–1851), a prominent figure in New York's Jewish community, edited several newspapers, among them the *Evening Star* and the *Sunday Times and Messenger*. Noah knew Poe well, as demonstrated by his testimony in Poe's libel suit against Hiram Fuller's *Evening Mirror* (17 February 1847); however, there is no evidence that Poe joined Noah "as subeditor" on the *Sunday Times* in 1844, a statement made by Thomas Ollive Mabbott in his 1969 edition of the *Poems* (p. 554). Mabbott's conclusion resulted from his mistaken attribution to Noah of an unsigned reminiscence in the January 1868 *Northern Monthly Magazine* (pp. 234–42); the author was actually Thomas C. Clarke; and the unnamed paper in question, his *Saturday Museum*.

LAUGHTON OSBORN (ca. 1809–1878), an eccentric New Yorker from a wealthy family, wrote many books, usually publishing them anonymously and at his own expense. Poe condemned Osborn's novel *Confessions of a Poet* (1835) in the April 1835 *Southern Literary Messenger*. They knew each other socially during Poe's later residence in New York; but Osborn was alienated when he discovered Poe's unflattering opinion of his satiric poem *The Vision of Rubeta* (1838), expressed in an unsigned article in the 15 March 1845 *Broadway Journal*.

FRANCES SARGENT OSGOOD (1811-1850), Massachusetts poetess, was the wife of the painter SAMUEL STILLMAN OS-GOOD (1808-1885), whom she married on 7 October 1835. They had three children, all girls, who were born in 1836, 1839, and 1846 respectively. During the early 1840's the family settled in New York City. Poe praised Mrs. Osgood's poetry in his 28 February 1845 lecture; he was introduced to her several days later. Although Poe and Mrs. Osgood addressed love poems to each other in the *Broadway Journal* and other periodicals, there is no evidence that their relationship was other than platonic. The kind of openness which characterized this romance has never been typical of adulterous liaisons, least of all in Victorian America. Amusing, charitable, and unpretentious, Mrs. Osgood was the only bluestocking whom Poe found totally congenial; she became a frequent visitor to his home and a close friend of his wife Virginia. She never saw him after the early 1846 scandal involving Elizabeth F. Ellet's letters, but she remained his steadfast admirer and defender. Shortly before her death from tuberculosis on 12 May 1850, Mrs. Osgood wrote a sympathetic reminiscence of Poe; Rufus W. Griswold inserted it in his "Memoir" (1850).

JOHN LOUIS O'SULLIVAN (1813-1895), journalist and diplomat, edited the *Democratic Review*, a political monthly begun in Washington in 1837 and transferred to New York City in 1841. O'Sullivan did much to encourage American literature, publishing contributions by Hawthorne, Poe, Walt Whitman, and other serious writers.

JAMES FREDERICK OTIS (1808-1867), Massachusetts-born journalist, was employed on the Washington *Daily National Intelligencer* in the mid-1830's; he frequently contributed to the early volumes of the *Southern Literary Messenger*. On 11 June 1836 Otis sent Poe a letter with a dozen autographs fastened to the margins: six of these were reproduced in the second installment of "Autography" (August *Messenger*), and still another as well as Otis' own closing signature were used in the December 1841 installment in *Graham's*.

WILLIAM JEWETT PABODIE (ca. 1815-1870), a native of Providence, Rhode Island, was admitted to the bar in 1837; having independent means, he soon abandoned the practice of law for the life of a gentleman litterateur. Several of his verses were anthologized in Rufus W. Griswold's *The Poets and Poetry of America* (1842). A friend and neighbor of Sarah Helen Whitman, Pabodie first met Poe at her home in the autumn of 1848. While he strenuously opposed Mrs. Whitman's ensuing engagement, he admired Poe as an author and treated him with great courtesy.

EDWARD HORTON NORTON PATTERSON (born 1828) was the junior editor of the *Oquawka Spectator,* a weekly newspaper in Oquawka, Illinois, owned and edited by his father John B. Patterson. On his twenty-first birthday, 27 January 1849, the younger Patterson was given control of the *Spectator*'s printing shop; he apparently came into a substantial inheritance at the same time. A few weeks before, on 18 December 1848, he had written Poe, offering to publish a national magazine with Poe as sole editor. After some hesitation Poe accepted this proposal, only stipulating that the publication be a "five-dollar magazine"— that is, a literary monthly designed for a sophisticated audience. In June 1849 Patterson sent him $50 to pay his travel expenses to Saint Louis. Their planned meeting there was delayed by Poe's drinking bout in Philadelphia and by his courtship of Elmira Shelton in Richmond, and then prevented altogether by his 7 October death in Baltimore. In 1859 Patterson emigrated to Colorado, where he became a prominent journalist.

SAMUEL DEWEES PATTERSON (died 1860), Philadelphia publisher and politician, became the principal proprietor of the *Saturday Evening Post*, George R. Graham's weekly, in March 1843. In July 1848 Patterson also acquired the controlling interest in *Graham's Magazine*; he published it until March 1850, when Graham temporarily resumed the proprietorship of the monthly he had founded.

JAMES KIRKE PAULDING (1778–1860), New York author, collaborated with his friend Washington Irving in writing and publishing the humorous periodical *Salmagundi* (1807–1808). Following a visit to Virginia in 1816, Paulding depicted the people and customs he had encountered in his gossipy *Letters from the South* (2 vols., 1817). In the summer of 1834 Paulding wrote Thomas Willis White to announce his support for the *Southern Literary Messenger*; he soon took an active interest in Poe's career. More sympathetic to the South than most Northern writers, Paulding defended its "peculiar institution" in his *Slavery in the United States* (1836); the favorable notice of this book in the April 1836 *Messenger* has often been ascribed to Poe, but the reviewer was Beverley Tucker. From July 1838 until March 1841 Paulding served as Secretary of the Navy, under President Van Buren.

JAMES PEDDER (1775–1859), English-born authority on agriculture and writer of children's books, emigrated to Philadelphia in 1832. Pedder seems to have aided Poe during his poverty-stricken early years in this city (ca. 1838–1839), but little is known of their relationship. Poe presented an inscribed copy of his *Tales of the Grotesque and Arabesque* to Pedder's daughters, ANNA and BESSIE PEDDER.

CHARLES JACOBS PETERSON (1819–1887), Philadelphia publisher, was George R. Graham's junior partner on the *Casket*, the *Saturday Evening Post*, and *Graham's*

Magazine. In December 1841 Peterson issued the first number of his own *Lady's World of Fashion* (dated January 1842); he subsequently withdrew from Graham's enterprises to devote himself to this flourishing monthly, which came to be known simply as *Peterson's Magazine* (1842–1898).

EDWARD COOTE PINKNEY (1802–1828), Baltimore poet, probably knew Poe's brother Henry. Poe greatly admired Pinkney's lyric "A Health," an apostrophe to a woman beginning "I fill this cup to one made up / Of loveliness alone."

DAVID POE, SR. (1742?–1816), Edgar's grandfather, was born in Ireland, the first child issuing from the September 1741 marriage of John Poe and Jane McBride. The family emigrated to Pennsylvania around 1748; they later moved to Cecil County, Maryland, and then settled in Baltimore, where John Poe died in 1756, and his wife in 1802. In the 1770's David Poe, Sr., operated a shop in Market Street, Baltimore, manufacturing spinning wheels and clock wheels. He married ELIZABETH CAIRNES (1756–1835), who had been born of Irish ancestry in Lancaster County, Pennsylvania. They had seven children: John Hancock (born 1776), William (born 1780), George Washington (born 1782), David, Jr. (1784–1811?), Samuel (born 1787), Maria (1790–1871), and Elizabeth (1792–1822). During the Revolutionary War David Poe, Sr., devoted himself to the cause of American independence. On 17 September 1779 he was commissioned Assistant Deputy Quartermaster General for Baltimore, with the rank of major; in 1780 he used his own funds to purchase supplies for the patriot forces. His services won him the friendship of Lafayette; in later years his fellow citizens referred to him as "General." After his death on 17 October 1816, his widow Elizabeth subsisted on an annuity of $240 granted her by the Maryland state government; for the last eight years of her life she was a bedridden paralytic, residing with her daughter Maria (Mrs. Clemm).

DAVID POE, JR., Edgar's father, was born

in Baltimore on 18 July 1784. Against the wishes of his family he abandoned the study of law to pursue a short-lived career as an actor, then an economically precarious and socially disreputable profession. He made his stage debut in Charleston, South Carolina, on 1 December 1803, at age nineteen. Early in April 1806 he married the English-born actress MRS. ELIZABETH ARNOLD HOPKINS (1787?–1811) in Richmond. Elizabeth Arnold had been brought to the United States by her mother, also an actress; they arrived in Boston on 3 January 1796. Elizabeth made her debut on the American stage later that year, at age nine. In the summer of 1802 she married the actor Charles Hopkins, who died on 26 October 1805. When she married David Poe, Jr., in the following spring, they were both members of Green's Virginia Company, then playing at the Richmond Theatre. In succeeding years the couple frequently appeared on the stage in Boston, New York, and Philadelphia. Of their three children, Henry and Edgar were born in Boston, on 30 January 1807 and 19 January 1809 respectively; Rosalie seems to have been born in Norfolk, Virginia, on 20 December 1810. Newspaper reports and reminiscences of contemporary observers establish that Mrs. Poe was a talented and popular actress; these same documents depict her husband as a hot-tempered, mediocre performer, occasionally hinting that he was given to excessive drinking. David Poe, Jr., made his last known stage appearance on 18 October 1809, in New York; sometime before 26 July 1811 he left his wife and children. Elizabeth Arnold Poe died in Richmond on 8 December 1811, after a lingering illness. According to tradition, her husband died several days later; the date and place of his death have never been documented.

GEORGE POE, SR. (1744–1823), born in Ireland, was the brother of Edgar's grandfather David Poe, Sr. Around 1774 he married Catherine Dawson (1742–1806) of Cecil County, Maryland; the couple settled in Baltimore, where all their children seem to have been born: Jacob (1775–1860),

George, Jr. (1778–1864), Harriet (1785–1815), and Stephen (died in infancy). Harriet became the first wife of William Clemm, Jr., who later married Maria Poe (Edgar's aunt). Jacob became a farmer, first in Baltimore County and after 1817 at Elmwood, Frederick County, Maryland. On 4 January 1803 he married Bridget Kennedy (1775–1844), an Irish emigrant; they had five children who lived to adulthood: George (1807–1879), the twins Amelia (1809–1888) and Neilson (1809–1884), James Mosher (1812–1885), and Harriet Clemm (1817–1878).

GEORGE POE, JR., was born in Baltimore on 14 November 1778. After an early career as a ship's officer, he became a well-to-do banker, first in Pittsburgh, Pennsylvania, and then in Mobile, Alabama; he finally settled in Georgetown in the District of Columbia, where he died on 21 July 1864. His prosperity did not go unnoticed by his impecunious relatives. A few days before 6 March 1809 he rejected a tactless request for money from his first cousin David Poe, Jr., Edgar's father. On 12 February 1836 he sent Edgar $100, intended to assist Mrs. Clemm in opening a Richmond boardinghouse; but he apparently declined the subsequent solicitations he received from this source. George Poe, Jr., married Anna Maria Potts, a member of a prominent Pennsylvania family, in December 1808. One of their six children, GEORGE W. POE, corresponded with Edgar in 1839.

HENRY POE (1807–1831), christened "William Henry Leonard," was Edgar's brother. As an infant Henry was left in the care of his Baltimore grandparents, David Poe, Sr., and Elizabeth Cairnes Poe; they continued to raise him after his mother's death. In the early 1820's Henry corresponded with Edgar, then in John Allan's custody; and he apparently paid at least one visit to Richmond. When he again went to this city in the summer of 1825, he accompanied his brother to the home of Elmira Royster (later Mrs. Shelton). In the next year or two Henry made one or more sea voyages; in February 1827 he visited Montevideo, South America, aboard the American frigate *Macedonian*. Shortly afterwards he returned to Baltimore; here he contributed sentimental verses and an account of Montevideo to the *North American*, an obscure weekly which ran from 19 May to 24 November 1827. The 15 September and 20 October issues contained brief excerpts from *Tamerlane and Other Poems* signed with Henry's initials ("W. H. P."); no doubt his brother Edgar had sent him a copy. In the late 1820's Henry and his grandmother took up residence with his aunt Maria Clemm. Edgar arrived in Baltimore early in May 1829; on 10 August he wrote John Allan that Henry was "entirely given up to drink & unable to help himself." Henry died on 1 August 1831, possibly from tuberculosis. A slender young man with dark eyes, he seems to have shared Edgar's inclinations toward dreamy romanticism and debilitating melancholy, while lacking this sibling's enthusiastic vigor and compelling genius.

NEILSON POE (1809–1884) was Edgar's second cousin, being the grandson of George Poe, Sr., and the son of Jacob Poe. Neilson joined the staff of William Gwynn's *Baltimore Gazette and Daily Advertiser* at age eighteen, beginning a three-year apprenticeship as a journalist. He almost certainly made Edgar's acquaintance shortly after this Richmond cousin arrived in Baltimore in 1829; their subsequent relations seem to have been characterized by civility and suspicion. In 1830 Neilson became owner and editor of the *Frederick Examiner*, a semiweekly newspaper in Frederick, Maryland; on 6 May 1831 Edgar wrote William Gwynn to apply for the *Gazette* post his cousin had vacated. In 1834 Neilson acquired the *Baltimore Chronicle*, an influential Whig daily; in the following year he offered to assume the guardianship of Mrs. Clemm's young daughter Virginia, a proposal which Edgar strenuously opposed. In the summer of 1838, after Edgar had taken up residence in Philadelphia, he solicited financial assistance from Neilson, who did not oblige him. Neilson's own difficulties

had placed him deeply in debt, eventually forcing him to sell the *Chronicle* on 2 December 1839. In 1840 he commenced the practice of law; he remained in the legal profession for the rest of his life. On 7 October 1849 Neilson made arrangements for Edgar's funeral; however indifferent he may have formerly been to his cousin's literary achievements, he had no qualms about sharing his posthumous fame. On 17 November 1875 he eulogized Edgar during the elaborate ceremonies dedicating his Baltimore monument. In 1878 Neilson was appointed Chief Judge of the Orphans' Court of Baltimore, a position he held until two months before his 3 January 1884 death. On 30 November 1831 Neilson had married his first cousin JOSEPHINE EMILY CLEMM (1808–1889), the daughter of William Clemm, Jr., by his first wife Harriet Poe, and thus the half sister of Edgar's wife Virginia. Seven children from this union were living at the time of Neilson's death, two daughters and five sons. One daughter MISS AMELIA FITZGERALD POE (1833?–1913) frequently corresponded with Edgar's biographers John Henry Ingram and George E. Woodberry.

ROSALIE POE (1810–1874), Edgar's sister, was adopted by William Mackenzie and his wife after the 8 December 1811 death of Elizabeth Arnold Poe. At her baptism on 3 September 1812, Rosalie was given the middle name "Mackenzie"; she remained with this prominent Richmond family for over half a century. In his will Joseph Gallego, the wealthy flour miller who died in 1818, left William Mackenzie $2,000 earmarked "for the benefit of Rosalie Poe"; no doubt Gallego felt especial compassion for this orphaned child of players, since his own wife had perished in the 26 December 1811 fire which destroyed the Richmond Theatre. Rosalie resembled her brother Edgar in physiognomy, having a broad pale forehead; and she shared his extreme susceptibility to alcohol, being adversely affected by even a glass of wine. Unlike her brother she was a simple, unsophisticated person of barely average intelligence. In childhood she attended the girls' school operated by

Miss Jane Mackenzie, William's sister; as an adult she taught penmanship at the school. Rosalie occasionally corresponded with Edgar when he resided in Philadelphia and New York, but neither her letters nor his have survived. Shortly before 1 April 1841 she visited him in Philadelphia, being chaperoned on the journey by her foster brother John Mackenzie. Her reputed visits to New York and Fordham, mentioned in some sources, have never been documented; but she was often in Edgar's company when he came to Richmond in 1848 and 1849. The Mackenzie family's wealth vanished with the collapse of the Confederacy in 1865; Rosalie subsequently supported herself by selling photographic likenesses of her brother in the streets of Richmond and Baltimore. In 1870 she gained admission to the Epiphany Church Home in Washington, an Episcopalian refuge for the indigent; she died in this institution on 22 July 1874.

WILLIAM POE (1755–1804) was the youngest brother of Edgar's grandfather David Poe, Sr. He almost certainly passed his childhood and youth in Baltimore; around 1789 or 1790 he emigrated to Georgia. He married Frances Winslow (died 1802), who bore him several sons. WASHINGTON (1800–1876) was the most prominent: a lawyer, he settled in Macon, Georgia, in 1825, later serving as the city's mayor. His brothers ROBERT FORSYTH (died 1854) and WILLIAM (born 1802) became bankers in Augusta, Georgia. The younger William corresponded occasionally with Edgar and Mrs. Clemm.

MICHAEL BENOÎT POITIAUX (1771–1854), a native of Brussels, came to Richmond in 1798 and prospered as a merchant until the panic of 1819. He then turned to teaching painting, music, and French in private classes as well as in the city's female academies. A talented violinist, Poitiaux performed in concerts held in the home of William Wirt. In 1804 he married Jane Charlton Russell; they had seven children. One daughter CATHERINE ELIZABETH POITIAUX was Frances Allan's godchild

and Poe's childhood playmate. In August 1849 Poe called on the Poitiauxs, then living in the city's "French Garden" section; in August 1852 Catherine published "Lines on the Death of Edgar A. Poe," prefacing her poem with a reminiscence of his visit to her family three years before.

ISRAEL POST (died 1849), New York City bookseller, founded the *Columbian Lady's and Gentleman's Magazine* in January 1844; he published it through 1846. In July 1847 Post began the *Union Magazine*, but he sold it to James L. DeGraw at the end of the year. His final venture was the *American Metropolitan Magazine*, which expired after only two numbers (January and February 1849).

JAMES PATTON PRESTON (1774–1843), soldier and public official, was a friend of Thomas Jefferson and a cousin of Senator William C. Preston of South Carolina; he served as Governor of Virginia (1816–1819) and Postmaster of Richmond (1824–1837). On 13 May 1829 Colonel Preston wrote Secretary of War John H. Eaton to recommend Poe for West Point, stating that he had seen evidence of "genius and talents" in the applicant's "own productions." He may have been thinking of a portfolio of Poe's adolescent poems which his son JOHN T. L. PRESTON (died 1890) brought home for his mother's appraisal. The younger Preston sat next to Poe at Joseph H. Clarke's school around 1822; in later life he became Professor of Latin at the Virginia Military Institute.

GEORGE PALMER PUTNAM (1814–1872), publisher, was John Wiley's partner in the New York firm of Wiley and Putnam. Around September 1838 Putnam, who had just opened a branch office in London, made the decision to reprint Poe's *The Narrative of Arthur Gordon Pym* in England, the novel having been issued by Harper & Brothers in New York on 30 July. After returning to the United States Putnam established an independent firm which bore his name; in 1848 he published Poe's *Eu-*

reka (ca. 11 July) and James Russell Lowell's *A Fable for Critics* (25 October).

MAYNE REID (1818–1883), Irish-born author of adventure novels, traveled widely throughout the United States; early in 1843 he settled temporarily in Philadelphia, where he made Poe's acquaintance. He published his recollections of Poe's Spring Garden home in the April 1869 issue of his *Onward*, a New York magazine for boys.

JEREMIAH N. REYNOLDS (1799–1858), American explorer, did much to create the public interest in Antarctic regions which Poe hoped to exploit with his concluding chapters of *The Narrative of Arthur Gordon Pym*. Reynolds' *Address on the Subject of a Surveying and Exploring Expedition to the Pacific Ocean and South Seas* (1836) provided material for this novel, as did his *Voyage of the U.S. Frigate Potomac* (1835). Poe favorably reviewed the *Address* in the January 1837 *Southern Literary Messenger*, implying that he had met and conversed with its author.

ANNIE RICHMOND (1820–1898), born Nancy Locke Heywood, was the wife of CHARLES B. RICHMOND (died 1873), a successful paper manufacturer in Lowell, Massachusetts. Poe met Annie at the time of his 10 July 1848 lecture in Lowell; they experienced a strong mutual attraction which rapidly developed into an intense but platonic romance. At the end of the summer Annie visited the Poe cottage at Fordham, beginning an affectionate, lasting friendship with his mother-in-law Maria Clemm. Poe, in turn, became an object of admiration and wonder for Annie's younger siblings, Bardwell and Sarah Heywood. In late October he returned to Lowell; after stopping briefly at the home of Jane Ermina Locke, he took lodging in the Richmond residence on Ames Street. At this time he also visited the Heywood family farm in nearby Westford. In early 1849 Poe wrote several intimate letters to Annie, explaining the termination of his engagement to Sarah Helen Whitman, but more often describing his current literary work or outlining his

plans for the future. To the *Flag of Our Union*, a Boston weekly, Poe contributed his poem "For Annie," simultaneously arranging for its republication in the more prestigious New York *Home Journal*; it appeared in the 28 April issues of both papers. The *Flag* for 9 June featured his "Landor's Cottage," a prose sketch containing a description of Annie. From late May to early June Poe paid his third and final visit to Lowell, again lodging with the Richmonds. On 10 October, three days after his death, Annie invited Mrs. Clemm to stay in her home, an offer the elderly woman promptly accepted. Mrs. Clemm later moved on to other temporary residences, but Annie continued to correspond. After her husband's death on 25 August 1873, she had her name legally changed to "Annie." In 1876 she began to provide John Henry Ingram with copies of Poe's letters to her; the English biographer soon offended her by publishing them, without her consent and greatly against her wishes. The Richmonds had one child, a daughter "Caddy" (later called "Carrie"); their only grandchild died in 1888 at the age of sixteen. Annie herself died in Lowell on 9 February 1898.

GEORGE ROBERTS (1807–1860) published the Boston *Daily Times* and the weekly *Boston Notion*.

EPES SARGENT (1813–1880), Massachusetts-born author, was associated with several New York journals during the 1840's; Poe included him in his sketches of the city's "Literati." In 1847 Sargent returned to Boston, where he succeeded Cornelia Wells Walter as editor of the *Evening Transcript*.

JOHN SARTAIN (1808–1897), Philadelphia engraver and publisher, furnished numerous steel plates for *Burton's* and *Graham's* during Poe's association with these monthlies. In January 1849 he began to publish the *Union Magazine*, now moved from New York to Philadelphia and rechristened *Sartain's*; he printed Poe's revised "Valentine" for Frances S. Osgood (March 1849), "The Bells" (November and December 1849), "Annabel Lee" (January 1850), and his lecture on "The Poetic Principle" (October 1850). When Poe stopped in Philadelphia early in July 1849, he called on Sartain in a state of delirium brought on by alcohol abuse. Sartain left several accounts of this episode, the most useful being found in his *Reminiscences of a Very Old Man* (1899).

ELMIRA SHELTON (1810–1888), born Sarah Elmira Royster, was the daughter of James H. Royster, a Richmond neighbor of Poe's foster father John Allan. Poe fell in love with Miss Royster in 1825, when he was sixteen. After he entered the University of Virginia on 14 February 1826, he frequently wrote her; but her father felt that the teenagers were too young for marriage and consequently intercepted his letters, thwarting the early romance. In late March 1827 Poe left Richmond for Boston; on 26 May he enlisted in the United States Army. On 6 December 1828, while he was stationed at Fort Moultrie outside Charleston, South Carolina, Elmira married ALEXANDER B. SHELTON (1807–1844), a Richmond businessman. The couple had four children: two (Sarah Elmira and Alexander Barret) died in infancy, but Southall Bohannan and Ann Elizabeth lived to have children of their own. Shelton died on 12 July 1844 at age thirty-seven; in his will he granted his widow control of his substantial estate and all the income from it, but stipulated that she must relinquish not only her executorship but also three-fourths of the income if she remarried. Poe and Mrs. Shelton had seen each other on one or more occasions shortly after his 16 May 1836 marriage to Virginia, when he was employed on the *Southern Literary Messenger*. He returned to Richmond in late July 1848, a widower with hopes of remarrying. Although he renewed his acquaintance with Elmira at this time, he left the city in early September to pursue an ill-fated romance with another widow, Sarah Helen Whitman. Poe arrived again in Richmond on 14 July 1849; within a few days he called on Elmira and proposed marriage. She hesitated for some weeks, no doubt pondering the needs of her two children and the loss of financial security which marriage with Poe would entail. By 22 September she had privately agreed to an engagement, for on this date she wrote a cordial letter introducing herself to Poe's mother-in-law Maria Clemm. Poe left for New York on 27 September, intending to resolve his affairs in the North and then return to Richmond with Mrs. Clemm. Elmira expressed her anguish over his unexpected death in an 11 October letter to Mrs. Clemm; she subsequently maintained a discreet silence regarding her relations with him for twenty-six years. On 19 November 1875 she granted a single interview to Edward V. Valentine, who recorded her spoken reminiscences (transcript now in Valentine Museum). Elmira died in Richmond on 11 February 1888 at age seventy-eight.

MARIE LOUISE SHEW (died 1877) was the daughter of Dr. Lowery Barney, a physician in Henderson, Jefferson County, New York, and the niece of Hiram Barney, a prominent attorney in New York City. A kindly, unsophisticated woman, Mrs. Shew occupied herself as an unpaid nurse and social worker to the poor and suffering. Around November 1846 Mary Gove informed her of the illness of Poe and his wife; she quickly devoted herself to alleviating their miseries, becoming a frequent visitor to their Fordham cottage. As an expression of gratitude Poe addressed several short poems to Mrs. Shew, one of which ("The Beloved Physician") she apparently destroyed to prevent its publication. Around June 1848 she withdrew from intimacy with Poe, the theology student John Henry Hopkins, Jr., having persuaded her that the forthcoming *Eureka* advocated dangerous heresies and that a continued association with its author would be detrimental to her spiritual welfare. Mrs. Shew divorced her first husband, the water-cure physician Joel Shew (1816–1855); in November 1850 she married Roland Stebbins Houghton (1824–1876), a Vermont-born physician and author living in New York City.

LYDIA HUNTLEY SIGOURNEY (1791–

1865) of Hartford, Connecticut, constantly produced saccharine, sententious verses for the magazines and newspapers of antebellum America. In the *Southern Literary Messenger* for January 1836, Poe reviewed Mrs. Sigourney's *Zinzendorff, and Other Poems*, graciously hinting that her poetry was imitative and her reputation overblown; in "Autography" he found that she possessed "fine taste, without genius" (*Graham's* for November 1841). When evaluating female authors, he generally modulated his criticisms to comply with the credo that a gentleman never spoke ill of a lady.

WILLIAM GILMORE SIMMS (1806–1870), South Carolina novelist, poet, and journalist, consistently admired Poe's power as an imaginative writer, while condemning the excesses of his literary criticism and his personal behavior. Simms edited several Charleston periodicals, among them the *Magnolia*, in which he noticed Poe's proposed *Stylus* (June 1843), and the *Southern and Western Magazine*, in which he reviewed the Wiley and Putnam edition of his *Tales* (December 1845). To the *Southern Patriot*, a Charleston newspaper, Simms contributed a defense of Poe's poetry reading before the Boston Lyceum (10 November 1845), a review of *The Raven and Other Poems* (2 March 1846), and a description of his physical appearance (20 July 1846). Simms made Poe's acquaintance during one of his frequent visits to New York City, probably in late August or early September 1845.

ELIZABETH OAKES SMITH (1806–1893), Maine-born poetess, figured prominently in the circle of bluestockings who surrounded Poe in New York City; she described him and other literati in her *Autobiography* (abridged version published in 1924). Her husband was the humorist SEBA SMITH (1792–1868), who wrote political satires under the pseudonym "Major Jack Downing."

RICHARD PENN SMITH (1799–1854), Philadelphia attorney and playwright, hosted an 1839 dinner party at which William E. Burton introduced Poe to the city's intelligentsia. His son HORACE WEMYSS SMITH (1825–1891) recalled this event and other less credible occurrences for the journalist Hyman Polock Rosenbach (1858–1892), who then published the reminiscences in the *American* of 26 February 1887.

THOMAS S. SMITH (ca. 1798–1873), Philadelphia lawyer and politician, was appointed that city's Collector of Customs on 10 September 1842. Four times during October and November Poe called on Smith to solicit a position in the Custom House. Smith ignored him, filling all the vacancies with nonentities who were politically reliable. On 3 March 1843 CALVIN BLYTHE (ca. 1792–1849), jurist and soldier, succeeded Smith; the change prompted Poe to make a hasty trip to Washington, with the impractical idea of laying his case personally before President John Tyler.

JOSEPH EVANS SNODGRASS (1813–1880), Virginia-born physician and editor, was a medical student at the University of Maryland in Baltimore during the early 1830's; he almost certainly made Poe's acquaintance at this time. Although Snodgrass received his M.D. degree in 1836, he embarked instead on an editorial career. With Nathan C. Brooks he began the *American Museum* (1838–1839), a Baltimore monthly to which Poe contributed "Ligeia" and other brief works. On 8 November 1841 Snodgrass succeeded John Beauchamp Jones as editor of the *Saturday Visiter*; on 15 January 1842 he became sole proprietor of this Baltimore newspaper, which he issued until April 1847. Poe frequently wrote Snodgrass from Philadelphia, sometimes thanking him for his favorable notices in the *Visiter*, but more often trying to enlist his financial backing for a magazine scheme. On 3 October 1849, when Poe was discovered fatally intoxicated in a Baltimore tavern, he managed to request that Snodgrass be sent for. A staunch temperance advocate, Snodgrass later could not resist the temptation to use his friend's example to demonstrate the evils of drink; his reminiscences of Poe's final hours are nonetheless factual, although characterized by emotive diction. Snodgrass' first account, written for the New York *Woman's Temperance Paper*, was reprinted by that city's *Life Illustrated*, 17 May 1856. He expanded his text for *Beadle's Monthly* of March 1867.

EDWARD VERNON SPARHAWK (1798–1838), Maine-born journalist, fought with DUFF GREEN (1791–1875) in the chambers of the United States Senate on 25 January 1828. At the time of this notorious brawl, Sparhawk was a reporter for the Washington *National Intelligencer*; Green edited and published a rival daily, the *United States Telegraph*. Sparhawk later settled in Richmond; in 1835 he prepared four issues of the *Southern Literary Messenger* (April, May, June, July) for Thomas Willis White. His editorship followed that of James E. Heath and preceded that of Poe; several of his contributions were signed with the pseudonym "Pertinax Placid."

JANE STITH CRAIG STANARD (1793–1824) was the daughter of Adam Craig (1760?–1808), who signed countless legal documents as the longtime clerk of the Richmond Hustings Court and the Henrico County Court. On 13 February 1812 she married ROBERT STANARD (1781–1846), a prominent Richmond attorney who was appointed a judge of the Virginia Supreme Court in 1839. Their son ROBERT CRAIG STANARD (1814–1857) also became a successful lawyer. In the spring of 1823 the boy was enrolled in William Burke's school, where he greatly admired Poe, a new student five years his senior. Young Stanard invited his schoolmate to the family's home on Ninth Street near Franklin, facing Capitol Square. Mrs. Stanard graciously welcomed her son's friend and gave him the words of sympathy and encouragement which were no doubt lacking in John Allan's household. Poe repeatedly sought her company and consolation; he was bereft when she died on 28 April 1824 at age thirty-one, after an illness said to have been accompanied by mental derangement. For months afterward he paid regular visits to her grave in the Shockoe Hill Cemetery. In 1848 he told Sarah Helen Whitman that the memory of Mrs. Stanard provided the inspiration for his 1831 poem "To Helen."

MARY STARR (ca. 1816–1887), the daughter of a Philadelphia engraver, had a brief romance with Poe in Baltimore during the early 1830's. She was then living with her uncle James Devereaux, on Exeter Street near Fayette. Mary subsequently married a New York merchant tailor named Jenning; the couple resided in Jersey City, New Jersey, across the Hudson River from Manhattan. Mary saw Poe on several occasions in later years; on 2 February 1847 she attended the funeral of his wife Virginia. Her reminiscences of him are authentic but exaggerated; they were published by her nephew Augustus Van Cleef in *Harper's* for March 1889.

ANDREW STEVENSON (1774–1857), Richmond soldier and congressman, studied law in the office of Adam Craig. From 1827 until 1834 he was Speaker of the United States House of Representatives; on 6 May 1829 he wrote a brief letter recommending Poe for West Point. Stevenson later served as Minister to Great Britain (1836–1841); one of his subordinates in London was Theodore S. Fay, the author of *Norman Leslie*.

WILLIAM TELFAIR STOCKTON (1812–1869), Philadelphia-born soldier and author, was one of Poe's West Point tentmates in the summer of 1830; he later became an officer in the Confederate Army. Stockton wrote hunting stories and sketches under the pen name "Cor-de-Chasse"; these were collected in a volume entitled *Dog and Gun*.

RICHARD HENRY STODDARD (1825–1903), poet and critic, attempted unsuccessfully to contribute to the *Broadway Journal* in the summer of 1845. He published several accounts of his visits to Poe's office and residence, and of this editor's unceremonious rejection of one of his juvenile poems.

WILLIAM LEETE STONE (1792–1844) edited the New York *Commercial Advertiser*, in which he vigorously denounced Poe's caustic reviews in the *Southern Literary Messenger*. By way of retaliation Poe dissected Stone's novel *Ups and Downs in the Life of a Distressed Gentleman* (*Messenger* for June 1836).

ROBERT MATTHEW SULLY (1803?–1855), Richmond portrait painter, was the son of the English-born actor Matthew Sully, who performed on the stage with Poe's mother. The younger Sully attended Joseph H. Clarke's school, where he possibly made Poe's acquaintance. According to tradition, Sully entertained Poe and his bride Virginia in 1836 and renewed his friendship with Poe in 1849. His uncle THOMAS SULLY (1783–1872), noted Philadelphia artist, painted a small portrait of Poe around 1839.

SUSAN ARCHER TALLEY (1822–1917), Richmond poetess, saw Poe on various occasions during his 1849 visit to that city. Under her married name (Mrs. Weiss), she contributed a perceptive memoir of him to *Scribner's Monthly* for March 1878. Her *Home Life of Poe* (1907) must be used with caution, being fraught with errors, fabrications, and unverifiable statements.

BAYARD TAYLOR (1825–1878), poet and author of travel books, temporarily edited New York's *Union Magazine* during the summer of 1848, while the regular editor (Caroline M. Kirkland) was in Europe.

SYLVANUS THAYER (1785–1872) reorganized the military and academic departments of West Point after he became its Superintendent in 1817, following closely the organization and curriculum of the French École Polytechnique. Poe seems to have admired Colonel Thayer; after leaving the Academy he wrote him to request a letter of introduction.

CALVIN FREDERICK STEPHEN THOMAS (1808–1876), printer, had his office at 70 Washington Street, Boston, when he issued Poe's *Tamerlane and Other* *Poems* (1827); he subsequently settled in Buffalo, New York. From 1846 to 1857 Thomas was part owner and publisher of Buffalo's *Western Literary Messenger*, which had reprinted Poe's "The Oblong Box" (7 September 1844) and "The Raven" (22 February 1845).

CREED THOMAS (1812–1889), Richmond physician, attended William Burke's school with Poe from 1823 until 1825; outside the classroom both boys participated in the Junior Volunteers and the Thespian Society. Dr. Thomas began to practice medicine in 1835.

EDWARD J. THOMAS, New York merchant, viewed Poe as his rival for the affections of Frances S. Osgood. Around June 1845 Thomas repeated to Mrs. Osgood an unfounded rumor that Poe had committed forgery; he tactfully retracted the accusation after Poe threatened to sue him.

FREDERICK WILLIAM THOMAS (1806–1866), novelist and poet, was born in Providence, Rhode Island, but spent his formative years in Charleston, South Carolina, and Baltimore. In 1828, while living in Baltimore, he became intimate with Poe's brother Henry. Around 1831 or 1832 Thomas settled in Cincinnati, where he wrote for the newspapers, practiced law, and dabbled in politics. He made Poe's acquaintance early in May 1840, while visiting Philadelphia; they became close friends and frequent correspondents. During the Presidential election of 1840 Thomas campaigned for William Henry Harrison; he went to Washington for the 4 March 1841 inauguration of Harrison, who died on 4 April and was succeeded two days later by his running mate, John Tyler of Virginia. In June 1841 Thomas obtained a clerkship in the Treasury Department; his example led Poe to dream of a political sinecure. Beginning in May 1842 Thomas sought to procure a position for Poe in the Philadelphia Custom House, relying on the influence of Robert Tyler, the President's son. Thomas visited Philadelphia in late September and assured Poe of the younger Tyler's goodwill. Unfortunately the authority to make the desired appointment did not rest with the administration in Washington, but with the Collector of Customs in Philadelphia. In this case two successive Collectors (Thomas S. Smith and Calvin Blythe) made their own choices for subordinate officeholders, simply ignoring Robert Tyler's repeated recommendations. Poe's March 1843 trip to Washington did not affect the situation, either one way or the other; nor did his abrasive drinking bout there later his cordial relationship with Thomas, who sympathized with his friend's struggle against alcoholism. The two men corresponded during Poe's subsequent residence in New York, but they did not meet again until Poe briefly visited Washington in July 1847. In later life Thomas lived in different parts of the country, finding employment as a professor of English literature, an Episcopalian minister, and a newspaper editor. He left manuscript "Recollections of Edgar A. Poe," which were quoted by James H. Whitty in his 1911 edition of Poe's poems.

JOHN REUBEN THOMPSON (1823–1873), Richmond journalist and poet, became editor and proprietor of the *Southern Literary Messenger* in November 1847, the magazine having been purchased for him by his father, a prosperous merchant. He continued to edit it until May 1860, enhancing its reputation as the leading Southern periodical. Although Thompson saw Poe in 1848 and 1849, his statements regarding him are not always trustworthy, being marred by sensationalism.

CHARLES WEST THOMSON (1798–1879), Philadelphia poet, contributed to *Burton's* and *Graham's* during Poe's association with these monthlies. Poe favorably noticed him in "Autography" (*Graham's* for December 1841).

JOHN TOMLIN (1806–1850), minor author and devout Southron, operated a retail store in Jackson, Tennessee, between 1834 and 1841. On 24 February 1841 he was appointed postmaster of Jackson, an office he held until 23 December 1847. During his tenure Tomlin used his franking privilege to correspond with some forty literary celebrities, including Poe, Dickens, Tennyson, and Longfellow; he published many of the letters he received in his pseudonymous serial "The Autobiography of a Monomaniac" by "Joe Bottom," which appeared in *Holden's Dollar Magazine* between November 1848 and November 1849. Tomlin first wrote Poe on 16 October 1839, forwarding a contribution for *Burton's*. He later enlisted subscribers for Poe's proposed *Penn Magazine* and the *Stylus*; in the autumn of 1845 he became an agent for the *Broadway Journal*.

JOHN KIRK TOWNSEND (1809–1851), Philadelphia ornithologist, held a post at the National Institute in Washington from 1842 until 1845. When Poe went to Washington in March 1843, he carried two letters for Townsend: these probably were related to Thomas C. Clarke's *Saturday Museum*, which was then serializing Townsend's revised *Narrative of a Journey Across the Rocky Mountains* (originally published in 1839).

NATHANIEL BEVERLEY TUCKER (1784–1851), jurist, novelist, and advocate of Southern secession, was the son of St. George Tucker (1752–1827) and the half brother of John Randolph of Roanoke (1773–1833). In 1834 Beverley Tucker (as he was usually called) became Professor of Law at his alma mater, the College of William and Mary; that same year he commenced a correspondence with Thomas Willis White, to whom he frequently offered advice as well as contributions for the *Southern Literary Messenger*. His first novel *The Partisan Leader* (1836), published in Washington by Duff Green, predicted a civil war between North and South. Abel P. Upshur praised the book in the January 1837 *Messenger*, which also carried Poe's favorable review of Tucker's second novel *George Balcombe* (1836). A third and final novel, *Gertrude*, was serialized in the *Messenger* between September 1844 and December 1845.

HENRY THEODORE TUCKERMAN (1813–1871), Boston author, was condemned as "insufferably tedious and dull" in Poe's "Autography" (*Graham's* for December 1841). Tuckerman may have recalled this criticism in late 1842, when, as the new editor of the *Boston Miscellany*, he rejected Poe's story "The Tell-Tale Heart." In 1845 Tuckerman settled in New York City; he was in Poe's company on 10 and 11 July, when they served together as judges of student compositions for the Rutgers Female Institute.

MARTIN FARQUHAR TUPPER (1810–1889), English author, was best known for his *Proverbial Philosophy* (1838), which he often revised and enlarged. He did much to extend Poe's reputation by favorably reviewing his *Tales* (1845) for the London *Literary Gazette* of 31 January 1846. *Littell's Living Age*, a Boston weekly, reprinted the review in its 23 May issue.

JOHN TYLER (1790–1862), Virginia statesman, succeeded to the Presidency on 6 April 1841, two days after the unexpected death of William Henry Harrison; he remained in office until March 1845. ROBERT TYLER (1816–1877), his eldest son and private secretary, was a minor poet who won some critical acclaim with a religious poem, *Ahasuerus*; in the summer of 1841 Robert became intimate with Poe's friend Frederick William Thomas.

ABEL PARKER UPSHUR (1790–1844), Virginia jurist, was a friend of Beverley Tucker and Thomas Willis White. In September 1841 Upshur became Secretary of the Navy; in May 1843 he succeeded Daniel Webster as Secretary of State.

ANN MOORE VALENTINE (1787?–1850) and her sister FRANCES KEELING VALENTINE (1785–1829) were the daughters of John Valentine of Princess Anne County, Virginia, by his marriage to Frances Thorowgood. Orphaned at an early age, the girls were raised in Richmond by the printer John Dixon, Jr., and his wife

Sarah Valentine (their half sister). On 9 February 1803 the *Virginia Gazette* (Richmond) announced the 5 February wedding of John Allan "to the much admired Miss Fanny Valentine." Ann Valentine never married, although she was at one time engaged to Jesse Higginbotham, an Ellis & Allan clerk. In 1803, or shortly thereafter, she became a permanent member of John Allan's household; in 1815 she accompanied the family to Great Britain. Long after the deaths of her sister and brother-in-law, she continued to reside in their imposing home "Moldavia," which she shared with Allan's second wife Louisa G. Patterson. The children of Charles Ellis referred to Ann Valentine as "Aunt Nancy"; Poe often mentioned her in his letters to Allan, addressing her more formally as "Miss Nancy," "Miss Valentine," or "Miss V." She died on 25 January 1850, in her sixty-third year.

EDWARD VIRGINIUS VALENTINE (1838–1930), Richmond sculptor, recalled seeing Poe during his 1849 visit to the city. In the 1870's Valentine forwarded the reminiscences of Elmira Shelton and others to the biographer John Henry Ingram.

HORACE BINNEY WALLACE (1817–1852), well-to-do Philadelphian, contributed articles and stories to *Burton's* and *Graham's* under the pseudonym "William Landor." Poe favorably noticed him in "Autography" (*Graham's* for November 1841).

WILLIAM ROSS WALLACE (1819–1881), Kentucky-born poet, settled in New York City in 1841. He probably made Poe's acquaintance in Philadelphia early in 1842. When Poe visited New York in late June, Wallace insisted that they drink mint juleps together, much to the former's detriment. Poe lauded Wallace in the *Columbia Spy* for 1 June 1844 and in the final installment of "Marginalia" (*Southern Literary Messenger* for September 1849).

ROBERT WALSH (1784–1859), Philadelphia scholar, was Professor of English at the University of Pennsylvania (1818–1828)

BIOGRAPHICAL NOTES

and editor of the *American Quarterly Review* (1827–1837). In May 1829 he gave Poe advice on his unpublished poetry.

CORNELIA WELLS WALTER (1815–1898) became editress of the Boston *Evening Transcript* following the 24 July 1842 death of its first editor, her brother Lynde M. Walter. As a "lady editor" Miss Walter was a great rarity among contemporary journalists, but she could be as combative and vitriolic as any of her masculine compeers. She strenuously objected to Poe's criticisms of Longfellow and other Boston literati; after his 16 October 1845 appearance before the city's Lyceum, she mercilessly ridiculed him in almost every issue, eventually goading him into making an excessive reply in the 22 November *Broadway Journal*. Miss Walter edited the *Transcript* until 2 September 1847, relinquishing her position to marry William B. Richards on 22 September; the couple had five children.

THOMAS WARD (1807–1873), wealthy New Yorker, contributed a series of verse tales to the *Knickerbocker Magazine* under the pseudonym "Flaccus." Poe's flippant treatment of him in "Our Amateur Poets, No. I" (*Graham's* for March 1843) evoked protests from James Kirke Paulding and Lewis Gaylord Clark.

HENRY COOD WATSON (1818–1875), music critic, emigrated to New York City from his native London in 1841. In 1845 he assisted Charles F. Briggs and Poe on the *Broadway Journal*, being announced as music editor in the 22 February issue. His name remained on the masthead through the 18 October issue.

JAMES WATSON WEBB (1802–1884) owned and edited the New York *Morning Courier* from 1827 until 1861. In December 1846 he collected funds for the relief of the Poe family.

AMELIA BALL WELBY (1819–1852), popular Kentucky poetess, published her verses under her first name alone; her contemporaries often referred to her simply as "Amelia." Poe favorably noticed Mrs. Welby in "Marginalia" (*Democratic Review* for December 1844).

WILLIAM WERTENBAKER (1797–1882), student and librarian at the University of Virginia, visited Poe in his dormitory room one evening in December 1826, just before his departure for Richmond. Wertenbaker published his recollections of Poe in the November–December 1868 issue of the *Virginia University Magazine*; these were reprinted in the January 1887 issue. The October 1879 issue carried a brief interview in which Wertenbaker, then "in his eighty-third year," reminisced about the University's early days.

EDWIN PERCY WHIPPLE (1819–1886), Massachusetts essayist and critic, scoffed at Poe's "Autography" in the Boston *Daily Times*, his attack being reprinted in the *Boston Notion* of 18 December 1841.

THOMAS WILLIS WHITE (1788–1843), Richmond printer, began to publish his *Southern Literary Messenger* in August 1834. The son of a tailor, White lacked both formal education and literary sophistication; as a consequence he relied heavily on editorial guidance from such Richmond authors as James E. Heath and Edward V. Sparhawk and on advice from such learned correspondents as Lucian Minor and Beverley Tucker. In August 1835 White employed Poe as his assistant. The younger man soon became the *de facto* editor of the *Messenger* and rapidly transformed it from a regional organ to a nationally respected journal. Like many of Poe's later associates, White admired his talents only to be appalled by his instability, his caustic book reviews, and his excessive drinking. One of Poe's repeated lapses from sobriety brought about his dismissal on 3 January 1837. White resumed control of his magazine; early in 1840 he engaged the Virginia naval officer Matthew Fontaine Maury (1806–1873) as assistant editor. Plagued with overwork, ill health, and financial problems, White eventually suffered a paralytic stroke in September 1842; he died in Richmond on 19 January 1843. From October 1842 until July 1843 Maury edited the *Messenger* with help from White's son-in-law PETER DUDLEY BERNARD (1805?–1889), the Richmond printer who had established the long-running *Southern Planter* in 1841. In August 1843 Benjamin Blake Minor became owner and editor of the *Messenger*; John R. Thompson succeeded him in November 1847. White married MARGARET ANN FERGUSON (1794?–1837) in Gates County, North Carolina, on 12 December 1809; she later opened a millinery shop in Richmond. Her death on 11 December 1837 left him deeply bereaved, as had the death of his only son THOMAS H. WHITE at age nineteen on 7 October 1832. One daughter SARAH ANN WHITE married Bernard in 1833. Another daughter ELIZA WHITE (1812–1888), called "Lizzie," contributed poetry to the *Messenger* and became a close friend of Poe. According to tradition, Poe and Eliza conducted a harmless flirtation shortly after he joined the *Messenger's* staff. She attended his wedding, and sometime in the late 1840's she seems to have visited his cottage at Fordham.

SARAH HELEN WHITMAN (1803–1878), poetess of Providence, Rhode Island, was born on 19 January, the same day as Poe, but six years earlier. Her parents were Nicholas Power (1769–1844), a roving seafarer, and Anna Marsh Power (died 1858); she had an older sister, Rebecca (1800–1825), and a younger, Susan Anna (1813–1877). On 10 July 1828 Sarah Helen Power married John Winslow Whitman (1799–1833), a Boston lawyer who wrote amateurish poetry. After her husband's death on 25 July 1833, Mrs. Whitman returned to the Power family's longtime residence in Providence, at the northwest corner of Benefit and Church (originally 50 Benefit Street, later numbered 76). In the early 1840's she became an avid reader of Poe's writings, which alternately terrified and enthralled her. Beginning in 1845 she began to learn about his literary career and his personal life

through her correspondence with Anne C. Lynch and Frances S. Osgood, two New York bluestockings who had formerly lived in Providence and whom she knew quite well. In January 1848, one year after the death of Poe's wife Virginia, Mrs. Whitman addressed an adulatory poem to him: it was read aloud at Miss Lynch's valentine party on 14 February and then published in the New York *Home Journal* for 18 March. By way of reply Poe sent her a manuscript poem written in her honor, the second "To Helen." On 21 September he presented himself at her home, bearing a letter of introduction. A romance ensued immediately; but Mrs. Whitman resisted Poe's proposal of marriage, later writing him to explain that she was in poor health and financially dependent on her mother. When Poe visited Providence in early November, he called on her in a state of near delirium brought on by an overnight drinking bout. Mrs. Whitman was dismayed to discover her suitor's alcoholism; but paradoxically this revelation led her to agree to marriage, since she felt pity for him and believed that as his wife she could influence him. Their engagement was brief and turbulent, with her friends warning her against him and her mother displaying an almost fanatical opposition to the proposed union. On 23 December, when Poe violated a promise to abstain from alcohol, Mrs. Whitman abruptly cancelled the preparations for their wedding. Although she did not see or write him again, she became his most steadfast defender after his death. In 1860 she published a perceptive interpretation of his personality, *Edgar Poe and His Critics*. Between 1874 and 1878 she corresponded voluminously with his English biographer John Henry Ingram, thus leaving a detailed account of her 1848 romance.

WALT WHITMAN (1819–1892), major American poet, was a relatively obscure journalist in 1845, when he contributed a brief essay to the *Broadway Journal*. He had a single interview with Poe shortly after its publication in the 29 November issue. From March 1846 until January 1848

Whitman edited the Brooklyn *Daily Eagle*.

NATHANIEL PARKER WILLIS (1806–1867), editor, poet, and European correspondent, rejected Poe's "Fairyland," commenting sarcastically on the verses in his *American Monthly Magazine* (Boston) for November 1829. Poe, in turn, satirized Willis' association with British nobility in "Lion-izing," a tale published in the *Southern Literary Messenger* for May 1835. Despite these early exchanges the two men proved compatible when they met each other in New York City in 1844. Willis employed Poe as his assistant on the *Evening Mirror* from October 1844 until February 1845. On 21 November 1846 Willis joined his longtime associate George P. Morris on the *Home Journal*, a weekly newspaper of folio size. As both editors admired Poe, the *Journal* consistently promoted his interests; but it was Willis alone whom Poe approached for special favors, notably the republication of his poems "Ulalume" and "For Annie" (1 January 1848 and 28 April 1849 issues). To the 20 October 1849 *Journal* Willis contributed a sympathetic memoir of Poe as a corrective to Rufus W. Griswold's malicious obituary in the 9 October *Daily Tribune*. For years Willis remained a watchdog of Poe's posthumous fame; he wrote a second reminiscence for the 30 October 1858 *Journal*.

LAMBERT A. WILMER (ca. 1805–1863), journalist, satirist, and poet, began his career in Baltimore; he almost certainly knew Poe's brother Henry in the late 1820's. In 1827 Wilmer contributed his *Merlin*, a verse drama based on Poe's romance with Elmira Royster, to the Baltimore *North American*. He subsequently went to Philadelphia, where he wrote for the *Saturday Evening Post* and the *Casket*. In January 1832 he returned to Baltimore and assumed the editorship of the *Saturday Visiter*, a weekly newspaper which commenced publication on 4 February. In August the *Visiter's* proprietors replaced him with John Hill Hewitt, who had volunteered to write editorials free of charge. Wilmer and Poe were frequent companions in 1832, seeing each other almost daily. In 1833 Wilmer became the editor of the *Cecil Courant* in Elkton, Cecil County, Maryland. Around 1839 he again moved to Philadelphia, where he was to be associated with a succession of newspapers. For the next few years Wilmer and Poe saw each other at least occasionally; their friendship probably came to an end in 1843. On 20 May Wilmer wrote John Tomlin, commenting frankly on Poe's excessive drinking; on 10 September Tomlin sent the letter to Poe. Wilmer described his fellow journalists in *Our Press Gang* (1859). *Merlin* and his "Recollections of Edgar A. Poe" (1866) were reprinted together in 1941. MARGARET E. WILMER, his daughter, defended Poe's character in *Beadle's Monthly* for April 1867.

JOHN WILSON (1785–1854), Scottish literary critic, was generally known by his pseudonym "Christopher North"; he edited *Blackwood's Magazine*, an influential Edinburgh monthly.

WILLIAM WIRT (1772–1834), Attorney General of the United States, also achieved literary distinction with several series of essays and a biography of Patrick Henry. On 11 May 1829 Poe called on Wirt in Baltimore and solicited his opinion of "Al Aaraaf."

JOHN W. WOODS, a Baltimore job printer, issued directories for that city with R. J. MATCHETT; the pair printed Poe's *Al Aaraaf, Tamerlane, and Minor Poems* (1829) for the publishers Hatch & Dunning.

WILLIAM JENKINS WORTH (1794–1849), a veteran of the War of 1812 and the Indian wars, was the commanding officer of Fortress Monroe in 1829; on 20 April he recommended Poe for West Point. Worth later distinguished himself in the Mexican War, achieving the rank of Major General.

THOMAS WYATT, English-born author

and lecturer, paid Poe $50 to help him prepare *The Conchologist's First Book* (Philadelphia, 1839), a scientific compilation designed primarily as a schoolbook. Poe's name was placed on the title page, Wyatt being unable to claim authorship because he had previously written another book on the subject for a New York publisher. Poe also seems to have assisted with *A Synopsis of Natural History* (Philadelphia, 1839), published under Wyatt's own name; but the extent of his role has never been determined. His friendship with Wyatt, begun in Philadelphia, was continued during his later residence in New York. Around January 1846 Wyatt separated Poe and Thomas Dunn English when a heated argument turned into fisticuffs.

MARTHA VAUGHN SHIELDS YARRINGTON (1796–1857), the wife of the carpenter James Yarrington, accepted boarders in her Richmond home, corner of Bank and Twelfth Streets, facing Capitol Square. On 3 October 1835 Poe brought Mrs. Clemm and her daughter Virginia to Mrs. Yarrington's.

THE
POE LOG

ELIZABETH ARNOLD POE
(from the miniature painting owned by her son Edgar)
Valentine Museum

CHAPTER ONE

A *Schoolboy* in *America* and *England*

1809–1825

Edgar Poe is born in Boston, Massachusetts, 19 January 1809. Soon after his birth his parents, both actors, take him to Baltimore, Maryland, where for a few months they leave him with his grandparents, David and Elizabeth Cairnes Poe, who have been caring for his older brother Henry. In 1810, possibly on 20 December, Rosalie, Poe's sister, is born at Norfolk, Virginia. On or about 11 December 1811 Poe's father may have died. On the death of his mother, 8 December 1811, in Richmond, Virginia, Poe is taken into the home of John Allan, of the merchant firm of Ellis & Allan, and Allan is added to his name. Rosalie is taken into the home of the William Mackenzies, neighbors of the Allans, and Mackenzie is added to hers. Accompanying John Allan to Scotland, where are visited his family and friends, and to London, England, where in 1815 a branch of the Richmond firm is established, are his wife Frances Keeling Valentine Allan, his wife's sister Ann Moore Valentine, and Poe. Poe is first tutored by the Misses Dubourg in London; later he attends the Manor House School of the Reverend John Bransby at Stoke Newington. Being unsuccessful in business abroad, John Allan returns to America with his family in 1820. Poe enters the Richmond schools of Joseph H. Clarke and William Burke. He is discouraged by Clarke and Allan in his attempts to publish a volume of poems. In 1825 John Allan inherits the larger part of the immense fortune of his uncle William Galt.

*

1809

*

19 JANUARY. BOSTON. Edgar Poe is born to Elizabeth Arnold Poe and David Poe, Jr., both actors, playing at the Boston Theatre and residing probably at No. 62 Carver Street (Quinn, pp. 30, 727–29).

[Poe's mother afterwards wrote on the back of her watercolor painting, "Boston Harbour, morning, 1808": "For my little son Edgar, who should ever love Boston, the place of his birth, and where his mother found her *best*, and *most sympathetic* friends." The painting has not survived (Miller [1977], pp. 121, 126).]

20 JANUARY. David Poe, Jr., appears as Leczinsky in T. J. Dibdin's *The Brazen Mask; or, Alberto and Rosabella*. Both he and his wife are members of Powell's Company playing at the Boston Theatre on Federal Street.

[A list of parts acted by Elizabeth and David Poe before and after their son's birth may be found in Quinn, pp. 697–724.]

9 FEBRUARY. The *Boston Gazette* in an editorial notice welcomes the return of Elizabeth Arnold Poe to the stage:

THEATRICAL COMMUNICATION.

We congratulate the frequenters of the Theatre on the recovery of Mrs. Poe from her recent confinement. . . . [periods in the original notice]. This charming little Actress will make her reappearance Tomorrow Evening, as ROSAMUNDA, in the popular play of ABAELLINO, the GREAT BANDIT, a part peculiarly adapted to her figure and talents.

10 FEBRUARY. The *New-England Palladium* of Boston reports Elizabeth Poe's recovery and runs an advertisement.

Theatrical Communication.

"ABAELLINO" and "LA PEROUSE," with the recovery of Mrs. POE, in the sweetly interesting character of *Rosamunda*[,] must certainly ensure a fashionable if not a very crowded house. Both these pieces will be inimitably performed; indeed it is one of the best bills for the season, and we hope the public will honour it *uno voce*.

THEATRE.

The time of the Curtain's rising is altered to 1/2 past 6

THIS EVENING,

Will be presented positively for the only time

this season, the popular Play, in 5 acts,

entitled

ABAELLINO;

THE GREAT BANDIT

[names of some of the cast omitted]

Contarino, Mr. Poe.

•••

Rosamunda, Mrs. Poe

•••

To which will be added, for the last time this season,

the much admired Pantomime of

LA PEROUSE;

OR, THE DESOLATE ISLAND.

[A similar advertisement appeared in the *Boston Gazette* of 9 February.]

LATE FEBRUARY? BALTIMORE. David and Elizabeth Arnold Poe take their son Edgar, then five weeks old, to Baltimore and leave him with his paternal grandparents, "General" (Major) David Poe, Sr., and Elizabeth Cairnes Poe, residing on Camden Street (Maria Clemm to Neilson Poe, 19 August 1860, Miller [1977], pp. 46–47; Allen, pp. 679–80; see LATE AUGUST?).

6 MARCH. STOCKERTON, PENNSYLVANIA. George Poe, Jr., writes his brother-in-law William Clemm, Jr.:

. . . I have been somewhat troubled within the last few days by a couple of Baltimoreans, connexions of *ours*—You may have heard my Father speak of a visit I had a few days ago from young Roscius. well, he is one of the Gentlemen alluded to; the other "tho' last not least" in my estimation for respectability in society, is Mr Thomas Williams. . . . The first mentioned Gentleman [David Poe] did not behave so well. One evening he came out to our house—having seen one of our servants (that is one of the two we keep) he had me called out to the door where he told me the most awful moment of his life was arrived, begged me to come and see him the next day at 11 o'clock at the Mansion house, said he came not to beg, & with a tragedy stride walked off after I had without reflection promised I would call—in obedience to my promise I went there the next day but found him not nor did I hear of him until yesterday, when a dirty little boy came to the door & said a man down at the tavern desired him to bring that paper and fetch back the answer—

[George Poe, Jr., copies this note to show his correspondent "the impertinence it contains."]

"Sir, *You* promised *me* on your honor to meet me at the Mansion house on the 23d—I promise *you* on *my* word of honor that if you will lend me 30, 20, 15, or even 10$ I will *remit* it to you *immediately* on my arrival in Baltimore. Be assured I will keep *my* promise at least as well as you did yours and that nothing but extreme distress would have *forc'd me* to make this application—Your answer by the bearer will prove whether I yet have 'favour in your eyes' or whether I am to be despised by (as I understand) a rich relation because when a *wild boy* I join'd a profession which I then thought and now think an honorable one. But which I would most willingly quit tomorrow if it gave satisfaction to your family provided I could do *any thing* else that would give bread to mine – Yr. politeness will no doubt enduce you to answer this note from Yrs &c

D. POE Jr."

To this impertinent note it is hardly necessary to tell you my answer—it merely went to assure him that he need not look to me for any countenance or support more especially after having written me such a letter as that and thus for the future I desired to hear not from or of him—so adieu to Davy— (Quinn, pp. 32–33).

6 JUNE. NEW YORK. The "sudden disappearance" of Elizabeth Poe causes the postponement of an entertainment at Mechanic's Hall (Odell, 2:324).

14 JUNE. BALTIMORE. Harriet Clemm, William Clemm's first wife, is baptized (St. Paul's Episcopal Church record; Quinn, p. 725).

11 AUGUST. Amelia and Neilson Poe, twins, are born to Jacob and Bridget Poe (First Presbyterian Church record; Quinn, p. 725).

LATE AUGUST? Poe's parents return to Baltimore for him.

["William [Poe's brother], the eldest, was cared for by his father's friends at Baltimore, by whom he appears to have been taken at an earlier date, not improbably soon after Edgar's birth, when, tradition asserts, the family visited the grandparents at Baltimore in the fall of 1809" (Woodberry,

1:16–17; see also Maria Clemm to Neilson Poe, 19 August 1860, Miller [1977], pp. 46–47; and Ingram, pp. 441–43).]

6 SEPTEMBER. NEW YORK. With Price and Cooper's Company at the Park Theatre David Poe, Jr., appears as Hassan and Elizabeth Poe as Angela in M. G. Lewis's *The Castle Spectre*, and David as Captain Sightly and Elizabeth as Priscilla Tomboy in T. A. Lloyd's *The Romp, or Love in a City* (Quinn, p. 719).

[Their New York engagement has been documented by Quinn, pp. 35–39, 719–22.]

18 SEPTEMBER. David Poe, Jr., plays Falieri in Cooper's *Abaellino*; he mispronounces the name "Dandoli" as "Dan Dilly" (Quinn, p. 36).

[The critic of the *Ramblers' Magazine and New-York Theatrical Register* was hereafter to refer scornfully to David Poe, Jr., as "Dan Dilly" (Quinn, pp. 36, 720).]

27 SEPTEMBER. David Poe, Jr., plays Alonzo in *Pizarro*.

[The critic of the *Ramblers' Magazine* adversely reviewed David Poe's performance: "By the sudden indisposition of Mr. Robertson, the entertainments announced for the evening (Pizarro and Princess and no Princess) necessarily gave place to the preceding. Mr. Poe was Mr. R's substitute in Alonzo; and a more wretched Alonzo have we never witnessed. This man was never destined for the high walks of the drama; —a footman is the extent of what he ought to attempt: and if by accident like that of this evening he is compelled to walk without his sphere, it would bespeak more of sense in him to read the part than attempt to act it; —his person, voice, and non-expression of countenance, all combine to stamp him—*poh! et praeterea nihil*." In a footnote to this criticism, the magazine's editor offered a few words of mitigation: "Here, as well as in some other passages of the Theatrical Register, our correspondent is too acrimonious; and I must take the liberty to differ from him, in some measure, respecting Mr. Poe's talents, who, *if he would take pains*, is by no means contemptible" (Quinn, pp. 36, 720). Here and elsewhere most misprints in quoted printed matter have been silently corrected to avoid the frequent use of *sic*.]

6 OCTOBER. David Poe, Jr., plays Amos, a black servant, in *To Marry or Not to Marry*.

[The critic of the *Ramblers' Magazine* commented: "*Dan Dilly* played *Amos*, and in spite of the coat of lampblack that covered his muffin face, there was no difficulty in penetrating the veil and discovering the worthy descendant of the illustrious Daniel. By the by, it has been said, that this *gentleman* has taken some of our former remarks very much in dudgeon; but whether this be true or not, we entertain very great doubts, for certainly we have said nothing but the truth, and that should give no man offence. If it is the case, however, we are sincerely sorry for it; for from his amiable *private character*, and high *professional standing*, he is among the last men we would justly offend. We owe this to our friend Dan from having heard much of his *spirit*; for, for men of high spirit, we have a high respect, though no *fear*. This we beg to be explicitly understood; for as there are men who will sometimes mistake motives, it may happen that this conciliatory conduct on our part be imputed to causes foreign from the truth" (Quinn, pp. 37, 720).]

18 OCTOBER. David Poe, Jr., makes his last known stage appearance as Captain Cypress in Richard Leigh's *Grieving's a Folly.*

20 OCTOBER. The *Ramblers' Magazine* reports: "It was not until the curtain was ready to rise that the audience was informed that, owing to the sudden indisposition of *Mr. Robertson* and *Mr. Poe*, the *Castle Spectre* was necessarily substituted for *Grieving's a Folly*" (Quinn, p. 37).

[The term "indisposition" was frequently used in theatrical notices of that day to cover intoxication.]

1 NOVEMBER. Elizabeth Poe plays Jessica in *The Merchant of Venice*. Mr. Bridges, an Englishman, records in his diary: "I saw Mrs. Poe and heard her sing two or three songs" (Phillips, 1:74–75).

16 DECEMBER. BOSTON. "Nemo Nobody, Esq." (James Fennell?), the editor of the Boston theatrical weekly *Something*, addresses the New York press: "We strongly and feelingly recommend to your encouragement and protection, the talents of Mr. Poe. —He *has* talents, and they may be improved or ruined by your just or incautious observations" (Quinn, p. 38).

[Buckingham (1:57) later observed that "Both he [David Poe, Jr.] and his wife were performers of considerable merit, but somewhat vain of their personal accomplishments."]

*

1810

*

4 JULY. NEW YORK. Elizabeth Poe makes her last New York stage appearance, as Ulrica in Frederick Reynolds' *The Free Knights; or, The Edict of Charlemagne* and as Rosa in Reynolds' *The Caravan; or, The Driver and his Dog* (*New York Evening Post* and *New York Commercial Advertiser*, 3 July 1810; Quinn, p. 39).

10 JULY? David Poe, Jr., is reported in New York City (unidentified letter cited in Phillips, 1:77, 219–20).

18 AUGUST. RICHMOND. The Placide and Green Company opens in Richmond, Virginia, with Elizabeth Poe as Angela in M. G. Lewis' *The Castle Spectre* and as Maria in T. J. Dibdin's *Of Age Tomorrow* (Shockley, pp. 307–08).

21 SEPTEMBER. Elizabeth Poe appears as Letitia Hardy in *The Belle's Stratagem*. A correspondent of the *Richmond Enquirer* applauds her:

But the object of these remarks, Mr. Editor, is yet behind the curtain. It is true, a man who has ever been acccustomed to esteem *modesty* and *woman* synonymous terms, and who has always been more ready to kneel at the shrine of beauty than before the image of a saint, feels some diffidence in introducing a lady in the columns of a newspaper. Yet he gathers strength from the resolution, that no observation of his shall tinge the cheek of modesty with a blush nor cast one stain on the vestal robe of virtue. Thus self justified, he enters on the task, confidently believing that the public will be prepared to welcome with the same approbation which marks her entrance on the stage, the introduction of Mrs. Poe. From an actress who possesses so eminently the faculty of pleasing, whose powers are so general and whose exertions are so ready, it would be unjust to withhold the tribute of applause. Were I to say simply that she is a valuable acquisition to the Theatre, I should dishonor her merit and do injustice to the feelings of the public. It is true she has never yet been called to the higher characters in tragedy, and it is proper that she never should be for she who is so well calculated to fill the heart with pleasure, should never be required to shroud it in gloom. On the first moment of her entrance on the Richmond boards, she was saluted with the plaudits of admiration, and at no one moment since has her reputation sunk. Her "exits and her entrances," equally operate their electric effects, for if we expect to be pleased when Mrs. Poe appears, when her part is ended, our admiration ever proclaims that our anticipations have been more than realized. It is needless to review the various characters in which her excellence has been displayed. I think I may be pardoned for asserting, that taking her performances from the commencement to the end, no one has acquitted himself with more distinguished honor. If it be excellent to satisfy the judgment and delight the heart, then Mrs. Poe is excellent. If it be the perfection of acting to conceal the actor, Mrs. Poe's name is a brilliant gem in the Theatrick crown. In a word, as no one has received more than she of the public applause, no one is better entitled to the public liberality.

Were I to say more, Mr. Editor, perhaps I should forget the character I have assumed. In regard to Mrs. Poe, for a reason which the glass will tell her, it is a difficult thing to separate the *actress* from the *woman*; no wonder then, if it should be also difficult to separate the *critic* from the *man*. Even were Aristarchus himself to rise from the dead to sit in judgment on her acting, he would find it necessary to put a strong curb upon his feelings. For if he did not, instead of criticising the *player*, he might find himself perhaps, in the situation of Shakspeare's Slender, dolefully heaving the lover's sigh and pathetically exclaiming, "Oh! Sweet Anna Page."

And now after thanking you for your complaisance, I will bid you good night—first however, assuring you that this is no *benefit puff* for the writer is a stranger to both Richmond and Mrs. Poe. Yet he sincerely hopes that on this night, the full horn of plenty may be emptied into her lap, and that she may moreover, reap in its fullest extent, the still richer reward of merited approbation (Shockley, pp. 318–19).

1 DECEMBER. BALTIMORE. Georgiana Maria Clemm is born to Harriet and William Clemm, Jr. (St. Paul's Protestant Episcopal Church record; Quinn, p. 726).

20 DECEMBER? NORFOLK, VIRGINIA. Rosalie, Poe's sister, is born at the old Forrest home, 16 Brewer Street, a boardinghouse run by Andrew Martin (Amelia F. Poe to John H. Ingram, 28 December 1908, ViU–I; "Rosalie Mackenzie Poe . . . (is said) was born 20 Decr. 1810" [Mackenzie Family Bible, ViHi]; Quinn, p. 40).

AFTER 20 DECEMBER? Elizabeth Poe writes a thank-you note to Mrs. Littleton Waller Tazewell, wife of the Governor of Virginia: "Mrs. Poe's respectfull [sic] compliments to Mrs. Taswell [sic] *returns* Mrs. Liverne thanks for her great kindness—Mrs. P.—being to sail this Eve Mrs. T will excuse the haste with which this is written / Tuesday Eve" (Quinn, p. 42).

*

1811

*

23 JANUARY. CHARLESTON, SOUTH CAROLINA. Elizabeth Poe performs with the Placide and Green Company at the Charleston Theatre (Quinn, pp. 40–41, 723–24).

26 FEBRUARY. RICHMOND. John Allan, a merchant of Richmond, Virginia, writes Margaret Nimmo, his wife's cousin, in Norfolk, Virginia: "Poor Frances has really been quite ill, and though by no means well now, yet she has much recovered. Nancy [Ann Moore Valentine, Frances' sister] sticks to the old thing. . . .So that we consider ourselves nearly fit for a frolic. . . .Write Fanny and tell her all the news of Norfolk" (ViRVal–THE).

28 APRIL. LISBON, PORTUGAL. On a business trip John Allan writes his partner Charles Ellis, in Richmond: "My mind is not sufficiently composed to tell you all I have seen. The truth is I have a journal in which I shall insert all my remarks" (DLC–EA).

11 JUNE. NORFOLK, VIRGINIA. The Placide and Green Company begins a theatrical season in Norfolk (Phillips, 1:80).

BEFORE 26 JULY. David Poe, Jr., deserts his wife and children (implied by "Floretta" to the *Norfolk Herald*, 26 July, and Samuel Mordecai to his sister Rachel, 2 November).

26 JULY. Elizabeth Poe is cast as Donna Violante in Susannah Centlivre's *The Wonder; or, A Woman Keeps a Secret*. "Floretta" writes a letter to the *Norfolk Herald*:

And now, Sir, permit me to call the attention of the public to the Benefit of Mrs. Poe and Miss Thomas for this Evening, and their claims on the liberality of the Norfolk audience are not small. The former of those ladies, I remember, (just as I was going in my teens) on her first appearance here, met with the most un-bounded applause—She was said to be one of the handsomest women in America; she was certainly the handsomest I had ever seen. She never came on Stage, but a general murmur ran through the house, "What an enchanting Creature! Heavens, what a form!—What an animated and expressive countenance!—and how well she performs! Her voice too! sure never anything was half so sweet!" Year after year did she continue to extort these involuntary bursts of rapture from the Norfolk audience, and to deserve them too; for never did one of her profession, take more pains to please than she. But now "The scene is changed,"—Misfortunes have pressed heavy on her. Left alone, the only support of herself and several small children—Friendless and unprotected, she no longer commands that admiration and attention she formerly did,—Shame on the world that can turn its back on the same person in distress, that it was wont to cherish in prosperity. And yet she is as assiduous to please as ever, and tho' grief may have stolen the roses from her cheeks, she still retains the same sweetness of expression, and symmetry of form and feature. She this evening hazards a Benefit, in the pleasing hope that the inhabitants of Norfolk will remember past services, And can they remember and not requite them generously?—Heaven forbid they should not (Quinn, pp. 41–42).

EARLY AUGUST. The Placide and Green Company departs from Norfolk for Richmond, leaving Elizabeth Poe and her two children behind (Phillips, 1:82; Shockley, p. 329).

12 AUGUST. RICHMOND. The Ellis & Allan firm writes William Holder (a customer?), in Bristol, England: "Mr. [John] Allan has returned from Lisbon in good health without visiting England" (DLC–EA).

14 AUGUST. The Richmond Theatre on Broad Street opens the twenty-ninth season with Susannah Centlivre's *The Wonder; or, A Woman Keeps a Secret* and John C. Cross's musical farce *The Purse or The Benevolent Tar* (*Richmond Enquirer*, 13 August; Shockley, p. 329).

LATE AUGUST OR EARLY SEPTEMBER. Manager Alexander Placide sends for Elizabeth Poe and her two children and finds them accommodations in or near the Washington Tavern, at the northwest corner of Ninth and Grace Streets (Phillips, 1:82; see also Quinn, pp. 45–46, 732–41).

9 SEPTEMBER. LYNCHBURG, VIRGINIA. William Galt, a prosperous Richmond merchant, writes his nephew John Allan on the day before his thirty-second birthday and instructs him about certain business transactions (DLC–EA).

19 SEPTEMBER. BALTIMORE. Georgianna Maria Clemm, daughter of Harriet and William Clemm, Jr., is baptized (St. Paul's Protestant Episcopal Church record; Quinn, p. 726).

20 SEPTEMBER. RICHMOND. Elizabeth Poe performs as one of three Graces in Byrne's *Cinderella; or The Little Glass Slipper* (*Virginia Patriot*; Shockley, pp. 331–32, 340).

[Shockley speculated that Edgar Poe may have played the part of one of the Cupids.]

25 SEPTEMBER. Elizabeth Poe is cast as Bridget in a farce *A Budget of Blunders* (*Virginia Patriot*, 24 September; Shockley, pp. 333–34).

27 SEPTEMBER. Elizabeth Poe is Emily Bloomfield in William Ioor's *The Battle of Eutaw Springs, and Evacuation of Charleston* (*Virginia Patriot*; Shockley, pp. 334–35).

7 OCTOBER. Elizabeth Poe's benefit on 9 October is advertised in the *Virginia Argus* (Shockley, p. 419 n. 52).

8 OCTOBER. Elizabeth Poe's benefit on 9 October is advertised in the *Richmond Enquirer* and the *Virginia Patriot* (Shockley, p. 419 n. 52).

9 OCTOBER. Elizabeth Poe has a benefit. The plays, with no casts listed, are Nathaniel Lee's *Alexander the Great* and George Colman the younger's *Love Laughs at Locksmiths* with a comic song by Mr. West, and the children's ballet *The Hunters and the Milkmaid* (Shockley, pp. 338 and 419 n. 52).

11 OCTOBER. Elizabeth Poe makes her last stage appearance, playing the part of the Countess Wintersen in August F. F. von Kotzebue's *The Stranger* (Quinn, p. 724).

22 OCTOBER. The Placide and Green Company returns from Fredericksburg and Petersburg, Virginia, to open the thirtieth season at the Richmond Theatre (Shockley, p. 342).

OCTOBER? Alexander Placide writes the Poe family in Baltimore.

["Mr. Placide wrote to her husband's [David Poe's] relatives in Baltimore in behalf of herself [Elizabeth Poe] and children, but received no satisfactory answer" (Weiss [1907], p. 5).]

2 NOVEMBER. Samuel Mordecai, a Richmond merchant and historian, residing on the west side of Thirteenth Street between Cary and Main Streets, writes his sister Rachel, in Warrenton, North Carolina:

A singular fashion prevails here this season—it is—charity—Mrs. Poe, who you know is a very handsome woman, happens to be very sick, and (having quarreled and parted with her husband) is destitute. The most fashionable place of resort, now is—her chamber—and the skill of cooks and nurses is exerted to procure her delicacies—Several other sick persons also receive a portion of these fashionable visits and delicacies—It is a very laudable fashion and I wish it may last long—I visited the Theatre last night for the first time—The Lady of the Lake was announced in a pompous bill—with *new Scenery* and decorations—and as *three horses* were to constitute a part of the dramatis personae the house was filled to over-flowing (NcD–M).

29 NOVEMBER. The *Richmond Enquirer* prints an appeal:

> TO THE HUMANE HEART,
> On this night, *Mrs. Poe*, lingering on the bed of disease and surrounded by her children, asks your *assistance*; and *asks it perhaps for the last time.*—The generosity of a Richmond Audience can need no other appeal.
> For particulars, see the Bills of the day.

29 NOVEMBER. The *Virginia Patriot* advertises Shakespeare's *Henry IV* and the afterpiece George Graham's *Telemachus in the Island of Calypso* with this announcement:

> MRS. POE'S BENEFIT
> In consequence of the serious and long continued indisposition of Mrs. Poe, and in compliance with the advice and solicitation of many of the most respectable families, the managers have been induced to appropriate another night for her benefit—Taking into consideration the state of her health, and the probability of this being the last time she will ever receive the patronage of the public, the appropriation of another night for her assistance, will certainly be grateful to their

feelings, as it will give them an opportunity to display their benevolent remembrance (Shockley, pp. 348–49).

NOVEMBER? Mr. and Mrs. Luke Noble Usher, actor friends of Elizabeth Poe, take care of her children (Mabbott [1969], 1:532).

Frances Allan, Jane Scott Mackenzie, and Mary Dixon Richard visit Elizabeth Poe.

On occasion of her [Jane Scott Mackenzie's] first visit to the Poes, she had observed that the children were thin and pale and very fretful. To quiet them, their old nurse—whom Mrs. Poe in her last days addressed as "Mother," while she called Mrs. Poe "Betty"—took them upon her lap and fed them liberally with bread soaked in gin, when they soon fell asleep. Subsequently, after the death of the parents, the old woman (who remained in Richmond until her death, not long after, devoting herself to the children) acknowledged to Mrs. Mackenzie that she had, from the very birth of the girl [Rosalie], freely administered to them gin and other spirituous liquors, with sometimes laudanum, "to make them strong and healthy," or to put them to sleep when restless. Mrs. Mackenzie was convinced that this woman, who was a simple, honest creature, was, in reality, the maternal grandmother of the children, and conscientiously acted for their good (Weiss [1883], p. 817).

[In his introductory note to "The Fall of the House of Usher," in which he commented on its theme and autobiographical elements, Mabbott (1978, 2:393) identified Luke Noble Usher and Harriet Ann L'Estrange Snowden Usher as the parents of James Campbell Usher and Agnes Pye Usher, who, orphaned in 1814, became neurotics. Phillips (1:53) reported that Harriet Usher died in 1832 at Lexington, Kentucky, during a cholera epidemic. See 27 OCTOBER 1827.]

8 DECEMBER. Elizabeth Poe dies (*Richmond Enquirer*, 10 December).

8 DECEMBER OR LATER. John and Frances Allan, living over a store on the northeast corner of Main and Thirteenth Streets, provide for Edgar Poe (Quinn, p. 53).

William and Jane Scott Mackenzie, friends of the Allans, take Rosalie into their home (Miller [1977], p. 58. "Rosalie Mackenzie Poe was delivered to the care of Wm & Jane Mackenzie 9 Decr 1811" [Mackenzie Family Bible, ViHi]).

"William [Poe], the eldest, was cared for by his father's friends at Baltimore" (Woodberry, 1:16–17).

Elizabeth Poe leaves her children two sketches and a bundle of letters. Edgar receives a small watercolor portrait of his mother, Rosalie a jewel case. John Allan acts as custodian of the few family trinkets, including some letters (Shew to Ingram, 3 April 1875, Miller [1977], p. 121; Ingram, p. 7; Weiss [1907], pp. 6–7).

10 DECEMBER. The *Richmond Enquirer* prints a notice: "Died on last Sunday morning [8 December], Mrs. Poe, one of the Actresses of the Company playing on the Richmond *Boards.*—By the death of this Lady the Stage has been deprived of one of its chief ornaments—And, to say the least of her, she was an interesting Actress; and never failed to catch the applause and command the admiration of the beholder."

The *Virginia Patriot* reports: "Mrs. Poe, of the Richmond Theatre. Her friends are requested to attend her funeral to day at ten o'clock."

Elizabeth Poe is buried in St. John's Church burial ground (Allen, p. 20).

11 DECEMBER OR LATER. The Reverend John Buchanan, D.D., baptizes Poe at the residence of John and Mary Dixon Richard.

[Campbell (1917), pp. 223–24, recorded: "There is a tradition that he was baptized soon after being adopted by the Allans at the home of a neighbor of the Allans, a Mr. John Richard (Richmond *Standard*, May 7, 1881), and it is said that he was confirmed at sometime in youth as a member of the Episcopal Church (Mrs. Weiss, p. 31)." T. H. Ellis stated that "the names of Edgar Allan and Rose Mackenzie were given in baptism by the Rev. John Buchanan, D.D., at the residence of Mr. John Richard, who was a friend of all the parties concerned" (*W*, 1:23). Whitty (pp. xxii–xxiii) reported: "It is said that Edgar was baptized December 11, 1811, but I am unable to find the church record."]

11 DECEMBER? NORFOLK, VIRGINIA? David Poe, Jr., dies.

[Phillips (1:77) gave the time and place as 19 October 1810 in Norfolk, Ingram (p. 6) early in 1811 in Richmond, Weiss ([1907], p. 4) 5 August 1811, and Amelia Poe (ViU–I) "A short time before his wife's death." Ellis (quoted by Harrison [1900], p. 2159) stated: "On the 8th of December, 1811, Mrs. Poe . . . died in Richmond, leaving three children. Her husband had died not long before, in Norfolk." John P. Poe (Mabbott [1969], 1:532) reported David a widower only two days. Gill (p. 20) recorded that three days after his wife's death David died as a consumptive or a victim of the Richmond Theatre fire! Poe himself wrote: "Our mother died a few weeks before him [my father]" (*L*, 1:68) and "Both died (as you [Nathaniel Beverley Tucker] may remember) within a few weeks of each other" (*L*, 1:78–79). "He [David Poe] was probably buried by the city [of Norfolk] in one of the obscure suburban cemeteries" (Weiss [1907], p. 4). See BEFORE 26 JULY 1811.]

18 DECEMBER. BOSTON. The *Boston Patriot* prints a notice of Elizabeth Poe's death:

DEATHS.

. . .In Richmond, on also 9th inst. Mrs. Poe, formerly of the Boston Theatre—She delighted a Boston audience but for one season—perhaps this was more owing to the eccentricity of her husband, than to her own volatility. Her remains were bedewed by the tears of strangers only. How transitory are the scenes of life!. . . .

CHRISTMAS HOLIDAYS. TURKEY ISLAND, VIRGINIA. John and Frances Allan and Poe spend the holidays at the Bowler Cocke plantation, on the James River, in Henrico County, southeast of Richmond (T. H. Ellis, *Richmond Standard*, 7 May 1881; ViRVal–THE).

26 DECEMBER. RICHMOND. Fire destroys the Richmond Theatre with a loss of seventy-two lives.

31 DECEMBER. Members of the Placide and Green Company express their sympathy through a letter in the *Richmond Enquirer*, and lament: "Never again shall we behold that feminine humanity which so eagerly displayed itself to soothe the victim of disease, nor view with exultation the benevolent who fostered the fatherless, and shed a ray of comfort on the departed soul of a dying mother" (Shockley, pp. 375–78).

The Burning of the Richmond Theatre
Virginia State Library

1812

*

3 JANUARY. BALTIMORE. James Mosher Poe, Poe's cousin, is born to Jacob and Bridget Poe (First Presbyterian Church record; Quinn, p. 725).

[A small typewritten book of memorabilia, entitled "The Family of George Poe, Oldest Son of Jacob Poe" (possessed by Mrs. J. Elliott Irvine, Durham, N. C., p. 11), has "James Mosher, born in Baltimore, January 3, 1812, died in South Carolina, October 1885."]

7 JANUARY. RICHMOND. John Allan pays the chairmakers John Hobday and William Seaton $8 for building a crib (DLC–EA).

8 JANUARY. NEW YORK. In a business letter W. Matlocke, Jr., writes John Allan: "How fortunate that yourself & family were out of town [the 26 December 1811]" (DLC–EA).

11 JANUARY. KILMARNOCK, SCOTLAND. Allan Fowlds writes his brother-in-law John Allan: "I had a letter from your Uncle William Galt and I cannot help thinking that he is one of the best hearted men. . . .and now my Dear Brother we are fully Expecting to see you and Mrs. Allan this summer. . . .Mrs. F. is keeping for you some fine Nappy Ale. I hope therefore you will not disappoint her for Mr. Ellis told her it was a favourite drink of yours" (DLC–EA).

10 APRIL. GREEN SPRING, VIRGINIA. Margaret Nimmo writes her brother James that plans for establishing a branch of the firm of Ellis & Allan in London, England, have been laid aside because of the Embargo (ViRVal–THE).

21–23 MAY. RICHMOND. Dr. Philip Thornton treats Poe for croup and bills John Allan $4 for three visits, "medicine," and "vial pectoral mint" (DLC–EA).

[Poe named a character Thornton in "The Journal of Julius Rodman."]

27 MAY. John Allan writes Charles Ellis: "Edgar has got quite well" (Phillips, 1:112).

18 JUNE. WASHINGTON. The United States Congress declares war on Great Britain.

[John Allan offered his services to his friend and customer General John

Hartwell Cocke (see 10 AUGUST 1815). Charles Ellis volunteered as a private in Richmond's Nineteenth Regiment (Quinn, p. 63).]

JULY? BALTIMORE. A letter from Poe's Aunt Elizabeth to Frances Allan goes astray (Elizabeth Poe to Frances Allan, 8 February 1813).

SUMMER. WHITE SULPHUR SPRINGS, VIRGINIA. Poe accompanies Frances and John Allan to the springs (Elizabeth Poe to Frances Allan, 8 February 1813, and John Allan to Poe, 18 May 1829).

["Edgar accompanied Mr. and Mrs. Allan to the White Sulphur in the summers of 1812, '13, '14, and '15. There are several persons now living in Richmond, who remember seeing him there in those years. They describe him as a lovely little fellow, with dark curls and brilliant eyes, dressed like a young prince, and charming every one by his childish grace, vivacity, and cleverness. His disposition was frank, affectionate, and generous, and he was very popular with his young companions" (Didier [1877], p. 28).]

AUGUST? STAUNTON, VIRGINIA. Poe accompanies the Allans to Staunton (Rosanna Dixon to John Allan, 6 September 1812).

3 SEPTEMBER. RICHMOND. Poe's sister Rosalie is christened Rosalie Mackenzie Poe (Rosanna Dixon to John Allan, 6 September 1812).

6 SEPTEMBER. Rosanna Dixon, Frances Allan's niece, writes distressing news to John Allan, in Staunton, Virginia: "I am very sorry to inform you that poor little Rosalie is not expected to live, altho' she is much better now than she has been for two weeks past; she was c[h]ristened on Thursday last and had Mackenzie added to her name. . . . Tell Edgar, Tib [a cat] is very well, also the Bird and Dog. . . . Kiss Edgar for me" (ViRVal–THE).

5 OCTOBER. John Allan pays William Richardson, a Richmond schoolmaster, $5 for tutoring his illegitimate son Edwin Collier for three months (DLC–EA; Allen, p. 36).

[The *Richmond Compiler*, 30 April 1822, reported the death of a Mrs. Eliza Richardson, "tutoress," perhaps the wife of William Richardson, on 26 April 1822.]

8 FEBRUARY. BALTIMORE. Elizabeth Poe writes Frances Allan a second letter, her first letter having gone astray:

'Tis the Aunt of Edgar that addresses Mrs. Allan for the second time, impressed with the idea that A letter if received could not remain unacknowledged so long as from the month of July; she is induced to write again in order to inquire in her family's as well as in her own name after the health of the Child of her Brother, as well as that of his adopted Parents. I cannot suppose my dear Mrs. Allan that A heart possessed of such original humanity as your's must without doubt be, could so long keep in suspence, the anxious inquiries made through the medium of my letter by the Grand Parents of the Orphan of an unfortunate son, surely e're this allowing that you did not wish to commence A correspondence with one who is utterly unknown to you had you received it. Mr. Allan would have written to my Father or Brother if it had been only to let them know how he was, but I am confident you never received it, for two reasons, the first is that not having the pleasure of knowing your christian name I merely addressed it to Mrs. Allan of Richmond, the second is as near as I can recollect you were about the time I wrote to you at the springs where Mr. Douglas saw you, permit me my dear madam to thank you for your kindness to the little Edgar—he is truly the Child of fortune to be placed under the fostering care of the amiable Mr. and Mrs. Allan, Oh how few meet with such A lot—the Almighty Father of the Universe grant that he may never abuse the kindness he has received and *that* from those who were not bound by any ties except those that the feeling and humane heart dictates—I fear that I have too long intruded on your patience, will you if so have the goodness to forgive me—and dare I venture to flatter myself with the hope that this will be received with any degree of pleasure or that you will gratify me so much as to answer it—give my love to the dear little Edgar and tell him tis his Aunt Eliza who writes this to you. my mother and family desire to be affectionately remembered to Mr. Allan and yourself—Henry frequently speaks of his little Brother and expresses A great desire to see him, tell him he sends his very best love to him and is greatly pleased to hear that he is so good as also so pretty A Boy as Mr. Douglas represented him to be—I feel as if I were wrighting to A sister and can scarcely even at the risk of your displeasure prevail on myself to lay aside my pen—with the hope of your indulgence in pardoning my temerity I remain my Dear Mrs. Allan yours with the greatest respect　　　　　Eliza Poe
Mrs. Allan the kind Benefactress
of the infant Orphan Edgar, Allan, Poe (DLC–EA).

[Here and elsewhere the name of John Allan and his family has been corrected to read with an "a."]

20 FEBRUARY. RICHMOND. Margaret Nimmo writes her brother James, in Norfolk: "Kiss my dear little [nephew] Mucius for me, and tell him that little Edgar Allan Poe sends his love to him" (ViRVal–THE).

14 MAY. John Allan writes his business partner Charles Ellis: "Edgar has caught the whooping cough. Frances has a swelled face" (DLC–EA).

17 MAY. John Allan reports that "poor Frances has not recovered. All the rest with the exception of Edgar & Hooping cough are well" (DLC–EA).

18 MAY. John Allan reports that Poe and Frances Allan "are getting better" (DLC–EA).

20 MAY. ELIZABETH, NEW JERSEY. Charles Ellis writes John Allan: "I am proud to know that Edgar has got the hooping cough. This may appear strange—but it wishes him well" (DLC–EA).

22 MAY. NEW YORK. Charles Ellis writes John Allan: "Sorry to hear of Mrs. Allan's illness. Tell her to keep up her spirits, its better than all the doctors in town" (DLC–EA).

22 MAY. RICHMOND. John Allan writes Charles Ellis that "all are well" (DLC–EA).

26 JULY. NORFOLK, VIRGINIA? Edward Valentine, Jr., writes his brother-in-law John Allan: "I am happy to hear that Edgar has recovered from an attack of the meazels" (DLC–EA).

10 AUGUST. RICHMOND? Charles Ellis writes John Allan that he is engaged to Margaret Nimmo (Quinn, p. 59).

SEPTEMBER. NORFOLK, VIRGINIA. Margaret Nimmo writes John Allan: "Remember me to the two Nancys, little Edgar and all inquiring friends" (DLC–EA).

[The "two Nancys" were Frances Allan and her sister Ann Moore Valentine.]

12 OCTOBER. RICHMOND. John Allan pays a bill of 75 cents for cutting "a suit for Edgar" (DLC–EA).

13 NOVEMBER. NORFOLK COUNTY, VIRGINIA. Margaret Nimmo marries Charles Ellis, John Allan's business partner.

2 DECEMBER. RICHMOND. Margaret Ellis writes her brother James Nimmo: "Mr. Allan has sprained his knee, and has been unable for several days to leave the house" (ViRVal–THE).

*

1814

*

20 JANUARY. RICHMOND. Mrs. Clotilda Fisher, a teacher, gives John Allan a receipt:

> Mr. John Allan
> To Clotilda Fisher, Dr.
> 1814. Janry the 20th To 1 quarters Tuition of
> Edgar A. Poe $4.00
> Received Payment
> Clotilda Fisher (DLC–EA).

[Listed in the Richmond City Directory of 1819, p. 47, is an Elizabeth Fisher "teacher, ss of E [Main] bt 9 and 10th sts. first from 9th st," who may have been Clotilda's sister. See Mabbott (1969), 1:533. More recently Denise Bethel discovered (in Rudd) a Mrs. Clotilda Fisher, at age 74, interred 14 January 1849 in Shockoe Hill Cemetery, Richmond.]

2 FEBRUARY. Daniel Ford sends John Allan a bill for Edwin Collier's education for one term, $5 (DLC–EA).

28 MARCH. John Allan receives a tailor's bill of 75 cents for cutting a new suit for Poe (DLC–EA).

13 APRIL. The Monumental Episcopal Church, built on the site of the Richmond Theatre, issues a notice: "The sale of the pews . . .will take place on this day, at 12 o'clock./*Wednesday*, April 13, 1814." John Allan purchases Pew No. 80 for $340 (G. D. Fisher, pp. 29, 37).

[The church, a memorial to the victims of the Richmond Theatre fire, was at first nondenominational.]

7 MAY. FREDERICKSBURG, VIRGINIA. Robert Craig Stanard is born to Robert and Jane Stith Craig Stanard (see 1 APRIL 1823 and 28 APRIL 1824).

SUMMER. BUFFALO CREEK, VIRGINIA. Poe accompanies John and Frances Allan to their estate "The Grove" at Buffalo Creek (Phillips, 1:119).

24 AUGUST. WASHINGTON. British forces capture Washington and burn the Capitol and other buildings.

1 SEPTEMBER. CAMPBELL COUNTY, VIRGINIA. Margaret Ellis writes her brother James Nimmo: "Mr. Allan and Cousin started for Staunton the day that we left Richmond" (ViRVal–THE).

6 SEPTEMBER. RICHMOND. John Allan writes Frances Allan, reassuring her that their friends are well and that Richmond is safe from the British (Frances Allan to John Allan, 11 September 1814).

11 SEPTEMBER. STAUNTON, VIRGINIA. Frances Allan writes John Allan, expressing her fears at the British landings (DLC–EA).

12–13 SEPTEMBER. BALTIMORE. British forces threaten Baltimore, but the Maryland Militia defeats them in the Battle of North Point. David Poe, Sr., Poe's grandfather, takes an active part in the city's defense (Phillips, 1:29).

14 OCTOBER. RICHMOND. John Allan writes James Nimmo:

I have great pleasure in informing you of the return of my family to our own fireside, after a pleasant trip to the mountains, not, as you well know, from choice, but compulsion. Frances has caught a bad cold, but is not confined by it. Nancy has seen one of the wonders of the world—the Blue Ridge Mountains . . . . Margaret and your grandson are hearty; she is beginning to recover her flesh. Thomas H. Ellis is a wonderful fellow; I can't distinctly comprehend him yet, but in a short time I have no doubt he will be an equal match for little Margaret . . . Now, my dear Sir, these things called privations—starvations—taxations—lastly, vexations, show the very age and figure of the times—their form and pressure, as Shakespeare says,—and he was a tolerable judge. God! what would I not give, if I had his talent for writing! and what use would I not make of the raw material at my command! (ViRVal–THE).

17 NOVEMBER. BALTIMORE. Elizabeth Poe, Edgar's aunt, marries Henry Herring, a lumber dealer (Quinn, p. 17).

1814. RICHMOND. The Ellis & Allan firm records assets of $223,133 and liabilities of $182,494.20 (DLC–EA).

1815

*

8 JANUARY. BALTIMORE. William Clemm's first wife Harriet is buried (St. Paul's Protestant Episcopal Church record; Quinn, p. 725).

15 JANUARY. RICHMOND. Hetherton, a tailor, charges John Allan $5 for "making a suit of Cloaths for son" (DLC–EA).

27 JANUARY. John Allan pays "duty" on a "4 wheeled carriage—a coacher" (DLC–EA).

CA. 1 FEBRUARY. Frances Allan has an accident (Mary Allan to John Allan, 24 March 1815).

EARLY MARCH. Poe attends the school of William Ewing (William Ewing to John Allan, 27 November 1817, and Allan to Ewing, 21 March 1818).

[The following year William Ewing removed "his school from Mr. M'Kechnies' to a brick tenement at the intersection of H [Broad] and Eighth streets near Mr. [William] Wirt's residence on Shockoe Hill," where he could "board three or four young men" (Meagher, pp. 55–56). He advertised his school in the *Richmond Compiler* for 17 January 1820:

EDUCATION.

THE friends of the subscriber in Richmond and Manchester and the public in general, are respectfully informed that on Monday the 17th inst. he will open SCHOOL at Summer Hill, on the plantation of the late John Lesslie, dec. about three miles distant from Manchester.

The Greek, Latin, French and English languages together with Writing, Arithmetic, and Mathematics, will be taught on the most approved principles. The tuition fees, which in all cases will be required in advance, are, viz:
For all or either of the above branches, per quarter $12.50
For board, washing and tuition   do.   [illegible]

In summer or fall, there will be 1 month's vacation; but to those who reside with the subscriber, throughout the year, it will be optional to continue during the vacation, for which no extra charge will be required. . . .

WM. EWING

In the *Compiler* for 10 January 1821 Ewing announced that he would continue to conduct his school at Summer Hill, near Manchester, across the James River from Richmond. At the sale of the late John Lesslie's estate William Galt bought land and a tenement house in Richmond, which he bequeathed to Elizabeth Galt. See Allen, p. 689.]

15 MARCH 1815–14 MARCH 1818. William Ewing charges John Allan tuition fees for Edwin Collier: "$42. per annum" (William Ewing to John Allan, 27 November 1817).

24 MARCH. KILMARNOCK, SCOTLAND. Mary Allan writes her brother John that "by your letter to Mrs. Fowlds I am sorry to read that Mrs. Allan had been so indisposed. I hope by this time she is quite well and that her face will not be injured by the fracture" (Allen, p. 683).

3 MAY. RICHMOND. John Allan has "a suit of cloeths [made for] Edgar $2.00" (DLC–EA).

1 JUNE. B. J. Macmurdo, a church treasurer, receives from John Allan $27.20, "being one half of an assessment of 16% on Pew, No. 80 in the Monumental Church" (Bondurant, p. 134).

15 JUNE. John Allan and his family plan to leave "in a day or two" for Norfolk, Virginia, where they will board the *Lothair*, bound for Liverpool, under Captain Stone "to sail next week" (DLC–EA; Phillips, 1:121).

BEFORE 22 JUNE. John Allan disposes of household furniture and personal effects through Moncure, Robinson & Pleasants, auctioneers at the corner of Cary and Thirteenth Streets, and draws from the firm of Ellis & Allan £335.10.6 (Allen, p. 54).

Jane and Michael Poitiaux, parents of Mary I. Dixon (nee Poitiaux) and Catherine Elizabeth Poitiaux (Frances Allan's godchild), give the Allans a farewell dinner. Poe shows great affection for Catherine (Phillips, 1:120).

22 JUNE. NORFOLK, VIRGINIA. John Allan writes Charles Ellis to sell Scipio, a slave, for $600 and to hire out others at $50 a year:

The Lothair & Steam Boat went off together today at 10 AM, the Boat moved off handsomely and with the tide, think she must have reached the Halfway House in an hour or a little better—to-morrow at 9 A. M will all go down to the Road to take our departure. I shall write by the Pilot Boat we have every thing comfortable. Frances & Nancey evince much fortitude; it has been a severe trial to them, their Spirit is good, Ned [Edgar] cared but little about it, poor fellow (DLC–EA; Quinn, p. 64).

23 JUNE. John Allan adds two postscripts to his letter of 22 June to Charles Ellis:

1/2 P. 3 P.M. Off the Horse Shoe. Inclosed you have $8.63 which to my Credit—we are trying to Beat out, I hope to succeed. Frances & Nancy rather qualmish Edgar and myself well.

5 P.M. We are now abreast of the Light House & are off. F. and Nancy sick Ed and myself well (DLC–EA).

23 JUNE–27 JULY. ATLANTIC OCEAN. Captain Stone of the *Lothair* is penurious. John Allan sleeps on the floor of the ship and complains that his wife and sister-in-law are "denied the privileges of Fire to broil a slice of Bacon" (DLC–EA; Quinn, p. 65).

28 JULY. LIVERPOOL. John and Frances Allan, Ann Valentine, and Poe disembark (Allan to Charles Ellis, 29 July 1815).

29 JULY. John Allan writes Charles Ellis: "I am now on English ground after an absence of more than 20 years. After a passage of 34 days all well—Frances and Nancey verry sick but are now perfectly Hearty. Edgar was a little sick but soon recovered. Capt. good seaman but too close. . . .We got here yesterday at 5 P.M. I took our abode at Mr. Lillymans Hotel today" (DLC–EA).

6 AUGUST. John Allan writes R. F. Gwathmey, an exporter, that he is still at Liverpool (DLC–EA; Quinn, p. 65).

10 AUGUST. RICHMOND. John Hartwell Cocke writes John Allan: "I . . . hope that you & Mrs. A. & your little adopted boy have happily arrived by this [time] at Liverpool—if not at London" (TxU–HRCL).

CA. 11 AUGUST. IRVINE, SCOTLAND. John and Frances Allan, Ann Valentine, and Poe visit John Allan's sisters Mary Allan and Jane Johnston. Perhaps for a few days Poe attends the Old Grammar School. Here Poe probably sees archers shooting the popinjay on the cathedral. Poe's playmates are James Anderson and a lad named Gregory (Chase, p. 303; Phillips, 1:125, 132, 136–42; Allen, p. 56; Quinn, pp. 65–66).

[Poe was to refer to the popinjay in "The Bargain Lost" and "Romance." See 6 AUGUST 1817.]

BEFORE 22 AUGUST. KILMARNOCK, SCOTLAND. For several days John Allan and his family visit his younger sister, Mrs. Allan Fowlds (nee Agnes Nancy Allan) on Nelson Street (DLC–EA; Quinn, pp. 65–66).

25 AUGUST. RICHMOND. William Galt writes his nephew John Allan:

I hope the Health of Mrs. Allan is very much improved by your passage and she has got quite strong and hearty & that I shl. soon hear from you to that effect. I hope the other Branches of your family are well & in good health also. I expect

Edgar was like Boys generally highly pleased with being at sea, and that it would add to his health very much. I hope Miss Nancey [Nancy] Valentine is in her usual good Health she was so Healthy there was but little room for improvement. I have miss'd you all very much hear [here] more than I thought I would have done—Since you left this nothing very particular has turn'd up to me nor unto your House of Ellis & Allan that I know of (TxU–HRCL).

21 SEPTEMBER. GREENOCK, SCOTLAND. John Allan writes Charles Ellis:

I arrived here about a half an hour ago . . .finding some American Vessels on the eve of sailing I avail myself of the chance to write a few lines, though I cannot say much about our business. . . .I flatter myself from the small quantity [of tobacco?] in London & the Posture of affairs on the Continent that our sales will be profitable.

It would appear that France and the Allies have concluded a Treaty but it has not been promulgated—the Allies will hold the strong posts for a while until the refractory spirit of some of the old adherents of Bonaparte has subsided. . . .Frances says she would like the Land o cakes better if it was warmer and less rain, she bids me say she will write Margaret [Ellis] as soon as she is settled but at present she is so bewildered with wonders that she *canna* write. Her best Love to Margaret & a thousand kisses to Thos [Ellis]. Nancy says give my love to them all—Edgar says Pa say something for me, say I was not afraid coming across the Sea. Kiss Thos. for him We all unite in best Love to my Uncle Galt & all our old Friends. Edgars love to Rosa & Mrs. Mackenzie (DLC–EA).

7 OCTOBER. LONDON. John and Frances Allan, Ann Valentine, and Poe arrive in London (Allan to Ellis, 10 October 1815).

10 OCTOBER. At Blake's Hotel John Allan writes Charles Ellis: "I arrived here on the evening of the 7th, from Kilmarnock by way of Greenock, Glasgow, Edinburg, New Castle, Sheffield. . . . Frances has been confined to her room with a bad cold—sore throat—the rest of us are well but cursedly dissatisfied" (DLC–EA).

13 OCTOBER. BALTIMORE. Elizabeth Rebecca Herring is born to Elizabeth Poe Herring and Henry Herring (Phillips, 1:514).

30 OCTOBER. LONDON. John Allan writes Charles Ellis:

. . .by a snug fire in a nice little sitting parlour in No. 47 Southampton Row, Russel[l] Square where I have procured Lodgings for the present with Frances and Nancy Sewing and Edgar reading a little Story Book. I feel quite in a comfortable mood for writing. I have no acquaintances that call upon me and none whom as yet I call on. 6 Guineas a week furnished lodgings is what I have agreed to for 6 months until I can find a more convenient and cheaper situation. I have no compting room yet of course. I cannot copy the Letters which I am obliged to write—everything is high it alarms Frances she has become a complete economist and has a most lively appetite. I begin to think London will agree with her (DLC–EA).

[No. 47 Southampton Row, Russell Square, Bloomsbury, was a house owned by Mrs. Martha How. The offices of Allan & Ellis, an inversion of the Richmond firm's name, were located at 18 Basinghall Street (DLC–EA; Quinn, pp. 67–68).]

7 NOVEMBER. John Allan writes: "We are all sick with colds. Doctor says we must all have a seasoning. Nancy, also poor Frances, confined to her room" (Phillips, 1:136).

11 NOVEMBER. KILMARNOCK, SCOTLAND. Mary Fowlds writes her uncle John Allan:

I hope Miss Valentine has got a beau to make a husband of by this time as she is in the Capitol. I suppose they will be as the midges in a summers' evening and when she is served herself I hope she will send them down a gross or two as they are a scarce commodity here and she may rely upon the thanks of all the ladies in Kilmarnock. I must finish this love story. Hope Mrs. Allan has got quite well again and able to go about and see all the curiosities as I understand they are great in number. . . . All the family join me in love to you, Mrs. Allan, Miss Valentine and little Edgar (ViRVal; Quinn, p. 67).

15 NOVEMBER. LONDON. John Allan writes Charles Ellis: "Glad to hear my little Thomas [Ellis' son] is getting better and none more delighted than Edgar" (DLC–EA).

20 NOVEMBER. John Allan writes Charles Ellis: "I told you I should stay here three years—this I gave you to understand was to remove Mrs. Allan's reluctance. You may count upon five years without an accident— the expense of making an establishment is too heavy for a shorter period. . . . I would not stay longer on any account" (DLC–EA).

21 NOVEMBER. John Allan writes William Holder: "Mrs. Allan who is now almost recovd. (and all the rest of us are well) bids me return you her (and in which Miss V. & myself unite) sincere thanks for the kind invitation you have given her & will avail ourselves of it, towards the Spring they request their compliments to the young Ladies & yourself, should you or them [they] visit London we shall be glad to see you in Southampton Row Russell Square" (typescript, ViRVal).

12 DECEMBER. RICHMOND. William Galt writes John Allan and acknowledges the receipt of Allan's letter of 22 August from Kilmarnock. He is anxious to know if Allan has commenced his business in London or has been prevented by sickness. "Please do remember me to my friends in

FRANCES ALLAN
(detail from the painting by Thomas Sully)
Valentine Museum

Scotland & to Mrs. Allan Miss Valentine & to Edgar & believe me to be your affectionate Uncle" (TxU–HRCL).

*

1816

*

7 JANUARY. KILMARNOCK, SCOTLAND. Allan Fowlds writes John Allan and sends his regards to Edgar (ViRVal; Quinn, p. 67).

11 JANUARY. RICHMOND. Catherine Wood writes John Allan: "How is my dear Mrs. Allan, Nancy and Edgar? Don't they look healthy and as sweet as ever?" (Stanard, p. 17).

19 JANUARY. Margaret Ellis writes her brother James: "We had a letter from Nancy [Valentine] a few days ago; she says they are all miserably dissatisfied with London" (ViRVal–THE)

19 JANUARY. LONDON. John Allan reports that "All [are] well" (Phillips, 1:142).

23 JANUARY. John Allan reports that Frances Allan is "complaining" (Phillips, 1:142).

FEBRUARY. LONDON? Josiah Ellis writes Charles Ellis that Frances Allan dislikes London and has had a fall (Phillips, 1:144–45).

3 MARCH. BALTIMORE. Jacob Poe and his son James Mosher Poe are baptized (First Presbyterian Church record; Quinn, p. 725).

27 MARCH. LONDON. John Allan writes William Galt: "I had a letter from Elizabeth Allan a day or two past. All our friends were well and boys busy at school poor Aunt Jeannie Bone had paid the Great Debt of nature. She was my Father's Sister and was very old and what is consoling a good Christian. . . . Frances does not enjoy good health but as the spring approaches I hope she will get better. Nancy Edgar and myself are all well and the whole unite in our best respects to you" (ViRVal).

EARLY APRIL Poe enters the boarding school of the Misses Dubourg, daughters of Francis Dubourg, 146 Sloan Street, Chelsea (Campbell [1916], p. 144).

[Their brother George was a bookkeeper and copyist for John Allan. Poe named the laundress in "The Murders in the Rue Morgue" Pauline Dubourg.]

18 MAY. RICHMOND. Catherine Poitiaux sends her love to Poe: "tell him I want to see him very much. . . .I expect Edgar does not know what to make of such a large City as London tell him Josephine and all the children want to see him" (Campbell [1916], p. 144).

MAY. LONDON. John Allan writes Charles Ellis: "If [I] get through the year I hope I shall not see such another" (DLC–EA; Quinn, p. 68).

6 JULY. John Allan receives a bill for Poe's tuition at the school kept by the Misses Dubourg. George Dubourg, Allan's clerk, signs the receipt.

Masr. Allan's School Acct. to Midsr. 1816.

Board & Tuition ¼ year	7	17	6
Separate Bed	1	1	0
Washing	0	10	6
Seat in Church	0	3	0
Teachers & Servants	0	5	0
Writing	0	15	0
Do. Entrance	0	10	6
Copy Book, Pens &c	0	3	0
Medicine, School Expences	0	5	0
Repairing Linen, shoe-strings &c	0	3	0
Mavor's Spelling	0	2	0
Fresnoy's Geography	0	2	0
Prayer Book	0	3	0
Church Catechism explained	0	0	9
Catechism of Hist. of England	0	0	9
	£12	2	0

(DLC–EA; Campbell [1916], p. 144).

17 JULY. John Allan writes William Galt that Frances Allan "complains a little but Nancy and Edgar enjoy excellent health and desire their united respects to you" (Phillips, 1:146).

22 JULY. The school of the Misses Dubourg recommences (Campbell [1916], p. 144).

12 AUGUST. RICHMOND. Charles Ellis writes John Allan: "Margaret Thomas and James unite with me in every good wish for you, Mrs. Allan and little Ed" (Stanard, p. 13).

15 AUGUST. LONDON. John Allan writes William Galt: "Frances, Nancy & Edgar beg to be kindly remembered to you" (typescript, ViRVal).

31 AUGUST. John Allan writes Charles Ellis: "Nancy weighs 146, Frances 104, myself 157 of good hard flesh—Edgar thin as a rasor." He plans to take Frances to Cheltenham "a few weeks for country air" (DLC–EA; Campbell [1912], p. 205; Quinn, p. 68).

2 OCTOBER. BALTIMORE. Harriet Mary Elizabeth Clemm, daughter of William Clemm, is baptized (St. Paul's Protestant Episcopal Church record; Quinn, p. 726).

2 OCTOBER. LONDON. John Allan writes William Galt: "Frances is beginning to enjoy much better health and better reconciled to Eng. Nancy is quite fat—Edgar is growing and of course thin and your Hble Servant as hard as a lightwood knot—we get fine Table Beer, now and then a good glass of Port" (DLC–EA; Campbell [1912], p. 205).

5 OCTOBER. John Allan, 18 Basinghall Street, gives advice to William Galt, Jr., in Kilmarnock, Scotland, who is preparing to go to America: "Now my good Boy you will soon be ushered into the World where your own exertions and good Sense will be put to the test, never fail to do your Duty to your Creator first, to your Employer next & by all means keep clear of bad company. mixing with improper characters tends only to make you the slave of vicious Habits which you will avoid as you shun the coiled Serpent" (NcD–G).

17 OCTOBER. BALTIMORE. David Poe, Sr., dies. He is survived by his widow Elizabeth Cairnes Poe.

18 OCTOBER. The *Federal Gazette* reports: "Died yesterday, in his 74th year, David Poe, a native of Ireland, and for the last 40 years a resident of Baltimore" (Quinn, p. 18 n. 38).

19 OCTOBER. The *American and Commercial Advertiser* prints an obituary: "Died on Thursday afternoon, in 74th year of his age, Mr. David Poe, a native of Ireland and for the last forty years a resident of Baltimore. Mr. Poe was an early and decided friend of American Liberty, and was actively engaged in promoting that cause during the Revolutionary War. He died as he lived, a zealous Republican, regretted by an extensive circle of relatives and friends" (ViU–I; Phillips, 1:29).

25 OCTOBER. KILMARNOCK, SCOTLAND. Allan Fowlds writes his brother-

in-law John Allan: "I hope Mrs. Allan['s] health is . . .Established and she is enjoying London with all its curiositys. . . . all here join me in warmest affection to Mrs A Miss Valentine Edgar and yourself" (TxU–HRCL).

22 NOVEMBER. LONDON. John Allan writes William Galt: "F.N.& E. are all well and desire their love to you" (Phillips, 1:147).

30 NOVEMBER. RICHMOND. William Galt, Sr., writes William Galt, Jr., in Kilmarnock, Scotland, holding up John Allan as a model: "to be both quick and correct is very desirable & such was [is] John Allan, he writes well & very fast, and he is very quick in both calculating exstending and adding; this he acquired when living with me he is now a clever man at business & I cannot allow myself to doubt but that you will be so also; Certain it is that much more pains has been taken in giving you an education than was taken for him and I hope that you are naturally clever as him" (NcD–G).

7 DECEMBER. LONDON. John Allan writes: "Frances complaining as usual. Nancy, Edgar and myself quite well" (Phillips, 1:147).

28 DECEMBER. John Allan receives a bill (£23.16s.) from the Misses Dubourg for teaching Poe during the preceding six months (Campbell [1916], p. 144).

*

1817

*

13 JANUARY. LONDON. John Allan writes William Galt: "Mrs. A. Miss N. and Edgar send their kindest regards" (Phillips, 1:147).

14 JANUARY. John Allan writes Charles Ellis: "Our property [assets] should now be worth 140,000 Dollars" (DLC–EA; Campbell [1912], p. 205).

30 JANUARY. John Allan writes William Galt: "Mrs. Allan, Miss Nancy and Edgar desire their kindest regards" (Stanard, p. 13).

3 FEBRUARY. John Allan writes James Fisher, a shipbroker, in Richmond: "Mrs. Allan is not well Miss Valentine myself & Edgar are perfectly so & unite in best respects to Mrs. Fisher the children & yourself" (typescript, ViRVal).

8 MARCH. John Allan writes William Galt, Jr., in Kilmarnock, Scotland: "you will recollect you are to have no Political Opinions, as you go to America as one of its foster Sons it is but right you should be neuter No man will blame your attachment to the country which gave you Birth, but prudence dictates that you should not say anything about the Government, but the best is to let Politics alone altogether" (NcD–G).

APRIL. RICHMOND. Thomas Willis White, a printer, returns to take up permanent residence (White to N. B. Tucker, 17 November 1834, Vi–W–TC. See 15 MAY 1834).

2 MAY. MANCHESTER, ENGLAND. John Allan writes his clerk George Dubourg: "I am pleased to hear that Mrs. Allan & the Family are well. . . .tell Mrs. Allan I am well & if I dont go to Liverpool I shall tell her so myself" (TxU–HRCL).

6 MAY. LONDON. John Allan writes Mrs. William Galt, Jr.: "Edgar is at school" (ViRVal; Quinn, p. 70. Stanard, p. 17, has 6 March. MS not accessible).

13 JULY. BALTIMORE. William Clemm, Jr., marries Maria Poe, Poe's aunt (St. Paul's Protestant Episcopal Church record. Quinn, p. 726, in error has 12 July, which was a Saturday. See 18 JULY).

18 JULY. An unidentified newspaper reports: "Married, on Sunday evening last, by the Rev. Mr. Wyatt, Mr. WILLIAM CLEMM to Miss MARIA POE" (clipping in a book of memorabilia possessed by Mrs. D. Skinner, Jr., Princeton, N. J.).

MIDSUMMER. LONDON. John Allan rents No. 39 Southampton Row from the Misses M. C. and M. A. Hows, subtenants of Charles Bleeks; but the Allans do not take possession of the house until September cr October (Phillips, 1:133, 147–48; Allan to Dubourg, 12 September).

2 AUGUST. KILMARNOCK, SCOTLAND. Mary Allan writes her brother John that she and Mrs. Galt plan to visit his family in the spring: "I was sorry to notice that Mrs. Allans Health was such as to require a change of Air but shall be extremely glad to hear that Cheltenham has been of service to her would a trip to Scotland not have answered the same purpose" (TxU–HRCL).

6 AUGUST. CHELTENHAM, ENGLAND. The day after his arrival at the Stiles Hotel John Allan writes George Dubourg: "Mrs. Allan desires me to add

that she expects a Parrot from Liverpool. Shd. it arrive she will be obliged by your taking care of it. . . .My Head feels a little confused from Drinking the Cheltenham Salts this morning but I hope to improve my Health eventually by a judicious use of them" (TxU–HRCL).

[Frances Allan's parrot spoke French and was lodged at least temporarily with the Dubourgs. In America the Allans had possessed a parrot that could speak the English alphabet. This English-speaking parrot, left with the Dixon family when the Allans went abroad, had sickened and died. Whitty (1935), pp. 188–90, thought the following lines from "Romance" were autobiographical: "To me a painted paroquet / Hath been—a most familiar bird— / Taught me my alphabet to say— / To lisp my very earliest word." Mabbott (1969), 1:128–29, linked "Romance" with the popinjay in Scotland and also called attention to the paroquet in "The Bargain Lost." In his "Philosophy of Composition" Poe stated that in planning "The Raven" he first considered a parrot, then an owl, and settled for a raven. See CA. 11 AUGUST 1815.]

9 AUGUST. John Allan writes George Dubourg: "Mrs. Allan has been using the waters and they agree verry well with her" (TxU–HRCL).

12 AUGUST. John Allan writes George Dubourg: "We are all well. . . . Mrs. Allan desires her love to Edgar. she has derived great benefit from the use of the waters" (TxU–HRCL).

14 AUGUST. John or Frances Allan writes Poe (Allan to Dubourg, 14 August).

14 AUGUST. John Allan writes George Dubourg: "Enclosed is a letter for Edgar, who, if he writes at all, must direct to his Mama, as I do not think she will return with me, as finding her health much improved, she wishes to give the waters a trial of greater duration" (Stanard, p. 17).

28 AUGUST. LONDON. A payment of £24 16s. "for Edgar's School" is charged to John Allan in the cash books of the Allan & Ellis firm (DLC–EA).

[Poe had been attending a school run by the Misses Dubourg.]

12 SEPTEMBER. CHELTENHAM, ENGLAND. John Allan writes George Dubourg: "I should hope to be with you by the 20th. inst therefore you will send no letters after the evening of the 18th., call on Mr. David Manley of 48 Southn. Row & present my Kind Respects & say I should like to have lodgings for a Month (or apartments) from the 20th. until I obtain possession of No. 39. . . .We are all well" (TxU–HRCL).

17 SEPTEMBER. CHELTENHAM, ENGLAND. Frances Allan writes John Allan that she is "better but not hearty." A bill for a dinner includes an "order for a child" (Phillips, 1:149).

20 SEPTEMBER? LONDON. John Allan returns from Cheltenham and takes lodgings until he can obtain possession of 39 Southampton Row (Allan to Dubourg, 12 September).

SEPTEMBER. RICHMOND. Ellis & Allan move their offices to Fifteenth Street, opposite the Bell Tavern (Allen, p. 76).

27 NOVEMBER. William Ewing writes John Allan:

. . .relative to Master Edwin Collier, whom you placed under my tuition in the spring of the year 1815 and who has regularly attended my school since that period. His mother informs me that she has frequently reminded your partner Mr. Ellis to mention Edwin's situation to you, but thinks that amid the hurry of important communications he had omitted the subject altogether. She has accordingly solicited me to write to you, and to present a statement of Edwin's account from his first entrance to the end of the year. It is as follows:

Mr. Allan	To Wm Ewing, Dr.	
For Master Edwin Collier's tuition from March 15th		
1815 to March 14 1818 at $42 per annum		$126.00
Cr. June 1815 by cash from Mr. Allan	$12.25	
Oct. 1816 by cash from Mr. Ellis	$29.75	42.00
To Balance		84.00

Thus there will be a balance due of $84 on the 14th of March next—You will confer a favor on me, and equally so on Mrs. Collier, by dropping a few lines to me through the medium of your firm, first opportunity, expressive of your concern for the tuition and education of the above child, as far as you may deem proper in regard to the future. . . .I trust Edgar continues to do well and to like his school as much as he used to when he was in Richmond. He is a charming boy and it will give me great pleasure to hear how he is, and where you have sent him to school, and also what he is reading. . . .remember me respectfully to your Lady Mrs. Allan and her Sister who I hope are well and do not forget to mention me to their august attendant Edgar (DLC–EA).

1817. Peter Cottom, a Richmond publisher and bookseller, brings out a second edition of *The American Star. Being a Choice Collection of the Most Approved Patriotic & Other Songs. Together with Many Original Ones Never Before Published.*

[One of the songs was "Nobody Coming to Marry Me" sung by Elizabeth Arnold Poe to "unbounded applause, at the New-York Theatre." See Hubbell (1941).]

21 MARCH. LONDON. John Allan writes William "Erwin [Ewing]":

I received your favr. of the 27th. Novr–last [by] the Albert that arrived here on
the 7th. inst handing your a/c for the Education of Edwin Collier making a
balance due you on the 15th. of March 1818 of $84 which sum Mr. Ellis will pay
you; but I cannot pay any more expense on a/c of Edwin. you will therefore not
consider me responsible for any expenses after the 15th. of this month I cannot
conceive who had a right to warrant Ellis & Allan on my a/c Accept my thanks for
the solicitude you have so kindly expressed about Edgar & the family. Edgar is a
fine Boy and I have no reason to complain of his progress (DLC–EA).

22 JUNE. John Allan writes home: "Edgar is a fine Boy and reads Latin
pretty sharply" (DLC–EA; Stanard, p. 17).

23 JUNE. John Allan writes Charles Ellis: "Frances has had an attack of
catarrh. Nancy is so attentive a nurse, she hasn't time to visit her friends"
(DLC–EA).

25 JUNE. John Allan writes Charles Ellis: "First frolic for a long time, was
a grand dinner on board the *Philip Tabb*. Mrs. A. in high spirits received
the ladies up and down the decks. She is much better and the rest of us all
well" (DLC–EA).

24 JULY. Poe's tuition fee (£16 14s. 3d.) is paid to the Reverend John
Bransby at the Manor House School, Stoke Newington (DLC–EA).

[In "William Wilson" (1839), Poe's fictional account of his experiences at
the Manor House School, the schoolmaster was part Bransby and part
George Gaskin, rector of St. Mary's Church. Poe perhaps knew three men
named William Wilson: two conducted business with John Allan and a
third taught school in Richmond (see Jackson, 1983, p. 13). "I [William
Elijah Hunter] spoke to Dr. Bransby about him [Poe] two or three times
during my school days. . . . Dr. Bransby seemed rather to shun the topic, I
suppose from some feeling with regard to his name being used distastefully
in the story of 'William Wilson.' In answer to my questions on one
occasion, he said, 'Edgar Allan' (the name he was known by at school) 'was
a quick and clever boy and would have been a very good boy if he had not
been spoilt by his parents,' meaning the Allans; 'but they spoilt him, and
allowed him an extravagant amount of pocket-money, which enabled him
to get into all manner of mischief—still I liked the boy—poor fellow, his
parents spoilt him!' " (Hunter, p. 497).]

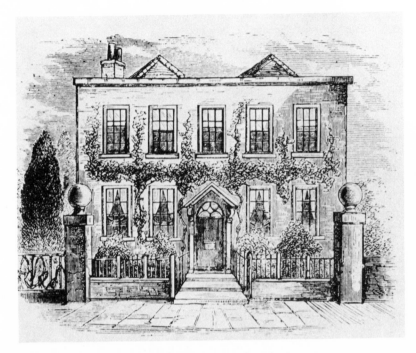

Manor House School, Stoke Newington
University of Virginia Library

17 AUGUST. John Allan plans a trip to the Isle of Wight "to see what effect sea air will have on" his wife (Phillips, 1:165).

31 AUGUST. STOKE NEWINGTON, LONDON. Poe hurts his hand badly. John Allan is charged 10*s*. 6*d*. for having the wound dressed, and several days later, 18 September, 2*s*. 6*d*. for ointment and lint (see 25 SEPTEMBER 1818).

BEFORE 10 SEPTEMBER. RIDE, ENGLAND. John Allan writes that Frances Allan is improving (Phillips, 1:165–66).

10 SEPTEMBER. LONDON. John and Frances Allan return from the Isle of Wight (Phillips, 1:166).

10 SEPTEMBER. BALTIMORE. Henry Clemm is born to Maria Poe Clemm and William Clemm, Jr. (St. Paul's Protestant Episcopal Church record; Quinn, p. 726).

25 SEPTEMBER. LONDON. John Allan is billed.

Mas Allan at Mr Bransbys.

1818. To Thos. Smith & Son Stoke Newington	£	s.	d.
Augt. 31 Dress Hand	–	10	6
Sept. 18 Ointment & Lint	–	2	6
	£	13.	

Mast. Allan———

Shoem	£.	s.	d.
1818			
July 27–Pair of Shoes	0.	7.	0
Aug 26–Mending	0.	1.	9
Sep. 21–Do	0.	2.	0
25–Do	0.	2.	0
New shoes &c as per bill	0.	12.	9
	£1.	15.	6

(Stanard, p. 327).

10 OCTOBER. John Allan reports that Frances Allan is visiting friends in Devonshire and has caught cold (Phillips, 1:166).

13 OCTOBER. John Allan writes Frances Allan (Frances Allan to John Allan, 15–16 October 1818).

15–16 OCTOBER. DAWLISH, ENGLAND. Frances Allan writes John Allan:

Your kind letter of the 13 was received this morning and you will perceive I have lost no time in replying to it, however pleasant a duty it may be I fear it will be long ere I shall write with any facility or ease to myself, as I fiend [find] you are determined to think my health better contrary to all I say it will be needless for me to say more on that subject but be assured I embrace every opportunity that offers for takeing [taking] air and exercies [exercises] but at this advanced season of the year we cant expect the weather to be very good I am this moment interupted [interrupted] with a message from Mrs. Dunlop requesting I would accompany her in a ride which I shall accept the Carriage is now at the door / Friday morning Octr 16 / we had a very long and pleasant ride we started at two o'clock and did not return until six the day was remarkably fine we had a beautyfull [beautiful] view of the surrounding Cuntry [country] we had a smart Beau with us who arrived here from London a few days ago I was very much pressed to go to the ball last night and nothing prevented me from going but the want of a little finery so you and the Doctr may lay aside some of your consequence for I really think you have a great deal of Vanity to immagien [imagine] you are the cause of all my misery, I only wish my health would admit of my entering into all the gaieties of this place I would soon let you see I could be as happy and contented without you as you appear to be in my absence as I hear of nothing but partyes [parties] at home and abroad but long may the Almighty grant my dear husband health and spirits to enjoy them now I must request my dear hubby to get me a nice piece of sheeting and a piece of shirting Cotton as they will be much wanted when I return tell Nancy she must get Abbatt to put up the tester and drapery to my bed and the parlour window Curtains to have the bedroom floors well cleaned before the Carpets are put down Miss G is very well and joins me in kind love to you the girls the Doctr Mrs. Rennolds & all friends and believe me my dear old man yours truely [truly] (ViRVal; Quinn, p. 78).

24 OCTOBER. Jane Galt, who is with Frances Allan, writes Mary Allan, who is visiting her brother John in London:

Mrs. Allan intended to have wrote herself today but is very Weak.—[?] and is afraid she will feel too much fatigued to write. We leave this on Monday for Sidmouth where Mrs. Elwell proposes staying two days we will let you know from there what day we shall have the pleasure of seeing you in Southampton Row. Mrs. Allan seems to dread very much the returning to London as she will enter it about the first of Nov. I think she regrets leaving this part of the country. Mr. Dunlop has been persuading her to remain here for some time. he will leave her in charge of two beaus who winter here, Major Court and Captain Donnell who he is sure will take good care of her and he would take a nice little cottage for her. What do you think of that arrangement don't you think we plan very well? Mrs. Allan drank tea last evening at Mr. Dunlops. They leave this Monday. Mr. [Charles Robert] Leslie who has been with them for some time is quite delighted with the country. He has been very busy taking views of the different places around. Mrs. Allan is much about the same as when I wrote (ViRVal; Allen, pp. 72, 682–83).

[Charles Robert Leslie (1794–1859) was the brother of Eliza Leslie (1787–1858), the editor of the *Gift* (1836), in which appeared Poe's "MS. Found in a Bottle," and of Thomas Jefferson Leslie (1796–1874), the paymaster at West Point in 1831. For a description of Dawlish, see Leslie, pp. 208–209.]

27 OCTOBER. TYDEMOUTH. Frances Allan and perhaps Jane Galt visit Tydemouth (ViRVal; Quinn, p. 79).

10 NOVEMBER. LONDON. Mary Allan writes her cousin William Galt, Jr., in Richmond: "Edgar is at School at Stock [Stoke] newington about four miles from London he is quite well he was in town for a day this week" (NcD–G).

12 NOVEMBER. John Allan writes William Galt, Jr.: "it [Virginia] abounds with natural Beauties in my eyes & I would not care how soon I was back among them" (NcD–G).

15 NOVEMBER. BALTIMORE. Henry Clemm, son of Maria Poe Clemm and William Clemm, Jr., is baptized (St. Paul's Protestant Episcopal Church record; Quinn, p. 726).

23 NOVEMBER. LONDON. John Allan reports that his wife Frances is "certainly improved" (Phillips, 1:166).

28 NOVEMBER OR BEFORE. Frances Allan joins her family in London (Quinn, p. 79).

25 DECEMBER. John Allan receives a bill from the Manor House School.

	£	S	D
Board & Education	23.	12.	6.
Washing £1:11:6 Single Bed			
£2:2:0	3	13	6
Allowance £0:5:0 Pew & Chary.			
Sermon £0:3:6	–	8	6
Books, Stationary &c	–	14	11
French	–	–	–
Dancing £2:2:0 Drawing £			
Music £	2	2	–
Shoemaker £1:15:6 Taylor £			
Hairdresser £ 0:2:0.	1	17	6
Sundries	–	1	–
Apothecary	0	13	0
Please to pay to Messrs. Sikes Snaith			
& Co. Mansion House St.	£33.	2.	11

The vacation will terminate Jany. 25th 1819.

(Stanard, p. 319).

*

1819

*

15 JANUARY. LONDON. Poe's tuition fees are paid to Fry and Bransby at the Manor House School: £69 16s. 4d. (DLC–EA; Campbell [1912], p. 206).

25 JANUARY. Poe's school vacation ends (see 25 DECEMBER 1818).

26 JANUARY. Poe's bill at the Manor House School is paid:

Mast. *Allan*				Mast. *Allan*			
Books	£	s	d	Sundries	£	s	d
Sep—Biglands				Postage	0.	0.	6
test—E. N.	0.	6.	6	Shoestrings ...	0.	0.	6
2 Large Slates	0.	2.	4		£0.	1.	0
Small copy book ...	0.	0.	10				
Tables	0.	0.	3				
Paper pens &c	0.	5.	0				
	£0.	14.	11				

London 26 Jany 1819
Recd of Mess's Allan & Ellis the Sum of Thirty
Three Pounds 2 / 11— on Acct. of the Revd Jno
Bransby for Messrs Sikes Snaith & Co
£33.2.11   P. *White* (Stanard, p. 323).

MAY OR BEFORE. The firm of Allan & Ellis suffers financial difficulties, and John Allan begins to think of returning home (Phillips, 1:167; Quinn, p. 79).

4 MAY. RICHMOND. For the purpose of securing to Messrs. Ewart, Taylor & Co. of London a certain sum of money, Ellis & Allan and Charles Ellis execute a deed of trust (recorded 4 October 1819 in the records of Henrico County, Virginia; *Richmond Compiler,* 13 and 14 May 1822).

BEFORE 22 MAY. LONDON. John Allan writes that "Frances begins to think she will never be able to cross the Atlantic" (Phillips, 1:168).

ABOUT 22 MAY. John Allan reports that his wife "is certainly improved in her general health" (Phillips, 1:168).

26 JUNE. IRVINE, SCOTLAND. John Allan and family attend the wedding of his sister Elizabeth to John Miller. Edgar Poe is left at Irvine until September (Phillips, 1:168).

6 SEPTEMBER. RICHMOND. In the *Richmond Compiler* Joseph H. Clarke advertises his school, which Poe enters the following year:

EDUCATION.

J. H. CLARKE tenders his best thanks to the patrons and friends of his ACADEMY, and begs leave to say that the English, French, Latin and Greek Languages are taught in his School, by a method, which equally facilitates the student's proficiency and diminishes his labour. By this *method*, which is the product of much study and research, Mr. C. has no hesitation to say, boys of ordinary capacity, may be taught to read, write, and speak the three first of these languages, with considerable accuracy and judgment, in a shorter space of time, than is usually allotted to the superficial attainment of but one. Mr. C. pledges himself to teach the French by this method in six months. Arithmetic, Geography, and the Elementary principles of Geometry and Astronomy form also an important appendage to his course of instruction.

28 SEPTEMBER. LONDON. John Allan writes his uncle William Galt: "Edgar is growing wonderfully, & enjoys a good reputation and is both able & willing to receive instruction" (Campbell [1912], p. 206; Phillips, 1:169. Quinn, p. 77, has 28 September 1818. MS. not accessible).

2 OCTOBER. Mr. Birch, landlord of a Southampton Row house, duns John Allan for rent (Campbell [1912], p. 205).

28 OCTOBER. KILMARNOCK, SCOTLAND. Mary Allan writes her cousin William Galt, Jr.: "I heard how very foolishly the young men in Virginia spend their time that they are much given to swearing, drinking, fighting with all the other vices that lead to destruction" (NcD–G; Guilds, pp. 5–7).

21 NOVEMBER. BRIGHTON, ENGLAND. An agent writes John Allan regarding a search for a house for "Mrs. Allan and another Lady to stay" (Quinn, p. 79).

27 NOVEMBER. LONDON. John Allan writes William Galt: "Edgar is in the Country at School, he is a verry fine Boy & a good Scholar" (DLC–EA).

29 NOVEMBER. John Allan, unable to return to America until he receives cash, writes "Messrs. Ellis and Allan": "Please bear in mind that I have only about £100 here in the world, and I depend upon you" (DLC–EA).

4 DECEMBER. John Allan writes Charles Ellis that Frances has "the greatest aversion to the sea and nothing but dire necessity and the prospect of a reunion with her old and dear Friends could induce her to attempt it. Ann submits with her wonted good nature and patience" (DLC–EA).

4 DECEMBER. RICHMOND. Ellis & Allan write Ewart, Myers & Company, referring to "their suspension and of their efforts to pay their creditors" (DLC–EA; Quinn, p. 79).

1819. The *Richmond Directory, Register and Almanac, for 1819* appears. Included in the directory are Martha Burling, a boardinghouse keeper; the Rev. John Buchanan; Peter Cottom; Peter V. Daniel; Charles Ellis; Elizabeth Fisher, teacher; William Galt; James E. Heath; Hetherton, tailor; John Hobday, chairmaker; William Lambert; William Mackenzie; Samuel Mordecai; Michael B. Poitiaux; Andrew Stevenson; John H. Strobia; Philip Thornton, physician; Carter Wills, bricklayer; and James Yarrington, carpenter.

*

1820

*

28 JANUARY. LONDON. John Allan writes his uncle William Galt: "Mrs. Allan & Miss Valentine are in good health & particularly request to be kindly remembered to you I am truly glad to hear of your good health—You are among the few that Edgar recollects perfectly Uncle Galt & Uncle Roland are his old Friends" (typescript, ViRVal). On this same day John Allan writes William Galt, Jr., that by his own exertions he has "repaired many Gaps [in his education] both in general literature and the Sciences" (NcD–G).

1 FEBRUARY. John Allan pays Poe's tuition fees of £70.9s.6d. to the Manor House School (DLC–EA; Campbell [1912], p. 206). He writes Charles Ellis, reporting the death of George III on 29 January and describing the immense crowds welcoming the reign of George IV (Phillips, 1:170).

19 FEBRUARY. John Allan writes about the assassination of Duke Charles Ferdinand of Berry on 13 February and concludes that "France appears in a terrible state" (Phillips, 1:170).

17 MARCH. John Allan writes Charles Ellis:

The truth is Charles we have erred through pride and ambition. I hope we shall yet have an opportunity to conduct our business like sensible and reflecting men. I shall leave the house and furniture standing, live it out for 12 or 18 months ready, should we be in condition, to prosecute our business. If impossible—it is easy getting rid of the furniture, home and all. . . . Rather than the old way—I would turn farmer or planter. This is a private letter. We must support and encourage each other. F. is getting better. She has to learn what a pleasing sensation is experienced on returning Home—even in Hot weather (Phillips, 1:170; see also 9 JUNE 1820).

MARCH. John Allan is seriously ill with dropsy (Allen, p. 72).

3 APRIL. John Allan winds up his affairs at the countinghouse (Allen, pp. 72–73).

18 APRIL. John Allan writes Charles Ellis that he has been robbed by his clerk Edward Tayle. He adds: "Would say we are all tolerably well, I certainly am much better. Frances complaining a good deal & Ann & Edgar are quite well" (Allen, p. 73).

20 MAY. John Allan writes a Richmond correspondent, probably Charles Ellis: "I trust to be off by the June Packet & when I arrive I shall use every exertion of which I am capable to complete our engagements to our creditors. . . . Mrs. Allan is in better health than usual, Ann quite well & so is Edgar, as for myself I was never better" (Allen, p. 73).

[Similar to a later entry, 16 JUNE 1820.]

26 MAY. John Allan pays Poe's bill of £35.4s.10d. for board and tuition to the Manor House School (DLC–EA; Campbell [1912], p. 206).

BEFORE 8 JUNE. IRVINE, SCOTLAND. John and Frances Allan, Ann Valentine, and Poe visit John Allan's sisters (Phillips, 1:171).

8 JUNE. LIVERPOOL. This evening the Allans and Poe arrive on their return journey to Richmond (Allan to Ellis, 9 June).

9 JUNE. John Allan writes Charles Ellis:

[Frances] . . . felt much indisposed. I hope the trip to Virginia [?] will be of service to her, she has yet to learn what a pleasing sensation is experienced on returning Home—Even in verry Hot weather. We will trust to God that our congratulations on the Birth of another Daughter to your family be . . . finally realized . . . make my best respects to our dear Margaret & all the children. Mrs. A. & Ann desire their love to you, Margaret & the young ones. Remember us all to Mr. and Mrs. Richard, Doct. and Mrs. Thornton, the children, Rose, Mr. and Mrs. Mackenzie. . . . Mrs. Mackenzie of Forest Hill called and addressed her love to Mrs. Mackenzie, they are all well (DLC–EA; Campbell [1912], p. 206; Allen, p. 73).

16 JUNE. The Allans and Poe leave aboard the sailing ship *Martha:* "The Martha Capt. Sketchly will not sail before Wednesday next the 14 int. I have made arrangements for all the Goods you ordered. . . . Mrs. Allan is in better Health than usual Ann is quite well so is Edgar. I for myself never was better" (DLC–EA; Allan to Ellis, 9 June; Quinn, p. 80).

[The *Martha* actually set sail 16 June. The voyage required thirty-six days.]

21 JULY. NEW YORK. The *Martha* arrives in the United States during the night (John Allan to Dr. Arnott, 22 August, and 26 JULY).

22 JULY. *The New-York Daily Advertiser* reports the arrival of the Allans and Poe:

DAILY ADVERTISER MARINE LIST
P O R T O F N E W - Y O R K
ARRIVED.
Ship Martha, Sketchely, 31 [36] days from Liverpool, with drygoods, hardware, &c. . . .
Passengers, J & F Allan, E A Poe, Ann Valentine, J Edgar, Henrietta Edgar, Lydia Parker, ...

26 JULY. RICHMOND. The *Compiler* prints the following news item:

LATEST FROM ENGLAND.
New York, July 22.————The quick sailing ship
MARTHA, Capt. *Sketchley,* which sailed from Liverpool
on the 16th ult. arrived at this port last evening.

27 JULY. NEW YORK. John Allan writes Charles Ellis that Frances Allan's illness has delayed their departure from New York: "I intended leaving this place today but Mrs. Allan was so unwell yesterday that I was obliged to call in Doctr. Horrock she is better today & I design starting tomorrow in the Steam Boat . . . by way of Norfolk" (DLC–EA).

27 JULY. RICHMOND. The *Compiler* prints three news items:

LATE FROM EUROPE.
The fine fast sailing ship MARTHA, capt. *Sketchley,*
arrived last night in 33 [36] days from Liverpool.

————

LATE AND IMPORTANT FROM ENGLAND AND
THE CONTINENT.
New York, July 22.————By the fast sailing ship
MARTHA, Capt. Sketchley, which arrived last night in
33 [36] days from Liverpool, the Editors of the *{New
York} Commercial Advertiser* have received Liverpool
papers to the 15th June.

————

MEMORANDA.

NEW YORK, JULY 22.————Arrd. ship Martha,
Sketchley, Liverpool————among the passengers, J.
Allen and lady, Edgar Allen, and Miss Valentine, of
Richmond, (Vir.).

[The *Compiler* misspelled the Allan name and changed "E A Poe" to "Edgar Allen" and "Ann Valentine" to "Miss Valentine" (cf. 22 JULY).]

28 JULY. NEW YORK. The Allans leave on a steamboat, bound for Richmond by way of Norfolk (implied by Allan to Ellis, 27 July).

[This trip normally required from three to four days.]

31 JULY. RICHMOND. Charles Ellis writes his wife Margaret, who is visiting in Concord, Virginia: "Mr. & Mrs. Allan has [have] at last arrived in New York, and as soon as they get on, and settled down a little I shall leave them the bag to hold and flee to the mountains . . . . Mr. Allan would set out from New York last Friday via Norfolk and I suppose will be here on next Friday or Saturday. Mrs. Allan was rather unwell & was resting. The rest were hearty, don't give yourself any uneasiness about my health" (DLC–EA).

2 AUGUST. The Allans and Poe return home and take up residence in the house of Charles Ellis (Woodberry, 2:361; T. H. Ellis, *Richmond Standard,* 7 May 1881).

["The square on the south side of Franklin, between First and Second Streets, was the residence of *Charles Ellis,* of the long existing firm of Ellis & Allan, worthy members of our community for nearly half a century. This unpretending mansion, now overtopped by those around, is still occupied by his family. The square opposite to it was Mr. Ellis's garden, embellished by a fine row of Linden trees along its front. Most of the Lindens have disappeared, but have given their name to the square, now built up with fine residences" (Mordecai, pp. 123–24).]

2 AUGUST. The *Richmond Compiler* prints a list of students who have excelled in the last session of Joseph H. Clarke's Academy. One is Ebenezer Burling, later Poe's friend.

> 2d Latin Class, 1st premium Benjamin Hooper.
> "Vain, very vain my weary search to find,
> "That bliss which only centres in the mind,
> "Why have I stray'd from *study* and repose,
> "To seek a good each well *spent hour* bestows."
> *Accesserunt* 1st. Alexander Rutherfoord, premium,
> 2. Jos. Stras, 3. Ebenezer Burling.

7 AUGUST. Charles Ellis writes his wife Margaret: "Your letter of the 4th inst. by last nights mail affords me great pleasure, and that of Mr. and Mrs. Allan who are at our home receiving the congratulations of their friends. Mrs. Allan could she be as even tempered and as accommodating as she has been sence [since] her return, she would make the path through life much more even to herself" (Allen, p. 77).

10 AUGUST. Charles Ellis writes his wife Margaret, who is visiting in Concord, Virginia: "Our friends Mr. & Mrs. Allan Nancy & Edgar are very well & you would be surprised to see what health and colour Mrs. A. has. They are quite well satisfied at our house, & I make out pretty well altho not as well as you would do. They are a little Englishised but it will soon wear off. They talk of going to Staunton" (DLC–EA). John Allan brings with him from England a telescope (Woodberry, 2:363).

22 AUGUST. John Allan writes his friend Dr. Neil Arnott, in London: "I arrived at New York July 21st, after a passage of 36 days. The ocean was very rough—Mrs. Allan and Miss Valentine suffered from seasickness" (Phillips, 1:171).

22 AUGUST. BALTIMORE. Virginia Sarah (or Maria) Clemm is born to Maria Clemm and William Clemm, Jr. (St. Paul's Protestant Episcopal Church record; Quinn, p. 726).

SEPTEMBER? RICHMOND. Poe enters the school of Joseph H. Clarke "over Dr. Leroy's store at Broad and Fifth."

Edgar Poe was five [three?] years in my school. During that time he read Ovid, Cæsar, Virgil, Cicero, and Horace in Latin, and Xenophon and Homer in Greek. . . . He had no love for mathematics. . . .While the other boys wrote mere mechanical verses, Poe wrote genuine poetry: the boy was a born poet. As a scholar, he was ambitious to excel, and although not conspicuously studious, he always acquitted himself well in his classes. He was remarkable for self-respect, without haughtiness. In his demeanor toward his playmates, he was strictly just and correct, which made him a general favorite. . . .His natural and predominant passion seemed to me to be an enthusiastic ardor in everything he undertook. . . .Even in those early years, Edgar Poe displayed the germs of that wonderfully rich and splendid imagination which has placed him in the front rank of the purely imaginative poets of the world. His school-boy verses were written *con amore,* and not as mere tasks. When he was ten years old, Mr. Allan came to me one day with a manuscript volume of verses, which he said Edgar had written, and which the little fellow wanted to have published. He asked my advice upon the subject. I told him that Edgar was of a very excitable temperament, that he possessed a great deal of self-esteem, and that it would be very injurious to the boy to allow him to be flattered and talked about as the author of a printed book at his age. . . .The verses, I remember, consisted chiefly of pieces addressed to the different little girls in Richmond (Didier [1877], pp. 30–31, quoting Clarke).

2 AND 4 OCTOBER. Joseph H. Clarke advertises his school in the *Richmond Compiler*.

Richmond Academy.

THE subscriber having engaged the assistance of a Gentleman late from Europe, offers to his patrons and friends in Richmond, Manchester, and their vicinities, the flattering prospect of a permanent Literary Institution,——where will be taught in the shortest possible time, not only the Learned Languages, but Writing and Arithmetic in its various departments, with Book-keeping by single and double entry; Geometry, Mensuration, Trigonometry plain and spherical; Navigation with the method of working Celestial and Lunar Observations; Land Surveying in theory and practice; Gunnery, and the doctrine of Projectiles, Gauging, Fortification and Optics with the use of the Instruments; Elementary and Physical Astronomy, Conic Sections, Algebra, Fluxions, Mechanics, &c. &c. Geography, with constant reference to Maps and Charts, and occasional illustrations from Astronomy, adapted to the student's capacity.

The subscriber, whose chief ambition is to be serviceable to the rising generation, will assure the present and future patrons of his Academy, that no literary labor shall be spared on his part or that of his assistant, to give universal satisfaction. The studies of the Academy will be conducted as formerly, by his direction and under his immediate supervision. There will be four exhibitions in the year, that the parents of the pupils and the public may judge of their proficiency; and one grand examination in the year, when the classical victors shall be honourably rewarded for pre-eminence in classical and mathematical acquirements.——The subscriber becomes responsible to parents for the progress of their children—both in science and polite manners. An accession of a few more scholars is desirable——no exceptions as to age.

TERMS.

For the Mathematics and			
Classics, *per quarter*,	$15		payable in
For plain English education,			advance.
per quarter,	10		

J. H. CLARKE.

[According to Meagher, p. 55, Clarke advertised his school as early as December 1818 in the *Compiler* and first had a "commodious room in the Old Capitol building" and later, in 1819, a classroom "over Dr. Leroy's store at Broad and Fifth."]

9 DECEMBER. John Allan is charged for "1 knife for Edgar" (DLC–EA; Campbell [1912], p. 207).

BEFORE 25 DECEMBER. John Allan and his family take a house on Fifth Street, fronting west, between Marshall and Clay Streets (Weiss [1907] , p. 20; Stanard, p. 19. See also 13 and 14 MAY 1822).

[The exact date of the Allans' leaving the Charles Ellis home for a house of their own on Fifth Street is not known. Both Weiss (1907), p. 20, and Quinn, p. 82, have "at the end of the year." Allen, p. 79, citing a July 1925 letter from E. V. Valentine, has "Autumn of 1820." T. H. Ellis wrote that the Allans lived with his family "the greater part of the year" (ViRVal–THE). Stanard, p. 19, states that the Allans spent several months in the Ellis home. Before moving to "Moldavia" in the summer of 1825, the Allans occupied in 1822 or 1823 a house at the corner of Fourteenth Street and Tobacco Alley (ViRVal–THE). See AFTER MAY 1822.]

25 DECEMBER 1820? The Charles Ellis family spends Christmas evening with the Allans (Harrison [1900], p. 2160, quoting T. H. Ellis).

[Thomas H. Ellis, son of Charles and Margaret Ellis, later recalled: "No boy ever had a greater influence over me than he [Poe] had. He was, indeed, a leader among boys; but my admiration for him scarcely knew bounds; the consequence was, he led me to many a forbidden thing, for which I was punished. The only whipping I ever knew Mr. Allan to give him was for carrying me out into the fields and woods beyond Belvidere, one Saturday, and keeping me there all day and until after dark, without anybody at home knowing where we were, and for shooting a lot of domestic fowls, belonging to the proprietor of Belvidere (who was at that time, I think, Judge Bushrod Washington). He taught me to shoot, to swim, and to skate, to play bandy, &c.; and I ought to mention that he once saved me from drowning—for having thrown me into the falls headlong, that I might strike out for myself, he presently found it necessary to come to my help, or it would have been too late" (*Richmond Standard*, 7 May 1881).]

*

1821

*

13 MARCH. BALTIMORE. Virginia Sarah (or Maria) Clemm, daughter of Maria Poe Clemm and William Clemm, Jr., is baptized (St. Paul's Protestant Episcopal Church record; Quinn, p. 726).

15 MAY. LONDON. Dr. Neil Arnott, of Bedford Square, writes John Allan: "You know that I have Master Edgar still inhabiting one of my rooms. Your not asking for him with these other things makes me hope that you do mean to come back again" (DLC–EA).

[Dr. Arnott may have been referring to a portrait of Poe by his daughter Anne or by Charles R. Leslie.]

BETWEEN 3 JUNE 1821 AND 31 OCTOBER 1825. RICHMOND. John Allan is charged eleven times for postage, from eighteen cents to a dollar and a half, for Poe, and several times for lesser amounts for Rosalie (DLC–EA; Campbell [1912], pp. 207–208).

11 JUNE. Poe continues to attend Joseph H. Clarke's school. John Allan pays $12.50 tuition in advance for the period 11 June to 11 September 1821 (DLC–EA; Campbell [1912], p. 207).

11 SEPTEMBER 1821–11 MARCH 1822. Poe attends Joseph H. Clarke's school during its fall quarter 11 September–11 December 1821 (see 11 MARCH 1822).

[Thomas H. Ellis later recalled: "Talent for declamation was one of his [Poe's] gifts. I well remember a public exhibition at the close of a course of instruction in elocution which he had attended (in the old frame building that stood high above the present grade of Governor street, at the southwest corner of Governor and Franklin streets,) and my delight when he bore off the prize in competition with Channing Moore, Cary Wickham, Andrew Johnston, Nat Howard, and others who were regarded as amongst the most promising of the Richmond boys" (*Richmond Standard*, 7 May 1881).]

*

1822

*

11 MARCH. RICHMOND. Poe continues to attend Joseph H. Clarke's school.

To tuition of Master Edgar Poe
  from Sept. 11th to March 11th. 1822
    at 12 50 pt. qt 25.00
      Portion of fuel. 1.00
  to Pens Ink & Paper   .75
                                        $26.75
Recd. payt Jos. H. Clarke
By a / c paid the 17th
Decr up to the 11th of that   14.–
            Month $12.75 (DLC–EA).

19 MARCH. Jesse Higginbotham of the late firm of Ellis & Higginbotham makes an effort to discharge his debts (*Richmond Compiler*, 19 March 1822).

["Miss [Ann] Valentine," wrote Thomas H. Ellis, "was at one time engaged to Jesse Higginbotham, a very clever and competent clerk, who had lived with Ellis and Allan and afterward became the partner of uncle Josiah Ellis, under the firm of Ellis and Higginbotham. The match was broken off, in consequence of his base and fraudulent treatment of my uncle" (ViRVal–THE).]

13 AND 14 MAY. Robert Gwathmey, as trustee, advertises for sale at auction properties owned by Ellis & Allan and Charles Ellis "for the purpose of securing to Messrs. Ewart, Taylor & Co. of London, a certain sum of money expressed in a deed of trust." These properties include a brick tenement occupied by Messrs. Ellis & Allan on Fifteenth Street, a part of a brick tenement next door to Robert Poore's Cabinet Warehouse, a "house and half acre lot on 5th and K [Leigh] street in handsome order, and now occupied by John Allan," "that beautiful half acre lot on F [Franklin] and 2d street, opposite to Mr. Charles Ellis's residence, which is well enclosed and laid out for a garden," land purchased from the Adam Craig heirs, a parcel of land commonly called "Mackenzie's Gardens," and "that highly improved and beautiful lot, containing about half an acre on F [Franklin] and 2d streets, the present residence of Mr. Charles Ellis" (*Richmond Compiler*. See 4 MAY 1819).

[All properties to be auctioned were bought in by an advance of $10,000 on a note endorsed by William Galt (Allen, p. 684). Apparently Quinn, p. 88, is referring to this endorsement: "in 1822 . . . he [John Allan] made a personal assignment with permission to retain his property." The Adam Craig mentioned in the advertisement was, of course, the father of Jane Stith Craig Stanard.]

AFTER MAY. John Allan and his family move from the house on Fifth Street, between Marshall and Clay Streets, to a house on Fourteenth Street and Tobacco Alley (Quinn, p. 88; Phillips, 1:187–88).

11 JUNE. John Allan pays Joseph H. Clarke.

To present quarter's tuition of	
Master Poe from June 11th to Sept 11–1822	$12.50
1. Horace 3 50, Cicero de Off. 62½——	4.12½
1. Copy book, paper Pen & Ink——————	.87½
	$17.50
to tuition of son Edgar Poe from June 11th	
to Sept 11th - - - - - - - - - - - - - - - - - -	$12.50

Recd payt. in advance

J. H. Clarke (DLC–EA).

12 JULY. *Timour the Tartar*, a horse-spectacle about Tamerlane by M. G. Lewis, is presented at the Richmond Theatre. It is repeated 17 July and 25 October (Both Shockley [1941], pp. 1103–06, and Mabbott [1969], 1:24, speculate that Poe may have seen it or surely heard about it. See 7 NOVEMBER 1829).

15 AUGUST. BALTIMORE. Virginia Eliza Clemm, Poe's cousin and future wife, is born to Maria Clemm and William Clemm, Jr. (St. Paul's Protestant Episcopal Church record; Quinn, p. 726. Mabbott [1969], 1:523, has 16 August and baptismal date 15 November).

31 AUGUST. RICHMOND. The following entry appears in the Ellis-Allan cash books: "postage to Miss [Rosalie] Poe .19" (DLC–EA; Campbell [1912], p. 208).

11 SEPTEMBER. John Allan pays in advance $13.25 to Joseph H. Clarke, $12.50 for the "Instruction of Edgar Poe" from 11 September to 11 December 1822, and $0.75 for "pens Ink & paper" (DLC–EA).

[This is the last payment that Allan is known to have made to Clarke.]

5 NOVEMBER. BALTIMORE. Virginia Eliza Clemm is baptized by Bishop James Kemp. Virginia Sarah (or Maria) Clemm, her sister, is buried (St. Paul's Protestant Episcopal Church record; Quinn, p. 726; Ingram List, p. 185).

3 DECEMBER. RICHMOND. In an advertisement dated 19 November in the *Enquirer* William Burke, a schoolmaster, "informs the public that the duties of his Seminary will be continued, the ensuing year, in its present situation or its vicinity." Poe enters his school the following year, 1 April.

8 DECEMBER. BALTIMORE. Elizabeth Poe Herring, wife of Henry Herring, dies, leaving a husband and five children (Maria Clemm to William Poe, 7 October 1836 [1835], *W*, 17:379–81).

17 DECEMBER. RICHMOND. John Allan pays his semiannual vestry assessment "for $20, on ac't of Pew, No. 80, in Monumental Church" (Phillips, 1:196).

DECEMBER. A tailor bills John Allan for $11.50: "coats, pantaloons & trimmings for Edgar" (Phillips, 1:196).

LATE 1822. In Joseph H. Clarke's school Poe is a good student and athlete.

[John T. L. Preston, a schoolmate, later recalled: "Although I was several years his junior, we sat together on the same form for a year or more, at a classical school in Richmond, Virginia. Our master was John [Joseph] Clark[e], of Trinity College, Dublin [Georgetown College] . . . a hot-tempered, pedantic, bachelor Irishman; but a Latinist of the first order, according to the style of scholarship of that date, he unquestionably was. I have often heard my mother amuse herself by repeating his pompous assurance, that in his school her boy should be taught 'only the pure Latinity of the Augustan age' . . . Edgar Poe might have been at this time fifteen or sixteen——he being one of the oldest boys in the school, and I one of the youngest. His power and accomplishments captivated me, and something in me or in him made him take a fancy to me. In the simple school athletics of those days, when a gymnasium had not been heard of, he was *facile princeps*. He was a swift runner, a wonderful leaper, and what was more rare, a boxer, with some slight training. . . . For swimming he was noted, being in many of his athletic proclivities surprisingly like Byron in his youth. . . . We selected Poe as our champion [in a foot-race] . . . The race came off one bright May morning at sunrise, on the Capitol Square. . . . our school was beaten. . . . In our Latin exercises in school, Poe was among the first. . . . One exercise of the school was a favorite one with Poe: it was what was called 'capping verses' . . . . He was very fond of the Odes of Horace, and repeated them so often in my hearing that I learned by sound the words of many, before I understood their meaning. . . . I remember that Poe was also a very fine French scholar. Yet with all his superiorities, he was not the master-spirit, nor even the favorite of the school. . . Poe, as I recall my impressions now, was self-willed, capricious, inclined to be imperious, and though of generous impulses, not steadily kind or even amiable. . . . Of Edgar Poe it was known that his parents were players, and that he was dependent upon the bounty that is bestowed upon an adopted son. All this had the effect of making the boys decline his leadership. . . . Not a little of Poe's time, in school and out of it, was occupied with writing verses. . . . My boyish admiration was so great for my schoolfellow's genius, that I requested him to give me permission to carry his portfolio home for the inspection of my mother. If her enthusiasm was less than mine, her judgment did not hesitate to praise the verses very highly; and her criticism might well gratify the boyish poet; for she was a lady who, to a natural love for literature, inherited from her father, Edmund Randolph, had added the most thorough and careful culture obtained by the most extensive reading of the English classics——the established mode of female education in those days. Here, then, you have the first critic to whom were submitted the verses of our world-famed poet. Her warm appreciation of the boy's genius and work, was proof of her own critical taste" (Rice, pp. 37–42).]

LATE 1822? Poe's fellow students elect him to compose and deliver a farewell ode to Joseph H. Clarke (Graves, p. 916).

["When Professor Clarke left Richmond in 1823 [1822], young Poe addressed to his beloved teacher a poem which was a remarkable production for a boy of fourteen [thirteen]. In after years the Professor was proud of his distinguished pupil, and referred, to his dying day, to the fact that Poe always called upon him when he visited Baltimore, to which city Mr. Clarke removed from Richmond" (Didier [1909], p. 222). Weiss (1907), pp. 24–25, records that Poe wrote Clarke a letter in Latin verse.]

1822? Poe addresses lines to schoolgirls at a school kept by Miss Jane Mackenzie, Mrs. William Mackenzie's sister-in-law (Mabbott [1969], 1:3–4. See Bondurant, pp. 86–88).

[In September 1828 Jane Mackenzie announced that on the reopening of her school in October she would accept boarding as well as day pupils. "During the six years that Miss M has been a Teacher, her day School has been abundantly supplied with Scholars" (advertisement, *Richmond Compiler*, 11, 13, 20, and 27 September 1828).]

*

1823

*

1 JANUARY. RICHMOND. John Allan begins making entries in his "general Note Book":

From long observation and experience I have been induced to commence a kind of dailey journal of events, which may have a bearing upon points in which I may be able to serve the cause of Truth & justice—to refresh my memory occasionally, to record the result of my reflections & observations note remarkable events or occurrences & lastly to enable me by bringing the transactions of every day before my Minds eye to correct any error either in my conversation or conduct (TxU–HRCL).

2 JANUARY. Another session of William Burke's school begins (see 7, 8, AND 9 JANUARY).

3 JANUARY. John Allan notes that against his better judgment he has made an arrangement for renting Rosanna Dixon's 240 acres of land in Hanover County to a Mr. Temple (TxU–HRCL).

The Maverick engraving of early Richmond
Virginia State Library

7, 8, AND 9 JANUARY. William Burke continues to promote his school in the *Richmond Enquirer* (7 and 9 January) and in the *Richmond Compiler* (8 January):

Education

THE subscriber respectfully informs the public that the duties of his Seminary will be resumed on the 2d Jan. in Southgate's buildings, opposite the City Hall. He has employed Mr. CAVIDALLY as Professor of French and Italian, and Mr. CHARLES O'FLINN, to conduct the Mathematical department. His own exertions united with the assistance of these gentlemen will, he hopes, make his Seminary worthy of public support. The course will be extensive, and such as to prepare young gentlemen for obtaining an honourable entrance in any University in the United States; or for acquiring any profession with advantage. At the close of each term there will be an examination at which gentlemen of literary acquirements will be requested to attend and award suitable premiums. The discipline will be mild but firm, and no youth of bad moral character will be received.————The subscriber will be found during the recess, at Mr. Southgate's boarding house. He requests all who wish to obtain places to make early application.

WM. BURKE.

Terms——payable in advance——

Greek, Latin, French, Italian
and Mathematics.   5 months, $30
   Do. do. do. do.   10 do. $55

Reading, Writing, Arithmetic, Grammar,
Geography, and the use of the Globes,   5 months   20
   Do. do. do. do   10 do   35

No extra charge for fuel   (*Richmond Compiler*, 8 January).

[Peyton Randolph, Thomas F. Ritchie, and Robert Stanard, whose sons attended Burke's school, endorsed it in an advertisement in the *Richmond Compiler*, 13 August 1828.]

21 JANUARY–10 MARCH. John Allan writes in his notebook:

Warm weather for the Season & so has continued to Jany 21st.. Early this morning the River James began to rise rapidly & unexpectedly. . . Mar 10, 1823 yesterday Sunday & the Day before quite Summer to day Monday cold enough for a Great coat. the Blossoms of Fruit Trees will be kept back done nothing in Horticulture yet but I augur favourably of the Spring and what depends on our fluctuating & variable climate (TxU–HRCL).

MARCH OR EARLIER? Poe and Robert Mayo, Jr., engage in a dangerous swimming feat, and both are ill for several weeks (Richmond *Evening Journal*, 1874; Baltimore *Sun*, 8 July 1875; clippings in ViRVal).

1 APRIL. John Allan records in his notebook: "Edgar was entered with Mr. Burke for a session of 5 mos. & $30 paid in advance" (TxU–HRCL).

[William Burke's "Seminary" for boys was founded by Charles O'Flinn (or O'Flynn), and was first located in the Mansion House on Main Street between Fifteenth and Sixteenth Streets (Meagher, p. 58). One of Poe's classmates was James Albert Clarke, of Manchester, Virginia, who was later suspended from the University of Virginia (Poe to Allan, 25 May 1826). Other classmates during the years 1823, 1824, and 1825 were Creed Thomas, Robert Gamble Cabell, William H. Howard, Andrew Johnston, Joseph Selden, Miles C. Selden, and Robert Craig Stanard (Didier [1877], p. 33). Thomas later recalled a fight Poe had with one of the Seldens:

Selden told somebody that Poe was a liar or a rascal. The embryo poet heard of it, and soon the boys were engaged in a fight. Selden was heavier than Poe whom he pommelled vigorously for some time. The delicate boy appeared to submit with little resistance. Finally Poe turned the tables on Selden, and much to the surprise of the spectators, administered a sound whipping. When asked why he permitted Selden to pommel his head so long, Poe replied that he was waiting for his adversary to get out of breath before showing him a few things in the art of fighting.

Poe was a quiet, peaceful youngster, and seldom got into a difficulty with his schoolmates. He was as plucky as any boy at school, however, and never permitted himself to be imposed upon. When it came to a question of looking after his individual rights, however, the young classic asserted himself. He was not at all popular with his schoolmates, being too retiring in disposition and singularly unsociable in manner. The only two boys he was intimate with were Monroe [Robert] Stanard, who afterwards became Judge Stanard, and Robert G. Cabell. He was quite fond of both of them, and the three boys were continually in each other's company. It was a noticeable fact that he never asked any of his school-mates to go home with him after school. Other boys would frequently spend the night or take dinner with each other at their homes, but Poe was seldom known to enter into this social intercourse. After he left the play-grounds at school that was an end of his sociability until the next day. Dr. Thomas was a member with Poe, Beverley Anderson, and William F. Ritchie, of the Thespian Society, that had its headquarters in the old wooden building which stood on the northeast corner of Sixth and Marshall Streets. Poe was a member of this society, contrary to the wishes of Mr. Allan. He had undoubted talent in this direction. The audience usually numbered about forty or fifty. A small admission fee was charged, and this was divided between the actors, who used it as pin money. A singular fact, Dr. Thomas used to say, was that Poe never got a whipping at school. He remembered that the other boys used to come in for a flogging quite frequently, and that he got his share. Mr. Burke believed in the moral power of the birch. He accepted the theory, "Spare the rod and spoil the child," as a matter of course, and the consequence was that whippings were so frequent that they created no sensation among the scholars who witnessed them (obituary notice of Dr. Creed Thomas, *Richmond Dispatch*, 24 February 1899; *W*, 1:27–29).]

AFTER 1 APRIL. Poe accompanies Robert Craig Stanard home and meets Robert's mother Jane Stith Craig Stanard (see 28 and 30 APRIL 1824).

["This lady, on entering the room, took his hand and spoke some gentle and gracious words of welcome, which so penetrated the sensitive heart of the orphan boy as to deprive him of the power of speech, and, for a time, almost of consciousness itself. He returned home in a dream, with but one thought, one hope in life—to hear again the sweet and gracious words that had made the desolate world so beautiful to him, and filled his lonely heart with the oppression of a new joy. This lady afterwards became the *confidant* of all his boyish sorrows, and her's was the one redeeming in-fluence that saved and guided him in the earlier days of his turbulent and passionate youth. . . . It was the image of this lady. . . that suggested the stanzas 'To Helen,' published among the poems written in his youth" (Whitman, pp. 49–51). On 14 April 1859 Maria Clemm wrote Sarah Helen Whitman: "It is true dear Eddie did love Mrs. Stannard [Stanard] with all the affectionate devotion of a son. When he was unhappy at home, (which was very often the case) he went to her for sympathy, and she always consoled and comforted him, you are mistaken when you say that you believe he saw her but *once* in her home. He visited there for years [months?]. He only saw her once while she was ill, which grieved him greatly, he was but a boy at that time. Robert has often told me, of his, and Eddie's visits to her grave, he has pointed to her last resting place to me often, when we would visit the [Shockoe] cemetery. It was a favorite drive of my darling Virginia's" (Miller [1977], p. 42).]

23 APRIL. John Allan writes that "though up and about" his wife Frances is "never clear of complaint." Allan himself, Ann Valentine, and Poe are well (Phillips, 1:197).

APRIL, MAY, AND JUNE. John Allan pays shoe bills for himself and Poe (DLC–EA; Phillips, 1:197).

JULY. A Richmond correspondent reports that "all are well John, Frances, Ann, Edgar" (DLC–EA; Phillips, 1:197).

15 SEPTEMBER. John Allan writes Charles Ellis about their financial affairs: "Mr. [William] Galt arrived Sunday, well, much pleased that we have a prospect of escape" (DLC–EA; Phillips, 1:197).

1 OCTOBER. Andrew Johnston enters Burke's school.

I [Johnston] knew him [Poe] before, but not well, there being two, if not three, years difference in our ages. We went to school together all through 1824 and the early part of 1825. Some time in the latter year (I cannot recollect at what time exactly) he left the school . . . Poe was a much more advanced scholar than any of us; but there was no other class for him—that being the highest—and he had nothing to do, or but little, to keep his headship of the class. I dare say he liked it well, for he was fond of desultory reading, and even then wrote verses. . . . We all recognized and admired his great and varied talents, and were proud of him as the most distinguished school-boy of the town. At that time, Poe was slight in person and figure, but well made, active, sinewy, and graceful. In athletic exercises he was foremost: especially, he was the best, the most daring, and most enduring swimmer that I ever saw in the water. . . . His disposition was amiable, and his manners pleasant and courteous (Didier [1877], pp. 33–34).

13 NOVEMBER. Poe witnesses a power of attorney granted to Joseph W. Dickenson by the Ellis & Allan firm (Phillips, 1:196).

1824

*

23 JANUARY. RICHMOND. John Allan makes an entry in his notebook: "My Uncle [William Galt] said that he was establishing his present business for all our Interests, that I was so hobbled [by creditors] that I could not be Known but that Wm. [Galt, Jr.] should have a third when James [Galt] became a Citizen he should have a third & when I was at Liberty I should have his third but this he did not wish mentioned" (TxU–HRCL).

26 JANUARY. William Burke is paid $10 for Poe's tuition (DLC–EA; Campbell [1912], p. 207).

FEBRUARY. A bill of $1.50 for "Boy's" shoes is entered in the Ellis & Allan office books (DLC–EA; Phillips, 1:211).

[Two other bills of $1.50 for a boy's shoes were recorded in March and May 1824 (Phillips, 1:211).]

5 MARCH. John Allan sends Charles Ellis a request: "If you have looked over the papers send them to me by Edgar—I have been looking over Bonds" (DLC–EA; Phillips, 1:211).

16 MARCH. In the Ellis & Allan office books John Allan is charged $10 "sent him by Edgar" (DLC–EA; Campbell [1912], p. 208).

28 APRIL. Jane Stith Craig Stanard, the mother of Poe's friend Robert Craig Stanard, dies.

30 APRIL. The *Richmond Enquirer* reports: "DIED—On Wednesday night in this city, Mrs. STANARD, the beloved and lamented lady of Robert Stanard, Esq."'
Mrs. Stanard is buried in the Shockoe Hill Cemetery (Rudd, 1:2; see also Allen, p. 90 n. 154, and Phillips, 1:205).

JUNE? 1824? Poe swims the James River from Mayo's Bridge (Ludlam's Wharf) to Warwick bar, a distance of six miles.

Robert Gamble Cabell recalled: "I was one of several who witnessed this swimming feat. We accompanied Mr. Poe in boats. Messrs. Robert Stannard [Robert Craig Stanard], John Lyle (since dead), Robert Saunders,

John Munford, I think, and one or two others, were also of the party. Mr. Poe did not seem at all fatigued, and *walked* back to Richmond immediately after the feat—which was undertaken for a wager" (Ingram, p. 23).

Robert Mayo, Jr., another participant, recalled that he "started with Poe in his celebrated swim from Richmond to Warwick bar, six miles down James River. . . . the day was oppressively hot." Mayo "concluded rather than endure the infliction to stop at Tree Hill, three miles from town. Poe, however, braved the sun and kept on, reaching the goal, but emerging from the water with blistered back, neck and face, and bearing the semblance of a boiled lobster" (Richmond *Evening Journal*, 1874; Baltimore *Sun*, 8 July 1875; clippings in ViRVal).

[Richard Carey Ambler indicated the feat probably took place in 1825 (Ambler to E. V. Valentine, 14 December 1874, ViRVal). Woodberry (1:26) has "when fifteen years old"; Mabbott (1969, 1:536), "June 1824." Robert Gamble Cabell (1809–1889), the grandfather of the novelist James Branch Cabell, should not be confused with Robert Henry Cabell, who married Julia Mayo 3 January 1823. Other witnesses to the feat were William Burke and T. G. Clarke. Clarke wrote Valentine in February 1878 (ViRVal). See CA. 10 FEBRUARY and 30 APRIL 1835, 12 FEBRUARY 1840.]

14 AUGUST. NEW YORK. Lafayette begins a triumphal tour of the United States.

1 SEPTEMBER? RICHMOND. John Allan pays William Burke $30 for Poe's tuition "for five months from 1st of April [1824] last" (DLC–EA; Campbell [1912], p. 207).

24 SEPTEMBER. William Galt, Jr., becomes a partner in the William Galt firm (Herndon, pp. 326–43).

8 OCTOBER. BALTIMORE. Lafayette notices the absence of David Poe, Sr.

The next day he [Lafayette] received visitors at the Exchange and dined with the corporation, &c., &c., and in the evening visited the Grand Lodge; after which he attended the splendid ball given in Holliday Street Theatre, which had been fitted up for the occasion. After the introduction of the surviving officers and soldiers of the Revolution who resided in and near Baltimore, to General LaFayette on Friday [8 October], he observed to one of the gentlemen near, "I have not seen among these my friendly and patriotic commissary, Mr. David Poe, who resided in Baltimore when I was here, and of his own very limited means supplied me with five hundred dollars to aid in clothing my troops, and whose wife, with her own hands, cut out five hundred pairs of pantaloons, and superintended the making of them for the use of my men." The General was informed that Mr. Poe was dead but that his widow [Elizabeth Cairnes Poe] was still living. He expressed an anxious wish to see her (Scharf, p. 415).

9 OCTOBER. Elizabeth Cairnes Poe calls on Lafayette.

The good old lady heard the intelligence with tears of joy, and the next day [9 October] visited the General, by whom she was received most affectionately; he spoke in grateful terms of the friendly assistance he had received from her and her husband: "Your husband," said he, pressing his hand on his breast, "was my friend, and the aid I received from you both was greatly beneficial to me and my troops." The effect of such an interview as this may be imagined but cannot be described. On the 11th General LaFayette left the city with an escort for Washington (Scharf, p. 415).

CA. 10 OCTOBER. On visiting the grave of David Poe, Sr., General Lafayette kneels and says: "Ici repose un cœur noble!" (*Philadelphia Saturday Museum*, 4 March 1843).

25 OCTOBER. Henry Poe writes his brother Edgar (Allan to Henry Poe, 1 November 1824).

26, 27, AND 28 OCTOBER. RICHMOND. The capital of Virginia welcomes Lafayette. Thomas H. Ellis is impressed by the role played by Poe in the ceremonies honoring the French hero.

["But never was I prouder of him [Poe] than when, dressed in the uniform of the 'Junior Morgan Riflemen' (a volunteer company composed of boys, and which General Lafayette, in his memorable visit to Richmond, selected as his bodyguard), he walked up and down in front of the marquee erected on the Capitol Square, under which the old general held a grand reception in October, 1824" (*W*, 1:25–26, quoting Ellis).]

31 OCTOBER. Lafayette attends a service in the Monumental Episcopal Church (*Richmond Enquirer*, 5 November 1824; G. D. Fisher, p. 92).

1 NOVEMBER. John Allan writes Henry Poe:

I have just seen your letter of the 25th ult. to Edgar and am much afflicted, that he has not written you. He has had little else to do for me he does nothing & seems quite miserable, sulky & ill-tempered to all the Family. How we have acted to produce this is beyond my conception—why I have put up so long with his conduct is little less wonderful. The boy possesses not a Spark of affection for us not a particle of gratitude for all my care and kindness towards him. I have given him a much superior Education than ever I received myself. If Rosalie has to relie on any affection from him God in his mercy preserve her—I fear his associates have led him to adopt a line of thinking & acting very contrary to what he possessed when in England. I feel proudly the difference between your principles

& his & have my desire to Stand as I ought to do in your Estimation. Had I done my duty as faithfully to my God as I have to Edgar, then had Death come when he will had no terrors for me, but I must end and this with a devout wish that God may yet bless him & you & that Success may crown all your endeavors & between you your poor Sister Rosalie may not suffer. At least She is half your Sister & God forbid my dear Henry that We should visit upon the living the Errors & frailties of the dead. Beleive [Believe] me Dear Henry we take an affectionate interest in your destinies and our United Prayers will be that the God of Heaven will bless & protect you. rely on him my Brave & excellent Boy who is willing & ready to save to the uttermost. May he keep you in Danger preserve you always is the prayer of your Friend & Servant (DLC–EA).

17 NOVEMBER. Poe, a lieutenant, and John Lyle, a captain of the Richmond Junior Volunteers, write the Governor and Council of Virginia, soliciting permission "to retain the arms which they lately were permitted to draw from the Armory" (L, 1:3).

20 NOVEMBER. Poe and John Lyle confer with Peter V. Daniel, one of three members of the Virginia State Council, regarding the arms which they have turned over to Dr. John Adams, the Mayor of Richmond (Poe and Lyle to Daniel, 23 November; see also Allen, p. 100).

23 NOVEMBER. Poe and John Lyle write Peter V. Daniel, referring to their Saturday meeting with him and soliciting his aid in retaining arms (L, 1:3–4).

2 DECEMBER. John Allan pays a tailor's bill: "Master Edgar Allan, making and trimming Blue Cloth Coat $8.50, Rec. payment, Bradley M. McCrery & Co. [Bradley, McCreery & Co.]" (DLC–EA; Phillips, 1:211. The tailor was Thomas H. Bradley).

25 DECEMBER. William Mackenzie, Secretary of the Marine Insurance Company of Richmond, notifies the stockholders of his company of a dividend declared by its President and Directors (Richmond Compiler, 25 December).

1824. The partnership of Ellis & Allan is dissolved by mutual consent (T. H. Ellis, Richmond Standard, 7 May 1881).

1824? Poe reads the part of Cassius in Shakespeare's Julius Caesar (Mabbott [1969], 1:536).

1824? Poe composes "Poetry."

[An undated sheet of paper placed in the Ellis & Allan files contains financial calculations by a person who estimates that he has $30,000 available for any emergency, and the earliest surviving poem by Poe.

—Poetry. by . Edgar A. Poe—
Last night with many cares & toils oppress'd
Weary, I laid me on a couch to rest—

Both Allen (facing p. 77) and Mabbott (1969, 1:5-6) ascribe the calculations to John Allan and the lines (which are in a different handwriting) to Poe, and date the lines November 1824.]

1824? Poe composes the satire "Oh, Tempora! Oh, Mores!"

[Mabbott (1969, 1:8–13) reprinted this satire. Campbell (1933, p. 203) and Stovall (1965, pp. 294–95) do not accept it as Poe's.]

*

1825

*

5 JANUARY. RICHMOND. John Allan is elected to the Board of Directors of the Richmond branch of the Bank of Virginia, of which his uncle William Galt is already a director (*Richmond Compiler*, 5 January 1825).

11 JANUARY. John Allan records a payment to Bradley & Co. of $8.50 for "Edgar's clothes" (DLC–EA; Campbell [1912], p. 208. Apparently this ledger entry refers to the 2 December 1824 bill).

25 FEBRUARY. William Galt, Jr., writes Mary Fowlds that his fiancee Rosanna Dixon is a niece of Frances Allan "but not exactly like her in temper & disposition" (NcD–G).

7 MARCH. CHARLOTTESVILLE. Thomas Jefferson's University of Virginia opens its doors.

25 MARCH. RICHMOND. William Galt, one of the wealthiest men in the State of Virginia, signs his will. The will is probated 29 March (MS, Deed Book 117–B, p. 99, in the Circuit Court of the City of Richmond, Va., Division I).

. . .I give, devise and bequeath to the said John Allan, my three landed estates, named the "Byrd," lying and being situate in the Counties of Goochland and Fluvanna, on the Byrd Creek, with the slaves, stocks and property of all kinds belonging thereto. . . . I give and bequeath to Mrs. Allan, the wife of said John, my Carriage and horses. . . . I give and bequeath to Miss Ann M. Valentine two thousand dollars. . . . I give and bequeath to Miss Rosanna Dixon, one thousand dollars. . . . I give my pew in the First Presbyterian Church to the said John Allan, William Galt, Jr., and James Galt.

26 MARCH. William Galt dies. John Allan writes an account of Galt's death (NcD–G).

28 MARCH. The *Richmond Compiler* prints an obituary.

DIED——In this City, on Saturday morning, WILLIAM GALT Esq. one of the oldest and most respectable Inhabitants. He breathed his last, profoundly impressed with the truths of the Christian Religion, and perfectly resigned to his lot.

The friends and acquaintances of the late WILLIAM GALT, are requested to attend his funeral this morning at 11 o'clock.

[The *Richmond Enquirer* printed an obituary on 1 April.]

MARCH. Poe leaves Burke's school (Woodberry, 1:29. See also 1 OCTOBER 1823).

AFTER MARCH? Poe attends the school of Dr. and Mrs. Ray Thomas (Didier [1877], p. 34; Ingram List, pp. 159–60).

[The *Richmond Compiler* for 1 September 1828 ran this advertisement: "Mr. & Mrs. Thomas's School, will be reopened on MONDAY, 1st September, at the Old Council Chamber, in the rear of Governor's st."]

2 APRIL. WASHINGTON. William Wirt writes Francis Walker Gilmer: "old Galt is dead and has enriched swivel-legged Allan Sic vos non nobis—I wish the old rascal had cut short my labours by giving me a hundred or two thousand dollars" (Davis, p. 132).

5 APRIL. RICHMOND. John Allan and William Galt, Jr., as executors, require notice of all claims against and payments of indebtedness to the estate of William Galt (*Enquirer*, 5 and 8 April; *Compiler*, 16 April).

28 JUNE. John Allan purchases at auction from Peter Joseph Chevallié, executor of the Joseph Gallego estate, and Mary Richard, executrix of the John Richard estate, three lots, including "Moldavia," a substantial brick house with a portico on the southeast corner of Main and Fifth Streets, for

$14,950 (Deed Book 24, page 96, Circuit Court, Division I, Richmond, Va. See also Scott [1941], pp. 46–49; Woodberry, 1:30–31, 2:362–64).

AFTER 28 JUNE. Poe falls in love with Sarah Elmira Royster, then about fifteen years of age.

[She was the daughter of the James Roysters, neighbors of the Allans. Later, as Mrs. Shelton, she recalled: "He [Edgar] was a beautiful boy— Not very talkative. When he did talk though he was pleasant but his general manner was sad—He was devoted to the first Mrs Allan and she to him. We lived opposite to Poe on 5th. I made his acquaintance so. Our acquaintance was kept up until he left to go to the University" (Edward V. Valentine, "Conversation with Mrs Shelton at Mr Smith's Corner 8th and Leigh Streets Nov. 19th 1875," ViRVal).]

SUMMER. Henry Poe makes the last of two visits to his brother Edgar. The two boys, with Henry in nautical uniform, and with Ebenezer Burling, Poe's friend, call at the home of Elmira Royster (Edward V. Valentine, "Conversation with Mrs Shelton at Mr Smith's Corner 8th and Leigh Streets Nov. 19th 1875," ViRVal; Whitty, p. xxxi. The date of Henry's first visit is not known).

14 SEPTEMBER. William Galt, Jr., marries Rosanna Dixon, Frances Allan's niece (NcD–G).

7 NOVEMBER. FRANKFORT, KENTUCKY. Jereboam O. Beauchamp, an attorney, fatally stabs Solomon P. Sharp, a politician. Beauchamp acts to avenge the honor of his wife Ann, who has been seduced by Sharp.

[This famous murder case, known as the "Kentucky Tragedy," provided the plot for Poe's unfinished and unsuccessful tragedy *Politian*. See CA. 26 NOVEMBER 1835.]

1825? RICHMOND. Poe composes a satire on the Junior Debating Society.

I remember to have heard some verses of his in the shape of a satire, upon some of the members of a debating society to which he belonged. This society held its meetings in a house known as Harris Building, situated at the corner of Main and 11th Streets (if I recollect it aright[)]—I cannot recall a line of these verses (R. C. Ambler to E. V. Valentine, 14 December 1874, ViRVal; see also Mabbott [1969], 1:6–7).

[By September 1828, when it celebrated its fourth anniversary, the Society was called the Richmond Athenaeum.]

JOHN ALLAN
Poe Museum of the Poe Foundation, Inc.

CHAPTER TWO

Student, Soldier, and Poet

1826–1830

From February to December 1826 Poe attends the University of Virginia, where he excels in Latin and French. He also incurs gambling debts which John Allan refuses to pay. In Poe's absence his sweetheart Sarah Elmira Royster becomes engaged to Alexander B. Shelton. After quarrels with John Allan Poe leaves the Allan household for Boston. Here he publishes *Tamerlane and Other Poems* (1827) and under the alias of Edgar A. Perry he enlists in the U. S. Army. His battalion is ordered to Fort Moultrie, South Carolina, and later to Fortress Monroe, Virginia. Poe becomes reconciled with John Allan after the death of Frances Allan, obtains an honorable discharge from the Army, and publishes *Al Aaraaf, Tamerlane, and Minor Poems* (Baltimore, 1829). With the assistance of Allan and the recommendations of others Poe receives an appointment to West Point. In October 1830, while Poe is a cadet at West Point, John Allan marries a second time.

*

1826

*

1 FEBRUARY. CHARLOTTESVILLE. The second session of the University of Virginia begins.

8 FEBRUARY. BALTIMORE. The *Baltimore Gazette* reports: "Died this morning, William Clemm, in 47th year."

9 FEBRUARY. William Clemm, Jr., is buried (St. Paul's Protestant Episcopal Church record; Quinn, p. 726).

13 FEBRUARY. Elizabeth Cairnes Poe draws up her will, bequeathing all her belongings to her daughter Maria Clemm (Baltimore Wills, 17:38–39, Maryland Hall of Records, Annapolis, Md.).

14 FEBRUARY. CHARLOTTESVILLE. Poe is one of five students who matriculate at the University of Virginia on this day. He is 136th on the list of 177 who attend this year. Of the 177, six withdraw, three are suspended, three are dismissed, and three are expelled during the year (Kent, pp. 10–11).

Poe pays his fees ($60) for attendance on two professors, George Long, School of Ancient Languages (Greek and Latin), and George Blaettermann, School of Modern Languages (French, German, Italian, and Spanish).

His class schedule is: Ancient Languages: Monday, Wednesday, and Friday, 7:30 to 9:30 A.M. Modern Languages: Tuesday, Thursday, and Saturday, 7:30 to 9:30 A.M.

Mr. Brockenborough, the Proctor, makes an entry in the Matriculation Books:

Name	Date of Birth	Parent or Guardian	Place of Residence	Professors Attended
Edgar A. Poe	19 Jan: 1809	John Allan	Richmond	Long Blaettermann

[George Long later recalled: "If Poe was at the University of Virginia in 1826, he was probably in my class which was the largest. . . . The beginning of the University of Virginia was very bad. There were some excellent young men, and some of the worst that ever I knew. . . .I remember the name of Poe, but the remembrance is very feeble; and if he was in my class, he could not be among the worst, and perhaps not among the best or I should certainly remember him" (Long to John H. Ingram, 15 April 1875, in Wilson [1923], p. 164).]

CA. 21 FEBRUARY. A week after his arrival Poe writes Allan "for some more money, and for books" (Poe to Allan, 3 January 1831).

CA. 24 OR 27 FEBRUARY. RICHMOND. A short time afterwards Allan, "in terms of the utmost abuse," replies to Poe (Poe to Allan, 3 January 1831).

MARCH? CHARLOTTESVILLE. Poe is "tolerably regular in attendance" at classes (Wertenbaker [1868], p. 114).

29 APRIL. William Matthews is "allowed the use of the Gymnasium . . .for the purpose of giving instruction upon military tactics to such of the students as may choose to be drilled. Mr. Matthews is held responsible to the faculty for all riots, or other disturbances of the peace, happening during his attendance upon the students composing his class" (Kent, p. 12).

APRIL OR LATER? "During the year 1826, there used to come into the

Library a handsome young student [Poe], perhaps eighteen years of age, in search of old French books, principally histories" (Wertenbaker [1879], p. 45).

[Quinn, p. 102, writes: "The library really began to function only in April, and was not properly catalogued until after Poe left college."]

BEFORE 9 MAY. John Allan visits Poe (Poe to Allan, 25 May 1826).

BEFORE 9 MAY? Poe scuffles with Miles George, whose home address is the north side of Grace Street adjoining the Washington Tavern, Richmond. Poe moves from the Lawn to No. 13 West Range.

[Denying the account of a fellow student, Thomas Goode Tucker, that he and Poe were roommates and had a fight, Miles George wrote E. V. Valentine, 18 May 1880: "Poe and myself were at no time room mates, therefore he did not leave me, or I him—Poe roomed on the West side of the Lawn, I on the East, he afterwards moved to the Western range—I was often in both rooms, & recall the many happy hours spent therein— Of the pugilistic combat so minutely described, I have some recollection; it was a boyish freak or frolic, & both fight & the feeling in which it originated were by consent buried in oblivion never again to be revived— Poe, as has been said, was fond of quoting poetic authors and reading poetic productions of his own, with which his friends were delighted & entertained, then suddenly a change would come over him & he would with a piece of charcoal evince his versatile genius, by sketching upon the walls of his dormitory, whimsical, fanciful, & grotesque figures, with so much artistic skill, as to leave us in doubt whether Poe in future life would be Painter or Poet; He was very excitable & restless, at times wayward, melancholic & morose, but again in his better moods frolicksome, full of fun & a most attractive & agreeable companion[.] To calm & quiet the excessive nervous excitability under which he labored, he would too often put himself under the influence of that 'Invisible Spirit of Wine' which the great Dramatist has said 'If known by no other names should be called Devil'—

"My impressions of Poe do not agree with the idea that he was 'short of stature, thick & somewhat compactly set'[.] On the contrary, he was of rather a delicate & slender mould[.] His legs not bowed, or so slightly so, as to escape notice, and did not detract either from the sym[m]etry of his person or the ease & grace of his carriage—To be practical & unpoetical I think his weight was between 130 & 140 pounds" (ViRVal. For Tucker's account, see Sherley, pp. 427–28).

Tucker reported: "Poe's passion for strong drink was as marked and as peculiar as that for cards. It was not the *taste* of the beverage that influenced him; without a sip or smack of the mouth he would seize a full glass, without water or sugar, and send it home at a single gulp. This frequently used him up; but if not, he rarely returned to the charge" (Tucker to Douglass Sherley, 5 April 1880; Woodberry, 1:33).

James Albert Clarke described Poe as "a pretty wild young man . . .[who] took much interest in athletic sports" (Richmond newspaper, 29 November 1885, ViU–I; Stovall {1967}, p. 309).]

BEFORE 9 MAY? Poe and Thomas Goode Tucker read the histories of Hume and Lingard (Sherley, p. 379; Kent, pp. 14–15).

9 MAY. Student disturbances at the University of Virginia cause the Faculty to issue a "proclamation," which is little heeded (Poe to Allan, 25 May 1826; Quinn, p. 105 n. 15).

10 MAY. Thomas Bolling, a University student, writes his father Colonel William Bolling: "We have lately lost a student by the name of Thomas Barclay, expelled for a very trivial offence, and suspended for the Session" (Allen, p. 714).

The Goodacre engraving of the University
University of Virginia Library

11 MAY. James Albert Clarke of Manchester, Poe's former schoolmate at William Burke's seminary, is suspended from the University for two months and J. Armstead Carter "for the remainder of the session" (Poe to Allan, 25 May 1826).

BEFORE 24 MAY. Sterling Edmunds, a University of Virginia student, loses $240 at a single sitting playing cards and horsewhips Charles Peyton, another student who he believes has cheated him. Peyton is later expelled and Edmunds is suspended until 1 July (Quinn, p. 106).

24–25 MAY. The University Faculty meets (Stovall [1967], p. 308).

BEFORE 25 MAY. Allan makes a second visit ("Soon after you left here") to Charlottesville (Poe to Allan, 25 May 1826).

25 MAY. Poe writes Allan, acknowledging the receipt of clothes, describing the disturbances at the University, and asking for "a copy of the Historiae of Tacitus—it is a small volume—also some more soap" (L, 1:4–5).

MAY? Poe meets Peter Pindar Pease.

["As a boy old Pease was apprenticed to an itinerant saddler, Hermann Tucker by name, and shortly before the early '30's arrived at Charlottesville, Virginia, where the worthy harnessmaker opened a shop, and my great-uncle [Pease] became his assistant.

"Trade was pretty brisk, and soon the little shop expanded into a sort of curio store filled with second-hand articles, including a library which had fallen under the auctioneer's hammer in order to satisfy a plantation debt and so came into the possession of Tucker. Among these books was a rare edition of Hogarth's prints, and this work the young assistant resolved to purchase on the installment plan from his employer.

"Two small payments had been made when Poe, then attending the college there, happened into the shop one day, noticed the book, and desired to buy it. Upon Tucker's telling Poe that his clerk was attempting to purchase the work out of his meager earnings, the poet asked to be made known to my great-uncle, and thus their acquaintance began.

"Poe immediately invited young Peter up to his room, asking him to bring the Hogarth along with him that they might look it over together, and the invitation was accepted.

"Next evening the call was made, and after some parley Poe suggested that they gamble for the book, agreeing to pay Peter the full price which Tucker asked in case he lost. If Peter lost, he was to continue paying off the debt to Tucker and Poe was to keep the Hogarth. My great-uncle had been brought up to fear the devil and all his works with Calvinistic severity, but he resolved to take the chance of getting the book for nothing, so the dice were thrown.

"Poe lost, and promptly paid over the money. Whatever became of the Hogarth I do not know. It is certainly not in the Pease family library and Peter probably sold it. This incident occurred some time in May, 1826, as nearly as the old Deacon remembers it" (Stearns, pp. 25–26).]

13 JUNE. Poe withdraws from the Library the "lst. 3d. 4th vols Rollin's A. hist. [*Historie Ancienne*]—[Charles Rollins, *Œuvres Complètes* . . . . Paris, 1807–10. 60 vols.]" (Cameron [1974], p. 33).

4 JULY. Thomas Jefferson and John Adams die.

5 JULY. CHARLOTTESVILLE. The University of Virginia bell tolls, for the first time, in honor of Jefferson.

7 JULY. FRANKFORT, KENTUCKY. Jereboam O. Beauchamp is hanged for the murder of Solomon P. Sharp (see CA. 26 NOVEMBER 1835).

15 JULY. PHILADELPHIA. John Lofland's poem "The Bride" with its first line "I saw her on the bridal day" appears in the *Saturday Evening Post*.

[This line Poe may have had in mind when he composed "Song" ("I saw thee on thy bridal day").]

8 AUGUST. CHARLOTTESVILLE. Poe withdraws from the University of Virginia Library: "33d. 34th vols Rollin (his. Romaine) [Charles Rollin, *Histoire Romaine*]" (Cameron [1974], p. 33).

15 AUGUST. Poe withdraws from the Library: "1st & 2d vols Robertson's America [William Robertson, *The History of America* . . ., Dublin, 1777. 2 vols.]" (Cameron [1974], p. 33).

29 AUGUST. Poe withdraws from the Library: "1st & 2d vols Marshall's Washington [John Marshall, *The Life of George Washington* . . ., Philadelphia, 1804–1807. 5 vols. and atlas]" (Cameron [1974], p. 33).

12 SEPTEMBER. Poe withdraws from the Library: "9. 10. Voltaire [Either volumes 9 and 10 of the complete works, 25 volumes, in French, Paris, 1817, or volumes 9 and 10 of a collection of letters, 12 volumes, in French, Paris, 1785]" (Cameron [1974], p. 33).

20 SEPTEMBER. Charles Wickcliffe, a student from Kentucky, is expelled

by the Faculty for fighting, the fight having taken place before Poe's door (Poe to Allan, 21 September 1826).

21 SEPTEMBER. Poe writes Allan that he is studying for an examination to be given from 1 to 15 December and that the Library has a "fine collection" of books (*L*, 1:6–7).

17 OCTOBER. The Library is open every day from 3:30 to 5 P.M. after this date, except Saturdays and Sundays (*W*, 1:52).

4 NOVEMBER. Poe withdraws from the Library: "lst and 2d Dufiefs Nature displayd [Nicholas Gouin Dufief's *Nature Displayed in Her Mode of Teaching Language to Man*]" (Cameron [1974], pp. 33–34).

4? DECEMBER. James Madison (rector), James Monroe, Joseph Cabell, and John Hartwell Cocke conduct an examination in ancient languages (Kent, p. 20).

4 DECEMBER. Poe makes some purchases.

Mr. Edgar A. Powe [*sic*]
In Acct. With Samuel Leitch, Jr., Dr.

Dec. 4 To 3 yds Super Blue Cloth $13.00	$39.00
" 3 " Linin 3 / 2 yds Cotten 1 / 6	$ 2.00
" 2 3 / 4 " Blk Bombazette 3 / Padding 3 /	1.88
" Staying 3 / 1 set Best Gilt Buttons 7 / 6	1.75
" 1 doz. Buttonmoulds 9d 1 Cut Velvet Vest 30 /	5.13
" 3 / 4 yd Blk Cassinette 27 /	3.38
" 1 " Staying 2 / 16 Hanks Silk 6d	1.63
" 9 Hanks Thread at 3c 1 Spool Cotten 1 /	.44
" 1 Peace Tape 9d 1 1 / 2 doz. Buttons 6d	.25 55.46
" 1 pr. Drab Pantaloones and Trimmings	13.00 13.00
	$68.46

(DLC–EA).

5 DECEMBER. An examination in modern languages is given at the University (Kent, p. 20).

15 DECEMBER. The University of Virginia Faculty meets. Poe is listed in Professor George Long's "report of the examinations of the classes belonging to the school of ancient languages and the names of the students who excelled at the examination of these classes" and in Professor George Blaettermann's report of "the names of the students who excelled in the Senior French Class" (Kent, p. 21).

20 DECEMBER. The University Faculty begins an investigation. Present are John T. Somes, Chairman; Dr. Robley Dunglison, Dr. George Blaettermann, Charles Bonnycastle, George Tucker, and J. Hewitt Key (Allen, p. 133).

The Chairman presented to the faculty a letter from the Proctor giving information that certain Hotel Keepers during the last session had been in the habit of playing at games of chance with the students in their Dormitories—he also gave the names of the following persons who he had been informed had some knowledge of the facts, Edgar Mason, Turner Dixon, William Seawell, E. LeBranche, Edgar Poe, [Edwin C.?] Drummond [,] Emmanuel Miller, Hugh Pleasants and E. G. Crump who having been summoned to appear (Allen, p. 133).

Edgar Poe never heard until now of any Hotel-Keepers playing cards or drinking with students (Faculty Minutes of the University of Virginia, ViU; Kent, p. 22; Quinn, p. 109).

BEFORE 21 DECEMBER. RICHMOND. Allan sends Poe $100. Poe's application to James Galt for a loan is refused (Poe to Allan, 3 January 1831).

21 DECEMBER. CHARLOTTESVILLE. Poe leaves for Richmond.

Mr. Allan went up to Charlottesville, inquired into his ways, paid every debt that he thought ought to be paid, and refusing to pay some gambling debts (which Mr. James Galt told me, in his lifetime, amounted to about $2,500) brought Edgar away in the month of December following, and for a time kept him in Ellis & Allan's countingroom (where they were engaged in winding up their old business)—thus attempting to give him some knowledge of book-keeping accounts, and commercial correspondence (T. H. Ellis, *Richmond Standard*, 7 May 1881).

AFTER 21 DECEMBER. RICHMOND. Poe's engagement to Elmira Royster is broken.

. . .during the time he was at the University he wrote to me frequently, but my father intercepted the letters because we were too young—no other reason . . . . I was about 15 or 16 when he first addressed me and I engaged myself to him, and I was not aware that he wrote to me until I was married to Mr Shelton when I was 17 (E. V. Valentine's "Conversation with Mrs. Shelton," ViRVal).

[The Royster-Shelton wedding did not take place until 6 December 1828, while Poe was stationed at Fort Moultrie.]

1826. CHARLOTTESVILLE. Poe signs a promissory note for $41.36 made payable to Dan'l S. Mosby & Co. (Stovall [1967], p. 311).

1826. Poe joins the Jefferson Literary Society and becomes its secretary (Stovall [1967], pp. 312 and 314; W, 1:60).

1826. Poe reads one of his stories to an audience of his friends.

On one occasion Poe read a story of great length to some of his friends who, in a spirit of jest, spoke lightly of its merits, and jokingly told him that his hero's name, "Gaffy," occurred too often. His proud spirit would not stand such, as he thought, open rebuke; so in a fit of anger, before his friends could prevent him, he had flung every sheet in a blazing fire, and thus was lost a story of more than ordinary parts, and, unlike most of his stories, was intensely amusing, entirely free from his usual sombre coloring and sad conclusions merged in a mist of impenetrable gloom. He was for a long time afterwards called by those in his particular circle "Gaffy" Poe, a name that he never altogether relished (Thomas Goode Tucker's account recorded by Sherley, p. 431).

1826. Poe excels in athletic exercises and has a fine talent for drawing.

I [Thomas Bolling] was acquainted with him, in his youthful days, for that was about all—My impression was and is that no one could say that he *knew* him—He wore . . . a sad, melancholy face always, and even a smile, for I dont remember his ever having laughed heartily, seemed to be forced—and when, as he sometimes engaged with others in athletic exercises, in which, so far as jumping high or far, he I think excelled all the rest. Poe, with the same sad face, appeared to participate in what was amusement to others more as a task, than sport—Upon one occasion on a slight declivity, he ran and jumpt 20 ft. which no other could reach, though there were two or three who made 18 & 19, and Euphemon Labranche, an especial friend of mine from Louisiana, of lower stature by several inches, was his chief competitor . . .educated in France, . . . where gymnastic feats were taught and practised as a part of the course. (Thomas Bolling to E. V. Valentine, 10 July 1875, ViRVal. Bolling with Thomas Powell, Jesse Maury, and John Willis recalled Poe's drawings (Kent, p. 13).]

Two classmates, William Wertenbaker and William Burwell, later recorded their recollections of Poe.

I [William Wertenbaker] was myself a member of the last three classes [French, Spanish, and Italian], and can testify that he [Poe] was tolerably regular in his attendance, and a successful student. . . .On one occasion Professor Blaettermann requested his Italian class to render into English Verse a portion of the lesson in Tasso, which he had assigned them for the next lecture. He did not require this of them as a regular class exercise, but recommended it as one from which he thought the student would derive benefit. At the next lecture on Italian, the Professor stated from his chair that Mr. Poe was the only member of the class who had responded to his suggestion, and paid a very high compliment to his performance.

As Librarian I had frequent official intercourse with Mr. Poe, but it was at or near the close of the Session before I met him in the social circle. After spending an evening together at a private house, he invited me, on our return, to his room. It was a cold night in December, and his fire having gone pretty nearly out, by the aid of some tallow candles, and the fragments of a small table which he broke up for the purpose, he soon rekindled it, and by its comfortable blaze I spent a very pleasant hour with him. On this occasion he spoke with regret of the large amount of money he had wasted and of the debts he had contracted during the Session. If my memory is not at fault, he estimated his indebtedness at $2,000, and though they were gaming debts, he was earnest and emphatic in the declaration, that he was bound by honor to pay at the earliest opportunity, every cent of them. He certainly was not habitually intemperate, but he may occasionally have entered into a frolick. I often saw him in the Lecture room and in the Library, but never in the slightest degree under the influence of intoxicating liquors. Among the Professors he had the reputation of being a sober, quiet and orderly young man, and to them and the officers, his deportment was uniformly that of an intelligent and polished gentleman. Although his practice of gaming did escape detection, the hardihood, intemperance and reckless wildness imputed to him by his Biographers, had he been guilty of them, must inevitably have come to the knowledge of the Faculty and met with merited punishment. The records of which I was then, and am still, the custodian, attest that at no time during the session did he fall under the censure of the faculty. . . . I think it probable that the night I visited him was the last he spent here. I draw this inference not from memory, but from the fact, that having no further use for his candles and table, he made fuel of them (Wertenbaker [1868], pp. 114–17).

My [William Burwell's] recollection of Poe, then little more than a boy, is that he was about five feet two or three inches in height, somewhat bandy-legged, but in no sense muscular or apt at any physical exercises. His face was feminine, with finely marked features, and eyes dark, liquid and expressive. He dressed well and neatly. He was a very attractive companion, genial in his nature and familiar, by the varied life that he had already led, with persons and scenes new to the unsophisticated provincials among whom he was thrown . . . . What, however, impressed his associates most were his remarkable attainments as a classical scholar. . . .

The particular dissipation of the university at this period was gaming with cards, and into this Poe plunged with a recklessness of nature which acknowledge[d] no restraint (Burwell, pp. 168–80).

*

1827

*

6 JANUARY. RICHMOND. The *Richmond Enquirer* lists John Allan as a director of the Bank of Virginia and its branches (Bondurant, p. 223).

20 JANUARY. PHILADELPHIA. The *Saturday Evening Post* prints Henry Poe's poem "Jacob's Dream."

JANUARY? RICHMOND. Perhaps Poe is employed without pay in the Ellis & Allan countinghouse (see 21 DECEMBER 1826).

JANUARY. Poe visits a guest of Mrs. Juliet J. Drew, an instructor in Miss Jane Mackenzie's school (Whitty, p. xxx; Phillips, 1:283).

FEBRUARY. MONTEVIDEO, SOUTH AMERICA. Aboard the *U.S.S. Macedonian* Henry Poe writes a travel letter (Allen and Mabbott, pp. 23, 31).

3 FEBRUARY. PHILADELPHIA. The *Saturday Evening Post* prints Henry Poe's "Psalm 139th."

FEBRUARY. GOOCHLAND COUNTY, VIRGINIA. Perhaps Poe spends a short time at the Allan plantation and studies law (Whitty, p. xxix; Phillips, 1:283).

3 MARCH. RICHMOND. Bernard Peyton writes Messrs. John Cochran & Co., Charlottesville, about his problems with Poe:

On the $30 note of Poe, I gave credit for $15 Dolls, & I have given the note to the constable, to warrant him for the residue, who has not yet made a return upon it;—for the dft: [draft] he gave you on Allan, I have taken his bond including interest from the date of the dft:, to the date of the bond—he says if these bonds had been held up & not presented to Allan, he would have returned to the University 1st Feb & discharged them all, but being pressed on Allan, he would not send him back there, but he thinks he will do so the next session & further, that after a while, he will discharge all these debts. I mention these things that you may consider of them, and if you still wish suit instituted against him on the bond, I will hand it to a lawyer forthwith—in writing, he is approaching to 21 years, when he will probably legally bind himself for these debts. I shall promptly obey any instructions you may give touching it (ViRVal).

[In the Richmond City Directory of 1819, p. 62, Peyton is listed as a merchant whose address is "ss [southside] of D [Cary] bt [between] 12 and 13th sts. sixth from 12th st." His name frequently appears in the pages of the *Richmond Compiler* in the 1820's. In 1822 Peyton was Secretary of the Board of Public Works of Virginia. In 1835 he was a Trustee of the Richmond Academy.]

14 MARCH. Bernard Peyton writes his client, Messrs. John Cochran & Co., Charlottesville, for instructions: "The constable informs me he has judgment against Poe, can find no property to levy execution on, & Mr. Allan assures him he will not pay that, or any other debt of his—under these circumstances shall I have him put to gaol, or compel him to plead nonage?" (ViRVal).

18 MARCH. Poe quarrels with Allan (Poe to Allan, 19 March).

19 MARCH. Poe quarrels again with Allan, takes a room at the Court-

house Tavern, and writes Allan that he has resolved to leave the Allan household, and begs for money and his trunk: "My determination is . . . to leave your house and indeavor to find some place in this wide world, where I will be treated—not as *you* have treated me. . . . A collegiate Education . . . was what I most ardently desired. . . . I have heard you say . . . that you had no affection for me" (*L*, 1:7–8).

20 MARCH. Poe writes Allan that he is roaming the streets. He begs for his trunk and passage money to Boston: "I sail on Saturday" (*L*, 1:8–9).

Allan writes Poe, refusing him financial aid: "I taught you to aspire, even to eminence in Public Life, but I never expected that Don Quixotte, Gil Blas, Jo: Miller & such works were calculated to promote the end . . . the charge of eating the Bread of idleness, was to urge you to perseverance & industry in receiving the classics, in perfecting yourself in the mathematics, mastering the French" (Stanard, p. 67).

24 MARCH. NORFOLK, VIRGINIA. Poe, perhaps accompanied by his friend Ebenezer Burling as far as Norfolk, takes passage in a coal vessel for Boston (Stanard, pp. 52–53; Mabbott [1969], 1:538; E. V. Valentine to J. H. Ingram, 10 December 1874, ViU–I; *Philadelphia Saturday Museum*, 4 March 1843).

25 MARCH. DINWIDDIE COUNTY, VIRGINIA. Edward G. Crump, a classmate of Poe at the University of Virginia, writes Poe:

When I saw you in Richmond a few days ago I should have mentioned the difference between us. . . .I must of course, as you did not mention it to me enquire of you if you ever intend to pay it. If you have not the money write me word that you have not, but do not be perfectly silent. I should be glad if you would write to me even as a friend. There can certainly be no harm in your avowing candidly that you have no money if you have none, but you can say when you can pay me if you cannot now. I heard when I was in Richmond that Mr. Allan would probably discharge all your debts. If mine was a gambling debt I should not think very strangely of it. But under the present circumstances I think very strangely of it. Write to me upon the receipt of this letter and tell me candidly what is the matter (DLC–EA).

27 MARCH. RICHMOND. John Allan writes one of his sisters, giving information about the settlement of William Galt's estate, and adds that "though Mrs. Allan occupuys one of the airiest & pretty places about Richmond it seems to make no improvement in hers [health]—it is indeed a lovely spot. . . . Miss Valentine is as fat & hearty as ever. Im thinking Edgar has gone to Sea to seek his own fortunes" (DLC–EA).

MARCH? Frances Allan writes Poe two letters (Phillips, 1:294).

MARCH? BALTIMORE. En route to Boston Poe perhaps stops off to see his brother Henry, to call upon Nathan C. Brooks, to become acquainted with Lambert A. Wilmer, and to meet Edward Coote Pinkney (Stanard, pp. 51–57; Woodberry, 1:67; Stovall [1969], p. 23; Mabbott [1969] 1:538). Poe composes "To Octavia" and writes an extract from Voltaire's *Princesse de Babylone* in Octavia Walton's album (Mabbott [1941], pp. xii–xv; [1969], 1:16–17; Leary, 9–15).

MARCH. BOSTON. Poe meets Peter Pindar Pease again.

It was while unloading a dray of hides on the waterfront one blustering March afternoon that my great-uncle [Peter Pindar Pease] recognized in a pale, rather stoop-shouldered clerk, emerging from a mercantile house hard by, his former acquaintance who had diced with him unsuccessfully in Virginia a year before. He was about to hail Poe when the latter, catching sight of him, turned away and hastily disappeared around the corner.

Thinking that Poe did not care to renew the friendship, Pease returned to his work, but when he had finished and was starting homeward, there was Poe waiting for him some distance down the street. He was very shabbily appareled.

Pease hailed him, but Poe hurriedly pushed him into an alleyway and begged him not to speak his name aloud, giving for his reason that "he had left home to seek his fortune, and until he had hit it hard he preferred to remain incognito."

As my great-uncle recounted it to Judge Pease: "He [Poe] told me that he had clerked for two months in a wholesale merchandise house on the water-front at a very small salary, the most of which he had been too proud to ask for, and his employer, taking advantage of this pride and being a man of brutal and unscrupulous character, the boy was easily done out of most of the money which he had earned.

"His landlady, too, was a woman of no attainments, and had no patience with a boarder who sat up nights writing on paper which he could not afterward sell. She soon turned him into the street.

"He then tried literary work, but failed to obtain employment on any of the large journals. Finally he secured work in the office of an obscure paper as market reporter; but, the proprietor being a man of shady reputation, the office soon got into debt, and soon after Poe joined it the paper stopped publication.

"He then told me that he was resolved to enlist in the army, for his resources were utterly exhausted, and he was determined not to write to former friends for help. I believe he remained in Boston several months altogether" (Stearns, pp. 25–26; see Mabbott [1969], 1:539).

2 APRIL. CHARLOTTESVILLE? George W. Spotswood, a hotelkeeper and a distant cousin of George Washington, writes John Allan:

My situation requires me again to request you will send the trifling sum I wrote for due by Mr Poe—for servants hire—every young man who comes to the Institution [the University of Virginia] has a servant—this of course is a necessary charge. Mr Poe did not live with me but hired my servant. . . .the amt. is $6.25 (DLC–EA).

24–25 APRIL. BOSTON. The *Boston Courier* advertises William Dimond's *The Foundling of the Forest*, a play in which Poe's mother once performed.

[It is purely speculative that Poe was the "young gentleman of Boston" in the cast who played the part of Bertrand in this 1827 performance. See Mabbott (1942), p. xxvii. T. H. Ellis wrote: "The occasional letters which he [Poe] wrote home . . . were written while he was on the stage in Boston" (ViRVal–THE).]

28 APRIL. RICHMOND. Bernard Peyton reports to John Cochran & Co., Charlottesville, on his collection problems with Hugh R. Pleasants, one of Poe's University of Virginia classmates, and with Poe: "Poe has gone off entirely, it is said, to join the Greeks—he had as well be there as any where else, I believe, for he appears to be worthless" (ViRVal).

APRIL OR LATER. BOSTON. Perhaps Poe meets the printer Calvin F. S. Thomas at 70 Washington Street (Woodberry, 1:38–39, 368; Wegelin, pp. 23–25; Quinn, pp. 119–22).

1 MAY. CHARLOTTESVILLE. George W. Spotswood writes John Allan:

I presume when *you sent* Mr Poe to the University of Virginia you felt yourself bound to pay all his necessary expences—one is that each young man is expected to have a servant to attend his room. Mr. Poe did not board with me but as I had hired a first rate Servant who cost me a high price—I consider him under greater obligations to pay me for the price of my Servant—I have written you two letters & have never recd. answer to eather—I beg again Sir that you will send me the small amt. due. I am distressed for money—& I am informed you are Rich both in purse & Honour (DLC–EA).

19 MAY. BALTIMORE. Samuel Sands begins the publication of the *North American or, Weekly Journal of Politics, Science and Literature.*

[Henry Poe's contributions to the *North American* included "The Pirate," a prose sketch based on his brother's love affair with Elmira Royster, and two of his brother's poems, "The Happiest Day" and "Dreams."]

26 MAY. CASTLE ISLAND, BOSTON HARBOR. Poe under the alias of Edgar A. Perry enlists in the U. S. Army for five years and is assigned to Battery H of the First Artillery in Fort Independence, Boston Harbor. He gives his age as 22, his birthplace Boston, occupation clerk, and personal description: grey eyes, brown hair, fair complexion, and 5 ft. 8 in. in height (National Archives—Register of Enlistments, 37:153).

[Kent (1917), p. 522, speculated that Poe may have borrowed the last name Perry from a University of Virginia classmate, Sidney A. Perry, who matriculated four days before him, on 10 February 1826.]

JUNE OR JULY. BOSTON. Calvin F. S. Thomas publishes *Tamerlane and Other Poems*.

[TAMERLANE / AND / OTHER POEMS. / (rule) / BY A BOSTONIAN. / (rule) / Young heads are giddy, and young hearts are warm, / And make mistakes for manhood to reform.—COWPER. / (printer's device) / BOSTON: / CALVIN F. S. THOMAS. . . .. PRINTER. / . . . . / 1827. 40 pages. paper wrappers.

Contents: "Preface"; "Tamerlane"; "Fugitive Pieces": "To— —" ("I saw thee on the bridal day"), "Dreams," "Visit of the Dead," "Evening Star," "Imitation," no title ("In youth have I known one with whom the Earth"), no title ("A wilder'd being from my birth"), no title ("The happiest day— the happiest hour"), "The Lake"; "Notes."

"*The* greater part of the Poems which compose this little volume, were written in the year 1821–2, when the author had not completed his fourteenth year" (from Poe's Preface).

Perhaps 50 copies printed. A facsimile edition with an Introduction by Thomas Ollive Mabbott was published for the Facsimile Text Society by Columbia University Press, New York, 1941.]

JUNE. BALTIMORE? Miss E. S. B., an acquaintance of Henry Poe, dies (see 28 JULY 1827).

28 JULY. BALTIMORE. Henry Poe's "On the Death of Miss E. S. B." appears in the *North American*.

JULY. LONDON. Sir Walter Scott reviews the works of E. T. A. Hoffman in the *Foreign Quarterly Review*, perhaps suggesting to Poe the title *Tales of the Grotesque and Arabesque* (Quinn, p. 289).

4 AND 11 AUGUST. BALTIMORE. Henry Poe's "Oh! Give that Smile" and "In a Pocket-Book" appear in the *North American*.

18 AUGUST. The first of three installments of Lambert A. Wilmer's *Merlin*, a verse drama based on Poe's unsuccessful romance with Elmira Royster, appears in the *North American*.

25 AUGUST. The second installment of Wilmer's *Merlin* appears in the *North American*.

AUGUST. BOSTON AND NEW YORK. The *United States Review and Literary Gazette* lists *Tamerlane and Other Poems* under "New Publications."

1 SEPTEMBER. BALTIMORE. The third and final installment of Wilmer's *Merlin* appears in the *North American*.

11 SEPTEMBER. Henry Poe enters "Woman" in the album of Margaret Bassett, which includes Poe's undated cento, "To Margaret" (Mabbott [1969], 1:14–16, 518).

15 SEPTEMBER. A variant of the stanzas entitled "The happiest day—the

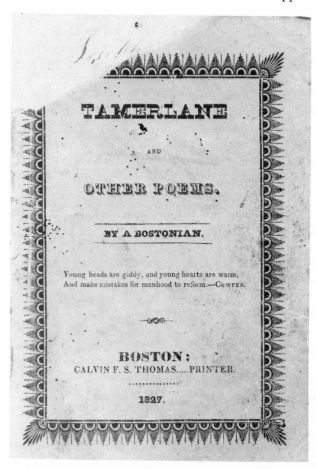

Front wrapper of *Tamerlane*
(copy in the Richard Gimbel Collection)
Philadelphia Free Library

happiest hour" (from Poe's *Tamerlane and Other Poems*) appears in the *North American* over the initials "W. H. P." (Mabbott [1969], 1:81).

21 SEPTEMBER. A pamphlet edition of Wilmer's *Merlin* is offered for sale (*North American*, 22 September).

22 SEPTEMBER. Henry Poe's "To R" and "To Montevideo" appear in the *North American*.

29 SEPTEMBER. Wilmer's "To Mary" (later printed as "To Mira" in the *Southern Literary Messenger* for December 1835) and Henry Poe's composition "I've lov'd thee" appear in the *North American*.

6 OCTOBER.. Henry Poe's composition of sixteen lines beginning "Scenes of my love" appears in the *North American*.

9 OCTOBER. PETERSBURG, VIRGINIA. Poe's friend John Hamilton Mackenzie marries Louisa Lanier (Mackenzie Family Bible, ViHi).

20 OCTOBER. BALTIMORE. Poe's "Dreams" (as "Extract—Dreams"), signed "W. H. P.," appears in the *North American*.

27 OCTOBER. Henry Poe's "The Pirate" appears in the *North American*.
    The *North American* prints a notice of the death of Elizabeth Usher: "Died . . . On Friday evening, the 12th inst. Elizabeth Usher, daughter of the late Thomas Usher, sen. of the county of Antrim, Ireland, and formerly a merchant of this city."

[According to Allen, p. 683, these Ushers, who settled in Baltimore, were friends of the Poes.]

31 OCTOBER. BOSTON. Poe's battery is ordered to Fort Moultrie, Sullivan's Island, Charleston Harbor, South Carolina (National Archives).

OCTOBER. The *North American Review* lists Poe's *Tamerlane and Other Poems* as a recent publication.

3 NOVEMBER. BALTIMORE. Henry Poe's "A Fragment" and "Despair" appear in the *North American*.

3 NOVEMBER. BOSTON. The *Boston Evening Gazette* reports that the brig *Waltham* has "Cleared."

6 NOVEMBER. The Boston *Palladium* reports: "Brig Waltham, Webb, for

Charleston, dropped down to Fort Independence, on Sunday [4 November], to take on board the garrison, &c. and proceed to Charleston. We learn that she returns to this port with the garrison of that place, as likewise one from another port, which she is to land at Portland" (*Charleston Courier*, 15 November, taken from the *Palladium*).

9 NOVEMBER. The Boston *Palladium* reports: "Went to sea, on Tuesday afternoon [6 November] . . .brig Waltham, Charleston, with a company of soldiers, in charge of Lt. Griswold" (H.C. Davis, p. 3).

10 NOVEMBER. BALTIMORE. Henry Poe's "Recollections" and "Lines" appear in the *North American*.

10 NOVEMBER. BOSTON. Captain Jacob Brown reports that the brig *Waltham* went to sea 6 November (H.C. Davis, p. 3).

The *Boston Evening Gazette* prints details of the sinking of the *Aurora* in a gale off the Hook (H.C. Davis, p. 3).

17 NOVEMBER. BALTIMORE. Henry Poe's "On Seeing a Lady Sleeping" appears in the *North American*.

19 NOVEMBER. CHARLESTON, SOUTH CAROLINA. Both the *Courier* and the *City Gazette* print the following "Ship News":

Arrived Yesterday

Brig *Waltham*, Webb, Boston 11 days. With a company of U.S. Troops for the Garrison at Fort Moultrie. *Passengers*, Lieut. H. W. Griswold, U.S.A., Lady and child, Lieut. J. Howard, U.S.A., Lady and three children, and Dr. J. Dodd, U.S.A.

(Hoole, p. 78).

20 NOVEMBER. The *Charleston Courier* prints a card of thanks, dated 18 November, under "Ship News":

The undersigned, officers of the 1st Regiment of Artillery, in behalf of ourselves, families, and a detachment of men, tender to Captain George Webb, our most unfeigned thanks, for his kind attention to us while on board the Brig Waltham, on her passage from the harbor of Boston to Charleston, South Carolina; more especially for his nautical abilities, under Divine Providence, in extricating the vessel under his command, from most imminent danger, when drifting on a lee shore, off the shoals of Cape Cod, as well as good management during several severe gales of wind, while on our passage. Wishing him the like success under every peril and danger, we subscribe ourselves, his most obedient and very humble servants.

H. W. Griswold, Lieut. and Adjt. 1st Regt Art'y.

J. Howard, Lieut 1st Regt. Art'y.
James Mann, Assistant Surgeon, U.S.A. (H.C. Davis, p. 3).

24 NOVEMBER. BALTIMORE. Henry Poe's "Waters of Life" appears in the final issue of the *North American*.

30 NOVEMBER. RICHMOND. The *Richmond Enquirer* reports that Charles Ellis has recommenced the drygoods business on his own account.

1827? CHARLESTON, SOUTH CAROLINA? Perhaps Poe meets Colonel William Drayton and Dr. Edmund Ravenel, a conchologist (Quinn, pp. 129 and 130).

1827? RICHMOND. Rosalie Poe composes two poems (Mabbott [1969], 1:521–22).

1827. BALTIMORE. Maria Clemm is listed in Matchett's Director, a directory, as the "precepteress of school, Stiles Street, North Side near Foot Bridge."

*

1828

*

25 JANUARY. WASHINGTON. In the rooms of the Senate Committee on Claims Duff Green accuses Edward Vernon Sparhawk, a reporter for the *National Intelligencer*, of maliciously misquoting the Washington *Telegraph's* report of a speech by John Randolph and then physically attacks Sparhawk (*Telegraph*, 1 and 11 February 1828; Ames, p. 161).

[Sparhawk preceded Poe as editor of the *Southern Literary Messenger*. See 11 JUNE 1835.]

17 APRIL. RICHMOND. Rosanna Dixon Galt, wife of William Galt, Jr., dies (NcD–G).

1 MAY. FORT MOULTRIE, SOUTH CAROLINA. Poe is appointed an artificer (National Archives).

28 JUNE. CHARLOTTESVILLE. Samuel Leitch writes Charles Ellis regarding Poe's debt incurred 4 December 1826: "Please let me know if Mr. Allan

[has] done anything with my account again[st] Mr. Poe" (DLC–EA; Quinn, p. 112 n. 26)

31 OCTOBER. RICHMOND. The firm of William Galt and William Galt, Jr., quits the drygoods business (*Compiler*, 31 October).

31 OCTOBER. FORT MOULTRIE, SOUTH CAROLINA. Poe's battery is ordered to Fortress Monroe, Old Point Comfort, Virginia (National Archives; *W*, 1:70).

28 NOVEMBER. RICHMOND. The *Richmond Enquirer* reports that John Allan is chairman of a group of merchants protesting auction sales (Bondurant, pp. 223–24).

BEFORE 1 DECEMBER. FORT MOULTRIE, SOUTH CAROLINA. Lieut. J. Howard writes a letter which John O. Lay, a Richmond insurance agent, leaves with John Allan for his perusal (Poe to Allan, 1 December 1828).

BEFORE 1 DECEMBER. RICHMOND. John Allan writes John O. Lay, who in turn writes Lieut. Howard, enclosing Allan's "note"—a note which gives Poe "concern" (Poe to Allan, 1 December 1828).

1 DECEMBER. FORT MOULTRIE, SOUTH CAROLINA. Poe writes Allan:

In that note [addressed to Lay] what chiefly gave me concern was hearing of your indisposition . . . . at no period of my life, have I regarded myself with a deeper satisfaction . . . . I have been in the American army as long as suits my ends or my inclination, and it is now time that I should leave it . . . I made known my circumstances to Lieut. Howard who promised me my discharge solely upon reconciliation with yourself . . . . He has always been kind to me, and, in many respects, reminds me forcibly of yourself. . . . I . . . am no longer a boy tossing about on the world without aim or consistency. . . . A letter addressed to Lieut: J. Howard assuring him of your reconciliation with myself (which you have never yet refused) & desiring my discharge would be all that is necessary—He is already acquainted with you from report & the high character given of you by Mr Lay . . . . My dearest love to Ma (*L*, 1:9–11).

3 DECEMBER. CHARLESTON, SOUTH CAROLINA. The *Charleston Courier* reports: "*In the offing*: The ship *Harriet*, (of Bath) Johnson, from Baltimore via Norfolk with two companies of U. S. Troops for the garrison in the harbor, anchored below yesterday" (Hoole, p. 79).

4 DECEMBER. The *Harriet* clears a day after her arrival and remains in the harbor one week (*Charleston Courier*, 5 December; Hoole, p. 79).

6 DECEMBER. RICHMOND. Elmira Royster marries Alexander Barret Shelton (Mabbott [1969], 1:65 and 539 n. 5).

11 DECEMBER. FORT MOULTRIE, SOUTH CAROLINA. Poe's battery sets sail on the *Harriet* for Fortress Monroe (Hoole, p. 79).

15 DECEMBER. FORTRESS MONROE, OLD POINT COMFORT, VIRGINIA. Poe's battery lands (Hoole, p. 79).

20 DECEMBER. Colonel James House issues an order:

Special Order No. 91—Private E. A. Perry of Company "H," and Private Joseph Moore of Company "E," are detailed for duty in the Adjutant's office until further orders. By order of Colonel House—H. W. Griswold, Adj't. Art'y. (National Archives).

22 DECEMBER. Poe writes Allan:

I wrote you shortly before leaving Fort Moultrie . . . Perhaps my letter has not reached you & under that supposition I will recapitulate its contents. . . .Lieut Howard has given me an introduction to Col: James House of the 1rst Arty to whom I was before personally known only as a soldier of his regiment. He spoke kindly to me. told me that he was personally acquainted with my Grandfather Genl Poe, with yourself & family, & reassured me of my immediate discharge upon your consent. . . .Richmond & the U. States were too narrow a sphere & the world shall be my theatre (*L*, 1:11–13).

22 DECEMBER. CHARLESTON, SOUTH CAROLINA. The *Gazette* prints a notice from a correspondent: "*Norfolk*. December 15: The ship *Harriet*, Johnson, fm *Charleston*, with two companies U. S. Artillery, anchored off Old Point this afternoon" (Hoole, p. 79).

BEFORE 23 DECEMBER–3 FEBRUARY 1829. RICHMOND. John Mackenzie writes Poe at Old Point Comfort (Poe to Allan, 4 February 1829).

BEFORE 23 DECEMBER–3 FEBRUARY 1829. FORTRESS MONROE, OLD POINT COMFORT, VIRGINIA. Poe writes his friend John Mackenzie and requests that he solicit Allan's aid in obtaining a West Point appointment for Poe (Poe to Allan, 4 February 1829).

1828. BALTIMORE. Frederick William Thomas, a young author, meets Henry Poe.

I was intimate with Poe's brother in Baltimore during the year 1828. He was a slim, feeble young man, with dark inexpressive eyes, and his forehead had nothing like the expansion of his brother's. His manners were fastidious. We visited lady acquaintances together, and he wrote Byron poetry in albums, which had little originality. He recited in private and was proud of his oratorical powers. He often deplored the early death of his mother, but pretended not to know what had become of his father. I was told by a lawyer intimate with the family that his father had deserted his mother in New York. Both his parents had visited Baltimore when he was a child, and they sent money from Boston to pay for his support (Thomas' "Recollections," Whitty, p. xxi).

*

1829

*

1 JANUARY. FORTRESS MONROE, OLD POINT COMFORT, VIRGINIA. Poe is promoted to the rank of Regimental Sergeant-Major (H. W. Griswold's note, 20 April).

JANUARY. Dr. Robert Archer, a post surgeon, attends Poe, who is ill in the military hospital (Allen, pp. 186–87).

JANUARY. BALTIMORE. Henry Poe, who is employed in the countinghouse of Henry Didier, lives with his aunt Maria Clemm in Mechanics Row, Wilks Street. Also living with Maria Clemm are her daughter Virginia and her mother Mrs. David Poe, Sr. (Allen and Mabbott, p. 31; Quinn, p. 188 n.6).

4 FEBRUARY. FORTRESS MONROE, OLD POINT COMFORT, VIRGINIA. Poe writes John Allan:

. . . the appointment [to West Point] could easily be obtained either by your personal acquaintance with Mr [William] Wirt—or by the recommendation of General [Winfield] Scott, or even of the officers residing at Fortress Monroe . . . . You will remember how much I had to suffer upon my return from the University. I never meant to offer a shadow of excuse for the infamous conduct of myself & others at that place.

It was however at the commencement of that year that I got deeply entangled in difficulty which all my after good conduct in the close of the session (to which all there can testify) could not clear away. I had never been from home before for any length of time (L, 1:13–14).

28 FEBRUARY. Poe answers roll-call (National Archives; Cameron [1973], p. 172).

28 FEBRUARY. RICHMOND. Frances Allan dies (*Richmond Whig*, 2 March 1829).

2 MARCH. Frances Allan is buried at Shockoe Hill Cemetery. The *Richmond Whig* reports: "Died on Saturday morning last, after a lingering and painful illness, Mrs. Frances K. Allan, consort of Mr. John Allan, aged 47 [44?] years. The friends and acquaintances of the family are respectfully invited to attend the funeral from the late residence on this day at 12 o'clock."

["Poe spoke of the first Mrs. Allan with the tenderest affection—of the second with admiration of her beauty & an avowed feeling that the [second] marriage was one of great discrepancy. *Entre nous* Mr. Allan was represented to me, by him, as a man of a gross & brutal temperament though *indulgent to him* & at *times* profusely lavish in the matter of money—at others, penurious and parsimonious" (Sarah Helen Whitman to John H. Ingram, 27 March 1874; Miller [1979], p. 95).]

2 MARCH. Poe, on leave, arrives the night after Frances Allan's burial (Poe to Allan, 3 January 1831).

3 MARCH. John Allan is charged with a bill of drygoods sold "p[er] order to E A P," including three yards of black cloth at twelve dollars a yard, three pairs of black hose at four shillings per pair, and one "London Hat" at ten dollars (DLC–EA; Campbell [1916], pp. 144–45; Stanard, p. 97).

4 MARCH. John Allan writes a younger brother of Charles Ellis, Powhatan Ellis, U. S. Senator from Mississippi, in Poe's behalf. He also addresses a note to Charles Ellis: "Please to furnish Edgar A. Poe with a suit of Black Clothes 3 pair Socks or Half Hose—McCreary [McCreery] will make them / —also a pr Suspenders / and Hat—& Knife / pair of Gloves" (DLC–EA).

9? MARCH. Poe leaves for Fortress Monroe (Poe to Allan, 10 March 1829).

10 MARCH. FORTRESS MONROE, OLD POINT COMFORT, VIRGINIA. Poe writes Allan:

I arrived on the point this morning . . . . Colonel [James House] has left the point this morning for Washington to congratulate . . . President [elect Andrew Jackson] so I have not yet seen him. He will return on Thursday week next. In the mean time I am employing myself in preparing for the tests which will engage my attention at W. Point if I should be so fortunate as to obtain an appointment. I am anxious to retrieve my good name with my friends & especially your good opinion. I think a letter of recommendation from Judge [John S.] Barber [Barbour], Major Gibbon, & Col: Preston forwarded to Washington with a letter to Mr. Patterson requesting that if nothing would prevent I may be regarded as a Bostonian (*L*, 1:15).

30 MARCH. Colonel House writes a letter in Poe's behalf to General E. P. Gaines, commanding the Eastern Department, U. S. Army.

I request your permission to discharge from the service Edgar A. Perry, at present the Sergeant Major of the 1t. Regt. of Artillery on his procuring a substitute—

The said Perry, is one of a family of orphans whose unfortunate parents were the victims of the conflagration of the Richmond theatre, in 1809.—The subject of this letter, was taken under the protection of a Mr Allan, a gentleman of wealth & respectability, of that city, who, as I understand, adopted his Protegé as his son & heir—with the intention of giving him a liberal education, he had placed him at the University of Virginia from which, after considerable progress in his studies, in a moment of youthful indiscretion he absconded and was not heard from by his Patron for several years—in the mean time, he became reduced to the necessity of enlisting into the Service and accordingly entered as a soldier in my Regiment, at Fort Independence in 1827.—Since the arrival of his company at this place, he has made his situation known to his Patron at whose request, the young man has been permitted to visit him—the result is, an entire reconciliation on the part of Mr. Allan, who reenstates him into his family & favor—and who in a letter I have recieved [received] from him request[s] that his son may be discharged on procuring a substitute—An experienced soldier & approved Sergeant, is ready to take the place of Perry so soon as his discharge can be obtained—The good of the Service, therefore cannot be materially injured by the exchange (National Archives; Cameron [1973], pp. 155–56).

4 APRIL. NEW YORK. General Gaines grants Colonel House's request. Under Special Order No. 28 "Edgar A. Perry," on furnishing an acceptable substitute without expense to the Government, is to be discharged on 15 April (National Archives).

15 APRIL. FORTRESS MONROE, OLD POINT COMFORT, VIRGINIA. Poe is officially discharged from the U. S. Army (Gaines to House, 4 April 1829).

17 APRIL. Sergeant Samuel Graves of Company H re-enlists as a substitute for Sgt.-Major Perry (National Archives; Quinn, p.742).

20 APRIL. J. Howard, Lieut. 1st Artillery, writes a letter of recommendation.

Edgar Poe, late Serg't Major in the 1st. Arty served under my command in H. Company 1st Regt of Artillery from June 1827 to Jan'y – 1829, during which time his conduct was unexceptionable—he at once performed the duties of company clerk and assistant in the Subsistent Department, both of which duties were promptly and faithfully done. his habits are good, and intirely free from drinking (National Archives; Cameron [1973], p. 158).

H. W. Griswold, Bt. Capt. & Adjt. 1st Arty., adds:

. . . I have to say that Edgar Poe was appointed Sergeant Major of the 1t Arty on the 1t of Jany. 1829. and up to this date has been exemplary in his deportment, prompt & faithful in the discharge of his duties—and is highly worthy of confidence (National Archives; Cameron [1973], pp. 158–59).

W. J. Worth, Lt. Col. Comd'g Fortress Monroe, writes his recommendation:

I have known & had an opportunity of observing the conduct of the above mentioned Serg't-Maj. Poe some three months during which his deportment has been highly praise worthy & deserving of confidence. His education is of a very high order and he appears to be free from bad habits in fact the testimony of Lt. Howard & Adjt. Griswold is full to that point—Understanding he is thro' his friends an applicant for cadets warrant, I unhesitatingly recommend him as promising to acquit himself of the obligations of that station studiously & faithfully (National Archives; Cameron [1973], p. 159).

[W. J. Worth was probably the commandant of West Point whom the cadets carried on their shoulders during a Fourth of July celebration in 1825 (Oelke, p. 2).]

AFTER 20 APRIL. RICHMOND. Poe visits the Allan home (Phillips, 1:329–30; Allen, p. 195).

6 MAY. Both Andrew Stevenson, Speaker of the House of Representatives, and Major John Campbell write Major John Henry Eaton, Secretary of War, Washington, D.C., in Poe's behalf.

I [Andrew Stevenson] beg leave to introduce to you Mr. Edgar Poe who wishes to be admitted into the Military Academy, & to stand the examination in June! He has been two years in the service of the U. States & carries with him the strongest testimonials, from the highest authority. He will be an acquisition to the service & I most earnestly recommend him to yr especial notice & approbation (National Archives; Cameron [1973], p. 160).

The history of the youth Edgar Allan Poe is a very interesting one as detailed to me [John Campbell] by gentlemen in whose veracity I have entire confidence and I unite with great pleasure with Mr. Stevenson & Col Worth in recommending him for a place in the Military Academy at West Point. My friend Mr. Allan of this city [Richmond] by whom this orphan & friendless youth was raised and educated is a gentleman in whose word you may place every confidence and can state to you more in detail the character of the youth & the circumstances which claim for him the patronage of the government (National Archives; Cameron [1973], p. 162).

6 MAY. John Allan writes Secretary John H. Eaton:

The youth who presents this, is the same alluded to by Lt. Howard Capt. Griswold Colo. Worth our representative & the speaker the Hon'ble Andrew Stevenson and my Friend Majr. Jno. Campbell. He left me in consequence of some Gambling at the university at Charlottesville, because (I presume) I refused to sanction a rule that the shopkeepers & others had adopted there, making Debts of

Honour, of all indiscretions—I have much pleasure in asserting that He stood his examination at the close of the year with great credit to himself. His History is short He is the Grandson of Quarter Master Genl Poe of Maryland; whose widow as I understand still receives a pension for the Services or disabilities of Her Husband—Frankly Sir, do I declare that He is no relation to me whatever; that I have many [in] whom I have taken an active Interest to promote thiers [theirs]; with no other feeling than that; every Man is my care, if he be in distress; for myself I ask nothing but I do request your kindness to aid this youth in the promotion of his future prospects—and it will offer me great pleasure to recipro-cate any kindness you can shew him—pardon my Frankness;—but I address a Soldier (National Archives; Cameron [1973], pp. 164–65).

AFTER 6 MAY. WASHINGTON. Poe brings testimonials of 20 April to Secretary John H. Eaton.

John S. Barbour interests himself in Poe's behalf (Allan to Poe, 18 May 1829).

7 OR 8 MAY. BALTIMORE. Poe reaches Baltimore and perhaps resides with his cousin Mrs. Beacham, in a house then No. 9 (now No. 28), Caroline Street, corner of Bounty Lane (Stovall [1969], p. 28; Mabbott [1969], 1:541).

AFTER 8 MAY. Poe writes "Alone" in the album of Lucy Holmes, later the wife of Judge Isaiah Balderston (Mabbott [1969], 1:145).

11 MAY. William Wirt gives Poe advice.

It occurred to me, after you left me this morning, that I was probably losing you a day on your journey to Philadelphia, by proposing to detain your poem ["Al Aaraaf"] even until tomorrow, as I understand the day-boat has commenced her spring trips between the cities. I thought it due to your convenience, therefore, to read the poem at once, and send it tonight.

I am sensible of the compliment you pay me in submitting it to my judgment and only regret that you have not a better counsellor. But the truth is that having never written poetry myself, nor read much poetry for many years, I consider myself as by no means a competent judge [of] poems. This is no doubt an old-fashioned idea resulting from the causes I have mentioned, my ignorance of modern poetry and modern taste. You perceive therefore that I am not qualified to judge of the merits of your poem. It will, I know, please modern readers—the notes contain a good deal of curious and useful information—but to deal candidly with you (as I am bound to do) I should doubt whether the poem will take with old-fashioned readers like myself. But this will be of little consequence—provided it be popular with modern readers—and of this, as I have already said, I am unqualified to judge. I would advise you, therefore, as a friend to get an introduc-tion to Mr. [Robert] Walsh or Mr. [Joseph] Hopkinson or some other critic in Philadelphia (Stanard, pp. 131–32).

12 MAY. Poe intends to leave for Philadelphia (Wirt to Poe, 11 May 1829).

AFTER 12 MAY. PHILADELPHIA. Robert Walsh, editor of the *American Quarterly Review*, points out to Poe "the difficulty of getting a poem published in this country" (Poe to Allan, 29 May 1829).

13 MAY. RICHMOND. Colonel James P. Preston, father of Poe's schoolmate John T. L. Preston, writes Secretary Eaton:

Some of the friends of young Mr Edgar Poe have solicited me to address a letter to you in his favor believing that it may be useful to him in his application to the Government for military service. I know Mr Poe and am acquainted with the fact of his having been born under circumstances of great adversity. I also know from his own productions and others undoubted proofs that he is a young gentleman of genius and talents. I believe he is destined to be distinguished, since he has already gained reputation for talents & attainments at the University of Virginia. I think him possessed of feelings & character peculiarly entitling him to public patronage. I am entirely satisfied that the salutary system of military discipline will soon develope his honorable feelings, and elevated spirit, and prove him worthy of confidence. I would not write in his recommendation if I did not believe that he would remunerate the Government at some future day, by his services and talents, for whatever may be done for him (National Archives; Cameron [1973], pp. 166–67).

CA. 14 MAY. BALTIMORE. Poe meets William Gwynn, editor of the *Federal Gazette and Baltimore Daily Advertiser*, to whom he shows "Al Aaraaf." Gwynn employs Neilson Poe, Poe's second cousin, and perhaps Poe himself (*W*, 1:73; Woodberry, 1:55 and 368).

CA. 14 MAY. Poe writes John Allan (Allan to Poe, 18 May 1829).

16 MAY. RICHMOND. Allan hands Poe's letter to Colonel James P. Preston (Allan to Poe, 18 May 1829).

18 MAY. Allan writes Poe:

I duly recd. your letter from Baltimore on Saturday but seeing Col. Preston I gave it to him to read, I have not yet recovered possession . . . . I was agreeably pleased to hear that the Honourable Jno. J. [S.] Barber [Barbour] did interest himself so much in your favour.

He perhaps remembered you when you were at the Springs in 1812, from the interest exhibited by the Secretary of War you stand a fair chance I think of being of those selected for Sept. Col. Preston wrote a warm letter in your favour to Major Eaton since your departure. Major Campbell left this for Washington on yesterday . . . . I cover a Bank check of Virga. on the Union Bank of Maryland (this date) of Baltimore for one Hundred Dollars payable to your order be prudent and careful (Stanard, p. 121).

18 MAY. BALTIMORE. Passages from Poe's "Al Aaraaf" ("Extract from Al Aaraaf, An Unpublished Poem"), signed Marlow, appear in the advertising columns of William Gwynn's *Federal Gazette and Baltimore Daily Advertiser* (Rede, pp. 49–54).

CA. 19 MAY. Poe writes "Elizabeth" and "An Acrostic" in the album of Elizabeth Rebecca Herring (Whitty, pp. xxxiii and 284–85; Campbell [1917], p. 297; Mabbott [1969], 1:147–50).

20 MAY. Poe writes Allan that he has received the draft for $100, that he has succeeded in finding his grandmother (Elizabeth Cairnes Poe) and other relations, and that he has introduced himself to William Wirt: "He treated me with great politeness, and invited me to call & see him frequently while I stay in Baltimore—I have called upon him several times. I have been introduced to many gentlemen of high standing in the city, who were formerly acquainted with my grandfather & have altogether been treated very handsomely" (*L*, 1:16–17).

BEFORE 27 MAY. PHILADELPHIA. At Heiskell's Indian Queen Hotel, 15 South Fourth Street, Poe writes Isaac Lea of Carey, Lea & Carey, publishers, regarding his manuscript "Al Aaraaf": "If the poem is published, succeed or not, I am 'irrecoverably a poet.' But to your opinion I leave it, and as I should be proud of the honor of your press, failing in that I will make no other application . . . the poem is by a minor & truly written under extraordinary disadvantages" (*L*, 1:18–19).

29 MAY. BALTIMORE. Poe writes Allan:

I have been several times to visit Mr Wirt, who has treated me with great kindness & attention. I sent him, for his opinion, a day or two ago, *a poem* which I have written since I left home . . . . if once noticed I can easily cut out a path to reputation . . . give me a letter to Mssrs Carey, Lea, & Carey saying that if in publishing the poem "Al Aaraaf" they shall incur any *loss*—you will make it good to them . . . . I have long given up *Byron* as a model—for which, I think, I deserve some credit (*L*, 1:20–21).

AFTER 29 MAY. Poe's distant cousin Edward Mosher robs him of about $46 at Beltzhoover's Hotel (Poe to Allan, 25 June 1829).

7 JUNE. NORFOLK, VIRGINIA. William Mackenzie dies.

[A brief account of Mackenzie's sudden death in the *Norfolk Beacon*, 8 June, was copied by the *Richmond Compiler*, 10 June. Surviving him were his wife Jane Scott and the following children: John Hamilton, Mary

Indian Queen Hotel, Philadelphia

Gallego, William Leslie, Thomas Gilliat, Richard Neil (or Neal), Martha H. Gilliat, and Rosalie Mackenzie Poe (Poe's sister).]

8 JUNE. RICHMOND. Allan censures Poe's conduct and refuses him any aid (*L*, 1:21).

10 JUNE. BALTIMORE. Poe writes Allan (Poe to Allan, 25 June 1829).

BEFORE 25 JUNE. Edward Mosher writes Poe, acknowledging his theft (Poe to Allan, 25 June and 26 July 1829).

25 JUNE. Poe writes Allan:

I should by no means publish it ["Al Aaraaf"] without your approbation . . . . The poem is now in the hands of Carey, Lea & Carey . . . . I have left untried no efforts to enter at W. Point . . . . it is only a little [money] that I now want . . . . A cousin of my own [Edward Mosher] robbed me at Beltzhoover's Hotel while I was asleep in the same room with him of all the money I had with me (about 46$) of which I recovered $10—by searching his pockets the ensuing night. . . . I have been moderate in my expences & $50 of the money which you sent me I applied in paying a debt contracted at Old Point for my substitute, for [which] I gave my note—the money necessary if Lt Howard had not gone on furlough would have been only 12$ as a bounty—but when he & Col: House left I had to scuffle for myself—I paid $25—& gave my note for $50—in all 75$

. . . . I have learnt . . . that I am the grandson of General Benedict Arnold (*L*, 1:21–23).

15 JULY. Poe writes Allan: "I am afraid that being up at the Byrd [plantation] you might probably not have received them [my two letters] . . . . I am incurring unnecessary expense as Grandmother is not in a situation to give me any accommodation . . . . You would relieve me from a great deal of anxiety by writing me soon—I think I have already had my share of trouble for one so young" (*L*, 1:23–24).

19 JULY. RICHMOND. Allan sends Poe money (Poe to Allan, 26 July 1829).

22 JULY. BALTIMORE. Poe receives Allan's letter of 19 July (Poe to Allan, 26 July 1829).

23 JULY. WASHINGTON. Poe walks from Baltimore to Washington to see Secretary John H. Eaton (Poe to Allan, 26 July 1829).

26 JULY. BALTIMORE. Poe writes Allan:

I received . . . the money which you sent me, notwithstanding the taunt with which it was given "that men of genius ought not to apply to your aid" . . . . As regards the substitute, the reason why I did not tell you that it would cost $75— was that I could not possibly foresee so improbable an event—The bounty is $12—& but for the absence of Col: House & Lt Howard at the time of my discharge it would have been all that I should have had to pay—The officer commanding a company can (if he pleases) enlist the first recruit who offers & muster him as a substitute for another, of course paying only the bounty of 12$ but as Lt Howard & Col: House were both absent, this arrangement could not be effected—As I told you it would only cost me $12 I did not wish to make you think me imposing upon you—so upon a substitute, offering for $75—I gave him $25 & gave him my note of hand for the balance—when you remitted me $100—thinking I had more than I should want. I thought it my best opportunity of taking up my note—which I did . . . . As regards the money which was stolen I have sent you the only proof in my possession a letter from Mosher . . . . On receiving your last letter, I went immediately to Washington, on foot, & have returned the same way, having paid away $40 for my bill & being unwilling to spend the balance when I might avoid it . . . . I saw Mr Eaton, he addressed me by name, & in reply to my questions told me—"that of the 47 surplus, on the roll, which I mentioned in my former letters, 19 were rejected [9] dismissed & 8 resigned—consequently there was yet a surplus of 10 before me on the roll . . . . if the number [of resignations] exceeded 10 I should be sure of the appt without farther application in Sepr if not I would at least be among the first on the next roll for the ensuing year. . . . he regretted my useless trip to Washington . . . . As regards the poem, I have offended only in asking your approbation (*L*, 1:24– 27).

28 JULY. Poe writes Carey, Lea & Carey: "Having made a better disposition of my poems than I had any right to expect . . . I would thank you to return me the Mss . . . Mr Lea, during our short interview, at your store, mentioned 'the Atlantic Souvenir' and spoke of my attempting something for that work . . . As I am unacquainted with the method of proceeding in offering any piece for acceptance (having been sometime absent from this country) would you, Gentlemen, have the kindness to set me in the right way" (*L*, 1:27–28).

3 AUGUST. PHILADELPHIA. Carey, Lea & Carey write Poe (cited on Poe's 28 July 1829 letter).

4 AUGUST. BALTIMORE. Poe writes Allan: "I repeat that I have done nothing to deserve your displeasure . . . . By your last letter I understood that it was not your wish that I should return home—I am anxious to do so—but if you think that I should not—I only wish to know what course I shall pursue" (*L*, 1:28–29).

CA. 7 AUGUST. RICHMOND. Allan writes Poe (Poe to Allan, 10 August 1829).

10 AUGUST. BALTIMORE. Poe writes Allan: "I knew that I had done nothing to deserve your anger, I was in a most uncomfortable situation— without one cent of money—in a strange place . . . . My grandmother is extremely poor & ill (paralytic). My aunt Maria if possible still worse & Henry entirely given up to drink & unable to help himself . . . . they will no longer enlist men for the *residue* of anothers' enlistment as formerly, consequently my substitute was enlisted for 5 years not 3 . . . . I left behind me in Richmond a small trunk containing books & some letters— will you forward it on to Baltimore to the care of *H–W. Bool Jr* & if you think I may ask so much perhaps you will put in it for me some few clothes as I am nearly without" (*L*, 1:29–30).

[H. W. Bool, Jr., was an eccentric auctioneer and second-hand bookdealer, whose business and residence address was 60 Baltimore Street (Jackson [1977], p. 44).]

19 AUGUST. RICHMOND. Allan writes Poe, sending him $50 (Stanard, p. 183).
Margaret Ellis writes her husband Charles: "Mr. Allan goes tomorrow to Virginia Springs, he has been sick, complains of being weak and nervous" (Phillips, 1:442).

AUGUST? BALTIMORE. Poe writes John Neal, perhaps at the suggestion of his cousin George Poe, the brother of Neilson Poe (*Yankee; and Boston Literary Gazette*, 3 [September 1829]:168; Phillips, 1:339).

LATE AUGUST OR EARLY SEPTEMBER. PORTLAND, MAINE. In the "To Correspondents" column of the *Yankee; and Boston Literary Gazette* for September John Neal addresses Poe:

If E. A. P. of Baltimore——whose lines about *Heaven*, though he professes to regard them as altogether superior to any thing in the whole range of American poetry, save two or three trifles referred to, are, though nonsense, rather exquisite nonsense—would but do himself justice, might make a beautiful and perhaps a magnificent poem. There is a good deal here to justify such a hope.

> Dim vales and shadowy floods,
> And cloudy-looking woods,
> Whose forms we can't discover,
> For the tears that—drip all over.
> The moonlight ——————————— falls
> Over hamlets, over halls,
> Wherever they may be,
> O'er the strange woods, o'er the sea——
> O'er spirits on the wing,
> O'er every drowsy thing——
> And buries them up quite,
> In a labyrinth of light,
> And then how deep!——*Oh deep!*
> *Is the passion of their sleep!*

He should have signed it Bah! We have no room for others.

SEPTEMBER. WASHINGTON. The quota for West Point does not include Poe (Poe to Allan, 10 August and 30 October 1829).

22 OCTOBER. BALTIMORE. Henry Poe is perhaps the author of the lines entitled "Life," written in the album of Miss Mary A. Hand (Mabbott [1969], 1:519).

CA. 27 OCTOBER. RICHMOND. Allan writes Poe (Poe to Allan, 30 October 1829).

30 OCTOBER. BALTIMORE. Poe writes Allan:

It is my intention upon the receipt of your letter to go again to Washington &, tho' contrary to the usual practice, I will get Mr Eaton to give me my letter of appt *now* . . . . I would have sent you the M. S. of my Poems long ago for your approval, but since I have collected them they have been continually in the hands of some person or another. & I have not had them in my own possession since Carey & Lea took them—I will send them to you at the first opportunity—I am sorry that your letters to me have still with them a tone of anger as if my former errors were not forgiven—if I knew how to regain your affection God knows I would do any thing I could (*L*, 1:30–32).

OCTOBER-NOVEMBER. Poe writes John Neal about *Al Aaraaf, Tamerlane, and Minor Poems*: "I am young——not yet twenty——*am* a poet——if deep worship of all beauty can make me one . . . I am about to publish a volume of 'Poems'——the greater part written before I was fifteen" (*Yankee*, VI, December 1829, 295; *L*, 1:32–33).

OCTOBER-NOVEMBER. Perhaps Poe writes Nathaniel Parker Willis, submitting "Heaven" (later "Fairyland") for publication in the *American Monthly*.

LATE OCTOBER OR EARLY NOVEMBER. PORTLAND, MAINE. A notice appears in John Neal's *Yankee* for November:

TO CORRESPONDENTS.

Many papers intended for this number have been put aside for the next, from necessity . . . . Among others are . . . . Unpublished Poetry (being specimens of a book about to appear at Baltimore), Death of James William Miller, our late highly gifted and most amiable associate, and a long piece of poetry which may or may not appear.

EARLY NOVEMBER. BOSTON. In his "The Editor's Table" of the *American Monthly* for November Nathaniel Parker Willis rejects Poe's "Fairyland" and confines the manuscript to the flames:

It is quite exciting to lean over eagerly as the flame eats in upon the letters, and make out the imperfect sentences and trace the faint strokes in the tinder as it trembles in the ascending air of the chimney. There, for instance, goes a gilt-edged sheet which we remember was covered with some sickly rhymes on Fairyland . . . . Now it [the flame] flashes up in a broad blaze, and now it reaches a marked verse—let us see—the fire devours as we read:

> "They use that moon no more
> For the same end as before—
> Videlicet, a tent,
> Which I think extravagant."

Burn on, good fire!

7 NOVEMBER. BALTIMORE. The *Baltimore Gazette* notices a performance of *Timour the Tartar* (Campbell [1917], p. 148. See 12 JULY 1822).

12 NOVEMBER. Poe writes Allan: "I wrote you about a fortnight ago and as I have not heard from you, I was afraid you had forgotten me . . . . I am almost without clothes—and, as I board by the month, the lady with whom I board is anxious for hey [her] money" (*L*, 1:33–34).

CA. 15 NOVEMBER. RICHMOND. Allan sends Poe $80 and states that his health has improved after a visit to the Virginia springs (Poe to Allan, 18 November 1829).

18 NOVEMBER. BALTIMORE. Poe writes Allan, thanking him for a check for $80 and asking him to obtain from the Galt store a piece of linen so that his Aunt Maria can make it up for him "gratis." He adds: "The Poems will be printed by Hatch & Dunning of this city upon terms advantageous to me they printing it & giving me 250 copies of the book:——I will send it on by Mr Dunning who is going immediately to Richmond——I am glad to hear that your trip to the springs was of service in recruiting your health & spirits" (L, 1:34).

LATE NOVEMBER OR EARLY DECEMBER. PORTLAND, MAINE. In "Unpublished Poetry" in the Yankee for December John Neal gives Poe advice:

The following passages are from the manuscript-works of a young author, about to be published in Baltimore. He is entirely a stranger to us, but with all their faults, if the remainder of Al Aaraaf and Tamerlane are as good as the body of the extracts here given——to say nothing of the more extraordinary parts, he will deserve to stand high——very high——in the estimation of the shining brotherhood. Whether he *will* do so however, must depend, not so much upon his worth now in mere poetry, as upon his worth hereafter in something yet loftier and more generous——we allude to the stronger properties of the mind, to the magnanimous determination that enables a youth to endure the present, whatever the present may be, in the hope, or rather in the belief, the fixed, unwavering belief, that in the future he will find his reward. [Neal quotes Poe's letter and extracts from his poems.]

Having allowed our youthful writer to be heard in his own behalf,——what more can we do for the lovers of genuine poetry? Nothing. They who are judges will not need more; and they who are not——why waste words upon them? We shall not (see L, 1:32–33; and 19, 21, and 23 JANUARY 1830).

10 DECEMBER. BALTIMORE. Perhaps Poe acts as Maria Clemm's agent in the assignment of a slave named Edwin to Henry Ridgway for a term of nine years (Jackson [1977], p. 44).

BEFORE 29 DECEMBER. Hatch & Dunning publish Poe's poems.

[AL AARAAF, / TAMERLANE, / AND / MINOR POEMS. / (rule) / BY EDGAR A. POE. / (rule) / BALTIMORE: / HATCH & DUNNING. / (rule) / 1829. Printed by Matchett & Woods. 71 pp.

Contents: no title ("Science! meet daughter of old Time thou art"); "Al Aaraaf"; "Tamerlane"; and "Miscellaneous Poems": "Preface" ("Romance who loves to nod and sing"), "To— —" ("Should my early life seem"),

"To— —" ("I saw thee on thy bridal day"), "To— —" ("The bowers whereat, in dreams, I see"), "To the River—," "The Lake—To—," "Spirits of the Dead," "A Dream," "To M—" ("Oh! I care not that my earthly lot"), "Fairyland."

Perhaps 250 copies printed. A facsimile edition with a bibliographical note by Thomas Ollive Mabbott was published for the Facsimile Text Society by the Columbia University Press, New York, in 1933.]

29 DECEMBER. Poe writes John Neal, forwarding a copy of *Al Aaraaf, Tamerlane, and Minor Poems*: "You will see that I have made the alterations you suggest '*ventur'd out*' in place of *peer-ed* . . . and other corrections of the same kind . . . I wait anxiously for your notice of the book" (*L*, 1:35–36).

[Before publication Poe had revised "Al Aaraaf" (line 33, Part II), following a suggestion Neal made in a footnote to the excerpts in the *Yankee* for December. The presentation copy he sent Neal contained holograph alterations to "Tamerlane" and "To— —" ("I saw thee on thy bridal day"); see Mabbott (1969), 1:25–26, 65–66, 577.]

AFTER 29 DECEMBER? An unknown critic, possibly William Gwynn or Lambert A. Wilmer, favorably reviews *Al Aaraaf, Tamerlane, and Minor Poems* in a Baltimore newspaper (Church, pp. 4–7).

AFTER 29 DECEMBER? Poe gives a copy of *Al Aaraaf, Tamerlane, and Minor Poems* to Elizabeth Rebecca Herring, inscribed "For my cousin Elizabeth" (presentation copy in NN–B; Wakeman, item 936; Mabbott [1942], pp. xxiii–xxv).

1829? Poe transcribes three stanzas by his brother Henry in the album of Lucy Holmes, later Mrs. Balderston. Henry writes several verses in an album belonging to Rosa Durham (Mabbott [1969], 1:518–19).

1829? Henry Poe's poems "To—" and "To Minnie" appear in the *Baltimore Minerva and Emerald*, a literary weekly edited by John Hill Hewitt (Gill, pp. 43–45).

1829. BOSTON. Poe's *Tamerlane and Other Poems* (1827) is listed in Samuel Kettell's "Catalogue of American Poetry," included in his three-volume anthology *Specimens of American Poetry*.

1829. NEW YORK. Lucretia Maria Davidson's *Amir Khan* contains a reference to "Israfil," a probable source for Poe's 1831 poem "Israfel" (Mabbott [1969], 1:173).

Title page of Poe's second volume
George Peabody Library of Johns Hopkins University

JANUARY? BALTIMORE. "S. S." (John Hill Hewitt) in the *Baltimore Minerva and Emerald* reviews unfavorably Poe's *Al Aaraaf, Tamerlane, and Minor Poems*: "The dead alive! Has the poet been struck with numb palsy? We believe not; for then it might only be said, that the poor fellow had but 'one foot in the grave,' where, as it appears by the above, that he has gone the whole————, and fairly kicked the bucket, still possessing the full enjoyment of his faculties. We have done with the book; what more is to be done remains with the public" (Hewitt [1949], pp. 22–24).

JANUARY? PORTLAND, MAINE? John Neal reviews *Al Aaraaf, Tamerlane, and Minor Poems* in an unidentified periodical: "If the young author now before us should fulfil his destiny . . . he will be *foremost* in the rank of *real* poets" (quoted in the *Philadelphia Saturday Museum*, 4 March 1843).

JANUARY. BOSTON. Sarah Josepha Hale publishes a review (not hers) of Poe's *Al Aaraaf, Tamerlane, and Minor Poems* in her *American Ladies' Magazine and Literary Gazette*: "It is very difficult to speak of these poems as they deserve. A part are exceedingly boyish, feeble, and altogether deficient in the common characteristics of poetry; but then we have parts, and parts too of considerable length, which remind us of no less a poet than Shelley. The author who appears to be very young, is evidently a fine genius, but he wants judgment, experience, tact."

EARLY JANUARY? BALTIMORE. Perhaps Poe writes Sarah Josepha Hale (*L*, 1:106).

Perhaps Poe accepts John Lofland's challenge to see who can write more verses in a given time and loses (Phillips, 1:457–58, 461; Mabbott [1969], 1:501–502).

Poe makes his earliest appearance in a satire in lines from *The Musiad or Ninead, by Diabolus*, edited by ME: "Next Poe who smil'd at reason, laugh'd at law, / And played a tune who should have play'd at taw . . ." (Stovall [1969], pp. 64–101; Mabbott [1969], 1:505, 541; ViU–I).

[That Poe was the author of this poem of eight pages is unlikely (Mabbott [1969], 1:541 n. 9).]

BEFORE 8 JANUARY. RICHMOND. Poe returns to Richmond and meets Thomas Bolling, a former classmate.

After being at College together, I never met with him [Poe] until his return having left Mr. A. on account of some disagreement. I happened there [at John Allan's residence] the second night after he got back——when he gave me a history of all he had experienced while away, how he had suffered and shifted to live, when finally as the only alternative for relief, he wrote Alaura-af ["Al Aaraaf"]——that Sanxy [Sanxay]——who kept a book store in Richd. at that time, had it for sale——to call on him for as many copies as I wished and should I meet with any of our old College mates, that would like to see it, give him one, as coming from *me* not Poe——The next day, he went with me, gave me a copy, leaving the above instructions with Sanxy (Thomas Bolling to E. V. Valentine, 10 July 1875, ViRVal).

8 JANUARY. Allan purchases a pair of gloves at $1.38 for Poe (DLC–EA; Campbell [1916], p. 145; Quinn, p. 166 n. 1).

19, 21, AND 23 JANUARY. The Richmond bookseller R. D. Sanxay runs an advertisement in the *Compiler*:

AL AARAAF—Just received Al Aaraaf[,] Tamerlane, and other minor poems, by Edgar A. Poe.
"The following passages are from the M. S. works of a young author, about to be published in Baltimore. If the remainder of Al Aaraaf and Tamerlane are as good as the body of the extracts here given [to say nothing of the more extraordinary parts,] he will deserve to stand high—very high, in the estimation of the brotherhood."——[*Yankee.*
For sale at the Book and Stationery store of

R. D. SANXAY.

[The *Richmond Whig* printed a similar advertisement on 19 January, according to Phillips, 1:358–59. These advertisements were probably supplied by Poe himself. See LATE NOVEMBER OR EARLY DECEMBER 1829.]

26 JANUARY. BALTIMORE. Neilson Poe writes his cousin Josephine Emily Clemm, later his wife: "Edgar Poe has published a volume of Poems one of which ['Tamerlane'] is dedicated to John Neal the great autocrat of critics—Neal has accordingly published Edgar as a Poet of great genius etc.—*Our* name will be a great one *yet*" (Quinn, p. 165).

30 JANUARY. RICHMOND. John Allan purchases for Poe "1/2 doz. Ret. L. Wool Hose. 4.50" (DLC–EA; Quinn, p. 166 n. 1).

2 FEBRUARY. William Galt, Jr., marries Mary Bell Taylor, daughter of Thomas Taylor and Lucy Harrison Singleton Taylor (NcD–G).

13 MARCH. WASHINGTON. Senator Powhatan Ellis of Mississippi writes Secretary of War John H. Eaton a letter in Poe's behalf: "I have recd. a letter from a young gentleman in Richmond by the name of Edgar A. Poe

stating that he was an applicant for a situation in the Military Academy at West Point. He requested me to ask you, if there was any probability of his receiving a warrant to enter that institution. I am not personally acquainted with Mr. Poe—but from information I would say his capacity & learning eminently qualify him to make in a few years a distinguished officer" (National Archives; Cameron [1973], p. 168).

31 MARCH. RICHMOND. Allan writes Secretary John H. Eaton: "As the Guardian of Edgar Allan Poe I hereby signify my assent to his signing articles by which he shall bind himself, to serve the United States for five years, unless sooner discharged, as Stipulated in your Official Letter appointing him a Cadet" (National Archives; Cameron [1973], p. 170).

BEFORE MAY. FORTRESS MONROE, OLD POINT COMFORT, VIRGINIA. Sergeant Samuel ("Bully") Graves writes Poe regarding Poe's debts to him and to Sergeant Griffith (Poe to Graves, 3 May 1830).

CA. 1 MAY. Sergeant Graves writes Poe again (Poe to Graves, 3 May 1830).

[Poe apparently had paid the $75 bounty due Graves for re-enlisting as his Army substitute on 17 April 1829 (see Poe to Allan, 25 June 1829). Graves may have been referring to other debts.]

3 MAY. RICHMOND. Poe writes Sergeant Graves:

I have just received your letter which is the first I have ever got from you . . . . As to what you say about [Thomas] Downey Mr A[llan] very evidently misunderstood me, and I wish you to understand that I never sent any money by Downey whatsoever—Mr A is not very often sober—which accounts for it—I mentioned to him that I had seen Downey at Balto., as I did, & that I wished to send it on by him, but he did not intend going to the point.

I have tried to get the money for you from Mr A a dozen times—but he always shuffles me off—I have been very sorry that I have never had it in my power as yet to pay either you or St Griffith . . . . I told St Benton why I never had it in my power . . . . Give my respects to the company to St Benton & wife & sister in la[w] . . . . remember me to Mrs Graves St Hooper & Charley—Duke &c (L, 1:36–37).

13? MAY. Allan buys "4 blankets, [$]5.34. 7[?] Hckfs. 4.63" for Poe (DLC–EA; Quinn, p. 166 n. 1. Campbell [1916], p. 145, has 12 May).

BEFORE 21 MAY. Poe leaves Richmond for West Point (Stanard, p. 231; Stovall [1969], pp. 43–44).

21 MAY. RICHMOND. Allan writes Poe and encloses $20 (Poe to Allan, 28 June 1830).

AFTER 21 MAY. BALTIMORE. Poe stops in Baltimore and promises Nathan Covington Brooks a poem for his forthcoming annual (Woodberry, 1:67).

CA. 20 JUNE. WEST POINT. Poe reaches the Military Academy (L, 1:38).

25 JUNE. Poe receives John Allan's letter dated 21 May and forwarded by Henry Poe from Baltimore (Poe to Allan, 28 June 1830).

28 JUNE. Poe writes Allan:

I received it [your letter of 21 May] 3 days ago—it has been lying some time in the W. P. post office where it was forwarded from Balto by Henry. As to what you say about the books &c I have taken nothing except what I considered my own property. Upon arriving here I delivered my letters of recommn & was very politely received by Capn [Ethan Allan] Hitchcock & Mr Ross—The examination for admission is just over—a great many cadets of good family &c have been rejected as deficient. Among these was Peyton Giles son of the Governor—James D Brown, son of Jas Brown Jr has also been dismissed for deficiency after staying here 3 years . . . . Of 130 Cadets appointed every year only 30 or 35 ever graduate—the rest being dismissed for bad conduct or deficiency the Regulations are rigid in the extreme . . . . I am in camp at present—my tent mates are Read [Reid?] & [John Eaton] Henderson (nephew of Major Eaton) & [William Telfair] Stockton of Phild (L, 1:37–38).

JULY. PHILADELPHIA. *Godey's Lady's Book* commences publication.

1 JULY. WEST POINT. Poe's name appears for the first time on the muster rolls of cadets. His age is recorded as nineteen years and five months (Cadet Alphabetic Cards, USMA).

CA. 1 JULY. RICHMOND. Twins are born to Mrs. Elizabeth Wills and John Allan, who is courting Louisa Gabriella Patterson, of Elizabethtown, New Jersey. ". . . it was when on a visit to her aunt Mrs. John Mayo that she [Louisa Patterson] first met Mr. Allan" (W 1:78; see 15 MARCH 1833).

JULY AND AUGUST. WEST POINT. Poe takes part in the encampment at Camp Eaton (Poe to Allan, 28 June 1830).

25 AUGUST. Cadet Jacob Whitman Bailey from Rhode Island writes his brother William and describes the masquerade ball at the end of Poe's summer camp (Oelke, p. 2).

30 AUGUST. The cadets move from camp to barracks (Oelke, p. 2). Poe rooms with Thomas W. Gibson (Indiana), Timothy Pickering Jones (Ten-

nessee), and perhaps John Eaton Henderson (Tennessee), Room 28 South Barracks.

31 AUGUST. The cadets receive their assignments (Oelke, p. 2).

1 SEPTEMBER. Classes begin at West Point. Poe takes two courses, French and mathematics (Oelke, p. 2).

11 SEPTEMBER. PHILADELPHIA. Poe's "Sonnet—To Science" appears in the *Saturday Evening Post*.

EARLY OCTOBER. Poe's "Sonnet—To Science" appears in the *Casket* for October.

5 OCTOBER. NEW YORK. John Allan marries Louisa Patterson (*W*, 1:78; transcript from Allan Family Bible, ViRVal).

6 NOVEMBER. WEST POINT. Poe writes Allan:

I was greatly in hopes you would have come on to W. Point while you were in N. York, and was very much disappointed when I heard you had gone on home without letting me hear from you. I have a very excellent standing in my class . . . . the study requisite is incessant, and the discipline exceedingly rigid. I have seen Genl [Winfield] Scott . . . he was very polite and attentive . . . I am very much pleased with Colonel [Sylvanus] Thayer . . . . Mr. [Edward] Cunningham was also on here some time since, and Mr J Chevalie (*L*, 1:38–39).

[Allan B. Magruder, a classmate from Virginia who left the Academy in 1831, later recalled:

He [Poe] was very shy and reserved in his intercourse with his fellow-cadets— his associates being confined almost exclusively to Virginians . . . . He was an accomplished French scholar, and had a wonderful aptitude for mathematics, so that he had no difficulty in preparing his recitations in his class and in obtaining the highest marks in these departments. He was a devourer of books, but his great fault was his neglect of and apparent contempt for military duties. His wayward and capricious temper made him at times utterly oblivious or indifferent to the ordinary routine of roll-call, drills, and guard duties. These habits subjected him often to arrest and punishment, and effectually prevented his learning or discharging the duties of a soldier (Woodberry, 1:70).

Timothy P. Jones recalled:

Poe and I were classmates, roommates, and tentmates. From the first time we met he took a fancy to me, and owing to his older years and extraordinary literary merits, I thought he was the greatest fellow on earth. From much that he told me of his previous life, he was dissipated before he ever entered for the West Point cadetship. He was certainly given to extreme dissipation within a very short time after he entered school. At first he studied hard and his ambition seemed to be to lead the class in all studies . . . . it was only a few weeks after the beginning of his career at West Point that he seemed to lose interest in his studies and to be disheartened and discouraged . . . .

There was one of the teachers there, Prof. Locke, who hated Poe, and the spirit of uncongeniality was mutual . . . .

Poe had evidenced considerable literary genius before he left West Point, and probably before he came there. He would often write some of the most forcible and vicious doggerel, have me copy it with my left hand in order that it might be disguised, and post it around the building. Locke was ordinarily one of the victims of his stinging pen. He would often play the roughest jokes on those he disliked. I have never seen a man whose hatred was so intense as that of Poe (*New York Sun*, 10 May 1903; 29 May 1904; Woodberry, 1:369–72)

Thomas W. Gibson recorded:

Number 28 South Barracks, in the last months of the year of our Lord 1830, was pretty generally regarded as a hard room. Cadets who aspired to high standing on the Merit Roll were not much given to visiting it, at least in daytime. To compensate in some measure for this neglect, however, the inspecting-officer was uncommonly punctual in his visits, and rarely failed to find some subject for his daily report of demerit . . . .

Edgar A. Poe was one of the occupants of the room. "Old P——" and the writer of this sketch completed the household. The first conversation I had with Poe after we became installed as room-mates was characteristic of the man. A volume of Campbell's Poems was lying upon my table, and he tossed it contemptuously aside, with the curt remark: "Campbell is a plagiarist;" then without waiting for a reply he picked up the book, and turned the leaves over rapidly until he found the passage he was looking for . . . .

Poe at that time, though only about twenty years of age, had the appearance of being much older. He had a worn, weary, discontented look, not easily forgotten by those who were intimate with him. Poe was easily fretted by any jest at his expense, and was not a little annoyed by a story that some of the class got up, to the effect that he had procured a cadet's appointment for his son, and the boy having died, the father had substituted himself in his place. Another report current in the corps was that he was a grandson of Benedict Arnold. Some good-natured friend told him of it; and Poe did not contradict it, but seemed rather pleased than otherwise at the mistake.

Very early in his brief career at the Point he established a high reputation for genius, and poems and squibs of local interest were daily issued from Number 28 and went the round of the Classes. One of the first things of the kind that he perpetrated was a diatribe in which all of the officers of the Academy, from Colonel Thayer down, were duly if not favorably noticed. I can recall but one stanza. It ran thus:

"John Locke was a very great name;

Joe Locke was a greater in short;
The former was well known to Fame,
The latter well known to Report."

Joe [Joseph Lorenzo] Locke, it may be remarked by way of explanation, was one of the instructors of tactics, and *ex-officio* Inspector of Barracks, and supervisor of the morals and deportment of cadets generally . . . .

The studies of the Academy Poe utterly ignored. I doubt if he ever studied a page of Lacroix [*Elements of Algebra*], unless it was to glance hastily over it in the lecture-room, while others of his section were reciting . . . .

I don't think he was ever intoxicated while at the Academy, but he had already acquired the more dangerous habit of constant drinking . . . .

Upon the whole the impression left by Poe in his short career at West Point was highly favorable to him. (Gibson, pp. 754–56).

Russell (p. 13 n. 23) points out that Gibson was "sixteen and a half years old when finally dismissed in 1832 after his second court-martial having been convicted of setting fire to a building near the barracks."]

15 NOVEMBER. Before a general court-martial Timothy P. Jones is found guilty for gross neglect of his academic and military duties (Allan, p. 451).

27 NOVEMBER. RICHMOND. The *Richmond Whig* reports that John Allan has been elected Secretary of the Amicable Society Club (Allen, p. 684).

["The AMICABLE SOCIETY was instituted in 1788, with the benevolent object of relieving strangers and wayfarers, in distress, for whom the law makes no provision" (Mordecai, p. 255). Its membership included Michael B. Poitiaux, Robert Greenhow, William Lambert, William Galt, Jr., Robert Gwathmey, T. Gwathmey, and W. Munford (Mordecai, pp. 257–58).]

27–28 DECEMBER. Allan writes Poe (Poe to Allan, 3 January 1831).

31 DECEMBER. WEST POINT. Timothy P. Jones, one of Poe's roommates, is dismissed from the Academy (Allan, p. 451).

MARIA CLEMM
(from the daguerreotype formerly owned by Annie Richmond)

CHAPTER THREE

Baltimore and the Early Fiction

1831–1834

Poe finds the life of a West Point cadet distasteful, disobeys orders, and is dismissed from the Academy, not before obtaining subscriptions to his *Poems* (1831). From West Point he journeys first to New York and then to Baltimore, where he joins the financially distressed family of his aunt Maria Clemm, a household that includes her daughter Virginia, her mother, and her nephew Henry Poe, Poe's brother. Henry dies in 1831. The following year Poe has five short stories published in the Philadelphia *Saturday Courier*: "Metzengerstein," "The Duke de L'Omelette," "A Tale of Jerusalem," "A Decided Loss," and "The Bargain Lost." In October 1833 Poe's "MS. Found in a Bottle" wins him a $50 prize offered by the *Baltimore Saturday Visiter* for the best short story, and the friendship of John Pendleton Kennedy, a Baltimore lawyer and novelist. Poe is left nothing when John Allan dies on 27 March 1834.

*

1831

*

3 JANUARY. WEST POINT. Midterm exams begin at the Academy (Allan, p. 453).

Poe writes John Allan, in Richmond:

Did I, when an infant, sollicit your charity and protection, or was it of your own free will, that you volunteered your services in my behalf? It is well known to respectable individuals in Baltimore, and elsewhere, that my Grandfather (my natural protector at the time you interposed) was wealthy, and that I was his favorite grandchild—But the promises of adoption, and liberal education which you held forth to him in a letter which is now in possession of my family, induced him to resign all care of me into your hands . . . . You would not let me return [to the University of Virginia] because bills were presented to you for payment which I never wished nor desired you to pay . . . . I will boldly say that it was wholly and entirely your own mistaken parsimony that caused all the difficulties in which I was involved while at Charlottesville . . . . Towards the close of the session you sent me $100—but it was too late . . . . I applied to James Galt—but he, I believe, from the best of motives refused to lend me any—I then became desperate, and gambled . . . . But these circumstances were all unknown to my friends when I returned home—They knew that I had been extravagant—but that was all—I had no hope of returning to Charlottesville, and I waited in vain in expectation that you would, at least, obtain me some employment. I saw no prospect of this . . . . Every day threatened with a warrant &c. I left home—and after nearly 2 years conduct . . . in the army, as a common soldier—I *earned*, myself, by the most humiliating privations—a Cadets' warrant . . . . I came home, you will remember, the night after the burial [of Frances Allan on 2 March 1829]—If she had not have died while I was away there would have been nothing for me to regret—*Your* love I never valued—but she I believed loved me as her own child. You sent me to W. Point like a beggar. The same difficulties are threatening me as before at Charlottesville—and I must resign . . . . When I parted from you—at the steamboat, I knew that I should never see you again.

As regards Sergt. Graves—I *did* write him that letter . . . . within a half hour after you had embittered every feeling of my heart against you by your abuse of my *family*, and myself, under your own roof—and at a time when you knew that my heart was almost breaking . . . . it is my intention to resign. For this end it will be necessary that you (as my nominal guardian) enclose me your written permission . . . . your refusal would only deprive me of the little pay which is now due as mileage.

From the time of writing this I shall neglect my studies and duties at the institution—if I do not receive your answer in 10 days—I will leave the point without—for otherwise I should subject myself to dismission (*L*, 1:39–43; letter is postmarked 5 January).

5 JANUARY. A general court-martial convenes and adjourns to 28 January (Quinn, p. 173). Poe mails his letter of 3 January to Allan (Poe to Allan, 3 January 1831).

7–27 JANUARY. Poe carries out his threat to neglect his duties (see 8 FEBRUARY 1831).

9 JANUARY. Poe ranks seventeenth among the eighty-seven fourth-classmen who take the mathematics examination and third in French ("Merit Roll of the 4th Class, Mathematics, 9 January 1831," in Post Order Book No. 5 [1827–32], USMA Archives, USMA Library; Quinn, p. 171).

10 JANUARY. RICHMOND. Allan receives Poe's letter of 3 January (see next entry).

13 JANUARY. Allan endorses Poe's letter of 3 January: "I do not think the

Boy has one good quality. He may do or act as he pleases, tho' I wd have saved him but on his own terms & conditions since I cannot believe a word he writes. His letter is the most barefaced one sided statement" (*L*, 2:471).

28 JANUARY. WEST POINT. Lieutenant Thomas J. Leslie, paymaster of the Academy, presides over a general court-martial. Lieutanant Charles F. Smith, the adjutant, as trial judge-advocate, prosecutes (Allan, pp. 453–54).

28 JANUARY OR LATER. Poe appears before the court-martial and is sentenced to dismissal (see next entry).

8 FEBRUARY. WASHINGTON. Secretary of War John Henry Eaton approves the court-martial proceedings to take effect after 6 March:

> Engineer Department
> Washington, February 8, 1831.

Military Academy Order, No. 7.

At the General Court-Martial, of which Lieutenant Thomas J. Leslie, of the Corps of Engineers, is President, convened at West Point, New York, on the 5th ult., in virtue of Military Academy Order No. 46 dated the 31st December 1830, was arraigned and tried . . . .

3. The Court next proceeded to the trial of Cadet E. A. Poe of the U. S. Military Academy on the following Charges and Specifications.

Charge 1st . . . . Gross neglect of duty.

Specification 1st . . . . In this, that he the said Cadet Poe did absent himself from the following parades and roll calls between the 7th of January and 27th January 1831, Viz. absent himself from evening parade on the 8, 9, 15, 20, 24 & 25 January 1831; absent from reveille roll call on the 8, 16, 17, 19, 20, 24 & 25 Jan'y 1831, absent from Class parade on the 17, 18, 19, 20, 24 & 25 Jan'y, absent from guard mounting on the 16 Jan'y 1831, and absent from Church parade on the 23d. Jan'y 1831; all of which at West Point N. Y.

Specification 2d . . . . In this, that he the said Cadet E. A. Poe, did absent himself from all his Academical duties between the 15th & 27 Jan'y 1831, viz. absent from Mathematical recitation on the 17, 18, 19, 20, 21, 22, 24, 25 & 26th Jan'y 1831, all of which at West Point N. Y.

Charge 2d . . . . Disobedience of Orders.

Specification 1st . . . . In this, that he the said Cadet Poe after having been directed by the officer of the day to attend church on the 23d January 1831, did fail to obey such order, this at West Point.

Specification 2d . . . . In this, that he the said Cadet Poe did fail to attend the Academy on the 25 Jany. 1831, after having been directed to do so by the officer of the day: This at West Point N. Y.

To which charges and specifications the prisoner pleaded as follows, to the 1st specification of the first charge "Not Guilty," to the 2nd specification of the lst charge "Guilty," and "Guilty" to the second charge and specification.

The court after mature deliberation on the testimony adduced find the prisoner "Guilty" of the lst specification of lst charge and confirm his plea to the remainder of the charges and specifications, and adjudge that he Cadet E. A. Poe be *dismissed* the service of the United States . . . .

7. . . . The proceedings of the General Court Martial of which Lieut. Thomas J. Leslie of the Corps of Engineers is President in the cases of Cadets L. [Llewellyn] Jones, H. [Henry] Swartwout, Thomas W. Gibson, W. [William] A. Parker, and Henry Minor [Jr.] have been laid before the Secretary of War and approved . . . .

Cadet E. A. Poe will be dismissed the service of the United States and cease to be considered a member of the Military Academy after the 6th March 1831 (USMA Archives, Post Order Book No. 5, 1827–38; ViU–I; *W,* 17:374–76; Quinn, pp. 743–44).

10 FEBRUARY. WEST POINT. Cadet David Emerson Hale (New Hampshire) writes his mother Sarah Josepha Hale: "I have communicated what you wrote to Mr. Poe, of whom perhaps you would like to know something. He ran away from his adopted father in Virginia who was very rich, has been in S. America, England and has graduated at one of the Colleges there. He returned to America again and enlisted as a private soldier but feeling, perhaps a soldier's pride, he obtained a cadet's appointment and entered this Academy last June. He is thought a fellow of talent here but he is too mad a poet to like Mathematics" (Quinn, p. 171).

18 FEBRUARY. The Academy releases Poe (Allan, p. 454).

19 FEBRUARY. Poe leaves West Point for New York (Poe to Allan, 21 February 1831).

[Timothy P. Jones, dismissed from the Academy 31 December 1830 before Poe's departure, recalled with exaggeration:

On the morning of the 6th [19th] of March [February], when Poe was ready to leave West Point, we were in our room together, and he told me I was one of the few true friends he had ever known, and as we talked the tears rolled down his cheeks . . . . He told me much of his past life, one part of which he said he had confided to no other living soul. This was that while it was generally believed that he had gone to Greece in 1827 to offer his services to assist in putting down the Turkish oppressors, he had done no such thing, that about as near Europe as he ever got was Fort Independence, Boston Harbor, where he enlisted, and was assigned to Battery H, First Artillery, which was afterward transferred to Fortress Monroe, Va. Poe told me that for nearly two years he let his kindred and friends believe that he was fighting with the Greeks, but all the while he was wearing the uniform of Uncle Sam's soldiers, and leading a sober and moral life (*New York Sun*, 29 May 1904, copied from the *Richmond Dispatch*; Woodberry, 1:372).

Cadet George Washington Cullum (Pennsylvania) recalled:

As Poe was of the succeeding class to mine at West Point, I remember him very well as a cadet. He was a slovenly, heedless boy, very eccentric, inclined to dissipation, and, of course, preferred making verses to solving equations. While at the Academy he published a small volume of poems, dedicated to Bulwer in a long, rambling letter. These verses were the source of great merriment with us boys, who considered the author cracked, and the verses ridiculous doggerel (Stoddard [1872], p. 561 n.).

Eugene L. Didier recorded:

General Lucius Bellinger Northrop [South Carolina], the last survivor of the classmates of Poe at West Point, told me [his son-in-law] that Edgar Poe, at West Point, was the wrong man in the wrong place—although, from an intellectual point of view, he stood high there, as elsewhere: the records of the academy show that he was third in French, and seventeenth in mathematics in a class of eighty-seven. The severe studies and dull routine duties were extremely distasteful to the young poet, and, at the end of six months, he applied to his adopted father, Mr. Allan, for permission to leave the academy, which request was promptly refused . . . . He was shy, proud, sensitive, and unsociable with the other cadets. He spent more time in reading than in study . . . . During his short stay at West Point, Poe made a high reputation for poetical genius, and when it was announced that he intended to publish his poems, great expectations were formed of the book. Gen. Northrop informed me that the cadets eagerly subscribed for the volume (Didier [1909], pp. 224, 225, 253, 254).]

CA. 20 FEBRUARY. NEW YORK. Poe writes his brother Henry (Poe to Allan, 21 February 1831).

21 FEBRUARY. Poe writes Allan: "I left [West] Point two days ago and travelling to N. York without a cloak or any other clothing of importance. I have caught a most violent cold and am confined to my bed—I have no money—no friends—I have written to my brother—but he cannot help me—I shall never rise from my bed—besides a most violent cold on my lungs my *ear* discharges blood and matter continually and my headache is distracting—I hardly know what I am writing—I will write no more— Please send me a little money—quickly—and forget what I said about you" (L, 1:43–44).

CA. 1 MARCH. Poe meets Peter Pindar Pease again.

Peter Pease did not see the poet again until 1831, when they met in New York, where Poe had gone, he said, to secure the publication of a book of his poems by Harpers. He claimed, almost boisterously, that he had "hit it hard" (evidently a favorite expression with him), meaning that his fortune was made. He told Pease that he was living in the vicinity of Madison Square, that he loved to walk beneath the elm trees there, and invited Pease to go with him for a refreshment. But my great-uncle was in a hurry to catch the boat for Amboy, so, after a short conversation, they shook hands and parted (Stearns, p. 25).

CA. 1 MARCH. Perhaps Henry Inman paints a portrait of Poe (Allen, pp. 245–46).

6 MARCH. WEST POINT. Poe's dismissal from the Academy takes effect (see 8 FEBRUARY 1831).

10 MARCH. NEW YORK. Poe writes Colonel Sylvanus Thayer, Superintendent of the U. S. Military Academy, West Point: "I intend by the first opportunity to proceed to Paris with the view of obtaining, thro' the interest of the Marquis de La Fayette, an appointment (if possible) in the Polish Army . . . . The object of this letter is . . . to request that you will give me such assistance as may lie in your power in furtherance of my views. A certificate of 'standing' in my class is all that I have any right to expect. Any thing farther—a letter to a friend in Paris—or to the Marquis—would be a kindness which I should never forget" (L, 1:44–45; also L, 2:472 n. 30).

MARCH. WEST POINT. One of the nineteen deductions for cadet accounts is "Edgar A. Poe's 'Poems' " (USMA Archives, Treasurer's Records; Russell, pp. 29–30).

APRIL? NEW YORK. Elam Bliss publishes Poe's *Poems*, printed by Henry Mason, 64 Nassau Street, and dedicated to "The U. S. Corps of Cadets." Poe sends a copy to John Neal, bearing the inscription on the flyleaf: "Mr. John Neal, with the author's best wishes" (Wakeman, item 935).

[POEMS / BY / EDGAR A. POE. / (rule) / TOUT LE MONDE A RAISON.—ROCHEFOUCAULT. / (rule) / SECOND EDITION. / (rule) / New York: / PUBLISHED BY ELAM BLISS. / (rule) / 1831. 124 pp.
  Contents: "Letter to Mr.——: Dear B—"; "Introduction" ("Romance, who loves to nod and sing"); "To Helen" ("Helen, thy beauty is to me"); "Israfel"; "The Doomed City"; "Fairy Land"; "Irene"; "A Paean"; "The Valley Nis"; "Al Aaraaf" (including "Science! meet daughter of old Time thou art"); "Tamerlane."
  Perhaps less than a thousand copies printed. A facsimile edition with a

bibliographical note by Killis Campbell was published for the Facsimile Text Society by the Columbia University Press, New York, 1936.]

APRIL. WEST POINT. One hundred and thirty-one out of 232 cadets subscribe to Poe's *Poems* at $1.25 per copy (Ledger records of the Treasurer of the U. S. Military Academy, Thomas J. Leslie; Russell, pp. 29–30). A check for $36.72 is drawn in Poe's favor for settlement of his account (USMA Archives, Treasurer's Office Cash Book, 1830–49, p. 8; Russell, p. 29 n. 41).

23 APRIL. A check for $170 is issued to Poe by Thomas J. Leslie, Treasurer of the U.S. Military Academy, transmitting Cadet subscription funds for *Poems*. Perhaps Colonel Sylvanus Thayer, Captain Ethan Allan Hitchcock, or Leslie contributes to the fund to make the amount $170 (Russell, pp. 30–31).

["Officer pay records were not retained at West Point. The USMA Treasurer kept the cadet records only, and there is no way one can determine who added the $1.25. I did check the report again. I would not indicate, as Mr. Russell did, that it could have been either Thayer, Hitchcock or Leslie. Any one of the instructors, professors or staff may have added the amount or it may have been a clerical error" (information from Mrs. Marie T. Capps, Map & Manuscript Librarian, USMA Library).

Allan B. Magruder (Virginia) later recalled:

The cadets, especially from the South, generally subscribed at seventy-five cents [$1.25] a copy, which the superintendent allowed to be deducted from our pay. I think the publisher came up from New York and bargained with Poe for its publication. The sum thus raised enabled him, I suppose, to save a small margin for his travelling expenses and necessities beyond the cost of publication. The book was not supplied to the subscribers until some time after he left the Point. It was a miserable production mechanically, bound in green boards and printed on inferior paper, evidently gotten up on the cheapest scale. The subscription was not fully paid until the book was delivered, and I remember a general expression of indignation at the inferior quality and condition of the book . . . . He went to New York, and there obtained, as I heard afterward, some literary employment which afforded him scant support (Woodberry, 1:78).

Thomas W. Gibson (Indiana) recalled:

Some month or two after he had left, it was announced that a volume of his poems would be published by subscription, at the price of two dollars and fifty cents [$1.25] per copy. Permission was granted by Colonel Thayer to the corps to subscribe for the book, and as no cadet was ever known to neglect any opportunity of spending his pay, the subscription was pretty near universal. The book was received with a general expression of disgust. It was a puny volume, of about fifty pages, bound in boards and badly printed on coarse paper, and worse than all, it contained not one of the squibs and satires upon which his reputation at the Academy had been built up. Few of the poems contained in that collection now appear in any of the editions of his works, and such as have been preserved have been very much altered for the better.

For months afterward quotations from Poe formed the standing material for jests in the corps, and his reputation for genius went down at once to zero. I doubt if even the "Raven" of his after-years ever entirely effaced from the minds of his class the impression received from that volume (Gibson, p. 755).]

BEFORE 6 MAY. BALTIMORE. Poe joins Maria Clemm, Mrs. David Poe, Sr., Henry Poe, Virginia Clemm, and Henry Clemm, Jr., at Mechanics Row, Wilks Street, now known as Eastern Avenue (*Matchett's Baltimore Directors* for 1831 and 1833, pp. 78 and 43; Woodberry, 1:375; Quinn, p. 188 n. 6).

6 MAY. Poe writes William Gwynn, editor of the *Baltimore Gazette and Daily Advertiser*:

Baltimore from Federal Hill

I am almost ashamed to ask any favour at your hands after my foolish conduct upon a former occasion . . . .

I am very anxious to remain and settle myself in Balto as Mr. Allan has married again and I no longer look upon Richmond as my place of residence . . . .

Perhaps (since I understand Neilson [Poe] has left you) you might be so kind as to employ me in your office in some capacity . . . . I would have waited upon you personally but am confined to my room with a severe sprain in my knee (*L*, 1:45).

AFTER 6 MAY. REISTERSTOWN, MARYLAND. Nathan Covington Brooks fails to obtain for Poe an usher's place in his school (Stanard, p. 277).

AFTER 6 MAY. BALTIMORE. Poe writes letters and verses to Kate Bleakley, whose father is proprietor of the Armistead Hotel. Henry Herring discourages Poe's attentions to his daughter Elizabeth (Woodberry, 1:89–90; Whitty, p. xxxvi; Phillips, 1:421, 425–26).

AFTER 6 MAY. Poe writes verses in the album of a friend of Poe's cousin Elizabeth Herring, a niece of Dr. James H. Miller (Phillips, 1:424).

7 MAY. NEW YORK. Either George P. Morris or Theodore S. Fay reviews Poe's *Poems* in the *New-York Mirror*.

THE poetry of this little volume has a plausible air of imagination, inconsistent with the general indefiniteness of the ideas. Every thing in the language betokens poetic inspiration, but it rather resembles the leaves of the sybil when scattered by the wind. The annexed lines, which close a short poem, entitled the "Doomed City," are less incomprehensible than most in the book, although the meaning is by no means perfectly clear . . . .

It sometimes happens that poetry, at first sight unintelligible, is discovered, upon a repeated and more careful examination, to be fraught with the treasure of thought and fancy. The "Rime of the Ancient Mariner" belongs to this class, but we can not flatter Mr. Poe with any similar hope respecting his own composition, although it occasionally sparkles with a true poetic expression, and sometimes a conflict of beauty and nonsense takes place, in which the latter seems to have the best of it. It is indeed encumbered by numerous obscurities, which we should be pleased to see either very much brightened or entirely expunged. What is the meaning of this?

> "A heaven that God doth not contemn
> With stars is like a diadem—
> We liken our ladies' eyes to them."

Or these lines, (with which we close the article,) from "Fairy Land?"

> "Huge moons—see! wax and wane
> Again—again—again—
> How they put out the starlight
> With the breath from their pale faces!

> Lo! one is coming down
> With its centre on the crown
> Of a mountain's eminence!
> Down—still down—and down—
> Now deep shall be—O deep!
> The passion of our sleep!
> For that wide circumference
> In easy drapery falls
> Drowsily over halls—
> Over ruin'd walls—
> Over waterfalls,
> (Silent waterfalls!)
> O'er the strange woods—o'er the sea—
> Alas! over the sea!"

21 MAY. PHILADELPHIA. Perhaps Lambert A. Wilmer briefly notices Poe's *Poems* in the *Saturday Evening Post* (Mabbott [1969], 1:542).

AFTER 21 MAY. The *Casket* for May reprints the *Saturday Evening Post* notice of 21 May.

28 MAY. The *Saturday Courier* announces a short story contest.

The publishers intend to devote annually a portion of the profits of their work, in the promotion of the Cause of LITERATURE.—As soon as proper arrangements can be effected, a premium of

ONE HUNDRED DOLLARS

will be awarded for the best AMERICAN TALE. The gentlemen who shall be selected to decide the award, shall be named at the time of offering the premium.

The publishers are aware of the difficulty of furnishing their paper in due season to subscribers residing at a distance—this obstacle will be remedied in the course of a few weeks, when such arrangements will be made as cannot fail to be perfectly satisfactory.

The Publishers request their country brethren to give the above notice a few insertions in their respective journals. The same favor will be reciprocated.

All orders for the S A T U R D A Y   C O U R I E R, (containing the price of subscription,) must be addressed to

WOODWARD & SPRAGG,
Philadelphia.

may 28–tf

4 JUNE. The *Saturday Courier* again announces its contest, an announcement which is repeated 31 July.

8 JULY. NEW YORK. A review of Poe's *Poems* appears in the *Morning Courier and New-York Enquirer*, edited by James Watson Webb:

"Poems by Edgar A. Poe." New-York. Elam Bliss (second edition,) page 124. —This is evidently a fellow of fine genius, but if one were disposed to believe to the contrary, and to sustain his belief, he need wish for nothing more than a passage or two, taken hap hazard from the book—as for example:

["To Irene" is quoted.]

Sheer nonsense, undoubtediy, yet *as* undoubtedly the author has the *gift*, and betrays the *presence*, here and there, that cannot be mistaken—for example:

["To Helen" ("Helen, thy beauty is to me") is quoted.]

And again—read the following sonnet, and then marvel at the strangeness of the mixture. Pure poetry in one page—pure absurdity in another—

["Sonnet—To Science" is quoted.]

But we are sick of poetry—so sick of it indeed, that we should not have meddled with this, but for a wish to prevent a young man—the author must be young, for there is the fever and the flush, and the strong delusion of youth about him, if not boyhood—from betraying himself unworthily. He has a fine genius, we repeat it, and may be distinguished, if he will not mistake oddity for excellence, or want of similitude to all others, for superiority over them. We have said as much to the confederacy of small poets around us, and they dont like our candour.

[Lease, p. 132, without explanation, attributes this review to John Neal.]

9 JULY–26 NOVEMBER. PHILADELPHIA. The *Saturday Courier* publishes its rules for a contest:

PREMIUM

The publishers of the Saturday Courier grateful for the liberal patronage they have received, and anxious to improve, as far as they possibly can, the character of American Literature, offer the following premium:—

ONE HUNDRED DOLLARS to the writer of the best ORIGINAL TALE, prepared for the Saturday Courier, and presented under the following restrictions and regulations.

All Tales intended to compete for this premium, must be addressed to Woodward and Spragg, Philadelphia, *free of postage*, on or before the first day of December, 1831.

Accompanying each Tale the writer must furnish his or her name, and address, in a separate sealed envelope, which will not be opened except in the case of the successful competitor.

Early in December the Tales presented will be submitted to a committee consisting of the following gentlemen, viz: —David Paul Brown, William M. Meredith, John Musgrave, Richard Penn Smith, Morton McMichael, and Charles Alexander, Esq'rs. who will award prior to the lst of January, 1832.

As soon as the award shall be determined, *public* information of the same will be given, and immediately thereafter the successful candidate may draw upon the publishers for the amount of the premium.

The publication of the Tales will be commenced in January, 1832, and continued at the discretion of the publishers.

Competitors for the premium are requested to use care in the preparation of their manuscripts, as it is very desirable that illegibility may be avoided.

Editors of papers which exchange with the Saturday Courier, by giving the above a few insertions will confer a favor upon the publishers, and probably advance the cause of Literature.

The Saturday Courier is published by Woodward and Spragg, No. 112 Chestnut street, Philadelphia, at $2 per annum, half yearly in advance.

july 9–tf

AFTER 9 JULY. BALTIMORE? Poe enters the Philadelphia *Saturday Courier* contest.

1 AUGUST. BALTIMORE. Henry Poe dies.

2 AUGUST. Henry Poe is buried in the churchyard of the First Presbyterian Church. A notice of his death and funeral appears in the *American and Commercial Daily Advertiser*: "Died last evening W. H. Poe aged 24 years. His friends and acquaintances are invited to attend his funeral this morning at 9 from the dwelling of Mrs. Clemm, in Wilks Street" (First Presbyterian Church record; Quinn, p. 725; Allen, p. 260).

3 AUGUST. The "List of Burials by Dr. William Nevins, 1831" includes the entry "3 Aug—W. H. Poe" (Phillips, 1:430).

13 AUGUST. PHILADELPHIA. The *Saturday Evening Post* publishes "A Dream," signed "P." (ascribed to Poe by Killis Campbell. See Mabbott [1978], 2:5–10).

23 AUGUST. RICHMOND. John Allan, Jr., is born to Louisa and John Allan.

SEPTEMBER. BALTIMORE. A cholera epidemic reaches its height.

16 OCTOBER. Poe writes John Allan:

It is a long time since I have written to you unless with an application for money or assistance . . . . I write merely because I am by myself and have been thinking over old times, and my only friends, until my heart is full—At such a time the conversation of new acquaintance is like ice, and I prefer writing to you altho' I know that you care nothing about me, and perhaps will not even read my letter. I have nothing more to say—and *this time*, no favour to ask—Altho I am wretchedly poor, I have managed to get clear of the difficulty I spoke of in my last, and am *out of debt*, at any rate . . . . Will you not write one word to me? (L, 1:46–47).

5 NOVEMBER. PHILADELPHIA. The editors of the *Saturday Courier* remind contestants to enter the contest promptly.

CA. 7 NOVEMBER. BALTIMORE. Poe is "arrested" for a debt of $80 incurred by his brother Henry (Poe to Allan, 18 November 1831).

BEFORE 18 NOVEMBER. RICHMOND. Allan writes Poe, perhaps sending him money (Poe to Allan, 18 November 1831).

18 NOVEMBER. BALTIMORE. Poe writes Allan:

I was arrested eleven days ago for a debt which I never expected to have to pay, and which was incurred as much on Hy's [Henry's] account as on my own about two years ago. I would rather have done any thing on earth than apply to you again after your late kindness . . . I am in bad health . . . If you will only send me this one time $80, by Wednesday next, I will never forget your kindness & generosity (*L*, 1:47–48).

[Quinn, p. 190, could find no evidence that Poe was arrested and put in jail.]

30 NOVEMBER. ELMWOOD, MARYLAND. Neilson Poe marries his cousin Josephine Emily Clemm, Maria Clemm's stepdaughter (Phillips, 1:419).

1 DECEMBER. PHILADELPHIA. The *Saturday Courier* contest closes.

5 DECEMBER. BALTIMORE. Maria Clemm writes John Allan:

As I am extremely distressed at Edgar's situation I take the liberty of writing to you once more in his behalf—We have made every exertion for his relief—but our circumstances are too poor to afford him any—I have with great difficulty procured $20 which I will reserve for him, with all my heart—but it is insufficient to extricate him—I beg that you will assist him out of this difficulty and I am sure that it will be a warning for him as long as he lives—to involve himself no further in debt—I am satisfied that except in this instance he does not owe one cent in the world, and would do well if you would relieve him—he is extremely distressed at your refusal to assist him—and has no other resource whatever—as not being a resident of this city he cannot take the benefit of the insolvent laws—I feel deeply interested in him, for he has been extremely kind to me as far as his opportunities would permit—I should consider it as one of the greatest obligations to myself and family if you will be so generous as to assist him for this time only (Stanard, pp. 295–97).

7 DECEMBER. RICHMOND. Allan writes John Walsh in Poe's behalf, but neglects to send his letter until 12 January 1832: "Wrote on the 7th Decr

1831 to John Walsh to procure his liberation & to give him $20 besides to keep him out of further difficulties & value on me for such amt as might be required—neglected sending it on till the 12th Jany 1832 Then put in the office myself" (Stanard, p. 300; *L*, 2:472).

15 DECEMBER. BALTIMORE. Poe writes Allan: "I know you have never turned a beggar from your door, and I apply to you in that light, I *beg* you for a little aid, and for the sake of all that was formerly dear to you I trust that you will relieve me" (*L*, 1:48–49).

24 DECEMBER. PHILADELPHIA. The *Saturday Courier* informs its readers: "The award of the prize committee will be announced in our next number."

29 DECEMBER. BALTIMORE. Poe writes John Allan: "for the sake of the love you bore me when I sat upon your knee and called you father do not forsake me this only time" (*L*, 1:49).

31 DECEMBER. PHILADELPHIA. The *Saturday Courier* announces the winner of its contest:

The Committee [David Paul Brown, Richard Penn Smith, William M. Meredith, Morton McMichael, John Musgrave, and Charles Alexander] to whom was referred the selection of a Tale from among those presented for the premium of *One Hundred Dollars*, offered by us, have awarded in favour of LOVE'S MARTYR, by Miss Delia S. Bacon, of the State of New York, author of "Tales of the Puritans," &c.

While we congratulate the fair author upon her success, we can at the same time promise our readers much gratification from the perusal of *Love's Martyr*, which is strongly characterized by taste, genius and feeling.

Many of the other Tales offered for the Premium, are distinguished by great merit, and we are assured by the Committee that they derived much pleasure from reading them.

The writer of the successful Tale, will be good enough to draw upon us at her earliest convenience, for the amount of the Premium.

1831? BALTIMORE. Maria Clemm writes Thomas Kell:

I am not myself personally known to you, but you were well acquainted with my late husband Mr. Wm. Clemm and also I believe, with many of my connexions. For their sakes as well as for my own I venture to solicit a little assistance at your hands. For a long time I have been prevented by continual ill health from making the exertions necessary for the support of myself and children, and we are now consequently enduring every privation. Under these circumstances I feel a hope that you will be inclined to give me some little aid. I do not ask for any material assistance, but the merest trifle to relieve my most immediate distress (Anon., "Letters and Documents," *Maryland Historical Magazine*, 6 [March 1911]: 44; Jackson [1979], p. 20).

1832

*

1832

*

7 JANUARY. PHILADELPHIA. The *Saturday Courier* publishes its prize-winning story, Delia S. Bacon's "Love's Martyr."

12 JANUARY. WEST POINT. The U. S. Military Academy dismisses Thomas W. Gibson "after his second court-martial having been convicted of setting fire to a building near the barracks" (Russell, p. 13 n. 23).

12 JANUARY. RICHMOND. Allan sends his letter written 7 December 1831 to John Walsh, in Baltimore.

14 JANUARY. PHILADELPHIA. The *Saturday Courier* publishes Poe's "Metzengerstein."

[It is doubtful that Poe received any financial reward for this tale and the four others published in the *Courier* following the contest.]

JANUARY. BALTIMORE. Lambert A. Wilmer returns to edit the *Baltimore Saturday Visiter,* a weekly established by Charles F. Cloud (Campbell [1916], p. 145).

[Wilmer later recalled his association with Poe:

He lived in a retired way with his aunt, Mrs. Clemm . . . . during an intimate acquaintance with him, which lasted for more than twelve years, I never saw him intoxicated in a single instance . . . . Poe's personal appearance was delicate and effeminate, but never sickly or ghastly, and I never saw him in any dress which was not fashionably neat with some approximation to elegance . . . . Almost every day we took long walks in the rural districts near Baltimore, and had long conversations on a great variety of subjects . . . . On one occasion, when I visited him at his lodgings, he produced a decanter of Jamaica spirits, in conformity with a practice which was very common in those days . . . . Poe made a moderate use of the liquor; and this is the only time that ever I saw him drink ardent spirits. On another occasion I was present when his aunt, Mrs. Clemm, scolded him with some severity for coming home intoxicated on the preceding evening. He excused himself by saying that he had met with some friends, who had persuaded him to take dinner with them at a tavern, where the whole party had become inebriated . . . . In conversation Poe was fluent, but not eloquent . . . . I never knew him to speak in warm terms of admiration of any poetical writer, except Alfred Tennyson. Among prose authors, Ben. Disraeli was his model. Poe was an amiable colloquist . . . . He was singularly effeminate in mind and person . . . One day, Poe, his cousin Virginia . . . and I were walking in the neighborhood of Baltimore when we happened to approach a graveyard, where a funeral was then in progress . . . . Virginia became affected and shed more tears than the chief mourner. Her emotion communicated itself to Poe ("Recollections of Edgar A. Poe," *Baltimore Daily Commercial*, 23 May 1866, reprinted in Wilmer [1941], pp. 29–32. See also M.E. Wilmer, pp. 385–86).]

3 MARCH. PHILADELPHIA. The *Saturday Courier* publishes Poe's "The Duke de L'Omelette."

10 MARCH. BALTIMORE. The *Minerva* reprints Poe's "The Duke de L'Omelette."

24 MARCH. ALBANY, NEW YORK. The *Literary Gazette* reprints "The Duke de L'Omelette."

EARLY APRIL? BALTIMORE. Poe visits his cousin Mrs. Beacham, the Henry Herrings, George Poe, the Cairnes, and Mrs. Samuel F. (Sarah P.) Simmons. To Mrs. Simmons, an Amity Street neighbor of Maria Clemm, Poe later gives the manuscript of "Morella" (Whitty, pp. xxxvi–xxxvii; Phillips, 1:478–79; Allen, pp. 275–76; Mabbott [1969], 1:541, and [1978], 2:224).

17 APRIL. RICHMOND. John Allan revises his will:

Item 2nd. I devise unto Miss Ann Moore Valentine, three hundred dollars annually and her board washing and lodging to be paid and found her by my executors out of my estate during her natural life, but this provision is to be in lieu and in discharge of the sum of two thousand dollars which I have in my possession belonging to her, and of which she is to discharge and acquit my estate in case she accepts of this bequest . . . .

Item 5th. I give and bequeath to my beloved wife Louisa Gabriella Allan, one third of the nett annual income of my whole estate during her natural life or until our eldest child becomes of age, to be paid her annually by my executors . . . .

Lastly I constitute and appoint my beloved wife Louisa Gabriella Allan and James Galt and Corbin Warwick executrix and executors of this my last will and testament . . . (extracts from MS, Will Book 2, p. 457, in the Circuit Court of the City of Richmond, Va., Division 1).

24 APRIL. The *Compiler* advertises the sale of Allan's "property on deed of trust, corner of Main and Fifth Streets, Clay Street house" (DLC–EA; Allen, p. 684).

SUMMER? BALTIMORE. Poe visits E. J. Coale's bookstore (Allen, p. 267).

Poe has a romantic affair with Mary Starr ("Baltimore Mary") (Van Cleef, pp. 634–40; Campbell [1916], pp. 145–46. Mabbott [1969], 1:232–33, dates this episode "about 1834").

9 JUNE. PHILADELPHIA. The *Saturday Courier* publishes Poe's "A Tale of Jerusalem."

JUNE. BALTIMORE. Perhaps Poe learns of Allan's illness through letters carried by a printer named Askew and returns to Richmond (Allen, pp. 272–73).

[If Poe made this visit, he did not see John Allan (Poe's statement, "more than three [years] since you have spoken to me," in his letter of 12 April 1833).]

23 JULY. RICHMOND. Thomas H. Ellis writes his brother James: "Uncle Allan has been in very bad health for some time: I have seldom seen a person so much [wasted]; his head is completely grey, and his step totter-[ing;] he [desi]gns going to the Springs on Wednesday next" (NcD–ME).

4 AUGUST. BALTIMORE. Wilmer writes in the *Saturday Visiter*: "Mr. Edgar A. Poe has favoured us with the perusal of some manuscript tales written by him" (Quinn, pp. 194–95).

[Poe gave to a proposed collection of his early stories the title of "Tales of the Folio Club."]

10 AUGUST. Wilmer brings suit against the proprietors of the *Baltimore Saturday Visiter* in chancery (Baltimore Court records; Campbell [1916], p. 145). John Hill Hewitt succeeds Wilmer as editor of the *Visiter*.

12 AUGUST. RICHMOND. Poe's boyhood friend Ebenezer Burling dies of cholera, and is buried in St. John's Church burial ground (Edward V. Valentine's notebook, ViRVal; Phillips, 1:440 and 2:1083).

25 AUGUST. BALTIMORE. The *Visiter* reports that Wilmer is now the editor of the *Morning Chronicle*.

29 SEPTEMBER. Wilmer's suit is transferred to the higher courts at Annapolis (Campbell [1916], p. 145).

EARLY FALL? Poe seeks employment as an editorial assistant and as a teacher. Perhaps Poe is a kiln worker (Weiss [1907], pp. 62–63; Campbell [1916], p. 146; R. T. P. Allen, pp. 142–43. See SEPTEMBER? 1834).

5 OCTOBER. RICHMOND. William Galt Allan is born to Louisa and John Allan.

BEFORE 31 OCTOBER. BALTIMORE. Wilmer leaves Baltimore (Campbell [1916], p. 145).

10 NOVEMBER. PHILADELPHIA. The *Saturday Courier* publishes Poe's "A Decided Loss" (later entitled "Loss of Breath").

1 DECEMBER. The *Saturday Courier* publishes Poe's "The Bargain Lost" (a draft for "Bon-Bon").

31 DECEMBER. RICHMOND. John Allan composes a memo to be added to his will (MS, Will Book 2, p. 457, in the Circuit Court of the City of Richmond, Va., Division 1; see Allen, pp. 691–98).

*

1833

*

JANUARY. NEW YORK. Charles Fenno Hoffman becomes the first editor of the *Knickerbocker Magazine*.

2 FEBRUARY. BALTIMORE. The *Saturday Visiter* publishes Poe's "Enigma (on Shakespeare)."

15 MARCH. RICHMOND. John Allan adds a codicil to his will:

This memo, in my own handwriting is to be taken as a codicil and can be easily proven by any of my friends.

The notes preceding [codicil of 31 December 1832] are in the hand writing of my friend Jno. G. Williams.

The twins were born sometime about the 1st of July 1830. I was married the 5th. October 1830 in New York, my fault therefore happened before I ever saw my present wife and I did not hide it from her. In case therefore these twins should reach the age of 21 years & from reasons they cannot get their share of the fifth reserved for them, they are to have $4000 each out of my whole estate to enable them to prosecute some honest pursuit, profession or calling. March 15th. 1833 I understand one of Mrs. Wills' twin sons died some weeks ago there is therefore only one to provide for. My wife is to have all my furniture, books, bedding, linin, plate, Wines, Spirits &c &c, Glass & China ware (MS, Will Book 2, p. 457, in the Circuit Court of the City of Richmond, Va., Division 1).

SPRING. BALTIMORE. Poe takes up residence with his aunt Maria Clemm, No. 3 Amity Street (later 203 North Amity Street). She has been supporting herself by dressmaking (Evans, pp. 363–80).

12 APRIL. Poe writes Allan: "It has now been more than two years since you have assisted me, and more than three since you have spoken to me . . . . without friends, without any means, consequently of obtaining employment, I am perishing—absolutely perishing for want of aid. And yet I am not idle—nor addicted to any vice—nor have I committed any offence against society which would render me deserving of so hard a fate. For God's sake pity me, and save me from destruction" (*L*, 1:49–50).

12 APRIL. RICHMOND. Allan endorses Poe's letter of 21 February 1831: "Apl 12, 1833 it is now upwards of 2 years since I received the above precious relict of the Blackest Heart & deepest ingratitude alike destitute of honour & principle every day of his life has only served to confirm his debased nature—Suffice it to say my only regret is in Pity for his failings—his Talents are of an order that can never prove a comfort to their possessor" (Stanard, p. 268).

13 APRIL. BALTIMORE. The *Saturday Visiter* acknowledges the receipt of "Serenade" from "E. A. P." (Mabbott [1969], 1:222).

20 APRIL. The *Saturday Visiter* publishes "Serenade" as "by E. A. Poe."

4 MAY. Poe writes Joseph T. and Edwin Buckingham, editors of the *New-England Magazine* (Boston), and submits the manuscript of "Epimanes" (later "Four Beasts in One"), one of eleven tales. "Epimanes" includes "Latin Hymn" (*L*, 1:53–54).

11 MAY. The *Saturday Visiter* publishes Poe's "To—('Sleep on')," signed "Tamerlane."

18 MAY. The *Saturday Visiter* publishes "Fanny," signed "Tamerlane."

15 JUNE. The *Saturday Visiter* announces the conditions of a contest:

PREMIUMS

The proprietors of the *Baltimore Saturday Visiter* feeling desirous of encouraging literature, and at the same time serving their readers with the best that lies within their reach, offer a premium of *50 dollars* for the best Tale and *25 dollars* for the best Poem, not exceeding one hundred lines, that shall be offered them between the present period and the first of October next.

The following gentlemen have been chosen to decide on the merits of the productions:

> John P. Kennedy, Esq.
> John H. B. Latrobe, Esq.
> Doctor James H. Miller

Those writers throughout the country who are desirous of entering the lists, will please forward their productions to [Charles Ferree] *Cloud and* [William P.] *Pouder*, Baltimore, before the first of October (postpaid) enclosed in an envelope bearing the name of the writer. If secrecy is preferred, the name may be enclosed in a separate envelope, which will not be opened, except in the case of the successful author. We wish those who may write for either of the premiums to understand that all manuscripts submitted will become the property of the Publishers.

Silver medals to the amount of the above rewards will be given in lieu of cash, if required (French, pp. 259–60).

[The offer of prizes was repeated at varying intervals until 7 September (French, p. 259).]

16 JULY. RICHMOND. Elizabeth Ellis writes her father Charles Ellis that "Mr. Allan [is] very unwell" (Phillips, 1:456).

18 JULY. CHARLOTTESVILLE. Thomas H. Ellis, son of Charles Ellis, graduates from the University of Virginia in French Language and Literature (NcD–ME).

27 JULY. RICHMOND. John Allan writes Charles Ellis: "Therm 95. My health greatly affected by it. I feel weak—I with all my family start Monday, stay 2 or 3 days at Byrd—then on to Sulphur Springs. Mrs. A. myself, Miss V. 2 children and 2 nurses, 2 drivers, five horses forms an expensive cavalcade. My sweet little Willie Galt is getting over his teething" (Phillips, 1:456–57)

7 SEPTEMBER. BALTIMORE. The *Saturday Visiter* repeats its offer of prizes.

26 SEPTEMBER. C. J. Durant makes his first ascension in a balloon.

[Ballooning, a nineteenth-century American fad, received fictional treatment by Poe in "Hans Phaall" and "The Balloon-Hoax." See 25 APRIL 1834.]

1 OCTOBER. The *Saturday Visiter* contest closes.

7 OCTOBER. The *Saturday Visiter* committee meets at the home of John H. B. Latrobe, 11 West Mulberry Street: "after dinner [J. P.] Kennedy and Dr. [James H.] Miller [and I] met at my house to decide the merits of certain compositions offered for premiums for the 'Saturday Visiter,' and made our selection of prose and poetry, and had altogether quite a pleasant afternoon and evening" (Latrobe, quoted in Semmes, p. 558).

[On 7 December 1852 Latrobe wrote Charles Chauncey Burr:

JOHN PENDLETON KENNEDY

The manuscripts, as received from the Editor, were laid in a pile on the table. Each one was opened as it came to hand. Sometimes, the first few sentences would condemn it as unworthy. Sometimes several pages were borne with. In some cases, the whole production was read. Two only of the prose pieces were laid aside for re-examination. I recollect them well. One was clever, but watery, evidently a woman's work. The other was terse, and the denouement terribly original. The poems were treated in the same way. But two of these were put by for review— one the Coliseum, by Poe, and the other, to which the prize was awarded, by J. H. Meritt [Hewitt], though the authorship was not known until afterwards. The loose MSS. having been gone through with, I turned to the Book, which contained many tales, and read it from beginning to end. It was so far, so very far, superior to anything before us, that we had no difficulty in awarding the first prize to the author. Our only difficulty was in selecting from the rich contents of the volume. We took the "Ms. Found in a Bottle" . . . .

To the committee, they [Poe's tales] were novelties for which they were wholly unprepared. Hence the admiration which, I well remember, the reading of them produced.

In this statement I hardly think I can be mistaken, so far as the action of the committee can be looked upon as a recognition of Mr. Poe's merits. Mr. Kennedy sent for him at once, and became his most useful friend. At my instance he called on me several times, and entered at length into the discussion of subjects on which he proposed to employ his pen. When he warmed up, he was most eloquent. He spoke, at that time, with eager action; and although, to judge from his outward man, the world was then going hard with him, and his look was *blaze* [*blasé?*], yet his appearance was forgotten, as he seemed to forget the world around him, as wild fancy, logical truth, mathematical analysis, and wonderful combinations of fact flowed, in strange commingling, from his lips, in words choice and appropriate as though the result of the closest study. I remember being particularly struck with the power that he seemed to possess of identifying himself with whatever he was describing. He related to me all the facts of a voyage to the moon, I think, which he proposed to put upon paper, with an accuracy of minute detail and a truthfulness as regarded philosophical phenomena, which impressed you with the idea, almost, that he had himself just returned from the journey which existed only in his imagination (Hubbell [1954], pp. 837–39).]

12 OCTOBER. The *Saturday Visiter* publishes the decision of the judges.

THE PREMIUMS

It will be seen by the following letter that the Committee have decided on the merits of the various productions sent for the premiums offered by us. The "Manuscript found in a bottle" is the production of Edgar A. Poe, of Baltimore.

The poem entitled "The Song of the Winds" by Henry Wilton, of Baltimore.

The prize pieces shall be published next week.

Messers. Cloud and Pouder—

Gentlemen:—We have received two pacquets containing the Poems and Tales submitted as competitors for the prizes offered by you in July last, and in accordance with your request have carefully perused them with a view to the award of the premiums.

Amongst the poems we have selected a short one, entitled "Song of the Winds," as the most finished production offered. There were several others of such a degree of merit as greatly to perplex our choice and cause some hesitation in the award we have made.

Of the tales submitted there were many of various and distinguished excellence; but the singular force and beauty of those offered by "The Tales of the Folio Club," it may be said without disparagement to the high merit of others presented in the competition, left us no ground for doubt in making choice of one from that collection. We have accordingly, awarded the prize in this department to the tale bearing the title of "A MS Found in a Bottle." It would scarcely be doing justice to the author of this collection to say the tale we have chosen is the best of the six offered by him. We have read them all with unusual interest, and can not refrain from the expression of the opinion that the writer owes it to his own reputation, as well as to the gratification of the community to publish the whole volume. These tales are eminently distinguished by a wild, vigorous and poetical imagination, a rich style, a fertile invention, and varied and curious learning. Our selection of "A MS Found in a bottle" was rather dictated by the originality of its conception and its length, than by any superior merit in its execution over the others by the same author.

The general excellence of the whole of the compositions offered for the prizes is very creditable to the rising literature of our country.

Very Respectfully Gentl'n
JOHN P. KENNEDY
JNO. H. B. LATROBE
J. H. MILLER

Baltimore, October 7, 1833 (French, pp. 260–61).

19 OCTOBER. The *Saturday Visiter* publishes Poe's "MS. Found in a Bottle" with an introductory note: "The following is the tale to which the Premium of Fifty Dollars has been awarded by the Committee. It will be found highly graphic in its style of composition." The editor of the *Visiter* comments: "It gives us great pleasure in stating for the literary credit of our city, that both the successful candidates are Baltimoreans" (French, p. 261).

21 OCTOBER. On the Monday following the publication of "MS. Found in a Bottle" Poe calls on John H. B. Latrobe.

[Later Latrobe described Poe:

His figure was remarkably good, and he carried himself erect and well, as one who had been trained to it. He was dressed in black, and his frock-coat was buttoned to the throat, where it met the black stock, then almost universally worn. Not a particle of white was visible. Coat, hat, boots and gloves had very evidently seen their best days, but so far as mending and brushing go, everything had been done apparently, to make them presentable. On most men his clothes would have looked shabby and seedy, but there was something about this man that prevented one from criticizing his garments, and the details I have mentioned were only recalled afterwards. The impression made, however, was that the award in Mr. Poe's favor was not inopportune (Rice, pp. 60–61).]

AFTER 21 OCTOBER. John Hill Hewitt, editor of the *Saturday Visiter* and the other successful contestant under the pseudonym of "Henry Wilton," winning the prize for the best poem, encounters Poe after the contest.

A few days after the publication of these prize pieces, as I [Hewitt] was about entering the office of the *Visiter*, on the S. E. corner of Baltimore and Gay Streets, I encountered Mr. Poe. He approached me with an ominous scowl on his features.

"You have used underhanded means, sir, to obtain that prize over me," said he, sternly.

"I deny it, sir," was my reply.

"Then why did you keep back your real name?'

"I had my reasons, and you have no right to question me."

"But you tampered with the committee, sir."

"The committee are gentlemen above being tampered with, sir; and if you say that you insult them," I replied, looking him full in the face.

"I agree that the committee are gentlemen," replied he, his dark eyes flashing with anger, "but I cannot place *you* in that category."

My blood mounted up to fever heat in a moment, and with my usual impulsiveness, I dealt him a blow which staggered him, for I was physically his superior.

There was every prospect of a very pretty fight, for Poe was full of pluck, but several gentlemen, friends to both parties, interfered, and the affair was "nipped in the bud." There was no duel—much to the disappointment of our friends and well-wishers (Hewitt [1949], p. 19).

26 OCTOBER. The *Saturday Visiter* publishes Poe's "The Coliseum" and reports that his *Tales of the Folio Club* will be issued by subscription.

THE FOLIO CLUB

This is the title of a volume of tales from the pen of Edgar A. Poe, the gentleman to whom the committee appointed by the proprietors of this paper awarded the premium of $50. The work is about being put to press, and is to be published by subscription. We have a list at our office, and any person wishing to subscribe will please call. The volume will cost but $1.

The prize tale is not the best of Mr. Poe's productions; among the tales of the Folio Club there are many possessing uncommon merit. They are all characterized by a raciness, originality of thought and brilliancy of conception which are rarely to be met with in the writings of our most favored American authors. In assisting Mr. Poe in the publication of the Folio Club, the friends of native literature will encourage a young author whose energies have been partially damped by the opposition of the press, and, we may say, by the lukewarmness of the public in appreciating American productions. He has studied and written much—his reward rested on public approbation—let us give him something more substantial than bare praise. We ask our friends to come forward and subscribe to the work—there are many anxious to see it before the public (French, pp. 262–63).

26 OCTOBER. NEWBURYPORT, MASSACHUSETTS. The *People's Advocate* prints an unauthorized version of Poe's "MS. Found in a Bottle."

2 NOVEMBER. BALTIMORE. The *Saturday Visiter* reports: "Mr. Poe has declined the publication of his Tales of the Folio Club in the manner stated in our last number. It is his intention, we understand, to bring them out in Philadelphia" (French, p. 262)

2 NOVEMBER. John Pendleton Kennedy makes an entry in his journal: "In July last I was appointed, together with John Latrobe and Dr. Miller, a committee, by the editors of the *Saturday Morning Visiter* to decide upon a prize tale and poem. Early in October we met for this purpose and having about a hundred tales and poems. The prize for the tale we gave to Edgar A. Poe, having selected that call[ed] 'A MS. Found in a Bottle' from a volume of tales furnished by him. The volume exhibits a great deal of talent, and we advised him to publish it. He has accordingly left it in my possession, to show it to [Henry C.] Carey in Philadelphia" (Campbell [1917a], p. 197; see Hammond, p. 27).

[Later, 13 April 1869, in a letter to George Wolff Fahnestock, Kennedy wrote: "I was very intimate with Poe, during the period of his residence in this city, and followed the story of his unhappy career with great interest after he left us. I have never known, nor heard of any one, whose life so curiously illustrated that twofold existence of the *spiritual* and the *carnal* disputing the control of the man, which has often been made the theme of fiction. His was debauched by the most grovelling appetites and exalted by the richest conceptions of genius.—In his special department of thought, our country has produced no poet or prose writer superior to him—indeed, I think, none equal to him" (Bohner [1958], pp. 220–22; Osborne, pp. 17–18).]

AFTER 2 NOVEMBER. John Pendleton Kennedy delivers Poe's manuscript to Carey & Lea, Philadelphia publishers (see 2 NOVEMBER).

NOVEMBER? Poe sustains "himself precariously by 'jobs' for the 'Visiter,' and for Mr. Kennedy" (W, 1:110–11; cf. Weiss [1907], pp. 68–69).

16 DECEMBER. RICHMOND. John Allan writes Charles Ellis that he is anxious to obtain a settlement of the business affairs of their firm: "My health is perhaps as good now as it ever will be. While therefore I can attend to these matters it were wise to do it" (DLC–EA; Quinn, p. 205).

CA. 1833. BALTIMORE. Poe writes "To Elizabeth" in the album of his cousin Elizabeth Rebecca Herring (Mabbott [1969], 1:233–36).

*

1834

*

JANUARY. PHILADELPHIA. *Godey's Lady's Book* publishes Poe's "The Visionary" (later called "The Assignation"), including "To One in Paradise."

1 JANUARY. BALTIMORE. John Pendleton Kennedy writes Henry C. Carey, in Philadelphia: "What have you done with Poe's MS?—When will you publish it, and what do you think of it?" (Hammond, pp. 27 and 41 n. 38).

26 JANUARY. RICHMOND. Patterson Allan is born to Louisa and John Allan.

"MOLDAVIA," the Allan house

CA. 14 FEBRUARY. Perhaps Poe pays his last visit to the ailing John Allan and meets Louisa Allan.

A short time previous to Mr. Allan's death, on the 27th of March, 1834, he was greatly distressed by dropsy, was unable to lie down, & sat in an arm-chair night & day; several times a day, by the advice of his physician, he walked across the room for exercise, leaning on his cane, and assisted by his wife & a manservant. During this illness of her husband, Mrs. Allan was on an occasion, passing through the hall of this house, when hearing the front doorbell ring, she opened the door herself. A man of remarkable appearance stood there, & without giving his name asked if he could see Mr. Allan. She replied that Mr. Allan's condition was such that his physicians had prohibited any person from seeing him except his nurses. The man was Edgar A. Poe, who was, of course, perfectly familiar with the house. Thrusting her aside & without noticing her reply, he passed rapidly upstairs to Mr. Allan's chamber, followed by Mrs. Allan. As soon as he entered the chamber, Mr. Allan raised his cane, & threatening to strike him if he came within his reach, ordered him out; upon which Poe withdrew, & that was the last time they ever met (Thomas H. Ellis, *Richmond Standard*, 7 May 1881).

1 MARCH. William Burke on leaving the Richmond Seminary writes a thank-you note to Charles Ellis, Jr., Montague Thompson, Charles Carter, and a Committee of Students:

I have received, with feelings of the utmost sensibility and gratitude, two beautiful Silver Tankards, presented by you, on behalf of the late students of the Richmond Seminary. . . . One exhortation, My Dr. Pupils, before you disperse— Cultivate a generous ambition—honour your parents—respect your Teachers—be industrious, docile and modest—love order and decency—frown down vicious companions—abhor meanness, and never forget that a virtuous and well spent youth affords the best prospect of a respectable and happy old age (NcD–ME).

10 MARCH. BALTIMORE. The *Baltimore American and Literary Gazette* reports that Henry Herring has bought Hampstead Hall (Phillips, 1:473).

19 MARCH. RICHMOND. Margaret Ellis writes her husband Charles that "Nancy Valentine called at the store today, & told Thomas [Ellis] that Mr. Allan was very sick" (Phillips, 1:473).

27 MARCH. John Allan dies, leaving a widow and three sons. Charles Ellis, Jr., writes his father: "I inform you of Uncle Allan's death—today at 11 o'clock very suddenly—he was sitting in his Easy-chair by himself and had not Mrs. Allan been called in by the cries of one of the children he would not have been known to be dead for some time. She found him laid back, noticed the difference in his appearance directly & brought assistance by her screams. The two Mr. Galts [William, Jr., and James] have arranged the funeral for Saturday" (Phillips, 1:474].

29 MARCH. Thomas Ellis writes his father Charles Ellis: "Uncle Allan was buried [in Shockoe Hill Cemetery] this morning at 12 o'clock. His death created much sensation & his family appear deeply distressed" (Phillips, 1:474).

On his tombstone appears the inscription:

SACRED TO THE MEMORY OF
JOHN ALLAN
WHO DEPARTED THIS LIFE
MARCH 27, 1834
IN THE 54TH YEAR OF HIS AGE.

He whose remains lie buried beneath
this tomb was a native of Ayrshire, Scotland.
Blessed with every social and benevolent
feeling, he fulfilled the duties of Husband,
Father, Brother, and Friend, with surpassing
Kindness, supported the ills of life with
Fortitude, and his Prosperity with Meekness.

A firm believer in Christ, and resigned to
the decrees of Almighty God, he gave up
life with all its enjoyments, without a murmur.

While affection mourns the great loss it
has sustained, the remembrance of his
virtues and the hope of a reunion hereafter
are the only sources of consolation to
the bereft heart.

1 APRIL. The *Richmond Enquirer* notices John Allan's death: "Died in this city on Thursday morning, in the 54th year of his age, John Allan, Esq., one of the worthiest citizens of Richmond. He has been long a resident of the city—and none was better known, none more highly respected— distinguished for his humanity, his hospitality, his attachment to his friends, his devotion to his family" (Bondurant, p. 209 n. 40).

11 APRIL. Jane Ellis writes her brother James, a cadet at West Point: "You have not heard of Uncle Allan's death I expect, as Father did not receive our letters until he reached Philadelphia; no one was with him and he died very suddenly sitting in his arm-chair. You can conceive how distressed Aunt Nancy is, the whole family are very much grieved, and I can say that Mrs. Allan looks as white as a sheet" (NcD–ME; Bondurant, p. 209).

15 APRIL. WEST POINT. James N. Ellis writes his brother Charles, Jr.: "I

have just heard the particulars of Uncle Allan's death. It was indeed a sudden call to one who has not although the newspapers say so, spent his time in a proper way. But peace be to his ashes for he was ever kind and affectionate to all and all his sins were against himself. No doubt his wife is very much afflicted at it. She should be for [an undecipherable deletion] man there could not be" (NcD–ME).

25 APRIL. BALTIMORE. The *Lutheran Observer, and Weekly Religious and Literary Visiter*, edited by Benjamin Hurtz and printed by Charles F. Cloud, makes an announcement:

Balloon Ascension

Mr. JAMES MILLS has the pleasure to inform the citizens of Baltimore that he will make his Second Grand Ascension on THURSDAY, 1st May, at Fair Mount Garden, East Baltimore st –

* * *

Mr. HERRING has at considerable expense, erected an Amphitheatre sufficient to contain from seven to eight thousand persons, where they can be comfortably seated and witness the whole of this interesting process.

[For an unknown reason the ascension was postponed to 26 May. In its 20 June issue the *Lutheran Observer* continued its interest in balloons. "Mr. Herring" was, of course, Henry Herring, the first husband of Poe's Aunt Elizabeth. See 17 NOVEMBER 1814.]

8 MAY. RICHMOND. John Allan's will is probated at a Circuit Superior Court of Law and Chancery held for Henrico County at the Capitol in the City of Richmond. His widow Louisa Allan renounces all her rights under the will and elects to take her share under the intestate law (Allen, pp. 695-98).

AFTER 8 MAY? Perhaps Poe calls on Louisa Allan.

. . . after Mr. Allan's death . . . she was sitting at one of the front windows of her chamber & seeing him [Poe] enter the gate & walk towards the door, she sent her chamber-maid down to say that she begged to be excused from receiving him (Thomas H. Ellis, *Richmond Standard*, 7 May 1881).

15 MAY. WASHINGTON. The *Daily National Intelligencer* carries a "PROSPEC-TUS of a Literary Paper to be published in Richmond, Va., by Thomas W. White, to be entitled THE SOUTHERN LITERARY MESSENGER, To be de-voted to every department of Literature and the Fine Arts."

["The *Southern Literary Messenger* originated from a remarkable combination in one individual of enterprise, industry and perseverance; one who could contribute little else than mechanical skill to such a periodical as he succeeded in establishing more to his honor than his profit. Thomas W. White commenced the publication in 1834, at a time when even our large cities sustained very few such enterprises. A local sale of 5,000 copies was more probable and feasible in New York or Philadelphia, than one of 250 in Richmond. . . .

"A short time after its commencement, he obtained the services of Edgar A. Poe as editor, which were continued for eighteen months—an unusually long period for that erratic genius to devote to one occupation" (Mordecai, pp. 241–43).]

16 MAY. BALTIMORE. John Pendleton Kennedy writes White, commending the *Messenger* venture and promising his aid (information from the late John C. Wyllie).

27 MAY. RICHMOND. Margaret Ellis writes her son James, at West Point: "I believe that Charles wrote you an account of the Coronation of the Queen of May, in Mr. [Genaro] Persico's School" (NcD–ME).

[Poe composed a "May Queen Ode." See APRIL? 1836.]

5 JUNE. White writes Mrs. Lydia Huntley Sigourney, a poetess of Hartford, Connecticut, and sends her a copy of James Ewell Heath's novel *Edge-Hill* (Mrs. Sigourney to White, 14 June 1834).

14 JUNE. HARTFORD, CONNECTICUT. Mrs. Sigourney writes White that she is "happy to announce the arrival of 'Edge-Hill'" and continues: "The proof-sheet of my poetical offering to the 'Southern Literary Messenger,' is correctly printed. I think it would improve its appearance to omit the dashes which occur in the orthography,—and which I am in the habit of making in the manuscript, with some inadvertence. I should be particularly pleased to attempt a sketch of the biography of Judge [John] Marshall. . . . I recollect taking great pains to get a sight of him, when in Richmond, in 1825, though ineffectually" (NHi).

JUNE OR JULY? NEW YORK? James Kirke Paulding, a novelist, writes White: "It gives me great pleasure to find that you are about establishing a literary paper in Richmond" (*Messenger*, 1 [August 1834]: 1).

[Other correspondents encouraging White at this time and earlier were Washington Irving, James Fenimore Cooper, John Pendleton Kennedy, John Quincy Adams, and Peter A. Browne. See *Messenger*, 1 [August 1834]: 1. Irving dated his letter 10 May.]

CA. 5 AUGUST. RICHMOND. The first number of the *Southern Literary*

Messenger appears (*Richmond Enquirer*, 5 August 1834; Washington *Daily National Intelligencer*, 9 August 1834).

24 AUGUST. Margaret Ellis writes her son James: "Friday was Elizabeths birth day, & Jane had Colombia Hudgins, Mary Shepherd & Rose McKenzie [Poe] to spend the day with her, in the evening William Robinson & William Perkins came in, & they spent quite a merry evening, playing with fortune cards & other amusements" (NcD–ME).

SEPTEMBER? BALTIMORE. Robert T. P. Allen, a West Point graduate, is informed that Poe is working in a brickyard (R.T.P. Allen, pp. 142–43. See EARLY FALL? 1832).

[John H. Ingram wrote Sarah Helen Whitman, 14 February 1877 (Miller [1979], p. 474): "By the way, did I tell you that the *Allen* who gave the story of Poe working in the brickyard 'late in the fall of 1834' was a witness *against* Poe in the West Point courtmartial . . . ?"]

24 OCTOBER. RICHMOND. Thomas H. Ellis writes his brother Charles that White would like to have the *Messenger* noticed in one of the Charlottesville papers and to have the names of any new subscribers (NcD–ME).

4 NOVEMBER. White invites Nathaniel Beverley Tucker, Professor of Law, College of William and Mary, to become a contributor to his *Messenger* (Vi–W–TC).

7 NOVEMBER. ESSEX COUNTY, VIRGINIA. James Mercer Garnett writes White, criticizing his editorial policies (ViHi).

13 NOVEMBER. ALEXANDRIA, VIRGINIA. Edgar Snowden, editor of the *Alexandria Gazette*, writes White: "I have been so busy that I have had hardly time to do any thing in your line—I send you a notice of and some extracts from a volume of Poems written by . . . [Thomas J.] Semmes of this place. . . . I shall try and be a regular contributor if my articles are worth publishing and if the [Richmond] Compiler! is not *too* hard upon me" (NcD–ME).

CA. 19 NOVEMBER. BALTIMORE. Poe writes John Pendleton Kennedy:

Since the day you first saw me my situation in life has altered materially. At that time I looked forward to the inheritance of a large fortune, and, in the meantime, was in receipt of an annuity sufficient for my support. This was allowed me by a gentleman of Virginia (Mr Jno Allan) who adopted me at the age of two years, (both my parents being dead) and who, until lately, always treated me with the affection of a father. But a second marriage on his part, and I dare say many follies on my own at length ended in a quarrel between us. He is now dead, and has left me nothing. . . . I could not help thinking that if my situation was stated—as you could state it—to Carey & Lea, they might be led to aid me with a small sum in consideration of my M.S. now in their hands. This would relieve my immediate wants (L, 1:54–55).

21 NOVEMBER. PHILADELPHIA. Henry C. Carey writes Kennedy: "I will see to your friend Poe this day or tomorrow. I have not had time since receipt of your letter this morning" (Campbell [1917a], p. 197).

26 NOVEMBER. Henry C. Carey writes Kennedy:

I should have written you sooner in relation to your friend, but that I have expected for several days to hear from you. The book shall go to press at once, but I have much doubt of his making anything by it. Such little things [?] rarely succeed, and if they do, their produce is small. I do not expect to make anything, but am perfectly willing to take the chance of it. As he, however, appears to want something immediately, I had thought of handing the volume to Miss [Eliza] Leslie to see if she could select something for her *Souvenir* [the *Gift*], for which he could be paid promptly. If he could dispose of them in that way, they would, I think, be more productive than in the form of a volume. Doubting, as I do, any extent of sale that will enable us to make anything by it, I am not very willing to increase the risque by paying the author in advance.

Say what I shall do, and it shall be done. It shall be printed as it stands—or I will hand it to Miss Leslie and print after she shall have selected one—or, in short, what you please shall be done. I should be exceedingly glad to promote your friend's objects if I knew how, but writing is a very poor business unless a man can find the way of taking the public attention, and *that is not often done by short stories*. People want something larger and longer. If, by the publication of these tales in the *Souvenir*—or the newspapers—he could obtain anything like a name, his book would afterwards—composed of the same tales—be worth more than it now is, unknown as he is. Direct me (Campell [1917a], pp. 197–98).

2 DECEMBER. BALTIMORE. Elizabeth Rebecca Herring, Poe's cousin, marries Andrew Turner Tutt of Virginia (Phillips, 1:425, 514; Mabbott [1969], 1:147–48).

19 DECEMBER. Poe writes Kennedy: "About four weeks ago I sent you a note respecting my Tales of the F. Club, and matters have since occurred to me that make me doubt whether you have recd. it. You would confer upon me the greatest favour by dropping a few words for me in the P. O." (L, 1:55–56).

22 DECEMBER. Kennedy writes Poe:

I have received your note, and should sooner have apprized you of what I had done, but that Carey's letter only reached me a few days ago as I was stepping into a carriage to go to Annapolis, whence I returned only a day or two since.

I requested Carey immediately upon the receipt of your first letter to do something for you as speedily as he might find an opportunity, and to make some advance on your book. His answer let me know that he would go on to publish, but the expectation of any profit from the undertaking he considered doubtful— not from want of merit in the production, but because small books of detached tales, however well written, seldom yield a sum sufficient to enable the bookseller to purchase a copyright. He recommended, however, that I should allow him to sell some of the tales to the publishers of the annuals. My reply was that I thought you would not object to this if the right to publish the same tale was reserved for the volume. He has accordingly sold one of the tales to Miss Leslie for the "Souvenir" [the *Gift*], at a dollar a page, I think with the reservation above mentioned—and has remitted me a draft for fifteen dollars which I will hand over to you as soon as you call upon me, which I hope you will do as soon as you can make it convenient. If the other tales can be sold in the same way, you will get more for the work than by an exclusive publication (*W*, 17:3; Woodberry, 1:105–06).

1834 OR EARLY 1835. Miss Mary Winfree of Chesterfield, Virginia, a friend of Elmira Shelton, meets Poe in Baltimore. For her he composes "To Mary" (later entitled "To One Departed" and "To Frances"), a poem first published in the July 1835 *Southern Literary Messenger* (Mabbott [1969], 1:236–37, 545).

THOMAS WILLIS WHITE

Humanities Research Center, University of Texas at Austin

CHAPTER FOUR

Richmond and the Messenger
1835–1837

Unsuccessful in finding employment as a teacher in the Baltimore area, Poe is encouraged by John Pendleton Kennedy to write for the *Southern Literary Messenger*, a monthly published by Thomas Willis White in Richmond. Poe returns to Richmond in August 1835, at a time when the Richmond Academy is advertising for a professor of English and White is seeking editorial assistance. When the professorship goes to another candidate, White employs Poe on a temporary basis and later as full-time editor. By his short stories and critical notices in the *Messenger* Poe attracts public attention. In October 1835 his aunt Maria Clemm and her daughter Virginia join him in Richmond. In May 1836 Poe marries his cousin Virginia, who is not quite fourteen years of age. White holds close reins on his *Messenger*, finds Poe's habits not good, and is reluctant to give Poe full editorial control. Late in 1836 White is beset by a printer's strike. In addition, his health is poor, and his wife has a terminal illness. Both Poe and White find themselves hard pressed financially and both are unhappy with their relationship. Poe's editorship terminates in January 1837. With Virginia and Maria Clemm, Poe moves to New York.

*

1835
*

19 JANUARY. WASHINGTON. The *Daily National Intelligencer* notices the December 1834 *Southern Literary Messenger*: "We have just received the 4th No. . . . and cannot refrain from occupying a few lines with a passing expression of our sense of its merits. . . . we are glad to find, in its acknowledgments of the number of subscriptions paid within the preceding month, evidence that it is liberally sustained by pecuniary contributors as well as literary ones."

[The *Messenger* did not appear regularly at the beginning of each month. With the December 1834 number White began to print on the covers the names of his subscribers and a time period in which their payments had been received. The December issue, for example, appeared after 8 January since subscription payments were acknowledged from "November 28, 1834, to January 8, 1835, inclusive." Press notices of the *Messenger* as well as White's correspondence help further to establish the approximate dates of issue. Many of the covers have press notices of the *Messenger*, letters from correspondents, and a few advertisements.]

29 JANUARY. RICHMOND. White writes Beverley Tucker that he is sending him for review the second and third volumes of Washington's letters and expresses his opposition "to the practice of taking whole chapters when noticing works" (Vi–W–TC).

5 FEBRUARY. White writes Beverley Tucker, instructing him to keep "Bancroft's 1st vol. History U. S. . . . for your Library. This is the disposition I wish you to make of every work you may review for my Messenger" (Vi–W–TC).

[Poe was to meet George Bancroft the following year. See 4 APRIL 1836.]

CA. 10 FEBRUARY. The January *Messenger* makes its appearance. In "The Doom," a tale by "Benedict," the pseudonymous author alludes to Poe's swimming feat in the James River:

One evening in June, 1832, when the thermometer stood at 94°, I had managed to convey myself about a mile up the river bank for the purpose of bathing, and going into the water I splashed about with great vigor, thinking about Leander's remarkable feat in crossing the Hellespont, until I felt a great desire to try whether I might not aspire to equal him, or at least E—P—, who swam from Mayo's Bridge to Warwick wharf some years ago (see JUNE? 1824? and 30 APRIL 1835).

[James Ewell Heath, who was then assisting White, expressed "doubts about the admission of 'The Doom' into our columns, not because of any inferiority in the style and composition, but because of the revolting character of the story. The writer, with apparent sincerity, states it to be founded upon actual occurrences; but we confess that it seems to us a wild and incredible fiction. . . . The hero of the tale . . . was in truth a remorseless fiend. . . . the 'Messenger' shall not be the vehicle of sentiments at war with the interests of virtue and sound morals" (*Messenger*, 1 [January 1835]:254–55). In a lengthy letter to the *Richmond Compiler* "Fra Diavolo" described "The Doom" as "vile balderdash." To this criticism "Benedict," apparently amused, pointed out that M. M. Noah of the *New York Evening Star* had found the tale "the effort of no ordinary pen." See *Compiler*, 6, 7, and 8 April 1835.]

17 FEBRUARY. White writes his friend Lucian Minor, a lawyer of Louisa County, Virginia, that James E. Heath "cannot find the leisure to do me half that service which he wishes; and continually importunes me to procure the assistance of a competent editor,—and no other name always assails me more than yours. . . . Professor [William Barton] Rogers [of the College of William and Mary] . . . is equally zealous that I should have you for my editor. . . . I will hand you a compensation of $800 per annum" (Jackson [1934], pp. 93–94).

17 FEBRUARY. ESSEX COUNTY, VIRGINIA. James Mercer Garnett, a contributor to the *Messenger*, writes White:

I have taken . . . a hasty glance at it [the January *Messenger*] which has enabled me to say, that it is at least equal, if not superior to its predecessor. Master Benedict [author of "The Doom"] however, has excited my most unqualified disgust & reprobation. Let me earnestly recommend to you, to wash your hands of him, as speedily as possible; unless he will, on some other occasion, strive to make amends, (for he seems capable of writing well,) for so gross an offence as he has committed both against good taste & good morals. I was much gratified by the editorial remarks on his communication, & hope such castigation may do him some good. Such a jumble of incredible, incongruous absurdities,—incongruous in every thing but the character of heartless, diabolical villainy which marks his Hero, I have scarcely ever seen (ViHi).

[Earlier White was indebted to John Marshall for writing a puff of a second edition of Garnett's *Lectures*. For Marshall's letter see White's advertisement in the *Richmond Compiler*, 4 December 1824.]

26 FEBRUARY. RICHMOND. James E. Heath writes Lucian Minor:

You are not at all mistaken in supposing yourself perfectly authorised to confer with me on the subject of Mr. White's proposition, and I take great pleasure in responding to your enquiries respecting it. In truth I am somewhat a party concerned, and strenuously advised White to engage your services if it were possible to do so. . . . I gave him that advice, because in perfect candor, I knew of no one whom I believed better qualified to make the "Messenger" an extensively useful and acceptable work in Virginia than yourself. . . . I felt that the humble aid I had rendered him must soon cease from the overwhelming demands upon my time to say nothing of other reasons why he should speedily have an *avowed* Editor to sustain his periodical. . . .

Although I know that White is *embarrassed* and (inter nos) of *fickle temperament*, yet I have great confidence in his honor and integrity—and under your *avowed auspices*—the success of the "Messenger" would be such as to insure the prompt payment of the proposed salary; nay more,—I think that with your Banner at the mast head—the present subscription, approaching 800, would be vastly increased. The question nevertheless presents itself whether you would be justified in abandoning a practice worth $1500—in the expectation of receiving an equivalent in your professional success here. That the editorial management of the "Messenger" in order to [make?] its firm and permanent establishment, would absorb much of your time, I think there can be no doubt;—From my little experience, I should be safe in asserting that *all the cares and duties* connected with the editorship would require at least 5 hours a day. Something more or less might answer, but this is my best conjecture. . . . it is difficult, very difficult to decide (ViHi).

2 MARCH. White writes Lucian Minor that he would expect to pay him $800 a year for his editorial services and that the *Messenger* has no less than 750 paying subscribers (Jackson [1936], pp. 226–28. See 14 MAY. RICHMOND).

12 MARCH. BALTIMORE. The *Baltimore Patriot* prints an advertisement for a public school teacher:

A Teacher Wanted—At male Public School No. 3 Aisquith St. The commissioners of Public Schools will appoint on Wednesday next, the 18th inst. a Teacher to supply a vacancy which has occurred at Male School No. 3. Satisfactory recommendations as to character, with testimonials of capacity for conducting a School on the Monitorial System, will be required. . . . Applications addressed to the commissioners, may be left with either of them or the Secretary, No. 8 Courtland Street (L, 2:474).

14 MARCH. RICHMOND. White writes Minor, expressing his disappointment that Minor has refused his offer and informing Minor that the February *Messenger* will make its appearance 16 March (Jackson [1936], pp. 228–29).

15 MARCH. BALTIMORE. Poe solicits Kennedy's help in obtaining employment as a teacher and encloses a copy of an advertisement in the *Baltimore Patriot* of 12 March or one similar to it: "In my present circumstances such a situation would be most desirable" (L, 1:56).

Kennedy invites Poe to dinner (Poe to Kennedy, 15 March 1835). Poe acknowledges Kennedy's invitation and requests a loan of $20: "Your kind invitation to dinner to day has wounded me to the quick. I cannot come— and for reasons of the most humiliating nature [in] my personal appearance. You may conceive my deep mortification in making this disclosure to you—but it was necessary. If you will be my friend so far as to loan me $20 I will call on you to morrow—otherwise it will be impossible, and I must submit to my fate" (L, 1:56–57).

16 MARCH. Poe calls on John Pendleton Kennedy (implied by Poe to Kennedy, second letter of March 15).

[On 10 October 1849 Kennedy wrote in his diary: "It is many years ago —

I think perhaps as early as 1833 or 4 – that I found him in Baltimore in a state of starvation. I gave him clothing, free access to my table, and the use of a horse for exercise whenever he chose—in fact brought him up from the very verge of despair" (Woodberry, 2:350).]

16 MARCH. RICHMOND. The February *Messenger* makes its appearance (White to Minor, 14 March 1835. See *Compiler*, 18, 25, and 31 March 1835).

13 APRIL. BALTIMORE. John Pendleton Kennedy writes White that Poe "is *very* poor. I told him to write something for every number of your magazine, and that you might find it to your advantage to give him some permanent employ. He has a volume of very bizarre tales in the hands of——[Henry C. Carey], in Philadelphia, who for a year past has been promising to publish them. He is at work upon a tragedy [*Politian*], but I have turned him to drudging upon whatever may make money" (Griswold [1850], p. xiii).

AFTER 13 APRIL? PHILADELPHIA. Perhaps Poe calls on Henry C. Carey (Poe to Kennedy, 11 September 1835).

CA. 17 APRIL. RICHMOND. The March *Messenger* appears with Poe's tale "Berenice" and Philip Pendleton Cooke's poem "Young Rosalie Lee" (*Compiler*, 17 April).

[The unsigned "Extract from an Unfinished Poem" in this issue is believed not to be Poe's. See Campbell (1933), p. 206, and Mabbott (1969), 1:506.]

18 APRIL. White writes Lucian Minor: "I have called E. V. Sparhawk's attention to that part of your letter touching his notice of [your] New-England Letter No. 4. He promises to look to it" (Jackson [1934], p. 95).

[Edward Vernon Sparhawk succeeded James E. Heath and during the months of April, May, June, and July 1835 assisted White. See 11 JUNE. RICHMOND and 12 JUNE. BALTIMORE.]

BEFORE 30 APRIL. White, perhaps influenced by James E. Heath, gives Poe his opinion of "Berenice" (Poe to White, 30 April 1835).

30 APRIL. BALTIMORE. Poe replies to White:

I noticed the allusion in the Doom. The writer seems to compare my swim with that of Lord Byron. . . . Any swimmer "in the falls" in my days, would have swum the Hellespont, and thought nothing of the matter. . . . A word or two in relation to Berenice. Your opinion of it is very just. The subject is by far too horrible, and I confess that I hesitated in sending it especially as a specimen of my capabilities. The Tale originated in a bet that I could produce nothing effective on a subject so singular, provided I treated it seriously. But what I wish to say relates to the character of your Magazine more than to any articles I may offer, and I beg you to believe that I have no intention of giving you *advice*, being fully confident that, upon consideration, you will agree with me. The history of all Magazines shows plainly that those which have attained celebrity were indebted for it to articles *similar in nature———to Berenice———*although, I grant you, far superior in style and execution. I say similar in *nature*. You ask me in what does this nature consist? In the ludicrous heightened into the grotesque: the fearful coloured into the horrible: the witty exaggerated into the burlesque: the singular wrought out into the strange and mystical. You may say all this is bad taste. I have my doubts about it. Nobody is more aware than I am that simplicity is the cant of the day— but take my word for it no one cares any thing about simplicity in their hearts. Believe me also, in spite of what people say to the contrary, that there is nothing easier in the world than to be extremely simple. But whether the articles of which I speak are, or are not in bad taste is little to the purpose. To be appreciated you must be *read*, and these things are invariably sought after with avidity. They are, if you will take notice, the articles which find their way into other periodicals, and into the papers, and in this manner, taking hold upon the public mind they augment the reputation of the source where they originated. Such articles are the "M. S. found in a Madhouse" and the "Monos and Daimonos" of the London New Monthly———the "Confessions of an Opium-Eater" and the "Man in the Bell" of Blackwood. The two first were written by no less a man than Bulwer———the *Confessions* [illegible] universally attributed to Coleridge—although unjustly. The first men in [England] have not thought writings of this nature unworthy of their talents, and I have good reason to believe that some very high names valued themselves *principally* upon this species of literature. To be sure originality is an essential in these things—great attention must be paid to style, and much labour spent in their composition, or they will degenerate into the tugid [*sic*] or the absurd. If I am not mistaken you will find Mr Kennedy, whose writings you admire, and whose Swallow-Barn is unrivalled for purity of style and thought of my opinion in this matter. It is unnecessary for you to pay much attention to the many who will no doubt favour you with their critiques. In respect to Berenice individually I allow that it approaches the very verge of bad taste—but I will not sin quite so egregiously again. I propose to furnish you every month with a Tale of the nature which I have alluded to. The effect—if any—will be estimated better by the circulation of the Magazine than by any comments upon its contents. This much, however, it is necessary to promise, that no two of these Tales will have the slightest resemblance one to the other either in matter or manner—still however preserving the character which I speak of (*L*, 1:57–59).

[A source for a part of this letter is a note entitled "Swimming" in the May *Messenger*.]

30? APRIL. RICHMOND. White writes Lucian Minor and expresses his concern about his failure to bring the April *Messenger* out on time (Jackson [1936], p. 230).

14 MAY. BALTIMORE. Poe notices the April *Messenger*, of which he has advance sheets, in the *Republican and Commercial Advertiser*, edited by Samuel Harker.

[This notice, copied in the *Richmond Compiler* of 20 May, and three other notices were published by Jackson (1935), pp. 251–56.]

14 MAY. RICHMOND. White writes Beverley Tucker: "I am pleased to tell you that I have nearly 1000 subscribers and my list is gradually increasing" (Vi–W–TC).

[In a letter to Charles Anthon, late October 1844, Poe wrote that when he joined the *Messenger* White had about 700 subscribers and 5,500 paying subscribers when he left; and in a letter, late April 1849, to E. H. N. Patterson that during its second year the circulation of the *Messenger* rose from less than 1,000 to 5,000 subscribers.]

CA. 14 MAY. The April *Messenger* makes its appearance with Poe's "Morella" (including "A Catholic Hymn") and his notices of the following works: the *North American Review* for April; the *London Quarterly Review* for February; *The Life of Samuel Drew* by his son; Volume I of H. Lee's *The Life of Emperor Napoleon*; *Celebrated Trials of all Countries, and remarkable cases of Criminal Jurisprudence, selected by a Member of the Philadelphia Bar*; Andrew Reed's *No Fiction*; Madame Junot's *Memoirs of Celebrated Women of all Countries*; *Influence*; Whitehead's *English Pirates, Highwaymen and Robbers*; Laughton Osborn's *Confessions of a Poet*; *The Language of Flowers;* Mr. [Richard Lovell] and Miss [Maria] Edgeworth's *Practical Education*; *The Highland Smugglers*; J. G. Lockhart's *Valerius*; *An Account of Col. Crockett's Tour to the North and Down East*, written by himself; *Illoraz de Courcy, an auto-biographical novel by Josiah Templeton, Esq.*; Charles Fenno Hoffman's *A Winter in the West, by a New Yorker*.

On the wrappers of the April issue White prints an extract from a letter by an anonymous correspondent, perhaps Tucker, who writes: "Poe's story ['Berenice'] is well written——very well written. . . . Tell me, when you next write, who are the authors of 'My Classmates,' and 'The Doom,' (the latter is a powerful and nervous writer—the censures hurled against him, will fall harmless at his feet,) that is, if you violate no confidence in so doing." Also a comment from the Augusta, Georgia, *Courier* is printed: "The singular tale of 'Berenice,' by EDGAR A. POE, developes much beauty and elegance of style, but is altogether too full of the wild, mysterious, horrible, and improbable." Poe's name appears in a list of subscribers making payments between 13 April and 9 May.

BEFORE 18 MAY. BALTIMORE. Poe writes Henry C. Carey, the Philadelphia publisher (Carey to Kennedy, 18 May 1835).

18 MAY. PHILADELPHIA. Henry C. Carey writes John Pendleton Kennedy: "Poe has written me to say that the tale ['MS. Found in a Bottle'] selected by Miss Leslie [editor of the *Gift* for 1836] has been printed already. That being the case, I should be glad [if] he would send her something good in its stead. Will you say so to him, and say that I would have written him but that his letter is only now received, and I am excessively occupied" (Campbell [1917a], pp. 197–98).

18 MAY. RICHMOND. "Fair Play" addresses a letter to the *Compiler*, in which he finds fault with Poe's brief notice of *The Language of Flowers* in the April *Messenger*: "The next time you review a work, would it not be more candid to give your *own* opinion of its merits, without casting sideway reflections on the *mental* or *moral* perceptions of its readers?"

20 MAY. "J." addresses a letter to the *Compiler*, sharply disagreeing with Poe's opinion of Laughton Osborn's *Confessions of a Poet*, a book reviewed in the April *Messenger*.
    The *Compiler* also reprints Poe's critique of the April *Messenger* from the *Baltimore Republican* of 14 May.

To The Editors of the Compiler.
    MESSRS. EDITORS:—A new publication entitled *Confessions of a Poet*, has received a brief critical notice in the last number of the Southern Literary Messenger. You are generally reputed to be untrammelled in literature as in politics; perhaps, then you will aid me in giving to the expression of my dissent from that criticism all the truth, force and dignity, which printing implies. I know not if the avowal of something like personal interest (not in the work itself, but simply as touched by the criticism) will be regarded as strengthening my claim to be heard.—The critic announces his assured conviction, that none but *le vulgaire* will go through with *The Confessions*. It happens that I have done so. My sin, I humbly hope, is the less for having been committed before the criticism appeared, and my pretensions to impartiality not materially weakened by a confession that might have been withheld.
    The readers of the Messenger can hardly fail to experience very great surprise at one or the other of two things suggested by the criticism; the critic's capacity of estimating a work which it must be intended that he never read,—or his activity in escaping the lash which he has been guilty of. Or taking yet a third direction, their astonishment, mingled with reverence, may be concentrated on the privileges of the critical ministry, allowed to perpetuate sin that the narrative of experience

may deter those who are yet uncontaminated. The critic may possibly allege that the tenor and tendency of a composition can be learned from less than the thorough perusal, and that his opinion has been formed in that way. In truth this is the best and the only explanation he can make. Supposing it to be what himself would reply if examined; and passing over the fact, apparent from the criticism itself, that he has read the first pages of the first volume and the concluding pages of the second, and is moreover acquainted with the outline of the whole story; I presume that the character of the work will not be regarded as stamped unalterably by the very few remarks he has vouchsafed to make directly upon its merits. These remarks are confined to a scoff at the catastrophe of the fable,—a beautifully tender alarm lest the Poet should have survived his own pistol-shot, and be yet in good ability to favour the world with a new series of his confessions,—a stout denial of the author's claim to the sacred title he has assumed,—and the aforesaid undoubting presumption that none but the vulgar will read the Confessions throughout. The complaint that the book is printed on singularly bad paper, and that the matter has been stretched into two volumes, when it might very well have been finished in one printed in the usual type of romances, cannot, I suppose, affect the merits of the composition. For the same reason the notes, which seem to have excited the critic's wrath must be discarded from the estimate of the *Confessions*. They are professedly written by the *editor*, as distinguished from the author and hero, who terminates his own wretched existence as soon as his confessions are completed. Whatever be the worth of the notes (and to them also I think great injustice has been done) they form too inconsiderable a portion of the book to determine whether it shall sink or swim. One part of the critic's objection to them is certainly very unfair. They are *not* added by way of explanation; they are avowedly written by an editor (whether a distinct person *in fact* from the author is very immaterial) and their principal object is or seems to be the counteraction of improper or extravagant sentiments in the confessions; so the circumstance that two or three of them are in French, cannot sustain the cavil that, professing to explain, they are wrapped in a foreign language, lest they should be understood. The text no where needs explanation.—What the editor's motive could have been for writing some of his notes in French, I do not pretend to comprehend; or rather, I cannot see the sufficiency of the motive he assigns. But admitting that the notes are added for explanation, their character, language or fate can only be important as connected with the work they explain. Here then, is the true question. Is the work itself such as the critic would have his readers believe that it is?

With something very like that inconsistency which he charges upon the author, the critic admits that the composition has merits; that very composition which he has so sweepingly denounced, and which he has forbidden to his readers, upon pain of *vulgarity*. What those merits are, he does not set forth. Perhaps they are too slight in his judgment, too entirely overborne by the defects and bad character of the Confessions, to be worth enumeration. But these defects and this character, what are they? Oh! the moral, doubtless the moral!—I should very much like to know what the critic's idea of a moral is. If he regards it as something nearly detached from the narrative, something not less distinct from the fable than the tail of a kite is from the kite itself, then certainly there is a want of moral in this book. At any rate, it can only be found in those notes which are deemed an incumbrance. But if the detail of errors overtaken by their consequences; of crimes deeply, severely, to the very extent of retribution, brought into reckoning and gathered around the last hours of the miserable autobiographer; of passions indulged from infancy to manhood, and until their strength became the sole support as it was the unceasing torment of existence;—if such a picture, relieved by two of the finest delineations that fancy ever wrought, can be said to carry with it a moral, the critic is assuredly unreasonable and unjust. For the style, it cannot be denied that extravagance of the wildest sort is frequently to be found in it. How far that exaggeration is appropriate to the character of the story, may form quite another question. Yet in very many portions there is no such defect, while the striking merits of intense compression, energy and rapidity force themselves on the admiration of the reader. If it be said that grossness is a characteristic of the Confessions, and that *therefore* they are condemned by the critic, I can only reply that the objection applies in no peculiar degree to this novel. There are many works of celebrity established long before the critic's time, and destined very long to survive him, which no man would ever think of recommending to ladies or children, and every man would be unwilling to see expunged from English literature. It would be easy to enumerate them; and there can be very little doubt as to the manner in which the critic would treat the question whether he has not read *every part* of every one of them. Indeed, if the last mentioned objection be specifically made to the Confessions, it is almost necessarily implied that the critic was addressing himself to women and children. To children I have nothing to say; and as for the ladies, I presume that the mysterious process by which, without reading a book, they become acquainted with its contents, will in due season be applied to this. I feel very sure that the prediction which the critic has made concerning *Valerius* will be true of the *Confessions*; they are destined to *live*. The slightness of the notice bestowed on them in the Messenger, leaves it uncertain what conjectures the critic had formed about the authorship; but if he supposed that he was reviewing the work of a nameless American, he is probably altogether mistaken. Internal evidence strongly favours the opinion that the author is an Englishman; there is some ground, however, for the conjecture that he is a Frenchman, and that the work has been merely translated into English. Whatever be the author's name or nation, both will in all probability be soon and extensively known. This appeal from the critic's decision is not needed for any influence upon the ultimate circulation of the Confessions, for ultimately they would force themselves into circulation. But there may be some persons within the sphere of the Messenger, willing to devolve on others the trouble of thinking for them, or afraid of being enrolled in the category of *le vulgaire* if they think for themselves. To such individuals it may be encouraging to perceive that there are two opinions respecting this new publication; the one of a critic who has not read it, the other of a person who has.

In conclusion, and for fear of misconstruction even more grievous than the stain of vulgarity already impressed upon me, I beg leave to assure yourselves, the critic, and all others whom it may concern, that I am not the unfortunate Fra Diavolo. His rejected rhymes I have never seen, but his printed *reasons* leave me no ambition to be identified with him. I hope, too, that my own observations are distinguished from his recent assault on the Messenger, not less by their tone and temper, than by the circumstance that he was fiercely for himself, while I am gently for an unknown and probably foreign writer.

[*Valerius* was J. G. Lockhart's novel described by Poe in the April *Messenger* as "a book *to live*." "Fra Diavolo" submitted "poetical communications" to the *Messenger* which James E. Heath found as offensive imitations of "such vicious models as Byron, Shelly [Shelley], and other gentlemen of the 'Satanic school.' " To Fra Diavolo's letter to the *Compiler*, 6 April, "Benedict," author of "The Doom," replied, 8 April.]

20 MAY. White sends Poe $5 and an order for $4.94 and calls attention to "J.'s" letter in the *Compiler* (Poe to White, 30 May 1835).

30 MAY. BALTIMORE. In a letter to White, Poe acknowledges the receipt of moneys; he apologizes for his review of Kennedy's *Horse-Shoe Robinson* in the May *Messenger*, pleading ill health. Poe has read the letter by "J." in the *Compiler*; he suggests their ignoring it. He is flattered by Beverley Tucker's favorable comments. He adds: "My notice of your Messenger in the [Baltimore] Republican was I am afraid too brief for your views" (*L*, 1:59–61).

2 JUNE. RICHMOND. White writes Beverley Tucker: "Bless me! I must also ask whether you cannot give me a Review of Chief Justices [John Marshall's] edition of Washington. I received your few hasty lines and read your compliment to Poe & Sparhawk with great pleasure.—They deserve it" (Vi–W–TC).

[For Tucker's "compliment to Poe & Sparhawk" see "Extracts from Letters of Correspondents: From Eastern Virginia" under 11 JUNE 1835.]

8 JUNE. White writes Poe, inquiring about his health and sending him magazines perhaps for review (Poe to White, 12 June 1835).

11 JUNE. The May number of the *Messenger* makes its appearance with Poe's "Lion-izing" and his review of Kennedy's *Horse-Shoe Robinson*.

In "Editorial Remarks" Edward V. Sparhawk writes: " 'Lionizing,' by Mr. Poe, is an inimitable piece of wit and satire and the man must be far gone in a melancholic humor, whose risibility is not moved by this tale. Although the scene of the story is laid in the foreign city of 'Fum Fudge,' the disposition which it satirizes is often displayed in the cities of this country—even in our own community, and will probably still continue to exist, unless Mrs. [Frances Anne] Butler's Journal should have disgusted the fashionable world with Lions."

Under the heading "Publisher's Notice," Sparhawk is introduced, not by name, as "manager of the editorial department." Also White acknowledges his indebtedness to Sparhawk's predecessor, James E. Heath, without mentioning his name.

On the wrappers of this issue White prints the following comments:

EXTRACTS FROM LETTERS OF CORRESPONDENTS.
From Eastern Virginia.

Mr. Poe possesses an extraordinary faculty. He paints the *palpable obscure*, with strange power; throwing over his pictures a sombre gloom, which is appalling. The images are dim but distinct; shadowy, but well defined. The outline indeed, is all we see; but there they stand, shrouded in darkness, and frighten us with the mystery that defies farther scrutiny. Mr. Pertinax Placid [Edward V. Sparhawk] has given us the best allegory in the language. Such things are commonly dull. But his "Content's Mishap" is ingenious and witty throughout. I have seen nothing of the sort so well sustained.

[A part of this letter was later printed in the biographical sketch of Poe in the *Philadelphia Saturday Museum*, 4 March 1843, where the correspondent is identified as N. B. Tucker.]

CRITICAL NOTICES.

"MORELLA, a Tale, by EDGAR A. POE," (like his "*Berenice,*" in the previous number,) is one of the best of those wild and gloomy exhibitions of passion, heretofore belonging almost peculiarly to the genius of the German school of romance. We cannot but think, that such over-wrought delineations of the passions are injurious to correct taste, however attractive they may be to the erratic mood, and unnatural imaginings of a poetically vivid mind. Mr. Poe is capable of higher and more useful flights; and will no doubt reach an enviable eminence, if he does not suffer the current of his genius to be choked by a morbid sensibility, or diverted from its natural channel by the destructive freshet of a superabundant fancy. . . .

"*A Tale of a Nose, by Pertinax Placid.*"—This is a nonpareil of humor, and loses nothing from its conveying a good moral, through a laughter-loving medium, irresistibly amusing. There is in it, a great deal of the broad, racy, and piquant humor which distinguishes IRVING and PAULDING, when they feel disposed to exercise our *risibles*, by introducing

"Mirth, that wrinkled care derides;
And Laughter, holding both his sides."

We present to our readers, entire, this inimitable "Tale of a Nose," confident that they will enjoy it with the deepest zest; for it is irresistibly comic and entertaining—*Augusta (Ga.) Chronicle.*

[The *Richmond Compiler* had reprinted the *Chronicle*'s notice earlier, 30 May 1835.]

We cannot accord much praise to "Morella," a tale, by Edgar A. Poe. It is the creation of a fancy unrestrained by judgment and undirected by design. The writer is truly imaginative and possesses great powers of language, while his production attracts and carries along the attention of the reader, it deals out to him in the end a sore and unmerited disappointment.—*Charleston (Va.) Kanawha Banner.*

Listed as a subscriber paying between 9 May and 6 June is Dr. Thomas Holley Chivers of Georgia.

11 JUNE. BALTIMORE. This morning Poe receives White's letter of 8 June with a number of magazines (Poe to White, 12 June 1835).

12 JUNE. RICHMOND. The *Richmond Enquirer* reprints Poe's "Lion-izing." John O. Lay, Secretary of the Board of Trustees of the Richmond Academy, announces a postponement of the choice of a Principal until 26 June (*Enquirer*, 12 June. See 24 JULY 1835).

12 JUNE. BALTIMORE. Poe, "entirely recovered," writes White that he will do his best to please White with a review of John Marshall's *Washington*: "I suppose you have recd Mr. [George H.] Calvert's communication. . . . I will send you on The American & Republican as soon as the *critiques* come out. What I can do farther to aid the circulation of your Magazine I will gladly do—but I must insist on your not sending me any remuneration for services of this nature. They are a pleasure to me & no trouble whatever." Poe congratulates White upon obtaining the assistance of Sparhawk: "He has a high reputation for talent" (*L*, 1:61–62).

AFTER 12 JUNE. At White's request Poe calls on John W. Woods, publisher and printer of the Baltimore directories (Poe to White, 22 June 1835).

13 JUNE. RICHMOND. White writes Beverley Tucker: "Your critical notices of Sparks and Bancroft are excellent. . . . The Review of the Italian novel [G. W. Featherstonhaugh's *I promessi sposi*] assuming an editorial appearance did not call for eulogy from us. . . . It is, in my opinion, as good a Review as you have penned for the Messenger" (Vi–W–TC).

13 JUNE. BALTIMORE. The *Baltimore Republican* publishes Poe's notice of the May *Messenger*: "*Lionizing*, a tale by Edgar A. Poe, is an admirable piece of burlesque, which displays much reading, a lively humor, and an ability to afford amusement or instruction, according to the direction he may choose to give to his pen, which should not be suffered to lie unemployed, and will not, we trust, be neglected. . . . We refer our readers confidently to the *Critical Notices* in the present Number. We have read with interest the remarks on the *Promessi Sposi* of Manzoni; on Mrs. Butler's Journal; and on our townsman Mr. Kennedy's new novel, Horse-

Shoe Robinson—of which latter the publication, although long anxiously expected, has been, for what reason we know not, deferred."

15 JUNE. The *Baltimore American* publishes Poe's notice of the May *Messenger*: "We are pleased to note a spirited contribution from our townsman Edgar A. Poe, Esq. It is an *extravaganza* called 'Lionizing,' and gives evidence of high powers of fancy and humor. . . . Among the literary notices is a good one of 'Horse-Shoe Robinson,' a work for which the public are eagerly looking, and for which we venture to predict universal popularity" (Mabbott [1920], p. 374; Jackson [1935], pp. 254–55).

16 JUNE. Perhaps Poe reviews *The Italian Sketch-Book* in the *Baltimore American* (Mabbott [1920], p. 374 n. 10).

16 JUNE. RICHMOND. The *Richmond Enquirer* reprints Poe's notice of the May *Messenger* from the *Baltimore Republican*.

18 JUNE. White sends Poe a reprint of the November 1834 *Messenger* (Poe to White, 22 June 1835).

21 JUNE. BALTIMORE. Poe receives White's letter of 18 June (Poe to White, 22 June 1835).

22 JUNE. Poe writes White, expressing doubt that a notice of the reprint of the November 1834 *Messenger* would be advantageous to White. He continues:

I would therefore look zealously to the future, letting the past take care of itself. . . . Many of the Contributors to No. 3 are familiarly known to me—most of them I have seen occasionally. Charles B. Shaw the author of the Alleghany Levels is an old acquaintance, and a most estimable and talented man. I cannot say with truth that I had any knowledge of your son. . . . I will pay especial attention to what you suggested in relation to the punctuation &c of my future M.S.S. You ask me if I would be willing to come on to Richmond if you should have occasion for my services during the coming winter. I reply that nothing would give me greater pleasure. I have been desirous, for some time past, of paying a visit to Richmond, and would be glad of any reasonable excuse for so doing. Indeed I am anxious to settle myself in that city, and if, by any chance, you hear of a situation likely to suit me, I would gladly accept it, were the salary even the merest trifle. . . . What you say, in the conclusion of your letter, in relation to the supervision of proof-sheets, gives me reason to hope that possibly you might find something for me to do in your office. If so I should be very glad—for at present a very small portion of my time is employed. . . . I called upon Mr. Wood[s] as you desired—but the Magazine was then completed. . . . I have heard it suggested that a lighter-faced type in the headings of your various articles would improve the appearance of the Messenger. Do you not think so likewise? Who is the author of the Doom? (*L*, 1:62–64).

22 JUNE. Perhaps Poe contributes a note on French tragedy to the *American* (Mabbott [1920], p. 374 n. 10).

22 JUNE. ESSEX COUNTY, VIRGINIA. James M. Garnett writes White:

With respect to Mr. Poe, if I am to judge by his last communication ["Lionizing"], I should determine that he will rather injure than benefit your Paper. His sole object in this seems to be, to inform your Readers how many Authors he knows,—at least by name. That he may be "a scholar of the very highest grade" I will not question; but it is not always the best scholars that write best, or have the best taste & judgment. Read his piece over again, & I think you will agree with me that it has neither wit nor humor; or, that if it has any, it lies too deep for common understandings to fathom it (ViHi).

23 JUNE. RICHMOND. The *Richmond Compiler* reprints a selection entitled "Beauchamp the Murderer" from Charles Fenno Hoffman's *A Winter in the West*, which Poe had briefly noticed in the April 1835 *Messenger*.

26 JUNE. NEW YORK. James Kirke Paulding writes White: " 'Lion-izing.' by Edgar A. Poe, [is] one of the most happy travesties of the coxcombical egotism of travelling scribblers I have ever seen" (inside front cover of the July 1835 *Messenger*; reprinted from the *Richmond Whig* by the *Richmond Compiler*, 21 July 1835, and by the Washington *Daily National Intelligencer*, 24 July 1835; reprinted in part in the *Philadelphia Saturday Museum*, 4 March 1843 and in the *Southern Literary Messenger*, N.S. 1 [August 1939]:549. The complete letter was printed by Jackson [1982], p. 41).

[For Poe's reference to Paulding's letter, see 20 JULY 1835.]

1 JULY. RICHMOND. Elmira Royster Shelton is baptized at age twenty-four (Mabbott [1969], 1:539 n. 5).

6 JULY. PHILADELPHIA. Chief Justice John Marshall dies.

8 JULY. BALTIMORE. The *Baltimore American* prints a notice of the death of Mrs. David Poe, Sr.: "Died yesterday morning, July 7th, in the 79th year of her age, MRS. ELIZABETH POE, relict of General Poe, of this city. Her friends are requested to attend her funeral, without further invitation, from the residence of her daughter, Mrs. William Clemm, in Amity Street, at 9 o'clock this morning."

BEFORE 10 JULY. RICHMOND. The June *Messenger* includes Poe's "Hans

Phaall—A Tale" and the following reviews by him: *The Italian Sketch-Book*, Henry W. Longfellow's *Outre-Mer*, J. N. Reynolds' *Voyage of the U. S. Frigate Potomac*, Thomas Moore's *The History of Ireland* (Volume I), *Blackbeard*, Eliza Leslie's *Pencil Sketches (Second Series)*, and the *American Quarterly Review* for June.

Edward V. Sparhawk furnishes "Hans Phaall" with an introduction:

Mr. Poe's story of *"Hans Phaall,"* will add much to his reputation as an imaginative writer. In these *ballooning* days, when every "puny whipster" is willing to risk his neck in an attempt to "leave dull earth behind him," and when we hear so much of the benefits which science is to derive from the art of aerostation, a journey to the moon may not be considered a matter of mere moonshine. Mr. Poe's scientific Dutch bellows-mender is certainly a prodigy, and the more to be admired, as he performs impossibilities, and details them with a minuteness so much like truth, that they seem quite probable. Indeed the *cause* of his great enterprise is in admirable harmony with the exploits which it encourages him to perform. There are thousands who, to escape the pertinacity of uncivil creditors, would be tempted to a flight as perilous as that of Hans Phaall. Mr. Poe's story is a long one, but it will appear short to the reader, whom it bears along with irresistible interest, through a region of which, of all others, we know least, but which his fancy has invested with peculiar charms. We trust that a future missive from the lunar voyager will give us a narrative of his adventures in the orb that he has been the first to explore.

On the inside front cover of the June *Messenger*, White reprints Poe's notice of the May *Messenger* from the *Baltimore American* of 15 June, and a notice of "Lion-izing" from the *Charlottesville Advocate*: "We cannot subscribe to the praise which we see lavished upon Mr. Edgar A. Poe's 'palpable obscure' effusions [Tucker's praise, 11 June]. His 'Lion-izing' is a feeble imitation of *Slawkenbergius*, and makes a very pedantic display of authors, which he may or may not have read, but of which no one else ever heard. It is, nevertheless, better than his 'Morella' of the preceding number."

10 JULY. BALTIMORE. The *Baltimore Republican*, edited by Samuel Harker, notices the June *Messenger*: "*Hans Phaal, a Tale*, by Edgar A. Poe, is a capital burlesque upon ballooning, which has recently been carried to a ridiculous extent, without much prospect of profit to the persons engaged in it, or advantage to the community."

10 JULY. CHARLESTON, SOUTH CAROLINA. In a notice of the June *Messenger* the *Daily Courier* praises Poe: "The article entitled 'Hans Phaal,' in which is narrated with all the minuteness of detail, which properly belongs to truth, a *balloon* voyage of a Dutch bellows' mender to the Moon, is one of

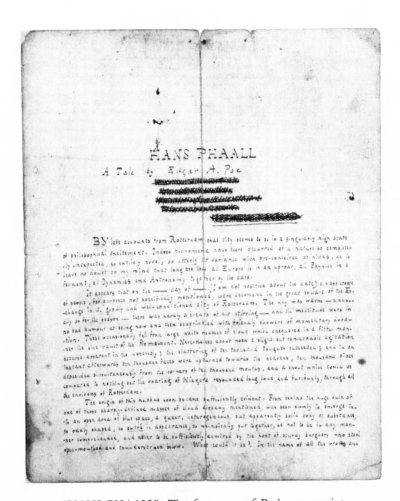

"HANS PHAALL": The first page of Poe's manuscript
Pierpont Morgan Library

the most exquisite specimens of blended humor and science that we have ever perused."

[This notice was reprinted on the covers of the July *Messenger*.]

11 JULY. BALTIMORE. The *Baltimore Athenaeum and Young Men's Paper*, edited by John N. McJilton and T. S. Arthur, comments: "The Story of Hans Phaall by Edgar A. Poe is well imagined. It details the incidents of a voyage to our lunar neighbor in a balloon. The writer attempts to meet all philosophical objections that might be brought against the journey and certainly displays much ingenuity in setting aside every reasonable barrier, to the prosecution of such an expedition."

11 JULY. NEW YORK. The *New-York Mirror* puffs Theodore S. Fay's novel *Norman Leslie*: "We this week present our readers with two detached passages from Mr. Fay's forthcoming novel—the first as a specimen of his powers of descriptive pathos, and his facility of touching the feelings, and the other as an example of his style of narrative."

[Poe was to create a sensation by damning both the novel and the *Mirror*'s puffery in the December *Messenger*. His devastating review led to a major battle of periodicals. For a full account see Moss (1963).]

14 AND 16 JULY. RICHMOND. In two letters White informs Poe that a trip has not improved his health and that perhaps "too close attention to business" caused his illness. White is anxious to know what opinion the *Martinsburg Gazette* has expressed of the *Messenger*. He reports that J. H. Pleasants of the *Richmond Whig* has criticized the commencement of "Hans Phaall" and that Paulding has praised "Lion-izing." He requests that Poe obtain a pound of ink and he advises Poe that because of "certain circumstances" his Chief Justice Marshall review will not appear in the July issue (Poe to White, 20 July 1835).

16 JULY. BALTIMORE. Perhaps Poe has a note on Samuel Taylor Coleridge's *Table Talk* in the *Baltimore American* (Mabbott [1920], p. 374 n. 10).

20 JULY. Poe writes White, whose letters of 14 and 16 July he has received. He has read the *Martinsburg Gazette*'s comments on the *Messenger* at Kennedy's home. He is pleased with John Hampden Pleasants' remarks ("What Mr Pleasants says in relation to the commencement of Hans Phaal is judicious. That part of the Tale is faulty indeed—so much so that I had often thought of remodelling it entirely") and with Paulding's letter of 26 June. He sends White a copy of the 12 October 1833 issue of the *Baltimore Saturday Visiter* and requests that White have the letter written

by Kennedy, Latrobe, and Miller, if possible, printed in the *Messenger* and in any Richmond newspapers. Then he adds: "Look over Hans Phaal, and the Literary Notices by me in No. 10 [the June *Messenger*], and see if you have not miscalculated the sum due me. There are 34 columns in all. Hans Phaal cost me nearly a fortnights hard labour and was written especially for the Messenger" (*L*, 1:64–66).

[For Paulding's letter, see 26 JUNE; for Pleasants' comments, AFTER 7 AUGUST. In his letters Poe spelled his title "Hans Phaal"; but in late 1839, when he reprinted the story in his *Tales of the Grotesque and Arabesque*, he again selected the "Hans Phaall" spelling found in his original manuscript written in early 1835 (NNPM), and used in the June 1835 *Messenger*. In 1842, when he prepared a tentative table of contents for his unrealized edition *Phantasy-Pieces*, he called this story "The Unparalleled Adventure of one Hans Pfaall," a title which has been adopted by his posthumous editors. For an explanation of these variants, see Pollin (1978a), pp. 519–27, and (1981), pp. 384–85.]

24 JULY. RICHMOND. The trustees of the Richmond Academy advertise in the *Enquirer* for a teacher of English.

RICHMOND ACADEMY.——By the direction of the Trustees, I give public notice that they will proceed on the 14th day of August next, to choose a Teacher for the English Department in said Institution. . . .

   The trustees announce to the public that they have engaged the services of Socrates Maupin, Esq. as Principal, and of Rowland Reynolds, Esq. as Teacher in the Academy: —the first will take charge of the school of Mathematics . . . and the last, the school of Ancient Languages . . .

WYNDHAM ROBERTSON,
President of the Board.

[This advertisement, which ran also in the Washington *Daily National Intelligencer*, the Philadelphia *National Gazette*, and the New York *Evening Post*, undoubtedly caught Poe's eye. See BEFORE 14 AUGUST and 19 AUGUST 1835. The job was awarded to Branch A. Saunders (Poe wrote in error "Branch T. Saunders" in his letter of 29 August 1835 to Maria Clemm), who in 1828 had his own school (advertisement, *Compiler*, 5 September 1828). In 1836 Saunders was head of the English Department of the Richmond Academy. Among the Academy trustees were John O. Lay, Charles Ellis, James E. Heath, and Bernard Peyton, with all of whom Poe was more or less acquainted. The school term was divided into two sessions of five months each, the first commencing 1 October and ending 21 February, and the second commencing 1 March.]

AFTER 7 AUGUST. The July *Messenger* appears with Poe's "To Mary" and

"The Visionary—A Tale" (later called "The Assignation"), including "To One in Paradise." White prints the following notices of the *Messenger*:

En passant—Mr. Paulding speaks only of the number before the last. We should like to see his judgment on an article in the last—the voyage to the Moon, by Edgar A. Poe. We see that extraordinary production ridiculed by some; but if the merits of a production may be estimated by the effect on the reader, we at least have never perused one which caused such a dizziness of sensation. There is a great deal of nonsense, trifling and bad taste before Hans Phaal quits the earth—but when he has blown up his creditors and mounted into the solitude of space, his speculations assume a true philosophical character, exhibit genius and invention, and if they shall ever be brought to the test of experiment, will, we are persuaded, be found wonderfully approximating to truth, and penetrative of the mysteries of creation. To our apprehension—uneducated, however, by the rules of art—there is much sublimity in his conceptions and his narrative.—[John Hampden Pleasants,] *Richmond Whig*.

[Then follows Paulding's letter of 26 June 1835.]

Hans Phaal, a Tale, by Edgar A. Poe, is full of hairbreadth 'scapes and stirring incidents, though not exactly by flood and field. It is an over long chapter in the annals of *Ballooning*—being no less than a true and authentic narration of a voyage made by Mynheer Phaal, from the city of Rotterdam to the Moon. The voyager did not return to mother earth, but remained in the satellite at the last dates. His bearer of despatches was an inhabitant of that far off region, who had politely consented to visit the authorities of Rotterdam, in that character. The thing to regret is, that there is no account appended touching the fate of the "quadrupeds," which, by an accident while on the journey, "too soon return'd to earth." We trust that Mr. PHAAL will not remain among the men in the moon, but will return ere long, and not forget to give an account of his "journey home." It will doubtless be as interesting as VANDERDECKEN'S.—*Baltimore Patriot*.

"*Lion-izing, a Tale, by Edgar A. Poe*." This tale we give entire this morning. The talents of the author are fine and varied; passing from "grave to gay" with pleasing facility. His Lion-izing has all the humor, animation, and satire of Sterne's man from the promontory of Noses, and creates as much sensation in Fum-Fudge, as Riego's did in Strasburg. The reader will take hold of Mr. Thomas Smith's nose with much pleasure and satisfaction.—*Augusta (Ga.) Chronicle*.

It [the *Messenger*] contains several stories of superior merit; that for instance, entitled Hans Phaal, is a capital burlesque upon the ballooning mania, which has recently driven a number of our good citizens beyond the confines of this nether world, to seek their fortunes in the unexplored aerial regions. The tale is a long one, but the sprightliness with which it is written, renders its length a recommendation. . . . —*Baltimore Gazette*.

8 AUGUST. NEW YORK. The *New-York Mirror* puffs Fay's *Norman Leslie*.

BEFORE 14 AUGUST. RICHMOND. Poe arrives and boards at Mrs. [Robert?]

Poore's boardinghouse on Bank Street. With Mrs. Poore live her daughter and son-in-law Thomas W. Cleland (Allen, p. 304; Phillips, 1:503–504).

Poe applies to the Richmond Academy for a job teaching English (Margaret Ellis to Charles Ellis, 19 August 1835).

14 AUGUST. The Trustees of the Richmond Academy begin the selection of a teacher for the English Department (see 24 JULY and 29 AUGUST 1835).

CA. 17 AUGUST. AUGUSTA, GEORGIA. William Poe writes Poe (Poe to William Poe, 20 August 1835).

18 AUGUST. RICHMOND. White writes Lucian Minor: "[The] Reviews [in the July *Messenger* are] all by Sparhawk . . . I have, my dear Sir, been compelled to part with Mr. Sparhawk, as regular editor—I have run too fast. He will however continue to assist me. Mr. Poe is here also.—He tarries one month—and will aid me all that lies in his power" (Jackson [1934], pp. 97–98).

19 AUGUST. Margaret Ellis writes her husband Charles, who is at White Sulphur Springs for his health, that "Edgar Poe is here & I understand has applied for one of the Professorships in the Academy." Also at White Sulphur are the second Mrs. John Allan, her sons, and Ann Moore Valentine (DLC–EA).

[Margaret Ellis was obviously referring to the Richmond Academy, and not to Genaro Persico's school as suggested by Killis Campbell (1936), pp. 487–88.]

20 AUGUST. Poe writes William Poe, relating his family history and making several false statements:

Mrs. [Elizabeth Poe] the widow of General D. Poe, and the mother of Maria [Clemm], died only 6 weeks ago, at the age of 79. She had for the last 8 years of her life been confined entirely to bed—never, in any instance, leaving it during that time. She had been paralyzed, and suffered from many other complaints—her daughter Maria attending her during her long & tedious illness. . . . My father David died when I was in the second year of my age and when my sister Rosalie was an infant in arms. Our mother died a few weeks before him. . . . At this period my grandfather's circumstances were at a low ebb, he from great wealth having been reduced to poverty. . . . My brother Henry he took . . . under his charge, while myself and Rosalie were adopted by gentlemen in Richmond. . . . I was adopted by Mr. Jno Allan. . . . The first Mrs. A. having died, and Mr A having married again I found my situation not so comfortable as before, and obtained a Cadet's appointment at W. Point. During my stay there Mr A died suddenly, and left me—nothing. No will was found among his papers. . . . I have lately obtained the Editorship of the Southern Messenger. . . . Mrs. Clemm . . . is now . . . struggling without friends, without money, and without health to support [herself] and 2 children (*L*, 1:66–69 and 2:672 [1966]).

[Poe's employment by White caused the "postponement" of Lambert A. Wilmer's and Poe's plans to publish "a monthly magazine of a superior intellectual character" (Wilmer [1859], pp. 35–36).]

CA. 20 AUGUST. Poe writes Maria Clemm (Poe to Maria Clemm, 29 August 1835).

20–26 AUGUST. BALTIMORE. Maria Clemm writes Poe (Poe to Maria Clemm, 29 August 1835).

21 AUGUST. RICHMOND. In a letter to the *Enquirer* a writer who signs himself "Pocosin" reviews the July *Messenger* and praises "The Visionary" without mentioning Poe's name.

[A part of this letter appeared on the covers of the August *Messenger*. See CA. 11 SEPTEMBER.]

25–31 AUGUST. NEW YORK. The *Sun* publishes Richard Adams Locke's hoax, "Great Astronomical Discoveries, Lately Made by Sir John Herschel," in five installments.

[In his letter to Kennedy, 11 September 1835, Poe expressed his belief that ideas in "Hans Phaall" had been stolen from him by Locke.]

27–28 AUGUST. BALTIMORE. Maria Clemm writes Poe (Poe to Maria Clemm, 29 August 1835).

29 AUGUST. RICHMOND. Poe writes Maria Clemm:

I have no desire to live and *will not*. . . . I love, *you know* I love Virginia passionately devotedly. . . . All my thoughts are occupied with the supposition that both you & she will prefer to go with N. [Neilson] Poe. . . . It is useless to disguise the truth that when Virginia goes with N. P. that I shall never behold her again. . . . I had procured a sweet little house in a retired situation on church hill—newly done up and with a large garden and every convenience—at only $5 per month. . . . Among strangers with *not one soul to love me*. The situation [at the Richmond Academy] has this morning been conferred upon another, Branch T. [A.] Saunders, but White has engaged to make my salary $60 a month. . . . She [Virginia] will have far—very far better opportunities of entering into society here than with N. P. Every one here receives me with open arms.

In a postscript Poe addresses both Virginia and her mother: "For Virginia, My love, my own sweetest Sissy, my darling little wifey, think well before you break the heart of your cousin. Eddy. . . . Dearest Aunty consider my happiness while you are thinking about your own" (*L*, 1:69–71).

29 AUGUST. NEW YORK. The *New-York Mirror* prints selections from T. S. Fay's *Norman Leslie* and reports: "In our present number we continue our extracts from this beautiful performance, which will make its appearance in this city and in London simultaneously."

29 AUGUST. CHARLESTON, SOUTH CAROLINA. The *Courier* expresses the belief that "The Visionary" demonstrates that Poe is "not as good at the purely romantic, as he is, supremely, in the humorous extravaganza. 'Hans Phaal,' even though it may have sold him to the Dutch, has *immortalized* him—and it may be but the brightness of his own previous merit that makes him now but seem obscure."

31 AUGUST. RICHMOND. White writes Lucian Minor: "It will be almost indispensably necessary that the [*Messenger*] Index (including No. 12 [August issue]) should reach me in a fortnight at farthest from this day" (Jackson [1936], p. 232).

2–5 SEPTEMBER. NEW YORK. Without identifying the author, the *New York Transcript* reprints Poe's "Hans Phaall" in four installments under the heading "Lunar Discoveries. Extraordinary Aerial Voyage by Baron Hans Phaal, the Celebrated Dutch Astronomer and Aeronaut."

4 SEPTEMBER. RICHMOND. Poe writes John Neal, in Boston: "Herewith I send a number of the Southern Literary Messenger, a Magazine of which I have lately obtained the Editorship. Do you think you could send me regularly in exchange, The [New-England] Galaxy or any other paper of wh: you have the control?" (*L*, 1:72).

BEFORE 8 SEPTEMBER. Poe writes Dr. James H. Miller, in Baltimore (Poe to Kennedy, 11 September 1835).

8 SEPTEMBER. White writes Lucian Minor: "I am now as it were my own editor—No. 12 [August 1835 issue] is made out of my *wits*. When we meet, I will tell you why I was obliged to part with Sparhawk. Poe is now in my employ—not as Editor. He is unfortunately rather dissipated,—and therefore I can place very little reliance upon him. His disposition is quite amiable. He will be some assistance to me in proof-reading—at least I hope so. . . . All the Critical & Literary Notices, by Mr. Poe" (Jackson [1934], p. 98).

[John W. Fergusson, employed by White as printer and messenger boy, later asserted: "Mr. Poe was a fine gentleman when he was sober. He was ever kind and courtly, and at such times every one liked him. But when he was drinking he was about one of the most disagreeable men I have ever met" (Woodberry, 2:443).]

8–9 SEPTEMBER. WESTMINSTER, MARYLAND. Dr. James H. Miller writes Poe (Poe to Kennedy, 11 September 1835).

10 SEPTEMBER. RICHMOND. Poe receives Dr. Miller's letter informing him that Kennedy has returned to Baltimore (Poe to Kennedy, 11 September 1835).

11 SEPTEMBER. Poe writes John Pendleton Kennedy:

Through your influence Mr White has been induced to employ me in assisting him with the Editorial duties of his Magazine at a salary of $520 per annum . . . *You will believe me* when I say that I am still miserable in spite of the great improvement in my circumstances. . . . I see *"the Gift"* [for 1836] is out. They have published the M.S. found in a Bottle (, the prize tale you will remember,) although I not only told Mr Carey myself that it had been published, but wrote him to that effect after my return to Baltimore, and sent him another tale in place of it (Epimanes). . . . Mr White is willing to publish my *Tales of the Folio Club*— that is to *print* them. Would you oblige me by ascertaining from Carey & Lea whether they would, in that case, appear nominally as the publishers, the books, when printed, being sent on to them, as in the case of H. S. Robinson? Have you seen the "Discoveries in the Moon"? Do you not think it altogether suggested by *Hans Phaal?*. . . . I am convinced that the idea was stolen from myself (*L*, 1:73– 75).

CA. 11 SEPTEMBER. Poe's "The Coliseum. A Prize Poem" (a reprint from the *Baltimore Saturday Visiter*), "Bon-Bon—A Tale," two fillers ("The Unities" and "By what *bizarrerie* . . ."), and "Critical Notices and Literary Intelligence" appear in the August *Messenger.* Under the heading "To Readers and Correspondents" appear the following remarks:

As one or two of the criticisms in relation to the Tales of our contributor, Mr. Poe, have been directly at variance with those generally expressed, we take the liberty of inserting here an extract from a *letter* (signed by three gentlemen of the highest standing in literary matters) which we find in the Baltimore Visiter. This paper having offered a premium for the best Prose Tale, and also one for the best Poem—*both* these premiums were awarded by the committee to Mr. Poe. The award was, however, subsequently altered, so as to exclude Mr. P. from the second premium, in consideration of his having obtained the higher one. Here follows the extract.

"Among the prose articles offered were many of various and distinguished merit; but the singular force and beauty of those sent by the author of the *Tales of the Folio Club,* leave us no room for hesitation in that department. We have accordingly awarded the premium to a Tale entitled *MS. found in a Bottle.* It would hardly be doing justice to the writer of this collection to say that the Tale we have chosen is the best of the six offered by him. We cannot refrain from saying that the author owes it to his own reputation, as well as to the gratification of the community, to publish the entire volume, (the Tales of the Folio Club.) These Tales are eminently distinguished by a wild, vigorous, and poetical imagination—a rich style—a fertile invention—and varied and curious learning.

(Signed)   JOHN P. KENNEDY,

                                                J. H. B. LATROBE,

                                                JAMES H. MILLER."

We presume this letter must set the question at rest. Lionizing is one of the Tales here spoken of—The Visionary is another. The *Tales of the Folio Club* are sixteen in all, and we believe it is the author's intention to publish them in the autumn. When such men as Miller, Latrobe, Kennedy, Tucker, and Paulding speak unanimously of any literary production in terms of exalted commendation, it is nearly unnecessary to say that we are willing to abide by their decision.

In another paragraph the "original filler" is introduced: "In every publication like ours, a brief sentence or paragraph is often wanted for the filling out a column, and in such cases it is customary to resort to selection. We think as well, therefore, to mention that, in all similar instances, we shall make use of original matter."

The publisher reprints on the inside covers of the *Messenger* the following notices under the heading "Opinions of the Press":

The editor, understood to be E. V. Sparhawk, Esq., a gentleman of fine literary taste and acquirements, most judiciously leaves in the number [July *Messenger*] before us, many of the best articles to speak for themselves.—*Richmond Compiler,* quoting the editor of the *Petersburg (Va.) Constellation.*

. . . and amid all the story writers of this story writing age, Mr. Poe deserves no small share of encomium. He first touches so beautifully on what is sure to interest the reader—no long-drawn tedious conversations between Polly and John about the weather and the news; no petty details of breakfast, dinner, and supper tables; his sketches are like the pencillings of some eminent painter, just the outline, with all left to the imagination that deserves to be filled by itself.—*Winchester (Va.) Republican.*

"The Visionary" is a vivid, inventive, and thrilling sketch—teeming with beautiful language, which has the freshness and volume of the mountain cataract, without its turbulence. There is no bombast in the offspring of this writer, though the dull man will look for it; and we defy the severest critic to find fault with the strength and delicacy of that pencil, which is alternately grasped by a master's hand, or which trembles with a woman's softness. The author has nothing to fear; his genius must light up his onward flight; and with labor and perseverance he will gain that proud fame so beautifully expressed by Beaumont and Fletcher:

> ———————————— "I have towered
> For victory, like a falcon in the clouds—
> Not dig'd for it, like a mole."

The Reviewer's and Editor's Department, is conducted with great ability, learning, and taste; while the typographical execution of the work happily unites the neatness of the Boston, with the elegance of the London press.—[from a lengthy review of the July *Messenger* by "Pocosin" in the] *Richmond Enquirer* [21 August].

The Visionary, a Tale, by Edgar A. Poe, sustains the high reputation the author has already won as a writer of fiction. The Visionary is decidedly one of his very best effusions. —[Washington] *National Intelligencer*.

"The Visionary," a Tale, by Edgar A. Poe, is a wild, imaginative, romantic tale, full of deep interest, which however is left too much ungratified.—*Augusta (Ga.) Chronicle*.

19 SEPTEMBER. BALTIMORE. John Pendleton Kennedy writes Poe:

I am sorry to see you in such plight as your letter shows you in.—It is strange that just at the time when every body is praising you and when Fortune has begun to smile upon your hitherto wretched circumstances you should be invaded by these villainous blue devils. . . . You will doubtless do well henceforth in literature and add to your *comforts* as well as to your reputation which, it gives me great pleasure to tell you, is every where rising in popular esteem. Can't you write some farces after the manner of the French Vaudevilles?. . . . More than yourself have remarked the coincidence between Hans Phaal & the Lunar Discoveries and I perceive that in New York they are republishing Hans for the sake of comparison. . . . I will write to Carey & Lea to know if they will allow you to publish The Tales of the Folio Club in their name. Of course, you will understand that if they do not *print* them they will not be required to be at the risk of the printing expenses. I suppose you mean that White shall take that risk upon himself and look for his indemnity to the sale. My own opinion is that White could publish them as advantageously as Carey (*W*, 17:19–20).

19 SEPTEMBER. John N. McJilton and T. S. Arthur, editors of the *Baltimore Athenaeum and Young Men's Paper*, observe: "Our townsman, Mr. E. A. Poe, is winning for himself a fair reputation by his contributions to the Messenger. He writes with a bold free hand, and is irresistibly interesting."

BEFORE 21 SEPTEMBER. RICHMOND. Poe leaves White and the *Messenger* and returns to Baltimore (White to Minor, 21 September).

21 SEPTEMBER. White writes his friend Lucian Minor: "Poe has flew [*sic*]

the track already. His habits were not good. —He is in addition the victim of melancholy. I should not be at all astonished to hear that he has been guilty of suicide" (Jackson [1934], p. 100).

22 SEPTEMBER. BALTIMORE. The Clerk of the Baltimore County Court issues a license for the marriage of Edgar A. Poe and Virginia E. Clemm (Woodberry, 1:143; Allen, pp. 704–05).

[Perhaps Poe and his cousin Virginia were privately married at this time, but conclusive evidence is lacking. Quinn, pp. 227–28, attempted to dismiss the possibility of a secret first marriage; Mabbott (1969), 1:546, argued for that possibility. See 16 MAY 1836.]

25 SEPTEMBER. BOSTON. The *Boston Courier* prints an unfavorable review of the *Gift* for 1836, without mentioning Poe and his "MS. Found in a Bottle": "*The Gift* contains articles by Miss Sedgewick [*sic*], Mrs. Sigourney, J. K. Paulding, W. L. Stone, Washington Irving, and others, less celebrated in the literary world. . . . The longer prose articles we have not read, except the closing sketch, by the veritable Miss Leslie, herself, who edited *The Gift*—a piece, which we venture to say no one will ever read twice. A more harmless concoction of skimmed-milk and rain-water, never was prepared for the stomach of a sick baby."

[For Poe's reaction, see LATE SEPTEMBER.]

BEFORE 29 SEPTEMBER. BALTIMORE. Poe writes White, asking for reinstatement (implied by White to Poe, 29 September).

29 SEPTEMBER. RICHMOND. White writes Poe:

Would that it were in my power to unbosom myself to you, in language such as I could on the present occasion, wish myself master of. I cannot do it—and therefore must be content to speak to you in my plain way.

That you are sincere in all your promises, I firmly believe. But, Edgar, when you once again tread these streets, I have my fears that your resolves would fall through,—and that you would again sip the juice, even till it stole away your senses. Rely on your own strength, and you are gone! Look to your Maker for help, and you are safe!

How much I regretted parting with you, is unknown to anyone on this earth, except myself. I was attached to you—and am still,—and willingly would I say return, if I did not dread the hour of separation very shortly again.

If you could make yourself contented to take up your quarters in my family, or in any other private family where liquor is not used, I should think there were hopes of you. But, if you go to a tavern, or to any other place where it is used at table, you are not safe. I speak from experience.

You have fine talents, Edgar—and you ought to have them respected as well as yourself. Learn to respect yourself, and you will very soon find that you are respected. Separate yourself from the bottle, and bottle-companions, for ever!

Tell me if you can and will do so—and let me hear that it is your fixed purpose never to yield to temptation.

If you should come to Richmond again, and again should be an assistant in my office, it must be expressly understood by us that all engagements on my part would be dissolved, the moment you get drunk.

No man is safe who drinks before breakfast! No man can do so, and attend to business properly.

I have thought over the matter seriously about the Autograph article, and have come to the conclusion that it will be best to omit it in its present dress. I should not be at all surprised, were I to send it out, to hear that [James Fenimore] Cooper had sued me for a libel.

The form containing it has been ready for press three days—and I have been just as many days deciding the question (W, 17:20–21).

SEPTEMBER? WINCHESTER, VIRGINIA? Philip Pendleton Cooke, praises Poe in a letter to White (see LATE SEPTEMBER).

LATE SEPTEMBER. RICHMOND. The September *Messenger* (the last issue of Volume I) publishes Poe's "Loss of Breath, a tale a la Blackwood," two fillers ("Milton is indebted for some of the finest passages in the Paradise Lost to Marino's 'Sospetti D'Herode' " and "The 'Acajou et Zirphile' of Du Clos is a whimsical and amusing Fairy Tale . . ."), "Lines Written in an Album" (originally entitled "To Elizabeth"), "King Pest the First. A Tale Containing an Allegory," "Shadow. A Fable," and critical notices: *Mephistopheles in England*, J. Orville Taylor's *The District School: or National Education*, the *New England Magazine* for September, the *Western Journal of the Medical and Physical Sciences*, *The Classical Family Library* (Nos. XV, XVI, and XVII), Robert Southey's *The Early Naval History of England*, and Eliza Leslie's *Gift* for 1836. Poe finds that "The Gift is highly creditable . . . this we say positively—the ill-mannered and worse-natured opinion of the Boston Courier to the contrary notwithstanding." He writes: "The present number closes the first volume of the Messenger; and accompanying it, the Publisher will transmit to each subscriber a title page and copious Index to the volume. Gratified that his past endeavors to please, have been crowned with success—the Publisher anticipates with confidence that, with the continued patronage of the public, the forthcoming volume shall in no respect be behind, if it does not greatly outstrip its predecessor." To readers and correspondents Poe reports that the whole edition of Volume I, consisting of fourteen hundred copies, has been exhausted. Extracts from "Opinions of the Press" follow:

We have been favored by the proprietor of the Southern Literary Messenger, with the perusal of a letter from the writer of articles on "English Poetry." The writer [Philip Pendleton Cooke], whose name we are not at liberty to give to the public, is unquestionably one of the most gifted and highly intellectual of Virginia's sons. He pays a deserved compliment to a fellow contributor to the Messenger; and we take great pleasure in spreading an extract from his letter before our readers.

"In looking over your list of contributors, I see the name of Mr. Poe. I have heard of some passages in his life, which have added to the interest with which I read his writings. *** For God's sake, value him according to his merits, which are exceeding great. I say this with deliberation, for I have been months in coming to the conclusion that he is the first genius, in his line, in Virginia. And when I say this, how many other States are included—certainly all South of us. The conversation in *Morella*—the description in *Berenice* of a mind dwelling with strained intensity upon some particular [trifling] object with which the eye meets—and the description of that Beckford of Venice, and his singular sanctum in the *Visionary*: as also the vague speculations of *Hans Phaal* upon the scenery of the moon—with its shadow-stained lakes and sombre vegetation—are compositions of rare beauty. I am too much hurried to write good English, but you may understand from what I have scribbled above, that I admire Poe greatly."—*Richmond Compiler*.

. . . The next article in order is *"Bon-Bon," a Tale*, by EDGAR A. POE. It is characterized by the quaint humor and eccentricity for which that gentleman's writings are usually remarkable, and by the antique lore, and happy talent for invention which distinguish some of his other tales. Bon-Bon is a most philosophical restaurateur, and the Devil, who appears to him, the most gentlemanly of his race. . . .—[Washington] *National Intelligencer*.

Of the preceding editor [Sparhawk] we know nothing. Of the present we know this, and we lose no time in saying so, he is *emphatically* a man of genius. Being a man of genius, it will depend *altogether* upon the sort of encouragement he receives, whether the work [the *Messenger*] be a matter of pride or of reproach to the south. . . .

But first—a word with the Richmond Enquirer, whose opinion of the work appears on the inside cover [of the August *Messenger*]. What the devil do you mean by the following passage? Speaking of the editor you say, "His notices are learned without pedantry, and his criticisms are *redolent* of a poet's taste, and beaming with a poet's fire." Hav'n't ye such a thing as an English Dictionary in your office? . . . Who will care a fig for your opinion of a literary work, if you are guilty of such unforgiveable nonsense?

To Sarah.—Boyish but sincere.
Bon-Bon: by Edgar A. Poe.—Excellent!—we need not say more—excellent!
Ballad.—Very sweet and affectionate.
The Coliseum: Edgar A. Poe.—Majestic and powerful poetry.
Critical Notices.—Rather too cautious, but lively.—[John Neal,] *New England Galaxy*.

Bon-Bon: by Edgar A. Poe—One of the most exquisite *jeu d'esprit* we have read in

many a day. It is equal, perhaps superior, to any thing Theodore Hook ever wrote.
. . .

The Critical Notices, though numerous, and generally correct, are too slight for our taste. . . .—*New York Courier & Enquirer*.

We have derived great pleasure from the contributions of our townsman E. A. Poe, Esq. who is fast building up for himself a high reputation as a writer of fiction.—[Neilson Poe?] *Baltimore Chronicle*.

Coliseum, a Prize Poem, by Edgar A. Poe, evinces no inconsiderable descriptive talent. Indeed, we think the author's fertile imagination can range the heights of Parnassus as well as the lofty mountains of our friendly and *now* highly interesting satellite. His Hans Phaal, published in a recent number of the Messenger, should be bound up in the same volume with the description of the sublime discoveries recently made by Dr. Herschell at the Cape of Good Hope. . . . [William Gwynn, editor,] *Baltimore Gazette*.

. . . Mr. Poe's Bon-Bon is quite a unique and racy affair.—*Winchester Republican*.

The number before us is made up of original matter, with the exception of a single article, "The Coliseum a Prize Poem," by E. A. Poe.—*Camden (S. C.) Journal*.

The articles of Edgar A. Poe, in this and previous numbers, give us a very high opinion of his talents. He invariably exhibits great research, a fund of rich thought, and a felicity of expression, scarcely equalled by one of his years. Experience and practice, under judicious criticism, will render him distinguished as a literary man.—*Richmond Compiler*.

. . . Edgar A. Poe, who, say what the captious may, has given the most conclusive evidence of genius and talent of no ordinary cast as a writer, in his *Hans Phaal* and several other productions, before the readers of the Messenger.—[Hiram Haines, editor,] *Petersburg (Va.) Constellation*.

Bon-Bon, a Tale by Edgar A. Poe, sustains the well established reputation of the author as a writer possessing a rich imaginative genius, and a free, flowing and very happy style.—[William Gwynn, editor,] *Baltimore Gazette*.

1 OCTOBER. CHARLESTON, SOUTH CAROLINA. The *Courier* acknowledges receipt of the *Messenger* for September.

1 OCTOBER. RICHMOND. White writes Lucian Minor, with whom he is indexing Volume I of the *Messenger*: "I have just seen Mr. Heath. He thinks he can manage the Autography for me. He proposes striking out Cooper's and Irving's names. I will not put the article in till I hear from you. Give me your candid opinion of it. Poe is its author. I should not like to shoot so sarcastic an arrow at poor Cooper—however much he deserves it" (Jackson [1934], pp. 101–02).

3 OCTOBER. Poe, Virginia, and Maria Clemm arrive from Baltimore and board at Mrs. James Yarrington's home (Maria Clemm to William Poe, 7

October 1835; *W*, 17:379–81; Poe to George Poe, Jr., 12 January 1836).

4 OCTOBER. PHILADELPHIA. Henry Carey writes John Pendleton Kennedy: "I do not know what to say respecting Poe. Is he not deranged? I should care nothing about aiding him as you propose, but I should like to be sure he was sane; let me hear from you" (Campbell [1917a], p. 198).

7 OCTOBER. RICHMOND. Maria Clemm writes William Poe, in Augusta, Georgia: "Edgar received a letter from you yesterday and requested me to answer it for him, as he is at present so much engaged. . . . We arrived here on Saturday evening last. Edgar went on to Baltimore for us. . . . My health is at present so bad that I have had no opportunity of seeing the place. . . . He [Poe] does not wish me to engage in any kind of business until my health is better. . . . [She relates their family history.] My daughter Virginia is with me here and we are entirely dependent on Edgar. He is, indeed a son to me & has always been so. . . . He requests me to say that he is obliged to you for the subscribers you procured him and says that all that you can obtain for the Messenger will be to his advantage" (*W*, 17:379–81, where it is misdated "1836").

8 OCTOBER. Poe writes Robert Montgomery Bird, a Philadelphia novelist and playwright: "At the request of Mr. Thomas W. White . . . I take the liberty of . . . soliciting your aid in the way of occasional or regular contributions to his Magazine" (*L*, 1:75–76).

10 OCTOBER. NEW YORK. The *New-York Mirror* puffs Theodore S. Fay's *Norman Leslie* a fourth time by quoting a passage from the novel.

17 OCTOBER. CHARLESTON, SOUTH CAROLINA. The *Courier* acknowledges receipt of Eliza Leslie's *The Gift: A Christmas and New Year's Present for 1836.*

[Four days later, the *Courier* printed a brief notice: "This is indeed a gem among the *Annuals.* . . . Among her [Miss Leslie's] contributors are Miss SEDGWICK, Mrs. SIGOURNEY, WASHINGTON IRVING, SIMMS, PAULDING, EDGAR A. POE, AND W. L. STONE—names well known to literature and poesy. . . . the 'Manuscript found in a Bottle,' is an *extravaganza*, somewhat of the terrific order, by EDGAR A. POE, whose eccentric genius delights in the creation of strange *possibilities*, and in making a play thing of science, and whose *fanciful* aim, in the production under consideration, seems to be to give the credulous well *bottled* proof of Capt. SYMMES' theory of polar apertures and concentric circles." John Cleves Symmes propounded the belief that the earth was hollow, open at both of the poles, and capable of habitation within. He and James McBride published

Symmes' Theory of Concentric Spheres (Cincinnati, 1826), which Poe drew on for "MS. Found in a Bottle," "Hans Phaall," and *The Narrative of Arthur Gordon Pym.*]

20 OCTOBER. RICHMOND. White writes Lucian Minor: "Mr. Poe, who is with me again, read it [Minor's 'Address'] over by copy with great care. He is very much pleased with it—in fact he . . . intends noticing it under the head of Reviews. . . . Critical Notices [in the September *Messenger*], all by Poe" (Jackson [1934], pp. 102–03).

22 OCTOBER. WASHINGTON. The *Daily National Intelligencer* reports: "We received a few days ago the thirteenth number (being the closing No. of the first volume) [the September issue] of Mr. White's Southern Literary Messenger." It has nothing but praise for the journal.

24 OCTOBER. RICHMOND. White writes Lucian Minor:

I very much fear that I shall not be able to issue the lst No. [December 1835] of my 2d Vol. till about the 25th Nov. Suppose you send me a modest paragraph—mentioning that the gentleman [Sparhawk] announced as my assistant in the 9th No. [May 1835] of the Messenger retired from its editorship with the 11th No. [July 1835]—that the paper is now under my own editorial management, assisted by several gentlemen of distinguished literary attainments.—You may introduce Mr. Poe's name as amongst those engaged to contribute for its columns—taking care not to say as editor. . . .I am in no little trouble.—My wife is very sick now, and has been for 10 days—though I think her much better to day (Jackson [1934], pp. 103–04).

31 OCTOBER. Poe, acting as amanuensis for White, writes Lucian Minor: "I will hand your translation to Mr. Poe in the morning, and will attend to your request touching keeping your name secret" (*L*, 1:76).

NOVEMBER. NEW YORK. The *Knickerbocker Magazine* publishes Lewis Gaylord Clark's notice of Fay's *Norman Leslie*: "With some faults, incident to a first attempt, this work of Mr. Fay is said by those critics who have perused it,—(a pleasure in which, owing to absence from town, we have been unable to participate,) to possess scenes of great power, and to be often characterized by that quiet ease of style and purity of diction for which the author is distinguished, and of which we have heretofore spoken in this Magazine. It may be taken as a conclusive evidence of the power of the novel to awaken interest, that in two weeks after the publication of the first large edition, not a copy remained in the hands of the publishers."

23 NOVEMBER. RICHMOND. White replies to Lucian Minor's letter of 20 November: "You are altogether right about the Leslie critique. Poe has

evidently shown himself *no lawyer*—whatever else he may be. The Editor of the Metropolitan has fallen into the same error.—Well, that blunder cannot be repaired.—It will pass undetected I hope. . . .if you really see talent in it ['The Broken Heart' in the December *Messenger*] I hope you will point it out. My daughter Eliza wrote it,—and it is her first attempt at blank verse" (Jackson [1934], pp. 105–06).

[Gossip linked Poe with White's daughter Eliza, called "Lizzie."

When I [Susan Archer Weiss] was a girl I more than once heard of Eliza White and her love affair with Edgar Poe. "She was the sweetest girl I ever knew," said a lady who had been her schoolmate; "a slender, graceful blonde, with deep blue eyes, who reminded you of the Watteau Shepherdesses upon fans. She was a great student, and very bright and intelligent. She was said to be engaged to Poe, but they never appeared anywhere together. It was soon broken off on account of his dissipation. I don't think she ever got over it" (Weiss [1907], pp. 78–79).

When Poe first went to Richmond, Mr. White, as a safeguard from the temptation to evil habits, received him as an inmate of his own home, where he immediately fell in love with the editor's youngest daughter. . . .the father, who idolized his daughter, and was also very fond of Poe, did not forbid the match, but made his consent conditional upon the young man's remaining perfectly sober for a certain length of time. All was going well, and the couple were looked upon as engaged when Mrs. Clemm . . . may have received information of the affair, and we have seen the result (Weiss [1907], pp. 77–78).

Maria Clemm in her letter of 22 April 1859 to Sarah Helen Whitman denied that Poe was ever engaged to Eliza White. See Harrison and Dailey, p. 448; Mabbott (1969), 1:545; Whitty, p. xxxix.]

CA. 26 NOVEMBER. The December *Messenger* appears with a publisher's notice written by Minor, reporting the departure of Sparhawk with the July issue and the engagement of Poe as an assistant:

The gentleman, referred to in the ninth number of the Messenger, as filling its editorial chair, retired thence with the eleventh number; and the intellectual department of the paper is now under the conduct of the Proprietor, assisted by a gentleman of distinguished literary talents. Thus seconded, he is sanguine in the hope of rendering the second volume which the present number commences, *at least* as deserving of support as the former was: nay, if he reads aright the tokens which are given him of the future, it teems with even richer banquets for his readers, than they have hitherto enjoyed at his board.

Some of the contributors, whose effusions have received the largest share of praise from critics, and (what is better still) have been read with most pleasure by that larger, unsophisticated class, whom Sterne loved for reading, and being pleased "they knew not why, and care not wherefore"—may be expected to continue their favors. Among these, we hope to be pardoned for singling out the name of MR. EDGAR A. POE; not with design to make any invidious distinction, but because such a mention of him finds numberless prece-

THE

SOUTHERN LITERARY MESSENGER

FOR

DECEMBER, 1835.

VOL. II.—T. W. WHITE, PROPRIETOR. RICHMOND. FIVE DOLLARS PER ANNUM.—NO. I.

CONTENTS.

☞ The LITERARY MESSENGER contains 64 pages, being 4 sheets to each number, the postage on which, according to law, is, for 100 miles and under, *five cents:* over 100 miles, *ten cents.*

RICHMOND, VA:

T. W. WHITE, PRINTER AND PROPRIETOR,

OPPOSITE THE BELL TAVERN.

1835.

Front wrapper of the December *Messenger*
University of Virginia Library

dents in the journals on every side, which have rung the praises of his uniquely original vein of imagination, and of humorous, delicate satire (White to Minor, 24 October 1835).

The December *Messenger* contains Poe's "Scenes from an Unpublished Drama" (*Politian*), two unsigned fillers ("Logic" and "Le Brun"), "MS. Found in a Bottle" (from the *Gift*), comment on Lucian Minor's "Greek Song," and critical notices: "The Heroine" (Eaton Stannard Barrett's *The Heroine: or Adventures of Cherubina*), "Hawks of Hawk-Hollow" (Robert Montgomery Bird's *The Hawks of Hawk-Hollow; a Tradition of Pennsylvania*), "Peerage and Peasantry" (*Tales of the Peerage and the Peasantry*, edited by Lady Barbarina Dacre), "Edinburgh Review," "Nuts to Crack" (anon., *Nuts to Crack: or Quips, Quirks, Anecdote and Facete of Oxford and Cambridge Scholars*), "Memoir of Dr. Rice" (William Maxwell's *A Memoir of the Reverend John H. Rice*), "Life of Dr. Caldwell" (Walter Anderson's *Oration on the Life and Character of the Rev. Joseph Caldwell, D.D., late President of the University of North Carolina*), "Washingtonii Vita" (Francis Glass's *A Life of George Washington, in Latin Prose*, edited by Jeremiah N. Reynolds), "Norman Leslie" (Theodore S. Fay's *Norman Leslie: A Tale of the Present Times*), "The Linwoods" (Catharine Maria Sedgwick's *The Linwoods; or, "Sixty Years Since" in America*), "Westminster Review," "London Quarterly Review," "North American Review," "Crayon Miscellany" (Washington Irving's *The Crayon Miscellany*), "Godwin's Necromancy" (William Godwin's *Lives of the Necromancers*), "Rev. D. L. Carroll's Address" (*Inaugural Address of the Rev. D. L. Carroll, D.D., President of Hampden-Sidney College*), "Minor's Address" (Lucian Minor's *An Address on Education, as connected with the Permanence of our Republican Institutions*), "Legends of a Log Cabin" (Chandler Gilman's *Legends of a Log Cabin*), "Traits of American Life" (Sarah Josepha Hale's *Traits of American Life*), "Western Sketches" (James Hall's *Sketches of History, Life, and Manners in the West*), "American Almanac" (*The American Almanac . . . for the year 1836*, edited by J. E. Worcester), "Clinton Bradshaw" (F. W. Thomas' *Clinton Bradshaw; or The Adventures of a Lawyer*), and "[Three] English Annuals" (*Friendship's Offering, The Forget Me Not for 1836*, and *Fisher's Drawing-Room Scrap-Book* for 1836). Also published are Eliza White's "The Broken Heart," Lambert A. Wilmer's "To Mira," and Lucian Minor's review of Conway Robinson's *Practice*. In the "To Correspondents" paragraph appears this notice: "A Cosmopolite, and Sylvio, we have declined after much hesitation."

["Sylvio" was the author of "To Sarah," a poem of twenty-four lines in the August 1835 *Messenger*, once attributed to Poe (see Mabbott [1969], 1:506). Poe's "Washingtonii Vita," a review of Jeremiah N. Reynolds' *A Life of George Washington*, later reappeared in part as a testimonial in a second edition of the book (Jackson [1976b], pp. 29–31). Poe called Fay's *Norman Leslie* "the most inestimable piece of balderdash with which the common sense of the good people of America was ever so openly or so villainously insulted," the plot "a monstrous piece of absurdity and incongruity," and the author's style "unworthy of a schoolboy." Poe's unsuccessful *Politian*, an unfinished play based on the real-life Sharp-Beauchamp tragedy of Kentucky in 1824–25 (see 7 NOVEMBER 1825), appeared as "Scenes from an Unpublished Drama" in the *Messenger* for December 1835 and January 1836. Poe, unhappy with it, wrote George W. Eveleth, 15 December 1846: "There *is* no more of Politian." On its appearance it was severely criticized by the press, especially the *Newbern (N. C.) Spectator* (see 15 JANUARY 1836). Beginning with the December issue Poe gave titles to the book reviews.]

The *Messenger* covers carry excerpts from newspapers:

"Loss of Breath: A Tale a la Blackwood, by Edgar A. Poe," is a capital burlesque of the wild, extravagant, disjointed rigmarole with which that much overrated and over-praised magazine is so redundant. The writer has hit off admirably the false, extravagant and exaggerated humor—the inconclusive nothings, and the rude baldness of so many of its articles, of which the beginning, the middle and the end is nothing. The reader finds it impossible to fathom the object, or could not develope it to the comprehension of common sense. We have our eye on Mr. Edgar A. Poe, and from what we have already seen of him, venture to predict it will not be long before his name will stand on a level with those of much higher pretensions. . . .

There is an air of independence about the criticisms, which is becoming in all who undertake to preside in the courts of literature. But we differ entirely from some of the principles adopted by the Messenger.—Most especially do we denounce the assertion of Victor Hugo, quoted, as we understand it, with approbation by the critic, that Racine, Bossuet, Pascal, Fenelon, LaFontaine, Corneille and Voltaire, would be but common writers, were it not for their "style." This is one of the new fangled French opinions fashionable in Paris, and in the true French spirit, places the ruffle before the shirt. It is an excrescence of the musical mania prevailing in that quarter, and is founded on the superiority of sound over sense, and of the ears over the understanding. It is analogous to the taste of a fine lady, who thinks much more of the dress of a man than of the man himself. Such opinions distinctly mark the decline of literature in France, and we do not wonder that Monsieur Victor Hugo should be considered a prodigy, among a people who prefer sound to sense.—*New York Courier and Enquirer.*

The entire volume [I] of which this number [13] forms the completion, is without an exception, (we do not forget the old Southern Review,) the most creditable to the literature of the South of any thing which in the shape of a periodical, has yet emanated from it. . . ."Loss of Breath" is really a capital thing, well imagined, well sustained, and well told; and with some triteness in the main incident, of sufficient novelty to attract highly. . . . "King Pest, the First" is told with spirit, and evinces talent though somewhat nonsensical towards the end. . . .It [the *Messenger*] is ably and judiciously edited. . . .—*Georgetown Metropolitan* [21 October].

. . .we must allude to an article in the last number, which gave us unalloyed amusement, and which we esteem one of the most admirable specimens of brilliant fancy, and apt description which we have ever read. It is "KING PEST THE FIRST," containing an Allegory. There can be no mistake in attributing it to the prolific pen of Edgar A. Poe, whose talent in imaginative productions, is not excelled by any writer of his age in this country. We say this from no motive of interest or partiality for we have scarcely an acquaintance with the author, but from the sincere opinion that he possesses talents and attainments of the first order, which he should persevere in using for the public benefit, regardless alike of the detractions of the envious, or the sneers of the critic race, who "hate the excellence they cannot reach."—*[Richmond] Compiler.*

It contains a number of well-written and interesting articles . . . we may mention . . . Mr. Poe's Tale of *"Loss of Breath".* . . . the critical notices are distinguished by candor and liberality.—*Philadelphia Saturday Evening Post.*

Magazines in America.—One *Poe* ("Phoebus! what a name!") is its [the *Messenger*'s] chief contributor, —perhaps its editor. . . . *Portland Advertiser.*

We were exceedingly amused with Poe's story *à la* Blackwood, entitled "Loss of Breath," and have been delighted with several of the poetical scraps, one of which will be given to-morrow . . .—*Richmond Compiler.*

We publish this morning from the Southern Literary Messenger the tale entitled *"King Pest the First,"* which we spoke of a few days since in noticing the last number of the Messenger. The article, seems generally, and we believe justly attributed to the pen of Mr. Edgar A. Poe, our townsman, whose productions have met almost universal approbation from the critical press. In King Pest, the evils and maladies attendant upon intemperance are well portrayed in the allegorical personages who group around the drinking table of the monarch "Tim Hurlygurly." Indeed few of Mr. P's tales are without aim or a moral; "Hans Phaal" was a burlesque upon the mania for ballooning—"Lionizing," upon the rage for making a Lion of every contemptible pretender to fashion, or small authorship—"Loss of Breath" is evidently a burlesque on the extravagant and rigmarole species of writing so prevalent in the pages of Blackwood.—*[Richmond] Compiler.*

BEFORE 29 NOVEMBER. Poe writes Carey & Lea (implied by Carey & Lea to Poe, 29 November).

29 NOVEMBER. PHILADELPHIA. A partner in Carey & Lea, probably Henry C. Carey, writes Poe: "I have called on Mess. E. L. Carey & A. Hart, who are the publishers of 'The Gift,' and they have examined among all the MS. and cannot find the story to which you allude. They think it very probable that Miss L. [Eliza Leslie] returned it with others but it cannot

now be found. Should it be hereafter they will return it" (Woodberry, 2:375, where dated "1836"; Hammond, pp. 32–33).

29 NOVEMBER. WILLIAMSBURG. Beverley Tucker writes White:

I am much flattered by Mr. Poe's opinion of my lines. Original thoughts come to me "like angels' visits few and far between." To Mr. P they come thronging unbidden, crowding themselves upon him in such numbers as to require the black rod of that master of ceremonies, Criticism, to keep them in order. I hope he will take this and other suggestions of mine kindly. I am interested in him, and am glad he has found a position in which his pursuit of fame may be neither retarded, nor, what is worse, hurried by necessity. His history, as I have heard it, reminds me of Coleridge's,—With the example of Coleridge's virtues and success before him, he can need no other guide. Yet a companion by the way to hint that "more haste makes less speed" may not be amiss. Will he admit me to this office? Without the tithe of his genius, I am old enough to be his father (if I do not mistake his filiation, I remember his beautiful mother when a girl), and I presume I have had advantages the want of which he feels. Now, if by aiding you, I can aid him too to disencumber himself of the clogs that have impeded his progress, I shall kill two birds with one stone. Let me tell you then why in the critique I prepared for [Duff] Green, I said nothing of his Tale ["MS. Found in a Bottle" reprinted in the December *Messenger*]. It was because I thought that he had been already praised as much as was good for him. And why? Because I am sure no man ever attained to that distinction to which Mr. P. may fairly aspire *by extravagance*. He is made for better things than to cater for the depraved taste of the literary vulgar, the most disgusting and impertinent of all vulgarians. Besides, I was disappointed in the tale; not because of the praises I had heard (for I make light of such things), but because Mr. P. had taught me to expect from him something more than the mere *physique* of the horrible. I had expected that the author of "Morella" on board the Flying Dutchman would have found a Dutch tongue in his head, would have thawed the silence of his shipmates, and have extracted from them a tale of thrilling interest, of the causes of that awful spell which has driven and still drives their ship careening safely through the innumerable horrors he has described. Cannot he rescue her yet from her perils, and send us another bottle full of intelligence of her escape, and of her former history? Cannot he, by way of episode, get himself sent on board of some fated ship, with letters from the spellbound mariners to their friends at home? Imaginations of this sort flocked to my mind as soon as I found him on her decks, and hence I was disappointed. I do not propose that he should work up these materials. He can do better in following the lead of his own fancy. But let him remember that fancy must be servant, not mistress. It must be made the minister of higher faculties. . . .

Now one word more. If Mr. P. takes well what I have said, he shall have as much more of it whenever occasion calls for it. If not, his silence alone will effectually rebuke my impertinence (Wilson [1924], pp. 652–53; Woodberry, 1:151–53; Quinn, pp. 234–35).

29 NOVEMBER. AUGUSTA, GEORGIA. William Poe writes Maria Clemm

about their family history and adds: "Remember me very affectionately to Edgar & his Sister & your daughter & say to Edgar that I hope to write him soon" (Quinn and Hart, pp. 11–12).

1 DECEMBER. RICHMOND. Poe, in his letter postmarked 3 December, writes Beverley Tucker:

Mr White was so kind as to read me some portions of your letter to himself, dated Nov 29. . . .in relation to your own verses. That they *are not poetry* I will not allow, even when judging them by your own rules. . . .What *is*, or *is not*, poetry must not be told in a mere epistle. I sincerely think your lines excellent. The distinction you make between levity, and wit or humour (that which produces a smile) I perfectly understand; but that levity is unbecoming the chair of the critic, must be taken, I think, cum grano salis. . . .Your opinion of "The MS. found in a Bottle" is just. The Tale was written some years ago, and was one among the first I ever wrote. I have met with no one, with the exception of yourself & P. P. Cooke of Winchester, whose judgment concerning these Tales I place any value upon. Generally, people praise extravagantly those of which I am ashamed, and pass in silence what I fancy to be praise worthy. The last tale I wrote was Morella and it was my best. . . .At present, having no time upon my hands, from my editorial duties, I can write nothing worth reading. What articles I have published *since Morella* were all written some time ago. . . . music is a most indefinite conception. . . .In short—I especially pride myself upon the accuracy of my ear. . . . In speaking of my mother you have touched a string to which my heart fully responds. To have known her is to be an object of great interest in my eyes. I myself never knew her—and never knew the affection of a father. Both died (as you may remember) within a few weeks of each other. I have many occasional dealings with Adversity—but the want of parental affection has been the heaviest of my trials (*L*, 1:76–79).

3 DECEMBER. White writes Beverley Tucker: "I have read to Mr. Poe such portions of your letter as related to himself. He is, I assure you, much pleased with the spirit breathed in every line,—and promises me that he will respond to all your arguments by the mail of this Evening" (Vi–W–TC).

5 DECEMBER. WILLIAMSBURG. Beverley Tucker writes Poe: "I have been congratulating myself on the success of my attempt to draw you into correspondence. . . .You are doubtless right in thinking that a mere flow of mellifluous lines is not the thing called for by the laws of metrical harmony. . . .Now in the 'fragment' [*Politian*] there are lines that cannot by any reading be forced into time. Take Baldazzar's speech at the bottom of the first column of p. 15 [December *Messenger*]. . . .I am glad you do not know who your dreamer is. He will keep his secret, and take care not to complain. [Here Tucker refers to the lines entitled "The Dream" by

"Sylvester" in the December *Messenger*.] Mr. White writes me that he is labouring under a woful lack of matter" (*W*, 17:21–24).

7 DECEMBER. NEW YORK. James Kirke Paulding praises Poe in a letter to White: "Your publication is decidedly superior to any Periodical in the United States, and Mr. Poe is decidedly the best of all our going writers. I dont Know but I might add all our Old Ones, with one or two exceptions" (Paulding, pp. 170–72; *Daily National Intelligencer*, 18 December 1835; *Messenger*, 2 [January 1836]:138).

9 DECEMBER. CHARLESTON, SOUTH CAROLINA. In its notice of the December *Messenger* the *Charleston Courier* singles Poe out for praise: "Among its contributors, EDGAR A. POE, equally ripe in graphic humour and various lore, seems by common consent, to have been awarded the laurel, and in the number before us, fully sustaining the reputation of its predecessors, will be found proofs of his distinguished merit."

11 DECEMBER. DISTRICT OF COLUMBIA. The *Georgetown Metropolitan* reports that "the unpublished drama by Poe, though crude, has both original thoughts, incidents and situations. . . .as we said before, [we] wish cordially that the bottle with that confounded manuscript had never been uncorked" (reprinted in the January 1836 *Messenger* supplement).

12 DECEMBER. NEW YORK. In the *New-Yorker* Horace Greeley gives Poe's *Politian* an "unenthusiastic" notice (Hyneman, p. 15).

15 DECEMBER. RICHMOND. The *Richmond Whig* quotes Mordecai M. Noah's comments on *Politian*: "Mr. Poe's 'Unpublished Drama' does not suit our taste. Why eternally ring the changes on those everlasting and hackneyed Venetian Doges and Italian Counts—latticed balconies, and verandas—time out of mind exhausted?" Noah finds: "The Critical Notices are full as they should be on American productions, and written with uncommon spirit. The decisions are generally correct, and we are glad to see the censures so unsparingly, but judiciously directed against the mawkish style and matter of those ephemeral productions with which, under the name of *chef-d'oeuvres* in novel writing, the poor humbugged public are so unmercifully gagged and bamboozled" (Hyneman, p. 18).

[White reprinted Noah's remarks in the January 1836 *Messenger* supplement.]

In still another notice the *Richmond Whig* quotes the postscript of Paulding's 7 December letter to White.

25 DECEMBER. White writes Lucian Minor that "All the Critical Notices [in the January 1836 *Messenger*] are from the pen of Poe—who I rejoice to tell you, still keeps from the Bottle. . . . The No. will be out on the 1st January, 1836" (Jackson [1934], p. 107).

*

1836

*

1? JANUARY. RICHMOND. In the January *Messenger* Poe publishes an editorial note on Robert Greenhow's "Sketches of the History and Present Condition of Tripoli, with Some Account of the Other Barbary States," "A Paean," a filler ("A. W. Schlegel says, that in a German drama . . ."), "Metzengerstein. A Tale in Imitation of the German," "Scenes from an Unpublished Drama" (*Politian*), and critical notices: "Mrs. Sigourney—Miss Gould—Mrs. Ellet" (Mrs. Lydia H. Sigourney's *Zinzendorff* . . . , Miss H. F. Gould's *Poems*, and Mrs. E. F. Ellet's *Poems*), "The Partisan" (William Gilmore Simms's *The Partisan: A Tale of the Revolution*), "Latrobe's Rambler" (Charles Joseph Latrobe's *The Rambler in North America, 1832–33*), "The South-West" (Joseph H. Ingraham's *The South-West*), "Poetry of Life" (Sarah Stickney's *The Poetry of Life*), "Miss Sedgwick's Sketches" (Catharine Maria Sedgwick's *Tales and Sketches*), "Reminiscences of Niebuhr" (Francis Lieber's *Reminiscences of an Intercourse with Mr. Niebuhr*), "Young Wife's Book," "Robinson Crusoe" (Daniel Defoe's *The Life and Surprising Adventures of Robinson Crusoe*), and "Christian Florist" (anon., *The Christian Florist*). Poe also writes an introductory Publisher's Notice and a footnote for the Supplement, which includes these testimonials:

The Critical Notices are much to our taste—decided in their character, correct (as we think) in judgment, and lashing dullness, as it always deserves to be lashed, with a cat-o'-nine-tails.—[John Hampden Pleasants, editor,] *Richmond Whig*.

The Editorial criticisms are generally just.—Whilst they "nothing extenuate," and refuse to deal out indiscriminate compliment and unremitted praise, they yet are free from even the semblance of that illiberal spirit which delights rather to triumph in the detection of an error than in the generous acknowledgment and commendation of a beauty. They embrace reviews of many new and popular works which have lately issued from the Press; among which is the Life of Washington, written in Latin, and said to be a production of extraordinary merit.—*Petersburg Intelligencer*.

. . . the notice of new works, in the Southern Messenger, are, we have no hesitation in saying it, the boldest, the most independent and unflinching, of all that appears in the periodical world. . . . the critiques on The Hawks of Hawk-Hollow—the Linwoods—and Norman Leslie we especially recommend to notice. They are evidently all written with equal sincerity, and force of *true* opinion, and as such command respect even where we differ from them in judgment. That on Dr. Bird's new book, for instance, is too favorable; and indeed we think that this gentleman is *always* overrated—that on "the Linwoods" is superlative, in truth, style, and taste; while that on Norman Leslie is severe to a fault; inasmuch as the criticism, though we cannot deny the truth of the greater portion of it, is paralyzed by the strong symptoms of *personal* hostility not to Mr. Fay only, but to all who may be supposed to favor or admire him.—*New York Courier and Enquirer.*

The tone of the criticisms differs widely from puffery, and is perfectly independent.—[Washington] *National Intelligencer.*

The contributions appear to be of an excellent kind; at least, those from Mr. Poe and others, whose reputations attracted our notice. The most striking feature of the number, however, is the critical department.—[Philadelphia] *Pennsylvanian.*

We perceive a considerable improvement in the editorial department, under which are contained several well written and judicious critical notices of new works.—*Alexandria Gazette.*

. . . among other things we must not forget that the author of the *Lunar Hoax* is indebted to the *Hans Phaal* of Mr. Poe (a regular contributor to the Messenger) for the conception and in a great measure for the execution of his discoveries. Indeed several passages in the two are nearly identical. . . . *The MS. found in a Bottle* is extracted from *The Gift*, Miss Leslie's beautiful Annual. It is from the pen of Edgar A. Poe, "whose eccentric genius," says the Charleston Courier, "delights in the creation of strange possibilities, and in investing the most intangible romances in an air of perfect verisimilitude." We have heard the *MS. found in a Bottle*, called the best of his Tales—but prefer *Lionizing* and *Morella.*—The highest praise, however, and from the very highest quarters, has been awarded to *all* he has written. . . . Among these, are Notices. . . .not forgetting Norman Leslie, which is utterly torn to pieces in a long and detailed Review of the most bitter and unsparing sarcasm. . . . The poetry is very excellent. . . . the *Scenes from an unpublished Drama by Edgar A. Poe.*—*Norfolk Herald.*

The MS. found in a bottle. By Edgar A. Poe, is good,—it is original and well told. Its wild impossibilities are pictured to the imagination with all the detail of circumstances, which truth and the fearful reality might be supposed to present. Whilst we do not agree to the justness of the praise which has been bestowed upon *some* of Mr. Poe's pieces, we concur in the general commendation which he has received as a writer of great originality and one who promises well. . . . The Review of Mr. Fay's novel Norman Leslie, is amusing and will be read, though we think some passages in it are in bad taste. The author is flayed, or to use a term more congenial with his taste, and with the Reviewer's article—*blistered.*—*Charlottesville Jeffersonian.*

The literary notices . . . are highly piquant and amusing. . . . There is an occasional severity in some of these strictures which we highly approve. . . . The number of works reviewed in this *monthly* periodical, shows how much the *cacoethes scribendi* needs to be restrained. . . . The longest of the metrical pieces ["The Dream"]. . . . deserves less lenient treatment. . . . We were disappointed in a "Dramatic Extract" from the pen of Mr. Edgar A. Poe. He had taught us to expect much, for his prose is often very high wrought poetry; but his poetry is prose, not in thought, but in measure. This is a defect of ear alone, which can only be corrected by more study than the thing is worth. As he has a large interest in all the praise that we have bestowed on the Messenger, we hope he will take this slight hint as kindly as it is meant.—[Beverley Tucker,] *Washington Telegraph*.

. . . the editorial criticism and reviews appear to be written in a spirit of candor quite unusual for the American Press.—*Philadelphia Saturday Evening Post.*

We condemned a day or two ago the *tone* of the notice of the North American Review in the Southern Literary Messenger for December. This number is strong in notice of new works, and we like the severity of some of them: there is much matter for "cutting up." But the cutter up must do his task like a neat carver, without smearing his own fingers. Our friend Mr. White and his editor should keep the tone and bearing of the Messenger elevated and cavalier-like. The higher the critic places himself, the more fatal will be his blows downwards.—[William Bose, editor,] *Baltimore American.*

Among its contributors, EDGAR A. POE, equally ripe in graphic humor and various lore, seems by common consent to have been awarded the laurel, and in the number before us fully sustaining the reputation of its predecessors, will be found proofs of his distinguished merit.—*Charleston Courier* [9 December 1835].

. . . we think the critical notices of this number, whether written by the old or new editor, more elevated in their tone than previously. There is a slight taint of pedantry about them, perhaps; and in one instance undue severity is shown towards a clever young author: yet they are, in the main, clever and just. . . . Mr. Edgar A. Poe, a writer of much versatility of talent, has contributed much to this number. He is a magazinist somewhat in the style of Willis: he needs condensation of thought. But this is too flippant criticism for us, and we will read him more.—*New York Spirit of the Times.*

The Critical Notices in the present number of the Messenger, particularly of the North American and the British Reviews are in bad taste. The review of Glass' Life of Washington is altogether unique. Some of the reviews are nevertheless good, and more than outweigh those that are bad.—[Hugh Blair Grigsby, editor,] *Norfolk Beacon.*

"Scenes from Politian," like the prose productions from the same pen (Mr. Poe) evince great powers, wasted on trifles. Why, (to adopt the catechetical style of his own criticisms,) why does Mr. Poe throw away his strength on shafts and columns, instead of building a temple to his fame? Can he not execute as well as design? No one can doubt it who is conversant with his writings. Eschew affectation, Mr. Poe. . . . Too much space is allotted to "Critical Notices" in the December No. of the Messenger—and several of the Notices themselves are too dogmatical and flippant.

. . . It should certainly not be occupied by *review of Reviews*—a dish of hash newly warmed, and served up, in all its insipidity, to an already palled appetite. Such reviews as that of Mr. Fay's "Norman Leslie" will be read. Men—and Women likewise—will always be attracted in crowds . . . to see a fellow creature flayed alive. And Mr. Fay—who, by the way, is a great favorite with us—fully deserves a *"blistering"* for putting forth such a book as Norman Leslie.—*Lynchburg Virginian.*

"*Scenes from an Unpublished Drama*, by Edgar A. Poe" contains one or two stirring and many beautiful passages—but we are not partial to dramatic poetry. . . . The critical department of the Messenger is managed with great candor, consideration and ability.—*New Yorker.*

The publisher has secured the assistance of a gentleman of eminent literary talents, with whose aid it may be fairly inferred that the Messenger will not only sustain but increase its already extensive and deserved popularity. The literary notices contained in this number are written with great ability, but in our opinion rather too great a space has been devoted to that subject.—[William Gwynn, editor,] *Baltimore Gazette.*

. . . the *critiques* are now precisely what they should be in such a work. . . . We have rarely read a review more caustic or more called for than the *flaying* which the new editor of the Messenger has so judiciously given Mr. Fay's "bepuffed, beplastered and be-*Mirrored*" novel of "Norman Leslie."—[Hiram Haines, editor,] *Petersburg Constellation.*

["A Fairy Tale" in the January 1836 *Messenger* (2:77–78) may have provided Poe with tone and color for his "The Island of the Fay" and "Eleonora." See Mabbott (1978), 2:598 and 636.]

12 JANUARY. The *Richmond Enquirer* reprints Poe's "A Paean."

12 JANUARY. Poe writes George Poe, Jr., in Mobile, Alabama, in behalf of Maria Clemm:

Having lately established myself in Richmond, and undertaken the Editorship of the Southern Literary Messenger, and my circumstances having thus become better than formerly, I have ventured to offer my aunt a home. She is now therefore in Richmond, with her daughter Virginia, and is, for the present boarding at the house of a Mrs Yarrington. My salary is only, at present, about $800 per ann: and the charge per week for our board, (Mrs Clemm's, her daughter's, and my own,) is $9. . . .

It is ascertained that if Mrs C could obtain the means of opening, herself, a boarding-house in this city, she could support herself and daughter comfortably with something to spare. But a small capital would be necessary for an undertaking of this nature, and many of the widows of our first people are engaged in it, and find it profitable. I am willing to advance, for my own part, $100, and I believe that Wm & R. Poe will advance $100. If then you would so far aid her in her design as to loan her, Yourself 100, she will have sufficient to commence with.

I will be responsible for the repayment of the sum, in a year from this date, if you can make it convenient to comply with her request (*L*, 1:79–80).

15 JANUARY. NEW BERN, NORTH CAROLINA. An editor of the *Newbern Spectator*, presumably Robert G. Moore, disapproves "of the unnecessary severity of the criticism [in the *Messenger*]. . . . this [January] number is a little more moderate, but yet not sufficiently so for a dignified and unbiassed periodical." Moore reprints parts of *Politian*, "italicising freely the incongruities in sense and sound, and the unprecedented instances of tautology."

21 JANUARY. RICHMOND. Poe writes Edward L. Carey and Abraham Hart, requesting a review copy of Bulwer-Lytton's *Rienzi* (*L*, 2:672–73 [1966]).

[Poe reviewed *Rienzi* in the February *Messenger*. Paulding thought Bulwer's novel "much overrated." See Paulding to White, 3 March 1836.]

22 JANUARY. Poe writes John Pendleton Kennedy:

My health is better than for years past . . . my pecuniary difficulties have vanished. . . . Mr White is very liberal, and besides my salary of 520$ pays me liberally for extra work, so that I receive nearly $800. Next year, that is at the commencement of the second volume, I am to get $1000 (*L*, 1:81–82).

26 JANUARY. WILLIAMSBURG. Beverley Tucker writes White:

Last night I received a letter from Mr. P. by which I learn that you may not feel as much confidence in his capacity for the duties of his station as is necessary for your mutual comfort. This doubt he attributes in part to what must have been a misconstruction by you of one of my letters. That I have not admired all Mr. P's productions, as much as some others, and that his writings are not so much to my taste as they would be were I (as would to God I were) as young as he, I do not deny. Thus much I expressed, and this so freely as to show that, had I meant more, I would have said more. You only know me on paper, but I think you can read this point in my character at the distance of sixty miles. I was equally sincere, I assure you, in what I said in his praise. . . . I do not agree with the reading (or rather the writing and printing) public in admiring Mrs. Sigourney & Co., or any of our native poets except Halleck. In this I know I shall stand condemned. But I appeal from contemporaneous and reciprocal puffing to the impartial judgment of posterity. Let that pass. I only mention this to say that Mr. P's review of the writings of a leash of these ladies, in your last number, is a specimen of criticism, which for niceness of discrimination, delicacy of expression, and all that shows familiarity with the art, may well compare with any I have ever seen. . . .

Mr. P. is young, and I thought him rash. I expressed this full as strongly as I thought it. I now repeat it, and apply to him the caution given by the God of Poets and Critics to his son when he permitted him to guide the Chariot that lights the world.

> "Parce, puer, stimulis, et fortiter utere loris."
> . . . . I write this letter at his request (Woodberry, 1:154–56).

5 FEBRUARY. RICHMOND. Poe writes Lucian Minor that, to preserve uniformity in the titles of articles, he has shortened the title of Minor's essay to read "Selection in Reading" and that he has omitted passages in Minor's "Liberian Literature" that might be taken as offensive (L, 1:83).

6 FEBRUARY. White writes Beverley Tucker:

My own impression is, that, on the whole the present No. is fully equal to any of its predecessors. My right hand man Poe thinks it superior—this is natural. . . .

I shall on some suitable occasion, tell you a great deal about my young friend and editor. It will be [only?] for your private ear (Vi–W–TC).

9 FEBRUARY. Poe solicits from Stephen Greenleaf Bulfinch, of Augusta, Georgia, a contribution to the *Messenger* and sends him a copy of the February issue (letter postmarked 13 February; L, 2:673 [1966]).

9 FEBRUARY. BALTIMORE. John Pendleton Kennedy writes Poe, gives him advice, and asks for his help in the recovery of a painting:

I am greatly rejoiced at your success not only in Richmond, but every where. . . . You are strong enough now to be criticized. Your fault is your love of the extravagant. Pray beware of it. You find a hundred *intense* writers for one *natural* one. Some of your *bizarreries* have been mistaken for satire—and admired too in that character. They deserved it, but *you* did not, for you did not intend them so. I like your grotesque—it is of the very best stamp, and I am sure you will do wonders for yourself in the comic, I mean the *serio tragi comic*. Do you easily keep pace with the demands of the magazine? I like the critical notices very well. . . . Your letter assures me that you have entirely conquered your late despondency. . . . There is a little scapegrace in Richmond, or its vicinity, to whom I have heretofore shown favour. I mean H——d [William James Hubard] the painter. He carried away from me four years ago nearly, a painting of myself & Mrs. K. and her sister, which I paid him $225 for, and which he never delivered to me. . . . Pray write to me if you can give me any information of H——d or the picture (W, 17:28–29).

11 FEBRUARY. RICHMOND. Poe fails to locate W. J. Hubard and writes John Pendleton Kennedy:

You are nearly, but not altogether right in relation to the satire of some of my Tales. Most of them were *intended* for half banter, half satire—although I might not have fully acknowledged this to be their aim even to myself. "Lionizing" and "Loss of Breath" were satires properly speaking—at least so meant—the one of the rage for Lions and the facility of becoming one—the other of the extravagancies of Blackwood. I find no difficulty in keeping pace with the demands of the Magazine. In the February number, which is now in the binder's hands, are no less than *40 pages* of Editorial. . . . There was *no* November number issued. . . . Mr. W. has increased my salary, since I wrote, 104$. for the present year. . . . He is exceedingly kind in every respect (*L*, 1:83–85).

[Earlier Poe had mentioned the artist Hubard in his "Memoir of Dr. Rice," a review in the December 1835 *Messenger*].

12 FEBRUARY. MOBILE, ALABAMA. George Poe, Jr., replies to Poe's letter of 12 January and sends $100 (endorsement, Poe to George Poe, Jr., 12 January 1836).

13 FEBRUARY. RICHMOND. The February *Messenger* publishes Poe's "The Gourd of Jonah," "The Duc de L'Omelette," "The Iliad," "Palaestine," "Martorelli," "The Valley Nis," "New Testament," "Gibbon and Fox," "Statius," "Greece," "Autography" (Part 1), and critical notices: "Paul Ulric" (Morris Mattson's *Paul Ulric: Or the Adventures of an Enthusiast*), "Martin's Gazetteer" (Joseph Martin's *A New and Comprehensive Gazetteer of Virginia, and the District of Columbia*), "Rose-Hill" (anon., *Rose-Hill, A Tale of the Old Dominion*), "Emilia Harrington" (Lambert A. Wilmer's *The Confessions of Emilia Harrington*), "American in England" (Alexander Slidell Mackenzie's *The American in England*), "Conti" (Henry F. Chorley's *Conti the Discarded*), "Noble Deeds of Woman" ([Jesse Clement's?] *Noble Deeds of Woman*), "Bulwer's Rienzi" (Edward Bulwer-Lytton's *Rienzi, The Last of the Tribunes*), and "Roget's Physiology" (Peter Mark Roget's *Animal and Vegetable Physiology*). Lucian Minor contributes a review entitled "Chief Justice Marshall."

17 FEBRUARY. WASHINGTON. James Frederick Otis reviews the February *Messenger* in the *Daily National Intelligencer* (Thomas [1975], p. 14 n. 1).

[Many signatures in Poe's "Autography" were those of subscribers (see *Messenger* wrappers) and contributors to the magazine. Others were sent to Poe by Otis, then a Washington journalist (see Thomas [1975], pp. 12–15, and Mabbott [1978], 2:259–91).]

BEFORE 20 FEBRUARY. RICHMOND. Poe writes Carey & Lea (Carey & Lea to Poe, 20 February 1836).

20 FEBRUARY. PHILADELPHIA. A partner in Carey & Lea, probably Henry C. Carey, writes Poe: "I received your letter this morning, having no knowledge of the MS. mentioned" (Woodberry, 2:375).

21 FEBRUARY. RICHMOND. Maria Clemm writes George Poe, Jr.: "I have received to-day from my nephew E A. Poe the sum of one hundred dollars—and which I learn I am to attribute to you. I beg you will accept my sincere gratitude and I now hope I may be enabled to surmount difficulties with which I have had to contend for a long time—particularly since my mothers death—myself and daughter are under the protection of Edgar—he is the Editor of the Southern Literary Messenger—and bids fair to be an honour to our name—he desires me to say any influence you may be able to exercise in behalf of the Messenger will be to his immediate advantage—he desires his respects to you" (Quinn and Hart, p. 15).

24 FEBRUARY. John Collins McCabe, a Virginia clergyman and poet, writes Poe (Poe to McCabe, 3 March 1836).

3 MARCH. Poe writes John Collins McCabe: "I need not speak to you of the difficulties I have to encounter, daily, in selecting from the mass of M.SS. handed in for The Messenger. Personal applications, from personal friends, of course embarrass me greatly. It is, indeed, almost impossible to refuse an article offered in this manner without giving mortal offence to the friend who offers it. This offence, however, is most frequently taken by those who have the fewest pretensions to merit. In the present instance I feel perfectly sure that I shall neither wound your feelings, nor cause you to think less of me as an acquaintance, by returning your Poem—which I now enclose [Poe declines "The Consumptive Girl"]. . . . I have frequently seen pieces from your pen which I would have been happy to insert. . . . and some lines lately printed in the Baltimore Athenaum—that great bowl of Editorial skimmed milk and water. . . . I know you will reply, and with some appearance of justice, that much worse verses have appeared in the Messenger since my Editorship, and are still appearing. But these are poems which have been long on hand, and to the publication of which Mr. W. [White] had bound himself, by promises to their respective authors, before my time" (L, 2:674–75).

3 MARCH. NEW YORK. James Kirke Paulding writes White:

I duly received the Book containing the Tales by Mr. Poe heretofore published in the "Messenger," and have delayed writing to you on the subject until I could communicate the final decision of the Messrs. Harpers as to their republication. By the way, you are entirely mistaken in your idea of my influence over these gentlemen in the transactions of their business. . . . I placed the work in their hands, giving my opinion of it, which was such as I believe I have heretofore expressed to you more than once, leaving them to their own decision.

The[y] have finally declined republishing it for the following reasons: They say the stories have so recently appeared before the Public in the "Messenger" that they would be no novelty—but most especially they object that there is a degree of obscurity in their application, which will prevent ordinary readers from comprehending their drift, and consequently from enjoying the fine satire they convey. It requires a degree of familiarity with various kinds of knowledge which they do not possess, to enable them to relish the joke; the dish is too refined for them to banquet on. They desire me, however, to state to Mr. Poe that if he will lower himself a little to the ordinary comprehension of the generality of readers, and prepare a series of original Tales, or a single work, and send them to the Publishers, previous to their appearance in the "Messenger," they will make such arrangements with him as will be liberal and satisfactory.

I regret this decision of the Harpers, though I have not opposed it, because I do not wish to lead them into any measure that might be accompanied by a loss, and felt as I would feel for myself in a similar case. I would not press a work of my own upon them, nor do I think Mr. Poe would be gratified at my doing so with one of his.

I hope Mr. Poe will pardon me if the interest I feel in his success should prompt me to take this occasion to suggest to him to apply his fine humor, and his extensive acquirements, to more familiar subjects of satire; to the faults and foibles of our own people, their peculiarities of habits and manners, and above all to the ridiculous affectations and extravagances of the fashionable English Literature of the day, which we copy with such admirable success and servility. His quiz on Willis ["Lion-izing"] , and the Burlesque of "Blackwood" ["Loss of Breath"] , were not only capital, but what is more, were understood by all. . . . Paul Ulric is treated as he should be, but I think Mr. Bulwer's much overrated in the notice of Rienzi. If Mr. Poe will analyze it, he will find it full of obscurities, incongruities, improbabilities, and affectations. Don't publish this at your Peril! (Paulding, pp. 173–75).

6 MARCH. AUGUSTA, GEORGIA. The *Chronicle* reacts unfavorably to Lucian Minor's article "Liberian Literature" in the February *Messenger* and disapproves of the *Baltimore American*'s acceptance of it.

SOUTHERN LITERARY MESSENGER.

The February No. of this beautiful and highly interesting work is one of the best, we think, that has yet appeared; and we take pleasure in earnestly recommending it to the attention of the public, and particularly the literary portion of it, as highly creditable to the literary character of the South, and deserving of the most liberal patronage of its people, who ought to cherish and foster such a work with peculiar pride and pleasure. We have one complaint, however, against the present No.; and in this we differ decidedly from the views of the Baltimore American, whose otherwise just and complimentary article we copy, below. We mean its very laudatory article on *"Liberian Literature,"* which we consider altogether unsuited to our Southern region, and as indicating a dangerous partiality for that most pestiferous and abominable parent of the Abolitionists, the *Colonization Society*. Such things may, perhaps, be tolerated in Maryland and Virginia; but we can assure the highly esteemed and respected publisher of the Messenger, (who we trust will not doubt the sincerity of our regard both for him and his valuable work,) that they cannot and will not be here, where the people look upon the Colonizationists as part and parcel of the Abolitionists, but more dangerous, because disguising the same infamous object under a pretence of *friendship*, while the Abolitionists at least deal openly and plainly with us, and are so far the more entitled to respect; and withal, the truly *Southern* people have no curiosity whatever, in Liberian, alias *Negro* Literature!! If Mr. WHITE would see the folly, absurdity, and utter futility of the ostensible object of the Colonization Society clearly exposed, let him read the admirable, and unanswerable Essay on Slavery, of his most valuable and able contributor, Professor DEW, which we beg leave earnestly to recommend to his attention, as also that of every other searcher after truth, who has not yet had the good fortune to peruse it.

From the Baltimore American.

"The *Southern Literary Messenger* for February is, we think, the best of the fifteen numbers that have been published. . . . "*The Duc de L'Omelette*, by *Edgar A. Poe*," is one of those light, spirited, fantastic inventions, of which we have had specimens before in the Messenger, betokening a fertility of imagination and power of execution, that with discipline, could, under a sustained effort, produce creations of enduring character. We are rejoiced to see in the Southern Literary Messenger, such an article as that headed "*Liberian Literature*," in which the prosperity of this Colony is spoken of with, we may say, enthusiastic approbation. ***** The best and also the largest portion of the present number of the Messenger, is the

JAMES KIRKE PAULDING

department of critical notices of books. These are the work of a vigorous, sportive, keen pen, that, whether you approve the judgments or not it records, takes captive your attention by the spirit with which it moves. The number ends with the amusing Miller correspondence [Poe's "Autography"], of which we have already spoken."

6 MARCH. LOUISA COURTHOUSE, VIRGINIA. Lucian Minor writes Poe or White (Poe to Minor, 10 March 1836).

10 MARCH. RICHMOND. Poe has read the *Augusta, Georgia, Chronicle* of 6 March and writes Lucian Minor: "Your Marshall article has been very well received in all directions. Grigesby [Hugh Blair Grigsby], of Norfolk, alone spoke ill of it and he speaks ill of every thing. . . . Professor Dew is now here, and thinks the whole article every thing it should be. Liberian Literature has met a fate very similar. Lauded by all men of sense, it has excited animadversion from the Augusta Chronicle. The scoundrel says it is sheer abolitionism" (*L*, 1:87–88).

BEFORE 17 MARCH. Poe writes James K. Paulding (Paulding to Poe, 17 March 1836).

17 MARCH. NEW YORK. James K. Paulding writes Poe in care of T. W. White:

In compliance with your wishes, it would have afforded me much pleasure to have proposed the publication of your Book to some respectable bookseller of this city. But the truth is, there is only one other, who publishes any thing but School Books, religious works and the like, and with him I am not on terms that would make it agreeable to me, to make any proposition of this nature, either in my own behalf or that of another. I have therefore placed your work in the hands of Messrs. Harper's to forward with a Box of Books they are sending to Richmond in a few days, and I hope it will come safely to hand.

I think it would be worth your while, if other engagements permit, to undertake a Tale in a couple of Volumes, for that is the magical number. There is a great dearth of good writers at present both in England and this Country, while the number of readers and purchasers of Books, is daily increasing, So that the demand is greater than the Supply, in mercantile phraze. Not one work in ten, now published in England, will bear republication here. You would be surprised at their excessive mediocrity. I am of opinion that a work of yours, would at least bring you a handsome remuneration, though it might not repay your labours, or meet its merits. Should you write such a work, your best way will be to forward the MS directly to the Harpers, who will be I presume, governed by the judgment of their *Reader*, who from long experience can tell almost to a certainty what will succeed. I am destitute of this valuable instinct, and my opinion counts for nothing with publishers (Paulding, pp. 177–78).

AFTER 26 MARCH. RICHMOND. The March *Messenger* publishes Poe's "Epimanes" (later "Four Beasts in One—The Homo-Cameleopard") including "Latin Hymn" and "Song of Triumph," "To Helen," "Bai" (a filler), "Authors" (a filler), and critical notices: "Episcopal Church in Virginia" (Francis L. Hawks's *Contributions to the Ecclesiastical History of the United States of America—Virginia*), "Phrenology" (Mrs. L. Miles's *Phrenology, and the Moral Influence of Phrenology*), "Mahmoud" (anon., *Mahmoud*), "Georgia Scenes" (Augustus Baldwin Longstreet's *Georgia Scenes*), and "The Tea Party" (anon., *Traits of the Tea Party*). Poe is probably the author of an advertisement for Thomas R. Dew's address, printed on the cover:

ADVERTISEMENT.

The Number of the Messenger now issued, has been delayed beyond its usual time, through the Proprietor's desire of publishing Professor Dew's Address. To counterbalance this delay, 16 pages of *extra* matter are given. The April Number (which will be speedily put to press) will contain, therefore, 16 pages *less* than usual.

PROFESSOR DEW'S ADDRESS.

☞Will be issued simultaneously with the present Number of the Messenger, a pamphlet edition of Mr. Dew's Address, which the Publisher proposes to dispose of at 25 cents per copy, or 25 copies for $5.☜

BEFORE 29 MARCH. MACON, GEORGIA. Washington Poe writes Poe (Poe to William Poe, 12 April 1836).

29 MARCH. AUGUSTA, GEORGIA. William Poe writes Poe, enclosing $50 for Maria Clemm (Poe to William Poe, 12 April 1836).

CA. 30 MARCH. RICHMOND. Poe writes Washington Poe (Poe to William Poe, 12 April 1836).

4 APRIL. RICHMOND. White writes Beverley Tucker: "I have just been introduced to Mr. [George] Bancroft. He wishes me to introduce him to Poe (which I have promised to do in the morning) who he says has unintentionally done him some injustice in my last No.—He has all the appearance of a gentleman,—and it strikes me he is one" (Vi–W–TC).

[In a review of Francis L. Hawks's *Ecclesiastical History* in the March *Messenger*, Poe criticized George Bancroft for intimating that the Colony of Virginia had been guilty of "disloyalty" during the Protectorate of Oliver Cromwell. In the April *Messenger* Poe apologized in an editorial on "The Loyalty of Virginia": "Since the publication of our remarks, a personal interview with Mr. Bancroft, and an examination, especially, of one or two passages in his History, have been sufficient to convince us that injustice (of course, unintentional) has been done that gentleman, not only by ourselves, but by Dr. Hawks and others."]

8 APRIL. NEW BERN, NORTH CAROLINA. The *Newbern Spectator* reprints the *New York Evening Star's* notice of the February *Messenger*: "The editor [Poe] is rather hard on 'Paul Ulric.' We make no comment except that the room appropriated to this subject might have been better occupied. The best and most decided humorous article, though its plan is not original, is the collection of autographs of some of our American authors, Halleck, Irving, &c."

8 APRIL. PHILADELPHIA. In the *Philadelphia Gazette* Willis Gaylord Clark attacks Poe:

The last number of the Southern Literary Messenger is very readable and respectable. Professor Dew's address is the best article in it, and was worth delaying the number for its insertion. The contributions to the Messenger are much better than the original matter. The critical department of this work,—much as it would seem to boast itself of impartiality and discernment,—is in our opinion, decidedly *quacky*. There is in it a great assumption of acumen, which is completely unsustained. Many a work has been slashingly condemned therein, of which the critic himself could not write a page, were he to die for it. This affectation of eccentric sternness in criticism, without the power to back one's suit withal, so far from deserving praise, as some suppose, merits the strongest reprehension.

9 APRIL. NEW YORK. Theodore S. Fay makes a satirical reply to Poe in the *New-York Mirror:*

☞Those who have read the notices of American books in a certain "southern" monthly which is striving to gain notoriety by the loudness of its abuse, may find amusement in the sketch, in another page, entitled "The Successful Novel." The "Southern Literary Messenger" knows ☞ *by experience* ☞ what it is to write a success*less* novel.☞

The *Mirror* publishes a squib ("The Successful Novel!!") in the style of Poe's "Lion-izing," in which Poe is given the name Bulldog and the *Messenger* the title *Passenger*.

[A part of the controversy that led Poe to satirize Fay's *Norman Leslie* in his "Mystification" (Pollin [1972a], pp. 111–30).]

11 APRIL. DISTRICT OF COLUMBIA. The *Georgetown Metropolitan* reprints Poe's "To Helen."

12 APRIL. RICHMOND. Poe writes William Poe: "A press of business has hitherto prevented my replying to your kind letter of the 29th March, enclosing $50 to Mrs. Clemm. Your . . . assistance so frequently manifested, is . . . appreciated by myself as well as by her. . . . On the day before receiving your letter I wrote to Washington Poe, Macon, in reply to

a favor of his. . . . He has become a subscriber to the *Messenger*. I hope you have received our March number. That for April will follow, I hope, soon" (*L*, 1:88).

12 APRIL. Maria Clemm writes William Poe: "Edgar, a few days since, handed me a note for $50, for which, I learn, I am indebted to your kindness. Accept my sincere gratitude. Will you have the goodness to present to your lady my respects" (Woodberry, 1:378).

12 APRIL. Poe replies to Mrs. Lydia H. Sigourney, the popular authoress of Hartford, Connecticut, who had complained that the review of her *Zinzendorff, and Other Poems* in the January *Messenger* was unduly severe:

At the request of Mr. T. W. White, I take the liberty of replying to your letter of the 6th ult. . . . To yourself, personally, we commit our review, with a perfect certainty of being understood. That we have evinced any "severity amounting to unkindness" is an accusation of which you will, I sincerely hope, unhesitatingly acquit us. . . . for the last six months, the Editorial duties have been undertaken by myself. Of course, therefore, I plead guilty to all the criticisms of the Journal during the period mentioned (*L*, 1:89–90).

12 APRIL. NEW YORK. In the *Commercial Advertiser* William Leete Stone reprints Willis Gaylord Clark's attack on Poe from the *Philadelphia Gazette* of 8 April and adds his own barbs:

We are entirely of opinion with the Philadelphia Gazette in relation to the Southern Literary Messenger, and take this occasion to express our total dissent from the numerous and lavish encomiums we have seen bestowed upon its critical notices. Some few of them have been judicious, fair and candid; bestowing praise and censure with judgment and impartiality; but by far the greatest number, of those we have read, have been flippant, unjust, untenable and uncritical. The duty of the critic is to act as judge, not as enemy, of the writer whom he reviews; a distinction of which the Zoilus of the Messenger seems not be aware. It is possible to review a book, severely, without bestowing opprobrious epithets upon the writer: to condemn with courtesy, if not with kindness. The critic of the Messenger has been eulogized for his scorching and scarifying abilities, and he thinks it incumbent upon him to keep up his reputation in that line, by sneers, sarcasm, and downright abuse; by straining his vision with microscopic intensity in search of faults, and shutting his eyes, with all his might, to beauties. Moreover, we have detected him, more than once, in blunders quite as gross as those on which it was his pleasure to descant.

15 APRIL. NEW BERN, NORTH CAROLINA. The *Newbern Spectator* praises the March *Messenger*: "One circumstance we cannot but congratulate the Editor upon—viz. the apparent relinquishment of unnecessary and cruel severity in the critical department. Who is there, that, if maimed he must

be, would not prefer the infliction from a polished instrument in the hands of a gentlemanlike and feeling operator, rather than from a rusty cleaver, in the hands of a practiced, but unfeeling, smithfield butcher?"

22 APRIL. The *Newbern Spectator* on its front page reprints from the *London Court Journal* a comic tale entitled "You Can't Marry Your Grandmother!" by Thomas Haynes Bayly.

[Mabbott (1978, 3:884) thought that Poe's "The Spectacles" might owe something to a farce *You Can't Marry Your Grandmother*, by Bayly, first performed in London on 1 March 1838. Poe may have seen this short-story version by Bayly either in the *London Court Journal* or in an American periodical such as the *Spectator*.]

23 APRIL. HARTFORD, CONNECTICUT. Mrs. Lydia H. Sigourney writes Poe:

Please to accept my thanks for your letter of the 12th. . . . I am happy to discover the present Editor of my favorite periodical, and also to perceive how much it profits by the guidance of that powerful pen, whose versatile and brilliant creations, I have often admired. . . . The contents of a volume of poems, published in 1814 & selected by a friend from journals, written in early youth, without a thought of publication, & another in 1821, were composed before I had heard of Mrs. Hemans, and likewise one of 1827,—most of whose poems were in existence, before I had enjoyed the pleasure of perusing any of hers,—can therefore not be classed as imitations of that pure model (W, 17:33–35).

BEFORE 26 APRIL. RICHMOND. White writes John Pendleton Kennedy (Kennedy to Poe, 26 April 1836).

26 APRIL. BALTIMORE. John Pendleton Kennedy writes Poe that James H. McCulloch, the attorney for William Clemm's children by his first wife, and he "had a long talk, the result of which was to show me that the heirs of Wm. Clemm have no claim to anything. There were debts, advances—and I know not what—that had utterly extinguished the claim of W. Clemm himself. . . . I believe he [Hubard] is in Norfolk and my picture perhaps is with him. . . . I heartily rejoice to see you thriving so well. Tell Mr. White that I recd. his letter informing me of his daughter's coming to Baltimore but was in Washington on the day he had named for her arrival" (W, 17:32–33).

AFTER 28 APRIL. RICHMOND. The April *Messenger* publishes Poe's note on "MSS. of Benj. Franklin," note to "Genius," "A Tale of Jerusalem," "Editorial" ("The Loyalty of Virginia" and a comment on "Chief Justice Marshall"), "Maelzel's Chess-Player," filler ("Lucian calls unmeaning verbosity, anemonae verborum . . ."), note on T. S. Fay's *Norman Leslie*, introduction to the "Supplement," and two critical notices: "Drake-Halleck" (Joseph Rodman Drake's *The Culprit Fay, and Other Poems* and Fitz-Greene Halleck's *Alnwick Castle, with Other Poems*) and "Brunnens of Nassau" (anon., *Bubbles from the Brunnens of Nassau*).

[In his "Drake-Halleck" review Poe replied to the attacks of T. S. Fay, W. G. Clark, and W. L. Stone and asserted that "it has been our constant endeavor, since assuming the Editorial duties of this Journal, to stem, with what little abilities we possess, a current so disastrously undermining the health and prosperity of our literature. . . . Mr. C. [Clark] has a right to think us *quacky* if he pleases. . . ." Stone's charges Poe answered in detail. "Slavery" (a review of William Drayton's *The South Vindicated . . .* and J. K. Paulding's *Slavery in the United States*) in this issue is the work of Beverley Tucker. Rosenthal, pp. 29–38, argued for Poe's authorship. Poe dedicated his *Tales of the Grotesque and Arabesque* to William Drayton. "Some Ancient Greek Authors," also in the April *Messenger*, has been assigned to Poe by Benjamin Blake Minor (p. 42), Margaret Alterton (p. 106), Campbell (1936: 487–88), Jackson (1933: 258–67; 1934a: 368), and Hull (p. 121).]

The Supplement includes these testimonials:

. . . a *jeu d'esprit* from Mr. Poe—some of the reviews—and a page or two of descriptions—together with a very few metrical lines—make the sum total of light reading. . . . The reviews are, as usual, piquant and lively, and in that style which will teach writers to value the praise and dread the censures of the critic.— *Charlottesville Advocate*, quoting the *Richmond Compiler*.

Epimanes.—This is one of Poe's queerities. He takes the reader back in supposition to the city of Antioch, in the year of the world 3830, and in that peculiar style, which after all must be called *Poe-tical*, because it is just that and nothing else, he feigns the enactment of a real scene of the times before your eyes. The actors "come like shadows, so depart,"—but yet assume a most vivid reality while they stay. We hope this powerful pen will be again similarly employed.

"To Helen" is a pretty little gem, and from the same mine. It shall glisten in the Patriot ere long. . . . Then follow *"Critical Notices."* These are written by POE. They are few and clever. The sledge-hammer and scimetar are laid aside, and not one poor devil of an author is touched, except one "Mahmoud," who is let off with a box on the ear for plagiarism. The review of "Georgia Scenes" has determined us to buy the book. The extracts are irresistible.—*Baltimore Patriot*.

Of the value of the [reading] matter, or rather of its value in comparison with such ephemera as those just mentioned [*Paul Ulric* and *Norman Leslie*], it is of course unnecessary to say much. . . . *Epimanes*. By Edgar A. Poe—an historical tale in which, by imaginary incidents, the character of Antiochus Epiphanes is vividly depicted. It differs essentially from all the other tales of Mr. Poe. Indeed no two of his articles bear more than a family resemblance to one another. They all differ widely in matter, and still more widely in manner. *Epimanes* will convince all who read it that Mr. P. is capable of even higher and better things.

To Helen—by the same author—a sonnet full of quiet grace—we quote it in full. . . . The *Critical Notices* maintain their lofty reputation. . . .—*Norfolk Herald.*

. . . its editor wields the gray goose quill like one who knows what he is about, and who has a right to. Commend us to the literary notices of this Magazine for genius, spice and spirit. Those which are commendatory, are supported by the real merit of the books themselves; but woe seize on the luckless wights who feel the savage skill with which the editor uses his tomahawk and scalping knife. The fact is, the Messenger is not given to the mincing of matter—what it has to say is said fearlessly.—*Cincinnati Mirror.*

Smarting under Criticism.—Fay can't bear criticism. The Southern Literary Messenger cut him up sharply—and Fay has retorted—evincing that the sting rankles. A pity.—[John Neal?] *Boston Galaxy.*

There is one department which we admire—the editorial criticisms. Racy, pungent, and reasonable, the editor writes as one disposed to test the true elements of authorship, and to weigh pretentions with achievements in the opposite scale. He has gently, yet with almost too daring a hand, taken apart the poetical attire of two or three ladies, whose writings have long been ranked among the better specimens of American poetry. . . . American prose writers and novelists are led under this keen critic's knife, as sheep to the slaughter. In the name of literature we thank Mr. White for his criticisms, that must purify the literary, as lightning does the natural atmosphere.—*Natchez Christian Herald.*

We are struck, in the *Messenger*, with this good point: the extent of literary intelligence which it affords, by an unusual number of critical notices of new publications, is exceedingly well judged. Its criticisms, too, are in a sounder and more discriminating taste, than that which infects the Magazines of the North, turning them all into the mere vehicles of puffery for each man's little set of associates in scribbling—and partners in literary iniquity. . . . its Editorial articles are decidedly the best that it contains. They seem to be almost uniformly good.—*Columbia (Ga.) Times.*

The critiques are particularly good, and evidence a mind feelingly alive to the literary reputation of our country. The collection of autographs will be examined with much interest.—*Washington Sun.*

The Critical Notices are peculiarly meritorious and sensible. The Messenger is now under the editorial guidance of Edgar A. Poe, a gentleman highly distinguished for his literary taste and talent.—*Tuscaloosa Flag of the Union.*

We miss the racy and condemnatory criticism that distinguishes the work [in the March issue], and which has been favorable to the production of good books.—[Philadelphia] *U.S. Gazette.*

That Mr. Poe, the reputed editor of the Messenger, is a gentleman of brilliant genius and endowments, is a truth which I believe, will not be controverted by a large majority of its readers. For one, however, I confess, that there are occasionally manifested some errors of judgment—or faults in taste—or whatever they may be called, which I should be glad to see corrected. I do not think, for example, that such an article as "the Duc De L'Omelette," in the number under consideration, ought to have appeared. That kind of writing, I know, may plead high precedents in its favor; but that it is calculated to produce effects permanently injurious to sound morals, I think will not be doubted by those who reflect seriously upon the subject. Mr. Poe is too fond of the wild—unnatural and horrible! Why will he not permit his fine genius to soar into purer, brighter, and happier regions? Why will he not disenthral himself from the spells of German enchantment and supernatural imagery? There is room enough for the exercise of the highest powers, upon the multiform relations of human life without descending into the dark mysterious and unutterable creations of licentious fancy. When Mr. Poe passes from the region of shadows, into the plain practical dissecting room of criticism, he manifests great dexterity and power. He exposes the imbecility and rottenness of our *ad captandum* popular literature, with the hand of a master. The public I believe was much delighted with the admirable scalping of "Norman Leslie," in the December number, and likewise of Mr. Simms' "Partisan," in the number for January; and it will be no less pleased at the caustic severity with which the puerile abortion of "Paul Ulric" is exposed in the present number. . . . The Review of "Rienzi," too, the last novel of Bulwer, is written in Mr. Poe's best style,—but I must be permitted to dissent *toto cœlo* from his opinion, that the author of that work is unsurpassed as a novelist by any writer living or dead.—There is no disputing about tastes, but according to my poor judgment, a single work might be selected from among the voluminous labors of Walter Scott, worth all that Bulwer has ever written, or ever will write—and this I believe will be the impartial verdict of posterity . . . The notices . . . are all very spirited articles, and are greatly superior to papers of the same description in the very best monthly periodicals of our country. The last article "Autography" is not exactly to my taste, though there are doubtless many who would find in it food for merriment . . . . there is a deep poetical inspiration about Mr. Poe's "Valley Nis," which would be more attractive if his verses were smoother, and his subject matter less obscure and unintelligible. Mr. Poe will not consent to abide with ordinary mortals.—A correspondent "X. Y. Z." in the *Richmond Compiler*.

["The Richmond papers were all friendly to the *Messenger*; but the *Compiler* particularly so. It was then edited by Gallagher [John Gallaher] and also had a correspondent, X. Y. Z., whose observations upon the *Messenger* were fair, discriminative and independent. They probably had some influence. I think X. Y. Z. was Judge John Robertson, the author of 'Riego, or the Spanish Martyr' " (Minor, p. 50). See also Bondurant, pp. 146, 169–70, 234.]

Our critical correspondent of the 22d, is not borne out, in some of his remarks, by public opinion. We allude to his observations on the *Duc de L'Omelette*, and Mr. Poe's *Autography*. These articles are eliciting the highest praise from the highest quarters. Of the Duc de L'Omelette, the Baltimore American, (a paper of the first authority and hitherto opposed to Mr. P.) says: "The Duc de L'Omelette, by Edgar A. Poe, is one of those light, spirited, fantastic inventions, of which we have had specimens before in the Messenger, betokening a fertility of imagination, and power of execution, that would, under a sustained effort, produce creations of an enduring character." The Petersburg Constellation copies the entire "*Autography*," with high commendations, and of the Duc de L'Omelette, says, "of the lighter contributions, of the diamonds which sparkle beside the more sombre gems, commend us, thou spirit of eccentricity! to our favorite, Edgar A. Poe's 'Duc de L'Omelette,' the best thing of the kind we ever have, or ever expect to read." These opinions seem to be universal. In justice to Mr. Poe, and as an offset to the remarks of our correspondent, we extract the following notice of the February number from the National Intelligencer.—*Richmond Compiler*.

"The Duc de L'Omelette" . . . is one of the best things of the kind we have ever read. *Mr. Poe* has great powers, and every line *tells* in all he writes. He is no spinner-out of long yarns, but chooses his subject, whimsically, perhaps, yet originally, and treats it in a manner peculiarly his own. . . . "Palæstine" is a useful article, containing geographical, topographical, and other statistical facts in the history of that interesting country, well put together and valuable as a reference. . . . [His] "Valley Nis" [is] characteristically wild, yet sweetly soft and smooth in measure as in mood. . . . In the "Editorial Department," we recognise the powerful discrimination of *Mr. Poe*. The dissection of "Paul Ulric," though well deserved, is perfectly savage. *Morris Mattson, Esq.* will hardly write again. This article will as surely kill him as one not half so scalpingly written did poor *Keats*, in the London Quarterly. The notice of *Lieutenant Slidell's* "American in England" we were glad to see. It is a fair offset to the coxcombical article (probably written by *Norman Leslie Fay*) which lately appeared in the New York Mirror, in reference to our countryman's really agreeable work. *Bulwer's* "Rienzi" is ably reviewed, and in a style to beget in him who reads it a strong desire to possess himself immediately of the book itself. . . . The number closes with a most amusing paper containing twenty-five admirably executed *fac simile* autographs of some of the most distinguished of our literati. The equivoque of *Mr. Joseph A. B. C. D. E. F. G. &c Miller* is admirably kept up, and the whimsical character of the pretended letters to which the signatures are attached is well preserved. Of almost all the autographs we can speak on our own authority, and are able to pronounce them capital.—[J. F. Otis in the Washington] *National Intelligencer* [17 February].

The editorial articles are vigorous and original, as usual. . . . . "Epimanes" displays a rich, but extravagant fancy. "To Helen," is pretty and classic, from the same hand—we give it in our next. . . . "Georgia Scenes" makes a capital article, and has excited, in our mind, a great curiosity to see the book.—*Georgetown Metropolitan* [8 April].

. . . Edgar A. Poe's sketch "The Duc de L'Omelette," is the best thing of the kind we have seen from him yet. . . . The Critical Notices are better by far, than those in any other magazine in the country. Paul Ulric is too small game for the tremendous demolition he has received—a club of iron has been used to smash a fly. . . . We agree with all the other critiques except that of Bulwer's Rienzi. The most extraordinary article in the book and the one which will excite most attention, is its tail piece, in which an American edition of Frazer's celebrated Miller hoax has been played off on the American Literati with great success—and better than all, an accurate fac simile of each autograph given along with it. This article is extremely amusing, and will excite more attention than probably any thing of the kind yet published in an American periodical. It is quite new for this part of the world.—*Georgetown Metropolitan.*

"The Duc de L'Omelette, by Edgar A. Poe" is one of those light, spirited, fantastic inventions, of which we have had specimens before in the Messenger, betokening a fertility of imagination and power of execution, that with discipline could, under a sustained effort, produce creations of an enduring character . . . . The best and also the largest portion of the present number of the Messenger is the department of critical notices of books . . . . The number ends with the amusing Miller correspondence, of which we have already spoken.—[William Bose, editor,] *Baltimore American.*

Of the lighter contributions, of the diamonds which sparkle beside the more sombre gems, commend us, thou spirit of eccentricity! forever and a day to our favorite Edgar A. Poe's *Duc de L'Omelette*—the best thing of the kind we ever have or ever expect to read . . . . Of the criticisms, the most are good; that on Mr. Morris Mattson's novel of "Paul Ulric," like a former criticism from the same pen on Fay's "Norman Leslie" is a literal "flaying alive!" a carving up into "ten thousand atoms!" a complete literary annihilation! If Mr. Morris Mattson is either courageous or wise, he will turn upon his merciless assailant as Byron turned upon Jeffrey, and prove that he can not only do better things, but that he deserves more lenient usage! . . . We copy the whole article ["Autography"] as a literary treat . . . .—[Hiram Haines, editor,] *Petersburg Constellation.*

The critical notices are written in a nervous style and with great impartiality and independence.—[Neilson Poe?] *Baltimore Chronicle.*

. . . the Southern Literary Messenger is equal in interest and excellence to any Monthly Periodical in the country . . . .—*Boston Mercantile Journal.*

The review of Paul Ulric is written with great freedom and unusual severity. The reviewer wields a formidable weapon . . . . the article on Autography is a treat of no common order. We have seen nothing of the kind before in an American periodical.—[Hugh Blair Grigsby, editor,] *Norfolk Beacon.*

. . . the 'great feature' of this [February] No. is an Editorial critique on Mr. Morris Mattson's novel of "Paul Ulric," which is tomahawked and scalped after the manner of a Winnebago . . . . The concluding paper . . . embraces the autographs, quaintly introduced and oddly accompanied, of twenty-four of the most distinguished literary personages of our country . . . .—*New Yorker.*

Its criticisms we pronounce to be at once the boldest and most generally correct of any we meet with.—*Natchez Courier.*

T. W. White prints a notice on the cover:

1836

There being a report, in New York and elsewhere, that Mr. Simms, Author of the Partisan, is the Editor of the Messenger, I take this method of stating that such is not the fact.

APRIL? Poe composes "May Queen Ode" for Harriet Virginia Scott, who lives on Main Street (Mabbott [1969], 1:302).

APRIL. CHARLESTON, SOUTH CAROLINA. The anonymous author of "Reminiscences of a Tour to the South-West. Number One" in the *Southern Literary Journal* writes: "We took up a number of the 'Southern Literary Messenger,' a Monthly published in the 'Old Dominion,' and a capital one it is—every way worthy of the place from which it is issued, and of the extensive patronage it has hitherto received."

2 MAY. RICHMOND. Poe writes Beverley Tucker:

At Mr. White's request I write to apologise for the omission of your verses "To a Coquette" in the present number of the Messenger . . . . I must also myself beg your pardon for making a few immaterial alterations in your article on Slavery, with a view of so condensing it as to get it in the space remaining at the end of the number. One very excellent passage in relation to the experience of a sick bed has been, necessarily, omitted altogether. It would give me great pleasure to hear your opinion of the *February*, and of the *April* number of the Messenger—I mean of the Editorial articles . . . . Please present my best respects to Professor Dew . . . . Will you ask Mr Saunders what has become of the article he promised us? (*L*, 1:90–91; Vi–W–TC).

[Here Poe may be referring to the "Slavery" review in the April *Messenger*. See AFTER 28 APRIL.]

3 MAY. AUGUSTA, GEORGIA. Stephen G. Bulfinch writes Poe (Poe to Bulfinch, 8 June 1836).

10 MAY. PHILADELPHIA. Willis Gaylord Clark in the *Philadelphia Gazette* attacks Poe again (Moss [1963], p. 50).

13 MAY. CHARLESTON, SOUTH CAROLINA. The *Charleston Courier*, without mentioning his name, finds in the April *Messenger* Poe's "highly ingenious attempt to shew that MAELZEL'S Chess Player is not a pure machine, but regulated by mind—by a human agent concealed within it."

[This notice was reprinted in the Supplement of the July *Messenger*, 2:523.]

14 MAY. ESSEX COUNTY, VIRGINIA. James M. Garnett writes White, complaining that his lectures have not been printed as promised (ViHi).

KNOW ALL MEN BY THESE PRESENTS, That we *Edgar A. Poe* (and) *Thomas W. Cleland* and acting as governor are held and firmly bound unto *Wyndham Robertson, Lieutenant* Governor of the Commonwealth of Virginia, in the just and full sum of ONE HUNDRED AND FIFTY DOLLARS, to the payment whereof, well and truly to be made to the said acting Governor, or his successors, for the use of the said Commonwealth, we bind ourselves and each of us, our and each of our heirs, executors and administrators, jointly and severally, firmly by these presents. Sealed with our seals, and dated this *16th* day of *May* — 183*6*.

THE CONDITION OF THE ABOVE OBLIGATION IS SUCH, That whereas a marriage is shortly intended to be had and solemnized between the above bound *Edgar A. Poe* and *Virginia E. Clemm* of the City of Richmond. Now if there is no lawful cause to obstruct said marriage, then the above obligation to be void, else to remain in full force and virtue.

Signed, sealed and delivered }
in the presence of }

Cha. Howard

Edgar A Poe SEAL.

Tho. W. Cleland SEAL.

CITY OF RICHMOND, To wit:

This day *Thomas W. Cleland* above named, made oath before me, as *Deputy* Clerk of the Court of Hustings for the said City, that *Virginia E. Clemm* is of the full age of twenty-one years, and a resident of the said City. Given under my hand, this *16* day of *May* 183*6*

Cha. Howard.

Poe's marriage bond

Poe Museum of the Poe Foundation, Inc.

16 MAY. RICHMOND. Poe and Thomas W. Cleland sign a marriage bond for Poe's marriage to Virginia E. Clemm, and Cleland gives an oath that Virginia is "of the full age of twenty-one years." The Reverend Amasa Converse, a Presbyterian minister and the editor of the *Southern Religious Telegraph*, marries Poe and Virginia in the presence of T. W. White and his daughter Eliza, Mr. and Mrs. Thomas W. Cleland, William McFarlane, John W. Fergusson, Mrs. James Yarrington, Maria Clemm, and Jane Foster (*W*, 1:115; Allen, pp. 318–20; Phillips, 1:529–34; Quinn, pp. 253–54).

17 MAY. PETERSBURG, VIRGINIA. Poe and Virginia are entertained by Hiram Haines, Dr. W. M. Robinson, and E. V. Sparhawk (Phillips, 1:532–33; Ostrom [1942], pp. 67–71).

17 MAY. BOSTON. Jared Sparks, Professor of History at Harvard University, writes Poe or White (Poe to Sparks, 23 May 1836).

20 MAY. RICHMOND. The *Richmond Whig* reports: "Married, on Monday May 16th, by the Reverend Mr. [Amasa] Converse, Mr. Edgar A. Poe to Miss Virginia Clemm."

[A similar announcement appeared in the *Richmond Enquirer*. The *Norfolk Herald* also called attention to the marriage (see the Supplement to the July *Messenger*, AFTER 13 JULY).]

21 MAY. NEW YORK. In his tale "The Three Editors of China," in the *New-York Mirror*, Theodore S. Fay criticizes Poe (Pollin [1972a], pp. 111–30).

23 MAY. RICHMOND. Poe writes Jared Sparks: "The M.S.S. from which we publish are not in our immediate possession—but in that of Mr Wm Duane Jr of Philadelphia . . . . I mean to say, of course, that this collection is in the hand-writing of [Benjamin] Franklin. Mr D. transcribes the M.S. for our use" (*L*, 1:91).

23 MAY. White writes Mathew Carey, of Philadelphia, soliciting his aid in increasing the circulation of the *Messenger* (Carey to White, 30 May, TxU–HRCL).

27 MAY. White writes B. Badger, editor of the *New York Weekly Messenger*: "I accidentally fell in with the 'New York Weekly Messenger' this morning,—and was pleased to recognize in its editor one with whom I was once personally acquainted during my sojourn in Boston—which city I most unluckily abandoned, in April 1817, for a residence in this my native place . . . . If . . . I can enter upon 3d Volume [of the *Messenger*]

with 12 or 1300 paying subscribers *all will be well*—otherwise my loss will be very great, for up to the present time my expenses in rearing it to what it is, have greatly run ahead of my actual receipts" (VtMiM).

CA. 27 MAY. The May *Messenger* publishes Poe's note to "MSS of Benj. Franklin," "Sonnet—To Science," "The Corpus Juris," "Alliteration," "Irene" ("The Sleeper"), "Editorial: Lynch's Law," and critical notices: "Spain Revisited" (Alexander Slidell Mackenzie's *Spain Revisited*), "Anthon's Sallust" (Charles Anthon's *Sallust's Jugurthine War . . .*), "Paris and the Parisians" (Frances Trollope's *Paris and the Parisians in 1835*), "Paulding's Washington" (James Kirke Paulding's *A Life of Washington*), "Walsh's Didactics" (Robert Walsh's *Didactics—Social, Literary, and Political*), and "Cooper's Switzerland" (James Fenimore Cooper's *Sketches of Switzerland*). To "Mellen's Poems" (a review of Grenville Mellen's *The Martyr's Triumph; Buried Valley; and other Poems*) Poe adds a footnote: "We have received this notice . . . from a personal friend [J. F. Otis?], in whose judgment we have implicit reliance—of course we cannot deviate from our rules by adopting the criticism as Editorial."

MAY? Poe, Virginia, and Maria Clemm move to a tenement on Seventh Street (Allen, p. 321).

MAY? Elmira Royster, now Mrs. Shelton, meets the Poes: "I remember seeing Edgar, & his lovely wife, very soon after they were married—I met them—I never shall forget my feelings at the time—They were indescribable, almost agonizing" (Sarah Elmira Royster Shelton to Maria Clemm, 22 September 1849; Quinn and Hart [1941], p. 27).

JUNE. CHARLESTON, SOUTH CAROLINA. The *Southern Literary Journal* publishes "The Puffing System," in which the editor Daniel K. Whitaker denounces the "puffing" practiced by American magazines. Whitaker alludes to the *Southern Literary Messenger* (see JULY 1836).

3 JUNE. RICHMOND. Poe writes James H. Causten of Washington, inquiring if he will "investigate and conduct" a claim which Maria Clemm may have against the United States Government for her father's services during the American Revolution (*L*, 1:91–93).

3 JUNE. Poe writes Harper & Brothers (Harper & Brothers to Poe, 19 June 1836).

3 JUNE. Poe signs a printed receipt issued to George W. Pollard of

Hanover C. H., Virginia, acknowledging his payment of five dollars for "Subscription to Vol. II" of the *Messenger* (document in ViRPM).

[The list of subscribers printed on the inside front cover of the June *Messenger* included Pollard and John Jacob Astor of New York.]

4 JUNE. Poe writes Mrs. Lydia H. Sigourney (Sigourney to Poe, 11 June 1836).

BEFORE 7 JUNE. PHILADELPHIA. Robert Montgomery Bird writes Poe (Poe to Bird, 7 June 1836).

CA. 7 JUNE. RICHMOND. Poe writes Sarah Josepha Hale (Poe to Hale, 20 October 1836).

7 JUNE. Poe writes Robert Montgomery Bird: "Can you not aid us—with a single page if no more?" (*L*, 1:93).

7 JUNE. Poe writes James Fenimore Cooper: "At the request of Mr. T. W. White, I take the liberty of addressing you and of soliciting some little contribution to our *Southern Literary Messenger*" (*L*, 1:94).

7 JUNE. Poe writes Fitz-Greene Halleck: "Send us any little scrap in your port-folio—it will be sure to answer" (*L*, 1:94–95).

7 JUNE. Poe writes Washington Irving and solicits a contribution to the *Messenger* (*L*, 2:676–77 [1966]).

7 JUNE. Poe writes John Pendleton Kennedy: "Mr White, having purchased a new house, at $10,000, made propositions to my aunt to rent it to her, and to board himself and family with her . . . . I obtained credit for some furniture &c to the amount of $200, above what little money I had . . . . it appears that the house will barely be large enough for one family, and the scheme is laid aside—leaving me now in debt . . . . I would be greatly indebted to you for the loan of $100 for 6 months . . . . It is our design to issue, as soon as possible, a number of the Magazine consisting entirely of articles from our most distinguished *literati* . . . . Could you . . . send a scrap . . . ? . . . I presume you have heard of my marriage" (*L*, 1:95–96).

7 JUNE? Poe writes James K. Paulding (Paulding to Poe; fragment in *Messenger*, 2 [July 1836]: 517).

AFTER 7 JUNE? NEW YORK. James K. Paulding writes Poe: "I should not hesitate in placing the 'Messenger' decidedly at the head of our periodicals, nor do I hesitate in expressing that opinion freely on all occasions. It is gradually growing in the public estimation, and under your conduct, and with your contributions, must soon, if it is not already, be known all over the land" (*Messenger*, 2 [July 1836]: 517).

AFTER 7 JUNE? NEW YORK? Fitz-Greene Halleck writes Poe: "There is no place where I shall be more desirous of seeing my humble writings than in the publication you so ably support and conduct. It is full of sound, good literature, and its frank, open, independent manliness of spirit, is characteristic of the land it hails from" (*Messenger*, 2 [July 1836]: 517).

AFTER 7 JUNE? NEWBURGH, NEW YORK? Washington Irving writes Poe: "You have given sufficient evidence on various occasions, not only of critical knowledge but of high independence; your praise is therefore of value, and your censure not to be slighted. Allow me to say that I think your article on Drake and Halleck one of the finest pieces of criticism ever published in this country" (*Messenger*, 2 [July 1836]: 517).

[This letter is ascribed to Irving without conclusive evidence. See Watts, pp. 249–51.]

8 JUNE. RICHMOND. Poe writes Stephen G. Bulfinch: "I look, with much interest, for your promised Notice of Mr Perdicaris' Lectures . . . . We would be glad, *indeed*, to publish any thing either from him [Perdicaris] or from yourself. Please give my best respects to my cousins, Robert F. Poe and William" (*L*, 2:677–78 [1966]).

BEFORE 11 JUNE. Poe writes James Frederick Otis, a reporter for the Washington *Daily National Intelligencer* (Otis to Poe, 11 June 1836).

11 JUNE. HARTFORD, CONNECTICUT. Mrs. Lydia H. Sigourney writes Poe: "I send at your request, what I happen to have by me" (*W*, 17:37–38).

11 JUNE. WASHINGTON. James Frederick Otis writes Poe, enclosing autographs for the August installment of Poe's "Autography":

I have just come out of the House of Reps. after a session of Twenty Five Hours—jaded, tired, and nipped. So pray bear this in mind as, you peruse my letter in reply to yours, apological. I pray you think no more of that. As regards all my pieces to you I say with Pope

> "—pray take 'em,—
> I'm all submission: what you'd have 'em, make 'em!"

Indeed I'll do something for you in the course of a week or two, but at present I am "used up."—

Tell our good friend T. W. White so, an you please—I actually could not get health, breath, or time, to do the notice he wrote about.—Shall write him soon.—

Also tell him, Evans relucts [*sic*] at having letters sent him when franked by distant correspondents, these people he does not know. I think this should not be.—

And now a word or two, autographical. I send you a collection.

The GEORGE LUNT is characteristic. He dwells in Newburyport, (Mass.)—is the author of "The Grave of Byron, and other Poems."—a clever fellow, a lawyer & Senator of Mass: about 30 years of age.

The WILLIS is all I can do for you. I have letters of his at my residence at home.—

JAMES BROOKS is something of a literary lion just now. This autograph is perfect.—Residence *Portland Maine.*

The G MELLEN is also good. He sometimes writes it as this—GRENVILLE MELLEN. The enclosed is genuine. His home is Cambridge Mass.

I send you one of Noah & Stone, which I happened to have.

WILLIAM CUTTER is genuine. Resides in Portland Maine. A merchant. Educated man. Young. Fine poet.

P. MELLEN's autograph is genuine. He was Chief Justice of Maine until last year, when he was legally disqualified from holding that office by reason of his having attained the age of 70. A fine writer: in the full vigor of his intellect. *Portland, Maine.*

Miss Gould's is only genuine in the initials.—The rest I believe I added some years ago.—It is at your service. *Newburyport, Mass.*

Mrs. Stephens is editress of the Portland Magazine. *Portland, Maine.*

The Downing is also positively genuine. I will vouch for its being from the pen of *the Veritable.—Downingville. Down East.*

Harrison Gray Otis's autograph may have some value with your readers. I need add nothing as to it. It is a fair specimen, & will be recognised all over the country.

Hoping this dozen will do you some good, and promising you my aid to obtain more . . . (Thomas [1975], pp. 12–13).

AFTER 16 JUNE. RICHMOND. The June *Messenger* publishes Poe's note to "Right of Instruction," note to "MSS. of Benjamin Franklin," "Otto Venius," "Editorial: Right of Instruction," note addressed to the editor of the *Southern Literary Journal*, Charleston, and critical notices: "Letters on Pennsylvania" (*A Pleasant Peregrination through the Prettiest Parts of Pennsylvania* by Peregrine Prolix [William Burke?]), "Armstrong's Notices" (John Armstrong's *Notices of the War of 1812*), "Recollections of Coleridge" (*Letters, Conversations and Recollections of S. T. Coleridge*), "Colton's New Work" (Calvin Colton's *Thoughts on the Religious State of the Country*), "Ups and Downs" (William Leete Stone's *Ups and Downs in the Life of a Distressed Gentleman*), "Watkins Tottle" (Charles Dickens' *Watkins Tottle, and Other Sketches*), "Flora and Thalia" (anon., *Flora and Thalia*).

17 JUNE. NEW BERN, NORTH CAROLINA. The *Newbern Spectator* reviews the May *Messenger* at great length, attacking Poe as a critic: "With the talent available in any particular spot in the southern country, it is out of the question, truly ridiculous to assume the tone of a Walsh, a Blackwood or a Jeffries; and to attempt it, without the means to support the pretension, tends to accelerate the downfall of so indiscreet an attempt."

[In the July *Messenger* Poe reprinted the *Spectator*'s review and replied to it. See AFTER 13 JULY.]

18 JUNE. RICHMOND. Poe writes Peter S. Du Ponceau, a Philadelphia lawyer, soliciting a contribution to the *Messenger* (*L*, 2:678–79 [1966]).

18 JUNE. Poe writes Francis Lieber, a distinguished scholar and professor of political economy at South Carolina College, soliciting a contribution to the *Messenger* (*Emerson Society Quarterly*, No. 51 [2nd Quarter 1968]: pt. 2, p. 51. See also Ostrom [1974], pp. 514–15).

19 JUNE. NEW YORK. Harper & Brothers write Poe:

. . . the MSS. to which you refer have reached you safely, as we learn from Mr. Paulding, who has been so informed we presume by Mr. White.

The reasons why we declined publishing them were threefold. First, because the greater portion of them had already appeared in print—Secondly, because they consisted of detached tales and pieces; and our long experience has taught us that both these are very serious objections to the success of any publication. Readers in this country have a decided and strong preference for works (especially fiction) in which a single and connected story occupies the whole volume, or number of volumes, as the case may be; and we have always found that republications of magazine articles, known to be such, are the most unsaleable of all literary performances. The third objection was equally cogent. The papers are too learned and mystical. They would be understood and relished only by a very few—not by the multitude . . . .

We are pleased with your criticisms generally—although we do not always agree with you in particulars, we like the bold, decided, energetic tone of your animadversions, and shall take pleasure in forwarding to you all the works we publish—or at least such of them as are worthy of your notice . . . . The last number of the Messenger came to hand last evening and in our opinion fully sustains the high character which it has acquired for itself. The notices of the Life of Washington, and Sallust we presume will prove highly pleasing to Mr. Paulding and Professor Anthon (Quinn, pp. 250–51).

28 JUNE. CHARLESTON, SOUTH CAROLINA. Francis Lieber, en route to Puerto Rico for a vacation, writes Poe (*Messenger*, 2 [August 1836]:535–38).

JUNE? NEW YORK AND OTHER CITIES. Charles Anthon, Robert Walsh, Alexander Slidell (later Mackenzie), and Mrs. Lydia H. Sigourney write Poe or White, promising to contribute to the *Messenger* and praising its "Editorial course" (cited by Poe, *Messenger*, 2 [July 1836]: 517)

1 JULY? CHARLESTON, SOUTH CAROLINA. In its "From Our Arm-Chair Department" the *Southern Literary Journal* for July prints an unsigned article on "American Criticism and Critics" by William Gilmore Simms:

A very able periodical published in Virginia, entitled the "Southern Literary Messenger" is the next on our list. It is probably superior in some of its departments to most of those of which we have spoken. It possesses decidedly more originality and is very spirited and racy. Its criticisms betray, in most cases, but little of the spirit of puffing—on the contrary, the editor [Poe] seems resolute to avoid any such charge, and knows no better way than to rush into the opposite extreme. He is harsh in his reviews of many of the popular writers, and allows none of their faults to escape him. He has his favorites, it is true, but his bias seems rather the result of intimacy and habitual deference, than of any mean or mercenary disposition to conciliate. So far from universally puffing, he does not often praise; and he discriminates more justly, where he does so, than all the rest of our periodicals. It is to this journal, however,—which is so resolute to avoid puffing others—that our editor's [Daniel K. Whitaker's] charge more directly refers of puffing itself, by publishing, on a fair proportion of its pages, the friendly opinion of other periodicals of its own pretensions. Justice should have prompted our editor, boldly to have designated the *one* journal, in blaming which, he has left a more general and unjustifiable charge against the whole.

Whitaker remarks:

In this connection, we will say that we are glad to see that the Southern Literary Messenger has abandoned the practice of reprinting in its own pages the voluminous newspaper encomiums that are every month so generously and so justly paid to it . . . . When it [the *Messenger*] intimates, however, that we are "disposed to unite with the Knickerbocker and New-York Mirror, in covert, and therefore unmanly thrusts at the Messenger," we confess, that we are quite unable to understand the meaning of such language . . . . There certainly is no concert between us and the Mirror to injure the Messenger, either by manly or "unmanly thrusts."

[Mott, pp. 664–65, identified the *Journal's* anonymous correspondent as Simms.]

4 JULY. RICHMOND. Poe writes Lewis Cass, a former governor of the Michigan Territory, soliciting an article for the *Messenger* (L, 2:679–80 [1966]).

7 JULY. NEW YORK. The *New York Transcript* attacks Poe (White to William Scott, 25 August 1836).

8 JULY. NEW BERN, NORTH CAROLINA. The *Newbern Spectator* finds the editorial criticisms in the June *Messenger* "unobjectionable and just."

AFTER 13 JULY. RICHMOND. The July *Messenger* publishes Poe's introduction to "MSS. of John Randolph," "Paradise Lost" (a filler), "Letter to B—," note to the "Supplement," and critical notices: "House of Lords" (Anne Grant's *Random Recollections of the House of Lords*), "Sigourney's Letters" (Mrs. Lydia H. Sigourney's *Letters to Young Ladies*), "The Doctor" (Robert Southey's *The Doctor, &c.*), "Raumer's England" (Frederick von Raumer's *England in 1835*, translated by Sarah Austin and H. E. Lloyd), "Memoirs of an American Lady" (Anne Grant's *Memoirs of an American Lady*), "Camperdown" (anon., *Camperdown*), "Erato" (William D. Gallagher's *Erato*), "Life on the Lakes" (anon., *Life on the Lakes*), and "Russia and the Russians" (Leigh Ritchie's *Russia and the Russians*).

In the Supplement Poe reprints the 17 June attack on his literary criticism from the *Newbern Spectator*. He replies: "We are at a loss to know who is the editor of the Spectator, but have a shrewd suspicion that he is the identical gentleman who once sent us from Newbern an unfortunate copy of verses . . . . If the Editor of this little paper does not behave himself we will positively publish his verses." Poe quotes commendatory letters he has received from Halleck, Paulding, and an unnamed author, probably Washington Irving.

[Both Benjamin Blake Minor and Margaret Alterton suggested that Poe might have written the tale "Erostratus" in the July *Messenger* (Minor, p. 49; Alterton, p. 107). Bandy (1982), p. 85, established that William Duane, Jr., was its author.]

The Supplement contains the following extracts from newspapers:

We do not agree by any means with some of its literary *conclusions*. For instance, it is very wide of our opinion on the merits of Halleck . . . but there is a vigor and manliness in most of the papers that appear in the Messenger, which we are most ready to admit, are found *no where* else in American periodicals . . . . its criticisms

. . . though sometimes a little too tomahawkish, have, generally speaking, a great deal of *justice* on their side.—*Augusta Chronicle*, quoting the *New York Courier and Enquirer*.

. . . in spite of the acknowledged ability with which it is conducted, and the admitted talents of its principal contributors (Judge Hopkinson, Professor Dew, Rbt. Greenhow, Heath, Timothy Flint, Edgar Poe, Judge Tucker, Groesbeck, Minor, Carter, Maxwell and a host of others) . . . we find our citizens regard the work with apathy . . . . "The Hall of Incholese" by J. N. McJilton should not have been admitted into the columns of the Messenger. It is an imitation of the Editor's tale of Bon-Bon, and like most imitations, utterly unworthy of being mentioned in comparison with its original . . . . The Editorial Department is (as it invariably is,) full, bold, vigorous and original . . . . Praise and blame are distributed with the soundest discrimination, and with an impartiality, (even in the case of known friends,) which it is impossible not to admire; or to impeach . . . . Two pieces by Mr. Poe are very beautiful; the one entitled "Irene," in especial, is full of his rich and well-disciplined imagination.—*Richmond Compiler*.

The long and able article on Maelzel's Chess Player . . . does credit to the close observation and acute reasoning of its author, who, as the article is published under the editorial head, we infer is the talented editor himself. The question whether or not the chess-player is a pure machine, is, we think, completely put to rest . . . . A Tale of Jerusalem, is one of those felicitous "hits," which are the forte of Edgar A. Poe. The "critical notices" . . . evince the usual ability of the editor in this department; though, what is more to our taste, not quite so caustic, as hitherto.—[William Gwynn, editor,] *Baltimore Gazette*.

The "Hall of Incholese" is decidedly bad, and moreover a direct imitation of Mr. Poe's tale of "Bon-Bon." The Editor should have refused to admit it in the Messenger, if for no other reason, on account of its barefaced flattery of himself . . . . we approve of the Editor's discrimination in not troubling himself, except in rare cases, with those [publications] of foreign countries. Both these pieces [the Drake and Halleck review and "Maelzel's Chess Player"] are unanswerable—and perhaps the two best articles of any kind which have ever appeared in an American Periodical . . . . we have heard the Editor challenges a reply from Maelzel himself, or from any source whatever.—*Norfolk Herald*.

. . . the Editor . . . opens with some spirited and just remarks on the puffing system, as practised in this country towards native writers, and a vindication of his own course.—[William Bose, editor,] *Baltimore American*.

. . . the poetry, judged by the Editor's own standard, that of Ideality, does not rank above the mediocrity. The critical notices . . . are in the Editor's best vein . . . . in general his dissections of "poor devil authors," though apparently severe, are well merited.—[John N. McJilton and T. S. Arthur, editors,] *Baltimore Athenæum*.

Some of the northern critics have intimated that Simms was the editor of the Messenger. This is an error. It is now edited, as we understand, by Edgar A. Poe, formerly of this city, a young gentleman of excellent talents, and untiring industry.—[John N. McJilton and T. S. Arthur, editors,] *Baltimore Athenæum*.

The Southern Literary Messenger is now under the editorial conduct of Edgar A. Poe, Esq. formerly of this city, and has been so, as we understand, since the commencement of the second volume. This gentleman has been, the while, a liberal contributor to its columns, and this thorough identification with a periodical, marked with unusual ability and attended with extraordinary success, must be satisfactory to the editor, and afford ample testimony at the same time that the conduct of the Messenger is in fit and competent hands.—*Baltimore Patriot.*

The [April] number now before us contains a long and ingenious editorial article, on the *modus operandi* of Maelzel's Chess Player.—*Baltimore Patriot.*

"Some Ancient Greek Authors Chronologically Considered [Arranged]," is an article evincing profitably directed research, which we shall copy . . . . The Editorials of the number are ably written, though some pages are devoted to a solution of the mystery of the Automaton Chess-Player, doubtless the correct one, viz. that, after all the scrutiny which it has undergone, there is actually a man concealed in the pretended machinery. We are not sure that the demonstration, conceding it be such, is worth the space it necessarily occupies.

In the matter of Criticism, the Messenger has involved itself in a difficulty with some of our Northern periodicals, either party, as is not unusual in such cases, being just about half right. The Southern Editor has quite too savage a way of pouncing upon unlucky wights who happen to have severally perpetrated any thing below par in the literary line, like the Indian, who cannot realize that an enemy is conquered till he is scalped, and some of the mangled have no more policy than to betray their soreness by attempts at retaliation, under very flimsy disguises, invariably making the matter worse. We think the Messenger often quite too severe, as in the case of 'Norman Leslie,' but still able and ingenuous. The Poems of Drake and Halleck are reviewed this month—neither of them after the fashion of an ardent and awed admirer—but faithfully, fairly, and with discrimination.—*New Yorker* [7 May].

. . . the "Critical Notices" of the Editor have afforded us by no means the least pleasure. They are acute, just, and pungent . . . . it [the *Messenger*] does not hold itself bound, like many of our journalists, to applaud everything that is American . . . .—*Charlottesville Advocate.*

The Editorial Criticisms are spirited but just . . . . Col. Stone's unfortunate "Ups and Downs in the Life of a Distressed Gentleman," is most unsparingly shown up.—*New Yorker.*

. . . a spirit characterizes its editorial department exceedingly gratifying.—*Boston Galaxy.*

The article upon Maelzel's Automaton Chess Player is the most successful attempt we have seen to explain the *modus operandi* of that wonderful production.—[Philadelphia] *United States Gazette.*

The "Editorial Notices" are, to us, the most interesting part of the periodical.—*Methodist Conference Sentinel.*

Let the New York Mirror snarl if it will; there are papers in each Messenger which will outlive all the Norman Leslies, [Willis'] "Pencillings by the Way," and [Morris'] "Wearies my Love of my Letters?" of its erudite editors. Kennel a stag-hound with a cur, and the latter will yelp in very fear. —[Hiram Haines, editor,] *Petersburg Constellation.*

. . . the critical notices are, as usual, able, candid and fearless. —*Winchester Virginian.*

. . . the *critiques* [are] precisely what they should be . . . . —*New Hampshire Patriot.*

Its criticisms are prepared with peculiar justness and acumen . . . . Edgar A. Poe sprinkles his gems among the leaves of the Messenger. —*Louisville City Gazette.*

We felt *then*, as we do *now*, that the editor's criticisms were unnecessarily, perhaps, strictly severe in some instances. The eagle who towers above all other birds, and even dares to look upon the sun, would not, unless hard pressed, condescend to notice the earthly flutterings of a tomtit—he aspires to higher game. —*Oxford* [N. C.] *Examiner.*

It ["Maelzel's Chess Player"] is exceedingly well written and interesting. —*Winchester Virginian.*

The "Critical Notices," though in themselves good, are not generally equal to the Editor's previous efforts. As it was however permitted Homer sometimes to nod, so should the really gifted mind which presides over the Messenger, be allowed occasionally a little repose. —*Richmond Whig.*

There is one article to which we object, the burlesque, or caricature, not criticism, on Fay's "Norman Leslie" . . . . —[B. Badger, editor,] *New York Weekly Messenger.*

The critical notices [in the May issue] are very good for the most part but then we could hardly expect Mr. Poe to be sour ere the honey moon be past. —*Norfolk Herald.*

The *Messenger* reprints the following newspaper notices on the covers:

The Critical Notices have the merit of brevity, (in our estimation always a high one,) and though they exhibit a piquancy not at all times agreeable to the authors reviewed, and somewhat characteristic of the editor, yet we are not prepared to say that they are void of a just discrimination. We have, however, a fraternal regard for Colonel Stone of the New York Commercial Advertiser, and therefore are not altogether satisfied with the manner in which his Ups and Downs has been noticed. But not having read the book, we cannot at present undertake an appeal from the critic's judgment. —*Richmond Compiler.*

The April number of the Southern Literary Messenger gives a very ingenious solution of Maelzel's Automaton Chess Player. The writer denies that it is a *pure* machine, and proves by positions which seem to be incontrovertible, that the automaton is regulated by *mind*, and worked by a man concealed in the interior. The arguments in favor of this opinion, carry with them the force of mathematical truth. —*Richmond Compiler.*

The June number of the Messenger sustains the excellent character of the work. Its critical notices are as ably written, and as fearless as usual, and the contributions are of a superior class.—*Pennsylvanian*.

The poetry of this number is far above mediocrity, and the editorial department evinces the usual talent of the keenly critical but judicious editor.—[William Gwynn, editor,] *Baltimore Gazette*.

The editorial department, which is at present under the supervision of Mr. Edgar A. Poe, heretofore, and now, an able and sprightly contributor to the Messenger, displays, in the main, enlarged and cultivated powers of judgment, much critical acumen, and certainly no ordinary share of boldness in wielding the rod of censure over the devoted author.

While concurring in many of the critical dicta of the editor, we differ very widely from those expressed in the present number, in his review of Drake's and Halleck's poems. He has fallen far short, as we conceive, of doing full justice to these writers. We should have assigned them both a much higher place than is allowed them, in the poetical temple of our country. The "Culprit Fay," a poem by Drake, is, in the opinion of Mr. Poe, quite an inferior and common-place production, altogether destitute of the higher attributes of true poetry. We have been accustomed to regard it as one of the most original poems in our language—a pure and sparkling gem of fancy, exquisitely wrought; but the total absence of human interest, and the deficiency of profound and touching sentiments, will prevent it from being a general favorite.

"The American Flag," another production of the same author, the reviewer thinks, owes its reputation chiefly to our patriotic sympathies and associations. The man who can read it, dispensing even with these aids of national glory and recollection, and not *feel* his heart thrill with deep and stirring emotions of delight and admiration—to him we would say, we envy you not your theories of *ideality*.*

Halleck meets with no better favor at the hands of our critic. His poetry, with some slight exceptions, comes under the ban of a pretty sweeping denunciation.† Here the reviewer, as we think, stands nearly alone in his judgment. The complaint against Halleck is, that he has written too little. All of that little is thought to be excellent in its way. It may be remarked of his poetry, as was said of the ashes of Alexander "it has shrunk to a narrow space, but is worthy of being deposited in a golden urn." Who can forget "Fanny," "The world is bright before thee," "Verses in the Album of an unknown Lady," "The Lines on Drake," "The tribute to Burns," suggested by the rose of Alloway, &c. &c. Halleck's minor pieces are, to our taste, extremely delightful; And his Lyric Muse has occasionally soared, as in "Marco Bozzaris," to "the highest heaven of invention," and displayed her bright and glancing plumes in the sun-light of freedom.

We shall expect to see a host of New York critics tilting at Mr. Poe for his bold disparagement of these twin favorites. His helmet must be made of good metal if he can stand the assault.—*Huntsville Southern Advocate*.

To the *Advocate* notice Poe appends two notes:

*A constituent of the poetical character in which Mr. Poe thinks both Drake and Halleck eminently deficient.

†The Advocate has misapprehended us—we refer our readers to the review in question—(*Ed. Mess.*

One of the distinguishing characteristics is the bold, independent tone of its criticism: a rare virtue in these modern times; and it has ability equal to its fearlessness . . . .—*Philadelphia Saturday News.*

15 JULY. NEW BERN, NORTH CAROLINA. The *Newbern Spectator* calls for Poe's resignation: " 'The way' the [Georgetown?] Metropolitan serves up the late number of the Southern Literary Messenger 'is a caution.' We think that Mr. Poe will soon see the necessity of resigning his chair, or of conforming to the rules of modern criticism. The Proprietor should look to this."

16 JULY. RICHMOND. Poe writes Littleton Waller Tazewell, Governor of Virginia, soliciting a contribution for the *Messenger*: "your Reasons for declining to transmit the instructions of the State Legislature to Mess. Tyler & Leigh" (*L*, 1:97–98).

27 JULY? NEW YORK. B. Badger, editor of the *New York Weekly Messenger*, notices favorably the *Southern Literary Messenger* (letter of White to Badger, 30 July, VtMiM).

29 JULY. NEW BERN, NORTH CAROLINA. The *Newbern Spectator* reprints a part of the July *Messenger* Supplement and replies:

Of the Supplement, however, we must say a word or two, if but to acknowledge, as early as possible, the debt of gratitude which we owe its profound editor, the author of the "Unpublished Drama," having taken "notice" of us in a manner so gentlemanlike and dignified, and so creditable to his own temper and erudition . . . . If this [Supplement] is not a precious treat for the readers of a dignified Monthly, we know not what is! Revelling in puffs, even ad nauseam, which the Messenger has the unexampled meanness to extract from every source, and to republish, yet it cannot permit a single voice to be raised against its errors without descending to scurrility and invective; thus showing conclusively the unfitness of its conductor for the task he has undertaken . . . . A perusal of "Politian, or Scenes from an Unpublished Drama" . . . would have cured us of verse writing, or of acknowledging the authorship of any thing in that way, had we been so inclined, but yet we will consent to father, however unworthy, the "unfortunate copy," if the Messenger will publish it in juxtaposition with the scenes from an Unpublished Drama, as we copied and remarked on them a few months ago . . . . we intend to take an early opportunity to give the Messenger some wholesome advice and some useful hints. We shall not do this either for the purpose of being noticed or of decrying the work, which is already estimated here at a value which we shall not name, notwithstanding the volume of nauseous puffs which accompanies almost every number.

BEFORE 30 JULY? PHILADELPHIA. Perhaps Mathew Carey, a contributor to the *Messenger*, writes Poe (Poe to Carey, 30 July 1836).

30 JULY. RICHMOND. Poe writes Mathew Carey, suggesting a new title for one of Carey's contibutions and referring to other writings by him (*L*, 1:98–99).

EARLY AUGUST? NEW YORK. Either the *Courier and Enquirer* or the *American* replies to an attack on Poe in the *Transcript* of 7 July (White to Scott, 25 August 1836).

2 AUGUST. RICHMOND. Poe writes an unknown correspondent (Ostrom [1981], p. 187).

5 AUGUST. White writes William Scott, proprietor of the *New York Weekly Messenger*, replying to Scott's letter of 3 August: "I have had a great deal of sickness in my office among my best hands, and since the 4th July . . . . Your opinion of the 'Mirror' is not an uncommon one" (VtMiM).

5 AUGUST. NEW BERN, NORTH CAROLINA. The *Newbern Spectator* finds Poe incapable of judging the writings of others, especially Robert Southey's *The Doctor*.

9 AUGUST. RICHMOND. In the *Richmond Compiler* John H. Mackenzie advertises for a partner in his business of selling horses, mules, wagons, drays, etc.

16 AUGUST. White writes William Scott: "If it be not too late, I should like to have you refer, in your preliminary remarks, to the mass of reading there is in the Messenger—and to speak also of the untiring industry and the immense expense it must cost the Publisher to collect together such a quantity of good matter monthly" (VtMiM).

19 AUGUST. The *Compiler* reports that the August *Messenger* "will be issued on Monday morning, 22d inst." and publishes its table of contents.

19 AUGUST. Poe writes Hiram Haines, publisher of the Petersburg, Virginia, tri-weekly *American Constellation*, and sends him an advance copy of the August *Messenger*: "Can you oblige me so far as to look it over and give your unbiassed opinion of its merits and demerits in the 'Constellation'? . . . All after the word *Editorial* is my own. If you copy any thing please take my Review of Willis' 'Inklings of Adventure'—or some other Review" (*L*, 1:99–100).

22 AUGUST. The August *Messenger* publishes Poe's three fillers ("In 'Dodsley's Collection' is an old play . . . ," "Wherever the Inquisition had power . . . ," and "Swift's 'Liliputian [Lilliputian] Ode' is an imitation . . ."), "Israfel," note to "Scenes in Campillo," note to "The Battle of Lodi," "The City of Sin," note to "MSS. of John Randolph," editorial section (including "Right of Instruction" and "Pinakidia"), "Autography," and critical notices: "The Old World and the New" (Orville Dewey's *The Old World and the New*), "Richardson's Dictionary" (Charles Richardson's *A New Dictionary of the English Language*), "Book of Gems" (*The Book of Gems*, edited by S. C. Hall), "South-Sea Expedition" (*Report of the Committee on Naval Affairs*), "Elkswatawa" (James S. French's *Elkswatawa*), "The Virginia Springs" (*Letters Descriptive of the Virginia Springs* by Peregrine Prolix [William Burke?]), "A Year in Spain" (Alexander Slidell Mackenzie's *A Year in Spain*), "Adventures in Search of a Horse" (anon., *The Adventures of a Gentleman in Search of a Horse*), "Lafitte" (Joseph H. Ingraham's *Lafitte: the Pirate of the Gulf*), "Draper's Lecture" (John W. Draper's *Introductory Lecture to a Course of Chemistry and Natural Philosophy*), "Lieber's Memorial" (*Memorial of Francis Lieber*), "History of Texas" (David B. Edward's *The History of Texas*), and "Inklings of Adventure" (N. P. Willis' *Inklings of Adventure*).

25 AUGUST. White writes William Scott: "Courtesy to Mr. Poe whom I employ to edit my paper makes it a matter of etiquette with me to submit all articles intended for the Messenger to his judgment and I abide by his dicta. I have heard there was reply to an attack made on Mr. Poe in the [New York] Transcript of July 7th either in the Enquirer or American. It must have appeared about three weeks ago. Will you do me the favor to call at the office of the American (Enquirer also) and look over their files. If such a piece appeared I should like to see it very much" (VtMiM).

26 AUGUST. The *Richmond Compiler* comments on Poe's review of James S. French's *Elkswatawa* in the August *Messenger*:

In running over some of the critical notices of the last Literary Messenger, we were much edified with a review of a new work, by a Virginian, entitled "ELKSWA-TAWA," in which the critic presents rather a ludicrous outline of the plot and characters. Mr. French himself cannot but be amused at the humorous style of the narrative portion of the criticism, and must admit that he has received several palpable hits. If, however, his sensibility has been wounded, he may find consolation in the reflection, that the best writers of every age have been excoriated by the critics, and have profited by the operation, and by the further reflection, that the critic has been compelled to admit that the "general style is intrinsically good." The criticism may have the effect upon others that it has had upon us—it may induce them to read a portion of the book, if not its whole contents. We were delighted with a scene in which the arts of western electioneering are most humorously depicted.

27 AUGUST. NEW YORK. The *Spirit of the Times* and the *New-Yorker* notice Poe's "Pinakidia" (Pollin [1985], p. 3).

30 AUGUST. RICHMOND. The *Compiler* suggests that Poe's criticism could be toned down:

The August No. of the Southern Literary Messenger has been well received by most of the editorial corps who have noticed it. These commendations may be valued, because they emanate from sources beyond the influence of private friendship; and therefore it is, that suggestions of improvement should be, and we have no doubt will be, duly regarded by the editor and publisher. No periodical in the country has been so successful in obtaining the aid of able and distinguished writers; and the quantity of matter is much greater than need be. We entirely agree with the editor of one of the prints, who thinks a *choice tale* in each number would add to its attraction; as something is due to the tastes of those who have neither time nor relish for the higher grades of literature. Specimens of the writing we refer to, have often been given in the Messenger, but the supply may not be as abundant as needful. The hint, we are sure, is enough to prompt the effort to obtain regular contributions of this sort.

The criticisms are pithy and often highly judicious, but the editors must remember that it is almost as injurious to obtain a character for regular cutting and slashing as for indiscriminate laudation.

BEFORE 2 SEPTEMBER. Poe writes the editor of the *Compiler*:

In a late paragraph respecting the "Southern Literary Messenger," you did injustice to that Magazine—and perhaps your words, if unanswered, may even do it an injury. As any such wrong is far from your thoughts, you will of course, allow the Editor of the Messenger the privilege of reply. The reputation of a young Journal, occupying a conspicuous post in the eye of the public, should be watched, by those who preside over its interests, with a jealous attention, and those interests defended when necessary and when possible. But it is not often possible. Custom debars a Magazine from answering in its own pages (except in rare cases,) contemporary misrepresentations and attacks. Against these it has seldom, therefore, any means of defence—the best of reasons why it should avail itself of the few which, through courtesy, may fall to its lot. I mean this as an apology for troubling you to-day. (*a*)

Your notice of the Messenger would generally be regarded as complimentary—especially so to myself. I would, however, prefer justice to a compliment, and the good name of the Magazine to any personal consideration. The concluding sentence of your paragraph runs thus: "The criticisms are pithy, and often highly judicious, but *the editors* must remember that it is almost as injurious to obtain a character for regular cutting and slashing, as for indiscriminate laudation." The italics are my own. I had supposed you aware of the fact that the Messenger has *but one* editor—it is not right that others should be saddled with demerits belonging only to myself. (*b*) But this is not the point to which I especially object. You assume that the Messenger has obtained a character for regular "cutting and slashing;" or if you do not mean to assume this, every one will suppose that you do—which, in effect, is the same. Were the assumption just, I would be silent, and set immediately about amending my editorial course. You are not sufficiently decided, I think, in saying that a career of "regular cutting and slashing is *almost* as bad as one of indiscriminate laudation." It is infinitely worse—it is horrible. The laudation may proceed from—philanthropy, if you please; but the "indiscriminate cutting and slashing" only from the vilest passions of our nature. But I wish briefly to examine two points—first, is the charge of indiscriminate "cutting and slashing" just, granting it adduced against the Messenger?—and, second, is such charge adduced at all? Since the commencement of my editorship in December last, 94 books have been reviewed. In 79 of these cases, the commendation has so largely predominated over the few sentences of censure, that every reader would pronounce the notices highly laudatory. In 7 instances, viz: in those of The Hawks of Hawk Hollow, The Old World and the New, Spain Revisited, the Poems of Mrs. Sigourney, of Miss Gould, of Mrs. Ellett [Ellet], and of Halleck, praise slightly prevails. In 5, viz: in those of Clinton Bradshaw, The Partisan, Elkswatawa, Lafitte, and the Poems of Drake, censure is greatly predominant; while the only reviews decidedly and harshly condemnatory are those of Norman Leslie, Paul Ulric, and the Ups and Downs.—The "Ups and Downs" alone is *unexceptionably* condemned. Of these facts you may satisfy yourself at any moment by reference. In such case the difficulty you will find, in *classing* these notices, as I have here done, according to the predominance of censure or commendation, will afford you sufficient evidence that they cannot justly be called "indiscriminate."

But this charge of indiscriminate "cutting and slashing" has *never been adduced*—except in 4 instances, while the rigid justice and impartiality of our Journal has been lauded even *ad nauseam* in more than four times four hundred. You should not therefore have assumed that the Messenger had obtained a reputation for this "cutting and slashing"—for the asserting a thing to be famous, is a well known method of rendering it so. The 4 instances to which I allude, are the *Newbern Spectator*, to which thing I replied in July—the *Commercial Advertiser* of Colonel Stone, whose Ups and Downs I had occasion (pardon me) to "use *up*"—the *N. Y. Mirror*, whose Editor's Norman Leslie did not please me—and the *Philadelphia Gazette,* which, being conducted by one of the sub-editors of the Knickerbocker, thinks it its duty to abuse all rival Magazines.

I have only to add that the inaccuracy of your expression in the words—"The August No. of the Southern Literary Messenger has been well received by *most* of the Editorial corps who have noticed it," is of a mischievous tendency in regard to the Messenger. You have seen, I presume, no notices which have not been seen by myself—and you must be aware that there is *not one*, so far, which has not spoken, in the highest terms, of the August number. I cannot, however, bring myself to doubt that your remarks, upon the whole, were meant to do the Messenger a service, and that you regard it with the most friendly feelings in the world. (*c*)

[The *Compiler* printed Poe's letter: see 2 SEPTEMBER.]

2 SEPTEMBER. NEW BERN, NORTH CAROLINA. The *Newbern Spectator* finds fault with Poe's "Israfel" in the August *Messenger*.

We cannot close this imperfect notice without congratulating the readers of the Messenger on the absence of the Puff Department . . . . As the Editor has failed to publish the "unfortunate copy of verses," which he honourably, and with a proper regard for truth, attributed to us, we will convince him that we do not resent his failure and our disappointment.

["Israfel" is reprinted.]

The editor of the *Spectator* then observes: "*Heart-strings of a spirit!* *Admirable conception* [on line 2] . . . . Beautiful! The light[n]ing of heaven pauses to *listen!* [on line 10] . . . This verse is so incomprehensibly beautiful, so purely English, and so perfectly connected with the context, that we know not how to express our admiration [on stanza 4] . . . . With all modesty we suggest that it would improve the sense of this line read thus: One half so childishly" [on line 41].

2 SEPTEMBER. RICHMOND. The *Richmond Compiler* replies to Poe's letter "To the Editor of the Compiler":

(*a.*) The idea that "injury" may accrue to the Messenger, from what we have said, may have arisen from the "jealous attention" above alluded to, but we doubt whether the public will concur in the opinion. At all events, we cannot appreciate that sort of jealousy which deems it proper to defend "reputation" for such slight causes.

(*b.*) We should have thought a critical eye would have observed that this was a mere typographical error. We did not mean to assume that the *editor* had *already* obtained "a character for regular cutting and slashing." We only *warned* him *against* that unenviable sort of reputation. He has chosen to transpose our words, and use the word "indiscriminate" instead of "regular," which makes us say what we did not say. There is surely a vast difference in the import of the terms. "Regular" dissection might be just and proper, from the nature of the subjects reviewed, but "indiscriminate" would imply the indulgence of a savage propensity in all cases whatsoever. The enumeration, therefore, of the cases in which praise predominated, was scarcely necessary to a defence, because this defence is "adduced" against *a charge which was never made by us.* The admission that the reviews of three works were "*harshly* condemnatory," is enough of itself to justify the *warning* which we had the temerity to utter, and the further avowal that Col. Stone's "Ups and Downs," was "*unexceptionably* condemned," would sustain the idea that the laudation *ad nauseam* of the "rigid justice and impartiality" of the editor was not entirely merited. No perfectly dispassionate mind can assent to the proposition that the works thus "harshly" and "unexceptionably" condemned, deserved a total and unqualified reprobation. The thing is not reasonable.

(*c.*) We are not ready to admit the "inaccuracy" of this expression. A single exception is enough to justify the use of the word "most," and that exception, if we remember aright, the Baltimore Chronicle [Neilson Poe?] furnished. We cannot therefore allow the "accuracy" of the intimation that our expression is of a "mischievous tendency in regard to the Messenger."

We make no professions here as to the nature of our "feelings" for that journal. If these have not been rightly understood, it is not probable we can now make them palpable. One thing, however, we will venture to remark in "rigid justice," and that is, that one so sensitive as the editor of the Messenger and so *tolerant* of a difference of opinion, may probably be led to reflect whether *any* provocation should induce the conductor of a grave literary work to censure harshly and "unexceptionably." Those who wield a ready and satirical pen, very rarely consider, that the subjects of their witticisms have nerves as sensitive as their own; and the instance before us shows the necessity of learning patiently to bear as well as "rigidly" to inflict the lash of criticism. It is not probable we shall ever again disturb the current of laudation, even by a hint, having had another confirmation of the truth, that giving advice, even with the best of motives, is rather an unthankful business.

2 SEPTEMBER. Poe writes Harrison Hall, a Philadelphia publisher:

Mr White duly received your letter of the 12th August, and I take the liberty of replying for him. The Latin Grammar and Mr [Basil] Hall's Sketches have come to hand . . . . I have also read the objectionable article in the N. A. Review and agree with you that some personal pique is at the bottom of it. I cannot republish the reply in the Am. D. Advertiser, but, with your leave, I will make it the basis of another notice for the Sep: Messenger . . . . At different times there has appeared in the Messenger a series of Tales, by myself—in all seventeen. They are of a bizarre and generally whimsical character, and were originally written to illustrate a large work "On the Imaginative Faculties." I have prepared them for republication, in book form, in the following manner. I imagine a company of 17 persons who call themselves the Folio Club. They meet once a month at the house of one of the members, and, at a late dinner, each member reads aloud a short prose tale of his own composition. The votes are taken in regard to the merits of each tale. The author of the worst tale, for the month, forfeits the dinner & wine at the next meeting. The author of the best, is President at the next meeting. The seventeen tales which appeared in the Messr are supposed to be narrated by the seventeen members at one of these monthly meetings. As soon as each tale is read—the other 16 members criticise it in turn—and these criticisms are intended as a burlesque upon criticism generally. The author of the tale adjudged to be the worst demurs from the general judgment, seizes the seventeen M.SS upon the table, and, rushing from the house, determines to appeal, by printing the whole, from the decision of the Club, to that of the public. The critical remarks, *which have never been published*, will make about ¼ of the whole . . . .

I refer you for the reputation of these tales to the covers of the 1rst & 2d vols. Lit Messr—A mass of eulogy, in the way of extracts from papers, might be appended if necessary, *such as have never appeared to any volume in the country* . . . . My object in stating the nature of these tales &c is to ascertain if you, or any bookseller of your acquaintance, would feel willing to undertake the publication (*L*, 1:103–05).

8 SEPTEMBER. NEW YORK. In the *Commercial Advertiser* W. L. Stone replies to Poe's letter in the *Richmond Compiler* of 2 September:

The natural and necessary inference is, that the charge [of cutting and slashing] was brought in the Commercial Advertiser because the editor of the Messenger had had occasion to *"use up"* a volume entitled "Ups and Downs"; this inference involving a charge of personal and interested feelings against one of the editors of the Commercial. The gentleman of the Messenger would have shown more candor if he had stated, as was the fact, that the "charge" was adduced in the Commercial Advertiser, long before "Ups and Downs" was either published or printed. So that if personal feelings had any influence in the matter, it must have been the editor of the Messenger who was governed by them, in his review of "Ups and Downs."

8 SEPTEMBER. CHARLESTON, SOUTH CAROLINA. The *Charleston Courier* acknowledges the receipt of the August *Messenger* "with a galaxy of bright things and bright names. Articles from . . . EDGAR A. POE, its gifted and versatile editor . . . . The critical notices . . . evince generally great critical discrimination, although we think that in seeking to avoid the common fault of heaping indiscriminate and injudicious praise on books of American parentage, there is sometimes a degree of harshness, bordering on disparagement."

9 SEPTEMBER. CANONSBURG, PENNSYLVANIA. The Franklin Literary Society of Jefferson College elects Poe an honorary member:

> No. 1556   Sept. 9th, 1836.
> A. E. [*sic*] Poe [was elected] Honorary Member.
> Nourse Semple & Thompson Jr., comm [committee].
> (Wells, p. 3; Ostrom [1981], pp. 187–88).

12 SEPTEMBER. DISTRICT OF COLUMBIA. The *Georgetown Metropolitan* finds that Poe's "critical notices in the *Messenger* are among the best pages of the book [magazine]. There is a manliness, candour, and critical ability and consciousness about them, to our mind of such high value in this department of a work, that we would forgive fifty other sins for such excellencies here alone."

16 SEPTEMBER. NEW BERN, NORTH CAROLINA. The *Newbern Spectator* reprints a *Camden (S. C.) Journal* notice of the *Messenger*: *"Throughout* the labors of the Editor, there is, it appears to us, *a vein of pedantry and sarcasm* which we confess we have not taste enough to admire."

21 SEPTEMBER. DISTRICT OF COLUMBIA. The *Georgetown Metropolitan* begins to reprint Poe's "Autography"; additional installments appear in the 7, 10, and 12 October issues.

AFTER 24 SEPTEMBER. RICHMOND. The September *Messenger* includes Poe's note to "Cromwell," note to "Memoirs of Mrs. Hemans" (a selection from advance sheets of *Memorials of Mrs. Hemans*), "Editorial," and critical notices: "Philothea" (Lydia Maria Child's *Philothea: A Romance*), "Sheppard Lee" (Robert Montgomery Bird's *Sheppard Lee: Written by Himself*), and "Hazlitt's Remains" (*Literary Remains of the Late William Hazlitt*, by his son, E. L. Bulwer, and Sergeant Talfourd). The following notice appears: "The illness of both Publisher and Editor will, we hope, prove a sufficient apology for the omission of many promised notices of new books."

[Both the *Georgetown Metropolitan* (7 October) and the *Newbern Spectator* (4 November) noticed the apology. White also planned a visit to New York in early October (White to William Scott, 23 September, VtMiM). Pollin (1985), pp. 439–41, questions Poe's authorship of "The Rainbow," a filler in this issue.]

26 SEPTEMBER. Poe writes the Reverend Samuel Gilman, a Unitarian minister of Charleston, South Carolina (Ostrom [1981], p. 188).

3 OCTOBER OR BEFORE. NEW YORK. Saunders and Otley, British publishers with a branch in New York City, write Poe (Johnston to White, 4 October 1836).

4 OCTOBER. Edward W. Johnston, a journalist and librarian, writes White, urging Poe to complete the writing of his tales:

By yesterday's post I sent you the proofs of my article on Classical Bibliography. You will find them corrected with great exactness.

I am likely to have upon my hands for a few days a little leisure, and shall probably employ a part of it in writing you another article or two. They shall be sent you—that is if I like them well enough when finished about the end of this week.

Have the goodness to tell Mr Poe that I had yesterday a second conversation with Saunders and Otley upon the affair of his MS, that they seem much disposed to become the publishers, here and in England, but cannot apparently take it upon themselves to decide for their paternal house abroad. They were anxious, therefore, to have the finished MS, in order to send it out by the next packet. To this general effect they had written him (Mr. P.). I told them that I felt sure that the writing of the tales in their final form had yet made too little progress to render so speedy a transcription of the Copy possible and that, as the months of Nov. and Decr. are those most advantageous in European publication, they had better send back the MS. in their hands, which may be of much importance to the rapid finishing of the work. This they at once promised to do, and Mr P. will receive it either through your bookseller Smith, or by the regular mode of conveyance. Tell him, further that I would advise him to send back the finished MS with all possible expedition in time enough for one of the earliest packets. Give him, at the same time, my sincere compliments and good wishes.

I am little likely to fix myself here, I think. I find the literary Journals—with which alone I have desired to connect myself—in such a wretched condition, both as to their management and resources. Political employment—the only alternative—I cannot willingly accept, unless it were in a region where other interests and more respectable principles prevail. It is probable that I shall finally accept a very fair offer made to me at Washington, in behalf of a Literary enterprize which is to be organized, in the South, this winter.

Give my very friendly respects to Mrs. White, and believe me very truly / Yours / Ed. W. Johnston. / PS. Direct any thing which you may have occasion to send me, to Mr. Ed. W. Johnston, No 30, Chapel Street, N. York. I shall probably go South in a week or 10 days. / E. W. J. (TxU–HRCL).

7 OCTOBER. DISTRICT OF COLUMBIA. The *Georgetown Metropolitan* reports that "The Southern Literary Messenger for September has just come out having been delayed by the sickness of both editor and publisher."

BEFORE 17 OCTOBER. RICHMOND. Poe writes Thomas R. Dew, of the College of William and Mary (Dew to Poe, 17 October 1836).

17 OCTOBER. WILLIAMSBURG. Thomas R. Dew writes Poe:

If you will read over my address you will be enabled to draw up a few editorial remarks of the character you desire. Our College is the oldest in the Union save one and older than that, if we might date back to the establishment of an Academy in this city of some note prior to the erection of the College. The numbers at Wm & Mary have rarely been great, & yet she has turned out more useful men, more great statesmen than any other college in the world in proportion to her alumni. The high political character of old Va. is due to this college. Some colleges may have equalled ours in Physics and Mathematics, but few have in Morals and Politics, & it is these last subjects that give the highest finish to the mind, and raise it to its greatest elevation. The scenery here, the hospitable population, the political atmosphere all conspire to give a utilitarian character to the mind of the student. Hence the alumni of this college have always been characterized by *business* minds & great efficiency of character. In conclusion I will say, that we never had more brilliant prospects than now, & I have no doubt that our numbers this year will be as great as have ever been known in this college. An editorial of the kind you mention would be highly gratifying to the friends of the college, & would be of great service . . . . Be sure you let me have the proof sheets as early as possible by steam boat or mail (*W*, 17:39–40).

BEFORE 20 OCTOBER. BOSTON. Sarah Josepha Hale addresses a letter to "W. G. Simms Esqr, Editor of the S. L. Messenger" (Poe to Hale, 20 October 1836).

20 OCTOBER. RICHMOND. Poe writes Sarah Josepha Hale:

I was somewhat astonished to day at receiving a letter addressed to "W. G. Simms Esqr, Editor of the S. L. Messenger" . . . . it is difficult to reply to one portion of your letter—that touching the prose article desired. If however, it was your wish that *I* should furnish it, I am grieved to say that it will be impossible for me to make a definite promise just now, as I am unfortunately overwhelmed with business, having been sadly thrown back by late illness . . . . I shall look anxiously for the "Ladies' Wreath." I am surprised and grieved to learn that your son (with whom I had a slight acquaintance at W. Point) should have been vexed about the autographs. So mere nonsense it was hardly worth while to find fault with. Most assuredly as regards yourself, Madam, I had no intention of giving offence—in respect to the "Mirror" I am somewhat less scrupulous (*L*, 1:105–106).

31 OCTOBER. WILLIAMSBURG. Thomas R. Dew writes Poe that he is returning the proof sheets of his address:

I wish you to have 50 additional copies struck off for me, which I wish to distribute. As soon as you have finished the publication send down the pamphlets to the students, & may I suggest the propriety of sending a copy of your next Messenger to each one of the committee, with the publisher's compliments. Little attentions of this kind are always flattering, & I should like to see the Messenger circulated among our young men. We have now more than 90 students, a number that perhaps has never been equalled so early in the course and the best possible spirit persists among them (MB–G. Dew's "Address Delivered at . . . William and Mary" was printed in the *Messenger*, 2 [November 1836]: 760–69).

OCTOBER? NEW YORK. White meets Charles Anthon, a Columbia College professor, and James Kirke Paulding (White to Tucker, 19 January 1837).

4 NOVEMBER. NEW BERN, NORTH CAROLINA. The editor of the *Newbern Spectator* borrows a copy of the September *Messenger* to write a review.

After waiting through the months of September and October without having received a number of the Messenger, we began to think that the Editor had "cut" us in consequence of our attempts to restrain his imprudence in the literary line. We went, therefore, to one of the subscribers in the town, and obtained the September number, that we might judge of the effects of the truths which we had told the Editor. We are happy to add, that they are visible in the increased moderation of the "Critical Notices," although there is yet just cause for a little "fault-finding," which we forbear this week on account of the plea of indisposition which the Editor puts in.—Even the "cut direct" will not prevent us hereafter from informing our readers of the merits of the Messenger.

[The *Spectator* received a copy of the October *Messenger* on 25 November.]

AFTER 8 NOVEMBER. RICHMOND. The October *Messenger* publishes Poe's footnote to Lindley Murray's poem "To My Wife," "Noms de Guerre," "Bibles," and critical notices: "The Swiss Heiress" (Susan Rigby Morgan's *The Swiss Heiress; or The Bride of Destiny*), "Roszel's Address" (*Address delivered . . . by S. A. Roszel*), "Wraxall's Memoirs" (Sir N. W. Wraxall's *Posthumous Memoirs of his Own Time*), "American Almanac" (*The American Almanac . . . for the Year 1837*), "Cooper's Switzerland" (James Fenimore Cooper's *Sketches of Switzerland*), "Professor Dew's Address" (*An Address . . . by Thomas R. Dew*), "Memorials of Mrs. Hemans" (Henry F. Chorley's *Memorials of Mrs. Hemans*), "Dr. Haxall's Dissertation" (Dr. Robert W. Haxall's *A Dissertation . . .*), "Schloss Hainfeld" (Basil Hall's *Skimmings*), "Peter Snook" (J. Dalton's *Peter Snook*), "Life of Richelieu" (G. P. R. James's *Lives of the Cardinal de Richelieu, Count Oxenstiern, Count Olivarez, and Cardinal Mazarin*), "Hall's Latin Grammar" (Baynard R. Hall's *A New and Compendious Latin Grammar . . .*), "Bland's Chancery Reports" (Theodorick Bland's *Reports of Cases . . .*), "Lucien Bonaparte" (*Memoirs of Lucien Bonaparte . . . by himself*), and "Madrid in 1835" (anon., *Madrid in 1835*).

In an "Advertisement" Poe apologizes for delays and announces future plans for the *Messenger*:

Various delays arising from sickness in our office, the difficulty of obtaining workmen at short notice in the South, and other causes unforeseen, have thrown us, during the progress of the last two numbers, more than a month behind our regular time of issue. We regret this, however, the less, since it will be desirable, at all events, not to commence our third volume until the beginning of the new year. The Messenger now published is No. XI [October 1836]. No. XII [November 1836] will follow as soon as possible, and complete Volume the Second. The first number of Volume III, in whose external appearance we hope to make some improvements, will be issued on the first of January next.

On the covers White exonerates Poe from a charge of vanity and publishes newspaper notices of the *Messenger*:

TO THE FRIENDS OF THE MESSENGER.

As Publisher and Proprietor of this Journal, I shall always consider it not only my right, but my duty, to advance its interests by any honorable means within my power. To show those who have favored me with their support, or who may deliberate about so doing, what the public think of the Messenger (as far as the voice of the public can be ascertained by means of the public press), I cannot be brought to think a censurable course, and shall accordingly pursue it at such intervals as may be thought proper. In the present instance, the high encomiums which have been lavished, from the loftiest source in the country, and lavished without exception, upon the exertions and talents of Mr. Poe, (and only a very few of which are here republished) render it incumbent upon me to exonerate *him* from the charge of vanity in giving farther circulation to the "Opinions of the Press." I, therefore, take this method of stating as distinctly as possible, that he has no part whatever in this proceeding—which is altogether a matter between reader and *Publisher*. The notices subjoined are taken, very nearly at random, from a mass lately received, amounting to more than one hundred, and which are, without exception, complimentary.

THOMAS W. WHITE.

. . . We desire once more to call public attention to this magazine, whose rare merits have by no means been overrated in the thousand and one laudatory notices with which the whole press of the country is teeming. The Messenger has had the good fortune to attain an unparalleled popularity, by striking out for itself a novel path, and by pursuing it with energy, steadfast perseverance, the greatest ability, and perfect fearlessness and independence. We allude, of course, to its editorial conduct, and especially to its department of Critical Notices. Throwing off, indignantly, the trammels of English opinions, the whole country, it seemed, was upon the point of rushing headlong into the opposite extreme, and giving exorbitant and indiscriminate praise to every American book. To such an extent was this pernicious feeling carried, that no sooner was a novel, poem, or any work of any species, published as the production of an American author, than the periodical press, unanimously, throughout the land, were occupied in singing its praises; and in this manner many a spurious and utterly untenable reputation has been attained. In December last, the "Messenger" boldly took up the cudgels against so pernicious an evil, and succeeded in shaking the throne of popular faith to its centre, by a series of attacks, bold, well-directed and irresistible, against a number of the most popular authors of the day. The system, too, has been followed up ever since, with an industry so untiring, an impartiality so unimpeachable, an ability so undeniable, as to have extorted admiration from all sources.

Nor in its powers of sarcasm alone has the Messenger obtained a decided advantage over all competitors. Its columns are equally renowned for sound scholarship, a just appreciation of real beauty, and a searching analysis of the principles of literary merit. These qualities have succeeded in drawing to its list of contributors a great number of the proudest literary names in our country—men, who, never having before contributed to any similar publication, thus evince their high appreciation of the Messenger. In the number before us (that for August) we see the names of Robert Greenhow, of this city; Judge Hopkinson, of Philadelphia; Professor Francis Lieber, editor of the Encyclopaedia Americana; James K. Paulding; Major Henry Lee, author of the Life of Napoleon; Dr. Robert M. Bird, author of "Calavar;" Lieutenant Slidell, author of "A Year in Spain;" Simms, author of the "Partisan;" the venerable Mathew Carey, of Philadelphia; James M. Garnett, of Virginia; Mrs. Ellet, Mrs. Sarah J. Hale, Mrs. Sigourney, and others. It has, besides, one or two contributions from Mr. Poe, by whom, we presume, all after the word "Editorial" is furnished. This department embraces, in the present instance, no less than thirty-two closely printed pages, in double columns, principally reviews of new works, among which are "The Old World and the New," "Richardson's Dictionary," "The Book of Gems," Mr. French's novel "Elkswatawa," "A Year in Spain," Professor Ingraham's novel "Lafitte," and Mr. Willis's "Inklings of Adventure." The reviews should be read to be appreciated. The number closes with an amusing article (also editorial) called "Autography," and embracing facsimile signatures of Sparks, Willis, Miss Gould, Professor Dew, Mellen, Simms, Slidell, Professor Anthon, Professor Lieber, Mrs. Hale, Jack Downing, Stone, and Fay. —[Washington] *National Intelligencer*.

We have not received the August number of the Southern Messenger; at least it has not as yet reached our peculiar desk. We always welcome the White Messenger, for it is always freighted with sweet poetry and lofty and intellectual prose.

Mayhap our senior has cabbaged it, and sits up after his dinner of politics, to take tea upon cakes of literature. The other papers say that Edgar Poe has committed murder upon a poor Virginia author [James S. French]. We feel anxious to see how he managed it.—[Washington] *United States Telegraph.*

The editor himself, Mr. Poe, has given his elegant, his powerful, and acute mind, to its [the *Messenger's*] advancement. Powerful in his own productions, he is just to those of others. His critical notices are always good or sometimes bordering on the brink of too much severity. There is no use in lashing authors, unfortunate race, as if they were highway robbers, horse thieves, and gallows birds. Mercy should smile upon the inkstand of the critic (forgive the sublime idea, Mr. Poe,)—should chasten the rod he had soaked in pickle, made doubly severe by his own consciousness of superiority—but we are running wild . . . . The critical notices are excellent, as usual. Mr. Poe has great *summary* powers. Witness his condensation, his summing up in so short a space, of the incidents in the life and death of Sheppard Lee.—*Washington Telegraph.*

The contributions to the [August] "Messenger" are all excellent, many of them first rate, as to matter as well as manner, without, so far as we remember, an atom of namby-pamby trash; but the titbits under the editorial department pleased us exceedingly. There is a raciness and scholarlike taste, a classical acumen, which made us feel as we have not felt for years, and brought back to us reminiscences that flitted like fire-flies athwart the gloom of our memory.—[William Bose, editor,] *Baltimore American.*

The August number of this journal is upon our table. It is published monthly at Richmond by T. W. White, Esq. and is edited, we believe, by Edgar A. Poe, Esq. a young man of brilliant talents and much promise . . . . Mr. Poe's poetical rhapsodies are quite equal to any thing in the works of Alfred Tennyson or John Keats. We are not admirers of this mystic school of poetry, but Mr. Poe has given evidence of considerable powers, which may be matured by study and practice. His versification is often incorrect, and we remember some blank verse of his, where all metrical rules were set at defiance, and some fine ideas were spoilt in the expression. The following stanza from a poem entitled "The City of Sin," could have preceeded only from high poetical impulses, but the epithet "Babylon-like" is harsh and inexpressive . . . .
   The "Critical Notices" are in general independent, just and discriminating. But Mr. Poe must be careful how he puffs the books of his contributors. It looks suspicious. The Messenger has taken a high stand among the literary periodicals of the country; and as its circulation increases, it will go on improving . . . .—*Boston Atlas.*

We however assure our readers that we do not *puff* . . . . How it is we cannot say, but the Messenger comes up to our *beau ideal* of a Southern Monthly, so well and so constantly, that we cannot (nor do we know why we should) refrain from, as well and as constantly, giving it what we consider to be its just due. Moreover, we are again compelled to allude to the excellence of its critical department, and excellent *we* at least must consider it; for so closely did its critique upon a certain "American Novel," yclept "Paul Ulric," resemble one we had been provoked into writing, and were waiting for Politics and Commerce to give us a chance to insert in our humble diurnal, that we suppressed it for fear of the charge of plagiarism; and we are sure that in relation to the strictures on "Lafitte," (Ingraham's new novel) and Willis' "Inklings of Adventure," in the number before us, had we attempted a similar task, a similar result must have followed. Under these circumstances then, although it will not do for us to deny too strenuously that we, and consequently the Messenger, may err, yet for the same reason, our commendation of that work must be taken for anything but the insincerity of puffing. On this point we are positively "committed," stand we by it or fall.— *Natchez Courier.*

If the Literary Messenger is always as well supported by its literary contributors, it need not fear the rivalry of any magazine, at home or abroad. We take an extract from a collection of thoughts, good sayings, and learned notes, entitled "Pinakidia."—*New York Evening Post.*

Besides the numerous contributions which it [the *Messenger*] contains, we observe that the pen editorial has been employed for the present [September] number, with industry, vigor and effect, upwards of thirty pages being apparently devoted to that department of the work. Undoubtedly, this Messenger must be "going ahead" with a rapidity or impetus suited to the era of locomotives and steam.— *Martinsburg Gazette,* quoting the *Baltimore Patriot.*

. . . we desire for the Editor continued health and strength, that he may not be obliged to remit his labors which in time must have a powerful influence.—*Boston Galaxy.*

One thing we do know assuredly, that this Magazine would do honor to any part of the world. If we had accidentally found any one number of it, without any knowledge of its source, we should unhesitatingly class it among the most chaste and brilliant productions of an age and place, more fruitful in literary and typographical excellence than our own. We are not surprised that this Magazine should have enemies—"Envy hatest that excellence it cannot reach"; and we are of the opinion that the time *has now arrived* when the covert insinuations of its foes, are as powerless as the eulogies of its friends are unnecessary.—[B. Badger, editor,] *New York Messenger.*

It [the *Messenger*] is conducted with courage, which, in such an undertaking, is more rare, if not more necessary than talent . . . . The Poetry by the editor is tolerable. The editorial and critical notices are written with animation and force, and exhibit a well regulated taste. The autography at the close of the volume, will be inspected with interest. The Messenger, take it all in all, is, perhaps, the most spirited, original and interesting periodical in the country, and though we cannot praise all its contents, we must own that it contains much which cannot be praised too highly.—*Pennsylvania Sentinel.*

We commend it as eminently worthy of patronage.—*Boston Aurora.*

It [the August *Messenger*] gives evidence of superior ability, and immense labor and research, particularly on the part of the editor, Mr. Edgar A. Poe. Paulding, Simms, Lieber, M. Carey, Mrs. Sigourney, Mrs. Hale, and other writers of acknowledged talents, contribute to its columns; and the publisher does his part of the work in a highly creditable manner.—*Portland Jeffersonian*.

Many of the articles are from persons of distinction: Mrs. Sigourney, Mr. Simms, Poe, Greenhow, Lee, and Judge Hopkinson.—*Raleigh Star*.

12 NOVEMBER. Poe writes Edgar S. Van Winkle, an attorney in New York City, soliciting an article on the "Study of Law in the U.S." for the *Messenger* (Ostrom [1974], pp. 515–16).

23 NOVEMBER. NEW YORK. Edgar S. Van Winkle writes Poe (Poe to Van Winkle, 26 November 1836).

24 NOVEMBER. RICHMOND. White writes William Scott, in New York: "When I reached home I found my wife very ill in bed, and all my office affairs in great confusion . . . . Let me know if you called on Miss Medina . . . . It is requisite I should have her first article here by the 10th Dec . . . . Send me the $15 in a $10 and $5 of one of your City Banks;—and send it on as soon as you can get it—for we are all without money in Richmond" (VtMiM).

26 NOVEMBER. Poe writes Edgar S. Van Winkle: " 'The Study of the Law,' has been duly received. I have read the essay with much interest, and shall be proud to have it in the 'Messenger' " (Ostrom [1974], pp. 515–16).

["Study of the Law," by a member of the New York bar, appeared in the January 1837 *Messenger*.]

26 NOVEMBER. CHARLESTON, SOUTH CAROLINA. The *Southern Rose* calls the *Messenger* "that admirable periodical."

2 DECEMBER. NEW BERN, NORTH CAROLINA. The *Newbern Spectator* gives Poe advice.

. . . an original dramatick sketch [the anonymous "Moses Pleading Before Pharaoh" in the October *Messenger*], of some four hundred lines in length, is well worth of perusal. Were it not that it so little resembles any of the previous productions of the Editor of the Messenger, except in its occasional irregularity and wildness of imagination, we would attribute the authorship to him. We have seldom read any thing more pleasing, indeed more sublime, than are some portions of the work, and whoever the author is, the whole does him credit . . . . we are arrested . . . by the imposing word "Editorial," over the "Critical Notices." The first work "scalped" is the "Swiss Heiress;" and never was poor devil treated with more downright coarseness of sneer and indiscriminating contemptuousness, than is the author of the unfortunate "Heiress" . . . we are perfectly convinced that the southern literati condemn the substitution of sneer and sarcasm for dignified reasoning and remark . . . . we contend that an editor has no more right, in his publick capacity, to bring an author into contempt by illiberal and contemptuous criticism on his writings, than he has to pursue a similar course in speech respecting the author's private character . . . . if the editors of newspapers would be a little more sparing of their gross flattery and indiscriminating praise, we have no doubt that the Messenger, in all its parts, will be a periodical to which the South may hereafter refer with pride.

3 DECEMBER. NEW YORK. The *New-Yorker* notices the *Messenger*.

7 DECEMBER. RICHMOND. White writes William Scott, in New York: "I shall forward to you by this evening's mail the sheets of my 12th No. It will be issued on Saturday morning [10 December]" (VtMiM).

9 DECEMBER. WASHINGTON. James H. Causten replies to Poe's 3 June letter (Causten's endorsement on Poe's letter, *L*, 2:478).

10 DECEMBER. RICHMOND. The November *Messenger* publishes Poe's introductory note to Thomas R. Dew's "Address," two fillers ("Walladmor" and "Sir John Hill . . ."), two unsigned notes (comment on Volumes II and III and "Erratum"), and critical notices: "Medical Review" (the *British and Foreign Medical Review* for January, February, and July 1836), "Mr. Lee's Address" (Z. Collins Lee's *Address*), and "The Pickwick Club" (Charles Dickens' *The Posthumous Papers of the Pickwick Club*). An announcement on the cover "To the Patrons of the Messenger, and the Public Generally," signed by White, may have been written by Poe:

The present number will conclude the second year of the Messenger, and the Publisher returns his sincere thanks to his numerous patrons for their friendly support. He has labored faithfully to create a Southern interest in favor of Literature, and he trusts that his efforts have not been unsuccessful. The generous spirits of the North and East, who have heretofore contributed to his pages, have for the most part pledged their continued support; and he feels assured from the interest awakened on this side of the Potomac, that Southern rivals will not be backward in that honorable literary strife which leads to excellence. If the Publisher's calculations are not oversanguine, the forthcoming Volume will surpass its predecessors. He has the promise of able pens, and pledges his unflinching exertions to accomplish that result. His efforts, however, must be aided by the pecuniary as well as intellectual assistance of his patrons. He earnestly therefore calls upon them to discharge their subscriptions, and if they feel any of the zeal which he does in the cause of the Messenger, he trusts that they will contribute to extend its circulation, so as to place it upon a solid and firm basis. The first Number of the next Volume will be issued in January.

15 DECEMBER. White writes William Scott, in New York: "Money is very

scarce here—Times very hard—and, what is still worse, I have a very sick wife,—and 'To mend of the matter' my Printing is nearly suspended, in consequence of as ruinous as a foolish strike of the young men Printers, a strike that will in all probability prevent my issuing the 1st No. of my 3d Volume earlier than the 1st February . . . . Will you call on Mr. Locke and tell him that I have not heard from him as yet,—and that this is the 10th" (VtMiM).

16 DECEMBER. NEW BERN, NORTH CAROLINA. The *Newbern Spectator* comments:

We have long said that the *frothy* part, that is, the editorial part, of the SOUTH-ERN LITERARY MESSENGER, would destroy that publication . . . . For the sake of the publisher, who is said to be a worthy, unpresuming man, we regret that such must eventually be the case. Every man of proper feelings, every lover of literature, who peruses the work, is disgusted with the superficial criticism and uneducated flippancy of its editorial contents, and with the low, egotistical means resorted to, to *force* it into notice . . . . We have been endeavouring for twelve months to convince the Editor of the Messenger that his course was erroneous, discreditable to the South, promotive of bad taste, and ruinous to Mr. WHITE's laudable enterprise, but we got from him in return anything but a column of abusive slang, which would be in place only in a Jackson newspaper.

The *Spectator* then reprints "Literary Forgeries" from Willis Gaylord Clark's *Philadelphia Gazette*: the article contains William Leete Stone's testy denial that he wrote the fictitious letter published over his signature in the August installment of Poe's "Autography."

24 DECEMBER. BUCHANAN, BOTETOURT COUNTY, VIRGINIA. The attorney Allan B. Magruder, a former classmate of Poe at West Point, writes him, submitting an essay for the *Messenger* (Poe to Magruder, 9 January 1837).

27 DECEMBER. RICHMOND. White writes Beverley Tucker:

Highly as I really think of Mr. Poe's talents, I shall be forced to give him notice, in a week or so at farthest, that I can no longer recognize him as editor of my Messenger. Three months ago I felt it my duty to give him a similar notice,—and was afterwards overpersuaded to restore him to his situation on certain conditions—which conditions he has again forfeited. Added to all this, I am cramped by him in the exercise of my own judgment, as to what articles I shall or shall not admit into my work. It is true that I neither have his sagacity, nor his learning—but I do believe I know a handspike from a saw . . . . I mean to dispense with Mr. Poe as my editor . . . if he chooses to write as a contributor, I will pay him well (Jackson [1934], pp. 109–10).

[R. M. T. Hunter, one of Poe's University of Virginia classmates, wrote Henry Tutwiler, another classmate, 20 May 1875: "Here [in Richmond] his [Poe's] habits were bad and as White did not appreciate his literary excellence I had hard work to save him from dismissal before it actually occurred. During a part of the time I was in Richmond, a member of the Legislature, and frequently volunteered to correct the press when pieces were being published with classical quotations. Poe was the only man on White's staff capable of doing this and when occasionally drinking (the habit was not constant) he was incapacitated for work. On such occasions I have done the work more than once to prevent a rupture between his employer and himself. He was reckless about money and subject to intoxication, but I was not aware of any other bad habit that he had" (Jacobs, p. 180).]

1836. Poe composes "Spiritual Song" (Mabbott [1969], 1:303–304).

LATE 1836 OR EARLY 1837. Poe writes Lambert A. Wilmer, in Baltimore (Ostrom [1981], p. 189).

[In *Our Press Gang* (1859) Wilmer gave this account: "A short time before I determined to [leave Baltimore] . . . I received a letter from my eccentric friend Edgar A. Poe,—who was then officiating as the editor and critic of the *Southern Literary Messenger* . . . . In his epistle, Poe gave me to understand that he was preparing to leave Richmond, and he advised me to come thither without delay,—as he was quite sure that I could obtain the situation he was about to vacate . . . . It was wholly out of my power to act in accordance with Mr. Poe's suggestion—for I could not raise money enough to pay for the transportation of myself and my family to Richmond" (pp. 39–40).]

*

1837

*

3 JANUARY. RICHMOND. Poe "retires" as editor of the *Messenger* (White to Tucker, 27 December 1836, and to Scott, 23 January 1837; *Messenger*, 3 [January 1837]: 72, 96).

AFTER 3 JANUARY? NEW YORK. Francis Lister Hawks writes Poe, offering him a position on a forthcoming magazine, the *New York Review*: "I wish you to fall in with your *broad-axe* amidst this miserable literary trash which surrounds us. I believe you have the will, and I know well you have the ability" (*Philadelphia Saturday Museum*, 4 March 1843).

VIRGINIA CLEMM POE
(from the watercolor formerly owned by Amelia F. Poe)
Humanities Research Center, University of Texas at Austin

[Poe reviewed Hawks's *Ecclesiastical History* in the March 1836 *Messenger*. Hawks was a native of New Bern, North Carolina. Occasional items about him appear in the *Newbern Spectator*.]

9 JANUARY. RICHMOND. Poe writes Allan B. Magruder: "Your kind letter of Christmas Eve was duly received—with the Essay . . . . It shall certainly appear, entire, in the February number of the Messenger . . . . Ill health, and a weight of various and harassing business will prove, I trust, a sufficient excuse [for not having replied before]" (*L*, 2:680).

14 JANUARY. White promises Poe financial assistance (White to Poe, 17 January 1837).

17 JANUARY. White writes Poe:

If it be possible, without breaking in on my previous arrangements, I will get more than the lst portion of Pym in—tho' I much fear that will be impossible.

If I had read even 10 lines of Magruder's manuscript, it would have saved me the expense of putting it in type.—It is all . . . bombast. He will have to live a little longer before he can write well enough to please the readers of the M.

Touching Carey's piece, gratitude to him for pecuniary assistance, obliges me to insert *it*.

You are certainly as well aware as I am that the last $20 I advanced to you was in consideration of what you were to write for me by the piece.

I also made you a promise on Saturday that I would do something more for you to-day,—and I never make even a promise without intending to perform it,—and though it is entirely out of my power to send you up any thing this morning, yet I will do something more for you before night, or early to-morrow,—if I have to borrow it from my friends (*W*, 17:41–42).

19 JANUARY. White writes Beverley Tucker:

Your Review of Bulwer will follow Judge [Abel P.] Upshur's of the Partisan [Leader] . . . . I really am delighted to learn that you design reviewing Blackwood. Professor Anthon, when I saw him in N. York last Oct. called my particular attention to the subject of Reviewing Reviews . . . which he thought wretchedly conducted—as he also said of the Knickerbocker, and American Monthly. I found Mr. Anthon, as I thought, not only a man of great acquirements but he really made a most favorable impression on me that he was a gentleman. With Paulding I was still more pleased—he is not a great man, but he is unquestionably a man of the strictest morality . . . . I am very sorry to hear that [J. N.] Reynolds is suspected even of being what he ought not be. I formed an acquaintance with him in this city about 10 years ago, and absolutely became almost devotedly attached to the fellow. He is a most fascinating dog,—and I think he has a great share of good common sense. —To me he owes the favor he has received in the Messenger—but if he is a corrupt man, I have done with him.

Tell me privately what you know of him . . . . I shall also send you a bundle of manuscripts which I have lately received—and get the favor of you to pass sentence on them . . . . I am glad to hear you say that you will stick to me in this my trying hour . . . . [Lucian] Minor will be here some time in Feb. when I shall hear what he says—But my dear Sir, I am so overwhelmed in debt that I scarcely dare think of such an editor as I know I ought to have . . . . Poe feels his situation at last—I see but little of him—but I hear a great deal about him and from him. I am tired out with hard work (Jackson [1934], pp. 111–12).

20 JANUARY. NEW BERN, NORTH CAROLINA. The *Newbern Spectator* praises the *Knickerbocker* while it condemns "inexperienced men who measurably control the critical press of the country."

23 JANUARY. RICHMOND. White writes William Scott, in New York:

It has been entirely out of my power to answer your kind favor of the 17th 'till today. Betwixt my office and my domicile, my whole time has been consumed—i.e. ever since my return to Richmond. At last, my poor wife seems to be better—and we begin to think we may yet conquer the disease, which is pronounced by the physicians cancer in her womb. She has had already a 5 months' siege of it. My hands are once more at work, but their "strike" has been a serious drawback as well as a great injury to me in a pecuniary point of view—one that will cost me months of hard labor to recover from. By to-morrow night's mail I will send you rough sheets of my Jan. No. in which you will find your article on the "Rights of Authors," though not in the part of the Messenger I promised you it should be placed. This was, however, intended, I assure you, in no ways as a mark of disrespect. But its getting where it now stands, was unavoidable, in consequence of arrangements which had been previously made by others—as well by the fact of my attention being called from my office when it was made up . . . . Previous to writing you I had submitted your manuscript to Mr. Poe, who handed it back to me as being suitable for the Messenger. After I had it put in type, I sent a corrected proof of it to him. He returned it, as you will see, making several corrections,—and amongst other things, striking out your first paragraph, or exordium. He also struck out your two concluding paragraphs—but I thought them worth preserving—and therefore took upon myself the "responsibility" of retaining them. I have no doubt whatever, that Mr. Poe done *what he has done* for the best. I hope, moreover, that you will think so also. Be that as it may, I assure you there was not the slightest intention on my part (nor do I believe there was on that of Mr. Poe's) to mar your production . . . . Mr. Poe retired from the editorship of my work on the 3d inst. I am once more at the head of my affairs. Nevertheless I have private friends to whom I submit all articles—and I have consented to abide by their judgment (VtMiM).

24 JANUARY. White writes Beverley Tucker: "stick to me . . . now [that] Poe is not my editor . . . . Except Walsh, Rights of Authors and Poe's

articles, no one would accept of cash for their articles" (Vi–W–TC; Jackson [1934], pp. 112–14).

White writes Tucker a second letter:

. . . the Messenger is safe. It shall live—and it shall outlive all the injury it has sustained from Mr. Poe's management,—unless Almighty God deprives me of health or of life . . . .

To yourself I am grateful in the extreme for what you have done, are doing, and I am sure will do for me. With two more friends like yourself, and I could get along for the 12 months to come, without any ostensible editor. At the end of that time, I should, I believe, be able to give a suitable reward for such talents as I ought to have.

At present help (original) is coming in more rapid than at any time since I have started the Messenger—all too since the fact has eked out that Poe is not to act as Judge or Judge Advocate—A great deal of it is good matter—and all far better than his Gordon Pym for which I apparently pay him now—$3 per page, but which in reality has and still costs me $20 per page. But him I shall soon be clear off [of.] His every movement shows me that he will be off in a short time . . . . I am, my friend, considerably inclined to melancholy—too much so, for my comfort or happiness—but I cannot help it (Vi–W–TC).

[Years later Benjamin Blake Minor wrote: "Mr. Poe besought the proprietor to reinstate him as editor, but Mr. White, in terms firm yet kindly, refused to do so" (Minor, p. 64).]

AFTER 26 JANUARY. The January 1837 *Messenger* makes its appearance with Poe's "Valedictory," first installment of *The Narrative of Arthur Gordon Pym*, "Ballad," "To Zante," and book reviews: Washington Irving's *Astoria*, William Cullen Bryant's *Poems*, Nathaniel Beverley Tucker's *George Balcombe*, Charles Anthon's *Select Orations of Cicero*, and Jeremiah N. Reynolds' *Address on the Subject of a Surveying and Exploring Expedition to the Pacific Ocean and South Seas*.

White announces:

To the Patrons of the Southern Literary Messenger: in issuing the present number of the "Messenger" (the first of a new volume) I deem it proper to inform my subscribers, and the public generally, that Mr. Poe, who has filled the editorial department for the last twelve months with so much ability, retired from that station on the 3d inst., and the entire management of the work again devolves on myself alone. Mr. P., however, will continue to furnish its columns, from time to time, with the effusions of his vigorous and popular pen,—and my old contributors among whom I am proud to number some of the best writers in our state and country, will doubtless continue to favor me with their valuable contributions. . . . It is perhaps due to Mr. Poe to state, that he is not responsible for any of the articles which appear in the present number, except the reviews of "Bryant's Poems," "George Balcombe," "Irving's Astoria," "Reynolds's Address on the South Sea Expedition," "Anthon's Cicero,"—the first number of "Arthur Gordon Pym," a sea story, and two poetical effusions to which his name is prefixed (2:96).

31 JANUARY. White writes Beverley Tucker:

You really have taken a great deal of trouble to read all the articles I sent you. —Poe always admitted the nonsense of Paulina [DuPré?].—You are right.—They will be well suited for the Ladies' Companion . . . . Poe pesters me no little—he is trying every manoeuvre to foist himself on some one at the North—at least I believe so.— He is continually after me for money. I am as sick of his writings, as I am of him, —and am rather more than half inclined to send him up another dozen dollars in the morning, and along with it all his unpublished manuscripts.

Tell me candidly what you think of his Pym (Marryatt's style I suppose) and his Poetry.

Treat all of this as private, which you think ought to be private—Let all be private about Poe (Vi–W–TC).

JANUARY? Poe transcribes "Irene" in John Collins McCabe's album (Mabbott [1969], 1:182–83).

7 FEBRUARY. Beverley Tucker arrives in Richmond (letter of White to Tucker, 7 February, Vi–W–TC).

EARLY FEBRUARY? NEW YORK. Poe, his wife Virginia, and Maria Clemm arrive here and take up residence at Sixth Avenue and Waverley Place, sharing a floor with William Gowans, a bookseller (Phillips, 1:549, 558–59).

[William Gowans later wrote: "For eight months or more, 'one house contained us, us one table fed!' During that time I saw much of him, and had an opportunity of conversing with him often, and I must say I never saw him the least affected with liquor, nor even descend to any known vice, while he was one of the most courteous, gentlemanly, and intelligent companions I have met with during my journeyings and haltings through divers divisions of the globe; besides, he had an extra inducement to be a good man as well as a good husband, for he had a wife of matchless beauty and loveliness, her eye could match that of any houri, and her face defy the genius of a Canova to imitate; a temper and disposition of surpassing sweetness; besides, she seemed as much devoted to him and his every interest as a young mother is to her first born . . . . Poe had a remarkably pleasing and prepossessing countenance, what the ladies would call decidedly handsome" (Quinn, p. 267, and Thomas [1978], pp. 773–74).]

3 FEBRUARY. NEW BERN, NORTH CAROLINA. The Newbern Spectator comments on Poe's departure from the Messenger:

We are glad to find that Mr. WHITE has resumed the sole management, as the unnecessary severity of the late Editor, Mr. Poe, had no doubt alienated from the work many who sincerely wished it success. Mr. POE is unquestionably a man of talents, and when these shall have been restricted by experience and moderation, there is no doubt that he will shine as a writer. He has a brilliant imagination, a free use of language, and corruscations of genius are not infrequent in his writings; but these gifts, to be useful, should not be under the impetuous guidance of youth. We seldom learn but from actual experience, what we owe to others: time alone can bestow this experience, and teach us to hold the scales of Justice with a hand as impartial as our common nature permits. We shall speak of the contents of the Messenger in our next.

10 FEBRUARY. The *Newbern Spectator* remarks that " 'Arthur Gordon Pym,' [is] apparently the first number of a series of the Pym family. We hope those to come will be more worthy of perusal."

14 FEBRUARY. CHARLESTON, SOUTH CAROLINA. The *Charleston Courier* censures the *Messenger* for printing in its January issue Abel P. Upshur's review of Beverley Tucker's *The Partisan Leader* and reports: "Mr. EDGAR A. POE, who has for some time past ably presided in the editorial department, has resigned the chair, but will continue to grace the work with his brilliant contributions."

BEFORE 28 FEBRUARY. BALTIMORE. W. H. Carpenter, J. S. Norris, and James Brown solicit from Poe a contribution to the *Baltimore Book* (Poe to Carpenter, Norris, and Brown, 28 February).

28 FEBRUARY. NEW YORK. Poe writes Carpenter, Norris, and Brown: "It would give me the greatest pleasure to aid you in your design of a 'Baltimore Book' and I would be quite willing to forward an article by the lst April if so late a period would answer. I am afraid my other engagements would not admit of my sending anything at an earlier date" (*L*, 1:111).

AFTER 3 MARCH. RICHMOND. The February *Messenger* appears with the second installment of Poe's *The Narrative of Arthur Gordon Pym*.

30 MARCH. NEW YORK. Poe attends the Booksellers Dinner sponsored by New York publishers at the City Hotel and proposes a toast: "The *Monthlies* of Gotham—Their distinguished Editors, and their vigorous Collaborateurs" (*American*, 3 April).

["Of the large number of literary men who were present at the famous dinner given to authors at the City Hotel, March 30, 1837, by the

booksellers of New-York, [Charles Fenno] Hoffman was the last survivor
. . . . among others who were present, Chancellor Kent, Colonel Trum-
bull, Albert Gallatin, Washington Irving, Fitz-Greene Halleck, James K.
Paulding, William Cullen Bryant, George P. Morris, William L. Stone,
Edgar A. Poe, Dr. John W. Francis, Dr. Orville Dewey, Matthew L. Davis,
Charles King, and Lewis Gaylord Clark" (J. G. Wilson [1893], 4:71).]

3 APRIL. The *New York American* carries an eight-column account of the
Booksellers Dinner; this is reprinted in the biweekly *American (For the
Country)* on 7 April.

5 APRIL. RICHMOND. White writes William Scott, in New York: "Tell
me, when you write what Poe is driving at—that is, if you know—but do
not put yourself out to gratify perhaps an idle curiosity. I have not heard
from him since he left here" (VtMiM).

26 APRIL. White writes Beverley Tucker:

I am very sure that you will give a just criticism of Paulding . . . . If he
[Paulding] would have been proud of praise from Poe, it would have been because
he really admired the fellow's talents. —Like myself he was completely gulled.
The truth is, Poe seldom or ever done what he knew was just to any book. He
read few through—unless it were some trashy novels,—and his only object in
reading even these, was to ridicule their authors. Read his eulogistic review of
of [your George] Balcombe—which he penned only because he believed you were
its author. He has scarcely selected a passage out of the two volumes which
warrants the praise he has lavished on it. But enough of this—this mortifying
subject (Vi–W–TC; Jackson [1934], p. 115).

29 APRIL. NEW YORK. The *New-Yorker* praises Poe's editorship of the
Messenger (Pollin [1974], p. 43).

MAY. The *Knickerbocker Magazine* announces that Harper & Brothers have
Poe's *The Narrative of Arthur Gordon Pym* "nearly ready for publication."

10 MAY. The New York City banks suspend specie payments, precipitating
the "Panic of 1837" and marking the beginning of one of the worst
depressions in American history.

BEFORE 27 MAY? Poe, Virginia, and Maria Clemm move to 113½ Carmine
Street (Phillips, 1:558–59; Quinn, p. 267).

27 MAY. Poe writes Charles Anthon and asks him to translate several
Hebrew phrases from the Old Testament. Poe believes that certain Biblical
quotations in John L. Stephens' *Incidents of Travel in Egypt, Arabia Petraea,*

and the Holy Land, which he is reviewing for the October *New York Review*, are inaccurate (Poe to Anthon, 1 June 1837; Thomas [1978], pp. 10–11).

MAY OR LATER? Perhaps Poe sees a performance of George Colman's *The Poor Gentleman* (Pollin [1970a], pp. 80–82).

1 JUNE. Charles Anthon writes Poe: "I owe you an apology for not having answered your letter of the 27th sooner, but I was occupied at the time with matters that admitted of no delay, and was compelled therefore to lay your communication on the table for a day or two. I hope you will find what is written below satisfactory. Do not wait to pay me a formal visit, but call and introduce yourself" (*W*, 17:42–43).

10 JUNE. Poe's *The Narrative of Arthur Gordon P.Y.M. of Nantucket* is copyrighted by the Harpers, although not published until 30 July 1838 (Exman, p. 96).

JUNE. The *American Monthly Magazine*, owned by Park Benjamin and Charles Fenno Hoffman, publishes Poe's "Von Jung, the Mystific" (later called "Mystification").

JULY. PHILADELPHIA. William Evans Burton launches the *Gentleman's Magazine*.

OCTOBER. NEW YORK. Poe's unsigned review of John L. Stephens' *Incidents of Travel in Egypt, Arabia Petraea, and the Holy Land* appears in the "2d number" of the *New York Review*.

NOVEMBER? BALTIMORE. Poe's "Siope—A Fable" (later "Silence") appears in the *Baltimore Book* for 1838.

2 DECEMBER. The *Baltimore Monument* reviews Poe's "Siope":

This fable, if we reck it right, is intended to indicate the horror of silence,—that man may not be entirely accursed while he can hear the sounds which hurtle in the bosom of nature; the curse of tumult is represented as happiness to the curse of silence. The strain is wild, the language beautiful and peculiar to Mr. Poe (Fisher, p. 56).

1837? NEW YORK. Poe appears at the Northern Dispensary, Waverley Place and Christopher Street, in Greenwich Village, to get remedies for a cold. Perhaps he meets Dr. Valentine Mott and Marie L. Shew at this time (Phillips, 1:556–57; Mabbott [1969], 1:547–48).

1837? Perhaps William Gowans introduces Poe, Virginia, and Maria Clemm to the James Pedder family (Allen, p. 339).

WILLIAM E. BURTON
Library of Congress

CHAPTER FIVE

Philadelphia: Tales of the Grotesque and Arabesque

1838–1840

The Poe family settles in Philadelphia early in 1838. On 30 July Harper & Brothers publish *The Narrative of Arthur Gordon Pym* in New York; in October Poe's novel is issued in England by the London office of Wiley and Putnam. Critics in both countries praise it for verisimilitude, but few regard it as authentic. In the autumn his tale "Ligeia" and other contributions appear in the *American Museum*, a Baltimore monthly begun by his friends Nathan C. Brooks and Joseph Evans Snodgrass. Still beset by poverty at the year's end, Poe agrees to assist Thomas Wyatt in preparing *The Conchologist's First Book* and *A Synopsis of Natural History*, two compilations published in April 1839. In the next month he solicits employment from William E. Burton, the popular English actor who owns and edits *Burton's Gentleman's Magazine*. Burton hires him as assistant editor on 11 May, at a salary of $10 a week. Poe performs most of the tiresome chores connected with the monthly's publication; Burton refuses to let him establish the tone of its book reviews. In September "The Fall of the House of Usher" appears in *Burton's*; the October number contains "William Wilson," reprinted from the *Gift* for 1840. These two stories and twenty-three others are collected in Poe's *Tales of the Grotesque and Arabesque*, issued by Lea & Blanchard around 4 December 1839. Although the book receives favorable reviews, few copies are sold. "The Journal of Julius Rodman," Poe's unsigned tale of Western exploration, is serialized in *Burton's* during the first six months of 1840; it proves a more successful hoax than *Pym*, being cited in an official report on the Oregon Territory prepared for the United States Senate. By May 1840 Burton is increasingly preoccupied with his National Theatre, then under construction; on 21 May he advertises his *Gentleman's Magazine* for sale. When Poe learns of the advertisement, he concludes that he will soon lose his position; he then prepares to announce his own journal, the *Penn Magazine*. Burton, learning of Poe's intention, sends him an angry letter of dismissal on 30 May. By 3 June Poe is distributing copies of his *Penn* prospectus to the Philadelphia newspapers, which comment favorably on the project. During the summer and autumn he enlists contributors and subscribers for the *Penn*, but fails to find adequate financial backing. Early in December he is bedridden by illness and consequently forced to postpone the first number until 1 March 1841.

*

1838

*

EARLY 1838. PHILADELPHIA. Poe, his wife Virginia, and his mother-in-law Mrs. Clemm leave New York and move to Philadelphia, where they take up residence in a boardinghouse operated by Mrs. C. Jones at 202 Mulberry (or Arch) Street (Thomas [1978], pp. 825–828).

EARLY 1838? Poe is intimate with the English-born writer James Pedder, who lives on Twelfth Street above Mulberry. Pedder's daughters Anna and Bessie frequently aid the Poe family, who are "literally suffering for want of food" and forced to live "on bread and molasses for weeks together" (Pedder's 1852 reminiscence quoted in Widener, 2:56).

SUMMER. BALTIMORE OR PHILADELPHIA. Poe sees Nathan C. Brooks, who solicits his contributions to the forthcoming *American Museum*. He unsuccessfully attempts to borrow money from his second cousin Neilson Poe, editor of the *Baltimore Chronicle* (Poe to Brooks, 4 September).

19 JULY. PHILADELPHIA. Poe writes James Kirke Paulding, who has been appointed the new Secretary of the Navy. He corrects a mistaken view of his character intimated in a previous letter from Paulding:

Intemperance, with me, has never amounted to a habit; and had it been ten times a habit it would have required scarcely an effort on my part to shake it from me at once and forever. I have been fully awakened to the impolicy and degradation of the course hitherto pursued, and have abandoned the vice altogether, and without a struggle. It was necessary that I should assure you of this before mentioning the request which is the object of this letter—that you would procure me some clerkship or other office in your Department.

Could I obtain the most unimportant Clerkship in your gift—*any thing, by sea or land*—to relieve me from the miserable life of literary drudgery to which I now, with a breaking heart, submit, and for which neither my temper nor my abilities have fitted me, I would never again repine at any dispensation of God. I feel that I could then, (having something beyond mere literature as a profession) quickly elevate myself to the station in society which is my due (PP-G; Ostrom [1974], pp. 517–18).

30 JULY. NEW YORK. Harper & Brothers publish a work with this title:

THE NARRATIVE / OF / ARTHUR GORDON PYM. / OF NANTUCKET. / COMPRISING THE DETAILS OF A MUTINY AND ATROCIOUS BUTCHERY / ON BOARD THE AMERICAN BRIG GRAMPUS, ON HER WAY TO / THE SOUTH SEAS, IN THE MONTH OF JUNE, 1827. / WITH AN AC-

COUNT OF THE RECAPTURE OF THE VESSEL BY THE / SURVIVERS; THEIR SHIPWRECK AND SUBSEQUENT HORRIBLE / SUFFERINGS FROM FAMINE; THEIR DELIVERANCE BY / MEANS OF THE BRITISH SCHOONER JANE GUY; THE / BRIEF CRUISE OF THIS LATTER VESSEL IN THE / ANTARCTIC OCEAN; HER CAPTURE, AND THE / MASSACRE OF HER CREW AMONG A / GROUP OF ISLANDS IN THE / EIGHTY-FOURTH PARALLEL OF SOUTHERN LATITUDE; / TOGETHER WITH THE INCREDIBLE ADVENTURES AND / DISCOVERIES / STILL FARTHER SOUTH / TO WHICH THAT DISTRESSING CALAMITY GAVE RISE.

The "Preface" is signed by "A. G. PYM," who acknowledges the assistance of "Mr. Poe, lately editor of the Southern Literary Messenger," in preparing this authentic narrative. A "Note" at the end of the text informs the reader of "the late sudden and distressing death of Mr. Pym," which has already been widely reported by the press. "It is feared that the few remaining chapters which were to have completed his narrative . . . have been irrecoverably lost through the accident by which he perished himself."

30 JULY. Two daily newspapers notice *Pym*'s publication. The *Morning Courier* reproduces the lengthy title: "There is certainly an array of horrors set forth in the title; but the volume is highly interesting in the story, well written, and to the lovers of marvellous fiction will be quite a treasure." The *New York Gazette* observes: "The Messrs. Harper have published a very extraordinary volume purporting to be a narrative of 'Arthur Gordon Pym,' who it is said [is] lately deceased in some melancholy way, and his adventures as well as his death are referred to as of perfect notoriety . . . . It is hinted that Mr. Poe, the accomplished Virginia writer, has something to do about the book. We should be more inclined to think that Mr. Lock[e], the very ingenious author of the Moon Marvel[,] was the author" (Pollin [1978b], pp. 8–9).

31 JULY. The *New York American* carries an advertisement for Israel Post, Bookseller, 89 Bowery, which lists *Pym* as published on 30 July and now available. The *Daily Whig* gives the novel's title, "from which the reader will be able to judge somewhat of the nature of the work" (Pollin [1978b], pp. 9–10; [1981], p. 13).

AUGUST. The *Knickerbocker Magazine* reviews *Pym*: "There are a great many tough stories in this book, told in a loose and slip-shod style, seldom chequered by any of the more common graces of composition, beyond a Robinson Crusoe-ish sort of simplicity of narration. The work is one of much interest, with all its defects, not the least of which is, that it is too liberally stuffed with 'horrid circumstance of blood and battle.' "

1 AUGUST. Horace Greeley's *New-Yorker* notices *Pym*: "This is a work of extraordinary, freezing interest beyond anything we ever read. It is more marvelous than the wildest fiction, yet is presented and supported as sober truth . . . . Mr. Edgar A. Poe is understood to have assisted in preparing the work for the press." In the *New Era* Richard Adams Locke, author of the "Moon Hoax" published in 1835, corrects the *New York Gazette* of 30 July: "Now this very ingenious person [Locke], duly thanking the editor of the Gazette for his double compliment, begs to say that he had no hand whatever in this new hoax [*Pym*], and verily believes that the merit of it, be it what it may, is entirely due to Mr. Edgar A. Poe" (Pollin [1974], p. 43; [1978b], pp. 9–10).

2 AUGUST. The *Gazette* replies to Locke's disclaimer: "Of course we were not very serious when we made the ascription, but really, the 'Man of the Moon' himself might have been willing to be considered the author. Mr. Gordon Pym's imagination ought to 'call and see' its cousin german at the Era Office, for they are as alike as two lumps of chalk, and we believe the one as faithfully as we do the other" (Pollin [1978b], p. 10).

2 AUGUST. PHILADELPHIA. The *Pennsylvania Inquirer*, the *Public Ledger*, and the *United States Gazette* notice *Pym*, quoting the complete title to give their readers an idea of its contents. A fourth daily paper, the *Pennsylvanian*, comments:

"*The Narrative of Arthur Gordon Pym, of Nantucket*," is the title of a new work just published by the Harpers, containing the details of the voyages, mutinies and other disastrous chances which befel said Pym in and about the year 1827. We have not yet had time to peruse the volume, which it is hinted is from the pen of an able American writer, but from what report says, we doubt not that it is replete with interest. It may be had of Mr. Perkins, Chesnut street, and of the other booksellers.

3 AUGUST. The *Pennsylvania Inquirer* mentions *Pym* again: "We have already noticed this entertaining and exciting narrative at some length, on the faith of paragraphs which have appeared in the columns of our New York contemporaries. The Harpers have favored us with a copy, and the adventures of Pym, though only occupying a small volume, are well calculated to enchain the interest and sympathies of every class of readers."

4 AUGUST. The *Saturday Courier* reviews *Pym*: "Here is a book with a title page as long as a table of contents, and as full of 'incredibles' as man can desire. The Harpers have given us an affair that throws Munchausen into the shade, and Jack the Giant Killer is a fool to 'Peters.' Pym professes to have been close to the South Pole, far beyond the 84th parallel of Southern

THE NARRATIVE

OF

ARTHUR GORDON PYM.

OF NANTUCKET.

COMPRISING THE DETAILS OF A MUTINY AND ATROCIOUS BUTCHERY
ON BOARD THE AMERICAN BRIG GRAMPUS, ON HER WAY TO
THE SOUTH SEAS, IN THE MONTH OF JUNE, 1827.

WITH AN ACCOUNT OF THE RECAPTURE OF THE VESSEL BY THE
SURVIVERS; THEIR SHIPWRECK AND SUBSEQUENT HORRIBLE
SUFFERINGS FROM FAMINE; THEIR DELIVERANCE BY
MEANS OF THE BRITISH SCHOONER JANE GUY; THE
BRIEF CRUISE OF THIS LATTER VESSEL IN THE
ANTARCTIC OCEAN; HER CAPTURE, AND THE
MASSACRE OF HER CREW AMONG A
GROUP OF ISLANDS IN THE

EIGHTY-FOURTH PARALLEL OF SOUTHERN LATITUDE;

TOGETHER WITH THE INCREDIBLE ADVENTURES AND
DISCOVERIES

STILL FARTHER SOUTH

TO WHICH THAT DISTRESSING CALAMITY GAVE RISE.

NEW-YORK:

HARPER & BROTHERS, 82 CLIFF-ST.

1838.

Title page of Poe's novel
University of Virginia Library

latitude, and to have undergone all manner of adventures . . . . When we can find a respectable endorser for Pym's statements, we will *think* of believing them" (Pollin [1974], p. 42).

5 AUGUST. NEW YORK. The *Sunday Morning News* reproduces the title of *Pym*, commenting: "We cannot pretend to subscribe to the truth of all the wonders therein related but the lovers of the marvellous will have a fine treat for a summer's day in its perusal" (Pollin [1975b], p. 33).

6 AUGUST. HARTFORD, CONNECTICUT. The *Daily Courant* announces *Pym* by reproducing the title (Pollin [1980], p. 21).

7 AUGUST. PHILADELPHIA. *Waldie's Select Circulating Library* notices *Pym*, quoting the complete title. "Part or all of this was published in the Southern Literary Messenger, and we are free to say it is a very ingenious affair—between Robinson Crusoe and Sir Edward Seaward. The air of truth is much like old Robinson, and the interest is very deep" (Pollin [1974], pp. 42–43).

8 AUGUST. NEW YORK. The *Evening Post* reviews *Pym*: "The air of reality in the narrative is assumed with no small skill. It is a fictitious journal of a voyage made in the Southern Ocean, in which Mr. Pym meets with adventures almost as surprising as those of Peter Wilkins, or Sinbad the Sailor" (Pollin [1974], p. 45).

10 AUGUST. Mordecai M. Noah's *Evening Star* summarizes the events described in *Pym*: "What are we to think of it?" There is "mystification about the author's trip" which the *Star* will not attempt to explain: "Let every man fathom Mr. Pym's secret for himself, say we. He tells some wonderful things, that's certain" (Pollin [1978b], p. 10).

11 AUGUST. The *New-York Mirror* reviews *Pym*: "The author would have shown his ingenuity to more purpose, if he had preserved the *vraisemblance* of his narrative. As it is, the gross improbabilit[i]es and preternatural adventures through which his hero passes, soon destroy the interest of the reader, and revolt the imagination. We are constantly tempted to exclaim: 'Ferdinand Mendez Pinto was but a type of thee, thou liar of the first magnitude!' At the same time we must concede to the author, the merit of a fine mastery over language, and powers of description rarely excelled."

11 AUGUST. PHILADELPHIA. The *Saturday Evening Post* publishes "Ode XXX.—To Edgar A. Poe" signed "Horace in Philadelphia," a pseudonym of the Baltimore journalist Lambert A. Wilmer. Apparently alluding to

Poe's current poverty, Wilmer observes that "the poet's prayer" does not petition "for houses or extended lands" or for "fair financial prospects in futurity." The poet seeks only fame:

> And yet, true genius, (like the sun
>   With bats and owls,) is little noted;
> But when his glorious course is run,
> His griefs forgot, his labors done,
>   Then is he prais'd, admired, and quoted!
>
> Dull mediocrity, meanwhile
>   Along his level turnpike speeds,
>   And fame and fortune are his meeds;
> While merit wants one cheering smile,
>   How bless'd stupidity succeeds!

The "heavenly gifted mind" should not be discouraged by this injustice. The passage of time, "sternly frowning on the *base*," will consign inferior poets to oblivion:

> So may it be.—tho' fortune now
>   Averts her face, and heedless crowds
> To blocks, like senseless Pagans, bow;—
>   Yet time shall dissipate the clouds,
>   Dissolve the mist which merit shrouds,
> And fix the laurel on *thy* brow.
>
>   There let it grow; and there 'twould be
>   If justice rul'd and men could see.
>   But reptiles are allow'd to sport
> Their scaly limbs in great Apollo's court.
> Thou once did whip some rascals from the fane
> O let thy vengeful arm be felt again.

18 AUGUST. NEW YORK. The *Albion* reviews *Pym*: "We are disposed to believe that the author is a second Capt. Lemuel Gulliver as regards authenticity, and think that although he does not deal in political and moral satire he has fabricated a volume which will be extensively read and very pleasing" (Pollin [1974], p. 45).

22 AUGUST. PHILADELPHIA. *Alexander's Weekly Messenger* reproduces *Pym*'s title, commenting:

Think of that, Master Brook! What say you, reader[,] to that for a title page? We assure you the book, if possible, is more marvellous still. Captain Riley's narrative was a tame affair, compared with it. "Incredible["] forsooth! The author should have said *impossible*. What will our nautical friends say to the feat of running a sloop with a jib, when her mast has been carried away in a gale of wind? What will the government say to the discoveries near the south pole? Will they not recal[l] the southern exploring expedition, which is rendered wholly unnecessary by Pym's discoveries? What will the Nantucket folks say to the miracle of a vessel being fitted out from that port, which had never been heard of there, by a mercantile house that never had an existence any where?

To be serious, this is a very clever extravaganza, after the manner of De Foe, understood to be written by Mr. Poe, of Virginia. It indicates great talent and vivacity, and will be perused with amusement by every class of readers.

SEPTEMBER. William E. Burton castigates *Pym* in his *Gentleman's Magazine*:

A more impudent attempt at humbugging the public has never been exercised; the voyages of Gulliver were politically satirical, and the adventures of Munchausen, the acknowledged caricature of a celebrated traveller. Sindbad the sailor, Peter Wilkins, and Moore's Utopia, are confessedly works of imagination; but Arthur Gordon Pym puts forth a series of travels outraging possibility, and coolly requires his insulted readers to believe his *ipse dixit*, although he confesses that the early portions of his precious effusion were published in the Southern Literary Messenger as a story written by the editor, Mr. Poe, because he believed that the public at large would pronounce his adventures to be "an impudent fiction." Mr. Poe, if not the author of Pym's book, is at least responsible for its publication, for it is stated in the preface that Mr. Poe assured the author that the shrewdness and common sense of the public would give it a chance of being received as truth. We regret to find Mr. Poe's name in connexion with such a mass of ignorance and effrontery.

SEPTEMBER. NEW YORK. William W. Snowden's *Ladies' Companion* reviews *Pym*: "There seems to be some diversity of opinion as to the *real* authorship of this work. It should be a matter of perfect indifference to the public, who the author is; the book *has been* written and *is* published, and that, certainly, is knowledge enough. It shows but poor taste that the *writer* of a book must be *known* before it can be appreciated. Pym's narrative is peculiarly amusing, although it borders on the marvellous" (Pollin [1975b], pp. 33–34).

SEPTEMBER? NEW YORK, BOSTON, PHILADELPHIA. The *Family Magazine* praises *Pym*: "Commend us to Arthur Gordon Pym! He is a genius and his *adventures* rare and wonderful. If the reader would like to take a voyage of discovery, or go on an exploring expedition to the south pole he has only to take up Arthur Gordon Pym's narrative and if he is not led off to the pole scientifically, he will at least find himself, when he gets there, in a situation where science is no longer useful or necessary, and ready and willing to admit that Arthur Gordon Pym's adventures have been infinitely more astonishing than any before recorded" (Pollin [1974], p. 46).

CA. SEPTEMBER. LONDON. The English office of the New York firm Wiley and Putnam decides to issue *Pym*. George P. Putnam recalls: "The late Mr. D. Appleton was sitting in our office in Paternoster Row. 'Here is an American contribution to geographical science,' I said to him. 'This man has reached a higher latitude than any European navigator. Let us reprint this for the benefit of Mr. Bull.' He assented, and took half share in the venture. The grave particularity of the title and of the narrative misled many of the critics as well as ourselves, and whole columns of these new 'discoveries,' including the hieroglyphics (!) found on the rocks, were copied by many of the English country papers as sober historical truth" (Putnam, p. 471).

4 SEPTEMBER. PHILADELPHIA. Poe writes Nathan C. Brooks in Baltimore, acknowledging a "favor with the $10." He must decline Brooks's invitation to review Washington Irving's writings for the forthcoming *American Museum*: "I should be most unwilling not to execute such a task well, and this I would not do at so short notice, at least now. I have two other engagements which it would be ruinous to defer. Besides this, I am just leaving Arch street for a small house, and, of course, somewhat in confusion . . . . Irving is much overrated, and a nice distinction might be drawn between his just and his surreptitious and adventitious reputation— between what is due to the pioneer solely, and what to the writer." Since Poe believes that a bold investigation of Irving's merits "would strike home," he regrets that he cannot write the critique: "Had you spoken decidedly when I first saw you, I would have adventured. If you can delay the 'Review' until the second number I would be most happy to do my best." Poe's financial situation has improved: "I have gotten nearly out of my late embarrassments. Neilson [Poe] would not aid me, being much pushed himself" (*L*, 1:111–13).

AFTER 4 SEPTEMBER. The Poe family moves to a small house on Sixteenth Street near Locust (Thomas [1978], pp. 25–27).

6 SEPTEMBER. BALTIMORE. The will of Poe's grandmother Elizabeth Cairnes Poe, who died on 7 July 1835, is probated. All her belongings are bequeathed to her daughter Mrs. Maria Clemm (Phillips, 1:494).

OCTOBER. NEW YORK. The *New York Review* notices *Pym*, quoting the complete title:

Notwithstanding this circumstantial and veracious looking length of title, the work is all a fiction. It is written with considerable talent, and an attempt is made, by simplicity of style, minuteness of nautical descriptions, and circumstantiality of narration, to throw over it that air of reality which constitutes the charm of Robinson Crusoe, and Sir Edward Seaward's Narrative. This work has, however, none of the agreeable interest of the two just named. It is not destitute of interest for the imagination, but the interest is painful; there are too many atrocities, too many strange horrors, and finally, there is no conclusion to it; it breaks off suddenly in a mysterious way, which is not only destitute of all *vraisemblance*, but is purely perplexing and vexatious. We cannot, therefore, but consider the author unfortunate in his plan (Pollin [1974], p. 44).

OCTOBER. LONDON. Wiley and Putnam publish an English edition of *Pym* with an abridged subtitle (Pollin [1981], p. 51).

EARLY OCTOBER. BALTIMORE. The first number of the *American Museum*, dated September, contains Poe's tale "Ligeia." A satire commencing in this issue, "The Atlantis, a Southern World—or a Wonderful Continent Discovered," may possibly be his work ("Atlantis" attribution in Quinn, pp. 757–61).

10 OCTOBER. The *Sun* notices the *Museum*: "Baltimore can at length boast of a monthly literary periodical, which, from the specimen before us, bids fair to rival in excellence those of her sister cities. This work . . . is edited by Nathan C. Brooks and Dr. J. E. Snodgrass, two gentlemen well known in the literary world."

13 OCTOBER. LONDON. The *Court Gazette* notices Wiley and Putnam's edition of *Pym*: "We apprehend it [*Pym*] has been produced as a sort of practical exposition and proof of Byron's assertion, that 'truth is stranger than fiction.' It is, in fact, a book of wonders, originally published in an American periodical, without any warranty of truth. It now appears that the exciting interest of the story which is told, and the intrinsic evidence of its veracity and general accuracy, have induced the London publishers to present it to the public in an entire form. The style of the narrative is not an indifferent imitation of that adopted by De Foe, in his best novel, 'Robinson Crusoe' " (Vann, p. 34).

13 OCTOBER. The *Torch* reviews *Pym* at length, disputing its authenticity:

Mr. Arthur Pym . . . stands up sturdily for the truth of his narrative; he is determined not to pass for the shadow of a name, for a mere eidolon, if he can help it, and in a preface of some tact maintains his identity against all unbelievers, while, to give a colour to the matter, his supposed editor slily despatches him in a note at the end of the volume. This no doubt is an excellent trick to coax belief, and one not altogether unworthy of Defoe himself; for it is hard to deny that a man has existed, when we see his coffin carried decently to the grave, and buried with all the fitting solemnities. But even this sacrifice will not, we fear, in our unbelieving age, establish the reality of Mr. Arthur Pym though it must be allowed that the eidolon has strung together as wonderful a set of adventures as lounger or invalid can desire to while away an hour at breakfast or on a sofa (Pollin [1974], p. 52).

20 OCTOBER. The *Naval and Military Gazette* notices *Pym*:

For those who possess a genuine love of the horrible, here is a rich and luxurious banquet; but let not the fastidious, the squeamish, the hypercritical, presume even to glance at such viands as brother Jonathan has in this instance spread forth; for they are to be digested only by the strongest of stomachs.

In this "Narrative" of Mr. Pym's are many "hair-breath 'scapes;" the incidents— some of them—are of a most appalling character; in parts, we find our feelings excited by powerful painting; but, as a whole, the story is very clumsily put together, and the discrepancies are so numerous, and so palpable, that, in its perusal, not even the merest child could be cheated into a belief of the page of truth being before him. For instance, what are we to think of a country (near the South Pole) where *everything is white* [black], and—where the inhabitants (jet black) *have a horror of everything that is white*;—where the *water* is *not* water, and yet it *is* water! . . . .

Here, and in hundreds of other places, we have not only the *improbable* but the *impossible*. It was not thus that De Foe wrote his *Robinson Crusoe*; it was not in such a spirit that Miss Porter conceived and executed her equally sweet and exquisite fiction of *Sir Edward Seaward*.

As we have intimated, however, this book will not be without its admirers (Vann, p. 43).

20 OCTOBER. The *Atlas* gives a detailed synopsis of *Pym*, observing that the story "would have been more entertaining, had the writer been a little more careful in subduing his tendency for the marvellous. He has so ridiculously overdone the recital, that the volume cannot impose upon anybody" (Pollin [1974], pp. 50–52).

21 OCTOBER. The *Era* quotes a long passage from *Pym*. This book "be-longs to the species of romance, which, not satisfied with relating proba-bilities, assumes the outward guise of authentic narrative. Its fault is, that it is too uniformly extravagant; but . . . the story is highly exciting, and leads one to regret that an author who has so evident a penchant for fiction should not lie boldly" (Vann, p. 43).

27 OCTOBER. The *Spectator* excerpts several passages from *Pym*, praising it as "a fiction of no mean skill; displaying much power, much nautical knowledge, and a Defoe-like appearance of reality. Its ease, simplicity, and natural effects, remind one of Marryat." The incidents described in the early chapters are "not physically impossible, and that is all: the later

discoveries are clearly fable: but both the one and the other are told with great appearance of truth . . . . Interest is also excited in the narrative—that kind of breathless and absorbing interest with which we may suppose our ancestors listened to stories of 'men whose heads do grow beneath their shoulders,' or with which we in our youth perused fairy tales. The disgusting though fearful scene of the passing vessel of the dead, the horrors of the tempest and the following famine, and the escape of Pym and Peters from the mountain in whose bowels they are entombed, are all examples of this kind" (Pollin [1974], pp. 53–54).

LATE OCTOBER? The *Monthly Review* for October recommends *Pym* to readers who "will have an *out and out* romance, and the marvels of an unprecedented voyager." While the *Review* praises the author's "originality, boldness, and skill," it observes "that some of the most elaborate scenes, and where no mean power is exhibited, are disgustingly horrible" (Pollin [1974], pp. 49–50).

NOVEMBER. The *Metropolitan Magazine* criticizes *Pym*: "The marvellous story—as we learn from the preface—was first published in an American periodical as a work of fiction. It is a pity it was not left as such. As a romance, some portions of it are sufficiently amusing and exciting; but, when palmed upon the public as a true thing, it cannot appear in any other light than that of a bungling business—an impudent attempt at imposing on the credulity of the ignorant." The *New Monthly Magazine* comments: "Arthur Pym is the American Robinson Crusoe, a man all over wonders, who sees nothing but wonders, vanquishes nothing but wonders, would, indeed, evidently, scorn to have anything to do but with wonders." The *Gentleman's Magazine* mentions *Pym*'s publication under "Literary and Scientific Intelligence" (Pollin [1974], pp. 47–49; [1980], p. 21).

NOVEMBER. BALTIMORE. The *American Museum* contains Poe's tandem stories "The Psyche Zenobia" and "The Scythe of Time" (later entitled "How to Write a Blackwood Article" and "A Predicament").

DECEMBER. PHILADELPHIA. The inside front cover of *Burton's* carries an announcement: "The Gentleman's Magazine has become the sole property of the Editor, William E. Burton" (Robbins [1947], p. 96).

1 DECEMBER. NEW YORK. The *New-York Mirror* publishes a dispatch from its British correspondent, Nathaniel P. Willis, who comments: "The 'American Museum' . . . has certainly put out a first number of uncom-

mon cleverness . . . . It has a paper on the fabulous Atlantis, full of ingenuity and humour; and in a tale called Ligeia, (by Mr. Poe,) there is a fine march of description, which has a touch of D'Israeli's quality, and is worthy of a more intelligible sequel."

CA. 25 DECEMBER. PHILADELPHIA. By making "the most painful sacrifices," Poe manages to pay Mrs. Jones, landlady of the Arch Street boardinghouse where his family resided earlier in the year (Poe to John C. Cox, 6 December 1839).

LATE 1838? Professor Thomas Wyatt, an English author and lecturer, engages Poe to assist in preparing *The Conchologist's First Book*, paying him $50. Poe writes "the Preface and Introduction," as well as translating "from Cuvier, the accounts of the animals" (Poe to G. W. Eveleth, 16 February 1847).

[The volume bore Poe's name on the title page, but was largely the work of Wyatt, whose *Manual of Conchology* had been issued by Harper & Brothers earlier in the year. John Gould Anthony of Harvard University explained Poe's role in an 1875 letter to John Parker of the Peabody Institute in Baltimore:

Some time about *1850* [in 1838] I think, there was published in N. Y. a book called Wyatts Manual of Conchology, illustrated by figures of shells and sold at I believe $6 [$8.00]. This price being somewhat above the means of beginners and too high also for a text-book it was soon apparent that a smaller and less costly work was needed and the author was beset to make an abridgement which could be sold for $1.50 and contain all that was actually needed, but no abridgement could be published without consent of the house that held the copy right of the larger work and they would not spoil the sale of their book by issuing a cheaper one so soon after its publication. So the only way was to get up the abridgement and have it published with the name of some irresponsible person whom it would be idle to sue for damages, and Poe was selected for the scape goat—A consideration of course was given for his assumption of paternity. The *facts* I had from Mr. Wyatt himself who was then lecturing on Conchology and using the abridgement as a help in that business—I think too he had them for sale at his lectures (quoted in Parker to J. H. Ingram, 7 July 1875, ViU–I).

The characterization of Poe as "some irresponsible person" is entirely Anthony's own. Wyatt was Poe's constant admirer and friend, as documented by Thomas (1978), pp. 947–56.]

LATE 1838? Poe assists Wyatt in preparing the latter's *Synopsis of Natural History* (implied by Poe's review in the July 1839 *Burton's*).

EARLY 1839. PHILADELPHIA. Poe borrows $50 from John C. Cox, a merchant living at 64 North Eleventh Street (Poe to Cox, 6 December 1839).

JANUARY. BALTIMORE. The *American Museum* contains Poe's "Literary Small Talk."

12 JANUARY. PHILADELPHIA. The *Saturday Evening Post* announces that its publisher Samuel C. Atkinson has given "the *Editorial* charge of the paper to GEORGE R. GRAHAM, Esq."

FEBRUARY. BALTIMORE. The *American Museum* contains a second installment of Poe's "Literary Small Talk."

20 FEBRUARY. NEW YORK. Harper & Brothers reply to Poe's 19 February letter of inquiry: "We are inclined to think that 'Pym' has not succeeded or been received as well in this country as it has in England. When we published the work, we sent 100 copies of it to London—And we presume they have been sold. In addition to which we understand that an English edition has been printed. We have not seen any review of it in the English papers yet—Should any come to hand, we will preserve and forward them to you. Are you connected with any of the newspapers in Philadelphia? If so, we should be pleased to send you a book for review occasionally" (MB–G).

BEFORE APRIL. PHILADELPHIA. Poe sends "The Haunted Palace" to the *Democratic Review*, then published in Washington. The editor John L. O'Sullivan finds the poem "impossible to comprehend" and rejects it (cited in the *Aristidean* for October 1845 [see BEFORE 8 NOVEMBER 1845]; corroborated by C. F. Briggs to J. R. Lowell, 27 January 1845).

APRIL. BALTIMORE. The *American Museum* contains "The Haunted Palace."

13 APRIL. PHILADELPHIA. The *Saturday Evening Post* carries a prospectus announcing that "GEORGE R. GRAHAM & CO." have purchased the *Casket* from Samuel C. Atkinson. The May number of this Philadelphia monthly "will be the first issued by the new proprietors."

BEFORE 20 APRIL. Haswell, Barrington, and Haswell publish:

THE / CONCHOLOGIST'S FIRST BOOK: / OR, / A SYSTEM / OF / TESTA-

CEOUS MALACOLOGY, / *Arranged expressly for the use of Schools*, / IN WHICH / THE ANIMALS, ACCORDING TO CUVIER, ARE GIVEN / WITH THE SHELLS, / A GREAT NUMBER OF NEW SPECIES ADDED, / AND THE WHOLE BROUGHT UP, AS ACCURATELY AS POSSIBLE, TO / THE PRESENT CONDITION OF THE SCIENCE. / [rule] / BY EDGAR A. POE. / [rule] / WITH ILLUSTRATIONS OF TWO HUNDRED AND FIFTEEN SHELLS, / PRESENTING A CORRECT TYPE OF EACH GENUS.

In the preface, signed "E. A. P.," Poe acknowledges his "great indebtedness" to the Philadelphia scientist and publisher Isaac Lea and to "Mr. Thomas Wyatt, and his late excellent *Manual of Conchology*."

20 APRIL. The *Saturday Courier* notices *The Conchologist's First Book*:.

The volume before us is from the pen of Edgar A. Poe, who was formerly editor of The Southern Literary Messenger, and who is the author of several works. The object of the present work is to furnish a system of Testaceous Malacology, set forth in a plain way, for a first book. It has been arranged expressly to introduce one of the most beautiful and interesting sciences into our schools, a science so connected with geology, and fraught with material for pleasurable investigation. This little work is based on the anatomy of the animals from Lamarck and Cuvier, and all the *new foreign species*, as well as our American, brought up to the present time. It is sold for the small sum of $1[.]75, by the principal booksellers in the city.

27 APRIL. The *Saturday Chronicle* notices *The Conchologist's First Book* (Pollin [1980], p. 22).

30 APRIL. The *United States Gazette* notices the publication of Wyatt's *Synopsis of Natural History*.

EARLY MAY? Carey & Hart send the *Gift* for 1840 to the printers. This annual, which contains Poe's tale "William Wilson," is prefaced by an advertisement dated 1 May.

EARLY MAY? Motivated by his continuing financial problems, Poe seeks employment as an assistant editor under William E. Burton.

11 MAY. Burton writes Poe: "I have given your proposals a fair consideration. I wish to form some such engagement as that which you have proposed, and know of no one more likely to suit my views than yourself." He mentions the difficulties his *Gentleman's Magazine* is encountering as "some slight reason" for his delay in accepting Poe's "indubitably liberal" proposal: "The expenses of the Magazine are already wofully heavy; more so than my circulation warrants. I am certain that my expenditure exceeds that of any publication now extant, including the monthlies which are

double in price. Competition is high,—new claimants are daily rising. I am therefore compelled to give expensive plates, thicker paper, and better printing than my antagonists, or allow them to win the goal." Burton offers Poe $10 a week for the remainder of the year: "Should we remain together, which I see no reason to negative, your proposition shall be in force for 1840 . . . . Two hours a day, except occasionally, will, I believe, be sufficient for all required, except in the production of any article of your own. At all events, you could easily find time for any other light avocation—supposing that you did not exercise your talents in behalf of any publication interfering with the prospects of the G. M." Burton will dine at his home, 100 North Ninth Street, today at 3 PM: "If you will cut your mutton with me, good. If not, write or see me at your leisure" (*W,* 17:45–46; Quinn, p. 278).

18 MAY. The *Saturday Chronicle* contains Poe's tale "The Devil in the Belfry."

BEFORE 30 MAY. Poe prepares a scathing critique of the Baltimore poetaster Rufus Dawes for the *Gentleman's Magazine.* Burton decides not to publish it; Poe then writes him in a state of depression.

30 MAY. Burton replies to Poe: "I am sorry that you thought [it] necessary to send me such a letter as your last. The troubles of the world have given a morbid tone to your feelings which it is your duty to discourage." He advises:

We shall agree very well, but you must get rid of your avowed ill-feelings towards your brother-authors—you see that I speak plainly—indeed, I cannot speak otherwise. Several of my friends, hearing of our connexion, have warned me of your uncalled for severity in criticism—and I confess that your article on Dawes is not written with that spirit of fairness which, in a more healthy state of mind, you would undoubtedly have used. The independence of my book reviews has been noticed throughout the Union—my remarks upon my friend [Robert M.] Bird's last novel evince my freedom from the trammels of expediency, but there is no necessity for undue severity. I wish particularly to deal leniently with the faults of genius, and feeling satisfied that Dawes possesses a portion of the true fire, I regretted the word-catching tone of your critique (MB–G).

JUNE. The outside back cover of *Burton's* carries an announcement: "William E. Burton, Editor and Proprietor, has much pleasure in stating that he has made arrangements with Edgar A. Poe, Esq., late Editor of the Southern Literary Messenger, to devote his abilities and experience to a portion of the Editorial duties of the Gentleman's Magazine." The inside front cover identifies Poe's position as "Assistant Editor." This number contains his first contribution, an unsigned review of Frederick Marryat's *The Phantom Ship*.

JUNE OR LATER? Burton introduces Poe to the Philadelphia literati at a dinner held at the home of the playwright Richard Penn Smith, 243 North Sixth Street, above Callowhill: "At this supper party were present Louis A. Godey, then owner and editor of *Godey's Magazine*, which had been started about five years previously; Robert M. Bird; Robert T. Conrad, editor of the *Daily Intelligencer*; Joseph R. Chandler, editor of the *United States Gazette*; Joseph C. Neal; Morton McMichael, then an alderman in Spring Garden; Adam Waldie, publisher of *Waldie's Circulating Library*, and a few others. Owing to the engagements of Mr. Burton at the Chestnut Street Theatre, the supper was not placed upon the table until midnight, at which time Mr. Burton, Mr. Wemyss, Mr. Wood and Mr. John R. Scott made their appearance. Edwin Forrest—who had but lately returned from England with his wife—was also present" (Smith's son, Horace Wemyss Smith, quoted by Rosenbach, p. 296).

JUNE OR LATER? Thomas Dunn English, a young poet who frequently contributes to *Burton's*, is introduced to Poe at the magazine's office on Dock Street, near the southeast corner of Walnut and Second:

I was in the office one day when Burton introduced me to Poe, and the two new acquaintances began to talk with each other. I was impressed favorably with the appearance and manner of the author. He was clad in a plain and rather worn suit of black which was carefully brushed, and his linen was especially notable for its cleanliness. His eyes at that time were large, bright and piercing, his manner easy and refined, and his tone and conversation winning. In a short while we went out of the office together and remained in conversation as we walked along the street. We parted in Chestnut Street some few blocks above Third, apparently well pleased with each other. There was no bond of sympathy between Poe and me, except the admiration I had for his undoubted genius; but our intimacy increased as months wore on, and I became a frequent visitor to his family. Mrs. Poe was a delicate gentlewoman, with an air of refinement and good breeding, and Mrs. Clemm had more of the mother than the mother-in-law about her. It was some time before I discovered anything about Poe's habits that was not proper . . . . I was passing along the street one night on my way homeward, when I saw some one struggling in a vain attempt to raise himself from the gutter. Supposing the person had tripped and fallen, I bent forward and assisted him to arise. To my utter astonishment I found it was Poe. He recognized me, and was very effusive in his recognition. I volunteered to see him home, but had some difficulty to prevent his apparent desire to survey the sidewalk by a series of triangles. I managed to get him through the front gate of his yard to the front door . . . . I knocked at the door, and Mrs. Clemm opened it. Raising her voice, she cried: "You make Eddie drunk, and then you bring him home." . . .

Three days after when I saw Poe—for if I remember rightly the next two days he was not at the office—he was heartily ashamed of the matter, and said that it was an unusual thing with him, and would never occur again.

For some weeks I saw Poe occasionally at the office and elsewhere, industrious as a beaver. I think it was several weeks before I observed any other aberration. Then I heard through two or three persons that Poe had been found gloriously drunk in the street after nightfall, and had been helped home (English, pp. 1415–16).

JUNE OR LATER? English introduces Poe to the poet Henry B. Hirst (Woodberry, 2:419).

1 JUNE. The *Saturday Courier* notices the first number of the *Literary Examiner*, dated May: "A new monthly, published at Pittsburg[h], has just commenced, under the auspices of E. Burke Fisher and Wm. H. Burleigh. They are gentlemen who have been several years known as writers for various periodicals in our country."

10 JUNE. PITTSBURGH. Fisher writes Poe, praising his "mode of handling authors," and soliciting his contributions for the *Examiner*: "terms of remuneration are $2 per page. And I shall make your case an exception and make the terms $3, or rather than not meet your favorable consideration $4 per page . . . . I pledge myself to send you the amount due for whatever you may write, immediately on the publication of each article. The quantity is discretionary with yourself. The choice of subjects could not be left in better hands" (Heartman and Canny, pp. 219–20).

20 JUNE. PHILADELPHIA. Nathaniel P. Willis' *Tortesa, the Usurer* opens at the Walnut Street Theatre, northeast corner of Ninth and Walnut. Poe probably attends the play, which he favorably reviews in the July *Examiner* and the August *Burton's* (Quinn, p. 284).

26 JUNE. Poe writes Nathan C. Brooks in Baltimore (cited *L*, 2:578).

LATE JUNE? PITTSBURGH. In the *Examiner* for June Fisher announces that Poe has been engaged as a regular contributor (Hull, p. 706).

JULY. PHILADELPHIA. *Burton's* contains Poe's poems "To Ianthe in Heaven," excerpted from his tale "The Visionary," and "Spirits of the Dead," formerly entitled "Visit of the Dead." Poe reviews James Fenimore Cooper's *History of the Navy of the United States*, Thomas Wyatt's *Synopsis of Natural History*, and other books. "As the work of Mr. Wyatt professes to be simply a translation of the well-known 'Tableaux' of M. Lemmonnier [Louis Ceran Lemonnier], we need say little more in the way of recommendation than that all the useful spirit of the original has been preserved—and this we say from personal knowledge, and the closest inspection and collation."

[On 21 September Poe wrote Philip Pendleton Cooke: "The critiques . . . are all mine in the July No—& all mine in the Aug & Sep. with the exception of the 3 first in each—which are by Burton."]

1 JULY. The *Pennsylvania Inquirer* reports: "An Ourang Outang. An animal of this species, and of a truly extraordinary character, has just arrived at this port, in the ship Saluda, from Africa.—We are told that it is more perfect in its proportions, and in its resemblance to the human form, than any specimen of the kind, ever seen in this country."

[Contemporary Philadelphians were captivated by the then unfamiliar animals of Africa and Asia. When Poe wrote "The Murders in the Rue Morgue," he would have been mindful of the popular sensation caused by the exhibition of the ourang outang at the Masonic Hall, Chestnut Street, during August and September 1839 (Thomas [1978], pp. 50–51, 57–59).]

3 JULY. The *Inquirer* notices *Burton's*, reprinting Poe's "To Ianthe in Heaven" as a "specimen" of the "excellent poetry" in this number.

4 JULY. NEW YORK. Burton, who is acting at Niblo's Gardens during the summer season, writes Poe about the *Gentleman's Magazine*:

Will you please see [the engraver Charles N.] Parmelee, and get him to do the enclosed directly, for this next number . . . . Desire [the magazine's clerk Charles R.] Morrell to obtain Mr. R. P. Smith's life from Mr. [James] Goodman, if he has not got it yet, but it must be done directly, because we want the matter to *begin* the September number, and consequently to *end* the next sheet. If the "Life" will not be ready, we must put in something else, with another plate, for I want the next number out immediately . . . .

I shall endeavor to send you an article (a short one) for this number, if you have three pages to spare. You will receive it by Monday, or not at all. I have so long been absent from the pages of the Maga. that if I do not make my appearance soon my readers will imagine a total absquatulation (MB–G).

6 JULY. PHILADELPHIA. The *Saturday Courier* comments: "We have omitted to name before that Edgar A. Poe has been associated with Mr. Burton, in the editorial control of 'Burton's Magazine.'—Mr. Poe was very favorably known as editor of the Southern Literary Messenger in its early days; and he has produced several works, which prove him a man of letters and industry. His accession is very valuable."

9 JULY. PITTSBURGH. E. Burke Fisher replies to Poe's letter of 5 July, which contained a review of Willis' *Tortesa, the Usurer*: "I am truly obliged by the receipt of your criticism admirable—scarcely severe enough, but still Willis is a kind of national pet and we must regard his faults as we do those of a spoiled stripling, in the hope that he will amend." Fisher discusses the prospects of the *Literary Examiner*: "With you to assist me in the department of reviews, that portion of the Magazine shall become what the Messenger was before you quitted . . . . You make the terms of compensation too low, but in my experimental stage I cannot do otherwise than accept the favor . . . of obliging myself to pay $3 per page" (Heartman and Canny, pp. 220–21).

10 JULY. PHILADELPHIA. *Alexander's Weekly Messenger* reviews *Burton's*, praising Poe: "he is a gentleman of superior ability and character, and we are glad to see that his name is associated with Mr. Burton in the future direction of the Gentleman's Magazine."

14 JULY. Poe writes George W. Poe, his second cousin: "Owing to my absence from Richmond for some time, I did not receive your letter until a few days ago, it having followed me from place to place, and at last caught me here." He discusses his own career and the history of the Poe family in America; he encloses a genealogical table listing his relatives. Although he will remain in Philadelphia "perhaps for a year," he considers Richmond his home (*L*, 2:682–86).

LATE JULY? PITTSBURGH. The *Literary Examiner* for July contains Poe's review of Willis' *Tortesa, the Usurer*.

AUGUST. PHILADELPHIA. *Burton's* contains Poe's tale "The Man that was Used Up," as well as his poems (all reprints) "Fairyland," "To———" (originally entitled "To Elizabeth"), and "To the River———." All the reviews are Poe's, except the first three; the notice of Willis' *Tortesa, the Usurer* is a condensation of his critique in the July *Examiner*. A brief essay, "An Opinion on Dreams," may be his work.

6 AUGUST. BALTIMORE. The *Sun* notices *Burton's*, alluding unfavorably to the proprietor's lengthy theatrical engagement in New York: "It is evident that the senior editor [Burton] has been busied elsewhere, and consequently, although this number contains many excellent articles, there is a palpable want of tact in the manner in which it has been gotten up."

8 AUGUST. PHILADELPHIA. Poe replies to the Baltimore journalist John Beauchamp Jones, whose 6 August letter cited the criticism in the *Sun*: "I

presume the 'Sun' has expressed the opinion that the August No: of the Mag: is not well edited, because it has been more than usually praised in this respect. No number ever issued from this office has recd 1/4 of the approbation which this has elicited. We are run down with puffs especially from the North—the South has not yet been so entirely heard from. Here lies the true secret of the spleen of the little fish." Since Poe has not seen the other attacks mentioned in the letter, he would be "much obliged" if Jones would forward them to him: "I intend to put up with nothing that I can *put down* (excuse the pun) and I am not aware that there is any one in Baltimore whom I have particular reason to fear in a regular set-to . . . . You speak of 'enemies'—could you give me their names? All the literary people in Baltimore, as far as I know them, have at least *professed* a friendship" (*L*, 1:113–14, 2:686; Moldenhauer [1973], pp. 45, 47).

17 AUGUST. LONDON. Under the heading "Sufferings from Thirst" *Franklin's Miscellany* excerpts "From *Gordon Pym's Narrative*," Chapter XIII, the diary entries for 31 July, 1 and 2 August 1827. This passage is reprinted in the *Free Press and Literary Times* on 24 August 1839 (Vann, pp. 43–44).

22 AUGUST. PETERSBURG, VIRGINIA. In *Th' Time o' Day* Hiram Haines comments: "The lines to '*Ianthe in Heaven*' from the pen of Edgar A. Poe, Esq., formerly Editor of the Southern Literary Messenger, but now co-Editor of the Gentleman's Magazine, are deeply touching and 'true to nature's feeling.' " Haines reprints this poem from the July *Burton's* (Ostrom [1942], p. 69).

LATE AUGUST? PITTSBURGH. The *Literary Examiner* for August contains Poe's article "American Novel-Writing."

SEPTEMBER. PHILADELPHIA. *Burton's* features Poe's tale "The Fall of the House of Usher," which incorporates his poem "The Haunted Palace." He also contributes the gymnastic article "A Chapter on Field Sports," a lengthy criticism of Friedrich de la Motte-Fouqué's romance *Undine*, and the other reviews (except the first three).

3 SEPTEMBER. In the *Pennsylvanian* Joseph C. Neal comments:

Burton's Gentleman's Magazine for September has been received, and as usual with that popular periodical, it contains a great variety of original matter, well written, varied in its character, and calculated to interest the general reader . . . . There is also a sketch of much power and peculiar interest entitled "The House of Usher," which cannot fail to attract attention. It is of the German cast, and is a remarkable specimen of a style of writing which possesses many attractions for those who love to dwell upon the terrible. It is from the pen of Edgar A. Poe, now the assistant editor of the Gentleman's Magazine, and well known to the public by his able editorship of the Southern Literary Messenger, to which he gave a high character, particularly by his fearless and independent criticisms.

4 SEPTEMBER. Reviewing *Burton's* in *Alexander's Weekly Messenger*, John Frost praises Poe's tale as a "finished picture":

We must say that we derive no small enjoyment from a delineation like this. We like to see the evidences of study and thought, as well as inspiration, in the design, and of careful and elaborate handling in the execution, as well as of grand and striking effect in the *tout ensemble*. "The Fall of the House of Usher," is what we denominate a stern and sombre, but at the same time, a noble and imposing picture, such as can be drawn only by a master hand. Such things are not produced by your slip-shod amateurs in composition, some of whom, in the character of critics, perhaps, may display their utter inability to perceive in this very performance any characteristic of its real design.

4 SEPTEMBER. Joseph R. Chandler reviews *Burton's* in the *United States Gazette*:

This periodical, the September number of which has been for some days upon our table, is, we perceive, under the editorial direction of Edgar A. Poe, not unknown to fame. The contents of this number of the work bear testimony to the industry of the editor as a writer, and to his judgment in selecting and sanctioning articles for publication . . . .

The story of "The Fall of the House of Usher" is from the pen of Mr. Poe, and is very interesting—a well told tale. Mr. Poe is, in our opinion, not only a good writer, but a good, though (if we ought not rather to say *because*) a severe judge; and has brought upon himself the ill will of certain writers, who have not, perhaps, the same estimate of their works that others have, and are rather under discipline. We have, we confess, seen some of Mr. Poe's remarks, that looked as if he had not sat down to *coax* young writers into correct imaginings or grammatical utterance; and when applying the lash of his criticism, it appeared to us (we may have been mistaken) as if he had determined to waken some dunce to a sensation of literary justice, by tying an extra knot on the lash. The noise made convinced us that justice was satisfied, however mercy may have fared . . . .

Mr. Poe praises when he thinks commendations are due, and censures whenever and wherever he thinks censure deserved; he will thus prove a blessing to the literature of the country, which needs a little wholesome discipline, and we trust that its true friends will treat with kindness and respect the man who has the courage to exhibit his friendship for the cause by sound severity.

5 SEPTEMBER. The *Public Ledger* notices *Burton's*: "Poe's contributions are unusually excellent."

5 SEPTEMBER. Poe sends the September *Burton's* to the Richmond author James E. Heath, who is assisting Thomas Willis White in editing the

Southern Literary Messenger. Although Poe recognizes that White has reason to harbor resentment toward him, he nonetheless hopes that the *Messenger* will notice *Burton's* and reprint "The Fall of the House of Usher." Poe assures Heath that he now abstains from alcohol (Heath's 12 September reply).

7 SEPTEMBER. The *Saturday Evening Post* notices *Burton's*: "There are some savage reviews in this number, possibly from the pen of Mr. Poe."

7 SEPTEMBER. NEW YORK. Mordecai M. Noah reviews *Burton's* in his *Evening Star*: "Mr. Poe's tale of 'The Fall of the House of Usher,' would have been considered a *chef d'oeuvre* if it had appeared in the pages of Blackwood."

BEFORE 11 SEPTEMBER. BALTIMORE. Joseph Evans Snodgrass sends Poe an issue of the Saint Louis *Commercial Bulletin* containing a favorable notice of his editorship of *Burton's*: "there are few writers in this country—take Neal, Irving, & Willis away and we would say *none*—who can compete successfully, in many respects, with Poe. With an acuteness of observation, a vigorous and effective style, and an independence that defies control, he unites a fervid fancy and a most beautiful enthusiasm. His is a high destiny" (*Bulletin* quoted in Poe's reply).

11 SEPTEMBER. PHILADELPHIA. Poe writes Snodgrass, thanking him for the *Bulletin*. He asks his friend to write a "rigidly just" notice of the September *Burton's*, which will incorporate the Saint Louis paper's praise: "The critique when written might be handed to Neilson Poe [editor of the *Baltimore Chronicle*]. If you ask him to insert it editorially, it is possible he may do it—but, in fact, I have no great faith in him. If he refuses—then upon your stating the fact to Mr [Samuel] Harker of the 'Republican'— you will secure its insertion there." Poe is about to publish a collection of his tales; he promises Snodgrass an early copy. "Did you see the 'Weekly Messenger' (Alexander's) or Noah's Evening Star? They spoke highly of my tale—'The House of Usher'.—as also the Pennsylvanian & The U.S. Gazette of this city" (*L*, 1:115–17).

11 SEPTEMBER. *Alexander's Weekly Messenger* notices the second edition of Poe's *Conchologist's First Book*:

The first very large edition of this work was exhausted in two months; a fact which speaks strongly in its favor. It has become a text-book in most of the larger Seminaries to the North and East, and is well received every where. It differs from the ordinary small books on the same subject in many essential respects—for example, in particularizing the American species; in the adoption of a modified

classification from La Marck and De Blainville; and, especially, in giving a suc-
cinct anatomical account of the animal which inhabits each shell—a point never
before attended to in a school Conchology. The author's versatile abilities are too
well known to the public to need comment from us; he acknowledges his indebtedness, in many respects, to Mr. Isaac Lea of this city. Colored copies of the work,
executed under the superintendence of Mr. James Ackerman, are for sale at our
principal bookstores.

12 SEPTEMBER. RICHMOND. Heath replies to Poe:

Since the receipt of yours of the 5 inst. I have been so exceedingly occupied and
withal so very much indisposed, that I could not until within the last day or two,
take a peep into the interesting magazine which you were good enough to send
me. I have read your article "The Fall of the House of Usher" with attention, and
I think it among the best of your compositions of that class which I have seen. A
man need not have a critical judgement nor a very refined taste to decide, that no
one could have written the tale, without possessing great scope of imagination,
vigorous thought, and a happy command of language; but I am sure you will
appreciate my candor when I say that I never could feel much interest in that class
of compositions. I mean that I never could experience pleasure in reading tales of
horror and mystery however much the narrative should be dignified by genius.
They leave a painful and melancholy impression on my mind, and I do not
perceive their tendency to improve the heart.

White "disclaims the existence of any unkind feeling" toward Poe; and he
will admit a notice of *Burton's* in the *Southern Literary Messenger*, "if possible
in the October number. He is apprehensive however that the 'Fall of the
House of Usher' would not only occupy more space than he can conven-
iently spare . . . but that the subject matter is not such as would be
acceptable to a large majority of his readers. He doubts whether the
readers of the Messenger have much relish for tales of the German School
although written with great power and ability." Heath is glad that Poe has
overcome "a seductive and dangerous treatment which too often prostrates
the wisest and best by its fatal grasp" (*W*, 17:47–48).

14 SEPTEMBER. PHILADELPHIA. The *Saturday Courier* notices *The Conchologist's First Book*: "This is the second edition of a work from the pen of
Edgar A. Poe, Esq., which we had occasion favourably to notice not long
ago. That the public have so soon demanded a second issue, is an evidence
that the book is properly appreciated."

16 SEPTEMBER. CHARLESTOWN, VIRGINIA. Philip Pendleton Cooke replies
to Poe's "friendly letter," which he received "a long time ago." He will
subscribe to *Burton's* and contribute to it occasionally, although "a profession & matrimony" have largely cured his "madness of scribbling." Complying with Poe's request, Cooke gives his opinion of "Ligeia":

The whole piece is but a sermon from the text of "Joseph Glanvil" which you cap it with—and your intent is to tell a tale of the "mighty will" contending with & finally vanquishing Death. The struggle is vigorously described—and I appreciated every sentence as I advanced, until the Lady Ligeia takes possession of the deserted *quarters* (I write like a butcher) of the Lady Rowena. There I was shocked by a violation of the ghostly proprieties—so to speak—and wondered how the Lady Ligeia—a wandering essence—could, in quickening *the body of the Lady Rowena* (such is the idea) become suddenly the visible, bodily, Ligeia. If Rowena's bodily form had been retained as a shell or case for the disembodied Lady Ligeia, and you had only become aware *gradually* that the blue Saxon eye of the "Lady Rowena of Tremaine" grew daily darker with the peculiar, intense expression of the "look" which had belonged to Ligeia—that a mind of grander powers, a soul of more glowing fires occupied the quickened body and gave an old familiar expression to its motions—if you had brooded and meditated upon the change until proof accumulated upon proof, making wonder certainty, and then, in the moment of some strangest of all evidence of the transition, broken out into the exclamation which ends the story—the *effect* would not have been lessened, and the "ghostly proprieties" would, I think, have been better observed (W, 17:49–51).

BEFORE 21 SEPTEMBER. TARRYTOWN, NEW YORK? Washington Irving replies to a letter from Poe, who has sent him the September *Burton's*: "I am much pleased with a tale called 'The House of Usher,' and should think that a collection of tales, equally well written, could not fail of being favorably received . . . . Its graphic effect is powerful" (quoted in the advertisement bound in the *Tales of the Grotesque and Arabesque*; cf. Poe to Irving, 12 October, and Irving to Poe, 6 November).

21 SEPTEMBER. PHILADELPHIA. Poe replies to Cooke's 16 September letter:

Touching Ligeia, you are right—all right—throughout. The *gradual* perception of the fact that Ligeia lives again in the person of Rowena, is a far loftier and more thrilling idea than the one I have embodied. It offers, in my opinion, the widest possible scope to the imagination—it might be rendered even sublime. And this idea was mine—had I never written before I should have adopted it—but then there is Morella. Do you remember, there, the *gradual* conviction on the part of the parent that the spirit of the first Morella tenants the person of the second? It was necessary, since Morella was written, to modify Ligeia. I was forced to be content with a sudden half-consciousness, on the part of the narrator, that Ligeia stood before him. One point I have not fully carried out—I should have intimated that the *will* did not perfect its intention—there shd have been a relapse—a final one—and Ligeia (who had only succeeded in so much as to convey an idea of the truth to the narrator) should be at length entombed as Rowena—the bodily alterations having gradually faded away.

Poe mentions that he has received a letter from Washington Irving praising "The Fall of the House of Usher," and that he will publish his tales in two volumes during autumn. He expresses dissatisfaction with Burton and his *Gentleman's Magazine*: "Do not think of subscribing. The criticisms are not worth your notice. Of course, I pay no attention to them—for there are 2 of us. It is not pleasant to be taxed with the twaddle of other people, or to let other people be taxed with ours . . . . As soon as Fate allows I will have a Magazine of my own—and will endeavor to kick up a dust" (*L*, 2:686–88).

21 SEPTEMBER. The *Saturday Evening Post* observes that the *Gift* for 1840 is "already published." The annual contains Poe's "William Wilson."

28 SEPTEMBER. PHILADELPHIA. The publishers Lea & Blanchard, southeast corner of Fourth and Chestnut Streets, write Poe: "As your wish in having your Tales printed is not immediately pecuniary, we will at our own risque & expense print a Small Ed[ition] say 1750 copies. This sum if sold—will pay but a small profit, which if realized is to be ours—The copy right will remain with you, and when ready a few copies for distribution among your friends, will be at your Service." The tales will make "2 vols. . . . say 240 pages each"; the printer Mr. Haswell will be ready to proceed by Tuesday (MB–G).

OCTOBER. *Burton's* reprints "William Wilson" from the *Gift*. "A Chapter on Field Sports" and all the reviews are by Poe. He criticizes Longfellow's *Hyperion: A Romance* as "a profusion of rich thought" which is "without design, without shape, without beginning, middle, or end."

OCTOBER. RICHMOND. James E. Heath notices the September *Burton's* in the *Southern Literary Messenger*:

We are pleased to find that our old assistant, Edgar A. Poe, is connected with Burton in the editorial management of the "Gentleman's Magazine." Mr. Poe, is favorably known to the readers of the Messenger, as a gentleman of fine endowments; possessing a taste classical and refined; an imagination affluent and splendid, and withall, a singular capacity for minute and mathematical detail. We always predicted that Mr. Poe would reach a high grade in American literature, but we also thought and still think, that he is too much attached to the gloomy German mysticism, to be a useful and effective writer, without a total divorce from that sombre school. Take for example, the tale of "the Fall of the House of Usher," in the September number of the Magazine, which is understood to be the production of his pen. It is written with great power, but leaves on the mind a painful and horrible impression, without any redeeming admonition to the heart. It resembles a finely sculptured statue, beautiful to the eye, but without an immortal spirit. We wish Mr. Poe would stick to the department of criticism; *there*, he is an able professor, and he uses up the vermin who are continually crawling, unbidden, into the literary arena, with the skill and *nonchalance* of a

HENRY WADSWORTH LONGFELLOW

practised surgeon. He cuts them up by piece-meal; and rids the republic of letters, of such nuisances, just as a good officer of police sentences to their proper destination, the night-strollers and vagabonds who infest our cities. We sincerely wish Mr. Poe well, and hope that he will take our advice in good part.

BEFORE 7 OCTOBER. BALTIMORE. Snodgrass writes Poe that he prepared the critique of the September *Burton's*, but that Neilson Poe would not print it in the *Baltimore Chronicle* (Poe's reply; cf. his 11 September request).

7 OCTOBER. PHILADELPHIA. Poe writes Snodgrass: "I *felt* that N. Poe, would not insert the article editorially. In your private ear, I believe him to be the bitterest enemy I have in the world. He is the more despicable in this, since he makes loud professions of friendship. Was it 'relationship &c.' which prevented him saying *any thing at all* of the 2 or 3 last Nos. of the Gents' Mag?" Poe is forwarding the current *Burton's*: "In the Octo. no: all the criticisms are mine—also the gymnastic article" (*L*, 1:120—21).

12 OCTOBER. Poe replies to Washington Irving's letter written before 21 September. Enclosing the October *Burton's*, he makes "another request," which he hopes Irving will not find importunate:

Mess: Lea & Blanchard are about publishing a collection of my Tales, in 2 vols, to be issued early next month. As these Tales, in their course of original publication from time to time, have received many high praises from gentlemen whose opinions are of weight; and as these encomiums have already been published in the papers of the day, (being comprised in notices of the Southern Lit: Messenger and other Magazines) Mess. L & B. think there would be nothing objectionable in *their* reprinting them, in the ordinary form of an advertisement appended to the various books which they may issue before mine. I do not speak altogether of editorial opinions, but of the personal opinions of some of our principal literary men, which have found their way into the papers. Among others, I may mention Mr Paulding, Mr Kennedy & Mr Willis. Now, if, to the very high encomiums which have been lavished upon some of my tales by these & others, I could be permitted to add *even a word or two* from yourself, in relation to the tale of "William Wilson" (which I consider my best effort) *my fortune would be made* (L, 2:688–90).

[The *Tales of the Grotesque and Arabesque* contained a four-page advertisement, usually inserted before the title page of the second volume. In it Poe quoted favorable opinions from newspapers and magazines, as well as from letters he had received from Irving and other literati.]

16? OCTOBER. John Frost reviews *Burton's* in *Alexander's Weekly Messenger*: " 'William Wilson,' by Mr. Poe, reminds us of Godwin and Brockden Brown. The writer is a kindred spirit of theirs in his style of art. He paints with sombre Rembrandt-like tints, and there is great force and vigor of conception in whatever he produces."

16 OCTOBER. JACKSON, TENNESSEE. John Tomlin, a minor poet, sends Poe a contribution for *Burton's*: "The Manuscript Story of 'Theodoric of the Amali' is with diffidence submitted to your better judgement for an opinion. A '*brither sinners*' [sic] hopes of future celebrity in *his* yet untrodden paths of Fiction, depends almost entirely on the success of 'Theodoric of the Amali.' " Tomlin "would feel proud in having Edgar A Poe as a correspondent" (MB–G).

30 OCTOBER. PHILADELPHIA. Lea & Blanchard reply to Poe: "The printing of a few extra copies of your tales on fine paper would be very troublesome to the printer. But if he is willing we have no objection to *six* copies being printed at your cost." They intend to send Poe "20 copies of the edition . . . on publication for private distribution" (Woodberry, 2:376).

NOVEMBER. *Burton's* reprints Poe's "Morella" from the forthcoming *Tales of the Grotesque and Arabesque*; the story incorporates his poem "Catholic Hymn." Poe reviews William Gilmore Simms's novel *The Damsel of Darien*, as well as *Shakespeare and His Friends*, *The Canons of Good Breeding*, and the *Literary Souvenir* for 1840.

2 NOVEMBER. The *Saturday Courier* reviews *Burton's*, praising "Morella" as "decidedly the most finished [story] in this month's issue." The weekly's co-editor, Ezra Holden, gives an advance notice:

> *"Tales of the Grotesque and Arabesque." Lea & Blanchard.*
> We purposed, a week or two ago, saying that our publishers had in press a collection of tales from the pen of Mr. Edgar A. Poe, now of the Gentleman's Magazine. It gives us much pleasure that these productions are forthcoming in the more substantial form of book publication.—They are richly worthy of it. Many of them are of a very high order of merit, and have been admired wherever they have been perused by men of mind. Mr. Poe is no imitator in story-telling. He has a peculiarity of his own—dealing often in rather wild imaginings; and yet he always contrives to sustain his plots with so much novelty of incident, that you must read him out in spite of any sober realities that may occasionally flit across the mind. And, as you read you are ever impressed with the truth that he has much fancy—great richness of description, and true poetry for his imagery and colorings.
> When Mr. Poe's tales shall appear, we are sure they will meet high appreciation, and be regarded as valuable contributions to the literature of our country.

2 NOVEMBER. The *Saturday Evening Post* reviews *Burton's*, observing that Poe "is deeply imbued with the spirit of German literature, and as one of that class of writers has few equals." The *Pennsylvanian* finds that "the editorial and critical department" of *Burton's* "is marked with spirit, talent and independence."

6 NOVEMBER. John Frost notices *Burton's* in *Alexander's Weekly Messenger*: "*Morella*, a Tale, by Edgar A. Poe, is worthy of the fame of the assistant editor of this Magazine."

6 NOVEMBER. GREENBURGH, NEW YORK. Washington Irving replies to Poe's 12 October letter: "I have read your little tale of William Wilson with much pleasure. It is managed in a highly picturesque Style and the Singular and Mysterious interest is well sustained throughout—I repeat what I have said in regard to a previous production, which you did me the favor to send me, that I cannot but think a Series of articles of like Style and merit would be extremely well received by the public." Irving prefers the present story to "The Fall of the House of Usher": "It is simpler. In your first you have been too anxious to present your pictures vividly to the eye, or too distrustful of your effect, and have laid on too much colouring. It is erring on the best side—the side of luxurance. That tale might be improved by relieving the Style from some of the epithets" (Irving, 3:24–25).

9 NOVEMBER. PHILADELPHIA. The *Saturday Evening Post* carries a valedictory by its publisher Samuel C. Atkinson, who announces that he has sold the paper to John S. Du Solle and George R. Graham.

BEFORE 11 NOVEMBER. BALTIMORE. Joseph Evans Snodgrass publishes a critique in the *Baltimore Post*: "Poe can throw a chain of enchantment around every scene he attempts to describe, and one of his peculiarities consists in the perfect harmony between each *locale* and the characters introduced. He has certainly written some of the most popular tales of American origin" (quoted in the advertisement bound in the *Tales of the Grotesque and Arabesque*).

11 NOVEMBER. PHILADELPHIA. Poe writes Snodgrass, acknowledging "the reception of *two* letters . . . one of which . . . has been lying *perdu* in the P. Office for some 10 days." Although he has not yet received the copy of the *Baltimore Post*, he saw Snodgrass' critique "on file in a friend's office." The only fault he can find in the article is that it is entirely too favorable:

I am sure you will be pleased to hear that Washington Irving has addressed me 2 letters, abounding in high passages of compliment in regard to my Tales—passages which he desires me to make public—if I think benefit may be derived. It is needless to say that I shall do so—it is a duty I owe myself—and which it would be wilful folly to neglect, through a false sense of modesty. L & Blanchard also urge the publication upon me—so the passages referred to, with others of a similar nature from Paulding, Anthon, &c will be printed in an Appendix of Advertisement to the book—such as publishers are in the habit of appending. Irving's name will afford me a complete triumph over those little critics who would endeavor to put me down by raising the hue & cry of *exaggeration* in style, of *Germanism* & such twaddle. You know Irving heads the school of the *quietists*.

Poe regrets that he "can say not a word touching compensation for articles" published in *Burton's*: "The intense pressure has obliged Mr B. with nearly every, if not with every, publisher in the country, to discontinue paying for contributions. Mr B. pays for nothing—and we are forced to *fill up* as we can" (*L*, 1:121–22).

17 NOVEMBER. MOUNT PLEASANT, PENNSYLVANIA. E. Burke Fisher writes Poe, whose draft on the *Literary Examiner* has been returned unpaid. Fisher explains that the draft would have been honored, except that he has been absent from the office (Hull, p. 708; *L*, 2:580).

20 NOVEMBER. PHILADELPHIA. Lea & Blanchard reply to Poe:

We have your note of today. The copyright of the Tales would be of no value to us; when we undertook their publication, it was solely to oblige you and not with any view to profit, and on this ground it was urged by you. We should not therefore be now called upon or expected to purchase the copyright when we have no expectation of realizing the Capital placed in the volumes. If the offer to publish was [*sic*] now before us we should certainly decline it, and would feel obliged if you knew and would urge some one to relieve us from the publication at cost, or even at a small abatement (Woodberry, 1:225).

[Because of troubled economic conditions, Lea & Blanchard were to issue an edition of only 750 copies, instead of the "1750 copies" proposed in their 28 September letter to Poe (Thomas [1978], pp. 73–74).]

20 NOVEMBER. *Alexander's Weekly Messenger* carries a large advertisement for volumes six and seven (1840) of *Burton's*, "WILLIAM E. BURTON & EDGAR A. POE, EDITORS." Poe's unsigned serial "The Journal of Julius Rodman" is announced in large capitals:

In the course of the next volume, the most interesting record ever written will be given to the public, in the Journal of the

FIRST WHITE MAN
THAT EVER CROSSED THE WESTERN WILDERNESS,

And passed the desert ridges of the Rocky Mountains. This eventful Journey, wherein a handful of men encountered perils scarcely to be believed, occurred a few years before the time of Lewis and Clarke. The MS. is now in the hands of the Editors, and in the January number we shall commence its publication.

In still larger capitals the advertisement describes an elaborate contest:

To render Burton's Magazine the most desirable monthly publication for the next year, the Proprietor, in addition to the promised articles from his powerful list of Contributors, ensures a series of Papers of Original value, from the pens of the best Authors in the United States. To perfect this arrangement, he offers

A PREMIUM OF $1,000!

In befitting sums, for articles of value, written expressly for the Magazine; and sent in, postage free, before the expiration of the month of February.

250 DOLLARS For a series of Five Short Tales, illustrating the events of distinct periods in the History of North America, or developing the habits and manners of the present day in various portions of the Union.	**100 DOLLARS** For the best Humorous or Satirical Poem. **100 DOLLARS** For the best Essay on any popular subject connected with Science or Belles Lettres.

200 DOLLARS
For the best Tale of pathos
or interest.

100 DOLLARS
For the most Humorous Story,
or Characteristic Sketch.

100 DOLLARS
For the best Serious Poem,
of not less than 200 lines.

100 DOLLARS
For the most graphic Memoir
of any living American of
celebrity, divested of all
political or sectarian
doctrines.

50 DOLLARS
For most interesting
Sketch of Foreign Travel.

The Editors do not intend to insult the competitors by referring their productions to the scrutiny of "a committee of literary gentlemen," who generally select, unread, the effusion of the most popular candidate as the easiest method of discharging their onerous duties. Every article sent in will be carefully perused by the Editors alone—and as they have hitherto catered successfully for the taste of their readers, and daily sit in judgment upon literary matters connected with the Review department, it is supposed that they possess sufficient capability to select the worthiest production offered to their notice. All papers, poems, tales, etcetera, sent in with a claim to the Premiums, will become the property of the Magazine— but no article will be printed without some return being made to the writer.

DECEMBER. On its outside back cover *Burton's* carries the same advertisement announcing "The Journal of Julius Rodman" and "A PREMIUM OF $1,000!" which had appeared in the *Weekly Messenger*. This number contains Poe's tale "The Conversation of Eiros and Charmion," as well as his reviews of Charles Dickens' *Nicholas Nickleby*, Joseph R. Chandler's *Address*, George P. Morris' *National Melodies of America*, and James Grant's *Walks and Wanderings in the World of Literature.*

2 DECEMBER. The *Public Ledger* reports: "BURTON'S GENTLEMAN'S MAGAZINE for December has come out, and offers a thousand dollars in premiums; which will set some persons to work."

CA. 4 DECEMBER. Lea & Blanchard publish Poe's *Tales of the Grotesque and Arabesque.* The collection of twenty-five stories is dedicated to the prominent Philadelphian Colonel William Drayton "with every Sentiment of Respect, Gratitude, and Esteem." In a brief preface Poe defends himself against those critics who have charged him "with what they have been pleased to term 'Germanism' and gloom. . . . If in many of my productions terror has been the thesis, I maintain that terror is not of Germany, but of the soul,—that I have deduced this terror only from its legitimate sources, and urged it only to its legitimate results."

The first volume contains fourteen stories: "Morella," "Lionizing," "William Wilson," "The Man that was Used Up," "The Fall of the House of

Usher," "The Duc de L'Omelette," "MS. Found in a Bottle," "Bon-Bon," "Shadow," "The Devil in the Belfry," "Ligeia," "King Pest," and "The Signora Zenobia" incorporating "The Scythe of Time."

The second volume contains these eleven: "Epimanes," "Siope," "Hans Phaall," "A Tale of Jerusalem," "Von Jung," "Loss of Breath," "Metzengerstein," "Berenice," "Why the Little Frenchman Wears His Hand in a Sling," "The Visionary," and "The Conversation of Eiros and Charmion."

AFTER 4 DECEMBER. Poe takes a copy of the *Tales* to Colonel Drayton at his residence, 13 Portico Square; he forwards another copy to Philip Pendleton Cooke in Charlestown, Virginia. The copy presented to Anna and Bessie Pedder, the daughters of James Pedder, is inscribed "from their most sincere friend, The Author" (Thomas [1978], pp. 91–92, 865–66).

5 DECEMBER. The *Public Ledger* lists the *Tales of the Grotesque and Arabesque* under "New Publications." The *Pennsylvania Inquirer* observes that several stories in the collection "are capital, while all afford agreeable reading. Indeed the subjects are so various, that few persons can peruse both volumes, without finding much to interest and amuse." In the *United States Gazette* Joseph R. Chandler comments: "These two volumes, though exceedingly well executed, and admirably explained by their title, rather show the versatility than the character of Mr. Poe's talents and while we read them with hearty pleasure, we feel a gratification in the knowledge, that he can do other things in literature equally as well. He is capable of much—and we trust that time and opportunity will be allowed, and ample encouragement afforded him."

AFTER 5? DECEMBER. NEW YORK. The *Knickerbocker Magazine* for December contains a promise (never fulfilled) to review Poe's *Tales* in the next number.

6 DECEMBER. PHILADELPHIA. Joseph C. Neal comments in the *Pennsylvanian*:

"TALES OF THE GROTESQUE AND ARABESQUE," is the title of a work just published by Messrs. Lea and Blanchard. It consists of tales and sketches from the pen of Edgar A. Poe, Esq. formerly of the Southern Literary Messenger, and now one of the editors of the Gentleman's Magazine in this city, a writer who adds to extensive acquirements, a remarkable vigor and originality of mind, the manifestations of which are strikingly displayed in the volumes of which we speak. These grotesque and arabesque delineations are full of variety, now irresistibly quaint and droll, and again marked with all the deep and painful interest of the German school, so that the reader, in whatever mood he may be, cannot fail to find something to suit his temper and absorb his attention. In every page, he will note matter unlike the productions of any other writer. Poe follows in nobody's track,—his imagination seems to have a domain of its own to revel in.

6 DECEMBER. Poe writes the merchant John C. Cox, forwarding a copy of his *Tales*. He regrets both that he has not been able to repay $50 which Cox "so kindly lent nearly a year ago," and that he has not seen him since that time to apologize for this failure. He invites Cox to visit his family: "We are still where we were. I could then speak to you more fully, and convince you that the embarrassments under which I have labored are not exaggerated." It was "only with the most painful sacrifices" that Poe managed to pay Mrs. Jones, the landlady of his Arch Street boarding-house, "about last Christmas" (*L*, 1:122–23).

7 DECEMBER. The *Saturday Evening Post* comments: " 'TALES OF THE GRO-TESQUE AND ARABESQUE' . . . These volumes contain the republished magazine articles of Mr. Poe. They are strongly infused with the German spirit, a metaphysical style to which the writer is ardently attached." In the same column the *Post* notices the December *Burton's*: "The reviews of the month, evince the taste, and judgment, and some of them the severity, for which Mr. Poe is distinguished."

9 DECEMBER. Poe writes Edward L. Carey and Abraham Hart, partners in the publishing firm Carey & Hart: "Mr Burton mentioned to me, before going to Charleston, that you were good enough to promise him a Chapter from Marryatt's forthcoming work [Frederick Marryat's *Diary in America*], for the Jan: No. of our Mag: The Chapter was, I believe, one on 'Migra-tion & Emigration'. Will you please let me have it, if convenient, by the bearer?" (*L*, 1:123–24).

[Burton had an acting engagement in Charleston, South Carolina, from 28 November to 9 December (Johnson, p. 129).]

10 DECEMBER. The *North American* notices Poe's *Tales of the Grotesque and Arabesque*: "These tales betoken ability on the part of the author to do better. Let him give up his imitation of German mysticism, throw away his extravagance, think and write in good sound sober English, and leave all touches of profanity to the bar room, and he will employ his talents to much better advantage."

11 DECEMBER. BALTIMORE. The *Sun* reviews the December *Burton's*: "We perceive that premiums, amounting in all to $1,000, are offered for articles of value written expressly for this Magazine. A rich treat may be expected in the January and February numbers."

12 DECEMBER. PHILADELPHIA. Poe writes Snodgrass that he is sending him a copy of *Tales of the Grotesque and Arabesque*. The package, addressed to "the office of the Baltimore American," also contains a second copy which Poe asks Snodgrass to present to John L. Carey, editor of this paper (*L*, 1:124–25).

12 DECEMBER. NEW YORK. The *Evening Star* lists Poe's *Tales* under "*New Books*."

13 DECEMBER. The *Evening Post* briefly notices Poe's collection: "a series of tales, grave and merry, in two duodecimo volumes."

14 DECEMBER. BALTIMORE. John L. Carey comments in the *American*:

"*Tales of the Grotesque and Arabesque*," by Edgar A. Poe—2 vols. The Tales comprising this series have before appeared from time to time in different periodicals; they are now given to the world in a more durable form. We know not many effusions of the imaginative class that better deserve such preservation. The impress of genius is marked upon them all—of genius erratic, it may be, but nevertheless of true quality. The several stories as they came forth singly were received with commendations by the press generally. The following will be recognized as familiar names—"The Fall of the House of Usher," "Bon Bon," "Mss. found in a Bottle," "William Wilson," "Hans Phaall," &c. &c.—Without particularizing others we will observe of the story entitled "*William Wilson*," that it contains a profounder meaning than will be gathered from regarding it as a mere fanciful invention.

14 DECEMBER. PHILADELPHIA. Ezra Holden reviews Poe's *Tales* in the *Saturday Courier*: "They are generally wildly imaginative in plot; fanciful in description, oftentimes to the full boundaries of the grotesque; but throughout indicating the polished writer, possessed of rare and varied learning. Some of them will bear good comparison with the productions of Coleridge, and it is not surprising that the author has often been compared with that author. The tale of 'William Wilson,' and that of 'The House of Usher,' are, to our judgment, the best in the volumes, and may be quoted as examples of the author's powers."

14 DECEMBER. NEW YORK. The *Spirit of the Times* notices the *Tales*, expressing a hope that "the premonitory encomiums . . . in the second volume, were placed there by the publisher, and not by the author" (Pollin [1980], pp. 17, 24).

14 DECEMBER. The *Albion* praises the *Tales*: "We have read them with great delight and can assure our readers of great satisfaction in their perusal."

14 DECEMBER. BOSTON. The *Boston Notion* condemns the *Tales*:

We have read a goodly number of these tales, and verily must say that they fall below the average of newspaper trash. They seem to be the offspring of a distempered, unregulated imagination, which needs a selection rather than "an ounce of civet." They consist of a wild, unmeaning, pointless, aimless set of stories, outraging all manner of probability, and without anything of elevated fancy or fine humor to redeem them. The style is slipshod, though the author says he has elaborated it carefully; and the congregation of nonsense is merely caricature run mad. But if any one is pleased with such stuff, it lies not in our humor to prevent it. *De gustibus*, etc (Pollin [1970b], p. 24).

17 DECEMBER. The *Morning Post* castigates the *Tales* (Pollin [1980], p. 23).

18 DECEMBER. PHILADELPHIA. John Frost reviews the *Tales* in *Alexander's Weekly Messenger*:

To say we have *read* this production attentively is not enough. We have *studied* it. It is every way worthy of such a distinction, and whoever shall give it a careful study and a philosop[h]ical analysis, will find in it the evidences of an original, vigorous, and independent mind, stored with rich and various learning and capable of su[c]cessful application to a great variety of subjects. As a writer of fiction, Mr. Poe passes "from grave to gay, from lively to severe," with an ease and buoyancy not less remarkable than the unfailing vigor of his style and prodigious extent of his resources for illustration and embellishment. He is capable of great things; and beautiful and interesting as the tales before us are, we deem them much less remarkable as actual performances than as evidences of ability for much more serious and sustained efforts. They seem to us the playful effusion of a remarkable and powerful intellect. We counsel the writer not to repose upon his laurels. He has placed himself in the foremost rank of American writers, as it respects ability. Let him maintain his position by untiring exertion and show that he fully deserves it by actual performance. He has raised the highest expectations. We trust he will not fail to fulfil them.

This issue of the *Messenger* contains two contributions by Poe, "Enigmatical and Conundrum-ical" and an untitled article praising James Pedder's plan to produce sugar from beets. In the former article Poe offers to solve any cryptogram his readers submit, "however unusual or arbitrary may be the characters employed" (Brigham, pp. 12–19).

[The *Messenger* was edited by Frost, Professor of Literature and Belles-Lettres in the Philadelphia High School, and published by Charles W.

Alexander, who had owned the *Gentleman's Magazine* before it was purchased by Burton. The *Messenger* was friendly to Burton, who would not have objected to the brief articles Poe contributed to it between 18 December 1839 and 6 May 1840.]

19 DECEMBER. Poe replies to a 16 December letter from Snodgrass, who inquired about the contest advertised on the covers of the December *Burton's*: "Touching the Premiums. The Advertisement respecting them was written by Mr. Burton, and is not, I think as explicit as might [be.] I can give you no information about their desig[nation furth]er than is shown in the advertisement itself. The tru[th is,] I object, in toto, to the whole scheme." He asks Snodgrass to forward any reviews of his *Tales of the Grotesque and Arabesque* which appear in the Baltimore newspapers: "The Philadelphians have given me the *very highest possible* praise—I cd desire nothing further. Have you seen the U. S. Gazette, the Pennsylvanian, or Alexander's Messenger. In the last is a notice by Professor Frost, which I forward you, today, with this. The books have just reached New York. The Star and the Evening Post have both capital notices." Poe believes "that the edition is already very nearly exhausted" (*L*, 1:125–26).

19 DECEMBER. CHARLESTOWN, VIRGINIA. Philip Pendleton Cooke replies to a letter from Poe, who requested an opinion of several stories collected in the *Tales*:

In your "Fall of the House of Usher", unconnected with style, I think you very happy in that part where you prolong the scene with Roderick Usher after the death of his sister; and the glare of the moon thro' the sundering house, and the electric gleam visible around it, I think admirably conceived.

Of "William Wilson" I am not sure that I perceive the true clew. From the "whispering voice" I would apprehend that you meant the second William Wilson as an embodying of the *conscience* of the first; but I am inclined to the notion that your intention was to convey the wilder idea that every mortal of us is attended with a shadow of himself—a duplicate of his own peculiar organization—differing from himself only in a certain angelic taint of the compound, derived from heaven, as our own wild humours are derived from Hell (figuratively);—I cannot make myself understood, as I am not used to the expression of a wild *half thought*. But, although I do not clearly comprehend, I certainly admire the story.

Of "Eiros & Charmion" I will only say that I consider the whole very singular and excellent, and the skill of one small part of it unapproachable. . . .

By the way you have selected an excellent title for your volume of Tales. "Tales of the grotesque and the Arabesque" expresses admirably the character of your wild stories—and as Tales of the grotesque & arabesque they were certainly never equalled (MB–G).

21 DECEMBER. NEW YORK. Timothy O. Porter reviews Poe's *Tales* in the

Corsair: "We have skimmed over the surface of these volumes and found them possessed of a fair claim upon our admiration. A sparkling dash of fancy, sentiment and wit intermingled,—clothed in rich language, and pink'd off with the latest gloss of transcendentalism, with little regard to definite plot or story-like dènouement, with an occasional burst of the 'grotesque' admirably sustained, recommend these Tales to those who hail with avidity a novelty in the literary mart." The book is also noticed by the *New-York American* and the *New-York Mirror* (Pollin [1972b], p. 56; [1980], p. 23).

25 DECEMBER. PHILADELPHIA. Poe replies to a 15 November letter from Joseph B. Boyd, a Cincinnati watchmaker, who requested a manuscript copy of one of his poems. He copies "Silence—A Sonnet" (*L*, 1:126–27).

28 DECEMBER. NEW YORK. An anonymous reviewer, possibly Louis F. Tasistro, lauds the *Tales* in the *New-York Mirror*:

Had Mr. Poe written nothing else but "Morella," "William Wilson," "The House of Usher," and the "MS. found in a Bottle," he would deserve a high place among imaginative writers, for there is fine poetic feeling, much brightness of fancy, an excellent taste, a ready eye for the picturesque, much quickness of observation, and great truth of sentiment and character in all these works. But there is scarcely one of the tales published in the two volumes before us, in which we do not find the development of great intellectual capacity, with a power for vivid description, an opulence of imagination, a fecundity of invention, and a command over the elegances of diction which have seldom been displayed, even by writers who have acquired the greatest distinction in the republic of letters. It would be, indeed, no easy matter to find another artist with ability equal to this writer for discussing the good and evil—the passions, dilemmas, and affectations—the self-sufficiency and the deplorable weakness, the light and darkness, the virtue and the vice by which mankind are by turns affected. These volumes present a succession of richly-coloured pictures in the magic lantern of invention.

CA. 1839. PHILADELPHIA. Poe attends informal social gatherings of artists, actors, and writers held in the Falstaff Hotel, Sixth Street above Chestnut. He becomes acquainted with three of the city's leading artists, Thomas Sully, John Sartain, and George R. Bonfield. Sully paints a portrait of Poe "in the Byron attitude" (Thomas [1978], pp. 805–08).

1840

*

JANUARY. PHILADELPHIA. *Burton's* publishes the first of six installments of Poe's unfinished serial "The Journal of Julius Rodman," as well as his critique of Thomas Moore's *Alciphron: A Poem*. This number contains a perfunctory notice of *Tales of the Grotesque and Arabesque*; the outside back cover carries the same advertisement announcing "Rodman" and "A PREMIUM OF $1,000!" found on the December 1839 covers and in *Alexander's Weekly Messenger* for 20 November 1839.

JANUARY. Morton McMichael reviews the *Tales* in *Godey's Lady's Book*:

Mr. Poe is a writer of rare and various abilities. He possesses a fine perception of the ludicrous, and his humorous stories are instinct with the principle of mirth. He possesses also a mind of unusual grasp—a vigorous power of analysis, and an acuteness of perception which have given to him high celebrity as a critic. These same faculties, moreover, aided by an unusually active imagination, and directed by familiar study of metaphysical writings, have led him to produce some of the most vivid scenes of the wild and wonderful which can be found in English literature. The volumes now published, contain favourable specimens of Mr. Poe's powers, and cannot fail to impress all who read them, with a conviction of his genius.

JANUARY. RICHMOND. James E. Heath reviews the *Tales* in the *Southern Literary Messenger*:

To say that we admire Mr. Poe's style, abstractly considered, is more than we can say and speak truly; neither can we perceive any particular beneficial tendency that is likely to flow from his writings. This, of course, is a mere matter of opinion, and we may differ, in saying so, from many. At the same time, the possession of high powers of invention and imagination—of genius—is undoubtedly his. His productions are, many of them, in Literature, somewhat like Martin's in the Fine Arts. His serious sketches all bear the marks of bold, fertile genius. There is the dark cloud hanging over all—there are the dim, misty, undefined shapes in the back-ground. But amid all these arise huge and magnificent columns, flashing lamps, rich banquetting vessels, gleaming tiaras, and sweet, expressive faces. But the writings of Mr. P. are well known to the readers of the Messenger.

The volumes before us, with a rather singular title, are composed of tales and sketches, which have appeared at different times before the public: many of them, in this journal. We have read but a portion of them. Of these, we like, as a specimen of the author's powers of humor, "The Man that was used Up," and "Why the Little Frenchman wears his hand in a Sling." "Siope," and "The MS.

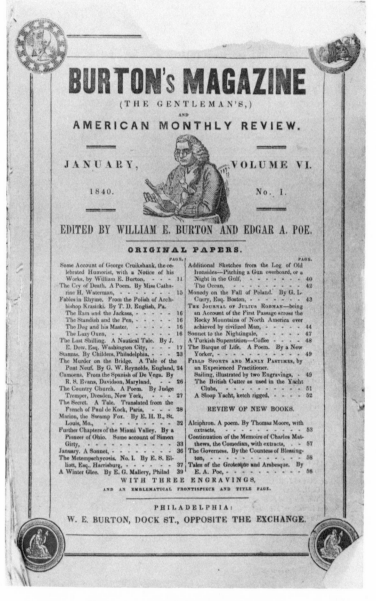

Front wrapper of the January *Burton's*
Philadelphia Free Library

found in a Bottle," afford good specimens of the author's stronger and more graphic powers.

We recommend Hans Phaal to every one who has not already read it—although our remembrance of it remains from a perusal some time since. The "opinions" prefixed to the second volume, are in bad taste. We do not intend to write a critique, but merely to bring to the notice of the public, the productions of a talented and powerful writer.

1 JANUARY. PHILADELPHIA. In *Alexander's Weekly Messenger* Poe notices the *New-York Mirror* for 28 December 1839, calling attention to its favorable review of his *Tales* (Brigham, pp. 19–20).

4 JANUARY. The *Saturday Courier* publishes Poe's "Silence—A Sonnet." In reviewing the January *Burton's*, the *Courier* remarks: "the most interesting article . . . is . . . a preliminary chapter of the Journal of Julius Rodman, an account of the first passage ever made by white men across the Rocky Mountains, and an exploring tour through a portion of the wilderness, then, and in fact now, entirely unknown. From what we learn, this Journal is one of the most extraordinary narratives ever penned."

4 JANUARY. NEW YORK. The *Madisonian* notices the publication of Poe's *Tales* (Pollin [1980], p. 23).

15 JANUARY. PHILADELPHIA. *Alexander's Weekly Messenger* contains Poe's articles "The Daguerreotype" and "Enigmatical." In the latter he deciphers a cryptogram a reader has submitted in response to his challenge in the 18 December 1839 issue (Brigham, pp. 20–24).

BEFORE 20 JANUARY. BALTIMORE. Snodgrass writes Poe. He apparently blames his former partner Nathan C. Brooks for the failure of their *American Museum*, which expired with its June 1839 number (Poe's reply; cf. Thomas [1978], pp. 549, 676).

20 JANUARY. PHILADELPHIA. During "a temporary lull in a storm of business," Poe replies to Snodgrass: "I am obliged to decline saying anything of the 'Museum' in the Gent's Mag: however much I feel anxious to oblige yourself, and to express my own views. You will understand me when I say that I have no proprietary interest in the Mag: and that Mr Burton is a warm friend of Brooks." Poe has heard "that an attempt is to be made by Some one of capital in Baltimore, to get up a Magazine"; and he asks Snodgrass to tell him "all about it *by return of mail*" (L, 1:127–28).

22 JANUARY. In *Alexander's Weekly Messenger* Poe deciphers two more cryp-

tograms submitted by readers in "Another Poser" and "Still Another" (Brigham, pp. 24–25).

29 JANUARY. *Alexander's Weekly Messenger* contains Poe's essay "Instinct VS Reason—A Black Cat"; he argues that the instinct of animals is in some ways superior to human reason, offering an example from his daily life:

The writer of this article is the owner of one of the most remarkable black cats in the world . . . . That portion of the kitchen which she most frequents is accessible only by a door, which closes with what is termed a thumb-latch; these latches are rude in construction, and some force and dexterity are always requisite to force them down. But puss is in the daily habit of opening the door, which she accomplishes in the following way. She first springs from the ground to the guard of the latch (which resembles the guard over a gun-trigger,) and through this she thrusts her left arm to hold on with. She now, with her right hand, presses the thumb-latch until it yields, and here several attempts are frequently requisite. Having forced it down, however, she seems to be aware that her task is but half accomplished, since, if the door is not pushed open before she lets go, the latch will again fall into its socket. She, therefore, screws her body round so as to bring her hind feet immediately beneath the latch, while she leaps with all her strength from the door—the impetus of the spring forcing it open, and her hind feet sustaining the latch until this impetus is fairly given.

To this issue Poe also contributes a news item "The Bloodhound Story" and a cryptogram solution "Yet Another Poser," as well as an advance notice of the February *Burton's*: "The Journal of Julius Rodman is continued, and a vivid description given of the persons and equipments of the travellers, who proceed up the Missouri as far as the mouth of the Platte. We prophecy that this will prove an intensely interesting narrative." One of the reviews in *Burton's* "shows up Professor Longfellow as a plagiarist of the first water" (Brigham, pp. 26–32).

FEBRUARY. *Burton's* contains the second installment of Poe's "Rodman" and his satiric tale "Peter Pendulum, the Business Man." He reviews Longfellow's *Voices of the Night*, suggesting that this poet's "Midnight Mass for the Dying Year" is a "plagiarism, which is too palpable to be mistaken," from Alfred Tennyson's "The Death of the Old Year."

1 FEBRUARY. The *Saturday Courier* reviews *Burton's*, describing "Rodman" as "A valuable piece of American history," and "Peter Pendulum" as "Funny and good, like all of Poe's writings."

4 FEBRUARY. In the *Philadelphia Gazette* Willis Gaylord Clark defends Longfellow against the accusation made in Poe's review of *Voices of the Night*:

A neighboring periodical [*Burton's*], we hear, has been attempting to prove that Professor LONGFELLOW's sublime and beautiful "Midnight Mass for the Dying Year," has been imitated from a poem by TENNYSON. Preposterous! There is nothing more alike in the two pieces than black and white, with the exception of the personification,—and *that* was LONGFELLOW's, long before the Scotch writer thought of "doing" his poem. Who does not remember that striking simile in one of the Professor's earlier lyrics,

> — "where Autumn, like a faint old man, sits down,
> By the wayside, aweary?"

This same beautiful piece was copied in Edinburgh, from an English periodical where it was *altered*, to suit the scenery of England; and it is fifty times more probable that TENNYSON thus got *his* idea. . . . We ask the Weekly Messenger, who [which] has repeated the charge of *abstraction*, to clip this *caveat*, and give it utterance.

5 FEBRUARY. *Alexander's Weekly Messenger* contains Poe's filler "Still Another," in which he translates "the ugliest hyeroglyphical puzzle we have yet received" (Brigham, p. 32).

10 FEBRUARY. WASHINGTON. Robert Greenhow, Translator and Librarian to the Department of State, mentions "Rodman" in his "Memoir, Historical and Political, on the Northwest Coast of North America," a document submitted to the United States Senate by its Select Committee on the Oregon Territory:

It is proper to notice here an account of an expedition across the American continent, made between 1791 and 1794, by a party of citizens of the United States, under the direction of Julius Rodman, whose journal has been recently discovered in Virginia, and is now in course of publication in a periodical magazine at Philadelphia. The portion which has yet appeared relates only to the voyage of the adventurer[s] up the Missouri during the summer of 1791; and no idea is communicated of their route beyond that river, except in the Introduction by the editor, where it is stated that they traversed the region "west of the Rocky Mountains, and north of the 60th parallel, which is still marked upon our maps as unexplored, and which, until this day, has been always so considered." From what has been published, it is impossible to form a definitive opinion as to the degree of credit which is due to the narrative, or as to the value of the statements, if they are true; and all that can be here said in addition is, that nothing as yet appears, either in the journal or relating to it, calculated to excite suspicions with regard to its authenticity (Jackson [1974], pp. 47–48).

12 FEBRUARY. PHILADELPHIA. In *Alexander's Weekly Messenger* Poe reprints the 4 February defense of Longfellow by the editor of the *Philadelphia Gazette*. He then comments:

In referring to the criticism mentioned [review of *Voices of the Night*], we find that Mr. Clark has made a little mistake—at which we are not a little astonished. Mr. Poe does not say that Professor Longfellow's poem is "imitated" from Tennyson. He calls it a bare-faced and barbarous plagiarism "belonging to that worst species of literary robbery, in which, while the words of the wronged author are avoided, his most intangible, and therefore his least defensible and least reclaimable property, is *purloined*." In support of this accusation he has printed the poems in question side by side—a proceeding, which, we must acknowledge, has an air of perfect fairness about it. That the reviewer, indeed, has nothing beyond truth as his object, is rendered quite apparent by the fact that nowhere has the fine genius of Professor Longfellow been so fully and so enthusiastically set forth, as in the '·~r portion of the very critique now made the subject of comment. . . .

In "Our Late Puzzles" Poe complains that the *Messenger* is receiving too many cryptograms: "Will any body tell us how to get out of this dilemma? If we don't solve all the puzzles forwarded, their concocters will think it is because we cannot—when we can." Under the heading "Swimming" he recalls his teenage feat of swimming the James River at Richmond for "a distance of seven miles and a half [six miles], in a hot June sun, and *against a tide of three miles per hour*" (Brigham, pp. 33–37).

18 FEBRUARY. PORTLAND, MAINE. Longfellow writes Samuel Ward in New York: "My brother told me yesterday that some paragraphs had appeared in some New York paper saying I stole the idea of the Midnight Mass from Tennison [*sic*]. Absurd. I did not even know that he had written a piece on this subject" (Longfellow [1966], 2:215–16).

19 FEBRUARY. In *Alexander's Weekly Messenger* Poe translates another cipher under the heading "Our Puzzles—Again!" (Brigham, pp. 38–40).

22 FEBRUARY. The *Saturday Evening Post* notices the February *Burton's*: " 'The Journal of Julius Rodman,' is a singular thing. 'Peter Pendulum,' by E. A. Poe, the junior editor, is highly amusing. We like the reviews, with the exception of that of the 'Midnight Mass of the Dying Year.' We cannot agree with the reviewers that the poem alluded to is a plagiarism."

26 FEBRUARY. In *Alexander's Weekly Messenger* Poe translates additional ciphers under the headings "More of the Puzzles" and "Our Puzzles Once More." Two fillers, "Thomas Paine" and "Advertising Oddities," may possibly be Poe's work (Brigham, pp. 40–52).

29 FEBRUARY. Poe writes the prominent physician Dr. John Kearsley Mitchell, 288 Walnut Street: "It will give me great pleasure to accept your invitation for Feb: 29th—this evening" (*L*, 1:128).

THE MOST POPULAR AND READABLE PERIODICAL OF THE DAY!

Burton's Magazine,

(THE GENTLEMAN'S,)

AND AMERICAN MONTHLY REVIEW,

Will present its Sixth and Seventh Volumes to the public during the course of the year 1840.

Terms, $3 per annum, in advance, or $5 for two years, or two separate Subscriptions; or ten copies for $20, cash.

Printed in large octavo, white thick paper, good type, etc. Each number contains as much matter as a volume of a novel; the illustrations are of the first quality. During the past year

Nearly Fifty of the most superior Engravings

Including three of Sartain's Splendid Mezzotints, were engraved expressly for this work. Each number contains TWO or more Engravings. New Designs, executed on steel, by the first Artists, are in progress for the coming Volume.

WILLIAM E. BURTON & EDGAR A. POE, EDITORS.

THE LIST OF CONTRIBUTORS

Embraces the names of most of the principal writers in America, with a respectable sprinkling of English authors. Original articles have appeared during the last year from the pens of the following:—

Professor Ingraham, *Author of La Fitte.*
" John Frost, Philadelphia.
" N. C. Brooks, Baltimore.
" C. F. Wines, Philadelphia, Author of Two Years in the Navy.
Captain Marryatt, Author of Peter Simple, etc.
General G. P. Morris, New York.
Leigh Hunt, England.
Mrs. Fanny Kemble Butler, Philadelphia.
Park Benjamin, New York.
Douglas Jerrold, England.
Joseph C. Neal, (Charcoal Sketches.) The American Boz!
James F. Otis, New York.
Hon. R. T. Conrad, Philadelphia.
David Hoffman, Baltimore.
Morton M'Michael, Philadelphia.
Charles West Thomson, Philadelphia.

Epes Sargent, Author of Velasco, New York.
Grenville Mellen, New York.
P. B. Elder, Editor of Columbia Spy, Pa.
The Author of " Stanley."
Mrs. L. Sigourney, Hartford.
Miss Catherine H. Waterman, Philadelphia.
Mrs. Ann Stephens, New York.
Benson Hill, England, Editor of the New Monthly Magazine.
Richard Penn Smith, Philadelphia.
Dr. J. K. Mitchell, Philadelphia.
James Montgomery, England.
T. G. Spear, Philadelphia.
A. M'Makin and E. Holden, Editors Saturday Courier, Phila.
J. Beauchamp Jones, Baltimore.
J. E. Dow, Washington City.
Mrs. E. F. Ellett, Boston.
Dr. Thomas Dunn English, Philadelphia.

To render Burton's Magazine the most desirable monthly publication for the next year, in addition to the promised articles from his powerful list of Contributors, ensures a series of Papers of Original value, from the pens of the best Authors in the United States. To perfect this arrangement, he offers

A PREMIUM OF $1,000!

In befitting sums, for articles of value, written expressly for the Magazine; and sent in, postage free, before the expiration of the month of February.

250 DOLLARS
For a series of Five Short Tales, illustrating the events of distinct periods in the History of North America, or developing the habits and manners of the present day in various portions of the Union.

200 DOLLARS
For the best Tale of pathos or interest.

100 DOLLARS
For the most Humorous Story, or Characteristic Sketch.

100 DOLLARS
For the best Serious Poem, of not less than 200 lines.

100 DOLLARS
For the best Humorous or Satirical Poem.

100 DOLLARS
For the best Essay on any popular subject connected with Science or Belles Lettres.

100 DOLLARS
For the most graphic Memoir of any living American of celebrity, divested of all political or sectarian doctrines.

50 DOLLARS
For the most interesting Sketch of Foreign Travel.

The Editors do not intend to insult the competitors by referring their productions to the scrutiny of "a committee of literary gentlemen," who generally select, unread, the effusion of the most popular candidate as the easiest method of discharging their onerous duties. Every article sent in will be carefully perused by the Editors alone—and as they have hitherto entered successfully for the taste of their readers, and daily sit in judgment upon literary matters connected with the Review department, it is supposed that they possess sufficient capability to select the worthiest production offered to their notice. All papers, poems, tales, etcetera, sent in with a claim to the Premiums, will become the property of the Magazine—but no article will be printed without some return being made to the writer.

ALL LETTERS SENT, POST PAID, TO

W. E. Burton, Dock street, opposite the Exchange, Philada.

*** To accommodate our country friends who may wish to subscribe for our work and many other Philadelphia periodicals, we will receive a Five Dollar Bill, postage free, for one year's subscription to Burton's Magazine and Godey's Lady's Book (also three dollars a year) or the Saturday Courier, or the Saturday Chronicle, or Alexander's Weekly Messenger.

In the course of the next volume, the most interesting record ever written will be given to the public, in the Journal of the

FIRST WHITE MAN

THAT EVER CROSSED THE WESTERN WILDERNESS,

And passed the desert ridges of the Rocky Mountains. This eventful Journey, wherein a handful of men encountered perils scarcely to be believed, occurred a few years before the time of Lewis and Clarke. The MS. is now in the hands of the Editors, and in the January number we shall commence its publication. Also, a series of HUMOROUS AND CHARACTERISTIC PAPERS, from the pen of Joseph C. Neal, whose inimitable " Charcoal Sketches" have justly gained him the title of " THE AMERICAN BOZ."

*** Our Editorial friends who receive our Magazine, will please notice our New Advertisement, and give publicity to the new arrangements. One copy of the paper containing the notice or advertisement, will be gladly received.

Back wrapper of the January *Burton's*
Philadelphia Free Library

MARCH. *Burton's* contains the third installment of Poe's "Rodman," his miscellany "A Chapter on Science and Art," and his reviews of Henry Duncan's *Sacred Philosophy of the Seasons* and Nathaniel P. Willis' *Romance of Travel*. On the inside front cover Burton announces a modification to his premium contest advertised on the December 1839 and January 1840 covers:

It is with the utmost regret that we announce to our friends that our liberal offer of Premiums, to the amount of One Thousand Dollars, has not been sufficiently attended to by the auctorial world. That the honesty of our intentions was thoroughly appreciated is evident from the various letters received from some of the most distinguished writers of the day; we have been complimented by the very highest members of the craft for the liberality of our scheme—and many cheering encomiums have been passed upon our plan as one divested of the usual humbug of the day. We have received a few manuscripts of invaluable worth, touching some of the subjects named; but we have nothing in the way of competition; our scheme or scale of premiums embraced a variety of sums and subjects— for various of these items we have no claimants; for others we have no competitors. We cannot award a premium for the *best* article, when we are without means of comparison. It has been suggested that the time originally allowed (to the end of February) was too short for the production of the articles required; as it is our earnest wish to carry our original plan into execution, we hereby extend the date of reception to the end of March—when, if we should still be unable to obtain a sufficiency of competitors, the articles sent will be returned to their owners, if a negotiation for their insertion should be unsuccessful in its issue.

4 MARCH. In *Alexander's Weekly Messenger* Poe comments briefly on "Revivals," which are "very much in fashion just at present in Philadelphia," and translates ciphers in "More of the Puzzles" and in a filler addressed "To T. S. of Boquet, Essex, N. Y." (Brigham, pp. 52–54).

11 MARCH. Poe solves additional ciphers for the *Messenger* in "Puzzles Again!" (Brigham, pp. 55–56).

18 MARCH. The *Messenger* contains Poe's news report "The Rail-Road War," as well as his favorable notices of the *Young Gardener's Assistant*, issued by his friends Henry B. Hirst and Henry A. Dreer "at their Seed store, No. 97 Chesnut street," and of the *Virginia Star*, a new paper published at Petersburg, Virginia, by Hiram Haines, "a gentleman of education and of unusually fine talents" (Brigham, pp. 56–60).

25 MARCH. The *Messenger* contains more cipher solutions by Poe under the heading "Puzzles Again!" (Brigham, pp. 60–62).

28 MARCH. The *Saturday Evening Post* announces that John S. Du Solle has

disposed of his interest in the paper: "Charles J. Peterson, Esq. will hereafter be associated . . . in the management of this paper. . . . The business will hereafter be conducted under the firm of G. R. GRAHAM & CO."

APRIL. NEW YORK. In the *Knickerbocker Magazine* Lewis Gaylord Clark reviews the March *Burton's*: "We observe . . . a continuation of the 'Journal of JULIUS RODMAN, being a minute account of the first passage across the Rocky Mountains ever achieved by civilized man.' We think we discover the clever hand of the resident editor of the 'Gentleman's Magazine,' Mr. E. A. POE, in these records; the more, perhaps, that the fabulous narrative of 'Mr. ARTHUR GORDON PYM,' of Nantucket, has shown us how deftly he can manage this species of [Robinson] Crusoe matériel."

APRIL. PHILADELPHIA. *Burton's* contains the fourth installment of Poe's "Rodman," his two miscellanies "A Chapter on Science and Art" and "Omniana," and his "Silence—A Sonnet" (reprint). On the inside front cover Burton reprints the first four sentences of his statement on the March covers; he then announces the cancellation of his premium contest:

We published the above statement on the cover of our last number, and, conceiving that the time originally fixed for the presentation of the articles was somewhat too brief for the purpose, we extended the date of reception to the end of March—but we might as well have settled the affair at the original period, for we have received but TWO articles during the whole of the month. We have therefore no resource but to acknowledge the failure of our plan, and to return, upon application, the few MSS. to their respective writers, who will individually be addressed by private letter from the editors. . . .

1 APRIL. Poe notices the publication of the April *Burton's* in *Alexander's Weekly Messenger*: "Mr. Poe has a clever Sonnet . . . . The 'Journal of Julius Rodman' progresses beautifully. The travellers are far on their way, and will soon enter a tract of country hitherto undescribed. A fine engraving illustrates this chapter." The *Messenger* also contains Poe's articles "The Trial of James Wood" and "Cabs." An editorial on "Disinterment" may possibly be his work (Brigham, pp. 63–68).

8 APRIL. The *Messenger* carries Poe's notice headed "Cyphers": he promises to answer "one or two letters from enigmatical friends" in the next issue (Brigham, p. 68).

15 APRIL. The *Messenger* contains Poe's articles on "Revivals" and "The Worm" (Brigham, pp. 68–70).

20 APRIL THROUGH 6 MAY. BALTIMORE. Burton has a successful acting engagement at the American Theatre on Front Street (advertisements and reviews in the *Sun*, 15 April through 6 May).

22 APRIL. PHILADELPHIA. The *Messenger* contains Poe's "Cyphers Again," in which he translates cryptograms submitted by readers. His other contributions are headed "A Long Leap" and "Changing Seats" (Brigham, pp. 70–75).

24 APRIL. Poe answers a 24 March letter from Hiram Haines of Petersburg, Virginia, who would like to give a pet fawn to Mrs. Poe: "She desires me to thank you with all her heart—but, unhappily, I cannot point out a mode of conveyance. What can be done? Perhaps some opportunity may offer itself hereafter—some friend from Petersburg may be about to pay us a visit. In the meantime accept our best acknowledgments, precisely as if the little fellow were already nibbling the grass before our windows in Philadelphia." Poe will do "anything in the world" to promote Haines's *Virginia Star* (L, 1:128–29).

27 APRIL. Poe writes Roland S. Houghton, a fifteen-year-old student at the University of Vermont in Burlington who submitted a story "John a' Combe" in the contest held by *Burton's*: "By reference to the last number (for April) you will perceive that the Premium scheme has proved a total failure, and that the M.S.S. sent await the commands of their authors. We should be glad, of course, to publish the piece, but are grieved to say that the absurd condition of our present copyright laws will not permit us to offer any compensation. We shall be pleased to hear from you in reply" (PP–G; Ostrom [1974], pp. 518–19).

29 APRIL. In *Alexander's Weekly Messenger* Poe solves a cryptogram in "Cyphers" and debunks the Philadelphia fortuneteller Thomas Hague in "A Charlatan!" (Brigham, pp. 75–80).

MAY. *Burton's* contains the fifth installment of Poe's "Rodman," his sketch "The Philosophy of Furniture," his two miscellanies "A Chapter on Science and Art" and "Omniana," and his "Notice of William Cullen Bryant," as well as his unsigned reviews of the *Memoirs and Letters of Madame Malibran*, Mrs. Grey's novel *The Duke*, Nathan C. Brooks's *Utility of Classical Studies*, Charles West Thomson's *Uncertainty of Literary Fame*, and James Pedder's *Frank; or Dialogues between Father and Son*.

EARLY MAY. Construction begins on William E. Burton's new project, the National Theatre on Chestnut Street near Ninth (*Daily Chronicle*, 30 May).

1 MAY. John S. Du Solle notices *Burton's* in the *Spirit of the Times*, praising Poe's article on Bryant. "The interesting Journal of Julius Rodman is continued" (Pollin [1981], p. 510).

4 MAY. *Burton's* is favorably reviewed in the *Daily Chronicle*, a new paper commenced today by Charles W. Alexander and a young associate, Andrew Scott.

4 MAY. A naval court-martial convenes in Philadelphia for the trial of the controversial Commodore Jesse D. Elliott. An important defense witness is Poe's friend Jesse E. Dow, a clerk in the Post Office Department in Washington who had formerly served as Elliott's private secretary.

[Dow's popular "Sketches from the Log of Old Ironsides," serialized in *Burton's* from July 1839 through April 1840, were based upon his experiences aboard Elliott's flagship, the frigate *Constitution*.]

4–5 MAY. BALTIMORE. The Whig National Convention ratifies the nomination of William Henry Harrison for President, to oppose the Democratic incumbent Martin Van Buren. One of the delegates is the novelist, lawyer, and journalist Frederick William Thomas, lately of Cincinnati, Ohio, who had been a friend of Poe's brother Henry in 1828.

AFTER 5 MAY. PHILADELPHIA. Thomas delivers the manuscript of his new novel *Howard Pinckney* to his publishers Lea & Blanchard. He makes Poe's acquaintance and solicits his opinion of the novel. Poe introduces Thomas to Dow; the three men become frequent companions, discussing literature, politics, and cryptograms at such fashionable resorts as John Sturdivant's Congress Hall Hotel, Chestnut and Third Streets, and Robert Harmer's Cornucopia Restaurant, 44 North Third above High (or Market) Street (Thomas [1978], pp. 125–27).

[In his 3 September 1841 letter to Poe, Thomas recalled: "I was a delegate to the Baltimore May convention in '40, where I held forth, and after which I made your acquaintance in Philadelphia and got pelted by the people as you remember—or rather by the Locos [Locofocos]." See 19 MAY.]

6 MAY. *Alexander's Weekly Messenger* contains five short articles by Poe: "Changing Seats," "Credulity," "The Daguerreotype," "Bulwer Used Up," and "Best Conundrum Yet" (Brigham, pp. 80–83).

AFTER 6 MAY. Burton returns from his engagement at the American Theatre in Baltimore. He instructs his clerk Charles R. Morrell to withhold three dollars each week from Poe's salary, until a debt of $100 is repaid (Poe to Burton, 1 June).

9 MAY. The *Saturday Courier* reviews *Burton's*: "Rodman's journey . . . is thought to bespeak the ready pen of Mr. Poe."

16 MAY. The *Spirit of the Times* reprints Poe's "Philosophy of Furniture" from *Burton's* (Mabbott [1978], 2:495).

19 MAY. Poe notices Thomas in Alexander's *Daily Chronicle*:

MR. THOMAS.—This gentleman, so well and so favorably known as the author of "East and West," "The Adventures of a Lawyer," "Clinton Bradshaw," and other minor productions of high merit, has now in the hands of Messieurs Lea and Blanchard a new novel called "Howard Pinckney," of which, from some loose pages which we had the pleasure of glancing at in MS, we entertain a high opinion. "Howard Pinckney," if we are not much mistaken, will place Mr. Thomas in a position which he should have occupied long ago—a position in the van of our literature. He has only to do himself justice (as he has here done) in his subject, and there is no better writer in America. Let him eschew "Pelham," and throw all mannerism to the dogs, and he will do honor to his country and to himself. He has the true soul of genius. We here wish to record a prophecy that in ten years from this date his works will be more extensively popular than those of any of our native writers. We would say even more than this—but we have a horror of being suspected of puffery.

In another column Poe comments:

J. E. DOW.—Among the witnesses attendant on the trial of Commodore El-liot[t], we notice *Jesse Erskine Dow, Esq.*, the very clever author of "The Log of Old Ironsides," and fifty other capital things, in a different vein, which have appeared from time to time at random in our Magazines. "The Log," it will be remembered, was for many months the "big fish" of Burton's Gentleman's Magazine. Mr. Dow, from a sad habit of being always in a hurry, has acquired a certain free and easy slip-shod sort of a style which ought to be amended; but he has true and peculiar talent, and as a man there is no one whom we more highly respect.

19 MAY. In the evening Poe attends a large Harrison rally "at the corner of Walnut and Schuylkill Front street," which is addressed by "Mr. Thomas Fitnam, Dr. Thomas Dunn English, and Mr. Thomas, of Cincinnati." The proceedings are disrupted "by some Van Buren men," who "throw brick-bats and stones among the people assembled" (*United States Gazette*, 21 May; see also Thomas [1978], pp. 130–31).

21 MAY. Burton advertises his *Gentleman's Magazine* for sale. In the *Daily Chronicle* Alexander, the monthly's original publisher, comments: "We have

an advertisement in to-day's paper, which presents peculiar advantages to gentlemen of a literary disposition; and from our knowledge of the character of the work, we have no hesitancy in saying, that it is the best speculation in the publishing way, that has been offered to the public for many years." Burton's advertisement appears on the next page:

LITERARY ENTERPRISE.

The entire purchase of a monthly publication of great popularity and profit, may now be made for cash, on the most advantageous terms. The price asked is but little more in sum than the profits of the past twelve months. The present publisher, who is about embarking in another business, is prepared to prove that he offers an investment of great eligibility, affording, for a small capital, an income of from three to four thousand dollars a year, to any industrious gentleman of literary acquirements.

Letters, stating real name, addressed box 306, Post Office, Philadelphia, will meet with instant attention.

The *United States Gazette* carries the same advertisement, which is repeated in subsequent issues of both papers.

AFTER 21 MAY. Learning of Burton's advertisement, Poe concludes that his employer intends to devote himself entirely to the National Theatre. Poe now prepares to circulate a prospectus announcing his own journal, the *Penn Magazine* (Poe to Burton, 1 June; entries for 3, 4 JUNE).

23 MAY. The *Saturday Courier* notices the presence of Thomas and Dow in Philadelphia.

30 MAY. The *Daily Chronicle* describes Burton's National Theatre, which will accommodate an audience of around two thousand: "we rejoice in the positive certainty of having a first-rate theatre of a larger size than any now in the city. . . . the workmen have been busily employed these three weeks, and in three months, the new theatre will be in operation." The report is reprinted in Alexander's other paper, the *Weekly Messenger*, on 3 June.

30 MAY. Burton sends Poe an angry letter of dismissal, rebuking him for attempting to start his own journal (Poe's reply).

[Burton had reason to be incensed: Poe's forthcoming announcement of the *Penn Magazine* would lessen the market value of the *Gentleman's Magazine*.]

1 JUNE. Poe replies to Burton's "very singular letter of Saturday." He resents the fact that three dollars have been retained from his salary each week for "the last 3 weeks." He does not owe Burton $100; he is indebted

"in the amount of about $60"; he will refuse to pay a larger sum. Burton's assertion that Poe contributes only "2 or 3 pp. of M.S." to each issue of the *Gentleman's Magazine* is also incorrect. He lists the number of pages he has provided each month since last July, claiming "an average of 11 pp per month." His monthly salary of $50 is not excessive, because he performs many services: "proofreading; general superintendence at the printing-office; reading, alteration, & preparation of M.S.S." Poe's plans for the *Penn Magazine* were prompted by Burton's own actions during this past month: "You first 'enforced', as you say, a deduction of salary: giving me to understand thereby that you thought of parting company—You next spoke disrespectfully of me behind my back—this as an habitual thing—to those whom you supposed your friends, and who punctually retailed me, as a matter of course, every ill-natured word which you uttered. Lastly you advertised your magazine for sale without saying a word to me about it. . . . Had I not firmly believed it your design to give up your Journal, with a view of attending to the [National] Theatre, I should [never] have dreamed of attempting one of my own. The opportunity of doing something for myself seemed a good one—(I was about to be thrown out of business)—and I embraced it." Poe will not agree to continue "The Journal of Julius Rodman" until he hears from Burton again (*L*, 1:129–33).

2 JUNE. The *United States Gazette* announces Thomas' third novel: "HO-WARD PINCKNEY, a novel by the author of Clinton Bradshaw, is in the press of Lea & Blanchard and will be published in October next."

3 JUNE. Poe writes John Neal, enclosing a printed prospectus of the *Penn Magazine*:

As you gave me the first jog in my literary career, you are in a measure bound to protect me & keep me rolling. I therefore now ask you to aid me with your influence, in whatever manner your experience shall suggest.

It strikes me that I never write you except to ask a favor, but my friend Thomas will assure you that I bear you always in mind—holding you in the highest respect and esteem (*L*, 1:137; Ostrom [1974], p. 519; Moldenhauer [1973], pp. 46–48).

3? JUNE. Poe sends copies of his prospectus to the Philadelphia newspapers.

4 JUNE. The *Pennsylvania Inquirer* reports: "Edgar A. Poe, Esq. has just issued proposals for a monthly literary journal, to be called the 'Penn Magazine.' " The *Inquirer* quotes two paragraphs from the prospectus. In the afternoon Willis Gaylord Clark notices Poe's plan in the *Philadelphia Gazette*, alluding to Burton as a "base" association:

Mr. EDGAR A. POE will issue in this city on the first of January next, and continue thereafter in monthly numbers, "The Penn Magazine." Mr. POE is a clear and vigorous writer; a discriminative and fearless critic,—and we shall be pleased to find him reigning in his own sphere, where his classic power and genuine good taste, untrammeled by base or palsying associations, shall have full scope and play. We do not doubt that the Penn Magazine will add to the reputation of its conductor, and do honor to its name (cf. Clark to Longfellow, 18 July).

5 JUNE. The *Daily Chronicle* reprints Clark's report. Alexander praises Poe and defends Burton:

We . . . are pleased to learn that Mr. Poe will again enter the field of literature, and give display to his sportive fancy and chaste imaginings. He has a fund of talent, and we ardently hope that he may succeed in his new enterprise, but he must recollect that the times are out of joint. We had understood that the Gentleman's Magazine was about to lose the benefit of his services.

The editor of the Gazette, in his article above, seems to infer that Mr. Poe, during a short residence in this city, has kept bad company—and been connected with men of no talent or taste. So far as *our* knowledge extends, it has been quite the contrary. Mr. Poe has, while among us, trod the classic fields with those who are eminent for their talent, good taste, and discernment; and a liberal facility, for a full display of his powers, has been extended to him, and due courtesy always tendered by those with whom he has been connected in business.

6 JUNE. In the *Saturday Evening Post* George R. Graham comments on Poe's project:

By reference to our advertising columns, it will be seen that a new magazine of a large class will be published in this city after the first of January next. The gentleman who issues the prospectus, and proposes to be publisher and editor, is so well known in the literary world, that commendation would be useless. He was for a long time connected with the Southern Literary Messenger, and won for himself an enviable distinction, as an able, vigorous, impartial, and a somewhat over caustic critic. His pen has been visible for some months past in the review department of the Gentleman's Magazine, of this city, *from which he has retired*. We wish him success in his new undertaking, and congratulate him; upon the *unique* title of his *magazine*. As we circulate widely among the Friends, we wish him no worse luck, than that he may make *friends indeed*, of many; as he will find none, should he live to have a thousand years' experience in publishing, who are more prompt, upright, and honest, in the performance of every obligation, and particularly of the one which we consider most imperious—*that of paying the Printer*.

The prospectus appears as a paid advertisement on the next page:

PROSPECTUS OF THE PENN MAGAZINE, A MONTHLY LITERARY JOURNAL, TO BE EDITED AND PUBLISHED IN THE CITY OF PHILADELPHIA, BY EDGAR A. POE.—*To the Public*.—Since resigning the conduct of The Southern Literary Messenger, at the commencement of its third year, I have constantly held in view the establishment of a Magazine which should retain some of the chief features of that Journal, abandoning the rest. . . .

I will be pardoned for speaking more directly of The Messenger. Having in it no proprietary right, my objects too, in many respects, being at variance with those of its very worthy owner, I found difficulty in stamping upon its pages that *individuality* which I believe essential to the perfect success of all similar publications. . . .

To those who remember the early years of the Messenger, it will be scarcely necessary to say that its main feature was [a] somewhat overdone causticity in its department of Critical Notices. The Penn Magazine will retain this trait of severity in so much only as the calmest and sternest sense of literary justice will permit. One or two years, since elapsed, may have mellowed down the petulance, without interfering with the rigor of the critic. . . . It shall be the first and chief purpose of the Magazine now proposed, to become known as one where may be found, at all times, and upon all subjects, an honest and a fearless opinion. . . .

In respect to the other general features of the Penn Magazine, a few words here will suffice. Upon matters of *very* grave moment, it will leave the task of instruction in better hands. Its aim, chiefly, shall be *to please*; and this through means of versatility, originality and pungency. It must not be supposed, however, that the intention is never to be serious. There *is* a species of grave writing, of which the spirit is novelty and vigor, and the immediate object the enkindling of the imagination. In such productions, belonging to the loftiest regions of literature, the journal shall abound. . . .

To the mechanical execution of the work the greatest attention will be given which such a matter can require. . . . The pictorial embellishments will be numerous, and by the leading artists of the country, but will be only introduced in the necessary illustration of the text.

The Penn Magazine will be published in Philadelphia, on the first of each month, and will form, half yearly, a volume of about 500 pages. The price will be $5 per annum, payable in advance, or upon the receipt of the first number, which will be issued on the first of January, 1841.

8 JUNE. PORTLAND, MAINE. John Neal writes Poe: "Yours of June 4 [3], directed to New York, reached me but yesterday. I am glad to hear of your new enterprize and hope it may be all that you desire; but I cannot help you. I have done with the newspapers—have abandoned the journals—and have involved so many of my friends of late by becoming editor, or associate editor of so many different things, for a few months at a time— and always against my will—that I haven't the face to ask any person to subscribe for anything on earth" (Neal, p. 2).

8 JUNE. PHILADELPHIA. The *North American* comments: "In the Prospectus of the Penn Magazine, now before us, . . . Edgar A. Poe, Esq. proposes to commence a work, which . . . shall endeavor to unite instruction with amusement. . . . Mr. Poe is himself a gentleman of richly imaginative powers."

my 30   36 Carter's Alley, Philadelphia.

PROSPECTUS OF THE PENN MAGA-ZINE, A MONTHLY LITERARY JOURNAL,

TO BE EDITED AND PUBLISHED IN THE CITY OF PHILADEL-PHIA, BY EDGAR A. POE.—*To the Public.*—Since re-signing the conduct of The Southern Literary Messenger, at the commencement of its third year, I have constantly held in view the establishment of a Magazine which should retain some of the chief features of that Journal, abandoning the rest. Delay, however, has been occa-sioned by a variety of causes, and not until now have I felt fully prepared to execute the intention.

I will be pardoned for speaking more directly of The Messenger. Having in it no proprietary right, my objects too, in many respects, being at variance with those of its very worthy owner, I found difficulty in stamping upon its pages that *individuality* which I believe essential to the perfect success of all similar publications. In regard to their permanent interest and influence, it has appeared to me that a continuous and definite character, with a marked certainty of purpose, was of the most vital impor-tance ; and these desiderata, it is obvious, can never be surely attained where more than one mind has the general direction of the undertaking. This consideration has been an inducement to found a Magazine of my own, as the only chance of carrying out to full completion what-ever peculiar designs I may have entertained.

To those who remember the early years of the Messen-ger, it will be scarcely necessary to say that its main feature was somewhat overdone causticity in its depart-ment of Critical Notices. The Penn Magazine will retain this trait of severity in so much only as the calmest and sternest sense of literary justice will permit. One or two years, since elapsed, may have mellowed down the petu-lance, without interfering with the rigor of the critic. Most surely they have not yet taught him to read through the medium of a publisher's interest, nor convinced him of the impolicy of speaking the truth. It shall be the first and chief purpose of the Magazine now proposed, to become known as one where may be found, at all times, and upon all subjects, an honest and a fearless opinion. This is a purpose of which no man need be ashamed It it one, moreover, whose novelty at least will give it in terest. For assurance that I will fulfil it in its best spirit

Poe's prospectus in the *Saturday Evening Post*, 6 June

9 JUNE. The *Public Ledger* quotes from the prospectus, praising Poe for his promise to be a rigorous but just critic. "As a writer of fiction, Mr. Poe possesses extraordinary powers, and with respect to originality of genius, he has few equals."

BEFORE 11 JUNE. *Burton's* for June contains the sixth and final installment of Poe's unfinished "Rodman," his plate article "Some Account of Stonehenge," his "Omniana," and his reviews of *The Youth of Shakspeare* and Henry Grattan's *High-Ways and By-Ways*. The inside front cover carries this announcement by Burton: "Our readers are respectfully informed that in future Edgar A. Poe will not be connected with this Magazine."

11 JUNE. The *United States Gazette* notices the publication of *Burton's*. In another column the editor Joseph R. Chandler welcomes the *Penn Magazine*: "There has been handed round a prospectus for a monthly magazine . . . to be published in this city by Edgar A. Poe, Esq., whose contributions to the literature of our country have been abundant and creditable." Poe is "a sound, and sometimes a severe critic—one who makes the shortcoming or over-reaching author feel that he has offended. Wholesome remembrances of this kind are good for the literary prospects of a country."

12 JUNE. The prospectus appears as a paid advertisement in the *Spirit of the Times*.

12 JUNE. BALTIMORE. Joseph Evans Snodgrass writes Poe, requesting his assistance in securing the return of an essay submitted in the *Gentleman's Magazine* premium contest. Snodgrass had previously contacted Burton, who wrote him that he could not locate the manuscript (Poe's 17 June reply).

13 JUNE. PHILADELPHIA. The *Saturday Chronicle* and the *Saturday Courier* favorably notice the forthcoming *Penn Magazine*, both papers quoting from Poe's prospectus.

17 JUNE. Poe replies to Snodgrass: "Touching your Essay. Burton not only *lies*, but deliberately and wilfully lies; for the last time but one that I saw him I called his attention to the M.S. which was then at the top of a pile of other M.S.S. sent for premiums, in a drawer of the office desk. . . . Were I in your place I would take some summary method of dealing with the scoundrel, whose infamous line of conduct in regard to this whole premium scheme merits, and shall receive exposure. I am firmly convinced that it was never his intention to pay one dollar of the money offered." Poe encloses a prospectus of the *Penn Magazine*: "I have every hope of success.

As yet I have done nothing more than send a few Prospectuses to the Philadelphia editors, and it is rather early to strike—six months in anticipation. My object, at present, is merely to call attention to the contemplated design." He does not know the "fate" of his *Tales of the Grotesque and Arabesque*, because he has "never spoken to the publishers concerning them since the day of their issue." He has "cause to think, however, that the edition was exhausted almost immediately" (*L*, 1:137–39).

20 JUNE. COLUMBIA, PENNSYLVANIA. The *Columbia Spy* quotes the *Penn* prospectus (Heartman and Canny, pp. 57, 174).

26 JUNE. PHILADELPHIA. The poet Charles West Thomson writes Poe, asking him to suggest some literary "employment" (Poe's reply).

27 JUNE. In the evening Poe calls twice at Thomson's residence, 70 North Tenth Street, in relation to his "note of the 26th," but fails to find him at home (Poe's reply).

28 JUNE. Poe replies to Thomson, writing on stationery bearing the *Penn* prospectus:

You may have heard that I have declined a farther connexion with the Gentleman's Magazine, and propose to establish one of my own. By the Prospectus you will see that the first number will not be issued until the first of January; th[is] delay being rendered necessary by my want of capital. It is, therefore, at present, altogether out of my power to suggest any employment of the nature you designate.

Desperate as my chances of success may appear, where so many have failed with every advantage of money, and monied interest—still I feel a perfect certainty of accomplishing the task I have deliberately undertaken. I am proposing to myself, however, to form a connexion, as soon as possible, with some gentleman of literary attainments, who could at the same time advance as much ready money as will be requisite for the first steps of the undertaking—to defray, for instance, the expences of visiting the chief northern cities, of printing and distributing circulars, of advertising &c &c—items which, altogether, would demand scarcely $500. Upon receipt of your note the idea suggested itself that you might feel willing to join me in the enterprise, and, if so, there is nothing [that] would give me greater pleasure. Will you let me hear from you upon this topic—if possible this afternoon? (*L*, 1:139–40; Moldenhauer [1973], pp. 46, 48–49).

JULY. NEW YORK. Lewis Gaylord Clark comments in the *Knickerbocker Magazine*:

The "GENTLEMAN'S MAGAZINE," issued monthly at Philadelphia, as we gather from the "Brother Jonathan," is offered for sale; "the proprietor being about to engage in a more profitable business." Mr. E. A. POE, a spirited writer, and hitherto the principal editor of the miscellany in question, announces his retirement from its supervision. He has issued proposals for a new monthly magazine, "to be executed in the neatest style, after the manner of the KNICKERBOCKER," to which he promises to bring great additions to the literary aid he has hitherto diverted into a different channel.

JULY. LONDON. *Bentley's Miscellany* reprints Poe's "Why the Little Frenchman Wears His Hand in a Sling" under the heading "The Irish Gentleman and the Little Frenchman." Neither the author nor the source (*Tales of the Grotesque and Arabesque*) is mentioned.

5 JULY. CAMBRIDGE, MASSACHUSETTS. Longfellow writes his friend Willis Gaylord Clark, editor of the *Philadelphia Gazette*, alluding to Poe's reviews of *Hyperion* and *Voices of the Night*: "Pray who is it that is attacking me so furiously in Philadelphia? I have never seen the attacks, but occasionally I receive a newspaper with a defense of [my] writings, from which I learn there has been an attack" (Longfellow [1966] 2:236–38).

BEFORE 10 JULY. PHILADELPHIA. *Burton's* for July contains Poe's "Omniana."

10 JULY. John S. Du Solle reviews *Burton's* in the *Spirit of the Times*, observing changes occasioned by Poe's departure: "The Review Department is rather of a more good natured, and less spicy character than usual. We have but one serious fault to find with this magazine; it is generally full of typographical errors."

18 JULY. Clark replies to Longfellow, erroneously attributing Poe's reviews to Burton: "You ask me who attacks you here? The only ones I have seen against you, have been in *Burton's* Magazine—a vagrant from England, who has left a wife and offspring behind him there, and plays the bigamist in '*this*,' with another wife, and his whore besides; one who cannot write a paragraph in English to save his life. I have answered *thoroughly*, any attack upon you—and shall continue to do so, whenever they appear" (Clark, pp. 57–59).

28 JULY. AUGUSTA, GEORGIA. William Poe writes Poe, inquiring about the *Penn Magazine* (Poe's 14 August reply).

[William Poe and his two brothers Robert and Washington were the first cousins of Poe's father David Poe, Jr., and his aunt Maria Clemm.]

AUGUST OR BEFORE. PHILADELPHIA. Poe revises the prospectus of the

Penn, adding a passage stating that the journal will be characterized by an "absolutely independent" criticism: "a criticism self-sustained; guiding itself only by the purest rules of Art; analyzing and urging these rules as it applies them; holding itself aloof from all personal bias; acknowledging no fear save that of outraging the right; yielding no point either to the vanity of the author, or to the assumptions of antique prejudice, or to the involute and anonymous cant of the Quarterlies, or to the arrogance of those organised *cliques*, which, hanging like nightmares upon American literature, manufacture, at the nod of our principal booksellers, a pseudo-public-opinion by wholesale" (Quinn, pp. 306–08; Thomas [1978], pp. 158–61).

AUGUST. *Burton's* contains Poe's "Omniana."

AUGUST. LONDON. *Bentley's Miscellany* reprints "The Fall of the House of Usher" from the *Tales of the Grotesque and Arabesque*, without identifying the author or his book.

14 AUGUST. PHILADELPHIA. Poe replies to William Poe's 28 July letter, writing on stationery bearing the *Penn* prospectus. He discusses this project: "The ambition which actuates me [is] now to be no ordinary nor unworthy sentiment, and, knowing this, I take pride in earnestly soliciting your support, and that of your brothers and friends. If I fully succeed in my purposes I will not fail to produce some lasting effect upon the growing literature of the country, while I establish for myself individually a name which that country 'will not willingly let die.' " Poe will rely chiefly "upon the South . . . for aid in the undertaking," and he has "every hope" that this region will not fail him: "I acknowledge to you that my prospects depend very much upon getting together a subscription list previously to the lrst of December. If, by this day, I can obtain 500 names, the w[or]k cannot fail to proceed, and I have no fear for the [resu]lt." He asks William Poe to act as agent for the *Penn* in Augusta; he is writing "a few lines also by this mail" to William's brothers, Robert and Washington. Mrs. Clemm is still living with him, "but for the last six weeks has been on a visit to a friend in the State of N. Jersey" (L, 1:140–43; 2:691).

14? AUGUST. Poe writes Robert Poe of Augusta, Georgia, requesting his support for the *Penn* (cited Poe to William Poe).

15 AUGUST. Poe writes Washington Poe of Macon, Georgia, using stationery bearing the *Penn* prospectus: "May I ask you to assist me in the present instance? Your brothers in Augusta have kindly offered me every aid in

their power . . . . Upon looking over my Prospectus I trust you will find my purposes, as expressed in it, of a character worthy your support. I am actuated by an ambition which I believe to be an honourable one—the ambition of serving the great cause of truth, while endeavouring to forward the literature of the country. . . . I think it very probable that your influence in Macon will procure for me several subscribers" (*L*, 1:143–44).

18 AUGUST. Poe writes Lucian Minor in Charlottesville, Virginia. Recalling that Minor evinced "many instances of good will" toward him during his editorship of the *Southern Literary Messenger*, Poe requests his assistance for the *Penn*: "The permanent success of the Magazine depends, chiefly, upon the number of subscribers I may obtain before the first of December. If, through any influence you will be kind enough to exert in my behalf, at Charlottesville, or elsewhere, you can procure me even one or two names, you will render me a service of the greatest importance, and one for which I shall be very grateful" (*L*, 1:144–45; Moldenhauer [1973], p. 49).

20 AUGUST. Poe writes Joseph B. Boyd of Cincinnati, using stationery with the *Penn* prospectus: "I believe that the purposes set forth in this Prospectus are such as your candor will approve; . . . the disadvantages under which I labor are, in some respects, exceedingly great—and, for these reasons, I have no hesitation in earnestly soliciting your assistance, even at the risk of being considered importunate" (*L*, 1:145–46).

27 AUGUST. NEW YORK. The eccentric Georgia poet Thomas Holley Chivers writes Poe: "In answer to your solicitation for my support for the forthcoming Journal, I must say, that I am much pleased with your 'Prospectus'—the plan which you have in view—and hope, sincerely, that you may realize all your antisipations. As it regards myself, I will support you as long as you may continue the Editor of the above-named work. In the Paradise of Literature, I do not know one better calculated than yourself, to prune the young scions of their exuberent [*sic*] thoughts." Chivers does not specify what form his support will take, but gives Poe a specimen of his own "exuberent thoughts":

I consider the publication of such a work as you have suggested, infinitely above any other undertaking. There can be no equivalent given to a man for the payment of divine thought. It is as far above every other consideration, as the soul is more immortal. He who has never wandered amid the labyrinthine vistas of the flower-gemed solitudes of thought, knows nothing of the capabilities of the soul, in its aspirations after the Beautiful in Natural Truth, which it, thereby, perceives will be fully manifested to it, in all its glory, in the enjoyment of the Hereafter. He knows nothing of that delightful Eden which remains immortal in the soul, whose flowers are the amaranths of celestial thought. The fruit of the ignorant seems sweet to the eye, but "turns to ashes on the lips." The garden of literature to the wise, is a *"Paradise Regained,"* wherein his thoughts, like the swan of Socrates, can soar up to the celestial regions, and become the soul's heralds of the divine To-come (Chivers [1957], pp. 7–11).

SEPTEMBER. PHILADELPHIA. Burton alludes to Poe's drinking in a reply to a Maine subscriber carried on the inside front cover of the *Gentleman's Magazine*: "Our friend at Portland may rest assured that we were ignorant of the non-transmission of his numbers. His name was erased from our list by the person whose 'infirmities' have caused us much annoyance. The back numbers will be forwarded forthwith."

5 SEPTEMBER. BOSTON. The *Boston Notion* reprints "The Fall of the House of Usher" without naming the author, "From Bentley's Miscellany for August" (Pollin [1970b], p. 25).

11 SEPTEMBER. PHILADELPHIA. In the *Daily Chronicle* Charles W. Alexander calls attention to the *Penn Magazine*, which "Mr. Edgar A. Poe, a gentleman well known in the literary world, will commence . . . on the first of January next. His ability as a writer will make the work interesting to readers and without doubt, cause it to have a large circulation. We wish him success, for he deserves it." Poe's revised prospectus appears in the advertising columns, followed by this postscript: "Those friends of the Editor who feel willing to give him their support in this enterprise, will aid his cause most essentially by sending in their names *before the 1st of December*, 1840."

[The prospectus was repeated in thirty-six subsequent issues of the *Chronicle*: eight times in September, five in October, and twenty-three in November.]

14 SEPTEMBER. The *Chronicle* reports that "the subscription list" for the *Penn* "is receiving rapidly a succession of names. A great number are from the Southern States, which is a proof that Mr. Poe's talents are appreciated, and that he gave satisfaction when editor of the Southern Literary Messenger. As a strictly chaste, clear, and vigorous writer, Mr. Poe stands pre-eminent."

16 SEPTEMBER. Poe replies to John Tomlin of Jackson, Tennessee, thanking him for his "kind letter, with the names of nine subscribers to the Penn Magazine." Tomlin's tale "The Devil's Visit to St Dunstan," offered for the *Penn*, will assuredly merit "a conspicuous place in the opening number" (*L*, 1:146–47).

30 SEPTEMBER. RICHMOND. Dr. Socrates Maupin, headmaster of the Richmond Academy, writes Poe:

Through the kindness of Miss [Jane] MacKenzie I learn that M[onsieur] C. Auguste Dubouchet, a gentleman of your acquaintance, would accept the situation of Teacher of the French Language at Mr. [Genaro] Persico's and the Academy but wishes to know the terms etc. definitely. . . .

We are willing to give five hundred dollars for the assistance of an experienced teacher. Three hours daily, say an hour and a half at each school for the session of ten months. Mrs. [Juliet J.] Drew and Miss MacKenzie have engaged a Lady to assist them. There is no gentleman engaged in teaching French in the city, so that the opening is very good for one qualified . . . .

Our session commences on the 1st day of October. May I ask of you the favour therefore to inform M. Dubouchet of our proposition and request of him the earliest answer that may suit his convenience (MB–G).

CA. OCTOBER. SAINT LOUIS. The *Commercial Bulletin* welcomes the proposed *Penn Magazine*: "From the success of this magazine we anticipate the happiest literary results. Mr. Poe is not only a man of genius and a ripe scholar, but he has an upright, a downright, and an outright honesty and fearlessness of purpose, which will guide his pen in the critical department of his work, without fear or favor. . . . Mr. Poe's career in the editorial department of the Messenger, while it made him some enemies among the pretenders to literature, won him the sincere respect of every man of eminence in the country. High testimonials to this effect were crowded upon him. Mr. Poe is, withal, a beautiful poet; and his late work 'Tales of the Grotesque and Arabesque' shows that his talents are as varied as they are profound" (*Daily Chronicle*, 8 October).

OCTOBER. LONDON. *Bentley's Miscellany* reprints "The Duc de L'Omelette" from the *Tales of the Grotesque and Arabesque*, without acknowledgment.

3 OCTOBER. PHILADELPHIA. The *Saturday Courier* and the *Saturday Evening Post* favorably notice the publication of Frederick William Thomas' novel *Howard Pinckney*, issued in two volumes by Lea & Blanchard.

8 OCTOBER. The *Daily Chronicle* reprints a notice of the *Penn M;agazine* "from a late number of the St. Louis Commercial Bulletin," commenting: "If Mr. Poe does not meet with the fullest success in the establishment of his contemplated Journal, it at least will not be the fault of his friends, who evince any thing but lukewarmness in his cause. The manner in which his attempt is spoken of by the southern and western papers especially, must be highly gratifying to himself."

10 OCTOBER. Poe replies to a 2 October letter from Pliny Earle, a physi-

cian and poet in Frankford, Pennsylvania: "I hasten to thank you for the interest you have taken in my contemplated Magazine, and for the beautiful lines 'By an Octogenarian'. They shall certainly appear in the first number. . . . Believe me that good poetry is far rarer, and therefore far more acceptable to the publisher of a journal, than even that rara avis money itself." Poe encloses a *Penn* prospectus, requesting Earle's aid in enlisting subscribers (*L*, 1:147; Moldenhauer [1973], pp. 49–50).

20 OCTOBER. Burton sells his *Gentleman's Magazine* for $3,500 to George R. Graham, publisher of the *Casket* and principal owner of the *Saturday Evening Post*. At this time the magazine has thirty-five hundred subscribers (November *Burton's*; Smyth, p. 217).

NOVEMBER. The inside front cover of the *Gentleman's Magazine* carries two cards. In the first Burton announces the magazine's sale; in the second Graham announces his intention to unite it with his monthly the *Casket* "on the 1st of December." The outside back cover carries a large advertisement for the first volume of *Graham's Magazine*, "The Casket and the Gentleman's United," which will commence on 1 January 1841. "The December [1840] number will, however, be a specimen of the New Volume."

6 NOVEMBER. Poe replies to a 10 October letter from Richard Henry Stoddard, a fifteen-year-old admirer in New York. He complies with Stoddard's "very flattering request" for a manuscript poem by transcribing his sonnet "To Zante" (*L*, 2:692–93).

6 NOVEMBER. SAINT LOUIS. Thomas writes Poe, promising an article for the *Penn Magazine*. He is forwarding, under separate cover, a favorable notice of Poe from the *Commercial Bulletin*. Mr. Bateman, who will soon visit Philadelphia, is to leave a copy of Thomas' *Howard Pinckney* for Poe at John Sturdivant's Congress Hall Hotel (Poe's 23 November reply).

22 NOVEMBER. JACKSON, TENNESSEE. John Tomlin writes Poe: "As the time will soon be here when the subscribers in this place will have to pay for your *Magazine*, I must beg of you . . . to inform me, if Tennessee money is current in the ordinary business transactions of your city. . . . If Virginia, N. Carolina or S. Carolina money is more current in Philadelphia, than Tennessee, I shall certainly obtain the one that you may mention, as preferable." Tomlin is certain that the *Penn* will succeed: "For the warm-hearted Southerners, by whom you are known, will not let the Work die for the want of patronage. They are your friends—for they know you well, and will sustain you." He asks Poe whether William Gilmore Simms

of Charleston, South Carolina, is doing anything for the *Penn*: "He can aid you materially, and I have no doubt but what he will. Some years ago, he was my friend and gave me much good advice." In two or three months Tomlin will visit Nashville: "While there I shall certainly procure other names to your work" (*W*, 17:61–62).

23 NOVEMBER. PHILADELPHIA. Poe replies to Thomas' 6 November letter. He has not received the Saint Louis *Commercial Bulletin*, but has seen this paper's favorable notice at the Merchants' Exchange: "The 'Bulletin' has always been very kind to me, and I am at a loss to know who edits it— will you let me into this secret when you write again? Neither did 'Howard Pin[c]kney' come to hand. Upon receipt of your letter, just now, I called at Congress Hall—but no books. Mr Bateman had been there, and gone, forgetting to leave them. I shall get them upon his return." Poe likes this novel "very well," but he prefers Thomas' earlier novel *Clinton Bradshaw*:

You give yourself up to your own nature (which is a noble one, upon my soul) in Clinton Bradshaw; but in Howard Pin[c]kney you abandon the broad rough road for the dainty by-paths of authorism. In the former you are interested in what you write & write to please, pleasantly; in the latter, having gained a name, you write

Philadelphia Merchants' Exchange

to maintain it, and [the] effort becomes apparent. This consciousness of reputation leads you so freq[uently] into those literary and other disquisitions about which we quarrell[e]d at Studevant's [Sturdivant's]. If you would send the public opinion to the devil, forgetting that a public existed, and writing from the natural promptings of your own spirit, you would do wonders. In a word, abandon is wanting in "Howard Pinkney"—and when I say this you must know that I mean a high compliment—for they to whom this very abandon may be safely suggested are very few indeed, and belong to the loftier class of writers.

Poe will review *Howard Pinckney* in the initial number of the *Penn Magazine*; he would like to have Thomas' promised article "in the first sheet, which goes to press early in December." He asks him to have the revised *Penn* prospectus "inserted once or twice" in several Saint Louis papers. "Mrs Clemm and Virginia unite with me in the kindest remembrances to yourself and sister [Frances Ann]—with whom your conversation (always turning upon the 'one-loved name') has already made us all so well acquainted" (*L*, 1:148–49; Moldenhauer [1973], p. 50).

BEFORE 28 NOVEMBER. The first number of *Graham's Magazine* contains Poe's tale "The Man of the Crowd."

28 NOVEMBER. The *Saturday Evening Post* notices *Graham's*: "This Magazine for December is already issued in a superior style of elegance, and contains a variety of beautiful embellishments, and articles from the pens of some of the first writers of the country."

BEFORE DECEMBER. ANDALUSIA. Poe calls on Nicholas Biddle, President of the United States Bank, at Andalusia, his country estate on the outskirts of Philadelphia. Biddle subscribes to the *Penn Magazine*, paying "four years in advance," but does not volunteer additional financial backing. Poe gives him a copy of the *Tales of the Grotesque and Arabesque*, inscribing it "For Mr. N. Biddle, with the author's respects" (*L*, 2:695; see 6 JANUARY 1841).

DECEMBER. LONDON. *Bentley's Miscellany* reprints "The Visionary" from Poe's *Tales of the Grotesque and Arabesque*, without acknowledgment.

EARLY DECEMBER. PHILADELPHIA. Poe is bedridden by illness and consequently forced to postpone the *Penn Magazine* until next March (*Daily Chronicle*, 29 December; Poe to L. J. Cist, 30 December).

7 DECEMBER. SAINT LOUIS. Thomas writes Poe:

Yours of the 23 of last month I received yesterday. I thought if I sat down to weave a tale for you that procrastination or a better apology might keep me from finishing the MS. till it was too late for your first number, for which you seemed to wish the communication. I therefore, as you like my "adventures of a Poet"— you remember I read it to you—thought I would give you extracts from it. Inclosed I send them. The "steamboat story" which I gave you is, you know, an extract from the same MS.

Thomas thanks Poe for his "good opinion" of *Howard Pinckney*; he admits that *Clinton Bradshaw* may be the better novel. He is glad that Poe will issue the *Penn Magazine* in January: "I went today to have an editorial notice &c taken of it and you, but found my friend out; to-morrow . . . I will see to it and duly send you a paper." Mr. Fowzer, a magazine agent of the firm Fowzer and Woodward, will agree to distribute the *Penn* in Saint Louis; Thomas transcribes the firm's "Terms of Agency." He is writing in the room of his sister Frances Ann: "she is indeed gratified at the kind manner in which Mrs. Clemm and your Lady mention her. She sends her regards while I look up from the paper to say that your letter is just as you talk" (*W*, 17:65–67).

19 DECEMBER. PHILADELPHIA. Graham's *Saturday Evening Post* lauds the second number of his monthly:

"GRAHAM'S LADYS' AND GENTLEMAN'S MAGAZINE *for January, 1841.*"—This Magazine is already issued and ready for delivery, embellished in a style which has not been equalled in this country before. The opening engraving is an *original* mezzotint on steel prepared expressly for the work by Mr. Sartain, of Philadelphia, the best engraver of the kind in the United States. . . . Next follows a plate of fashions of three figures, exquisitely colored, and we stake our reputation on the assertion, that they are unequalled by any. Then follow two pages of music, the popular song of "The Indian Maid." And lastly we have Angling illustrated, making with the three fashion figures *eight embellishments*. Truly enough for a three dollar magazine.

[For Graham, as for Burton, Louis A. Godey, and other commercial publishers of the day, "embellishments" were the crux of a magazine, even more important than its literary contents. Poe had nothing but contempt for these adventitious and expensive decorations (cf. his 25 May 1842 letter to Thomas). In his *Penn* prospectus he declared his intention to use engravings only "in the necessary illustration of the text."]

29 DECEMBER. The *Daily Chronicle* carries this announcement: "THE PENN MAGAZINE.—Owing to the severe and continued illness of Mr. Poe, the issue of the first number of this journal is postponed until the first of March next."

30 DECEMBER. Poe replies to the Cincinnati poet Lewis J. Cist: "Your letter of the 7th found me labouring under a severe illness, which has

confined me to bed for the last month, and from which I am now only slowly recovering." As the "worst result of this illness" he has been forced to postpone the *Penn Magazine* until the first of March; he asks Cist to mention this delay to Joseph B. Boyd and to insert a brief announcement of it in one of the Cincinnati papers. Cist's poem "Bachelor Philosophy" will not appear in the *Penn* until the second number, "as at the time of its reception, all the poetry for the first number was already in type" (*L*, 1:150).

31 DECEMBER. Poe writes John P. Kennedy of Baltimore, soliciting his contributions for the *Penn*:

Since you gave me my first start in the literary world, and since indeed I seriously say that without the timely kindness you once evinced towards me, I should not at this moment be among the living—you will not feel surprise that I look anxiously to you for encouragement in this new enterprise—the first of any importance which I have undertaken on my own account. What I most seriously need, in the commencement, is caste for the journal—I need the countenance of those who stand well in the social not less than in the literary world. I know that you have never yet written for Magazines—and this is a main reason for my now begging you to give me something for my own. I care not what the article be, nor of what length—what I wish is the weight of your name. Any unused scrap lying by you will fully answer my purpose (*L*, 1:150–51).

LATE 1840. NEW YORK. George P. Morris reprints Poe's "To Ianthe in Heaven" in his anthology *American Melodies*, from the July 1839 *Burton's* (Heartman and Canny, p. 62; Mabbott [1969], 1:214–15, 584).

CA. 1840? PHILADELPHIA. Silas Weir Mitchell, the future novelist, encounters Poe in the office of his father Dr. John Kearsley Mitchell (A. R. Burr, pp. 21, 298).

CA. 1840? Henry Herring, who had married Poe's aunt Eliza Poe, settles in Philadelphia with his daughter by a subsequent marriage, Mary Estelle Herring. They frequently see the Poe family (Thomas [1978], pp. 802–04).

CA. 1840? Poe's early Baltimore friend Mary Starr, who is now married to a New York merchant tailor named Jenning, spends "a pleasant evening" with the Poe family while "on a visit to Philadelphia" (Van Cleef, p. 639; Mabbott [1969], 1:232–33).

CA. 1840? BALTIMORE. Poe visits Baltimore on "legal business" for his wife Virginia, who has inherited a portion of the estate of her grandparents, William Clemm, Sr., and his wife (Phillips, 1:640).

FREDERICK WILLIAM THOMAS
(detail from the painting by Thomas D. Jones)
American Antiquarian Society

CHAPTER SIX

Graham's Magazine *and*
the Custom House

1841–1842

In January 1841 Poe renews his efforts to enlist contributors a..d subscribers for the *Penn Magazine*, now scheduled to appear on 1 March; but in early February a financial crisis involving the Philadelphia banks forces him to postpone its publication indefinitely. He then accepts the position of book review editor on *Graham's Magazine*, newly established by George R. Graham. The April *Graham's* contains Poe's tale "The Murders in the Rue Morgue"; the May number, "A Descent into the Maelström." In the last half of 1841 he contributes two serials to *Graham's* which excite much attention, "Secret Writing" and "Autography." Around 20 January 1842 Virginia Poe suffers a pulmonary hemorrhage, marking the onset of tuberculosis. Poe, who has largely abstained from alcohol for several years, resumes drinking under the stress occasioned by her recurrent illness. Around 1 April he resigns from *Graham's*, disgusted with its emphasis on fashion plates and sentimental literature. In May his friend Frederick William Thomas, a novelist holding a minor office in the Treasury Department, intercedes on his behalf with Robert Tyler, eldest son of President John Tyler. Thomas writes Poe from Washington on 21 May, giving him hope of a political sinecure in the Philadelphia Custom House. In late June Poe visits New York in an unsuccessful attempt to find a publisher for a new collection of his tales, tentatively entitled *Phantasy-Pieces*. After returning to Philadelphia he prepares a judicious critique of Rufus W. Griswold's anthology *The Poets and Poetry of America*, and he once again plans to issue the *Penn Magazine*. On 17 September Thomas visits Poe at his residence in the Fairmount district, assuring him that Robert Tyler wishes to see him given a government appointment. In October and November the new Collector of Customs, Thomas S. Smith, appoints several dozen supporters of the Tyler administration to offices in the Custom House. As Poe is not included, he solicits four interviews with Smith, who at first evades his questions and finally, on 19 November, informs him that all the vacancies have been filled. At the end of 1842 Poe's novelette "The Mystery of Marie Rogêt" is serialized in William W. Snowden's *Ladies' Companion*, and his short story "The Tell-Tale Heart" is accepted for the first number of James Russell Lowell's *Pioneer*.

*

1841

*

EARLY JANUARY? PHILADELPHIA. Poe makes "a most advantageous arrangement" with J. R. Pollock, a periodical agent and publisher at 205 Chestnut Street, who agrees to handle "the business department" of the *Penn Magazine*. He has printed a new supply of *Penn* prospectuses ated 1 January, which promise the initial number on 1 March (Poe to Thomas Wyatt, 1 April; Heartman and Canny, pp. 62–65).

CA. 1 JANUARY. Poe writes Nathan C. Brooks in Baltimore, inquiring about a new magazine to be established in that city (Poe to Snodgrass, 17 January).

2 JANUARY. William Burke Wood, manager of the Walnut Street Theatre, sends Poe a brief note. He apologizes for his failure to see or write Poe "before the end of the past week"; he begs his "further patience for a few days" (PHi).

6 JANUARY. Poe writes the banker Nicholas Biddle at his residence in the city, 215 Spruce Street, discussing the *Penn Magazine*: "My cousins in Augusta, [Georgia,] who had led me to hope that they would aid me materially, have been unable to do so, and could not even obtain me a few subscribers in that place. On the other hand I have received a great many names from villages, in the South and West, of whose existence even I was not aware. . . . The kind manner in which you received me when I called upon you at Andalusia—upon so very equivocal an errand—has emboldened me to ask of you a still greater favor than the one you then granted. . . . The favor I would ask is that you would lend me the influence of your name in a brief article for my opening number." Poe explains this request:

I need not suggest to you, as a man of the world, the great benefit I would derive from your obliging me in this matter. Without friends in Philadelphia, except among literary men as uninfluential as myself, I would at once be put in a good position—I mean in respect to that all important point, *caste*—by having it known that you were not indifferent to my success. You will not accuse me of intending the meanness of flattery to serve as a selfish purpose, when I say that your name has an almost illimitable influence in the city, and a vast influence in all quarters of the country, and that, would you allow me its use as I propose, it would be of more actual value to me in my enterprise than perhaps a thousand dollars in money—this too more especially as the favor thus granted would be one you are not in the habit of granting (*L*, 2:693–95).

9 JANUARY. The *Saturday Evening Post* reprints Poe's "To Ianthe in Heaven," giving it the title "To One Beloved" (Mabbott [1969], 1:214–15).

17 JANUARY. Poe replies to a letter from Joseph Evans Snodgrass in Baltimore: "You wish to know my prospects with the 'Penn'. They are *glorious*—notwithstanding the world of difficulties under which I labored and labor. My illness (from which I have now entirely recovered) has been, for various reasons, a benefit to my scheme, rather than a disadvantage; and, upon the whole, if I do not eminently succeed in this enterprize, the fault will be altogether mine own. Still, I am using every exertion to ensure success, and, among other maneuvres, I have cut down the bridges behind me." Poe thanks Snodgrass for offering to contribute; he has an abundance of poetry, but will welcome "any *prose* article." He especially wants an article on the need for an international copyright law or on "the Laws of Libel in regard to Literary Criticism." The Baltimore lawyer David Hoffman has promised to aid the *Penn*; perhaps Snodgrass can persuade him to prepare an article on one of these topics. Any contribution for the opening number should be on hand soon: "I am about to put the first sheet to press immediately; and the others will follow in rapid succession." Tomorrow Poe will see George R. Graham and inquire about the essay Snodgrass submitted in the premium contest conducted by the *Gentleman's Magazine* last year; he suspects that "to prevent detection, Burton may have destroyed it." Poe requests details about "a new Magazine to be established in Baltimore by a Virginian & a practical printer"; he inquired of Nathan C. Brooks "about a fortnight ago," but has received no reply to his letter (*L*, 1:151–53).

22 JANUARY. Poe writes the playwright and lawyer Robert T. Conrad, using stationery bearing the *Penn* prospectus: "As a man of the world you will at once understand that what I most need for my work in its commencement (since I am comparatively a stranger in Philadelphia) is *caste*. I need the countenance of those who stand well not less in the social than in the literary world. I, certainly, have no claim whatever upon your attention, and have scarcely the honor of your personal acquaintance—but if I could obtain the influence of your name in an article (however brief) for my opening number, I feel that it would assist me beyond measure." Poe hopes to publish articles on "the International Copy-Right Law, and The Laws of Libel in their relation to Literary Criticism"; he doubts that anyone is more qualified than Conrad to discuss these subjects. He is "rash, however, in making any suggestions"; he will be "only too much delighted" to receive "an article upon any question whatever." The first number of the *Penn* "will be put to press on the first of February" (*L*, 1:153–55).

25 JANUARY. Judge Joseph Hopkinson replies to Poe's letter soliciting contributions for the *Penn*:

It has always been my desire that we should concentrate in Philadelphia as much literary talent as possible, and be distinguished by works of science and genius issuing from ourselves—I have therefore never been reluctant to afford the little aid in my power to such enterprizes—My time and attention, however, are much occupied by my official duties, so that I avoid making engagements which may interfare with them, or may themselves be neglected—I wish your Magazine may succeed, and with the talent you can of yourself bring into it, your prospect is encouraging—I will keep it in my view, & shall be happy to contribute to its support when I have any communications which may be acceptable to your readers—Allow me to remind you that the ruin of our periodicals has been *distant subscribers*, who never send their money, and the collection of which costs more than is received (MB–G).

4 FEBRUARY. A financial crisis disrupts the operations of the Philadelphia banks. In the morning the United States Bank suspends specie payments; by night most of the city's other banks have "suspended paying notes, of a higher denomination than five dollars." The Southern banks, "beginning at Baltimore," follow the example of the Philadelphia banks and suspend payments (*Saturday Evening Post*, 13 February).

[On 20 February the *Post* reported: "The suspension of the Banks still continues, and, as a consequence, the financial world is considerably embarrassed. Money is difficult to obtain, even at a high premium."

AFTER 4 FEBRUARY. Because of the bank suspensions Poe is forced to postpone the *Penn*. He accepts an offer from George R. Graham to conduct the book review department of *Graham's Magazine*, at a salary of $800 a year (Poe's 1 April letters to Snodgrass and Thomas Wyatt; Sartain, p. 200).

20 FEBRUARY. In the *Saturday Evening Post* Graham comments:

Mr. Poe, we are sorry to say, has been forced, at the last moment, to abandon finally, or at least to postpone indefinitely, his project of the Penn Magazine. This is the more to be regretted as he had the finest prospects of success in the establishment of the journal—such prospects as are seldom enjoyed—an excellent list of subscribers, and, what is equally to the purpose, the universal good-will of the public press. The south and west were especially warm in his cause, and, under ordinary circumstances, he could not have failed of receiving the most gratifying support. In the present disorder of all monetary affairs, however, it was but common prudence to give up the enterprise—in fact it would have been madness to attempt it. Periodicals are among the principal sufferers by these pecuniary convulsions, and to *commence* one just now would be exceedingly hazardous. It is, beyond doubt, fortunate for Mr. P. that his late illness induced the postponement of his first number; which, it will be remembered, was to have appeared in January.

It is with pleasure we add, that we have secured the services of Mr. Poe as one of the editors of Graham's Magazine. As a stern, just and impartial critic Mr. Poe holds a pen second to none in the country, and we have the confident assurance, that with such editorial strength as the Magazine now possesses, the literary department of the work will be of the very highest character.

22 FEBRUARY. Edward L. Carey writes Charles West Thomson that the *Gift* for 1842 "is now in the hands of the printer" (Heartman and Canny, p. 68).

[This edition of Carey & Hart's annual contained Poe's tale "Eleonora."]

EARLY MARCH. Poe's tale "The Murders in the Rue Morgue" is set in type for the April *Graham's* by Barrett & Thrasher, Printers, No. 33 Carter's Alley. The manuscript, afterwards thrown "into the waste-basket," is rescued by a young apprentice printer, W. J. Johnston, who preserves it (Thomas [1978], pp. 822–24).

CA. 1 MARCH. WASHINGTON. Frederick William Thomas arrives in the capital for the inauguration of the victorious Whig candidate, William Henry Harrison. Thomas renews his acquaintance with Jesse E. Dow, whom he met in Philadelphia last May (Thomas to Poe, 7 March).

4 MARCH. Harrison is inaugurated as President. John Tyler of Virginia, his running mate, becomes Vice-President.

7 MARCH. Thomas writes Poe: "I have been in Washington this week past. Dow, whom I see frequently, told me that you had given up the idea of the Penn and was [*sic*] engaged with Graham. I regret that you have been prevented from carrying out that glorious enterprise at present, but you'll do it yet." Thomas wishes "to write for some periodical a novel in numbers, say two or three chapters per month, as Marryat and Boz write their novels." He asks Poe whether this serial would be appropriate for *Graham's Magazine*: "Write me . . . if Mr. Graham likes the proposition[,] what he would give—all about it. Of course a continuous story is worth more per page than a mere sketch, as it would create a desire in the reader to see the conclusion of it and consequently make him the purchaser of the subsequent numbers of the Magazine." Thomas hopes, "in a month or so," to take Poe "by the hand"; he sends his respects to Poe's "mother and lady" (W, 17:81–82).

10 MARCH. CINCINNATI. William Davis Gallagher, editor of the *Cincinnati Gazette*, writes Poe:

> Will you be good enough to favor me so much as to enter the name of the Daily paper with which I am connected upon the exchange list of the "Penn Magazine?" The independence of critical remark which characterized the "Southern Literary Messenger" while under your control, and the *individuality* of that department of the work, make me anxious to get your new magazine. If this proposition suit you, please direct "Daily Gazette." If it do not, send me the work any how, and I will pay you in money, or, what is more plenty[ful] with me, *scribbler-coin*.

A copy of Gallagher's anthology *Selections from the Poetical Literature of the West*, just issued "by an enterprising Western publisher," accompanies this letter: "I trust you may find in it something to your liking" (MB–G).

12 MARCH. JACKSON, TENNESSEE. John Tomlin writes Poe, expressing disappointment that the *Penn Magazine* has been "indefinitely postponed." He offers his assistance in any future project Poe may undertake (W, 17:82–83: L, 2:584).

22 MARCH. CAMBRIDGE, MASSACHUSETTS. James Russell Lowell writes Charles J. Peterson, who performs many editorial duties on *Graham's Magazine*. Lowell is annoyed that his "Callirhöe" has been published in the March number without his consent. This poem was submitted as an entry in the premium contest conducted by the *Gentleman's Magazine* last year; William E. Burton should have returned it (Peterson's 29 March reply).

25 MARCH. PHILADELPHIA. Poe signs a receipt: "Recd . . . of Geo. R. Graham Sixty dollars" (PP-G).

BEFORE 26 MARCH. *Graham's* for April carries an announcement on its inside front cover:

> It is with pleasure the Proprietor announces, that he has made arrangements with EDGAR A. POE, Esq., commencing with the present number, by which he secures his valuable pen, as one of the editors of the Magazine. Mr. POE is too well known in the literary world to require a word of commendation. As a critic he is surpassed by no man in the country; and as in this Magazine his critical abilities shall have free scope, the rod will be very generously, and at the same time, justly administered.
>
> With this additional editorial strength, the Magazine may be expected to take a high position in literary merit, among the periodicals of the day. In the beauty of its embellishments, it is now on all hands confessed, to be superior to any Magazine published in this country. It is the wish of the editors, however, to make the literary department the great attraction of the Magazine, and to enlist the pride of the American people and writers, in the support of a work creditable to National Literature.

This number contains "The Murders in the Rue Morgue," as well as Poe's reviews of Edward Bulwer-Lytton's novel *Night and Morning* and R. M. Walsh's translation *Sketches of Conspicuous Living Characters of France*. Observing that one of Walsh's sketches deals with a cipher, Poe rejects the notion that its solution required "extraordinary penetration." In this case both the cipher and its key were in French and addressed to Frenchmen: "The difficulty of decyphering may well be supposed much greater had the key been in a foreign tongue; yet any one who will take the trouble may address us a note in the same manner as here proposed, and the key-phrase may be either in French, Italian, Spanish, German, Latin, or Greek (or in any of the dialects of these languages), and we pledge ourselves for the solution of the riddle. The experiment may afford our readers some amusement—let them try it."

26 MARCH. The *Daily Chronicle* notices the April *Graham's*. "The Murders in the Rue Morgue" is one of "its most interesting articles."

27 MARCH. The *Pennsylvanian* notices *Graham's*: "We observe that Mr E. A. Poe is now associated with Mr Graham in the editorial management of the work, and besides having contributed a tale of powerful interest, the traces of his able pen will attract much attention in the critical department, which contains several reviews of late publications written with remarkable vigor and discrimination."

27 MARCH. NEW YORK. Horace Greeley's *New-Yorker* reviews *Graham's*: "the article entitled 'The Murders in the Rue Morgue' is of deep but repulsive interest; . . . the Literary Notices are much more able and carefully prepared than usual."

29 MARCH. PHILADELPHIA. Peterson replies to Lowell's 22 March letter:

When Mr Graham purchased Burton's Magazine he bought also a bundle of articles, many of which Mr B[urton] said he had already paid for. In this bundle I found yours. I was struck with it, and inserted it in March. Since, as you say, it was offered for a prize, Mr B had no right to dispose of it, but should have returned it to you. Believe me *such* a piece of (I must say it) fraud I could not knowingly countenance. You will do me the justice to exonerate me from any imputation of having participated in it. Of Mr B, or *his* magazine I knew little more than yourself (MH–H).

31 MARCH. GERMANTOWN, PENNSYLVANIA. The *Germantown Telegraph* notices *Graham's*: "Among the number, there is a powerful article from Mr. POE, one of our very best writers, who is permanently connected with this magazine. The Reviews which are from the pen of Mr. P., are of an able, spirited and independent order—such as all reviews ought to be."

1 APRIL. PHILADELPHIA. Poe replies to an 8 March letter from Snodgrass. He is grateful for permission to give Graham the essay Snodgrass submitted in the *Burton's* premium contest. It will appear in the June *Graham's*: "In order to understand this apparent delay, you must be informed that we go to press at a singularly early period. The *May* number is now within two days of being ready for delivery to the mails." Poe thanks Snodgrass for "the kind interest" he has shown in regard to the malicious rumors spread by Burton: "My situation is embarrassing. It is impossible, as you say, to notice a buffoon and a felon, as one gentleman would notice another." Burton's assertions that Poe is a drunkard are totally false:

It is, however, due to candor that I inform you upon what foundation he has erected his slanders. At no period of my life was I ever what men call intemperate. I never was in the *habit* of intoxication. I never drunk drams, &c. But, for a brief period, while I resided in Richmond, and edited the *Messenger*, I certainly did give way, at long intervals, to the temptation held out on all sides by the spirit of Southern conviviality. My sensitive temperament could not stand an excitement which was an everyday matter to my companions. In short, it sometimes happened that I was completely intoxicated. For some days after each excess I was invariably confined to bed. But it is now quite four years since I have abandoned every kind of alcoholic drink—four years, with the exception of a single deviation, which occurred shortly *after* my leaving Burton, and when I was induced to resort to the occasional use of *cider*, with the hope of relieving a nervous attack.

In a postscript Poe states that the *Penn Magazine* "would have appeared under glorious auspices, and with capital at command, in March, as advertised, but for the unexpected bank suspensions. . . . The *Penn* project will unquestionably be resumed hereafter" (L, 1:155–58).

1 APRIL. Poe replies to his friend Thomas Wyatt, now in New Brunswick, New Jersey, whose letter he received "yesterday morning." Complying with Wyatt's request, Poe called on the lithographer Peter S. Duval later in the day: "He says that it will be *impossible* to execute the alterations mentioned in Prof. Millington's letter, without ruining the drawing—and that the cost of them, even if executed, would exceed that of a new drawing. . . . In truth the drawing by Mr Pinkerton is shockingly botched and 'touched up'—so that it would be useless to attempt doing anything farther with it. Mr D. refuses to put his name to it—so you may imagine how bad it is—for Mr D. has put his name to some of the most execrable things." Were Poe in Wyatt's place, he would refuse to pay E. J. Pinkerton "and get the design executed by some competent artist." He invites Wyatt to visit his family when passing through Philadelphia: "We are still at the old place." Rosalie Poe, his sister, has recently spent a week with them. Her foster brother John Mackenzie accompanied her up from Richmond and left her in Philadelphia "while he went to Boston." The *Penn Magazine* has been deferred, but not abandoned:

I had made a most advantageous arrangement with Mr Pollock to enter into partnership, and attend to the business department—when just as I was putting the first sheet to press—there came like a clap of thunder, the bank suspensions. No periodical could be *commenced* under such circumstances—and I therefore made up my mind to accept for the present year an engagement with Mr Graham, of Graham's Magazine (3d & Chesnut). He gives me an excellent salary, far more than I had with Burton—and I have a good deal less to do—so that I can afford to lay on my oars for a time, as regards the "Penn Magazine" project (TxU–HRCL; Moldenhauer [1971], pp. 468–77).

1 APRIL. Poe replies to Thomas' 7 March letter. Graham would not serialize Thomas' proposed novel in his magazine. Poe solicits his friend's opinion of "The Murders in the Rue Morgue" (Thomas' 11 May reply).

3 APRIL. The *Saturday Evening Post* quotes favorable notices of the April *Graham's* by the New York *Weekly Dispatch*, which stated that Poe's association with the magazine was "an acquisition to its interest Mr. G. may well be proud of," and by the Providence, Rhode Island, *Patriot*, which described Poe's "Rue Morgue" as "a well written and highly interesting article . . . one of that author's best efforts."

3 APRIL. Poe signs a receipt: "Recd . . . of Geo. R. Graham Fifty four dollars" (PP–G).

4 APRIL. WASHINGTON. President Harrison dies, having been in office only one month. The Vice-President John Tyler succeeds him on 6 April.

15 APRIL. PHILADELPHIA. Poe writes John Tomlin in Jackson, Tennessee (Tomlin's 30 April reply).

BEFORE 21 APRIL. *Graham's* for May contains Poe's tale "A Descent into the Maelström," as well as his reviews of Dickens' *The Old Curiosity Shop* and *Master Humphrey's Clock*, Charles Sprague's *Writings*, and John N. McJilton's poem *The Sovereignty of Mind*.

The inside front cover carries an announcement: "Writers who send articles to this Magazine for publication, *must state distinctly at the time of sending them*, whether they expect *pay*. We cannot allow compensation unless by special contract *before* publication. This rule will hereafter be rigidly enforced."

21 APRIL. STONINGTON, CONNECTICUT. A reader signing himself "S. D. L." writes *"the Editor of Graham's Magazine,"* quoting Poe's offer to solve ciphers made in the April number. He submits two ciphers, the first having a key-phrase in English, and the second, one in Latin: "As I did

not see (by the number for May,) that any of your correspondents had availed himself of your offer, I take the liberty to send the enclosed, on which, if you should think it worth your while, you can exercise your ingenuity" (*W*, 14:124–25).

AFTER 21? APRIL. NEW YORK. Mordecai M. Noah's *Evening Star* notices *Graham's*: "Edgar A. Poe, Esq. has furnished a narrative entitled 'A Descent into the Maelstrom,' which appears to be equal in interest with the powerful article from his pen in the last number, 'The Murder[s] in the Rue Morgue' " (quoted in the *Saturday Evening Post*, 1 May).

24 APRIL. PHILADELPHIA. Poe signs a receipt: "Recd . . . of Geo. R. Graham Forty dollars" (PP–G).

28 APRIL. The *Daily Chronicle* notices *Graham's*: "The 'Descent into the Maelstroom' [*sic*] by Edgar A. Poe, Esq., is unworthy of the pen of one whose talents allow him a wider and more ample range."

30 APRIL. JACKSON, TENNESSEE. Tomlin acknowledges a 15 April letter from Poe, "received on yesterday." He hopes that his tale "The Devil's Visit to St Dunstan," submitted for the *Penn Magazine*, can be published in *Graham's*. Having been appointed the postmaster of Jackson on 24 February by President Van Buren, Tomlin wonders how he will fare under the new administration: "If John Tyler Esq, President of the United States, removes me from office for being a *loco-foco*, I will certainly be opposed to him—and the measure" (MB–G).

1 MAY. PHILADELPHIA. Charles West Thomson writes Poe about *Graham's*:

I observe a notice on the cover of the May Mag. in reference to payment of writers, which perhaps may be intended for my information—I have merely to remark in regard to the matter, that I do not expect payment for anything heretofore published or now in your possession, but I should like to know from Mr. Graham whether he is willing to pay for future contributions and at what rate. It is time for me to think of making my efforts a little more productive than they have heretofore been.—I have preferred addressing you on this occasion, as we have before spoken together on the subject (MB–G).

1 MAY. In the *Saturday Evening Post* Poe reviews Dickens' novel *Barnaby Rudge*, now being published serially. He correctly predicts that the subsequent installments will reveal "that Barnaby, the idiot, is the murderer's own son." Poe praises Dickens' "creation of the hero Barnaby Rudge, and the commingling with his character, as accessory, that of the human-looking raven."

3 MAY. Poe writes Henry Wadsworth Longfellow in Cambridge, Massachusetts: "Mr Geo: R. Graham, proprietor of 'Graham's Magazine', a monthly journal published in this city, and edited by myself, desires me to beg of you the honor of your contribution to its pages. . . . I should be overjoyed if we could get from you an article each month—either poetry or prose—length and subject à discretion. In respect to terms we would gladly offer you carte blanche—and the periods of payment should also be made to suit yourself." Poe is forwarding the April and May numbers in order that Longfellow "may form some judgment of the character of the work." If he decides to contribute, "it would be an important object with us to have something, as soon as convenient, for the July number, which commences a new volume, and with part of which we are already going to press." Poe expresses his "fervent admiration" for Longellow's writings (L, 1:158–59).

BEFORE 8 MAY. Poe meets Rufus W. Griswold, a young editor and journalist.

[In his 1850 "Memoir," p. v, Griswold recalled: "My acquaintance with Mr. POE commenced in the spring of 1841. He called at my hotel, and not finding me at home, left two letters of introduction. The next morning I visited him, and we had a long conversation about literature and literary men, pertinent to the subject of a book, 'The Poets and Poetry of America,' which I was then preparing for the press." No doubt Poe hoped to have his poems featured in the new anthology; Griswold, in turn, would have realized that a favorable review by Poe in Graham's would enhance the book's chances of success.]

BEFORE 8 MAY. Poe writes Griswold: "Will you be kind enough to lend me the No. of the Family Magazine of which we spoke—if you have received it?" He also hopes to borrow John L. Stephens' Incidents of Travel in Central America, Chiapas, and Yucatan or some other "new book of interest" (L, 1:159–60).

8 MAY. BOSTON. Griswold begins an editorial engagement on the Boston Notion, a weekly newspaper of folio size published by George Roberts (Griswold [1898], pp. 65–66).

11 MAY. WASHINGTON. Thomas replies to Poe's 1 April letter. He encloses an article for Graham's, requesting payment as soon as possible: "A gentleman of address, if not of character . . . did me the honor to borrow feloniously my coat with an hundred and ten dollars in it—This has shortened my finances." Thomas thinks that he may move to New Orleans, where he would practice law. "Speaking of law reminds me of your tale

'The Murders in the Rue Morgue' and your wish to know how I like it in 'my capacity of a lawyer'—I must speak frankly, and without flattery[.] I think it the most ingenious thing of the kind on record—It is managed with a tact, ability and subtlety that is wonderful—I do not know what in the devil to make of your intellectuals." Yesterday Thomas read Poe's critique of *Barnaby Rudge* in the *Saturday Evening Post*, but he will not comment on it because he has not yet read Dickens' novel. "Poe don't forget that Henry Clay said that at the extra session of Congress he meant to bring up the copy right law—Are you not going to give an editorial on the subject—Do prick the Senator's memory and I will have the article copied here—I think when Congress meets that your humble servant will lecture on the subject." Thomas reprimands Poe for not keeping his promise to review *Howard Pinckney*: "By the bye you are a shabby fellow—Do you think by love! that I thought you . . . to get over 'Howard Pinckney' with out 'abusing it'—No sir, and be it known to you that I consider this no good reason in the eye of friendship why you should not notice it— Better be damned &c—Dont you know that to be before the public is the thing—Poe I dont like that—and that's flat." Their mutual friend Jesse E. Dow, a Democratic appointee under the Van Buren administration, has been removed from his clerkship in the Post Office Department: "I am more than sorry for it—It is though what he ought to have expected . . . . Dow has a wife and three children, with soon [to] have a fourth, and yet he bears up like a man . . . . He boards next door to me. I see him daily. We walk often together and I do not think we have ever taken a walk without speaking of you" (MB–G).

19 MAY. CAMBRIDGE, MASSACHUSETTS. Longfellow replies to Poe's 3 May letter:

I am much obliged to you for your kind expressions of regard, and to Mr. Graham for his very generous offer, of which I should gladly avail myself under other circumstances. But I am so much occupied at present that I could not do it with any satisfaction either to you or to myself. I must therefore respectfully decline his proposition.

You are mistaken in supposing that you are not "favorably known to me." On the contrary, all that I have read from your pen has inspired me with a high idea of your power; and I think you are destined to stand among the first romance-writers of the country, if such be your aim (Longfellow [1966], 2:302).

20 MAY. WASHINGTON. Thomas writes Poe again, complaining that he has not received payment for his article: "I have been disappointed in receiving a remittance from St. Louis from an editor for whom I have been writing and I feel constrained to request, my dear friend, that you would jog Mr. Graham's memory. Don't fail me—for my pocket is at a low ebb." Thomas

fears that "with the failure of the banks and the death of General Harrison, . . . it will be some time before publishing resumes its former busy existence. Dam[n] Locofocoism there was some little money to be made by books before that—but nowadays!" Dow is now "getting along well as an agent for post-masters—or rather for those who wish to make contracts with the post office department. He seems cheerful and has quit drinking even hard cider. The Locofocos here seem to think or wish to think that President Tyler will go with them—or at least be half and half." Thomas suggests that Poe come to Washington and apply for a clerkship:

How would you like to be an office holder here at $1500 per year payable monthly by Uncle Sam who, however slack he may be to his general creditors, pays his officials with due punctuality. How would you like it? You stroll to your office a little after nine in the morning leisurely, and you stroll from it a little after two in the afternoon homeward to dinner, and return no more that day. If during office hours you have anything to do it is an agreeable relaxation from the monstrous laziness of the day. You have on your desk everything in the writing line in apple-pie order, and if you choose to lucubrate in a literary way, why you can lucubrate (W, 17:84–85).

BEFORE 22 MAY. PHILADELPHIA. *Graham's* for June contains Poe's sketch "The Island of the Fay," written to accompany the frontispiece, a steel engraving by John Sartain with the same title. Poe reviews Macaulay's *Essays*, T. S. Arthur's tale *Insubordination*, Pliny Earle's *Marathon, and Other Poems*, William Davis Gallagher's *Selections from the Poetical Literature of the West*, and Joseph Holt Ingraham's novel *The Quadroone*.

22 MAY. BOSTON. Griswold notices *Graham's* in the *Boston Notion*, condemning Poe's favorable review of Earle's poetry: "we never saw anything more ineffably senseless and bombastic, than these verses so lauded by the editor of *Graham's Magazine*—the same editor who pronounced Charles Sprague's *Shakspeare Ode* 'a specimen of commonplace,' and *Curiosity* a 'tolerable occasional poem'!" (Cohen, pp. 98–99).

22 MAY. PHILADELPHIA. The *Saturday Chronicle* publishes Poe's poem "The Sleeper" (Mabbott [1969], 1:183).

28 MAY. WASHINGTON. Thomas replies to Poe: "Yours of the 26 enclosing a draft upon F[ranck] Taylor, periodical agent of this place, drawn in my favour by Mr Graham for twenty dollars, I received yesterday." He went "forthwith to Mr Taylor's book store and presented the draft," but Taylor declined to honor it because "he had not that amount . . . due Mr Graham." Thomas again reminds Poe that he urgently needs money. He appreciates his friend's good opinion of his article: "I don't know why it is,

but frankly I like your approval of my little efforts better than any other critic's whatsoever—firstly because you are a critic—and secondly because you are outright downright and upright in your criticism." Turning to the June *Graham's*, Thomas endorses Poe's unfavorable verdict on Gallagher's anthology: "I am glad you 'rapped Gallagher over the knuckles[']—He deserved it . . . He is between you and me as morbid an egotist and as envious a fellow as you will find in the sea's compass." In "The Island of the Fay" Poe has "struck a new vein" (MB–G).

29 MAY. PHILADELPHIA. Poe writes Griswold in Boston, forwarding a number of his poems for possible inclusion in *The Poets and Poetry of America*: "I should be proud to see one or two of them in your book." The poem entitled "The Haunted Palace" is the one Poe discussed with Griswold "in reference to Prof. Longfellow's plagiarism." It was first published in the Baltimore *American Museum*. Poe afterwards incorporated it in "The Fall of the House of Usher," which appeared in *Burton's Gentleman's Magazine* in September 1839: "Here it was, I suppose, that Prof. Longfellow saw it; for, about 6 weeks afterwards, there appeared in the South. Lit. Mess: a poem by him called 'The Beleaguered City' . . . . The identity in title is striking; for by the Haunted Palace I mean to imply a mind haunted by phantoms—a disordered brain—and by the Beleaguered City Prof. L. means just the same. But the whole tournure of the poem is based upon mine . . . . Its allegorical conduct, the style of its versification & expression—all are mine." As Poe understands that Griswold intends "to preface each set of poems by some biographical notice," he is enclosing a "memo" outlining "the particulars" of his life (*L*, 1:160–61; facsimile of memo in Robertson, 2:284–85).

AFTER 29 MAY? BOSTON. Griswold writes Poe, requesting assistance in obtaining biographical sketches of the Maryland poet Edward Coote Pinkney and the Kentucky poetess Amelia Welby for his anthology (Thomas to Griswold, 8 June).

EARLY JUNE? PHILADELPHIA. Poe writes Griswold that Thomas can provide suitable sketches. He then informs Thomas of Griswold's request (Thomas to Griswold, 8 June).

8 JUNE. WASHINGTON. Thomas writes Griswold in Boston:

My friend Edgar A. Poe, of Graham's Magazine, Philadelphia, wrote me the other day informing me that you were about publishing a volume of American poetry, and that you were desirous of having sketches biographical of Pinckney [Pinkney] of Baltimore and "Amelia" of Kentucky. He also stated to me that he had replied to you that I could furnish you the sketches, and he advised me to write to you on the subject.

Pinckney I formerly knew, and I have the pleasure of knowing personally as well as poetically "Amelia." Having been a Baltimorean and being lately of the West I feel a natural interest in the fame of both those individuals.

It would give me pleasure to furnish you the sketches, as my friend Poe writes me that you "pay well and promptly." A thing as excellent in a man, as silence, according to old Lear, is excellent in a woman. If you should like me to furnish you the sketches aforesaid I should be glad to hear from you in the premises (Griswold [1898], pp. 66–67).

12 JUNE. PHILADELPHIA. The *Saturday Evening Post* reprints Poe's poem "The Coliseum" (Mabbott [1969], 1:227).

14 JUNE. WASHINGTON. Thomas replies to two recent letters from Poe. Because he has been suffering from a fever "these four days past," he was not able to return the proof sheets of his article until yesterday. He simply added several lines to replace the sheet which was lost: "To require me to furnish that lost copy would be like requiring me without the aid of astronomy or telescope to discuss the lost Pleiad." Graham's order on the periodical agent Thomas R. Hampton was paid, "at least the last ten dollars of it," only four days ago. Thomas would be very willing to join Poe in establishing a magazine: "Let me hear from you again on the subject—I have friends throughout the broad west, [who] would be glad to advance my literary interest in the west—and who have a high regard for your literary reputation." He answers Poe's questions:

Yes I have read your "Descent into a Maelstrom": I did not like it as much as several of your other articles; but I must say to you that a friend, of mine, whose ability I respect, in the highest degree, thinks it one of your best papers—and he has the "tallest" kind of opinion of you—

I saw your challenge about decyphering—I feel satisfied that you can fullfil [*sic*] it—so do it and excite the wonder of the people (MB–G).

21 JUNE. PHILADELPHIA. Poe writes Washington Irving in Tarrytown, New York: "Mr George R. Graham of this city, and myself, design to establish a Monthly Magazine, upon certain conditions, one of which is the procuring your assistance in the enterprise. Will you pardon me for saying a few words upon the subject?" The foremost authors of Europe now contribute to magazines: "In this country, unhappily, we have not any journal of the class, which either can afford to offer pecuniary inducement to the highest talent, or which would be, in all respects, a fitting vehicle for its thoughts." The magazine Poe envisions to remedy this deficiency will be "an octavo of 96 pages," with paper "of excellent quality" and "clear and bold" type: "The printing will be done upon a hand press, in the best manner. There will be a broad margin. We shall have no engravings, except occasional wood-cuts (by Adams) when demanded in obvious

illustration of the text; and, when so required, they will be worked in with the type—not upon separate pages, as in 'Arcturus.' . . . The price will be $5." In the new journal Poe and Graham intend to publish "contributions from the most distinguished pens (of America) *exclusively*," admitting few articles from other sources:

We shall endeavour to engage the permanent services of yourself, Mr Cooper, Mr Paulding, Mr Kennedy, Mr Longfellow, Mr Bryant, Mr Halleck, Mr Willis, and perhaps, one or two others. In fact, as before said, our ability to make these arrangements is a condition without which the Magazine will not go into operation . . . .

It would be desirable that you agree to furnish one paper each month—either absolute or serial—and of such length as you might deem proper. We leave terms entirely to your own decision. . . . It would be necessary that an agreement should be made for one year, during which period you should be pledged not to write for any other American Magazine. The journal will be commenced on the first of January 1842 . . . .

With this letter I despatch one of similar tenor to each of the gentlemen above named (*L*, 1:161–63).

[Poe's letters to Cooper, Kennedy, Longfellow, and Halleck are basically identical with his letter to Irving, revealing only minor variations. The letters sent to Paulding, Bryant, and Willis have not been located.]

21 JUNE. Poe writes Kennedy in Baltimore, adding several sentences not found in the other letters:

I believe I sent you, some time ago, a Prospectus of the "Penn Magazine", the scheme of which was broken up by the breaking up of the banks. The name will be preserved—and the general intentions, of that journal. . . .

I look most anxiously for your answer; for it is of vital importance to me, personally. This you will see at once. Mr Graham is to furnish all supplies, and will give me, merely for editorial service, and my list of subscribers to the old "Penn", a half interest in the proposed Magazine—but he will only engage in the enterprize on the conditions before stated—on condition that I can obtain as contributors the gentlemen above named—or at least the most of them—giving them carte blanche as to terms. Your name will enable me, I know, to get several of the others (*L*, 1:163–66).

CA. 21 JUNE. Poe writes Cooper in Cooperstown, New York (Thomas [1978], pp. 234–37).

22 JUNE. Poe writes Longfellow in Cambridge, Massachusetts: "Your letter of the 19th May was received. I regret to find my anticipations confirmed, and that you cannot make it convenient to accept Mr Graham's proposition. Will you now pardon me for making another?" He solicits Longfellow's contributions, adding an inducement not offered in the other letters:

GEORGE R. GRAHAM
Humanities Research Center, University of Texas at Austin

"Should illustrations be desired by you, these will be engraved at our expense, from designs at your own, superintended by yourself." Observing that Longfellow spoke of "present engagements" in last month's letter, Poe points out: "The proposed journal will not be commenced until the 1st January 1842" (*L*, 1:166–68).

24 JUNE. Poe writes Halleck in New York (*L*, 1:168–70).

24 JUNE. TARRYTOWN, NEW YORK. Irving replies to Poe (cited on Poe's 21 June letter).

AFTER 24 JUNE. NEW YORK. Halleck replies to Poe. However eminent the magazine's contributors may be, it is on Poe's "own fine taste, sound judgment, and great general ability for the task, that the public will place the firmest reliance" (fragment quoted in the *Philadelphia Saturday Museum*, 4 March 1843).

26 JUNE. BALTIMORE. In the *Saturday Visiter* the editor John Beauchamp Jones comments: "F. W. Thomas, Esq., the author of several popular novels, and a fine poet withal, has recently received an appointment in the Treasury Department. We are glad to find that this administration is inclined to reward literary as well as political talent; for in our opinion a literary man may confer as much honor on his native country as a politician—the united strength of both form national character."

26 JUNE. PHILADELPHIA. Poe writes Thomas:

I have just heard through Graham, who obtained his information from Ingraham, that you have stepped into an office at Washington—salary $1000. From the bottom of my heart I wish you joy. You can now lucubrate more at your ease & will infallibly do something worthy yourself.

For my own part, notwithstanding Graham's unceasing civility, and real kindness, I feel more & more disgusted with my situation. Would to God, I could do as you have done. Do you seriously think that an application on my part to Tyler would have a good result? My claims, to be sure, are few. I am a Virginian—at least I call myself one, for I have resided all my life, until within the last few years, in Richmond. My political principles have always been as nearly as may be, with the existing administration, and I battled with right good will for Harrison, when opportunity offered. With Mr Tyler I have some slight personal acquaintance—although this is a matter which he has possibly forgotten. For the rest, I am a literary man—and I see a disposition in government to cherish letters. Have I any chance? (*L*, 1:170–71).

JULY. *Graham's* contains "A Few Words on Secret Writing," in which Poe solves the two ciphers submitted by "S. D. L." in his 21 April letter. Poe reviews Hugh A. Pue's *Grammar of the English Language*, Seba Smith's *Powhatan*, and the other books noticed in this issue (except *The Works of Lord Bolingbroke*).

1 JULY. WASHINGTON. Thomas replies to Poe's 26 June letter:

I trust, my dear friend, that you can obtain an appointment. President Tyler I have not seen except in passing in his carriage—never having called at the White House since the death of Harrison except to see the sons of the President, and then they were not in—could n't you slip on here and see the president yourself—or if you would prefer it I will see him for you—but perhaps your application had better be made through someone who has influence with the executive. I have heard you say that J. P. Kennedy has a regard for you—he is here a Congressman and would serve you—would he not? My employment is merely temporary. I had a letter of introduction to the Secretary of the Treasury, [Thomas Ewing,] from my friend Governor Corwin of Ohio, merely introducing me as a "literary character"—I did not then expect to ask office, but finding that publishing was at a low ebb, I waited on Mr. Ewing and told him frankly how I was situated and that I should like to be making something; he with great kindness installed me here.

Thomas encloses a cipher composed by his friend Dr. Charles S. Frailey, a clerk in the General Land Office: "If you decypher it then you are a magician—for he has used as I think much art in making it" (*W*, 17:92–93).

2 JULY. PHILADELPHIA. Poe signs a receipt: "Recd . . . of Geo R Graham Fifty Five doll[ar]s" (PP–G).

4 JULY. Poe replies to Thomas:

Call upon Kennedy—you know him, I believe—if not introduce yourself—he is a perfect gentleman and will give you cordial welcome. Speak to him of my wishes, and urge him to see the Secretary of War in my behalf—or one of the other Secretaries—or President Tyler. I mention in particular the Secretary of War, because I have been to W. Point, and this may stand me in some stead. I would be glad to get almost any appointment—even a $500 one—so that I have something independent of letters for a subsistence. To coin one's brain into silver, at the nod of a master, is to my thinking the hardest task in the world.

Poe deciphers Frailey's cryptograph, pointing out that it exceeds the limits of his challenge "because it cannot be readily decyphered by the person to whom it is addressed, and who possesses the key. In proof of this, I will publish it in the Mag: with a reward to any one who shall read it *with the key*, and I am pretty sure that no one will be found to do it. . . . will you be kind enough to get from his own hand an acknowledgment of my solution, adding your own acknowledgment, in such form that I may append both to the cipher by way of note. I wish to do this because I am seriously accused of humbug in this matter—a thing I despise. People *will not* believe I really decipher the puzzles" (*L*, 1:171–74; Moldenhauer [1973], p. 51).

6 JULY. WASHINGTON. In the morning Thomas receives Poe's letter and forwards his solution to Frailey.

6 JULY. Frailey writes Thomas:

It gives me pleasure to state that the reading by Mr. Poe of the cryptograph which I gave you a few days since for transmission to him is correct.

I am the more astonished at this, since for various words of two, three and four letters, a distinct character was used for each in order to prevent the discovery of some of those words, by their frequent repetition in a cryptograph of any length and applying them to other words. I also used a distinct character for the terminations *tion* and *sion*, and substituted in every word where it was possible, some of the characters above alluded to. Where the same word of two of those letters occurred frequently, the letters of the key phrase and the characters were alternately used, to increase the difficulty (*W*, 14:139–40).

6 JULY. Thomas forwards Frailey's letter of acknowledgment to Poe, adding his own statement:

Doctor Frailey had heard me speak of your having deciphered a letter which our mutual friend, Dow, wrote upon a challenge from you last year, at my lodgings in your city, when Aaron Burr's correspondence in cipher was the subject of our conversation. You laughed at what you termed Burr's shallow artifice, and said you could decipher any such cryptography easily. To test you on the spot, Dow withdrew to the corner of the room, and wrote a letter in cipher, which you solved in a much shorter time than it took him to indite it.

As Doctor Frailey seemed to doubt your skill to the extent of my belief in it, when your article on "Secret Writing" appeared in the last number of your Magazine, I showed it to him. After reading it, he remarked that he thought he could puzzle you, and the next day he handed me the cryptograph which I transmitted to you. He did not tell me the key (*W*, 14:136–37).

7 JULY. Thomas writes Poe again. Since Congress is in session, he may not be able to see Kennedy for several days. He will, however, see President Tyler on Friday, having been invited to dine with him by "his son" [presumably Robert Tyler]. Thomas stresses that he lacks "address" with the administration, and that there are "thousands of applicants"; but he feels certain of Poe's eventual success in obtaining a clerkship. "I know very few of the 'bigbugs' here, having kept myself to myself, but I think I have skill enough to commit your merits to those, who, though not women, will be more skilful advocates of your claims" (*W*, 17:94–95).

7 JULY. PHILADELPHIA. Poe writes William Landor, a contributor to *Graham's*: "I duly received both your notes, and, daily, since the reception of the first, have been intending to reply. The cause of my not having done so is my failure to obtain certain definite information from the printer to whom I had allusion, and who still keeps me in momentary expectation of an answer. I merely write these few words now, lest you should think my silence proceeds from discourtesy." In a postscript Poe mentions that he wrote all the reviews in the July *Graham's*, except that on Bolingbroke: "There are passages in that critique which I am sure are *stolen*, although I cannot put my hand upon the original. Your acquaintance with Bolingbroke's commentators is more extensive than my own. Can you aid me in tracing the theft?" (*L*, 1:174).

["William Landor" was actually the pseudonym of the wealthy Philadelphian Horace Binney Wallace.]

10 JULY. The *Saturday Evening Post* carries an advertisement for the "New Volume" of *Graham's*, which commences with the July number. "We print now per month an edition of 17,000 Copies."

12 JULY. Poe replies to a 10 July letter from Joseph Evans Snodgrass in Baltimore:

You flatter me about the Maelström. It was finished in a hurry, and therefore its conclusion is imperfect. Upon the whole it is neither so good, nor has it been 1/2 so popular as "The Murders in the Rue Morgue". I have a paper in the August no: which will please you.

Among the Reviews (for August) I have one which will, at least, surprise you. It is a *long* notice of a satire by a quondam Baltimorean L. A. Wilmer. You must get this satire & read it—it is really good—good in the old-fashioned Dryden style. It blazes away, too, to the right & left—sparing not. I have made it the text from which to preach a fire–&–fury sermon upon critical independence, and the general literary humbuggery of the day.

A portion of this review previously appeared in the defunct Pittsburgh *Literary Examiner*: "It was edited by E. Burke Fisher Esqre—th[a]n whom a greater scamp never walked. He wrote to me offering 4$ per page for criticisms, promising to put them in as contributions—not editorially. The first thing I saw was one of my articles under the editorial head, so altered that I hardly recognized it, and interlarded with all manner of bad English and ridiculous opinions of his own." Poe asks Snodgrass to call at the Baltimore Post Office and inquire for the letter he sent Kennedy on 21 June: "By some absence of mind I directed it to that city in place of Washington. If still in the P.O. will you forward it to Washington?" (*L*, 1:175–77).

13 JULY. In the *Daily Chronicle* Charles W. Alexander discusses Poe's article on "Secret Writing" in the July *Graham's*:

The subject is altogether a remarkable one, and we cannot wonder that it has excited interest and surprise. In a previous number of the magazine, Mr. P. put forth what may be termed a challenge, in respect to secret writing; offering to read any cipher of a species designated—this species, in itself, being the most difficult of all. This challenge met with but a single response, and the cypher sent in this case is deciphered in the July number.

Pursuing the subject, Mr. P. speaks of a weekly paper of this city, to which, about two years ago, similar ciphers were sent upon a similar challenge, and promptly deciphered by himself. The paper alluded to is "Alexander's Messenger," the proprietor of which is also one of the proprietors and editors of the "Daily Chronicle." Mr. Poe's statements need no endorsement; but the article in question, in its reference to us, would seem to call for some acknowledgment at our hands. We, therefore, take occasion to say that what he has asserted, however difficult of belief, is *true to the letter*. Ciphers *were* poured in upon us from all parts of the country, and in every instance promptly unriddled. It was found nearly impossible to convince our readers that we were not humbugging them; and as a great many of them would be satisfied with nothing short of demonstration in their own persons, the consequence was that we were overflooded with communications, and had, at length, to put a stop to the matter.

The cyphers *now* solved by Mr. Poe, are far more abstruse than even those to which we allude. How it is *possible* to read them, is a mystery.

19 JULY. WASHINGTON. Thomas writes Poe. He has gone twice to ask Kennedy to aid Poe, but as yet he has not succeeded in seeing him because the House of Representatives is in session. "President Tyler is opposed to removals in office here—Twelve Locofocos were turned out on Saturday late, and it is said the President has reinstated all but 5—But this is a mere rumor." Thomas reports his attendance at the dinner mentioned in his 7 July letter: "I enjoyed myself much at the Presidents [*sic*], but as it was a formal dinner party I had not an opportunity of speaking to him especially of you—These public men are occupied so much that it is difficult to see them" (MB–G).

AFTER 19 JULY. Thomas writes Poe again. He has met with Kennedy, who expressed a willingness to aid Poe (Thomas to Poe, 30 August).

24 JULY. PHILADELPHIA. Poe signs a receipt: "Recd . . . of Geo R Graham One hundred & five . . . $105 to November 17th" (PP–G).

28 JULY. HOBOKEN, NEW JERSEY. The body of Miss Mary Rogers, a salesgirl in a Manhattan cigar store, is found in the Hudson River. She has been brutally murdered by persons unknown.

[This famous unsolved crime provided the basis for Poe's novelette "The Mystery of Marie Rogêt." See Walsh, *passim*, and Mabbott (1978), 3:715–22.]

31 JULY. PHILADELPHIA. The *Saturday Evening Post* reprints Poe's "Ballad" from the *Southern Literary Messenger* for January 1837. The heading wrongfully describes the poem as "Written for the Saturday Evening Post" (cf. Poe to L. J. Cist, 18 September).

AUGUST. *Graham's* contains Poe's tale "The Colloquy of Monos and Una," as well as his reviews of Lambert A. Wilmer's verse satire *The Quacks of Helicon*, Washington Irving's *Biography and Poetical Remains of the late Margaret Miller Davidson*, John L. Stephens' *Incidents of Travel in Central America, Chiapas, and Yucatan*, and several other works. In a second installment of "Secret Writing," Poe prints Charles S. Frailey's cipher and the 6 July acknowledgments of his solution from Frailey and Thomas. He offers a year's subscription to *Graham's* and the *Saturday Evening Post* to any reader who solves it: "We have no expectation that it will be read; and, therefore, should the month pass without an answer forthcoming, we will furnish the key to the cipher, and again offer a year's subscription to the Magazine, to any person who shall solve it *with the key*."

7 AUGUST. The *Saturday Evening Post* reports that the proprietor of *Graham's* spent $1,300 on "embellishments" for the August number: "The embellishments consist of the 'Penitent Son,' one of Sartain's exquisite Mezzotinto's [*sic*] on steel. A Lace pattern with a boquett [*sic*] of flowers, handsomely colored:—A plate of elegantly colored Fashions for the month, compiled from the late arrivals from London and Paris, consisting of *four figures*, a Gentleman and three Ladies, and two pages of music."

[This report does much to explain why Poe felt "more & more disgusted" with his position (26 June letter to Thomas).]

10 AUGUST. BALTIMORE. A correspondent who signs himself "Timotheus Whackemwell" writes Poe, enclosing two ciphers (*W*, 14:138).

11 AUGUST. PHILADELPHIA. Believing that the handwriting of "Whackemwell" is that of John N. McJilton, Poe addresses a reply to this Baltimore author:

Your letter of yesterday is this moment received. A glance at the cipher which you suppose the more difficult of the two sent, assures me that its translation must run thus—

"This specimen of secret writing is sent you for explanation. If you succeed in divining its meaning, I will believe that you are some kin to Old Nick."

As my solution in this case will fully convince you of my ability to decipher the longer but i[n]f[ini]tely more simple cryptograph, you will perhaps exc[use] me from attempting it—as I am exceedingly occupied with business (*L*, 1:177).

13 AUGUST. BALTIMORE. McJilton returns Poe's letter with a brief comment written on the bottom: "This is certainly intended for some one else, I know nothing of the matter whatever, nor should I be able to tell how the thing happened, but having seen the piece headed secret writing pubd in Graham's mag. noticed somewhere, I suppose some wag has addressed you anonymously whom you have mistaken for me" (*W*, 17:100).

13 AUGUST. PHILADELPHIA. Poe writes Lea & Blanchard. He wishes to publish a new edition of his prose tales, which would include the eight stories he has completed since this firm issued his *Tales of the Grotesque and Arabesque*. The proposed collection would consist of thirty-three tales and "would occupy two *thick* novel volumes." Poe is anxious that Lea & Blanchard continue to be his publishers: "I should be glad to accept the terms which you allowed me before—that is—you receive all profits, and allow me twenty copies for distribution to friends" (*L*, 1:178).

14 AUGUST. Poe writes Horatio Hastings Weld, editor of the *Brother Jonathan*, a New York weekly. He solicits Weld's autograph for inclusion in his "Autography" articles, soon to be published in *Graham's Magazine*: "The design is three-fold: first, to give the Autograph signature—that is, a fac-simile in woodcut—of each of our most distinguished literati; second, to maintain that the character is, to a certain extent, indicated by the chirography; and thirdly, to embody, under each Autograph, some literary gossip about the individual, with a brief comment on his writings. . . . We are still in want of the Autographs of Sprague, Hoffman, Dawes, Bancroft, Emerson, Whittier, R. A. Locke, and Stephens, the traveller." If Weld has one of these autographs, and will permit an engraving to be taken from it, Poe "will endeavor to reciprocate the obligation" (*L*, 1:179–80).

16 AUGUST. Lea & Blanchard reply to Poe's 13 August letter: "In answer we very much regret to say that the state of affairs is such as to give little encouragement to new undertakings. As yet we have not got through the edition of the other work & up to this time it has not returned to us the expense of its publication. We assure you that we regret this on your account as well as our own, as it would give us great pleasure to promote your views in relation to publication" (*W*, 17:101–02; Ostrom [1981], p. 202).

18 AUGUST. NEW YORK. Rufus W. Griswold writes his Philadelphia publishers Carey & Hart: "I have resigned the conduct of the papers with which I have been connected in Boston, to superintend in person the stereotyping of 'The Poets and Poetry of America.' . . . I shall be in Philadelphia next week" (NNPM).

21 AUGUST. WASHINGTON. The *Index*, a new Democratic paper edited by Poe's friend Jesse E. Dow, commences publication.

AFTER 25? AUGUST. PHILADELPHIA. Griswold visits the office of *Graham's* and leaves a note for Poe, requesting him to furnish a biographical sketch of Thomas for *The Poets and Poetry of America* (Poe to Thomas, 1 September).

30 AUGUST. WASHINGTON. Thomas writes Poe, explaining that he has not corresponded because of illness. Previously, he wrote that he contacted John P. Kennedy, who offered to assist Poe in obtaining a government position. "Sure I have conversed with the President's sons about you—they think the president will be able and willing to give you a situation, but they say, and I felt the truth of the remark before it was made, that at the present crisis when everything is 'hurlyburly' it would be of no avail to apply to him. He is much perplexed, as you may suppose amidst the conflicting parties, the anticipated cabinet break up, etc." Thomas promises to see President Tyler when the crisis has passed and to write Poe describing the interview. The articles on cryptography have caused "quite a talk" in Washington; Hampton, the bookseller, had a heavy demand for the August number of *Graham's*. Thomas asks a favor: "Poe, I have a song that has been set to a very pretty tune, by a gentleman here. I would like to have it published, and will give it to any music publisher who would undertake it. . . . Will you make some inquiry with regard to the publishing it" (*W*, 17:102–03).

SEPTEMBER. PHILADELPHIA. *Graham's* contains Poe's "Never Bet Your Head: A Moral Tale," his revised poem "To Helen," and his reviews of Frederick Marryat's novel *Joseph Rushbrook* and Thomas Campbell's *Life of Petrarch*.

CA. 1 SEPTEMBER. Carey & Hart issue the *Gift* for 1842, which contains Poe's tale "Eleonora."

1 SEPTEMBER. Poe writes Thomas: "Griswold left a note for me at the office, the other day, requesting me to furnish him with some memoranda of your life [for *The Poets and Poetry of America*]; and it will, of course, give

me great pleasure to do so; but . . . I find that neither myself, nor Mrs Clemm, upon whom I mainly depend for information, can give all the necessary points with sufficient precision." Poe needs more details as soon as possible, because Griswold's anthology is already in press: "When & where were you born? With whom did you study law? What was (exactly) the cause of your lameness? How did you first become known to the literary world? Who were your most intimate associates in Baltimore? When did you remove to Cincinnati? With what papers have you been occasionally connected—if with any?" Poe inquires about Jesse E. Dow and his newspaper. He himself will probably remain with Graham, even if he starts the *Penn Magazine* in January; he has had "some excellent offers respecting the 'Penn' and it is more than probable that it will go on." The success of *Graham's Magazine* is astonishing: "we shall print 20,000 copies shortly" (*L*, 1:180–81).

3 SEPTEMBER. WASHINGTON. Thomas replies to Poe, forwarding a long account of his career (*W*, 17:95–100).

4 SEPTEMBER. BOSTON. The *Boston Notion* reprints "Eleonora" on its front page. On another page the *Notion* reviews the *Gift*, praising this story: "Poe's contribution is written with much power, and in that gentleman's peculiar style" (Pollin [1970b], p. 26).

4 SEPTEMBER. NEW YORK. The oversize weekly *Brother Jonathan* reprints "Never Bet Your Head" from *Graham's*. Poe's tale appears in the 7 September issue of the weekly's quarto edition, *Jonathan's Miscellany* (Heartman and Canny, pp. 168, 215–16).

9 SEPTEMBER. PONTOTOC, MISSISSIPPI. Richard Bolton, a reader of *Graham's*, writes Poe, enclosing the solution to the Frailey cipher published in the August number (Bolton to Poe, 4 November).

11 SEPTEMBER. BALTIMORE. John Beauchamp Jones reviews the September *Graham's* in the *Saturday Visiter*: "If one half the dollars laid out for engravings were only expended on authors of genius, these flashy things would live longer, be more profitable to the publishers, and do more credit to the country."

[In the *Saturday Evening Post* for 28 August, Graham had boasted that the number's "leading embellishment" was "a magnificent steel line engraving, entitled 'Cottage Fireside,' " which "cost the proprietor of the Magazine over *four hundred dollars*."]

15 SEPTEMBER. BOSTON. *Roberts' Semi-Monthly Magazine* reprints Poe's "Eleonora" (Pollin [1970b], p. 26).

18 SEPTEMBER. NEW YORK. The *Weekly Tribune* reprints "Eleonora." The tale appears in the *Daily Tribune* on 20 September (Heartman and Canny, p. 228).

18 SEPTEMBER. PHILADELPHIA. Poe replies to a 30 August letter from Lewis J. Cist of Cincinnati, who complained that his poem "Bachelor Philosophy," submitted for the *Penn Magazine*, has been published in the *Saturday Evening Post* under the caption "written for The Post." Although Poe has been "guilty of a sad neglect," he is innocent of "any intentional disrespect or discourtesy." When he joined *Graham's Magazine*, he delivered Cist's poem and other manuscripts submitted for the *Penn* into the custody of Charles J. Peterson, "the then editor of that journal" whose duties included "revising MSS for press and attending to the general *arrangement* of the matter." Poe intended to obtain permission from the *Penn* contributors to publish their articles in *Graham's*, and his impression was that he had secured Cist's consent. "Mr. Peterson, however, (who has a third interest in the 'Saturday Evening Post' and superintends the 'getting up' of that paper also) has taken the unwarrantable liberty, it seems, of using the poem to suit his own views—leaving out of question my positive understanding and intention on the subject." In extenuation Poe cites "the *confusion* attendant upon the joint issue of a paper and Magazine," adding that his duties on *Graham's* have nothing to do with the disposition of manuscripts: "I merely write the Reviews, with a tale monthly, and read the last proofs." Peterson, in using Cist's poem for the *Post*, is guilty of "a falsehood wilfully perpetrated—of a kind which he is in the *habit* of perpetrating." Recently Poe gave his poem "A Ballad" to Peterson for "republication" in the *Post*, with the understanding that it was to appear under the caption "From the *Southern Literary Messenger*." Peterson published it under the same caption as Cist's "Bachelor Philosophy" (*L*, 1:181–82; Moldenhauer [1973], p. 52).

19 SEPTEMBER. Poe replies to a 6 September letter from Snodgrass, who discussed "Never Bet Your Head" in this month's *Graham's*: "You are mistaken about 'The Dial'. I have no quarrel in the world with that illustrious journal, nor it with me. I am not aware that it ever mentioned my name, or alluded to me either directly or indirectly. My slaps at it were only in 'a general way.' The tale in question is a mere Extravaganza levelled at no one in particular, but hitting right & left at things in

general." Poe thanks Snodgrass for inquiring after the 21 June letter he directed to John P. Kennedy at Baltimore. "It is not impossible that Graham will join me in The 'Penn.' He has money. By the way, is it impossible to start a first-class Mag: in Baltimore? Is there no publisher or gentleman of moderate capital who would join me in the scheme?" (*L*, 1:183–84).

20 SEPTEMBER. Poe replies to Thomas' 30 August letter, offering to publish his song in *Graham's*. Poe inquires whether Thomas can provide the signatures of Joseph Rodman Drake and George D. Prentice for his forthcoming "Autography" series (Thomas' reply).

22 SEPTEMBER. WASHINGTON. Thomas writes Poe:

Yours postmarked the 20th I received yesterday. I do not wonder that you have been annoyed by cryptographic connoisseurs. Your astonishing power of de-cyphering secret writing is to me a puzzle which I can't solve. Thats a curious head-piece of yours, and I should like to know what phrenologists say about it. Did you ever have your head examined? And what said the examiner? . . .

I remember well your autographic articles in the Southern Literary Messenger— They were very interesting—No, I have not either Prentice's or Drake's auto-graph's here—but I could get them for you—The President's Mr Webster's and others of the eminent politicians and statesmen here I can easily obtain for you—if you include them in your plan—About my song—(don't put yourself to any trouble in the matter)—I should like to have it published in a sheet, by some publishers or other—I don't ask anything for it—and only want a few copies to give to a fair friend or so, which I am willing to buy—If you cannot get any publisher to publish it as I here propose, will you a[s]certain for me what it will cost to publish it on my own account—It is a song of four verses of four lines each—There is no music publishers here or I would not trouble you in the matter—My only objection to publishing it in the magazine is that I could not present copies of it—and if it should be popular . . . it could not be obtained in a form likely to give it . . . circulation.

Thomas discusses the political climate of Washington; he regrets "the break up in the cabinet," especially the resignation of his patron Thomas Ewing, the Secretary of the Treasury. On the other hand, he is heartened by his growing intimacy with the Tylers: "I think that the President and family have a kind feeling towards me, and I shall put my trust there. . . . I have just received an invitation to dinner there to day." Thomas and his friend Robert Tyler, the President's oldest son, frequently speak of Poe (MB–G).

24 SEPTEMBER. PHILADELPHIA. Poe replies to Thomas. He has arranged for the music publisher George Willig, 171 Chestnut Street, to issue Thomas' song: "He says he cannot afford to give anything for it beyond a

few copies—but will promise to get it up handsomely. I suppose you had better send it through me." Poe still needs the autographs of Drake, Prentice, and Amelia Welby: "If you can get them *soon* I would be greatly obliged. Our design includes only literary people" (*L*, 2:696).

BEFORE 25 SEPTEMBER. *Graham's* for October contains Poe's revised poem "Israfel" and the third installment of his "Secret Writing," which reveals the solution and the key to the Frailey cipher. A footnote appears on the first page of the review section: "Owing to the temporary absence of Mr. Poe, the reviews in this number are from another hand. That department is exclusively under the control of Mr. Poe. C. J. Peterson, his coadjutor, has the charge of the other departments of the work."

25 SEPTEMBER. Poe signs a receipt: "Recd . . . of Geo R Graham Thirty Three Doll[ar]s and fifty Cents on acct of editing Magazine" (TxU–HRCL).

25 SEPTEMBER. WASHINGTON. Jesse E. Dow reviews the October *Graham's* in the *Index*, commenting that "its main editor, Edgar A. Poe, Esq., a Richmond boy by adoption, is the severest critic, the best writer, and the most unassuming little fellow in the United States."

27 SEPTEMBER. WASHINGTON. Thomas replies to Poe's 24 September letter, apparently forwarding his song (cited on Poe's letter).

9 OCTOBER. BOSTON. The *Boston Notion* reviews the October *Graham's*, describing Poe's poem ["Israfel"] as praiseworthy (Pollin [1970b], p. 26).

13 OCTOBER. PHILADELPHIA. Poe signs a receipt: "Recd . . . of Geo. R. Graham Sixty Dollars and Ninety Cents on acct of editing Magazine" (TxU–HRCL).

14 OCTOBER. WASHINGTON. Thomas writes Poe: "Did you receive the MS: music I sent you the other day—What says Willig of it—How does your lady and mother like the tune? . . . Dow is well—He has gone to housekeeping—does better out of office he says than in—He edits the 'Index' . . . . Do you know Judge [Abel Parker] Upshur the new secretary of the Navy? He could be of service to you in your views here—Let me know if you do" (MB–G).

BEFORE 19 OCTOBER. PHILADELPHIA. The November *Graham's* is ready for circulation. It contains the first installment of Poe's "A Chapter on Autography," as well as his reviews of William Harrison Ainsworth's novel *Guy*

Fawkes, Isaac D'Israeli's *Amenities of Literature*, Edward Bulwer-Lytton's *Critical and Miscellaneous Writings*, Charles Dickens' *Pic-Nic Papers*, W. F. Napier's *History of the War in the Peninsula*, and Samuel Warren's novel *Ten Thousand a Year*. In noticing the *Gift* for 1842, Poe describes his own "Eleonora" as a tale "which is not ended so well as it might be—a good subject spoiled by hurry in the handling."

BEFORE 19 OCTOBER. George R. Graham sends his November number to Park Benjamin, editor of the *New World* (implied by Benjamin's 19 October letter).

19 OCTOBER. NEW YORK. Benjamin writes Graham, proposing to reprint "Autography":

> Will you loan the New World the wood-blocks of the autographs, which appear in your Magazine for November? If you will cause them to be placed in the hands of Mr. G. B. Zieber, agent of the New World, he will safely forward them to us and they shall be as safely returned. I should be glad to receive them as early as Monday of next week. If you will have the goodness to comply with this request, it will spare us some expense, and it will afford us much pleasure to reciprocate by printing your table of contents and by noticing the admirable style in which your Magazine is presented to the public.

Benjamin is glad to hear of Graham's success. "I thank Mr Poe heartily for his just notice" (MB–G).

23 OCTOBER. The *New World* contains Benjamin's review:

> THE NOVEMBER NUMBER OF GRAHAM'S LADY'S AND GENTLEMAN'S MAGAZINE which we have received, anticipatory of its day of publication, is marked equally by the richness of its embellishments and the excellence of its literature. It seems to us that this periodical is edited with singular ability and vigor; although characteristics like these every reader has a right to expect from so accomplished and forcible a writer and critic as Mr. Edgar A. Poe. . . .
>
> The most interesting article in this number, though, perhaps, we say it that should not, since our own vile chirography figures among the rest—is one by Mr. Poe on autography. His remarks display great acumen and some severity; but they are honest and kind, and, for the most part, correct.

26 OCTOBER. PHILADELPHIA. Charles J. Peterson writes James Russell Lowell in Boston, forwarding *Graham's* for November. Lowell will find Poe's "Autography" of interest. Next month's installment will feature "sixty more signatures"; some of the subjects will be very minor writers; "and the public will be not a little like the wonderers at flies in amber, as Pope has it—they'll 'wonder how the d—d things got there.' " Lowell's autograph will appear in this December installment: "However you must

keep your temper & not scout for the company you are in . . . . I send you
the sheet on which it will appear enclosed in your Nov. number. I hope
the notice appended to your name will please you. It is by Poe. He lost
your *Scrip* or your name would have figured in Novr" (MH–H).

27 OCTOBER. Poe replies to Thomas' 14 October letter: "I received your
last some days ago, and have delayed answering it, in hope that I might
say your song was out, and that I might give you my opinion and
Virginia's about its merits." Yesterday Poe called on the music publisher
George Willig, who promised that the song would be ready by next
Monday: "As soon as it is done, he will forward some copies (he did not
say how many) to your address at Washington." Although Poe is not
personally acquainted with Judge Upshur, he has a high opinion of the
new Secretary of the Navy: "He is not only the most graceful speaker I
ever heard, but one of the most graceful & luminous writers. His head is a
model for statuary." Poe answers Thomas' query in his 22 September letter:
"Speaking of heads—my own *has been* examined by several phrenologists—
all of whom spoke of me in a species of extravaganza which I should be
ashamed to repeat." Thomas' name was omitted from the November installment of "Autography" because of "the length of the comment upon it.
It heads the list in the December no; which is already finished." Poe is glad
to learn of Dow's prosperity: "I wonder he never sends me an 'Index'."
When Graham combined *Burton's Gentleman's Magazine* and the *Casket* last
December, "the joint list of both Mags. was 5000. In January we print
25000. Such a thing was never heard of before. Ah, if we could only get
up the 'Penn'! I have made a definite engagement with Graham for
1842—but nothing to interfere with my own scheme, should I be able by
any good luck, to go into it. Graham holds out a hope of his joining me
in July. Is there no one among your friends at Washington—no one having
both brains & funds who would engage in such an enterprise?" (*L*, 1:184–
85).

29 OCTOBER. The *Public Ledger* publishes "Three Thursdays in One Week,"
an unsigned article which is a source for Poe's story "A Succession of
Sundays" (see 27 NOVEMBER).

29 OCTOBER. Robert Morris reviews the November *Graham's* in the *Pennsylvania Inquirer*: "The most singular, and at the same time, the most
interesting article in the work, is the chapter on autographs, which
present[s] '*fac similes*' of the signatures of about one half of the best authors
of our country, with a brief critical notice of the style of each—the other
half to be given in December. We predict, therefore, that the November
and December numbers of this Miscellany, will be carefully treasured up
by many of its readers."

29 OCTOBER. JACKSON, TENNESSEE. John Tomlin writes Poe:

Sergeant N Talfourd Esq of London, says to me in his letter of August the 11th 1841—"I transcribe my last Effusion—on an occasion very dear to me." The following Sonnet, composed in view of Eton College after leaving his Eldest Son there for the first time, is the Effusion he alluded to.

I feel proud of having it in my power, of sending to you for for [*sic*] publication in Graham's Magazine "an Original Article["] from the pen of this high minded and gifted individual. Powerful as his intellect is, it is not more powerful, than his heart is tender, and warmed by a parent's feeling! From the buried treasures of his heart gushes [*sic*] Sentiments full of tenderness and love—and with a father's feeling he is carried to that distant day when his Son takes his place in the toiling struggles of life (MB–G).

[Sir Thomas Noon Talfourd was a British jurist, playwright, and poet; his "Sonnet," transcribed by Tomlin, appeared in the January 1842 *Graham's*. Tomlin submitted other "contributions" to *Graham's* taken from personal letters he had received. See his 1 and 12 December 1841 letters to Poe.]

BEFORE 30 OCTOBER. NEW YORK. The *Evening Mail* notices the November *Graham's*: "Among the articles which interested us most was the article on autography, by E. A. Poe. We wish we had the cuts, so that we might transfer it."

30 OCTOBER. PHILADELPHIA. The *Saturday Evening Post* reviews *Graham's*: "A most capital chapter on Autography, by Edgar A. Poe, graces the number. The article contains forty-two signatures of our best American writers, engraved expressly for the Magazine; and we understand, that the publisher intends to complete, in the next number, the en[t]erprize, by adding over sixty more, which will embrace the signature of *every writer in America*, at all known. This will be the most finished collection ever issued." The *Post* quotes favorable notices of the current number by the *Evening Mail* and other papers.

NOVEMBER. LOWELL, MASSACHUSETTS. The *Lady's Pearl* reprints Poe's "Israfel" from the October *Graham's* (Heartman and Canny, pp. 217–18).

2 NOVEMBER. WASHINGTON. Dow reviews the November *Graham's* in the *Index*:

Mr. Poe, the talented critic of the Magazine, gives us a new chapter of wonders. He has gathered together a goodly list of autographs of authors, male and female, and served them up with vinegar and sweet sauce to be rolled upon the tongue of memory for no inconsiderable portion of time. Mr. Poe is a wonderful man. He can read the hieroglyphics of the Pharoahs, tell you what you are thinking about while he walks beside you, and criticise you into shape without giving offence.

We trust that he will soon come out with his Penn Magazine, a work which, if carried out as he designs it, will do away with the monopoly of puffing and break the fetters which a corps of pensioned blockheads have bound so long around the brows of young intellects who are too proud to pay a literary pimp for a favorable notice in a mammoth six penny or a good word with the fathers of the Row, who drink wine out of the skulls of authors and grow fat upon the geese that feed upon the grass that waves over their early tomb stones.

4 NOVEMBER. PONTOTOC, MISSISSIPPI. Richard Bolton writes Poe:

The November number of your valuable magazine has just arrived. To my great surprise no notice is taken of my solution of the cryptograph proposed to your readers in the August number. This I can attribute only to accident or oversight. As you had thrown the gauntlet which I took up, I must call upon you as a true man and no craven to render me according to the terms of the defiance the honours of a field worthily contested and fairly won.

A friend lent me for perusal your magazine for that month. On the ninth of September, within a month after the arrival of the magazine my solution was mailed postage paid, addressed to the editor. Accompanying it were certificates of two subscribers, Messrs. Glokenau and L. C. Draper (the latter assistant postmaster) that I had effected the solution unaided by the key and that the September [October] number in which the key was exposed had not arrived.

My solution fully agrees with your published solution except in two words about which I will soon take occasion to remark. I therefore claim to have fully complied with the terms of the challenge and to be entitled to all the rights, privileges and honours therein expressed.

Bolton transcribes his solution, adding extensive notes to indicate how he arrived at it. He identifies two words incorrectly translated in Poe's solution, as published in the October *Graham's* (Thomas [1978], pp. 279–81).

6 NOVEMBER. NEW YORK. Park Benjamin's *New World* reprints Poe's "Autography" from the November *Graham's*.

6 NOVEMBER. WASHINGTON. The author and jurist Henry Marie Brackenridge writes Thomas. Brackenridge has written a new biography of his father, the novelist Hugh Henry Brackenridge. He intends to publish it in a well-known periodical "as a precursor" to a new edition of his father's *Modern Chivalry* "now about to be put to press." Some ten days ago he gave the biography to his friend Walter Colton, editor of the Philadelphia *North American*; he has since decided that *Graham's Magazine* would be a more suitable journal for it. Brackenridge asks Thomas to send his letter to Poe, who can then obtain the biography for his consideration: "Mr. Colton on seeing this letter will hand over the MSS. to Mr. E. A. Poe, the editor of the Magazine, unless the publication shall have been announced in the N. American" (MB–G).

6 NOVEMBER. Thomas forwards Brackenridge's letter to Poe, writing on the bottom:

The above will explain itself—The Judge . . . was speaking to me of his father's biography which he said he had written and which he handed me for perusal—I thought it would be the thing for your work, and advised him to send it to you . . . Write me frankly about it—(get it forthwith)[.] If it does not suit your Magazine, let us know quickly and I will send it to the Southern Literary Messenger.

I have not got my song yet—though I got your letter [of 27 October]—and had been wondering for a long time why I had not gotten one from you before. . . .

I write this in great haste . . . . I wish indeed that you had a friend here who had "both brains and funds," as you say, to embark in the Penn. It will all come right some day. I believe you can make the best Magazine extant; and your friends, if you were embarked in your own boat, would feel much deeper interest, and give more aid to your exclusive work than to any other (MB–G).

10 NOVEMBER. Thomas replies to a letter from Poe declining Brackenridge's manuscript: "Thanks for your punctuality and promptness—I read the Judge what you said (of course leaving out what Graham said about its 'heaviness') at which he seemed much pleased." Since Brackenridge wishes to submit the biography to the *Southern Literary Messenger*, Poe should return it to him as soon as possible. "I am sorry that your lady likes not the music to which my song is married . . . . Well—I like 'Virginia's' frankness, my dear friend, as I have always liked yours . . . . You, my dear Poe, have a very high reputation here among the literatti [*sic*], and more than once in 'dining out' I have discussed you and made conversational capital out of you" (MB–G).

10 NOVEMBER. PHILADELPHIA. Poe writes the popular poetess Mrs. Lydia H. Sigourney in Hartford, Connecticut: "Since my connexion, as editor, with 'Graham's Magazine', of this city, I have been sadly disappointed to find that you deem us unworthy your correspondence. . . . Is there no mode of tempting you to send us an occasional contribution? Mr Graham desires me to say that he would be *very especially* obliged if you could furnish . . . a poem, however brief, for the January number. His compensation . . . will be at least as liberal as that of any publisher in America" (L, 1:186).

13 NOVEMBER. GLEN MARY, NEW YORK. Nathaniel P. Willis replies to Poe:

Your letter of the 10th finds me under an engagement to your neighbor Mr Godey to write for no other periodical in Philadelphia during the year 1842. In that year I am to write him an article a month. I see however by his literary notices that he is bon ami with Mr Graham, and with Mr Godey's "let-up," I am very happy to promise you the best I can do for your Magazine. My predilections I may say are very much with you—but my quill must eke out my short crops, & Mr. Godey's very liberal engagement holds me. As he wants only *prose* however, perhaps he will release me in rhyme.

Would you think it too much trouble to send me the No. of your Maga. containing my own autograph. I hear of it; but have not seen it (TxU–HRCL).

13 NOVEMBER. BALTIMORE. The *Saturday Visiter* announces that John Beauchamp Jones retired from its editorship on 8 November. The *Visiter* is now edited by Joseph Evans Snodgrass, who has been "favorably known as one of the editors of the AMERICAN MUSEUM" and "as a contributor to the SOUTHERN LITERARY MESSENGER, and many other leading magazines."

13 NOVEMBER. LOWELL, MASSACHUSETTS. The *Literary Souvenir* reprints Poe's "Eleonora" (Heartman and Canny, p. 222).

16 NOVEMBER. PHILADELPHIA. Poe replies to a 13 November letter from Mrs. Sigourney in Hartford, thanking her for agreeing to contribute to the January *Graham's*: "We are forced to go to press at a very early period . . . so that it would be desirable we should have your article in hand by the 1rst December. We shall look for it with much anxiety, as we are using every exertion to prepare a number of more than ordinary attraction. . . . We shall have papers from Longfellow, Benjamin, Willis, Fay, Herbert, Mrs Stephens, Mrs Embury, Dr Reynell Coates, and (what will surprise you) from Sergeant Talfourd, author of 'Ion'—besides others of nearly equal celebrity." Poe and Graham hope that Mrs. Sigourney will consent to become a regular contributor: "Is it not possible that we can make an arrangement with yourself for an article *each* month? It would give us the greatest pleasure to do so" (*L*, 1:186–87).

18 NOVEMBER. Poe replies to Richard Bolton's 4 November letter: "I hasten to exonerate myself from . . . the suspicion, no doubt long since entertained by yourself, that I wished to deny you the honors of victory— and a participation in its spoils." Bolton's solution of the Frailey cipher is given "an unqualified acknowledgment" in the December *Graham's*, which has been ready for ten days. His letter of 9 September arrived too late for his solution to be acknowledged in the November issue: "We print 25000 copies. Of course much time is required to prepare them. Our last 'form' necessarily goes to press a full month in advance of the day of issue. It often happens, moreover, that the last form *in order* is not the last in press. Our *first* form is usually held back until the last moment on account of the 'plate article.' Upon this hint you will easily see the possibility of your

letter not having come to hand in season for acknowledgment in the November number." Poe admits that Bolton's solution *"astonished"* him: "I make no question that it even astonished yourself—and well it might—for from among at least 100,000 readers—a great number of whom, to my certain knowledge busied themselves in the investigation—you and I are the only persons who have succeeded" (*L*, 1:187–89).

23 NOVEMBER. WASHINGTON. Thomas writes Poe:

I looked in my trunk in hopes of obtaining an autograph of Prentice; but I find I have none by me—I have written to Louisville and wonder I do not hear from there, from him. . . .

Poe, I have commenced the study of the French language, and wish that you would give me some advice as to [the] best manner of pursuing it—Do you consider its acquirement very difficult? . . .

Can I be of any service to the Magazine here? Command me if I can—Have you heard from John P Kennedy since I wrote you—His Whig "Manifesto" I suspect, has "used up" as we say in the West, all the influence he might have had at the White House—Cant you slip on here and see us—

I have not succeeded in being permanently fixed yet in my situation . . . If I had a permanent situation, which I am promised, I could get leave of absence, my salary still continuing, and I could slip on to the City of Brotherly love and shake you by the hand, which I certainly should—I long to have a talk with you, Poe— On my conscience I know no man whom I would rather meet than you—No! I would rather meet you than any "feller" as Sam Weller says that I know (MB–G).

26 NOVEMBER. PHILADELPHIA. Poe replies to Thomas:

You need not put yourself to trouble about Prentice's autograph, as we have now closed that business. I suppose you have not the December number yet—it has been ready for several weeks. The January no: is nearly prepared—we have an autograph article in each. . . .

Touching your study of the French language. You will, I fear, find it difficult— as, (if I rightly understood you,) you have not received what is called a "classical" education. To the Latin & Greek proficient, the study of all additional languages is mere play—but to the non-proficient it is anything else. The best advice I can give you, under the circumstances, is to busy yourself with the theory or grammar of the language as little as possible & to read *side-by-side* translations continually, of which there are many to be found. I mean French books in which the literal English version is annexed page per page. Board, also, at a French boarding-house, and force yourself to speak French—bad or good—whether you can or whether you *cannot*.

I have *not* heard from Kennedy for a long time, and I think, upon the whole, he has treated me somewhat cavalierly—professing to be *a friend*.

I would give the world to see you once again and have a little chat. Dow you & I—"when shall we three meet again?" Soon, I hope (*L*, 1:189–91).

1841

26 NOVEMBER. Charles J. Peterson writes James Russell Lowell in Boston, discussing the December installment of "Autography":

Your autograph, *as printed*, is indeed but in its slippers. I gave Poe a better one, but he lost it, and then I had none but this. His remarks on your poetry were well meant; but you know Poe prides himself on severity, and, except in rare instances, his commendation is wrung out like an eye-tooth. He did not, however, know that your occassional [*sic*] ruggedness was the result of choice—besides he has a great fancy for numbers "In linked sweetness long drawn out[.]"

He has one creed: you and I another. I must say however, in justice to Poe, that I have read some of your poems where I would have liked less ruggedness (MH–H).

BEFORE 27 NOVEMBER. *Graham's* for December contains the second installment of "A Chapter on Autography," as well as Poe's reviews of the *Poetical Remains of the late Lucretia Maria Davidson, The Seaman's Friend* by Richard Henry Dana, Jr., and William Gilmore Simms's novel *Confession*. In the fourth and final installment of "Secret Writing," Poe prints a letter on cryptography he received from W. B. Tyler, a reader who has composed an especially complicated cipher. He acknowledges Bolton's solution of the Frailey cipher.

The issue contains an announcement that "the graceful pens of two lady-editors," Mrs. Emma C. Embury and Mrs. Ann S. Stephens, will be added to the magazine's "editorial list," which already includes Graham, Peterson, and Poe.

[The women were never more than nominal editors. See 5 FEBRUARY 1842.]

27 NOVEMBER. BALTIMORE. In the *Saturday Visiter* Snodgrass notices the December *Graham's*, criticizing its engravings and poetry:

But the reader must not infer that there is nothing worth valuing, in this number. To the contrary—the *sixty-eight autographs*, and the multiplicity of information given by Mr. Poe, relating to the whereabouts, employments, and qualities of American writers, will insure a large sale of this issue. They are selling rapidly already. The whole article on autographs, has been interesting, and excels anything of the kind yet attempted. No pen but Mr. P.'s, could probably have afforded so general a sketch of American literary character. We say all this, while having no faith in the notion of *character* being denoted by the scratchings of an author! The talented collator is carried away with an innocent belief of the science of autography. His own *MS.*, being exceedingly neat and unvaried, refutes his theory—for a more excentric genius cannot be found in a search of half a dozen months.

284　　　　　AUTOGRAPHY.

Mr. J. R. LOWELL, of Massachusetts, is entitled, in our opinion, to at least the second or third place among the poets of America. We say this on account of the vigor of his *imagination*—a faculty to be first considered in all criticism upon poetry. In this respect he surpasses, we think, any of our writers (at least any of those who have put themselves prominently forth as poets) with the exception of Longfellow, and perhaps one other. His ear for rhythm, nevertheless, is imperfect, and he is very far from possessing the artistic ability of either Longfellow,

Bryant, Halleck, Sprague or Pierpont. The reader desirous of properly estimating the powers of Mr. Lowell will find a very beautiful little poem from his pen in the October number of this Magazine. There is one also (not quite so fine) in the number for last month. He will contribute regularly.

His MS. is strongly indicative of the vigor and precision of his poetical thought. The man who writes thus, for example, will never be guilty of metaphorical extravagance, and there will be found *terseness* as well as strength in all that he does.

Mr. L. J. CIST, of Cincinnati, has not written much prose, and is known especially by his poetical compositions, many of which have been very popular, although they are at times disfigured by false meta-

phor, and by a meretricious straining after effect. This latter foible makes itself clearly apparent in his chirography, which abounds in ornamental flourishes, not illy executed, to be sure, but in very bad taste.

Mr. ARTHUR is not without a rich talent for description of scenes in low life, but is uneducated, and too fond of mere vulgarities to please a refined taste. He has published "The Subordinate", and "Insubordination", two tales distinguished by the

peculiarities above mentioned. He has also written much for our weekly papers, and the "Lady's Book."

His hand is a common-place clerk's hand, such as we might expect him to write. The signature is much better than the general MS.

Mr. HEATH is almost the only person of any literary distinction residing in the chief city of the Old Dominion. He edited the "Southern Literary Messenger" in the five or six first months of its existence; and, since the secession of the writer of this article, has frequently aided in its editorial conduct.

He is the author of "Edge-Hill", a well-written novel, which, owing to the circumstances of its publication, did not meet with the reception it deserved. His writings are rather polished and graceful, than forcible or original; and these peculiarities can be traced in his chirography.

Dr. THOMAS HOLLEY CHIVERS, of New York, is at the same time one of the best and one of the worst poets in America. His productions affect one as a wild dream—strange, incongruous, full of images of more than arabesque monstrosity, and snatches of sweet unsustained song. Even his worst nonsense (and some of it is horrible) has an indefinite charm of sentiment and melody. We can never be sure that there is *any* meaning in his words—neither is there any meaning in many of our finest musical airs—

but the effect is very similar in both. His figures of speech are metaphor run mad, and his grammar is often none at all. Yet there are as fine individual passages to be found in the poems of Dr. Chivers, as in those of any poet whatsoever.

His MS. resembles that of P. P. Cooke very nearly, and in poetical character the two gentlemen are closely akin. Mr. Cooke is, by much, the more *correct*; while Dr. Chivers is sometimes the more poetic. Mr. C. always sustains himself; Dr. C. never.

A page from the December "Autobiography"

27 NOVEMBER. PHILADELPHIA. The *Saturday Evening Post* contains Poe's tale "A Succession of Sundays," subsequently entitled "Three Sundays in a Week."

30 NOVEMBER. GLEN MARY, NEW YORK. Willis replies to a second letter from Poe: "You cannot have received my letter written in answer to yours some time since (say a month ago) in which I stated that I was under contract to Mr. Godey to write for no other periodical in Philadelphia than the Lady's Book, for one year—1842. I said also that if he were willing, I should be very happy to send you *poetry*, (he bargaining for *prose*,) but that without his consent I could do nothing. . . . I am very sorry to refuse anything to a writer whom I so much admire as yourself, & to a Magazine as good as Graham's" (*W*, 17:104; cf. Willis' 13 November letter).

DECEMBER? NEW YORK? Thomas Holley Chivers writes Poe, objecting to the notice of him given in "Autography" (Poe's reply, 6 July 1842).

[In the December installment Poe had described this Georgian as "one of the best and one of the worst poets in America. . . . Even his worst nonsense (and some of it is horrible) has an indefinite charm of sentiment and melody."]

1 DECEMBER. PHILADELPHIA. Poe signs a promissory note for $104, payable "Ninety days after date" to John W. Albright, a tailor, 16 South Third Street (TxU–HRCL).

1 DECEMBER. JACKSON, TENNESSEE. John Tomlin writes Poe, discussing a letter he received from Charles Dickens:

I have Mr. Poe in my possession a communication from "Boz", in its nature so perfectly *unique*—and in its construction so full of the most beautiful thoughts, that I can scarcely get my own consent for any other to see a sparkle of the rich gems in which it is embedded. He sent it to me as a token of his remembrance—and gratefully did I receive it—and most sacredly have I preserved it.

As he is about visiting this country, I have concluded to suffer some of his own bright thoughts that have never yet seen the light of a garish day, to meet him on its thresh-hold. In permitting other eyes than my own to see it, I have yielded an unwilling consent to duty, and but justice to the Author, which under ordinary circumstances would not have been done. *This* original communication will be sent to you in time for publication in the February issue of "Graham's Magazine." If you see "Boz", while he is in America, give him my thanks for his notice of his distant countryman (MB–G).

[Dickens' 23 February 1841 letter to Tomlin was published in the February 1842 *Graham's*. When noticing the number in the *Saturday Visiter* on 5 February, Snodgrass expressed a hope "that Mr. Graham will not obtrude any more such common-place private letters upon his readers, to gratify the vanity of a contributor, who cannot feel that he is as good as Boz."]

12 DECEMBER. Tomlin writes Poe again, enclosing a twenty-line poem headed "To John Tomlin, Esq." He explains that the poem was sent to him anonymously "a few days since," accompanied by a request that he should have it published in *Graham's*. "You will not Mr. Poe for one moment believe that it was my Vanity that caused the *producing* of the Eulogy—nor will you believe that your warm-hearted friend, with all of his Southern chivalry, can, or will ever act in derogation of the high name of man" (MB–G).

BEFORE 18 DECEMBER. BOSTON. Edwin P. Whipple attacks Poe in an unsigned article in the *Daily Times*:

The last number of Graham's Gentlemen's Magazine contains a chapter on autography, by Edgar A. Poe. As all the world, however, is probably aware of this fact, we must beg the pardon of that large portion of it which it is presumed reads the Times, for tacitly taking it for granted that they are ignorant of so important an intellectual phenomenon. In this "chapter" fac-similes of the autographs of many great and small American authors are given, and an attempt is made to trace a connection between their mental character and the character of the chirography—damnation being dealt out liberally to all whose penmanship displays no genius, and praise awarded to those whose hand-writing pleases the said Mr. Poe. . . .

In the article . . . there are manifested many qualities of disposition which reflect little credit upon the author . . . . We refer to the dogmatism, egotism, and other *isms* equally as offensive, from which a good portion of the production appears to spring. It is certainly a collossal [*sic*] piece of impertinence for Mr. Edgar A. Poe to exalt himself into a literary dictator, and under his own name deal out his opinions on American authors as authoritative. . . . He does not appear to form his opinions on enlarged principles of taste, but judges of an author by the manner his own particular feelings are affected. . . . We would as soon go to a New Zealander for correct views of Christianity as to Mr. Poe for correct criticism on certain authors. . . .

But the sins of commission in the article are nearly overbalanced by the sins of omission. We are favored with the autographs of men of inferior talent and reputation, while we look in vain for some of the most prominent of American authors. . . .

The Germans would call a profound and comprehensive critic many-sided, but Mr. Poe is decidedly one-sided. . . . One peculiarity of his article is, that the contributors to Graham's Magazine, from the proprietor downwards, or from the proprietor upwards, are praised with singular benevolence. As long as Mr. Poe is allowed to retain his position as censor general of American authors, it is well to know that the path to immortality lies through Graham's Magazine (Gerber, pp. 111–13).

18 DECEMBER. Whipple's attack is reprinted in the *Boston Notion*, a weekly issued from the same office as the *Daily Times*, both papers being published by George Roberts.

20 DECEMBER. Whipple writes Rufus W. Griswold in Philadelphia: "I perceive that Poe did you justice in the Chapter on Autography, published in Graham's Magazine, although he was unjust to others. If you see the Notion, you will perceive a rather savage article on his impertinence. You are no particular friend of his, I believe, and therefore it can hardly shock you. How he cuts up [Henry T.] Tuckerman! *That* set my pen in motion. He does not mention Sprague, Holmes, Sargent, and many other 'good poets and true,' but finds space for Johnny M'Jilton, Dr. Snodgrass, *Pliny Earle*, and other lights of the age" (Gerber, pp. 110–11).

25 DECEMBER. PHILADELPHIA. The *Saturday Evening Post* reviews the first number of the *Lady's World of Fashion*, a saccharine monthly begun by Charles J. Peterson.

LATE DECEMBER. In the *Spirit of the Times* John S. Du Solle defends Poe against Whipple's unsigned attack in the Boston *Daily Times* (see 10 JANUARY 1842).

1841. LONDON. John Cunningham, Crown-Court, Fleet-Street, reprints Poe's novel, altering its title to *Arthur Gordon Pym: Or, Shipwreck, Mutiny, and Famine* (Pollin [1981], pp. 3, 43–44).

*

1842

*

EARLY 1842? PHILADELPHIA. Poe becomes acquainted with the young Kentucky poet William Ross Wallace, who is a frequent visitor at the offices of *Graham's Magazine*, southwest corner of Chestnut and Third Streets (Poe in the *Columbia Spy*, 1 June 1844).

EARLY 1842? Poe becomes acquainted with the young journalist and satirist George Lippard, recently employed on Du Solle's daily paper, the *Spirit of the Times*, whose offices at the northwest corner of Chestnut and Third are directly across from those of *Graham's* (Thomas [1978], pp. 325, 835–38).

JANUARY. *Graham's* contains "An Appendix of Autographs," which concludes the "Autography" series with nineteen additional signatures, as well as Poe's reviews of Henry Cockton's novel *Stanley Thorn*, Oliver Goldsmith's *The Vicar of Wakefield*, the *Critical and Miscellaneous Essays* of "Christopher North" (John Wilson), and Mrs. Sigourney's *Pocahontas, and Other Poems*. The review section is prefaced by a cogent "Exordium," in which Poe defines his concept of literary criticism.

JANUARY. NEW ORLEANS. Daniel K. Whitaker's *Southern Quarterly Review* discusses the American magazines, recalling the early days of the *Southern Literary Messenger*: "Edgar A. Poe, Esq., a gentleman of brilliant but eccentric powers, and the author of some works of fiction, composed in a very original vein of thought, was for a short time its editor, and it throve under his auspices."

1 JANUARY. BALTIMORE. In the *Saturday Visiter* Snodgrass finds that the January *Graham's* represents a significant improvement over the December number: "We enjoyed a rich treat reading the poetry of Talfourd, Longfellow, 'Amelia' [Welby] and others, the other night—and we made a hearty supper with Poe's devil-may-care criticisms."

1 JANUARY. NEW YORK. The *New-York Mirror* reports: "The November and December numbers of 'Graham's Magazine' contain engraved facsimiles of the signatures of the most distinguished American authors, with very sprightly comments by Mr. E. A. Poe; and we understand they have excited a great deal of interest. The collecting of autographs has been a great rage among people of fashion for some years past in England . . . . The fondness for these trifles seems to be extending to this country."

10 JANUARY. PHILADELPHIA. In the *Spirit of the Times* Du Solle replies to the Boston *Daily Times*:

MR. POE'S AUTOGRAPHY.—The editor of the "Boston Times," who is indignant at our calling him an "afflicted genius," (for which we beg his pardon, as he really is no genius of any kind,) takes us to task, in quite a cavalier tone, for having dared to defend Mr. Poe from his disingenious and scurrilous attacks—attacks which have elicited rebuke not only from ourselves, and two or three other papers of this city, but from many other journals throughout the country, and which have been repudiated, in effect, even by its own immediate friends and neighbours. Never dreaming that any one *may* be actuated by honest motives, the "Times" is at great pains to imagine a reason for the few comments we made, and can find none better than the following passage in the second "Chapter on Autography":

"Mr. Du Solle is well known through his connection with the 'Spirit of the Times.' His prose is forcible and often excellent in other respects. As a poet he is entitled to higher consideration. Some of his Pindaric pieces are unusually good, and it may be doubted if we have a better versifier in America."

And these few words of commendation, (which assuredly do not amount to much, and would seem insufficient to drive any man mad through vanity,) have been regarded as our *motive* in this matter.—But, we may well ask—is it permitted to *no one* of the numerous individuals who happen to have been favorably noticed in these articles, to rebut the malignant and ignorant slanders of the "Times," lest, peradventure, that print should accuse him of interested motive? . . .

As regards its opinion of ourself, it is really a point of no consequence. Mr. Poe has thought proper to speak well of us in certain respects. That Mr. P. has expressed his *honest* opinion, we are as sure as we are that the "Times" is no judge of honesty. The question then, upon this point, resolves itself into a nut-shell. It is nothing more than opinion against opinion—Mr. Poe against the "Times." Now Mr. Poe is well known and appreciated. At all events, he is no anonymous and skulking defamer. The editor of the "Boston Times"! Who, in the name of Beelzebub, *is* the editor of the "Boston Times"? Who, or what, even, is the "Boston Times" itself?—and of what possible consequence, to any living being, can be the *opinion* of the "Boston Times," except to the "Boston Times" in its own individuality?

10 JANUARY. PONTOTOC, MISSISSIPPI. Richard Bolton replies to Poe's "very complimentary letter" of 18 November:

As to the process by which I effected the solution of Dr. Frailey's cypher it is useless to repeat all my abortive efforts and guesses. Suffice it to say that from a comparison of various words reduced to syllables I ascertained the vowels and particularly e from its frequent use and u from its unfrequent [*sic*] occurrence. I and a from their being used per se. If representing "ed" a common terminal syllable in long words next became known. Having advanced thus far the cipher fi-fvti and nia-fvti representing reduce and produce gave me a thread to the labyrinth after which my progress was comparatively easy. . . . The grammatical sequence of long and short words incident to language was of much assistance to me. Candour compels me to add that had the letters been continuous and not divided into words I should probably have failed. I therefore pay homage to you as King of Secret Readers (Thomas [1978], pp. 309–10).

13 JANUARY. WASHINGTON. Frederick William Thomas writes Poe:

I thought I had made arrangements whereby about the middle of last month I might visit Philadelphia, and spend a week or two—but I was prevented by being compelled to attend to my duties here, for the meeting of Congress has accumulated the papers upon my desk faster than I expected—

I have felt the truth of your advice about the study of the french [*sic*]—My teacher thinks that I can easily acquire the pronunciation, but I fear fear [*sic*] it will tax my industry fearfully to master the language gram[m]atically.—I believe that if I were thrown among the French that I could learn it orally, much sooner than one who by book would beat me by all odds.—

January 14, My dear Poe, just as I had finished the word "odds" above I was taken off to "schedule" some fellows' claims to office—Think of it in comparison to the "primrose path of dalliance" in literature—but that "primrose path of dalliance" how beset with the thorns of poverty—and there's the consolation. Many thanks to you for your kind notice of me among your autographs—I owe you one . . . .

Dow is well and cheerful[.] I saw him yesterday, but somehow I don't think he gets on as well as when in office—He is a violent politician as you see by his paper (MB–G).

CA. 20 JANUARY. PHILADELPHIA. Poe's wife Virginia begins to cough up blood while singing. She is seriously ill (Poe to Thomas, 3 February).

[The pulmonary hemorrhaging marked the onset of tuberculosis or "consumption," the then incurable disease which eventually claimed Virginia's life five years later, on 30 January 1847. A neighbor of the Poe family left this reminiscence in 1852:

Mrs. Poe, while singing one evening, ruptured a blood-vessel, and after that she suffered a hundred deaths. She could not bear the slightest exposure, and needed the utmost care; and all those conveniences as to apartment and surroundings which are so important in the care of an invalid were almost [a] matter of life and death to her. And yet the room where she lay for weeks, hardly able to breathe except as she was fanned, was a little place with the ceiling so low over the narrow bed that her head almost touched it. But no one dared to speak—Mr. Poe was so sensitive and irritable; "quick as steel and flint," said one who knew him in those days. And he would not allow a word about the danger of her dying—the mention of it drove him wild (Harris, p. 24).

The hemorrhages were recurrent and progressive. In his 4 January 1848 letter to George W. Eveleth, Poe stated that Virginia's prolonged illness, with its "horrible never-ending oscillation between hope & despair," led him to seek solace in excessive drinking.]

22 JANUARY. BOSTON. Charles Dickens arrives for a tour of the United States.

[The best-known author in the English-speaking world was accorded a tumultuous welcome in Boston, New York, Philadelphia, and other cities. For the reactions of the Philadelphia literati to his visit, see Thomas (1978), pp. 308, 318–52.]

FEBRUARY. PHILADELPHIA. *Graham's* contains Poe's "Harper's Ferry" (an unsigned sketch accompanying the frontispiece) and his signed essay "A Few Words About Brainard," in which he examines an overrated American poet from the preceding generation, John G. C. Brainard. Poe contributes long reviews of Dickens' *Barnaby Rudge* and Cornelius Mathews' *Wakondah*. Giving a detailed synopsis of Dickens' novel, he recalls that he correctly predicted its denouement in the *Saturday Evening Post* of 1 May 1841, after having read only its first few pages. He condemns Mathews' epic poem as "trash": "its faults, more numerous than the leaves of Vallombrosa, are of that rampant class which, if any schoolboy *could* be found so uninformed as to commit them, any schoolboy should be remorselessly flogged for committing."

3 FEBRUARY. Poe replies to Thomas' 13 January letter: "I am sure you will pardon me for my seeming neglect in not replying to your last when you learn what has been the cause of the delay. My dear little wife has been dangerously ill. About a fortnight since, in singing, she ruptured a blood-vessel, and it was only on yesterday that the physicians gave me any hope of her recovery. You might imagine the agony I have suffered, for you know how devotedly I love her." Poe's relationship with Graham has begun to deteriorate: "On the morning subsequent to the accident I called upon him, and, being entirely out of his debt, asked an advance of two months salary—when he not only flatly but discourteously refused. Now that man *knows* that I have rendered him the most important services . . . . If, instead of a paltry salary, Graham had given me a tenth of his Magazine, I should feel myself a rich man to-day." Although the "Autography" articles have "had a great run" and "done wonders for the Journal," Poe fears that they have harmed his reputation as a critic: "I was weak enough to permit Graham to modify my opinions (or at least their expression) in many of the notices. In the case of Conrad, for example; he insisted upon *praise* and worried me into speaking well of such ninnies as Holden, Peterson, Spear, &c., &c." Still intending to begin his own magazine, Poe inquires whether President Tyler's eldest son would aid the project: "You are personally acquainted with Robert Tyler, author of 'Ahasuerus.' In this poem there are many evidences of power, and, what is better, of nobility of thought & feeling. In reading it, an idea struck me—'Might it not,' I thought, 'be possible that *he* would, or rather might be induced to feel some interest in my contemplated scheme . . . ?' The Magazine might be made to play even an important part in the politics of the day, like Blackwood; and in this view might be worthy his consideration. Could you contrive to suggest the matter to him?" (*L*, 1:191–93).

5 FEBRUARY. BALTIMORE. Snodgrass reviews the February *Graham's* in the *Saturday Visiter:*

Graham announces too many editors—if they be *really* editors! We find the names of Mrs. A. S. Stevens [*sic*], Mrs. Embury, Mr. Peterson, besides Messrs. Poe and Graham. So many cooks will spoil his broth for him. In the way of the critical dishes, we want no French or fashionable cooks. Poe is sufficient. He may give homely fare, but it will be honestly served. We are glad to find that, owning to the aforenamed arrangement, or some other cause, Mr. Poe has given real *reviews* this month. All the better. Give him room. He will do much good. We want just such fearless fellows.

8 FEBRUARY. PHILADELPHIA. Charles J. Peterson writes James Russell Lowell in Boston, praising his contribution in the February *Graham's*: "Rosaline *is* a fine poem. Poe, Griswold, all of us say so. In the March no. in a review of Longfellow, Poe, after doing justice to you, says of Rosaline *'that no American poem equals it in the higher elements of song.'* . . . Poe wishes to be remembered to you" (MH–H).

17 FEBRUARY. Peterson replies to a letter from Lowell in Boston:

Poe laughed heartily when I told him you thought that he had a pique against Wakondah & its author. He says he pleads guilty as to the poem, but asks for a *nolle prosequi* so far as Matthews [*sic*] is concerned. He thinks the poem is on a par with Sheridan's statesmanship as Brougham describes it—"neither good, bad, nor indifferent, but no statesmanship at all." Matthews is a sociable kind-hearted man & has many friends: so the criticism has woke up quite a tempest. I understand he has said that, if he ever gets a chance, he will not spare Poe. Poe sends his respects & says that he never allows personal love or hate to warp his criticisms (MH–H).

26 FEBRUARY. WASHINGTON. Thomas replies to Poe's 3 February letter, explaining that he "delayed writing so long" in the hope that he could offer suggestions about the magazine project: "Mr. Robert Tyler would assist you with his pen all he could, but I suppose he could not assist you in any other way, unless government patronage in the way of printing blanks &c could be given to you. Anything that I could do for you you know will be done. Robert Tyler expressed himself highly gratified with your favorable opinion of his poem which I mentioned to him. He observed that he valued your opinion more than any other critic's in the country—to which I subscribed." Thomas agrees that in "Autography" Poe lowered his standards: "I must confess that I was more than surprised at the eulogistic notices which you took of certain writers—but I attributed it to a monomania partiality. I am glad to see that you still retain the unbiassed possession of your mental faculties. But, Poe, for the sake of that high independence of character which you possess you should not have let Graham influence you into such notices. There, that in complete imitation of your frankness." Thomas deeply regrets Virginia's illness: "Though I have no wife, yet I have sisters, and have experienced the tenderness of woman's nature. I can therefore, in part, sympathise with you" (W, 17:105–06; L, 2:591).

28 FEBRUARY. PHILADELPHIA. Poe signs a receipt: "Received of Mr G. R. Graham Fifty eights [*sic*] Dollars, in full for salary as Editor, up to this date" (TxU–HRCL).

MARCH. *Graham's* contains Poe's revised poem "To One Departed," formerly entitled "To Mary," as well as his preliminary notice of Longfellow's *Ballads and Other Poems* and his reviews of Harry Lorrequer's novel *Charles O'Malley*, Roswell Park's *Pantology*, and *The Critical and Miscellaneous Writings of Henry Lord Brougham*.

5 MARCH. The *Saturday Evening Post* notices the March *Graham's*: "The publisher now issues over forty thousand copies monthly, which is the strongest evidence of merit,—and he purposes opening the new volume in July next with *fifty thousand copies*, which will be made the regular and standing edition, being as many as any steel line engraving will yield impressions."

5 MARCH. In the evening Charles Dickens arrives in Philadelphia, taking lodgings at the United States Hotel, Chestnut Street above Fourth (Dickens, 3:100).

6 MARCH OR BEFORE. Poe writes Dickens, requesting an interview. With

CHARLES DICKENS

the letter he sends his *Tales of the Grotesque and Arabesque* as well as his two reviews of *Barnaby Rudge*, in the *Saturday Evening Post* of 1 May 1841 and *Graham's* for February 1842 (Dickens' reply).

6 MARCH. Dickens writes Poe:

> I shall be very glad to see you, whenever you will do me the favor to call. I think I am more likely to be in the way between half past eleven and twelve, than at any other time.
>
> I have glanced over the books you have been so kind as to send me; and more particularly at the papers to which you called my attention. I have the greater pleasure in expressing my desire to see you, on their account.
>
> Apropos of the "construction" of Caleb Williams. Do you know that Godwin wrote it *backwards*—the last Volume first—and that when he had produced the hunting-down of Caleb, and the Catastrophe, he waited for months, casting about for a means of accounting for what he had done? (Dickens, 3:106–07).

[In the *Graham's* review of *Barnaby Rudge*, Poe had compared the novelist and philosopher William Godwin with Dickens: " 'Caleb Williams' is a far less noble work than 'The Old Curiosity-Shop;' but Mr. Dickens could no more have constructed the one than Mr. Godwin could have dreamed of the other."]

7? MARCH. Poe has "two long interviews" with Dickens, presumably at the United States Hotel. They discuss the state of American poetry; Poe reads Emerson's poem "To the Humble Bee." Dickens promises to seek an English publisher for the *Tales of the Grotesque and Arabesque*. Apparently, Poe brings an invitation from George R. Graham; Dickens agrees to write for *Graham's*, if he contributes to any American magazine (Poe to Lowell, 2 July 1844; see also Moss [1978], pp. 10–12, and Thomas [1978], pp. 341–44).

9 MARCH. In the morning Dickens leaves Philadelphia for Washington (*Public Ledger*, 10 March).

13 MARCH. Poe writes Thomas in Washington, inquiring whether his friend had an opportunity to meet Dickens there (Thomas' 21 May reply).

13 MARCH. Poe replies to a 14 February letter from the Baltimore author John N. McJilton, who submitted to *Graham's* Esther Wetherald's translation of a tale in French: "My silence, for so long an interval, will have assured you that the article is accepted with pleasure. Mr Graham, however, desires me to say that it will be out of his power to pay more than 2$ per printed page for translations. Should these terms meet the views of Miss Wetherald, we should be glad to receive from her, each month, an

article similar to the one sent, and not exceeding three or four pages in length." Poe wonders why he does not occasionally hear from McJilton, as in "the olden time" (L, 1:194).

31 MARCH. Poe signs a receipt: "Received of Mr G. R. Graham Fifty eight dollars in full for salary, up to this date" (TxU—HRCL).

APRIL. *Graham's* contains Poe's tale "Life in Death," subsequently entitled "The Oval Portrait," as well as his detailed criticism of Longfellow's *Ballads and Other Poems*, his reviews of *Ideals and Other Poems* by "Algernon" and of Patrick S. Casserly's *Translation of Jacob's Greek Reader*, and his preliminary notice of Hawthorne's *Twice-Told Tales*.

1 APRIL. Charles J. Peterson writes Lowell in Boston, urging him to read Poe's article on Longfellow in the April *Graham's*: "It is, in my opinion, the most masterly critique, as a whole, I ever saw from an American pen" (MH—H).

CA. 1 APRIL. Poe resigns from the staff of *Graham's* (Poe to Thomas, 25 May, and to Daniel Bryan, 6 July).

2 APRIL. BALTIMORE. In the *Saturday Visiter* Snodgrass observes that the April *Graham's* reveals "a decided improvement" over previous numbers: "We allude to the insertion of reviews. We speak of this class of writings, as distinct from mere critical notices. We think they add greatly to the value of the work,—being useful, at the same time, in no slight degree. We are, furthermore, very sure the editor, Mr. Poe, is gratified by the change he has been permitted to make in this respect. He is fond of reviewing, and, though, at times, provokingly *hypercritical*, is an excellent reviewer."

18 APRIL. PHILADELPHIA. The publishers Carey & Hart write Rufus W. Griswold in New York: "We have at last published the 'Poets & Poetry of America' & a handsome Book it is" (MB—G).

[The anthology contained Poe's "The Coliseum," "The Haunted Palace," and "The Sleeper." The three poems were preceded by a brief and somewhat inaccurate biographical sketch.]

19 APRIL. Graham writes Griswold in New York, offering him the position vacated by Poe:

Have you fully determined on assuming the Chaplaincy and to *abandon* the editorial chair? Or could you find it in your heart to locate in Philadelphia? Let me hear from you, as I have a proposal to make.

I like your book much. We received it from Carey & Hart on yesterday, and although it will give offense to a few, it must be popular, and will please every man of taste (MB–G).

23 APRIL. Graham's *Saturday Evening Post* reviews *The Poets and Poetry of America*:

This is the most valuable publication of the season. No collection of American Poetry has ever been made, at all comparable to this, whether we regard the completeness of the work, or the taste displayed in the selections. Few men in the country were so well qualified for the task of editor as the Rev. Mr. Griswold . . . .

The work comprises selections from eighty-eight of our poets, whose productions are prefaced by neat biographies. . . . In an Appendix are contained selections from "Various Authors," who, without pretending to the rank of poets, have yet written occasional verses. We see more than one writer in this department, whose friends will think him entitled to a more extended notice. . . . We fear more for the success of the work on this account than on any other.

BEFORE 30 APRIL. *Graham's* for May contains Poe's tale "The Mask of the Red Death," as well as his long criticism of Hawthorne's *Twice-Told Tales* and his briefer reviews of Charles Fenno Hoffman's *The Vigil of Faith, and Other Poems* and William Gilmore Simms's novel *Beauchampe*.

30 APRIL. The *Saturday Evening Post* notices the May *Graham's*: "It is doubtful, if engravings of equal beauty ever adorned an American work,—and as the publisher expended *over two thousand dollars on the engravings of the May number alone*, some idea may be formed of their excellency, and of the patronage of a work that can amply afford it."

30 APRIL. BALTIMORE. In the *Saturday Visiter* Snodgrass reprints "The Mask of the Red Death" from *Graham's*. He finds that Poe's tale "exhibits his love of the mysterious and his artistical ability—tho' not so much as his stories generally."

MAY. NEW YORK. *Arcturus*, edited by Cornelius Mathews and Evert A. Duyckinck, contains an unsigned essay on "Criticism in America":

Mr. Poe, editor of Graham's Magazine, has lately written several elaborate criticisms in that periodical, which are richly deserving of attention. He is somewhat over literal and minute, looking oftener to the letter than the spirit; but in the full examination of a book, we know of no one who will take the same pains. His recent review of Barnaby Rudge is a masterpiece of ingenuity.

MAY. COLUMBIA, TENNESSEE. In the *Guardian* John Tomlin favorably reviews Lambert A. Wilmer's satire on American poets, *The Quacks of Heli-*

con. Observing that the nation's poetry is inferior to that produced by Europeans, Tomlin points out that in fiction Americans "can *now* compete, and successfully too, with the Bulwers of England, and De Kocks of France. J. Fenimore Cooper is Bulwer's equal—and Edgar A. Poe in 'The Murders in the Rue Morgue,' has exhibited powers of mind, equal to any living writer."

3 MAY. PHILADELPHIA. Graham replies to a letter from Griswold in New York, who has accepted the editorial position on *Graham's* left vacant by Poe's departure: "I am glad that you agree to our proposal, and we shall be ready to give you the 'right hand of fellowship,' as soon as 'orders are taken.' Mr. P[eterson] is right. The salary to be $1,000 per annum" (MB–G).

13 MAY. ALEXANDRIA, DISTRICT OF COLUMBIA. Daniel Bryan writes Poe, forwarding his "Crowning of the May Queen" and other poems for possible publication in *Graham's*: "Although I have not the happiness to be personally acquainted with you, yet my intimate acquaintance with your lamented Brother [Henry Poe], the occasional correspondence which has taken place between us, and the favourable sentiments which you have expressed towards my poetical pretensions, embolden me to regard you in a very different light from that of a stranger.—Hence I write to you with freedom and frankness, and I desire you to deal with me in the same spirit.—If you believe my verses to be unsuitable to your Journal, I beg you to return them to me" (MB–G).

14 MAY. PHILADELPHIA. Graham's *Saturday Evening Post* carries an announcement: "Mr. R. W. Griswold, a gentleman of acknowledged taste and ability, has become associated with us, as one of the Editors of the Saturday Evening Post and Graham's Magazine."

18 MAY. The *Public Ledger* reports: "E. A. Poe, Esq, has retired from the editorship of *Graham's Magazine*, and has been succeeded by Rev. R. W. Griswold."

21 MAY. WASHINGTON. In the *Index* Jesse E. Dow comments: "Edgar A. Poe, Esq., has resigned the charge of Graham's Magazine. We regret this exceedingly. We trust the Penn Magazine will now be started by Mr. Poe."

21 MAY. Thomas replies to Poe's 13 March letter. Although Robert Tyler, the President's son, could not provide any financial assistance to Poe's proposed magazine, he may be able to assist the project indirectly:

Last night I was speaking of you [to Robert Tyler], and took occasion to suggest that a situation in the Custom House, Philadelphia, might be acceptable to you, as Lamb (Charles) had held a somewhat similar appointment, etc., and as it would leave you leisure to pursue your literary pursuits. Robert replied that he felt confident that such a situation could be obtained for you in the course of two or three months at farthest, as certain vacancies would then occur.

What say you to such a place? Official life is not laborious, and a situation that would suit you and place you beyond the necessity of employing your pen, he says, he can obtain for you there. Let me hear from you as soon as convenient upon this subject.

Thomas answers Poe's question: "Yes, I saw Dickens, but only at the dinner which a few of us gave him here—I liked him very much though." Thomas inquires whether there is any truth in the report that Poe has "parted company" with Graham (*W*, 17:108–10).

[At the beginning of his administration President Tyler opposed the then prevalent "spoils system," whereby the party victorious in an election rewarded its followers with government appointments; but by early 1842, after his break with the Whigs, he himself adopted this policy to build a political base for his candidacy in the 1844 Presidential election. The installation of Tyler supporters in the Philadelphia Custom House had been temporarily thwarted by the Collector of Customs, Jonathan Roberts, a loyal Whig who refused to remove the incumbents. The vacancies Thomas mentioned to Poe were not to occur for "two or three months" because President Tyler was waiting until the adjournment of the Whig-dominated Congress before replacing Roberts with a new Collector who would make the changes. Poe probably knew of the situation before Thomas wrote him, since it was fully described in the Philadelphia newspapers. See Thomas (1978), pp. 366–67, 371, 373–75, 388–89.]

25 MAY. PHILADELPHIA. Poe replies to Thomas: "What you say respecting a situation in the Custom House here gives me new life. Nothing could more precisely meet my views. Could I obtain such an appointment, I would be enabled thoroughly to carry out all my ambitious projects. It would relieve me of all care as regards a mere subsistence, and thus allow me time for thought, which, in fact, is action. . . . If the salary will barely enable me to live I shall be content. Will you say as much for me to Mr [Robert] Tyler, and express to him my sincere gratitude for the interest he takes in my welfare?" Poe answers Thomas' question:

The report of my having parted company with Graham, is correct; although, in the forthcoming June number, there is no announcement to that effect; nor had the papers any authority for the statement made. My duties ceased with the May number. I shall continue to contribute occasionally. Griswold succeeds me. My reason for resigning was disgust with the namby-pamby character of the Magazine—a character which it was impossible to eradicate—I allude to the contemptible pictures, fashion-plates, music and love tales. The salary, moreover, did not pay me for the labor which I was forced to bestow. With Graham who is really a very gentlemanly, although an exceedingly weak man, I had no misunderstanding.

The Poe family has moved from "the old place"; if Thomas should visit Philadelphia, he can find their new address by inquiring at the office of *Graham's* (*L*, 1:197–99; Moldenhauer [1973], p. 54).

25 MAY. Poe signs a promissory note for $32.85, payable to Swain, Abell, and Simmons, publishers of the *Public Ledger*, "for value received" (Phillips, 1:742; Ostrom [1981], p. 206).

31 MAY. Charles J. Peterson writes James Russell Lowell in Boston: "I suppose you know Poe has left us. He's a splendid fellow, but 'unstable as water.' In his place we have taken Griswold, who is an indefatigable fellow & knows more about the literary men of this country than they do themselves" (MH–H).

JUNE. *Graham's* contains Peterson's favorable review of Griswold's *Poets and Poetry of America*, which stresses that Lowell should have been accorded "a

A fashion plate from *Graham's*
Humanities Research Center, University of Texas at Austin

more liberal notice" (attribution implied by Peterson to Lowell, 25 April, MH–H).

[Harrison mistakenly reprinted this review and that of Bulwer-Lytton's novel *Zanoni* as Poe's (*W*, 11:115–26). See also Poe to Snodgrass, 4 June.]

JUNE? ALBANY, NEW YORK. The *Poet's Magazine* reviews Griswold's anthology, criticizing the "undue prominence" given to various poetasters: "We have neither time or space to specify, but who ever thought before Mr. Griswold informed them of the fact, that Edgar A. Poe was entitled to a place among the Poets of America? Who ever dreamed that the cynical critic, the hunter up of small things, journeyman editor of periodicals, and Apollo's man of all work, was a favourite of the Muses, or wrote *Poetry?* It is certainly a 'grotesque' discovery, and, we conjecture, had not Mr. P. taken particular pains to impress the fact upon Mr. Griswold's mind, the world would have remained in happy ignorance of his (Mr. P's) poetical abilities" (Mabbott [1949], pp. 122–23).

EARLY JUNE. PHILADELPHIA. Poe replies to a letter from the civil engineer and inventor James Herron, a Virginian now living in Washington:

You have learned, perhaps, that I have retired from "Graham's Magazine". The state of my mind has, in fact, forced me to abandon for the present, all mental exertion. The renewed and hopeless illness of my wife, ill health on my own part, and pecuniary embarrassments, have nearly driven me to distraction. My only hope of relief is the "Bankrupt Act", of which I shall avail myself as soon as possible. . . .

You will be pleased to hear that I have the promise of a situation in our Custom-House. The offer was entirely unexpected & gratuitous. I am to receive the appointment upon removal of several incumbents—the removal to be certainly made in a month. I am indebted to the personal friendship of Robert Tyler. If I *really* receive the appointment all may yet go well. . . .

Mrs Poe is again dangerously ill with hemorrhage from the lungs (*L*, 1:198–99).

4 JUNE. NEW YORK. In the *New World* Park Benjamin comments: "EDGAR A. POE—We regard this gentleman as one of the best writers of the English language now living. His style is singularly pure and idiomatic. He never condescends to affectations, but writes with a nervous clearness, that inspires the reader with a perpetual confidence in his powers. Mr. Poe has left Mr. Graham's Magazine; but in whatever sphere he moves, he will surely be distinguished."

4 JUNE. LOWELL, MASSACHUSETTS. The *Literary Souvenir* reprints Poe's "The Mask of the Red Death" from the May *Graham's* (Heartman and Canny, p. 222).

4 JUNE. PHILADELPHIA. Poe writes George Roberts, publisher of the *Boston Notion*, describing a long tale he has just completed, "The Mystery of Marie Rogêt—a Sequel to the Murders in the Rue Morgue":

The story is based upon the assassination of Mary Cecilia Rogers, which created so vast an excitement, some months ago, in New-York. I have, however, handled my design in a manner altogether *novel* in literature. I have imagined a series of nearly exact *coincidences* occurring in Paris. A young grisette, one Marie Rogêt, has been murdered under precisely similar circumstances with Mary Rogers. Thus, under pretence of showing how Dupin (the hero of "The Rue Morgue[")] unravelled the mystery of Marie's assassination, I, in reality, enter into a very long and rigorous analysis of the New-York tragedy. No point is omitted. I examine, each by each, the opinions and arguments of the press upon the subject, and show that this subject has been, hitherto, *unapproached*. In fact, I believe not only that I have demonstrated the fallacy of the general idea—that the girl was the victim of a gang of ruffians—but have *indicated the assassin* in a manner which will give renewed impetus to investigation.

Because of "the nature of the subject," the tale will "excite attention." It would occupy twenty-five pages of *Graham's*, and "at the usual price" it would be worth $100 to Poe: "For reasons, however, which I need not specify, I am desirous of having this tale printed in Boston, and, if you like it, I will say $50. Will you please write me upon this point?—by return of mail, if possible" (*L*, 1:199–200).

4 JUNE. Poe writes Joseph Evans Snodgrass in Baltimore, offering him "The Mystery of Marie Rogêt" for the *Saturday Visiter*: "Of course I could not afford to make you an absolute present of it—but if you are willing to take it, I will say $40." Poe is glad that Snodgrass has become the sole proprietor of the *Visiter*: "I have to thank your partiality for many flattering notices of myself. How is it, nevertheless, that a *Magazine* of the highest class has never yet succeeded in Baltimore? I have often thought, of late, how much better it would have been had you joined me in a Magazine project in the Monumental City, rather than engage with the 'Visiter'—a journal which has never yet been able to recover from the *mauvais odeur* imparted to it by [John Hill] Hewitt. . . . Have you seen Griswold's Book of Poetry? It is a most outrageous humbug, and I sincerely wish you would 'use it up'." Poe composes a notice of his withdrawal from *Graham's*, which he asks Snodgrass to publish in the *Visiter*:

We have it from *undoubted authority* that Mr Poe *has* retired from the editorship of 'Graham's Magazine', and that his withdrawal took place with the *May* number, notwithstanding the omission of all announcement to this effect in the number for June. We observe that the "Boston Post", in finding just fault with an exceedingly ignorant and flippant review of "Zanoni" which appears in the June number, has spoken of it as from the pen of Mr Poe[.] We will take it upon ourselves to say that Mr P. neither did write the article, nor could have written any such absurdity. . . . The article appears to be the handiwork of some underling who has become imbued with th[e] fancy of *aping* Mr Poe's peculiarities of diction. . . . Not to announce Mr P's withdrawal in the June number, was an act of the rankest injustice; and as such we denounce it (*L*, 1:201–03).

BEFORE 7 JUNE. Poe writes Charles Dickens at New York, reminding him of a "mission . . . already entrusted . . . by word of mouth" (Dickens to Poe, 27 November).

[Dickens left for England on 7 June; the "mission" he accepted was to find a London publisher for a collection of Poe's tales.]

11 JUNE. MIDDLETOWN, CONNECTICUT. Thomas Holley Chivers writes Poe, enclosing his "Invocation to Spring" and several other poems for possible publication in *Graham's* (Poe's reply, 6 July).

17 JUNE. WASHINGTON. The *Independent* publishes a letter from "FLASH," a correspondent in Philadelphia who denies that "genius" was required to produce *The Poets and Poetry of America*: "I am willing to admit that Mr. Griswold has shown a proper discrimination in his selections, and that his biographical notices are satisfactory—that the binder and printer have done their duty; but beyond this, I do not see that Mr. Griswold has much to boast of. Mr. Griswold is a lively and elegant writer of prose and poetry, and a very fair and impartial critic, though the sponsor, as editor of Graham's Magazine, of the malignant, unjust, and disgraceful attacks on the literary character of its former editor, Mr. Poe."

23 JUNE. In the *Index* Dow comments on the change in the editorial staff of *Graham's*: "We would give more for Edgar A. Poe's toe nail, than we would for Rueful Grizzle's soul, unless we wanted a milk-strainer. Them's our sentiments."

BEFORE 24 JUNE? PHILADELPHIA. Poe prepares the title page and a table of contents for a new edition of his stories, *Phantasy-Pieces*. The three-volume collection is to contain the twenty-five stories in his *Tales of the Grotesque and Arabesque*, as well as the thirteen he has since written (facsimiles in Quinn, pp. 338–39, and Mabbott [1978], 2:474 ff.).

[The collection never appeared. On the title page Poe subsequently changed the projected volumes from "Three" to "Two"; from the table of contents he crossed out his two latest tales, "The Pit and the Pendulum" and "The Mystery of Marie Rogêt," both of which were still unpublished.]

CA. 24 JUNE. NEW YORK. Poe visits New York in an unsuccessful attempt to secure employment and to find a publisher for *Phantasy-Pieces*. He begins drinking while in the company of the young poet William Ross Wallace, who insists on mint juleps. In an intoxicated state he visits J. and H. G. Langley, publishers of the *Democratic Review*, and Robert Hamilton, editor of William W. Snowden's *Ladies' Companion* (Poe's statement to Thomas on 17 September; Poe to the Langleys, 18 July, and to Hamilton, 3 October).

24 JUNE. Poe scribbles a curt letter to Thomas in Washington:

New York June 24.

My dear Thomas,
   If there [i]s anything in the world to be done for my friend W. Wallace with Rob. Tyler do it, and charge it to my account. Use your influence to its ultimate extent. No better man ever lived. Write me by return of mail. Why have I not heard from you lately?

Truly yours
Edgar A Poe.

Wallace has informed me that he has made application for a Consulship.

[This letter has not been previously published; the badly faded manuscript was purchased by the Philadelphia Free Library in 1976 (PP–G). See also Poe to Thomas, 27 August 1842.]

25 JUNE. Poe's letter is postmarked.

AFTER 25 JUNE? JERSEY CITY, NEW JERSEY. Mary Starr, now Mrs. Jenning, receives a visit from Poe:

He came to New York, and went to my husband's place of business to find out where we lived. He was on a spree, however, and forgot the address before he got across the river. He made several trips backward and forward on the ferry-boat. . . .
   When Mr. Poe reached our house I was out with my sister, and he opened the door for us when we got back. We saw he was on one of his sprees, and he had been away from home for several days. . . .
   Mr. Poe staid to tea with us, but ate nothing; only drank a cup of tea. . . . He then went away. A few days afterward Mrs. Clemm came to see me, much worried about "Eddie dear," as she always addressed him. She did not know where he was, and his wife was almost crazy with anxiety. I told Mrs. Clemm that he had been to see me. A search was made, and he was finally found in the woods on the outskirts of Jersey City, wandering about like a crazy man. Mrs. Clemm took him back with her to Philadelphia (Mary's reminiscence, possibly exaggerated, quoted by Van Cleef, p. 639).

27 JUNE. ALEXANDRIA, DISTRICT OF COLUMBIA. Daniel Bryan writes Poe:

"As your connexion with Graham's Mag. has ceased, you may feel some difficulty about the disposal of the verses which I some weeks ago [on 13 May] enclosed to you. They were transmitted for that work under an impression,—and because I believed,—that you were still one of its editors. But now that you have withdrawn from it, I prefer having the verses returned to me, or retained by you,—if you deem them worthy of preservation,—for your future use" (MB–G).

30 JUNE. PHILADELPHIA. Poe writes James Herron in Washington:

Upon return from a brief visit to New-York, last night, I found here your kind letter from Washington, enclosing a check for $20, and giving me new life in every way. I am more deeply indebted to you than I can express, and in this I really mean what I say. Without your prompt and unexpected interposition with Mr [Robert] Tyler, it is by no means improbable that I should have failed in obtaining the appointment which has become so vitally necessary to me; but now I feel assured of success. . . .

My wife's health has slightly improved and my spirits have risen in proportion; but I am still *very* unwell—so much so that I shall be forced to give up and go to bed (L, 1:204).

JULY. *Graham's* contains an announcement on its last page:

RUFUS WILMOT GRISWOLD, a gentleman of fine taste and well known literary abilities, has become associated with us as one of the editors of this Magazine. The extensive literary knowledge of Mr. G. renders him a most valuable coadjutor.

The connection of E. A. POE, Esq., with this work ceased with the *May Number*. Mr. P. bears with him our warmest wishes for success in whatever he may undertake.

The outside back cover carries this notice: "The circulation of this Magazine has increased over Seventeen Thousand during the last six months, and the publisher issues, of the July number, and will continue to issue, until the close of the present volume, OVER FIFTY THOUSAND COPIES!—a circulation never attained before by any European or American periodical—the best evidence that can be offered of merit."

JULY. Griswold commissions Poe to prepare a review of *The Poets and Poetry of America*, promising to pay him his "usual" fee for the criticism, and to arrange for its publication "in some reputable work" (Poe to Thomas, 12 September; cf. Griswold to J. T. Fields, 12 August and 7 September).

6 JULY. WASHINGTON. The *Index* carries a valedictory by Poe's friend Jesse E. Dow, who is resigning the editorship because of ill health.

6 JULY. PHILADELPHIA. Poe replies to Daniel Bryan's 27 June letter. He

has not received the "verses" Bryan sent him on 13 May: "My connexion with 'Graham's Magazine' ceased with the May number, which was completed by the 1rst of April . . . Can it be possible that the present editors have thought it proper to open letters addressed to myself, because addressed to myself as 'Editor of Graham's Magazine'? I know not how to escape from this conclusion." Although Poe has "no quarrel" with either Graham or Griswold, he holds neither man "in especial respect." Therefore it might be best if Bryan were to write them himself, requesting the return of his manuscripts. Poe is now making "earnest although *secret* exertions" to resume his project of the *Penn Magazine*:

You may remember that it was my original design to issue it on the first of January 1841. I was induced to abandon the project at that period by the representations of Mr Graham. He said that if I would join him as a salaried editor, giving up, for the time, my own scheme, he himself would unite with me at the expiration of 6 months, or certainly at the end of a year. As Mr G. was a man of capital and I had no money, I thought it most prudent to fall in with his views. The result has proved his want of faith and my own folly. In fact, I was continually laboring against myself. Every exertion made by myself for the benefit of "Graham", by rendering that Mag: a greater source of profit, rendered its owner, at the same time, less willing to keep his word with me. At the time of our bargain (a verbal one) he had 6000 subscribers—when I left him he had more than 40,000. It is no wonder that he has been tempted to leave me in the lurch.

Poe had "nearly 1000 subscribers with which to have started the 'Penn' "; from his original list perhaps "3 or 4 hundred" will still support the magazine. Between now and 1 January 1843, when he plans to issue the first number, he must enlist additional subscribers: "If, therefore, you can aid me in Alexandria, with even a single name, I shall feel deeply indebted to your friendship" (*L*, 1:204–07).

6 JULY. Poe writes Thomas Holley Chivers in Middletown, Connecticut, apologizing for not replying to his last three letters: "A world of perplexing business has led me to postpone, from day to day, a duty which it is always a pleasure to perform." In the first letter Chivers had spoken of the notice he received in the December 1841 installment of "Autography." Poe wishes to modify this evaluation of Chivers' merits: "The paper had scarcely gone to press before I saw and acknowledged to myself the injustice I had done you—an injustice which it is my full purpose to repair at the first opportunity. What I said of your grammatical errors arose from some imperfect recollections of one or two poems sent to the first volume of the S. L. Messenger. But in more important respects I now deeply feel that I have wronged you by a hasty opinion. You will not suppose me insincere in saying that I look upon some of your late pieces as the finest I have *ever read*." When Chivers wrote his most recent letter, dated 11 June,

he was unaware of Poe's resignation from *Graham's*: "What disposition shall I make of the 'Invocation to Spring'? The other pieces are in the hands of my successor, Mr Griswold." Poe now intends to resume the *Penn Magazine* project: "As I have no money myself, it will be absolutely necessary that I procure a partner who has some pecuniary means. I mention this to you—for it is not impossible that you yourself may have both the will & the ability to join me" (*L*, 2:697–98).

7 JULY. Poe writes his first cousin Elizabeth Rebecca Herring, now the widow of Andrew Turner Tutt, in Woodville, Rappahannock County, Virginia: "My dear little wife grew much better from the very first day after taking the Jew's Beer. It seemed to have the most instantaneous and miraculous effect. . . . About ten days ago, however, I was obliged to go on to New York on business . . . she began to fret . . . because she did not hear from me twice a day" (*L*, 1:209).

9 JULY. LOWELL, MASSACHUSETTS. The *Literary Souvenir* reprints Poe's tale "Eleonora" (Heartman and Canny, p. 222).

11 JULY. ALEXANDRIA, DISTRICT OF COLUMBIA. Bryan replies to Poe's 6 July letter, promising to enlist subscribers for the *Penn Magazine*: "We stand in need of a literary journal of the character which you propose to give to yours; a character based on principles uninfluenced by selfish monopolising *cliques*, and stamped with the impress of justice and truth, regardless of sectional partialities and the indiscriminate puffery and exclusiveness of a combination of self-constituted critics. . . . I am convinced that you occupy a very favourable position as an editor in the estimation of the public; and when you get your journal fully established, I believe that its independence and the spirit and genius which you will be able to infuse into its columns will insure it success." Bryan is unable to understand why Poe failed to receive his 13 May letter and the accompanying poems, since he addressed these items simply to "Edgar A Poe, Esq. Philada.," not in care of *Graham's Magazine*: "If, therefore, they were taken from the P.O. and opened by any other person, without your authority, the person opening them, was guilty of an act of baseness, for which he deserves to have his ears cut off, or a brand of infamy stamped on his front" (MB–G).

12 JULY. NEW YORK. Chivers replies to Poe's 6 July letter: "I am now on my way to the South, and had not time to answer your letter from Middletown, as I received it only a few moments before I started. My brother has written me a letter informing me that the division of my father's estate will take place on the first of August, and I must hasten to my plantation to receive my portion," Chivers thanks Poe for his "polite

remarks" in regard to "Autography": "I had always spoken so highly of your talents as a poet, and the best critic in this Country, that, when my friends saw it [Poe's notice of Chivers], believing you were what I represented you to be, they came almost to the conclusion that they were not only mistaken, but that I was a bad writer, and a fit subject for the Insane Hospital." If the editor of *Graham's* likes Chivers' poem "Invocation to Spring," Poe has permission to give it to him. "In regard to the 'Penn Magazine,' all I can say at present is, that I will do all I can to aid you in the procurement of subscribers for it" (Chivers [1957], pp. 14–15).

18 JULY. PHILADELPHIA. Poe writes the New York publishers J. and H. G. Langley:

Enclosed I have the honor to send you an article which I should be pleased if you would accept for the "Democratic Review." I am *desperately* pushed for money; and, in the event of Mr [John L.] O'Sullivan's liking the "Landscape-Garden," I would take it as an especial favor if you could mail me the amount due for it, so as to reach me here by the 21rst, on which day I shall need it. . . .

Will you be kind enough to put the best possible interpretation upon my behavior while in N-York? You must have conceived a *queer* idea of me—but the simple truth is that [William Ross] Wallace would insist upon *the juleps*, and I knew not what I was either doing or saying. The Review of [Rufus] Dawes which I offered you was deficient in a 1/2 page of commencement, which I had written to supersede the old beginning, and which gave the article the character of a general & retrospective review. No wonder you did not take it (*L*, 2:698–99).

AFTER 18 JULY. NEW YORK. The Langleys return "The Landscape Garden" to Poe. He then sells the story to Robert Hamilton, editor of Snowden's *Ladies' Companion* (Poe to Hamilton, 3 October).

26 JULY. ALEXANDRIA, DISTRICT OF COLUMBIA. Bryan writes Poe again, inquiring whether he located the poems forwarded on 13 May: "I don't care much about the loss of the M.S. as I have the rough originals, and am not sure, any how, that they merit preservation.—But the violation of your sealed packages and the detention of their contents wd. be a very different matter. I venture to hope, however, that I shall hear from you that the parties to whom suspicion pointed as being guilty of the presumed offence are innocent thereof." Bryan has seen a report in the Philadelphia *Evening Journal* that a new edition of Griswold's *Poets and Poetry of America* is being issued:

Is there not some of the "trickery of trade" in this?—What was the am[oun]t of the 1st edition—and may not the 2nd ed. have been printed at the same time the 1st was?—By the bye have you read any of Griswold's own verses?—The only sample I have seen of them is mere doggerel in my humble estimation. I allude to

"Sights from my window—Alice"—printed in the May or June No. of Graham.—I have at my disposal a MS *critique* on this production, wh[ich] I wd. be pleased to see printed in some respectable newspaper, or periodical, published in one [of] the large cities.—Would it comport with your views & feelings to take charge of it, and, if you deemed it just and worthy of publication, have it transferred to the columns of some journal over which you have influence? (MB–G).

AFTER 26 JULY. PHILADELPHIA. Poe replies to Bryan's letters of 11 and 26 July. He has finally received Bryan's 13 May letter: someone on the staff of *Graham's* obtained it from the post office and opened it. The letter then passed into the possession of Griswold, who apparently read it, but did not bother to forward it. Poe suggests that Bryan contact either Thomas or Dow about publishing his criticism of Griswold's poem in the June *Graham's*, "Sights from My Window—Alice" (Bryan's 4 August reply).

30 JULY. NEW YORK. The *New-York Mirror* reports: "Edgar A. Poe, whose capabilities as an analytical critic are so generally acknowledged, is about to have a new field for their display in his proposed 'Penn Magazine.' "

30 JULY. BALTIMORE. Joseph Evans Snodgrass reviews the August *Graham's* in the *Saturday Visiter*: "A decided change in the tone of book notices. They are more laudatory than when Mr. Poe presided over the critical department."

4 AUGUST. ALEXANDRIA, DISTRICT OF COLUMBIA. Bryan replies to a letter from Poe:

I feel equally surprised and indignant at the conduct of the wretch by whom the sanctity of my letter to you was invaded: and, while I desire to exercise charity in relation to Mr Griswold in this matter, I cannot abstain from the indulgence of a suspicion that there has been at least a culpable disregard by him of our rights and of honourable principle in his connivance at the perpetration of this act of baseness; or in his failure to communicate to you the fact of the existence of such a letter, with an explanation of the circumstances connected with the invasion of its seal and the removal of its enclosures.

In a postscript Bryan acknowledges Poe's advice: "I will take into consideration yr suggestion with regard to the publication of the *critique* through Mr Dow or Mr Thomas. Not having any personal or epistolary acquaintance with either of them, I feel some hesitation about the introduction of the subject to them" (MB–G).

BEFORE 12 AUGUST. PHILADELPHIA. Poe delivers his review of *The Poets and Poetry of America* to Griswold, receiving from him the promised "compensation" (Poe to Thomas, 12 September).

12 AUGUST. Griswold writes his friend James T. Fields in Boston: "I have sent to-day the article by Poe, about my book, to Bradbury & Soden for their magazine [the *Boston Miscellany*], with a request that if it be not acceptable, they will return it to you. I thought likely the name of Poe—gratuitously furnished—might be of some consequence, though I care not a fig about the publication of the criticism, as the author and myself not being on the best terms, it is not decidedly as favorable as it might have been. Will you see to it, though" (MH–H).

[Poe's criticism was judiciously favorable, but Griswold had expected pure laudation. He seems to have regarded reviews as advertisements or favors, rather than impartial evaluations. On 10 July, for example, he had written Fields, the junior partner in Ticknor & Company, discussing this firm's new edition of Tennyson's poetry: "Did you see what a puff I gave Tennyson in the Sat. Eve. Post? . . . I puff your books, you know, without any regard to their quality" (CSmH).]

17 AUGUST. In the *Spirit of the Times* John S. Du Solle reports: "We understand that Edgar A. Poe, Esq., has made all his arrangements and will positively bring out the first number of the 'Penn Magazine' on 1st January. It will assume a high tone, and take a bold stand among our literary periodicals. God knows! something of the kind is needed."

19 AUGUST. Du Solle's *Times* carries a second report: "NOT SO.—The Eastern and Southern papers all state Edgar A. Poe is about to start a *Penny* Magazine. It is the 'Penn' Magazine, gentlemen—$5 per annum."

27 AUGUST. Poe writes Frederick William Thomas in Washington: "How happens it that I have received not a line from you for these four months? . . . I wrote a few words to you, about two months since, from New York, at the importunate demand of W. Wallace, in which you were requested to use your influence, &c. He overlooked me while I wrote, & therefore I could not speak of private matters. I presume you gave the point as much consideration as it demanded, & no more." Poe is anxious to learn of Thomas' activities: "Since I heard from you I have had a reiteration of the promise, about the Custom-House appointment, from Rob Tyler. A friend of mine, Mr. Jas. Herron, having heard from me casually, that I had some hope of an appointment, called upon R. T., who assured him that I should *certainly* have it & desired him so to inform me. I have, also, paid my respects to Gen. J. W. Tyson, the leader of the T. party in the city, who seems especially well disposed—but, notwithstanding *all this*, I have my doubts. A few days will end them. If I do not get the office, I am just where I started. Nothing more can be done to secure it than has been

already done." Virginia Poe is still ill: "I have scarcely a faint hope of her recovery" (*L*, 1:209–10).

[During the summer the Philadelphia papers carried reports of impending removals and appointments in the Custom House, which were expected to occur as soon as Thomas S. Smith, a lawyer and politician active in the city's Tyler organization, became the new Collector. See Thomas (1978), pp. 415, 428.]

2 SEPTEMBER. WASHINGTON. Thomas writes Poe, describing his continuing efforts to secure an appointment for his friend. Mr. Beard, who will visit Philadelphia in a few days, wishes to make Poe's acquaintance (Poe's 12 September reply).

7 SEPTEMBER. PHILADELPHIA. Griswold replies to a letter from James T. Fields in Boston: "Perhaps Poe's article will not affect the book at all, but I am rather pleased that it is to appear, lest Poe should think I had prevented its publication" (Griswold [1898], pp. 120–21).

10 SEPTEMBER. In the *Spirit of the Times* Du Solle reports: "It seems that there is a little backwater somewhere in relation to the *Collectorship* of this

RUFUS W. GRISWOLD
New York Public Library

Port. T. S. Smith has not gotten his commission yet, or had not yesterday morning, and per consequence the expectants of office under him (and so far, we perceive by the list, he has had only 1124 applicants for about 30 berths,) are in a state of most inextricable confusion."

10 SEPTEMBER. WASHINGTON. Walter Forward, the Secretary of the Treasury, writes Jonathan Roberts, Collector of the Port of Philadelphia: "I am directed by the President to inform you that he has appointed Thomas S. Smith to be Collector of the Customs for the District of Philadelphia, in your place" (printed in the Philadelphia *United States Gazette*, 14 September).

BEFORE 12 SEPTEMBER. PHILADELPHIA. The Poe family moves to a small row house on Coates Street, in the Fairmount district (*McElroy's Philadelphia Directory* for 1843; Phillips, 1:747–49).

12 SEPTEMBER. Poe replies to Thomas' 2 September letter. He has not seen Mr. Beard, who may have had difficulty in locating his residence: "since you were here I have moved out in the neighborhood of Fairmount." Poe thanks Thomas for his "kind offices in the matter of the appointment" to the Custom House: "So far, nothing has been done here in the way of *reform*. Thos. S. Smith is to have the Collectorship, but it appears has not yet received his commission—a fact which occasions much surprise among the quid-nuncs." Graham has made Poe "a good offer" to return to his magazine:

He [Graham] is not especially pleased with Griswold—nor is any one else, with the exception of the Rev. gentleman himself, who has gotten himself into quite a hornet's nest, by his "Poets & Poetry". It appears you gave him personal offence by *delay* in replying to his demand for information touching Mrs Welby, I believe, or somebody else. Hence his omission of you in the body of the book; for he had prepared quite a long article from my MS. and had selected several pages for quotation. . . . About two months since, we were talking about the book, when I said that I had thought of reviewing it in full for the "Democratic Review", but found my design anticipated by an article from that ass [John L.] O'Sullivan, and that I knew no other work in which a notice would be readily admissible. Griswold said, in reply—"You need not trouble yourself about the publication of the review, should you decide upon writing it; for I will attend to all that. I will get it in some reputable work, and look to it for the usual pay; in the meantime handing you whatever your charge would be". This, you see, was an ingenious insinuation of a *bribe* to puff his book. I accepted his offer forthwith, wrote the review, handed it to him and received from him the compensation:—he never daring to look over the M.S. in my presence, and taking it for granted that all was right. But that review has not yet appeared, and I am doubtful if it ever will (*L*, 1:210–13).

[Griswold had asked Poe to prepare a sketch of Thomas; later he decided to relegate Thomas to the appendix reserved for lesser poets, who were not accorded biographical notices or extensive quotation. In this letter Poe overemphasized the severity of his review in order to assure Thomas that he disapproved of Griswold's decision.]

13 SEPTEMBER. The *Spirit of the Times* reports: "So Mr. Smith is Collector of the Port at last. . . . The applications for office under him yesterday were innumerable."

15 SEPTEMBER. The *United States Gazette* reports: "Thos. S. Smith, Esq., the recently appointed Collector, took possession of his office on Monday last [12 September], and on the same day removed eleven of the Measurers and Inspectors."

15 SEPTEMBER. NEW YORK. Chivers writes Poe, forwarding the names of four subscribers to the *Penn Magazine* (Poe's 27 September reply).

16? SEPTEMBER. PHILADELPHIA. Thomas arrives from Washington for a brief visit, taking lodgings in John Sturdivant's Congress Hall Hotel, Chestnut and Third Streets.

17 SEPTEMBER. SATURDAY. Thomas visits the Poe residence on Coates Street:

I met Poe in Philadelphia during September, 1842. He lived in a rural home on the outskirts of the city. His house was small, but comfortable inside for one of the kind. The rooms looked neat and orderly, but everything about the place wore an air of pecuniary want. Although I arrived late in the morning Mrs. Clemm, Poe's mother-in-law, was busy preparing for his breakfast. My presence possibly caused some confusion, but I noticed that there was delay and evident difficulty in procuring the meal. His wife entertained me. Her manners were agreeable and graceful. She had well formed, regular features, with the most expressive and intelligent eyes I ever beheld. Her pale complexion, the deep lines in her face and a consumptive cough made me regard her as the victim for an early grave. She and her mother showed much concern about Eddie, as they called Poe, and were anxious to have him secure work. I afterwards learned from Poe that he had been to New York in search of employment and had also made effort to get out an edition of his tales, but was unsuccessful.

When Poe appeared his dark hair hung carelessly over his high forehead, and his dress was a little slovenly. He met me cordially, but was reserved, and complained of feeling unwell. His pathetic tenderness and loving manners towards his wife greatly impressed me. I was not long in observing with deep regret that he had fallen again into habits of intemperance. I ventured to remonstrate with him. He admitted yielding to temptation to drink while in New York and turned the subject off by telling an amusing dialogue of Lucian, the Greek writer. We visited the city together and had an engagement for the following day. I left him sober, but he did not keep the engagement and wrote me that he was ill (Thomas quoted by Whitty [1911], pp. xliii–xliv).

17 SEPTEMBER. Poe and Thomas visit the city. Poe describes his plans for the *Penn Magazine*. Thomas discusses Poe's prospects of obtaining a position in the Custom House, assuring him that Robert Tyler wishes to see him appointed. Poe promises to meet Thomas at his hotel tomorrow morning (Poe's letters to Thomas, 21 September 1842 and 8 September 1844).

18 SEPTEMBER. Thomas sees John S. Du Solle, editor of the *Spirit of the Times*.

19 SEPTEMBER. Du Solle's *Times* reports: "Mr. Thomas[,] the gifted author of 'Clinton Bradshaw,' was in town yesterday, and left last evening for Washington, where he has an official situation."

21 SEPTEMBER. Poe writes Thomas in Washington:

I am afraid you will think that I keep my promises but indifferently well, since I failed to make my appearance at Congress Hall on Sunday, and I now, therefore, write to apologise. The will to be with you was not wanting—but, upon reaching home on Saturday night, I was taken with a severe chill and fever—the latter keeping me company all next day. I found myself too ill to venture out, but, nevertheless, would have done so had I been able to obtain the consent of all parties. . . . I was much in hope that you would have made your way out in the afternoon. Virginia & Mrs C. were much grieved at not being able to bid you farewell.

I perceive by Du Solle's paper that you saw him. He announced your presence in the city on Sunday, in very handsome terms (*L*, 1:213–14).

24 SEPTEMBER. The *Saturday Evening Post* notices the publication of the *Gift* for 1843, observing that it contains a contribution by Poe ["The Pit and the Pendulum"].

26 SEPTEMBER. NEW YORK. Chivers writes Poe: "Just before I started to the South, I gave Mr Hunt a poem entitled 'The Mighty Dead,' which I directed him to give to Israel Post, to be directed to you. I have just seen Post, and he informs me that the Package was never handed to him. I am very uneasy to know what disposition he [Hunt] made of the poem, as I am fearful that he has caused you to pay the postage on it . . . . I do wish that if you received the poem that you will let me know immediately whether or not you were so imposed upon" (Chivers [1957], p. 16).

27 SEPTEMBER. PHILADELPHIA. Poe writes Chivers in New York: "Through some accident, I did not receive your letter of the 15th inst: until this morning, and now hasten to reply." The "four names" Chivers forwarded for the *Penn Magazine* will aid the project "most materially in this early stage." As yet Poe has not even prepared a new prospectus; he does not wish to announce the "positive resumption of the original scheme" until the middle of October:

Before that period I have reason to believe that I shall have received an appointment in the Philadelphia Custom House, which will afford me a good salary and leave the greater portion of my time unemployed. With this appointment to fall back upon, as a certain resource, I shall be enabled to start the Magazine without difficulty, provided I can make an arrangement with either a practical printer possessing a small office, or some one not a printer, with about $1000 at command.

It would, of course, be better for the permanent influence and success of the journal that I unite myself with a gentleman of education & similarity of thought and feeling. It was this consciousness which induced me to suggest the enterprise to yourself. I know no one with whom I would more readily enter into association than yourself.

I am not aware what are your political views. My own have reference to no one of the present parties; but it has been hinted to me that I will receive the most effectual patronage from Government, for a journal which will admit occasional papers in support of the Administration. For Mr [John] Tyler personally, & as an honest statesman, I have the highest respect. Of the government patronage, upon the condition specified, *I am assured* and this alone will more than sustain the Magazine (*L*, 1:214–16).

OCTOBER. *Graham's Magazine* contains Poe's scathing evaluation of a Baltimore poetaster, "The Poetry of Rufus Dawes—A Retrospective Criticism."

OCTOBER. NEW YORK. Snowden's *Ladies' Companion* contains Poe's story "The Landscape Garden."

1 OCTOBER. Horace Greeley's *Daily Tribune* reviews the October *Graham's*, describing Poe's criticism of Dawes as "true in the main but supercilious and rather commonplace" (Griswold [1898], pp. 117–18).

1 OCTOBER. BALTIMORE. Snodgrass notices *Graham's* in the *Saturday Visiter*: "Edgar A. Poe completely 'uses up' Rufus Dawes in a review. Dawes, in poetry, *is* pretty much of a humbug, it must be confessed."

3 OCTOBER. PHILADELPHIA. Poe writes Robert Hamilton, editor of the *Ladies' Companion*:

I see that you have my Landscape-Garden in your last number—but, oh

Jupiter! the typographical blunders. Have you been sick, or what is the matter? I wrote you, some time since, saying that if, upon perusal of the "Mystery of Marie Rogêt," you found anything not precisely suited to your pages, I would gladly re-purchase it; but, should you conclude to retain it, for God's sake contrive to send me the proofs; or, at all events read them yourself. Such errors as occur in the "Landscape-Garden" would completely *ruin* a tale such as "Marie Rogêt."

How about the $5 due? Try and get it for me & send it by return mail and "as in duty bound we shall ever pray" &c &c.

Apparently alluding to his drinking bout in New York in late June, Poe assures Hamilton: "I am as straight as judges—somewhat more straight indeed than some of our Phil: dignitaries—and, what is more, I intend to keep straight" (TxU–HRCL; Moldenhauer [1973], pp. 55–56).

5 OCTOBER. Poe replies to a 21 September letter from John Tomlin in Jackson, Tennessee, who had inquired about the *Penn Magazine*. Poe is determined to begin publication on 1 January 1843: "I am to receive an office in the Custom House in this city . . . . With this to fall back upon as a certain resource until the Magazine is fairly afloat, all must go well. . . . Every new name, in the *beginning* of the enterprise, is worth five afterwards. My list of subscribers is getting to be quite respectable, although, as yet, I have positively taken no overt steps to procure names" (*L*, 1:216–17).

5 OCTOBER. Lambert A. Wilmer replies to two letters from Tomlin: "I believe the tightness of the times and the uncertain state of the currency have prevented Poe's Magazine enterprise and my own,—at least for the present." Wilmer has never seen Tomlin's review of *The Quacks of Helicon*, which appeared in the Columbia, Tennessee, *Guardian* for May: "The copy you sent fell into the hands of Poe, who lost or mislaid it before I could set eyes on it. I was vexed at this circumstance, as I intended to have the article copied into some of our city papers" (published by Tomlin in *Holden's Dollar Magazine*, November 1848).

AFTER 11 OCTOBER. Poe has three interviews with Thomas S. Smith, the new Collector of Customs.

[In his 19 November letter to Thomas, Poe recalled:

As for me, he [Smith] has treated me most shamefully. In my case, there was no need of any political shuffling or lying. I professed my willingness to postpone my claims to those of political claimants; but he told me, upon my first interview after the election, that if I would call on the fourth day he would swear me in. I called & he was not at home. On the next day I called again & saw him, when he told me that he would send a Messenger for me when ready:—this without even inquiring my place of residence—showing that he had, from the first, no design of appointing me. Well, I waited nearly a month, when, finding nearly all the appts made, I again called. He did not even ask me to be seated—scarcely spoke—muttered the words "I will *send* for you Mr Poe"—and that was all.

A municipal election was held in Philadelphia on 11 October. During October and November the city's newspapers carried frequent reports of the removals and appointments in the Custom House.]

BEFORE 21 OCTOBER. BOSTON. The *Boston Miscellany* for November contains Poe's review of *The Poets and Poetry of America*. Although Poe expresses disagreement with some of Griswold's critical judgments and with his partiality for New England writers, he describes this anthology as "*the most important addition which our literature has for many years received.* . . . Mr. Griswold . . . has entitled himself to the thanks of his countrymen, while showing himself a man of taste, talent, *and tact*."

21 OCTOBER. NEW YORK. Henry J. Raymond writes Griswold in Philadelphia: "The Boston Miscellany, I see, has a good puff of your Poets by Poe" (Griswold [1898], p. 125).

NOVEMBER. Snowden's *Ladies' Companion* contains the first installment of Poe's long tale "The Mystery of Marie Rogêt."

9 NOVEMBER. PHILADELPHIA. The *Pennsylvanian* reports the publication of Dickens' *American Notes for General Circulation*, an account of his tour of the United States earlier this year: "There was quite an excitement about town yesterday in reference to the new word by 'Boz.' The news boys did a smashing business in selling what it pleased them to call 'Dickinson's Works on Amerikey,' and Zieber, at the corner of Third and Dock streets, disposed of fifteen hundred extras of the 'New World,' containing this literary novelty, in the course of an hour."

11 NOVEMBER. Charles J. Peterson replies to a letter from John Tomlin in Jackson, Tennessee:

You ask me for a line of literary news. There is little afloat, and of that little the "Notes for General Circulation" contribute the chief topic. Boz has done as much justice to this country as we deserve, and quite as much as any dispassionate American would ask for. He has been as impartial as he could be considering the character of his mind, for while he notices details accurately he is not capable of comprehensive views, and his imagination, like a woman's, conquers his more reasoning faculties. . . . I didn't see Boz, but Poe did, and he said at the time that my estimate of Dickens' character was correct. You have great faith in Poe, and if you will read the "Notes" you will agree with me (published by Tomlin in *Holden's Dollar Magazine*, August 1849).

14 NOVEMBER. WASHINGTON. Thomas writes Poe, giving him "new hope" of a Custom House appointment (Poe's 19 November reply).

16 NOVEMBER. PHILADELPHIA. Poe writes James Russell Lowell in Boston:

Learning your design of commencing a Magazine [the *Pioneer*], in Boston, upon the first of January next, I take the liberty of asking whether some arrangement might not be made, by which I should become a regular contributor.

I should be glad to furnish a short article each month—of such character as might be suggested by yourself—and upon such terms as you could afford "in the beginning".

That your success will be marked and permanent I will not doubt. At all events, I most sincerely wish you well; for no man in America has excited in me so much of admiration—and, therefore, none so much of respect and esteem—as the author of "Rosaline" (*L*, 1:217).

17 NOVEMBER. The *National Forum* reports: "The following removals and appointments have been made in the Custom House. Removals—Peter B. Curry, Henry Schell, Robert Neal, J. Hullings, and Urban R. Titterville. Appointments—George Guthrie, Jesse Waln, Sandy Harris, and—Pogue" (cf. Poe to Thomas, 19 November).

17 NOVEMBER. LONDON. Charles Dickens writes the prominent publisher Edward Moxon, concerning a possible English edition of Poe's fiction: "Pray write me such a reply as I can send to the author of the volumes [*Tales of the Grotesque and Arabesque*] and to get absolution for my conscience in this matter" (Dickens, 3:375).

18 NOVEMBER. NEW YORK. The influential *Daily Tribune* reports the solution of the Mary Rogers mystery: the pretty "cigar girl" was not murdered, but had died during an illegal abortion (Walsh, pp. 55–56; Mabbott [1978], 3:719–20).

19 NOVEMBER. PHILADELPHIA. The *Spirit of the Times*, the *Daily Chronicle*, and the *Public Ledger* announce the solution of the Mary Rogers case, basing their reports on the account in yesterday's *Tribune*. The *North American* simply reprints this account:

The terrible mystery which for more than a year has hung over the fate of Mary Rogers, whose body was found, as our readers will well remember, in the North River, under circumstances such as convinced every one that she was the victim of hellish lust and then of murder, is at last explained—to the satisfaction we doubt not of all. It may be recollected that associated with the tale of her disappearance was the name of Mrs. Loss, the woman who kept the refreshment house nearest the scene of her death. About a week since, as we have already stated, this woman was accidentally wounded by the premature discharge of a gun in the hands of her son; the wound proved fatal; but before she died she sent for Justice Merritt, of New Jersey, and told him the following facts.

On the Sunday of Miss Rogers' disappearance she came to her house from this city in company with a young physician, who undertook to procure for her a premature delivery.

While in the hands of the physician she died, and a consultation was then held as to the disposal of her body. It was finally taken at night by the son of Mrs. Loss and sunk in the river where it was found. . . .

[These reports would have been unsettling to Poe, who believed that he had indicated Mary's murderer in "The Mystery of Marie Rogêt," then being serialized in Snowden's *Ladies' Companion*. Although the *Tribune's* account soon proved without foundation, Poe revised "Marie Rogêt" to accommodate the possibility of a bungled abortion before including it in the 1845 edition of his *Tales* (Walsh, pp. 69–73). On 4 January 1848 he wrote George W. Eveleth that Mary's death had resulted "from an attempt at abortion."]

19 NOVEMBER. Presumably disturbed by the new development in the Mary Rogers case, Poe calls on Thomas S. Smith in search of an occupation other than literature.

19 NOVEMBER. Poe writes Thomas in Washington:

Your letter of the 14th gave me new hope—only to be dashed to the ground. On the day of its receipt, some of the papers announced four removals and appointments. Among the latter I observed the name——Pogue. Upon inquiry among those behind the curtain, I soon found that no such person as——Pogue had any expectation of an appt and that the name was a misprint or rather a misunderstanding of the reporters, who had heard *my own* name spoken of at the Custom-House. I waited 2 days without calling upon Mr Smith, as he had twice told me that "he would send for me when he wished to swear me in." To-day, however, hearing nothing from him, I called. I asked him if he had no good news for me yet. He replied—"No, I am instructed to make no more removals." At this, being much astonished, I mentioned that I had heard, through a friend, from Mr Rob. Tyler, that he was requested to appoint me. At these words he said, roughly,—"From *whom* did you say?" I replied from Mr Robert Tyler. I wish you could have seen the scoundrel—for scoundrel, my Dear Thomas in your private ear, *he is*—"From *Robert* Tyler!" says he—"hem! I have received orders from *President* Tyler to make no more appts and shall make none." Immediately afterwards he acknowledged that he *had* made one appt *since* these instructions.

Poe describes three previous interviews in which Smith treated him "most shamefully"; but he has not been insulted so much as Thomas' friend Robert Tyler, who requested his appointment. "It seems to me that the only way to serve me *now*, is to lay the matter once again before Mr T. and, if possible, through him, to procure a few lines *from the President* directing Mr Smith to give me the place" (*L*, 2:699–701).

19 NOVEMBER. BOSTON. Lowell writes Poe: "Your letter [of 16 November] has given me great pleasure in two ways;—first, as it assures me of the friendship and approbation of almost the only *fearless* American critic, and second (to be Irish) since it contains your acquiescence to a request which I had already many times mentally preferred to you. Had you not written you would soon have heard from me." Lowell gives Poe *"carte blanche"* to contribute either prose or verse to the *Pioneer*, with a single exception: "namely I do not wish an article like that of yours on Dawes, who, although I think with you that he is a bad poet, has yet I doubt not tender feelings as a man which I should be chary of wounding. I think that I shall be hardest pushed for good stories (imaginative ones) & if you are inspired to anything of the kind I should be glad to get it." Although the magazine is already in press, "anything sent *'right away'* will be in season for the first number." Lowell offers Poe "$10 for every article at first" (*W*, 17:120–21).

19 NOVEMBER. NEW YORK. The *Morning Courier* publishes a letter from Justice Gilbert Merritt of Hudson County, New Jersey, who denies the report that Mary Rogers had died during an abortion: "I noticed a statement in the Tribune of this morning [18 November], relative to a confession said to have been made before me by the late Mrs. Loss, which is entirely incorrect, as no such examination took place, nor could it, from the deranged state of Mrs. Loss' mind" (Walsh, p. 56).

21 NOVEMBER. PHILADELPHIA. The *Spirit of the Times* reports that the article published in Friday's New York *Daily Tribune* has proven to be a hoax: "On Saturday last [19 November] an examination was held before a magistrate. The sons of Mrs. Loss, and a number of other persons were examined on oath, but nothing was elicited tending in the least to throw any light on the death of Mary C. Rogers."

BEFORE 27 NOVEMBER. LONDON. Edward Moxon replies to Dickens' 17 November letter: he is unable to publish Poe's tales (Dickens to Poe).

27 NOVEMBER. Dickens writes Poe:

I have never been able to find among my papers, since I came to England, the letter you wrote to me at New York. But I read it there, and think I am correct in believing that it charged me with no other mission than that which you had already entrusted to me by word of mouth. Believe me that it never, for a moment, escaped my recollection . . . .

I should have forwarded you the accompanying letter from Mr. Moxon before now, but that I have delayed doing so in the hope that some other channel for the publication of [y]our book on this side of the water would present itself to me. I am, however, unable to report any success. I have mentioned it to publishers with whom I have influence, but they have, one and all, declined the venture. And the only consolation I can give you is that I do not believe any collection of detached pieces by an unknown writer, even though he were an Englishman, would be at all likely to find a publisher in this metropolis just now (Dickens, 3:384–85).

DECEMBER. NEW YORK. Snowden's *Ladies' Companion* contains the second installment of Poe's "Mystery of Marie Rogêt."

EARLY DECEMBER? PHILADELPHIA. Poe submits his story "The Tell-Tale Heart" to the *Boston Miscellany* (Lowell to Poe, 17 December).

7 DECEMBER. AUGUSTA, GEORGIA. Chivers writes Poe: he has returned to his home state to receive his share of his father's estate. He gives his reactions to the death of his daughter, Allegra Florence Chivers, on 18 October: "Now my hope is dead—the beautiful saintly winged dove which soared so high from the earth—luring my impatient soul to wander, delighted, from prospect to prospect—has been wounded in her midway flight to heaven by the keen icy arrows of Death! . . . She was sick only two days—*sick* when I was not near to render her assistence! My God! there is a darkness gathering round [my] soul of the deepest sorrow, which the light of no future joy can ever illumine! . . . My little daughter of three years old—my blue eyed child—is gone!" (Chivers [1957], pp. 19–21).

10 DECEMBER. PHILADELPHIA. The *Saturday Museum*, a weekly newspaper edited and published by Poe's friend Thomas C. Clarke, issues its first number.

BEFORE 12 DECEMBER. BOSTON. Henry T. Tuckerman, the new editor of the *Boston Miscellany*, rejects "The Tell-Tale Heart," having the publishers Bradbury & Soden write the author: "if Mr Poe would condescend to furnish more quiet articles he would be a most desirable correspondent." Lowell obtains Poe's story for the *Pioneer* (Lowell to Poe, 17 December, and Poe's reply, 25 December).

12 DECEMBER. Lowell writes Charles J. Peterson. He is due money for a

contribution to *Graham's Magazine*; he requests that $10 of this sum be given to Poe as payment for "The Tell-Tale Heart" (Peterson's reply; Poe to Lowell, 4 February 1843).

15 DECEMBER. PHILADELPHIA. Peterson replies to Lowell: "As soon as your poem is in print I will pay Poe and take the receipt as you wish" (MH–H).

17 DECEMBER. BOSTON. Lowell writes Poe: "Your story of 'The Tell-Tale Heart' will appear in my first number. Mr. Tuckerman (perhaps your chapter on Autographs is to blame) would not print it in the Miscellany, & I was very glad to get it for myself. It may argue presumptuousness in me to dissent from his verdict. I should be glad to hear from you soon. You must send me another article, as my second number will soon go to press" (W, 17:125).

25 DECEMBER. PHILADELPHIA. Poe replies to Lowell, enclosing his poem "Lenore" for the second number of the *Pioneer*. He thanks Lowell for reversing Tuckerman's judgment: "Touching the 'Miscellany'—had I known of Mr T's accession, I should not have ventured to send an article. Should he, at any time, accept an effusion of mine, I should ask myself what twattle I had been perpetrating, so flat as to come within the scope of his approbation." Poe quotes a letter he received from the publishers which reflects Tuckerman's opinion of his story: "All I have to say is that if Mr T. persists in his *quietude*, he will put a quietus to the Magazine of which Mess. Bradbury & Soden have been so stupid as to give him control" (L, 1:220).

27 DECEMBER. Poe writes Lowell again, proposing a minor revision in the fourth stanza of "Lenore" (L, 1:221).

1842. John S. Detwiler, the son of Poe's next-door neighbor Benjamin Detwiler, recalls: "This property [Poe's residence in the Fairmount district] was owned in those days by a Mr. Michael Bouvier . . . who seemed to be [a] very warm friend of Mr. Poe, because both his wife and himself used to visit Mr. Poe and Mrs. Clem[m] . . . . Poe often visited the Wissahickon because he was a great lover of nature and fond of roving about the country . . . . Mr. Bouvier was a mahogany and marble merchant at 2d and Walnut streets" (Detwiler to E. C. Jellett, undated letter in Joseph Jackson Collection, PHi; cf. Phillips, 1:748–49).

[The Wissahiccon was a stream on the outskirts of Philadelphia which Poe described in his sketch "Morning on the Wissahiccon" (later entitled "The Elk").]

CA. 1842. George R. Graham recalls:

He [Poe] was quick, it is true, to perceive mere quacks in literature, and somewhat apt to be hasty when pestered with them; but upon most other questions his natural amiability was not easily disturbed. Upon a subject that he understood thoroughly, he felt some right to be positive, if not arrogant, when addressing pretenders. . . . Literature with him was religion; and he, its high-priest, with a whip of scorpions scourged the money-changers from the temple. In all else he had the docility and kind-heartedness of a child. . . .

I shall never forget how solicitous of the happiness of his wife and mother-in-law he was, whilst one of the editors of Graham's Magazine—his whole efforts seemed to be to procure the comfort and welfare of his home. Except for their happiness—and the natural ambition of having a magazine of his own—I never heard him deplore the want of wealth. The truth is, he cared little for money, and knew less of its value, for he seemed to have no personal expenses. What he received from me in regular monthly instalments, went directly into the hands of his mother-in-law . . . . His love for his wife was a sort of rapturous worship of the spirit of beauty which he felt was fading before his eyes. I have seen him hovering around her when she was ill, with all the fond fear and tender anxiety of a mother for her first-born—her slightest cough causing in him a shudder, a heart-chill that was visible. I rode out one summer evening with them, and the remembrance of his watchful eyes eagerly bent upon the slightest change of hue in that loved face, haunts me yet as the memory of a sad strain (Graham, p. 225).

CA. 1842. BALTIMORE. William Whitelock, a businessman, receives a presentation copy of *The Conchologist's First Book* from Professor Thomas Wyatt, who inscribes it "From the author." Whitelock recalls:

Turning to the title page, where Poe was so named, the Professor informed me he had prepared the work, but paid Poe $50 for the use of his name. This naturally led him to speak of the poet, whose neighbor he was in Philadelphia—the sickness of his wife, his pecuniary straits at times, and his assistance in enabling him to bridge these over. He alluded to him in the kindest manner, and while conceding to the poet a brilliant genius, attributed his troubles to a want of thrift and prudence in his domestic affairs (Baltimore *American*, 7 April 1881; see also Thomas [1978], pp. 951–54).

JAMES RUSSELL LOWELL
(from a daguerreotype taken in 1844)

CHAPTER SEVEN

"The Gold-Bug" and
"The Balloon-Hoax"

1843–1844

At the beginning of 1843 Poe reaches agreement with Thomas C. Clarke, a Philadelphia publisher, to issue his long-planned monthly journal, its proposed title now changed from the *Penn Magazine* to the *Stylus*. The 25 February issue of the *Saturday Museum*, Clarke's weekly newspaper, contains a biographical sketch of Poe accompanied by his portrait and copious extracts from his poetry; the article is reprinted in the 4 March issue. During the first week of March the United States Senate confirms Calvin Blythe as Collector of Customs in Philadelphia, to succeed Thomas S. Smith. On 8 March Poe hastily leaves for Washington in hopes of obtaining one of the Custom House appointments that Blythe will make. His visit is brought to an abrupt end by his excessive drinking, which alarms his friends Frederick William Thomas and Jesse E. Dow; the promised appointment never materializes. Around April the Poe family moves to a small house on North Seventh Street, in the Spring Garden district of Philadelphia. In May Clarke withdraws from the *Stylus* because of the financial difficulties besetting his *Saturday Museum*. Poe's fortunes improve in the following month, when "The Gold-Bug" receives the $100 first prize in a contest conducted by the *Dollar Newspaper*. The tale is immediately popular, being reprinted three times by the *Dollar Newspaper* and subsequently being dramatized at the Walnut Street Theatre. In July the magazine agent William H. Graham issues *The Prose Romances of Edgar A. Poe*, a pamphlet containing "The Murders in the Rue Morgue" and "The Man that was Used Up." In spite of the success of "The Gold-Bug" and the *Prose Romances*, Poe remains impoverished; on 13 September he is forced to write James Russell Lowell and request payment for his contributions to the defunct *Pioneer*. On 21 November Poe embarks on a new career, delivering his lecture on "American Poetry" before the William Wirt Institute. He later addresses audiences in Wilmington and Newark, Delaware, in Baltimore, and in Reading, Pennsylvania. The lecture is repeated in Philadelphia on 10 January 1844. On 6 April Poe and his wife Virginia move to New York City. A week later his "Balloon-Hoax," published anonymously in the *Sun*, temporarily fools New Yorkers into believing that the Atlantic has been crossed by voyagers in a balloon. During May and June Poe furnishes the New York correspondence, "Doings of Gotham," for the *Columbia Spy*, a weekly newspaper in Columbia, Pennsylvania. In October he finds employment as an assistant to Nathaniel P. Willis, editor of the *Evening Mirror*.

*

1843

*

JANUARY. BOSTON. The first number of the *Pioneer* contains Poe's story "The Tell-Tale Heart."

JANUARY. PHILADELPHIA. *Graham's Magazine* contains Poe's poem "The Conqueror Worm."

EARLY JANUARY? Poe enlists Thomas C. Clarke, publisher of the *Saturday Museum*, as his partner in issuing his long-planned magazine, now entitled the *Stylus* and scheduled to appear on 1 July (31 January contract; Poe to Thomas, 25 February).

EARLY JANUARY? Poe reviews the *Pioneer* in Clarke's *Museum*:

In these days of self-bepuffed and glorified magazines, it is positively refreshing to look upon a publication that comes to us modestly, promising nothing, but wearing on its face the stamp of intrinsic merit. We hail the PIONEER as the first in the great work of reform. But how could it be otherwise, edited as it is by a man whose genius and originality is at once the praise and wonder of his countrymen. We mean JAMES RUSSEL[L] LOWELL. . . .

The contributors are J. Russell Lowell, ("a man of men!")[,] Edgar Allan Poe, John Neal, who contributes an excellent article on Aaron Burr, with others whose names are known and respected by all true lovers of sound literature. The Reviews are good and just, with the sole exception of one, on Matthews' [*sic*] "Puffer Hopkins," a qualified puff when it should have been an unqualified condemnation: "Puffer Hopkins" being one of the most trashy novels that ever emanated from an American press (notice reprinted on inside back cover of February *Pioneer*).

EARLY JANUARY? Poe writes Frederick William Thomas in Washington, forwarding memoranda of his life. Poe will appear in the *Saturday Museum*'s forthcoming series entitled "The Poets & Poetry of Philadelphia," which will feature biographical sketches of the city's poets as well as excerpts from their poetry. He asks Thomas to write his biography for the series (Thomas' 1 February reply).

6 JANUARY. The *United States Gazette* reprints "The Tell-Tale Heart" from the *Pioneer*.

7 JANUARY. NEW YORK. Nathaniel P. Willis notices the *Pioneer* in the *Brother Jonathan*:

J. R. Lowell, a man of original and decided genius has started a monthly magazine in Boston. The first number lies before us, and it justifies our expectation, viz.:—that a man of genius, who is merely a man of genius, is a very unfit editor of a periodical. . . . In the first No. of the Pioneer are half a dozen articles which will fall still-born under the notice of the nineteen in twenty of the readers *who pay* for what they read, yet they are articles of a very refined and elevated character and will do the magazine credit with here and there a man of very refined taste—for example Mr. Dwight's article on Beethoven's Symphonies and Mr. Lowell's own paper on the "Plays of Middleton." Mr. Poe's contribution is very wild and very readable, and that is the only thing in the number that most people would read and remember.

13 JANUARY. Horace Greeley reviews the *Pioneer* in the *Daily Tribune*: "Poe contributes a strong and skilful, but to our minds overstrained and repulsive, analysis of the feelings and promptings of an insane homicide. The painting of the terror of the victim while he sat upright in his bed feeling that death was near him is most powerful and fearfully vivid."

19 JANUARY. RICHMOND. Thomas Willis White, the proprietor of the *Southern Literary Messenger*, dies after a long illness.

23 JANUARY. PHILADELPHIA. The *Pennsylvania Inquirer* and other papers report White's death.

25 JANUARY. "The Tell-Tale Heart" is reprinted in the first number of the *Dollar Newspaper*, an oversize weekly published by A. H. Simmons & Co.

28 JANUARY. The *Saturday Museum* contains Henry B. Hirst's blistering review of the third edition of Rufus W. Griswold's *Poets and Poetry of America*.

[Harrison reprinted this review in his Poe edition (*W*, 11:220–43); but it is unquestionably by Hirst, Poe's admirer and companion who repeated many of his opinions. See Thomas (1978), pp. 495–98.]

31 JANUARY. An agreement is reached "between Felix O. C. Darley, on the one hand and Thomas C. Clarke with Edgar A. Poe on the other." Darley,

a young Philadelphia artist, "agrees to furnish original designs, or drawings (on wood or paper as required) of his own composition, in his best manner, and from subjects supplied him by Mess: Clarke and Poe; the said designs to be employed in illustration of the Magazine entitled 'The Stylus' . . . . Mess: Clarke and Poe agree to demand of Mr Darley not more than five of these designs in any one month . . . . And, for each design so furnished, Mess: Clarke and Poe agree to pay the said Darley the sum of Seven Dollars ($7)." The contract, in Poe's hand, bears the signatures of the principals as well as two witnesses, Henry B. Hirst and W. D. Riebsam (facsimile in Gill, after p. 118).

LATE JANUARY. Poe writes Thomas in Washington. He imagines that Thomas has postponed correspondence while waiting for the United States Senate to act on Thomas S. Smith's nomination as Collector of Customs in Philadelphia. Poe asks whether Thomas will be able to write the biographical sketch he requested several weeks ago; if not, he should return the memoranda, as Poe's biography and poems are scheduled for early publication in the *Saturday Museum*. Although Hirst wrote the review of Griswold's *Poets and Poetry of America* in the 28 January *Museum*, Poe emphasizes that he was responsible for the portion condemning the anthologer's treatment of Thomas and Robert Tyler (Thomas' 1 February reply).

[Poe and Thomas were hoping that the Senate would reject Smith's nomination and that the Tyler administration would then replace him with a new Collector, who might be more willing to appoint Poe to a position in the Custom House.]

BEFORE FEBRUARY? Poe sits for a daguerreotype; apparently it is used in making the engraved portrait which is to accompany his biography in the *Museum* ("McKee" daguerreotype discussed by George E. Woodberry, *Century Magazine*, NS 26 [1894]: 725, 854; information supplied by Michael J. Deas, from his forthcoming book on Poe portraiture).

FEBRUARY. NEW YORK. Snowden's *Ladies' Companion* contains the third and final installment of Poe's "Mystery of Marie Rogêt."

FEBRUARY. BOSTON. The *Pioneer* contains Poe's poem "Lenore" and Nathaniel Hawthorne's humorous sketch of his contemporaries, "The Hall of Fantasy." Hawthorne describes Poe's standing among American literati: "Mr. Poe had gained ready admittance [into the Hall of Fantasy] for the sake of his imagination, but was threatened with ejectment, as belonging to the obnoxious class of critics."

1 FEBRUARY. WASHINGTON. Thomas replies to Poe:

You judged rightly I did not write to you waiting "for some definite action of Congress on Smith's case." I feel most anxious in the matter for you, my friend.

About the biography. I duly received your notes, and determined at the earliest hour to take it in hand. Congress is now, you know, in session, and my labors at the department are treble while it continues. Thrice I have set myself about writing out the notes and thrice I have been taken off. It would be a labor of love with me, Poe, as you know, and let who will do it now some of these days I will do it better unless they do it damned well. I could not do it until Congress adjourns, and not speedily then—I am so much occupied. Therefore [I] think it best to send you the MS. as you request, but I do it with regret. . . .

Yes, I saw the "Saturday's Museum" in Mr. Robert Tyler's room, and happened to light upon the article in which we are mentioned. I read that portion of it to him and shall take care that he is not misinformed on the subject. I remember Mr. Hirst (*W*, 17:128–29).

4 FEBRUARY. PHILADELPHIA. Poe writes Lowell, thanking him for forwarding the *Pioneer*:

As far as a $3 Magazine can please me at all, I am delighted with yours. I am especially gratified with what seems to me a certain coincidence of opinion & of taste, between yourself and your humble servant, in the minor arrangements, as well as in the more important details of the journal. For example—the poetry in the same type as the prose—the designs from [John] Flaxman—&c. As regards the contributors our thoughts are one. Do you know that when, some time since, I dreamed of establishing a Magazine of my own, I said to myself—"If I can but succeed in engaging, as permanent contributors, Mr Hawthorne, Mr Neal, and two others, with a certain young poet of Boston, who shall be nameless, I will engage to produce the best journal in America." At the same time, while I thought and still think highly of Mr Bryant, Mr Cooper, and others, I said nothing of *them*.

Poe received $10 on Lowell's account from George R. Graham: "I would prefer, however, that you would remit directly to myself through the P. Office." About two weeks ago he sent his "Notes Upon English Verse" to Lowell by Harnden's Express Company; if the article proves "too long, or perhaps too dull," for the *Pioneer*, he will be glad to "send something in its place" (*L*, 1:221–23).

11 FEBRUARY. BALTIMORE. Joseph Evans Snodgrass reviews the *Ladies' Companion* in the *Saturday Visiter*: "Mr. Poe's 'Mystery of Marie Roget,' founded on the murder of Mary Rogers, is concluded—and will add to his reputation for a *sui generis* play of imagination with an exercise of rare powers of analysis."

BEFORE 16 FEBRUARY. BOSTON. Robert Carter, Lowell's partner on the *Pioneer*, writes Poe. Lowell is suffering from a serious eye ailment and has gone to New York for treatment; Carter will edit the magazine in his absence (Poe's reply).

16 FEBRUARY. PHILADELPHIA. Poe writes Carter: "What you tell me about Mr Lowell's health, grieves me most sincerely—but we will hope for the best. Diseases of an opthalmic character, are, by no means, so intractable now, as they were a few years ago. When you write, remember me kindly to him." Poe transcribes his poem "Eulalie" for the fourth number of the *Pioneer* (*L*, 1:223).

CA. 18 FEBRUARY. Poe writes his friend Thomas Wyatt, now in Washington, enclosing a letter of introduction to Thomas (Poe to Thomas, 25 February).

BEFORE 22 FEBRUARY. *Graham's Magazine* for March contains Poe's "Our Amateur Poets, No. I.—Flaccus." He demolishes the poetic claims of Thomas Ward, a wealthy New Yorker who contributes to the *Knickerbocker Magazine* under the pseudonym "Flaccus."

22 FEBRUARY. John S. Du Solle reviews *Graham's* in the *Spirit of the Times*: "Poe's review of 'Flaccus' is really exquisite."

BEFORE 24 FEBRUARY. The *Saturday Museum* for 25 February contains "The Poets & Poetry of Philadelphia, No. II: Edgar Allan Poe." The article, apparently prepared by Poe in collaboration with Hirst, occupies the entire front page. It consists of a lengthy, often inaccurate biographical sketch accompanied by laudatory opinions on Poe's writings excerpted from newspapers and magazines, and from letters he received. The following poems, most of them revised, are reprinted: "To Helen," portions of "Al Aaraaf," "Sonnet—To Science," "Romance," "To the River———," "The Conqueror Worm," "Lenore," "Sonnet to Zante," "The Sleeper," "To One in Paradise" (formerly "To Ianthe in Heaven"), "Sonnet—Silence," "Israfel," "Song of the Newly-Wedded" (formerly "Ballad"), "To One Departed," "The Coliseum," and "The Haunted Palace."

On its fourth page the *Museum* carries a prospectus for the *Stylus*, written by Poe and signed "CLARKE & POE":

The Prospectus of a Monthly Journal to have been called "THE PENN MAGAZINE," has already been partially circulated. Circumstances, in which the public have no interest, induced a suspension of the project, which is now, under the best auspices, resumed, with no other modification than that of the title. "The Penn Magazine," it has been thought, was a name somewhat too local in its suggestions . . . .

"The Stylus" will include about one hundred royal octavo pages, in single column, per month; forming two thick volumes per year. . . . Engravings, when used, will be in the highest style of Art, but are promised only in obvious illustration of the text, and in strict keeping with the Magazine character. . . . As, for many reasons, it is inexpedient to commence a journal of this kind at any other period than the beginning or middle of the year, the first number of "The Stylus" will not be regularly issued until the first of July, 1843. . . . The price will be *Five Dollars* per annum, or *Three Dollar*s per single volume, in advance. Letters which concern only the Editorial management may be addressed to Edgar A. Poe, individually; all others to Clarke & Poe.

24 FEBRUARY. In the *Spirit of the Times* Du Solle comments: "The Saturday Museum of this week contains a very fair likeness of our friend Edgar A. Poe, Esq., with a full account of his truly eventful life. We look upon Mr. Poe as one of the most powerful, chaste, and erudite writers of the day, and it gives us pleasure to see him placed, through the public spirit of our neighbor of the Museum, in his proper position before the world." The *Daily Chronicle, Pennsylvania Inquirer*, and *United States Gazette* also praise the *Museum*'s article on Poe.

25 FEBRUARY. The *Pennsylvanian* reports: " 'THE PHILADELPHIA SATURDAY MUSEUM' of to-day . . . contains the second of a series of articles on 'The Poets and Poetry of Philadelphia,' giving a sketch of the life and writings of Edgar Allan Poe, accompanied by a portrait."

25 FEBRUARY. Poe writes Thomas in Washington:

Herewith I forward a "Saturday Museum" containing a Biography and carica-ture, both of myself. I am ugly enough God knows, but not *quite* so bad as that. The biographer is H. W. [Henry B.] Hirst, of this city. I put into his hands your package, as returned, and he has taken the liberty of stating his indebtedness for memoranda to yourself—a slight extension of the truth . . . .

On the outside of the paper you will see a Prospectus of "The Stylus"—my old "Penn" revived & remodelled under better auspices. I am anxious to hear your opinion of it. I have managed, *at last*, to secure, I think, the great object—a partner possessing ample capital, and, at the same time, so little self-esteem, as to allow me entire control of the editorial conduct. He gives me, also, a half interest, and is to furnish funds for all the business operations—I agreeing to supply, for the first year, the literary matter. This will puzzle me no little, but I must do my best—write as much as possible myself, under my own name and pseudonyms, and hope for the casual aid of my friends, until the first stage of infancy is surpassed.

Poe asks Thomas to furnish an article for his opening number and to solicit contributions from Robert Tyler and Judge Abel Parker Upshur, the new Secretary of the Navy. "About a week since I enclosed an introductory

Poe's biography in the *Saturday Museum*, 25 February
(printer's copy, somewhat mutilated)

Poe Museum of the Poe Foundation, Inc.

400

letter to yourself in one to a friend of mine (Professor Wyatt) now in Washington. I presume you have seen him" (*L*, 1:223–25).

25 FEBRUARY. NEW YORK. James Kirke Paulding writes Rufus W. Griswold, editor of *Graham's Magazine*:.

I observe in your last number the commencement of what seems to be a series of numbers, on our American Poets. A critical analysis of our Poetry, given with proper judgement, taste, and temper would be not only interesting but useful; and Mr. Poe has I Know both the two first, but certainly has not given a good sample of the last in his notice of Mr Ward. I Know nothing of that Gentleman, but have read his little collection, and am of opinion it does not merit the—I will not dignify them with the honors of severity—but the scurrilous strictures bestowed on them by Mr. Poe. Such articles will do no credit to your Magazine, and make many deadly enemies, among a race proverbial for their irritability. If he continues this Series, I would advise you to "Restrain and aggravate his choler," as Nic Bottom says—or he will bring a Nest of Hornets about your Ears. Let Mr. Poe proceed coolly, impartially & dispassionately, and I am of opinion there are few, if any, writers among us more capable of doing justice to the subject. I have formerly seen some criticisms of his on poetical productions, equally distinguished by profound analysis, and cultivated Taste (PHi; Paulding, pp. 329–30).

BEFORE MARCH? PHILADELPHIA. Poe writes a member of the Mackenzie family in Richmond, probably John Mackenzie. He asks his correspondent to determine whether the "subscription list" of the *Southern Literary Messenger* is for sale: "A capitalist of this place [Clarke] is anxious to purchase, if possible, and, as I am interested, I will take it as a *very* great favor if you will make the necessary inquiries . . . . Virginia is nearly recovered—indeed I may say quite so—with the exception of a slight cough . . . . Tell Rose [Rosalie Poe] I hope to see her before long, and that I will write her soon" (manuscript fragment in TxU–HRCL).

[The letter was mutilated in such a way that the date and the correspondent's first name were removed. Ostrom reconstructed the name as "[Willia]m Mackenzie" (*L*, 1:233); a more plausible reading would be "[Joh]n Mackenzie." The elder William Mackenzie died on 7 June 1829; William Leslie Mackenzie, one of his sons, died on 5 June 1834 (Mackenzie Family Bible, ViHi).]

BEFORE MARCH? RICHMOND. Thomas Mackenzie, one of John Mackenzie's younger brothers, writes Poe that the heirs of Thomas Willis White have not yet decided upon a disposition for the *Messenger* (Poe to Thomas Mackenzie, 22 April).

MARCH. BOSTON. The *Pioneer* ceases publication because of financial difficulties; the third and final number contains Poe's "Notes Upon English Verse."

1 MARCH. JACKSON, TENNESSEE. John Tomlin writes Poe: "Since the death of Mr. White of the 'Literary Messenger,' I have often thought if you would take charge of it, what a great Journal it would become, under your conduct and supervision. With you at the head of the 'Messenger,' and Simms of the 'Magnolia' (my two most valued friends), we of the South would then have a pride in talking about our Periodical Literature" (*W*, 17:133).

BEFORE 3 MARCH. PHILADELPHIA. The *Saturday Museum* for 4 March features Poe's biography and poems on its first page, reprinted from the 25 February issue. Poe's prospectus for the *Stylus* appears on the third page. On the second page Thomas C. Clarke quotes Du Solle's report from the 24 February *Spirit of the Times*, commenting:

We are glad to hear so good a paper as the Times speak thus highly of Mr. Poe, not only from the justice which it renders that powerful writer, but because we have been so fortunate as to secure his services as assistant Editor of the Saturday Museum. We have the pleasure of announcing this week, this association, from which our paper cannot fail to reap the most brilliant advantages. . . .

So great was the interest excited by the Biography and Poems of Mr. Poe, published in the Museum of last week, that to supply those who were disappointed in obtaining copies, we shall be at the expense of an extra Museum, in which the whole article will be re-printed, with corrections and additions. Of this extra we shall publish an edition on fine white paper. It will be ready for delivery at this office on Saturday morning.

[Notwithstanding Clarke's announcement, Poe never officially joined the *Museum* staff (cf. Poe to Lowell, 27 March).]

3 MARCH. The *Pennsylvania Inquirer* reviews this week's *Museum*: "E. A. Poe, Esq. is now associated in the editorial department. This is an important acquisition, Mr. Poe being an able and spirited writer, a profound critic, and well calculated to add interest to the columns of the Museum." The *United States Gazette* also welcomes Poe's editorship: "His new position will afford another field for the exercise of his fine talents."

4 MARCH. The *Pennsylvanian* and the *Spirit of the Times* notice the *Museum*, both papers praising the announcement of Poe's editorship.

4 MARCH. Samuel D. Patterson replaces Charles J. Peterson as one of the editors and proprietors of the *Saturday Evening Post*. The name of the firm

is changed from "George R. Graham & Co." to "Samuel D. Patterson & Co."

6 MARCH. WASHINGTON. The *Daily Madisonian* reports that on Friday, 3 March, the United States Senate rejected the nomination of Thomas S. Smith as Collector of Customs in Philadelphia. Judge Calvin Blythe has been confirmed in his place.

6 MARCH. PHILADELPHIA. Du Solle comments in the *Spirit of the Times*: "The appointment of Hon. Calvin Blythe is everything we could wish. He is honest, capable, Democratic and popular. He was Collector under Van Buren, and the post was never filled to greater advantage, than on that occasion. . . . Shocking long faces at the Custom House on Saturday. Strange! The officers there should look happy. Don't they all intend to be *Blythe* as possible?"

[Blythe's confirmation was believed to signal another round of removals and appointments in the Custom House. Poe made a hasty trip to Washington in hopes of securing one of the anticipated vacancies.]

7 MARCH. Poe writes Robert Carter in Boston: "Could you do me a *very* great favor? I am obliged to go on to Washington on Saturday morning— this is Tuesday—and am in sad need of means. I believe there is due me from 'The Pioneer' $30, and if you could, by any management, send me the amount so as to reach me, here, by that period, I would feel myself under deep obligation. If you cannot spare 30$ I would be exceedingly glad of $20" (*L*, 1:225–26).

8 MARCH. WASHINGTON. Poe leaves Philadelphia in the morning and travels to Washington, taking lodgings in the evening at Fuller's City Hotel, where his friend Thomas rooms, on the north side of Pennsylvania Avenue between Fourteenth and Fifteenth Streets.

8 MARCH. Thomas addresses a letter of introduction to Robert Tyler at the White House:

This will be handed to you by my friend, Poe, of Philadelphia, who is anxious to know the author of "Ahasuerus."

I would have presented Poe in person to you, but I have been confined to my bed for the last week with congestive fever, and am covered all over with the marks of cupping and blistering and am not able to go out, though I am convalescing.—When you are down town do call and see me—I feel as lonely as a cat in a strange garret (MB–G; see also Thomas [1978], pp. 526–27).

8 MARCH. "On the first evening" Poe is "over-persuaded to take some Port wine" and seems to be "somewhat excited." On the next day, 9 March, he avoids excessive drinking, keeping "pretty steady" (J. E. Dow to Clarke, 12 March).

9 MARCH. PHILADELPHIA. The *Spirit of the Times* reports: "There are over twelve hundred applicants for situations in the Custom House, under the new Collector already."

9 MARCH. WASHINGTON. At Fuller's Hotel in the morning, Poe writes the scientist John Kirk Townsend, a leading contributor to Clarke's *Saturday Museum*: "I have the honor to enclose two letters, and the bearer will deliver a case containing an air-gun." Poe promises to call on Townsend in "a day or two" (Thomas [1978], pp. 527–28).

CA. 10 MARCH. Poe begins to drink excessively; "at intervals" he becomes "quite unreliable" (Dow to Clarke, 12 March).

CA. 10 MARCH. The musician and journalist John Hill Hewitt encounters Poe on Pennsylvania Avenue: "He [Poe] was then *un homme blasée*—seedy in his appearance and woe-begone. He came boldly up to me, and, offering me his hand, which I willingly took, asked me if I would forget the past. He said he had not had a mouthful of food since the day previous, and begged me to lend him fifty cents to obtain a meal. Though he looked the used-up man all over—still he showed the gentleman. I gave him the money—and I never saw him afterwards" (Hewitt [1949], p. 19; cf. [1877], p. 43).

CA. 10 MARCH? Perhaps Poe is introduced to the photographer Mathew B. Brady (Mabbott [1969], 1:353).

11 MARCH. BALTIMORE. In the *Saturday Visiter* Snodgrass comments:

EDGAR ALLAN POE.—A late number of the Philadelphia Museum, contains a long biographical sketch of this far famed writer, accompanied by a portrait, which is perhaps as good as a wood-cut could make it—but not very truthful we think. We observe that the proprietors of the Museum, intend to unite with Mr. Poe, in the establishment of a new magazine to be called *The Stylus*. We have seen the design of the title page—which represents a hand inscribing the greek [*sic*] of *truth*, with a *stylus*. The form of the work, will be a large *octavo* of single column.—The text will be illustrated by one of the best artists.

Snodgrass predicts that the *Stylus* "will make a sensation" when it appears: "True criticism we need much—and of true criticism Poe has proved himself the only master in the land."

11 MARCH. WASHINGTON. Poe writes Clarke in Philadelphia:

I write merely to inform you of my will-doing [sic]—for, so far, I have done nothing. My friend Thomas, upon whom I depended, is sick. I suppose he will be well in a few days. In the meantime, I shall have to do the best I can. I have not seen the President yet.

My expenses were more than I thought they would be, although I have economised in every respect, and this *delay* (Thomas' being sick) puts me out sadly. *However* all is going right. I have got the subscriptions of *all* the Departments—President, [illegible] &c[.] I believe that I am making a *sensation* which will tend to the benefit of the Magazine.

Day [after] to-morrow I am to lecture.

Rob. Tyler is to give me an article—also Upsher [Upshur].

Send me $10 by mail, as soon as you get this. I am grieved to ask you for money, in this way.—but you will find your account in it—twice over (facsimile in Gill, after p. 120).

CA. 12 MARCH. Poe's behavior is adversely affected by excessive drinking. He displays "petulance" toward Thomas and occasions "vexation" to Jesse E. Dow's wife Eliza. At a social gathering at Fuller's Hotel, Poe becomes drunk from the proprietor's port wine. While intoxicated he makes fun of Thomas Dunn English, a Philadelphia supporter of the Tyler administration who is visiting Washington on political business (Poe to Thomas and Dow, 16 March; see also Gravely, pp. 352–54).

[Thomas later recalled: "I was confined to my room by sickness when Poe came to Washington early in 1843. He was sober when I saw him, but afterward in the company of old friends he drank to excess. My physician attended him for several days, and he suffered much from his indiscretion" (quoted by Whitty [1911], p. xlvii).]

12 MARCH. Jesse E. Dow writes Clarke in Philadelphia:

He [Poe] arrived here a few days since. On the first evening he seemed some-what excited, having been over-persuaded to take some Port wine.

On the second day he kept pretty steady, but since then he has been, at intervals, quite unreliable.

He exposes himself here to those who may injure him very much with the President, and thus prevents us from doing for him what we wish to do and what we can do if he is himself again in Philadelphia. He does not understand the ways of politicians, nor the manner of dealing with them to advantage. How should he?

Mr. Thomas is not well and cannot go home with Mr. P. My business and the health of my family will prevent me from so doing.

Under all the circumstances of the case, I think it advisable for you to come on and see him safely back to his home. Mrs. Poe is in a bad state of health, and I charge you, as you have a soul to be saved, to say not one word to her about him until he arrives with you. I shall expect you or an answer to this letter by return of mail.

Should you not come, we will see him on board the cars bound to Phila., but we fear he might be detained in Baltimore and not be out of harm's way (Gill, pp. 120–22).

CA. 14 MARCH. PHILADELPHIA. Clarke replies to Dow (Poe to Thomas and Dow, 16 March).

15 MARCH. Poe leaves Washington in the morning; he arrives in Philadelphia around 4:30 PM, finding Mrs. Clemm waiting for him at the train station. In the evening he visits Clarke at his residence, 56 South Twelfth Street (Poe to Thomas and Dow).

[Poe was understandably worried about the impression that his partner on the *Stylus* received from Dow's letter. Clarke's editorials in the *Saturday Museum* reveal him to have been a staunch temperance advocate. His daughter Anne E. C. Clarke recalled that "he never drank liquor nor used tobacco" (Sartain, p. 217).]

16 MARCH. Poe sends a single letter to Thomas and Dow, describing his return trip to Philadelphia yesterday. After "a warm bath & supper" he called on Clarke:

I never saw a man in my life more surprised to see another. He thought by Dow's epistle that I must not only be dead but buried & would as soon have thought of seeing his great-great-great grandmother. He received me, therefore, very cordially & made light of the matter. I told him what had been agreed upon—that I was a little sick & that Dow, knowing I had been, in times passed, given to spreeing upon an extensive scale, had become unduly alarmed &c&c.—that when I found he had written I thought it best to come home. . . .

Clarke, it appears, wrote to Dow, who must have received the letter this morning. Please re-inclose the letter to me, here—so that I may know how to guide myself.

Poe has not yet received the payment for his *Pioneer* contributions he requested in his 7 March letter to Robert Carter: "Immediately upon receipt of it, or before, I will forward the money you were both so kind as to lend—which is 8 to Dow—and 3 1/2 to Thomas." Poe addresses a paragraph to Dow alone: "My dear fellow—Thank you a thousand times for your kindness & great forbearance, and don't say a word about the cloak turned inside out, or other peccadilloes of that nature. Also, express to your wife my deep regret for the vexation I must have occasioned her." He similarly addresses his other correspondent:

And this is for Thomas. My dear friend. Forgive me my petulance & don't believe I think all I said. Believe me I am very grateful to you for your many attentions &

forbearances—and the time will never come when I shall forget either them or you. Remember me most kindly to Dr Lacey—also to the Don [Thomas Dunn English], whose mustachios I *do* admire after all, and who has about the finest figure I ever beheld—also to Dr Frailey. Please express my regret to Mr Fuller for making such a fool of myself in his house, and say to him (if you think it necessary) that I should not have got half so drunk on his excellent Port wine but for the rummy coffee with which I was forced to wash it down.

Poe promises to join the Washingtonians, a national temperance society, if Robert Tyler can obtain "the Inspectorship" for him (*L*, 1:228–30; see also Quinn and Hart, pp. 16–18).

16 MARCH. The *Spirit of the Times* reports that yesterday Calvin Blythe assumed his duties as the new Collector of Customs: "No removals have taken place as yet, though a great number we believe are in contempla-tion. . . . In the meantime the Custom House is beset with an army of eager applicants for office, and name after name is diligently sought after to append to petitions and recommendations. All this indicates the hard-ness of the times. Thousands of men are ready and anxious to take a public office now, who, in ordinary times, would rather trust to their own inde-pendent exertions for a living."

24 MARCH. Poe writes Peter D. Bernard, the son-in-law of Thomas W. White, in Richmond. He is forwarding an issue of the *Saturday Museum* containing a prospectus of the *Stylus*, a magazine which he intends to begin "in connexion with Mr Thomas C. Clarke" on 1 July: "My object in addressing you is to ascertain if the list [of subscribers] of 'The South: Lit: Messenger' is to be disposed of, and, if so, upon what terms. We are anxious to purchase the list and unite it with that of 'The Stylus,' provided a suitable arrangement could be made" (*L*, 1:230–31).

24 MARCH. BOSTON. Lowell writes Poe, promising to pay him for his contributions to the *Pioneer* as soon as possible:. "The magazine was started on my own responsibility, & I relied on the payments I should receive from my publishers to keep me even with my creditors until the Magazine should be firmly established. You may conceive my distress when the very first note given me by my publishers has been protested for nonpayment, & the magazine ruined. For I was unable to go on any farther, having already incurred a debt of $1,800 or more." Lowell is now making arrange-ments to borrow money to cover his debts. "The loss of my eyes at this juncture (for I am as yet unable to use them to any extent) adds to my distress" (*W*, 17:138–39).

25 MARCH. The *Saturday Museum* contains Poe's "Original Conundrums" (Mabbott [1943], pp. 328–29).

27 MARCH. WASHINGTON. Thomas replies to Poe's 16 March letter: "I would have answered it immediately, but my desk got so behindhand, during my illness when you were here, that every moment of my time has been engaged in bringing it up." He hopes that Poe will yet receive a position in the Custom House:

I cannot leave the office at present to see Robert Tyler, as you suggest, to get a line from him. But this I can tell you that the President, yesterday, asked me many questions about you, and spoke of you kindly. John Tyler, who was by, told the President that he wished he would give you an office in Philadelphia, and before he could reply a servant entered and called him out. John had heard of your frolic from a man who saw you in it, but I made light of the matter when he mentioned it to me; and he seemed to think nothing of it himself. He seems to feel a deep interest in you. Robert was not by. I feel satisfied that I can get you something from his pen for your Magazine (W, 17:140–41).

27 MARCH. PHILADELPHIA. Poe replies to Lowell's 24 March letter: "As for the few dollars you owe me—give yourself not one moment's concern about *them*. I am poor, but must be very much poorer, indeed, when I even think of demanding them." He hopes that Lowell has overestimated his financial difficulties and will be able to continue the *Pioneer*: "I have looked upon your Magazine, from its outset, as the best in America, and have lost no opportunity of expressing the opinion. Herewith I send a paper, 'The Phil: Sat. Museum', in which I have said a few words on the topic." Poe is not editing the *Museum*, "although an announcement was prematurely made to that effect," but has the privilege of inserting what he likes. He hopes to begin the *Stylus* on 1 July: "I am anxious to get a poem from yourself for the opening number, but, until you recover your health, I fear that I should be wrong in making the request. . . . When you find yourself in condition to write, I would be indebted to you if you could put me in the way of procuring a brief article (also for my opening number) from Mr Hawthorne—whom I believe you know personally. . . . You will see by the Prospectus that we intend to give a series of portraits of the American literati, with critical sketches. . . . Could you put me in possession of any likeness of yourself?—or could you do me the same favor in regard to Mr Hawthorne?" (L, 1:231–33).

28 MARCH. The *Spirit of the Times* reprints Poe's "Original Conundrums" from the *Saturday Museum* of 25 March.

29 MARCH. The *Dollar Newspaper* announces a literary contest, offering $100 for the best story submitted. The announcement is repeated in the 5 April issue (cf. Phillips, 1:793).

AFTER 29 MARCH. Poe retrieves his unpublished tale "The Gold-Bug" from George R. Graham, who had purchased it for $52, and enters it in the *Dollar Newspaper* contest (Poe to Graham, 10 March 1845).

30 MARCH. The *Spirit of the Times* reports: "The Dollar Newspaper offers $200 premiums for first-rate tales."

31 MARCH. BALTIMORE. The *Sun* reports:

PRIZES.—*Important to Literary Writers—Very Liberal Offers and No Humbug.*—We perceive by an advertisement in the last number of the Philadelphia Dollar Newspaper, that the publishers have come out with an offer of $200 for the three best stories that shall be furnished them by the first day of June next. One hundred for the best, sixty for the second, and forty for the third best. The only conditions imposed upon the writers, are that the subjects of the stories shall be American, and that they shall not be less than a certain length. This exhibits a liberality rarely met with among the publishers of our weekly sheets.

[The *Sun* was published by A. H. Simmons & Co., the same firm that issued the *Dollar Newspaper* and the *Public Ledger* in Philadelphia.]

31 MARCH. WASHINGTON. Robert Tyler writes Poe: "I have received your letter in which you express your belief that Judge Blythe would appoint you to a situation in the Custom House provided you have a reiteration of my former recommendation of you. It gives me pleasure to say to you that it would gratify me very sensibly, to see you appointed by Judge Blythe. I am satisfied that no one is more competent, or would be more satisfactory in the discharge of any duty connected with the office" (*W*, 17:141).

CA. APRIL? PHILADELPHIA. The Poe family rents a small house at 234 North Seventh Street (now numbered 530) in the Spring Garden district, then a largely undeveloped suburb north of the city proper. Their landlord is William M. Alburger, a wealthy plumber.

CA. APRIL? The novelist Mayne Reid recalls:

When I first became acquainted with Poe he was living in a suburban district of Philadelphia, called "Spring Garden." . . . It was then a quiet residential neighborhood, noted as the chosen quarter of the Quakers.

Poe was no Quaker; but, I remember well, he was next-door neighbor to one. And in this wise: that while the wealthy co-religionist of William Penn dwelt in a splendid four-story house, built of the beautiful coral-colored bricks for which Philadelphia is celebrated, the poet lived in a lean-to of three rooms, (there may have been a garret with a closet,) of painted plank construction, supported against the gable of the more pretentious dwelling. . . .

In this humble domicile I can say, that I have spent some of the pleasantest hours of my life—certainly some of the most intellectual. They were passed in the company of the poet himself, and his wife—a lady angelically beautiful in person and not less beautiful in spirit. . . . I remember how we, the friends of the poet, used to talk of her high qualities. And when we talked of her beauty, I well knew that the rose-tint upon her cheek was too bright, too pure to be of Earth. It was consumption's color—that sadly beautiful light that beckons to an early tomb.

In the little lean-to, besides the poet and his interesting wife, there was but one other dweller. This was a woman of middle age, and almost masculine aspect. She had the size and figure of a man, with a countenance that, at first sight, seemed scarce feminine. A stranger would have been incredulous—surprised, as I was, when introduced to her as the mother of that angelic creature who had accepted Edgar Poe as the partner of her life.

Such was the relationship; and when you came to know this woman better, the masculinity of her person disappeared before the truly feminine nature of her mind . . . . She was the ever-vigilant guardian of the house, watching it against the silent but continuous sap of necessity, that appeared every day to be approaching closer and nearer. She was the sole servant, keeping every thing clean; the sole messenger, doing the errands, making pilgrimages between the poet and his publishers, frequently bringing back such chilling responses as "The article not accepted," or, "The check not to be given until such and such a day"—often too late for his necessities (Reid, pp. 305–08).

1 APRIL. The *Saturday Museum* contains Poe's tale "The Conversation of Eiros and Charmion," reprinted under the heading "The Destruction of the World," and a second installment of his "Original Conundrums." An editorial by Poe on the second page calls attention to his story on the first:

The views embodied in this conversation are in strict accordance with philosophical speculation. The danger to be apprehended from collision with a comet is, to be sure, very little, and, from the gaseous nature of these erratic bodies, it has been contended that even actual contact would not have a fatal result; but the purport of the article in question seems to be the suggestion of a mode in which, through the cometary influence, the destruction of the earth might be brought about, and brought about in accordance with Prophecy.

From the celestial visitant now present [the comet of 1843], we have, of course, nothing to fear. It is now receding from the earth with a rapidity absolutely inconceivable, and, in a very short period, will be lost, and perhaps forever, to human eyes. But it came unheralded, and to-morrow its counterpart, or some wonder even more startling, *may* make its appearance. A firm reliance upon the wisdom and goodness of the Deity is by no means inconsistent with a due sense of the manifold and multiform perils by which we are so fearfully environed.

8 APRIL. NEW YORK. George P. Morris and Nathaniel P. Willis issue the first number of their *New Mirror*, a revival of the old *New-York Mirror*, which had expired in December 1842.

17 APRIL. BOSTON. Lowell replies to Poe's 27 March letter. Hawthorne has agreed to contribute to the *Stylus* and will forward an article in a week or two: "His terms are $5 a page, but probably, as your pages will 'eat up' Copy with a less anaconda-like appetite than the fine print magazines, your best plan would be to pay him so much by the article. His wife will make a drawing of his head or he will have a Daguerreotype taken, so that you can have a likeness of him." Lowell discusses a likeness of himself which Poe might use for the series on American authors to be published in the *Stylus*: "[William] Page has painted a head of me which is called very fine, & which is now Exhibiting (I believe) at the National Academy in New York. This might be Daguerreotyped—or I might have one taken from my head as it is now—namely in a more civilized condition—the portrait by Page having *very* long hair, not to mention a beard and some symptoms of moustache, & looking altogether, perhaps, too antique to be palatable to the gentle public" (*W*, 17:142–43).

BEFORE 22 APRIL? PHILADELPHIA. Poe writes his sister Rosalie in Richmond, discussing Virginia's health (implied by Poe to John Mackenzie, before March, and to Thomas Mackenzie, 22 April).

22 APRIL. Poe writes Thomas Mackenzie in Richmond: "About a fortnight ago [on 24 March], I wrote to Peter D. Bernard, who married one of T. W. White's daughters, and made inquiry about 'The Southern Literary Messenger', but have received no reply. . . . You wrote me, some time ago, that the heirs had not made up their minds respecting it." Poe requests that Mackenzie call upon Bernard, "or upon some one of the other heirs," and inquire about the *Messenger's* subscription list: "If the list is for sale I would make arrangements for its immediate purchase upon terms which would be fully satisfactory to the heirs. But do not let them suppose I am *too* anxious. By the bye, there may be some prejudice, on the part of the heirs, against me individually, on account of my quitting White—suppose, then, you get some one of your friends to negotiate for you and don't let me be known in the business at all. . . . Tell Rose that Virginia is much better, toe and all, & that she has been out lately, several times, taking long walks" (*L*, 2:702–03).

29 APRIL. BOSTON. In the *Boston Notion* Robert Carter publishes an abridgment of the *Saturday Museum* biography of Poe, quoting as well a long excerpt from his prospectus for the *Stylus* (Pollin [1969], pp. 585–89).

8 MAY. CAMBRIDGE, MASSACHUSETTS. Lowell writes Poe: "I have been

delaying to write to you from day to day in the expectation that I should have received an article from Hawthorne to send with my letter." Hawthorne has not yet furnished the promised contribution for the *Stylus*: "I have got the idea of Hawthorne's article so fixed in my mind that I forgot that I did not send you a poem in my last. I have such a reluctance to go into the city that though I have been here nearly three weeks I have not even brought out my MSS. yet. But I mean to do it in a day or two & shall then send you something which I hope will be to your liking." Lowell thanks Poe for forwarding a copy of the *Saturday Museum* with his biography and poetry: "Your early poems display a maturity which astonished me & I recollect no individual (& I believe I have all the poetry that was ever written) whose early poems were anything like as good. Shelley is nearest, perhaps" (*W*, 17:143–44).

BEFORE 15 MAY? PHILADELPHIA. Thomas C. Clarke withdraws his support from the *Stylus* (Poe to Lowell, 20 June).

[While Clarke may have felt uncomfortable with Poe's drinking, his decision was almost certainly prompted by the facts that his *Saturday Museum* was encountering financial difficulties and that his publishing experience had been limited to "family newspapers," inexpensive and innocuous weeklies intended for mass circulation. See Thomas (1978), pp. 558–59, 624–27.]

BEFORE 15 MAY. Poe sends a despondent letter to his Georgia cousin William Poe, describing "many recent reverses" (William's 16 June letter).

15 MAY. BALTIMORE? William Poe replies to Poe, admonishing him (William's 16 June letter).

16 MAY. BOSTON. Lowell writes Poe: "I send you this little poem with some fears that you will be disappointed therein. But it is on the whole the most likely to please of any that I could lay my hands on . . . . You must tell me frankly how you like what I sent & what you should like better. Will you give me your address more particularly so that in case I have a package to send you I can forward it by express?" (*W*, 17:144–45).

20 MAY. PHILADELPHIA. Lambert A. Wilmer writes John Tomlin in Jackson, Tennessee: "Edgar A. Poe (you know him by character, no doubt, if not personally), has become one of the strangest of our literati. He and I are old friends,—have known each other since boyhood, and it gives me inexpressible pain to notice the vagaries to which he has lately become subject. Poor fellow! he is not a teetotaller by any means, and I fear he is

going headlong to destruction, moral, physical and intellectual" (Quinn, pp. 401–02).

31 MAY. In the *Citizen Soldier*, a weekly of limited circulation, George Lippard commences "The Spermaceti Papers," his satires aimed at Graham, Griswold, Peterson, and other literati connected with the editorship of *Graham's Magazine* and the *Saturday Evening Post*.

LATE MAY? The *Saturday Museum* carries Clarke's announcement that he cannot publish the *Stylus* (Tomlin to Poe, 2 July).

LATE MAY? CONCORD, MASSACHUSETTS. Hawthorne writes Lowell:

I am greatly troubled about that contribution for Mr. Poe. Hitherto, I have never been accustomed to write during summer weather; and now I find that my thoughts fly out of the open window, and will not be enticed back again. I am compelled, indeed, to write a monthly article for the Democratic [Review], but it is with great pain and dolor, and only by the utmost force of self-compulsion. If I am to send anything to Mr. Poe, I should wish it to be worth his reception; but I am conscious of no power to produce anything good, at present. When you write to him, do make my apologies, and tell him that I have no more brains than a cabbage—which is absolutely true. He shall hear from me after the first frost— possibly sooner (NN–B).

JUNE OR BEFORE. PHILADELPHIA. Felix O. C. Darley recalls Poe:

He [Poe] impressed me as a refined and very gentlemanly man; exceedingly neat in his person; interesting always, from the intellectual character of his mind, which appeared to me to be tinged with sadness. His manner was quiet and reserved; he rarely smiled. I remember his reading his "Gold Bug" and "Black Cat" to me before they were published. The form of his manuscript was peculiar: he wrote on half sheets of note paper, which he pasted together at the ends, making one continuous piece, which he rolled up tightly. As he read he dropped it upon the floor. It was very neatly written, and without corrections, apparently (Darley quoted by Woodberry, 2:2–3).

JUNE OR BEFORE. OAKY GROVE, GEORGIA. Thomas Holley Chivers writes Poe (Chivers to Poe, 15 June 1844).

JUNE. CHARLESTON, SOUTH CAROLINA. In the *Magnolia* William Gilmore Simms reports that Poe will soon establish a new magazine called the *Stylus*: "Mr. Poe is well calculated to conduct a literary magazine. He is acknowledged as one of our best writers and critics. If any fault is to be found with him, it is in the latter capacity. He is, we fancy, not unfrequently tempted into the utterance of a smart thing, without troubling himself to ask if it be a just one. But the error may well find its excuse, in a day of such lamentable magazine puffery as the present." The *Magnolia* also contains a notice of Mrs. Caroline Lee Hentz written by the Alabama author Alexander Beaufort Meek, who favorably mentions Poe in passing.

BEFORE 10 JUNE. PHILADELPHIA. Thomas Dunn English completes *The Doom of the Drinker*, a temperance novel commissioned by Clarke for his *Saturday Museum*. The novel contains a malicious caricature of Poe under the influence of alcohol (Thomas [1979], pp. 259–60).

10 JUNE. In the *Museum* Clarke announces that the serialization of English's novel has been postponed: "The DRUNKARD'S DOOM, it would have afforded us great pleasure to have commenced with this No., but the sickness of Mr. R. S. Gilbert, who is to furnish the engravings from Mr. Darley's admirable designs [illustrating the novel], has prevented our opening the work in season."

14 JUNE. The *Dollar Newspaper* carries an announcement by the publishers:

Early after the first of June, we placed in the hands of the "Committee of Decision" all the stories which had reached us pursuant to our offer of premiums, and hoped to be able in the present number of our paper to publish their award, announcing all the premiums. The temporary indisposition of one of the Committee, and the necessary absence of another from town for a few days, have precluded them from concluding their labours as they expected. They have not, however, been idle, and inform us that they have gone over all the stories presented to them, and have awarded the *first prize* of ONE HUNDRED DOLLARS to "THE GOLD BUG," which we find, on examination of the private notes sent us, and which no one of the members of the Committee has seen, was written by Edgar A. Poe, Esq., of this city—and a capital story the Committee pronounce it to be.

15 JUNE. Robert Morris reprints the announcement "from the 'Dollar Newspaper' of yesterday" in his *Pennsylvania Inquirer*: "We congratulate the successful competitor. The story alluded to will no doubt prove worthy the reputation of its gifted author, and the high distinction which has been conferred upon it by the Committee."

15 JUNE. The *Spirit of the Times* publishes a letter from the well-known balloonist John Wise of Lancaster, Pennsylvania, who describes his plan "to make a trip across the Atlantic Ocean in a Balloon, in the summer of 1844."

[Wise's letter in the *Times*, a paper Poe read, is a probable source for "The Balloon-Hoax."]

16 JUNE. BALTIMORE. The *Sun* reports:

A PRIZE TALE.—Some time since, as announced in this paper, the proprietors of the "Dollar Newspaper" made an offer of premiums more liberal in amount we believe than has hitherto been done by any newspaper in the country, for the best stories which should be sent them before the first of June. The premiums thus submitted to the writers of light literature, were $100 for the best, $60 for the next, and $40 for the third in merit; the tales to be placed in the hands of a committee for decision, whose names were not made known, while the names of the candidates were received in sealed notes by the publishers. We learn by the last number of "The Dollar" that the committee have decided upon a story entitled "The Gold Bug," as the best, which proves to have been written by Edgar A. Poe, Esq., of Philadelphia; it is announced to appear in the next number of the above paper, and with the added commendation of the committee that it is an excellent tale, will be no doubt universally sought. The committee have not yet decided on the second and third prizes, some difficulty being experienced in the fact that there are several of the tales of nearly equal merit. The decision is, however, expected next week.

16 JUNE. William Poe writes Poe:

I wrote you on the 15th ulto since which time I have rec'd nothing from you, mine was in answer to a letter rec'd giving an a/c of yr many recent reverses, & I fear it was in a style not relished by you, but in great sincerity of feeling for you & yours I wrote it, and the reason why I presumed to be so free in my expressions was, in consequence of the great friendship, I feel for you & interest I take in yr welfare, & therefore hoped to hear again from you, & of yr wife's being better, & yr recovery from the sickness & despondency you were suffering when you last wrote.

William has seen a report in the *Sun* that Poe has been awarded a prize of $100 for "The Gold-Bug"; he hopes that this money will alleviate his cousin's financial problems. "Ought you ever to give up in despair when you have such resources as yr well stored mind to apply to? . . . There is one thing I am anxious to caution you against, & which has been a great enemy to our family, I hope, however, in yr case, it may prove unnecessary, 'A too free use of the Bottle.' Too many & especially Literary Characters, have sought to drown their sorrows & disappointments by this means, but in vain, and only, when it has been too late, discovered it to be a deeper source of misery" (*W*, 17:145–46; Ostrom [1981], p. 212).

17 JUNE. PHILADELPHIA. The *Saturday Courier* reports that Poe has won a prize of $100 "for a story entitled 'The Gold Bug,' which is said to be every way worthy his high reputation."

19 JUNE. The *Public Ledger* reports:

AWARD OF PRIZES.—Some few months ago, the publishers of the "Dollar News-paper" offered their prizes, amounting in the aggregate to $200, for the three best tales for that paper. The Committee to award the prizes was composed of the following gentlemen:—R. T. Conrad, Esq., H. S. Patterson, M.D., and W. L. Lane, and in order that they should not be influenced by names, those of the writers were withheld from the Committee.

These gentlemen, after a full examination of the various stories submitted to them, have made the following award:—The prize of $100 to the tale entitled "The Gold Bug," written by E. A. Poe, Esq.; the second prize, of $60, to the "Banker's Daughter," by Robert Morris, Esq.; the third prize, of $40, to "Marry-ing for Money," by a lady in New York, whose name does not accompany her production; she is known as a contributor to several of the magazines by initials only.

[Like the *Dollar Newspaper*, the *Ledger* was issued by A. H. Simmons & Co.: its report apparently represents the first official announcement by the publishers of the contest results and the names of the judges, though of course Poe's tale had been announced on 14 June. Robert T. Conrad was a playwright and jurist; Henry S. Patterson, a physician and author; and Washington L. Lane, managing editor of the *Ledger*.]

19 JUNE. CAMBRIDGE, MASSACHUSETTS. Robert Carter writes Poe, for-warding the abridgment of the *Saturday Museum* biography he published in the *Boston Notion* of 29 April: "I was absent from the city when it was printed and did not see the proof; consequently it is full of atrocious errors. What has become of the Stylus? I trust that it has not been found prudent to relinquish the enterprise though I fear that such is the case." Carter discusses *The Narrative of Arthur Gordon Pym*, which he read for the first time within the past week:

I lent it [*Pym*] to a friend who lives in the house with me, and who is a lawyer, a graduate of Harvard, and a brother of Dr. O. W. Holmes, yet he is so completely deceived by the minute accuracy of some of the details, the remarks about the statements of the press, the names of people at New Bedford, &c. that, though an intelligent and shrewd man he will not be persuaded that it is a fictitious work, by any arguments drawn from the book itself. . . . I dislike to tell him that I *know* it to be fictitious, for to test its truthfulness I gave it to him without remark and he has so committed himself by grave criticisms on its details that I dread to undeceive him. He has crossed the Atlantic twice and commented on an inaccu-racy in the description of Pym's midnight voyage with his drunken friend. I have not the book in the house and knowing nothing of the sea, did not clearly comprehend the objection, but I think it was upon setting a "jib" or some such thing upon a dismasted *sloop*—I know that the words "jib," "sloop" & "only one mast" occurred in his remarks (*W*, 17:146–48).

20 JUNE. PHILADELPHIA. Poe writes Lowell in Boston:

I owe you fifty apologies for not having written you before—but sickness and domestic affliction will suffice for all.

I received your poem, which you undervalue, and which I think truly beautiful—as, in fact, I do all you have ever written—but, alas! my Magazine scheme has exploded—or, at least, I have been deprived, through the imbecility, or rather through the idiocy of my partner, of all means of prosecuting it for the present. . . .

My address is 234, North Seventh St above Spring Garden, West Side. Should you ever pay a visit to Philadelphia, you will remember that there is no one in America whom I would rather hold by the hand than yourself (*L*, 1:234–35).

20 JUNE. Poe writes John Tomlin in Jackson, Tennessee, informing him that the *Stylus* has been postponed (Tomlin to Poe, 2 July).

20 JUNE. Poe writes Miss Lucy D. Henry of Red Mill, Charlotte County, Virginia, a granddaughter of Patrick Henry. "It gives me pleasure to comply with the very flattering request [for an autograph] contained in your letter to my sister [Rosalie] of March 26th" (*L*, 1:234).

21 JUNE. The *Dollar Newspaper* contains the first half of "The Gold-Bug."

[Each installment was illustrated with an engraving by Darley; both designs are reproduced in Phillips, 1:790–91.]

21 JUNE. The *Public Ledger* reports:

ONE HUNDRED DOLLAR PRIZE STORY.—"The Dollar Newspaper" for this week, this day published, contains the prize story of "THE GOLD BUG," written by Edgar A. Poe, Esq., which is pronounced, by every man of taste who has read it, a production of superior merit. For ourselves, we never read a fiction that in its plot runs more in the line of probability, and consequently never one that more closely rivetted [*sic*] our attention from its opening to its close; and this, as much from the fact that, as we read, we frequently found ourselves yielding to it credence as a matter of fact, as that the several incidents are in themselves highly interesting and the whole story chastely written.

The *Pennsylvania Inquirer* also notices the *Dollar Newspaper*, which "contains the first part of 'The Gold Bug' . . . . Single copies may be obtained at the S.W. corner of Third and Chesnut streets [location of *Ledger* and *Dollar Newspaper* offices]."

22 JUNE. John S. Du Solle comments in the *Spirit of the Times*: "We forgot to notice the 'Dollar Newspaper' yesterday, with its new prize tale by our friend Poe, entitled the 'Gold Bug.' The story is illustrated by an engraving, and is highly praised. We shall read it attentively, and advise others to 'go and do likewise.' " The *Public Ledger* reports:

The Poe house on North Seventh Street
(photograph by Dwight Thomas)

A GREAT RUSH FOR THE PRIZE STORY!—As largely as the publishers provided for the supposed demand for "The Dollar Newspaper," containing the prize story of "THE GOLD-BUG," written by Mr. Poe, the rush to obtain the paper yesterday greatly exceeded their expectation, and there is every probability that they will have forthwith to republish it. We have yet to meet the first man who has read it, that does not pronounce it a production of superior merit—one, which, besides being finely written, possesses more the air of truth than any we have ever read.

23 JUNE. The publishers A. H. Simmons & Co. register "The Gold-Bug" for copyright in the United States District Court, Eastern District of Pennsylvania (Mabbott [1978], 3:804).

24 JUNE. The *Public Ledger* reports:

THE PRIZE STORY OF THE GOLD-BUG.—"The Dollar Newspaper" of this week, containing this capital story, has been in unexampled request, and notwithstanding the large extra edition printed, the supply is nearly exhausted, and the publishers will probably be compelled to put the story to press in pamphlet form. With the view of protecting their own interest in this respect, they have taken out a COPY RIGHT for the Tale, and will endeavor to supply the public demand for it, be it ever so large.

The *Saturday Courier* comments: "We give to-day, the first part of Mr. Poe's Prize Tale. The conclusion will be immediately published, and will be sought for with great interest."

[The *Courier* reprinted all three prize stories from the *Dollar Newspaper*, apparently by prior agreement with A. H. Simmons & Co. "The Gold-Bug" appeared in three installments (24 June, 1 and 8 July), Darley's two illustrations being reproduced in the 8 July issue.]

27 JUNE. The editors of the *Daily Forum* comment:

We give place to the following, but at the same time feel convinced that perfect fairness must have been used in the distribution of prizes, as the character of the Committee precludes any possibility of collusion.

COMMUNICATED.
The "Gold Bug"—A Decided Humbug.

We have no hesitation in stating the fact, that *humbug* beyond all question is at last the "Philosopher's stone," in the discovery of which so many geniuses have heretofore been bewildered. In this opinion we are more fully confirmed by the recent *literary* production entitled the "Gold Bug," which has been paraded in flourishing capitals by the publishers of the "Dollar Magazine," [*sic*] and pronounced *by them* as the most entertaining and *superbly written* "prize tale" of modern times! That "one hundred dollars" was paid for this signal *abortion* we believe to be an arrant falsehood, and in this sentiment we are not singular, for several of our friends who have read the portion which has already appeared, pronounce upon it the verdict of *unmitigated trash*! We are inclined to think that ten or fifteen dollars satisfied "*the talented Edgar A. Poe, Esq.*" for this excruciating effort in the *tale* line.

In the publication of this *unique* affair, the proprietors of the "Dollar Magazine" know how to give the public "two bites of a cherry["]; but they will find it a *very* difficult task to point out hereafter even "*the man in a claret coat*" who has read the *second* part of the "Gold Bug." The writer threw away three cents in the purchase of the commencement of the tale, but will be exceedingly careful in not getting *blistered* by the ensuing dose of *cantharides*, which is usually made out of *Gold Bugs*. The public are little aware of the humbug heretofore practised in this "prize tale" business. . . .

[The communication, signed only with the initial "D.," was written by Francis H. Duffee, a minor Philadelphia journalist and playwright.]

CA. 28 JUNE. Poe commences a libel suit against Duffee (*Public Ledger*, 4 July).

28 JUNE. The *Dollar Newspaper* contains the second half of "The Gold-Bug." The *Public Ledger* advises readers:

DON'T BE DISAPPOINTED—Those who, by delay, were last week disappointed in obtaining a copy of "The Dollar Newspaper," in consequence of the large supply having been early exhausted, will take care this week to call early and secure a copy. It contains the conclusion of that excellent prize story, "The Gold-Bug," the merits of which we spoke fully last week. The public demand for the paper bears out all that we have said of the Tale. All who have read it through, so far as we have heard it spoken of, pronounce it superior to any American production that they ever before read. The interest given to the story in working up the mystery to the point at which it stopped last week, is successfully maintained to the conclusion in elucidating it.

In the *Citizen Soldier* George Lippard comments:

THE DOLLAR NEWSPAPER.—A capital sheet. The "Gold-bug, a Prize Story," by Edgar A. Poe, Esq., is written in the most popular style of the gifted author, characterised by thrilling interest and a graphic though sketchy power of description. It is one of the best stories that Poe ever wrote. And with regard to the matter of the "Prize," it is a humbug—a transparent, gauze-lace, cobweb-tissue humbug. The public well know that name and not merit, constitute the criterion of the board of secret critics. . . . The idea that the board of judges do not know the hand writing of all literary men of celebrity, is—with respect we say it—all fudge. In such a system, the man of notoriety has all the chances—the man of genius none. However, with regard to Mr. Poe, we can have but one opinion. This story is worth the "Prize money," ten times told.

29 JUNE. In the *Spirit of the Times* John S. Du Solle reports: "We learn that

an action for damages has been brought against Mr. F. H. Duffee, No. 3 South Third street, for publishing a communication in the Forum, in which it was insinuated that the publishers of the Dollar Newspaper had defrauded the public, by paying that talented writer, Edgar A. Poe, Esq., $15 for his admirable tale of the 'Gold Bug,' instead of paying the prize of $100, as announced, to the author of the best production offered them." The *Pennsylvania Inquirer* observes that yesterday's *Dollar Newspaper* "contains the conclusion of the 'GOLD BUG,' . . . which has excited much attention. The entire story, printed in an extra, may be obtained at the office of the 'Newspaper' . . . . A large edition will no doubt be called for."

30 JUNE. The *Public Ledger* reports:

THE GOLD-BUG.—A second edition of "The Dollar Newspaper," containing the whole of this prize story, as written by Mr. POE, has been published and will be for sale to-day at the counter of the Ledger office. The story is illustrated with two finely executed engravings, and the paper, besides containing another excellent story, by Willis, with much other news matter, is afforded at THREE CENTS per copy, with or without wrappers. The prize story, in every direction, elicits unqualified commendation.

30 JUNE. NEW YORK. The *New York Herald* mentions Poe's suit against Duffee, basing its account on Du Solle's report yesterday (Mabbott [1978], 3:804).

JULY. In the "Editor's Table" of the *Knickerbocker Magazine*, Lewis Gaylord Clark quotes an anonymous correspondent who defends "Flaccus" (Thomas Ward) from Poe's attack in the March *Graham's*: "His [Ward's] 'Epistle from my Arm-chair' was in good hexameters, and his 'Address to the President of the New-England Temperance Society' had a TOM MOORE-ish spice of elegant wit about it, and might have been written by Mr. POE in about a century of leap-years."

1 JULY. PHILADELPHIA. The *Spirit of the Times* publishes a letter to its editor from Duffee, who retracts his assertion in the *Daily Forum* of 27 June that Poe did not receive $100 for "The Gold-Bug":

Mr. Du Solle—Dear Sir:—You say in your paper of yesterday [29 June], that an action for damages has been brought against Mr. F. H. Duffee . . . .

In justice to myself, whatever may be the result of this unpleasant business, will you give place to the following extract from the publication in question? The language used by me is as follows:—"That one hundred dollars was paid for this signal abortion, we believe to be an arrant falsehood," &c. &c. "We incline to think that ten or fifteen dollars satisfied the talented," &c. &c. My position, you will perceive, is qualified by a doubt, and is stated merely as an opinion, the contradiction of which publicly given by the publishers, sets the matter at rest, and merely goes to show that I, in my criticism, have committed an error.

In the same column Du Solle himself begins another controversy by facetiously accusing Poe of plagiarizing "The Gold-Bug" from a story written by a schoolgirl:

> In Miss Sherburne's "Imogine," the "treasure" found on Long Island Sound, as once belonging to the noted "Kidd," [is] buried under an "old oak." Figures are traced on the tree—1, 7, 1, 2—with a hand pointing to the ground near the tree. At some distance from the tree, is the figure of another hand pointing to an old stone wall; while under the tree a "dead limb falls and stands upright in the ground," to the surprise of the hero, &c. page 57. Again the treasure is found under the old tree. A skeleton also lies buried on the treasure, which is removed. Then a few pieces of gold are seen. On digging, the men find the treasure, which is all taken away. Spades and mattacks are used. A "damp piece of leather" (not parchment) is also found, tied with tarred twine, which on being opened is discovered to be the "journal of the Pirate,"—pages 102, 104, 105, &c. &c.
>
> We need say no more. Mr. Poe is a good-hearted, clever man, a most able and talented writer, and we would not for the world accuse him of plagiarism, but we cannot help thinking how curious a thing it is that two such persons should hit on such exactly corresponding ideas.

[The *Tales* of George Ann Humphreys Sherburne, a slender volume published in Washington in 1839, contained only two stories, "Imogine; or the Pirate's Treasure" and "The Demon's Cave." In her preface the author stated that she had "numbered but thirteen summers."]

2 JULY. JACKSON, TENNESSEE. John Tomlin writes Poe: "I had seen, before I received your letter of the 20 ult, Mr. Clark[e]'s announcement in the 'Museum,' of his withdrawal from the Stylus *proje[c]t*;—and even before then, from your long and protracted silence, and in the absence of all evidence, save this, had the belief that the devilish machinations of a *certain* clique in Philadelphia, had completely baulked your laudable designs." Tomlin had asked Simms to notice the *Stylus* in the *Magnolia*, which he did in the June number. "I had caused to be noticed in various newspapers of the South and West, your project; and did see thro' these sources, the high admiration in which my friends in those places, held your Endowments. . . . Have you not in your City, some, that thro' a friendship which they feel not, are doing you much evil? I have had a letter quite lately [from Lambert A. Wilmer on 20 May], from one professing all friendship for you, in which some allusions are made to you in a manner greatly astonishing me" (W, 17:149–51).

AFTER 2 JULY. PHILADELPHIA. Poe replies to Tomlin, asking to be sent the letter containing the unflattering references to him (Poe to Tomlin, 28 August).

4 JULY. NEW YORK. The *New York Herald* repeats Du Solle's charge that Poe plagiarized "The Gold-Bug" from Miss Sherburne's "Imogine" (Mabbott [1978], 3:802–03).

4 JULY. PHILADELPHIA. The *Public Ledger* reports:

We are informed that Edgar A. Poe, Esq., author of the prize story entitled the "Gold-Bug," published in the Dollar Newspaper, has commenced a suit for libel against one Francis H. Duffee, a person formerly connected in some official capacity, we understand, with several of the small savings institutions of our city now no more, and at present in some capacity in connection with a broker's office, No. 3 S. Third st. The alleged libel consisted in the publication of an anonymous communication in the Forum of the 27th of June, reflecting upon the character for integrity of Mr. P., as well as upon the committee of decision appointed to award the premiums lately offered by the publishers of the Dollar Newspaper, and also upon the publishers. The article in question charges the parties, if not directly, at least by implication, with collusion and positive fraud.

Mr. P. will, of course, allow the gentleman every opportunity he may desire to substantiate his charges, or any portion of them, and as he will necessarily fail in every particular to do so, or to show the least shadow or particle of the appearance of anything to justify the charges he has made, he will hold himself ready to bear the consequences of an act which must have been prompted solely and entirely by his own mere suspicions . . . .

The card purporting to be an apology, over the signature of the gentleman himself, in the Spirit of the Times of Saturday last, amounts to nothing more than an exposure of his own attempted injustice to the parties concerned.

The *Ledger* criticizes the *Daily Forum* for publishing Duffee's "foul slander."

4, 6, 7 JULY. The *Pennsylvania Inquirer* reprints "The Gold-Bug" in three installments, without Darley's illustrations.

6 JULY. The *Daily Forum* replies to the *Ledger*'s editorial of 4 July, defending its decision to publish Duffee's communication: "We stated that the character of the gentlemen composing the committe[e] to award the premiums, precluded the possibility of any collusion between the editors of the Dollar Weekly and Mr. Poe, and as we were of this opinion, we rejected one communication from the same source, and even cut out sentences from the published one. The correspondent spoke with certainty, and having a responsible name, we felt it a *duty* to lend our colemns [*sic*] to expose what was characterized as a humbug. Upon the first application made to us, we gave the name of our correspondent."

In another column the *Forum* publishes a long letter from Duffee:

I have yet received no intimation that a suit has been commenced. If, however, to receive a polite note from a highly talented and amiable member of the bar—if to be waited upon by Mr. Edgar A. Poe, accompanied by two gentlemen with big sticks—if to meet them boldly and candidly acknowledge myself the author of the *critique*—if to be again waited on by the said Poe, accompanied by another gentleman with a big stick, and presented with a paper for me to sign calculated to make me acknowledge myself a liar and a scoundrel in the face of the public— if this is the commencement of legal proceedings, it is a way so *outre*, so *"grotesque and arabesque,"* that it could only emanate from the *clique*, and not from the proper tribunal, the law! . . .

If Poe is so excrutiating [*sic*] sensitive, how is it that he passes over the *in{n}uendoes* so delicately aimed at him by his caustic friend, the author of a poem entitled Recantation? Is not this Poe notorious for his severe and scorching criticisms? Has he not driven from the field of poetry the timid and aspiring son of genius? and that too with a withering scorn, which has paled the cheek of many a poor wight! Has he ever shown mercy to others? Then why so *"demm'd"* sensitive now? Will not the young lady, (scarcely sixteen,) the accomplished Miss Sherburne, the talented authoress of "Imogene, or the Pirate's Treasure," feel aggrieved to find that the Gold Bug is partly built upon the beautiful materials her imagination collected together . . . .

[One of Poe's legal advisers was almost certainly Henry B. Hirst, who had been admitted to the Philadelphia bar on 4 February; another may have been the prominent lawyer and playwright David Paul Brown (see Thomas [1978], pp. 503–04, 607–08, and Miller [1979], p. 440). Poe's "caustic friend" was Lambert A. Wilmer, whose *Recantation* (1843) was a tongue-in-cheek denial of the satiric observations on American poets he had made in *The Quacks of Helicon* (1841).]

8 JULY. BALTIMORE. In the *Saturday Visiter* Snodgrass reports: "E. A. POE has carried a prize of $100 from the proprietors of the 'Dollar Newspaper,' with a story entitled the 'Gold Bug.' It has had a tremendous run."

8 JULY. PHILADELPHIA. Clarke comments in the *Saturday Museum*:

THE GOLD BUG. This is the title of the story written by our friend Edgar A. Poe, Esq., which has been very justly designated as the most remarkable "American work of fiction that has been published within the last fifteen years." The period might very safely have been extended back to a period much more remote[,] for so singular a concatenation of incongruous and improbable, nay, impossible absurdities, were never before interwoven in any single or half dozen works of fancy, fact or fiction; and never before, we venture to say, were such mysterious materials so adroitly managed, or a train of incongruities dovetailed together with such masterly ingenuity. Indeed the intense interest which the fiction awakens arises from the skillful management of the several improbabilities, which are so presented as to wear all the semblance of sober reality. It is the unique work of a singularly constituted, but indubitably great intellect, and we give, in another part of our paper, the substance of the "Gold Bug," omitting the ab[s]truse and elaborate details in which the plot is involved. We may add that the train of reasoning is throughout of a clear, strong, and highly ingenious character, such in fact as would do credit to the highest order of talent that ever puzzled a judge or mystified a jury.

[In this issue Clarke published a plot summary of Poe's tale, about one-fourth the length of the original. The *Museum* and the *Dollar Newspaper* were in direct competition with each other, both being weekly "family newspapers"; and the publishers of the latter presumably did not give Clarke permission to reprint the story which they had copyrighted.]

12 JULY. The *Public Ledger* reports a third edition of Poe's tale: " 'THE GOLD-BUG' AND 'THE BANKER'S DAUGHTER.'—The second edition of this first prize story, and the first edition of the second, having been exhausted, an additional supply has been printed in extra sheets, and are now for sale at the Office of the Public Ledger. Price, *three cents* each, with or without wrappers."

13 JULY. The *Daily Forum* comments: "The third prize tale of the Dollar Weekly, 'Marrying for Money,' is delightfully written. It is worth a whole library of such entomological productions as the Gold Bug. We have not seen Mr. Morris' production, which took the second prize."

14 JULY. The *Forum* adds: "We have read the second prize tale . . . . Having now read the three productions, with all deference to the Committee who adjudged the prizes, we think they were exactly reversed in the order of merit; the last should have been first, and the first last." The *Public Ledger* reports: "ALL THE PRIZE STORIES TOGETHER.—The publishers of 'The Dollar Newspaper,' in order to supply the demand for the three prize stories, for which they recently paid two hundred dollars, have issued them together, on a large sheet, as a 'supplement' to their regular paper, which will be for sale at the Ledger Office to-day. This sheet . . . is sold at SIX CENTS . . . . this is the *fourth edition* of 'The Gold-Bug.' "

15 JULY. In the *Spirit of the Times* Du Solle retracts his accusation of plagiarism: "THE GOLD BUG.—We have read this prize tale by Mr. Poe carefully, and also the 'Pirate's Treasure' by Miss Sherburne, and while we confess that the Gold Bug pleases us much, is exceedingly well-written and ingenious, we are constrained to add that it bears no further resemblance to Miss Sherburne's tale, than it must necessarily bear from the fact of touching upon the same general grounds. Mr. Poe well deserved the prize of $100."

18 JULY. The *Public Ledger* observes that the *New York Herald* has perpetrated "one of the most barefaced plagiarisms," its 16 July editorial "on the decline of the drama" being copied "word for word" from *Blackwood's Magazine* for June. "This same paper charged Mr. Poe with having committed plagiarism in writing the prize story for the Dollar Newspaper, the Gold-Bug, by stealing the plot from a tale by Miss Sherbourne [*sic*]. Even this idea of the Herald was stolen from another paper, which has since retracted the charge in a handsome manner; but the Herald holds on to the stolen idea as if it was its own and honestly come by, even after the owner himself has repudiated it as unjust to Mr. Poe. For shame!"

CA. 18 JULY. William H. Graham, No. 98 Chestnut Street, publishes a pamphlet with this title on the outside front cover:

THE / PROSE ROMANCES OF EDGAR A. POE, / AUTHOR OF "THE GOLD-BUG," "ARTHUR GORDON PYM," "TALES / OF THE GROTESQUE AND ARABESQUE," / ETC. ETC. ETC. / [rule] / UNIFORM SERIAL EDITION. / EACH NUMBER COMPLETE IN ITSELF. / [rule] / No. I. / CONTAINING THE / MURDERS IN THE RUE MORGUE, / AND THE / MAN THAT WAS USED UP.

19 JULY. In the *Dollar Newspaper* the editor Joseph Sailer compares "The Gold-Bug" and "Imogine," exonerating Poe of plagiarism. Miss Sherburne's tale contains "not a word about Kidd—not a word about secret writing—not a syllable about a Gold-Bug—not a syllable about anything that is found in Mr. Poe's story; the only point of coincidence being *the finding of money*—a subject which has been handled not only by Miss Sherburne, but by some fifty, if not by some five hundred talewriters." Sailer surmises that the accusation in the *Spirit of the Times* "was, no doubt, hurriedly written, before a full perusal of both tales"; he reprints Du Solle's 15 July retraction, "in which the *amende honorable* is magnanimously made" (Mabbott [1978], 3:802).

19 JULY. In the *Pennsylvania Inquirer* Robert Morris comments:

Mr. W. H. Graham, No. 98 Chesnut street, has just commenced the publication in a series of numbers, of the Prose Romances of Edgar A. Poe, Esq. We bespeak for this work more than ordinary attention. Mr. Poe is an able and a popular writer, and we notice with sincere pleasure, an undertaking which will collect his admirable stories together, and afford the public an opportunity of possessing them in a convenient form. The first number, which is sold at 12½ cents, contains two articles entitled "Murders in the Rue Morgue," and the "Man that was used up"—both of them excellent.

The *Daily Chronicle* also notices "the first number" of Poe's *Prose Romances*: "The stories are very interesting, and writ[t]en in the peculiar graphic and forcible style of the distinguished author."

19 JULY? Poe signs a document in the District Court.

[The document cannot presently be located. According to an anonymous and often unreliable article on "Poe in Philadelphia" in the Philadelphia *Press*, 19 June 1892, p. 26, Poe "signed a blank form, and had himself registered . . . as a student of law, with H. B. Hirst for legal preceptor." It seems very unlikely that Poe would have chosen to study law under Hirst; perhaps the "blank form" was related to his current suit against Duffee, in which Hirst seems to have played a part. See 27 JULY.]

AFTER 19 JULY. Poe gives an autographed copy of his *Prose Romances* to Francis J. Grund, a politician and journalist holding an office in the Custom House (presentation copy in DLC–RB).

20 JULY. The *Daily Forum* notices the *Prose Romances*: "We are pleased to have this opportunity of expressing our general admiration of Mr. P's writings, and although we cannot see the merit of the 'Gold Bug,' and esteem it entirely unworthy of his name and reputation, still every oyster we know does not contain a pearl. The tales in the present number are the 'Murders in the Rue Morgue,' and the 'Man that was used up;'—differing as they do most essentially in style, they evince the varied powers of the author, and the facility with which he travels 'from grave to gay.' "

21 JULY. Three daily papers notice the *Prose Romances*. The *Public Ledger* finds that the two stories in this first number "will repay anybody by entertainment for their perusal." The *Pennsylvanian* comments: "Mr. Poe is a man of remarkable and peculiar ability, and his prose romances are not only original in style and conception, but, in the main, possess singular merit. They will be found well worth reading, and this edition gives them in a neat and agreeable form." In the *United States Gazette* Joseph R. Chandler comments: "Whether Mr. Poe has been too much occupied, or too indifferent to his own fame, we do not know; but we have often, in our own mind, doubted which was the cause that prevented him from issuing a uniform edition of his interesting and vigorous writings. The number before us shows that the work has been well commenced, and we cannot doubt that it will be well received, and amply rewarded."

22 JULY. Two weekly papers notice the *Prose Romances*. In the *Saturday*

THE

PROSE ROMANCES OF EDGAR A. POE,

AUTHOR OF "THE GOLD-BUG," "ARTHUR GORDON PYM," "TALES
OF THE GROTESQUE AND ARABESQUE,"
ETC. ETC. ETC.

UNIFORM SERIAL EDITION.

EACH NUMBER COMPLETE IN ITSELF.

No. I.

CONTAINING THE

MURDERS IN THE RUE MORGUE,

AND THE

MAN THAT WAS USED UP.

PHILADELPHIA:
PUBLISHED BY WILLIAM H. GRAHAM,
NO. 98 CHESTNUT STREET.
1843.

Price 12½ cents.

Front wrapper of Poe's *Prose Romances*
Pierpont Morgan Library

Museum Clarke comments: "Those who have a relish for the wild and wonderful—who would 'sup their full of horrors,' revel in mysteries and riot in the deep, dark, recesses which an iron intellect is capable of investing with intense interest, have a full feast spread for them in the pages of the Prose Romances. But above all has the man of legal lore an opportunity of acquiring an insight into his profession, more thorough than his long days and studious nights could ever glean from all the records of criminal practices in the courts, or the pages of Blackstone or Coke. Mr. Poe has the power, more than any other writer within our knowledge, not only of creating the most intricate mysteries, but unravelling them too." The *Saturday Evening Post* welcomes "the commencement of a re publication of the Stories and Sketches of E. A. Poe, Esq, in a neat form, such as will make, when completed, a very handsome volume. . . . To the readers of the Saturday Post, or indeed to any one acquainted with the periodical literature of our country, Mr. Poe requires no introduction."

24 JULY. In the morning Poe meets Duffee; they sign an agreement ending their dispute. Later in the day, Duffee sends a letter describing their meeting to the *New York Cynosure* (see 27 JULY).

25 JULY. The *Daily Forum* publishes the agreement:

A CARD.—The undersigned avail themselves of this opportunity to announce to their friends and the literary public, that all differences between them have been amicably and satisfactorily arranged. In regard to the article on the "Gold Bug," published in the "Forum," Mr. Duffee sincerely regrets that it should have been misconstrued into a *collusion* between Mr. Poe and the publishers of the "Dollar Newspaper," as well as the committee appointed to award the premiums lately offered by that paper, in which Mr. Poe was the successful competitor, and consequently retracts any alleged construction on his part to that effect.

With this admission, they conjointly waive all matter of dispute heretofore in existence, by Mr. Poe withdrawing *his libel suit*, which was instituted in consequence of the above misunderstanding. (Signed)

F. H. DUFFEE,
EDGAR A. POE.

Philadelphia, July 24th, 1843.

The editors of the *Forum* comment: "We are pleased . . . that a very foolish quarrel has been amicably arranged. We do not believe in a resort to libel suits—the reputation that requires the law to mend it, is hardly worth tinkering, and we must all expect knocks and bruises in this world of politics and literature."

25 JULY. The *Public Ledger*, the *Daily Forum*, and the *Spirit of the Times* report that the bookseller J. R. Colon, 203½ Chestnut Street, is now

offering for sale Miss Sherburne's *Tales*, containing "Imogine" and "The Demon's Cave."

25 JULY. Rufus W. Griswold writes Fitz-Greene Halleck in New York, discussing the notice of this poet to be published in the "Our Contributors" series of *Graham's Magazine*: "Instead of attempting an illustrative sketch myself, I employed Mr. Edgar A. Poe to write an essay on your poetry and a sketch of your history. I have just read his manuscript, and think that your friends will be gratified with the article" (J. G. Wilson [1869], pp. 441–42).

26 JULY. In the *Pennsylvania Inquirer* Robert Morris comments:

We learn that the first number of the Prose Romances of Edgar A. Poe, Esq., has met with a ready sale. This was to be expected. Mr. Poe has distinguished himself in every walk of literature; and it may be doubted whether the country boasts a writer of greater favor and more varied and finished accomplishments. As an editor of the Southern Literary Messenger he acquired and deserved a reputation, [of] which any living writer might be proud. In the field of romance, he has the rare merit of originality. Most of the tales of the day are copies of copies,—a reiteration of incidents a hundred times recited, and a repetition of sentiments, which, however commendable, are as well known as the Lord's Prayer. Mr. Poe's Romances are of a character entirely dissimilar. There is no apparent effort; no straining after sentiment; no daubing of red and white antithesis; no copied descriptions, a thousand times repeated, and weakened like circles in the water, with every repetition. In the present number, *The Murders in the Rue Morgue* is the better of the two tales. Of itself it proves Mr. Poe to be a man of genius. The inventive power exhibited is truly wonderful[.] At every step it whets the curiosity of the reader, until the interest is heightened to a point from which the mind shrinks with something like incredul[i]ty; when with an inventive power and skill, of which we know no parallel, he reconciles every difficulty, and, with the most winning *vraisemblance* brings the mind to admit the truth of every marvel related. . . .

26 JULY. In the *Citizen Soldier* George Lippard briefly notices Poe's *Prose Romances*: "The number before us, containing 'The Murders in the Rue Morgue,' and 'The man that was used up,' strikingly develope [*sic*] the analytic talent of the gifted author, as well as his powers of cutting and sarcastic humor. The first story is, like the 'Gold Bug,' *unique*, original and impressive in its style and character."

The issue also contains the seventh installment of Lippard's "Spermaceti Papers," in which the "Grey Ham" [George R. Graham] discusses his magazine with the engraver "Phelix Phillegrim" [possibly John Sartain], "Rumpus Grizzel" [Rufus W. Griswold], and "Peter Sun" [Charles J. Peterson]:

"And then with regard to the Contributors to my Babe—"

"Yer Babe? Och, Whalaloo!—what's that?" [asks Phelix Phillegrim.]

"A familiar name for my magazine . . . . With regard to my contributors—
'*Pay the rich, insult the poor*' is my motto; it[']s a safe one. There's Ex-Secretary
Paulding, there's Hoffman, there's Herbert, there's Fay—I pay 'em all. There's
some dozens of poor devils whom I treat with proper scorn—the *poor* devils!"

"The saints presarve me—here's the August number of your Babe. All rich
authors—gilded geniuses, seven of the Riverend Clergy—Grizzle, noble, 'Be-
thune the Beautiful'—etcetera. Yet here's one poor author—I'll be split if there
isn't! Edgar A. Poe—isn't he one o' th' poor devils?"

"Aye, aye, but my dear Mr. Phillegrim, this same Edgar A. Poe is—is—rather
a bitter fellow, and has a way of his own of using up all humbugs. He carries a
Tomahawk—does Poe. A very bad Tomahawk, a very nasty Tomahawk. Poe is
poor—but we have to get him to write for the Babe."

"It isn't meself as is much of a judge of caracter, but it seems to me, ye fear the
man? By the big bull-frog of Athlone! ye've a wholesome fear of this same poor
author—Misther Poe?"

"He doesn't think I'm a great man," quoth Rumpus.

"I suspect he thinks I steal the gems of my stories," cries little Peter.

BEFORE 27 JULY. *Graham's* for August contains Poe's "Our Amateur Poets,
No. III [No. II]: William Ellery Channing."

27 JULY. The *Pennsylvanian* reviews *Graham's*:

There is a slashing critique . . . upon the poetry of William Ellery Channing,
written by Mr. E. A. Poe, in his sharpest manner, which on such occasions is apt
to be sharp enough. How far the censure is deserved, we cannot pretend to say,
not being familiar with the poetry in question, but certainly some people will be
not a little surprised to learn from the article referred to, that Thomas Carlyle is
"an ass," such being the reviewer's private opinion—now first made public. This is
rather a startling announcement, when, in the opinion of multitudes on both sides
of the Atlantic, the "Past and Present" of this "ass" had placed him first, immea-
surably first, among living essayists.

27 JULY. In the *Spirit of the Times* Du Solle reports:

THE GOLD BUG DIFFICULTY.—The difficulty between Mr. Poe and Mr. F. H.
Duffee, we are pleased to learn, has been settled. The Philadelphia correspondent
of the New York Cynosure, (who is Mr. F. H. Duffee himself,) says in his letter of
Monday—

> It appears that the Petty-fogger about whom I wrote you in my last,
> has been at the bottom of all the mischief which existed between the
> belligerents in the matter of the "Gold Bug." This morning Edgar A.
> Poe, Esqr, waited upon Mr. F. H. Duffee, and in the most honorable
> manner waived all matter of dispute, by attaching his name to a card,

dictated by the other, which will appear in the Forum of tomorrow, when you will have an opportunity of perusing the termination of this *critical* squabble. Duffee, you know, handles a literary dissecting knife as well as Poe, and when "diamond cuts diamond" there is sure to be sharp work . . . .

I have several "rods in pickle" for the *creature* who rejoices in the *soubriquet* of "golden locks," which were I once to flourish around his insignificant person it would produce a strain of music sufficient to affright even the veritable pegas-asses, that browse upon nothing else but "spondee and dactyls."

[The "Petty-fogger" may well have been Henry B. Hirst. Duffee's second paragraph clearly refers to Hirst, whose red hair ("golden locks") and vaunted knowledge of versification were frequently satirized in the city's newspapers.]

27 JULY. The *Daily Forum* comments: *"Miss Sherburne's Tales.*—We have reperused the story of 'Imogene, or the Pirate's Treasure,['] with a view to detect whether Mr. Poe had borrowed any of its incidents for his Gold Bug. There are men and women, pirates and a concealed treasure in each, and there the resemblance ends. They are no more alike than the Gold Bug is like the 'Man that was used up.' "

[In the *Saturday Museum* of 29 July Clarke also observed that the "supposed resemblance" between the two stories was "altogether imaginary."]

28 JULY. The *Daily Forum* reviews the August *Graham's*:

Mr. Poe, the most hyper-critical writer of this meridian, cuts the poetry of William Ellery Channing, *Junior*, if not into inches, at least into feet. Mr. C.'s poetry is very trashy, and we should as soon expect to hear Bryant writing sonnets on a lollypop as to see Mr. Poe gravely attempt to criticise the volume. But there is method in it—it is not so absurd as one might suppose—Mr. Channing's weakness gives Mr. Poe an excellent opportunity of showing his strength! Your critical Olivers—your wrestlers in the rough and tumble of the *quasi*-chair editorial of a magazine, are never afraid to knock a chip off the shoulder of any pigmy of them all! . . . Mr. Poe is *the* critic, beyond dispute, of the age. Mr. Channing is the greatest po-etaster, Mr. Poe the greatest small po-tatoe! Bah! How this humbug pretension sickens us! Such nonsensical stuff to be dignified as a criticism upon "Our *Amateur* Poets" as antithetical to the *professional* merits of the cutter up, we presume! . . . Altogether the number is an excellent one, and even if disposed to find fault, we could hardly find occasion, when we allow ourselves to suppose that Mr. Poe's contribution was intended as a jeu d'esprit and not a grave criticism.

29 JULY. The *Saturday Courier* notices the *Prose Romances*:

Is there a man, woman, or child, "read up," as they phrase it in American Literature, who is unacquainted with Edgar A. Poe? We take it for granted that there is not . . . .

Had we space and time, we should delight to enter into an extended critique of Mr. Poe's productions: and yet, should we do so, some might—perhaps justly—charge us with egotism, even in such an attempt. . . . That Edgar A. Poe, has a peculiar mind, everybody admits. That he is original, all know. That he is learned—very learned—is equally well established. That he is one of the severest of critics, none deny—but many have felt. That he is one of the very best of the American Critics, we think only a few would undertake to deny. Yet, it is very certain that he sometimes wields a broad-axe, where a hatchet might have been equally efficacious. Besides, we have sometimes inclined to the opinion, that some of his book criticisms were infused with a little too much of worm-wood, with a sprinkling of gall, in doses far from being Homeopathic.

29 JULY. BALTIMORE. The *Saturday Visiter* contains an abridgment of the *Saturday Museum* biography of Poe. Snodgrass comments:

The extraordinary "run" which the "Gold Bug" has enjoyed, has naturally attracted general attention to its author, and caused many to desire to learn something of his parentage, character, and career—as well as personal appearance. Inasmuch as we have, for years, enjoyed the acquaintance of the subject of this sketch, we might speak of our own knowledge; but finding the facts to our hands, in the "Philadelphia Saturday Museum," we merely assume to the office of an *editor* on the present occasion—not having room nor leisure for enlarging upon his unquestioned abilities and characteristics as a writer of pure fiction, and as a critic—in which latter capacity he is unequalled in this country, be his faults what they may.

BEFORE AUGUST? PHILADELPHIA. Samuel D. Patterson, editor of the *Saturday Evening Post*, pays Poe $20 for his tale "The Black Cat" (Poe to Ezra Holden, 26 August).

3, 10, 17 AUGUST. MONTROSE, PENNSYLVANIA. The *Volunteer* reprints "The Gold-Bug" in three installments (Heartman and Canny, p. 271).

5 AUGUST. BALTIMORE. In the *Saturday Visiter* Snodgrass briefly notices "number *one* of a neat serial issue of the prose romances of Edgar Allan Poe, . . . containing the 'Murders of the Rue Morgue' complete—certainly one of his greatest efforts."

5, 7 AUGUST. PHILADELPHIA. The *Public Ledger* carries an advertisement for the Walnut Street Theatre, northeast corner of Ninth and Walnut, announcing the "FAREWELL BENEFIT" of the actor and playwright Silas S. Steele, "Prior to his departure for England," on "TUESDAY EVENING, August 8th." The benefit will feature a performance of Steele's drama *Clandare*: "To conclude with an entire new piece, entitled THE GOLD-BUG, Or, The Pirate's Treasure. Dramatized from the Prize Story of Edgar A. Poe, Esq., published in the DOLLAR NEWSPAPER, which for several weeks has had an unprecedented run. BLACK JUPITER by the celebrated COAL WHITE."

8 AUGUST. The *Ledger* carries a second advertisement for Steele's benefit which lists the casts of the two dramas: "THE GOLD-BUG.—Friendling, Mr. Charles; Legrand, Mr. Thompson; Jupiter, Mr. J. H. White; Old Martha of the Isle, Mrs. Knight." A similar advertisement naming the actors appears in the *Pennsylvanian*.

9 AUGUST. JACKSON, TENNESSEE. John Tomlin writes Poe, enclosing a letter in cipher which he received from Alexander B. Meek of Tuscaloosa, Alabama: "Believing that many things are possible with you, that is not believed in the World's Phylosophy [*sic*], I have taken the liberty, which you will excuse, of sending the letter to you, with the belief that you will make some thing out of it. In conclusion allow me to say, that very many of our learned Citizens, have endeavored, but in vain to solve it" (MB–G).

10 AUGUST. PHILADELPHIA. In the *Spirit of the Times* Du Solle comments: "MR. STEELE had a good house at his benefit on Tuesday night, and the performances were generally good. The Gold Bug, however, dragged, and was rather tedious. The frame work was well enough, but wanted filling up."

BEFORE 18 AUGUST. The *Saturday Evening Post* for 19 August features "The Black Cat" on its first page. On the second the editors comment:

"The Black Cat," by Mr. Poe, is written in that vein of his which no other American writer can imitate, or has, successfully. The accompaniment of probable events with improbable circumstances, so blended with the real that all seems plausible; and the investiture of the whole with a shadowy mythic atmosphere, leaving a strong and ineffaceable impression upon the reader's mind, is an effort of imagination to which few are equal. For our own part, we are bound to give the *pas* to all black cats, henceforth and forever; and to treat them with most obsequeous [*sic*] consideration. Cruelty to animals is a sin which deserves a punishment as severe as Mr. Poe has inflicted upon his hero.

18 AUGUST. The *United States Gazette* reports: "A thrilling original tale, from the pen of Edgar A. Poe Esq, leads off this week in the Post."

18 AUGUST. LENOX, MASSACHUSETTS. The novelist Catharine Maria

Sedgwick writes George R. Graham in Philadelphia: "Will you be kind enough through your magazine to inform Mr Poe & those who may have fallen into the error he has committed in his review of the Poems of William Ellery Channing that this young gentleman is not the son but the nephew of the illustrious Dr [William Ellery] Channing?" (MB–G).

BEFORE 26 AUGUST. PHILADELPHIA. Poe gives his tale "Raising the Wind; or, Diddling Considered as One of the Exact Sciences" to Ezra Holden, co-editor of the *Saturday Courier*.

26 AUGUST. Poe has Mrs. Clemm deliver a letter to Holden: "I am obliged to go to Richmond for a few weeks, on pressing business, and all the money I can raise I am forced to take with me. . . . If you can spare the amount for the article I left with you, please to do so . . . . Patterson, of The 'Post,' gave me, some weeks ago, for 'The Black Cat', 20$. I presume the article you have is worth as much—being longer &, I think, better" (Ostrom, [1974], pp. 521–22).

28 AUGUST. Poe replies to Tomlin's 9 August letter, providing a translation of Meek's cipher. He explains that he was "at one time absolutely overwhelmed" by ciphers sent to test his powers and that consequently he has vowed to solve no more: "You will hardly believe me when I tell you that I have lost, in time, which to me is money, more than a thousand dollars, in solving ciphers." Poe repeats his request for the slanderous letter Tomlin mentioned in his 2 July letter:

And now, my dear friend, have you forgotten that I asked you, some time since, to render me an important favor? You can surely have no scruples in a case of this kind. I have reason to believe that I have been maligned by some envious scoundrel in this city, who has written you a letter respecting myself. I believe I know the villain's name. It is Wilmer. In Philadelphia no one speaks to him. He is avoided by all as a reprobate of the lowest class. Feeling a deep pity for him, I endeavoured to befriend him, and you remember that I rendered myself liable to some censure by writing a review of his filthy pamphlet called the "Quacks of Helicon." He has returned my good offices by slander behind my back. *All* here are anxious to have him convicted—for there is scarcely a gentleman in Phila whom he has not libelled, through the gross malignity of his nature. Now, I ask you, as a friend and as a man of noble feelings, to send me his letter to you (*L*, 1:235–37).

SUMMER? SARATOGA SPRINGS, NEW YORK. Poe reputedly visits the resort at Saratoga, where he makes the acquaintance of John Barhyte and his wife Ann, a minor poetess. Mrs. Barhyte offers Poe advice on a poem he is writing, "The Raven" (Thomas [1978], pp. 707–11, 856–57).

BEFORE SEPTEMBER? PHILADELPHIA. Poe sells an unfavorable review of Longfellow's dramatic poem *The Spanish Student* to George R. Graham (R. W. Griswold to Longfellow, 26 December 1843; Graham to Longfellow, 9 February 1844).

BEFORE SEPTEMBER? Rufus W. Griswold resigns the editorship of *Graham's* (announcement in October number).

SEPTEMBER. *Graham's* contains Poe's signed article "Our Contributors, No. VIII: Fitz-Greene Halleck." In his unsigned review of *A Brief Account of the Discoveries and Results of the United States' Exploring Expedition*, he praises Jeremiah N. Reynolds, who organized the expedition (attribution in Hull, pp. 386–87).

SEPTEMBER. *Godey's Lady's Book* reviews Poe's *Prose Romances*: "The reputation of this author is deservedly high for originality, independence, a perfect command of the English language, and a certain easy and assured mastery of every subject which he handles. The first number contains the '*Murders in the Rue Morgue*,' and the '*Man that was Used Up*,' stories in totally different styles, showing versatility of power, but affording only a glimpse of the rich resources of his invention."

SEPTEMBER. In his *Ladies' National Magazine* Charles J. Peterson favorably reviews the *Prose Romances* (Pollin [1980], p. 24).

9 SEPTEMBER. NEW YORK. In their *New Mirror* George P. Morris and Nathaniel P. Willis welcome Poe's *Prose Romances*: "few writers of fiction are at all comparable with this fine author for clearness of plot and individuality of character." The first number contains "a most thrilling story, entitled, 'The Murders in the Rue Morgue,' " as well as "a laughable sketch." Morris and Willis reprint "The Man that was Used Up" to demonstrate the truth of their "commendatory remarks."

10 SEPTEMBER. JACKSON, TENNESSEE. Tomlin answers Poe's 28 August letter. He is enclosing Wilmer's 20 May letter to him. Although he fears that he has "violated somewhat the rules that govern correspondents," he believes that Poe's "great good sense" will protect his honor (*W*, 17:152).

12–13 SEPTEMBER. PHILADELPHIA. In the *Spirit of the Times* Du Solle reprints "The Man that was Used Up" in two installments.

13 SEPTEMBER. Poe writes James Russell Lowell in Boston: "Since I last wrote you I have suffered much from domestic and pecuniary troubles,

and, at one period, had nearly succumbed. I mention this by way of apology to the request I am forced to make—that you would send me, if possible, $10—which, I believe, is the amount you owe me for contribution. You cannot imagine how sincerely I grieve that any necessity can urge me to ask this of you—but I ask it in the hope that you are now in much better position than myself, and can spare me the sum without inconvenience" (*L*, 1:237–38).

LATE SEPTEMBER. BOSTON? Robert Carter writes Poe on Lowell's behalf, enclosing five dollars of the ten due for his contributions to the *Pioneer* (Poe to Lowell, 19 October).

EARLY AUTUMN? PHILADELPHIA. Horace Wemyss Smith recalls:

I read the "Raven" long before it was published, and was in Mr. George R. Graham's office when the poem was offered to him. Poe said that his wife and Mrs. Clemm were starving, and that he was in very pressing need of money. I carried him fifteen dollars, contributed by Mr. Graham, Mr. Godey, Mr. McMichael and others, who condemned the poem, but gave the money as a charity. An hour afterward he was found in a state of intoxication in Decatur street, where now is the alley running from the rear of Charles Joly's, No. 9 South Seventh Street, then occupied as a tavern and kept by a man named Dicky Harbut, an Irish shoemaker (Smith quoted by Rosenbach, p. 296).

[Richard Harbord's "Decatur Coffee House" was located at 6 Decatur Street, about half a block south of High (or Market) Street, between Sixth and Seventh. According to an advertisement in the *Daily Chronicle*, 22 May 1840, the establishment featured the "choicest Liquors," with "Mint Juleps, Cobblers, Egg Noggs, &c, served in a superior style."]

OCTOBER. *Graham's* carries an announcement: "Mr. GRISWOLD . . . withdraws after the present number from his editorial connection, but will continue to be an occasional contributor."

OCTOBER. The *Cold Water Magazine*, a temperance organ, begins to serialize Thomas Dunn English's *The Doom of the Drinker*.

[The novel, containing a malicious caricature of Poe, was commissioned by Thomas C. Clarke for his *Saturday Museum*. Its publication in the *Museum* being delayed, Clarke, an ardent temperance advocate, permitted the prior serialization in the *Cold Water Magazine*, a monthly of limited circulation which was not in competition with his weekly. The novel occupied three entire numbers—October, November, December—with the attack on Poe appearing in October (Thomas [1979], pp. 261–62). See 25 NOVEMBER, 9, 23 DECEMBER.]

OCTOBER. NEW YORK. In the "Editor's Table" of the *Knickerbocker Magazine*, Lewis Gaylord Clark quotes George D. Prentice, the editor of the Louisville, Kentucky, *Daily Journal*:

MR. PRENTICE, the well-known Louisville Journalist, is "down upon" a "gentleman of some smartness who rejoices in the euphonious name of POE," (a correspondent of ours spells it "Poh!") for terming CARLYLE, in one of his thousand-and-one MAC-GRAWLER critiques, "an ass." The Kentucky poet and politician thus rejoins: "We have no more doubt that Mr. EDGAR A. POE is a very good judge of an ass, than we have that he is a very poor judge of such a man as THOMAS CARLYLE. He has no sympathies with the great and wonderful operations of CARLYLE's mind, and is therefore unable to appreciate him. A blind man can describe a rainbow as accurately as Mr. POE can CARLYLE's mind. What Mr. POE lacks in Carlyleism he makes up in jackassism. It is very likely that Mr. CARLYLE's disciples are as poor judges of an ass as Mr. POE is of CARLYLE. Let them not abuse each other, or strive to overcome obstacles which are utterly irremovable. That Mr. POE has all the native tendencies necessary to qualify him to be a judge of asses, he has given repeated evidences to the public."

1 OCTOBER. SOUTH ATTLEBOROUGH, MASSACHUSETTS. Abijah M. Ide, Jr., an eighteen-year-old poet, writes Poe. He explains that he has received only a limited education "from the 'Schoolmasters and Schoolma'ams' of our District School," and that by occupation he is a farmer:

I want but one thing:—an acquaintance and fellowship with other Poets. Men are brothers, and man must, if he be a Poet, have some to cherish and love. Now there are not in the regions around about Old Attleboro' ten men who know Poetry from prose.—Not one who has any sympathy with the hopes and dreams of the poet's heart. This utter loneliness and complete want of some in whom to confide such secrets as a Poet has, has driven me to seek friends among strangers.

You now understand my position, and why I have written to you; and if you will give me your hand in friendship, you will make one heart glad. Upon the next page I copy a few lines from some poems, that I have lately written and, I shall value your opinion of their merit, higher than that of others (*W*, 17:153–55).

10 OCTOBER. PHILADELPHIA. Poe writes the attorney John B. Morris in Baltimore:

In a lot of ground, owned by yourself, and lying upon Clemm's Lot, fronting upon Park Lane, Baltimore, Mrs Maria Clemm, now of this city, retains her right of dower, as the widow of the late William Clemm. The object of this letter is to ascertain if you will be willing to purchase the right.

Mrs Clemm is in excellent health, and may live forty years. At the same time she is in indigent circumstances, and would regard your purchase of the Right as a favor for which she would be grateful. May I ask you, on her behalf, what would be the value of the Right to yourself? (*L*, 2:703–04).

11 OCTOBER. The *Citizen Soldier* contains an installment of George Lippard's "Walnut Coffin Papers," a sequel to his "Spermaceti Papers." Professor "Peter Sun" [Charles J. Peterson] describes his literary compositions to the engraver "Phelix Phillegrim":

"I turn out a first rate, Original American Novel—'Marion and his Sweet Potato'—illustrative of the 'Domestic Life of the Revolution.'—Grey Ham here says I'm a genius—"

"And Misther Edgar Allan Poe—what does he say of you, Pather?" [asks Phillegrim.]

"Why—why—in fact—Poe—is—a—a—great reader of Bulwer, and—he looks at me—as if—he thought, you know—oh, d—n the thing, *he knows* I steal my stories—that's all!"

"Is that all! What an inconsiderate crathur that Poe is to be shure!"

13 OCTOBER. CAMBRIDGE, MASSACHUSETTS. Lowell writes Poe, enclosing the remaining five dollars due for his contributions to the *Pioneer* (Poe's 19 October reply).

14 OCTOBER. PHILADELPHIA. The *Saturday Courier* contains Poe's "Raising the Wind; or, Diddling Considered as One of the Exact Sciences."

19 OCTOBER. Poe replies to Lowell: "I was upon the point of fulfilling a long neglected duty and replying to Mr Carter's letter, enclosing $5, when I received yours of the 13th, remitting 5 more. Believe me I am sincerely grateful to you both for your uniform kindness and consideration." Carter has written that Lowell has recovered his health, and Poe finds evidence in his correspondent's handwriting that his vision has returned: "I need not say that I am rejoiced at this—for you must know and feel that I am. When I thought of the possible loss of your eye-sight, I grieved as if some dreadful misfortune were about happening to myself." Poe will await "with much anxiety" Lowell's forthcoming volume of poetry: "I am seeking an opportunity to do you justice in a review, and may find it, in 'Graham,' when your book appears. No poet in America has done so much." Longfellow has genius, but he does not equal Lowell "in the true spirit." Poe has written "quite a long notice" of Longfellow's *Spanish Student* for the December *Graham's*: "The play is a poor composition, with some fine poetical passages" (*L*, 1:238–40).

19 OCTOBER. Poe replies to Ide's 1 October letter, giving him words of "friendship, approval and encouragement" (Ide to Poe, 2 November).

23 OCTOBER. The *Democratic Argus* carries an advertisement announcing the "WILLIAM WIRT INSTITUTE LECTURES AND DEBATES" for the 1843–

1844 season, "to be held in the usual place, viz, in the Juliana Street Church, between Fifth and Sixth, and Vine and Callowhill streets." There will be "Eight Lectures and Two Debates, commencing on Tuesday Evening, October 24." The advertisement lists the speakers engaged: "November 21 . . . Lecture, by Edgar A. Poe, Esq. Subject—American Poetry."

24 OCTOBER. In the *Spirit of the Times* Du Solle reports the commencement of the lectures: "Several powerful names are on the list. We notice Edgar A. Poe."

NOVEMBER. *Graham's Magazine* contains Poe's review of James Fenimore Cooper's novel *Wyandotté*.

EARLY NOVEMBER. NEW YORK. The *Opal* for 1844, edited by Nathaniel P. Willis, contains Poe's sketch "Morning on the Wissahiccon" (publication noticed in the Philadelphia *Pennsylvanian*, 8 November).

2 NOVEMBER. SOUTH ATTLEBOROUGH, MASSACHUSETTS. Ide replies to Poe's 19 October letter: "I need not tell you that I am grateful for your willing friendship, approval and encouragement. You have given me some confidence in myself which I think may be a very good matter for a Poet." Poe has apparently discussed his intention of establishing a magazine; Ide assures him: "I do not wish to pass judgment upon others, but no one has a more ardent wish than myself to see somewhat of a Revolution in American Literature. Our country supports too many of these *Dish-water Magazines*:—& *reads too much blank paper*! . . . I am glad to learn that *you* intend to attempt the overthrow of Humbug! If my hand can aid in the deed, it shall labor willingly. . . . I wish to learn something more of your plans whenever it pleases you to communicate them" (*W*, 17:156–57).

15 NOVEMBER. PHILADELPHIA. George Lippard comments in the *Citizen Soldier*:

. . . it gives us pleasure to announce a "Lecture on American Poetry" by Edgar A. Poe, Esq., on Tuesday next. Poe was born a poet, his mind is stamped with the impress of genius. He is, perhaps, the most original writer that ever existed in America. Delighting in the wild and visionary, his mind penetrates the inmost recesses of the human soul, creating vast and magnificent dreams, eloquent fancies and terrible mysteries. Again, he indulges in a felicitous vein of humor, that copies no writer in the language, and yet strikes the reader with the genuine impression of refined wit; and yet again, he constructs such works as "Arthur Gordon Pym," which disclose perceptive and descriptive powers that rival De Foe, combined with an analytical depth of reasoning in no manner inferior to Godwin or Brockden Brown.

It was Mr. Poe that made Graham's Magazine what *it was* a year ago; it was his intellect that gave this now weak and flimsy periodical a tone of refinement and mental vigor, which all the imbecility of its conductors for a year past, could not entirely erase or utterly annihilate.

We can promise the audience a refined intellectual repast in the lecture of Edgar Allan Poe.

16 NOVEMBER. Poe writes Joseph H. Hedges: "I presume the request you make, in your note of the 14th, has reference to my grandfather Gen. David Poe, and not to my father David Poe, Jr. I regret to say, however, that, owing to peculiar circumstances, I have in my possession no autograph of either" (*L*, 1:240).

18 NOVEMBER. The *Public Ledger* and the *Pennsylvania Inquirer* carry an advertisement:

WM. WIRT INSTITUTE LECTURES.—The Third Lecture of the Course will be delivered in the JULIANNA STREET CHURCH, on TUESDAY EVENING NEXT, Nov. 21st, by EDGAR A. POE, Esq., author of the Gold-Bug, &c.; Subject, American Poetry. To commence at 7½ o'clock. Tickets to the Course, to admit a Gentleman and two Ladies, $1; single Evening Tickets, to admit a Gentleman and two Ladies, 25 cents; single Evening Tickets, to admit one person, 12½ cents. To be had of S. SNYDER LEIDY, No. 199 NORTH SIXTH Street, above Vine, and at the door on the evening of the Lecture.

21 NOVEMBER. The advertisement is repeated in the *Ledger* and the *Inquirer*, both papers also according Poe's lecture brief editorial notices. Robert Morris of the *Inquirer* observes: "A large and intellectual audience will no doubt be in attendance."

21 NOVEMBER. Poe lectures to an overflow audience, "hundreds" being "unable to gain admission" (*United States Gazette*, 8 January 1844).

25 NOVEMBER. In the *Saturday Courier* the editors Ezra Holden and Andrew McMakin notice Poe's lecture: "We regret that we could not attend, but we are told it was a very learned critique, marked by the severity of illustration for which the author is so ably known." In the *Saturday Museum* Clarke comments:

Quite a large, and certainly highly intelligent audience, attended the Lecture on American Poetry, delivered by Edgar A. Poe, Esq., on Tuesday evening, before the William Wirt Literary Institute. We have not leisure this week to give even a brief outline of the lecture, the character of which may be inferred from the reputation which Mr. Poe has so extensively enjoyed, as a severe and impartial critic. Added to this important qualification, the fact of the Lecturer himself possessing talents, as a poet, of a high order, and therefore capable of more truly appreciating his subject, with great analytical power, and that command of language and strength of voice which enables a speaker to give full expression to whatever he may desire to say, it will readily be perceived that the Lecturer on Tuesday evening, combined qualities which are rarely associated in a public speaker.—With the exception of some occasional severity, which however merited, may have appeared somewhat too personal, the lecture gave general satisfaction, especially the portions in which the eloquent Sonnets of Judge Conrad, on "The Lord's Prayer," were introduced. The judicious reading of these created a marked sensation.

We hear it suggested that an attempt will be made to prevail on Mr. Poe to re-deliver this Lecture in a more central place in the city. With some modification, it would bear repetition, and we dare say the press will unite in forwarding these views, notwithstanding the cool manner in which Mr. P. laid bare its system of almost universal and indiscrim[in]ate eulogy, bestowed alike upon anything and everything—"from the most elaborate quarto of Noah Webster, down to a penny edition of Tom Thumb."

25 NOVEMBER. The *Museum* commences a serial with this heading: "ORIGINAL TALE, / Written expressly for the 'Philadel- / phia Saturday Museum.' / [rule] / THE / DOOM OF THE DRINKER; / OR, / Revel and Retribution. / [rule] / ILLUSTRATED BY ENGRAVINGS ON WOOD, / AFTER ORIGINAL DESIGNS, BY FELIX O. C. / DARLEY."

[English's long-awaited novel, which Clarke had repeatedly announced both in his *Museum* editorials and in paid advertisements in other Philadelphia papers, was published in eleven consecutive installments, being concluded in the 3 February 1844 issue (Thomas [1979], pp. 262–63).]

28 NOVEMBER. WILMINGTON, DELAWARE. The *Delaware State Journal* reports:

LECTURE BEFORE THE FRANKLIN LYCEUM.—The first lecture of the course which the members of the Franklin Lyceum have procured to be delivered before them this winter, will take place this evening at Temperance Hall. *Edgar A. Poe*, the lecturer, is well and favorably known in the literary world as a poet and magazine writer of high standing, whose powers in describing the thrilling and adventurous scenes of life are perhaps unrivalled. The subject is *"American Poetry,"* upon which, we understand, Mr. Poe has very peculiar notions, he will therefore probably be the more entertaining, as he will travel out of the usual track.

In another column the *Journal* carries an advertisement for tonight's lecture, "commencing at 1/2 past 7 o'clock . . . tickets 12 1/2 [cts]—2 tickets will admit a gentleman and two ladies."

[On 6 January 1844 the Philadelphia *Spirit of the Times* published a letter from a Wilmington correspondent who remarked: "Edgar A. Poe, Esq., delivered a lecture here several weeks since, on 'American Poetry.' Good, but rather severe."]

29 NOVEMBER. PHILADELPHIA. In the *Citizen Soldier* Lippard comments on Poe's 21 November lecture:

The subject, "American Poetry," was handled in a manner, that placed all the pseudo-critics, the Rev. Mr. Rufus Griswold, Esq. among others, to the blush, and showed the audience, how a man born a poet, could describe the true nature and object, [a]s well as the principles of poetry. The sentences of the Lecturer were vigorous, energetic and impassioned, his criticisms scathingly severe in some cases, and des[e]rvedly eulogistic in others. Ex-Judge Conrad, received a merited compliment from Mr. Poe, who recited the whole of his version of the Lord's Prayer, and Mr. Morris of the Inquirer, was noticed with cordial approbation. As a general thing, the Lecture was received with the most enthusiastic demonstrations of applause, and it was agreed by all, that it was second to none, if not superior to all lectures ever delivered before the Wirt Institute.

DECEMBER. *Graham's* contains Poe's favorable review of Robert Tyler's poem *Death* (attribution in Hull, pp. 388–89).

9 DECEMBER. The *Saturday Museum* publishes the third installment of English's *The Doom of the Drinker*, containing Chapter VI, entitled "The Revellers." The novel's protagonist Walter Woolfe attends a fictional drinking party at the home of his father's friend John Purdon; one of the guests is Poe, unnamed but easily recognizable:

At the head of the table sat the master of the mansion. John Purdon was a rosy, burly man, apparently the very personification of good health. . . . The wine bottle never rested a moment in his hands, and he urged the tardy drinkers by voice and example.

Next to him sat a pale, gentlemanly looking personage [Poe], with a quick, piercing, restless eye, and a very broad and peculiarly shaped forehead. He would occasionally, under the excitement of the wine, utter some brilliant jests, which fell all unheeded on the ears of the majority of the drinkers, for they could appreciate no witticisms that were not coarse and open. This man seemed hardly in his element, and no doubt wished himself away at least a dozen times during the evening. He was an extraordinary being, one of the few who arise among us with a power to steal judiciously. He was a writer of tact, which is of a higher order than ordinary genius. But he was better known as a critic than as any thing else. His fine analytical powers, together with his bitter and apparently candid style, made him the terror of dunces and the evil spirit of wealthy blockheads, who create books without possessing brains. He made no ceremony though, in appropriating the ideas of others when it suited his turn, and, as a man, was the very incarnation of treachery and falsehood.

23 DECEMBER. In the *Museum* Clarke discusses *The Doom of the Drinker*: "The effect of this narrative would be materially enhanced were we permitted to designate the different characters, and point out the particular scenes which are drawn from life. Among the daring adventures and exciting passages, there are more real, actual occurrences than we dare specify—far more, in fact, of painful, instructive reality, than is [are] to be found in the host of ordinary novels of the day." The author is "one of the most remarkable men in the country, destined, at no distant period, to create a sensation."

[The *Museum* never mentioned English by name, but his authorship was no secret. He had been identified in three numbers of the *Cold Water Magazine*, as well as in the influential Washington *Daily National Intelligencer* and in two important Philadelphia papers, the *Pennsylvania Inquirer* and the *Public Ledger* (Thomas [1979], pp. 266–68).]

23 DECEMBER. NEWARK, DELAWARE. In the evening Poe delivers his lecture on "American Poetry" at the Newark Academy, a boys' preparatory school (Moyne, pp. 1–19; see 2 JANUARY 1844).

26 DECEMBER. PHILADELPHIA. Rufus W. Griswold writes Longfellow in Cambridge, Massachusetts:

Mr Graham has requested me to write to you on the subject of contributing to the current volume of his magazine. It is a long time since the public have heard from you, and doubtless you have more than one finished poem in your portfolio. It is needless to say that anything you may send will be gladly received and promptly paid for by Mr Graham.

You may remember some conversation we once held at Cambridge in regard to Poe. He has recently written an elaborate review of your "Student," in his customary vein, but if anything a little more personal and malignant than usual. This was offered to Graham before I left, and has since been given to him—so anxious is the poor critic for its appearance; but of course Mr Graham refused it. I mention the circumstance because it would be very like Poe, since he cannot find a publisher for his "criticism," to attempt again to win your friendship with his praise (MH–H).

[Graham actually paid $30 for Poe's review of *The Spanish Student*. He never intended to publish it; but in this letter, and his own 9 February 1844 letter to Longfellow, he used the implicit threat of its publication to prod a valued but reluctant contributor.]

29 DECEMBER. READING, PENNSYLVANIA. John C. Myers, Samuel Williams, and William Greaff, Jr., write Poe, inviting him to deliver his lecture on "American Poetry" before the Mechanics' Institute of Reading (Poe's 1 March 1844 reply).

CA. 1843. PHILADELPHIA. Clarke's young daughter, Miss Anne E. C. Clarke, frequently visits the Poe home, amusing Virginia by singing "the old song of *Gaffer-Poe*" (Miss Clarke quoted by Sartain, p. 216; cf. T. C. Clarke quoted by Gill, pp. 100–03).

CA. 1843. Miss Clarke recalls the visitors to her father's residence at 56 South Twelfth Street: "Among the callers or stoppers-in would be 'Tom' as he was called, Dr. Thomas Dunn English, who, after being *bon camarade* with Hirst and Poe, quarrelled with one or both. All three of them happening in early one evening, they had to be kept apart lest they come to deadly strife. English was put in the parlour, Hirst in the library, where he was in the habit of lying prone on a lounge by the hour, dreaming dreams and seeing visions, and Poe was shown as usual into the dining-room" (quoted by Sartain, p. 226).

CA. 1843. A schoolgirl in the Spring Garden district recalls the Poe family:

Twice a day, on my way to and from school, . . . I had to pass their house, and in summer time often saw them. In the mornings Mrs. Clemm and her daughter would be generally watering the flowers, which they had in a bed under the windows. They seemed always cheerful and happy, and I could hear Mrs. Poe's laugh before I turned the corner. Mrs. Clemm was always busy. I have seen her of mornings clearing the front yard, washing the windows and the stoop, and even white-washing the palings. You would notice how clean and orderly everything looked. She rented out her front room to lodgers, and used the middle room, next to the kitchen, for their own living room or parlor. They must have slept under the roof (quoted by Weiss [1907], pp. 95–97).

CA. 1843. Miss Lydia Hart Garrigues, a young girl living on North Seventh Street, recalls Poe:

Dozens of times have I seen him [Poe] pass my father's windows going down Seventh St., into the city. He wore a Spanish cloak; they, at that time, were much used instead of overcoats. I was always impressed with the grave and thoughtful aspect of his face. He looked to be much older than I now know him to have been. Tho' little over thirty he had the appearance of middle age. To his neighbors his name meant very little. It was not until after "The Raven" was published, and that was subsequent to his removal to New York, that we knew him as a literary figure. Then, we felt sorry we had not taken more notice of him. He, his wife and Mrs. Clemm, kept to themselves. They had the reputation of being very reserved,—we thought because of their poverty and his great want of success. We knew he did not pay his rent to Mr. Alburger, who, however, was not disposed to cause him distress (quoted by Phillips, 1:827).

CA. 1843. The artist A. C. Smith, 86 Chestnut Street, paints a portrait of Poe, which is then engraved for use in the "Our Contributors" series of *Graham's Magazine* (Poe to Lowell, 30 March 1844).

*

1844

*

JANUARY. LONDON. The *Foreign Quarterly Review* contains a long, patronizing critique of "American Poetry." The reviewer, probably Dickens' friend John Forster, praises Bryant, Emerson, and Longfellow, while dismissing other American poets as mere imitators of English verse. "Poe is a capital artist after the manner of Tennyson; and approaches the spirit of his original more closely than any of them." Quoting from "The Haunted Palace" and "The Sleeper" to illustrate Poe's "metrical imitation," the reviewer observes: "These passages have a spirituality in them, usually denied to imitators; who rarely possess the property recently discovered in the mocking-birds—a solitary note of their own."

JANUARY. PHILADELPHIA. *Graham's* contains Poe's review of James Fenimore Cooper's *Ned Myers* and his preliminary notice of Richard Henry Horne's *Orion* (attributions in Mabbott [1932], p. 441, and Hull, pp. 390–92).

2 JANUARY. WILMINGTON, DELAWARE. The *Delaware State Journal* publishes a letter from "Academicus," a correspondent in Newark, Delaware, who describes the lecture on "American Poetry" Poe delivered to the students and faculty of the Newark Academy, "as well as a considerable number of the more intelligent of the citizens of the place," on 23 December 1843:

After a graceful exordium and prospective apology for the foreseen necessary length of remarks designed to cover so wide a field, our Lecturer approached the body of his theme. The proper criterion by which we may safely judge of the present state of the poetic art in America and of the comparative excellence of the productions of our different bards first occupied his attention. In this part of the subject the system of *puffery* at present common with our newspapers, magazines, and even dignified reviews was most clearly and indignantly exposed and condemned. Editors of newspapers building up large Libraries for which they pay by wholesale and indiscriminate puffs of works whose title pages they have hardly had time to copy.—Authors reviewing and praising their own writings, or securing the bespoken praises of a friend—booksellers and publishers promoting the sale of their goods by measures equally corrupt, all received their full share of severe rebuke. . . .

After showing the incompetency of our criticism, as at present managed, to present a true picture of American Poetry, our Lecturer turned to an inspection of the works themselves of our poets—and especially to the several *"collections"* of American poetry which have successively appeared as *representing* the state of the art in our country. After a cursory examination and criticism of some five or six such "collections" in the order of their publication, the late compilation of Rev. Rufus W. Griswold, styled the *"Poets and Poetry of America,"* was introduced—as the last and best—tho' by no means unobjectionable. This book and its author were handled by the critical Lecturer in not the most gentle manner. Many names had been inserted which Apollo would have refused and some (such as Morris and Conrad) left out, which the muses have acknowledged. The selections from those admitted have been made with a miserable want of judgment—the worst specimens being often chosen instead of the best,—and an extravagant proportion of space allotted to personal friends—altho' inferior poets—(as in the case of Mr. Hoffman)—while superior merit has been put off with a single page. After thus preparing the way, some eight or ten of our lady poets were introduced one by one and dismissed to their appropriate seats in the temple of Fame, after whom, came the *five* steel plate faces of Mr. Griswold's frontispiece, in their order—Dana, Bryant, Halleck, Sprague and Longfellow.

The whole was closed with a highly philosophical and eloquent discourse on the true end and province of poetry and condemnation of what the Lecturer was pleased to term the *"didacticism"* of modern Poetry.

6 JANUARY. PHILADELPHIA. The *Irish Citizen*, a weekly newspaper now edited by Thomas Dunn English, contains "several chapters of a tale entitled 'The Doom of the Drinker, or Revel and Retribution' " (*Public Ledger*, 10 January).

8 JANUARY. In the *United States Gazette* Joseph R. Chandler reports: "We learn that Edgar A. Poe, Esq., has consented to repeat, at the Museum, on Wednesday night, his admired lecture on the *Poets and Poetry of America*. His first lecture was attended by one of the largest and most fashionable audiences of the season; and the Museum will doubtless be crowded by hundreds who were then unable to gain admission." In the *Spirit of the Times* John S. Du Solle comments: "Mr. Poe is a correct and graceful reader, and his lecture is not only beautifully written, but commends itself by its good sense and good judgment to the attention of every person of taste." Robert Morris of the *Pennsylvania Inquirer* also reports that Poe "will repeat his lecture . . . with further illustrations."

9 JANUARY. In the *Inquirer* Morris comments:

The lecture of Mr. Poe on the Poets and Poetry of America,—one of the most brilliant and successful of the season, will be repeated to-morrow evening, at the Museum. Mr. Poe is one of the most vigorous and beautiful writers in the country, and as a critic, has won great reputation, by the ability, independence, and boldness of his strictures. His style of delivery is finished and effective, and his lecture, which was listened to by a very large and fashionable audience with delight, is certainly one of the best ever delivered in this city. He will doubtless be greeted by a crowded auditory.

Chandler also gives a second notice in his *United States Gazette*: "Those who would hear a good lecture well delivered should go to the Museum TO-MORROW evening . . . . Mr. Poe is himself a poet, an acute critic, and a vigorous prose writer. It is well occasionally to hear such an one upon his own craft, and his fellow craftsmen." The *Public Ledger* comments: "The subject [of the lecture] is one of much interest, and in Mr. Poe the audience will find one well qualified by judgment, good taste and perfect independence, to do full justice to it." In another column the *Ledger* carries an advertisement:

LECTURE ON AMERICAN POETRY. —The *Lecture* on "American Poetry," lately delivered before the William Wirt Institute, by EDGAR A. POE, Esq., will be repeated, with additional illustrations, TO-MORROW (Wednesday) EVENING, at the Lecture Room of the Museum, in GEORGE Street. Tickets may be had at Graham's Periodical Depot, or at Berford's "Publishers' Hall," or at the Museum on the night of the Lecture. Single tickets, 25 cents; tickets admitting a gentleman and two ladies, 50 cents. Doors open at half past 6. Lecture to commence at a quarter past 7.

10 JANUARY. The advertisement is repeated in the *Ledger*. Du Solle of the *Times* notices the lecture for a second time, describing it as "full of vigorous thought, surpassing taste, and sparkling images." Morris of the *Inquirer* mentions it for a third time: "A literary treat of no common kind may be looked for." Two daily papers, the *Philadelphia Gazette* and the *Pennsylvanian*, announce the lecture for the first time. In the weekly *Citizen Soldier* George Lippard comments:

LECTURE BY MR. POE. —It is with sincere pleasure we perceive that the excellent lecture lately delivered before the Wm. Wirt Institute by Edgar A. Poe, will be repeated this evening at the Lecture Room of the Philadelphia Museum. The subject "American Poetry," was handled in the lecture, in an able, effective and original manner, calling forth the most enthusiastic demonstrations of applause from the audience. Mr. Poe is rapidly adding to his towering fame as Poet, Author, Critic, in his new capacity of lecturer; and all friends of a correct and healthy national literature hail with delight, the appearance of an able and eloquent advocate of the right and caustic censor of the wrong. We hope in a short time, to have it in our power to welcome the appearance of a sound Magazine, devoted to all the higher objects of American Literature, edited, owned and controlled by Mr. Poe, and do now most heartily bid him "God-speed" in the cause.

10 JANUARY. Poe lectures in the Philadelphia Museum, northeast corner of Ninth and George (or Sansom) Streets (implied by advance notices).

11 JANUARY. Thomas C. Clarke resigns the editorship of the *Saturday Museum* (valedictory in 20 January issue).

13 JANUARY. Poe writes Joel B. Sutherland, a former Congressman now serving as the naval officer of the Custom House: "Will you permit me to introduce to you my friend Mr Robert Travers, of this city, who will hand you this note? He is an applicant for a post in the Revenue Service. If you could further his views in any regard, I would consider myself as under the *very deepest* personal obligation." Travers is not only "an experienced seaman," but a member "of the Hughes' family," from the Philadelphia suburb of Southwark, who have "always possessed much political influence" (*L*, 1:240–41).

BEFORE 20 JANUARY. *Graham's Magazine* for February contains Poe's review of Eugène Sue's novel *The Mysteries of Paris* (attribution in Mabbott [1932], p. 441).

20 JANUARY. COLUMBIA, PENNSYLVANIA. The *Columbia Spy* reviews the February *Graham's* (Spannuth and Mabbott, p. 121).

24 JANUARY. BALTIMORE. The *Sun* reports:

LECTURE BY EDGAR A. POE, ESQ.—We have authority to promise our readers an evening's entertainment within a short time, to consist of a lecture by Mr. Edgar A. Poe, the subject of which we learn will be "American Poetry." It is scarcely necessary for us to do more than introduce this gentleman by name, as he is so well and popularly known to every admirer of modern literature, not only by the exquisite productions of his own imaginative genius, but by his elaborate, daring and caustic criticisms, which have from time to time enriched the pages of the most popular magazines of the day, and proved him abundantly capable of the task he now proposes. The author of "Tales of the Arabesque and the Picturesque," and within a short time past admired in that ingenious production of his pen, "The Gold Bug," which took the first prize of "The Dollar Newspaper," is sure of a hearty welcome in this city, and equally sure to be honored with, as he is to entertain, a crowded audience on his lecture night.

27 JANUARY. Snodgrass reviews the February *Graham's* in the *Saturday Visiter*: "We note an improvement in the critical department. Is not E. A. POE back again? The long article on Eugene Sue's 'Mysteries of Paris,' could scarcely have been written by such a common-place critic as R. W. Griswold."

27 JANUARY, 3 FEBRUARY. NEW YORK. Park Benjamin's *New World* reprints, in two installments, the critique of "American Poetry" from the London *Foreign Quarterly Review*.

27? JANUARY. PHILADELPHIA. The *Irish Citizen* contains "The Ghost of a Grey Tadpole, by Edgar A. Poe," a clever burlesque of Poe's fiction by Thomas Dunn English (Gravely, pp. 362–67; reprints of 31 January and 1 February).

BEFORE 29 JANUARY. Poe writes "Mr Clark" [presumably Thomas C. Clarke], asking to borrow money: "I am exceedingly anxious to try my fortune in Baltimore with a lecture or two, and wish, if possible, to go immediately" (*L*, 1:241).

CA. 29 JANUARY. BALTIMORE. Poe asks the editors of several newspapers to publish advance notices of his lecture (Poe to Isaac Munroe, 31 January).

30 JANUARY. The *Republican and Daily Argus* comments: "*Mr. Poe's lecture—American poetry.*—It affords us much pleasure at being able to announce to our readers that our esteemed friend, Edgar A. Poe, Esq., will deliver a lecture on the above very interesting subject to-morrow evening at the Odd Fellows' Hall. It will be remembered that Mr. Poe is the author of several excellent prize essays, which have afforded so much pleasure to all who have read them. The literary attainments and eminent talent of this gentleman, are of themselves sufficiently indicatory that the subject selected by him will be most ably handled."

31 JANUARY. Three morning papers mention Poe's lecture. The editors of the *Sun* comment:

LECTURE OF EDGAR A. POE, ESQ.—It will be seen by a notice in another part of our paper, that the lecture of Mr. Poe, on "American Poetry," heretofore announced, will be delivered this evening, in the Egyptian Saloon of [the] Odd Fellows' Hall. The name of the lecturer, the subject of the lecture, and the well known adaptation of the talents of the one to the material of the other, form a combination of attractions which will irresistibly result in a crowded audience— and our word for it a delighted one.—We have never yet confessed to the sin of poetry—jogging along steadily in humble prose with now and then the guilt of a poetic quotation only on our heads, we say boldly, "Let the galled jade wince; our withers are unwrung."

An advertisement appears on the first page:

A LECTURE ON "AMERICAN POETRY" will be delivered by EDGAR A. POE, in the ODD FELLOWS' HALL, in Gay street, on THIS (Wednesday) EVENING, 31st, at half past 7 o'clock, Single tickets 25 cents; admitting a gentleman and two ladies, 50 cents—to be had at Mr. Hickman's book store, at Mr. Isaac P. Cook's, and at the door.

The *American* observes that Poe's subject "affords an excellent and interesting theme; and will, without doubt, be treated with ability." The *Baltimore Clipper* requests attendance at this lecture by a well-known author.

31 JANUARY. Poe writes Isaac Munroe, editor of the *Baltimore Patriot*: "I have been endeavouring for the last two days to see you and beg of you to do me the kindness to call attention, in the 'Patriot' to a lecture on 'American Poetry' . . . . If not too late, will you say a good word for me in this afternoon's paper" (*L*, 1:241–42).

31 JANUARY. Two afternoon papers notice Poe's lecture. In the *Patriot* Munroe prints a brief announcement. The *Republican and Daily Argus* reminds its readers of the lecture it mentioned yesterday: "The lecture will doubtless be an able one, and we doubt not will attract a numerous audience."

31 JANUARY. In the evening Poe lectures at the Odd Fellows' Hall, 30 North Gay Street (corner of Gay and Fayette).

31 JANUARY. PHILADELPHIA. In the *Citizen Soldier* Lippard reprints "The Ghost of a Grey Tadpole, by Edgar A. Poe" from the *Irish Citizen*, without comment and presumably without recognizing it as a hoax by English.

1 FEBRUARY. BALTIMORE. The *Republican and Daily Argus* reprints "The Ghost of a Grey Tadpole, by Edgar A. Poe" from the *Irish Citizen*, without comment.

1 FEBRUARY. At 7:00 AM Poe writes his early benefactor John P. Kennedy: "Some matters which would not be put off, have taken me to Elkton [Maryland]—so that I shall not have the pleasure of dining with you to-day, as proposed. Before leaving Baltimore, however, I hope to give you another call" (*L*, 2:704).

3 FEBRUARY. In the *Saturday Visiter* Snodgrass comments:

Edgar A. Poe delivered a lecture in Odd-Fellows Hall, on Wednesday evening—theme "American poetry." He was very entertaining, and enforced his views well—though to some of them we cannot assent. For instance—that the inculcation of truth is not the highest aim of poetry! He was witheringly severe upon Rufus W. Griswold, and declared it was a *shame* that he placed the name of N. C. Brooks in the "*appendix*"—and so it was a "shame"—but we think we should have prefer[r]ed silence on the topic, had we been placed among the *ephemera* of a volume *large* enough certainly to admit of putting all in the body of the work! But such alas, is often the fate of "undiscovered genius."

BEFORE 9 FEBRUARY? PHILADELPHIA. Poe writes Lowell in Cambridge, Massachusetts. He wishes to deliver his lecture on "American Poetry" in Boston, and he asks Lowell to ascertain whether any learned society in that city would be willing to sponsor it (Lowell's 6 March reply).

9 FEBRUARY. George R. Graham writes Longfellow in Cambridge, Massachusetts:

I send the proof here with [of a contribution to the April *Graham's*.] I wish it had been *original*, as such are worth three times the sum to a magazine. A translation is merely noticed by the press while an original from your pen is *always* widely copied and commented on.

However I hold you to your promise of an original *soon*, and am obliged to you for sending the enclosed. . . .

I have a *savage* review of your "Spanish Student" from the pen of Poe, which shall *not* appear in Graham. I do not know what your crime may be in the eyes of Poe, but suppose it may be a better, and more widely established reputation. Or if you have wealth—which I hope you *have*—that is sufficient to settle your damnation so far as Mr Poe may be presumed capable of effecting it[.]

The rascal borrowed some money of me the other day to take him to Boston and I learned within the hour afterward abused me at the next corner as an exclusive. I am so unfortunate as to have many of his MSS. to cover loans, but we part company as soon as I publish some of the least venomous. I had to suffer $30 for the review of you and you shall have it for as many cents when you come along this way. I do not suppose it will ever be redeemed, and I doubt if the writer of it will be (MH–H; cf. Poe to Graham, 10 March 1845).

18 FEBRUARY. Poe writes Lippard, evaluating his latest novel *The Ladye Annabel*: "The opinion I expressed to you, personally, was based, as I told you, upon a very cursory examination. It has been confirmed, however, by a subsequent reading at leisure. You seem to have been in too desperate a hurry to give due attention to details; and thus your style, although generally nervous, is at times somewhat exuberant—but the work, as a whole, will be admitted, by all but your personal enemies, to be richly inventive and imaginative—indicative of *genius* in its author." Poe advises Lippard not to worry about these enemies: "Let a fool alone—especially if he be both a scoundrel and a fool—and he will kill himself far sooner than you can kill him by any active exertion" (*L*, 1:242–43).

BEFORE 22 FEBRUARY. *Graham's Magazine* for March contains Poe's laudatory critique of Richard Henry Horne's epic *Orion* and his unsigned review of Lowell's *Poems* (Hull, p. 394).

22 FEBRUARY. Du Solle notices *Graham's* in the *Spirit of the Times*: "The review of 'Orion,' by Edgar A. Poe, is a rare production—one of those strong, thoughtful, intelligible, and truth-telling papers, which only come across us about once in a century."

23 FEBRUARY. JACKSON, TENNESSEE. John Tomlin writes Poe. He forwarded "the libellous letter" of Lambert A. Wilmer on 10 September 1843; since then he has not heard from Poe:

Did you inflict on him [Wilmer] a chastisement equal to the injury he designed, by the publication of such scandals? Previous to the reception of that letter, I had entertained a good opinion of the "Quacks of Helicon" man, and it had been brought about in a great measure by your Review of the Book. In his former letters, he not only spoke kindly of you, but seemed disposed to become your advocate, against the *littérateurs* of Philadelphia. I hope that you will forgive him, and that he will go, and "Sin no more."

Your Review of "Orion" . . . I have read with much pleasure. The article is one of great ability (*W*, 17:158).

CA. MARCH. PHILADELPHIA. In the company of Henry B. Hirst, Poe expresses a desire to see an article in an early volume of the *Southern Literary Messenger*. Hirst borrows the volume for Poe from the private library of William Duane, Jr., a Philadelphia scholar. Poe subsequently asks Mrs. Clemm to return it to Hirst; instead of complying, she sells it to the bookseller William A. Leary, 158 North Second Street (Poe to Duane, 28 October 1844 and 28 January 1845; Duane's annotations on these letters; see also Bandy [1982], pp. 81–95).

1 MARCH. Poe replies to John C. Myers, Samuel Williams, and William Greaff, Jr., of Reading, Pennsylvania, who have invited him to deliver his lecture on "American Poetry" before the Mechanics' Institute there: "Through some accident which I am at a loss to understand, your letter dated and postmarked Decr 29, has only this moment come to hand; having been lying, ever since, in the Phila P. Office. . . . I presume that your Lectures are over for the season; but, should this not be the case, it will give me great pleasure to deliver a Discourse before your Society" (*L*, 1:244).

5 MARCH. READING, PENNSYLVANIA. Williams and Greaff reply to Poe, inviting him to lecture on 12 March (Poe's 7 March reply).

6 MARCH. CAMBRIDGE, MASSACHUSETTS. Lowell replies to Poe's "last letter." He does not believe that Poe's lecture on "American Poetry" would succeed in Boston at the present time. The lectures "of a more literary

class" have been concluded for the year: "I spoke to the secretary of the Boston Lyceum about the probability of your success if you came experimentally, and he shook his head. It is not a matter in which I feel myself competent to judge—my bump of hope being quite too large. I asked him about engaging you for next year & he seemed very much pleased with the plan & said that the Society would be glad to do it." The lectures sponsored by the Lyceum hold "the highest rank"; the Society pays each speaker "from fifty to a hundred dollars, as their purse is full or empty." Lowell will soon forward a sketch of his life to Poe, who has offered to write the notice of him for the "Our Contributors" series now appearing in *Graham's Magazine*: "*Outwardly* it [Lowell's life] has been simple enough, but inwardly every man's life must be more or less of a curiosity. . . . When will Graham give us your portrait? I hope you will have it done well when it is done, & quickly too" (*W*, 17:158–60).

7 MARCH. PHILADELPHIA. Poe replies to the 5 March letter from Williams and Greaff of Reading, agreeing to lecture there on next Tuesday, 12 March: "Please reply by return of mail and let me know at what place I shall meet the Committee" (*L*, 1:244–45).

9 MARCH. READING, PENNSYLVANIA. The *Berks and Schuylkill Journal* announces that "A stated meeting of the Mechanics' Institute . . . on Tuesday evening next at 7:00 o'clock" will feature a "lecture by Edgar A. Poe of Philadelphia." Another notice appears in the *Reading Gazette*: "Lecture—Edgar A. Poe, Esq. will deliver a Lecture before the Mechanics' Institute, and the public, on Tuesday evening, next at the Academy Hall. Subject.—'American Poetry' " (Nolan, p. 15).

11 MARCH. PHILADELPHIA. The *Public Ledger* reports that Poe will lecture in Reading: "The people of that borough will be pleased with the lecture."

12 MARCH. Du Solle announces Poe's lecture in the *Spirit of the Times*: "Mr. P. is a finished scholar; a man of taste, genius, and nice discrimination."

12? MARCH. READING. Poe delivers his lecture (see 21 MARCH).

15 MARCH. PHILADELPHIA. Poe writes Cornelius Mathews in New York: "I have a letter and small parcel for Mr Horne, your friend, and the author of 'Orion'. Would you be so kind as to furnish me with his address?" Poe thanks Mathews for copies of his "able pamphlet on the International Copy-Right Question" and his novel *Puffer Hopkins*; he apologizes for the "impudent and flippant critique" of Mathews' epic poem *Wakondah* published in *Graham's Magazine* for February 1842. "Since I scribbled the

article in question, you yourself have given me fifty good reasons for being ashamed of it" (*L*, 1:245–46).

AFTER 15 MARCH. Poe writes Richard Henry Horne in London, forwarding a manuscript of his new tale "The Spectacles." He asks Horne to secure its publication in a British magazine (Horne to Poe, 16 and 27 April; Moldenhauer [1977], p. 186).

21 MARCH. BALTIMORE. The *Sun* reports: "EDGAR A. POE, ESQ.—This distinguished writer delivered his much extolled lecture on the 'Poets and Poetry of America,' at Reading, Pa., on Wednesday [Tuesday?] evening last. He was greeted by a large and highly respectable audience, and they testified their approbation of the lecture by repeated bursts of applause."

22 MARCH. SOUTH ATTLEBOROUGH, MASSACHUSETTS. Abijah M. Ide, Jr., writes Poe: "I am now at *my old home* again and, in the coming Spring and Summer, I shall plough the same old fields, and make hay on the greensward, that first gave me lessons in labor." Recently Ide had the good fortune to acquire some money, and he purchased volumes of poetry by Longfellow, Lowell, Whittier, and George Lunt. "I wish you would mention to me, such volumes as you think would do me most profit to read." In spite of "the wearisome tasks" Ide had to perform during the past winter, he managed to write many poems: "I have published *little*. A total lack of acquaintance with gentlemen connected with the literary Magazines & newspapers, has withheld me from offering but few lines for publication.—I sent a brief poem to John Inman, (for the Columbian), which was immediately published; (*in the March no.*). You will find it on page 139—'Strife.' . . . What publication would you advise me to send my poetry to; and ought I to send it anonymously, or not? You know better about those things than I do" (*W*, 17:162–64).

BEFORE 23 MARCH. PHILADELPHIA. *Godey's Lady's Book* contains Poe's "A Tale of the Ragged Mountains."

23 MARCH. BALTIMORE. The *Weekly Sun* reprints this story from *Godey's* (Phillips, 1:859).

27 MARCH. PHILADELPHIA. The *Dollar Newspaper* contains "The Spectacles." On another page the editor Joseph Sailer comments: "We publish this week from the pen of Edgar A. Poe, Esq., a story under the title of 'The Spectacles', to which we call the attention of the readers of the 'Newspaper' under the assurance that they will join us in the opinion that it is one of the best from his chaste and able pen and second only to the

popular prize production, 'The Gold Bug.' Who will go without 'Spectacles' when an article so handsomely furnished may be obtained for 3 cents?" (Moldenhauer [1977], pp. 179, 183).

27, 28, 29 MARCH. In the *Spirit of the Times* Du Solle reprints "A Tale of the Ragged Mountains" in three installments, from *Godey's*.

28 MARCH. Du Solle comments: "THE DOLLAR NEWSPAPER of this week is a choice number. Poe's Story of 'The Spectacles' is alone worth double the price of the paper."

30 MARCH. Poe replies to Lowell's 6 March letter. He discusses the "Our Contributors" series of *Graham's Magazine*: "Graham has been speaking to me, lately, about your Biography, and I am anxious to write it at once—always provided you have no objection. Could you forward me the materials within a day or two? . . . You inquire about my own portrait. It has been done for some time—but is better as an engraving, than as a portrait. It scarcely resembles me at all. When it will appear I cannot say. . . . My Life is not yet written, and I am at a sad loss for a Biographer—for Graham insists upon leaving the matter to myself." Poe asks: "Have you seen the article on 'American Poetry' in the 'London Foreign Quarterly'? It has been denied that Dickens wrote it—but, to me, the article affords so strong internal evidence of his hand that I would as soon think of doubting my existence. He tells much truth—although he evinces much ignorance and more spleen." Like the British critic, however, Poe believes that the present condition of American literature is "dreadful." The remedy is "a well-founded Monthly Journal" which could set the tone for the nation's letters: "Such a journal might, perhaps, be set on foot by a coalition, and, thus set on foot, with proper understanding, would be irresistible. Suppose, for example, that the élite of our men of letters should combine secretly. . . . The articles to be supplied by the members solely, and upon a concerted plan of action. A nominal editor to be elected from among the number. . . . If we do *not* defend ourselves by some such coalition, we shall be devoured, without mercy, by the Godeys, the Snowdens, et id genus omne" (*L*, 1:246–48).

6 APRIL. NEW YORK. Early in the morning Poe and Virginia leave Philadelphia, travelling by train to Perth Amboy, New Jersey, where they take the steamer to New York. Poe rents a room in a boardinghouse at 130 Greenwich Street in lower Manhattan, near the Hudson River (Quinn, pp. 406–08).

7 APRIL. Poe writes Mrs. Clemm in Philadelphia, describing yesterday's trip:

We started in good spirits, but did not get here until nearly 3 o'clock. We went in the cars to Amboy about 40 miles from N. York, and then took the steamboat the rest of the way.—Sissy [Virginia] coughed none at all. When we got to the wharf it was raining hard. I left her on board the boat, after putting the trunks in the Ladies' Cabin, and set off to buy an umbrella and look for a boarding-house. . . . When we got to the house we had to wait about ½ an hour before the room was ready. . . . Last night, for supper, we had the nicest tea you ever drank, strong & hot—wheat bread & rye bread—cheese—tea-cakes (elegant) a great dish (2 dishes) of elegant ham, and 2 of cold veal, piled up like a mountain and large slices—3 dishes of the cakes, and every thing in the greatest profusion. No fear of starving here. The landlady seemed as if she could'nt press us enough, and we were at home directly. . . . We have now got 4 $ and a half left. Tomorrow I am going to try & borrow 3 $—so that I may have a fortnight to go upon. I feel in excellent spirits & have'nt drank a drop—so that I hope soon to get out of trouble. The very instant I scrape together enough money I will send it on. You ca'nt imagine how much we both do miss you. Sissy had a hearty cry last night, because you and Catterina [the family cat] weren't here.

In a postscript Poe reminds Mrs. Clemm to return the volume of the *Southern Literary Messenger* which Hirst borrowed for him from William Duane, Jr. (*L*, 1:251–53; facsimile in Quinn and Hart, pp. 19–21).

BEFORE 13 APRIL. Poe sells "The Balloon-Hoax" to Moses Y. Beach, editor of the *Sun*.

13 APRIL. The regular morning edition of the *Sun* carries an announcement under the heading "Postscript":

ASTOUNDING INTELLIGENCE BY PRIVATE EXPRESS FROM CHARLES-TON VIA NORFOLK!—THE ATLANTIC OCEAN CROSSED IN THREE DAYS!!—ARRIVAL AT SULLIVAN'S ISLAND OF A STEERING BALLOON INVENTED BY MR. MONCK MASON!!
We stop the press at a late hour, to announce that, by a Private Express from Charleston, S. C., we are just put in possession of full details of the most extraordinary adventure ever accomplished by man. *The Atlantic Ocean has been actually traversed in a balloon, and in the incredibly brief period of Three Days!* Eight persons have crossed in the machine—among others Sir Everard Bringhurst and Mr. Monck Mason.—We have barely time now to announce this most novel and unexpected intelligence; but we hope by 10 this morning to have ready an Extra with a detailed account of the voyage.
P.S.—The Extra will be positively ready, and for sale at our counter, by 10 o'clock this morning. It will embrace all the particulars yet known. We have also placed in the hands of an excellent artist a representation of the "STEERING BALLOON," which will accompany the particulars of the voyage.

13 APRIL. MID-DAY. Poe's story is issued as a one-page broadside under the masthead "THE EXTRA SUN":

ASTOUNDING / NEWS! / BY EXPRESS VIA NORFOLK! / [rule] / THE / ATLANTIC CROSSED / IN / THREE DAYS! / [rule] / SIGNAL TRIUMPH / OF / MR. MONCK MASON'S / *FLYING* / MACHINE!!! / [rule] / Arrival at Sullivan's Island, / near Charleston, S. C., of / Mr. Mason, Mr. Robert Hol–/ land, Mr. Henson, Mr. Har–/ rison Ainsworth, and four / others, in the / STEERING BALLOON / "VICTORIA," / AFTER A PASSAGE OF / SEVENTY-FIVE HOURS / FROM LAND TO LAND. / [rule] / FULL PARTICULARS / OF THE / *VOYAGE*!!!

[In his second dispatch to the *Columbia Spy*, published on 25 May, Poe commented:

Talking of "expresses"—the "Balloon-Hoax" made a far more intense sensation than anything of that character since the "Moon-Story" of Locke. On the morning (Saturday) of its announcement, the whole square surrounding the "Sun" building was literally besieged, blocked up—ingress and egress being alike impossible, from a period soon after sunrise until about two o'clock P.M. In Saturday's regular issue, it was stated that the news had been just received, and that an "Extra" was then in preparation, which would be ready at ten. It was not delivered, however, until nearly noon. In the meantime I never witnessed more intense excitement to get possession of a newspaper. As soon as the few first copies made their way into the streets, they were bought up, at almost any price, from the news-boys, who made a profitable speculation beyond doubt. I saw a half-dollar given, in one instance, for a single paper, and a shilling [12½ cents] was a frequent price. I tried, in vain, during the whole day, to get possession of a copy. It was excessively amusing, however, to hear the comments of those who had read the "Extra." Of course there was great discrepancy of opinion as regards the authenticity of the story; but I observed that the more intelligent believed, while the rabble, for the most part, rejected the whole with disdain (Spannuth and Mabbott, p. 33).

Richard Adams Locke's famous "Moon-Hoax" had appeared in the *Sun* in August 1835.]

14 APRIL. Major Mordecai M. Noah reprints "The Balloon-Hoax" in his *Sunday Times*. Another Sunday paper, the *Mercury*, carries a spoof of Poe's story headed "Astounding Intelligence from the Man in the Moon" (Mabbott [1978], 3:1067).

15 APRIL. In its daily and semiweekly editions the *New York American* reports:

The Sun has issued an *Extra* with a poor imitation of the Moon Hoax in the shape of a narrative of a *balloon voyage* across the Atlantic in three days—the particulars of which, it purports to have received express from Charleston, where the balloon landed on Tuesday.

The express, which has hardly outstripped the ordinary mail, must also have brought along a woodcut of the balloon, as the Sun has the picture as well as the story—one as good as the other.

"The Balloon-Hoax" in the *Sun*, 13 April

Richard Gimbel Collection, *Philadelphia Free Library*

James Gordon Bennett of the *New York Herald* castigates an editorial adversary:

BEACH'S LAST HOAX.—On Saturday last the community were very much exasperated by being imposed upon by a ridiculous hoax, issued by that manufacturer of hoaxes of all kinds, whether in banking or anything else, that offers the prospect of "turning a penny," Moses Y. Beach. This hoax was in the form of an extra, giving an account of the arrival at Charleston, S. C., of a balloon from England, and extracts from the journal of the *voyageurs*. When this blundering blockhead had an intention of getting up something in the hoaxing line, he ought to have engaged some person who had common sense and who had information enough to preserve localities and other necessary circumstances in such a narrative. But it was so blunderingly got up—so ridiculously put together—so preposterously issued . . . .

The *Sun* carries this retraction:

BALLOON.—The mails from the South last Saturday night not having brought a confirmation of the arrival of the Balloon from England, the particulars of which from our correspondent we detailed in our Extra, we are inclined to believe that the intelligence is erroneous. The description of the Balloon and the voyage was written with a minuteness, and scientific ability calculated to obtain credit every where, and was read with great pleasure and satisfaction. We by no means think such a project impossible.

15 APRIL. PHILADELPHIA. The *Native American* publishes a humorous commentary on "The Balloon-Hoax" (Mabbott [1978], 3:1067).

16 APRIL. LONDON. Horne replies to Poe's letter written from Philadelphia after 15 March. Many British literati have been displeased by Horne's *New Spirit of the Age*, containing his critical essays on living authors; therefore he can do little at present to promote Poe's interests in this country. Perhaps Horne can insert "The Spectacles," the manuscript Poe forwarded, in *Jerrold's Illuminated Magazine*: "Jerrold has always spoken and written very handsomely and eloquently about me, and there would be no difficulty. But—I fear this magazine is not doing at all well. I tell you this *in confidence*. They have a large but inadequate circulation. The remuneration would be scarcely worth having—ten guineas a sheet is poor pay for such a page! And now, perhaps, they do not even give that. . . . Your name is well known to me in the critical literature of America, although I have not seen any American magazine for some months" (Woodberry, 2:50–52).

[Horne was unable to place Poe's tale. "I tried several magazines. Not an editor would touch it" (Horne to S. S. Rice, 8 April 1876, in Rice, pp. 81–84).]

20 APRIL. PHILADELPHIA. The *Saturday Courier* reprints a portion of "The Balloon-Hoax," explaining:

We make the short extracts above for the purpose of showing very briefly to our readers the nature of the narrative. It is stated that about 50,000 of the extras were sold, notwithstanding the absurdity of the details which it contained.

We think every intelligent reader will be disposed to regard this attempt to hoax as not even possessing the character of pleasantry. The celebrated "Moon Hoax," issued from the office of the New York Sun, many years ago, was an ingenious essay; but that is more than can be said of this "Balloon Story."

20 APRIL. COLUMBIA, PENNSYLVANIA. The *Columbia Spy* reports that the *Sun* has issued an extra describing a transatlantic balloon voyage: "The joke is an imitation of the *moon hoax* published in the same paper several years since" (Spannuth and Mabbott, p. 121).

27 APRIL. The *Spy* reprints Poe's "A Tale of the Ragged Mountains" (Spannuth and Mabbott, p. 121).

27 APRIL. LONDON. Horne writes Poe again: "When I replied to your letter (which I did by the next post of the day on which I received it) I had not seen the number of 'Graham's' for March, containing the review of 'Orion.' . . . It would be uncandid in me to appear to agree to all the objections; and, amidst such high praise, so independently and courageously awarded, it would be ungrateful in me to offer any self-justificatory remark on any such objections. I shall, therefore, only observe that there are *some* objections from which I can *derive advantage* in the way of revision—which is more than I can say of any of the critiques written on this side of the water. . . . Would any American bookseller like to reprint 'Orion,' do you think?" (Woodberry, 2:52–55).

MAY? NEW YORK. Mrs. Clemm joins Poe and Virginia.

BEFORE 14 MAY. Poe receives Horne's 16 April letter, forwarded from Philadelphia (*Columbia Spy*, 18 May).

18 MAY. COLUMBIA, PENNSYLVANIA. In the *Columbia Spy*, a weekly newspaper of limited circulation, the editor Eli Bowen remarks: "Edgar A. Poe, Esq., well known to the Literary public as an eminent scholar and a distinguished critic, we are pleased to announce to our readers, will, in future, be a regular contributor to the Spy. Besides other matters, he will furnish us with a weekly 'Correspondence' from the City of New York, where he has taken up his residence for the present." The issue contains

Poe's first dispatch, dated 14 May, in which he describes his wanderings "far and wide over this island of Mannahatta" and quotes from Horne's 16 April letter (Spannuth and Mabbott, pp. 23–29, 121).

20 MAY. PHILADELPHIA. Horne's 27 April letter is forwarded to New York (Ostrom [1981], p. 216).

CA. 20 MAY. *Graham's Magazine* for June contains Poe's signed poem "Dream-Land" as well as two unsigned criticisms, "Our Contributors, No. XII: Robert T. Conrad" and a review of Epes Sargent's *The Light of the Light House, and Other Poems* (attributions in Hull, pp. 394–95, and Mabbott [1932], p. 441).

21 MAY. NEW YORK. Poe writes Nathaniel P. Willis at the office of the *New Mirror*:

Seeing that you, now and then, published Original Papers in the "New Mirror," I have ventured to send you a Tale ["The Oblong Box"] and an Essay for consideration. If you could afford me anything for them, or for either of them, I would feel highly honored by their appearance in your paper. I have long been exceedingly anxious to make the acquaintance of the author of "Melanie," and, more especially, of a little poem entitled "Unseen Spirits," and would have called upon you personally, but that I am ill in health and wretchedly depressed in spirits. By and bye I will try and find you at the office of the "Mirror." Will you please reply, at your leisure, through the P. Office? Should you not be able to accept the articles, I would be obliged if you would retain them until I see you (Crocker, p. 232).

AFTER 21 MAY. Willis either sees or writes Poe: he praises "The Oblong Box" but explains that the *Mirror* cannot pay for original contributions (Poe to Mrs. S. J. Hale, 29 May).

25 MAY. COLUMBIA, PENNSYLVANIA. The *Spy* contains Poe's second dispatch, dated 21 May, in which he describes the reception of "The Balloon-Hoax," acknowledges the sketch of Conrad in the June *Graham's*, and discusses Willis and the *Mirror* (Spannuth and Mabbott, pp. 31–37).

28 MAY. NEW YORK. Poe replies to a letter from Lowell in Cambridge, Massachusetts, who has offered to write his biography for the "Our Contributors" series of *Graham's*. "I received yours last night—forwarded from Philadelphia to this city, where I intend living for the future: Touching the Biography—I would be very proud, indeed, if you would write it—and did, certainly, say to myself, and I believe to Graham—that such was my wish; but as I fancied the job might be disagreeable, I did not venture to suggest it to yourself." Poe encloses a copy of the *Saturday Museum*

containing his biography and poems: "Besides the Tales enumerated in the foot-note, I have written 'The Spectacles'; *'The Oblong Box'*; 'A Tale of the Ragged Mountains'; *'The Premature Burial'*; *'The Purloined Letter'*; *'The System of Doctors Tar and Fether'*; 'The Black Cat'; 'The Elk'; 'Diddling Considered as one of the Exact Sciences;' *'Mesmeric Revelation'*; 'The Gold-Bug;' *'Thou art the Man* . . . . Those Italicized are as yet unpublished . . . . Of the 'Gold-Bug' (my most successful tale) more than 300,000 copies have been circulated" (*L*, 1:253–54).

29 MAY. Poe writes Mrs. Sarah J. Hale in Philadelphia: "A day or two ago, I handed an article, 'The Oblong Box', to Mr Willis, under the impression that he occasionally purchased original papers for 'The New-Mirror'. This I found, however, not to be the case." Willis recommended the story for the *Opal*, a New York annual which he formerly edited. Poe called on the publisher, John C. Riker, who told him that Mrs. Hale, the new editor, would be solely responsible for the contents of the next volume. "Under these circumstances, I have thought it best to write you this letter, and to ask you if you could accept an article from me—whether you would wish to see the one in question—or whether you could be so kind as to take it, unseen, upon Mr Willis' testimony in its favor" (*L*, 2:705).

31 MAY. Poe replies to a "kind and very satisfactory letter" from Mrs. Hale in Philadelphia: "if you will be so good as to keep open for me the ten pages of which you speak, I will forward you, in 2 or 3 days, an article which will about occupy that space, and which I will endeavour to adapt to the character of 'The Opal.' The price you mention—50 cts per page— will be amply sufficient . . . ." Poe will soon forward "a package" to Louis A. Godey (*L*, 1:255).

31 MAY. Poe writes Edward L. Carey, partner in Carey & Hart, in Philadelphia: "I would take it as a very great favor if you could let me see the proof of my tale, 'The Purloined Letter', which will be in the next 'Gift'. I am not, usually, solicitous about proofs; but, in this instance, the MS. had many interlineations and erasures, which may render my seeing one, necessary" (*L*, 2:706).

EARLY JUNE. Poe forwards his stories "The Oblong Box" and "Thou Art the Man" to Godey for the *Lady's Book* (implied by Poe to Mrs. Hale, 31 May, and by Godey's acknowledgment in the August number).

EARLY JUNE? The Poe family takes lodging in the two-story farmhouse of Patrick and Mary Brennan, located on Eighty-fourth Street between Amsterdam Avenue and Broadway, then a rural neighborhood. Poe revises his unpublished poem "The Raven" while the Brennan's young daughter Martha arranges his manuscripts (New York *Mail and Express*, 21 April 1900, p. 15; see also Gill, pp. 148–50, Phillips, 2:882–98, and *W*, 1:223–27).

1 JUNE. COLUMBIA, PENNSYLVANIA. In the *Spy* Eli Bowen comments: "if the *puffs* of our contemporaries, etc., be any evidence, Mr. Poe's letters are the best things afloat at present." This issue contains Poe's third dispatch, dated 27 May, in which he describes his visit to Blackwell's Island (now Roosevelt Island) in the East River, a "day or two since" in "a light skiff." Poe praises his friend William Ross Wallace; he condemns William W. Snowden's *Ladies' Companion* as "the *ne plus ultra* of ill-taste, impudence, and vulgar humbuggery" (Spannuth and Mabbott, pp. 39–45, 121–22).

2 OR 3? JUNE. NEW YORK. Poe forwards "A Chapter of Suggestions," his contribution to the *Opal*, to Mrs. Hale in Philadelphia (implied by Poe to Hale, 31 May).

3 JUNE. Poe writes the poet Lewis J. Cist in Cincinnati: "Yours, dated April 30th, has only this moment reached me; having been lying, ever since, at Graham's office. I have removed to New-York, where I intend residing for the next year or two—and this will account, in part, for my not receiving the package sooner." He was deeply interested in "the memoirs" Cist sent him of another Cincinnati poet, Mrs. Rebecca S. Reed Nichols: "I have long admired her writings." Poe promises to write George R. Graham today about the disposition of Cist's poem "The Beaten Path" (*L*, 2:706–07).

4 JUNE. Poe sends Bowen his fourth dispatch for the *Columbia Spy*, pencilling this request on the manuscript: "I would take it as a very great favor if you could mail me an X [$10] by return of mail, if possible" (*L*, 1:255–56; Spannuth and Mabbott, p. 55).

5 JUNE. PHILADELPHIA. The *Public Ledger* contains "Singular Death," a paragraph describing the death of an Englishman who accidentally swallowed a dart while playing "puff the dart."

[Poe quoted the paragraph in his tale "The Angel of the Odd."]

8 JUNE. COLUMBIA, PENNSYLVANIA. The *Spy* contains Poe's fourth dispatch, dated 4 June, in which he discusses Locke's "Moon-Hoax," the German-American novelist Charles Sealsfield, and the Antarctic Exploring Expedition originated by Jeremiah N. Reynolds (Spannuth and Mabbott, pp. 47–57).

15 JUNE. The *Spy* contains Poe's fifth dispatch, dated 12 June, in which he describes the architecture of Brooklyn and street pavements of Kyanized wood (Spannuth and Mabbott, pp. 59–64).

15 JUNE. OAKY GROVE, GEORGIA. Thomas Holley Chivers writes Poe. He has received no answer to his last two letters, the first written on 7 December 1842 and the second about a year ago. "I see you still write for 'Graham's Magazine.' He ought to give you ten thousand dollars a year for supervising it. . . . It is not my opinion that you ever have been, or ever will be, paid for your intellectual labour. You need never expect it, until you establish a Magazine of your own. . . . Your criticism of 'Orion' pleased me very much. . . . Your conception of the uses, or excellence, of Poetry is the loftiest I have seen. There is, in the perspicuous flow of your pure English, a subtle delicacy of expression which always pleases me— *except when you tomahawk people*! I cannot say that I like very much your *dis*like to Transcendentalism" (Chivers [1957], pp. 21–25).

22 JUNE. COLUMBIA, PENNSYLVANIA. In the *Spy* Bowen remarks: "The Letter of our New York Correspondent [Poe's 18 June dispatch] arrived too late for insertion in to-day's paper" (Spannuth and Mabbott, p. 122).

27 JUNE. ELMWOOD HOUSE, CAMBRIDGE, MASSACHUSETTS. Lowell replies to Poe's 28 May letter. For the past month he has been "stealing a kind of vacation from the pen," but he is now resolved to begin work on Poe's biography for *Graham's*. "The newspaper you sent me will give me enough outward facts—but I want *your own estimate* of your life. Of course you need not write it as if for my use merely in the writing of this article— but as to a friend. I believe that the opinion a man has of himself (if he be accustomed to self-analysis) is of more worth than that of all the rest of the world." Although Lowell agrees that the unsigned critique of "American Poetry" in the January *Foreign Quarterly Review* "was fair enough as far as the Conclusions the author came to were concerned," he disputes the attribution Poe gave in his 30 March and 28 May letters: "It was not (I am quite sure) written by Dickens, but by a friend of his named Forster . . . . Dickens may have given him hints. Forster is a friend of some of the Longfellow clique here which perhaps accounts for his putting L. at the top of our Parnassus" (Woodberry, 2:87–89; Moss [1963], p. 158).

29 JUNE. COLUMBIA, PENNSYLVANIA. The *Spy* contains Poe's sixth dispatch, dated 18 June, in which he discusses the case of the accused murderess Polly Bodine and the forthcoming 1845 editions of the *Opal* and the *Gift*. Poe regrets that Nathaniel P. Willis left the seclusion of Glen Mary, New York: "In its retirement he might have accomplished much,

both for himself and for posterity; but, chained to the oar of a mere weekly paper [the *New Mirror*], professedly addressing the frivolous and the fashionable, what can he now hope for but a gradual sinking into the slough of the Public Disregard?" (Spannuth and Mabbott, pp. 65–71).

JULY. NEW YORK. The "Editor's Table" of the *Knickerbocker Magazine* contains a fictitious interview with "the great SEATSFIELD" [Charles Sealsfield]. This European commentator on American life is made to compare Poe with the anonymous author of *Washington: A National Poem* (1843). "POE is a man of nearly equal ability, but his genius condescends to dally with the diminutive. His soul-grasp is indeed vigorous, but his relish for the beautiful breaks up the wholeness of his life-imagery into brilliancy of detail. There is a splendor in his general survey of outward things which too often decoys him from the stern filling-up and elaborate job-work which is absolutely demanded to render a work truly artistical."

[The purported observations parody Poe's critical dicta; cf. *W*, 10:39–40, and L. G. Clark to Longfellow, 5 July.]

2 JULY. Poe answers Lowell's 27 June letter, complying with the request for an estimate of his life: "I am *not* ambitious—unless negatively. I, now and then feel stirred up to excel a fool, merely because I hate to let a fool imagine that he may excel me. Beyond this I feel nothing of ambition. I really perceive that vanity about which most men merely prate—the vanity of the human or temporal life. I live continually in a reverie of the future. I have no faith in human perfectibility. I think that human exertion will have no appreciable effect upon humanity. Man is now only more active—not more happy—nor more wise, than he was 6000 years ago." Poe still believes that Dickens wrote the article in the *Foreign Quarterly Review*: "I had two long interviews with Mr D. when here. Nearly every thing in the critique, I heard from him or suggested to him, personally. The poem of Emerson I read to him" (*L*, 1:256–59).

5 JULY. Lewis Gaylord Clark writes Longfellow in Cambridge, Massachusetts, discussing the July *Knickerbocker*: "You'll find those Seatsfield notices capital, I think. The [meaning?] of the writer was not so apparent at first. I can see that in his *Standards* (such as Poe and the author of 'Washington!') he designs to crucify the commenting and non-producing asses, who are nothing if *not* critical, and very little at that" (Clark, pp. 120–21).

6 JULY. COLUMBIA, PENNSYLVANIA. The *Spy* contains Poe's seventh and final dispatch, dated 25 June, in which he praises John Inman, editor of the *Columbian Magazine*, and quotes "the best" of Willis' poems, "Unseen Spirits" (Spannuth and Mabbott, pp. 73–77).

10 JULY. NEW YORK. Poe writes Chivers in Oaky Grove, Georgia: "Yours of June 15 was forwarded here to me [from Philadelphia] on the 25th [ul]t. . . . The two letters of which you speak were received; but, in the hurry of mere business, I chanced to file them away among a package of letters endorsed 'answered,' and thus it was that I failed to reply." He still intends to establish his own magazine, to be called the *Stylus*: "Should you conclude to join me, we will not fail to make fame and fortune. . . . A Magazine like Graham's will never do." Chivers is mistaken in his belief that Poe dislikes the Transcendentalists: "it is only the pretenders and sophists among them." Poe's personal philosophy is "somewhat detailed" in "Mesmeric Revelation," forthcoming in the *Columbian Magazine*. He paraphrases the cosmology revealed in this article: "There is no such thing as spirituality. God is material. All things are material; yet the matter of God has all the qualities which we attribute to spirit: thus the difference is scarcely more than of words. There is a matter without particles—of no atomic composition: this is God. It permeates and impels all things, and thus *is* all things in itself. Its agitation is the thought of God, and creates" (*L*, 1:259–60).

12 JULY. RICHMOND. Alexander B. Shelton, who married Poe's early love Elmira Royster, dies at age thirty-seven, leaving his widow an estate estimated at $100,000 (Rudd, 1:31; see CA. 22? SEPTEMBER 1849).

17–18 JULY. PHILADELPHIA. The *Public Ledger* publishes "A Moving Chapter," Poe's unsigned article on omnibuses and cabs, in two installments (attribution in the *Columbia Spy*, 14 August; Mabbott [1978], 3:1088–95).

19 JULY. The *Ledger* contains "Desultory Notes on Cats," an unsigned playful essay by Poe (Mabbott [1978], 3:1095–98).

CA. 20 JULY. In a notice to correspondents *Godey's Lady's Book* for August lists "The Oblong Box" and "Thou Art the Man" among the "articles on file for publication."

30 JULY. The *Dollar Newspaper* for 31 July contains "The Premature Burial." The editor Joseph Sailer comments: "the original story by Edgar A. Poe is not only powerfully worked up but the interests are set forth in the choicest and most beautiful language that we almost ever placed in print" (Robertson, 2:210).

31 JULY. The *Public Ledger* notices this week's *Dollar Newspaper*, which went on sale at the *Ledger* office yesterday afternoon. "The genius and power of

Mr P. as a writer is [are] well known, and 'The Premature Burial' exhibits both in a striking degree. It is a highly exciting production, and will be widely read."

31 JULY. COLUMBIA, PENNSYLVANIA. The *Spy* contains a possible Poe contribution, a paragraph headed "Literary Theft" (Spannuth and Mabbott, p. 111).

AUGUST. NEW YORK. The *Columbian Magazine* contains Poe's philosophic tale "Mesmeric Revelation."

AUGUST OR LATER. PHILADELPHIA. The Swedenborgians write Poe that at first they doubted the authenticity of "Mesmeric Revelation" but have since discovered it to be completely true (Poe in "Marginal Notes," August 1845 *Godey's*; T. D. English in October 1845 *Aristidean* [see BEFORE 8 NOVEMBER 1845]).

3 AUGUST. NEW YORK. The *New World* reprints "Mesmeric Revelation" from the *Columbian Magazine*, prefacing it with this disclaimer: "Mr. Poe cannot, on so serious a subject, trifle with his readers: yet more extraordinary statements can hardly be conceived. We *do* believe in the facts of mesmerism, although we have not yet been able to arrive at any theory sufficient to explain them. Here, however, we are almost staggered. Of course, the narrative will be universally circulated; so we recommend it to the perusal of our readers and invite them to draw their own conclusions."

6 AUGUST. OAKY GROVE, GEORGIA. Chivers writes Poe: "I have just received your beautiful, friendly, abstruse, and transcendental letter of July the 10*th* . . . . I should like very much to see your article entitled 'Mesmeric Revelation.' Will you be so good as to forward the Number of the 'Columbian Magazine' on to me containing it? If you will, I will do ten times as much for you." Chivers disputes Poe's concept that everything is material: "Then the matter of God *is* spirit. We must either attribute to spirit properties which it does not possess, or '*God is a spirit*'—as the substance of any thing cannot be less than the qualities of which it is composed. If you mean by matter what I mean by spirit, then your matter is my spirit, and God is material; but if you mean by matter no more than what is *usually* meant by it, then, my spirit is *not* your matter, and '*God is a spirit*.' All the alchimy [alchemy] of your refined genius cannot transmute 'unparticled matter' into my idea of spirit" (Chivers [1957], pp. 27–32).

14 AUGUST. COLUMBIA, PENNSYLVANIA. The *Spy* reprints the second installment of Poe's "A Moving Chapter," with this preface by Eli Bowen: "If

the following article from the Philadelphia Ledger [of 18 July] does not set our readers into a broad laugh, we know not human nature. From the style and manner, we should infer that the paper was written by Edgar A. Poe, who, it is whispered, indites many of the *leaders* of that able journal. It looks very much like him" (Spannuth and Mabbott, pp. 88–90).

17 AUGUST. NEW YORK. Under the heading "Burying Alive" the *Rover*, a weekly magazine, reprints several paragraphs from Poe's "The Premature Burial" in the 31 July *Dollar Newspaper* (Heartman and Canny, pp. 242–43; Mabbott [1978], 3:954).

18 AUGUST. Poe writes Lowell in Cambridge, Massachusetts, forwarding a corrected copy of his "Mesmeric Revelation" contained in the August *Columbian Magazine*: "In fact the article was wofully misprinted; and my principal object in boring you with it now, is to beg of you the favor to get it copied (with corrections) in the Brother Jonathan—I mean the Boston Notion—or any other paper where you have interest. . . . In what are you occupied? . . . For myself I am very industrious—collecting and arranging materials for a Critical History of Am. Literature. Do you ever see Mr Hawthorne? He is a man of rare genius. . . . How fares it with the Biography?" (*L*, 1:261).

BEFORE 28 AUGUST. PHILADELPHIA. *Godey's Lady's Book* for September contains "The Oblong Box."

28 AUGUST. The *Dollar Newspaper* reprints Poe's tale from *Godey's*, adding the subtitle "A Capital Story" (Mabbott [1978], 3:922).

31 AUGUST. The *Saturday Museum* reprints "Mesmeric Revelation" from the *New World* of 3 August (Mabbott [1978], 3:1026, 1029).

2 SEPTEMBER. WASHINGTON. Frederick William Thomas writes Poe, addressing his letter to Philadelphia:

Some months since, in passing through Philadelphia, where I tarried a day, I tried to find you, and learned that you were absent in New York. I regretted I did not see you—I saw Mr [Rufus W.] Griswold, and had quite a talk with him.

Poe, you remember that you wrote me that you liked my poem which I call "The Beechen Tree" very much—Well, my good friend, it is just published—I have no copy by me or I would contrive to send you one—You know how much I value a good word from you my friend—and a word to [the wise] &c. . . .

Why, my old friend, have you not written to me—often when I grow tired of my daily dull task I turn to your letters, which I have carefully put away, and have a talk with you . . . .

My particular friend (heaven save the mark!) Thomas Dunn English, is I see editor of the [New York] Aurora—The only notice, except from Clarke of the Knickerbocker, from whom I have had a very kind letter, that I have seen of my poem is in the columns of the Aforesaid Aurora—The editor says it gave him "nausea" and that it was all "twattle" (MB–G).

7 SEPTEMBER. BUFFALO, NEW YORK. The *Western Literary Messenger* reprints "The Oblong Box" from the September *Godey's* (Jackson [1981], pp. 109–10).

8 SEPTEMBER. NEW YORK. Poe answers Thomas' letter:

I have left Philadelphia, and am living, at present, about five miles out of New-York. For the last seven or eight months I have been playing hermit in earnest—nor have I seen a living soul out of my family—who are well, and desire to be kindly remembered. . . .

Touching the "Beechen Tree", I remember it well and pleasantly. I have not yet seen a published copy—but will get one forthwith, and notice it as it deserves—and it deserves much of high praise—at the very first opportunity I get. . . .

You said to me, hurriedly, when we last met on the wharf in Philadelphia, that you believed Robert Tyler really wished to give me the post in the Custom-House. This I also really think; and I am confirmed in the opinion that he could not, at all times, do as he wished in such matters, by seeing Dunn English at the head of the "Aurora"—a bullet-headed and malicious villain who has brought more odium upon the Administration than any fellow (of equal littleness) in its ranks (L, 2:708–09).

BEFORE 24 SEPTEMBER. PHILADELPHIA. Carey & Hart publish the *Gift* for 1845, containing Poe's tale "The Purloined Letter."

24 SEPTEMBER. NEW YORK. The *Daily Tribune* carries an advertisement for the *Gift*.

24 SEPTEMBER. OAKY GROVE, GEORGIA. Chivers writes Poe, who has not corresponded since 10 July: "Your last letter gave me such intellectual delight—the highest pleasure that a man can enjoy on earth—such as the Angels feel in heaven—that I desire, very much, to receive another one from you. I have been studying it ever since I received it." Chivers discusses at length the "twofold nature in man," physical and spiritual. "It is, therefore, plain that the body, to glorify God, must be redeemed as well as the soul. This redemption consists in its *perfection*. It is the instrument of the soul. Without a perfect instrument, how can the soul elicit its functions? . . . This soul and body, perfected, constitute the *beautified* person of man. . . . If you will write me in what Number of the 'Columbian Magazine' your 'Mesmeric Revelation' is published, I can get it in Augusta" (Chivers [1957], pp. 32–36).

27 SEPTEMBER. ELMWOOD HOUSE, CAMBRIDGE, MASSACHUSETTS. Lowell writes Poe: "I kept back the biography a short time in order to send it on by a private hand. It is not half so good as it ought to be, but it was written under many disadvantages, not the least of which was depression of spirits which unfits a man for anything. . . . You will find the package at No. 1 Nassau Street, *up stairs*. It was addressed to the care of *C. F. Briggs*" (Woodberry, 2:100).

28 SEPTEMBER. NEW YORK. The *New Mirror*, a weekly magazine, ceases publication. The editors George P. Morris and Nathaniel P. Willis explain that the *Mirror* will henceforth be issued as a daily newspaper with a weekly edition, thus avoiding the higher postage rates charged for magazines.

LATE SEPTEMBER? Mrs. Clemm calls on Willis, seeking employment for Poe: "she excused her errand by mentioning that he [Poe] was ill, that her daughter was a confirmed invalid, and that their circumstances were such as compelled her taking it upon herself" (Willis in the *Home Journal*, 20 October 1849).

OCTOBER? Poe writes his satire "The Literary Life of Thingum Bob, Esq.," which incorporates a phrase applied to him in Lowell's biography, "that

GEORGE P. MORRIS and NATHANIEL P. WILLIS
Humanities Research Center, University of Texas at Austin

indescribable something which men have agreed to call *genius*" (Mabbott [1978], 3:1125, 1145, 1149).

OCTOBER? The artist Gabriel Harrison recalls his first acquaintance with Poe:

At that time I was the President of the White Eagle Club [a Democratic political organization], New York, and kept a tea store on the southeast corner of Broadway and Prince street, then Mr. William Niblo's property. One evening I observed a person looking intently through my windows at a display of some Virginia leaf tobacco. After some minutes he entered the store, spoke of the beauty of the leaf and its quality. He took a very small bit of it in his mouth, and further remarked that he might be considered a small user of the Solace. In a few days after he called again. On this occasion I was endeavoring to compose a campaign song for my club. I acquainted him with the fact, and while I was waiting upon a customer, he had composed a song to the measure and time of the "Star Spangled Banner." It was used by the club successfully through the campaign of 1844. I was exceedingly pleased with it and ready to present him with all the tobacco I had in my store, the most of which he respectfully declined.

On his departure, I requested the name of my stranger friend, which he left as Thaddeus K. Peasly. Here, to keep my story whole, I must introduce the celebrated poet, FITZ GREEN[E] HALLECK, with whom I was well acquainted, and who at that time was in the office of John Jacob Astor, a little brick building, then situated on the north side of Prince street, west of Broadway. In the evenings, Mr. Halleck frequently visited me, and behind a pile of tea chests, with which I had partitioned off a little room, we would sit in company with old Grant Thorburn, who kept a floral depot next door to me, and would listen to his stories of old New York.

Incidentally, we three lords of the hour, snugly ensconced behind our China walls, would embellish our evening's entertainment with occasional tastes of my several wines, for which I had not a very large sale, and about which, both the wine and the slow sale, none of us three were much troubled. On one of these occasions, when Mr. Halleck was leaving my store, he met the socalled Peasly entering it, whom he hailed as Poe. An explanation was soon made, and in a few moments we were behind those blessed walls, smiling over the *nom de plume* of Thaddeus K. Peasley [Peasly]. From this moment Poe and I became well acquainted with each other, and from 1844 to 1847, whenever he was in the city we frequently met (*Brooklyn Daily Eagle*, 17 November 1875, p. 4; cf. second reminiscence in the *New York Times Saturday Review*, 4 March 1899, p. 144).

OCTOBER. The *Columbian Magazine* contains Poe's "The Angel of the Odd—An Extravaganza."

3 OCTOBER. COLUMBIA, PENNSYLVANIA. Eli Bowen notices the *Columbian* in the *Spy*: "We are gratified to see the name of our friend, Edgar A. Poe, Esq., among the contributors to this Magazine. Mr. Poe is one of the

ablest and most original writers of the day. A capital article from his pen, entitled the 'Angel of the Odd' (an *odd* title, by the way,) is contained in the number for the present month" (Spannuth and Mabbott, p. 122).

7 OCTOBER. NEW YORK. Morris and Willis sign a contract with Hiram Fuller, formerly a teacher and bookseller in Providence, Rhode Island, who is to "attend to the publication" and "the general business" of the *Evening Mirror* and the *Weekly Mirror* (Dedmond, pp. 253–54).

7 OCTOBER. The *Evening Mirror*, edited by Willis, commences publication, "corner of Nassau and Ann-Sts."

CA. 7 OCTOBER. Willis hires Poe as his assistant on the *Evening Mirror*.

[According to Hiram Fuller, Poe's salary was $15 a week (*Evening Mirror*, 5 January 1847). With the exception of "The Raven" in the 29 January 1845 issue, Poe's contributions were unsigned. Although he began to write lead editorials in January and February 1845, his articles in the closing months of 1844 were routine and usually indistinguishable. Willis recalled Poe's editorship in a 17 October 1858 letter to Morris:

It was rather a step downward, after being the chief editor of several monthlies, as Poe had been, to come into the office of a daily journal as a mechanical paragraphist. It was his business to sit at a desk, in a corner of the editorial room, ready to be called upon for any of the miscellaneous work of the moment— announcing news, condensing statements, answering correspondents, noticing amusements—everything but the writing of a "leader," or constructing any article upon which his peculiar idiosyncrasy of mind could be impressed. Yet you remember how absolutely and how good-humoredly ready he was for any suggestion, how punctually and industriously reliable, in the following out of the wish once expressed, how cheerful and present-minded in his work when he might excusably have been so listless and abstracted. We loved the man for the entireness of fidelity with which he served us—himself, or any vanity of his own, so utterly put aside. When he left us we were very reluctant to part with him, but we could not object, as it was to better his fortunes. He was to take the lead in another periodical (*Home Journal*, 30 October 1858).]

8 OCTOBER. The *Evening Mirror* contains Willis' unsigned critique of Elizabeth Barrett Barrett (wrongly attributed to Poe by Woodberry, 2:102; see Hull, p. 414).

10 OCTOBER. The *Mirror* contains Willis' unsigned editorial "Authors' Pay in America." He argues that authors, not publishers, should receive the bulk of the profits from the sale of books: "we wish to light beacons for an authors' crusade and we have no leisure to be more than its Peter the

Hermit. We solemnly summon Edgar Poe to do the devoir of Coeur de Lion—no man's weapon half so trenchant!" This issue contains Poe's first recognizable contribution, "The Swiss Bell-ringers," in which he describes these popular performers—"white-plumed and fancifully costumed, and each armed with four or five hand-bells of various sizes"—and then face-tiously suggests that they are really automatons. Both Willis' editorial and Poe's *jeu d'esprit* are reprinted in the first issue of the *Weekly Mirror*, dated 12 October.

10 OCTOBER. WASHINGTON. Thomas replies to Poe's 8 September letter:

> I would have written you in answer before, but I delayed until I could send you a copy of my little book, [*The Beechen Tree*,] which please accept as a slight testimony of my faithful friendship and regard.
>
> I have seen my book favorably noticed so far, with the exception of Dunn English, and, as I am told, Park Benjamin, who, a friend informs me, has mounted me without mittens—Do, if you can obtain a copy of the "New World" which contains the aforesaid criticism, send send [*sic*] it to me . . . .
>
> As to Dunn English—what you say of him I believed long ago—it would not be consistent with self-love for me to think otherwise now . . . .
>
> Our friend [Jesse E.] Dow is very well and deeper immersed in politics than ever. . . . Dow is door keeper to the House of Representatives, has a good salary, and has succeeded as agents for various claimants in making money, and he has purchased himself a house, and is living very comfortably, indeed I may say luxuriously (MB–G).

12 OCTOBER. NEW YORK. The *Evening Mirror* contains Willis' unsigned editorial "The Pay for Periodical Writing" (attributed to Poe by Heartman and Canny, p. 230, but author refers to his former editorship of the *New Mirror*).

15 OCTOBER. PHILADELPHIA. William Duane, Jr., writes Poe. He com-plains that Poe has not returned the volume of the *Southern Literary Messen-ger* he borrowed around March (Poe's 28 October reply).

19 OCTOBER. NEW YORK. In the *Evening Mirror* Willis publishes a con-gratulatory letter he received from a young author who read his 10 Octo-ber editorial "Authors' Pay in America," reprinted in the *Weekly Mirror* of 12 October. The anonymous correspondent comments: "I am glad to see that Edgar Poe is in your clearings. He is a man of the finest ideal intellect in the land—carries a nasty tomahawk as a critic—bitter as gall to the literary flies who have been buzzing around his windows. Do give Poe a corner (or a column, or ten o' 'em) in your 'Strong-ly' Mirror, and let him fire away at the humbugs of our literature."

BEFORE 24 OCTOBER. QUOGUE, LONG ISLAND, NEW YORK. Samuel D. Craig, a lawyer, writes Poe, possibly threatening legal action because of an article in the *Evening Mirror* (Poe's reply).

24 OCTOBER. NEW YORK. Poe answers Craig: "Proceed. There are few things which could afford me more pleasure than an opportunity of holding you up to that public admiration which you have so long courted . . . . The tissue of written lies which you have addressed to myself individually, I deem it as well to retain. It is a specimen of attorney grammar too rich to be lost. As for the letter designed for Mr Willis (who, beyond doubt, (will feel honoured by your correspondence), I take the liberty of re-inclosing it. The fact is, I am neither your footman nor the penny-post" (*L*, 1:263).

28 OCTOBER. Poe replies to Duane's 15 October letter: "I regret exceedingly that circumstances should have led you to think me negligent, or uncourteous, in not returning the volume . . . . The facts are these: Some eight months ago, I believe, I chanced to mention, in Mr Hirst's hearing, that I wished to look over a particular article in the 'Messenger'. He immediately volunteered to procure me the desired volume from you. . . . Soon afterwards he handed me the book, which I retained a very short time. It is now certainly more than seven months since I returned it to Mr Hirst, through my mother in law (Mrs Clemm), who informs me that she left it at his office, with one of his brothers" (*L*, 1:263–64).

28 OCTOBER. Poe writes Lowell in Cambridge, Massachusetts: "A host of small troubles growing from the *one* trouble of poverty, but which I will not trouble you with in detail, have hitherto prevented me from thanking you for the Biography and all the well-intended flatteries which it contains. . . . I sent it to Graham on the day I received it—taking with it only one liberty in the way of modification. . . . It was merely the substitution of another brief poem for the last you have done me the honor to quote." He inquires whether Lowell has yet married his fiancée Maria White: "At all events I can wish you no better wish than that you may derive from your marriage as substantial happiness as I have derived from mine." Since Poe has received no response from Lowell to his call for a national magazine controlled by "a coalition" of eminent authors, he again outlines the plan proposed in his 30 March letter (*L*, 1:264–66).

LATE OCTOBER. The *American Review: A Whig Journal of Politics, Literature, Art and Science* issues its first number, dated January 1845 (Mott, p. 750).

LATE OCTOBER. Poe sends a long letter to Charles Anthon, forwarding his biography in the *Saturday Museum* and one of his tales. He recalls that Anthon first corresponded with him during his editorship of the *Southern Literary Messenger*. Before leaving the *Messenger* Poe perceived the opportunity offered to the man who could establish a "bold & noble" magazine in America:

Of "Graham's Magazine" you have no doubt heard. It had been in existence under the name of the "Casket" for 8 years, when I became its editor with a subscribption [*sic*] list of about 5000. In about 18 months afterward its circulation amounted to no less than *50.000*—astonishi[n]g as this may appear. . . . The nature of this journal, however, was such, that even its 50.000 subscribers could not make it very profitable to its proprietor. Its price was $3—but not only were its expenses immense owing to the employment of absurd steel plates & other extravagances which tell not at all but recourse was had to innumerable agents who recd it at a discount of no less th[a]n 50 per cent . . . . But, if 50000 *can* be obtained for a 3$ Maga— among a class of readers who really read little, why may not 50,000. be procured for a $5 journal among the true and permanent readers of the land?

Poe's "ultimate purpose" has always been the establishment of his own magazine, but in the meantime he has been concerned to establish a literary reputation which would further this end. Unfortunately, he has not published books but articles; he has been "essentially a Magazinist . . . liable to be grossly misconceived & misjudged by men . . . who see, perhaps, only a paper here & there, by accident,—often only one of his mere extravaganzas." Poe wishes to remedy this deficiency by issuing a new collection of his tales, now sixty-six in number: "They would make, perhaps, 5 of the ordinary novel volumes. I have them prepared in every respect for the press; but, alas, I have no money, nor that influence which would enable me to get a publisher—although I seek *no* pecuniary remuneration. . . . I know that you have unbounde[d] influence with the Harpers—& I know that if you would exert it in my behalf you could procure me the publication I desire" (*L*, 1:266–72).

NOVEMBER. PHILADELPHIA. *Godey's Lady's Book* contains Poe's detective story "Thou Art the Man."

NOVEMBER. NEW YORK. The *Democratic Review* contains the first installment of Poe's "Marginalia."

CA. NOVEMBER. The *Opal* for 1845 contains Poe's "A Chapter of Suggestions."

2 NOVEMBER. Anthon writes Poe: "I have called upon the Harpers, as you requested, and have cheerfully exerted with them what influence I possess,

but without accomplishing anything of importance. They have *complaints* against you, grounded on certain movements of yours, when they acted as your publishers some years ago . . . . However, they have retained, for a second and more careful perusal, the letter which you sent to me . . . . My *own advice* to you is to call in person at their store, and talk over the matter with them." Anthon subscribed to the *Messenger* solely because Poe was connected with it, and since then he has read and admired many of Poe's subsequent writings: "The Harpers also entertain, as I heard from their own lips, the highest opinion of your talents" (Quinn, p. 427).

19 NOVEMBER. In the *Evening Mirror* Poe notices Thomas' poem *The Beechen Tree*:

A modest and acceptable offering to the muse, by one of our popular authors, who has heretofore given us little but good prose. His story, "told in rhyme," however, convinces us of his qualifications as a poet. He has [a] fine command of all forms of expression, a true eye to the beautiful, a deep and natural sense of the affections, and possesses, withal, the rarer power of curbing both his imagination and his language at the point this side [of] redundancy. His r[h]ythmus is smooth and musical, and his choice of epithets peculiarly true and artistic. We do not know but we could find some blemishes in this sweet little poem, if we should look very critically over its fair pages; but, at any rate, we shall not make the experiment (attribution in Hull, pp. 409–10, 425–27).

23, 30 NOVEMBER. COLUMBIA, PENNSYLVANIA. The *Spy* contains two installments of a satiric article on "Puffing," somewhat in Poe's manner (Spannuth and Mabbott, pp. 103–09).

BEFORE 28 NOVEMBER. LOUISVILLE, KENTUCKY. The poetess Amelia B. Welby writes Willis: "I copy the subjoined lines 'By Mr. Willis,' from an old number of the Jackson (Tenn.) Advocate, where they are evidently out of place, and at all events so grossly misprinted that I must ask you to republish them, the more especially as they do not appear in the late collection by Mr. W. It can scarcely be possible that there are *two Dromios*."

28 NOVEMBER. NEW YORK. In the *Evening Mirror* Willis prints Mrs. Welby's letter and the poem she transcribed, Poe's "Lenore." He comments: "We thank our friend, *the* 'Amelia,' for supposing us capable of the authorship of these majestic-paced stanzas. They are not ours—we wish they were! But, (if they are not 'Amelia's[']—and they are very much in the *measure* of the 'Step-son'), we do not know whose they are; and we trust that our sail is not filled by *many* such mis-labelled breezes."

30 NOVEMBER. EDINBURGH, SCOTLAND. *Chambers' Edinburgh Journal* pub-

lishes an abridged version of "The Purloined Letter," with this introduction:

The Gift is an American annual of great typographical elegance, and embellished with many beautiful engravings. It contains an article, which, for several reasons, appears to us so remarkable, that we leave aside several effusions of our ordinary contributors in order to make room for an abridgment of it. The writer, Mr. Edgar A. Poe, is evidently an acute observer of mental phenomena; and we have to thank him for one of the aptest illustrations which could well be conceived, of that curious play of two minds, in which one person, let us call him A, guesses what another, B, will do, judging that B will adopt a particular line of policy to circumvent A (Mabbott [1978], 3:972–73).

DECEMBER. NEW YORK. The *Democratic Review* contains a second installment of "Marginalia," in which Poe discusses the *Undine* of Friedrich de la Motte-Fouqué and Mrs. Welby's poetry.

DECEMBER. The *Columbian Magazine* contains Poe's signed plate article "Byron and Miss Chaworth," accompanying an engraving with the same title.

DECEMBER. RICHMOND. The *Southern Literary Messenger* contains Poe's unsigned satire on magazine editors, "The Literary Life of Thingum Bob, Esq."

3–4 DECEMBER. PARIS. The newspaper *La Quotidienne* publishes in two installments Gustave Brunet's "James Dixon, ou la funeste resemblance," an adaptation of Poe's tale "William Wilson" which is the first known rendition of any of his writings into a foreign language (Mabbott [1978], 2:425).

7 DECEMBER. NEW YORK. The *Evening Mirror* contains a second Willis criticism of "Miss Barrett," which alludes to his previous notice in the 8 October issue. The *Weekly Mirror* contains his "Personal Notices of Elizabeth Barrett" (articles wrongly attributed to Poe by Woodberry, 2:102, and others; see Hull, pp. 434, 484–85).

7 DECEMBER. Charles F. Briggs, the satiric novelist popularly known as "Harry Franco," writes Lowell in Cambridge, Massachusetts:

I have made arrangements for publishing the first number of my long talked of paper in January. It will be published by John Biscoe [Bisco], a shrewd yankee from Worcester, who has been a school teacher in New Jersey, and was once the publisher of the Knickerbocker. . . . I have promise of good support here, but I rather hope to draw out something better than we have yet seen afloat on the surface of our literature in this quarter. Do you know of any available talent, or genius rather, in your neighborhood? . . . I shall issue a prospectus in a day or two; the name will be, for the sake of individuality and a-part-from-other-people-ness, the Broadway Journal, or Review, or Chronicle, or Broadway Something. . . . If you know Poe's address, send it on to me when you write (MiDAAA–P).

10 DECEMBER. WASHINGTON. Thomas writes Poe: "Two months ago I wrote to you enclosing a copy of my poem [*The Beechen Tree*]. Since which I have not heard one word from you—not even a line of acknowledgement. . . . I send this to know if you are in the land of the living, and if I do not soon get an answer I shall conclude you have departed, and proceed forthwith to write your obituary" (MB–G).

12 DECEMBER. ELMWOOD HOUSE, CAMBRIDGE, MASSACHUSETTS. Lowell writes Poe:

My object in writing this is to introduce you to my friend, Charles F. Briggs, who is about to start a literary weekly paper in New York & desires your aid. He was here a month or two since, & I took the liberty of reading to him what I had written about you & today I received a letter from him announcing his plan & asking your address. Not knowing it, & not having time to write him I thought that the shortest way would be to introduce you to him. He will pay & I thought from something you said in your last letter that pay would be useful to you. I also took the liberty of praising you to a Mr. [George H.] Colton, . . . whom I suspect, from some wry faces he made on first hearing your name, you have cut up. He is publishing a magazine [the *American Review*] & I think I convinced him that it would be for his interest to engage you permanently (*W*, 17:194–95).

19 DECEMBER. NEW YORK. Briggs writes Lowell in Cambridge: "Mr Poe called upon me with yr. note" (MiDAAA–P).

23 DECEMBER. Briggs and John Bisco sign a contract to issue the *Broadway Journal*. Briggs is to control "the editorial department . . . and attend to all communications relating to the same"; Bisco "shall have charge of the publishing department" and handle all financial transactions. "Neither party shall dispose of his interest in the publication without the consent of the other" (Ehrlich, pp. 77–78).

26 DECEMBER. WATERTOWN, MASSACHUSETTS. Lowell marries Maria White (Scudder, 1:150).

BEFORE 27 DECEMBER. NEW YORK. Poe gives Briggs a lengthy critique of Miss Barrett for the first number of the *Broadway Journal*.

27 DECEMBER. Briggs writes Evert A. Duyckinck, enclosing Poe's critique and asking Duyckinck to emend an ambiguous passage (Ehrlich, p. 79).

LATE 1844. PHILADELPHIA. The publisher R. G. Berford issues George Lippard's novel *Herbert Tracy*, containing the text of Poe's 18 February letter to the author (Heartman and Canny, pp. 86–87).

FRANCES SARGENT OSGOOD
(John Sartain's engraving of a portrait by Samuel S. Osgood)

CHAPTER EIGHT

New York: "The Raven" and the Broadway Journal

1845

During the opening months of 1845 Poe makes his presence felt in literary New York. The *Evening Mirror* for 29 January contains the first publication of "The Raven," copied in advance from the *American Review* for February: the poem is an immediate sensation, reprinted by journals throughout the country and followed by numerous parodies. *Graham's Magazine* for February contains a laudatory biography of Poe by James Russell Lowell. With the appearance of "The Raven" and the *Graham's* biography, Poe becomes a popular celebrity. In late February he leaves the staff of Nathaniel P. Willis' *Evening Mirror* and acquires a third interest in the *Broadway Journal*, a new weekly begun by Charles F. Briggs with John Bisco as publisher. In the *Journal* Poe continues the discussion of plagiarism begun in his unfavorable review of Longfellow's *The Waif* in the *Mirror* of 13–14 January. Some three hundred New Yorkers attend his biting lecture on the "Poets and Poetry of America," delivered at the Society Library on 28 February. Throughout 1845 Poe makes frequent appearances at social gatherings held in the homes of Miss Anne C. Lynch and other minor literati; in March he is introduced to the poetess Mrs. Frances S. Osgood, wife of the painter Samuel S. Osgood. Poe and Mrs. Osgood conduct a flirtation by means of playfully romantic poems addressed to each other and published in the *Broadway Journal*. While Briggs, the *Journal's* founder, is initially impressed with Poe, he soon becomes disillusioned with his partner's obsession with plagiarism and his recurrent drinking bouts. By late June Briggs plans to acquire control of the magazine and remove Poe's name from its masthead; but he is unable to purchase the interest of its publisher John Bisco, and he consequently withdraws from the concern. The second volume of the *Journal* commences with the 12 July issue, with Poe as sole editor and Bisco as publisher. In 1845 Wiley and Putnam publish two volumes by Poe in their "Library of American Books": his *Tales* on 25 June and *The Raven and Other Poems* on 19 November. On 16 October Poe reads his poem "Al Aaraaf" before the Boston Lyceum; since many Bostonians still resent his attacks on their native poet Longfellow, his Lyceum appearance is derisively reviewed by the city's newspapers. On 24 October he acquires Bisco's interest in the *Broadway Journal* and becomes its sole proprietor. Because the *Journal* is experiencing financial difficulties, he attempts to borrow money from his friends; but on 3 December he is forced to sell a half interest in the magazine to Thomas H. Lane, publisher of Thomas Dunn English's *Aristidean*. In spite of Poe's efforts the *Journal* perishes at the end of the year: the last issue, dated 3 January 1846, contains his "Valedictory."

*

1845

*

EARLY 1845? NEW YORK. Miss Anne C. Lynch, a schoolteacher and poetess, begins to invite Poe to the literary soirees she conducts at her home, 116 Waverley Place: "During the time that he [Poe] habitually visited me, a period of two or three years, I saw him almost always on my reception evenings, when many other guests were present. . . . In society, so far as my observation went, Poe had always the bearing and manners of a gentleman—interesting in conversation, but not monopolising; polite and engaging, and never, when I saw him, abstracted or dreamy. He was always elegant in his toilet, quiet and unaffected, unpretentious, in his manner; and he would not have attracted any particular attention from a stranger, except from his strikingly intellectual head and features, which bore the unmistakable character of genius" (Lynch to G. W. Eveleth, 8 and 19 March 1854, Miller [1977], pp. 202–05).

JANUARY OR BEFORE. Poe sells "The Raven" to the *American Review*.

[On 7 April the young editor George H. Colton wrote James Russell Lowell: "I paid Mr. Poe for the Raven not *over* $20" (Colton, p. 325). Donald Grant Mitchell remembered hearing Colton, a college friend at Yale, read the poem aloud "in his ramshackle Nassau Street office . . . before yet it had gone into type; and as he closed with oratorical effect the last refrain, [he] declared with an emphasis that shook the whole mass of his flaxen locks—'that is amazing—amazing!' " (Mitchell, 2:387).]

JANUARY. The *Columbian Magazine* lists Poe's "Some Words with a Mummy" among the articles it has accepted for publication.

[The story did not appear in the *Columbian*, but in the *American Review* for April: Poe presumably retrieved it and sold it to the *Review*, which may have paid better.]

BEFORE MID-JANUARY. Poe and Rufus W. Griswold encounter each other in the office of the *Daily Tribune* (Poe to Griswold, 16 January).

CA. 1 JANUARY. James Russell Lowell and his wife Maria visit New York on their way to Philadelphia, where they intend to spend the winter. Charles F. Briggs is unable to see his friends (Briggs to Lowell, 6 January).

4 JANUARY. SATURDAY. Briggs's *Broadway Journal*, 153 Broadway, issues its opening number, which contains the first half of Poe's lengthy review of Elizabeth Barrett Barrett's *The Drama of Exile, and Other Poems*. In a "Prospectus" the publisher John Bisco promises that the *Journal* "will be made up entirely of original matter"; it will be published every Saturday, "TERMS $3.00 per annum—Single numbers 6¼ cts."

4 JANUARY. Poe replies to Frederick William Thomas' letters of 10 October and 10 December 1844. He has received Thomas' poem *The Beechen Tree*, forwarded with the 10 October letter; but he has not reviewed it: "I could find no good opportunity of putting in a word anywhere that would have done you service. You know I do not live in town—very seldom visit it—and, of course, am not in the way of matters and things as I used to be. . . . In about three weeks, I shall move into the City, and recommence a life of activity under better auspices, I hope, than ever before. *Then* I may be able to do something." Virginia and Mrs. Clemm are "about as usual"; Poe is "truly glad to hear of Dow's well-doing" (*L*, 1:274–75).

[Poe's explanation of his failure to review *The Beechen Tree* is unconvincing. At the time he was connected with the *Evening Mirror*; he wrote the unsigned notice of Thomas' poem in the 19 November 1844 issue.]

4 JANUARY. Poe writes George Bush, Professor of Hebrew at the New York University. He encloses his tale "Mesmeric Revelation," reprinted in the New York *Dollar Weekly* from its original publication in the *Columbian Magazine* for August 1844: "I have ventured to send you the article because there are many points in it which bear upon the subject matter of your late admirable work on the Future Condition of Man—and therefore I am induced to hope that you will do me the honor to look over what I have said." Although "the article is purely a fiction," Poe believes it contains "some thoughts which are original"; he is "exceedingly anxious to learn if they have claim to absolute originality" (*L*, 1:273–74, 2:709; Moldenhauer [1973], p. 59; Mabbott [1978], 3:1029).

4 JANUARY. LONDON. *Lloyd's Entertaining Journal*, a penny publication, reprints Poe's "Raising the Wind; or, Diddling Considered as One of the Exact Sciences" (Moldenhauer [1977], p. 188).

AFTER 4 JANUARY. NEW YORK. George Bush replies to Poe's 4 January letter, giving a favorable opinion of "Mesmeric Revelation" (implied in the *Aristidean* for October; see BEFORE 8 NOVEMBER).

6 JANUARY. Briggs writes Lowell in Philadelphia. He plans to feature a series on "American prose writers" in the *Broadway Journal*: "Cannot you give me a paper on Hawthorn[e], or Emerson, or somebody else whose writings you are familiar with? You have done up Poe so thoroughly in Graham [the forthcoming *Graham's Magazine* for February] that I suppose you do not feel like saying anything further on his style. . . . Poe is going to assist Willis in the Mirror. I like Poe exceedingly well; Mr Griswold had told me shocking bad stories about him, which his whole demeanor contradicts" (MiDAAA–P).

9 JANUARY. The *Evening Mirror* contains Poe's "Does the Drama of the Day Deserve Support?"; the editorial is reprinted in the *Weekly Mirror* for 18 January.

11 JANUARY. The *Broadway Journal* contains the conclusion of Poe's review of Miss Barrett.

11 JANUARY. The *Evening Mirror* contains Poe's satiric notice of the *Alphadelphia Tocsin*, "the title of a new journal published at Alphadelphia, Michigan," and his review of James Russell Lowell's *Conversations on Some of the Old Poets*. Although Poe praises Lowell's "fine taste and critical power," he objects to his suggestion that the clever stratagems used by writers generally fail to capture the reader's heart: "In all cases, if the practice fail, it is because theory is imperfect. If Mr. Lowell's heart is not caught in the pitfall or trap, then the pitfall is ill-concealed, and the trap is not properly baited and set." Both contributions are reprinted in the *Weekly Mirror* for 18 January.

13–14 JANUARY. The *Evening Mirror* contains Poe's unfavorable review of Henry Wadsworth Longfellow's *The Waif*, an anthology of little-known poetry. In the 13 January installment Poe attributes the anonymous poems in *The Waif* to Longfellow himself, suggesting "that Mr. Longfellow's real design has been to make a book of his 'waifs,' and his own late compositions conjointly; since these late compositions are not enough in number to make a book of themselves." Poe concludes the 14 January installment by observing that "this exquisite little volume" reveals "a very careful avoidance of all American poets who may be supposed especially to interfere with the claims of Mr. Longfellow. These men Mr. Longfellow can continuously *imitate* (*is* that the word?) and yet never even incidentally commend." The review is reprinted in the *Weekly Mirror* for 25 January.

14 JANUARY. In the *Morning News* Evert A. Duyckinck notices the *Broadway Journal*, which "holds out the promise of a very bright, spirited affair. . . . Miss Barrett (rather painfully to us) is put to the question by Mr. Poe, with his usual critical acumen and force of style" (attribution in Duyckinck to Poe, 17 or 18 January).

14 JANUARY. In the *Evening Mirror* Poe discusses his most recent story, published anonymously: "A broadly satirical article, oddly entitled 'The Literary Life of Thingum Bob, Esq., late Editor of the Goosetherumfoodle,' and which appeared originally in the 'Southern Literary Messenger' for December, has been the subject of much comment, lately, in the Southern and Western papers, and the query is put to *us* especially, here in the North,—'who wrote it?' Who *did?*—can any one tell?"

14 JANUARY. Rufus W. Griswold writes Poe: "Although I have some cause of personal quarrel with you, which you will easily enough remember, I do not under any circumstances permit, as you have repeatedly charged, my private griefs to influence my judgment as a critic, or its expression." Griswold therefore retains his "early formed and well founded favorable opinions" of Poe's writings; and he hopes to render Poe "very perfect justice" in his new anthology *The Prose Writers of America*, which will be published by Carey & Hart of Philadelphia. "I shall feel myself yr debtor if there being any writings of yours with wh. I may be unacquainted, you will advise of their titles, and where they may be purchased; and if, in the brief biography of you in my Poets &c. of America, there are any inaccuracies, you will point them out to me" (*W*, 17:197–98).

15 JANUARY. BOSTON. A correspondent who signs himself "H." [George S. Hillard] writes the *Evening Mirror*, protesting Poe's unsigned review of *The Waif* in the 13–14 January issues. The reviewer's assertion that Longfellow composed the anonymous poems in the collection is unwarranted:

Not one of them was written by him. But my principal concern, however, is with the sting in the tail of the second communication, in which Mr. Longfellow is charged with omitting, from discreditable motives, any extracts from American poets, though he continuously imitates some of them. . . . Were Mr. Longfellow wholly unknown to me, my reply to such a charge would be, that the editor of such a compilation had a perfect right to select or reject, as he saw fit, and from no better reason than Corporal Nym's, that such was his humor . . . . But from long and intimate knowledge of Mr. Longfellow, I pronounce the charge wholly untrue. He is remarkable, among his friends, for his warm and generous commendation of the poetical efforts of his contemporaries. . . . If it be asked, why has he not given public demonstration of this kindness of spirit towards his poetical brethren, the answer is obvious. He is a poet himself, and addresses the public in that capacity, and not as a critic (printed in the 20 January *Mirror*; attribution in Longfellow to Lowell, 15 March).

15 JANUARY. NEW YORK. A commentator in the *Daily Tribune*, possibly Margaret Fuller, objects to Poe's review of Lowell in the 11 January *Mirror*: "Mr. Lowell's idea plainly is, that simplicity and nature are more successful than pit falls and traps. . . . We do not believe that traps of any kind, bait them as you may, can ever succeed in the long run, or impose on the heart. Tricks in literature are no better than tricks in morals" (unverified attribution in Briggs to Lowell, 17 January).

16 JANUARY. Poe replies to Griswold's 14 January letter, which gave him both pain and pleasure: "pain because it gave me to see that I had lost, through my own folly, an honorable friend:—pleasure, because I saw in it a hope of reconciliation." Since Poe believed Griswold to have been "irreparably offended" by his strictures on *The Poets and Poetry of America*, he "could make no advances" when they "met at the Tribune Office." Poe asks Griswold to accept his apologies: "If you *can* do this and forget the past, let me know where I shall call on you—or come and see me at the Mirror Office, any morning about 10. We can then talk over the other matters, which, to me at least, are far less important than your good will" (*L*, 1:275–76).

16 JANUARY. PHILADELPHIA. Lowell writes Briggs: "I received this morning the two numbers of your 'Broadway Journal,' & am in haste to tell you how much I like it. . . . The article upon Miss Barrett is extremely well written, I suppose by Poe. It is a good *telling* article, though I do not agree with it in its conclusion. From a paragraph I saw yesterday in the 'Tribune' I find that Poe has been at me in the 'Mirror.' He has at least the chief element of a critic—a disregard of persons. He will be a very valuable contributor to you" (Woodberry, 2:368–69).

AFTER 16 JANUARY. NEW YORK. Poe and Griswold meet. Griswold invites Poe to furnish selections from his poetry for a revised edition of *The Poets and Poetry of America*, as well as excerpts from his prose for the forthcoming *Prose Writers of America* (Poe to Griswold, 16 January and 24 February; Briggs to Lowell, 6 February).

17 JANUARY. Briggs replies to Lowell: "Poe's criticism about your Conversations was extremely laudatory and discriminating; it was the female ass of the Tribune [Margaret Fuller] that misunderstood him. . . . Poe writes for me, at the rate of one dollar a column. If you will do so, I shall esteem it a capital barg[a]in" (MiDAAA–P).

17 JANUARY. The *Evening Mirror* contains Poe's editorial "Nature and Art," a reply to the *Daily Tribune* of 15 January:

We grant that "Mr. Lowell's idea plainly" is, that simplicity and Nature are more successful than Art; but we do *not* grant that this idea is set forth *more* plainly in the Tribune's repetition than in the English of Mr. Lowell himself. . . .

There being then no dispute about Mr. L's meaning, we object that, in Letters, he improperly distinguishes Nature from Art.—The latter *is*—(or, lest the Tribune may have a difficulty in comprehending that we speak absolutely, and of the *perfected* Art)—the latter *should be* nothing more than the arranging, the methodizing, the rendering easily available so as to carry into successful application, the suggestions, the laws, and the general intentions of the former.

In a briefer article headed "Criticism," Poe replies to Evert A. Duyckinck's notice of the *Broadway Journal* in *"The Tribune"* [*Morning News*] of 14 January: "Mr. D. . . . speaks of a Review of Miss Barrett's Poems as if it were condemnatory. We should be sorry indeed, if any general disparagement were intended of the most extraordinary woman of her age—perhaps of any age. Our impression, however, is that the critic of the Broadway Journal meant only, by a few unimportant objections, to place her preeminent merits in the best light." The *Weekly Mirror* for 25 January reprints "Nature and Art."

17 OR 18 JANUARY. Duyckinck writes Poe:

This is a world of presumption. I first presumed, mentally, that you were the author of the Barrett criticism in [the] Broadway Journal. I then presumed, morally, or rather immorally to say so in print. And I am pleasantly punished for my sins by a complimentary fillip—if I presume rightly again—*from Mr Poe*, in the Evening Mirror. But he has mistaken the Tribune for the Morning News which E A D regrets as there are excellent anonymous literary articles in the former paper (said to be written by Miss S M Fuller and W E Channing) which he may unjustly get the credit of. Will Mr Poe take the trouble to correct the matter by stating Morning News for Tribune (Reece [1954], p. 90).

BEFORE 18 JANUARY. BOSTON. *Littell's Living Age* for 18 January contains an abridgment of Poe's "The Purloined Letter," reprinted from *Chambers' Edinburgh Journal* of 30 November 1844 with this magazine's introduction.

18 JANUARY. NEW YORK. The *Broadway Journal* contains Poe's "American Prose Writers, No. 2: N. P. Willis."

18 JANUARY. The *Morning News* comments: "LITTELL'S LIVING AGE, for this week, contains a story by Edgar A. Poe, *copied from an English paper* and accompanied by a complimentary criticism, *English also*, entitled 'The Purloined Letter.' It originally appeared in the Gift for 1845, and has

attracted far less attention at home than abroad. We shall give our readers an early opportunity of reading it for themselves."

18 JANUARY. The *Evening Mirror* carries a paragraph headed "A Mistake," in which Poe complies with Duyckinck's request: "Through inadvertence . . . yesterday . . . we wrote 'Tribune,' when we should have written 'Morning News.'"

BEFORE 20 JANUARY. PHILADELPHIA. *Graham's Magazine* for February contains Lowell's "Our Contributors, No. XVII: Edgar Allan Poe," accompanied by a portrait of Poe by the Philadelphia artist A. C. Smith. Lowell observes:

Mr. Poe is at once the most discriminating, philosophical, and fearless critic upon imaginative works who has written in America. It may be that we should qualify our remark a little, and say that he *might be*, rather than that he always *is*, for he seems sometimes to mistake his phial of prussic-acid for his inkstand. If we do not always agree with him in his premises, we are, at least, satisfied that his deductions are logical, and that we are reading the thoughts of a man who thinks for himself, and says what he thinks, and knows well what he is talking about. His analytic power would furnish forth bravely some score of ordinary critics. . . . Had Mr. Poe had the control of a magazine of his own, in which to display his critical abilities, he would have been as autocratic, ere this, in America, as Professor Wilson has been in England . . . . As it is, he has squared out blocks enough to build an enduring pyramid, but has left them lying carelessly and unclaimed in many different quarries.

Lowell outlines Poe's early life, following the inaccurate biography published in the *Saturday Museum* of 25 February and 4 March 1843. "Mr. Poe has that indescribable something which men have agreed to call *genius*. No man could ever tell us precisely what it is, and yet there is none who is not inevitably aware of its presence and its power." Lowell reprints Poe's poems "To Helen," "Ligeia" (from "Al Aaraaf," lines 100–11), "The Haunted Palace," and "Lenore"; the first of these was "written when the author was only *fourteen*!" In fiction the "analyzing tendency" of Poe's mind "balances the poetical, and, by giving him the patience to be minute, enables him to throw a wonderful reality into his most unreal fancies." Lowell lists the thirty stories Poe has written since his *Tales of the Grotesque and Arabesque*, identifying him as the author of the anonymously published "Balloon-Hoax" and "Literary Life of Thingum Bob."

20–21 JANUARY. NEW YORK. The *Evening Mirror* reprints Lowell's sketch in two installments, both on its front page. On the second page of the 20 January issue, Nathaniel P. Willis comments:

From Graham's Magazine . . . we copy . . . a biographical and critical sketch of the American Rhadamanthus, done with Lowell's broad and honest appreciation, and giving us a *coup d'oeil*, of the position and powers of Mr. Poe, which is of great interest to the public that *feels* him. We wonder, by the way, that, with so fine a critic at command for an editor, some New York publisher does not establish a Monthly Review, devoted exclusively to high critical purposes. Poe has genius and taste of his own, as well as the necessary science, and the finest discriminative powers; and such a wheel of literature should not be without axle and linch-pin. Mr. Poe is now residing in New York, and ready, we presume, for propositions.

20 JANUARY. In the *Evening Mirror* Willis discusses the paper's 13–14 January review of Longfellow's *The Waif*: "The criticisms . . . were written in our office by an able though very critical hand [Poe] . . . . We judge the poet [Longfellow] by ourself when we presume that he prefers *rubbing* to *rust*—sure of being more brightened than fretted." Willis prints the 15 January letter protesting the review from "H." [George S. Hillard] in Boston. In "Post-Notes by the Critic," appended to the letter, Poe replies to Hillard's objections, commenting: "If ever a man had cause to ejaculate, 'Heaven preserve me from my friends!' it is Mr. Longfellow." Willis' remarks, the letter, and Poe's reply are reprinted in the *Weekly Mirror* for 25 January.

20 JANUARY. Poe signs a receipt: "Recd of Mr John Bisco eighteen dollars, in full for two articles in Broadway Journal" (*L*, 2:520–21).

20, 22 JANUARY. PHILADELPHIA. The *Spirit of the Times* reprints the abridgment of "The Purloined Letter" in two installments, from *Littell's* for 18 January (Mabbott [1978], 3:974).

21, 24 JANUARY. NEW YORK. The *Morning News* reprints "The Purloined Letter" in two installments, "*From Chambers' Journal, via Littell's Living Age.*" The abridgment appears in the *Weekly News* for 25 January.

22 JANUARY. The *Evening Mirror* contains Poe's essay "American Diffuseness—Objectionable Concision."

24 JANUARY. In the *Daily Tribune* Margaret Fuller notices Lowell's sketch of Poe in *Graham's Magazine* for February: "This article is frank, earnest, and contains many just thoughts, expressed with force and point. . . . Among the poems quoted from Mr. Poe, before unknown to ourselves, two please us so much, that they must be inserted here." Fuller reprints "The Haunted Palace" and "To Helen"; the latter poem, "written at the age of *fourteen*," is "of such distinguished beauty in thought, feeling, and expression, that we might expect the life unfolded from such a bud to have the sweetness and soft lustre of a rose." She relates the portrait in *Graham's* to

Poe's writings: "A person of fine perceptions, and unacquainted with the writings of Mr. Poe, observed, on looking at this head of him, that the lower part of the face is that of the critic, cold, hard, and self-sufficient; while the upper part, especially the brows, expresses great feeling, and tenderness of feeling. We wish the 'Psyche' had taken him far enough in that 'Nicéan bark,' to give the expression of the upper part of the face a larger preponderance than we find in his reviews of the poets." The notice is reprinted in the *Weekly Tribune* for 1 February.

24, 25, 27, 31 JANUARY. The *Evening Mirror* publishes Poe's "Pay of American Authors" in four installments. This editorial calling for an international copyright law is reprinted in the *Weekly Mirror* for 1 and 8 February.

BEFORE 25 JANUARY. PHILADELPHIA. *Godey's Lady's Book* for February contains Poe's "The Thousand-and-Second Tale of Scheherazade."

25 JANUARY. NEW YORK. In the *Broadway Journal* Briggs reviews the February numbers of *Godey's* and *Graham's*. *Godey's* features "ten ladies and six gentlemen, besides the editors," as contributors:

But the great marvel is that so many writers should have been able to produce so small an amount of readable matter. The only article in the Magazine that will ever be read a second time, except by the writers of them, is the New Arabian Nights' Tale by Mr. Poe. The idea of this tale is a very happy one, and it afforded the author a wide scope for displaying his exact knowledge and lively imagination; two qualities that we rarely find united in the same person. Scheherazade tells a new story, more wondrous than any that she had related before, a continuation of Sinbad's adventures, wherein are related some of the modern discoveries in science, which startle the king more than any of the doings of the Genii. At last, when the narrator tells of women who wear artificial humps on their backs [bustles], he grows impatient, and believing that his Queen is imposing upon his credulity, orders her to be bow-strung.

Graham's contains "a something which is called a portrait of Edgar A. Poe. . . . It bears no more resemblance to that gentleman than to any other of Mr. Graham's contributors. But if it were much worse than it is, which is hardly conceivable, it would be amply compensated by the fine sketch of Mr. Poe's genius, by Lowell, which accompanies it."

25 JANUARY. In the *Morning News* Evert A. Duyckinck notices the portrait and sketch in *Graham's*:

We cordially give a welcome to this distinct recognition of Mr. Poe's merits. Whenever his name is mentioned it has been with the comment that he is a remarkable man, a man of genius. Few knew precisely what he had written, his

Poe's portrait in the February *Graham's*
National Portrait Gallery, Smithsonian Institution, Washington, D. C.

name was not on Library catalogues or any of his books on the shelves. His influence has been felt while the man was unknown. Lowell's article removes the anonymous and exhibits the author of some of the most peculiar and characteristic productions in our literature. Metaphysical acuteness of perception, resting on imagination, might be no unapt description of the powers developed in the creation of tales remarkable for touching the extreme of mystery and the most faithful literalness of daily life, and criticisms, profoundly constructed and original in the mind of the critic, and calling forth the same faculties as the production of the best books themselves.

The notice is reprinted in the *Weekly News* for 1 February (attribution implied in W. G. Simms to Duyckinck, 15 March).

25 JANUARY. PHILADELPHIA. The *Saturday Courier* reports that *Graham's* features "a striking likeness of Edgar A. Poe."

25 JANUARY. BALTIMORE. In the *Saturday Visiter* Joseph Evans Snodgrass evaluates the portrait in *Graham's*: "The likeness is good, though rather wanting in that *nervousness* of expression so peculiar to Mr. Poe."

25 JANUARY. NEW YORK. Poe writes Richard Henry Horne in London. He encloses the *Broadway Journal* for 4 and 11 January, containing his review of Elizabeth Barrett Barrett, and a copy of "The Raven." He solicits Horne's opinion of this yet unpublished poem, also asking him to obtain opinions on it from Miss Barrett and Alfred Tennyson. Poe expresses his admiration for Miss Barrett: his review should be forwarded to her. Answering Horne's query in his 27 April 1844 letter, Poe states that an American publisher might be willing to reprint his correspondent's epic *Orion* (Horne to Poe, 17 May; Barrett to Horne, 12 May).

25 JANUARY OR LATER? The Poe family leaves the farmhouse of Patrick Brennan in upper Manhattan and moves into New York City proper, taking lodgings at 154 Greenwich Street (Poe to Thomas, 4 January; Poe to Mrs. Mowatt, 20 March).

27 JANUARY. Briggs writes Lowell in Philadelphia:

Poe tells me that Graham refused to print his tale of the Gold Bug, and kept it in his possession nine months. I never read it before last week, and it strikes me as among the most ingenious pieces of Fiction, that I have ever seen. If you have not read it, it will repay you for the trouble when you do. He told me furthermore that the poem which you have quoted from the House of Usher,

> "In a valley fair and shady
> By good angels tenanted &c,"

He sent to O'Sullivan for the Democratic, and it was returned to him. You see by these what the judgments of magazine editors amount to. . . . I have always strangely misunderstood Poe, from thinking him one of the Graham and Godey species, but I find him as different as possible. I think that you will like him well when you come to know him personally (MiDAAA–P).

BEFORE 28 JANUARY. PHILADELPHIA. William Duane, Jr., writes Poe. He has recovered the volume of the *Southern Literary Messenger* he lent Poe last year; it was found in Richmond (Poe's reply).

28 JANUARY. NEW YORK. Poe writes Duane:

Richmond is the last place in which I should have hoped to find a copy of either the lrst 2d or 3d volumes of the Messenger. For this reason I did not apply there. I have been putting myself, however, to some trouble in endeavouring to collect among my friends here the separate numbers of the missing volume. I am glad that your last letter relieves me from all such trouble in future. I do not choose to recognize you in this matter at all. To the person of whom I borrowed the book, or rather who insisted upon forcing it on me, I have sufficient reason to believe that it was returned. Settle your difficulties with him, and insult me with no more of your communications (*L*, 1:276).

[Duane wrote this explanation on Poe's letter: "The volume . . . was lent by me to E. A. Poe, through Henry B. Hirst, Esq., and was sold by the said Poe [actually Mrs. Clemm] among a lot of books belonging to himself to William A. Leary, a bookseller on North Seventh Street [in Philadelphia]. Mr. Leary sold it to a bookseller in Richmond, Va., who sold it to the publishers of the 'Messenger,' who sold it to a friend of mine who was visiting Richmond, and whom I had commissioned to purchase me a copy. My name was on the title-page during all these sales" (Woodberry, 2:367–68).]

BEFORE 29 JANUARY. Poe encounters his friend William Ross Wallace, to whom he has been in the habit of reading his "not yet published poetical work." He solicits Wallace's opinion of "The Raven":

"Wallace," said Poe, "I have just written the greatest poem that ever was written."
"Have you?" said Wallace. "That is a fine achievement."
"Would you like to hear it?" said Poe.
"Most certainly," said Wallace.
Thereupon Poe began to read the soon to-be famous verses in his best way—which . . . was always an impressive and captivating way. When he had finished it he turned to Wallace for his approval of them—when Wallace said:
"Poe—they are fine; uncommonly fine."

"Fine?" said Poe, contemptuously. "Is that all you can say for this poem? I tell you it's the greatest poem that was ever written" (Benton, p. 733).

29 JANUARY. The *Evening Mirror* publishes "The Raven" with this introduction by Nathaniel P. Willis:

We are permitted to copy (in advance of publication) from the 2d No. of the American Review, the following remarkable poem by EDGAR POE. In our opinion, it is the most effective single example of "fugitive poetry" ever published in this country; and unsurpassed in English poetry for subtle conception, masterly ingenuity of versification, and consistent, sustaining of imaginative lift and "pokerishness." It is one of these "dainties bred in a book" which we *feed* on. It will stick to the memory of everybody who reads it.

Both poem and introduction are reprinted in the *Weekly Mirror* for 8 February.

FEBRUARY. The *American Review* contains "THE RAVEN, BY——QUARLES," with this preface by George H. Colton:

The following lines from a correspondent—besides the deep quaint strain of the sentiment, and the curious introduction of some ludicrous touches amidst the serious and impressive, as was doubtless intended by the author—appear to us one of the most felicitous specimens of unique rhyming which has for some time met our eye. The resources of English rhythm for varieties of melody, measure, and sound, producing corresponding diversities of effect, have been thoroughly studied, much more perceived, by very few poets in the language. While the classic tongues, especially the Greek, possess, by power of accent, several advantages for versification over our own, chiefly through greater abundance of spondaic feet, we have other and very great advantages of sound by the modern usage of rhyme. Alliteration is nearly the only effect of that kind which the ancients had in common with us. It will be seen that much of the melody of "The Raven" arises from alliteration, and the studious use of similar sounds in unusual places. In regard to its measure, it may be noted that if all the verses were like the second, they might properly be placed merely in short lines, producing a not uncommon form; but the presence in all the others of one line—mostly the second in the verse—which flows continuously, with only an aspirate pause in the middle, like that before the short line in the Sapphic Adonic, while the fifth has at the middle pause no similarity of sound with any part beside, gives the versification an entirely different effect. We could wish the capacities of our noble language, in prosody, were better understood.—ED. AM. REV.

[The first publication of "The Raven" probably occurred in the *Evening Mirror* of 29 January, which seems to have appeared on the streets of New York a day or two before the *American Review* for February. The first printing almost certainly occurred in the *Review*: this number was set in type before the end of January, since it was published on or before 1

February (*Daily Tribune*, 1 February). Poe's use of the pseudonym "——— Quarles" was in keeping with the practice of the *Review*, which was "to publish poems either unsigned or with pseudonyms" (Colton, p. 324).]

FEBRUARY. RICHMOND. The *Southern Literary Messenger* favorably notices the *Broadway Journal*. As a sample of the new weekly's literary criticism, the *Messenger* quotes the reviews of *Godey's* and *Graham's* from the *Journal* for 25 January; the excerpts contain Briggs's praise of Poe's "The Thousand-and-Second Tale of Scheherazade" and his condemnation of the Poe portrait accompanying Lowell's biography.

EARLY FEBRUARY. NEW YORK. Poe writes Benjamin Blake Minor, editor and proprietor of the *Southern Literary Messenger*, enclosing a revised copy of "The Raven." Poe asks Minor to relax his magazine's rule against reprints and to publish this poem "in the beautiful typography of the *Messenger*" (Minor, p. 138).

EARLY FEBRUARY. Elizabeth Oakes Smith, a popular poetess, recalls:

The *Raven* was first published in the *New York Review* [*American Review*]. I had not yet seen it, when one evening Charles Fenno Hoffman called with the *Review*, and read it to me. He was a fine reader, and read the poem with great feeling. His reading affected me so much I arose and walked the floor, and said to him, "It is Edgar Poe himself." He had not told me who the author was; indeed, it was published anonymously. "Well," said I, "every production of genius has an internal life as well as its external. Now, how do you interpret this, Mr. Hoffman?" The latter, who had had many disappointments and griefs in life, replied, "It is despair brooding over wisdom."

The next evening who should call but Mr. Poe. I told him what Mr. Hoffman had said. Poe folded his arms and looked down, saying, "That is a recognition." Soon the Raven became known everywhere, and everyone was saying 'Nevermore.'

One afternoon Poe called on me and said, "I find my Raven is really being talked about a great deal. I was at the theatre last night, and the actor interpolated the word 'Nevermore,' and it did add force to the sentiment that was given, and the audience immediately (he looked so pleased when he said this), evidently took the allusion" (Mrs. Smith quoted by Derby, pp. 547–48).

EARLY? FEBRUARY. Poe makes "a most favorable impression" at a reception at the home of Mrs. Caroline M. Kirkland: "there were a good many of the New York literati [present], not one of whom had ever before seen him, and only a few had ever read anything of his writings except 'The Raven,' which had just been published . . . . there was great curiosity to see the writer of that wonderful poem" (Briggs, pp. 1–2).

FEBRUARY OR LATER. Henry T. Tuckerman recalls a social gathering at the home of Dr. John W. Francis, a prominent New York physician:

. . . a card was brought the Doctor, while we were all seated at the tea-table; the expression of his face, as he left the room, betokened the visit of a celebrity; in a few moments he ushered into the room a pale, thin, and most grave-looking man, whose dark dress and solemn air, with the Doctor's own look of ceremonious gravity, produced an ominous silence, where, a moment before, all was hilarity; slowly conducting his guest around the table, and turning to his wife, he waved his hand, and, with elaborate courtesy, made this unique announcement: "The Raven!" and certainly no human physiognomy more resembled that bird than the stranger's, who, without a smile or a word, bowed slightly and slowly; with a fixed, and, it almost seemed, a portentous gaze, as if complacently accepting the character thus thrust upon him. Instantly, the fancy of all present began to conjure up all the ravens they had ever heard of or seen, from those that fed Elijah to the one in "Barnaby Rudge"; and it was not for some minutes that Edgar A. Poe was recognized, in the "fearful guest," to be "evermore" associated in the minds of all present, not with the "lost Lenore," but with that extraordinary presentation of the Doctor's (Tuckerman, pp. lxxix–lxxx).

1 FEBRUARY. The *Daily Tribune* comments: "THE AMERICAN JOURNAL AND WHIG REVIEW [*American Review*] for February is published. We shall notice its contents when we have had time to read them."

1 FEBRUARY. The *New World* reprints "The Haunted Palace" with this introduction by the editor Charles Eames: "The following exquisite Poem, from the pen of Edgar A. Poe, is new to us. We can hardly call to mind in the whole compass of American Poetry, a picture of more intense and glowing Ideality. It portrays with admirable power and pathos, a noble mind given over to wreck and desolation."

1 FEBRUARY. The *Broadway Journal* contains a passage from the French historian Froissart describing a fatal fire at a costume ball in the court of Charles VI; it prints a letter from the New York physician Dr. A. Sidney Doane, who describes a surgical operation performed while the patient was "in a *magnetic sleep*" (or mesmerized). The Froissart is a source for Poe's tale "Hop-Frog"; the letter, a source for his hoax "The Facts in the Case of M. Valdemar."

3 FEBRUARY. A writer in the *Daily Tribune*, probably Horace Greeley, notices the *American Review*: " 'The Raven' is a poem which would have enriched Blackwood." The *Morning News* reprints the poem from the *Evening Mirror*, along with Willis' introduction identifying Poe as its author. It appears in the *Weekly News* for 8 February.

3 FEBRUARY. The *Evening Mirror* contains Poe's "Increase of the Poetical Heresy—Didacticism"; the article is reprinted in the *Weekly Mirror* for 8 February.

3 FEBRUARY. Poe writes his friend J. Augustus Shea, a journalist and poet connected with the *Daily Tribune*, describing two alterations he wishes to make in "The Raven" (*L*, 1:279).

4 FEBRUARY. The *Daily Tribune* reprints "The Raven" from the *American Review*. This printing omits George H. Colton's introduction, identifies "Edgar A. Poe" as the author, and incorporates the revisions Poe indicated to Shea. The poem appears in the *Weekly Tribune* for 8 February.

5 FEBRUARY. In the *Morning Express* James Brooks notices the *American Review*: "There is a poem in this book which may well defy competition in its way from the whole circle of cotemporary verse writers; though Alfred Tennyson might, perhaps, enter for the prize,—but to be excelled out of measure. We allude to 'The Raven,' in which deep settled grief, bordering on sullen despair, is personified, in the chance visitor of the poet, perching over his door, to leave his presence 'Nevermore.' As a piece of versification it is as curious as it is, psychologically, a wonder. We think we are right in our guess that 'Quarles' means Edgar Poe."

5 FEBRUARY. In the *Evening Mirror* Willis defends his decision to publish Poe's unfavorable review of Longfellow's *The Waif*. He quotes Poe's closing paragraph from the 14 January *Mirror*, which questions Longfellow's motives for omitting extracts from other American poets; and he observes: "It was a literary charge, by a pen that never records an opinion without some supposed good reason, and only injurious to Longfellow, (to our belief) while circulating, un-replied-to, in *conversation-dom*." Since the Boston newspapers have not replied to this accusation, Willis prints the following defense of *The Waif* from a letter "a friend" [Charles Sumner] has sent him:

> It has been asked, perhaps, why Lowell was neglected in this collection? Might it not as well be asked why Bryant, Dana and Halleck were neglected? The answer is obvious to any one who candidly considers the character of the collection. It professed to be, according to the Proem, from the humbler poets; and it was intended to embrace pieces that were anonymous, or which were not easily accessible to the general reader—the *waifs* and *estrays* of literature. To put anything of Lowell's, for example, into a collection of *waifs*, would be a peculiar liberty with pieces which are all collected and christened.

Willis' article is reprinted in the *Weekly Mirror* for 8 February (Sumner identified in Longfellow to Lowell, 15 March).

6 FEBRUARY. Briggs writes Lowell in Philadelphia: "You will see in this week's [Broadway] Journal a grand poem by Poe ['The Raven'], which I think you will like. You will see that it is framed according to his notions of poetry. A mere beautiful something entirely free from didacticism and

sentiment. . . . Griswold is going to give a life and character of Poe in his prose writers with a portrait, which Poe is desirous that [William] Page should paint" (MiDAAA–P).

6 FEBRUARY. Briggs writes the portrait painter William Page in Boston, discussing his correspondent's essay on the use of color in painting: "I have put the whole of it into my Journal. . . . Edgar A. Poe, whom Lowell has glorified, and whose fine verses in my Journal ['The Raven'] you will like better than anything in Tennyson, says it is exceedingly fine, and the only true piece of writing which he has ever seen upon the subject. He knows something about color, and his opinion is worth a vast deal more than mine. He had no sooner read it, than he said he wanted you to paint his portrait. . . . He is as good a fellow as yourself but very different, and I know that you would like him highly" (MiDAAA–P).

6 FEBRUARY. The *Evening Mirror* contains Poe's "Literary Intelligence." He complains that Nathaniel Hawthorne's *Twice-Told Tales* are out of print: "Why will no one give us a new impression, and the modest author a couple of thousands?"

7 FEBRUARY. In the *Mirror* Poe favorably notices the *American Review* for February, praising Evert A. Duyckinck's article on the nation's "Literary Prospects." He reports: "Mr. J. S. Redfield, of this city, has in press . . . the Poetical Writings of Mrs. Elizabeth Oakes Smith, (better known, perhaps, as Mrs. Seba Smith)."

BEFORE 8 FEBRUARY. Alexander T. Crane, the office boy of the *Broadway Journal*, hears James E. Murdoch recite "The Raven":

It was one cold day in winter, when everybody in the Literary [Broadway] Journal office, from myself on up, was busily at work, that Poe came into the office, accompanied by the great actor named Murdock [*sic*]. . . . Mr. Poe summoned the entire force, including myself, about him. There were less than a dozen of us, and I was the only boy.

When we were all together Poe drew the manuscript of "The Raven" from his pocket and handed it to Murdock. He had called us to hear the great elocutionist read his newly written poem. Murdock read, and what with the combined art of two masters, I was entranced. It is the most cherished memory of my life that I heard the immortal poem read by one whose voice was like a chime of silver bells. . . . In the next issue of the Literary Journal "The Raven" appeared in the place of honor (Crane, p. 34).

8 FEBRUARY. The *Broadway Journal* publishes a corrected version of "The Raven," identifying Poe as its author. Briggs observes: "It will have been

read by many of our city subscribers, we have no doubt, before it reaches them in our columns, but there are others to whom it will be as welcome as it is new." The *Journal* contains Poe's unfavorable reviews of Edward Bulwer-Lytton's *Poems* and Joseph Rocchietti's *Why a National Literature Cannot Flourish in the United States*.

8 FEBRUARY. The *Evening Mirror* contains Poe's editorial "Why Not Try a Mineralized Pavement?" (cf. his discussion of street pavements in the *Columbia Spy*, 15 June 1844).

BEFORE 12 FEBRUARY. The *Aristidean* commences publication: this new monthly is edited by Thomas Dunn English and published by T. H. Lane & Co., 304 Broadway. The first number, dated March, contains Poe's satiric review of George Jones's *Ancient America*, a book which attempts "to demonstrate the identity of our Aborigines with the Tyrians and Israelites, and the introduction of Christianity into the Western Hemisphere by one of the twelve Apostles in person."

12 FEBRUARY. The *Evening Mirror* contains Poe's "Magazine Literature," in which he notices English's *Aristidean*. With tongue in cheek he lauds the contents of the opening number, which include an essay and a poem expressing opposition to capital punishment: "Much is done in small compass. 'Whom shall we hang?' is a vigorous paper of just the right length, on a topic of precisely the right kind. 'The Ropemaker' [by English] is in verse, just such a paper as 'Whom shall we hang?' is in prose, and by this we intend a compliment, beyond doubt." Poe's editorial is reprinted in the *Weekly Mirror* for 15 February.

13 FEBRUARY. CAMBRIDGE, MASSACHUSETTS. Longfellow's wife, Fanny Appleton Longfellow, writes his brother Samuel Longfellow, alluding to Nathaniel P. Willis' 5 February defense of Poe's review of *The Waif*: "If you see the *Mirror*, you know how shabbily Willis tries to excuse Poe's insolence. Have you seen a curious poem by the latter entitled 'The Raven,' most artistically rhythmical but 'nothing more,' to quote its burden?" (Mrs. Longfellow, p. 116).

14 FEBRUARY OR BEFORE. NEW YORK. George R. Graham asks Willis to publish a retraction of Poe's criticisms of Longfellow (Graham to Longfellow, 11 March).

14 FEBRUARY. The *Evening Mirror* contains Willis' flippant retraction:

To gratify a friend [Graham] we say that if our playful notice of our assistant critic's notice of "Longfellow's Waif," a few days since, did not give the impression that we (Willis) fully dissented from our assistant as to the charge against Longfellow for enviously leaving out of his book such poets as competed with himself—dissented from *all* the disparagement of Longfellow in this review, and only let it pass for good reasons given at length in this same article—if that impression was not given, it was not the fault of the fullest intention to that effect. We meant to do so, and we think it was so understood,—but for a friend for whom we would do a much more unreasonable thing, we thus draw the nail and drive it again.

In another column Willis notices Graham's presence "in town." The retraction is reprinted in the *Weekly Mirror* for 22 February.

15 FEBRUARY. The *Broadway Journal* contains Poe's sketch "Some Secrets of the Magazine Prison-House," which relates the history of a "poor-devil author" who starves to death while waiting for a magazine publisher to pay him for his contribution. In an editorial headed "Thefts of American Authors," Briggs objects to an accusation of plagiarism Poe brought against the American poet James Aldrich when reviewing Longfellow's *The Waif*. There is no similarity "sufficient to warrant the charge" between Aldrich's "A Death-Bed" and Thomas Hood's "The Death-Bed," except "the measure and the subject, which are certainly not peculiar to Hood; the thoughts are by no means identical."

15 FEBRUARY. The *Evening Mirror* publishes Poe's "Imitation—Plagiarism." He explains his abhorrence of plagiarism, a "sin" which "involves the quintessence of meanness," especially if committed by an established author. The article is reprinted in the *Weekly Mirror* for 22 February.

15 FEBRUARY. The *Town*, a weekly magazine devoted to satirizing the New York literati, reports: "Mr. EDGAR A. POE, has it in contemplation to publish a new five dollar Magazine. If a wide celebrity, as the most interesting and original of Magazine writers, and a fearless critic be of any avail, it may succeed—unless prevented by the overshadowing popularity of the Aristidean, by 'Doctor *Thomas* DUNN ENGLISH, M.D.' as he whilom wrote his name."

15 FEBRUARY. The *New World* publishes Poe's revised tale "Ligeia," which now incorporates for the first time his poem "The Conqueror Worm." The weekly's editor Charles Eames comments:

We call attention to the powerful tale in this number of our paper by Edgar A. Poe, entitled LIGEIA. The force and boldness of the conception and the high artistic skill, with which the writer's purpose is wrought out, are equally admirable. Mark the exquisite art, which keeps constantly before the reader the ruined and spectre-haunted mind of the narrator, and so suggests a *possible explanation* of the marvels of the story, without in the least weakening its vigor as an exposition of the mystical *thesis* which the tale is designed to illustrate and enforce.

The story will be, we presume, entirely new to most of our readers. . . . In our copy of LIGEIA, the author has put the last hand to his work, and improved it by several important changes and additions.

In this issue Eames also notices the *American Review* for February: "Edgar A. Poe, we believe under the '*nom de plume*' of Quarles, gives a wild and *shivery* poem, which he calls the Raven. It is written in a Stanza unknown before to gods, men, and booksellers, but it fills and delights the ear strangely with its wild and clashing music. Everybody reads the Poem and praises it—justly we think, for it seems to us full of originality and power."

15 FEBRUARY. PHILADELPHIA. Robert Morris' *Pennsylvania Inquirer* reprints "The Raven" from the *Broadway Journal* of 8 February, under the heading "A BEAUTIFUL POEM."

15 FEBRUARY. ELLICOTT CITY, MARYLAND. The *Howard District Press*, a weekly newspaper, reprints "The Raven" and Willis' introduction from the *Evening Mirror*.

BEFORE 16 FEBRUARY. SOUTH ATTLEBOROUGH, MASSACHUSETTS. The young poet Abijah M. Ide, Jr., sends his "Bunker's Hill" to Poe, soliciting his opinion (Ide to Poe, 16 February).

16 FEBRUARY. Ide replies to a letter from Poe:

I am very thankful to you for the manner in which you wrote to me of my Poem; and feel flattered by your opinion of its general merits. I feel your suggestions to be most appropriate, but I wish you had given your reason to [for] thinking the last stanza should be *omitted*. . . . I am glad to learn that you have established yourself in New York; because I have learned to regard it as producing a better order of literature, than Philadelphia, and also, that in the former city, I may the more likely have the good fortune to meet you at some future time. I learn by a friend that you are connected with a publication, called the "Broadway Journal" which I have never seen. Your new magazine I presume is to be of a similar character:—*a fearless critical monthly.*

Since Ide's last letter to Poe, he has seen *Graham's Magazine* for February: "tho' my praise may be little worth to you, I cannot refrain from saying that I have been exceedingly pleased with the 'Haunted Palace,' quoted in Mr. Lowell's article" (MB–G).

17 FEBRUARY. NEW YORK. The *Evening Mirror* publishes Poe's "Plagia-

rism," a reply to Briggs's editorial in the *Broadway Journal* of 15 February. Poe prints both Aldrich's poem and Hood's, pointing out ten similarities between them. He repeats his accusation: "somebody *is* a thief." The *Mirror* also contains "The Owl: A Capital Parody on Mr. Poe's Raven" by "Sarles." In this eighteen-stanza poem the narrator is disturbed "upon a midnight dreary" by "a flapping, flapping, flapping, flapping, flapping" outside his chamber door. He opens his shutter: "In there stepped a staring owl, one of the saintly days of yore." The owl perches "upon a bursted band-box" above the chamber door and utters a single word— "nevermore":

But the owl he looked so lonely, saying that word and that only,
That a thimble-full of whiskey I did speedily outpour
In a tea-cup on the table, which, as well as I was able,
I invited him to drink of, saying there was plenty more—
But the owl he shook his head, and threw the whiskey on the floor,
               Plainly saying, "nevermore!"

"What? a temperance owl, by thunder! Well, indeed 'tis no great wonder;—
He has doubtless just now come from out the 'Tabernacle' door,
Where he's heard a temperance lecture, and has seen a fearful picture
Of the consequences of running up a whiskey-toddy score—
Of the evils brought by sixpence worth inside the pothouse door—
               That it is, and nothing more.

Or this word so full of meaning is perhaps his only gleaning
In the field of human lore—doubtless his only stock and store,
Taught him by some drunken master, who by bailiffs and disaster
Aye was followed fast and faster, while the friends him did adjure,
Friends and cash, and hope which now he did no longer dare adjure,
               Left him, and forevermore."

Poe's article and the parody are reprinted in the *Weekly Mirror* for 22 February.

19 FEBRUARY. PHILADELPHIA. The *Sun* protests that Poe's "Some Secrets of the Magazine Prison-House," published in the *Broadway Journal* of 15 February, is unfair to magazine publishers, citing the liberal payments given authors by George R. Graham and Louis A. Godey (Mabbott [1978], 3:1205).

21 FEBRUARY. NEW YORK. Poe and John Bisco sign a contract. "Edgar A. Poe agrees to assist C. F. Briggs in the editorship of the 'Broadway Journal' published by John Bisco, to allow his name to be published as one of the Editors of said paper, to furnish each and every week original matter to the amount of, at least, one page of said paper, and to give his faithful

superintendence to the general conduct of the same." Bisco agrees to pay Poe "one-third of the profits arising from the said 'Broadway Journal' and to allow him to inspect the Books of the same whenever he may wish to do so" (Quinn, p. 751; Moldenhauer [1973], pp. 79–80).

22 FEBRUARY. The *Broadway Journal* announces "that hereafter, EDGAR A. POE and HENRY C. WATSON, will be associated with the Editorial department . . . . MR. WATSON will have entire control of the Musical department." Poe replies to the Philadelphia *Sun* of 19 February: "We are extremely happy to learn that GRAHAM paid COOPER fifteen hundred dollars in seventeen months, and that GODEY keeps almost as many ladies in his pay as the Grand Turk; but we have heard of writers, whose articles are certainly equal to any thing of COOPER'S that we have seen in Graham, to whom that munificent publisher pays nothing."

22 FEBRUARY. The *Town* reports:

EDGAR A. POE. This gentleman has become one of the editors of the "Evening Mirror." We rejoice at the fact. We hope to see the columns of that paper relieved of much of the Miss Nancyism of Willis, and a more manly vigor infused into them. Poe must starch up "Mi-boy and the Brigadier," [N. P. Willis and "General" George P. Morris] but at the same time keep the Mirror clean of all "Gold Bugs."
P.S. EDGAR has since gone into the Broadway Journal.

On another page the *Town* scoffs at Poe's review of Bulwer-Lytton's *Poems*: "A YOUNG MAN in the Broadway Journal of last week [actually 8 February issue], solemnly declares that BULWER is not a man of genius, but rather a clever little fellow, as a general thing. This young man in the Broadway Journal ought to hurry express haste to Washington and get out a patent right for his Discovery."

22 FEBRUARY. The *New World* reprints "THE RAVEN: By Quarles" from the *American Review*. In an adjoining column it publishes "THE VETO: By Snarles," a satire on municipal politicians; each of the eighteen stanzas parodies the adjacent stanza in Poe's poem:

Once upon an evening dreary, the Council pondered weak and weary,
Over many a long petition which was voted down a bore.
While they nodded, mostly napping, suddenly there came a tapping,
As of some one gently rapping at the Corporation's door—
" 'Tis some petition," then they muttered, "come to ask for something more—
        Only this and nothing more."

Ah, distinctly I remember it was in the bleak December,
When the Tenth's respected member had possession of the floor,

When the rest were mostly napping—'twas the President was tapping,
And so stoutly he was rapping, to drown the sleepers' snore—
And this was all the rapping that they fancied at the door,—
           Only this and nothing more.

22 FEBRUARY. BUFFALO, NEW YORK. The *Western Literary Messenger* reprints "The Raven" with this introduction: "The following remarkable and powerful poem, by EDGAR A. POE, is from the second number of the *American Review*. It is a bold and original conception, sustained and wrought out with most admirable skill. The versification is new and 'fills the ear with a wild and delightful music.' "

24 FEBRUARY. NEW YORK. Poe writes Rufus W. Griswold in Philadelphia. Shortly after his meeting with Griswold, Poe sent him all his poems "worth re-publishing" for possible inclusion in a revised edition of *The Poets and Poetry of America*. He is forwarding with this letter his "Mesmeric Revelation" and an excerpt from "Marginalia" for Griswold's forthcoming *Prose Writers of America*. He does not have ready access to samples of his literary criticism, but Griswold will find his reviews of "Flaccus" (Thomas Ward) and of Dickens' novel *Barnaby Rudge* in *Graham's Magazine*. "In the tale line I send you 'The Murders in the Rue Morgue' and 'The Man that was used up'—far more than enough, you will say—but you can select to suit yourself. I would prefer having in the 'Gold Bug' . . . but have not a copy just now. If there is no immediate hurry for it, however, I will get one & send it you corrected" (*L*, 1:279–80).

25 FEBRUARY. PHILADELPHIA. Lowell writes Briggs, commenting on the announcement in the *Broadway Journal* for 22 February: "I do not know whether to be glad or sorry that you have associated Poe and [Henry C.] Watson with you as editors. I do not know the last; the first is certainly able, but I think that there should never be more than one editor with any proprietary control over the paper. Its individuality is not generally so well preserved" (Lowell, 1:85).

27 FEBRUARY. NEW YORK. The *Daily Tribune* reports:

THE POETS AND POETRY OF AMERICA.—Mr. Edgar A. Poe, so favorably known in many quarters as a Critic, lectures to-morrow evening, at the Society Library. To Mr. Poe's numerous admirers this announcement will be sufficient, and to those who may not have come within the sphere of his influence we recommend an attendance upon the lecture of this evening. Mr. Poe has shown himself to be a poet of no mean order, and it may hence be concluded that he will freely sympathize with the "Poets and Poetry of America."

In the *Evening Mirror* Willis observes: "The decapitation of the criminal who did not know his head was off till it fell into his hand . . . conveys an idea of the Damascene slicing of the critical blade of Mr. Poe. On Friday night we are to have his 'Lecture on the Poets of America,' and those who would witness fine carving will probably be there."

BEFORE 28 FEBRUARY. In the *New World* for 1 March Charles Eames announces Poe's lecture: "We shall listen with great pleasure, and, we doubt not, with profit to Mr. Poe's views of the efforts of his brethren in an art, the theory and practice of which he knows so well."

28 FEBRUARY. In the *Morning News* Evert A. Duyckinck comments:

MR. POE'S LECTURE AT THE SOCIETY LIBRARY FOR THIS EVENING.—We learn with pleasure that we are to have an opportunity of listening to this celebrated author to-night, on a topic which will bring out his rare and peculiar merits— nothing less than the Poets and Poetry of America. There are enough of poets in this city alone to fill the lecture room, and allowing the proportion of three *claquers* to each male, and five to each female author (a reasonable allowance), the house will overflow. We remember a good deal of noise being made about this lecture, on its delivery some time since in Philadelphia—proof presumptive that the author spoke his own mind and was worth listening to. . . . What mode of discussion Mr. Poe will adopt, we cannot pretend to say; but the lecture will differ from anything he has ever done before, if it do[es] not prove novel, ingenious, and a capital antidote to dullness.

THE SOCIETY LIBRARY
New York Public Library

The *Daily Tribune* reminds its readers: "Those who love to see the blade of criticism wielded by a competent hand, will go and hear Mr. POE'S Lecture." The *New York Herald* predicts that the lecture "will doubtless be a great literary treat."

28 FEBRUARY. In the evening "some three hundred" persons attend Poe's lecture at the Society Library, corner of Broadway and Leonard Street (*Daily Tribune*, 1 March).

MARCH. In the "Editor's Table" of the *Knickerbocker Magazine*, Lewis Gaylord Clark notices the *American Review* for February: "The very best thing in its pages is an unique, singularly imaginative, and most musical effusion, entitled 'The Raven.' We have never before, to our knowledge, met the author, Mr. EDGAR A. POE, as a poet; but if the poem to which we allude be a specimen of his powers in this kind, we shall always be glad to welcome him in his new department."

MARCH. RICHMOND. The *Southern Literary Messenger* reprints "The Raven" with an introduction by Benjamin Blake Minor: "The following poem first appeared, we think, in the Evening Mirror; though intended for the American Review. It has since been frequently republished with the highest approbation. Still we take pleasure in presenting it to our readers, who must remember with delight many of the contributions of Mr. Poe to the Messenger." Minor quotes the praise James Brooks accorded "The Raven" in the New York *Morning Express* of 5 February.

CA. MARCH. Minor writes Poe, inviting him to contribute a critical article to the *Messenger* each month, at "$3 a printed page" (implied by Minor's announcement in the April *Messenger* and by his letter to J. A. Harrison, *W*, 1:220–21).

1 MARCH. NEW YORK. A reviewer in the *Daily Tribune*, probably Horace Greeley, comments:

EDGAR A. POE delivered a remarkable Lecture on American Poets and Poetry last evening, at the Society Library. It embodied much acute and fearless criticism, with some that did not strike us so favorably. The worst portion of the Lecture was the introduction, wherein Mr. P. indulged in indiscriminate and often unjust censure on whatever has hitherto aspired to be criticism in this Country, whether in the shape of Reviews, Magazines or Newspapers. . . . But what he said of American Poetry, his proper theme, was generally well said, and was very direct and hearty. We object to his intimation that Sprague, and his broad assertion that Longfellow is a plagiarist. Of all critical cant, this hunting after coincidence of idea or phrase, often unavoidable, between authors, is the least endurable. . . .

On Bryant, Halleck, Dana, and Mrs. Osgood, Mr. P. discoursed satisfactorily, but we do think his quarter of an hour employed in demolishing the Poetical reputation of the Misses Davidson might have been better bestowed. . . .

Mr. Poe writes better than he reads. His Lecture gained nothing from the graces of his elocution, and in one or two instances we thought the Poets suffered more from his recitation of their verses than from his most savage criticism. "Florence Vane" [by Philip Pendleton Cooke] was especially ill done. And this reminds us that Mr. P. closed with three [re]citations—"Unseen Spirits" by Willis, "Florence Vane," (two admirable poems) and a "Heavenly" something ["The Heavenly Vision"] by Dr. Thomas Holley Chivers, which seemed to us very middling sing song. . . .

We are rather ashamed to add that this Lecture by a Poet and critic of genius and established reputation, was listened to but by some three hundred of our four hundred thousand people. Any dancing dog or summerseting monkey would have drawn a larger house. Why is this? Have we no taste? Merely as a source of information with regard to our National Poetry, the bare announcement should have sufficed to crown the house.—Shall we not have a repetition?

The review is reprinted in the *Weekly Tribune* for 8 March.

In the *Morning News* Evert A. Duyckinck comments:

A notice of Poe's lecture . . . cannot of necessity be coldly discriminating, for it is written while under the spell of his genius and eloquence. In the exordium he gave a great and cutting description of the arts which are practised, with the aid of the periodical press, in obtaining unmerited reputation for literary worth. His observations upon this division of his subject extended also to the pernicious influence of coteries, and he did not hesitate to point to the Capital of New England [Boston] as the chief habitation, in this country, of literary hucksters and phrase mongers. Mr. Poe's manner was that of a versed and resolute man, applying to a hideous sore a keen and serviceable knife.

In speaking of the sisters Lucretia and Margaret Davidson, two sentimental poetesses who died before reaching adulthood, Poe observed that the "remarkable mental powers" they displayed in childhood "afforded no promise of their maturing to such splendid genius," because "precocity is more apt to be followed by mediocrity than otherwise." He evaluated the several anthologies of American poetry, pronouncing "Griswold's to be the best" and selecting "some ten or twelve" poets from it for further discussion. Poe's recitations displayed "force and pathos" and gave "undissembled pleasure" to the audience. "It would be difficult to exaggerate the merit of his closing disquisition on the general purposes and construction of poetical composition. Competent persons who heard it, will perhaps not decline to rank the author with a Hazlitt or a Coleridge."

In the *Evening Mirror* Nathaniel P. Willis reviews the lecture:

After some general remarks on poetry and the uses of impartial criticism, Mr. Poe gently waked up the American Poetesses. He began with Mrs. Sigourney, whom he considered the best known, and who, he seemed to think, owed her famousness to the same cause as "old Boss Richards"—the being "kept before the people." He spoke well of her poetry abstractly, but intimated that it was strongly be-Hemans'd . . . . He next came to Mrs. Welby as No. 2, and gave her whole-some muse some very stiff laudation. Mrs. Osgood came next, and for her he prophesied a rosy future of increasing power and renown. He spoke well of Mrs. Seba Smith . . . .

Of the inspired males Mr. Poe only took up the Copperplate Five—BRYANT, HALLECK, LONGFELLOW, SPRAGUE and DANA. These, as having their portraits engraved in the frontispiece of Griswold's "Poets and Poetry of America," were taken to represent the country's poetry, and dropped into the melting-pot accord-ingly. Mr. BRYANT came first as the allowed best poet; but Mr. Poe, after giving him high praise, expressed a contempt for "public opinion," and for the opinion of all majorities, in matters of taste, and intimated that Mr. Bryant's universality of approval lay in his keeping within very narrow limits, where it was easy to have no faults. HALLECK, Mr. Poe praised exceedingly, repeating with great beauty of elocution his "Marco Bozzaris." LONGFELLOW, Mr. Poe said, had more genius than any other of the five, but his fatal alacrity at imitation made him borrow, when he had better at home. SPRAGUE, but for one drop of genuine poetry in a fugitive piece, was described by Poe as Pope and water. DANA found very little favour. Mr. Poe thought his metre harsh and awkward, his narrative ill-managed, and his conceptions eggs from other people's nests. With the Copperplate Five, the criti-cisms abruptly broke off, Mr. Poe concluding his lecture with the recitation of three pieces of poetry which he thought had been mistakenly put away, by the housekeeper of the Temple of Fame, among the empty bottles. Two of them were by authors we did not know, and the third was by . . . ourself!

Poe's audience numbered "between two and three hundred" and consisted "of critics and poets," who heard him "with breathless attention." Willis describes Poe's manner on the rostrum: "He becomes a desk,—his beauti-ful head showing like a statuary embodiment of Discrimination; his accent drops like a knife through water, and his style is so much purer and clearer than the pulpit commonly gets or requires, that the effect of what he says, besides other things, pampers the ear." The review is reprinted in the *Weekly Mirror* for 8 March.

1 MARCH. In the *Evening Mirror* Willis publishes a long letter from a correspondent who signs himself "Outis," the Greek word for "Nobody." Outis strenuously objects to Poe's efforts "to convict Longfellow of imita-tion, and Aldrich and others, of plagiarism. . . . Did no two men ever think alike, without stealing one from the other? or, thinking alike, did no two men ever use the same, or similar words, to convey the thoughts, and that, without any communication with each other?" Outis sees no evidence of plagiarism either in James Aldrich's "A Death-Bed" or Thomas

Hood's "The Death-Bed"; he disputes Poe's demonstration of similarities in the 17 February *Mirror*. Parodying the procedure in Poe's article, Outis quotes "The Bird of the Dream," an anonymous poem written years before; and he then enumerates fifteen *"identities"* between it and "The Raven," showing how Poe himself might be convicted of plagiarism. "Now I shall not charge Mr. Poe with plagiarism . . . . Such criticisms only make the *author* of them contemptible, without soiling a plume in the cap of his victim. I have selected this poem of Mr. Poe's, for illustrating my remarks, because it is recent, and must be familiar to all the lovers of true poetry hereabouts." The letter is reprinted in the *Weekly Mirror* for 8 March.

1 MARCH. The *Rover* notices the controversy about Aldrich's reputed plagiarism from Hood, as debated in Briggs's editorial in the 15 February *Broadway Journal* and in Poe's reply in the 17 February *Evening Mirror*. The *Rover* observes that Hood's poem was published in 1831, nine years before Aldrich's: "We do not put our fingers in the charge against Mr. Aldrich, further than to remove suspicion of stain from the reputation of Mr. Hood; and, furthermore, we do not approve the Mirror's standard of criticism, for it leaves not a foundation stone on which to rest the reputation of most modern poets."

1 MARCH. The *Broadway Journal* contains Poe's review of *Graham's Magazine* for March.

1 MARCH. William M. Gillespie, a minor author, writes Poe, discussing his lecture on the "Poets and Poetry of America":

> I was one of your delighted hearers last night, but have to complain that you tempted me to load my memory with so many points of thought and expression, that I carried off very imperfectly one passage which I particularly desired to remember—your characterization of Mrs. Osgood.
>
> I had left her in the Astor house with her hat on awaiting the friend with whom she was coming to the lecture; but she was disappointed, and lost the pleasure of hearing you, which she had so eagerly anticipated, though not knowing that she would be noticed. I fear that she was not sufficiently *en rapport* with me to share my thrill of pleasure at the passage, and the applause which followed it; and therefore I ask of you the favor of giving me an opportunity to *copy* it from your manuscript, as I should be unwilling to give you that trouble (MB–G).

AFTER 1 MARCH. Mrs. Frances S. Osgood, an attractive poetess of thirty-three, meets Poe. She recalls:

> My first meeting with the poet was at the Astor House. A few days previous, Mr. Willis had handed me, at the *table d'hôte*, that strange and thrilling poem entitled "The Raven," saying that the author wanted my opinion of it. Its effect

upon me was so singular, so like that of "wierd, unearthly music," that it was with a feeling almost of dread, I heard he desired an introduction. Yet I could not refuse without seeming ungrateful, because I had just heard of his enthusiastic and partial eulogy of my writings, in his lecture on American Literature. I shall never forget the morning when I was summoned to the drawing-room by Mr. Willis to receive him. With his proud and beautiful head erect, his dark eyes flashing with the elective light of feeling and of thought, a peculiar, an inimitable blending of sweetness and hauteur in his expression and manner, he greeted me, calmly, gravely, almost coldly; yet with so marked an earnestness that I could not help being deeply impressed by it. From that moment until his death we were friends; although we met only during the first year of our acquaintance. . . .

During that year, while travelling for my health, I maintained a correspondence with Mr. Poe, in accordance with the earnest entreaties of his wife, who imagined that my influence over him had a restraining and beneficial effect. It *had*, as far as this—that having solemnly promised me to give up the use of stimulants, he so firmly respected his promise and me, as never once, during our whole acquaintance, to appear in my presence when in the slightest degree affected by them (letter to R. W. Griswold, early 1850, quoted in Griswold [1850], p. xxxvii).

2 MARCH. The *New York Herald* comments:

POETS AND POETRY OF AMERICA. —There was a goodly muster of the *literati* and the would-bes of this city on Friday evening, at the Society Library, to hear Mr. E. A. Poe deliver a lecture on this subject. More than one of them appeared to wince under the severity of his remarks, which were not a few . . . . The newspaper press, the monthly magazines, and the quarterlies came in alike for a meed of his censure, as being venal, ignorant, and entirely unfit to form a judgment on the most humblest [*sic*] productions of the writers of this country—of course, his own included—and [he] was particularly severe on "the Dunderheaded critics of Boston," as he termed certain writers of that city. He then proceeded to criticise several writers personally—the ladies having the preference—and certainly they came in for no small share of his bile—each and every one to whom the public had awarded their approbation (among whom were some of the ablest writers of the old and new world) he censured the most. Mrs. Sigourney had been placed on a pinnacle of fame she did not merit—she was but a poor imitator of Mrs. Hemans—the writings of Misses Davidson were not worthy of the character they had received. —After treating the principal of the female writers of the country in this style generally at some length, and giving extracts from their writings as specimens—but for every good passage pointing out what he deemed ten bad ones—he proceeded to attack the male portion, if possible, in stronger terms. Kettle, Morris, Bryant, Keese, Griswold, Gaynor, Taylor, &c., came in for a share of his lash. There was not one, in his judgment, that came up to the proper standard of a poet—their writings, more or less, abounded in faults to a much greater extent than in beauties. The lecture throughout was the severest piece of criticism that has come within our recollection for some time, but in a very many instances we have yet to learn how far it is just. What the lecturer lacked in dispassionate judgment and expression, was made up by Latin and French adages and extracts; and certainly, if we are to judge from what he advanced on this occasion, and take him at his own valuation, he is the only man in the country that is able to write a poem, or form a proper judgment of the writings of others.

3 MARCH. BOSTON. The *Daily Atlas* reports:

A chap named Poe, has been engaged in delivering a lecture on American Poets and Poetry, in the city of New York. In the course of some remarks upon this lecture, the New York Tribune says: "We are rather ashamed to add, that this lecture, by a poet and critic of genius and established reputation, was listened to but by some three hundred of our four hundred thousand people. Any dancing dog or sommerseting monkey would have drawn a larger house."

The Tribune may think as it pleases—but we commend the taste of the 399,700 people, as far preferable to that of the 300, in this case. We should much prefer the dancing dog, or sommerseting monkey, to the man who could utter such remarks as this Poe is said to have made, in reference to the poetry of Sprague and Longfellow. If he was [*sic*] to come before a Boston audience with such stuff, they would *poh* at him at once.

5 MARCH. The *Evening Transcript* reprints the report of Poe's lecture from the "Atlas of Monday." Miss Cornelia Wells Walter, the editor of the *Transcript*, adds:

Somebody sent us the other day, an epitaph on a man named POE, of which the above [report from the *Atlas*] has reminded us. We know not in what burial place the record is made, but it runs as follows:

> There lies, by Death's relentless blow,
> A would-be critic here below;
>   His name was Poe
>   His life was woe:
> You ask, "What of this Mister Poe?"
> Why nothing of him that I know;
> But echo, answering, saith—"*Poh!*"

6 MARCH OR LATER. NEW YORK. Poe writes William M. Gillespie that he will be unable to keep his appointment with Mrs. Osgood:

An unlucky *contretemps*, connected with the getting out of the "Journal" will, I fear, detain me until after 10 to night—too late for the appointment.

If you can (this evening) see Mrs O. & make any decent apology for me, I will be greatly obliged. Any evening (except to-morrow) I shall be disengaged, and will be happy to accompany you (*L*, 1:306).

BEFORE 8 MARCH. The publishers Wiley and Putnam agree to issue a new edition of Poe's tales in their forthcoming "Library of American Books" (Briggs to Lowell, 8 March).

8 MARCH. The *Town* evaluates Poe's lecture: "It was worthy of its author—keen, cutting and withering, when it touched on the mountebanks of American literature; and full of faith and hope, when it spoke of the future. Among the mountebanks, a man named GRISWOLD, who *is* a Reverend and who is *not* a Reverend, received his proper share of castigation." In the *New World* Charles Eames comments: "We were unable to hear Mr. Poe's lecture . . . but it has been universally spoken of as a strong and spirited performance. Mr. Poe has been urged to repeat it, and we trust he will comply with the request."

8 MARCH. The *Broadway Journal* now identifies its staff on its masthead: "C. F. BRIGGS, EDGAR A. POE, H. C. WATSON, EDITORS." The *Journal* publishes the first of five installments of "IMITATION—PLAGIARISM—MR. POE'S REPLY TO THE LETTER OF OUTIS—A LARGE ACCOUNT OF A SMALL MATTER—A VOLUMINOUS HISTORY OF THE LITTLE LONGFELLOW WAR." Poe reprints the letter of "Outis" from the *Evening Mirror* of 1 March, asking: "Is it altogether impossible that a critic be instigated to the exposure of a plagiarism, or still better, of plagiarism generally wherever he meets it, by a strictly honorable and even charitable motive?" The *Journal* also carries a letter "to the Editor" from Poe, who discusses his 28 February lecture. On this occasion he told "an audience made up chiefly of editors and their connexions" an unpleasant truth: "I told these gentlemen to their teeth that, with a *very* few noble exceptions, they had been engaged for many years in a system of indiscriminate laudation of American books—a system which, more than any other one thing in the world, had tended to the depression of that 'American Literature' whose elevation it was designed to effect. . . . Could I, at the moment, have invented any terms *more* explicit, wherewith to express my contempt of our general editorial course of corruption and puffery, I should have employed them."

8 MARCH. Briggs writes Lowell in Philadelphia:

Poe is only an assistant to me, and will in no manner interfere with my own way of doing things. It was requisite that I should have his or some other person's assistance on account of my liability to be taken off from the business of the paper, and as his name is of some authority I thought it advisable to announce him as an editor. . . . Poe has left the Mirror. Willis was too Willisy for him. Unfortunately for him (Poe) he has mounted a very ticklish hobby just now, Plagiarism which he is bent on riding to death, and I think the better way is to let him run down as soon as possible by giving him no check. Wiley & Putnam are going to publish a new edition of his tales and sketches. Every body has been raven mad about his last poem, and his lecture, which W[illiam Wetmore] Story went with me to hear, has gained him a dozen or two of waspish foes who will do him more good than harm (MiDAAA–P).

8 MARCH. PHILADELPHIA. Lowell writes Longfellow in Cambridge, Massachusetts: "Somebody has been mixing *me* up with the foolish controversy about the 'Waif.' " Lowell never dreamed of attributing his omission from Longfellow's anthology to the cause implied by Poe in his review for the *Evening Mirror*: "But as I had written a life of Mr. Poe I thought some of your friends might imagine I jogged Mr. Poe's elbow in the criticism. I have had no communication with him, . . . since nearly two months before the appearance of the 'Waif.' I say frankly your copying any verse of mine into that pleasant little volume never occurred to me" (Phillips, 2:972–73).

10 MARCH. NEW YORK. Poe writes George R. Graham in Philadelphia:

> I believe that you feel a delicacy in publishing my criticism on Longfellow's "Spanish Student"; and, perhaps, upon the whole, it would be for your interest *not* to do it, as, in a Magazine such as yours, you could not well manage to fight out the battle with Longfellow's coterie in Boston, which would be the result of your publishing it. But, with me, the case is very different, and if I can only get them all fairly down upon me, I shall know precisely what to do. I will, therefore, be very grateful to you if you will let me have the article back. I will write you, in place of it, any thing you may suggest—or I will advertise your Magazine conspicuously in the "Broadway Journal" to the amount of the $30—or I will refund you the money, as soon as I can place my hands upon it.

On a separate sheet Poe itemizes his financial dealings with *Graham's Magazine*:

> We were square when I sold you the "Versification" article; for which you gave me first 25, and afterward 7—
> in all $32.00
> Then you bought "The Gold Bug" for 52.00
> I got both these back, so that I owed $84.00
> You lent Mrs. Clemm 12.50
> Making in all $96.50
> The review of "Flaccus" was 3 3/4 pp, which, at $4, is 15.00
> Lowell's poem is 10.00
> The review of Channing, 4 pp. is 16, of which I got 6,
>   leaving 10.00
> The review of Halleck, 4 pp. is 16, of which I got 10,
>   leaving 6.00
> The review of Reynolds, 2 pp. 8.00
> The review of Longfellow, 5 pp. is 20, of which I got 10, leaving 10.00
> So that I have paid in all 59.00
> Which leaves still due by me $37.50
> (*L*, 1:272–73, 2:710–11).

11 MARCH. PHILADELPHIA. Graham writes Longfellow in Cambridge, Massachusetts: "What has 'broke loose' in Poe? I see he is down on you in New York papers and has written demanding return of Review I mentioned he had written for me. If he sends money or another article I shall be obliged to let him have it. . . . Mr. Willis made a disclaimer of being an endorser of Poe's views, at my request. I cannot see what Poe says *now*, can hurt you" (Phillips, 2:978).

13 MARCH. ITHACA, NEW YORK. Jedediah Hunt, Jr., the editor of the *National Archives*, reviews the *Broadway Journal* for 8 March in his weekly newspaper. Hunt praises the *Journal* as "a prize" among periodicals:

As a critical tattler, we know of none other which seems to give a more candid review of the works of *authors*. We own, notwithstanding, that we have cherished rather of a sour feeling towards one of the editors—Mr. POE in times past, for his sarcastic, and what to us then appeared malicious criticism on others' productions. All who have read "Graham" for the last two or three years—will corroborate our statement, and there breathes not a man, having any pretensions to authorship, who so flinchingly squirms at the strictures of others, than does Mr. POE. This may be seen in the No. now before us. (No. 10, vol. 1) One quarter of the paper is made use of by Mr. POE, endeavoring to smooth over and give diminutiveness to what a writer for the Mirror, calling himself "Outis," and some of the other papers have said of him, respecting his late lecture on the "Poets and Poetry of America," and his Plagiarisms. It is a very true remark, that a Joker will rarely ever receive one in return, good naturedly; and this is to a great extent true of Mr. POE. But we will "pass all his imperfections by" and to show that we are not blind to his good qualities, we will say that, as a writer, on general topics, Mr. POE, undoubtedly, stands on an equal with the best of his class.

15 MARCH. NEW YORK. The *Rover* announces that it will publish "an original poem by the lamented and highly gifted Margaret Davidson" in its next number: "By-the-bye—was it not rather uncalled for—the manner in which Mr. Poe spoke of these talented girls [Lucretia and Margaret Davidson] in his late Lecture? We think so. They did not write for criticism—at least such criticism as his; and it is a pity that a lamb shall not stray beyond its fold without being pounced upon by an undiscriminating wolf. Mr. Poe must not be too *raven*ous, lest he provoke the judgment of the gods."

15 MARCH. The *Broadway Journal* contains the second installment of Poe's reply to "Outis." He agrees with Outis' position that two persons can "think alike" without one or the other being guilty of plagiarism. As an example, Poe observes that Outis no doubt considers him "a fool" and that this same idea is independently "entertained by Mr. Aldrich, and by Mr. Longfellow—and by Mrs. Outis and her seven children—and by Mrs.

Aldrich and hers—and by Mrs. Longfellow and hers." In an article on "Satirical Poems," Poe condemns such crude American satires as John Trumbull's *M'Fingal* and Laughton Osborn's *The Vision of Rubeta*, which manifest the colonial tendency to imitate the mother country. The former is "a faint echo from 'Hudibras' "; the latter, "an illimitable gilded swill-trough overflowing with Dunciad and water." The *Journal* reprints Poe's revised tale "Lionizing" (under the heading "Some Passages in the Life of a Lion") and Philip Pendleton Cooke's "Florence Vane," a poem "recited by Mr. Poe in his late Lecture."

15 MARCH. The poetess Mary E. Hewitt writes Poe from her quarters at the Athenaeum Hotel: "Mr. [William M.] Gillespie tells me that he has mentioned to you the singular coincidence that I related to him, of the simultaneous appearance of your admirable poem, 'The Raven,' and the receipt of a letter by myself from a very dear brother resident in Manilla, containing a marvelous history of a 'white bird,' the which, although the very opposite of the 'raven,' struck me as being so singularly like it in groundwork as to constitute a 'remarkable coincidence.' " Mrs. Hewitt has composed a verse "paraphrase" of this fable, entitled "A Tale of Luzon," which she encloses. She is also forwarding her brother's letter, thinking that Poe might like "to see the story as told in the original prose" (Mabbott [1937], pp. 116–17).

15 MARCH. WOODLANDS, SOUTH CAROLINA. William Gilmore Simms writes Evert A. Duyckinck in New York:

I am glad that you think and speak well of Poe, which [Cornelius] Mathews was not disposed to do though I tried to open his eyes to the singular merits of that person. Poe is no friend of mine, as I believe. He began by a very savage attack on one of my novels—the Partisan. . . . I do not puff the man when I say I consider him a remarkable one. He has more real imaginative power than 99 in the 100 of our poets & tale writers. His style is clear & correct, his conceptions bold & fanciful, his fancies vivid, and his taste generally good. His bolder effects are impaired by his fondness for *detail* & this hurts his criticism which is too frequently given to the analysis of the inferior points of style, making him somewhat regardless of the more noble features of the work. But, I repeat, he is a man of remarkable power, to whom I shall strive one day to do that justice which a great portion of our public seems desirous to withhold (Simms, 2:42–43).

15 MARCH. CAMBRIDGE, MASSACHUSETTS. Longfellow replies to Lowell's 8 March letter:

I regret as much as you do, that your name should have been dragged into the "Waif Controversy." Willis, and he alone, is to blame for this. He first connected you with the matter in a letter to [Charles] Sumner; and then published an extract from Sumner's answer, which was private, and not intended for any eye but Willis's. In fact, I have from the beginning, known as little about this whole affair, as you. [George S.] Hillard wrote the first letter, without my knowledge. Then Summer wrote three or four private letters of expostulation to Willis, partly without my knowledge and partly against my request to the contrary. Who wrote the long epistle copied into the "Broadway Journal" I do not know. I have had nothing to do with the discussion, and shall have nothing to do with it; as I consider, with you, life too precious to be wasted in street brawls (Shuman, pp. 155–56; also in Longfellow [1972], 3:57–58).

16 MARCH. STATEN ISLAND, NEW YORK. Briggs writes Lowell in Philadelphia:

Poe is a monomaniac on the subject of plagiarism, and I thought it best to allow him to ride his hobby to death in the outset and be done with it. It all commenced with myself. When he was in the Mirror office he made, what I thought, a very unjustifiable charge against my friend Aldrich, who is one of the best fellows in the world, and I replied to it as you saw. Somebody in Boston, "Outis," whose name I forget, replied to P[oe] on behalf of Longfellow and Aldrich, and so the war began. It will end, as it began, in smoke. But it will do us some good by calling public attention to our paper. Poe is a much better fellow than you have an idea of. Wiley and Putnam have a new edition of his tales in press (MiDAAA–P).

16 MARCH. NEW YORK. Mrs. Frances S. Osgood writes a friend, possibly Mrs. Sarah Helen Whitman of Providence, Rhode Island:

Did you see how beautifully Mr Edgar Poe spoke of me in his lecture on the Poets—the other night?—He recited a long poem of mine exquisitely, they said—& praised me very highly—He is called the severest critic of the day—so it was a real compliment—& he did not know me then—I was introduced to him afterwards—& like him very much—They say when mine was recited—the audience applauded for the first time. I had four invitations to go—but had company & couldn't (RPB–W).

17 MARCH. Poe writes Jedediah Hunt, Jr., in Ithaca, New York: "There is something in the tone of your article on 'The Broadway Journal' (contained in the 'Archives' of the 13th.) which induces me to trouble you with this letter." Poe recognizes the author of this article as "an educated, an honest, a chivalrous, but . . . a somewhat over-hasty man." He explains his conduct as a critic in order that Hunt may be his friend without reservations: "Let me put it to you as to a frank man of honor—Can you suppose it possible that any human being could pursue a strictly impartial course of criticism for 10 years (as I have done in the S. L. Messenger and in Graham's Magazine) without offending irreparably a host of authors and their connexions?—but because these *were* offended, and gave vent at every

opportunity to their spleen, would you consider my course an iota the less honorable on that account?" (*L*, 1:282–84).

19 MARCH. STATEN ISLAND, NEW YORK. Briggs replies to a letter from Lowell in Philadelphia, who has objected to Poe's reference to "Mrs. Longfellow" in the 15 March *Broadway Journal*:

I think that you are too sensitive in regard to Longfellow; I really do not see that he [Poe] has said anything offensive about him, I am sure not half as bad as I have heard you say, and the allusion to Mrs L[ongfellow], was only a playful allusion to an abstract Mrs L, for Poe did not know even that L was married; look at the thing again and you will see that it contains nothing offensive. Poe has, indeed, a very high admiration for Longfellow and so he will say before he is done. For my own part I did not use to think well of Poe, but my love for you, and implicit confidence in your judgment, led me to abandon all my prejudices against him, when I read your account of him. The Rev Mr Griswold of Phila told me some abominable lies about him, but a personal acquaintance with him has induced me to think highly of him (MiDAAA–P).

20 MARCH. NEW YORK. Poe acknowledges Mrs. Hewitt's letter and "little package" of 15 March:

The coincidence to which you call my attention is certainly remarkable, and the story as narrated by your brother is full of a rich interest, no particle of which, most assuredly, is lost in your truly admirable paraphrase. I fear, indeed, that my enthusiasm for all that I *feel* to be poetry, has hurried me into some indiscretion touching the "Tale of Luzon". Immediately upon reading it, I took it to the printer, and it is now in type for the "Broadway Journal" of this week [22 March issue]. As I re-peruse your note, however, (before depositing it among my most valued autographs) I find no positive warrant for the act—I am by no means sure that you designed the poem for our paper (Ostrom [1974], p. 523).

20 MARCH. Poe apparently writes the actress Anna Cora Mowatt, identifying himself as the drama critic of the *Broadway Journal* and asking to see the manuscript of her forthcoming comedy *Fashion*. Her reply should be addressed to 154 Greenwich Street (Ostrom [1974], pp. 524–25).

20 MARCH. In the evening Mrs. Mowatt sends Poe a copy of *Fashion*: "I have not a more legible manuscript of the Comedy to submit to your perusal, or even one containing all the corrections made at the suggestion of critical advisers. The only fair copy is in the hands of the managers, and that I could not procure. Your criticisms will be prized—I am sorry that they could not have been made before preparations for the performance of the Comedy had progressed so far" (*W*, 17:207–08; also in E. W. Barnes, pp. 104–05).

21 MARCH. PHILADELPHIA. Lowell replies to Briggs's letter of 19 March:

The Rev. Mr. Griswold is an ass & what's more a knave, & even if he had said anything against Poe, I should not have believed it. But neither he nor any one else ever did. I remain of my old opinion about the allusion to Mrs. Longfellow. I remain of my old opinion about Poe, & I have no doubt that Poe estimates L's poetical abilities more highly than I do, perhaps, but I nevertheless do not like his two last articles. I still think Poe an invaluable contributor, but I like such articles as his review of Miss Barrett better than these last (Hull, pp. 496–97).

21 MARCH. NEW YORK. Mrs. Hewitt replies to Poe's letter of 20 March: "I certainly intended to place the 'Tale of Luzon' quite at your disposal— and beg you to believe that I appreciate highly the kindness that has prompted your favorable notice of my lines. After the 'RAVEN,' my verse seemed to me but a broken chime—and since sending it to you, I have wondered at my own temerity. I shall be proud to see it published in the columns of the 'Broadway Journal' " (Mabbott [1937], pp. 117–18).

22 MARCH. The *Broadway Journal* contains the third installment of Poe's reply to "Outis," as well as his notice of the *Southern Literary Messenger*:

The Messenger has always been a favorite with the people of the South and West, who take a singular pride in its support. Its subscribers are almost without exception the *élite*, both as regards wealth and intellectual culture, of the Southern aristocracy, and its corps of contributors are generally men who control the public opinion of the Southerners on *all* topics. . . .

Mr. [Benjamin Blake] Minor is about to make some important improvements in the work, with a view of extending the circulation among ourselves here in the North and East, and we shall not fail to do our part in this endeavour. The New-York agent is *Mr. John Bisco, publisher of the "Broadway Journal," 153 Broadway.* Any communications or subscriptions for the Messenger, may be forwarded either to him or to *Edgar A. Poe*, at the same office.

On another page the *Journal* carries an advertisement for the *Messenger*.

22 MARCH. The *Weekly News* reports: "Wiley & Putnam have in press a volume of 'Tales by Edgar A. Poe' " (Tanselle [1962], p. 252).

24 MARCH. Briggs writes Lowell in Philadelphia: "Poe's Longfellow war, which, by the way, is all on one side, has annoyed a good deal, but since I allowed him to begin it, without any expectation of his making more than one article on it, I could not cut it off until he had made a finish of it in his own way. . . . I presume it will in some quarters do us an injury, but I hope that Longfellow is too good a fellow to take it much to heart. . . . I had supposed from what I have heard you say about the Longfellow clique that you were entirely out of the reach of its circles and cared not the snap of your finger about any of them" (MiDAAA–P).

25 MARCH. The *Evening Mirror* contains "The Craven: BY POH!"—an advertisement:

Once upon a midnight dreary, while with toil and care quite weary,
I was pondering on man's proneness to deceitfulness and guile,
Soon I fell into a seeming state 'twixt wakefulness and dreaming,
When my mind's eye saw a scheming fellow counterfeiting Soap—
Yes! counterfeiting GOURAUD'S matchless *Medicated Soap;*
                Twisting sand into a rope! . . .

I said—"thou man of evil (I will not call thee devil,)
Get thee back into the darkness and the night's Plutonian shore!
By *my fame* thou hast a token, that the spells which thou hast spoken,
Are scattered all, and broken! Craven, wilt thou now give o'er,
And never counterfeit my *Soap* or *Poudres* any more?"
            Quoth the craven—"Never more!"

    Dr. F. FELIX GOURAUD, of 67 Walker street, again deems it necessary to caution the public against purchasing any *imitations* of his matchless *Italian Medicated Soap*, incomparable *Poudres Subtiles* and marvellous *Grecian Hair Dye*.

26 MARCH. Mrs. Mowatt's comedy *Fashion* opens at the Park Theatre; Poe attends the first performance as well as several successive repetitions (E. W. Barnes, pp. 96–115; Poe in *Broadway Journal*, 5 April).

28 MARCH. BOSTON. The *Liberator*, a weekly newspaper devoted to the cause of abolition, publishes a letter from Robert Carter, Lowell's friend and former partner. Carter denounces the *Broadway Journal* for favorably noticing the *Southern Literary Messenger* in its 22 March issue:

The style and matter of the Messenger, are chiefly of the kind expressively denominated "sophomoric" . . . . Its principles are of the vilest sort, its aim being to uphold the "peculiar institution," to decry the colored race, to libel the abolitionists . . . . This miserable magazine, the Broadway Journal not only puffs, but gratuitously solicits and offers to receive subscriptions for it, besides inserting a standing advertisement; and with contemptible cunning, to catch the aristocrats among its readers, it repeatedly makes the alluring statement, that the supporters of the Messenger are "the *elite* of the Southern aristocracy," and that "it is the principal organ of Southern opinion"!! Precious inducements, truly, to Northern democratic freemen!

28 MARCH. NEW YORK. Briggs writes the painter William Page in Boston:

I have received a letter from Carter, in which the gentle creature informs me that he has been abusing me in the Emancipator [the *Liberator*], or rather abusing the Journal, because the last number contained an advertisement of the South Lit. Messenger. I must confess that I never read the advertisement, and did not know that it was in the Journal until I got Carter's letter. He speaks of my course in regard to reform. In God's name I would like to know what he means. I have half a mind, indeed, I have a whole mind to turn reformer and try to reform the abolitionists of their wretched bad manners and worse principles. . . .

The Southern Lit Messenger, as far as I know, is as innocent of meaning of any kind as a blank sheet of paper. I really believe, upon my soul, that the abolitionists care no more about slavery than the devil himself does. . . . Don't stay in Boston until the atmosphere of the place infects you (MiDAAA–P).

29 MARCH. The *Broadway Journal* contains Poe's lengthy review of Mrs. Mowatt's *Fashion*, as well as the fourth installment of his reply to "Outis." Poe defends himself against Outis' accusation that he has been given to the "wholesale mangling" of authors: "no man can point to a single *critique*, among the very numerous ones which I have written during the last ten years, which is either wholly fault-finding or wholly in approbation; nor is there an instance to be discovered, among all that I have published, of my having set forth, either in praise or censure, a single opinion upon any critical topic of moment, without attempting, at least, to give it authority by something that wore the semblance of a reason." In a notice "To Correspondents," the editors of the *Journal* acknowledge the poems contributed by "Kate Carol" and "Violet Vane" (pseudonyms used by Mrs. Osgood).

APRIL. The *American Review* contains Poe's tale "Some Words with a Mummy" and his two revised poems "The Valley of Unrest" and "The City in the Sea."

APRIL. In the *Democratic Review* Evert A. Duyckinck comments: "There were some things in Mr. Poe's Lecture on the American Poets at the Society Library which appeared out of harmony with the general tone of his remarks, but they were slight, unworthy of being mentioned alongside of the devoted spirit in which he advocated the claims and urged the responsibilities of literature." In another article Duyckinck notices the discussion of plagiarism Poe has been conducting "for some weeks past" in the *Broadway Journal*: "While it is necessary that something should be said on this point, there is also great danger that the thing may be carried too far. There is no literary question which requires more discrimination, greater nicety of apprehension and occasionally more courage. We appreciate the latter quality in Mr. Poe."

APRIL. In his *Merchants' Magazine* Freeman Hunt praises the *Broadway Journal*: "Its criticisms are discriminating and just, and impress the reader with the conviction that they are made in all fairness, sincerity, and candor. We admire its elevated tone, and independent and manly bearing, and are gratified to learn that it is in 'the full tide of successful experiment.' It is the nearest approach to our *beau ideal* of what a literary Journal should be."

APRIL. In the "Editor's Table" of the *Knickerbocker Magazine*, Lewis Gaylord Clark comments: "We have already encountered one or two parodies upon Mr. POE'S '*Raven*,' but have seen nothing so faithful to the original . . . as one which has been sent us, entitled '*The Black Cat*.' " This parody features "a huge *Black Cat*, . . . between 'whom' and the writer there ensues a colloquy, which is quite like the conversation carried on between Mr. POE and 'The Raven.' " Clark excerpts six stanzas from "The Black Cat."

APRIL. RICHMOND. The *Southern Literary Messenger* carries an announcement by its editor Benjamin Blake Minor: "we have engaged the services of Mr. Poe; who will contribute monthly a *critique raisonnée* of the most important forthcoming works in this Country and in Europe."

[Poe did not become a regular contributor at this time, although he forwarded two reviews published in the May *Messenger*.]

2 APRIL. NEW YORK. Duyckinck writes William Gilmore Simms in Woodlands, South Carolina. He has become the literary editor of the *Democratic Review*; Simms will see his "initial efforts" in the April number. "The articles on . . . Poe's Lecture, Longfellow's Plagiarism &c are mine" (NNC).

2 APRIL. Poe writes W. Dinneford, manager of Palmo's Theatre, requesting the customary free admission accorded representatives of the press. As the drama critic of the *Broadway Journal*, Poe is anxious "to do *Justice*" to Palmo's forthcoming production of Sophocles' tragedy *Antigone* (Dinneford to Poe, 15 April).

5 APRIL. The *Broadway Journal* contains the fifth and final installment of Poe's reply to "Outis," as well as his revised tale "Berenice" and his favorable review of W. Newnham's *Human Magnetism*, a treatise on mesmerism. He modifies the opinion he expressed of Mrs. Mowatt's *Fashion* in last week's *Journal*, based only on the manuscript of this comedy and its first performance. Having "been to see it every night since," Poe now believes its thesis to be original: "We can call to mind no drama, just now, in which the design can be properly stated as the satirizing of fashion *as* fashion." In "So Let It Be" by "Violet Vane," Mrs. Osgood addresses Poe, alluding to his happy marriage with Virginia:

The fair, fond girl, who at your side,
   Within your soul's dear light, doth live,
Could hardly have the heart to chide
   The ray that Friendship well might give.

But if you deem it right and just,
   Blessed as you are in your glad lot,
To greet me with that heartless tone,
   So let it be! I blame you not!

5 APRIL. BALTIMORE. In the *Saturday Visiter* Joseph Evans Snodgrass notices this month's *Southern Literary Messenger*: "We observe with approbation, that the powerful pen of Edgar A. Poe has been engaged for the critical department."

7 APRIL. NEW YORK. Poe signs a receipt: "Received of John Bisco ten dollars, on account of the Southern Literary Messenger" (*L*, 2:521).

10 APRIL. Briggs writes William Page in Boston. He has just read Robert Carter's attack on the *Broadway Journal* in the *Liberator* of 28 March: "The poor fellow [Carter] is certainly crazy . . . . I never had the most remote idea of making the B.J. an abolition paper . . . . I cannot afford to publish a radical reform paper, for I could get no readers if I did. . . . I engaged Poe's services almost entirely on the score of Lowell's and Carter's recommendations . . . . It was he who wrote the notice about the Southern Magazine which Carter objects to" (MiDAAA–P).

11 APRIL. PHILADELPHIA. The *Spirit of the Times* reprints Poe's "Berenice" from the *Broadway Journal* of 5 April (Mabbott [1978], 2:208).

BEFORE 12 APRIL. NEW YORK. C. Shepard, Publisher, 191 Broadway, issues the second edition of George Vandenhoff's *A Plain System of Elocution*, which contains compositions in prose and verse suitable for "Practice in Oratorical, Poetical, and Dramatic Reading and Recitation." Among the works selected is "The Raven," now printed in a book for the first time.

12 APRIL. The *Morning News* notices Vandenhoff's *Elocution*: "We are pleased to see Mr. Poe's 'Raven' thus early domesticated as a classic production in a work of this kind." The review is reprinted in the *Weekly News* for 19 April.

12 APRIL. The *Broadway Journal* contains Poe's essay "Anastatic Printing," as well as his favorable reviews of Charles Anthon's *A Dictionary of Greek and Roman Antiquities*, Francis Fauvel-Gouraud's *Phreno-Mnemotechny; Or,*

The Art of Memory, and Vandenhoff's *Elocution*. In noticing the *Southern Literary Messenger* for April, he objects to its unperceptive critique of Elizabeth Barrett Barrett: "The critic merely shows that her poetry is no poetry *to him*. She is unquestionably, in spite of her numerous faults, the most glorious woman of her age—the queen of all female poets." Poe condemns the contemporary version of Sophocles' *Antigone* being performed at Palmo's Theatre: "The idea of reproducing a Greek play before a modern audience is the idea of a pedant and nothing beyond . . . . Many persons will be curious to understand the mode in which the Greeks wrote dramas and performed them—but, alas! no person should go to Palmo's for such understanding." The *Journal* prints two poems by Mrs. Osgood, "Love's Reply" under her own name and "Spring" under the pseudonym "Violet Vane."

12 APRIL. Briggs writes Lowell in Philadelphia:

Carter's strange letter in the Boston Liberator has annoyed me excessively. . . . The [New York agency of the] Southern Literary Messenger was offered to Mr Bisco, and he asked me if he had better accept of the agency, I told him by all means . . . . Bisco asked Poe to write an advertisement for him and having once been the editor of the Messenger he glorified it, perhaps, a little too much. . . . Poe's criticisms upon Longfellow I thought unjust, improper and in bad taste, but he thought otherwise, of course (MiDAAA–P).

AFTER 12? APRIL. Poe forwards reviews of Anthon's *Dictionary* and Fauvel-Gouraud's *Phreno-Mnemotechny* to the *Southern Literary Messenger*. In these notices he enlarges upon his favorable comments on the two books in the *Broadway Journal* of 12 and 19 April.

[Benjamin Blake Minor later wrote J. A. Harrison: "He [Poe] sent me two or three articles entirely unworthy of him, and the magazine. Still, they were published and paid for" (*W*, 1:220–21).]

15 APRIL. W. Dinneford, the manager of Palmo's Theatre, writes Poe:

In your note of the 2d inst. you request of me the *favor* of being placed on the *free list* of this theatre, because (as your letter says) you were anxious "to do *Justice* to 'Antigone' on its representation." Your name was accordingly placed on the free list. Your *Critique* has appeared, in the Broadway Journal, *characterized*, much *more* by *ill nature* and an *illiberal* spirit, than by fair and candid, or even *just* criticism. —

In *justice* therefore to MYSELF, I have withdrawn your name *from* the free list. I am always prepar'd to submit, as a catererer [*sic*] for public amusement, to any *just* remarks, though they may be severe, but I do not feel MYSELF called upon to offer *facilities* to any one, to do me *injury* by *animadversions* evidently marked by ill *feeling* (printed in the 19 April *Journal*).

16 APRIL. Poe signs a receipt: "Received of John Bisco three dollars on a/c of Southern L. Messenger" (L, 2:521).

16 APRIL. The *Evening Mirror* comments: "Those who would like to hear a fine specimen of unsparing critical analysis and good delivery, have the opportunity in Mr. Poe's repetition of his famous Lecture to-morrow evening at the Society Library."

17 APRIL. The *Daily Tribune*, the *New York Herald*, and the *Evening Mirror* carry this advertisement:

THE LECTURE ON AMERICAN POETRY, lately delivered by Edgar A. Poe, will be repeated by him This Evening (Thursday), at 7 1/2 o'clock, at the Society Library. Tickets 25 cents—to be had at the door.

In a brief editorial the *Tribune* describes the lecture as "pungent and amusing although perhaps not in all respects judicious."

17 APRIL. Alexander T. Crane, the office boy of the *Broadway Journal*, witnesses the cancellation of Poe's lecture:

The night set for the second lecture was a very bad one. It stormed incessantly, with mingled rain and hail and sleet. In consequence there were scarcely a dozen persons present when Poe came upon the platform and announced that, under the circumstances, the lecture could not be given, and those in the audience would receive their money back at the door. I was one of those present, as Poe had given me a complimentary ticket to the lecture, and badly as I was disappointed, I could see upon his face that my master was much more so. It was a little thing, it is true, but he was a man easily upset by little things. The next morning he came to the office, leaning on the arm of a friend, intoxicated with wine (Crane, p. 34).

18 APRIL. The *New York Herald* reports: "POSTPONED.—Mr. Poe did not deliver his lecture on Shakspeare [*sic*] last night—there not being more than between thirty and forty persons present at the appointed hour, which was probably owing to the state of the weather." The *Evening Mirror* comments: "Mr. Poe postponed his lecture . . . in consequence of the inclemency of the weather."

[The *Daily Tribune*, 19 April, complained that New Yorkers had been subjected to "sour, spitting North-East weather" for the past "two or three days."]

19 APRIL. The *Broadway Journal* contains Poe's essay "Street-Paving" and his revised tale "Bon-Bon." He concludes his review of Fauvel-Gouraud's *Phreno-Mnemotechny*, begun in last week's issue. Under the heading "Achilles' Wrath," he prints W. Dinneford's 15 April letter with a pungent commentary: "We told him [Dinneford] that we meant to do him

justice—and *we did it.*" Poe wishes to call public attention "to the peculiar character of the *conditions* which managers such as this have the impudence to *avow,* as attached to the privilege of the free list. No puff no privilege, is the contract."

19 APRIL. The *New World* publishes "A Vision" by "Snarles," a parody of "The Raven" satirizing "all the City's Press," in which "Each paper seemed personified, by goblins strange and tall." The narrator's description of the *Broadway Journal* refers to Poe's fearless criticism:

Then with step sedate and stately, as if thrones had borne him lately,
Came a bold and daring warrior up the distant echoing floor;
As he passed the COURIER'S Colonel, then I saw THE BROADWAY JOURNAL,
In a character supernal, on his gallant front he bore,
And with stately step and solemn marched he proudly through the door,
        As if he pondered, evermore.

With his keen sardonic smiling, every other care beguiling,
Right and left he bravely wielded a double-edged and broad claymore,
And with gallant presence dashing, 'mid his confreres stoutly clashing,
He unpityingly went slashing, as he keenly scanned them o'er,
While with eye and mien undaunted, such a gallant presence bore,
        As might awe them, evermore.

Neither rank nor station heeding, with his foes around him bleeding,
Sternly, singly, and alone, his course he kept upon that floor;
While the countless foes attacking, neither strength nor valor lacking,
On his goodly armor hacking, wrought no change his visage o'er,
As with high and honest aim, he still his falchion proudly bore,
        Resisting error, evermore.

19 APRIL. The *Evening Mirror* publishes an anonymous satire entitled "Criticism on Poe's 'Raven,'" preceded by Nathaniel P. Willis' note: "The following contemplative and droll criticism of this *poem that has made a mark,* will amuse our friend Poe quite as much as our other readers—perhaps more." The satire is reprinted in the *Weekly Mirror* for 26 April.

19 APRIL. Poe writes Rufus W. Griswold in Philadelphia, returning proof sheets: "The poems look quite as well in the short metre as in the long, and I am quite content as it is." Four lines in "The Raven" have been divided "at the wrong place"; Poe copies them in the short metre, indicating the correct divisions. In "The Sleeper" the line "Forever with uncloséd eye" should be changed to read "Forever with unopen'd eye." Poe adds a conciliatory postscript: "I presume you understand that in the repetition of my Lecture on the Poets (in N. Y.) I left out *all* that was offensive to yourself?" (*L*, 1:284–86).

[This letter seems to indicate that Griswold hoped to insert "The Raven" in the sixth edition of *The Poets and Poetry of America* (1845); but the poem was not included until the enlarged eighth edition, published shortly before 29 May 1847. The reviews of Poe's 28 February lecture in the *New York Herald*, 2 March, and the *Town*, 8 March, suggest that it still contained much that Griswold would have found "offensive."]

26 APRIL. The *Broadway Journal* carries Poe's revised tale "The Oval Portrait," formerly entitled "Life in Death." Under the heading "A Gentle Puff," Poe reprints the stanzas on the *Journal* from the *New World* of 19 April. He addresses Frances S. Osgood in a short poem "To F———," originally published as "To Mary" in the *Southern Literary Messenger* for July 1835. The *Journal's* editorial "Miscellany" contains a new stanza by Poe, playfully addressing Mrs. Osgood by one of her pseudonyms:

IMPROMPTU.
TO KATE CAROL.

When from your gems of thought I turn
To those pure orbs, your heart to learn,
I scarce know which to prize most high—
The bright *i-dea*, or bright *dear-eye*.

26 APRIL. The *Town* obliquely alludes to Poe's drinking in a fictitious list of forthcoming books: "A treatise on 'Aqua Pura,' its uses and abuses, by Edgar A. Poe, is to be issued at the Broadway Journal office."

26 APRIL. BALTIMORE. In the *Saturday Visiter* Joseph Evans Snodgrass notices the *Broadway Journal*: "Its peculiar feature is the boldness of its book-criticisms, for which it is, doubtless, mainly indebted to Mr. Poe, who *seems* to revel in a work which he knows so well how to perform. It strikes us, that it would be more significant to call this 'The Broad-*axe* Journal'!"

AFTER 26 APRIL. NEW YORK. Mrs. Osgood transcribes Poe's "Impromptu" from the *Broadway Journal* of 26 April; she later presents her manuscript copy to her friend Mrs. Elizabeth Oakes Smith, giving it the title "To the Sinless Child," in allusion to Mrs. Smith's poem "The Sinless Child" (Mabbott [1969], 1:380n; Smith, pp. 87, 99–100, 124–26).

29 APRIL. The *Evening Mirror* publishes "The Gazelle (After the Manner of Poe's 'Raven')" by C. C. Cooke. This parody is preceded by an editorial note identifying its author as a "new-found boy-poet of fifteen"; it is reprinted in the *Weekly Mirror* for 3 May.

29 APRIL. BAINBRIDGE, NEW YORK. Jedediah Hunt, Jr., the former editor of the Ithaca, New York, *National Archives*, commences a new weekly paper, the *Bainbridge Eagle*. In the first number he publishes Poe's 17 March letter to him. Hunt rejects Poe's suggestion that he is "a somewhat over-hasty man"; he has been instead "a somewhat over-*tardy* man," who is "still obliged to insist that Mr. POE is a too severe critic." Hunt's objections to Poe's criticism have not been made out of malice or envy; on the contrary, he admires "his untiring energy; his discriminating genius; his well improved intellect." Poe is "a star in the literary galaxy of our country, whose light no other 'twinkling world' in the least diminishes. There are those whose beam is more dazzling—but none which bids fairer to be ultimately, more lasting."

30 APRIL. Hunt writes Longfellow in Cambridge, Massachusetts: "I send you my paper this week in which I have answered Mr. Edgar A. Poe touching severity of his strictures on productions of others" (Phillips, 2:979).

30 APRIL. NEW YORK. Poe signs a receipt: "Received of John Bisco five dollars account of the Southern Literary Messenger" (*L*, 2:521).

LATE APRIL. The *Aristidean* for April contains an abusive article on "Longfellow's Poems," unsigned but written by the editor Thomas Dunn English, apparently after some consultation with Poe. English describes Poe in "Notes About Men of Note," a sketch characterizing seven New York editors:

EDGAR A. POE, ONE OF THE EDITORS OF THE BROADWAY JOURNAL. He never rests. There is a small steam-engine in his brain, which not only sets the cerebral mass in motion, but keeps the owner in hot water. His face is a fine one, and well gifted with intellectual beauty. Ideality, with the power of analysis, is shown in his very broad, high and massive forehead—a forehead which would have delighted GALL beyond measure. He would have made a capital lawyer—not a very good advocate, perhaps, but a famous unraveller of all subtleties. He can thread his way through a labyrinth of absurdities, and pick out the sound thread of sense from the tangled skein with which it is connected. He means to be candid, and labours under the strange hallucination that he is so; but he has strong prejudices, and, without the least intention of irreverence, would wage war with the DEITY, if the divine canons militated against his notions. His sarcasm is subtle and searching. He can do nothing in the common way; and buttons his coat after a fashion peculiarly his own. If we ever caught him doing a thing like any body else, or found him reading a book any other way than upside down, we should implore his friends to send for a straitjacket, and a Bedlam doctor. He were mad, then, to a certainty.

CA. MAY. The Poe family moves to a boardinghouse at 195 East Broadway, renting several rooms on the second floor (Quinn, p. 463; Chivers [1952], pp. 58, 60, 108).

CA. MAY. Poe, who has abstained from alcohol for over eighteen months, resumes drinking and frequently becomes incapacitated. Briggs is dismayed by his partner's conduct (Briggs to Lowell, 27 June and 16 July).

MAY. RICHMOND. The *Southern Literary Messenger* publishes Poe's reviews of Anthon's *Dictionary* and Fauvel-Gouraud's *Phreno-Mnemotechny*.

1 MAY. NEW YORK. The *Morning News* reprints "The Oval Portrait" from the *Broadway Journal* of 26 April. Poe's tale appears in the *Weekly News* for 10 May.

1 MAY. Alexander T. Crane's "Water," a poem revised by Poe, is published in the *Youth's Cabinet* (Mabbott [1969], 1:491–92).

3 MAY. The *Broadway Journal* announces that its office "*has been removed from 153 Broadway to 135 Nassau Street, Clinton Hall Buildings.*" The *Journal* contains Poe's poem "The Sleeper" (reprint) and his revised sketch "House Furniture," formerly entitled "The Philosophy of Furniture." Poe favorably reviews the *Aristidean* for April, discussing the article on Longfellow: "It is, perhaps, a little coarse, but we are not disposed to call it unjust; although there are in it some opinions which, by implication, are attributed to ourselves individually, and with which we cannot altogether coincide."

3 MAY. LONDON. *Lloyd's Entertaining Journal* reprints Poe's tale "The Spectacles" from the Philadelphia *Dollar Newspaper* for 27 March 1844 (Moldenhauer [1977], p. 188).

4 MAY. NEW YORK. Poe writes Frederick William Thomas in Washington, apologizing for his tardiness in answering Thomas' last two letters: "For the last three or four months I have been working 14 or 15 hours a day— hard at it all the time—and so, whenever I took pen in hand to write, I found that I was neglecting something that *would be* attended to." In spite of his industry, Poe has made no money: "I am as poor now as ever I was in my life—except in hope, which is by no means bankable." Since he has "a 3d pecuniary interest" in the *Broadway Journal*, everything he has written for it has been "so much out of pocket." He is forwarding "The Raven," contained in the *Journal* for 8 February: "It was copied by Briggs, my associate, before I joined the paper. 'The Raven' has had a great 'run ,

Thomas—but I wrote it for the express purpose of running—just as I did the 'Gold-Bug', you know. The bird beat the bug, though, all hollow" (*L*, 1:286–87).

7 MAY. The *Evening Mirror* reprints Poe's "House Furniture" with a preface: "The following Essay on a subject of that, in New York, at least, has more of May-day in it than dog-wood blossoms, birds or willow buds, is well worth copying entire from our excellent contemporary, the Broadway Journal." The sketch appears in the *Weekly Mirror* for 17 May.

10 MAY. The *Broadway Journal* contains Poe's poem "To One in Paradise," formerly entitled "To Ianthe in Heaven," and his revised tale "Three Sundays in a Week," formerly entitled "A Succession of Sundays." Poe notices "The Gazelle," published in the *Evening Mirror* of 29 April: "It is the composition of a mere boy of fifteen, C. C. Cooke, and, although professedly an imitation of 'The Raven,' has a very great deal of original power."

BEFORE 12 MAY. LONDON. Richard Henry Horne writes Elizabeth Barrett Barrett, enclosing "The Raven," Poe's review of her poems in the *Broadway Journal* for 4 and 11 January, and Poe's 25 January letter to him (Barrett to Horne, 12 May; Horne to Poe, 17 May).

12 MAY. Miss Barrett writes Horne:

Your friend, Mr. Poe, is a speaker of strong words "in both kinds." But I hope you will assure him from me that I am grateful for his reviews, and in no complaining humour at all. As to the "Raven" tell me what you shall say about it! There is certainly a power—but it does not appear to me the natural expression of a sane intellect in whatever mood; and I think that this should be specified in the title of the poem. There is a fantasticalness about the "sir or madam," and things of the sort, which is ludicrous, unless there is a specified insanity to justify the straws. Probably he—the author—intended it to be read in the poem, and he ought to have intended it. The rhythm acts excellently upon the imagination, and the "nevermore" has a solemn chime with it. . . . And I am of opinion that there is an uncommon force and effect in the poem (*W*, 17:385–86).

12 MAY. Later in the day Miss Barrett sends a second letter to Horne: "I am uncomfortable about my message to Mr. Poe, lest it should not be grateful enough in the sound of it. Will you tell him, what is quite the truth,—that, in my own opinion, he has dealt with me most generously, and that I thank him for his candour as for a part of his kindness. . . . Also, the review is very ably written,—and the reviewer has so obviously & thoroughly *read* my poems, as to be a wonder among critics" (*W*, 17:387).

THE BROADWAY JOURNAL.

VOL. I.   NEW YORK, SATURDAY, MAY 10, 1845.   NO. 19.

Three Dollars per Annum.
Single Copies, 6 1-4 Cents.

C. F. BRIGGS, EDGAR A. POE, H. C. WATSON, EDITORS.

Published at 135 Nassau St.
By JOHN BISCO.

GLIMPSES OF BROADWAY.

NO. I.

FROM UNION SQUARE LOOKING DOWN BROADWAY

Rushton's Apothecary's Shop.   Houses of—C. V. S. Roosevelt.   James Phalen.   J. F. Penniman.

THE NATIONAL ACADEMY.

PORTRAITS.

EVERY year upon the opening of the exhibition, we hear the senseless cry repeated from shallow-thoughted writers, "too many portraits—who wants to see men's faces—why don't they give us more historical works?" as if historical pictures were anything but groups of men's faces. A portrait is to a historical composition what a biography is to history, or a legend to a novel. For ourselves, we prefer portraiture to historical compositions; and we regard a good portrait as the very highest reach of art; and so does the world at large regard it. The most valuable paintings in the world are portraits; they sell at higher prices than any other pictures, and give the highest degree of pleasure. Even the gross beauties of Rubens are valued more highly than any other of his paintings, and the portraits of Van Dyke and Titian are the most esteemed of their productions. Take the portraits from the list of Reynolds' works, and there would be nothing left worth having. Among our own painters, Copley, Stewart, Trumbull, and Alston's portraitures comprise the best and most numerous of their productions. Perhaps the finest collection of pictures in the country, is the Portrait Gallery of Harvard College, which contains some of the finest of Copley's and Stuart's heads. A bad portrait of a bad subject is certainly not a pleasant thing to contemplate; but a fine portrait of a fine head, is one of the most charming and profitable objects in Art. A portrait of Shakspeare by such an artist as Van Dyke, would be worth more than all the historical pictures painted in his century. It is the true object of

First page of the *Broadway Journal*, 10 May

12 MAY. WASHINGTON. Thomas writes Poe: "Your letter of May 4th gave me great pleasure. . . . I am glad you have embarked in the editorial way again and I thank you for the journal and the 'Raven.' . . . Do you ever see Willis? Make my kindest regards to him." Thomas' letter is written on a sheet of paper containing a cryptogram and this note by his friend Charles S. Frailey: "The subjoined piece of secret writing was received at the Genl Land Office in connection with a letter having relation to a claim for bounty land due a soldier, which letter was without address on its face, but from other evidence appeared designed for a person out of office." Thomas explains that Frailey asked him to send the cipher to Poe for a translation: "At your earliest leisure (as it may be a matter of importance) will you do me the favor to let me know what it means" (MB–G).

14 MAY. NEW YORK. Poe writes Thomas, giving this translation of Frailey's cryptogram: "In September 1843, our respected friend Colonel T. C. Gardner, auditor of the Post office Department, applied at the Land office with his warrant. His patent did not render it necessary to reside at the place. Richard Douglas." Poe complains that the cipher was composed "by some barbarously ignorant person" who wrote "neseserri" for "necessary," "puwst ofis" for "post office," and "tuw" for "to." Nathaniel P. Willis is "going to England next month" (*L*, 1:288–89; Moldenhauer [1973], pp. 59–60).

14 MAY. PHILADELPHIA. The *Spirit of the Times* reprints Poe's "Three Sundays in a Week" from the *Broadway Journal* of 10 May (Mabbott [1978], 2:649).

14 MAY. FRUIT HILLS, OHIO. The *Regenerator* reprints Poe's "Mesmeric Revelation" (Mabbott [1978], 3:1026).

17 MAY. NEW YORK. The *Broadway Journal* contains Poe's revised tale "The Pit and the Pendulum" and his revised criticism of S. C. Hall's *The Book of Gems*, an anthology of English poetry he reviewed in the *Southern Literary Messenger* for August 1836. Poe notices *Graham's Magazine* for June, criticizing its portrait of Rufus W. Griswold, who "has a much finer face in every respect. The biography attached is written, we fancy, by Mr. C. F. Hoffman, and does Mr. G. no more than justice, either in regard to his acquirements or character as a man."

17 MAY. The *Town* satirizes Poe's literary criticism in a mock review, "Astray from the office of the Broadway Journal," of *The Adventures, Life and Opinions of John Smith*. The review describes this fictitious title as "a mass of insufferable trash, without one redeeming quality," which is none-

theless "one of the most delightful books . . . printed in a beautiful arabesque style by Wiley & Putnam."

17 MAY. LONDON. The *Critic* notices the *Broadway Journal*, which exhibits "excellent taste and high principle." The *Journal* is "the best procurable record of American literature and art"; its criticisms "are distinguished for the largeness and liberality of their views."

17 MAY. Richard Henry Horne replies to Poe's 25 January letter, which he did not receive until "the latter end of April." He encloses a portion of the second letter that Miss Barrett sent him on 12 May, in order that Poe "may see in what a good and noble spirit she receives the critique." She has said that "The Raven" has "a fine lyrical melody." Horne believes that Poe "intends to represent a very painful condition of mind, as of an imagination that was liable to topple over into some delirium or an abyss of melancholy, from the continuity of one unvaried emotion." He has not been able to obtain Tennyson's opinion of the poem: "It is curious that you should ask me for opinions of the only two poets with whom I am especially intimate. Most of the others I am acquainted with, but am not upon such terms of intellectual sympathy and friendship as with Miss Barrett and Tennyson. But I do not at this moment know where Tennyson is." Since Poe has mentioned that an American publisher might be willing to reprint *Orion*, Horne is forwarding a copy of his epic for this purpose: "I also send a copy, in which I have written your name" (*W*, 17:208–10).

BEFORE 24 MAY. NEW YORK. John Keese, who has edited *The Poetical Writings of Mrs. Elizabeth Oakes Smith*, sends this book and several others to Poe (Poe to Keese, 26 May).

BEFORE 24 MAY. D. Appleton & Co., 200 Broadway, publish the *Poems* of William Wilberforce Lord, a student at the Princeton Theological Seminary. The volume includes "The New Castalia," which parodies "The Raven" and other poems by Poe.

24 MAY. The *Broadway Journal* contains Poe's revised tale "Eleonora" and his poem "The Conqueror Worm" (reprint). Reviewing Lord's *Poems*, Poe objects to the publisher's description of the volume as "very remarkable." He finds that "the only remarkable things about Mr. Lord's compositions, are their remarkable conceit, ignorance, impudence, platitude, stupidity and bombast." The *Journal* prints a sixteen-line poem "To——," by "M.," which may be Poe's reply to Mrs. Osgood's "So Let It Be" in the 5 April issue:

We both have found a life-long love
  Wherein our weary souls may rest,
Yet may we not, my gentle friend
  Be each to each the *second best?*

[The poem was attributed to Poe by Mabbott (1969), 1:380–82.]

24 MAY. John Keese, who is editing the *Opal* for 1846, writes Poe, apparently to solicit a contribution for this forthcoming annual (Poe's reply).

26 MAY. Poe writes Keese: "Permit me to thank you for the many expressions of good will in your letter of the 24th—also for the books you were so kind as to send me a few days before—very especially for Mrs Smith's beautiful Poems." He will give Keese "a brief article" for the *Opal* "in the course of this week" (*L*, 1:289).

29 MAY. Mrs. Mary E. Hewitt writes Poe, enclosing a translation "from the old French edition (1716) of Madame Dacier" for the *Broadway Journal*. She asks him to present her "compliments to Mrs. Poe," whose acquaintance she is "happy to have made" (Mabbott [1937], p. 118).

30 MAY. The *Evening Mirror* publishes "The Whippoorwill: A Parody on Mr. Poe's 'Raven.' " The poem appears in the *Weekly Mirror* for 7 June.

31 MAY. The *Town* notices Poe's review of Lord's *Poems*: "The last Broadway Journal contains one of Poe's most destructive attacks upon the poetical defences of a Mr. W. W. Lord, who, it seems, has been guilty of all sorts of enormities in rhyme. We pitied the man at first, and were disposed to defend him; but as a finishing stroke Mr. Poe proves that Mr. Lord has stolen from Edgar A. Poe. This is too much—and we abandon him to his fate!"

31 MAY. The *Alleghanian*, a new weekly, objects to Poe's review of Lord in an article on "The Poe-dom of Poetry" (Lord, p. ix).

31 MAY. The *Broadway Journal* contains Poe's revised tale "Shadow—A Parable," formerly entitled "Shadow: A Fable," and his revised criticism of Mrs. Lydia Maria Child's romance *Philothea*, originally reviewed in the *Southern Literary Messenger* for September 1836.

31 MAY. CINCINNATI, OHIO. The *Western Luminary* reprints Poe's "Mesmeric Revelation" (Mabbott [1978], 3:1026).

LATE MAY. NEW YORK. James Russell Lowell and his wife Maria spend several days in New York, on their return from Philadelphia to Elmwood, the Lowell family home in Cambridge, Massachusetts. Lowell has a single interview with Poe:

I have a clear recollection of my first sight of him [Poe]—in his own lodgings in New York. I went by appointment & found him a little tipsy, as if he were recovering from a fit of drunkenness, & with that over-solemnity with which men in such cases try to convince you of their sobriety. I well remember (for it pained me) the anxious expression of his wife. . . . The shape of his head was peculiar, broad at the temples, & the forehead sloping backward almost sharply. I cannot describe it better than by giving the impression which I took then & which has remained ever since—that there was something snakelike about it. I do not intend to convey any moral but only a physical suggestion (Lowell to J. H. Ingram, 12 May 1879, Cauthen, pp. 231–32; cf. Lowell to G. W. Woodberry, 12 March 1884, Woodberry, 2:137, and Quinn, p. 461).

[On 9 March 1850 Mrs. Clemm wrote Lowell: "I wish . . . I could remove your wrong impression of my darling Eddie. The day you saw him in New York *he was not himself*. Do you not remember that I never left the room. Oh if you only knew his bitter sorrow when I told him how unlike himself he was" (Quinn, pp. 461–62). See also Poe's remark to T. H. Chivers, after 15? June, and Briggs to Lowell, 16 July.]

JUNE OR BEFORE. Thomas Dunn English listens to Poe's remarks on the *Broadway Journal*: "It [the *Journal*] did not achieve success; and Poe, who had frequently given me glowing prophecies as to its future circulation, told me one day that its comparative failure was owing to the fact that he had it not all in his own hands. 'Give me,' said he, 'the entire control, and it will be the great literary journal of the future.' During this time he reiterated this expression of discontent on his visits to my rooms" (English, p. 1416).

JUNE OR BEFORE. Charles F. Briggs decides to obtain sole control of the *Broadway Journal*. He informs John Bisco of his intention to find a new publisher; he tells Poe that he "should drop his [Poe's] name from the 'Journal' " (Briggs to Lowell, 1 August).

JUNE OR BEFORE. Anne C. Lynch describes the poetess Sarah Helen Whitman to Poe.

[On 1 October 1848 Poe wrote Mrs. Whitman: "some few casual words spoken of you—not very kindly—by Miss Lynch, were the first in which I had ever heard your name mentioned. . . . She alluded to what she called your 'eccentricities' and hinted at your sorrows. Her description of the former strangely arrested—her half sneers at the latter enchained and riveted, my attention. She had referred to thoughts, sentiments, traits, *moods* which I knew to be my own, but which, until that moment, I had believed to be my own solely—unshared by any human being. A profound sympathy took immediate possession of my soul." Cf. Poe to Anna Blackwell, 14 June 1848.]

JUNE. The *Democratic Review* publishes Poe's philosophic tale "The Power of Words."

JUNE. Henry B. Hirst, the Philadelphia poet, gives Poe a presentation copy of *The Coming of the Mammoth*, his newly published volume of verse (Mabbott [1969], 1:348).

1 JUNE. SOUTH ATTLEBOROUGH, MASSACHUSETTS. Abijah M. Ide, Jr., writes Poe, submitting a poem for the *Broadway Journal* (MB–G).

7 JUNE. NEW YORK. The *Town* praises the article "The Poe-dom of Poetry" in the *Alleghanian* for 31 May as "a slashing affair—*very much in Poe's way* . . . . Let us be always understood, however, as yielding and recording our great admiration of Poe's genius—his great critical acumen, and the perfect aquafortis of his satire. We will say, however, that his censure is too indiscriminate and his egotism *sometimes* uncalled for."

7 JUNE. The *Broadway Journal* contains Poe's revised tale "The Assignation," formerly entitled "The Visionary." In his revised essay "Magazine-Writing—Peter Snook," originally published in the *Southern Literary Messenger* for October 1836, he complains that the articles in American magazines are decidedly inferior to those in British and French periodicals; he gives a detailed summary of an English tale, "Peter Snook" by James Forbes Dalton, which presents "many striking points for the consideration of the Magazinist."

7 JUNE. LOWELL, MASSACHUSETTS. The *Star of Bethlehem* reprints Poe's "Three Sundays in a Week" from the *Broadway Journal* of 10 May (Mabbott [1978], 2:649).

9 JUNE. NEW YORK. Poe writes John Keese: "With this note I have the honor to send you a brief sketch for 'The Opal'—and hope that I am not too late" (*L*, 1:289–90).

[Poe's article did not appear in the *Opal* for 1846.]

13 JUNE. Wiley and Putnam register Poe's forthcoming *Tales* in the Clerk's

Office of the United States District Court, Southern District of New York State (Heartman and Canny, p. 94).

14 JUNE. LONDON. The *Critic* copies "The Raven" from the *American Review*, "on account of its unusual beauty." This reprinting is prefaced by Willis' introduction, from the *Evening Mirror* of 29 January.

14 JUNE. NEW YORK. The *Broadway Journal* contains Poe's tale "The Premature Burial" (corrected reprint).

BEFORE 15? JUNE. The Georgia poet Thomas Holley Chivers arrives in New York to oversee the publication of his forthcoming volume of poetry, *The Lost Pleiad*. He writes Poe that he would like to make his acquaintance (Chivers [1952], p. 11, and [1957], pp. 37–38).

15? JUNE. Poe writes Chivers: "I have just received your very polite letter informing me that you are in the city. How *could* you have remained here so long without calling to see me? Call upon me immediately . . . . You will find me at 195, East Broadway" (Chivers [1957], pp. 37–38).

AFTER 15? JUNE. Chivers visits Poe at home; they have an extensive conversation on current literature. Poe displays two copies of Horne's *Orion*, which the British poet recently sent him: "I have taken this book to every respectable Publisher in this City, and not one of them is willing to take upon himself the responsibility of the publication. Here is a work which is, at best, five hundred years in advance of the Age . . . if it were a book of romance, full of absurd improbabilities, bad grammar, and wanting in every other thing necessary to make it a book at all, I could find a Publisher at every corner." Turning to American poets, Poe observes that Lowell "has written some fine things," especially the poem "Rosaline." "He [Lowell] called to see me, the other day . . . I was very much disappointed in his appearance as an intellectual man. He was not half the noble-looking person that I expected to see." Poe introduces Chivers to his wife Virginia and Mrs. Clemm. Observing Virginia "attacked with a terrible paroxysm of coughing," Chivers asks Mrs. Clemm whether she has "caught cold" or suffers from "a consumption." Mrs. Clemm replies: "No—it is not a cold—Dr. [John Kearsley] Mitchell, of Philadelphia, says that she has the Bronchitis. She ruptured a blood vessel while singing, in Philadelphia, and has never been well since" (Chivers [1952], pp. 39–52).

BEFORE 20 JUNE. Charles E. West, Principal of the Rutgers Female Institute, sends two letters to Poe, asking him to serve on a committee to judge the literary compositions of the girls at this secondary school. The winning compositions are to be read at the Annual Commencement on 11 July (Poe to West, 20 June; see also 11 JULY).

20 JUNE. Poe writes West:

The previous letter to which you allude did not reach me—I trust, therefore, that you will exonerate me from the charge of discourtesy.

I shall be happy to oblige you in any way—and it will give me very great pleasure to act as one of a Committee in which I shall be associated with two gentlemen whom I so highly respect as Drs [Rufus W.] Griswold and [W. D.] Snodgrass (Ostrom [1974], pp. 525–26).

20 JUNE. The "University of the City of New-York" issues an engraved invitation: "The honor of your company is respectfully requested at the University-Place Church, (Dr. Potts') on Tuesday Evening, July 1st, at half-past seven o'clock, when the Annual Oration before the Philomathean and Eucleian Societies, will be delivered by the Hon. Daniel D. Barnard, and the Annual Poem by Edgar A. Poe, Esq." (PP–G).

[According to the New York Herald, 2 July, these Societies were "composed of the young students of the New York University" who wished to "promote their literary education."]

20 JUNE. Wiley and Putnam deposit a copy of the title page of Poe's Tales in the Clerk's Office of the United States District Court (Heartman and Canny, p. 94).

20–21 JUNE. The Daily Tribune carries a Wiley and Putnam advertisement: "TALES BY EDGAR A. POE: Will appear on WEDNESDAY next."

AFTER 20? JUNE. Edward J. Thomas, a New York merchant who is enamored of Frances S. Osgood, hears a rumor that Poe has been guilty of forgery. Apparently viewing Poe as a rival for Mrs. Osgood's affection and hoping to discredit him, Thomas repeats the rumor to her. She, in turn, repeats it to Poe, who calls upon Thomas at his business office in Broad Street, denies the rumor, and asks him to retract it. Thomas promises to trace the rumor to its source. Poe describes the situation to Thomas Dunn English, who counsels him to sue Thomas for libel. Poe writes Thomas: "As I have not had the pleasure of hearing from you since our interview at your office, may I ask of you to state to me distinctly, whether I am to consider the charge of *forgery* urged by you against myself, in the presence of a common friend [Mrs. Osgood], as originating with yourself or Mr. [Park] Benjamin?" Poe's letter is personally delivered by English, who brings him a "verbal and somewhat vague" reply. Poe now considers commencing a suit against Thomas ("Mr. Poe's Reply to Mr. English," 10 July 1846; see documents in Moss [1970], pp. 36, 57–59, 167–68, 177, 181–82).

21 JUNE. The *Broadway Journal* contains Poe's revised tale "Morella" and his review of *Plato Contra Atheos—Plato Against the Atheists*. The *Journal* reprints two poems by Miss Anne C. Lynch, preceded by Poe's note: "We have no excuse to offer for copying them . . . except that we have been profoundly impressed with their excellence." In a notice "To Correspondents" Poe expresses indebtedness "to J. T. of Jackson" (John Tomlin) and "to T. H. C." (Thomas Holley Chivers).

CA. 24 JUNE. Thomas Dunn English recalls: "Mr. Poe accepted an invitation to deliver a poem before a society [Philomathean and Eucleian Societies] of the New York University. About a week before the time when this poem was to be pronounced, he called on me, appearing to be much troubled—said he could not write the poem, and begged me to help him out with some idea of the course to pursue. I suggested that he had better write a note to the society, and frankly state his inability to compose a poem on a stated subject. He did not do this, but—as he always does when troubled—drank until intoxicated; and remained in a state of intoxication during the week" (English in *Morning Telegraph*, 23 June 1846).

25 JUNE. Wiley and Putnam publish Poe's *Tales*, the second volume in their "Library of American Books" (*Daily Tribune*, 20–21, 26 June).

[Twelve stories appear in the *Tales*, in this order: "The Gold-Bug," "The Black Cat," "Mesmeric Revelation," "Lionizing," "The Fall of the House of Usher," "A Descent into the Maelström," "The Colloquy of Monos and Una," "The Conversation of Eiros and Charmion," "The Murders in the Rue Morgue," "The Mystery of Marie Rogêt," "The Purloined Letter," and "The Man of the Crowd."]

25 JUNE. PHILADELPHIA. *Alexander's Weekly Messenger* reprints "The Turkey," a parody of "The Raven," from the Boston *Jester* (Mabbott [1969], 1:352).

25 JUNE OR LATER. NEW YORK. Poe gives a presentation copy of his *Tales* to John Bisco (copy in NN–B).

26 JUNE. The *Daily Tribune* carries an advertisement for Wm. Taylor, Bookseller, No. 2 Astor House, who offers for sale "Tales by Edgar A. Poe. 1 vol. beautifully printed in large clear type, on fine paper—50 cents."

" *Sundry citizens of this good land, meaning well, and hoping well, prompted by a certain something in their nature, have trained themselves to do service in various Essays, Poems, Histories, and books of Art, Fancy, and Truth.*"

ADDRESS OF THE AMERICAN COPY-RIGHT CLUB.

WILEY AND PUTNAM'S

LIBRARY OF AMERICAN BOOKS.

NO. II.

T A L E S.

BY

EDGAR A. POE.

NEW YORK AND LONDON.

WILEY AND PUTNAM, 161 BROADWAY: 6 WATERLOO PLACE.

Price, Fifty Cents.

Front cover of Poe's *Tales*
Richard Gimbel Collection, Philadelphia Free Library

26 JUNE. Poe writes Evert A. Duyckinck, Wiley and Putnam's editor: "I am still dreadfully unwell, and fear that I shall be very seriously ill. . . . I have resolved to give up the B. Journal and retire to the country for six months, or perhaps a year, as the sole means of recruiting my health and spirits. Is it not possible that yourself or Mr Matthews [Cornelius Mathews] might give me a trifle for my interest in the paper? Or, if this cannot be effected, might I venture to ask you for an advance of $50 on the faith of the 'American Parnassus'?—which I will finish as soon as possible" (L, 1:290).

["American Parnassus" was Poe's long-contemplated but never completed work on American authors, partially realized in "The Literati of New York City." In his 13 November letter to Duyckinck, he acknowledged receipt of $50 "on account of the 'Parnassus.' "]

26 JUNE. The *Evening Mirror* reprints English's "Notes About Men of Note," with its characterization of Poe, from the *Aristidean* for April. The article appears in the *Weekly Mirror* for 5 July.

BEFORE 27 JUNE. Poe sends Anne C. Lynch a copy of his *Tales* and a despondent letter (Lynch to Poe, 27 June).

27 JUNE. Miss Lynch writes Poe, thanking him for his "very kind notice" of her poems in the *Broadway Journal* of 21 June, as well as for his "kind and friendly" letter: "But I am exceedingly pained at the desponding tone in which you write. Life is too short & there is too much to be done in it, to give one time to *despair*. Exorcise that devil, I beg of you, as speedily as possible. . . . At all events come over and see me to-morrow evening (Saturday) & we will talk the matter over." Since Miss Lynch will not be in town to hear Poe's poem before the Philomathean and Eucleian Societies "on Tuesday evening," she hopes he will bring it and "read a few passages." She thanks him for his *Tales* (W, 17:258–59; dating established by Reece [1954], p. 19).

27 JUNE. Briggs writes Lowell in Cambridge, Massachusetts:

I have arrangements on foot with a new publisher for the Journal who will enable me to give it a fresh start; and I trust very soon to be able to give you an earnest of its profits. I shall haul down Poe's name; he has lately got into his old habits and I fear will injure himself irretrievably. I was rather taken at first with a certain appearance of independence and learning in his criticisms, but they are so verbal, and so purely selfish that I can no longer have any sympathy with him. In all that he has ever written there is not benevolent thought. . . . Poe is a good proof reader and a good scanner of verses, but his merits as a critic hardly reach further (MiDAAA–P).

[Briggs hoped to replace John Bisco, the original publisher, with J. Smith Homans, a bookseller who advertised in the *Journal* (cf. Homans to Bisco, 12 July; Briggs to Lowell, 16 July).]

28 JUNE. The *Broadway Journal* reprints Poe's poem "Dream-Land." His *Tales* are listed in a Wiley and Putnam advertisement: this "excellent collection" contains "the most characteristic of the peculiar series of Tales written by Mr. Poe."

28 JUNE. In the *Morning News* Evert A. Duyckinck reviews the *Tales*:

Mr. Poe's tales will be welcomed in this neat convenient form. They have hitherto been scattered over the newspapers and magazines of the country, chiefly of the South, and have been scarcely, if at all, known to Northern and Eastern readers. Singly, the most remarkable have been received with great favor. The Gold Bug received a prize of five [one] hundred dollars. The Fall of the House of Usher was pirated in Bentley's (London) Magazine, and the Murders of the Rue Morgue appeared translated in one of the Parisian journals. The Purloined Letter appeared in this year's Gift, and was not copied into any American paper, we believe, till it had been produced in Chambers's Edinburgh Journal, and been republished here in Littell's Living Age of Foreign Literature! It is to be presumed that our American readers will not be ashamed of the volume after these circumstances. It is eminently original and characteristic of the peculiar idiosyncrasy of the author. The subtle ingenuity exhibited in the construction will strike every one; the analysis of this power is a subject worthy of the maturest critic. The Gold Bug is a tale of Captain Kid[d]'s treasure, the interest of which depends upon the solution of an intricate cypher. . . .

The murders of the Rue Morgue, the History of Marie Roget and the Purloined Letter turn upon matters of police, and would do credit either to the sagacity of an Indian hunter or the civilized skill of a Fouché for their ingenuity and keenness of scent. Marie Roget is the story of Mary Rogers, the Cigar Girl, the scene being transferred from the banks of the Hudson to those of the Seine.

The review appears in the *Weekly News* for 5 July.

[Duyckinck was probably indebted to Poe himself for the information on European reprintings (cf. Poe to Duyckinck, 30 December 1846). The earliest known French translation of the "Rue Morgue" was not published until 11–13 June 1846.]

28 JUNE. The *Rover* carries a review by its editor Lawrence Labree: "TALES . . . Mr. Poe has acquired the reputation of a powerful and vigorous writer, though occasionally delighting in biting sarcasm and highly-strained and unreasonable criticism. But in this instance he has given the public a pleasant volume of tales rather above the medium of that style of writing, each one of which possesses the power of holding the reader to the end—tales of absorbing interest."

28 JUNE. BIRMINGHAM, ENGLAND. The *Birmingham Journal* reprints "The Raven" (Phillips, 2:1079).

BEFORE 29? JUNE. PROVIDENCE, RHODE ISLAND. Mrs. Osgood, who is visiting Providence, writes Poe, asking him to come to this city (Poe's remark to Chivers, 29? June).

BEFORE 29? JUNE. NEW YORK. In the "Editor's Table" of the *Knickerbocker Magazine* for July, Lewis Gaylord Clark condemns Poe's essay "Magazine-Writing—Peter Snook," published in the *Broadway Journal* of 7 June without the author's name. "Some sage correspondent of the 'Broadway Journal' has temporarily resuscitated from oblivion an article from an old English magazine, entitled '*Mr. Peter Snook*,' which it [he] lauds without stint, but the very 'plums' of which we defy any person of taste to swallow with pleasure." Had it not been for "an indiscrim[in]ate fling at American periodicals," Clark would not have denounced "the nil-admirari critic" of the *Journal*. "Judging from the taste exhibited by the critic in his 'foreign' selection, we should say that the less *he* was struck with an American magazine article, the more credit would it reflect upon the periodical which contained it."

29? JUNE. Thomas Holley Chivers recalls:

I was once going down Nassau street . . . when who should I meet but Edgar A. Poe coming along the pavement, tottering from side to side, as drunk as an Indian, while at the corner of Ann I saw a man standing on the steps of either a Whiskey-Shop, or a Restaurant, Spouting at the top of his voice in his praise— calling him the "*Shakespeare of America.*" As soon as he met me, he grasped me by the coat collar, exclaiming, "*By G-d! here is my friend now! Where are you going? Come, you must go home with me!*"

Chivers takes Poe by the arm. As he is leading him home, they encounter Lewis Gaylord Clark in the street: "The moment Poe saw him—maddened by the remembrance of something that he had said in a recent Number of the [*Knickerbocker*] Magazine touching one of his own articles which had appeared in the *Broadway Journal*—he swore, while attempting to rush away from my hold, that he would attack him." Chivers restrains Poe, who then introduces him to Clark. Poe asks Clark belligerently, "What business had you to abuse me in the last Number of your Magazine?" Clark protests, "how did I know the Article referred to, was yours? You had always attached your name to all your articles before, and how, in H—l, did I know it was yours?" After Clark departs Poe tells Chivers that he is involved "in the d—dst amour," asking him not to mention it to Virginia Poe. Chivers asks, "where is the lady [Mrs. Osgood] with whom you are so in love?" Poe replies, "In Providence, by G-d! I have just received a letter from her, in which she requests me to come on there this afternoon on the four o'clock Boat. Her husband [Samuel S. Osgood] is a Painter—always from home" (Chivers [1952], pp. 57–61).

30? JUNE. On the "next day" Chivers calls at Poe's boardinghouse, 195 East Broadway; but Poe is "not to be found" (Chivers [1952], p. 61).

30? JUNE. Chivers writes Clark, apologizing for Poe's conduct on the day before, "while he was laboring under such an '*excitement*' " (letter quoted by Clark in October 1846 *Knickerbocker*).

JULY. The *American Review* publishes Poe's poem "Eulalie."

JULY. PHILADELPHIA. *Graham's Magazine* publishes Poe's tale "The Imp of the Perverse."

EARLY JULY? NEW YORK. Richard Henry Stoddard, an aspirant poet aged nineteen, writes Poe, submitting his "Ode on a Grecian Flute" for the *Broadway Journal* (Stoddard [1872], pp. 564–65; [1884], 1:127–28; [1889], p. 107; [1903], p. 146).

1 JULY. The *Daily Tribune* reports: "The Philomathean and Eucleian Societies will meet this evening at half-past 7 o'clock in Dr. Potts's Church to hear an Oration from Hon. D. D. BARNARD and a Poem from EDGAR A. POE, Esq."

1? JULY. On the second day after he encountered Poe in Nassau Street, Chivers visits his residence and finds him "in bed pretending to be sick, but with nothing in the world the matter with him—his sole object for lying there being to avoid the delivering of the Poem which he had promised—for he was reading Macaul[a]y's *Miscellanies*" (Chivers [1952], p. 61).

2 JULY. The *New York Herald* describes the meeting of the Philomathean and Eucleian Societies last night, which was attended by "all the beauty and fashion of the city, also all the students of the University." After the "most excellent discourse" by the Hon. Daniel D. Barnard, "Professor MASON . . . announced . . . that through indisposition, Mr. Poe would be unable to deliver the poem that had been set down in the programme. Mr. Poe had been severely ill for a week past, and it had not been judged prudent for him to exert himself." The *Daily Tribune* and the *Evening*

Mirror carry brief accounts of the meeting which state that the scheduled poem was omitted "owing to the sickness of Mr. Poe."

2? JULY. On the day after finding Poe in bed, Chivers meets him "about half past three o'clock . . . drest in his finest clothes, going down towards the *Broadway Journal Office*." Poe shows Chivers "an advertisement" which he plans to insert in the *Journal*, announcing the dissolution of his partnership with Briggs; Chivers persuades him not to publish it. "He [Poe] was then on his way to Providence—had not a dollar in the world—borrowed ten from me—requesting me at the same time not to let his wife or Mrs Clemm know anything about his going—and left me. Some body [Mrs. Osgood], he said, had written to him to come on there" (Chivers [1952], pp. 61–62).

[In "Mr. Poe's Reply to Mr. English," 10 July 1846, Poe stated that he "left town to procure evidence" for use in his anticipated libel suit against Edward J. Thomas. Presumably, the evidence he wanted was the testimony of Mrs. Osgood, then in Providence.]

2 JULY OR LATER. PROVIDENCE, RHODE ISLAND. Poe sees Sarah Helen Whitman, a poetess who has strongly aroused his curiosity, as she is walking outside her home at 76 Benefit Street.

[Poe alluded to this first unplanned encounter with Mrs. Whitman in his second "To Helen," a poem he sent her around 1 June 1848. Mrs. Whitman, aged forty-two in 1845, was widowed; but Poe then believed her to be happily married. "For this reason," he explained to her in his 1 October 1848 letter, "when I passed through Providence with Mrs Osgood [in July 1845], I positively refused to accompany her to your house, and even provoked her into a quarrel by the obstinacy and seeming unreasonableness of my refusal." On 27 February 1865 Mrs. Whitman wrote George W. Eveleth:

Mrs. Osgood . . . was at the hotel in Providence, where Mr. Poe stopped on that "July midnight." Her account of the incident, given me in the autumn of 1848, agreed with what Mr. Poe had himself told me. Mrs. Osgood informed me that the night was exceedingly hot and sultry; that Mr. Poe told her, in the morning, he had passed the greater part of the night in rambling over the hills that command a fine view of the City from the east; that, at a late hour, he passed the house where I then lived, whose situation he had previously ascertained from her, and saw me walking up and down the lime-shaded side-walk in the neighborhood of my home. He told her that I wore a white dress, with a thin white shawl or scarf thrown over my head, and that he knew me through her description of me. The moon was at, or near, the full. I knew nothing of his having seen me at that time, till the summer of 1848, when he sent me, anonymously, the poem (in Ms) beginning:—"I saw thee once, once only—" (Miller [1977], pp. 217–19).]

2 JULY OR LATER. BOSTON. Poe visits Boston, where he is impressed by "the number of intrinsically valuable works" offered for sale by the city's booksellers (Poe in "Editorial Miscellany," *Broadway Journal*, 23 August; Boston visit also mentioned in Whitman to Eveleth, 27 February 1865).

3 JULY. NEW YORK. Intending to gain sole control of the *Broadway Journal*, Charles F. Briggs prepares a "memorandum of agreement" for Bisco to sign. "John Bisco agrees to dispose of his entire interest in . . . the Broadway Journal . . . for the consideration of Fifty Dollars." Bisco is to retain "all back numbers" and the office furniture, but he must "furnish the said Briggs with fifty complete sets of the paper . . . at one cent per single number." Briggs will "assume all debts incurred and now due by the said Bisco as publisher" (two drafts of agreement, ViRPM).

3 JULY OR LATER. Bisco declines to sign Briggs's agreement; he wants more money for his share of the *Journal* (Briggs to Lowell, 16 July).

5 JULY. The *Journal* is not issued this Saturday.

5 JULY. Edward J. Thomas writes Poe. He has traced the rumor that Poe has been guilty of forgery: "I saw the person on Friday evening last [27 June], from whom the report originated. . . . He denies it *in toto*—says he does *not know it* and never said so—and it undoubtedly arose from the misunderstanding of some word used. It gives me pleasure thus to trace it, and still more to find it destitute of foundation in truth . . . . I have told Mr. [Park] Benjamin the result of my inquiries, and shall do so to [Mrs. Osgood] by a very early opportunity—the only two persons who know anything of the matter" (W, 17:251; also in Moss [1970], p. 58).

5 JULY. The *Town* comments: "POH! The audience at the Eucleian Society celebration were very much delighted with the oration of Mr. Barnard; but they were thrown into perfect exstacies [*sic*] at the poem of the critic of the Broadway Journal, which was *not* delivered—the distinguished author being indisposed. We understand that the receipts of the Journal are now so large that it takes both editors and publishers all the week to get rid of them." This squib is accompanied by an illustration of a humanized raven with a peacock's tail feathers.

5 JULY OR LATER. Poe returns to New York and finds the 5 July letter from Edward J. Thomas awaiting him at his boardinghouse. He is satisfied with Thomas' explanation and decides not to bring suit against him ("Mr. Poe's Reply to Mr. English," 10 July 1846).

8 JULY. Evert A. Duyckinck writes Lowell in Cambridge, Massachusetts: "There's trouble in the camp of the Broadway Journal—no number Saturday. Briggs I believe has fallen in love with a new publisher and finds it difficult to be off with the old. I suppose it will work itself clear & that we shall live (at least I hope so) to see another Journal soon" (Ehrlich, p. 83).

8 JULY. BOSTON. The *Morning Post* notices Poe's *Tales*, praising his curious learning and the ingenuity of his detective stories (Pollin [1980], p. 26).

9 JULY. NEW YORK. The *Evening Post* notices Poe's *Tales*, praising his powers of analysis (Pollin [1980], p. 26).

10 JULY. Henry T. Tuckerman writes Rufus W. Griswold in Philadelphia: "This P.M. I have promised to take yr place on the Rutgers Institute Com[mittee]. What a fellow you are to shift responsibilities!" (MB–G).

10 JULY. In the evening Poe and Tuckerman meet each other for the first time at the Rutgers Female Institute, 240 Madison Avenue, where they judge student compositions (C. F. Hoffman to Griswold, 11 July).

10 JULY. WASHINGTON. Frederick William Thomas writes Poe, thanking him for the translation of the cipher forwarded on 14 May: "It [the translation] comports with the facts in the case—It made you quite the talk among the officials—I have obtained your book [*Tales*] published by Wiley and Putnam and have been delighted with it—I have just loaned it to a lady friend of mine who is an admirer of yours." Thomas submitted a series of biographical sketches to Wiley and Putnam for their "Library of American Books," but this firm has written him that they find the sketches too fragmentary: "A polite way of saying, you know, that they dont think the sketches will sell. . . . Poe, if I do not give you too much trouble I should be glad if you would obtain the MS, from Wiley & Putnam, and put it in a safe place for me—If any of the sketches suit your journal they are very much at your service." Thomas asks Poe whether he knows the last editor of the *New World*: "Do you know a Gentleman formerly of New York, who is now here in office, named [Charles] Eames? He was a fellow boarder of mine . . . . Mr [George] Bancroft has given him a Fourteen hundred dollar situation" (MB–G).

BEFORE 11 JULY. NEW YORK. Briggs is unable to come to terms with John Bisco, who has raised the price for his interest in the *Broadway Journal* still higher. Briggs withdraws from the *Journal*; Bisco and Poe decide to continue its publication without him (C. F. Hoffman to Griswold, 11 July; Briggs to Lowell, 16 July).

11 JULY. The *Daily Tribune* carries a first-page review of Poe's *Tales* by Margaret Fuller:

No form of literary activity has so terribly degenerated among us as the tale. Now that every body who wants a new hat or bonnet takes this way to earn one from the magazines or annuals, we are inundated with the very flimsiest fabrics ever spun by mortal brain. . . .

In such a state of things, the writings of Mr. Poe are a refreshment, for they are the fruit of genuine observations and experience, combined with an invention, which is not "making up," as children call *their* way of contriving stories, but a penetration into the causes of things which leads to original but credible results. His narrative proceeds with vigor, his colors are applied with discrimination, and where the effects are fantastic they are not unmeaningly so.

The "Murders of the Rue Morgue" especially made a great impression upon those who did not know its author and were not familiar with his mode of treatment. Several of his stories make us wish he would enter the higher walk of the metaphysical novel, and, taking a mind of the self-possessed and deeply marked sort that suits him, give us a deeper and longer acquaintance with its life and the springs of its life than is possible in the compass of these tales.

The review appears in the *Weekly Tribune* for 19 July.

11 JULY. Charles Fenno Hoffman writes Griswold in Philadelphia: "The Broadway Journal stopped for a week to let Briggs step ashore with his luggage and they are now getting up steam to drive it ahead under captains Poe & [Henry C.] Watson—I think it will soon stop again to land one of these. Let me tell you a good joke. Poe & Tuckerman met for the first time last night—& how? They each upon invitation repaired to the Rutgers Institute where they sat alone together as a committee upon young Ladies compositions—Odd isnt it that the women who divide so many should bring these two together!" (H. F. Barnes, pp. 263–64).

11 JULY. The "Sixth Anniversary Commencement" of the Rutgers Female Institute is held "in that commodious edifice, the Rutgers Street Church," which is filled to capacity in spite of the intense heat. The ceremony begins "about the hour of three" with the procession of the distinguished guests and of "the pupils of the Institution, in number between four and five hundred." Henry T. Tuckerman reads the report of "the Committee on Compositions of the 1st Department," which consisted of himself, Poe, and W. D. Snodgrass, D.D. Poe recites the "Prize Composition" selected by the committee, a poem by Miss Louise O. Hunter beginning "Deep in a glade by trees o'erhung" (long report in the *Weekly Mirror*, 19 July).

12 JULY. The *Broadway Journal* resumes publication, beginning its second volume. On the first page John Bisco announces the new arrangements:

"The editorial conduct . . . is under the sole charge of EDGAR A. POE—Mr. H. C. WATSON, as heretofore, controlling the Musical Department." The number contains Poe's revised tale containing a tale, "How to Write a Blackwood Article" containing "A Predicament" (formerly entitled "The Psyche Zenobia" and "The Scythe of Time"), his poem "The Coliseum" (reprint), and his critique of Henry B. Hirst's *The Coming of the Mammoth*. He briefly reviews his own *Tales*, complaining that this "mere selection of twelve" does not adequately represent the "variety of subject and manner" revealed in the series of "about seventy tales, of similar length, written by Mr. Poe." In noticing the *Knickerbocker Magazine* for July, he reacts to Lewis Gaylord Clark's attack on his "Magazine-Writing—Peter Snook." Clark's "Editor's Table" is "a monthly *farrago* of type so small as to be nearly invisible, and so stupid as to make us wish it were quite so. . . . he talks about a *nil admirari* critic [Poe]; some person, we presume, having quizzed him with the information that the meaning of *nil admirari* is 'to *admire* nothing.' We certainly do not admire Mr. Clarke [*sic*]—nor his wig—but the true English of the Latin phrase is 'to *wonder* at nothing.' "

12 JULY. The *Evening Mirror* reports that the *Broadway Journal* "has reappeared after the suspension of a week." It "comes forth 'like a giant refreshed.' "

12 JULY. J. Smith Homans, the bookseller whom Briggs selected as his new publisher, writes Bisco: "I am willing to take your interest in the Broadway Journal and pay you for the same One Hundred Fifty Dollars, in my note at 60 days" (ViRPM; cf. Briggs to Lowell, 16 July).

12 JULY. WEST ROXBURY, MASSACHUSETTS. The *Harbinger*, the organ of the Brook Farm Transcendentalists, contains a review of Poe's *Tales* by Charles A. Dana, who wonders about the "strange means" by which "the present volume finds its way into a library of American Books." These tales exhibit "a peculiar order of genius," which might be called "the intense order": "They remind us of the blue lights, the blood and thunder, and corked eyebrows of that boast of modern dramatic achievements, the melodrama." Dana quotes the conclusion of "The Fall of the House of Usher" to illustrate Poe's style: "If our readers can get through this passage unmoved they have a most remarkable degree of insensibility." As a specimen of several "Philosophic Sketches" found in the *Tales*, Dana quotes a passage from "Mesmeric Revelation," which he has previously "seen in the newspapers." He believes that he has spent "too much time upon this book. Its tales are clumsily contrived, unnatural, and every way in bad taste. There is still a kind of power in them; it is the power of disease; there is no health about them; they are like the vagaries of an opium eater."

14 JULY. NEW YORK. Poe and John Bisco sign a new contract: "Edgar A. Poe is to be the sole editor of the said 'Broadway Journal,' furnishing the matter therefor, from week to week, uninterfered with by any party whatever, and to receive, for said editorial conduct, one half of the entire profits." Bisco is to publish the *Journal* and pay its expenses, receiving the other half of the profits. The contract, written in Poe's hand, is witnessed by Cornelius Mathews (Quinn, pp. 751–52).

16 JULY. Briggs writes Lowell in Cambridge, Massachusetts:

The non-appearance of the Broadway Journal [on 5 July] has probably surprised you. I had made arrangements with a new publisher, a very good business man, and had agreed upon terms with Bisco to buy his interest, but when I came to close with him he exacted more than I had stipulated for, and finding that he was determined to give me trouble I refused to do anything more with the Journal. I had the first number of the new volume already to be issued with a handsomely engraved title &c, but as I could not put the new publisher's name upon it without Bisco's consent, I let it go a week, meaning to issue a double number, not doubting that I could agree with him upon some terms, but he had fallen into the hands of evil advisers, and became more extortionate than ever. Poe in the mean time got into a drunken spree, and conceived an idea that I had not treated him well, for which he had no other grounds than my having loaned him money, and persuaded Bisco to carry on the Journal himself. . . .

Mr Homans[,] the publisher with whom I had agreed to undertake the publication of the Journal[,] is an educated man and a thorough good fellow with a very extensive book-selling connexion. He is still desirous of taking hold of the Journal, and has made me a very liberal offer to go on with him if he can purchase Bisco's share. . . .

Poe's mother in law told me that he was quite tipsy the day that you called upon him, and that he acted very strangely, but I perceived nothing of it when I saw him in the morning. He was to have delivered a poem before the societies of the New York University, a few weeks since, but drunkenness prevented him. I believe that he had not drunk anything for more than 18 months until within the past 3 months, but in this time he has been very frequently carried home in a wretched condition. I am sorry for him. He has some good points, but taken altogether he is badly made up (MiDAAA–P).

17 JULY. Anne C. Lynch writes Poe:

I was very sorry not to find you at home when I called on Mrs Poe the other day—I wanted to ask you what I am now going to write—that is, if you will not come here on Saturday evening & read your poem [presumably "The Raven"] or some passages from it. Of course you will say "it is too warm"—but I do not believe it will ever be any cooler so if that is all your objection you must not refuse me. Let me hear your decision so that I may ask a few friends if you consent. Do you know Mr William Wallace? I should be happy to make his acquaintance.

Miss Lynch derived "much pleasure" from Poe's *Tales*: "They are unsurpassed by any stories I have ever read in poetry of language & force of imagination" (NNPM).

18 JULY. ROCHESTER, NEW YORK. John S. Clackner writes the *Regenerator* of Fruit Hills, Ohio, which had reprinted Poe's "Mesmeric Revelation" on 14 May. Clackner regards the tale as a factual account of a mesmeric experiment, but doubts the truth of the revelation said to be given while the subject was under hypnosis: "I am not yet so great a novice, or so credulous, as to believe that Deity condescended to reveal such astounding mysteries to a clairvoyant [the subject of the experiment], which have hitherto been withheld from the intelligent mass of mankind." Clackner argues that these "revelations" could have resulted from the subject's illness and imagination (Mabbott [1978], 3:1026–27).

19 JULY. NEW YORK. The *Town* comments:

POE'S PREDICAMENT.—In Poe's last effort in the Broadway Journal, speaking of sensations, he contrives to get a lady to a considerable height into the tower of a church, where she discovers a small aperture in the wall, through which she feels an irresistible desire of forcing her head; but the hole is so high that she cannot reach it without assistance. To obviate this difficulty she mounts *astride the head of her black attendant, Pompey*; with her feet upon his shoulders, projects her head through the opening, which proves to be a small door in the dial of the church-clock, and remains there till the approaching minute hand arrives and severs it from her shoulders.

On another page the *Town* notices Poe's attack on Lewis Gaylord Clark: "BROADWAY JOURNAL AND KNICKERBOCKER.—There is the beginning of a Kilkenny-cat business between the editorial critics of these two redoubtable journals. The last Broadway contains a very severe rap at old Knick."

19 JULY. The *Broadway Journal* contains Poe's revised tale "The Masque of the Red Death" and his sonnet "To Zante" (reprint). In an article headed "The Drama," he reviews Mrs. Mowatt's engagement at Niblo's Gardens. The *Journal* prints a long excerpt from Cornelius Mathews' lecture on American literature, preceded by Poe's editorial endorsement.

19 JULY? Poe reads "The Raven" at Miss Lynch's home, 116 Waverley Place (implied by Lynch to Poe, 17 July).

[Thomas Dunn English described Poe at one of Miss Lynch's soirees, possibly the present occasion:

I remember one evening in particular at the house of Mrs. Botta, then Miss Lynch, when he [Poe] and I were the only gentlemen present. I let him as much as possible monopolize the male share of the talk, and finally he gave quite a lecture on literary matters, to which we all listened attentively. To my surprise and delight he did not attempt to pick flaws anywhere, but confined himself to commendation of such poems as the "Florence Vane" of Philip P. Cook[e], and a number of others written by men of lesser note, on whose beauties he expatiated at length. . . .

So strongly was the scene impressed upon my memory that I can at any time close my eyes and, by a species of retinism, behold it in all its colors. In the plainly furnished room at one corner stands Miss Lynch with her round, cheery face, and Mrs. Ellet, decorous and ladylike, who had ceased their conversation when Poe broke into his lecture. On a sofa on the side of the room I sit with Miss Fuller, afterward the Countess Ossoli, on my right side, and Mrs. Elizabeth Oakes Smith on my left. At my feet little Mrs. Osgood, doing the infantile act, is seated on a footstool, her face upturned to Poe, as it had been previously to Miss Fuller and myself. In the center stands Poe, giving his opinions in a judicial tone and occasionally reciting passages with telling effect (English, p. 1448).]

AFTER 19 JULY? Miss Lynch writes Mrs. Sarah Helen Whitman in Providence, describing the "electrifying" effect that Poe's recitation of "The Raven" had upon her guests (Whitman, pp. 21–22; Whitman to J. H. Ingram, 17 April 1874, Miller [1979], p. 123).

AFTER 19? JULY. Having waited several weeks for his "Ode on a Grecian Flute" to appear in the Broadway Journal, Richard Henry Stoddard decides to see its editor:

When I could bear my disappointment no longer I made time to take a long walk to the office of the Broadway Journal, in Clinton Hall, and asked for Mr. Poe. He was not in. Might I inquire where he lived? I was directed to a street and a number that I have forgotten, but it was in the eastern part of the city, I think in East Broadway, near Clinton Street . . . . I knocked at the street-door, and was presently shown up to Poe's apartments on the second or third floor. He received me kindly. I told my errand, and he promised that my ode should be printed next week. I was struck with his polite manner toward me, and with the elegance of his appearance. He was slight and pale, I saw, with large, luminous eyes, and was dressed in black. When I quitted the room I could not but see Mrs. Poe, who was lying on a bed, apparently asleep. She too was dressed in black, and was pale and wasted. "Poor lady," I thought; "she is dying of consumption." I was sad on her account, but glad on my own; for had I not seen a real live author, the great Edgar Allan Poe, and was not my ode to be published at once in his paper? (Stoddard [1872], p. 565).

22–23 JULY. PHILADELPHIA. The Spirit of the Times reprints Poe's tale "Bon-Bon" from the Broadway Journal of 19 April (Mabbott [1978], 2:85).

24 JULY. NEW YORK. In the Morning News Evert A. Duyckinck notices the

Broadway Journal: "We regret that any circumstances should have deprived it of the valuable services of Mr. Briggs (Harry Franco) . . . . A journal, however, from the hands of Mr. Poe, is right welcome. His subtle powers of analysis have been displayed in the work from the appearance of the first number, which opened with an elaborate criticism on Miss Barrett, perhaps the minutest, closest survey of her volumes which has been written, and which we have reason to know, though anything but a mere eulogy, called forth an expression of pleasure from the authoress for the evident faithfulness and ability with which it was written." The notice appears in the *Weekly News* for 26 July.

26 JULY. BOSTON. *Littell's Living Age* reprints "The Raven" and the accompanying introduction from the London *Critic* of 14 June.

26 JULY. NEW YORK. The *Town* carries an illustration of a humanized raven, said to be the "portrait of a distinguished poet, critic and writer of tales." With tongue in cheek the *Town* characterizes this author: "He [Poe] is remarkable for his great powers of originality which have been evinced in his great work, the 'Raven,' showing no resemblance to an old English ballad or to the 'Ancient Mariner' in its construction. His tales are equally original; his 'Pit and Pendulum' has no resemblance to an old tale of an Italian place of torment, or to the accounts of the tortures of the Inquisition. As a critic, he is mild, judicious, and rigidly just, and never allows personal predilections or prejudices to interfere with his examination of the productions of others."

26 JULY. The *Broadway Journal* publishes Poe's revised poems "Israfel" and "Sonnet—Silence," as well as his revised tale "The Literary Life of Thingum Bob, Esq.," which now contains several sarcastic references to Lewis Gaylord Clark. Poe favorably reviews Ralph Hoyt's *A Chaunt of Life and Other Poems*; he continues his notice of Mrs. Mowatt's engagement at Niblo's, begun in the 19 July issue. The *Journal* carries this message for Stoddard: "TO THE AUTHOR OF THE 'LINES ON THE GRECIAN FLUTE.' We fear that we have mislaid the poem."

26 JULY. Briggs writes William Page in Albany, New York:

You over estimate my losses by the Broadway Journal, although they are pretty large; for instance: I lost my temper, I lost my good opinion of the public, and what was infinitely greater, my good opinion of myself. . . . I have nothing to regret but that I did not start with a different kind of a publisher, for with a suitable partner the paper would have been profitable and pleasant. I am indebted to Lowell for my connexion with Poe. I should never have dreamed of him but for James' extravagant praise of him; and when I first became intimate with him I liked him exceedingly well, but I soon discovered that he was the merest shell of a man, but I could not, then, easily get rid of him. In addition to his other unpleasant qualities he is a drunken sot, and the most purely selfish of human beings (MiDAAA–P).

30 JULY. CINCINNATI, OHIO. The *Daily Cincinnati Gazette* publishes a dispatch, dated 19 July, from its New York correspondent:

There has been a flare up in the Broadway Journal, which prevented the appearance of one number a week or two since, and may break up the paper. It originated in some difference between one of the Editors and the Publisher. The Editor [Briggs] undertook to get a new publisher on the paper, and so the publisher turned round and put the name of the other editor [Poe] on his sheet. Where the merits or demerits of the case lie we do not pretend to determine. The Journal has force—some good criticism and a good deal of bad. It needs more catholicity—more liberality and a little less attempt at severity. With its flashy name exchanged for something more dignified, and its main plan retained, it would soon be the most able and entertaining weekly in the country (Ehrlich, pp. 85–86).

30 JULY. RICHMOND. The *Richmond Compiler* reviews Poe's *Tales*:

For our part, we think these tales manifest unusual talent, and indeed genius—but of a morbid, unpoised character; they resemble the strange outpourings of an opium eater, while under the influence of that stimulating drug, and we may properly adopt a part of the language of a critic, who, when speaking of Poe, says his book "appears to us a collection of visions of some one to whom Fancy only comes in a fit of the nightmare. The man has mounted the wrong peak of Parnassus. We were never there; but they tell us that there were two: they who clim[b]ed the one became poets, and they who scaled the other, madmen" (Pollin [1985a], p. 6).

LATE JULY? NEW HAVEN, CONNECTICUT. The *Morning Courier* reviews Poe's *Tales*: "These Tales . . . will be hailed as a rare treat by all lovers of the exciting and the marvellous. Full of more than German mysticism, grotesque, strange, improbable, but intensely interesting, they will be read and remembered when better things are forgotten" (Gimbel, p. 162).

LATE JULY. LONDON. Wiley and Putnam, 6 Waterloo Place, issue the *Tales* in England. The English edition is identical to the American, except that the title page names London as the place of publication (*Spectator*, 2 August).

AUGUST. NEW YORK. Freeman Hunt reviews the *Tales* in his *Merchants' Magazine*. The volume contains "fine specimens of the genius of that author, who takes so high a stand among our American fiction writers and poets. A glance at some of the tales convinces us that Mr. Poe's exuberance of fancy displays itself in these, as in his previous writings."

AUGUST. The *Democratic Review* notices the *Tales*, listing the twelve stories collected.

AUGUST. The *American Review* contains Poe's essay "The American Drama," in which he analyzes two recent plays, Willis' *Tortesa, the Usurer* and Longfellow's *The Spanish Student*.

[His discussion of Longfellow could be either the 1843 review which George R. Graham would not publish or a reconstruction of it (cf. Poe to Lowell, 19 October 1843, and to Graham, 10 March 1845).]

AUGUST. PHILADELPHIA. *Godey's Lady's Book* contains Poe's "Marginal Notes—No. 1: A Sequel to the 'Marginalia' of the 'Democratic Review.' " He observes: "The Swedenborgians inform me that they have discovered all that I said in a magazine article, entitled 'Mesmeric Revelation,' to be absolutely true, although at first they were very strongly inclined to doubt my veracity."

AUGUST. *Graham's Magazine* contains Mrs. Osgood's "Ida Grey," which seems to be loosely based on her relationship with Poe. The story describes the unfulfilled love of a young coquette for a married man.

AUGUST. CHARLESTON, SOUTH CAROLINA. In his *Southern and Western Magazine* William Gilmore Simms discusses Wiley and Putnam's "Library of American Books," mentioning Poe's *Tales*: "This volume has not yet reached us;—but, from a previous knowledge of the writings of this gentleman [Poe], we venture to assert that his book possesses more sterling genius, more genuine imaginative power, more art, and more analysis, than can be found in five-eighths of the tale writers of Great Britain put together. He is too original, perhaps, to be a highly successful writer. The people are not prepared for him yet."

AUGUST. PARIS. The *Magasin pittoresque* publishes a French adaptation of "The Purloined Letter" under the title "Une Lettre volée." Neither Poe's name nor the translator's is given (Mabbott [1978], 3:973–74; Heartman and Canny, p. 277).

CA. AUGUST. NEW YORK. Alexander T. Crane faints in the office of the *Broadway Journal*:

Not a great while after I had gone to work on the paper, on a hot August afternoon while wrapping and addressing Journals, I was overcome with the heat and fainted dead away. Poe was writing at his desk. When I recovered consciousness I was stretched out on the long table at which I had been at work and Poe was bending over me bathing my wrists and temples in cold water. He ministered to me until I was able to stand up, and then he sent me home in a carriage.

This act of kindness, coupled with his uniform gentle greetings, when he entered the office of a morning, together with frequent personal inquiries and words of encouragement, made me love and trust my editor (Crane, p. 33).

1 AUGUST. Briggs writes Lowell in Cambridge, Massachusetts:

I did not give you sufficient particulars to enable you to understand my difficulties with Bisco and Poe. Neither has done anything without my full consent, and I have nothing to complain of but their meanness . . . . I had told P. a month before that I should drop his name from the "Journal." He said I might keep it there if I wanted to, although he intended to go into the country and devote his time to getting up books . . . . I had also told Bisco that I would have nothing more to do with him after the close of the first volume, and that I would not carry it on unless I could find a publisher to my mind. I did find such a publisher, and Bisco, thinking that I was very anxious to go on with it, was more exacting in his demands for his share of the "Journal" than I thought just, so I told him I would not take it; and he, thinking to spite me, and Poe, thinking to glorify himself in having overmastered me, agreed to go on with it. . . . I still hold the same right that I ever did, and could displace them both if I wished to do so. But seeing so much poltroonery and littleness in the business gave me a disgust to it (Woodberry, 2:143–44).

2 AUGUST. LONDON. The *Spectator* reviews Poe's *Tales*, a publication it received during the period *"From July 25th to July 31st"*:

This volume contains a dozen tales, mostly tinged with a spirit of diablerie or mystery, not always of a supernatural character, but such as caterers for news delight to head "mysterious occurrence." To unfold the wonderful, to show that what seems miraculous is amenable to almost mathematical reasoning, is a real delight of Mr. Poe: and though he may probably contrive the mystery he is about to unravel, this is not always the case—as in the tale of the murder of Marie Roget; and in all cases he exhibits great analytical skill in seizing upon the points of circumstantial evidence and connecting them together. He has also the faculty essential to the story-teller by "the winter's fire," who would send the hearers trembling to their beds—despite a profusion of minute circumstances if not of mere words, he holds the attention of the reader and sometimes thrills him. As a novelist, Mr. Poe has little art; depending for his effects chiefly upon the character of his subject, and his skill in working out the chain of proofs to solve the mystery. Both art and effects are of a *magazinish* kind; and in an American periodical some if not all of the tales appear to have been published. The volume is an importation, though issued in London.

2 AUGUST. NEW ORLEANS. The *Daily Picayune* notices Poe's *Tales* (Pollin [1980], p. 25).

2 AUGUST. NEW YORK. The *Broadway Journal* contains Poe's revised tale "The Business Man" and his poems "Sonnet—To Science" and "Bridal Ballad" (reprints). He favorably reviews Thomas Holley Chivers' *The Lost Pleiad*; in an article on "The Drama" he describes Mrs. Mowatt's concluding performance at Niblo's Gardens "on the 26th ult." In the "Editorial Miscellany" he quotes a favorable review of Cornelius Mathews' *Poems on Man* from *Tait's Edinburgh Magazine*; and he praises Frederick William Thomas' sketch of William Wirt, reprinted in this number of the *Journal*. In a notice "To Correspondents" Poe addresses Richard Henry Stoddard: "We doubt the originality of the 'Grecian Flute,' for the reason that it is *too good* at some points to be so bad at others. Unless the author can re-assure us, we decline it."

AFTER 2 AUGUST. Stoddard visits the office of the *Broadway Journal*:

Poe was in his *sanctum*. He was awakened either by myself or his publisher, and was in a very stormy mood. When summoned back to earth he was slumbering uneasily in a very easy chair. He was irascible, surly, and in his cups.

"Mr. Poe," I ventured to remark, meekly, "I saw you two or three weeks ago, and I read in your paper that you doubted my ability to write——"

"I know," he answered, starting up wildly. "You never wrote the Ode to which I lately referred. You never——" But the reader may imagine the rest of this unfortunate sentence. I was comminated, and threatened with condign personal chastisement. I left quickly, but was not, as I remember, downcast. On the contrary, I was complimented, flattered. The great American Critic had declared that I could not write what I *had* written (Stoddard [1889], p. 108).

AFTER 2 AUGUST. Chivers, who is departing New York for his plantation in Georgia, writes Poe: "I leave with you a M.s. Play in Five Acts, which I wish you to read carefully—not to run over—and notice all those passages which you think praiseworthy—if any there be—in your Paper, and send the Numbers on to me in which you notice it . . . . The article entitled *'Luciferian Revelation,'* was suggested by reading your *'Mesmeric Revelation.'* This, I wish you to publish in your paper the *very first thing*. . . . I send you also some poems, which you can publish in your paper also. But I wish you not to forget to read my *printed* poems [*The Lost Pleiad*] carefully, and review them as you ought to do—for there are many good ones you have not noticed" (Chivers [1957], pp. 38–39).

BEFORE 8 AUGUST. Evert A. Duyckinck writes Simms in Charleston, South Carolina, describing Poe's intemperance (Simms's reply, 8 August).

[Duyckinck left this undated entry in a notebook: "There is Poe with coolness, immaculate personal cleanliness, sensitiveness, the gentleman, continually putting himself on a level with the lowest blackguard through a combination of moral, mental and physical drunkenness" (Reece [1954], p. 95).]

8 AUGUST. Poe writes his second cousin Neilson Poe in Baltimore: "It gave me sincere pleasure to receive a letter from you—but I fear you will think me very discourteous in not sooner replying. I have deferred my answer, however, from day to day, in hope of procuring some papers relating to my grandfather [David Poe, Sr.]. In this I have failed. Mrs C. has no memoranda of the kind you mention, and all of which I have any knowledge are on file at Annapolis." Poe discusses his family: "Virginia . . . has been, and is still, in precarious health. About four years ago she ruptured a blood-vessel, in singing, and has never recovered from the accident. I fear that she never will. Mrs Clemm is quite well:—both beg to be kindly remembered" (L, 1:291–92).

8 AUGUST. The *Evening Gazette* notices the *American Review* for August, discussing Poe's analysis of *The Spanish Student*: "Mr. Longfellow does not seem to please Mr. Poe in anything that he writes" (Moss [1963], p. 155).

8 AUGUST. CAMBRIDGE, MASSACHUSETTS. Lowell replies to Briggs's letter of 1 August: "I am glad to hear that the conduct of Poe and Bisco about the B.J. was not so bad as I had feared" (Woodberry, 2:369; also in Ehrlich, p. 87).

8 AUGUST. CHARLESTON, SOUTH CAROLINA. Simms replies to Duyckinck, whose letter he received today: "What you tell me of Poe distresses me. But, in his circumstances, & for such a man, it is difficult to devise anything,—unless it be to control his infirmities with a moral countenance which coerces while it soothes & seems to solicit. This should be the care of the circle in which he moves" (Simms, 2:97–99).

BEFORE 9 AUGUST. BOSTON. Robert Hamilton sends Poe proof sheets of his tale "The Imp of the Perverse," which is to be reprinted in the *May-Flower* for 1846 (implied in the *Broadway Journal*, 9 August; cf. Poe to Hamilton, 3 October 1842).

9 AUGUST. NEW YORK. The *Broadway Journal* contains Poe's revised tale "The Man That Was Used Up" and his poem "Eulalie" (reprint). He favorably reviews Hunt's *Merchants' Magazine* for August, as well as two

books issued by Wiley and Putnam, Joel T. Headley's *Letters from Italy* and Thomas Hood's *Prose and Verse, Part 1*. In his "Editorial Miscellany" he praises several forthcoming annuals: "*Mr. Robert Hamilton*, is getting ready 'The May-Flower,' of which we have seen some specimen sheets which promise remarkably well. . . . Saxton and Kelt, of Boston, are the publishers." Poe takes issue with the New York correspondence in the *Daily Cincinnati Gazette* of 30 July: "What does he [the correspondent] mean by calling 'The Broadway Journal' 'a *flashy* name'? What does he mean by 'putting the name of the other editor [Poe] on the paper'? The name of the 'other editor' was never *off* the paper."

9 AUGUST. Poe writes Thomas W. Field, a poet: "It is nearly a month since I received a note from you, requesting an interview—but, by some inadvertence, I placed it (your note) among my pile of 'answered letters'. This will account to you for my seeming discourtesy in not sooner giving you an answer." He invites Field to call upon him at 195 East Broadway: "You will generally find me at home in the morning before 10" (*L*, 1:292).

9 AUGUST. A correspondent who signs herself "X," possibly Margaret Fuller, sends a letter "To the Editors of The Broadway Journal," enclosing a satiric poem: "The object of the present communication [the poem] speaks for itself. It is to ridicule a style of writing very common in your sex, when discoursing of ours, but which deserves no better epithet than *ineffable silliness*. I am aware that Longfellow is a popular poet & deservedly so, but I am sure he will not be offended at such a mere piece of pleasantry, coming as it does from one of the party to whom such soft nonsense is addressed" (MB–G).

[The letter is not in Fuller's hand, but docketed "Miss Fuller" by Poe. The poem, entitled "The Whole Duty of Woman," appeared in the *Broadway Journal* for 23 August; it satirizes Longfellow's lines "What most I prize in woman / Is her affection, not her intellect."]

9 AUGUST. BALTIMORE. Snodgrass' *Saturday Visiter* publishes an article by Edward H. Docwra, a Baltimore law student who is a frequent contributor: " 'The Haunted Palace' by Edgar A. Poe is a gem of the most brilliant and beautiful caste . . . . Its beauty has enchanted me, and has led me to attempt, in the same measure, a sort of 'companion-piece.' I know not, if Mr. P. intended to have it inferred that the wreck of the mind alluded to in 'The Haunted Palace,' had been caused by intemperance; but it certainly will bear such a construction. And, whether or not that was the writer's idea, my construction will afford a good opportunity for the teaching of a lesson." Docwra quotes Poe's poem in its entirety; he then appends his own

sententious poem "The Restoration," which depicts "that palace, once so ruin'd," being restored by "Temperance with her heaven-like care."

9 AUGUST. LONDON. The *Critic* lists Poe's *Tales*, price "3s. 6d.," in its "Register of New Publications." The *Literary Gazette* carries this review:

There is considerable interest in these Tales, the plots of most of them partaking of mysterious ingredients, and, where the ground is laid in America, the local descriptions being ably written. The style is not disfigured by any gross Yankeeisms, but blemished by some common instances. For example, we are told that the chief amusements of a person were "gunning and fishing." Now we cannot see why it should not be shooting and fishing; or, if they will say gunning, why, it should be all of a piece, and *"gunning and rodding"* the expression. In spite of such trifling defects, the volume will be read with satisfaction to amuse the vacant hour.

9 AUGUST. The *Atlas* notices the *Tales*, quoting a long passage from "A Descent into the Maelström" (Pollin [1980], p. 24).

BEFORE 11 AUGUST. PHILADELPHIA. Thomas Holley Chivers, returning to Georgia, writes Poe, who fails to receive the letter (Poe to Chivers, 29 August; Chivers to Poe, 9 September).

11 AUGUST. OAKY GROVE, GEORGIA. Chivers writes Poe again (Poe to Chivers, 29 August).

11 AUGUST. NEW YORK. Poe writes Chivers at Oaky Grove: "Mr Bisco says to me that, with the loan of $50, for a couple of months, he would be put out of all difficulty in respect to the publication of the 'Broadway Journal'. Its success is decided, and will eventually make us a fortune. . . . You know that I have no money at command myself, and therefore I venture to ask you for the loan required. . . . In 2 months certainly the money will be repaid" (*L*, 1:292–93).

13 AUGUST. SOUTH ATTLEBOROUGH, MASSACHUSETTS. Abijah M. Ide, Jr., writes John Bisco, enclosing one dollar to begin his subscription to the *Broadway Journal*: "I beg pardon for not sending the whole subscription price [three dollars per annum] *at once*; but you shall receive all—free of postage, and in good time, and be *thrice thanked*." Ide asks to be sent "the no. [8 February] that contains Mr. Poe's 'Raven' " (ViRPM).

14 AUGUST. NEW YORK. Laughton Osborn, an eccentric author, writes Poe. In the *Broadway Journal* for 15 March, Osborn has chanced upon an unsigned article condemning *The Vision of Rubeta*, his satiric poem aimed at malicious literary critics: "Whoever of yr. associates was the writer (for I

will not do you the injustice to suppose that you were more than cognizant of the matter) I shall never take any public notice of it though I should now be able to complete the *Vision*, but I can no more forget it than I can any other act of wilful injustice." Osborn regrets to find Poe allied with his foes: "Our former positions towards each other must now be restored: as I sought yr acquaintance under the impress[io]n that you were one of my truest defenders, I cannot of course profit by what was so mere a mistake. With what sadness this is said you may conceive, when I assure you, without the least reluctance, that had I had the choice, of all the literary men of my country there is none, with the exception of the author of *Ferdinand & Isab{ell}a* [William H. Prescott], whose friendship I should have preferred to yours." Osborn has been reading the copy of the *Tales* Poe gave him "with unalloyed satisfaction"; he has the highest opinion of Poe's abilities (PP–G).

15 AUGUST. Poe replies to Osborn: "I am neither disposed, nor can I afford, to give up your friendship so easily." During the first volume of the *Broadway Journal*, Poe was only a contributor: "With the making up of the journal—with the reception or rejection of communications—I had no more to do than yourself. The article to which you refer had never been seen by me until you pointed it out. . . . It is quite a coincidence that,

CHARLES F. BRIGGS

although Halleck is the only poet of whom we both spoke cordially in approbation, on the night when I saw you, I should in his case, also, have been subjected to just such misconception as arose in your own." Because Poe "had been known to write previous criticisms on poetical works, for the Journal," the attack on Halleck's *Alnwick Castle* in the 3 May issue was "universally attributed" to him: "I endured the loss of Mr Halleck's good will, until, by mere accident, he discovered that the offensive article had been written by a brother poet, Lowell, at the malicious instigation of my former associate, Mr Briggs" (*L*, 1:293–94; Ostrom [1974], pp. 527–28).

[Notwithstanding his denial, Poe wrote the article which offended Osborn (Hull, pp. 562–63). On 31 March Briggs sent "Halleck's poems" to Lowell, giving him this license: "Please abuse them to your hearts contents" (MiDAAA–P).]

16 AUGUST. The *Broadway Journal* contains Poe's revised tale "Never Bet the Devil Your Head" and his poems "Lenore," "A Dream," and "Catholic Hymn" (reprints). He favorably reviews William Hazlitt's *The Characters of Shakspeare*, published in Wiley and Putnam's "Library of Choice Reading." In noticing *Graham's Magazine* for August, he praises Lowell's poem "To the Future" as "a noble composition," but points out that the last stanza is "a palpable plagiarism" from Wordsworth. He copies four lines from this stanza and then quotes, "altogether from memory," a parallel passage by the English poet. In his "Editorial Miscellany" Poe replies to the *Evening Gazette* of 8 August: "because we are not so childish as to suppose that every book is thoroughly good or thoroughly bad . . . because upon several occasions we have thought proper to *demonstrate* the sins, while displaying the virtues of Professor Longfellow, is it just, or proper, or even courteous on the part of 'The Gazette' to accuse us, in round terms, of uncompromising hostility to this poet?"

18 AUGUST. Evert A. Duyckinck writes Charles Eames in Washington: "Poe's Tales are worthy of your comment. It is only to the first class of critics that he can look for any notice at all, for, like a man of genius he spins his thread too fine for common readers" (Reece [1954], p. 92).

21 AUGUST. CAMBRIDGE, MASSACHUSETTS. Lowell writes Briggs: "Poe, I am afraid, is wholly lacking in that element of manhood which, for want of a better name, we call *character*. It is something quite distinct from genius,—though all great geniuses are endowed with it. . . . As I prognosticated, I have made Poe my enemy by doing him a service. In the last B.J. he has accused me of plagiarism, and *misquoted* Wordsworth to sustain his charge. . . . My metaphor was drawn from some old Greek or Roman

story which was in my mind, and which Poe, who makes such a scholar of himself, ought to have known. . . . Any one who had ever read the *whole* of Wordsworth's poem would see that there was no resemblance between the two passages. Poe wishes to kick down the ladder by which he rose" (Woodberry, 2:369–70; also in Lowell, 1:99–102).

21 AUGUST. NEW YORK. Briggs replies to Lowell:

You have formed a correct estimate of Poe's characterless character. I have never met a person so utterly deficient of high motive. He cannot conceive of anybody's doing anything, except for his own personal advantage; and he says, with perfect sincerity, and entire unconsciousness of the exposition which it makes of his own mind and heart, that he looks upon all reformers as madmen . . . . His presumption is beyond the liveliest imagination. He has no reverence for Homer, Shakespeare, or Milton, but thinks that [Horne's] "Orion" is the greatest poem in the language. . . . The Bible, he says, is all rigmarole. As to his Greek,—you might see very well if it were put in your eye. He does not read Wordsworth (Woodberry, 2:145–46).

23 AUGUST. The *Broadway Journal* contains Poe's revised story "The Tell-Tale Heart." He favorably reviews *The Poetical Writings of Mrs. Elizabeth Oakes Smith*, Thomas Hood's *Prose and Verse, Part II*, and Nathaniel P. Willis' *Dashes at Life with a Free Pencil*. In his "Editorial Miscellany" he praises the booksellers of Boston, whose stores he inspected during "a recent visit" to that city: "Among other booksellers in Boston, whose publications deserve to be better known here, are James Munroe & Co. The inimitable 'Twice Told Tales' of Hawthorne, were published by this house. . . . Hawthorne, it appears to us, has fulfilled all the conditions which should insure success, and yet he has reaped but a scanty harvest. He is a prose poet, full of originality, beauty and refinement of style and conception, while many of his subjects are thoroughly American. He is frugal and industrious, but the profit[s] of his writings are inadequate to his support."

23 AUGUST. PHILADELPHIA. The *Saturday Courier* reprints Poe's "Bridal Ballad" (Heartman and Canny, p. 244).

25 AUGUST. PARIS. *L'Echo de la Presse* reprints "Une Lettre volée," an adaptation of "The Purloined Letter," from the *Magasin pittoresque* for August (Mabbott [1978], 3:974).

25 AUGUST. OAKY GROVE, GEORGIA. Chivers writes Poe, complaining that he has received no reply to the letter he sent him from Philadelphia before 11 August. Chivers promises to send Poe the $50 he requested in

his 11 August letter (Poe to Chivers, 29 August; Chivers to Poe, 9 September).

27 AUGUST. PHILADELPHIA. The *Spirit of the Times* reprints "The Tell-Tale Heart," presumably from the *Broadway Journal* of 23 August (Mabbott [1978], 3:792).

29 AUGUST. NEW YORK. Poe replies to Chivers' 25 August letter: "What can you be thinking about? You complain of me for not doing things which I had no idea that you wanted done. Do you not see that my short letter [of 11 August] to you was written on the very day in which yours was addressed to me? How, then, could you expect mine to be a reply to yours?" Poe is puzzled by Chivers' reference to the $50: "You write—'Well I suppose you must have it'—but it does not come." He asks Chivers to forward the money immediately, because "almost everything" with regard to the *Broadway Journal* "depends upon it." As soon as Poe can complete "Wiley & Putnam's book" [*The Raven and Other Poems*], he will have "plenty of money—$500 at least"; and he will then repay Chivers. "I have not touched a drop of the 'ashes' [alcohol] since you left N. Y.—& I am resolved not to touch a drop as long as I live" (*L*, 1:295–97).

30 AUGUST. The *Broadway Journal* contains Poe's revised tale "William Wilson" and his revised poem "The City in the Sea." He concludes his review of Thomas Hood's *Prose and Verse, Part II*, begun in last week's issue; and he favorably notices William Gilmore Simms's *Southern and Western Magazine*. The *Journal* prints Mrs. Osgood's poem "Slander," which may possibly allude to rumors occasioned by her open affection for Poe.

30 AUGUST. WASHINGTON. The *Daily National Intelligencer* contains Rufus W. Griswold's essay "Tale Writers." He identifies the leading American story writers as Washington Irving, Richard Henry Dana, Sr., Hawthorne, Willis, Charles Fenno Hoffman, and Poe:

The reader of Mr. POE'S tales is compelled, almost at the outset, to surrender his mind to his author's control. . . . Unlike that of the greater number of *suggestive* authors, his narrative is most *minute*; and, unlike most who attend so carefully to detail, he has nothing superfluous—nothing which does not tend to the common centre—nothing which is not absolutely necessary to the production of the desired result. His stories seem to be written *currente calamo*, but, if examined, will be found to be the results of consummate art. . . . Mr. POE resembles BROCKDEN BROWN in his intimacy with mental pathology, but surpasses that author in delineation. No one ever delighted more, or was more successful, in oppressing the brain with anxiety, or startling it with images of horror. GEORGE WALKER, ANN RADCLIFFE, MARIA ROCHE, could alarm with dire chimeras, could lead their characters into difficulties and perils—but they extricated them so clumsily as to destroy every impression of *reality*. Mr. POE'S scenes all seem to be actual.

30 AUGUST, 6 SEPTEMBER. MONTPELIER, VERMONT. The *Universalist Watchman*, a religious weekly, reprints Poe's "Mesmeric Revelation" in two installments, with an introduction by its editor Eli Ballou: "We do not take the following article as an historical account, nor, as a burlesque on mesmerism; but, as a presentation of the writer's philosophical theory which he wished to commend to the attention of his readers" (Mabbott [1978], 3:1027).

SEPTEMBER. NEW YORK. The *American Review* contains a four-page critique of Poe's *Tales* by its editor George H. Colton. Although Poe has made many enemies with his criticisms, "even an enemy would be found to acknowledge, that the present volume is one of the most original and peculiar ever published in the United States, and eminently worthy of an extensive circulation, and a cordial recognition." The "peculiarity" of Poe's stories "consists in developing new sources of interest. Addressed to the intellect, or the more recondite sympathies and emotions of our nature, they fix attention by the force and refinement of reasoning employed in elucidating some mystery which sets the curiosity of the reader on an edge, or in representing, with the utmost exactness, and in the sharpest outlines, the inward life of beings, under the control of perverse and morbid passions. As specimens of subtle dialectics, and the anatomy of the heart, they are no less valuable and interesting, than as tales."

SEPTEMBER. The *Columbian Magazine* briefly notices the first three volumes in Wiley and Putnam's "Library of American Books," including Poe's *Tales*: "These books are all worthy of a place in the best selected library."

SEPTEMBER. The *Democratic Review* contains an essay on "American Humor" by William A. Jones, a close friend of Evert A. Duyckinck. Jones praises the humorous writings of Cornelius Mathews, "Felix Merry" (Duyckinck), "Harry Franco" (Briggs), and other Americans. In passing he describes Poe as "one of the most ingenious critics, and a prose poet of much force, imagination, invention and versatility."

SEPTEMBER. PHILADELPHIA. The *American Phrenological Journal* reprints "Mesmeric Revelation" with an introduction by the editor Orson Squire Fowler: "As chroniclers of magnetic occurrences, we cannot well refuse admission to our pages of an article as important as the *subject matter* of the following 'MAGNETIC REVELATION,' as it is headed, claims to be. In copying it, however, we must not be understood as endorsing it, nor yet as repudiating it. We simply lay it before our readers, soliciting that they do by it as we have done, *think it over fully*, and form their own conclusions." It is "written by Edgar A. Poe, a man favorably known in the literary world; so that it may be *relied* upon as authentic. Its mere literary merit, the reader will perceive, is by no means inconsiderable. Read and re-read."

SEPTEMBER. *Godey's Lady's Book* publishes Poe's "Marginal Notes—No. 2."

SEPTEMBER. *Graham's Magazine* reviews Poe's *Tales*:

These tales are among the most original and characteristic compositions in American letters. . . . "The Gold Bug" attracted great attention at the time it appeared, and is quite remarkable as an instance of intellectual acuteness and subtlety of reasoning. "The Fall of the House of Usher" is a story of horror and gloom, in which the feeling of supernatural fear is represented with great power. The pertinacity with which Mr. Poe probes a terror to its depths, and spreads it out to the reader, so that it can be seen as well as felt, is a peculiarity of his tales. He is an anatomist of the horrible and ghastly, and trusts for effect, not so much in exciting a vague feeling of fear and terror, as in leading the mind through the whole framework of crime and perversity, and enabling the intellect to comprehend their laws and relations. . . . "The Murders in the Rue Morgue," and "The Mystery of Marie Roget," are fine instances of the interest which may be given to subtle speculations and reasonings, when they are exercised to penetrate mysteries which the mind aches to know.

SEPTEMBER. EDINBURGH, SCOTLAND. *Tait's Edinburgh Magazine* reviews the *Tales*:

We take for granted that Edgar A. Poe is an American. His tales are of a peculiar, we had almost said, of an original character; and though monstrosities, often revolting, nay, disgusting, and chargeable with all kinds of bad taste, there is a rude power and a subtlety about them which is not without a fascination of the hideous or disagreeable sort. Some of the Tales, or Sketches, are attempts at philosophizing, in the safe way of making imaginary personages broach wild hypotheses, and conjectural systems, as supernatural revelations. The records of every court of criminal justice furnish, in doubtful and perplexing cases, or conflicting testimony and contradictions, much more curious tales than those which Mr. Poe has invented, and the type of which is [Voltaire's] *Zadig*.

CA. SEPTEMBER. WASHINGTON, GEORGIA. Chivers writes the editor of the *Southern Courant*, a Washington, Georgia, newspaper, objecting to a review of *The Lost Pleiad* published in the *Bee*, another Washington newspaper. In noticing Chivers' volume Thomas W. Lane, the editor of the *Bee*, has foolishly criticized Poe's favorable review of it in the *Broadway Journal* of 2

August: "Not satisfied with *misquoting* me, he [Lane] must *libel* Mr Poe, than whom a more perfect gentleman never existed. He is not only one of the best Critics, but one of the most versatile and accomplished scholars in the world. . . . He [Lane] talks about Mr Poe's '*puffing*,' and would, no doubt, make the People believe it; but *no man ever was farther from it*. His greatest fault is, that he is *too severe*. This has become proverbial" (Chivers [1957], pp. 44–51).

1 SEPTEMBER. FRUIT HILLS, OHIO. The *Regenerator* publishes John S. Clackner's 18 July letter discussing Poe's "Mesmeric Revelation" (Mabbott [1978], 3:1026–27).

5, 6, 8 SEPTEMBER. PHILADELPHIA. The *Spirit of the Times* reprints Poe's "William Wilson" in three installments, from the *Broadway Journal* of 30 August (Mabbott [1978], 2:426).

6 SEPTEMBER. LONDON. The *Critic* reviews the *Tales*:

Mr. POE is familiar to us as a poet of considerable power. We remember the fine conception and the musical execution of some of his stanzas, and, with these fresh in our mind, we confess ourselves disappointed by the present volume of Tales. The first story, "The Gold Bug," is only interesting from its strangeness. It tells of the discovery of some hidden treasure, by the solving of certain enigmatical figures. Viewed with the moral, the tale *may* be useful, as showing what a patient, earnest mind may accomplish. . . .

Of a piece with "The Gold Bug" are the "Mystery of Marie Roget," and the "Murders of the Rue Morgue." The author seems here to have amused himself by following the plan of those philosophers who trace a series of references between every minute act, and so upward to the making and dethroning of kings. Mr. POE has been as assiduous in this scheme as an Indian who follows the trail of a foe. . . .

Perhaps of even less utility is Mr. POE's tale of the "Black Cat." The Black Cat would have been a proper inmate for the "Castle of Otranto," and a most valuable counterpart to the mysterious plume and helmet. . . .

We object, for the most part, to the tales we have instanced, because they uncurtain horrors and cruelties. It is enough, and perhaps too much, for public benefit, that minute details of murders and other horrors find their way into newspapers. . . .

Mr. POE could not possibly send forth a book without some marks of his genius, and mixed up with the dross we find much sterling ore.

To demonstrate that Poe is "a deep thinker," the *Critic* reprints his "Mesmeric Revelation" in its entirety.

6 SEPTEMBER. NEW YORK. The *Broadway Journal* reprints Poe's tales "Why

the Little Frenchman Wears His Hand in a Sling" and "Silence—A Fable" (formerly entitled "Siope"), and his poems "To the River" and "The Valley of Unrest." He reviews the American editions of two English books, Philip James Bailey's *Festus* and John Wilson's *Genius and Character of Burns.* On its first page the *Journal* carries Mrs. Osgood's poem "Echo-Song," addressed to Poe and quoting his poem "Israfel":

> I know a noble heart that beats
> For one it loves how "wildly well!"
> *I* only know for *whom* it beats;
> But I must never tell!
> Never tell!
> Hush! hark! how Echo soft repeats,—
> Ah! *never* tell! . . .

9 SEPTEMBER. OAKY GROVE, GEORGIA. Chivers replies to Poe's 29 August letter: "What can *you* be thinking about to ask me what *I* could have been thinking about, when I referred to the letter I wrote from Philadelphia [before 11 August], and also from this place [on 11 August], immediately after my return home?" He regrets that he has not been able to send Poe the $50 for the *Broadway Journal*: "I will send it to you as soon as possible, but to *you* alone. You are always talking to me about the '*paper*' [the *Journal*]. '*Cuss*' the paper! what do *I* care for the '*paper?*' The 'paper' will do me no more good than it will any body else. I have no interest in it—it is in your *individual* welfare and happiness that I have an interest—an abiding, disinterested, heartborn interest." Chivers, a temperance advocate, endorses Poe's decision to abstain from drinking: "For God's sake, but *more* for your own, *never touch another drop*. Why should a Man whom God, by nature, has endowed with such transcendent abilities, so degrade himself into the verriest automaton as to be moved only by the poisonous stream of Hell-fire?" He encloses five dollars for Poe "to swear by" (Chivers [1957], pp. 51–56).

10 SEPTEMBER. NEW YORK. Poe writes Evert A. Duyckinck, Wiley and Putnam's editor, forwarding "the best" of his poems for his forthcoming *The Raven and Other Poems*: "They [the poems] are *very* few—including those only which have not been published in volume form. If they can be made to fill a book, it will be better to publish them alone—but if not, I can hand you some 'Dramatic Scenes' [*Politian*] from the S.L. Messenger (2d Vol) and 'Al Aaraaf' and 'Tamerlane,' two juvenile poems of some length" (*L*, 1:297).

11 SEPTEMBER? Poe writes Duyckinck: "Your note of yesterday was not

received until this morning." He will call at Duyckinck's home tonight, "about 8" (*L,* 1:297).

13 SEPTEMBER. The *Broadway Journal* contains Poe's revised tale "Diddling Considered as One of the Exact Sciences." He replies to Mrs. Osgood's "Echo-Song" in the 6 September issue by printing, under the heading "To F———," the first four lines of his eight-line poem "To Elizabeth," originally written for his cousin Elizabeth Rebecca Herring:

> Thou wouldst be loved?—then let thy heart
> From its present pathway part not!
> Being everything which now thou art,
> Be nothing which thou art not!

In his "Editorial Miscellany" Poe criticizes a Pennsylvania newspaper, the *Chambersburg Times,* which made up "the whole of its first page from a single number of 'The Broadway Journal.' This would be all very well, had it not forgotten to give us credit for our articles, contributed and editorial—and had it not forgotten *not* to make certain improvements in our compositions to suit its own fancy. Copying, for example, a little poem of our own called 'Lenore' [from the 16 August *Journal*], the Chambersburg editor alters 'the damnèd earth' into 'the cursed earth.' Now, we prefer it damned, and will have it so."

20 SEPTEMBER. The *Broadway Journal* contains Poe's revised tales "The Landscape Garden" and "A Tale of Jerusalem," and his poems "To———" ("The bowers whereat, in dreams, I see") and "Song" ("I saw thee on thy bridal day"), both reprints. In noticing the *Democratic Review* for September, Poe condemns William A. Jones's essay on "American Humor," which "is insufferable: nor do we think it the less a nuisance because it inflicts upon ourselves individually a passage of maudlin compliment." He especially objects to Jones's praise of Charles F. Briggs: "A vulgar driveller, . . . (Harry Franco), . . . our essayist places 'on a par with Paulding and much above Miss Leslie and Joseph Neal.' " In the "Editorial Miscellany" Poe observes: "The Mesmeric journals, and some others, are still making a to-do about the tenability of Mr. Vankirk's doctrines as broached in a late Magazine paper of our own, entitled 'Mesmeric Revelation.' " He quotes John S. Clackner's "very curious comments" on the story from the *Regenerator* of 1 September.

24 SEPTEMBER. SAINT LOUIS. The *Daily Reveille* quotes with approval Poe's rebuke to the *Chambersburg Times* from the 13 September *Journal* (Moss [1968], p. 18).

25 SEPTEMBER. NEW YORK. Duyckinck writes Joel T. Headley: Poe's

remarks on Jones in the last *Journal* constitute "so bad a specimen of the 'onslaught' in criticism . . . that I cry out more than ever for the man who is not passion's or whim's or prejudice's man—*for arguments before adjectives*" (Reece [1954], p. 95).

BEFORE 27 SEPTEMBER. BOSTON. Saxton and Kelt issue the *May-Flower* for 1846, containing Poe's revised tale "The Imp of the Perverse," originally published in *Graham's Magazine* for July.

27 SEPTEMBER. NEW YORK. The *Broadway Journal* contains Poe's revised tale "Ligeia," as well as his favorable reviews of Rufus W. Griswold's edition of *The Prose Works of John Milton* and Cornelius Mathews' novel *Big Abel and the Little Manhattan*, the fifth volume in Wiley and Putnam's "Library of American Books." Poe briefly notices the *May-Flower*, the "first published Annual . . . of the season." In his "Editorial Miscellany" he prints a defense of William A. Jones he received from "a warm personal friend of Mr. Jones" [presumably Duyckinck] in the past week.

28 SEPTEMBER. Poe writes Griswold. He wishes to borrow the second volume of the *Southern Literary Messenger*, presumably to obtain his "Scenes from an Unpublished Drama" (*Politian*) for *The Raven and Other Poems* (L, 1:298; cf. Poe to Duyckinck, 10 September).

29 SEPTEMBER. WASHINGTON. Frederick William Thomas writes Poe: "I received your journal regularly—Thank you for it.—I see you have published two of my sketches (Randolph-Wirt)." He also receives a copy of the *Broadway Journal* intended for his friend Dr. Lacy of the Post Office Department: "I am not now boarding at Fuller's [Hotel] with Lacy, having taken private lodging in another part of the town; so that I seldom see him—I therefore have to redirect the 'Journal' and drop it in the post office, for him—You had better tell your 'folks' to send it direct to the doctor." Although Thomas had hoped to see Poe during the summer, circumstances compelled him "to remain in Washington, in these stressing times for officials." He praises Poe's *Tales*: "I have made myself popular with several few ladies by reading portions of them to the persons in question" (MB–G).

29 SEPTEMBER. William Fairman, a traveling representative for the *Broadway Journal*, writes John Bisco, describing his efforts to enlist magazine agents and individual subscribers in Baltimore and Washington:

The general impression in Balto and this city was that your paper had stopped. In Balto when I arrived there had been no papers for three weeks. In this city there have been none for some months. The agent says he has had several calls for it lately. The complaint in Ba[l]to and this city has been that it came too late and very irregularly, seldom getting in Saturday and sometimes a week behind. . . . I hope to be able in Richmond to make out my expenses and to make up the amount of my defalcations in your half [of the *Journal*'s profits]. . . . Mr Poe has a great many friends and is held in the highest estimation both by those who know him as a man and as a writer. My only hopes is [*sic*] among his friends. The prospects of the Journal I think are good. But the day of canvassing for periodicals is over. . . . The truth is many of those disposed to take [subscribe] either have not the money to pay in advance or are afraid to do so. . . .

I am convinced that if in every considerable place there was an agent who would advertise the Journal weekly, if every considerable newspaper in the Union should recieve [*sic*] the Journal and notice it editorially, that it would eventually become extensively circulated. I do not think any person can make it for his interest to travel and solicit subscribers (ViRPM).

BEFORE 30 SEPTEMBER. NEW YORK. Poe accepts an invitation to deliver an original poem before the Boston Lyceum, for an honorarium of $50 (Phillips, 2:1050–51).

30 SEPTEMBER. BOSTON. The *Evening Transcript* carries an advertisement, which is repeated in subsequent issues: "BOSTON LYCEUM. The Anniversary of this Institution will occur on THURSDAY, the 16th of October, on which occasion an Address will be pronounced by HON CALEB CUSHING, and a Poem by EDGAR A. POE Esq, of New York; to be followed by Lectures on each succeeding Thursday evening. . . . The introductory exercises will take place at the Odeon, . . . at 7 1/2 P.M. Doors open at 6 1/2."

BEFORE OCTOBER. NEW YORK. The Poe family moves from 195 East Broadway to a three-story house at 85 Amity Street, near Washington Square (*L*, 1:301; Quinn, p. 475).

OCTOBER. In the "Editor's Table" of the *Knickerbocker Magazine*, Lewis Gaylord Clark condemns William A. Jones's essay on "American Humor," quoting Poe's opinion from the 20 September *Journal* that it is "contemptible, both in a moral and literary sense."

OCTOBER. The *Biblical Repository* notices Wiley and Putnam's "Library of American Books": "Poe's Tales are much praised by some, as indicating superior genius; for ourselves, while a portion of them are well-wrought and fascinating, others of them are extravagant, and one, at least, of hurtful tendency."

OCTOBER. PHILADELPHIA. The *American Phrenological Journal* carries a retraction by its editor Orson Squire Fowler, who has discovered that "Mesmeric Revelation" is a fiction:

Retraction, when convinced of error, is due on its own account, and evinces a highminded love of *truth*. The Editor intends to be so cautious as seldom to have occasion to make an apology now due to his readers. The article in his last [September] number, quoted from Mr. Poe, proves not to be that "magnetic revelation" it claims for itself, but simply the production of its author's own brain.

The Editor was first led into the error of supposing it a veritable magnetic disclosure, by a verbal account given of it by a magnetizer; which was such as to induce him to procure and peruse it; and secondly, by knowing that the literary clique to which Poe belongs, Joseph C. Neal included, had given much attention to magnetism [mesmerism]. Without the least suspicion, therefore, that it was not genuine—he did not examine it in this respect, but being obligated by his prospectus to lay before his readers whatever appeared to be *particularly* interesting or important—he gave it the insertion it really merited, provided it had been genuine.

OCTOBER. *Graham's Magazine* publishes "The Divine Right of Kings," a twelve-line poem signed with the initial "P."

[The December *Graham's* contained another brief poem signed with "P." Both were collected by Mabbott, who believed that they may have been Poe's response to Mrs. Osgood's "Ida Grey" in the August *Graham's*; but the evidence supporting this attribution is not conclusive. See Campbell (1933), pp. 208–09, and Mabbott (1969), 1:382–86.]

CA. OCTOBER? Uriah Hunt & Son issue *The Poetry of the Sentiments*, which contains Poe's poem "The Coliseum," a reprint (Heartman and Canny, p. 112).

EARLY OCTOBER. NEW YORK. Poe borrows $30 from Thomas Dunn English as "a part of the money necessary" to purchase John Bisco's share of the *Broadway Journal*. In return he promises English an interest in the *Journal*, assuring him that the paper "would be profitable to those concerned in it" (English's 11 February 1847 deposition).

EARLY OCTOBER? Poe finds himself unable to write an original poem to read before the Boston Lyceum, as required by the rules of that institution; and he asks Mrs. Osgood for help in composing one. Because of illness she is unable to assist him (assertion by Griswold [1850], p. xxii).

1 OCTOBER. Laughton Osborn writes Poe, alluding to Poe's new address, 85 Amity Street (*L*, 1:301).

CA. 1 OCTOBER. Copy for *The Raven and Other Poems* is sent to the printer (Mabbott [1942], p. ix).

BEFORE 4 OCTOBER. The *Aristidean* for September contains English's devastating ten-page critique of Henry B. Hirst's *The Coming of the Mammoth*. "Our Book-Shelves," the review section proper, reveals Poe's influence. English echoes Poe's opinions when noticing his *Tales*: "Mr. P. should never have consented to so brief a selection—unless, indeed, he proposes to continue it in a series of similar volumes. . . . Most of the pieces in the present volume, too, are of one kind—analytical. Of his (serious) imaginative tales a class may be said to be represented by 'The House of Usher,' but his numerous extravaganzas and nondescripts (his most characteristic compositions,) are left quite unrepresented."

4 OCTOBER. The *Broadway Journal* contains Poe's revised tale "The Island of the Fay" and his revised poem "Fairy-Land." He favorably reviews William Gilmore Simms's *The Wigwam and the Cabin*, a collection of stories, and Nathan C. Brooks's edition of James Ross's *Latin Grammar*. In noticing the *Aristidean* he observes that English's "scorching review of Hirst's Poems" is "a good thing for everybody but Mr. Hirst," ambiguously pronouncing it "a *very* laughable article." In his "Editorial Miscellany" he reports that the composer Joseph P. Webster has perpetrated "a most vile fraud" by setting English's popular ballad "Ben Bolt" to music and then attempting "to claim the authorship of the words as well as the music." Poe defends Lowell, "one of the noblest of our poets," from an attack by the "ignorant and egotistical" British critic John Wilson in *Blackwood's Magazine* for September. He is delighted that Wiley and Putnam's "Library of American Books" has proven successful: "Even of our own book, [*Tales*,] more than fifteen hundred copies have been sold here."

4 OCTOBER. BUFFALO, NEW YORK. The *Western Literary Messenger* comments: "THE BROADWAY JOURNAL . . . is the most valuable weekly paper which we receive. Why is there no agent in this city?"

4 OCTOBER. LOWELL, MASSACHUSETTS. The *Star of Bethlehem* reprints Poe's "Mesmeric Revelation" with this introduction: "The following extraordinary article was, we believe, originally published in the 'Columbian Magazine.' Whether it is a statement of facts, or merely a development of the writer's system of mental philosophy we know not. Be that as it may it is worthy of a careful perusal. The reader can draw his own conclusions" (Mabbott [1978], 3:1028).

6 OCTOBER. NEW YORK. The *Evening Mirror* carries an editorial headed "POE-LEMICAL" and signed with an asterisk, indicating its author to be Hiram Fuller, the paper's junior editor. Fuller quotes Poe's statement in the last *Broadway Journal* that Simms is "the best novelist which this country

has, upon the whole, produced"; and he then gives his own dissenting opinion:

. . . we are inclined to believe that it is above the power of any single critic—or of all the critics in the country combined, to convince the world that William Gilmore Simms is a better novelist than Cooper, or Brockden Brown. He is certainly less known and read, at home and abroad. We doubt if the copy-right of all Mr. Simms's collected works would bring as good a price in America or England, as the "Norman Leslie" of Fay, or the "Sketch Book" of Irving. But our surprise at Mr. Poe's estimate is somewhat diminished, when, on turning to another article, we find him speaking of our old friend, "Christopher North," as "the *ignorant* and egotistical Wilson"! And adding, that, "with the exception of Macaulay and Dilke, and one or two others, there is not in Great Britain a critic who can be fairly considered worthy the name!" This is indeed, "bearding the lion in his den"; and as Mr. Poe is preparing to publish an edition of his "Tales" in England, (omitting the story of the Gold *Bug*, we suppose,) he can expect but little mercy from the *back*-biting reviews of the Lockharts and Fonblanques, those bull-dogs of the English press.

The article is reprinted in the *Weekly Mirror* for 11 October (asterisk identified as Fuller's signature in the *Evening Mirror*, 31 October).

11 OCTOBER. The *Broadway Journal* contains Poe's revised tales "MS. Found in a Bottle" and "The Duc de L'Omelette." He reviews Amanda M. Edmond's *The Broken Vow and Other Poems*, Caroline Gilman's *Oracles from the Poets*, and William Hazlitt's *Table-Talk*. In his "Editorial Miscellany" he replies to the *Evening Mirror* of 6 October:

Mr. Simms is "better known" than Brockden Brown.

Putting the author of "Norman Leslie" by the side of the author of the "Sketch-Book," is like speaking of "The King and I"—of Pop Emmons and Homer—of a Mastodon and a mouse. If we were asked which was the most ridiculous book ever written upon the face of the earth—we should answer at once, "Norman Leslie."

We are *not* "preparing to publish" our Tales in England; we leave such manoeuvres to those who are in the habit of bowing down to the Golden Calf of the British opinion. Our book, to be sure, *has been* re-published in England—long ago—but we had nothing to do with its re-publication. Should we ever think of such a thing, however, we should undoubtedly give The "Bug" a more prominent position than it even occupies at present. We should call the book "The Gold-Bug and Other Tales"—instead of "Tales," as its title stands.

Poe is curious about the identity of the *Mirror*'s columnist, hidden behind the asterisk.

11 OCTOBER. In the *Evening Mirror* Hiram Fuller replies to Poe:

THE BROADWAY JOURNAL of to-day is down upon us. But we *s are above being troubled at such things; and only wink at the arrows of criticism however sharp or well aimed. . . . The Journal ridicules the idea of our naming the author of "Norman Leslie" on the same page with the author of the "Sketch Book." We did not make any *comparison* between them; but merely ventured a doubt, if the collected works of Mr. Simms . . . would bring as much money as the publishers in this city paid to the author of "Norman Leslie," as his proportion of the profits of the book—viz: $1500—and inferred that Mr. Fay is at least as well known, and as extensively read as Mr. Simms; and estimating books by the *common standard*, taking success as the measure of men, we come to the very natural conclusion that the author of "Norman Leslie," is as good a novelist as the author of "The Wigwam and the Cabin"—the latter being in our opinion a very excellent book.

11 OCTOBER. The *New York Illustrated Magazine*, edited by Lawrence Labree, endorses Poe's rebuke to John Wilson in the *Broadway Journal* of 4 October: "In the September number of Blackwood, we have another ferocious growl from its Editor [Wilson] toward a young American Author [Lowell], which we are happy to see is meeting with a just response. Among others, Mr. Poe, has taken up the gauntlet, and reciprocates his savageisms with proper severity."

11 OCTOBER. DERBY, CONNECTICUT. A correspondent who signs himself "E. S." writes Poe, exonerating Joseph P. Webster from the charge of plagiarism made in the 4 October *Journal*: "The song [English's 'Ben Bolt'] was in a New-Haven paper . . . . It was without signature or reference of any kind, to the author. I was pleased with the poetry, and gave it to Mr. Webster, as he said he would compose some music for it. . . . As Mr. W. did not know the author's name, he could not of course give it. . . . I am certain that no thoughts of claiming the authorship ever crossed his mind; and what may so appear in the publication, is the result of carelessness" (letter published in 25 October *Journal*).

13 OCTOBER. NEW YORK. Briggs writes Lowell in Cambridge, Massachusetts, discussing Poe's criticism of William A. Jones in the 20 September *Journal*:

> You take Poe's *niaiseries* too seriously. I only cared for his unhandsome allusion to me in the B.J. because it proved him a baser man than I thought him before. . . . The truth is that I have not given him the shadow of a cause for ill-feeling; on the contrary he owes me now for money that I lent him to pay his board and keep him from being turned into the street. . . . I did not much blame him for the matter of his remarks about Jones, although the manner of them was exceeding[ly] improper and unjust; the real cause of his ire was Jones' neglecting to enumerate him among the humorous writers of the country, for he has an inconceivably extravagant idea of his capacities as a humorist (Woodberry, 2:146–47).

13 OCTOBER. The *Evening Mirror* reports that Poe is to deliver a poem before the Boston Lyceum on "Thursday evening" [16 October].

15 OCTOBER. On the evening before his Lyceum appearance, Poe reads "the last proofs" of *The Raven and Other Poems* ("Editorial Miscellany," 13 December *Journal*).

BEFORE 16 OCTOBER. Poe makes several attempts to see John P. Kennedy, his early benefactor, who is visiting New York. Failing to see Kennedy, Poe leaves his card. On the day Kennedy receives the card, he calls at the *Broadway Journal* office, where he is informed that Poe is just leaving the city (Poe to Kennedy, 26 October; Kennedy to Poe, 1 December).

16 OCTOBER. BOSTON. The *Daily Times* comments:

BOSTON LYCEUM.—Our readers will not forget that the series of lectures before the Boston Lyceum is to commence this evening. A lecture by Caleb Cushing, and a poem by Edgar A. Poe, will form the introductory exercises; and a full house will testify the public appreciation of these distinguish-ed writers.

We learn that the sale of tickets by the Lyceum has been most encouraging and satisfactory.

Similar editorials appear in the *Boston Courier*, *Daily Atlas*, and *Evening Transcript*.

16 OCTOBER. At 7:30 PM the Lyceum commences its new season of lectures at the Odeon Theatre. Caleb Cushing, a Massachusetts politician and diplomat, delivers a long address on Great Britain. After Cushing's lecture Poe is introduced to the large audience. He occupies "some fifteen minutes with an apology for not 'delivering,' as is usual in such cases, a didactic poem," explaining his belief that poetry cannot be primarily didactic. He then reads his early poem "Al Aaraaf," renamed "The Messenger Star" for this occasion. After the reading, as some members of the audience are beginning to leave, N. W. Coffin, the corresponding secretary of the Lyceum, announces that Poe has been requested to recite "The Raven." Poe concludes the evening's entertainment by reciting this poem. Afterwards he attends a social gathering of the Boston literati. "Over a bottle of champagne" he reveals to Cushing, Edwin P. Whipple, Henry Norman Hudson, James T. Fields, "and a few other natives" that his poem "The Messenger Star" was not a new composition prepared especially for the Lyceum, but a "juvenile poem" (Poe's own account in the *Broadway Journal*, 1 November).

Thomas Wentworth Higginson, a Harvard student in 1845, recalls Poe's poetry reading before the Lyceum:

There was much curiosity to see him [Poe], for his prose-writings had been eagerly read, at least among college students, and his poems were just beginning to excite still greater attention. . . . I distinctly recall his face, with its ample forehead, brilliant eyes, and narrowness of nose and chin; an essentially ideal face, not noble, yet anything but coarse; with the look of oversensitiveness which when uncontrolled may prove more debasing than coarseness. It was a face to rivet one's attention in any crowd; yet a face that no one would feel safe in loving. . . .

I remember that when introduced he stood with a sort of shrinking before the audience and then began in a thin, tremulous, hardly musical voice, an apology for his poem, and a deprecation of the expected criticism of a Boston audience; reiterating this in a sort of persistent, querulous way, which did not seem like satire, but impressed me at the time as nauseous flattery. . . . When, at the end, he abruptly began the recitation of his rather perplexing poem, the audience looked thoroughly mystified. The verses had long since been printed in his youthful volume [*Al Aaraaf, Tamerlane, and Minor Poems* (1829)], and had reappeared within a few days [on 19 November], if I mistake not, in Wiley & Putnam's edition of his poems; and they produced no very distinct impression on the audience until Poe began to read the maiden's song in the second part. Already his tones had been softening to a finer melody than at first, and when he came to the verse:

> Ligeia! Ligeia!
> My beautiful one!
> Whose harshest idea
> Will to melody run,
> O! is it thy will
> On the breezes to toss?
> Or, capriciously still,
> Like the lone Albatross,
> Incumbent on night
> (As she on the air)
> To keep watch with delight
> On the harmony there?

his voice seemed attenuated to the finest golden thread; the audience became hushed, and, as it were, breathless; there seemed no life in the hall but his; and every syllable was accentuated with such delicacy, and sustained with such sweetness as I never heard equaled by other lips. . . . I remember nothing more, except that in walking back to Cambridge my comrades and I felt that we had been under the spell of some wizard (Higginson, p. 89).

17 OCTOBER. The *Daily Evening Traveller* reports that last night's Lyceum exercises were "densely crowded"; it describes Cushing's lecture at length. "After the lecture was concluded, Mr. Poe rose and made a long and prosy preface to an imaginative poem, which, however beautiful in itself, was hardly adapted to the occasion." Poe's poem was, "Tarpeia like, literally *crushed* with ornaments"; and "the greater portion of the audience, being rather fatigued at its close, . . . could not be detained," even by the promise that he would recite "The Raven." The audience "seemed to have had *poetry* enough for one night."

In the *Evening Transcript* the editor Cornelia Wells Walter condemns the Lyceum exercises as "heavy and uninteresting." Cushing's lecture was "one long laudation upon America at the expense of Great Britain." At its conclusion "an officer of the society" introduced Poe:

The poet immediately arose; but, if he uttered poesy in the first instance, it was certainly of a most prosaic order. The audience listened in amazement to a singularly didactic exordium, and finally commenced the noisy expedient of removing from the hall, and this long before they had discovered the style of the measure, or whether it was rhythm or blank verse. We believe, however, it was a prose introductory to a poem on the "Star discovered by Tycho Brahe," considered figuratively as the "Messenger of the Deity," out of which idea Edgar A. Poe had constructed a sentimental and imaginative poem. The audience now thinned so rapidly and made so much commotion in their departure that we lost the beauties of the composition.

18 OCTOBER. In the *Boston Courier* the editor Joseph T. Buckingham comments:

On Thursday evening, Mr. Poe delivered his poem before the Boston Lyceum, to (what we should have conceived, from first appearances) a highly intelligent and respectable audience. He prefaced it with twenty minutes of introductory prose, showing that there existed no such thing as didactic poetry, and that all *real* poetry must proceed and emanate directly from truth, dictated by a pure taste. The poem, called the "Messenger Star," was an elegant and classic production, based on the right principles, containing the essence of *true* poetry, mingled with a gorgeous imagination, exquisite painting, every charm of metre, and a graceful delivery. It strongly reminded us of Mr. Horne's "Orion," and resembled it in the majesty of its design, the nobleness of its incidents, and its freedom from the trammels of productions usual on these occasions. The delicious word-painting of some of its scenes brought vividly to our recollection, Keats' "Eve of St. Agnes," and parts of "Paradise Lost."

That it was not appreciated by the audience, was very evident, by their uneasiness and continual exits in numbers at a time. Common courtesy, we should think, would have suggested to them the politeness of hearing it through, though it should have proved "Heathen Greek" to them; after, too, the author had expressed his doubts of his ability, in preparing a poem for a Boston audience.

In the *Evening Transcript* Miss Walter comments:

A PRODIGY. It has been said by "those who know," that the poem delivered by EDGAR A. POE before the Lyceum, on Thursday evening, was written *before its author was twelve years old*. If the poet felt "doubts of his ability in preparing a poem for a Boston audience" at that early age, it is not to be wondered at that they were openly *expressed* (as a correspondent of a morning paper states) on Thursday evening. A poem delivered before a literary association of adults, as written by *a boy*! Only think of it! Poh! Poh!

The *Transcript* also prints an attack on Poe by a correspondent who signs himself "P," possibly Henry Norman Hudson. Poe's theory that poetry *"has nothing to do with truth*, and is concerned only with beauty," is applicable to his verses alone: "Whether his theory be devised to explain his poetry, or his poetry be written to exemplify his theory, certainly no one will question the intimate correspondence between them. His poetry, accordingly, has neither truth nor falsehood in it; is not chargeable, indeed, with having any ideas whatever; but is simply beautiful. His poem of Thursday evening, *at whatever age it may have been written, and for what purpose soever he may have given it in Boston*, was fully equal to anything we have ever seen from him" (Hudson attribution suggested by Hudson to E. A. Duyckinck, 24 November).

18 OCTOBER. NEW YORK. In the *Evening Mirror* Hiram Fuller reviews *Graham's Magazine* for November, which contains Poe's tale "The System of Dr. Tarr and Prof. Fether." "The leading article . . . belongs to . . . the new school of Poe-lite literature. The scene is laid in a French mad-house, and the characters, of course, are very odd, and very funny. One of them 'thinks himself a pinch of snuff, and is truly distressed because he cannot take himself between his own thumb and finger.' " The review appears in the *Weekly Mirror* for 25 October.

18 OCTOBER. The *Broadway Journal* contains Poe's revised tale "King Pest," signed with the pseudonym "Littleton Barry." He excerpts a long passage from Cornelius Mathews' *Big Abel and the Little Manhattan* "by way of instancing the author's very peculiar style and tone."

BEFORE 19 OCTOBER. PHILADELPHIA. Mrs. Sarah J. Hale, the literary editor of *Godey's Lady's Book*, writes Poe, apparently enclosing her verse romance *Alice Ray* for him to review in the *Broadway Journal*. She asks him whether she should approach the New York publishers Clark and Austin with a collection of her poems she is now preparing (Poe's 26 October reply; 1 November *Journal*).

20 OCTOBER. NEWBURYPORT, MASSACHUSETTS. William W. Caldwell, Jr., writes Poe: "Enclosed are three dollars, entitling me to the honor of being, with your sovereign permission, a subscriber to your very excellent Journal! . . . Will you gratify your friends at the East, by publishing the 'Messenger Star' in the Journal?—The silly abuse of the Boston Press, would then need no other champion—opponent—Like 'Hesper in the glowing west', let it rise pure and clear from out their 'muddy impurities' " (ViRPM).

22 OCTOBER. WASHINGTON. The *United States Journal*, a daily newspaper edited by Theophilus Fisk and Poe's friend Jesse E. Dow, quotes a writer in the Boston *Mercantile Journal*, who gave this unfavorable report on Poe's Lyceum appearance: "The poet, an utter stranger to me, was a phenomena [*sic*] in his way. He delivered a dissertation which he was not invited to deliver before he commenced his poem. The principles of his preliminary discourse were his own, and will never belong to anyone else; and his poem was a tangled tissue of bright words and confused imagery. It seems to me that this production must have been an infantile effort of his, and that he brought it to Boston to see how far the patience of our citizens could be tried" (Chivers [1957], p. 60).

BEFORE 24 OCTOBER? NEW YORK. Horace Greeley, editor of the *Daily Tribune*, loans Poe $50 in cash, apparently to be applied toward the purchase of the *Broadway Journal*. Poe gives Greeley his "note of hand" for this sum (Greeley, pp. 196–97).

24 OCTOBER. Poe acquires John Bisco's share of the *Broadway Journal*. The two men sign a contract: "Edgar A. Poe agrees to pay the said Bisco Fifty Dollars in cash on Signing agreement, to give the said Bisco his note at three months for the full amount of debts due the paper" (Quinn, pp. 752–53).

Poe signs a promissory note for $100, payable to Bisco three months from this date (Moldenhauer [1973], p. 80).

Horace Greeley signs a promissory note: "Sixty days after date I promise to pay Edgar A. Poe, or his order, Fifty dollars for value received" (Phillips, 2:1063–64).

25 OCTOBER. The masthead of the *Broadway Journal* identifies Poe as "EDITOR AND PROPRIETOR." This issue contains his stories "The Thousand-and-Second Tale of Scheherazade" and "The Power of Words" (reprints), as well as his favorable review of Mary E. Hewitt's *The Songs of Our Land, and Other Poems*. In his "Editorial Miscellany" he announces that he has assumed "sole control" of the *Journal*: "May we hope for the support of our friends?" He alludes to his Lyceum appearance: "We have been quizzing the Bostonians, and one or two of the more stupid of their editors and editresses have taken it in high dudgeon. We will attend to them all in good time."

26 OCTOBER. In the *Sunday Times and Messenger* Mordecai M. Noah reports Poe's Lyceum appearance, quoting the favorable description of his poem from the *Boston Courier* of 18 October. "And yet the papers abused him,

and the audience were fidgety—made their exit one by one, and did not at all appreciate the efforts of a man of admitted ability, whom they had invited to deliver a poem before them. . . . We presume Mr. Poe will not accept another invitation to recite poetry, original or selected, in that section of the Union."

26 OCTOBER. Poe writes Mrs. Hale in Philadelphia, replying to a letter written before 19 October: "I have been a week absent from the city, and have been overwhelmed with business since my return—may I beg you, therefore, to pardon my seeming discourtesy in not sooner thanking you for your sweet poem, and for the high honor you confer on me in the matter of your proposed volume? . . . I *have* some acquaintance with Mess. Clark and Austin, and believe that you will find them, as publishers, every thing that you could wish" (*L*, 1:298–99).

26 OCTOBER. Poe writes Rufus W. Griswold in Philadelphia: "After a prodigious deal of manoeuvring, I have succeeded in getting the 'Broadway Journal' entirely within my own control. It will be a fortune to me if I can hold it—and I can do it easily with a very trifling aid from my friends. May I count you as one? Lend me $50 and you shall never have cause to regret it" (*L*, 1:298).

26 OCTOBER. Poe writes John P. Kennedy in Baltimore: "When you were in New-York I made frequent endeavours to meet you—but in vain—as I was forced to go to Boston." Recalling that Kennedy assisted him at the outset of his career, Poe again asks for help: "I have succeeded in getting rid, one by one, of all my associates in 'The Broadway Journal' . . . . I have exhausted all my immediate resources in the purchase—and I now write to ask you for a small loan—say $50" (*L*, 1:299–300).

28 OCTOBER. BOSTON. In the *Evening Transcript* Cornelia Wells Walter scoffs at Poe's remarks in the last *Broadway Journal*. Quoting his promise to "attend to" the Boston "editors and editresses," she observes: "The promise . . . is certainly very poe-tential. We thought the poet might possibly be *poe-dagrical*, but it seems he is intending to take time enough to become a poe-ser!" Noticing his call for "the support" of his friends, she obliquely alludes to his drinking: "What a question to ask! Edgar A. Poe to be in a condition to require *support*! It is indeed remarkable."

29 OCTOBER. Miss Walter again mocks Poe: "We showed our readers yesterday that the editor of the Broadway Journal called his childish effort for the amusement of the members of the Lyceum a '*quizz*' upon the Bostonians. If it were so, we say like honest Sancho—God bless the giver

nor look the gift horse in the mouth. We would gently hint, however, to the editor of the Broadway Journal, that while he is perfectly at liberty to think he has quizzed the Bostonians, the quizzer sometimes turns out to be the *quizzee*."

29 OCTOBER. SAINT LOUIS. The *Daily Reveille* reports: "The Boston papers are rather down upon Poe—a little bit of retaliation, perhaps." The *Reveille* quotes the *Boston Courier* of 18 October, which had observed that the Lyceum audience should have been polite enough to hear Poe's poem to its end, even if they found it "Heathen Greek" (Moss [1968], p. 19).

30 OCTOBER. OAKY GROVE, GEORGIA. Thomas Holley Chivers writes Poe, complaining that his correspondent has not written him: "You are in arrears two or three letters at least." The *United States Journal* of 22 October contains "a mean notice" of the poem Poe delivered in Boston; Chivers wonders about Poe's friendship with this Washington paper's co-editor, Jesse E. Dow: "No man can be the friend of another who would give publicity to any such foul slander." If Poe will forward a copy of his poem, Chivers "will give it a handsome notice here in the South." Having sent Poe, on 9 September, $5 of the $50 he requested in his 11 August letter, Chivers now promises him: "I will send the money you spoke of soon—$45.00" (Chivers [1957], pp. 58–61).

30 OCTOBER. BOSTON. In the *Evening Transcript* Miss Walter comments: "In 'E. A. Poe's Poems,' *second edition*, published in New York in 1831, is the entire poem recently delivered before the Lyceum of this city, and for the attempt of speaking before which association, the author made an apology as regards his *capacity*. This *capacity*, it seems, has been deteriorating since Mr Poe was ten years of age, his best poems having been written before that period."

31 OCTOBER. Miss Walter publishes a letter she has received:

MR EDITOR: It seems that Mr Edgar A. Poe is claiming for his *poe*tical soul, the flattering unction that a Gotham Editor has at last succeeded in "quizzing the Bostonians." It must be confessed that he did *out-Yankee* the managers of the Lyceum since he not only emptied their pockets but emptied the house. Still the thing was worth all its cost, since several "*jeu d'esprits*" were founded upon the results of his antic gallopings around Mount Parnassus. So curious a Pegasus as his, disturbed even the equilibrium of one of our grave jurists who relieved himself in this wise. The departing audience was fast making manifest a beggarly display of empty boxes when "*His Honor*" turning to a professional brother sitting near, remarked, that he "could not judge of the merit of the speaker's poetry as it was above his comprehension, but it must be confessed that his *numbers were*

THOMAS HOLLEY CHIVERS

flowing." How soon may we hope that the whole scene will be dramatized for the Olympic? A QUIZZEE.

LATE OCTOBER? NEW YORK. Poe writes Mrs. Osgood, thanking her for her "kind and altogether delightful note" and for her poem: "Business, of late, has made of me so great a slave that I shall not be able to spend an evening with you until Thursday next" (*L*, 1:300).

NOVEMBER OR BEFORE. Walker & Co. issue the *Missionary Memorial* for 1846, containing Poe's revised poem "The Lake" (annual noticed in the *Broadway Journal*, 15 November).

NOVEMBER OR BEFORE. LONDON? George P. Putnam, a partner in Wiley and Putnam, gives a copy of Poe's *Tales* to Martin Farquhar Tupper, whose popular *Proverbial Philosophy* has been selected for this firm's "Library of Choice Reading." Tupper writes Putnam, proposing to review the *Tales*: "Shall we make Edgar Poe famous by a notice in the Literary Gazette?" (Putnam, pp. 470–71; cf. Tupper's 25 November and 23 December letters).

NOVEMBER. PARIS. The *Revue britannique* publishes "Le Scarabée d'or" ["The Gold-Bug"], the first literal translation of a Poe story into a foreign language. Poe is identified as the original author; the French text is signed with the initials "A. B.," standing for "Alphonse Borghers," apparently a pseudonym used by Amédée Pichot, the *Revue*'s editor (Bandy [1964], pp. 277–80).

NOVEMBER. PHILADELPHIA. *Godey's Lady's Book* contains Poe's favorable review of Cornelius Mathews' novel *Big Abel and the Little Manhattan*, an expansion of his notice in the 27 September *Broadway Journal*.

NOVEMBER. In its "Monthly Literary Bulletin" the *Democratic Review* reports: "Messrs. Wiley and Putnam's Series of American Books will shortly include . . . Mr. Poe's volume, 'The Raven and other Poems,' including 'Poems of Youth,' No. VIII."

CA. NOVEMBER [1845?]. Richard Henry Stoddard passes Poe in the streets: "The last time that I remember to have seen him [Poe] was in the afternoon of a dreary autumn day. A heavy shower had come up suddenly, and he was standing under an awning. I had an umbrella, and my impulse was to share it with him on his way home, but something—certainly not unkindness—withheld me. I went on and left him there in the rain, pale, shivering, miserable . . . . There I still see him, and always shall,—poor, penniless, but proud, reliant, dominant" (Stoddard [1903], p. 151).

1 NOVEMBER. The *Broadway Journal* contains Poe's tale "Some Words with a Mummy" (reprint) and his favorable review of Mrs. Sarah J. Hale's *Alice Ray*. In the "Editorial Miscellany" he reprints the account of his Lyceum appearance from Noah's *Sunday Times and Messenger* of 26 October. He complains: "Our excellent friend Major Noah has suffered himself to be cajoled by that most beguiling of all beguiling little divinities, Miss Walters [Walter], of 'The Transcript.' . . . The adorable creature has been telling a parcel of fibs about us, by way of revenge for something that we did to Mr. Longfellow (who admires her very much) and for calling her 'a pretty little witch' into the bargain." Poe gives his version of events, stressing that his appearance was actually a success. He was "most cordially received" when introduced to the audience, and his reading of "Al Aaraaf" was punctuated "with many interruptions of applause." "When we had made an end, the audience, of course, arose to depart—and about one-tenth of them, probably, had really departed, when Mr. Coffin, one of the managing committee, arrested those who remained, by the announcement that we had been requested to deliver 'The Raven.' " Poe's recitation of this poem was "very cordially applauded again—and this was the end of it."

1 NOVEMBER. OAKY GROVE, GEORGIA. Chivers writes his friend Herschel V. Johnson in Milledgeville, Georgia. He has submitted a manuscript play in five acts to "Mr Poe, one of the greatest men that ever lived." Two poems collected in his volume *The Lost Pleiad*, "To Isa Singing" and "The Heavenly Vision," have been "selected by Mr Poe in his recitations, while lecturing on Poetry" (Chivers [1957], pp. 61–65; cf. Chivers to Poe, after 2 August).

4 NOVEMBER. BOSTON. The *Evening Transcript* reprints Poe's account of his Lyceum appearance from Saturday's *Broadway Journal*, preceded by Miss Walter's rejoinder: "The editor of the Journal probably found himself in a po-kerish po-sition when he took his pen to commence the annexed article. He determined to do the thing magnanimously however, and if he had but sent a copy of the following to the managers of the Lyceum enclosing the fifty dollars which he *poke*d out of them for his *childish* effort in versification, he would have exhibited the only proof now wanting of his excessive *po*-liteness."

5 NOVEMBER. The *Daily Star* reprints Poe's "Al Aaraaf" from the 1831 edition of his *Poems* (Mabbott [1969], 1:559).

BEFORE 8 NOVEMBER. NEW YORK. The *Aristidean* for October contains a long critique of Poe's *Tales* by the editor Thomas Dunn English, who repeats some things Poe has told him. "The Gold-Bug," the first story in the volume, was "circulated to a greater extent than any American tale, before or since. . . . Perhaps it is the most *ingenious* story Mr. POE has written; but in the higher attributes—a great invention—an invention proper—it is not at all comparable to the 'Tell-tale Heart'—and more especially to 'Ligeia,' the most extraordinary, of its kind, of his productions." The third story, "Mesmeric Revelation," has "excited much discussion. A large number of the mesmerists, queerly enough, take it all for gospel. Some of the Swedenborgians, at PHILADELPHIA, wrote word to POE, that at first they doubted, but in the end became convinced, of its truth. . . . It is evidently meant to be nothing more than the vehicle of the author's views concerning the DEITY, immateriality, spirit, &c., which he apparently believes to be true, in which belief he is joined by Professor [George] BUSH." Among "literary people" the most popular tale seems to be "The Fall of the House of Usher," which depicts "the revulsion of feeling consequent upon discovering that for a long period of time we have been mistaking sounds of agony, for those of mirth or indifference." The poem introduced in this story, "The Haunted Palace," was "originally sent to [John L.] O'SULLIVAN, of the 'Democratic Review,' and by him rejected, because 'he found it impossible to comprehend it.' "

The *Aristidean* also carries English's hoax "The American Poets." He explains that he "addressed notes to various of our poets," requesting them to furnish poems, "without charge," for the magazine; he then prints farcical letters of reply and absurd poems said to have been written by Bryant, Longfellow, and others. Poe's "contribution" is entitled "The Mammoth Squash."

8 NOVEMBER. The *Broadway Journal* contains Poe's revised tale "The Devil in the Belfry." He favorably reviews Freeman Hunt's *Merchants' Magazine* for November; he briefly notices the publication of the October *Aristidean*. He complains: "*The Knickerbocker Magazine*, for November, is really beneath notice and beneath contempt. . . . We should regret, for the sake of New York literature, that a journal of this kind should perish, and through sheer imbecility on the part of its conductors."

[In the November *Knickerbocker* Lewis Gaylord Clark had condemned Cornelius Mathews' *Big Abel and the Little Manhattan*, published in Wiley and Putnam's "Library of American Books." Privately Poe also held a low opinion of Mathews' writings; but since he was indebted to Mathews' friend and admirer Evert A. Duyckinck, he was obliged to reply to Clark's attack. Duyckinck published his own protests against Clark in the 7 November *Evening Mirror* (reprinted 15 November *Weekly Mirror*) and in the 8 November *Morning News*. See W. G. Simms to Duyckinck, 13 November, and the 15 November *Broadway Journal*.]

9 NOVEMBER. SAINT LOUIS. The *Daily Reveille* reprints this report from another paper: " 'The *Broadway Journal* is edited and owned solely by Mr. Edgar A. Poe. If he had as much tact as talent, he would make success for half a dozen papers.' " The *Reveille* observes: "Poe, reliant upon his talent, has too much contempt for tact; he is wrong, but his error makes his career the more remarkable. He is full of eccentricity." Quoting Poe's statement that he has been "quizzing the Bostonians" from the 25 October *Journal*, the *Reveille* asks: "Does he mean . . . that his late Boston poem, was intended by him as a *hoax?*" (Moss [1968], p. 19).

10 NOVEMBER. CHARLESTON, SOUTH CAROLINA. In the *Southern Patriot* William Gilmore Simms comments on Poe's Lyceum appearance:

As a Poet, Mr. Poe's imagination becomes remarkably conspicuous . . . . He seems to dislike the merely practical, and to shrink from the concrete. His fancy takes the ascendant in his Poetry, and wings his thoughts to such superior elevations, as to render it too intensely spiritual for the ordinary reader. With a genius thus endowed and constituted, it was a blunder with Mr. Poe to accept the appointment, which called him to deliver himself in poetry before the Boston Lyceum. Highly imaginative men can scarcely succeed in such exhibitions. The sort of poetry called for on such occasions, is the very reverse of the spiritual, the fanciful or the metaphysical. To win the ears of a mixed audience, nothing more is required than moral or patriotic commonplaces in rhyming heroics. . . . In obeying this call, to Boston, Mr. Poe committed another mistake. He had been mercilessly exercising himself as a critic at the expense of some of their favorite writers. The swans of New-England, under his delineation, had been described as mere geese, and those too of none of the whitest. He had been exposing the shortcomings and the plagiarisms of Mr. Longfellow, who is supposed, along the banks of the Penobscot, to be about the comeliest bird that ever dipped his bill in Pieria. . . . It is positively amusing to see how eagerly all the little witlings of the press, in the old purlieus of the Puritan, flourish the critical tomahawk about the head of their critic. In their eagerness for retribution, one of the newspapers before us actually congratulates itself and readers, on the (asserted) failure of the poet. The good Editor himself was not present, but he hammers away not the less lustily at the victim, because his objections are to be made at second hand.

10 NOVEMBER. NEW YORK. Mary E. Hewitt writes Poe, thanking him for his "very, very kind and encouraging notice" of her *Songs of Our Land* in his paper for 25 October: "The Broadway Journal was the Scylla and Charybdis of my fear, and its editor's criticism more to be dreaded than that of fifty Blackwoods. Judge then of the measure and quality of my delight on finding that I had passed the strait in safety!" Mrs. Hewitt encloses "a little song" for possible publication in the *Journal* (Mabbott [1937], p. 119).

12 NOVEMBER. Wiley and Putnam deposit a complete copy of *The Raven*

and Other Poems, for copyright, in the Clerk's Office of the United States District Court, Southern District of New York State (Mabbott [1942], p. xi).

12 NOVEMBER. Laughton Osborn writes Poe at 85 Amity Street: "The copy of translated sonnets from certain old & little known Ital. poets which I did myself the honor to send you some time since in accordance with my promise, were intended, by their publication in yr. 'Journal', not to benefit myself, (quite the contrary,) but to be of service to you in the irksome part of yr. labors as an editor. As several weeks have elapsed without my rec[eivin]g. any intimation of their being in type, I am forced to conclude that they are not so important as my vanity had led me to believe, & I must therefore be permitted to solicit their return" (copy by T. O. Mabbott, MB–G).

13 NOVEMBER. Poe writes Evert A. Duyckinck: "I seem to have just awakened from some horrible dream, in which all was confusion, and suffering—relieved only by the constant sense of your kindness, and that of one or two other considerate friends." Most of Poe's troubles will disappear once the *Broadway Journal* is firmly established. As Wiley and Putnam's editor, Duyckinck can help him: "Of course I need not say to you that my most urgent trouble is the want of ready money. . . . I have already drawn from Mr [John] Wiley, first $30—then 10 (from yourself)—then 50 (on account of the 'Parnassus')—then 20 (when I went to Boston)—and finally 25—in all 135. Mr Wiley owes me, for the Poems, 75, and admitting that 1500 of the Tales have been sold, and that I am to receive 8 cts a copy—the amount which you named, if I remember—admitting this, he will owe me $120 on them:—in all 195. Deducting what I have received there is a balance of 60 in my favor." Although Poe understands that Wiley had planned to settle with him in February, he urges Duyckinck to obtain an immediate payment: "So dreadfully am I pressed, that I would willingly take even the $60 actually due, (in lieu of all farther demand) than wait" (*L*, 1:300–301).

13 NOVEMBER. WOODLANDS, SOUTH CAROLINA. William Gilmore Simms writes Duyckinck in New York. He has read the protests against Lewis Gaylord Clark's review of Cornelius Mathews that Duyckinck inserted in the 7 November *Evening Mirror* and the 8 November *Morning News*: "No doubt you should long ago have silenced or crushed the miserable reptile in question [Clark]. . . . But you have erred in making his assault upon Mathews the particular text. You should have anticipated that assault, and had you all turned in & hammered him when Poe began the game, you would have timed it rightly" (Simms, 2:116–19; cf. Poe's initial attack on Clark in the *Broadway Journal*, 12 July).

13 NOVEMBER. BOSTON. In the *Evening Transcript* Cornelia Wells Walter quotes George D. Prentice, editor of the Louisville, Kentucky, *Daily Journal*:

"HOW HE IS CATCHING IT." The Louisville Journal says: "Mr Edgar A. Poe, of the New York Broadway Journal, recently delivered a poem by invitation, before the Boston Lyceum. The Boston papers spoke of it as a miserable production, and Poe tries to take his revenge by saying that he meant it as a hoax on the people of Boston. We think there is precious little of Poe's rhyme or prose that wouldn't pass better as a hoax, than as anything else."

14 NOVEMBER. PHILADELPHIA. Mrs. Sarah J. Hale writes Poe, apparently forwarding copies of her drama "Ormond Grosvenor" and her verse romance "Harry Guy." She asks his advice about finding a publisher for these works (Poe's reply, 16 January 1846).

BEFORE 15 NOVEMBER. BOSTON. In the *New England Washingtonian*, a temperance journal, the editor Edmund Burke condemns Poe's Lyceum appearance, wrongfully intimating that he was drunk on stage: "he [Poe] should bow down his head with shame at the thought that he, in this day of light, presented himself before a moral and intelligent audience *intoxicated*! and that he made himself afterwards, in another public place, a living testimony to the fact that the man of talents, when drunk, is no more than a *fool*."

15 NOVEMBER. NEW YORK. The *Crystal Fount and Rechabite Recorder* quotes Burke's remarks, observing: "That lets the cat out of the bag, and if Mr. Poe says any thing about Boston after that, we shall put him down as a little more than green" (Pollin [1972c], pp. 124–26).

15 NOVEMBER. The *Broadway Journal* contains Poe's favorable reviews of C. Edwards Lester's *The Artist, the Merchant, and the Statesman* and Charles Lamb's *Specimens of English Dramatic Poets*. In a front-page editorial headed "A New Mode of Collecting a Library," Poe attacks Lewis Gaylord Clark: "The *Knickerbocker Magazine* has received a severe rebuke from the city press, during the last week, for some peculiarities in its general conduct, and especially for the spirit and letter of an article in the last number, upon MR. MATHEWS. . . . Of what literary or social offences has he been guilty, that he should be pilloried in the small print and pelted with the pleasant missives of the 'Editor's Table'?" Poe relates an anecdote about a subscriber to the *Knickerbocker* who builds "one of the best libraries in town" by buying the books Clark condemns.

15 NOVEMBER. Poe writes Thomas Holley Chivers in Oaky Grove, Geor-

gia, replying to his 30 October letter. He apologizes for his failure to correspond: "The Broadway Journals I now send, will give you some idea of the reason. I have been buying out the paper, and of course you must be aware that I have had a tough time of it—making all kind of maneuvres . . . . I have succeeded, however, as you see—bought it out entirely, and *paid for it all*, with the exception of 140$ which will fall due on the lrst of January next. . . . If you *can* send me the $45, for Heaven's sake do it, *by return of mail*—or if not all, a part." Poe wishes he could explain his "hopes & prospects," but he has not time: "I have to do *everything* myself edit the paper—get it to press—and attend to the multitudinous *business* besides. . . . the moments I now spend in penning these words are gold themselves—& more." He is sending Chivers an advance copy of *The Raven and Other Poems* (*L*, 1:302–03).

15 NOVEMBER. BOSTON. *Littell's Living Age* reprints the review of Poe's *Tales* from the London *Critic* of 6 September.

AFTER 15? NOVEMBER. NEW YORK. Poe visits Thomas Dunn English's chambers and asks his advice on the *Broadway Journal*, which is "fast decreasing in circulation." English suggests that Poe go into partnership with Thomas H. Lane, the publisher of the *Aristidean*. Poe and Lane agree to an arrangement which allows Poe to remain the *Journal's* sole editor while Lane assumes responsibility for its financial management. The office is moved from 135 Nassau Street to 304 Broadway, corner of Duane Street, in the building housing English's chambers and the *Aristidean* (English, p. 1382).

[The removal of the *Journal* office was mentioned in its 22 November issue and formally announced in its 29 November issue.]

19 NOVEMBER. Wiley and Putnam issue *The Raven and Other Poems*, a small volume with stiff paper covers. It contains this dedication: "TO THE NOBLEST OF HER SEX— / TO THE AUTHOR OF / 'THE DRAMA OF EXILE'— / TO MISS ELIZABETH BARRETT BARRETT, / OF ENGLAND, / I DEDICATE THIS VOLUME, / WITH THE MOST ENTHUSIASTIC ADMIRATION / AND WITH THE MOST SINCERE ESTEEM. / E. A. P." Poe's preface is self-deprecatory:

These trifles are collected and republished chiefly with a view to their redemption from the many improvements to which they have been subjected while going at random "the rounds of the press." If what I have written is to circulate at all, I am naturally anxious that it should circulate as I wrote it. In defence of my own taste, nevertheless, it is incumbent upon me to say, that I think nothing in this volume of much value to the public, or very creditable to myself. Events not to be controlled have prevented me from making, at any time, any serious effort in what, under happier circumstances, would have been the field of my choice. With me poetry has been not a purpose, but a passion; and the passions should be held in reverence; they must not—they cannot at will be excited with an eye to the paltry compensations, or the more paltry commendations, of mankind.

19 NOVEMBER. The *Daily Tribune* carries an advertisement for Wiley and Putnam's "Library of American Books," with the heading "THIS DAY IS PUBLISHED":

No. 8—The Raven, and other Poems: By Edgar A. Poe. 1 vol. Beautifully printed. 31 cents.
Contents—The Raven; The Valley of Unrest; Bridal Ballad; The Sleeper; The Coliseum; Lenore; Catholic Hymn; Israfel; Dream Land; Sonnet to Zante; The City in the Sea; To One in Paradise; Eulalie, A Song; The Conqueror Worm; The Haunted Palace; Scenes from Politian; Poems written in Youth. Published and for sale by WILEY & PUTNAM, 161 Broadway.

AFTER 19 NOVEMBER? Poe gives a presentation copy of *The Raven and Other Poems* to John Bisco (copy in NN–B).

21 NOVEMBER. In the *Evening Mirror* George P. Morris reviews *The Raven and Other Poems*: "In spite of Mr. Poe's majestic disclaimer of any great interest in this book, we must venture to think it contains a good deal of that which we call poetry—an element too *rare* in these days of frigid verse-making to be treated with disregard." He describes the effect of Poe's poems on the reader:

Tall shadows and a sighing silence seem to close around us as we read. We feel dream land to be more real and more touching than the actual life we have left . . . . The Raven, for instance, which we have been surprised to hear called, in spite of its exquisite versification, somewhat aimless and unsatisfactory, leaves with us no such impression; but on the contrary, the shadowy and indistinct implied resemblance of the material and immaterial throughout, gives an indescribable charm to the poem . . . . The reader who cannot feel some of the poet's "fantastic terrors," hear the "whisper'd word, LENORE," perceive the air grow denser "per-fum'd from an unseen censer," and at least catch some dim vanishing glimpse of the deathly beauty of "The rare and radiant maiden" mourned so agonizingly, can have pondered but little over those "quaint and curious volumes of forgotten lore" which so well introduce this "stately raven of the saintly days of yore." We recommend to him a year's regimen of monkish legends, and chronicles with which Warton and Scott fed the poetic fire . . . .
The ballad of Lenore is in the same tone—a wild wail, melancholy, as the sound of the clarion to the captive knight who knew that its departing tones bore with them his last earthly hope. "Mariana" [by Tennyson] is not more intensely mournful. The *"peccavimus,"* the passing bell, the hair natural and life-like above *closed* eyes hollow with the death-change—leave pictures and echoes within the heart, which allows no doubt as to the power of the poet.

The review is reprinted in the *Weekly Mirror* for 29 November.

22 NOVEMBER. The *Anglo-American* and the *Morning Courier* review *The Raven and Other Poems*. The *Anglo-American* complains that the juvenile poems of an established author should not be circulated; the *Courier* praises Poe's imagination and versification (Pollin [1980], p. 26).

22 NOVEMBER. The *Broadway Journal* contains Poe's revised tale "The Spectacles" and Mrs. Osgood's poem "To——," apparently addressed to him ("Oh! they never can know that heart of thine, / Who dare accuse *thee* of flirtation!"). Because of "the bustle consequent upon removing our office," this issue has no reviews, only "a mere announcement of the books on hand," one of which is *The Raven and Other Poems*. In the "Editorial Miscellany" Poe reprints Simms's account of his Lyceum appearance from the Charleston *Southern Patriot* of 10 November, observing that "our friends in the Southern and Western country (*true* friends, and *tried*,) are taking up arms in our cause." He quotes the Saint Louis *Daily Reveille* of 9 November, which had inquired whether his Lyceum poem was intended as a hoax. He explains: "We knew very well that, among a certain *clique* of the Frogpondians [Bostonians], there existed a predetermination to abuse us under *any* circumstances. . . . It would have been very weak in us, then, to put ourselves to the trouble of attempting to please these people. . . . We read before them a 'juvenile'—a *very* 'juvenile' poem—and thus the Frogpondians were *had*—were delivered up to the enemy bound hand and foot." Poe has been told "that as many as three or four of the personal friends of the little old lady entitled Miss Walters [Walter], did actually leave the hall during the recitation"; but he did not see them depart: "they belong to a class of people that we make it a point *never to see*." Miss Walter "defends our poem on the ground of its being 'juvenile,' and we think the more of her defence because she herself has been juvenile so long as to be a judge of juvenility. Well, upon the whole we must forgive her—and do. Say no more about it, you little darling!"

22 NOVEMBER. In the *Evening Mirror* Hiram Fuller comments: "The Broadway Journal of to-day contains a long tale, by the editor, a long attack by the editor, and a long defence *of* the editor—each excellent *of its kind*!" The *Weekly Mirror* reprints English's hoax "The American Poets" from the *Aristidean* for October.

22 NOVEMBER. BALTIMORE. In the *Saturday Visiter* Joseph Evans Snodgrass reports that *The Raven and Other Poems* is available from "TAYLOR, WILDE & CO. . . . at their new establishment, next door, . . . for thirty one cts." The first poem, "The Raven," is by itself "worth the cost of the book."

24 NOVEMBER. BOSTON. Henry Norman Hudson writes Evert A. Duyck-inck in New York:

> I write you this at the suggestion of some of Mr. Poe's friends in this city, who are shocked and alarmed at his late remarks on Miss Walter. I do not recollect ever to have seen anything so mean, and dirty, and wicked, as his last paper. Miss Walter is one of the most respectable young ladies in Boston; and her paper circulates among the very best people of the place; is, indeed, *the* family newspaper of the city. Said one of the best friends Mr. Poe has in Boston, "the course he is taking is perfectly damnable, and, if persisted in, will inevitably damn him and everybody that has any connection with him. He may call the rest of us what he pleases; fools, frogpondians, hypocrites, or anything; but such grossly brutal treatment of a lady, there is not a man in the United States but had better be in his grave, than be guilty of it." Such are substantially the remarks Mr. [Edwin P.] Whipple made to me; and I trust I need not say, I entirely agree with him. Can you not, Mr. Poe's friend and adviser, dissuade him from this vile blackguardism? . . . So far as the remarks on Mr. Poe in the Transcript, the most offensive of them were not written by Miss Walter but by myself. The truth is, I did think, and still think, that Mr. Poe's conduct here, whatever may have been its merit as a hoax, was utterly beneath the dignity of a gentleman; a disgrace to the name of literature (NN–D).

25 NOVEMBER. ALBURY, GUILDFORD, ENGLAND. Martin Farquhar Tupper writes William Jerdan, editor of the London *Literary Gazette*, enclosing a review of Poe's *Tales*: "I volunteer a critique for your Gazette: the book is worth all I say of it: if you find the extracts too long, you can shorten them; but perhaps you will find room for all. I have no other cause to serve in this bit of 'offered service' (you know the adage) except to give a foreign genius some encouragement amongst us Britishers . . . . How say you? shall we, or shall we not, make Edgar A. Poe, famous?" (PP–G).

25 NOVEMBER. NEW YORK. The *Evening Mirror* reprints the review of Poe's *Tales* from the London *Critic* of 6 September. The review appears in the *Weekly Mirror* for 6 December.

26 NOVEMBER. The *Daily Tribune* contains Margaret Fuller's long critique of *The Raven and Other Poems*. She quotes from Poe's preface his assertion that he has no high regard for these poems; she is inclined to believe him, because "the productions in this volume indicate a power to do something far better. With the exception of The Raven, which seems intended chiefly to show the writer's artistic skill, and is in its way a rare and finished specimen, they are all fragments—*fyttes* upon the lyre, almost all of which leave us something to desire or demand." Fuller reprints "To One in Paradise," observing that Poe's poems "breathe a passionate sadness, re-lieved sometimes by touches very lovely and tender . . . . This kind of

beauty is especially conspicuous, then rising into dignity, in the poem called 'The Haunted Palace.' " His imagination expresses itself "in a sweep of images, thronging and distant like a procession of moonlight clouds on the horizon, but like them characteristic and harmonious one with another, according to their office. The descriptive power is greatest when it takes a shape not unlike an incantation, as in the first part of 'The Sleeper.' " Fuller understands that the "Poems Written in Youth" were composed "before the author was ten years old"; as such they represent "a great psychological curiosity. Is it the delirium of a prematurely excited brain that causes such a rapture of words?" She concludes by reprinting "Israfel." Her review appears in the *Weekly Tribune* for 29 November.

26 NOVEMBER. PHILADELPHIA. The *North American* reviews *The Raven and Other Poems*, welcoming a collection of Poe's poetry, but objecting to the inclusion of his juvenilia. "The Raven," "Lenore," and a few other poems will endure (Pollin [1980], p. 27).

BEFORE 27 NOVEMBER. *Godey's Lady's Book* for December contains Poe's expanded critique of *The Poetical Writings of Mrs. Elizabeth Oakes Smith*, which he had initially reviewed in the *Broadway Journal* for 23 August. In its "Editors' Book Table" *Godey's* notices "Nos. 2, 3, 4, and 5" of Wiley and Putnam's "Library of American Books":

No. 2 is a collection of "*Tales*," by Edgar A. Poe. Our readers know him to be one of the most accomplished authors in America. In England he is ranked among the classic writers of the mother tongue. In his narrative pieces he exhibits qualities of mind deemed incompatible with each other—such as a talent for profound analysis, and a most brilliant fancy—a power of rigidly minute and exact detail in description, like testimony on oath; and, contrasted with this, a skill in the "building" of marvelous and grotesque stories, which make the Arabian Tales seem tame and prosaic in comparison. We like a writer of this character and calibre. We are tired of being merely *satisfied*; and we like occasionally to be *astonished*. Talent and learning can satisfy. It takes genius to astonish. This Poe possesses, and he has exhibited some of its most decisive proofs in the volume before us.

27 NOVEMBER. NEW YORK. In the *Evening Mirror* Hiram Fuller reprints the notice of Poe's *Tales* from *Godey's*, appending a squib aimed at the reviewer: "We *are* astonished that the Arabian Tales should seem 'tame and prosaic in comparison' with Poe's 'grotesque and arabesque'—therefore, the writer of the above paragraph must be a genius. 'It takes genius to astonish.' "

27 NOVEMBER. The *New-York Evangelist*, a religious newspaper, reviews *The Raven and Other Poems*: "There is great diversity of opinion respecting

Mr. Poe's poetry—more so than respecting his talents as a prose writer, or temper as a critic. But the reader of the Raven will never deny him originality and great power both of thought and versification. It is an extraordinary performance, and of itself is enough to establish the author's reputation as a poet. The other poems are various in subject and merit; but usually evince great skill in versification. And if obscurity is the test, uncommon originality. The collection of these poems is a public favor and we doubt not it will be popular" (Mabbott [1942], p. xv).

28 NOVEMBER. In the *Evening Mirror* George P. Morris quotes Poe's statement in the preface to *The Raven and Other Poems* that for him "poetry has been not a purpose, but a passion." For Morris this assertion represents the "sentiments of a true poet. . . . We like the spirit that dictated it."

28 NOVEMBER. LONDON. Elizabeth Barrett Barrett writes Robert Browning at New Cross, Hatcham, Surrey: "And think of Mr. Poe, with that great Roman justice of his, (if not rather American!), dedicating a book to one & abusing one in the preface of the same. He wrote a review of me in just that spirit—the two extremes of laudation & reprehension, folded in on one another—You would have thought that it had been written by a friend & foe, each stark mad with love & hate, & writing the alternate paragraphs—a most curious production indeed" (Browning [1969], 1:296–99).

[Miss Barrett is not mentioned in Poe's preface to *The Raven and Other Poems*: conceivably, she may have seen an earlier version of the preface which was not published; but it seems more likely that she was misinformed.]

29 NOVEMBER. The *Popular Record of Modern Science* reprints "Mesmeric Revelation" under the heading "The Last Conversation of a Somnambule." The editor of this London weekly prefaces the tale with his verification: "The following is an article communicated to the Columbian Magazine, a journal of respectability and influence in the United States, by Mr. Edgar A. Poe. It bears internal evidence of authenticity" (Mabbott [1978], 3:1028; *Record* quoted by Poe in "Marginalia," *Graham's Magazine*, March 1848).

29 NOVEMBER. NEW YORK. The *Broadway Journal* contains Poe's revised story "A Tale of the Ragged Mountains." He favorably reviews Caroline M. Kirkland's *Western Clearings*, the seventh volume in Wiley and Putnam's "Library of American Books," and the *Aristidean* for October, whose reception he had acknowledged in the 8 November issue. In noticing a translation of Frederick von Raumer's *America and the American People*, he objects

to this German writer's opinion of *The Poets and Poetry of America*: "If Dr. Griswold's book is *really* to be received as a fair representation of our poetical literature, then are we in a very lamentable—or rather in a very ridiculous condition indeed." Poe welcomes William D. Ticknor's new edition of *Poems* by Alfred Tennyson, "a poet, who (in our own humble, but sincere opinion,) is *the greatest* that ever lived."

The *Journal* carries Mrs. Osgood's salutation to Poe:

To——

"In Heaven a spirit doth dwell,
Whose heart-strings are a lute."

I cannot tell *the world* how thrills my heart
To every touch that flies thy lyre along;
How the wild Nature and the wondrous Art,
Blend into Beauty in thy passionate song—
But this *I know*—in thine enchanted slumbers,
Heaven's poet, Israfel,—with minstrel fire—
Taught thee the music of his own sweet numbers,
And tuned—to chord with *his*—thy glorious lyre!

This issue contains Walt Whitman's essay on music, "Art-Singing and Heart-Singing," accompanied by Poe's footnote: "The author desires us to say, for him, that he pretends to no scientific knowledge of music. He merely claims to appreciate so much of it (a sadly disdained department, just now) as affects, in the language of the deacons, 'the natural heart of man.' It is scarcely necessary to add that we agree with our correspondent throughout."

AFTER 29 NOVEMBER. Whitman visits 304 Broadway: "I also remember seeing Edgar A. Poe, and having a short interview with him, (it must have been in 1845 or '6,) in his office, second story of a corner building, (Duane or Pearl street.) . . . The visit was about a piece of mine he had publish'd. Poe was very cordial, in a quiet way, appear'd well in person, dress, &c. I have a distinct and pleasing remembrance of his looks, voice, manner and matter; very kindly and human, but subdued, perhaps a little jaded" ("Broadway Sights" in *Specimen Days*, Walt Whitman, 1:17).

30 NOVEMBER. Poe writes George Poe, Jr., his father's first cousin and a well-to-do banker, formerly of Mobile, Alabama, but now resident in Georgetown in the District of Columbia: "Since the period when (no doubt for good reasons) you declined aiding me with the loan of $50, I have perseveringly struggled, against a thousand difficulties, and have succeeded, although not in making money, still in attaining a position in the world of Letters." Because Poe believes that his correspondent will appreci-

ate his "efforts to elevate the family name," he ventures to request assistance "once more." He has become the proprietor of the *Broadway Journal*: "if I can retain it, it will be a fortune to me in a short time:—but I have exhausted all my resources in the purchase. . . . The loan of $200 would put me above all difficulty" (*L*, 1:303–04).

DECEMBER. In the "Editor's Table" of the *Knickerbocker Magazine*, Lewis Gaylord Clark replies to Duyckinck, Poe, and other friends of Cornelius Mathews: "What a pudder our last number has created among two or three inferior members of the small 'Mutual Admiration Society,' who for 'mutual' ends swear just now by the author [Mathews] of 'Puffer Hopkins' and 'Great Abel,' but usually by each other reciprocally!" Clark scoffs at "the Forcible-Feeble [Poe] of a weekly sheet" who "in one number [8 November] deems the KNICKERBOCKER 'utterly beneath notice and beneath contempt,' and in a succeeding issue [15 November] . . . contends that the censure of this Magazine has been and is of the greatest service." Mathews' *Big Abel and the Little Manhattan* "is an utterly incomprehensible farrago." To prove his point, Clark quotes and italicizes a sentence from Poe's review of the novel in the November *Godey's*: " '*Out of ten readers, nine will be totally at a loss to comprehend the meaning of the author!*' "

DECEMBER. The *American Review* contains Poe's tale "The Facts of M. Valdemar's Case." The *Review* lists *The Raven and Other Poems* among the "Publications of the Month," making a promise, never fulfilled, to discuss the volume "at another time."

DECEMBER. The *Democratic Review* notices Wiley and Putnam's "Library of American Books": "Mr. Poe's Poems appear in this series; and we doubt not the popularity of 'The Raven,' will give them a large sale, as we hear copies of that spirited and ingenious poem continually demanded."

DECEMBER. The *Literary Emporium*, a religious magazine, reprints "The Raven."

DECEMBER. CHARLESTON, SOUTH CAROLINA. In his *Southern and Western Magazine* William Gilmore Simms reviews Poe's *Tales*:

Mr. Poe is a mystic, and rises constantly into an atmosphere which as continually loses him the sympathy of the unimaginative reader. But, with those who can go with him without scruple to the elevation to which his visions are summoned, and from which they may all be beheld, he is an acknowledged master,—a Prospero, whose wand is one of wonderful properties. . . . At a period of greater space and leisure, we propose to subject the writings of Mr. Poe, with which we have been more or less familiar for several years, to a close and searching criticism. . . . We must content ourselves here, with simply regretting that, in the first tale in this collection ["The Gold-Bug"], he has been so grievously regardless of the geographical peculiarities of his *locale*. It is fatal to the success of the tale, in the mind of him who reads only for the story's sake, to offend his experience in any thing that concerns the scene of action. Every Charlestonian, for example, who does not see that the writer is aiming at nothing more than an ingenious solution of what might be held as a strange cryptographical difficulty, will be revolted when required to believe in the rocks and highlands in and about Sullivan's Island.

CA. DECEMBER. NEW YORK. The *Aristidean* for November contains Poe's long essay "American Poetry," which is largely composed of excerpts from his reviews of Lambert A. Wilmer's *The Quacks of Helicon* (August 1841 *Graham's*), Rufus W. Griswold's *The Poets and Poetry of America* (November 1842 *Boston Miscellany*), and Richard Henry Horne's *Orion* (March 1844 *Graham's*).

Thomas Dunn English reviews *The Raven and Other Poems*. In "The Raven" Poe has attempted "to evolve interest from a common-place incident, and by means of the mechanism of verse, to throw beauty around a simple narration, while the very borders of the ludicrous are visited. . . . That much of the effect depends upon the mode of construction, and the peculiar arrangement of words and incidents, there can be no doubt; but, the power to conceive and execute the effect, betokens the highest genius." Although some of these poems seem to be included simply "to fill up the book," others are more notable:

The commencement of "The Sleeper," is one of the finest pictures of sleepy calm, in the language. . . . "The Coliseum," written at an early age, has force—and contains well-managed apostrophe and antithesis. The close is unsatisfactory and incomplete. "Lenore" is musical and melancholy—it tells a tale without seeming to attempt narration. "Israfel," is a very pretty specimen of fiddle-de-dee. "Dreamland," "The City in the sea," "The Haunted Palace," and "The Conqueror Worm," are well-managed allegories—the first and last, especially fine. The scenes from "Politian," are not of any great account. They are very well in their way—and their way, is not remarkable. The Sonnet to "Zante" is beautiful.

English "cannot help pronouncing Mr. POE, the first poet of his school . . . . As such we admire him, and look with wonder on his productions; yet they have little power over our spirit. The sensations we feel in reading his poems are more those of admiration than sympathy. . . . He is the poet of the idler, the scholar and dreamer. He has nothing to do with every day life."

1 DECEMBER. BOSTON. The *Morning Post* reviews *The Raven and Other Poems*. "The Raven" is ingenious, but most of these poems are mediocre or

absurd. "Al Aaraaf," Poe's Lyceum poem, remains incomprehensible (Pollin [1980], p. 27).

1 DECEMBER. BALTIMORE. John P. Kennedy writes Poe: "I was in Virginia when your letter [of 26 October] came to Baltimore and did not return until very recently, which will account for my delay in acknowledging it." Kennedy is "an attentive reader" of Poe's writings and takes "great pleasure" in hearing of his career: "When in New York . . . I called at your Broadway Journal establishment in the hope of meeting you, but was told you were just setting out for Providence [Boston?], and as I received your card the same day I took it for granted you had left it only in the moment of your departure and I therefore made no further effort to see you." While Kennedy hopes that the *Broadway Journal* will prove successful, he is unable to support it financially: "Good wishes are pretty nearly all the capital I have for such speculations. . . . When it falls in your way to visit Baltimore both Mrs Kennedy and myself would be much pleased to receive you on our old terms of familiar acquaintance and regard" (*W*, 17:224–25).

1 DECEMBER. NEW YORK. Poe writes Fitz-Greene Halleck: "On the part of one or two persons who are much imbittered against me, there is a deliberate attempt now being made to involve me in ruin, by destroying *The Broadway Journal*." To resolve "this emergency" Poe needs $100: "If you could loan me for three months any portion of it, I will not be ungrateful" (*L*, 1:304–05).

AFTER 1 DECEMBER? Halleck loans Poe $100 (assertion by J. G. Wilson [1869], pp. 430–31).

2 DECEMBER. BOSTON. In the *Evening Transcript* Cornelia Wells Walter reprints a letter from a Baltimore correspondent published in the Boston *Daily Atlas* on 29 November:

I remember, it is now near about fifteen years, when this poem [Poe's "Al Aaraaf"] was first published, in this city [Baltimore], I believe. It was very handsomely printed, in a volume with another poem called Tamerlane, but did not sell—people could not understand it, or Tamerlane. A friend of mine, who felt it to be his duty to read what nobody else would, purchased a copy, read it, and recorded his opinion of it in this epigram, which I take leave to transcribe for the benefit of your readers:

> "If Tamerlane and Al Aaraff
> Were rendered subject to a tariff,
> Of cent per centum ad valorem,
> On every copy leaves the store-room,

How many centuries would roll
To their eternal cemetery,
Before the poor collector, fool,
Would in his purse find one *obole*,
To pay the passage of his soul
Across the infernal Stygean ferry?"

The question then propounded has never been answered here, and perhaps some of your *calculating* citizens may deem the problem worthy of their efforts to solve.

2, 5, 8 DECEMBER. NEW YORK. Poe sends anastatic copies of a letter, dated "Nov. 1845," to George Watterston in Washington, D. C., Charles Campbell in Petersburg, Virginia, and William Green in Culpeper, Virginia. In this letter Poe recalls that his correspondent was "one of the earliest subscribers to 'The Southern Literary Messenger' " and supported this magazine during his editorship. "I venture now frankly to solicit your subscription and influence for 'The Broadway Journal', of which I send you a specimen number" (*L*, 1:304, 2:514–15; cf. Poe's article on "Anastatic Printing," *Broadway Journal*, 12 April).

3 DECEMBER. Poe and Thomas H. Lane sign a contract, witnessed by Samuel Fleet and George H. Colton. Poe transfers to Lane one half of his "interest and property" in the *Broadway Journal*. Lane agrees to pay "all dues" contracted against the *Journal* since 17 November, provided "that the said debts do not amount to more than the sum of forty dollars"; he will supply the magazine's "necessary expenses" and attend to its "business conduct." The editorial conduct will remain "under the sole charge of the said Edgar A. Poe" (Rede, pp. 53–54).

3 DECEMBER. PHILADELPHIA. *Smith's Weekly Volume* notices *The Raven and Other Poems*, praising, with tongue in cheek, the unfavorable judgment on the book Poe gave in his preface (Pollin [1980], p. 27).

3 DECEMBER. SAINT LOUIS. The *Daily Reveille* favorably notices *The Raven and Other Poems* (Pollin [1980], p. 27).

4 DECEMBER. The *Reveille* reports that Poe has given "the history of the poem *hoax*." It quotes from the 22 November *Broadway Journal* a portion of his reply to the Bostonians (Moss [1968], p. 19).

6 DECEMBER. WEST ROXBURY, MASSACHUSETTS. In the *Harbinger* John S. Dwight reviews *The Raven and Other Poems*:

Mr. Poe has earned some fame by various tales and poems, which of late has become notoriety through a certain blackguard warfare which he has been waging against the poets and newspaper critics of New England, and which it would be most charitable to impute to insanity. Judging from the tone of his late articles in the Broadway Journal, he seems to think that the whole literary South and West are doing anxious battle in his person against the old time-honored tyrant of the North. . . .

The present volume is not entirely pure of this controversy, else we should ignore the late scandalous courses of the man, and speak only of the "Poems." The motive of the publication is too apparent; it contains the famous Boston poem ["Al Aaraaf"], together with other juvenilities . . . .

In a sober attempt to get at the meaning and worth of these poems as poetry, we have been not a little puzzled. We must confess they have a great deal of power, a great deal of beauty, (of thought frequently, and always of rhythm and diction,) originality, and dramatic effect. But they have more of *effect*, than of *expression*, to adopt a distinction from musical criticism; and if they attract you to a certain length, it is only to repulse you the more coldly at last. There is a wild unearthliness, and unheavenliness, in the tone of all his pictures, a strange unreality in all his thoughts; they seem to stand shivering, begging admission to our hearts in vain, because they look not as if they came from the heart. That ill-boding "Raven," which you meet at the threshold of his edifice, is a fit warning of the hospitality you will find inside. . . . Mr. Poe has made a critical study of the matter of versification, and succeeded in the art rather at the expense of nature. Indeed the impression of a very *studied* effect is always uppermost after reading him. . . . What is the fancy which is merely fancy, the beauty which springs from no feeling, which neither illustrates nor promotes the great truths and purposes of life, which glimmers strangely only because it is aside from the path of human destiny?

6 DECEMBER. NEW YORK. Lawrence Labree reviews *The Raven and Other Poems* in his *Illustrated Magazine*: "We have but few poets whose works we care to see in 'book form,' and Mr. Poe is one of these. His 'Raven' is more remarkable for its mechanical construction than for its spirit of poetry, though any one who has read it several times over, as we have, must confess it to have some merit."

6 DECEMBER. The *Broadway Journal* contains Poe's revised tale "Four Beasts in One—The Homo-Cameleopard," formerly entitled "Epimanes." He favorably reviews two biographies, Thomas Carlyle's *Life of Frederick Schiller* and Lord Mahon's *Life of Louis de Bourbon*. In the "Editorial Miscellany" he facetiously complains of maltreatment by other periodicals: "Every body is at us—little dogs and all." An example is provided by the *Nassau Monthly* of Princeton College, possibly the "littlest of all the dogs." From it Poe quotes this criticism of his tale "The Imp of the Perverse":

If asked to what species of the genus humbug this article properly attaches itself, we should reply to the humbug philosophical. We have not time to analyze, but would say that the author introduces himself as in pursuit of an idea; this he chases from the wilderness of phrenology into that of transcendentalism, then into that of metaphysics generally; then through many weary pages into the open field of inductive philosophy, where he at last corners the poor thing, and then most unmercifully pokes it to death with a long stick. This idea he calls the "Perverse."

6, 10 DECEMBER. NEW ORLEANS. The *Daily Picayune* notices *The Raven and Other Poems* (Pollin [1980], p. 27).

10 DECEMBER. NEW YORK. In the *Daily Tribune* Horace Greeley comments: "The article in the American Review of this month entitled 'The Facts of M. Valdemar's Case,* by EDGAR A. POE,' is of course a romance— who could have supposed it otherwise? Those who have read Mr. Poe's Visit to the Maelstrom, South Pole, &c. have not been puzzled by it, yet we learn that several good matter-of-fact citizens have been, sorely. It is a pretty good specimen of Poe's style of giving an air of reality to fictions, and we utterly condemn the choice of a subject, but whoever thought it a veracious recital must have the bump of Faith large, very large indeed."

10 DECEMBER. Poe writes Evert A. Duyckinck, forwarding an article by Mrs. Elizabeth F. Ellet. He asks Duyckinck to have it published as an unsigned editorial in the *Morning News* (L, 1:305; cf. Ellet to Poe, ca. 15 December and 16 December).

10 DECEMBER. CAMBRIDGE, MASSACHUSETTS. Longfellow writes in his journal: "In Graham's Magazine for January, received this morning, is a superb poem by Lowell . . . . If he goes on in this vein, Poe will soon begin to pound him" (Longfellow [1886], 2:26).

13 DECEMBER. BOSTON. *Littell's Living Age* lists *The Raven and Other Poems* among the "New Books."

13 DECEMBER. BROOKLYN. The *Daily Eagle* notices *The Raven and Other Poems*, objecting to Poe's self-deprecatory preface. He is one of the best American writers, both in prose and verse (Pollin [1980], p. 26).

13 DECEMBER. NEW YORK. The *Golden Rule* briefly reviews *The Raven and Other Poems* (Mabbott [1942], p. xv).

13 DECEMBER. The *Broadway Journal* contains Poe's tale "The Oblong Box" (reprint) and his laudatory review of Mrs. Osgood's *Poems*. In the "Editorial Miscellany" he reprints John S. Dwight's review of *The Raven and Other Poems* from the 6 December *Harbinger*, identifying this Brook Farm weekly

as "the most reputable organ of the Crazyites" and characterizing its opinion of his poetry as "all leather and prunella." He corrects the reviewer's impression that the book's publication was related to his 16 October Lyceum appearance: " 'The Raven, etc.,' was in the publishers' hands a month or six weeks before we received the invitation from the Lyceum— and we read the last proofs on the evening before that on which we 'insulted the Boston audience.' " Poe condemns Henry Norman Hudson's lecture on Shakespeare's *King Lear*, which he heard delivered at the Society Library "on Tuesday evening last"; the lecturer's defects include "an elocution that would disgrace a pig, and an odd species of gesticulation of which a baboon would have excellent reason to be ashamed." He notices Margaret Fuller's "very just review" of Longfellow's *Poems*, published in the *Daily Tribune* on 10 December. From it he quotes several passages in which she argues that Longfellow is not a creative genius but a derivative writer largely indebted to the works of others. This issue of the *Broadway Journal* also contains Mrs. Ellet's "Coquette's Song" and Mrs. Osgood's "A Shipwreck": both poems seem to express the affection these poetesses feel for Poe.

13 DECEMBER. John Bisco transfers Poe's promissory note for $100, dated 24 October, to W. H. Starr (Moldenhauer [1973], p. 81).

CA. 15 DECEMBER. Mrs. Elizabeth F. Ellet writes Poe to describe an editorial she wishes him to publish in the *Broadway Journal*, condemning the dismissal of the former President of the South Carolina College in Columbia:

> It might be well to mention the fact *admitted* in all the southern papers—that Revd Dr [Robert] Henry was removed simply on the ground that he was "unpopular" without a single charge being alleged against his character, qualifications or scholarship. In the latter he has no equal in the state. To be "unpopular" in South Carolina is as fatal as the cry of "mad dog" or the accusation of "pricer" at the west. . . . It might do also to mention how much the Trustees are fettered by their fear of not pleasing the Legislature. . . . I would write the article, but am afraid of displeasing Dr E. [her husband Dr. William H. Ellet, a professor at the College] as the Broadway Journal goes to Columbia—& I should be discovered at once.

The verso of the manuscript carries a postscript written in German, in which Mrs. Ellet tells Poe that she has a letter for him ("einen Brief für Sie") and asks him to send for it, or to call for it at her residence this evening (MB-G).

[In the "Editorial Miscellany" of the 13 December *Journal*, Poe had congratulated the College on the accession of William C. Preston to its

Presidency, but indicated that "the late President" had been the victim of "some injustice," which he promised to discuss "more fully in our next." The *Journal* did not publish a second report.]

16 DECEMBER. Mrs. Ellet sends an unsigned note via "Dispatch Post" to Poe, who has not complied with the request made in her postscript: "Do not use in any way the memorandum about the So. Ca. College. Excuse the repeated injunction—but as you would not decipher my German manuscript—I am fearful of some other mistake" (MB–G).

16 DECEMBER. BOSTON. Robert H. Collyer writes Poe:

Your account of M. Valdemar's Case has been universally copied in this city, and has created a very great sensation. It requires from me no apology, in stating, that I have not the least doubt of the *possibility* of such a phenomenon; for, I did actually restore to active animation a person who died from excessive drinking of ardent spirits. He was placed in his coffin ready for interment. . . .

I will give you the detailed account on your reply to this, which I require for publication, in order to put at rest the growing impression that your account is merely a *splendid creation* of your own brain, not having any truth in fact. My dear sir, I have battled the storm of public derision too long on the subject of Mesmerism, to be now found in the rear ranks (printed in 27 December *Broadway Journal*).

19 DECEMBER. UTICA, NEW YORK. Charles G. Percival writes Poe, enclosing a cypher for him to translate (Poe to Percival, 3 January 1846; see also *L*, 2:610).

20 DECEMBER. NEW YORK. The *Broadway Journal* reprints Poe's most recent tale, its title altered to "The Facts in the Case of M. Valdemar." In a prefatory note Poe comments that the story "has given rise to some discussion—especially in regard to the truth or falsity of the statements made. It does not become *us*, of course, to offer one word on the point at issue. . . . We may observe, however, that there are a certain class of people who pride themselves upon Doubt, as a profession." He favorably reviews William H. Prescott's *Biographical and Critical Miscellanies*, Lewis J. Cist's *Trifles in Verse*, and the *Diadem* for 1846, quoting from this annual Ralph Waldo Emerson's "A Fable," a poem "exceedingly *piquant* and *naive*." The *Journal* contains Mrs. Osgood's poem "To 'The Lady Geraldine,' " possibly intended as a reproach to Mrs. Ellet, her rival for Poe's affection: "Was it so blest—my life's estate—/ That you with envy viewed me?"

20 DECEMBER. BALTIMORE. On its first page the *Saturday Visiter* reprints Poe's tale under the heading "Valdemar's Case," from the *American Review*

for December. In noticing the *Review* Joseph Evans Snodgrass comments: "That there is something more and better than mere party politics in this journal, our first page will show. Its literary contents are of a high standard."

AFTER 20 DECEMBER? NEW YORK. Poe goes "off on one of his fits of drunkenness," leaving the next issue of the *Broadway Journal* only "partly finished," with "about a column or a column and a half of matter lacking." After vainly attempting "for several days to get Poe into sobriety," Thomas H. Lane decides "to close the publication entirely" with the 3 January 1846 issue (assertions by English, p. 1382).

21 DECEMBER. PHILLIPS, MAINE. George W. Eveleth, a young medical student, writes Poe. He explains that he became a subscriber to *Graham's Magazine* early in 1842. At that time he was puzzled by the writings of Poe, then its editor:

His criticisms, I thought, were sheer pedantries, and his tales very perplexities, very enigmas which I could not unravel. His "Mask of the Red Death," in particular, seemed a complete mystery. I could find neither beginning, middle, nor end to it—neither design nor meaning. But I was only a boy, and unused to much thinking, or to analyzing . . . . I am but little better fitted for the station of judge of literary merit than I was three years ago . . . . I merely give my feeling. I have gone back to that old volume of the magazine, and read over and over again the reviews there, and have read, as carefully, those that have appeared in all the later volumes. But it has appeared to my mind that there was less of real, sound, philosophical criticism in the whole of these latter, than even in the one little notice of Hawthorne's "Twice-told Tales" among the former. And I should find more pleasure in perusing now, for the twentieth time, the fantasy condemned above, than in reading a story by Mrs. Osgood, Mrs. Embury, Mr. Peterson, or any of the host of fanciful news-paper contributors, for the first time.

To be short and direct, Mr. Poe is the one I have selected from all the writers of whom I know any thing, for my especial favorite. I am passionately fond of reading his productions of all kinds.

Eveleth appreciatively discusses those stories and poems he has read. He owns the Wiley and Putnam edition of Poe's *Tales*; he wants to obtain all his other publications, especially "The Raven" and the *Tales of the Grotesque and Arabesque*: "I wish Mr. Poe would 'stoop so low' as to address by letter a rustic youngster of the backwoods of Maine, and tell him where he can get those things which he covets so much." Eveleth would like to subscribe to the *Broadway Journal*, "if the expence is not too much"; he asks to be sent "a specimen-number or two" (Eveleth, pp. 4–6).

22 DECEMBER. NEW YORK. Mrs. Mary E. Hewitt writes Poe, submitting a sonnet for the *Broadway Journal* (Mabbott [1937], p. 119).

22 DECEMBER. WOODLANDS, SOUTH CAROLINA. William Gilmore Simms writes Evert A. Duyckinck in New York: "Will you see Poe & ask him what became of a little poem that was left with an elderly gentleman at his desk (the Bookkeeper) I believe, just before I left New York." Simms is disappointed that Poe has not published his poem. "Request Poe to send the Broadway Journal to me hereafter at this place, & discontinue it at Charleston, except to the '[Southern] Patriot' " (Simms, 2:124–26).

[Simms was in New York from late August to early October.]

23 DECEMBER. ALBURY, GUILDFORD, ENGLAND. Martin Farquhar Tupper writes William Jerdan, editor of the London *Literary Gazette*, inquiring why his review of Poe's *Tales* has not been published. "What on earth's become of Poe?" (PP–G).

23, 24 DECEMBER. PHILADELPHIA. The *Spirit of the Times* reprints "The Facts in the Case of M. Valdemar" in two installments, from the *Broadway Journal* of 20 December (Mabbott [1978], 3:1232).

CA. 25 DECEMBER [1845?]. The health reformer Mrs. Mary Gove, later Mrs. Nichols, hears Poe recite "The Raven" at a Christmas party (Nichols [1855], p. 340).

27 DECEMBER. The *Broadway Journal* contains Poe's revised tale "Mystification," formerly entitled "Von Jung, the Mystific." He favorably reviews the *Opal* for 1846, *The Poems of Alfred B. Street*, Joel T. Headley's *The Alps and the Rhine*, and J. S. Reffield's edition of Shelley's *Poetical Works*. Although he praises the second edition of Longfellow's *Hyperion* as "tastefully printed," he condemns the romance for its lack of suggestiveness: "Mr. Longfellow's works seem to some minds greater than they are, on account of their perfection of finish—on account of the thoroughness with which their designs are carried out. They exhaust limited subjects. His books are books and no more. Those of men of genius are books and a dream to boot." In the "Editorial Miscellany" Poe prints the 16 December letter from "Dr. Collyer, the eminent Mesmerist," appending an ambiguous corroboration: "We have no doubt that Mr. Collyer is perfectly correct in all that he says—and all that he desires us to say—but the truth is, there was a very small modicum of truth in the case of M. Valdemar."

27 DECEMBER. Hiram Fuller becomes the editor of the *Evening Mirror* and *Weekly Mirror*, his former partners George P. Morris and Nathaniel P. Willis "retiring from the concern" (announcement in the *Evening Mirror* for this date).

31 DECEMBER. The *Evening Mirror* reports that Poe has withdrawn from the *Broadway Journal*.

CA. 31 DECEMBER [1845?]. Mrs. Mary Gove attends a New Year's party: "Poor Poe was there, and his image rises in memory, with those of common men, like a marble shaft among wooden pillars. He was very beautiful, though it was a pale, cold beauty . . . . His life was not the life of a man, but an artist" (Nichols [1855], pp. 341–42).

1845? Poe frequents Bartlett and Welford's bookstore in the Astor House. John R. Bartlett observes that Poe is "very fond" of strong coffee (Miller [1979], pp. 232–33; cf. Haskell, p. 47).

1845? Parke Godwin, William Cullen Bryant's son-in-law, recalls seeing Poe and Bryant "together at an evening party, given by Mrs. C. M. Kirkland, when they talked with each other for a long time. Poe was slim in person, neatly dressed, clean shaven, with a large head, dark hair, and the most wonderfully luminous eyes. Mr. Bryant was not so slight, but his head was also large, and he wore a venerable white beard. Poe approached him as some Grecian youth might be imagined to approach an image of Plato—with a look and attitude full of the profoundest reverence" (Godwin, 2:22).

1845? Samuel S. Osgood paints a portrait of Poe (Schulte, p. 43).

LATE 1845? Poe gives Mrs. Gove a copy of his *Tales*, inscribing it "from her most sincere friend" (presentation copy in InU–L).

LATE 1845? PHILADELPHIA. Haswell, Barrington, and Haswell publish the third edition of *The Conchologist's First Book*, dated 1845. Poe's name is removed from the cover and the title page, although his initials are retained at the end of the preface.

LATE 1845? LONDON. *Churton's Literary Register* for 1845, an annual, favorably reviews Poe's *Tales*, summarizing "The Murders in the Rue Morgue" (Pollin [1980], p. 25).

LATE 1845? George P. Putnam writes Wiley and Putnam's home office in New York, stating that Tupper will notice the *Tales* in the *Literary Gazette*. Poe is subsequently informed of the forthcoming review (implied by Poe to E. A. Duyckinck, 30 January 1846).

THOMAS DUNN ENGLISH

CHAPTER NINE

The War of the Literati

1846–1847

The years 1846 and 1847 bring Poe increasing recognition in Europe. The London *Sunday Times* and other British journals reprint his hoax "The Facts in the Case of M. Valdemar," creating a controversy over its authenticity. In France "The Murders in the Rue Morgue" and other stories attract such able translators as E. D. Forgues and Isabelle Meunier. Two European critics convinced of Poe's importance review the Wiley and Putnam edition of his *Tales*: Martin Farquhar Tupper in the London *Literary Gazette* of 31 January 1846 and Forgues in the Paris *Revue des Deux Mondes* of 15 October 1846. At home Poe is troubled by ill health, poverty, and quarrels with minor literati. Mrs. Elizabeth F. Ellet, a jealous and vindictive woman, interferes with his innocent correspondence with Mrs. Frances S. Osgood; he is forced to return the letters he received from both these rivals for his attention. The ensuing scandal in January and February 1846 damages his standing with the circle of bluestockings headed by Miss Anne C. Lynch, who no longer invites him to her popular soirees. Around May, seeking seclusion and inexpensive lodging, Poe moves his family to a small cottage at Fordham, some thirteen miles outside New York. His sketches of "The Literati of New York City," then being serialized in *Godey's Lady's Book*, keep his name before the public. The July installment contains his flippant notice of his enemy Thomas Dunn English, who responds by inserting a vitriolic "Reply" in the *Evening Mirror* of 23 June. Since this attack falsely accuses Poe of forgery and pecuniary fraud, he sues the *Mirror* for publishing it. Around November 1846 Mrs. Mary Gove visits Poe and his wife at Fordham and finds them both seriously ill, without adequate food or clothing. On 15 December the New York *Morning Express* carries a report of their plight, which is reprinted by many newspapers. On 30 January 1847 Virginia Poe dies of tuberculosis, aged twenty-four years and five months. Although Poe becomes dangerously ill after her death, he is nursed back to health by Mrs. Marie Louise Shew, a kindly, unsophisticated woman with medical training, but no interest in literature. His libel suit against the *Mirror* is heard in Superior Court on 17 February; a twelve-man jury awards him $225 damages as well as legal costs. He discusses his judicial victory and his proposed magazine the *Stylus* in several letters to a young admirer, George W. Eveleth of Phillips, Maine.

In 1847 Mrs. Sarah Anna Lewis, an ambitious but mediocre poetess, becomes a frequent visitor to Fordham, occasionally providing Poe and Mrs. Clemm with financial assistance. The *American Review* for December contains Poe's melodic but puzzling poem "Ulalume."

*

1846

*

WINTER. NEW YORK. Mrs. Elizabeth Oakes Smith encounters Poe at various social gatherings held in the homes of Anne C. Lynch, Orville Dewey, James Lawson, and other literati. She recalls: "He [Poe] delighted in the society of superior women, and had an exquisite perception of all graces of manner, and shades of expression. He was an admiring listener, and an unobtrusive observer. We all recollect the interest felt at the time in everything emanating from his pen—the relief it was from the dulness of ordinary writers—the certainty of something fresh and suggestive. His critiques were read with avidity; not that he convinced the judgment, but that people felt their ability and their courage" (Smith quoted by Whitman, p. 23; cf. Smith, p. 121).

JANUARY. The *Columbian Magazine* mentions *The Raven and Other Poems* among the "Books of the Month" (Pollin [1980], p. 26).

JANUARY. Freeman Hunt reviews *The Raven and Other Poems* in his *Merchants' Magazine*:

This is the second volume of Mr. Poe's productions that have appeared in Wiley & Putnam's American Library. The characteristics of his poetry are a quick, subtle conception, and a severe taste of what is harmonious in expression. Exhibiting all the nervous, impatient marks of true genius, an unbridled playfulness of fancy, it is, while seemingly riding havoc in thought, metre and harmony, restrained throughout by a skilful rein, that guides sentiment and style by well defined rules, never allowing it to border upon the ridiculous, or ill judged sublimity. This union of the faculties of a *critic* and *genius*, making cultivation a second nature, and unconsciously governing the style, is a rare gift and power in a writer. The passion and sentiment are also original, while the style has a fragmentary character, like the architecture of the ruins of Chiapas, where frescoes, and rude, but beautiful workmanship, are scattered about in the wildest profusion. The Raven is rather a production of artistic cleverness than genius, while the poems that follow breathe such pure passion, and are embodied in such beautiful imagery, and the etherial speculations given with so much descriptive, thought-awakening power, that we regret Mr. Poe should do aught else than write poetry.

JANUARY. The *Knickerbocker Magazine* contains Lewis Gaylord Clark's abusive review of *The Raven and Other Poems*. Clark can readily accept Poe's assertion that he composed some of these poems in childhood:

At what period he [Poe] commenced writing verses we do not know; but he tells us in a note that it was in his "earliest boyhood," which begins we believe with the jacket-and-trousers, generally at three or four years. If Mr. POE wrote the Ode to Science ["Sonnet—To Science"] at that early period, he was certainly a remarkable boy, but hardly a poet. We have heard that, in the paper [*Broadway Journal*] of which he is the editor, he has stated that he wrote "Al Aaraaf," the poem with which he professes to have humbugged the poor Bostonians, in his tenth year. The "Boston Post" thought it must have been produced at a much earlier age. We have no opinion on the subject ourselves, not having read it, but are disposed to believe the author, and should believe him if he said the same of the poems which we have read. We see no reason why they might not have been written at the age of ten: children are more apt, in remembering words, than men; and as there have been infant violinists, pianists, mimics and dancers, we see no reason why there should not be an infant rhythmist.

JANUARY. PHILADELPHIA. *Godey's Lady's Book* contains Poe's favorable criticism of William Gilmore Simms's *The Wigwam and the Cabin*, which he had initially reviewed in the *Broadway Journal* for 4 October 1845. *Godey's* also carries a brief notice of *The Raven and Other Poems*, "a collection of fugitive pieces which fully sustain the high reputation which the author had previously gained by his prose works for power of imagination and command over the English language. Indeed, Poe's masterly facility in diction may be supposed to have occasioned the only fault which we perceive in any of these poems, an appearance of careless wantonness in rhythm, which, perhaps, after all, may be merely the independent freedom of one who cannot but feel his own power."

JANUARY. *Arthur's Ladies' Magazine* contains Poe's tale "The Sphinx."

JANUARY. CINCINNATI. The *Quarterly Journal and Review*, edited by Lucius A. Hine, notices *The Raven and Other Poems*: "Edgar A. Poe occupies a conspicuous position in the literary world. . . . He is—what can be said of few—*sui generis*, stamped with his own originality. . . . He is a man of genius rather than talents,—though were his genius less, and his talents greater, he would do more for the good of the world, and his own reputation." The reviewer quotes six stanzas from "The Raven"; he objects to the poem's "general tenor," because "it associates the author with the people of ancient times, when the fate of man was seen by the perverted imagination in the flight and song of ominous birds." The second poem, "The Valley of Unrest," lacks "every mark of poetry, except its rhyme, which is very imperfect, and the capitals that commence each line." An example of wretched taste occurs in "The Sleeper," in the line "Soft may the worms about her creep!" While "The Coliseum" is excellent, "Israfel" is unworthy of Poe's talents. "Dream-Land," "To One in Paradise," and "The Conqueror Worm" all contain poetry "of a high order." None of the other pieces is "particularly striking," except the "Scenes" from *Politian*: "The part given forces a desire to see the whole; which we hope Mr. Poe will not be backward in handing over to the printer."

EARLY JANUARY? LONDON. Wiley and Putnam, 6 Waterloo Place, issue *The Raven and Other Poems* in England. The volume, bound in green cloth, is made up of the American sheets and an inserted title page giving London as the place of publication (Mabbott [1942], p. xviii; *Spectator*, 24 January).

CA. 1 JANUARY? PROVIDENCE, RHODE ISLAND. Sarah Helen Whitman writes Anne C. Lynch in New York, inquiring about Poe. She wishes to obtain his review of Elizabeth Barrett Barrett, published in the *Broadway Journal* for 4 and 11 January 1845 (implied by Lynch to Whitman, 7 January).

[Mrs. Whitman was fascinated by Poe and his writings for several years before she actually met him. On 10 October 1850 she wrote Mary E. Hewitt: "I can never forget the impressions I felt in reading a story of his for the first time about six or seven years ago. I experienced a sensation of such intense horror that I dared neither look at anything he had written nor even utter his name. . . . By degrees this terror took the character of fascination—I devoured with a half-reluctant and fearful avidity every line that fell from his pen" (Williams, pp. 769–71).]

2 JANUARY. BOSTON. In the *Evening Transcript* Cornelia Wells Walter comments:

> EDGAR A. POE. In October last, Mr Poe notified the public that he had assumed the whole control, (proprietary and editorial) of the Broadway Journal, on which occasion he appended the interrogative, "may we not hope for the support of our friends?" Now Mr Poe either has no friends (which we won't believe) or they have proved hard hearted and uncharitable, for we learn from the New York Mirror of Wednesday, that "he has disposed of his interest in the Broadway Journal, and will hereafter devote his time and pen to some better paying business."

> To trust in friends is but so so,
> Especially when cash is low;
> The Broadway Journal's proved *"no go"*—
> *Friends* would not pay the pen of POE.

3 JANUARY. NEW YORK. Poe replies to Charles G. Percival of Utica, New York, who had sent him a cipher to translate on 19 December 1845: "It is an illegitimate cryptograph—that is to say, the chances are, that, even *with* the key, it would be insoluble by the authorized correspondent. Upon analysis, however, independent of the key-solution, I find the translation to be the 3 first verses of the 2d chapter of St John" (*L*, 2:309).

3 JANUARY. The *Broadway Journal* ceases publication. The final issue contains Poe's revised tale "Loss of Breath," as well as his reviews of Thomas Carlyle's edition of the *Letters and Speeches of Oliver Cromwell*, published by Wiley and Putnam, and of the November and December 1845 numbers of the *Aristidean*, received "some time" ago. The "Editorial Miscellany" contains Poe's "Valedictory":

Unexpected engagements demanding my whole attention, and the objects being fulfilled, so far as regards myself personally, for which "The Broadway Journal" was established, I now, as its editor, bid farewell—as cordially to foes as to friends.

Mr. Thomas H. Lane is authorized to collect all money due the Journal.

4 JANUARY. LONDON. The *Sunday Times* reprints "The Facts in the Case of M. Valdemar" from the *American Review*, under the heading "Mesmerism in America: Astounding and Horrifying Narrative" (Mabbott [1978], 3:1232).

5 JANUARY. The *Morning Post* reprints Poe's tale under the heading "Mesmerism in America." The editors comment: "For our own parts we do not believe it; and there are several statements made, more especially with regard to the disease of which the patient died, which at once prove the case to be either a fabrication, or the work of one little acquainted with consumption. The story, however, is wonderful, and we therefore give it" (Mabbott [1978], 3:1232; *Post* quoted by Poe in "Marginalia," *Graham's Magazine*, March 1848).

5 JANUARY. PHILLIPS, MAINE. George W. Eveleth writes Poe that he has received the *Broadway Journal* for 20 December 1845: "I like it in some respects, and in some, do not. The quality of the paper is pretty good, and the sheet is in a form such as I would have it. . . . Your 'Facts in the Case of M. Valdemar' are wonderful, if true—if false, you are a genius of wonderfully curious fancies, I must confess. The article suits me very well whether it *is* fact or fiction. . . . I do not value your critical notices so highly as I should if they were more lengthy. There cannot be much *criticism* in so few words." Eveleth encloses three dollars for his subscription, "commencing with the new volume" (Eveleth, p. 6).

6 JANUARY. PRINCETON, NEW JERSEY. A correspondent who signs himself "T. L. C." writes the *Richmond Compiler*, reporting that Poe has left the *Broadway Journal* and "is to annoy the public, or the small portion of it who saw his paper—through its columns no longer. He signalized the close of his career by declaring lately that he considered *Tennyson* (the man whom he imitates) *'the greatest poet that ever lived!'* and by declaring farther that he was 'willing to bear all the reproach this might call down on him.' His vanity might have spared itself this bravado." The letter appears in the Virginia paper on 9 January (Pollin [1985a], pp. 6-7).

7 JANUARY. NEW YORK. Anne C. Lynch writes Sarah Helen Whitman in Providence: "I sent you a few days ago Mr Poe's review of Miss Barrett which he gave me for that purpose. . . . I see Mr Poe very often. I think his stories are, some of them, very remarkable" (RPB–W).

7 JANUARY. Another New York correspondent, possibly Mrs. Frances S. Osgood, writes Mrs. Whitman, apparently in response to her inquiry: "I meet Mr. Poe very often at the receptions. He is the observed of all observers. His stories are thought wonderful, and to hear him repeat the Raven, which he does very quietly, is an event in one's life. People seem to think there is something uncanny about him, and the strangest stories are told, and, what is more, *believed*, about his mesmeric experiences, at the mention of which he always smiles. His smile is captivating! . . . Everybody wants to know him; but only a very few people seem to get well acquainted with him" (Didier [1877], p. 13).

CA. 7 JANUARY? A correspondent writes Mrs. Whitman, describing a literary soiree at which Poe bested Margaret Fuller in conversation: "The Raven has perched upon the casque of Pallas, and pulled all the feathers out of her cap" (Didier [1877], p. 12).

8 JANUARY. Poe writes Evert A. Duyckinck, Wiley and Putnam's editor: "For 'particular reasons' I am anxious to have another volume of my Tales published before the lrst of March. . . . Would not Mr. Wiley give me, say $50, in full for the copyright of the collection I now send. It is a far better one than the first—containing, for instance, 'Ligeia', which is undoubtedly the best story I have written—besides 'Sheherazade', 'The Spectacles', 'Tarr and Fether,' etc." Poe requests "an early answer, by note, addressed 85 Amity St." (*L*, 2:309–10).

8 JANUARY. LONDON. Wiley and Putnam deposit a copy of Poe's *Tales* in the British Museum, for copyright (Mabbott [1942], p. xix).

9 JANUARY. Elizabeth Barrett Barrett writes Robert Browning at New Cross, Hatcham, Surrey: "I have just received Mr. Edgar Poe's book [*The Raven and Other Poems*]—& I see that the deteriorating preface which was to have saved me from the vanity-fever produceable by the dedication, is cut down & away—perhaps in this particular copy only!" (Browning [1969], 1:372–74; cf. Barrett to Browning, 28 November 1845).

10 JANUARY. The *Popular Record of Modern Science* reprints Poe's "Valdemar" from the *Morning Post* of 5 January, giving it the heading "Mesmerism in America. Death of M. Valdemar of New York." The *Record* quotes the *Post*'s observation that the article seems to be a fabrication; it objects that the *Post* "does not point out the especial statements which are inconsistent with what we know of the progress of consumption." The *Record* is inclined to accept the account as factual, because "credence is understood to be given to it at New York." Corroboration of its details can surely be obtained:

The initials of the medical men and of the young medical student must be sufficient in the immediate locality, to establish their identity, especially as M. Valdemar was well known, and had been so long ill as to render it out of the question that there should be any difficulty in ascertaining the names of the physicians by whom he had been attended. In the same way the nurses and servants under whose cognizance the case must have come during the seven months which it occupied, are of course accessible to all sorts of inquiries. . . . The angry excitement and various rumors which have at length rendered a public statement necessary, are also sufficient to show that *something* extraordinary must have taken place. . . . Under this view we shall take steps to procure from some of the most intelligent and influential citizens of New York all the evidence that can be had upon the subject. No steamer will leave England for America till the 3d of February, but within a few weeks of that time we doubt not it will be possible to lay before the readers of the *Record* information which will enable them to come to a pretty accurate conclusion (Mabbott [1978], 3:1232; *Record* quoted in "Marginalia," *Graham's Magazine*, March 1848).

10 JANUARY. PHILADELPHIA. The *Saturday Courier* reprints the report of Poe's retirement from the *Broadway Journal* published in the Boston *Evening Transcript* on 2 January. The *Courier* explains: "Miss Walter, editor of that spicy little journal, . . . has not liked Edgar A. Poe much since he was indiscreet enough, last fall, to say he attempted to hoax the Bostonians by pronouncing a poem, written when he was 13."

10 JANUARY. BUFFALO, NEW YORK. In the *Western Literary Messenger* Jesse Clement, the editor, reviews *The Raven and Other Poems*:

As a poet, Mr. Poe is a peculiar writer. His style and his manner of thinking are purely his own. . . . We have an instance of this in the "Raven." . . . In artistic grace it is excelled by no poem ever composed in this country; and did more to elevate the reputation of the author as a poet, than all else he has written. It is a poem whose beauties every one can appreciate, and which every one likes to read. We wish as much could be said of the productions of the same pen generally; but the major quantity, though they possess the genuine melody of high[ly] wrought verse, find no response in the reader's heart. Their tone is foreign to the ordinary feeling of mankind. For this reason but few of them have been widely circulated through the medium of the newspaper press.

Clement quotes the first stanza of "Dream-Land," observing that few "can appreciate such lines as these." Of the nineteen poems in the first part of the book, only two or three "approach the naturalness and simplicity which, when combined with fervor and strength, are so certain to move the universal heart." Clement reprints "To One in Paradise," the "best of the minor poems." The second part "contains eleven poems written in the author's youth . . . . Two of these early effusions, 'Al Aaraaf' and 'Ta-merlane,' are long and tedious; most of the others are short and tedious. In all of them, however, is here and there a line or a brief passage, which is strikingly beautiful."

10 JANUARY. NEW YORK. At the request of Anne C. Lynch, Poe writes the poet Fitz-Greene Halleck and the clergyman Charles Edwards Lester. In each letter Poe extends Miss Lynch's invitation to her soiree this evening, remarking that the New England novelist Catharine M. Sedgwick, the Kentucky abolitionist Cassius M. Clay, "and some other notabilities" are expected to attend (*L*, 2:310–11).

10 JANUARY. 7:00 PM. Poe attends Miss Lynch's soiree at 116 Waverley Place (Lynch to Mrs. Whitman, 20 January).

12 JANUARY. Poe writes Philip Pendleton Cooke at The Vineyard, Clarke County, Virginia (cited Moldenhauer [1973], p. 62, and Ostrom [1974], p. 528).

14 JANUARY. BOSTON. The *Morning Post* praises Lewis Gaylord Clark's hostile review of *The Raven and Other Poems* in the January *Knickerbocker*, while objecting to the suggestion that Poe "humbugged" the Bostonians with his Lyceum poem: "Nearly if not quite half the audience actually left the hall before the conclusion of the reading, and those who remained were actuated by feelings of politeness toward a *stranger*, who, though sadly disappointing them, had done perhaps *as well as he was able*. . . . It is true that the audience did not know that the poem was written in the 'tenth year' of the author; they only knew that it was sad stuff" (Moss [1963], pp. 109–10; *Post* quoted in February *Knickerbocker*).

15 JANUARY. NEW CROSS, HATCHAM, SURREY. Robert Browning writes Miss Barrett in London: "Will you let Mr. Poe's book [*The Raven and Other Poems*] lie on the table on Monday, if you please, that I may read what he *does* say, with my own eyes?" (Browning [1969], 1:388–90).

16 JANUARY. NEW YORK. Poe writes Sarah J. Hale in Philadelphia, replying to her 14 November 1845 letter. He had already seen Mrs. Hale's drama "Ormond Grosvenor" in *Godey's Lady's Book*; but upon receiving her manuscript, he gave it "a second careful reading." Although he retains his "first impression of its remarkable vigor and dramaticism," he suggests that it would be improved by "a curtailment of some of the mere dialogue." For her romance "Harry Guy" he would prefer the subtitle "A Tale in Verse" instead of "A Tale in Rhyme": "I think Clark & Austin or Paine & Burgess would be more willing to publish it, and afford you more liberal terms, than Wiley & Putnam—although, in point of caste, the latter are to be preferred, and their issues are sure of *some* notice in England" (*L*, 2:311–12).

16 JANUARY. PROVIDENCE, RHODE ISLAND. Sarah Helen Whitman writes Anne C. Lynch in New York, asking whether Poe's tales about mesmerism are based on actual occurrences (Lynch to Whitman, 20 January).

CA. 16 JANUARY? Mrs. Whitman writes her friend George William Curtis, an emergent author of twenty-one, in New York. She discusses Poe's review of Miss Barrett (Curtis to Whitman, 20 January).

19 JANUARY. NEW YORK. Andrew Jackson Davis, a clairvoyant known as the "Poughkeepsie Seer," receives a visitor: "His remarkable face bore traces of feminine mental characteristics; but upon his spacious brow there sparkled the gems of rare endowments. . . . At length he informed us that his name was 'Edgar A. Poe.' . . . I recollect of assuring him that, though he had poetically imagined the whole of his published article upon the answers of a clairvoyant ['Mesmeric Revelation'], the main ideas conveyed by it concerning 'ultimates' were strictly and philosophically true. At the close of this interview he departed, and never came again" (Davis quoted by Damon, pp. 157–58).

20 JANUARY. Miss Lynch replies to Mrs. Whitman: "Mr Poe's mesmeric revelations are mere fancies of his own without the least shadow of foundation in fact." She describes her 10 January soiree:

I will tell you who were here . . . Cassius Clay, Mr Hart the Sculptor who is going to *do* Henry Clay, full length in marble, & who has great genius I think— and is just fresh from Kentucky for the first time—Halleck, Locke (the man in the moon) Hunt of the merchants' magazine Hudson, Mr Bellows, Poe, Headley Miss Sedgwick Mrs Kirkland Mrs Ellet Mrs Seba Smith Miss Fuller Mrs Osgood & a great many others distinguished & undistinguished that I do not now remember. I wish very much that I could have numbered you among them. They come at seven & break up early & I give no entertainment except what they find in each other. My evening[s] however are by no means always as full and pleasant as this was. Many came to meet Mr Clay who do[es] not come very often (RPB–W).

20 JANUARY. Curtis replies to Mrs. Whitman: "You speak of Poe's article upon Miss Barrett. I should much like to see anything really good of his. With the exception of his volume of poems I know nothing of him save a tale ['Valdemar'] in one of the reviews a month ago, which was only like an offensive odor. There seems to be a vein of something in him, but if of gold he is laboring thro' many baser veins, and may at last reach it" (Curtis, pp. 371–73).

24 JANUARY. LONDON. The *Spectator* reviews the books it received *"From January 16th to January 22d,"* perfunctorily noticing *The Raven and Other Poems*: "A collection of fugitive American poems, which their author, Mr. Poe, has reprinted; not that he thinks the 'volume will be of much value to the public or very creditable to himself,' but with a view to 'their redemption from the many improvements to which they have been subjected while going at random the rounds of the press.' "

24–25 JANUARY. Elizabeth Barrett Barrett writes Robert Browning at New Cross, Hatcham, Surrey, forwarding "The Facts in the Case of M. Valdemar" and *The Raven and Other Poems*:

I send you besides a most frightful extract from an American magazine sent to me yesterday . . . no, the day before . . . on the subject of mesmerism—& you are to understand, if you please, that the Mr. Edgar Poe who stands committed in it, is my dedicator . . . whose dedication I forgot, by the way, with the rest—so, while I am sending, you shall have his poems with his mesmeric experience & decide whether the outrageous compliment to me EBB or the experiment on M. Vandeleur [*sic*] goes furthest to prove him mad. There is poetry in the man, though, now & then, seen between the great gaps of bathos . . . "Politian" will make you laugh—as the "Raven" made *me* laugh, though with something in it which accounts for the hold it took upon people such as Mr. N. P. Willis & his peers—it was sent to me from *four* different quarters besides the author himself, before its publication in this form, & when it had only a newspaper life. Some of the other lyrics have power of a less questionable sort. For the author, I do not know him at all—never heard from him nor wrote to him—and in my opinion, there is more faculty shown in the account of that horrible mesmeric experience (mad or not mad) than in his poems. Now do read it from the beginning to the end. That *"going out"* of the hectic, struck me very much . . . & the writhing *away* of the upper lip. Most horrible! (Browning [1969], 1:415–19).

620

30 JANUARY. NEW YORK. Poe writes Evert A. Duyckinck, requesting information on various authors he intends to discuss in his forthcoming sketches of "The Literati of New York City." He asks whether Duyckinck has seen Martin Farquhar Tupper's promised review of his *Tales*: "if so—how is it? long or short—sweet or sour?—if you have it, please lend it me." This letter will be delivered by Mrs. Clemm: "Should she not see you, can't you contrive to step in at 85 Amity St—some time to-day or tomorrow?" (*L*, 2:312–13).

31 JANUARY. LONDON. The *Literary Gazette* contains Tupper's long critique of Poe's *Tales*: "His work has come to our shores recommended by success upon its own; and . . . such success is no more than it deserves." Before discussing Poe's virtues, Tupper applies "a light and wholesome touch of censure" to "The Black Cat," which is "impossible and revolting," and to "Mesmeric Revelation," which "far too daringly attempts a solution of that deepest of riddles, the nature of the Deity." He characterizes "Lionizing" as "simply foolish" and "The Fall of the House of Usher" as "a juvenile production." While these four stories are "not without their own flashes of genius," they could have been omitted. Poe's "pervading characteristics" are "induction, and a microscopic power of analysis." As an illustration Tupper quotes a passage from "The Gold-Bug" describing Legrand's solution of Captain Kidd's cryptograph. This "bit of ingenious calculation" parallels the deciphering of the Rosetta stone. "The Murders in the Rue Morgue" reveals a "marvellous train of analytical reasoning"; in this tale "the horror of the incidents is overborne by the acuteness of the arguments." Poe displays similar powers in "The Mystery of Marie Rogêt." Other stories in this volume are "equally brightened by genius" while "untarnished with the dread details of crime." From "A Descent into the Maelström" Tupper quotes a long passage of "magnificent writing" describing the narrator's experiences inside the whirlpool. "The Conversation of Eiros and Charmion" is "full of terror and instruction; true to philosophy and to holy writ." Tupper prints an excerpt which "details the probable mode of the final conflagration." To conclude his review he reprints "The Haunted Palace," the book's sole specimen of poetry: "It occurs in the otherwise condemned tale of 'Usher'; and not only half redeems that ill-considered production, but makes us wish for many more such staves."

LATE JANUARY? Short & Co., 8 King Street, Bloomsbury, publish a sixteen-page pamphlet: "MESMERISM / 'IN ARTICULO MORTIS.' / AN / AS-TOUNDING & HORRIFYING NARRATIVE, / SHEWING THE EXTRAORDINARY POWER OF MESMERISM / IN ARRESTING THE / PROGRESS OF DEATH. / BY EDGAR A. POE, ESQ. / OF NEW YORK / . . . / *Price Threepence*." The inside front cover contains an "Advertisement":

The following astonishing narrative first appeared in the *American Magazine* [*American Review*], a work of some standing in the United States, where the case has excited the most intense interest.

The effects of the mesmeric influence, in this case, were so astounding, so contrary to all past experience, that no one could have possibly anticipated the final result. The narrative, though only a plain recital of facts, is of so extraordinary a nature as almost to surpass belief. It is only necessary to add, that credence is given to it in America, where the occurrence took place (copy in NN–B; cf. Arch Ramsay to Poe, 30 November).

LATE JANUARY? NEW YORK. Mrs. Frances S. Osgood visits Poe:

Virginia, his sweet wife, had written me a pressing invitation to come to them; and I, who never could resist her affectionate summons, and who enjoyed his society far more in his own home than elsewhere, hastened to Amity-street. I found him just completing his series of papers entitled "The Literati of New-York." "See," said he, displaying, in laughing triumph, several little rolls of narrow paper, (he always wrote thus for the press,) "I am going to show you, by the difference of length in these, the different degrees of estimation in which I hold all you literary people. In each of these, one of you is rolled up and fully discussed. Come, Virginia, help me!" And one by one they unfolded them. At last they came to one which seemed interminable. Virginia laughingly ran to one corner of the room with one end, and her husband to the opposite with the other. "And whose lengthened sweetness long drawn out is that?" said I. "Hear her!" he cried, "just as if her little vain heart didn't tell her it's herself!" (Mrs. Osgood to R. W. Griswold, early 1850, quoted in Griswold [1850], p. xxxvii).

LATE JANUARY? A Poe correspondent, probably Mrs. Elizabeth F. Ellet, is irritated by the treatment accorded one of her letters: "A certain lady . . . fell in love with Poe and wrote a love-letter to him. Every letter he received he showed to his little wife. This lady went to his house one day; she heard Fanny Osgood and Mrs. Poe having a hearty laugh, they were fairly shouting, as they read over a letter. The lady listened, and found it was hers, when she walked into the room and snatched it from their hands" (Elizabeth Oakes Smith quoted by Derby, p. 548).

LATE JANUARY? While visiting Poe's home at 85 Amity Street, Mrs. Ellet sees a letter to him from Mrs. Osgood which she considers indiscreet. She later persuades Mrs. Osgood to seek the return of all her letters to Poe. Margaret Fuller and Anne C. Lynch call upon him to present Mrs. Osgood's request. Annoyed at this intrusion into his personal life, Poe testily remarks that Mrs. Ellet should be more concerned about her own letters to him. As soon as Misses Fuller and Lynch depart with Mrs. Osgood's letters, Poe collects Mrs. Ellet's letters into a bundle, which he leaves at her residence. Mrs. Ellet schemes to free herself from Poe's imputation that

ELIZABETH F. ELLET

she sent him compromising letters: she has her brother William M. Lummis call upon him and demand her letters. Having already returned them, Poe is unable to comply; Lummis threatens his life unless he produces them. Poe visits Thomas Dunn English and asks to borrow a pistol to defend himself. English refuses to assist him, suggesting that he never possessed letters from Mrs. Ellet in the first place. Incensed, Poe engages in fisticuffs with English; the two men are quickly separated by Poe's friend Thomas Wyatt. Poe is subsequently confined to bed by illness; he has his physician, Dr. John W. Francis, deliver a letter of apology to Mrs. Ellet. In it Poe apparently denies any recollection of having charged her with an indiscreet correspondence; and he suggests that if he made such an accusation, he must have been suffering from temporary insanity (Poe to Mrs. Whitman, 24 November 1848; Mrs. Whitman to J. H. Ingram, 11 February and 11 May 1874, Miller [1979], pp. 20–22, 154–55; English in the *Morning Telegraph*, 23 June 1846; "Mr. Poe's Reply to Mr. English," 10 July 1846; Mrs. Ellet to Mrs. Osgood, 8 July 1846; Griswold [1850], pp. xxiii–xxiv; English, p. 1448; Reece [1970], pp. 157–64).

[As a result of this episode, Poe ceased to see or write Mrs. Osgood; and Miss Lynch removed his name from her guest list. He gained the lasting enmity of English and Mrs. Ellet. Reports of his "insanity," possibly spread by Mrs. Ellet, were printed by newspapers in New York and elsewhere. See W.G. Simms to E. A. Duyckinck, 27 March, and to James Lawson, 15 May; Mrs. Hewitt to Poe, 15 April; reports published on 12, 18 April, 9, 14 May 1846; Miss Lynch to Mrs. Whitman, 31 January and 21 February 1848.]

FEBRUARY? Virginia Poe writes Mrs. Osgood.

[Early in 1850 Mrs. Osgood wrote Rufus W. Griswold, asking him to declare her "innocence" in his forthcoming biography of Poe: "You have the proof in Mrs. Poe's letter to me, and in *his* [Poe's] to Mrs. Ellet, either of which would fully establish my innocence in a court of justice— certainly *hers* would. Neither of them, as you know, were persons likely to take much trouble to prove a woman's innocence, and it was only because she felt that I had been cruelly and shamefully wronged by her mother and Mrs. E[llet] that she impulsively rendered me that justice" (Griswold [1898], p. 256).]

FEBRUARY. In the "Editor's Table" of the *Knickerbocker Magazine*, Lewis Gaylord Clark quotes the Boston *Morning Post* of 14 January, which has denied that Poe actually deceived the Lyceum audience with "Al Aaraaf."

FEBRUARY. PHILADELPHIA. *Godey's Lady's Book* contains Poe's expanded criticism of Mrs. Mary E. Hewitt's *The Songs of Our Land, and Other Poems*, which he had initially reviewed in the *Broadway Journal* for 25 October 1845.

3 FEBRUARY OR BEFORE. LONDON? Acting on the request of the editor of the *Popular Record of Modern Science*, a "gentleman" writes "direct to Mr. Poe," inquiring whether his "Mesmeric Revelation" and "The Facts in the Case of M. Valdemar" are authentic accounts. This correspondent encloses the *Record* for 29 November 1845, containing the former tale, and for 10 January 1846, containing the latter (the *Record*, 10 January and 11 April).

13 FEBRUARY. NEW YORK. Poe composes an acrostic poem of twenty-one lines, dated "Valentine's Eve," which conceals the name "Frances Sergeant [Sargent] Osgood" (facsimile in Quinn and Hart, pp. 1–2).

14 FEBRUARY. George P. Morris issues the first number of his *National Press: A Journal for Home*, a weekly subsequently named the *Home Journal*.

14 FEBRUARY. Virginia Poe composes an acrostic valentine which conceals the name "Edgar Allan Poe." The poem, addressed to Poe at 85 Amity

Street, reveals her desire to escape the petty rumors occasioned by his association with Mrs. Osgood, Mrs. Ellet, and other bluestockings:

> Ever with thee I wish to roam—
> Dearest my life is thine.
> Give me a cottage for my home
> And a rich old cypress vine,
> Removed from the world with its sin and care
> And the tattling of many tongues.
> Love alone shall guide us when we are there—
> Love shall heal my weakened lungs;
> And Oh, the tranquil hours we'll spend,
> Never wishing that others may see!
> Perfect ease we'll enjoy, without thinking to lend
> Ourselves to the world and its glee—
> Ever peaceful and blissful we'll be
> (facsimile in Phillips, 2:1096).

14 FEBRUARY [1846?]. Poe composes a valentine poem "To Miss Louise Olivia Hunter," addressed to the schoolgirl whose "Prize Composition" he read at the commencement of the Rutgers Female Institute on 11 July 1845 (Mabbott [1969], 1:396–99; Moldenhauer [1973], pp. 8–9).

14 FEBRUARY. A revised manuscript of Poe's acrostic valentine for Mrs. Osgood, dated "Saturday, February 14," is read at Anne C. Lynch's soiree at 116 Waverley Place (Mabbott [1969], 1:386–91).

[On 16 January 1847 Miss Lynch wrote Mrs. Whitman: "Last year, on the evening of valentines day which came on Saturday, I had a valentine party—that is there were valentines written for all present—mostly original & in general merely complimentary verses—The best of them were selected & read & some of them afterwards published. . . . Mrs Osgood Mrs Ellet & a good many were here" (RPB–W). While Poe contributed a valentine to this soiree, it seems unlikely that he would have attended, considering the current scandal over Mrs. Ellet's letters.]

AFTER 14 FEBRUARY. The Poe family leaves 85 Amity Street and moves "in the country" (Poe to P. P. Cooke, 16 April).

[The family seems to have lived near the East River for several months, close to the home of Mr. and Mrs. John C. Miller. In 1909 Miss Sarah F. Miller, their daughter, left this reminiscence:

When I was a little girl we lived in a house facing Turtle Bay, on the East River, near the present 47th Street. Among our nearest neighbors was a charming family trio consisting of Mr. Poe, his wife Virginia, and his mother-in-law, Mrs. Clemm. Poor Virginia Poe was very ill at the time, and I never saw her leave her home.

Poe and Mrs. Clemm would very frequently call on us. He would also run over every little while to ask my father to lend him our rowboat, and then how he would enjoy himself pulling at the oars over to the little islands just south of Blackwell's Island, for his afternoon swim.

Mrs. Clemm and my mother soon became the best of friends, and she found mother a sympathetic listener to all her sad tales of poverty and want. I would often see her shedding tears as she talked. In the midst of this friendship they came and told us they were going to move to a distant place called Fordham, where they had rented a little cottage, feeling sure the pure country air would do Mrs. Poe a world of good (Whitty [1911], p. lvii; see also Phillips, 2:1109–13).]

21 FEBRUARY. The *Evening Mirror* prints twenty short poems from Miss Lynch's 14 February soiree; Poe's acrostic for Mrs. Osgood appears under the heading "TO HER WHOSE NAME IS WRITTEN BELOW." The final valentine is addressed to Poe:

TO THE AUTHOR OF THE RAVEN.

I asked the raven on his bust, above
  the chamber-door,
If that your fame could ever die—he answered
  "Nevermore."

The article is reprinted in the *Weekly Mirror* for 28 February.

23 FEBRUARY. PORTLAND, MAINE. Mary Neal, the daughter of John Neal, writes Mrs. Osgood in New York: "I am making a collection of the hair of our distinguished authors, poets, and painters . . . . May I hope to possess yours?" (MB–G).

26 FEBRUARY. SOUTH ATTLEBOROUGH, MASSACHUSETTS. Abijah M. Ide, Jr., writes Poe. He needs "certain numbers" of the *Broadway Journal* to make his set complete. Although he sent 50 cents to the magazine's office by a friend, he never received these issues: "Perhaps you may have the papers reserved for me in your possession" (MB–G).

27 FEBRUARY. NEW YORK. Mrs. Osgood writes Mary Neal, enclosing a lock of her hair. If Mary would also like a lock of Poe's hair, Mrs. Osgood can obtain it for her (Mary's reply, 25 April).

28 FEBRUARY. LONDON. The *Athenaeum* notices *The Raven and Other Poems*. The reviewer, probably the editor Thomas K. Hervey, complains that American poetry is merely an imitation of English verse. Since "Mr. Poe's fancy" is "to be original," it is unfortunate that he has not chosen "to be so after a native fashion. The instinct of borrowing must be unconquerable

amongst a people who borrow even their *originality*. . . . Electing to be mystical, we should have been grateful to Mr. Poe for a mysticism caught up on his own mountains,—fed on the far prairie,—watered by the mighty rivers of the land . . . . But Mr. Poe has taken his mystical degree in one of the worst of our London schools; where the art, as taught, consists in saying plain things enough after a fashion which makes them hard to be understood, and commonplaces in a sort of mysterious form which causes them to sound oracular." While Poe's poems occasionally reveal "a breathing of the Muse," he often "approaches dangerously near to the verge of the childish, and wanders on the very confines of the absurd." In the "Scenes" from *Politian* "the excess of the puerile . . . amounts to dramatic imbecility." The reviewer reprints "The Raven" ("a strange speci-men of the author's mannerisms") and "Dream-Land." Poe has "both music and imagination," yet his poetry is not altogether comprehensible: "The sense of the vague and mysterious, no doubt, may be conveyed by mysteri-ous music; but the character and meaning of the mystery wants some more intelligible exponent."

LATE FEBRUARY? NEW YORK. Wiley and Putnam reissue Poe's *Tales* and *The Raven and Other Poems*, bound together in a cloth volume which is priced at one dollar (Mabbott [1942], pp. xvi–xviii).

LATE FEBRUARY? Poe writes Charles Dickens in London. He understands that Dickens has become the editor of a London paper, the *Daily News*; he offers to furnish American correspondence for it. In another package Poe is sending Dickens the volume containing his *Tales* and *The Raven and Other Poems* (Dickens to Poe, 19 March).

LATE FEBRUARY? Poe sends a copy of his tales and poems to Miss Barrett in London, inscribed "To Miss Elisabeth Barrett Barrett / With the Re-spects of / Edgar A Poe" (presentation copy in NN–B; Barrett's letters to Robert Browning and John Kenyon, 20 March).

MARCH. PHILADELPHIA. *Graham's Magazine* contains an installment of Poe's "Marginalia."

MARCH. *Godey's Lady's Book* contains Poe's laudatory criticism of Mrs. Osgood's *A Wreath of Wild Flowers from New England*, a volume of verse published in 1842, and of her *Poems*, a new collection which he had initially noticed in the *Broadway Journal* for 13 December 1845.

MARCH. LONDON. *Churton's Literary Register* reviews *The Raven and Other Poems*, quoting three stanzas from the title poem (Pollin [1980], p. 26).

CA. MARCH. BALTIMORE. Robert DeUnger, an apprentice printer, becomes acquainted with Poe, who is visiting Baltimore:

I first met him [Poe] in 1846, about a year previous to his wife's death. He was probably 12 or 15 years my elder at that time, as I was nearing my majority. [We were introduced by] Mr. John N. Millington, then foreman of the Baltimore *Patriot*, an evening paper, (also publishing a morning edition.) The introduction took place in Guy's Coffee House, corner of Monument Square and Fayette street, but our conversation was quite brief, Mr. Poe being of a nervous, melancholy, glum disposition and not much inclined to converse. He spoke to Mr. Millington of the illness of his wife—she had then been an invalid for some years—and remarked that there was a slight improvement in her condition. I do not remember where he said she was, but she certainly was not in Baltimore at that time. As Mr. Poe stood up to the "Bar" and drank off a *big* drink of whiskey, (I believe this was his favorite tipple), Mr. Millington and myself joining him—my drink "California Pop," as it was called, I formed the opinion that the poet had, in his time, seen many a barkeeper's countenance; and, really, I pitied him, for I had read a number of his short stories, printed if my memory serves me correctly, in Graham's Gentlemen's Magazine, a Philadelphia monthly, and greatly admired his style of composition. I was "courting" those days and the men in the *Patriot* office, on account of my youth, twitted me a good deal about it. At that time I was assisting Mr. John Wills, who managed the commercial column of the *Patriot*. Mr. Millington joked me and mentioned the matter of my "courting" to Mr. Poe, who, with the gravity of a Church beadle, remarked—"My young friend—don't hurry yourself as to marriage. It has its joys, but its sorrows overbalance those." His manner, when he uttered this sentence, actually *chilled* me. A second drink—called for by Mr. Millington,—was indulged in and we separated. It is fresh in mind that Mr. Poe, on this occasion, was entirely destitute of funds, because he took Mr. Millington aside and borrowed a trifle from him (DeUnger to E. R. Reynolds, 29 October 1899, ViU–I; cf. Mrs. Hewitt to Poe, 15 April 1846).

2 MARCH. CHARLESTON, SOUTH CAROLINA. In the *Southern Patriot* William Gilmore Simms reviews *The Raven and Other Poems*: "The wild, fanciful and utterly abstract character of these poems, will prove incomprehensible to him who requires that poetry shall embody an axiom in morals, or a maxim in philosophy or society." While Simms will not go "so far as to approve wholly of the scheme and tenor of Mr. Poe's performances in verse," he cautions those readers who would condemn this book: "Mr. Poe is a fantastic and a mystic—a man of dreamy mood and wandering fancies. His scheme of a poem requires that his reader shall surrender himself to influences of pure imagination. He demands as a preliminary that you should recognize totally unreal premises—that you should yield yourself wholly to the witch element, as implicitly as Mephistopheles requires it of Faust, ascending the wizard eminences of the Brocken. Unless you can make him this concession you had better have nothing to do with his volume." Having space for "but a single extract," Simms

reprints "The Valley of Unrest," which aptly illustrates Poe's genius: "The music of the verse, the vagueness of the delineation, its mystical character, and dreamy and spiritual fancies, are all highly characteristic."

6 MARCH. LONDON. Miss Barrett writes Robert Browning at New Cross, Hatcham, Surrey: "I forgot to tell you that Mr. [John] Kenyon was in an immoderate joy the day I saw him last, about Mr. Poe's 'Raven' as seen in the Athenaeum extracts [of 28 February], & came to ask what I knew of the poet & his poetry, & took away the book [*The Raven and Other Poems*]. It's the rhythm which has taken him with 'glamour' I fancy" (Browning [1969], 1:521–22).

7 MARCH. NEW YORK. The *Daily Tribune* reports: "The New-York correspondent of a Washington paper says that Mr. Poe is engaged on a work which will embrace his opinions of the various New-York literati, and thinks that it will create a sensation, and that the uproar which attended Pope's Dunciad was nothing to the stormy confusion of the literary elements which will war and rage, 'with red lightning winged,' when that book makes its appearance."

14 MARCH. LONDON. The *Literary Gazette* contains a hostile review of *The Raven and Other Poems* by the editor William Jerdan: "The genius of Edgar Poe, such as it is, had its full exposition and place assigned to it [by Martin F. Tupper] in the *Literary Gazette* of 31st January." Jerdan prints a letter he received afterwards from William Petrie, a reader of the *Gazette* who ingeniously pointed out several inaccuracies in Poe's description of the whirlpool in "A Descent into the Maelström." Jerdan observes: "If such objections can justly be raised against his [Poe's] prose, we fear we must allow that some of his poetry is not less wild; or, in other words, that there is not so much method in his *furor* as could be desired by readers not inflamed and carried away by his vague thoughts and diction." As "a specimen of bad taste and exaggeration," Jerdan quotes the last stanza of "The Sleeper," italicizing the line "*Soft may the worms about her creep!*" He then reprints "The Conqueror Worm": "another sample of the morbid." Miss Barrett's style seems to have had "considerable influence" on Poe: "In some points it might have been better had he studied her more closely."

14 MARCH. PHILADELPHIA. The *Saturday Evening Post* cites *The Conchologist's First Book* in an editorial discussing plagiarism:

One of the most remarkable plagiarisms was perpetrated by Mr. Poe, late of the Broadway Journal, whose harshness as a critic and assumption of peculiar originality makes [make] the fault, in his case, more glaring. This gentleman, a few years ago, in Philadelphia, published a work on Conchology as original, when in reality it was a copy, nearly verbatim, of "The Text-Book of Conchology, by Capt. Thomas Brown," printed in Glasgow in 1833, a duplicate of which we have in our library. Mr. Poe actually took out a copy-right for the American edition of Capt. Brown's work, and, omitting all mention of the English original, pretended, in the preface, to have been under great obligations to several scientific gentlemen of this city. It is but justice to add, that in the second [third] edition of this book, published lately in Philadelphia, the name of Mr. Poe is withdrawn from the title-page, and his initials only affixed to the preface. But the affair is one of the most curious on record, and we recommend it to Mr. Griswold as a rare morsel for his forthcoming "Curiosities of American Literature."

[Poe's book was actually an undertaking of his friend Thomas Wyatt, who paid him for the use of his name. While it contained some original material, it was largely compiled from various European sources, like most American textbooks and scientific manuals of the time. All its illustrations were reproduced from Brown's book; the other borrowings from this source are much less obvious.]

17 MARCH. WOODLANDS, SOUTH CAROLINA. Simms writes Evert A. Duyckinck in New York, mentioning his 2 March review of *The Raven and Other Poems*: "Did you receive a notice of Poe's & Headley's Vols. that I sent you . . . ? Where is Poe now & what doing" (Simms, 2:151–53).

18 MARCH. QUINCY, ILLINOIS. The *Whig* publishes "The Pole-Cat," a parody of "The Raven" (Lincoln, 1:377).

18 MARCH OR LATER. Andrew Johnston, a Quincy lawyer, writes his friend Abraham Lincoln, an amateur poet as well as an emergent Illinois politician, forwarding the newspaper containing "The Pole-Cat" (Lincoln to Johnston, 18 April).

19 MARCH. LONDON. Charles Dickens replies to Poe's recent letter. Although he has not yet received the volume containing the *Tales* and *The Raven and Other Poems*, he avails himself "of a leisure moment" to thank Poe "for the gift of it." Dickens cannot consider Poe's offer to furnish American correspondence for the London *Daily News*: "I am not in any way connected with the Editorship or current management of that Paper. I have an interest in it, and write such papers for it as I attach my name to. This is the whole amount of my connexion" (PHi).

20 MARCH. Elizabeth Barrett Barrett writes Robert Browning at New Cross, Hatchman, Surrey: "Mr. Poe has sent me his poems & tales . . . . Just now I have the book" (Browning [1969], 1:546–48).

20 MARCH. Miss Barrett writes her friend John Kenyon: "To-day Mr. Poe

sent me a volume containing his poems and tales collected, so now I *must* write and thank him for his dedication. What is to be said, I wonder, when a man calls you the 'noblest of your sex'? 'Sir, you are the most discerning of yours' " (Browning [1898], pp. 248–49).

21 MARCH. The *London Journal* reprints "The Raven" (Tanselle [1963], pp. 229–30).

27 MARCH. WOODLANDS, SOUTH CAROLINA. Simms writes Duyckinck, who has alluded to the scandal involving Mrs. Ellet's letters: "Your hints with regard to Poe, the Ladies, Billet doux &c quite provoke my curiosity. What is the mischief—who the victims &c. *Entre nous*, I half suspected that mischief would grow out of all those fine critical discriminations &c. It is dangerous to the poetess when the critic teaches her the use of spondees, and trochaics, dactyls, trimeters & dimeters" (Simms, 2:157–59).

BEFORE 28 MARCH. PHILADELPHIA. *Godey's Lady's Book* for April contains Poe's essay on William Cullen Bryant.

28 MARCH. NEW YORK. In the *Evening Mirror* Hiram Fuller reviews *Godey's*, citing the "very discriminating *critique* on the poetical works of Bryant, from the pen of Mr. Poe." The review appears in the *Weekly Mirror* for 4 April.

BEFORE APRIL. Poe replies to a correspondent in England, who had inquired whether the two tales of his reprinted in the London *Popular Record of Modern Science* are fact or fiction:

The philosophy detailed in the "Last Conversation of a Somnambule," [the *Record's* title for "Mesmeric Revelation"] is my own—original, I mean, with myself, and had long impressed me. I was anxious to introduce it to the world in a manner that should insure for it attention. I thought that by presenting my speculations in a garb of vraisemblance—giving them as revelations—I would secure for them a hearing . . . . In the case of Valdemar, I was actuated by similar motives, but in this latter paper, I made a more pronounced effort at verisimilitude for the sake of effect. The only material difference between the two articles is, that in one I believe actual truth to be involved; in the other I have aimed at merely suggestion and speculation. I find the Valdemar case universally copied and *received as truth*, even in spite of my disclaimer (quoted in the *Record*, 11 April).

APRIL. LONDON. Miss Barrett writes Poe, thanking him for the volume containing his *Tales* and *The Raven and Other Poems*. She expresses her "sense of the high honor" Poe has done her by dedicating his poems to her: "It is too great a distinction, conferred by a hand of too liberal generosity. I wish for my own sake I were worthy of it." She also thanks him, "as another reader," for "this vivid writing, this power which is felt! Your 'Raven' has produced a sensation, a 'fit horror,' here in England. Some of my friends are taken by the fear of it and some by the music. I hear of persons haunted by the 'Nevermore,' and one acquaintance of mine who has the misfortune of possessing a 'bust of Pallas' never can bear to look at it in the twilight." Poe's "Valdemar" is now "going the round of the newspapers, about mesmerism, throwing us all into 'most admired disorder,' and dreadful doubts as to whether 'it can be true,' as the children say of ghost stories" (*W*, 17:229–30).

APRIL. NEW YORK. Wiley and Putnam's *Literary News-Letter*, published free of charge, advertises the cloth volume containing Poe's tales and poems (Mabbott [1942], pp. xvi–xvii).

APRIL. In the *Knickerbocker Magazine* Lewis Gaylord Clark unfavorably reviews Simms's novel *Count Julian*, alluding to Poe as a "small magazine 'critic-ling' " and as "the besotted driveller who called CARLYLE an ass."

APRIL. The *Democratic Review* contains an installment of Poe's "Marginalia."

APRIL. PHILADELPHIA. *Graham's Magazine* contains "The Philosophy of Composition," in which Poe describes the writing of "The Raven."

APRIL. RICHMOND. The *Southern Literary Messenger* contains Philip Pendleton Cooke's essay "Old Books and New Authors," which argues that "Fairly, or unfairly, every new writer makes extensive use of old books." Cooke quotes Poe's review of the January 1846 *Graham's*, found in the *Broadway Journal* for 27 December 1845, which suggested that "Emily: Proem to the Froissart Ballads" revealed an indebtedness to Richard Lovelace's "To Althea, From Prison." As the author of the poem in *Graham's*, Cooke can testify that if there was imitation, it was unconscious. He observes that the verse "None sing so wildly well," in Poe's "Israfel," bears a similarity to Byron's line "He sings so wild and well," from "The Bride of Abydos." "Of course this was, as in my own case, an unconscious appropriation—or, if conscious, still perfectly innocent. The man who goes out of his way to *avoid* such trivial imitations, is over dainty to do manly work."

3 APRIL. PHILLIPS, MAINE. George W. Eveleth writes Poe: "I am not to believe that the three letters which have been addressed to you concerning the Broadway Journal have all failed to reach you. . . . If you did not get the letter [of 5 January] in which were enclosed three dollars for your

paper, why have you not let me know it after having learned that I sent the money to you?. . . as it is hardly possible that every one of the letters which have been sent to you (two by myself, and one by our post master) miscarried, and as I have not heard a word from you, so it is probable that you have received them all, the money with them, and no thanks to me for it." Eveleth has seen an editorial in the Philadelphia *Saturday Evening Post* for 14 March, "speaking of plagiarisms (another kind of swindling)," which referred to Poe as "*late* of the Broadway Journal"; from this he supposes that his correspondent has left this paper. "Well, am I going to receive my money back again, or any thing in recompense? It is not the money that I care about so much, although three dollars is something to lose. I was in hopes that I had found the opportunity of becoming a permanent subscriber to a publication conducted by my favorite, Edgar A. Poe Esq. It is for this that I care principally" (Eveleth, pp. 6–7).

4 APRIL. LONDON. The *Critic* reviews *The Raven and Other Poems*: "In an early number [14 June 1845] . . . we presented . . . a very remarkable poem, entitled *The Raven*, which had been sent to us from America. It was its first appearance in England, and it attracted a great deal of notice, and went the round of the provincial papers." Judging from the subjects Poe has selected for his poetry, he is still a young man: "If so, there is good stuff in him. He has the foundation of the poet, and industry and experience may raise a structure that will be an honour to his own country, and the admiration of ours." The reviewer reprints three poems, "which are among the most favourable specimens of his genius contained in the collection." "The Valley of Unrest" is unquestionably poetry; it reminds the reader "forcibly of TENNYSON." Although "The Sleeper" is beautiful, it is "after the manner of COLERIDGE" and thus illustrates "the imitative character of American literature." The third poem, "Dream-Land," reveals Poe's "power of painting." More than half the book is devoted to "Poems Written in Youth," which "serve, at least, to mark the great progress the author has made; otherwise they are not worth the paper on which they are printed." This reviewer will be "glad to meet Mr. POE again, both in prose and poetry."

11 APRIL. The *Popular Record of Modern Science* informs its readers that "Mesmeric Revelation" and "The Facts in the Case of M. Valdemar," which it had initially regarded as authentic, are only fictions. The *Record* quotes Poe's recent letter discussing these stories, which was sent to "a gentleman" who wrote him at the editor's request (Ostrom [1974], pp. 528–29).

12 APRIL. SAINT LOUIS. The *Daily Reveille* reports: "A rumor is in circula-

tion in New York, to the effect that Mr. Edgar A. Poe, the poet and author, has become deranged, and his friends are about to place him under the charge of Dr. Brigham, of the Insane Retreat at Utica. We sincerely hope that this is not true; indeed we feel assured that it is altogether an invention" (Moss [1968], p. 19, and [1970], p. 92).

14 APRIL. NEW YORK. Poe receives three letters from Philip Pendleton Cooke, as well as the manuscripts of Cooke's poem "The Power of the Bards" and his prose sketch "The Turkey-hunter in the Closet" (Poe to Cooke, 16 April).

CA. 15 APRIL. Poe sends Cooke's poem to George H. Colton, editor of the *American Review*, and his sketch to William T. Porter, editor of the *Spirit of the Times*, a New York sporting journal (Poe to Cooke, 16 April).

15 APRIL. Mrs. Mary E. Hewitt writes Poe. Not knowing his current address, she has had to entrust this letter to the Post Office, hoping that "by some favorable chance" he will receive it:

We [the bluestockings associated with Poe] were all exceedingly sorry to hear of your illness in Baltimore, and glad when we heard that you had so far recovered as to be able to return to our latitude, though it were to play hide-and-seek with your friends. Our charming friend Mrs. Osgood, and myself, indulge often in talking of you and your dear wife. Next to seeing those we remember, is the luxury of talking of them—and you know the power of the femenine [*sic*] organ at *laudation*, as well as its opposite.

All Bluedom misses you from its charmed circle, and we often ask when we are to have Mr. Poe back again among us. Will you not favor me with a reply, should this reach you? (Mabbott [1937], p. 120).

16 APRIL. Poe writes Cooke at The Vineyard, Clarke County, Virginia, acknowledging receipt of three letters, "all at once," on 14 April: "I have been living in the country for the last two months (having been quite sick) and all letters addressed to 85 Amity St. were very sillily retained there, until their accumulation induced the people to send them to the P. Office." At present Poe is preparing sketches of the New York literati for *Godey's Lady's Book*: "Pending the issue of this series, I am getting ready similar papers to include American littérateurs generally—and, by the beginning of December, I hope to put to press (here and in England) a volume embracing *all* the articles under the common head 'The Living Literati of the U S.'—or something similar." The forthcoming book will be prefaced by James Russell Lowell's sketch of Poe, which appeared in *Graham's Magazine* for February 1845: "This Memoir, however, is defective, inasmuch as it says nothing of my latest & I think my best things—'The

Raven' (for instance), 'The Valdemar Case', etc. May I ask of you the great favor to add a P.S. to Lowell's article—bringing up affairs as you well know how. . . . If you are willing to oblige me—speak frankly above all—speak of my *faults*, too, as forcibly as you can" (*L*, 2:313–15).

16 APRIL. Poe replies to Eveleth's 3 April letter: "Your letters, one and all, reached me in due course of mail—and I attended to them, *as far as I could*." Poe explains that he is "in no degree to blame" for failing to return Eveleth's three dollars, because the person to whom the *Broadway Journal* was transferred, "and in whose hands it perished," was responsible for handling subscriptions: "Of course, I feel no less in honor bound to refund you your money, and now do so, with many thanks for your promptness & courtesy" (*L*, 2:315).

18 APRIL. BOSTON. *Littell's Living Age* reprints the review of *The Raven and Other Poems* from the London *Athenaeum* of 28 February.

18 APRIL. BALTIMORE. In the *Saturday Visiter* Joseph Evans Snodgrass comments: "EDGAR A. POE, according to a New York letter writer, labors under mental derangement, to such a degree that it has been determined to consign him to the Insane Retreat at Utica.—This will be a painful piece of intelligence to thousands."

18 APRIL. TREMONT, ILLINOIS. Abraham Lincoln writes Andrew Johnston in Quincy, Illinois: "Your letter, written some six weeks since [actually on 18 March or later], was received in due course, and also the paper with the parody [Quincy *Whig* of 18 March with 'The Pole-Cat']. It is true, as suggested it might be, that I have never seen Poe's 'Raven'; and I very well know that a parody is almost entirely dependent for its interest upon the reader's acquaintance with the original. Still there is enough in the pole-cat, self-considered, to afford one several hearty laughs. I think four or five of the last stanzas are decidedly funny" (Lincoln, 1:377–79).

18 APRIL. NEW YORK. Poe replies to an inquiry from James E. Root: "A complete copy of the B.J. [*Broadway Journal*] can be obtained of Mr. Cornelius Mathews, 400 Nassau St. N. Y. *up stairs*—or, if you prefer it, enclose me the subscription price ($3.) and I will leave a copy for you at any place you shall designate in this city" (*L*, 2:713–14).

18 APRIL. The *Evening Mirror* carries an advertisement for "Edgar A. Poe's Opinions of the Literary People of New York," which will appear in *Godey's Lady's Book*: "Look out for the first number on Monday, the 20th. Something piquant may be expected."

20 APRIL OR BEFORE. PHILADELPHIA. *Godey's* for May contains "The Literati of New York City: Some Honest Opinions at Random Respecting Their Autorial Merits, with Occasional Words of Personality." In this first installment Poe discusses George Bush, George H. Colton, Nathaniel P. Willis, William M. Gillespie, Charles F. Briggs, William Kirkland, and John W. Francis. His sketches are favorable, except that of his former partner: "Mr. Briggs has never composed in his life three consecutive sentences of grammatical English. He is grossly uneducated." In the "Editors' Book Table" Louis A. Godey calls attention to the series: "We are much mistaken if these papers of Mr. P. do not raise some commotion in the literary emporium."

20 APRIL. NEW YORK. Hiram Fuller reviews *Godey's* in the *Evening Mirror*, praising Poe's "Literati" as the article "calculated to make the most noise." The "juxtaposition of names" in this installment "is quite amusing. But as personalities are always popular, we think this kind of gossip will prove a happy hit for the publisher—though the friends of the gentlemen discussed would have been puzzled to recognize the portraits had the names been omitted. . . . Mr. Poe makes sad mistakes in his attempts at minute description of personal appearance, height, figure, age, foreheads, noses, &c. But he always writes with spirit, and a commendable degree of independence, and we hope that next month, he will dish us up a lady or two, just by way of adding a plum to his pudding."

21 APRIL. The *Gazette and Times* notices *Godey's*, condemning Poe's "Literati" as "a piece of gratuitous and unpardonable impertinence" consisting of "ungentlemanly and unpardonable personalities, and intrusion into the private matters of living men." The *Gazette* recalls that the "unfortunate writer of this paper" has recently "attracted some attention and compassion" because of his idiosyncrasies. He is "at present in a state of health which renders him not completely accountable for all his peculiarities."

24 APRIL. The *Evening Mirror* carries an advertisement for the magazine agent W. H. Graham, located in the Tribune Buildings:

EDGAR A. POE AND THE NEW YORK LITERATI.—The great excitement caused by the publication of No. 1 of the above remarkable papers, exhausted our supply of the May number of Godey's Lady's Book. We have this morning received a few more, and will be in the constant receipt of them until the extraordinary demand is fully supplied.

The June number will contain several more notices, and they will continue monthly.

25 APRIL. The *Daily Tribune* carries the same advertisement.

25 APRIL. PORTLAND, MAINE. Mary Neal replies to Mrs. Frances S. Osgood, whose letter of 27 February was not received until today: "I guess I *do* want a lock of Mr Poe's hair! and I guess I *am* an admirer of his Raven; I think it is—I hardly know what word to use—it is strange grotesque and very beautiful;—but as I also want a line of his writing with a lock of his hair, I will enclose in this letter a note for him and then I shall be sure of having an answer;—don't you think so?"

John Neal writes Mrs. Osgood on the verso of his daughter's letter: "say to Mr Poe, that for old acquaintance sake, if for no other reason, I hope he will furnish my girl with a bit of the raven plumage and a word or two of writing" (MB–G).

27 APRIL. PHILADELPHIA. Louis A. Godey replies to the magazine agents Burgess, Stringer & Co., 222 Broadway, New York, who have requested additional copies of the May *Lady's Book*: "Your order will be attended to as soon as we can get the numbers ready to send, which will be in a day or two. Portions of the book we have been obliged to reprint" (New York *Evening Mirror*, 28 April).

28 APRIL. NEW YORK. Poe replies to Jerome A. Maubey, whose letter has been forwarded to him from Philadelphia: "You have, evidently, supposed me editor of 'Godey's Magazine' and sent me the poem (a very beautiful one) under that supposition. . . . I am not connected, at present, with any journal in which I could avail myself of your talents" (L, 2:317).

28 APRIL. Poe replies to George F. Barstow and Fayette Jewett of Burlington, Vermont, who have written him that he has been elected commencement poet: "Will you be so kind as [to] express to the Societies of the University of Vermont, my profound sense of the honor they have done me, and at the same time my deep regret that a multiplicity of engagements, with serious and, I fear, permanent ill health, will not permit me to avail myself of their flattering invitation?" (L, 2:714).

28? APRIL. Poe writes John Keese, a New York author and editor (Poe to Duyckinck).

28 APRIL. Poe writes Evert A. Duyckinck, enclosing his letter to Keese: "May I ask of you the favor to look it over and then seal it and send it to him?" Poe also encloses the letter he received "from the Lit. Societies of the Vermont University." He asks Duyckinck to insert a report in the *Morning News* or another paper, stating that he has been elected poet for the University's "ensuing Anniversary in August next," but cannot accept

because of "continued ill health, with a pressure of engagements" (*L*, 2:316–17).

28 APRIL. Poe writes Godey in Philadelphia, enclosing forty-seven autographs. He believes that he can supply autographs for almost all the authors to be discussed in his "Literati" articles: "You will see that I send an autograph of all included in the May No. with the exception of Dr Francis:—and him I will supply *to-morrow*. For the article intended for the June No. there are 3 signatures wanting—viz: Maroncelli, Verplanck, and Cheever; and unless you have these, or can get them at once, perhaps it will be better to leave out these names for the present." Poe thanks Godey for "the prompt payment of the 4 drafts" (Ostrom [1974], pp. 529–31).

28 APRIL. The *Evening Mirror* carries an advertisement for Burgess, Stringer & Co.: "THE DEMAND STILL CONTINUES for the May number of Godey's Lady's Book, containing No. 1 of Edgar A. Poe's 'Notices of the Literary People of New York.' " These magazine agents quote Godey's 27 April letter, which reveals that "we will be enabled to serve our customers as soon as the new supply is received." The advertisement appears in the *Daily Tribune* on 29 April.

BEFORE 29 APRIL. Lewis Gaylord Clark attacks Poe in the "Editor's Table" of the May *Knickerbocker Magazine*: "There is a wandering specimen of '*The Literary Snob*' continually obtruding himself upon public notice; to-day in the gutter, to-morrow in some milliner's magazine . . . . Mrs. LOUISA GODEY has lately taken this snob into her service in a neighboring city, where he is doing his best to prove his title to the distinction of being one of the lowest of his class at present infesting the literary world." Clark asserts that Poe's "Literati" sketches are "so notoriously false that they destroy themselves. The sketch for example of Mr. BRIGGS, ('HARRY FRANCO,') . . . is *ludicrously* untrue, in almost every particular."

29 APRIL. In the *Evening Mirror* Hiram Fuller reviews the *Knickerbocker*: "The way old 'Knick' touches up Poe is 'a caution.' By the way, we notice that the article on the 'New York Literati' in the April [May] number of Godey's Lady's Book has compelled the publisher to print a second edition. There is nothing in this country that sells so well as literary scandal."

29 APRIL? Poe sends Godey the autograph of Dr. John W. Francis (implied by Poe to Godey, 28 April, and by the autograph's publication in the June *Lady's Book*).

CA. MAY. FORDHAM. The Poe family moves to Fordham, a village some thirteen miles north of New York proper, where they rent a small cottage owned by John Valentine for $100 a year (Phillips, 2:1114–18, 1546–49; Quinn, pp. 506–07).

[Mrs. Whitman recalled that Poe told her "that he took Virginia out there in the spring of the year to see the cottage, & that it was half-buried in fruit trees, which were then all in blossom. That she was charmed with the little place, which was rented for a very trifling sum" (Whitman to J. H. Ingram, 21 April 1874, Miller [1979], p. 124).]

1 MAY. NEW YORK. The *Daily Tribune* reports: "EDGAR A. POE.—By a concurrent vote of the Literary Societies of the University of Vermont, Mr. Poe has been elected Poet for their ensuing Anniversary in August next; but we are sorry to hear that continued ill health, with a pressure of engagements, will force him to decline the office."

1 MAY. PHILADELPHIA. Godey writes Poe (cited on Poe's 28 April letter to him).

3 MAY. LONDON. Wiley and Putnam deposit a copy of *The Raven and Other Poems* in the British Museum, for copyright (Mabbott [1942], p. xix).

5 MAY. BOSTON. In the *Evening Transcript* Cornelia Wells Walter observes: "The Knickerbocker occasionally serves up in its 'editor's table' rare bits of opinion which well answer the purpose of palpable *hits* for individuals." She quotes Clark's attack on Poe from the May number, adding: "This same individual [Poe] is famous for indulging in gross falsehoods, and these have become so common with him that whenever seen in print they are ever met by the reader, with the simple exclamation Poh! POE!"

6 MAY. LONDON. Elizabeth Barrett Barrett writes Robert Browning at New Cross, Hatcham, Surrey: "Today I had a book sent to me from America by the poetess Mrs. Osgood. . . . her note was of the very most affectionate, & her book is of the most gorgeous, all purple & gold—and she tells me . . . that I ought to go to New York, only 'to see Mr. Poe's wild eyes flash through tears' when he reads my verses" (Browning [1969], 2:683–84).

7 MAY. BOSTON. Horace Greeley, who is visiting Boston, writes his friend William H. C. Hosmer, a poet in upstate New York:

Poe—who is a brilliant writer when neither too drunk nor too sober—and might be somebody if he were not an incorrigible rascal and vagabond—has published in the last Godey some sketches of New York literati, which are said to be pungent. I have not seen them, but they are exciting a sensation, so that every copy is bought up in the City [New York]. I have applied twice for one without success. Godey advertises that this series is to be reprinted and accompanied by another in his June number. I presume the reprint will appear in the edition of our City alone. Poe has run all out in New York, and gone South, but his writings will sell, for he has genius. I presume he ran in debt $1,000 during the time he stopped in our City, scandalized two eminent literary ladies [Mrs. Ellet and Mrs. Osgood], and came near getting horsewhipped or pistoled. He insulted the Bostonians grossly, having been engaged to deliver a Poem here, which he did rather drunk and the poem an old and poor one. That chap will be getting into scrapes all his life until the sexton gets him into one that he cannot get out of (Mabbott [1933], pp. 14–16).

8 MAY. NEW YORK. The *Evening Mirror* carries a paid insertion, headed "A CARD," signed by Louis A. Godey: "When during a recent visit to New York, the subscriber [Godey] informed Mr. Lewis Gaylord Clark that Mr. Poe had him 'booked' in his 'Opinions of the New York Literati,' he supposed that he was giving Mr. Lewis Gaylord Clark a very agreeable piece of information; as it must have been quite apparent to the gentleman himself, that his natural position was not among the literati, but *subliterati* of New York." This information seems instead to have put Clark "in a perfect agony of terror. His desperation is laughably exhibited in the insane attack he has made on Mr. Poe, in the Knickerbocker for May." Godey has been "repeatedly advised" to discontinue Poe's sketches; but this course "would be as indelicate and unjust towards Mr. Poe, as it would be ungrateful towards the public, who have expressed distinct and decisive approbation of the articles in that unmistakeable way which a publisher is always happy to recognize."

9 MAY. BALTIMORE. Snodgrass' *Saturday Visiter* reports: "EDGAR A. POE has been elected Anniversary Poet, by the University of Vermont, but has been obliged to decline on account of continued ill health. He is sojourning in a retired part of Long Island, where he is still severely suffering from an attack of 'brain fever.' "

14 MAY. NEW ORLEANS. The *Daily Picayune* reports that Poe is "sojourning" on Long Island, "still suffering from an attack of brain fever. So says the correspondent of the North American" (Moss [1970], p. 92).

15 MAY. WOODLANDS, SOUTH CAROLINA. William Gilmore Simms writes James Lawson in New York: "Hints have reached me that Poe had been dealing in mischief, &c. Duyckinck talks of strange doings, & I see by one of the papers that it was gravely thought to send P. to Bedlam" (Simms, 2:161–63).

16 MAY. NEW YORK. In the *Weekly Mirror* Hiram Fuller reprints Poe's sketches of William Kirkland and Dr. John W. Francis from the May installment of "The Literati."

18 MAY. The *Evening Mirror* carries Godey's advertisement for the June *Lady's Book*, which will contain both "Nos. 1 & 2 of Edgar Poe's opinions of the New York Literati. . . . The demand has been so great that a reprint has become necessary." Godey offers to repurchase copies of the May number at "25 CTS." each.

20 MAY OR BEFORE. PHILADELPHIA. *Godey's* for June features the second installment of Poe's "Literati," with sketches of Anna Cora Mowatt, George B. Cheever, Charles Anthon, Ralph Hoyt, Gulian C. Verplanck, Freeman Hunt, Piero Maroncelli, and Laughton Osborn. This issue contains a supplement in which the first installment is reprinted, followed by facsimiles of the autographs of Hoyt, Francis, Colton, Gillespie, Willis, Bush, and Mowatt.

In the "Editors' Book Table" Louis A. Godey acknowledges "several letters from New York, anonymous and from personal friends," which asked him to moderate Poe's sketches: "We reply to one and all, that we have nothing to do but publish Mr. Poe's opinions, *not our own*. . . . Our course is onward. The May edition was exhausted before the first of May, and we have had orders for hundreds from Boston and New York which we could not supply." Godey observes that "various persons" are attempting to turn public opinion against Poe: "We have the name of one person,— others are busy with reports of Mr. Poe's illness. Mr. Poe has been ill, but we have letters from him of very recent dates, also a new batch of the Literati, which show anything but feebleness either of body or mind."

20 MAY. NEW YORK. In the *Evening Mirror* Hiram Fuller notices the publication of the June *Godey's*: "we purpose giving in a day or two a thorough review of 'Poe's Literati' . . . . The writer of course would not object to the same treatment which he so liberally deals to others."

22 MAY. The *Evening Mirror* reprints a pseudonymous poem, by "Mustard Mace," from the Philadelphia *Saturday Gazette*:

> Dictator Poe,
> Of Scribblers' Row!
> (I name you so
> Because you show
> You're fain to crow
> O'er every foe
> Who will not go

Your feet below.)
Beware lest you
A storm may brew
That harm may do
Yourself unto,
And you may rue,
And learn to sue
For quarter too. . . .

23 MAY. BOSTON. *Littell's Living Age* reprints Martin Farquhar Tupper's review of Poe's *Tales* from the London *Literary Gazette* of 31 January.

AFTER 23 MAY. Eliakim Littell writes Poe that Tupper's review has been reprinted in the *Living Age* (Poe to E. A. Duyckinck, 29 June).

25 MAY. Cornelia Wells Walter comments in the *Evening Transcript*:

EDGAR A. POE AND THE BOSTON LYCEUM. The 18th Annual Report of the Boston Lyceum has recently been given to the public, with a mention of the different literary exercises of the past year. THE POEM by Mr Poe is alluded to in a very proper manner, whilst explanatory of the causes which brought him person-ally before the Boston people. The report says, "the Board had invited this person on the strength of his literary reputation, and were not aware of his personal habits or the eccentricities of his character. For the merit or faults of his literary productions, he, of course, is alone responsible. The public were disappointed as well as ourselves in the poem, and his subsequent abuse of our city and its institutions, show[s] him to be an unprincipled man, while the venom which he ejected against us, only defiled himself."

25 MAY. NEW YORK. Poe writes T. Honland, complying with his "very flattering request for an autograph" (*L*, 2:317).

26 MAY. In the *Evening Mirror* Hiram Fuller publishes a savage attack on Poe's "Literati" articles, unsigned but written by Charles F. Briggs. Last month, through "advertisements and placards," Louis A. Godey informed the public "that Mr. Poe was coming down, upon the New York literati, in a series of papers in a Philadelphia magazine." This announcement caused quite "an uproar": it is said that "the students in Dr. Anthon's grammar school made a pilgrimage to Bloomingdale to gaze upon the asylum where Mr. Poe was reported to be confined . . . and a certain great writer on small subjects, in Ann street, had serious thoughts of calling him the American Tasso." Although Godey has asserted that Poe's articles "are creating a great sensation throughout the country," the only sensation Briggs has observed "has been one of disgust." Of the fifteen authors noticed in the first two installments, "not more than half were ever heard

of before as literati." Only the sketch of Nathaniel P. Willis "makes any show of ability of analysis, or of knowledge." Alluding to Willis' reputation as a dandy and as the intimate of English aristocrats, Briggs scoffs: "Mr. Poe thinks that Mr. Willis . . . gave the best evidence of possessing genius, by publishing a string of affidavits and certificates from my Lord knows who, in London, and the proprietors of certain tailors shops and boarding-houses in New York, in favor of his moral character." Poe is "the last man in the country who should undertake the task of writing 'honest opinions' of the literati. His infirmities of mind and body, his petty jealousies, his necessities even, which allow him neither time nor serenity . . . all unfit him for the performance of such a duty." Briggs concludes, "after the fashion of our Thersitical Magazinist," by describing the author's appearance:

Mr. Poe is about 39. . . . In height he is about 5 feet 1 or two inches, perhaps 2 inches and a half [actually 5 ft. 8 in.]. His face is pale and rather thin; eyes gray, watery, and always dull; nose rather prominent, pointed and sharp; nostrils wide; hair thin and cropped short; mouth not very well chiselled, nor very sweet; his tongue shows itself unpleasantly when he speaks earnestly, and seems too large for his mouth; teeth indifferent; forehead rather broad, and in the region of ideality decidedly large, but low, and in that part where phrenology places conscientiousness and the group of moral sentiments it is quite flat; chin narrow and pointed, which gives his head, upon the whole, a balloonish appearance, which may account for his supposed light-headedness.

The article is reprinted in the *Weekly Mirror* for 30 May (attribution demonstrated by Reece [1954], pp. 34–36, and Weidman [1968], pp. 163–64, 179; cf. Poe to E. A. Duyckinck, 16 June).

AFTER 26 MAY. Willis writes Poe, who has suggested that they respond to the article in the *Evening Mirror*: "Why reply *directly* to Mr. Briggs? If you want a shuttlecock squib to fall on the ground, never battledore it *straight back*. Mr. B's attacks on me I never saw, & never shall see. I keep a good-sense-ometer who reads the papers & tells me if there is anything worth replying to, but *nothing is* that is written by a man who will be honor'd by the reply. A reply from *me* to Mr. Briggs would make the man. So will *yours*, if you exalt him into your mate by contending on equal terms" (*W*, 17:206).

30 MAY. In the *National Press* George P. Morris reprints four paragraphs "from Mr. Poe's Sketch of Willis in Godey's Lady's Book [for May]. It is able, as all Mr. Poe's sketches are, but shows, in one or two points, that he does not quite understand Willis, especially as to the latter's 'pushing himself.' If Poe had seen a little more of our friend, he would have known that Willis is rather remarkable for never seeking an acquaintance."

SUMMER. FORDHAM. The health reformer Mrs. Mary Gove, later Mrs. Nichols, recalls:

We made one excursion to Fordham to see Poe. We found him, and his wife, and his wife's mother—who was his aunt—living in a little cottage at the top of a hill. There was an acre or two of greensward, fenced in about the house, as smooth as velvet and as clean as the best kept carpet. There were some grand old cherry-trees in the yard, that threw a massive shade around them. The house had three rooms—a kitchen, a sitting-room, and a bed-chamber over the sitting-room. There was a piazza in front of the house that was a lovely place to sit in in summer . . . .

On this occasion I was introduced to the young wife of the poet, and to the mother, then more than sixty years of age [actually fifty-six]. She was a tall, dignified old lady, with a most ladylike manner, and her black dress, though old and much worn, looked really elegant on her. She wore a widow's cap of the genuine pattern, and it suited exquisitely with her snow-white hair. Her features were large, and corresponded with her stature, and it seemed strange how such a stalwart and queenly woman could be the mother of her almost petite daughter. Mrs. Poe looked very young; she had large black eyes, and a pearly whiteness of complexion, which was a perfect pallor. Her pale face, her brilliant eyes, and her raven hair gave her an unearthly look. One felt that she was almost a disrobed spirit, and when she coughed it was made certain that she was rapidly passing away. . . .

The cottage had an air of taste and gentility that must have been lent to it by the presence of its inmates. So neat, so poor, so unfurnished, and yet so charming a dwelling I never saw. The floor of the kitchen was white as wheaten flour. A table, a chair, and a little stove that it contained, seemed to furnish it perfectly. The sitting-room floor was laid with check matting; four chairs, a light stand, and a hanging bookshelf completed its furniture. There were pretty presentation copies of books on the little shelves, and the Brownings had posts of honour on the stand. With quiet exultation Poe drew from his side pocket a letter that he had recently received from Elizabeth Barrett Browning. He read it to us. It was very flattering. She told Poe that his "poem of the Raven had awakened a fit of horror in England" (Nichols [1863], pp. 7–9; cf. description of cottage in *W*, 1:253–54).

SUMMER? [1846?] Poe commences a friendship with Father Edward Doucet, S.J., a faculty member at nearby St. John's College, later Fordham University. Poe frequently visits the college campus (Quinn, p. 520; Phillips, 2:1240–44).

[John H. Hopkins recalled that Poe had words of praise for "his near neighbors, the Jesuit Fathers at Fordham College . . . 'They were highly cultivated gentlemen and scholars,' he said, 'smoked, drank, and played cards like gentlemen, and never said a word about religion' " (Hopkins to Mrs. M. L. Shew, later Mrs. Houghton, 9 February 1875, Miller [1977], pp. 100–01).]

4 JUNE. STATEN ISLAND, NEW YORK. Charles F. Briggs writes William Page in Boston:

I am thankful also for your generous offer to hammer Poe on my account. But I would hammer him myself if I cared anything about him. He is altogether the poorest devil (I beg the devil's pardon) I ever knew. I was indebted to James [Russell Lowell] for an introduction to him and having his ideas in my mind all the while thought I had a great liking for him [Poe]. But, as I gradually discovered his poltroonish character and at last saw what a humbug I had imposed upon myself[,] my disgust was so strong that I could not tolerate him, and passed him without returning his how d'ye do when I saw him. This, together with the favors I had done him, and the instigations of some of the friends to whom I had introduced him and who had become my enemies by the lies which he told them about me, led to his making what [Robert] Carter told you was an attack upon me in Godey's Lady's Book. . . . The amount of the ill which he said of me was that I have a low narrow forehead, a Flemish taste in art and had never written three sentences of grammatical English (MiDAAA–P).

6 JUNE. BALTIMORE. Snodgrass' *Saturday Visiter* reviews *Godey's* for June. Poe's sketches "of the New York Literati" are attracting much attention, "especially in the city where the great noticed reside. The 'Book' is consequently in great demand."

9 JUNE. PHILLIPS, MAINE. George W. Eveleth writes Poe. He has acquired a copy of *The Raven and Other Poems*; he discusses appreciatively "The Raven," "The Sleeper," and "The Valley of Unrest" (Poe to Eveleth, 15 December).

11, 12, 13 JUNE. PARIS. The newspaper *La Quotidienne* publishes a free translation of "The Murders in the Rue Morgue" under the heading "Un Meurtre sans exemple dans les Fastes de la Justice: Histoire trouvée dans les papiers d'un Américain." This version is signed "G. B."; Poe is not mentioned (Seylaz, p. 39).

12 JUNE. NEW YORK? Poe writes his wife at Fordham: "My Dear Heart, My dear Virginia! our Mother will explain to you why I stay away from you this night. I trust the interview I am promised, will result in some *substantial good* for me, for your dear sake, and hers—Keep up your heart in all hopefulness, and trust yet a little longer . . . I shall be with you tomorrow P.M. and be assured until I see you, I will keep in *loving remembrance* your *last words* and your fervant prayer!" (L, 2:318).

15 JUNE. NEW YORK. Poe writes his friend Joseph M. Field, editor of the Saint Louis *Daily Reveille*. He encloses Briggs's attack on him from the 26 May *Evening Mirror*, asking Field "to say a few words in condemnation of

it" and to correct the false impression of his appearance it conveys: "You have seen me and can describe me as I am. Will you do me this act of justice, and influence one or two of your editorial friends to do the same?" Poe believes that the New Orleans *Daily Picayune*, "which has always been friendly," will act in conjunction with the *Reveille*. He composes several paragraphs discussing the reception of his writings in England, which he hopes Field will publish "editorially":

A long and highly laudatory review of his Tales, written by *Martin Farquhar Tupper*, . . . appeared in a late number of "The London Literary Gazette". "The Athenaeum," "The British Critic,["] "The Spectator", "The Popular Record"[,] "Churton's Literary Register", and various other journals, scientific as well as literary, have united in approbation of Tales & Poems. "The Raven" is copied in full in the "British Critic" and "The Athenaeum". "The Times"—the matter of fact "*Times!*"—copies the "Valdemar Case". The world's greatest poetess, *Elizabeth Barrett Barrett*, says of Mr Poe:—"This *vivid* writing!—this power *which is felt!* 'The Raven' has produced a *sensation*—a 'fit horror'—here in England" (L, 2:318–21).

16 JUNE. FORDHAM? Poe writes a friend, presumably Evert A. Duyck-inck. He composes a news item, requesting his correspondent to arrange for its insertion in the *Daily Tribune* or some other paper: "MR POE has been invited by the Literary Societies of Dickinson College, Carlisle, Pa. to deliver a poem at their approaching anniversary, but this invitation, as well as that of the University of Vermont, he is forced to decline through continued illness and a pressure of other engagements." Poe asks: "Who is the 'great writer of small things in Ann St' referred to by Briggs in the article about me in the Mirror of the 26? Has anything concerning me appeared lately in Morris' 'National Press[']? (L, 2:321, 715; Moldenhauer [1973], pp. 63–64).

[Briggs might have been referring to Poe's friend George P. Morris, whose *National Press* was published at the corner of Broadway and Ann; but it seems more likely that he simply intended to suggest a hypothetical journalistic hack, several New York newspapers having their offices on Ann Street, including the *Evening Mirror*.]

17 JUNE. SALEM, MASSACHUSETTS. Nathaniel Hawthorne writes Poe. He presumes his publishers have sent Poe a copy of *Mosses from an Old Manse*, his latest collection of tales: "I have read your occasional notices of my productions with great interest—not so much because your judgment was, upon the whole, favorable, as because it seemed to be given in earnest. I care for nothing but the truth; and shall always much more readily accept a harsh truth, in regard to my writings, than a sugared falsehood." Hawthorne nonetheless admires Poe more as a writer of tales than as a

critic of them: "I might often—and often do—dissent from your opinions, in the latter capacity, but could never fail to recognize your force and originality, in the former" (facsimile in Gimbel, p. 171).

19 JUNE. NEW YORK? Frances S. Osgood writes Elizabeth F. Ellet, protesting the rumors her correspondent has spread regarding her relationship with Poe. Mrs. Osgood denies sending him an indiscreet letter (Mrs. Ellet's reply, 8 July).

CA. 20 JUNE. PHILADELPHIA. *Godey's Lady's Book* for July features the third installment of "The Literati," containing sketches of Fitz-Greene Halleck, Ann S. Stephens, Evert A. Duyckinck, Mary Gove, James Aldrich, Thomas Dunn English, Henry Cary, and Christopher Pearse Cranch. Poe's remarks on English are flippantly contemptuous:

No spectacle can be more pitiable than that of a man without the commonest school education busying himself in attempts to instruct mankind on topics of polite literature. The absurdity in such cases does not lie merely in the ignorance displayed by the would-be instructor, but in the transparency of the shifts by which he endeavours to keep this ignorance concealed. The editor of "The Aristidean," for example, was not laughed at . . . *so much* for his excusable deficiencies in English grammar (although an editor should certainly be able to write *his own name*) as that, in the hope of disguising such deficiency, he was perpetually lamenting the "typographical blunders" that "in the most unaccountable manner *would* creep into his work." Nobody was so stupid as to suppose for a moment that there existed in New York a single proof-reader—or even a single printer's devil— who would have permitted *such* errors to escape.

With tongue in cheek Poe claims to be unacquainted with his subject: "I do not personally know Mr. English."

23 JUNE. NEW YORK. The *Morning Telegraph*, edited by S. DeWitt Bloodgood, publishes "Mr. English's Reply to Mr. Poe." After quoting Poe's facetious statement that he is unacquainted, English explains that he knows Poe through "a succession of his acts," all disreputable. One of these has proven "rather costly." Alluding to the $30 Poe borrowed for the *Broadway Journal* early in October 1845, English asserts: "I hold Mr. Poe's acknowledgement for a sum of money which he obtained from me under false pretences." He gives another example of Poe's financial dishonesty, referring to the unfounded rumor circulated by Edward J. Thomas around 20 June 1845: "A merchant of this city [Thomas] had accused him of committing forgery. He consulted me on the mode of punishing his accuser . . . I suggested a legal prosecution as his sole remedy. At his request I obtained a counsellor who was willing, as a compliment to me, to conduct his suit without the customary retaining fee. But, though so

eager at first to commence proceedings, he dropped the matter altogether, when the time came for him to act, thus virtually admitting the truth of the charge." English now recounts "a series of events . . . in January last," which "provoked the exhibition of impotent malice" found in the "Literati" sketch of him. At that time Poe visited him in his lodgings, requesting a private interview:

Then he told me that he had vilified a certain well known and esteemed authoress [Mrs. Ellet], of the South, then on a visit to New York; that he had accused her of having written letters to him which compromised her reputation; and that her brother (her husband being absent) had threatened his life unless he produced the letters he named. . . . He then begged the loan of a pistol to defend himself against attack. This request I refused, saying that his surest defence was a retraction of unfounded charges. He, at last, grew exasperated, and using offensive language, was expelled from the room. In a day or so, afterwards, being confined to his bed from the effect of fright and the blows he had received from me, he sent a letter to the brother [probably to Mrs. Ellet herself] . . . denying all recollection of having made any charges of the kind alleged, and stating that, if he had made them, he was laboring under a fit of insanity to which he was periodically subject.

English characterizes Poe as a drunkard who is "thoroughly unprincipled, base and depraved . . . not alone an assassin in morals, but a quack in literature."

23 JUNE. English takes his "Reply," printed in the *Morning Telegraph*, to Hiram Fuller. Assuring Fuller that the article is "to be published in every newspaper in the city" and that every word in it is true, he asks him to reprint it in the *Evening Mirror* (Fuller in the *Mirror*, 18 February 1847).

23 JUNE. The *Mirror* carries English's "Reply," preceded by Fuller's explanation: "THE WAR OF THE LITERATI.—We publish the following terrific rejoinder of one of Mr. Poe's abused *literati*, with a twinge of pity for the object of its severity. But as Mr. Godey, 'for a consideration,' lends the use of his battery for an attack on the one side, it is but fair that we allow our friends an opportunity to exercise a little 'self-defence' on the other." The "Reply" is reprinted in the *Weekly Mirror* for 27 June.

24 JUNE. The *Morning News* reports: "Edgar A. Poe attacked Thomas Dunn English most ridiculously in a late number of Godey's Lady's Book, and Mr. English, in the papers of yesterday, replied in a most caustic and fearful article."

CA. 24 JUNE. PHILADELPHIA. Louis A. Godey sends Poe a copy of English's "Reply," suggesting that portions of it might require a response ("Mr. Poe's Reply to Mr. English," 10 July).

25 JUNE. The *Public Ledger* reports: "The New York Literati are by the ears again, and are saying all sorts of complimentary things of each other in the tartest possible manner." When Poe attacked English in *Godey's*, he "caught a tartar, for Mr. English is out in a terrific rejoinder." Observing that this exchange is but "the first brush between the literary combatants," the *Ledger* predicts that Poe "will muster his intellectual forces, and give his adversary another battle."

26 JUNE. NEW YORK. The *Evening Mirror* publishes a letter to its editor from "Justitia," a correspondent in Troy, New York: "In inserting Mr. English's card relative to Edgar A. Poe, you have 'done the State some service.' Mr. P. may consider his 'position defined.' " In another column Hiram Fuller notices the July *Godey's*, condemning "the insane riff-raff, which Mr. Poe calls his 'honest opinions' of the New York Literati." His review appears in the *Weekly Mirror* for 4 July.

27 JUNE. In his *National Press* George P. Morris comments: "The reply of Mr. English to Mr. Poe is one of the most savage and bitter things we ever read—so much so that we are obliged to decline the requests of several correspondents to publish it in these columns. We condemn all literary squabbles—they are in very bad taste; but when attacks are made, rejoinders will follow."

27 JUNE. PHILADELPHIA. In the *Spirit of the Times* John S. Du Solle reports that Poe made "an ungenerous attack" upon English in the July *Godey's*, "and among other things asserted that he did not know Mr. E. The latter is back upon the literary meat-axe in a style which shows pretty conclusively that he knows Mr. Poe very well."

27 JUNE. NEW YORK. Poe writes the poetaster Henry B. Hirst in Philadelphia: "I presume you have seen . . . an attack made on me by English." Poe asks for an account of Hirst's reputed duel with English, as well as for information on English's quarrels with the Philadelphia politician Sandy Harris and the Virginia congressman Henry A. Wise. "See Du Solle, also, if you can & ask him if he is willing to give me, for publication, an account of his kicking E. out of his office" (*L*, 2:321–22).

29 JUNE. Poe writes Evert A. Duyckinck: "I am about to send the 'Reply to English' (accompanying this note) to Mr Godey—but feel anxious that some friend should read it before it goes. Will you be kind enough to look it over & show it to [Cornelius] Mathews?" The number of *Littell's Living Age* containing Tupper's review of Poe's *Tales* "is 106—so he [Eliakim Littell] writes me" (*L*, 2:323).

EVERT A. DUYCKINCK

New York Public Library

29 JUNE OR LATER. Poe sends his "Reply" to Louis A. Godey, asking him to publish it in his *Lady's Book* (Poe to Godey, 16 July).

30 JUNE. SAINT LOUIS. Complying with Poe's request in his 15 June letter, Joseph M. Field defends him in the *Daily Reveille*:

Certainly one of the most original geniuses of the country is Edgar A. Poe, and the only fault we have to find with him is, that he is wasting his time at present in giving his "*honest* opinions" touching his contemporaries—the maddest *kind* of honesty, in our opinion. Poe's papers upon the "New York Literati," published in Godey's Magazine, have stirred up, as might have been expected, any amount of ill temper. The *Evening Mirror* takes the lead in the attack upon the author, who is very sick, by-the-bye, and unable to make battle, as is his wont. The Mirror, among other things, seeks to make Poe ridiculous by a false description of his personal appearance. We won't stand this. Instead of being "five foot one," &c, the poet is a figure to compare with any in manliness, while his features are not only intellectual, but handsome.

Field publishes the paragraphs Poe composed on his favorable reception in England, featuring excerpts from Miss Barrett's April letter to him, and citing notices in eight British journals. The article is reprinted in the *Weekly Reveille* for 6 July (Moss [1968], pp. 19–20, and [1970], pp. 20–25; Heartman and Canny, p. 243).

CA. JULY. PHILLIPS, MAINE. George W. Eveleth writes George H. Colton in New York, requesting "a specimen number" of his *American Review*, preferably that for September 1845 containing the critique of Poe's *Tales*. Colton sends Eveleth this issue as well as the current July 1846 number, requesting his aid in increasing the magazine's circulation in Maine (Eveleth to Poe, 11 January 1848).

JULY. NEW YORK. The *Democratic Review* contains a brief installment of Poe's "Marginalia."

8 JULY. Mrs. Elizabeth F. Ellet replies to a 19 June letter from Mrs. Osgood, which she has only "this moment" received, having been out of town. She discusses the letter from Mrs. Osgood to Poe which she saw at his residence and which prompted her to intervene in this innocent correspondence:

The letter shown me by Mrs Poe *must have* been a forgery, and any man capable of offering to show notes he never possessed [Mrs. Ellet's own letters to Poe], would not, I think, hesitate at such a crime. Had you seen the fearful paragraphs which Mrs Poe first repeated and afterwards pointed out—which haunted me night and day like a terrifying spectre—you would not wonder I regarded you as I did. But her husband will not *dare* to work further mischief with the letter;—nor have either of us any thing to apprehend from the verbal calumnies of a wretch so steeped in infamy as he is now. . . .

Most fervently do I hope you may soon forget the whole painful affair . . . . What I have suffered—and the keen anguish of thinking how much pain I have been instrumental in causing to one of my own sex—to one whose genius and grace I have so much admired will be a lesson never again to listen to a tale of scandal. May Heaven forgive me—as you have—for having done so! . . .

It is most unfortunate both for you & me that we ever had any acquaintance with such people as the Poes—but I trust the evil is now at an end (MB–G).

BEFORE 10 JULY. PHILADELPHIA. Accepting the advice of friends, Godey decides not to publish Poe's "Reply" in the *Lady's Book*; instead he pays $10 to have it printed in the *Spirit of the Times*, the daily paper edited by English's longstanding foe John S. Du Solle (Poe to Godey, 16 July).

10 JULY. Du Solle's *Times* contains "Mr. Poe's Reply to Mr. English and Others." Since Poe has been in "perfect seclusion in the country," he would not have noticed Thomas Dunn English's attack in the New York *Evening Mirror* of 23 June, except that Godey sent it to him and suggested a reply. Poe will not allow "any profundity of disgust" to induce him to violate the truth: "What is *not false*, amid the scurrility of this man's statements, it is not in my nature to brand as false, although oozing from the filthy lips of which a lie is the only natural language." Poe's "weakness" [drinking] has been a calamity rather than a crime, and Dr. John W. Francis and other physicians can testify "that the irregularities so profoundly lamented were the *effect* of a terrible evil rather than its cause." He will not deny English's account of their conversation in January, "because *every* portion of it *may* be true, by a very desperate possibility." Poe would have preferred to ignore English's attack, except that two of the accusations are "criminal" and thus demand a rebuttal. He strenuously denies either that he obtained money from English under false pretenses or that he committed forgery. He prints a 5 July 1845 letter retracting the latter charge from Edward J. Thomas, the merchant involved. Poe proposes to demonstrate his innocence "in a court of justice"; he condemns English as a "wretch" who has attempted to stigmatize him as a felon. Hiram Fuller, the editor of the *Mirror*, is also at fault, having "prostituted his filthy sheet to the circulation of this calumny" (Moss [1970], pp. 49–59).

10 JULY. NEW YORK. In the *Evening Mirror* Fuller quotes one of the Philadelphia newspapers: " 'The New York Mirror has published one number without once referring to Poe's Notices of the New York Literati. Who is it about this establishment winces so dreadfully? Can it be Mr. Harry Franco Briggs?' " Fuller replies: "We are not aware of harboring any body about our establishment who would be likely to 'wince' at anything which

can emanate from Mr. Poe, who was once employed upon our paper, and of course is well known to us. . . . The gentleman whose name is unwarrantably used by our Philadelphia contemporary is not, nor ever was, attached to our establishment."

11 JULY. PHILADELPHIA. On its first page the *Saturday Gazette* reprints "Mr. Poe's Reply to Mr. English and Others" from the *Spirit of the Times*. On the second page the editor Joseph C. Neal explains that "some of Mr. Poe's friends in this city" asked him to copy the article: "Mr. E.'s letter was very severe upon the private character of Mr. Poe, and the latter retaliates in the same spirit. All this is, to our notion, in bad taste, yet we cannot well refuse the assailed an opportunity to exculpate himself. . . . Their friends will probably watch the progress of affairs with some interest, and the public, if it reads them, will enjoy a laugh for which they must jointly pay unless the victorious party—as is proposed in our war with Mexico— makes the vanquished foot the bill."

11 JULY. NEW YORK. The *Morning News* reports: "Poe has at last replied to the card of Mr. English, and it is a most terrific, [*sic*] absolutely bitterness and satire unadulterated. Poe states that he will prosecute the *Mirror* for publishing the card of Mr. E. This is rather small business for a man who has reviled nearly every literary man of eminence in the United States."

13 JULY. The *Evening Mirror* contains "A Card, in Reply to Mr. Poe's Rejoinder," signed by English: "In the 'Times,' a Philadelphia journal of considerable circulation, there appears a communication, headed—'Mr. Poe's reply to Mr. English, and others.' As it is dated '27th of June,' and the newspaper containing it is dated 10th July; and as it appears in another city than this,—it is to be inferred that Mr. Poe had some difficulty in obtaining a respectable journal to give currency to his scurrilous article." English excerpts numerous derogatory words from the article to give his readers an idea of its style. He comments: "Actuated by a desire for the public good, I charged Mr. Poe with the commission of certain misdemeanors, which prove him to be profligate in habits and depraved in mind. The most serious of these he admits by silence—the remainder he attempts to palliate; and winds up his tedious disquisition by a threat to resort to a legal prosecution. That is my full desire. Let him institute a suit, if he dare, and I pledge myself to make my charges good by the most ample and satisfactory evidence."

14 JULY. The *Morning News* reports: "T. D. English replies to Poe's bulletin No. 2, in last evening's *Mirror*. He dares Poe to a legal battle, and threatens to prove all the assertions made in his first official despatch."

14 JULY. PHILADELPHIA. The *Public Ledger* comments: "The war between the literati increases in violence. Mr. Poe, whose 'Sketches of the New York Literati' drew from Mr. English such a caustic attack, has replied in a manner equally biting and severe. We suggest a truce or treaty of peace among these ecclesiastics of the church literary; for Billingsgate is not the wide *gate* or the straight *gait* to Parnassus or Helicon, any more than to the White Mountains or Saratoga." Critics should exercise better breeding, taste, and judgment "than is exhibited by vituperative personalities." Bringing authors "before the public in relations exclusively private" violates the precepts of a gentleman: "It exposes the assailant to the imputation of envy, malignity, falsehood, and other vices of the heart, and to that of having exhausted his whole stock in the literary trade, and consequently of being driven to slander for raw material."

BEFORE 15 JULY. FORDHAM? Poe writes William Gilmore Simms, who is visiting New York. He asks Simms to publish an article in a South Carolina newspaper which will correct the exaggerated account of his appearance given in the *Evening Mirror* of 26 May (Simms to Poe, 30 July; cf. Poe to J. M. Field, 15 June).

15 JULY. NEW YORK. Simms sends the Charleston *Southern Patriot* a dispatch containing an accurate description of Poe (*Patriot*, 20 July).

15 JULY. NEW ORLEANS. The *Daily Picayune* reports that Poe's "Literati" articles have involved him in "personal differences of the most rancorous description. He has been assailed in terms of unmeasured severity, and not content with efforts to impugn his critical judgments and to ridicule his literary pretensions, his enemies have assailed his personal character, and dragged his private affairs before the eyes of the public. . . . With this no right-minded man can sympathize." In any case, it is "quite idle" to question Poe's abilities: "He has been one of the most successful contributors to our literary periodicals, and his tales have been extensively copied both here and in England. . . . That production of his which critics and his personal enemies have most frequently endeavored to deride is 'The Raven,' but the oft repeated efforts have been entirely harmless. . . . This single poem is a complete vindication of his possession of genius of the most sterling quality" (Moss [1968], p. 20, and [1970], pp. 65–66).

16 JULY. NEW YORK. The *Morning News* reprints the *Public Ledger's* editorial of 14 July, omitting only the first three sentences, which refer specifically to Poe and English. The *News* praises the article for "so much good sense . . . and such a brief yet wholesome rebuke administered to those who deserve it."

16 JULY. Poe testily replies to a letter from Louis A. Godey in Philadelphia. He regrets that Godey paid to have his "Reply" published in the *Spirit of the Times*; he could have had it printed "in a *respectable* paper" in New York without charge:

I am rather ashamed that, knowing me to be as poor as I am, you should have thought it advisable to make the demand *on me* of the $10. . . .

The man, or men, who told you that there was anything wrong in *the tone* of my reply, were either my enemies, or your enemies, or asses. When you see them, tell them so from me. I have never written an article upon which I more confidently depend for *literary* reputation than that Reply. Its merit lay in being *precisely* adapted to its purpose. In this city I have had, upon it, the favorable judgments of the best men. All the error about it was yours. You should have done as I requested—published it in the "Book".

Poe has "put this matter in the hands of a competent attorney"; Godey's charge of $10 "will of course be brought before the court, as an item" (*L*, 2:323–24).

17 JULY. Poe writes John Bisco: "You will confer a *very* great favor on me by stepping in, when you have leisure, at the office of E. L. Fancher, Attorney-at-Law, 33 John St. Please mention to him that I requested you to call in relation to Mr English. He will, also, show you my Reply to some attacks lately made upon me by this gentleman" (*L*, 2:325).

BEFORE 20 JULY. Poe, accompanied by Mrs. Clemm, visits Hiram Fuller at the *Evening Mirror* office, corner of Nassau and Ann Streets (*Mirror*, 20 July).

20 JULY. CHARLESTON, SOUTH CAROLINA. The *Southern Patriot* publishes a 15 July dispatch from its correspondent [Simms], who discusses literary affairs in New York:

Among the petty excitements common to authorship is that which Mr. Edgar A. Poe is producing by his pencil sketches of the New York Literati in Godey's Ladies Magazine. He has succeeded most happily (if such was his object) in fluttering the pigeons of this dove cote. His sketches, of which we have seen but a few, are given to a delineation as well of the persons as of the performances of his subjects. Some of them are amusing enough. I am not prepared to say how true are his sketches, but they have caused no little rattling among the dry bones of our Grub street. Of Poe, as a writer, we know something. He is undoubtedly a man of very peculiar and very considerable genius—but is irregular and exceedingly mercurial in his temperament. He is fond of mystifying in his stories, and they tell me, practises upon this plan even in his sketches; more solicitous, as they assert, of a striking picture than a likeness. Poe, himself, is a very good looking fellow. I have seen him on two or three occasions, and have enjoyed a good opportunity of examining him carefully. He is probably thirty three or four years old [actually thirty-seven], some five feet, eight inches in height, of rather slender person, with a good eye, and a broad intelligent forehead.

20 JULY. NEW YORK. Enoch L. Fancher prepares Poe's declaration of grievances against Hiram Fuller and Augustus W. Clason, Jr., proprietors of the *Evening* and *Weekly Mirror*. Through his attorney Poe accuses these defendants of "wickedly and maliciously intending to injure . . . his good name, fame and credit" by publishing in both editions of the *Mirror* "a certain false, scandalous, malicious and defamatory libel over the name of one Thomas Dunn English." This article contained two libelous statements: that Poe obtained money under false pretenses and that he committed forgery. The suit asks that the plaintiff, Poe, be awarded damages of $5,000 (Moss [1970], pp. 77–85).

[Moss explained this document: "Why Poe sued the owners of the *Mirror* and not English, or why he didn't sue the owners of the *Mirror and* English, can only be conjectured. . . . Very likely his attorney had advised him that the proprietors of the *Mirror* had incurred a greater degree of culpability . . . and that typically one always sued the deeper pocket . . . . Perhaps, too, Poe wanted to be vindicated more than he wanted to avenge himself upon everyone implicated in the libel. If he could achieve this clearly by a legal victory in one case, there would be no point in bringing concurrent, consolidated, or subsequent suits against English and, for that matter, the owners of the *Morning Telegraph* who first published English's reply" (p. 77).]

20 JULY. In the *Evening Mirror* Fuller depicts Poe as a degenerate, without actually naming him:

A poor creature . . . called at our office the other day, in a condition of sad, wretched imbecility, bearing in his feeble body the evidences of evil living, and betraying by his talk, such radical obliquity of sense, that every spark of harsh feeling towards him was extinguished, and we could not even entertain a feeling of contempt for one who was evidently committing a suicide upon his body, as he had already done upon his character. Unhappy man! He was accompanied by an aged female relative, who was going a weary round in the hot streets, following his steps to prevent his indulging in a love of drink; but he had eluded her watchful eye by some means, and was already far gone in a state of inebriation. After listening awhile with painful feelings to his profane ribaldry, he left the office, accompanied by his good genius, to whom he owed the duties which she was discharging for him, and we muttered involuntarily, "*remote, unfriended, solitary alone*," &c. &c. And this is the poor man who has been hired by a mammon-worshipping publisher to do execution upon the gifted, noble-minded and pure-hearted men and women, whose works are cherished by their contemporaries as their dearest national treasure.

The attack is reprinted in the *Weekly Mirror* for 25 July.

21 JULY. The *Morning News* objects to Fuller's article: "We are pained by having read a most inexcusable and vindictive editorial attack upon Mr. Poe and his personal, ay! his domestic relations. That gentleman may have discoursed coarsely of others, but that furnishes no reason for those that have been attacked to make blackguards of themselves, and to offend the public by a wanton display of backwoods vituperation. . . . It is a melancholy fact that the literary profession is divided against itself. Instead of being a fraternity, it is like the athletae of old.—Gladiator like, we meet that we may destroy."

22 JULY. Poe writes Thomas Holley Chivers in Oaky Grove, Georgia:

I had long given you up . . . when this morning I received no less than 6 letters from you, all of them addressed 195 East Broadway. Did you not know that I merely boarded at this house? It is a very long while since I left it, and as I did not leave it on very good terms with the landlady, she has given herself no concern about my letters . . . . I am living out of town about 13 miles, at a village called Fordham, on the rail-road leading north. We are in a snug little cottage, keeping house, and would be very comfortable, but that I have been for a long time dreadfully ill. I am getting better, however, although slowly, and shall get *well*. In the meantime the flocks of little birds of prey that always take the opportunity of illness to peck at a sick fowl of larger dimensions, have been endeavoring with all their power to effect my ruin.

Although Poe is "ground into the very dust with poverty," he does not despair "even of worldly prosperity." He encloses Joseph M. Field's article from the Saint Louis *Daily Reveille* of 30 June: "You will be pleased to see how they appreciate me in England" (*L*, 2:325–27).

BEFORE 23 JULY. PHILADELPHIA. *Godey's Lady's Book* for August features the fourth installment of "The Literati," containing Poe's extensive sketch of Margaret Fuller and his shorter notices of James Lawson, Caroline M. Kirkland, Prosper M. Wetmore, Emma C. Embury, and Epes Sargent. He grants Miss Fuller possession of "high genius," praising especially her critique of Longfellow published in the New York *Daily Tribune* on 10 December 1845: "In my opinion it is one of the very few reviews of Longfellow's poems, ever published in America, of which the critics have not had abundant reason to be ashamed. Mr. Longfellow is entitled to a certain and very distinguished rank among the poets of his country, but that country is disgraced by the evident toadyism which would award to his social position and influence . . . that amount of indiscriminate approbation which neither could nor would have been given to the poems themselves."

23 JULY. NEW YORK. Hiram Fuller notices *Godey's* in the *Evening Mirror*: "Mr. Poe's habit of misrepresentation is so confirmed, and malignity is so much a part of his nature, that he continually goes out of his way to do ill-natured things, when nothing can be gained by it." As an example, Fuller quotes the "lying insinuations about Mr. Longfellow" found in Poe's sketch of Margaret Fuller. "He also speaks of 'Professor Longfellow's magnificent edition of his own works, with a portrait,' meaning to insinuate that Carey & Hart's edition of Longfellow's Poems was published at the expense of the author." The review is reprinted in the *Weekly Mirror* for 1 August.

23 JULY. Poe's declaration of grievances against Hiram Fuller and Augustus W. Clason, Jr., is filed in the Superior Court of the City of New York (Moss [1970], p. 77).

CA. 23 JULY. FORDHAM? Poe writes William Gilmore Simms in New York. He apparently inquires whether Simms has published a defense of him in a South Carolina paper (Simms to Poe, 30 July).

24 JULY. NEW YORK. In the *Evening Mirror* Fuller comments: "EDGAR A. POE has commenced a suit against us for a libel contained in a Card of *Thomas Dunn English*, which was copied from the *Morning Telegraph*, and published in the Mirror as an advertisement. We do not hold ourselves responsible for Mr. English's charges against Mr. Poe, but if the latter gentleman chooses to take the matter into Court, we shall not shrink from the trial. We are confident that his attorney cannot be aware of the testimony he will have to meet in the progress of the suit."

[Fuller published English's attack free of charge, not as a paid advertisement. The commencement of Poe's suit was also reported in today's *Daily Tribune*.]

24 JULY. PHILADELPHIA. Rufus W. Griswold writes Evert A. Duyckinck in New York, asking to borrow his "Paris edition of Irving" when Poe returns it. "Speaking of Poe reminds me of the brutal article in the Mirror, [by English,] which it is impossible on any grounds whatsoever to justify in the slightest degree." Although Griswold has "as much cause as any man to quarrel with Poe," he would rather cut off his hand than use it "to write such an ungentlemanly card, though every word were true" (NN–D).

25 JULY. NEW YORK. In his *National Press* George P. Morris praises the August *Godey's*: "The notices of the New-York Literati, by Poe, which have excited so lively a sensation, are continued."

25 JULY. In the *Evening Mirror* Fuller facetiously attributes to Poe an unsigned filler on etiquette in the August *Godey's*: "It does not bear his signature, but it was written by him, and is almost equal to . . . Chesterfield." Poe's excellent recommendations and prohibitions "should be immediately stereotyped, and hung up in all our primary schools and seminaries for young gentlemen. Think of the enormity of wearing white trowsers of a Sunday! or green spectacles on any day, or of touching any part of a lady but her fingers! But to use the word genteel, Good gracious! We didn't know before that that was such a profane word. To get drunk, to curse and swear, to slander innocent women, to betray your friend, are trifles, in comparison with such an offence."

25 JULY. The *Weekly Mirror* commences its serialization of English's unsigned novel *1844, or, The Power of the "S.F."* This *roman à clef* satirizes Poe and other prominent New Yorkers; the installments are reprinted in the *Evening Mirror*, beginning on 27 July.

25 JULY. PHILADELPHIA. The *Saturday Courier* reprints "The Raven" in its poetry column "Our Classic Niche," preceded by a sketch of the author:

EDGAR A. POE, Esq. The occupant of our "Classic Niche" to-day, is acknowledged by all his cotemporaries one of the most original and gifted *geniuses* of his times . . . .

Mr. Poe's *forte* is in the mystical philosophy of nature, and his powerfully analytic and penetrating mind gives him the facility of revelling in the supernatural or forbidden fields of occult science. His most remarkable efforts, aside from "The Raven," are his very numerous Prose Tales, some of which have elicited very high encomiums from the first British critics, and continue to attract no little attention at home. He is at present creating quite an excitement by his sketches of literary people of New York, now being published in Godey's Lady's Book, and which we hear are to be extended to embrace the whole Union, and the whole to be issued in book form, simultaneously here and in England,—with autographs.

26 JULY. NEW YORK. The *Sunday Mercury* reports: "We hear that Poe has sued the Mirror in an action of libel, by which he seeks to recover damages for injuries sustained by the publication of Mr. Thos. Dunn English's defence. This is about the most imprudent and most impudent thing of the kind we ever heard of. The Mirror will, of course, justify."

27 JULY. Fuller reprints the *Mercury*'s report in the *Evening Mirror*.

30 JULY. William Gilmore Simms writes Poe at Fordham, replying to a note he received a week ago:

I surely need not tell you how deeply & sincerely I deplore the misfortunes which attend you—the more so as I see no process for your relief and extrication but such as must result from your own decision and resolve. . . . Money, no doubt, can be procured; but this is not altogether what you require. . . . Suffer me to tell you frankly, taking the privilege of a true friend, that you are now perhaps in the most perilous period of your career—just in that position—just at that time of life—when a false step becomes a capital error—when a single leading mistake is fatal in its consequences. You are no longer a boy. "At thirty wise or never!"

Simms has heard that Poe reproaches Louis A. Godey: "But how can you expect a Magazine proprietor to encourage contributions which embroil him with all his neighbours. These broils do you no good—vex your temper, destroy your peace of mind, and hurt your reputation. . . .

Change your tactics & begin a new series of papers with your publisher." Simms encloses the Charleston *Southern Patriot* of 20 July, in which he has discussed "the matter" Poe "suggested in a previous letter" (Simms, 2:174–77).

AUGUST. The *Knickerbocker Magazine* contains Charles F. Briggs's "City Articles: Number Two." He condemns "the imbecile snarlings of the Zoilus of a Milliner's Magazine," who has recently accused him "of vulgarity and a Flemish taste" (cf. Briggs to William Page, 4 June).

4 AUGUST. A preliminary hearing for Poe's libel suit is held at the City Hall before the Justices of Superior Court. Through their attorney Hiram Fuller and Augustus W. Clason, Jr., plead not guilty to the charges in Poe's 20 July declaration of grievances. "Therefore the issue above joined is ordered . . . to be tried . . . before the Justices aforesaid on the first Monday of September" (Moss [1970], pp. 95–98).

4 AUGUST. MILLWOOD, CLARKE COUNTY, VIRGINIA. Philip Pendleton Cooke answers Poe's 16 April letter, explaining his tardiness: "I have been a good deal away from home, and whilst *at* home greatly drawn off from literature and its adjuncts by business, social interruptions, &c." Cooke will be pleased to bring Lowell's sketch of Poe up to date: "I, however, have not Graham's Mag. for February 1845, and if you still wish me to continue the memoir you must send that number to me." Some months ago he obtained Poe's "Tales & Poems" and "read them collectively with great pleasure." Of the poems he admires "The City in the Sea," "Lenore," "To One in Paradise," and "The Raven"; he has more to say about the tales:

John [P.] Kennedy, talking with me about your stories, old & recent, said, "the man's imagination is as truth-like and minutely accurate as De Foe's"—and went on to talk of your "Descent into the Maelström," "MS. found in a Bottle," "Gold

Bug," &c. I think this last the most ingenious thing I ever read. Those stories of criminal detection, "Murders of the Rue Morgue," &c., a prosecuting attorney in the neighborhood here declares are miraculous. I think your French friend, for the most part, fine in his deductions from over-laid & unnoticed small facts, but sometimes too minute & hair-splitting. The stories are certainly as interesting as any ever written. The "Valdemar Case" I read in a number of your Broadway Journal last winter—as I lay in a Turkey blind, muffled to the eyes in overcoats, &c., and pronounce it without hesitation the most damnable, vraisemblable, horrible, hair-lifting, shocking, ingenious chapter of fiction that any brain ever conceived, or hands traced (W, 17:262–64).

9 AUGUST. NEW YORK. Poe replies to Cooke. He appreciates Cooke's praise of his writings more than that awarded by other critics, because he feels that Cooke understands and discriminates: "You are right about the hair-splitting of my French friend:—that is all done for effect. These tales of ratiocination owe most of their popularity to being something in a new key. I do not mean to say that they are not ingenious—but people think them more ingenious than they are—on account of their method and *air* of method." Cooke remains Poe's choice to continue Lowell's sketch. If he undertakes this project, he should mention the injustice done Poe by Wiley and Putnam's editor Evert A. Duyckinck, who prepared the 1845 edition of his *Tales*: "He has what he thinks a taste for ratiocination, and has accordingly made up the book mostly of analytic stories. But this is not *representing* my mind in its various phases . . . . Were all my tales now before me in a large volume and as the composition of another—the merit which would principally arrest my attention would be the wide *diversity and* variety" (L, 2:327–30).

14 AUGUST. WASHINGTON. Frederick William Thomas writes Poe. Mr. Heape, his "fellow-boarder and friend," is coming to New York for a week. Thomas has asked Heape to bring him the manuscript of biographical sketches he placed in Poe's keeping last year: "May I trouble you to leave it, directed to the care of Mr Heape, at the counting room of Fitch & co. No. 14. Wall street, within the week?" Thomas has "suffered a terrible affliction lately." Two years ago his sister Fanny, whom Mrs. Clemm "remembers well," went to India to be with her husband, "who is naval agent for the India Company in Calcutta." Since she suffered from the climate, "her medical adviser recommended that she should return to the U States for her health." Fanny and her two children, "a little boy & girl," left Calcutta in February. In April the ship in which they had embarked ran aground and disintegrated: "my sister and her children were washed off and lost. Only 7 lives were saved of the whole ship company" (NN–Mss; cf. Thomas to Poe, 10 July 1845).

24 AUGUST. Thomas writes Poe again, sending his letter to Philadelphia:

I wrote to you directing to New York some time since requesting you to send me my MS. by Mr Heap[e?] who would soon leave N York for Washington. To day I received a letter from Mr Heap, written from Philadelphia, in which he tells me that he was informed in New York that you had returned to Philadelphia to reside.

Will you be so kind, my dear Poe, as to leave the MS. for me at *Mr Charles Field's, Front St, near Pine*, and Mr Heap will get it for me. . . . How I long to see you Poe—How is Mrs Clemm and your lady (MB–G).

BEFORE 27 AUGUST. PHILADELPHIA. *Godey's Lady's Book* for September features the fifth installment of "The Literati," containing Poe's favorable notices of Frances S. Osgood, Lydia M. Child, Elizabeth Bogart, Catharine M. Sedgwick, and Anne C. Lynch, as well as his flippant attack on Lewis Gaylord Clark. Although Clark edits the *Knickerbocker Magazine*, he is "known principally as the twin brother of the late *Willis* Gaylord Clark, the poet, of Philadelphia." The *Knickerbocker* has able contributors, but it lacks individuality: "As the editor has no precise character, the magazine, as a matter of course, can have none. When I say 'no precise character,' I mean that Mr. C., as a literary man, has about him no determinateness, no distinctiveness, no saliency of point;—an apple, in fact, or a pumpkin, has more angles. He is as smooth as oil or a sermon from Doctor Hawks; he is noticeable for nothing in the world except for the markedness by which he is noticeable for nothing."

27 AUGUST. NEW YORK. Hiram Fuller notices *Godey's* in the *Evening Mirror*: "Mr. Poe will go on with his pedantic sketches of our literati. His remarks on Mrs. Child are evidently well intended. He describes her personal appearance with a flippant inaccuracy: it is possible that he has never seen her. In scanning the verses of Mrs. Osgood he is quite at home. His remarks about Mr. Clark of the *Knickerbocker* are probably intended to be sarcastic, but sarcasm is Mr. Poe's weakness." The review is reprinted in the *Weekly Mirror* for 5 September.

29 AUGUST. BALTIMORE. In the *Saturday Visiter* Joseph Evans Snodgrass reprints Poe's sketch of Mrs. Child from "the Lady's Book."

SEPTEMBER. PARIS. The *Revue britannique* publishes "Une Descente au Maelstrom," accompanied by a footnote: "Cet article est de M. Edgar Poe, auteur américain dont nous avons publié le *Scarabée d'or*." The translation is signed with the initials "O. N.," standing for "Old Nick," the pseudonym of E. D. Forgues (Seylaz, p. 40).

1846

SEPTEMBER. PHILADELPHIA AND NEW YORK. The *Talisman and Odd Fellows' Magazine* refers to Poe as "the tomahawk man" and "the Comanche of literature" (Campbell [1933], p. 59).

5 SEPTEMBER. NEW YORK. The *Weekly Mirror* contains the seventh installment of Thomas Dunn English's novel *1844, or, The Power of the "S.F."* Poe makes his first appearance, as "Marmaduke Hammerhead," at the "weekly conversazione" hosted by the "Misses Veryblue." Two gentlemen bystanders discuss him:

"Do you see that man standing by the smiling little woman in black, engaged, by his manner, in laying down some proposition, which he conceives it would be madness to doubt, yet believes it to be known by himself only?"

"Him with the broad, low, receding, and deformed forehead, and a peculiar expression of conceit in his face?"

"The same."

"That is Marmaduke Hammerhead—a very well known writer for the sixpenny periodicals, who aspires to be a critic, but never presumes himself a gentleman. He is the author of a poem, called the 'Black Crow,' now making some stir, in the literary circles."

"What kind of man is he?" . . .

"Oh! passable; he never gets drunk more than five days out of the seven; tells the truth sometimes by mistake; has moral courage sufficient to flog his wife, when he thinks she deserves it, and occasionally without any thought upon the subject merely to keep his hand in; and has never, that I know of, been convicted of petit larceny. He has been horsewhipped occasionally, and has had his nose pulled so often as to considerably lengthen that prominent and necessary appendage to the human face."

This installment is reprinted in the *Evening Mirror*, 8–9 September.

7 SEPTEMBER. Poe's libel suit against Fuller and Clason, scheduled to be heard in Superior Court today, is postponed until 1 February 1847 (Moss [1970], p. 105).

10 SEPTEMBER. The *Evening Mirror* contains a filler alluding to Poe and his suit:

EPIGRAM
ON AN INDIGENT POET.

P— money wants to "buy a bed,"—
His case is surely trying;
It must be hard to want a bed,
For one so used to *lying*.

The verses are reprinted in the *Weekly Mirror* for 19 September.

12 SEPTEMBER. The *Weekly Mirror* publishes a letter from "Ferdinand Mendez Pinto," a fictitious American correspondent in Europe created by Charles F. Briggs. In this dispatch "Pinto" recounts an interview he purportedly had with Richard Henry Horne, whose *Orion* Poe had lauded in *Graham's Magazine* for March 1844: "Horne enquired after Mr. Poe, and said that he had received from him a review of 'Orion,' in some wishywashy Magazine—the name of which he had forgotten. I asked what he thought of Poe as a critic? He replied, 'He is a very good critic for a lady's magazine' " (Weidman [1979], pp. 105, 144–46).

19 SEPTEMBER. The *Weekly Mirror* contains the ninth installment of English's *1844*, which depicts Poe ("Hammerhead") staggering down Broadway:

> The truth is that Hammerhead was drunk—though that was no wonder, for he was never sober over twenty-four hours at a time; but he was in a most beastly state of intoxication. His cups had given him a kind of courage; and though naturally the most abject poltroon in existence, he felt an irresistible inclination to fight with some one. Such a propensity can always be gratified in the city of New York, which is blessed with as pugnacious a population as any other city in the world. True to his purpose, Hammerhead accosted the first comer, and taking him by the button, said—
>
> "Did—did—did you ever read my review of L—L—Longfellow?"
>
> "No!" said the one addressed—a quiet, sober looking personage, "I dare say it's very severe; but I never read it."
>
> "Well," said Hammerhead, "you lost a gr—gr—eat pleasure. Your'e an ass!"

The installment appears in the *Evening Mirror*, 23, 26, 28 September.

OCTOBER. PHILADELPHIA. *Godey's Lady's Book* features the sixth and final installment of "The Literati," containing sketches of Charles Fenno Hoffman, Mary E. Hewitt, and Richard Adams Locke. Poe observes: "Mr. Hoffman was the original editor of 'The Knickerbocker Magazine,' and gave it . . . an impetus which has sufficed to bear it on alive, although tottering, month after month, through even that dense region of unmitigated and unmitigable fog—that dreary realm of outer darkness, of utter and inconceivable dunderheadism, over which has so long ruled King Log the Second, in the august person of one Lewis Gaylord Clark."

OCTOBER. NEW YORK. In the "Editor's Table" of the *Knickerbocker* Clark reacts to Poe's attack in the September *Godey's*: "Our thanks are due to 'J. G. H.,' of Springfield, (Mass.,) for his communication touching the course and the capabilities of the wretched inebriate whose personalities disgrace a certain Milliner's Magazine in Philadelphia; but bless your heart, man! you can't expect us to publish it. The jaded hack who runs a broken pace for common hire, upon whom you have wasted powder, might revel in his congenial abuse of this Magazine and its EDITOR from now till next October without disturbing our complacency for a single moment. He is too mean for hate, and hardly worthy scorn." From the *Evening Mirror* of 20 July Clark quotes Hiram Fuller's "faithful picture" of Poe as a degenerate alcoholic, and he asks: "Now what can one gain by a victory over a person such as this?" In his "Literati" sketches Poe "professes to know many to whom he is altogether unknown." Clark himself has seen Poe only twice: "In the one case, we met him in the street with a gentleman [Thomas Holley Chivers], who apologized the next day, in a note now before us, for having been seen in his company."

OCTOBER. BOSTON. The *North American Review* contains a hostile criticism of William Gilmore Simms's *The Wigwam and the Cabin* and *Views and Reviews*, both issued in Wiley and Putnam's "Library of American Books." In passing, the critic condemns several other volumes in this series, including the "Tales by Edgar A. Poe," who belongs "to the forcible-feeble and the shallow-profound school."

3 OCTOBER. NEW YORK. The *Weekly Mirror* contains the eleventh installment of English's *1844*, which depicts Poe ("Hammerhead") on a visit to the office of Horace Greeley ("Satisfaction Sawdust"):

Hammerhead . . . had drank sufficiently to make him quarrelsome. He took Sawdust by the buttonhole, and drawing him aside, requested—as the latter had predicted, the loan of some money. This was denied, and Hammerhead waxed indignant. . . .

"D—n you! I made you. You owe all your reputation to me. I wrote you up. I'll criticise you—I'll extinguish you—you ungrateful eater of bran pudding—you—you—galvanized squash."

"Undoubtedly," replied Sawdust, "and now let me go."

He disengaged his coat from Hammerhead's grasp, as he spoke, and the poet, fastening on a stranger, informed him that he was the great critic, Hammerhead, at that moment in want of a loan—of a shilling.

The installment appears in the *Evening Mirror*, 8–9 October.

9–10 OCTOBER. BROOKLYN. In the *Daily Eagle* Walt Whitman reprints Poe's "A Tale of the Ragged Mountains" (Mabbott [1978], 3:939).

10 OCTOBER. NEW YORK. In his *National Press* George P. Morris admonishes Poe in a purported review of *The Raven and Other Poems*:

We take this work, not so much with a view to a particular examination of its merits, as for the purpose of saying to Mr. Poe, how much greater pleasure it gives us to meet him in his own proper field of poetical creation, than in the uncomfortable regions of criticism and controversy.

Mr. Poe is, unquestionably, a man of genius. Narratives which rivet the interest, and sway the passions, as powerfully as his do, indicate a vigour of imagination that might send its productions forward far along the line of future life. Many of these tales, we have no doubt, will long survive, as among the ablest and most remarkable of American productions. . . . To one who possesses the powers of close, logical reasoning, and of pointed and piercing sarcasm, the "*torva voluptas*" of literary and social controversy is often a fatal fascination. But a man who is conscious within himself of faculties which indicate to him that he was born, not to wrangle with the men of his own times, but to speak truth and peace to distant ages and a remote posterity, ought to make a covenant with himself, that he will be drawn aside by no temptation . . . .

As an analytical critic, Mr. Poe possesses abilities, in our opinion, quite unrivaled in this country, and perhaps on either side of the water. We have scarcely ever taken up one of his more careful critical papers, on some author or work worthy of his strength, without a sense of surprise at the novel and profound views . . . . But in the case of inventive genius so brilliant and vigorous as is shown in these poems, and in the tales to which we have alluded, we feel that even criticism of the highest kind is an employment below the true measure of its dignity, and, we may say, its duty . . . . A man who can produce such a work as "The Raven," ought to feel that it was his office to afford subjects, and not models, to criticism.

12 OCTOBER. PARIS. The newspaper *Le Commerce* publishes an abridged translation of "The Murders in the Rue Morgue" by the journalist and critic E. D. Forgues. This version is entitled "Une sanglante énigme" and signed with Forgues's pseudonym "Old Nick"; Poe is not mentioned (Seylaz, p. 40).

13 OCTOBER. PHILLIPS, MAINE. George W. Eveleth writes Poe. He has been reading Poe's "Literati" articles, which the newspapers describe as "Satires." Since he wants to collect "a choice library of American books," he hopes Poe will be outspoken in these sketches: "I know not whose judgment than yours, if it be unbiased, is better for me to depend upon in my selection. . . . Are you going to notice all the Authors of our Country in your series?" Eveleth wonders whether Poe wrote the unsigned review of James Russell Lowell's *Poems* in *Graham's* for March 1844: "The idea with respect to Lowell's merit as a poet, is the same that you have advanced—and the criticism is something in your manner, though not so lengthy and analytical as I should expect." He asks when Poe will issue his own magazine: "I am earnest to receive it" (Eveleth, pp. 7–8).

14 OCTOBER. PARIS. The newspaper *La Presse* accuses Forgues of plagiarism: "le feuilleton qu'il a publié dans le *Commerce* . . . est, à quelques mots près, entièrement pris et textuellement copié dans le feuilleton de *La*

Quotidienne qui a para les 11, 12 et 13 juin dernier." *La Presse* prints excerpts from Forgues's translation of "The Murders in the Rue Morgue" and that published by *La Quotidienne* in June (Seylaz, pp. 40–41).

15 OCTOBER. The *Revue des Deux Mondes* contains Forgues's laudatory twenty-page critique of the Wiley and Putnam edition of Poe's *Tales* (Quinn, pp. 517–19; condensed translation in Moss [1970], pp. 143–54).

15 OCTOBER. Forgues publishes a statement in two Paris papers, *Le Commerce* and *Le National*, explaining that his feuilleton was actually a translation: "Et la source de l'article en question n'est pas celle qu'indique *La Presse*. . . . Ainsi donc ce n'est pas dans *La Quotidienne*, mais dans les Contes d'E. Poe, littérateur américain, que j'ai pris quoi?" (Seylaz, p. 41).

AFTER 15 OCTOBER. M. de Girardin, editor of *La Presse*, refuses to publish Forgues's statement declaring his innocence. Forgues consequently sues him for libel (Seylaz, p. 41).

20 OCTOBER. *L'Entre-Acte*, a theatrical journal, humorously reports the controversy over Forgues's feuilleton: "M. Old-Nick [Forgues] l'avait emprunté à un romancier américain qu'il est en train d'inventer dans la *Revue des Deux-Mondes*. Ce romancier s'appelle Poe"; je ne dis pas le contraire. Voilà donc un écrivain qui use du droit légitime d'arranger les nouvelles d'un romancier américain qu'il a inventé, et on l'accuse de plagiat, de vol au feuilleton; on alarme ses amis en leur faisant croire que cet écrivain est possédé de la monomanie des orangs-outangs. . . . En attendant que la vérité se découvre, nous sommes forcés de convenir que ce Poë est un gaillard bien fin, bien spirituel, quand il est arrangé par M. Old-Nick" (Griswold [1850], p. xix; Cambiaire, pp. 23–24).

CA. 20 OCTOBER. PHILADELPHIA. *Godey's Lady's Book* for November contains Poe's tale "The Cask of Amontillado." In the "Editors' Book Table" Louis A. Godey responds to Clark's attack on Poe in the October *Knickerbocker*: " 'H. G. J.,' of Springfield, Mass., is respectfully informed that we cannot republish any article in our 'Book,' especially the one he refers to—biographical notice of L. Gaylord Clark. He is referred to the September number of our magazine, which he can either buy or borrow."

21 OCTOBER. NEW YORK. In the *Evening Mirror* Hiram Fuller favorably reviews *Godey's*: "What adds particularly to the value of the magazine, is the absence of the rigmarole papers on the literati of New York city, which, we are happy to hear, for his own sake, Mr. Godey has determined to discontinue."

24 OCTOBER. The *Weekly Mirror* contains the fourteenth installment of English's *1844*, which describes the deterioration of Poe ("Hammerhead"): "The bloated face—blood-shotten eyes—trembling figure and attenuated frame, showed how rapidly he [Hammerhead] was sinking into a drunkard's grave; and the drivelling smile, and meaningless nonsense he constantly uttered, showed the approaching wreck of his fine abilities." Delirium tremens, "under which he had nearly sunk," was rapidly followed "by confirmed insanity, or rather mono-mania. He deemed himself the object of persecution on the part of the combined literati of the country, and commenced writing criticisms upon their character as writers, and their peculiarities as men. In this he gave the first inkling of his insanity, by discovering that there were over eighty eminent writers in the city of New York." The installment appears in the *Evening Mirror*, 31 October.

31 OCTOBER. The *Weekly Mirror* contains the fifteenth installment of English's *1844*, which places Poe ("Hammerhead") in the Lunatic Asylum at Utica, New York. John and Mary Melton, a newly married couple honeymooning in Utica, are permitted to visit him in his cell. Melton introduces his bride to "the celebrated writer" of "The Black Crow," a poem, and *The Humbug and Other Tales*:

Hammerhead bowed, and went on to say—"Pray, take a seat, madam. Melton, my dear fellow, I am really glad to see you, indeed I am." Here he took Melton aside, and said confidentially—"You haven't such a thing as a shilling about you, have you? The fact is that I'm devilish hard up, till I get some money for the article I'm writing."

Melton produced the required small coin, and Hammerhead continued—

"I'm engaged on a critique on Carlyle, and the transcendentalists. I'll read a little to you, in order to show you how I use the fellows up." Here he read in a sing-song tone of voice—"The fact is that Mr. Carlyle, is an ass—yet it is not in the calculus of probabilities to explain why he has not discovered, what the whole world long since knew. Perhaps—and for this suggestion I am indebted to the wit of my friend, M. Dupin, with whose fine powers, the whole world, thanks to my friendship, are acquainted—perhaps, I say, it could not be beaten into his noddle."

The installment appears in the *Evening Mirror*, 2 November.

NOVEMBER. PHILADELPHIA. *Graham's Magazine* contains an installment of "Marginalia." Poe states, almost certainly erroneously, that the Paris *Charivari* copied "The Murders in the Rue Morgue" and that the French novelist Eugène Sue drew upon the story for his *Mysteries of Paris*.

NOVEMBER. RICHMOND. The *Southern Literary Messenger* contains "The Priestess of Beauty: A Dramatic Sketch" by Miss H. B. MacDonald, who quotes with approval Poe's definition of poetry as "a thirsting after a wilder beauty than earth can afford" (cf. Poe's review of Horne's *Orion*, W, 11:256).

NOVEMBER. NEW YORK. The *Knickerbocker Magazine* contains this unsigned doggerel satirizing Poe as Aristarchus, the prolific Greek grammarian and critic:

EPITAPH ON A MODERN "CRITIC."
"P'OH PUDOR!"

"HERE ARISTARCHUS LIES!" (a pregnant phrase,
And greatly hackneyed, in his earthly days,
By those who saw him in his maudlin scenes,
And those who read him in the magazines.)
Here ARISTARCHUS lies, (nay, never smile,)
Cold as his muse, and stiffer than his style;
But whether BACCHUS or MINERVA claims
The crusty critic, all conjecture shames;
Nor shall the world know which the mortal sin,
Excessive genius or excessive gin!

In the "Editor's Table" Lewis Gaylord Clark praises the *North American Review* for October; he quotes a portion of its unfavorable critique of Simms, including the derogatory reference to Poe's *Tales*.

CA. NOVEMBER. Mrs. Clemm tells Mary Gove that her daughter Virginia is "dying of want" and that Poe is "very ill" (Nichols [1855], p. 342).

CA. NOVEMBER. FORDHAM. Mrs. Gove visits the Poe cottage:

The autumn came, and Mrs. Poe sank rapidly in consumption, and I saw her in her bed chamber. Everything here was so neat, so purely clean, so scant and poverty-stricken, that I saw the sufferer with such a heartache as the poor feel for the poor. There was no clothing on the bed, which was only straw, but a snow white spread and sheets. The weather was cold, and the sick lady had the dreadful chills that accompany the hectic fever of consumption. She lay on the straw bed, wrapped in her husband's great-coat, with a large tortoise-shell cat on her bosom. The wonderful cat seemed conscious of her great usefulness. The coat and the cat were the sufferer's only means of warmth, except as her husband held her hands, and her mother her feet. . . .

As soon as I was made aware of these painful facts, I came to New York, and enlisted the sympathies and services of a lady [Marie Louise Shew], whose heart and hand were ever open to the poor and miserable. A featherbed and abundance of bed-clothing and other comforts were the first fruits of my labour of love. The lady headed a subscription, and carried them sixty dollars the next week. From the day this kind lady first saw the suffering family of the poet, she watched over them as a mother watches over her babe. She saw them often and ministered to the comfort of the dying and the living (Nichols [1863], pp. 12–13; details corroborated by Mrs. Shew, then Mrs. Houghton, to J. H. Ingram, 16 February and 16 May 1875, Miller [1977], pp. 108, 138).

7 NOVEMBER. NEW YORK. The *Weekly Mirror* contains the sixteenth and final installment of *1844*, in which English summarizes the fates of the novel's major characters: "Hammerhead [Poe] is still in the mad house, writing as vigorously as ever." The conclusion appears in the *Evening Mirror*, 6 November.

8 NOVEMBER. THE VINEYARD, CLARKE COUNTY, VIRGINIA. Philip Pendleton Cooke writes Rufus W. Griswold, requesting assistance in finding a publisher for his volume of poetry, *Froissart Ballads*. "Mr. Poe holds himself ready to review my book—saying all that fairness will let him say in favor of it" (Griswold [1898], p. 191).

18 NOVEMBER. NEW YORK. Poe signs a promissory note for $14.00, payable to Harnden's Express Company from his account with Louis A. Godey (Moldenhauer [1973], p. 81).

21 NOVEMBER. The *National Press* changes its name to the *Home Journal*; as of this date, the weekly is jointly edited by George P. Morris and Nathaniel P. Willis.

23 NOVEMBER. Mrs. Mary L. Seward, a minor poetess, writes Mrs. Frances S. Osgood in Philadelphia, discussing Anne C. Lynch, Mary E. Hewitt, and other literati: "I have heard nothing of the Poe family except that they are in great poverty" (MB–G).

BEFORE 30 NOVEMBER. Mary Gove writes John Neal, discussing Poe (implied by Neal's 30 November letter).

30 NOVEMBER. PORTLAND, MAINE. Neal writes Mrs. Gove in New York: "How Mr. Poe may feel towards me, I do not know: we have had no correspondence for many years; but there was a time when he thought as highly of my doings, I believe, as any body, & was only prevented from dedicating his first volume of poems to me by my assurances that such a dedication would be a positive injury both to him and to his book. . . . Of Mr. Poe's talents and genius, I have always thought & spoken highly: but of his liability to be influenced by personal feelings, for or against his fellow authors—although I have spoken—in private conversation, as a lamentable disqualification for the high duties which he is other wise remarkably well qualified to perform in the country of literature, I have never written a word, or never till now" (MB–G).

30 NOVEMBER. STONEHAVEN, SCOTLAND. Arch Ramsay, a druggist, writes Poe:

As a believer in Mesmerism I respectfully take the liberty of addressing you to know, if a pamphlet lately published in London (by Short & Co., Bloomsbury) under the authority of your name & entitled *Mesmerism, in Articulo-Mortis*, is genuine.

It details an acc't of some *most extraordinary circumstances*, connected with the death of a M M Valdemar under mesmeric influence, *by you*. *Hoax* has been emphatically pronounced upon the pamphlet by all who have seen it here, & for the sake of the Science & of truth a note from you on the subject would truly oblige (*W*, 17:268–69).

BEFORE DECEMBER? FORDHAM. Poe sends his critique "Tale-Writing— Nathaniel Hawthorne" to *Godey's Lady's Book* and his essay "The Rationale of Verse" to the *American Review* (Poe to Eveleth, 15 December).

DECEMBER. PHILADELPHIA. *Graham's Magazine* features an installment of "Marginalia." This issue also contains a squib signed with the initial "W.," aimed at Poe's "Philosophy of Composition" in the April number:

P——, THE VERSIFIER, REVIEWING HIS OWN POETRY.

> When critics scourged him, there was scope
> For self-amendment, and for hope:
> Reviewing his own verses, he
> Has done the deed—*felo-de-se*!

DECEMBER. RICHMOND. In the *Southern Literary Messenger* the anonymous author of an essay on Shelley's poetry quotes with approval this dictum from "The Philosophy of Composition": *"the death . . . of a beautiful woman, is unquestionably the most poetical topic in the world."*

DECEMBER. BOSTON. The *Ladies' Wreath* reprints "The Raven" (Heartman and Canny, p. 218).

DECEMBER OR LATER. FORDHAM. Poe begins a pseudonymous letter to the editor of *Graham's Magazine*, entitled "A Reviewer Reviewed: By Walter G. Bowen." In it he quotes the squib on him from the December *Graham's*; he then gives an adverse criticism of his own writings, identifying flaws in his reviews, tales, and poems. He briefly describes the favorable European reactions to his work in 1846, citing the praises accorded him by Martin Farquhar Tupper and Miss Barrett, and the reprints of "The Facts in the Case of M. Valdemar" in London and "The Murders in the Rue Morgue" in Paris. Although the letter is never completed, Poe preserves the manuscript (text in Mabbott [1978], 3:1377–88).

9 DECEMBER. PARIS. E. D. Forgues's libel suit against M. de Girardin, editor of *La Presse*, comes to trial. A letter to Forgues from Amédée Pichot, editor of the *Revue britannique*, is read to the court: "Je vois que vous avez pris dans Poe une idée pour le *Commerce*." Forgues testifies: "Ce n'est pas dans *La Quotidienne* que j'ai puisé, c'est dans Edgar Poe, littérateur américain. Avez-vous lu Edgar Poe? Lisez Edgar Poe." M. Langlois, counsel for the defense, retorts: "Tout cela me paraît charmant pour E. Poe. Grâce à M. Forgues, tout le monde va savoir que M. E. Poe fait des contes en Amérique." The case is dismissed (*Gazette des Tribunaux*, 10 December, quoted by Seylaz, pp. 41–42).

BEFORE 15 DECEMBER. NEW YORK. Mrs. Mary E. Hewitt learns of the Poe family's straitened circumstances; she begins to collect money for them, bringing their plight to the attention of the city's newspaper editors (Hewitt to Mrs. Osgood, 20 December).

15 DECEMBER. The *Morning Express* reports:

ILLNESS OF EDGAR A. POE.—We regret to learn that this gentleman and his wife are both dangerously ill with the consumption, and that the hand of misfortune lies heavy upon their temporal affairs.—We are sorry to mention the fact that they are so far reduced as to be barely able to obtain the necessaries of life. This is, indeed, a hard lot, and we do hope that the friends and admirers of Mr. Poe will come promptly to his assistance in his bitterest hour of need. Mr. Poe is the author of several tales and poems, of which Messrs. Wiley & Putnam are the publishers, and, as it is believed, the profitable publishers. At least, his friends say that the publishers ought to start a movement in his behalf.

The paragraph is reprinted in the *Evening Express* this afternoon and in the *Semi-Weekly Express* on 18 December.

15 DECEMBER. Poe writes George W. Eveleth in Phillips, Maine, apologizing for not having answered his letters of 9 June and 13 October: "For more than six months I have been ill—for the greater part of that time dangerously so." He discusses "The Raven," "The Sleeper," and "The Valley of Unrest," responding to Eveleth's remarks on these poems in his 9 June letter: "Ten times the praise you bestow on me would not please me half so much, were it not for the intermingled scraps of censure, or objection, which show me that you well know what you are talking about." Answering Eveleth's question in the 13 October letter, Poe explains that he has discontinued his "Literati" articles: "I was forced to do so, because I found that people insisted on considering them elaborate criticisms when I had no other design than critical *gossip*. The unexpected circulation of the series, also, suggested to me that I might make a hit and some profit, as well as proper fame, by extending the plan into that of *a book* on American

Letters generally . . . . You may get an idea of the manner in which I propose to write the whole book, by reading the notice of Hawthorne which will appear in the January 'Godey', as well as the article on 'The Rationale of Verse' which will be out in the March or April no: of Colton's Am. Magazine, or Review." Although Poe's "grand purpose" in life is to issue his own magazine, the *Stylus*, he has postponed this project until he completes his book. He acknowledges the unsigned review of Lowell's *Poems* in the March 1844 *Graham's* (L, 2:331–34).

15 DECEMBER OR LATER. James Watson Webb, editor of the *Morning Courier*, collects "fifty or sixty dollars" for Poe at the Metropolitan Club. Sylvanus D. Lewis, a Brooklyn lawyer, donates "a similar sum" after reading "the statement of the poet's poverty" (R. W. Griswold in the *Daily Tribune*, 9 October 1849).

16 DECEMBER. The *Evening Mirror* reprints the report of Poe's illness from yesterday's *Morning Express*. Hiram Fuller comments: "Mr. Poe is undeniably a man of fine talents, and in his peculiar vein has written stories unequalled. We have no doubt but that with a fair field for exertion, he could produce a series of tales in grotesqueness and force equal to those of the German Hoffman. His friends ought not to wait for publishers to start a movement in his behalf, and if they do not, we, whom he has quarrelled with, will take the lead."

AFTER 16 DECEMBER. PHILLIPS, MAINE. Eveleth receives Poe's 15 December letter, mailed on 16 December. He writes Louis A. Godey in Philadelphia, stating that Poe has told him his reason for discontinuing the "Literati" articles (Eveleth to Poe, 21 February 1847).

18 DECEMBER. BROOKLYN. In the *Daily Eagle* Walt Whitman reports: "It is stated that Mr. Poe, the poet and author, now lies dangerously ill with the brain fever, and that his wife is in the last stages of consumption.— They are said to be 'without money and without friends, actually suffering from disease and destitution in New York.'"

19? DECEMBER. PHILADELPHIA. The *Saturday Evening Post* reports the illness of Poe and his wife. They are "without money, and without friends" (Eveleth to Poe, 19 January 1847).

20 DECEMBER. NEW YORK. Mrs. Hewitt writes Mrs. Osgood in Philadelphia:

The Poe's are in the same state of physical & pecuniary suffering—indeed worse than they were last summer, for now the cold weather is added to their accumulation of ills. I went to enquire of Mr Post [Israel Post, publisher of the *Columbian Magazine*] about them. He confirmed all that I had previously heard of their condition. Although he says Mrs Clem[m] has never told him that they were in want, yet she borrows a shilling often, *to get a letter from the* [post] *office*—but Mrs Gove had been to see the Poe's & found them living in the greatest wretchedness. I am endeavoring to get up a contribution for them among the editors, & the matter has got into print—very much to my regret, as I fear it will hurt Poe's pride to have his affairs made so public (MB–G).

BEFORE 23? DECEMBER. LOWELL, MASSACHUSETTS. Mrs. Jane Ermina Locke, a middle-aged poetess with a husband and five children, sends Nathaniel P. Willis her poem "An Invocation for Suffering Genius," inspired by press reports of Poe's illness (Poe to Willis, 30 December 1846, and to Mrs. Locke, 10 March 1847; Reilly [1972], pp. 206–09).

CA. 23 DECEMBER. NEW YORK. The *Home Journal* for 26 December contains Willis' editorial headed "HOSPITAL FOR DISABLED LABOURERS WITH THE BRAIN." Willis has long believed that there should be an institution to assist educated and refined persons who become disabled or impoverished. His belief has been strengthened "by a recent paragraph in the *Express*, announcing that Mr. EDGAR A. POE, and his wife, were both dangerously ill and suffering for want of the common necessaries of life. Here is one of the finest scholars, one of the most original men of genius, and one of the most industrious of the literary profession of our country, whose temporary suspension of labour, from bodily illness, drops him immediately to a level with the common objects of public charity." Since Poe lives outside the city, Willis has not been able to determine how much of the report is true: "We received yesterday a letter from an *anonymous hand*, mentioning the paragraph in question, expressing high admiration for Mr. Poe's genius, and enclosing a sum of money, with a request that we would forward it to him." During former illnesses Poe has been "deeply mortified and distressed by the discovery that his friends had been called upon"; but since "a generous gift could hardly be better applied than to him," Willis offers "to forward any other similar tribute of sympathy."

23 DECEMBER. Willis writes Poe at Fordham, enclosing his editorial, the anonymous letter mentioned in it, and apparently Mrs. Locke's poem: "The enclosed speaks for itself—the letter, that is to say. Have I done right or wrong in the enclosed editorial? It was a kind of thing I could *only* do *without asking* you, & you *may express anger about it if you like in print*. . . . Please write me whether you are suffering or not, & if so, let us do something systematically for you" (W, 17:272).

24 DECEMBER. FORDHAM. Poe writes Evert A. Duyckinck in New York:

"You remember showing me about a year ago, at your house, some English stanzas—by a lady I think—from the rhythm of which Longfellow had imitated the rhythm of the Proem to his 'Waif.' I wish very much to see the poem—do you think you could loan me the book, or (which will answer as well) give me the title of the book in full, and copy me the 2 first stanzas?" He also hopes to borrow George Gilfillan's two-volume *Sketches of Modern Literature*, or at least "the vol. containing the sketch of Emerson." Poe is taking good care of the Paris edition of Washington Irving and the magazine *Arcturus*; he asks "to keep them some time longer," unless Duyckinck needs them (*L*, 2:334; cf. R. W. Griswold to Duyckinck, 24 July).

24 DECEMBER. Poe writes William D. Ticknor, senior partner in the Boston firm Ticknor & Company. He is preparing a book tentatively entitled "Literary America," which will offer a survey of the nation's literature: "I wish, of course, to speak of Oliver Wendell Holmes, and as I can say nothing of him to which you, as his publisher, could object, I venture to ask you for a copy of his Poems, and any memoranda, literary or personal, which may serve my purpose . . . . Please send anything for me, to the care of Freeman Hunt Esq, Merchants' Magazine Office, N. York" (*L*, 2:335).

26 DECEMBER. NEW YORK. The *Morning Express* comments: "The Home Journal of this week contains an article about Mr. Poe, suggested by the paragraph in our paper, and to which we would call the attention of the public. It would appear from the article in question, that what we said of Mr. Poe's condition was strictly true; and it also appears that Mr. Willis has received certain monies for his benefit, and that he is willing to act as agent in receiving more. We trust that the admirers of genius will remember the unfortunate but gifted author." This plea is reprinted in today's *Evening Express*.

26 DECEMBER. In the *Evening Mirror* Hiram Fuller sarcastically endorses Willis' proposed "hospital" for impoverished authors: "This is all very well; we approve of charity in any shape. But we propose to add to the building, an asylum for those who have been ruined by the diddlers of the quill. We think it quite possible that *this* apartment might be soonest filled, as we cannot now call to mind a single instance of a man of real literary ability suffering from poverty, who has always lived an industrious, honest and honorable life; while of the other class of indigents, we know of numerous melancholy specimens, of both sexes."

26 DECEMBER. BOSTON. The *Bostonian*, a weekly paper, comments: "Great God! is it possible, that the literary people of the Union, will let poor Poe

perish by starvation and lean faced beggary in New York? For so we are led to believe, from frequent notices in the papers, stating that Poe and his wife are both down upon a bed of misery, death and disease, with not a ducat in the world . . . . This is really too bad to be looked for in a christian land, where *millions*! are wasted in a heathenish war, in rum, in toasting and feasting swindlers, robbers of the public purse and squandering thousands for dress and parade, in ungodly finery, jewelry and such profanity . . . . *Christians* for shame" (Moss [1970], pp. 126–27).

27 DECEMBER. SAINT LOUIS. The *Daily Reveille* observes: "If Poe has made enemies, his misfortunes, unhappily, have afforded them ample revenge; and not all of them have had magnanimity enough to forego it. We still see his infirmities alluded to uncharitably." The *Reveille* quotes the New York *Morning Express* of 15 December, whose "painful announcement" of Poe's illness should be sufficient "to sweeten the bitterest disposition" (Moss [1968], p. 21, and [1970], p. 133).

29 DECEMBER. NEW YORK. The *Daily Tribune* reprints the plea for Poe's relief from the *Morning Express* of 26 December, appending this corrective comment: "We are glad to be able to state that the distressing accounts regarding Mr. POE, if they have not been from the first greatly exaggerated, are no longer applicable to his situation. He is steadily, though slowly, recovering his health, and is engaged at his usual literary avocations."

29 DECEMBER. BOSTON. Oliver Wendell Holmes writes William D. Ticknor: "I hope you will do whatever you can to favor Mr. Poe in the matter of which he spoke to you in his letter [of 24 December]. I suppose you will send him a copy of my poems and one of 'Urania,' and refer him for the little facts of my outward existence to the preface to my volume and to Mr. Griswold's book. . . . I have always thought Mr. Poe entertained a favorable opinion of me since he taught me how to scan one of my own poems. And I am not ashamed, though it may be very unphilosophical, to be grateful for his good opinion" (Griswold [1898], pp. 220–21).

30 DECEMBER. FORDHAM. Poe writes Nathaniel P. Willis: "The paragraph which has been put in circulation respecting my wife's illness, my own, my poverty etc., is now lying before me; together with the beautiful lines by Mrs. Locke and those by Mrs.——, to which the paragraph has given rise, as well as your kind and manly comments in 'THE HOME JOURNAL.' " Since the private affairs of Poe's family have been "thus pitilessly thrust before the public," he must make a statement clarifying "what is true and what erroneous in the report alluded to." It is true that his wife is

hopelessly ill and that he himself has been "long and dangerously ill." Because of his illness Poe has been in want of money, but he has never suffered from privation beyond his powers of endurance. The statement that he is "without friends" is a complete falsehood: "Even in the city of New York I could have no difficulty in naming a hundred persons, to each of whom—when the hour for speaking had arrived—I could and would have applied for aid." Poe is now recovering his health: "The truth is, I have a great deal to do; and I have made up my mind not to die till it is done" (published in the *Home Journal* for 9 January 1847).

30 DECEMBER. Poe replies to the 30 November letter from Arch Ramsay of Stonehaven, Scotland: " 'Hoax' *is* precisely the word suited to M. Valdemar's case. The story appeared originally in 'The American Review' . . . . The London papers, commencing with the 'Morning Post' and the 'Popular Record of Science', took up the theme. The article was generally copied in England and is now circulating in France. Some few persons believe it—but *I* do not—and don't you." Poe thinks that he may have relatives in Stonehaven, "of the name of Allan, who again are connected with the Allans and Galts of Kilmarnock"; his full name is "Edgar *Allan* Poe." If Ramsay knows the Allans, Poe would be grateful for "some account of the family" (*L*, 2:337; facsimiles in Gimbel, p. 172, and Robertson, 2:234–35).

30 DECEMBER. Poe writes Evert A. Duyckinck: "Mrs Clemm mentioned to me, this morning, that some of the Parisian papers had been speaking about my 'Murders in the Rue Morgue'. She could not give me the details—merely saying that you had told her." He encloses two letters he has received from Great Britain, Miss Barrett's April letter and Ramsay's 30 November letter. From "the Scotch letter" Duyckinck will learn "that the 'Valdemar Case' still makes a talk, and that a pamphlet edition of it has been published by Short & co. of London." Poe requests an important favor: "It is, to make a paragraph or two for some one of the city papers, stating the facts here given, in connexion with what you know about the 'Murders in the Rue Morgue' . . . . If you think it advisable, there is no objection to your copying any portion of Miss B's letter" (*L*, 2:336–37).

31 DECEMBER. BOSTON. In the *Evening Transcript* Cornelia Wells Walter comments: "The '*Bostonian*' has opened a subscription for the relief of Mr Poe, and so has the *Home Journal* of New York. This is all very proper; no object of humanity should be permitted to die of hunger, or to lay upon the couch of sickness without some ministering angel to relieve distress." Miss Walter quotes the New York *Daily Tribune* of 29 December, which has stated that Poe is recovering his health. She offers a prescription for his

continued well-being: *"Reformation of habits and proper principle exerted to others* is what is requisite to free him in future from the necessity of pity. . . . Let him remember how much of his pecuniary distress he has brought on through the indulgence of his own *weaknesses."*

1846. PHILADELPHIA. Carey & Hart publish Thomas Wyatt's *History of the Kings of France.* The title page identifies Wyatt as the author of several earlier volumes, including *The Conchologist's First Book* (cf. Poe to Eveleth, 16 February 1847).

1846? NEW YORK? Poe writes Mrs. Sarah Anna Lewis, expressing admiration for her poem "The Forsaken," which he has seen "floating the round of the Press." He subsequently meets this young poetess (Mrs. Lewis to J. H. Ingram, 15 April 1879, Miller [1977], pp. 200–01; cf. Poe's praise of the poem, *W*, 13:158–61, 217–19, 225).

SARAH ANNA LEWIS

1846? The attorney Sylvanus D. Lewis, Sarah Anna's husband, recalls: "Shortly after I moved here [Brooklyn], in 1845, Mr. Poe and I became personal friends. His last residence, and where I visited him oftenest, was in a beautifully secluded cottage at Fordham, fourteen miles above New

York. It was there that I often saw his dear wife during her last illness, and attended her funeral. It was from there that he and his 'dear Muddie' (Mrs. Clemm) often visited me at my house, frequently, and at my urgent solicitation, remaining many days" (Lewis to S. S. Rice, 11 October 1875, Rice, pp. 86–87).

LATE 1846? LONDON. "The Gold-Bug" is issued as a pamphlet by A. Dyson, Paul's Alley, Paternoster-Row (Heartman and Canny, pp. 114–15).

LATE 1846? FORDHAM. Augustine O'Neil, a notary public, sees Poe at the train station:

I once went down to the City in the same train and waited a considerable time for the car on the same platform. I had ample opportunity to observe him [Poe]. . . . He was very neatly dressed in black. He was rather small, slender, pale and had the air of a finished gentleman. . . . I once saw him and his wife on the Piazza of their little cottage at Fordham. There was much quiet dignity in his manner. In my opinion neither Shakespeare nor Byron could have been handsomer and I am not a woman that I should be impressed by beauty in a man. . . . Poe must have been at that time about thirty-six years old, but he looked to be forty. His exterior was very pleasing. There was nothing forbidding in his manner. He simply looked like one who had a decent self-respect (Birss, p. 440).

1846 OR 1847? Eliza White, daughter of Thomas Willis White, visits the Poe cottage. "She [Eliza] passed many months with us at Fordham, before and after Virginia's death, but he [Poe] never *felt* or *professed* other than friendship for her" (Maria Clemm to Mrs. Whitman, 22 April 1859, Harrison and Dailey, p. 448).

*

1847

*

JANUARY. NEW YORK. In its "Notices to Correspondents" the *Columbian Magazine* reports its acceptance of Poe's sketch "The Domain of Arnheim."

CA. JANUARY. FORDHAM. Sarah Anna Lewis becomes a frequent visitor to the Poe cottage: "I was in the habit of seeing Mr. Poe once or twice a month from Jan. 1847, to the 29th of June, 1849" (Mrs. Lewis to Eveleth, 6 November 1854, Miller [1977], pp. 199–200).

EARLY JANUARY? PHILADELPHIA. Louis A. Godey replies to George W. Eveleth's letter written after 16 December 1846. He asks to be given Poe's reason for discontinuing the "Literati" articles, explaining that he does not know it (Eveleth to Poe, 21 February).

EARLY JANUARY? PHILLIPS, MAINE. Eveleth replies to Godey. He quotes the reason Poe gave in his 15 December 1846 letter to him: "namely, 'because people insisted on considering them [the articles] elaborate criticisms.' " Eveleth wonders why the *Lady's Book* for January does not contain Poe's critique of Hawthorne (Godey to Eveleth, 30 January; Eveleth to Poe, 21 February).

5 JANUARY. EASTON, PENNSYLVANIA. The *Easton Star* reprints an appeal for Poe's relief from a Philadelphia paper (Quinn, pp. 526–27).

5 JANUARY. NEW YORK. The *Evening Mirror* reprints Miss Walter's prescription for Poe's reformation from the Boston *Evening Transcript* of 31 December 1846. Hiram Fuller comments: "We sincerely hope this good advice will be heeded. Mr. Poe, after libelling half the literary men in the country, commenced a libel suit against us for publishing as an *advertisement* an article which originally appeared in a morning paper in reply to one of his own coarse attacks. This suit was commenced *after* he had grossly abused us in a Philadelphia paper in one of the most scurrilous articles that we ever saw in print; and all this, too, after we had been paying him for some months a salary of $15 a week for *assisting* Morris and Willis, and two or three other 'able bodied men,' in the Herculean task of editing the Evening Mirror."

BEFORE 8 JANUARY. In the *Home Journal* for 9 January, Nathaniel P. Willis publishes Poe's 30 December 1846 letter to him, commenting: "What was the under-current of feeling in his [Poe's] mind while it was written, can be easily understood by the few; but it carries enough on its surface to be sufficiently understood."

In another column the *Journal* carries Evert A. Duyckinck's article "An Author in Europe and America," written in response to Poe's 30 December 1846 letter to him. There is a curious contrast between Poe's position at home, where he is attacked "by penny-a-liners," and his reputation in Europe, "where distance suffers only the prominent features of his genius to be visible." The favorable reception of his stories in England is a recognized fact. "The mystification of M. Valdemar was taken up by a mesmeric journal as a literal verity . . . . A London publisher has got it out, in pamphlet, under the title of 'Mesmerism in Articulo Mortis,' and a Scotchman in Stonehaven has recently paid a postage by steamer, in a letter to the author, to test the matter-of-factness of the affair." Duyckinck quotes Miss Barrett's April 1846 letter to Poe, which contains "a handsome compliment on this story." Another tale, "The Murders in the Rue Morgue," is now attracting attention in Paris: "It has been translated in the feuilletons, local personal allusion discovered and the American authorship denied. One of the journals says 'if there turn out to be such an American author, it will prove that America has at least one novelist besides Mr. Cooper'—and this, in France, is praise. The *Revue des deux Mondes*, in the meantime, has an elaborate review of the 'Tales.' "

8 JANUARY. PHILADELPHIA. In the *Spirit of the Times* John S. Du Solle notices the Poe letter published in this week's *Home Journal*: "If Mr. P. had not been gifted with considerable gall, he would have been devoured long ago by the host of enemies his genius has created." Du Solle quotes with approval Poe's statement that he has "a great deal to do" and has decided "not to die till it is done."

AFTER 8? JANUARY. WEST FARMS, NEW YORK? Poe mails the *Home Journal* for 9 January to George W. Eveleth in Phillips, Maine, and to Thomas Holley Chivers in Oaky Grove, Georgia (Eveleth and Chivers letters to Poe, 21 February).

11 JANUARY. BROOKLYN. The *Daily Eagle* reprints "The Dove" by J. J. Martin, D.D., a religious poem inspired by "The Raven." Walt Whitman provides a brief preface: "Although not possessing the artistic beauty of Mr. Poe's celebrated 'Raven,' the following production, which we find in an exchange [paper], commends itself to every reader by its graceful spirit of Christianity. Mr. Poe's piece was wild and mysterious; this is perhaps less poetic, but its influence . . . will be more apt to soften and ameliorate the heart" (Brasher, pp. 30–31; Mabbott [1969], 1:352).

16 JANUARY. NEW YORK. William T. Porter's *Spirit of the Times* publishes a translation of the 20 October 1846 article in *L'Entre-Acte*, reporting the charge of plagiarism brought against E. D. Forgues. In a footnote the translator repeats Poe's assertions about the story's French reception made in *Graham's Magazine* for November 1846: "The tale referred to, about the Orang-Outang, is '*The Murders in the Rue Morgue*.' It appeared originally in 'Graham's Magazine' for April, 1841; was copied immediately, or at all events noticed, and a digest given of it, in the 'Charivari,' and Sue, in his '*Mysteries of Paris*,' has been largely indebted to it for the epistle of 'Gringalêt et Coupe en Deux.' Subsequently, the story was included in the volume of Poe's Tales, published by Wiley & Putnam. There is an elaborate review of this book in the '*Revue des Deux Mondes*,' and from this latter source [the

Tales], probably, the French journals have, each and all, taken the story" (Pollin [1977], pp. 235–36).

16 JANUARY. The satiric weekly *Yankee Doodle* comments: "We have been inexpressibly delighted with the considerate delicacy and forbearance with which the temporary misfortunes of a distinguished author [Poe] have been recently dragged before the public by the newspapers. Every mean-spirited cur, who dared not bark when his tormentor had strength, feeds fat his ancient grudge, now that he sees his enemy prostrate and powerless—with heart crushed and brain shattered by the sickness and suffering of those most dear to him in life."

16 JANUARY. Anne C. Lynch writes Sarah Helen Whitman in Providence, Rhode Island, asking her to contribute valentines in verse to be read at a "valentine party" next month. After describing the similar party she held last year, Miss Lynch names some of the persons she expects to attend this year: "if you will write you can select your victims from the list" (RPB–W; see also 14 and 21 FEBRUARY 1846).

AFTER 16 JANUARY. PROVIDENCE. Mrs. Whitman replies to Miss Lynch, agreeing to furnish valentines. She apparently asks whether she can address one to Poe, whom Miss Lynch failed to mention (Lynch to Whitman, 31 January).

17 JANUARY. FORDHAM. Poe writes Charles Astor Bristed, a young, well-to-do New Yorker who contributes to George H. Colton's *American Review*: "Permit me to thank you, from the bottom of my heart, for the ten dollars which you were so considerate and generous as to send me through Mr. Colton. I shall now cease to regard my difficulties as misfortune, since they have shown me that I possessed such friends" (L, 2:339–40).

19 JANUARY. PHILLIPS, MAINE. George W. Eveleth replies to Poe's 15 December 1846 letter:

Perusing your Tales, Poems, Criticisms etc. I set you down a man of mighty intellect, and possessed of a soul which might almost claim kindred with the disembodied spirits of heaven, but wanting somewhat—considerably perhaps—in heart, that principle in the human breast which constitutes it human—without which man would be a brute or a God—your letter came and I judged you differently. I could call you *my friend* as well as my favorite author . . . . I never *hoped* to be so favorably noticed by you, and had often feared that you would consider me too presuming for scribbling to you in the manner that I did.

Eveleth quotes the Philadelphia *Saturday Evening Post*, which has reported that Poe and his wife are desperately ill. He believes that the facts in this case have been exaggerated by a journal given to "misrepresentations" of Poe. Alluding to the editorial in the *Post* for 14 March 1846, Eveleth wonders how much of *The Conchologist's First Book* was taken from the British volume: "did you copy it *bodily*, and put your name to it? If so, it *was* a 'bold step' . . . . But it seems strange to me that so daring a deed should have been kept thus secret" (Eveleth, pp. 9–12).

20 JANUARY. Eveleth receives the *Home Journal* for 9 January, forwarded by Poe (Eveleth to Poe, 21 February).

27 JANUARY. PARIS. *La Démocratie pacifique* publishes an able translation of "The Black Cat" by Isabelle Meunier. Since Poe's story seems to illustrate principles contrary to those advocated by this socialist newspaper, the editors offer a brief explanation: "Le morceau que nous publions aujourd'hui est traduit d'un auteur fort connu au delà de l'Atlantique et dont on commence à s'occuper en France. Nous donnons cette Nouvelle pour montrer à quels singuliers arguments sont réduits les derniers partisans du dogme de la perversité native" (Seylaz, p. 42).

29 JANUARY. FORDHAM. Poe writes Marie Louise Shew: "My poor Virginia still lives, although failing fast and now suffering much pain. May God grant her life until she sees you and thanks you once again! Her bosom is full to overflowing—like my own—with a boundless—inexpressible gratitude to you. Lest she may never see you more—she bids me say that she sends you her sweetest kiss of love and will die blessing you[.] But come—oh come to-morrow!" Mrs. Clemm would like Mrs. Shew to stay overnight at the Poe cottage (*L*, 2:340; facsimile in Ingram, p. 323).

29? JANUARY. Mary Starr, the early Baltimore friend of Poe and Virginia, visits them: "The day before Virginia died I found her in the parlor. I said to her, 'Do you feel any better to-day?' and sat down by the big arm-chair in which she was placed. Mr. Poe sat on the other side of her. I had my hand in hers, and she took it and placed it in Mr. Poe's, saying, 'Mary, be a friend to Eddie, and don't forsake him; he always loved you—didn't you, Eddie?' We three were alone, Mrs. Clemm being in the kitchen" (Van Cleef, p. 639; Mary's presence at Fordham confirmed by Mrs. Shew to J. H. Ingram, 23 January and 16 February 1875, Miller [1977], pp. 97, 103).

30 JANUARY. NEW YORK. The *Home Journal* reprints this report from the Paris correspondent of *Willmer and Smith's European Times*, a London paper:

The name of Mr. Edgar A. Poe the American novelist, has figured rather prominently of late before the law courts. A newspaper, which, for the sake of clearness,
I will call No. 1 [*Le Commerce*], gave a *feuilleton*, in which one of Mr. Poe's tales of
a horrible murder in the United States was dressed up to suit the French palate;
but no acknowledgement was made of the story being taken from Mr. Poe.
Another newspaper, No. 2 [*La Presse*], stated that the said *feuilleton* was stolen
from one previously published in another journal. This led to a squabble between
the writer of *feuilleton* No. 1 [E. D. Forgues] and the editor of the newspaper No.
2 [M. de Girardin], that accused him of plagiary from newspaper No. 3 [*La
Quotidienne*]. This squabble resulted in a process [law suit], in the course of which
the *feuilletoniste* No. 1 proved that he had stolen it from Mr. Poe. It was proved,
too, that No. 3 was himself an impudent plagiarist, for he had filched Mr. Poe's
tale without one word of acknowledgement; whilst, as to No. 2, he was forced to
admit that not only had he never read Mr. Poe, but had never heard of him in his
life. All this, it will be perceived, is anything but creditable to the three newspapers in question.

30 JANUARY. PHILADELPHIA. Louis A. Godey replies to a letter from
Eveleth: " 'Hawthorne' by Poe will soon appear" (Eveleth to Poe, 27 July).

30? JANUARY. FORDHAM. Mrs. Shew attends Virginia: "She called me to
her bedside, took a picture of her husband from under her pillow kissed it
and gave it to me. . . . She took from her portfolio a worn letter and
showed it to her husband, he read it and weeping heavy tears gave it to me
to read. It was a letter from *Mr. Allan's wife* after his death. It expressed a
desire to see him, acknowledged that she alone had been the cause of his
adopted Father's neglect" (Shew to Ingram, 28 March 1875, Miller
[1977], p. 116).

30 JANUARY. Virginia dies (obituary, 1 February).

31 JANUARY. NEW YORK. Anne C. Lynch writes Sarah Helen Whitman in
Providence, thanking her for agreeing to contribute to her valentine party.
Replying to Mrs. Whitman's inquiry, Miss Lynch apparently states that
she has not seen Poe recently. She quotes someone in her circle who has
visited Fordham:

Of Mr Poe & his wife she says. I saw him a few days ago for the first time in
several months. He is living about 14 miles from town & has been ill for some
time—his wife also has been dying of Consumption. Hearing that she wished to
see me I went out but the cars returned so soon that they left me only a few
moments there. I found Mrs Poe apparently in the last stages of Consumption &
not expected to survive the day—he was well to all appearance. I have not heard
from them since. They have been suffering from pecuniary distress as well as
sickness (RPB–W).

[The bottom of the letter's first sheet has been cut off, presumably by Mrs. Whitman. It seems likely that in the excised passages Miss Lynch discouraged her from addressing a valentine to Poe. The extant comments on Poe are given in their entirety.]

31 JANUARY. PARIS. *La Démocratie pacifique* publishes Isabelle Meunier's abridged translation of "The Murders in the Rue Morgue" (Seylaz, p. 43).

FEBRUARY. NEW YORK. The *Illustrated Magazine* contains Lawrence Labree's editorial "What Is a National Literature Worth?" As long as American authors are doomed to poverty, there is little hope for literature: "Has not the fact been recently trumpeted through the papers that an unfortunate child of genius [Poe] was lying at the point of death in this city, without the means of making his last hours (if such should be the finale) comfortable; and that his wife was in scarcely better condition? Carried that no heartache to the thousands who have dwelt delighted over the inspirations of his genius? . . . Must we come to this inevitable conclusion, that a poor man has no right to be a literary one?"

CA. 1 FEBRUARY. FORDHAM. Marie Louise Shew makes arrangements for Virginia's funeral: "I bought her coffin, her grave clothes, and Edgars mourning, except the little help Mary Star[r] gave me" (Shew to Ingram, 23 January 1875, Miller [1977], p. 97).

[According to Mary Gove, Mrs. Clemm described Mrs. Shew's care of Virginia in these words: "She [Mrs. Shew] tendered her while she lived, as if she had been her dear sister, and when she was dead she dressed her for the grave in beautiful linen. If it had not been for her, my darling Virginia would have been laid in her grave in cotton" (Nichols [1863], p. 13).]

1 FEBRUARY. NEW YORK. The *Daily Tribune* and the *New York Herald* carry this notice in their obituary columns:

> On Saturday, the 30th ult., of pulmonary consumption, in the 25th year of her age, VIRGINIA ELIZA, wife of EDGAR A. POE.
> Her friends are invited to attend her funeral at Fordham, Westchester county, on Tuesday next, (to-morrow,) at 2 P.M. The cars leave New-York for Fordham, from the City Hall, at 12 [P.]M.—returning at 4 P.M.

1 FEBRUARY. The Superior Court convenes to hear Poe's libel suit against Hiram Fuller and Augustus W. Clason, Jr., publishers of the *Evening* and *Weekly Mirror*. William H. Paine, counsel for the defense, moves that a commission be created to obtain a deposition from Thomas Dunn English, who is now a journalist in Washington. Justice Aaron H. Vanderpoel

appoints as commissioners three residents of that city, John Ross Browne, John Lorimer Graham, Jr., and J. B. H. Smith, any or all of whom being authorized to examine English under oath. Further proceedings in the case are postponed until 15 February (Gravely, pp. 644–45; Moss [1970], pp. 160–62).

1 FEBRUARY. BROOKLYN. In the *Daily Eagle* Walt Whitman notices the death of Poe's wife, which "is mentioned in the New York prints."

2 FEBRUARY. NEW YORK. The *Morning Express*, the *Evening Express*, and the *Semi-Weekly Express* carry this report: "DEATH OF MRS POE.—The death of Edgar A. Poe's wife is recorded in the city papers. She died of pulmonary consumption, on Saturday of last week."

2 FEBRUARY. FORDHAM. In the afternoon Virginia is buried in the family vault of John Valentine, owner of the Poe cottage, in the graveyard of the Old Dutch Reformed Church (Phillips, 2:1204–05).

[Mary Starr recalled: "On the day of the funeral I remember meeting at the cottage Mrs. Ann S. Stephens, Mrs. Shew, N. P. Willis and his partner Morris, and some of the neighbors. It was very cold, and I did not go to the grave, but staid at the house" (Van Cleef, pp. 639–40). Other persons present included Valentine's adopted daughter Mary, Sylvanus D. Lewis and presumably his wife Sarah Anna, and reputedly Poe's first cousin Elizabeth Rebecca Herring (Phillips, 2:1202–03; Rice, p. 86). The funeral was almost certainly attended by Poe's close friends among the New York literati, such as Evert A. Duyckinck, Mrs. Gove, Mrs. Hewitt, Freeman Hunt, and Cornelius Mathews.]

AFTER 2 FEBRUARY? Poe writes these two lines on a manuscript copy of his "Eulalie," a poem celebrating a happy marriage: "Deep in earth my love is lying / And I must weep alone" (Mabbott [1969], 1:396).

5 FEBRUARY. RICHMOND. The *Richmond Whig* reports the death of "Virginia E. Poe, wife of Edgar A. Poe, . . . at Fordham, Westchester county, New York."

6 FEBRUARY. NEW YORK. In the *Home Journal* Morris and Willis notice Virginia's death: "Mrs. Poe was an estimable woman and an excellent wife. Her loss is mourned by a numerous circle of friends."

6 FEBRUARY. The *Literary World*, a weekly edited by Evert A. Duyckinck, commences publication.

8 FEBRUARY. Justice Vanderpoel approves the written questions to be put to Thomas Dunn English in Washington, six "interrogatories" prepared by the defense attorney William H. Paine and ten "cross-interrogatories" drawn up by Poe's attorney Enoch L. Fancher (Moss [1970], pp. 162–65).

11 FEBRUARY. WASHINGTON. English's deposition under oath is taken by J. B. H. Smith, an attorney. Answering the fourth interrogatory, English explains his statement in the *Evening Mirror* of 23 June 1846 that Poe obtained money under false pretenses. In "the early part of October 1845" Poe borrowed $30 from him to be applied toward the purchase of the *Broadway Journal*, offering him an interest in this paper and promising to repay him from its profits. "Mr Poe not only never repaid me the money but never conveyed nor offered to convey to me an interest in said journal. This and the fact that I afterwards learned that the said journal was not a profitable investment constituted the false pretenses." Answering the seventh cross-interrogatory, English admits that he cannot produce Poe's acknowledgment for the loan, having mislaid it since last June. To the fifth interrogatory he testifies:

The charge of forgery referred to was made against Mr Poe by a merchant in Broad street [Edward J. Thomas], whose name I forget. Mr Poe stated to me that this gentleman was jealous of him and of his visits to Mrs Frances S. Osgood, the writer, the wife of S. S. Osgood, the artist; that this gentleman was desirous of having criminal connection with Mrs Osgood; and that, supposing he, Mr Poe, to be a favored rival, he had cautioned Mrs Osgood against receiving his, Poe's, visits, alleging to her that he, Poe, had been guilty of forgery upon his, Poe's, uncle. . . . I called on the gentleman, who would not on his own responsibility avow the truth of the charge nor would he retract . . . . On communicating these facts to Mr Poe, he asked my advice . . . . I told him that he had his alternative, as long as his adversary would not retract, either to fight or bring suit. The latter he preferred; &, as he said he had no money to fee a lawyer, I induced a friend of mine to take charge of his suit without a fee to oblige me. Mr Poe afterwards informed me that he had received an unsatisfactory apology from his adversary (Moss [1970], pp. 165–70).

14 FEBRUARY. FORDHAM. Poe presents Marie Louise Shew with a valentine poem expressing his deep gratitude, "To M. L. S———" (Mabbott [1969], 1:399–401).

14 FEBRUARY. NEW YORK. Anne C. Lynch writes Sarah Helen Whitman in Providence: "The valentines you sent were admirable. They were nearly all read last night . . . . There were about 80 to 90 people here & the evening passed off delightfully" (RPB–W).

15 FEBRUARY. English's 11 February deposition is filed in Superior Court (Gravely, p. 651).

16 FEBRUARY. Poe replies to George W. Eveleth's 19 January letter, enclosing several newspaper announcements of Virginia's death to avoid "writing on painful topics." He has not previously heard "about the accusation of plagiarism" made by the *Saturday Evening Post*. The work in question is *The Conchologist's First Book*: "I wrote it, in conjunction with Professor Thomas Wyatt, and Professor [Henry] McMurtrie of Ph[il]a— my name being put to the work, as best known and most likely to aid its circulation. I wrote the Preface and Introduction, and translated from Cuvier, the accounts of the animals etc. *All* school-books are necessarily made in a similar way." The *Post*'s charge is an infamous falsehood: "I shall prosecute for it, as soon as I settle my accounts with the 'Mirror' " (*L*, 2:343–44).

17 FEBRUARY. In the *Evening Mirror* Hiram Fuller comments: "We are undergoing the luxury to-day of a trial for libel on *Edgar A Poe*, contained in a card of Thomas Dunn English."

17 FEBRUARY. Poe's suit against Fuller and Augustus W. Clason, Jr., is tried before a twelve-man jury in Superior Court, Chief Justice Samuel Jones presiding. As evidence for the plaintiff, Enoch L. Fancher introduces the *Evening Mirror* of 23 June 1846 and the *Weekly Mirror* of 27 June 1846. English's statements that Poe obtained money under false pretenses and that he committed forgery are read to the court. Edward J. Thomas testifies for the plaintiff, identifying himself as the merchant mentioned in English's article. His 5 July 1845 letter to Poe, retracting all imputation of forgery, is introduced and read. Thomas and two other witnesses, Freeman Hunt and Mordecai Manuel Noah, testify that Poe is of good character. The defense is conducted by Clason, who moves for dismissal on the ground that it has not been demonstrated that he is a proprietor of the *Mirror*. In rebuttal Fancher testifies that Clason told him privately that he owns the paper and that Fuller is merely a nominal proprietor. The motion being denied, Clason introduces English's deposition, which he reads to the court. After closing arguments by Fancher and Clason, the jury returns a verdict in Poe's favor, awarding $225 damages and six cents costs ("Rough Minutes" of trial in Moss [1970], pp. 174–75; summary in morning papers, 18 February).

[Gravely, p. 654, pointed out that the award of six cents for costs indicated "that the jury considered the plaintiff to be entitled to the expenses that he had incurred, over and above what he had been awarded for damages."]

18 FEBRUARY. In the morning the *Daily Tribune*, the *Morning Express*, and the *Sun* publish an identical summary of the trial, written by a court reporter. The summary quotes English's accusations in the *Mirror* and his testimony in his deposition. "Mr. English, in that deposition, also stated that 'the general character of said Poe is that of a notorious liar, a common drunkard, and of one utterly lost to all the obligations of honor.' " Mr. Thomas, "the merchant named," testified that Poe called upon him in relation to the charge of forgery: "witness immediately sought out the person who told him, that person denied that he had ever made any such charge about Mr. Poe, and I supposed, said the witness, that I had misunderstood him. . . . This witness, also Judge Noah, and Mr. Freeman Hunt, testified as to the character of Mr. Poe.—Never heard anything against him except that he is occasionally addicted to intoxication." Chief Justice Jones charged the jurors to decide "whether the publications were true or not, or if there is mitigation in relation to them as to the character of Mr. P."; they "returned a verdict for plaintiff of $225." Poe was represented by Mr. Fancher, who "stated that Mr. P. has recently buried his wife, and his own health was such as to prevent him being present."

18 FEBRUARY. In the *Evening Mirror* Hiram Fuller describes the trial, which had its origin in *Godey's Lady's Book*: "Mr. Poe published sundry unliterary articles on literary men, including in the latter category Mr. Thomas Dunn English. Although the sketch of Mr. E. was a mere scratch, still the latter, being quite as sharp a marksman with the quill as the former, determined to give a shot for a shot, and selected as his revolver the Evening Mirror. Mr. Poe's attack was a mere snapping of a percussion cap, compared to Mr. English's fusee, and as he found the pen fight an unequal one, he resorted to a libel suit." English's deposition, read at yesterday's trial, confirms "all his charges." Fuller quotes English's characterization of Poe as a liar and drunkard. "Judge Noah and Mr. Freeman Hunt also testified that Mr. Poe was addicted to intoxication, and notwithstanding this, the jury returned a verdict for *the plaintiff of two hundred and twenty five dollars, and costs!*" Before the trial Mr. Fancher "offered to settle the suit by the payment of $100—thus proving that even he . . . was by no means confident of the justice of his cause."

In another editorial, headed "Law and Libel," Fuller defends his decision to publish English's card: "it was brought to us *printed in a morning paper* [the *Telegraph*], and we were assured that it was to be published in every newspaper in the city on the day that it appeared in the Mirror, and that every word it contained was true." Fuller offered Poe "the free use" of the

Mirror's columns to refute "the charges contained in the 'card,' an offer which he at the time accepted, but was probably advised differently by counsel, who hoped to find something worth picking from this 'bone of contention.'"

19 FEBRUARY. The *Daily Tribune* comments:

GENIUS AND THE LAW OF LIBEL.—Mr. Edgar A. Poe, well known as a Poet, having of course more wit than wisdom, and we think making no pretensions to exemplary faultlessness in morals, still less to the scrupulous fulfillment of his pecuniary engagements, wrote for Godey's Lady's Book a series of Literary Portraits of New-York notables, both of the major and minor order.—They were plain, sincere, free, off-hand criticisms—seldom flattering, sometimes savagely otherwise. Of this latter class was an account of Mr. Thomas Dunn English, which seemed to us impelled by personal spite. To this birching Mr. English very naturally replied, charging Mr. Poe with gross pecuniary delinquency and personal dishonesty, and the *Evening Mirror* was so good-natured as to give him a hearing. Mr. English is a disbeliever in Capital Punishment, but you would hardly have suspected the fact from the tenor of this retort acidulous upon Poe. Mr. P. therefore threw away the goose-quill, (though the columns of the Mirror were impartially tendered him for a rejoinder,) and most commendably refrained from catching up instead the horse-whip or the pistol; but he did something equally mistaken and silly, if not equally wicked, in suing—not his self-roused castigator, but the harmless publisher, for a libel! The case came to trial on Wednesday, and the Jury condemned the Mirror to pay Mr. P. $225 damages and six cents costs.— This was all wrong; $25 would have been a liberal estimate of damages, all things considered, including the severe provocation; and this should have been rendered, not against the Mirror, but against English, if, upon a fair comparison of the two articles, it appeared that Mr. P. had got more than he gave. . . .

19 FEBRUARY. In the *Evening Mirror* Fuller sarcastically inquires: "WHAT HAS BECOME OF THE FUNDS?—We know of three several persons—an old lady, a Christian minister, and a benevolent editor, who have during the past winter been about soliciting money for the support of poor *Poe*. In a recent communication to *N. P. Willis*, *Poe* declares that he has *never been in want of pecuniary assistance*, and in case he had, he knew of a hundred persons to whom he could apply with confidence for aid. We again ask, with some emphasis, what has become of the funds?"

19 FEBRUARY. PHILADELPHIA. In the *Spirit of the Times* John S. Du Solle reports that Poe "has just recovered in New York $225 and costs in an action for libel . . . . We regret to see Mr. Poe bring libel suits against authors, for with all his consummate ability he is not himself apt to speak mincingly of other writers."

19 FEBRUARY. SPRINGFIELD, OHIO. The Philosophian Society of Wittenberg College elects Poe to honorary membership (*L*, 2:523).

21 FEBRUARY. NEW YORK. Poe writes Horace Greeley, editor of the *Daily Tribune*, in Washington, enclosing this paper's 19 February editorial: "When I first saw it I did not know you were in Washington and yet I said to myself—'this misrepresentation is *not* the work of Horace Greeley'." In *Godey's* Poe published "a *literary criticism*" on English, who retaliated by publicly accusing him of two criminal offenses. A court of law has established Poe's innocence of "these foul accusations"; he now wishes to clear himself from two falsehoods circulated by the *Tribune*. Although Poe owes Greeley money, he knows that this editor would never accuse him of being unscrupulous in fulfilling his financial obligations: "The charge is *horribly false*—I have a hundred times left myself destitute of bread for myself and family that I might discharge debts." Poe also did not "throw away the quill"; instead he wrote a reply to English which appeared in the Philadelphia *Spirit of the Times*. "The 'columns of the Mirror' were tendered to me—with a proviso that I should forego a suit and omit this passage and that passage, to suit the purposes of Mr Fuller." The *Tribune's* editorial does Poe "a vital injury," because it bears Greeley's reputation for "truth and love of justice." He asks Greeley to disavow it (*L*, 2:344–46).

21 FEBRUARY. LOWELL, MASSACHUSETTS. Mrs. Jane Ermina Locke writes Poe, expressing sympathy and admiration (Poe's reply, 10 March).

21 FEBRUARY. PHILLIPS, MAINE. George W. Eveleth replies to Poe's 16 February letter. Before receiving it he had seen a notice of Virginia's death in a Boston newspaper: "You will believe me when I say that *I* deeply sympathise with you in your loss." On 20 January, the day after he mailed his last letter, Eveleth received the *Home Journal* for 9 January, containing Poe's letter to Willis and Duyckinck's article on Poe's reputation in Europe. He is forwarding the *Saturday Evening Post* for 14 March 1846, which accuses Poe of plagiarizing *The Conchologist's First Book*. "Will you inform me what is the substance of English's letter published in the 'Mirror,' and when the affair is to be settled?" Eveleth wonders why Poe's critique of Hawthorne has not appeared in *Godey's Lady's Book*; he describes several letters he exchanged with Louis A. Godey regarding the discontinuance of Poe's "Literati" articles (Eveleth, pp. 13–14).

21 FEBRUARY. WASHINGTON, GEORGIA. Thomas Holley Chivers writes Poe: "I received the paper [*Home Journal* for 9 January], containing your letter and the notice of your writings, some time ago. I was delighted with your letter—that is, with the idea that you had got well again . . . .

If you will come to the South to live, I will take care of you as long as you live—although, if ever there was a perfect mystery on earth, you are one—and one of the most *mysterious*." Some time ago he sent Poe "The Return from the Dead," a manuscript tale: "Well, I wish you to look over it, and correct any error you may see in it, and envelope it, as at first, and direct it to Frederick W. Bartlett, Esqr., Atlanta, Ga." Chivers' friend Bartlett edits the *Atlanta Luminary*, a newspaper: "I will notice your poems in the next No. I have spoken to him of you, and he likes you" (Chivers [1957], pp. 69–71; facsimile in Damon, after p. 234).

AFTER 21 FEBRUARY. Chivers has Duyckinck's article "An Author in Europe and America" reprinted in the *Atlanta Enterprise*, asking the paper's editor Dr. William Henry Fonerden to send Poe this issue (Chivers to Poe, 4 April).

22 FEBRUARY. NEW YORK. J. Oakley, clerk of Superior Court, enters the verdict in Poe's libel suit in the Judgment Record. The plaintiff has been awarded $225 for damages "and also the sum of One Hundred and One Dollars, and forty-two cents, for his said costs and charges . . . which said damages, costs and charges in the whole amount to Three Hundred and twenty-six Dollars and forty-eight cents" (Gravely, p. 654; also in Moss [1970], pp. 173–74).

24 FEBRUARY. SPRINGFIELD, OHIO. J. F. Reinman and J. H. Walker of Wittenberg College write Poe that he has been elected an honorary member of the Philosophian Society (Poe's reply, 11 March).

24 FEBRUARY. CAMBRIDGE, MASSACHUSETTS. Henry Wadsworth Longfellow writes these verses in his journal: "In Hexameter sings serenely a Harvard Professor, / In Pentameter him damns censorious Poe" (Phillips, 2:1220).

25 FEBRUARY. NEW YORK. Hiram Fuller writes Louis A. Godey in Philadelphia, discussing Poe's suit against the *Evening Mirror* (cited catalog of American Autograph Shop, Merion Station, Pa. [April 1942], p. 111).

27 FEBRUARY. The *Weekly Mirror* carries an installment of its new serial, Charles F. Briggs's satiric novel *The Trippings of Tom Pepper*. Briggs describes a fictitious soiree at the home of "Lizzy Gilson," a character based on Anne C. Lynch and Elizabeth F. Ellet; he introduces Poe as "the celebrated critic, Austin Wicks," who is accompanied by "Mr. Ferocious" [Cornelius Mathews] and "Tibbings" [Evert A. Duyckinck]:

Mr. Wicks [Poe] entered the room like an automaton just set a going; he was a small man, with a very pale, small face, which terminated at a narrow point in the place of a chin; the shape of the lower part of his face gave to his head the appearance of a balloon, and as he had but little hair, his forehead had an intellectual appearance, but in that part of it which phrenologists appropriate for the home of the moral sentiments, it was quite flat . . . . Pauline was excessively amused at the monstrously absurd air of superiority with which this little creature carried himself, and was vexed with her sister Lizzy for receiving him with such marked respect. But the truth was, he had praised some of Lizzy's verses, and had talked to her about spondees and dactyls until she thought him a miracle of learning. . . . Mr. Ferocious, and his follower, Mr. Tibbings, listened with open-mouthed admiration to Wicks, and declared he was the most profound critic of the age.

When refreshments are served, Wicks takes a glass of wine, becomes intoxicated, then abusive, and finally has to be escorted home. Briggs now introduces a distorted account of last year's controversy over Mrs. Ellet's letters. In this episode Wicks exhibits a letter from Lizzy "as an evidence that she had made improper advances to him." Being threatened by one of her male relatives, he persuades "a good natured physician to give him a certificate to the effect that he was of unsound mind, and not responsible for his actions." The installment is reprinted in the *Evening Mirror*, 4–5 March.

27 FEBRUARY. In the *Evening Mirror* Hiram Fuller comments: " 'B.' [Briggs?] wishes to know why we do not publish the whole of the testimony in *Poe's libel suit*. We answer, because it involves a good deal of delicate matter, and introduces the names of several literary ladies, for whom we have too much respect to publish their names in the connection in which they unfortunately appear."

LATE FEBRUARY? FORDHAM. Mrs. Clemm writes Marie Louise Shew in New York:

> I write to say that the medicines arrived the next train after you left today, and a kind friend brought them up to us, that same hour—The cooling application was very grateful to my poor Eddie's head, and the flowers were lovely, not "frozen" as you feared they would be. I very much fear this illness will be a serious one. The fever came on at the same time today as you said and I am giving the "sedative mixture". He did not rouse to talk to Mr. C. [H. D. Chapin] as he would naturally do to so kind a friend—Eddie made me promise to write you a note about the wine (which I neglected to tell you about this morning.) He desires me to return the last box of wine you sent my sweet Virginia, (there being some left of the first package, which I will put away for any emergency)—The wine was a great blessing to us while *she needed it*, and by its cheering and tonic influence we were enabled to keep her a few days longer with us.

Mrs. Clemm expects Mrs. Shew to return "in an early train" tomorrow morning: "Eddie says you promised Virginia to come every *other* day, for a long time, or until he was able to go to work again. I hope and believe *you will not fail him*" (Miller [1977], pp. 23–24).

CA. MARCH. NEW YORK. Mrs. Shew takes Poe in a closed carriage to Dr. Valentine Mott of the New York University School of Medicine. She recalls: "I made my Diagnosis and went to the great Dr. Mott with it. I told him that *at best* when he was well Mr. Poe's pulse beat only ten regular beats after which it suspended or intermitted (as Doctors say). I decided that in his best health, he had leasion [lesion] on one side of the brain, and as he could not bear stimulants or tonics, without producing insanity, I did not feel much hope, that he could be raised up from a brain fever, brought on by extreme suffering of mind and body . . . sedatives even had to be administered with caution" (Shew to J. H. Ingram, 23 January 1875, Miller [1977], pp. 92–94).

MARCH. The *Columbian Magazine* contains Poe's sketch "The Domain of Arnheim," an expansion of "The Landscape Garden."

MARCH. The *Democratic Review*, now edited by Thomas Prentice Kettell, criticizes Wiley and Putnam's "Library of American Books." It would be better for the national literature if these publishers were to refrain from issuing an American series, "rather than put forth such imperfect efforts as those of Simms, Poe, Matthews [*sic*], Headl[e]y, and last and worst, [George B.] Cheever. . . . there is not one of these writers whose books really do honor to our letters."

3 MARCH. SAINT LOUIS. The *Daily Reveille* reports that Poe "has recovered in New York $225 and costs in an action for libel against the proprietors of the Evening Mirror" (Moss [1968], p. 21).

3 MARCH. PHILADELPHIA. Carey & Hart publish Rufus W. Griswold's *The Prose Writers of America*; the anthology contains "The Fall of the House of Usher," reprinted from Poe's *Tales* (1845). In a prefatory essay on American literature, Griswold reproduces his critique of Poe's fiction originally published in the Washington *National Intelligencer* on 30 August 1845. The biographical sketch preceding "Usher," based on that in *The Poets and Poetry of America* (1842), has been expanded to cover Poe's career through 1845. Here Griswold briefly evaluates Poe's achievements in three genres:

It is as a writer of tales that Mr. Poe has most reputation . . . . A subtle power of analysis is his distinguishing characteristic, and the minuteness of detail and refinement of reasoning which he frequently displays in the anatomy of mystery give to his most improbable inventions a wonderful reality. . . . The analytical subtlety and the singular skill shown in the management of revolting and terrible circumstances in The Murders of the Rue Morgue produced a deep impression, and made this story perhaps the most popular that Mr. Poe has written. An equal degree of intellectual acuteness marks The Gold Bug and The Purloined Letter, which are more pleasing and scarcely less interesting. The Fall of the House of Usher is characterized by a sombre beauty of style, and is an instance of the power with which he paints a disease of the mind.

Griswold shares Poe's regret, expressed in the preface to *The Raven and Other Poems*, that events have prevented him from making a "serious effort" in poetry: "The Raven is imaginative and spiritual . . . . This and many of the minor pieces are pervaded by a touching sadness, and they are all more or less indicative of his habits of dreamy speculation." Poe leaves much to be desired as a critic: "His chief skill lies in the dissection of sentences."

3 MARCH. In his diary Griswold records that his anthology was "published today" (Griswold [1898], p. 223).

10 MARCH. FORDHAM. Poe replies to a 21 February letter from Mrs. Jane Ermina Locke of Lowell, Massachusetts, which he has "only this moment" received. He explains his tardiness in acknowledging her poem "An Invocation for Suffering Genius," inspired by last December's newspaper reports of his illness and poverty: "Your beautiful lines appeared at a time when I was indeed very ill, and might never have seen them but f[or th]e kindness of Mr Willis who enclosed them to me." Poe had feared that if Mrs. Locke should see his letter to Willis in the *Home Journal* for 9 January, she would regret having written this poem: "my first impulse was to write you and assure you even at the risk of doing so too warmly of the sweet emotion made up of respect and gratitude alone with which, my heart was filled to overflowing. While I was hesitating, however, in regard to the propriety of this step—I w[as o]verwhelmed by a sorrow so poignant as to deprive me for several weeks of all power of thought or action." Her letter, now lying before him, convinces him that he should not have hesitated to address her: "believe me, dear Mrs Locke, that I am alreading [already] ceasing to regard those difficulties as misfortune which have led me to even this partial correspondence" (L, 2:346–48; facsimile in Phillips, 2:1215–19).

11 MARCH. Although Poe is "still quite sick and overwhelmed with business," he takes "a few moments" to reply to Eveleth's 21 February letter. Because of "law technicalities" the editorial in the *Saturday Evening Post* accusing him of plagiarizing *The Conchologist's First Book* is not action-

able; he nonetheless will make this paper retract "by *some* means." Poe's suit against the *Evening Mirror* has ended with a verdict in his favor. He encloses his 10 July 1846 "Reply to Mr. English," which will enable Eveleth to understand the nature of English's slanders: "The vagabond, at the period of the suit's coming on, ran off to Washington for fear of being criminally prosecuted." Poe does not know why his article on Hawthorne has not appeared in *Godey's Lady's Book*; he has "no business to ask about it," since Godey paid for it upon acceptance (*L*, 2:348–49).

11 MARCH. Poe replies to a 24 February letter from J. F. Reinman and J. H. Walker of Springfield, Ohio, notifying him that he has been elected an honorary member of the Philosophian Society of Wittenberg College: "May I now beg you to express to your society my grateful acceptance and appreciation of the honor they have conferred on me?" (*L*, 2:349–50).

13 MARCH. NEW YORK. In the *Home Journal* Morris and Willis publish "To M. L. S——," Poe's poetic tribute to Mrs. Shew, with this introduction: "The following seems said over a hand clasped in the speaker's two. It is by Edgar A. Poe, and is evidently the pouring out of a very deep feeling of gratitude."

15 MARCH. Edward J. Thomas writes Mrs. Osgood in Philadelphia:

You know the result of Poe's suit vs Fuller. It went as I thought it would for I always believed the article a *libel* in reality. I had strong apprehension that your name would come out under English's affadavit [*sic*] in a way I would not like for I believed Poe had told him things (when they were friends) that English would sweare to; but they left the names blank in reading his testimony so that a "Mrs——" and "a merchant in Broad St" were all the Jury knew, except on the latter point which I made clear by swearing on the stand that I was "the merchant in Broad St". I got fifty cents as a witness for which sum I swore that Poe frequently "got drunk" and that was all I could afford to sweare to for fifty cents.

Poor Poe—he has lost his wife—his home—may the folly of the past make him contrite for the future—may he live to be what he can be if he has but the will. He is now alone & his good or his evil will not so much afflict others (MB–G).

20 MARCH. The *Home Journal* reports: "EDGAR A. POE is preparing for the press a series of 'The Authors of America'—in prose and verse."

21 MARCH. The *Sunday Dispatch* reports: "The Philadelphia *Galaxy* promises another action growing out of Mr. Poe's suit against the *Mirror*, in which several literary ladies will figure" (Moss [1970], pp. 204–05).

24 MARCH. In the *Evening Mirror* Hiram Fuller copies this unfounded report from the *Dispatch*, commenting: "We shouldn't wonder. Mr. Poe

and his lawyer having made so good a speculation by their infamous prosecution of the Mirror, will very naturally be tempted to try their hand upon some other victim."

28 MARCH. FORDHAM. Poe writes his attorney Enoch L. Fancher: "Mrs. Maria Clemm is hereby authorized to receive the amount of damages lately awarded in my suit, conducted by yourself, against the proprietors of the New-York Evening Mirror, and to give a receipt for the same" (L, 2:716).

CA. APRIL. Poe composes a poem "The Beloved Physician" for Mrs. Shew. Learning that he has been offered $20 for it, she purchases it for $25 to prevent its publication: "every body would know, *who it was* [addressed to], and it was so very personal and complimentary I dreaded the ordeal" (Mrs. Shew to J. H. Ingram, 23 January 1875, Miller [1977], pp. 92–94; Mabbott [1969], 1:401–04).

APRIL. PHILADELPHIA. *Godey's Lady's Book* contains a ten-stanza panegyric "To Edgar A. Poe" by "The Lynn Bard" [Alonzo Lewis of Lynn, Massachusetts]:

> I read thy "Song of the Raven," Poe:
> The thrilling notes of its magic flow
> Sunk into my heart, like the summer rain
> In the thirsty earth, till it glowed again.
>
> When I read the first lines of that wondrous song,
> That doth to a brighter world belong,
> I said—no poet of Freedom's land
> On the summit of such a height can stand. . . .
>
> Another verse, and I seemed to stand
> On the verge of limitless Fairy Land,
> While spirits were passing to and fro,
> And the earth lay far and dark below. . . .
>
> Could I have my choice of the treasured lore
> Of classic land, I would give more
> The author of that strange song to be,
> Than of volumes of unread casuistry. . . .
>
> A thousand brilliant years may flit,
> And still that classic bird will sit,
> As he sat in the golden days of yore,
> On the bust of Pallas above the door.

4 APRIL. WASHINGTON, GEORGIA. Thomas Holley Chivers writes Poe, who has not replied to his 21 February letter: "Are you in the Cave of

Trophonius, or where, that I cannot get the mere scratch of a pen from you?" Chivers has had "the Home-Journal-Article" reprinted in the *Atlanta Enterprise*: "You will see a Poem on you in the next No . . . which will show you what I think of *you*. I wrote you to send '*The Return from the Dead*,' to Bartlette of the Luminary; but if you have not sent it to him, send it to Dr W*m* Henry Fonerden, of the '*Atlanta Enterprise*' . . . . I have made you an ocean of friends since I saw you last." Chivers plans to arrive in New York on 1 May: "if you don't write to me before then, you may expect to be passed in the street without ever being recognized by me" (Chivers [1957], pp. 71–73).

14 APRIL. STONEHAVEN, SCOTLAND. Arch Ramsay replies to Poe's 30 December 1846 letter. He has been unable to identify any persons "of the name of Allan" who might be related to Poe: "There are a good number of the name here & hereabout, & I have made enquiry at all of them I could find but none of them appear to be connected with the families or place you mention." As a believer in mesmerism, Ramsay regrets that Poe could not give a more conclusive answer to his 30 November 1846 letter: "The Pamphlet on Valdemar is published in your name as *the sole conductor & operator in the case* so that I thought you could at once affirm or deny it, but from the tenor of your letter to me this appears not to be the fact" (*W*, 17:284–85).

BEFORE MAY. NEW YORK. Poe visits Mrs. Marie Louise Shew's home at 47 Bond Street, near Washington Square (Poe to Shew, May).

MAY. SATURDAY NIGHT. Mrs. Shew writes Poe, inviting him to select furnishings for the new house of her uncle, the attorney Hiram Barney, at 51 Tenth Street, west of Fifth Avenue (Poe's reply; see also Ingram, p. 361, and Phillips, 2:1267–69).

MAY. SUNDAY NIGHT. FORDHAM. Poe replies to Mrs. Shew: "Nothing for months, has given me so much real pleasure, as your note of last night. I have been engaged all day on some promised work—otherwise I should have replied immediately as my heart inclined. . . . How kind of you to let me do even *this small service* for you, in return for the great debt I owe you. . . . I know I can please you in the purchases." When Poe first visited Marie Louise Shew's home, he was immediately impressed by its decoration: "I wondered that a little country maiden like you had developed so classic a taste & atmosphere. Please present my kind regards to your uncle & say that I am at his service any or every day this week" (*L*, 2:350–51).

MAY? Poe writes Hiram Barney (cited *L*, 2:617).

8 MAY. NEW YORK. In the *Literary World* the publishers announce that Charles Fenno Hoffman has become the weekly's editor, replacing Evert A. Duyckinck.

BEFORE 29 MAY. PHILADELPHIA. Carey & Hart publish the eighth edition of Rufus W. Griswold's *The Poets and Poetry of America*, now significantly revised and enlarged for the first time since it appeared in 1842. The volume contains two new selections from Poe, "The Raven" and "The Conqueror Worm," as well as the three poems included in the original edition ("The Coliseum," "The Haunted Palace," and "The Sleeper").

29 MAY. NEW YORK. The *Literary World* carries an advertisement for Griswold's anthology.

The Poe cottage at Fordham

CA. JUNE. FORDHAM. Some of Poe's friends and admirers spend the day at his cottage; the party includes Professor Cotesworth P. Bronson, a lecturer on elocution, and his daughter Mary Elizabeth, then only a schoolgirl. Mary describes the occasion, recalling that she had expected Poe to be "grave and melancholy":

We saw Mr. Poe walking in his yard, and most agreeably was I surprised to see a very handsome and elegant-appearing gentleman, who welcomed us with a quiet, cordial, and graceful politeness that ill accorded with my imaginary sombre poet. I dare say I looked the surprise I felt, for I saw an amused look on his face as I raised my eyes a second time, to be assured that his were the handsomest hazel eyes I ever saw. . . .

Mrs. Clem[m]—Poe's mother-in-law—whose face bore the traces of many sorrows, but who was always refined and ladylike, met us on the veranda. I noticed, in speaking to Mr. Poe, she always called him Eddie; and in her voice and actions showed all a mother's love. . . . They kept no servant, but the house was a model of neatness and order; the parlor floor was covered with matting, and was simply furnished. A round table, with writing materials, some magazines, a few books, light chairs, and a pretty French print of a young girl hanging on the wall completed the furniture of the room. . . .

After dinner, we all walked along the banks of the Bronx, Mr. Poe pointing out his favorite ramble, where he was seldom interrupted, saying he liked it even on a rainy day. Tired with the walk, we sat under the trees, and while the gentlemen criticized the new books of the day and their authors, the ladies listened in admiring silence for the most part. Mr. Poe spoke much and well of the science of composition, more particularly of his own style—of "The Raven"—mentioning that he had recently written an article for one of the magazines on this subject. As a critic, I thought him severe to himself as well as others of whom he spoke . . . .

Among a number of other authoresses mentioned by Mr. Poe, was the name of Mrs. Osgood. Her poetry was characterized as sometimes careless, but always graceful and natural . . . . In one of the pauses of this pleasant talk, one of the ladies placed on the head of the poet an oak-leaf wreath; and as he stood beneath the tree, half in the shade, the sun's rays glancing through the dark-green leaves, and lighting up his broad white forehead, with a pleasant, gratified smile on his face, my memory recalls a charming picture of the poet, then in his best days (Mary's 1860 reminiscence, Laverty [1948], pp. 165–66).

JUNE OR LATER. NEW YORK. Poe and Mrs. Clemm visit Professor Bronson and his daughter. Accompanied by Bronson, Poe goes "to the daguerreian's," where he sits for a daguerreotype (Mary's reminiscence, pp. 166–67).

[The daguerreotype taken at this sitting may have been the one formerly owned by the playwright Augustin Daly, which was sold at auction in 1903, but is now unlocated (information supplied by Michael J. Deas, from his forthcoming book on Poe portraiture; cf. *carte de visite* used as frontispiece in Allen).]

5 JUNE. The *Literary World* reviews Thomas Dunn English's *1844, or, The Power of the "S.F.,"* now issued as a book bearing the author's name. The novel "attracted no little attention when published as a *feuilleton* in the New York Mirror, and its present cheap form is probably destined to still more general circulation."

1847

7 JUNE. Poe visits the office of the *Evening Mirror*, corner of Nassau and Ann Streets. In the afternoon the paper carries Hiram Fuller's reaction:

PRENEZ GARDE, CHRONY.—We regret to learn that the bold, clever, and rather reckless editor of the Boston *Chronotype* has been sued for a libel. He had better apologize and compromise at once. We speak from experience—having now before our eyes a document (which we intend to frame and hang up in our sanctum as a perpetual caution) showing the utter folly of trusting for justice to the law . . . . The interesting document we allude to certifies that we have paid to *Edgar A. Poe* and his attorney, *E. L. Fancher*, the sum of *three hundred and fifty-three dollars* . . . . Since writing the above we have had a striking demonstration of the truth of our remarks: the poor wretch [Poe] who succeeded by aid of the law and a sharp attorney in filching our money, staggered into our publishing office this morning, clad in a decent suit of black, which had doubtless been purchased by the money so infamously obtained, and behaved himself in so indecent a manner that we were compelled to send for a posse of the police to take him away.

The last that we heard him say, as they took him up Nassau street, was something about *home*, and we suppose that he wanted to go to his friend [Willis] of the *Home Journal*, who a short time since proposed founding an Asylum for used-up authors. Poor wretch! We looked upon him with sincere pity, and forgave him all the wrong he had done us, only reserving our wrath for the instruments which give such people power to inflict injury upon innocent victims.

24 JUNE. Evert A. Duyckinck writes in his diary: "With Mathews, visited Poe at Fordham whom the wondrous Mrs Clem[m] has domiciliated in a neat cottage near a rock overlooking the pretty valley with its St John's College of Jesuits, contiguous hill and forest, the Sound and the blue distance of Long Island. The purity of the air, delicious. At night the whole agreeable impression of the afternoon reversed by dreams, into which it might have been supposed Poe had put an infusion of his Mons Valdemar with the green tea, the probable cause of them. All the evil I had ever heard of him took bodily shape in a series of most malignant scenes" (Yannella, p. 223).

[Many years later Cornelius Mathews described this occasion in a letter to J. C. Derby: "There was quite a little party gathered to take tea with Poe and his mother-in-law and aunt, Mrs. Clemm. When we were summoned into the supper-room we found to the open-eyed wonder of the company, the floor laid with a brand-new rag carpet, an ample table, sumptuous with delicacies, and Mrs. Clemm at the head of the table, decanting, from a new silver-plated urn, amber coffee, which glowed as it fell in the light of the setting sun. All this was in strong contravention of Poe's proclaimed abject poverty, unless observers had brought to mind that the equipage represented in part of the proceeds of a libel suit collected by the poet in the previous week from Hiram Fuller, editor of the *Evening Mirror*" (Derby, pp. 588–89).]

30 JUNE. Rufus W. Griswold writes in his diary: "In the street today met Poe, who was extremely civil" (Griswold [1898], p. 230).

JULY. The *Union Magazine*, edited by Mrs. Caroline M. Kirkland, commences publication.

EARLY JULY. PHILLIPS, MAINE. George W. Eveleth replies to a letter from George H. Colton, editor of the *American Review*. Eveleth would be willing to subscribe to Colton's monthly, except that in the near future he expects to subscribe to a magazine conducted by Poe. He inquires why Poe's essay "The Rationale of Verse" has not appeared in the *Review* (Colton to Eveleth, 24 July; Eveleth to Poe, 27 July 1847 and 11 January 1848).

3 JULY. PARIS. *La Démocratie pacifique* publishes "Fragment d'Eiros et Charmion," a translation of Poe's tale by Isabelle Meunier (Seylaz, p. 43).

24 JULY. NEW YORK. Colton replies to Eveleth: "As to Poe's Journal— supposing you take my Review at $4, a year, till his appears;—candidly I do not at all believe you will see a Magazine from him this four years—a mere literary Maga. cannot live—I understand the matter perfectly . . . . Mr. Poe's MS was so long I could not publish it" (Eveleth to Poe, 11 January 1848).

27 JULY. PHILLIPS, MAINE. Eveleth answers Poe's 11 March letter. He explains that he delayed his reply in the hope of being able to discuss Poe's critique of Hawthorne and his "Rationale of Verse," but neither article has been published. On 30 January Louis A. Godey wrote Eveleth that the notice of Hawthorne would soon appear in the *Lady's Book*: "his 'soon' seems to embrace quite a period of time." Colton wrote him "about three weeks since," but failed to mention "The Rationale of Verse." Although Poe's "Reply to Mr. English" needed to be severe, it is not altogether in good taste: "In some instances you have *come down* too nearly on a level with English himself. . . . You laid yourself liable to be laughed at by answering in such a spirit, more than you would have done if you had kept calm . . . . do you think proper to *hint* to me what the 'terrible evil' is which caused those 'irregularities so profoundly lamented'?" Eveleth inquires about Poe's forthcoming magazine, the *Stylus* (Eveleth, pp. 14–16).

AFTER 27 JULY. Eveleth receives Colton's 24 July letter. Questioning the reason given for "the non-appearance" of "The Rationale of Verse," Eveleth writes him, reminding him of the space accorded a critique of Joel T. Headley's *Washington and his Generals* in his May number, "which article contained 17 pages, the principal part extract" (Eveleth to Poe, 11 January 1848).

31 JULY. NEW YORK. The *Literary World* notices the book publication of Charles F. Briggs's *Trippings of Tom Pepper*: "meditating over the author's life-like sketches of character, we could not help, despite the disclaimer of all personalities in his preface, questioning whether his means of giving such verisimilitude was perfectly fair and above-board; whether, in fact, his book was not a gallery of portraits of well-known living people."

LATE JULY? WASHINGTON. Poe visits the capital, where he sees his friend Frederick William Thomas as well as Charles Eames, former editor of the *New World* (suggested by Poe to Thomas, 14 February 1849).

LATE JULY? VIRGINIA, NEAR WASHINGTON. Poe attends the commencement of the Episcopal High School: "In the year 1847, while the final exercises were going on out under the trees, Edgar Allan Poe was seen standing near the rostrum. He had come out to the school from Alexandria with a party of friends. But when he was discovered he was at once the object of universal attention and obligingly went forward and recited 'The Raven', to the delight of all who were present" (Goodwin, 2:420).

LATE JULY. PHILADELPHIA. Poe takes lodgings in William Arbuckle's Western Hotel, 288 High (or Market) Street. He calls on Louis A. Godey and on Robert T. Conrad, who is now sharing the editorial duties of *Graham's Magazine* with George R. Graham. Later he sees Graham himself, who is just leaving for the summer resort at Cape May, New Jersey (Godey to Eveleth, 6 August; Poe to Conrad, 10 and 31 August).

6 AUGUST. Godey replies to a letter from Eveleth, who asked him to publish Poe's critique of Hawthorne in the *Lady's Book*: "I assure you that 'Hawthorne' has been in the printer's hands for three months—your letter acted as a hint, and I have sent to the office, *commanding* its insertion in either the Oct. or Nov. number—Mr. Poe has been on here—but it were better for his fame to have staid away. I don't like to say much about him—he called on me quite sober—but I have heard from him elsewhere, when he was not so" (Eveleth to Poe, 11 January 1848).

10 AUGUST. NEW YORK. Poe writes Robert T. Conrad:

Permit me to thank you, in the first place, very sincerely, for your considerate kindness to me while in Philadelphia. Without your aid, at the precise moment and in the precise manner in which you rendered it, it is more than probable that I should not now be alive to write you this letter. Finding myself exceedingly ill— so much so that I had no hope except in getting home immediately—I made several attempts to see Mr Graham and at last saw him for a few minutes just as he was about returning to Cape May. He was very friendly—more so than I have ever known him, and requested me to write continuously for the Mag. As you were not present, however, and it was uncertain when I could see you, I obtained an advance of $10 from Mr G. in order that I might return home at once.

Poe hopes that Conrad can give him a prompt decision on the two articles he left at *Graham's Magazine*: "Should you take both, it will render me, just now, the most important service. I owe Mr G. about $50. The articles, at the old price ($4 per page) will come to $90—so that, if you write me that they are accepted, I propose to draw on Mr G. for $40—thus squaring our account" (*L*, 2:351–52).

[One of the articles was probably "The Rationale of Verse." On 4 January 1848 Poe wrote Eveleth that he "sold it to 'Graham' at a round advance on Colton's price."]

17 AUGUST. Williamson & Burns, publishers of the *Weekly Universe*, reply to a letter from Eveleth, who inquired about Poe's drinking habits and his proposed *Stylus*:

Edgar A. Poe, in the estimation of the editors of the "Universe," holds a high rank, regarded either as an elegant tale-writer, a poet, or a critic. He will be more fairly judged after his death than during his life. His habits have been shockingly irregular, but what amendment they have undergone within the past six months we cannot say, for Mr. Poe, during that time, has been in the country—we know him personally—he is a gentleman—a man of fine taste and of warm impulses, with a generous heart. The little eccentricities of his character are never offensive except when he is drunk. We do not hear that he has any enterprise of the description intimated by you, in hand. A Magazine conducted as he is capable of conducting a Magazine, could hardly fail of success (Eveleth to Poe, 11 January 1848).

31 AUGUST. Poe writes Conrad, who has not replied to his 10 August letter: "I can only suppose that my letter has not reached you—or, at all events, that, in the press of other business, you have forgotten it and me." He repeats his request for a prompt answer "about the two articles" (*L*, 2:352).

SEPTEMBER. Returning to New York after an absence, Professor Cotesworth P. Bronson and his daughter Mary Elizabeth see Poe and Mrs. Clemm again. Mary recalls Mrs. Clemm as "looking very anxious," but speaking "hopefully of what Eddie could do if he only could obtain some regular employment worthy of his abilities." Professor Bronson asks Poe to compose a poem for him, which he could recite when lecturing on elocution (Laverty [1948], p. 167).

4 SEPTEMBER. BUFFALO, NEW YORK. The *Western Literary Messenger* reports: "Edwin Forrest offers a liberal opportunity for the production of something worthy of American literature . . . proposing to give the sum of three thousand dollars for the best original tragedy, in five acts, the production of an American Citizen; or in case no good acting play should be produced, one thousand dollars for the best tragedy sent in" (Chivers [1957], p. 75).

9 SEPTEMBER. NEW YORK. Evert A. Duyckinck writes in his diary: "Forrest's offer of $3000 for a new tragedy to suit him, or $1000 for the best sent in, if he does not act it will probably consume a great deal of paper by the American Poets. Poe to day in town wonder struck wanting to know if there was really such an offer" (Yannella, p. 236).

23–24 SEPTEMBER. PARIS. *La Démocratie pacifique* publishes Poe's "Une descente au Maelstrom," translated by Isabelle Meunier, in two installments (Seylaz, p. 43).

CA. OCTOBER. FORDHAM. Miss Anna Blackwell boards at the Poe cottage.

[In her *Edgar Poe and his Critics* (1860), pp. 30–32, Sarah Helen Whitman gave an account of the cottage related to her by an unnamed English authoress: "It was at the time bordered by a flower-garden, whose clumps of rare dahlias and brilliant beds of fall flowers showed, in the careful culture bestowed upon them, the fine floral taste of the inmates. . . . He [Poe] had some rare tropical birds in cages, which he cherished and petted with assiduous care. . . . A favourite cat, too, enjoyed his friendly patronage, and often when he was engaged in composition it seated itself on his shoulder, purring as in complacent approval of the work proceeding under its supervision." In her 17 April 1874 letter to J. H. Ingram, Mrs. Whitman identified her informant as Anna Blackwell: "She was in very delicate health at the time, & a friend of hers [Mary Gove] who chanced to know Mrs. Clemm prevailed upon that lady to receive her as a boarder for a few weeks" (Miller [1979], p. 124; see also pp. 162, 234–35, 246, 255).]

CA. OCTOBER. NEW YORK. Mary Elizabeth Bronson encounters Mrs. Clemm, who tells her "that Mr. Poe had written a beautiful poem—better than anything before" (Laverty [1948], p. 167).

CA. OCTOBER. FORDHAM. Poe writes Professor Cotesworth P. Bronson in New York: "I wish to ascertain if the poem which, at your suggestion, I have written, is of the len[g]th, the character &c you desire:—if not I will write another and dispose of this one to Mrs Kirkland. Cannot Miss

Ulalume — A Ballad.
By Edgar A. Poe.

The skies they were ashen and sober;
    The leaves they were crisped and sere —
    The leaves they were withering and sere:
It was night, in the lonesome October
    Of my most immemorial year:
It was hard by the dim lake of Auber,
    In the misty mid region of Weir: —
It was down by the dank tarn of Auber,
    In the ghoul-haunted woodland of Weir.

Here once, through an alley Titanic,
    Of cypress, I roamed with my Soul —
    Of cypress, with Psyche, my Soul.
These were days when my heart was volcanic
    As the scoriac rivers that roll —.
    As the lavas that restlessly roll
Their sulphurous currents down Yaanek,
    In the ultimate climes of the Pole —
That groan as they roll down Mount Yaanek,
    In the realms of the Boreal Pole.

Our talk had been serious and sober,
    But our thoughts they were palsied and sere —
    Our memories were treacherous and sere;

"ULALUME"
(detail from the manuscript Poe gave Susan V. C. Ingram)
Pierpont Morgan Library

Bronson and yourself, pay us a visit at Fordham—say this afternoon or tomorrow?" (Mabbott [1969], 1:412; see also Moldenhauer [1973], pp. 64–65).

CA. OCTOBER. NEW YORK. Professor Bronson is unable to visit Fordham; Poe therefore delivers the poem to his home. Bronson being out, his daughter Mary Elizabeth receives the manuscript from Poe: "I asked if I might read it. He not only assented, but opened the roll, which consisted of leaves of paper wafered neatly together, and I noticed then and afterward that the writing was beautifully distinct and regular, almost like engraving. It was the 'Ballad of Ulalume.' He made one or two remarks in regard to the ideas intended to be embodied, answering my questions while he read it to me, and expressing his own entire satisfaction with it" (Laverty [1948], pp. 167–68).

CA. OCTOBER. Poe submits "Ulalume" to Mrs. Caroline M. Kirkland, editor of the *Union Magazine*. She asks the rising poet Richard Henry Stoddard to read the poem. "After complying with her request, he told her, he could not understand it." She returns it to Poe (Derby, p. 597).

15 OCTOBER. George H. Colton replies to Eveleth's letter of inquiry: "I hope Mr. Poe has done drinking—I don't think he has drank any thing this long time. He is living in a quiet way out in the beautiful county of Westchester" (Eveleth to Poe, 11 January 1848).

CA. NOVEMBER. FORDHAM. Mary Gove visits the Poe cottage, accompanied by several other literati. She recalls:

We strolled away into the woods, and had a very cheerful time, till some one proposed a game at leaping. I think it must have been Poe, as he was expert in the exercise. Two or three gentlemen agreed to leap with him, and though one of them was tall, and had been a hunter in times past, Poe still distanced them all. But alas! his gaiters, long worn and carefully kept, were both burst in the grand leap that made him victor. . . . I pitied Poe more now. I was certain he had no other shoes, boots, or gaiters. Who amongst us could offer him money to buy a new pair? . . . When we reached the cottage, I think all felt that we must not go in, to see the shoeless unfortunate sitting or standing in our midst. . . . The poor old mother looked at his feet, with a dismay that I shall never forget.

Mrs. Gove tells Mrs. Clemm "the cause of the mishap"; they then have a private conversation in the kitchen. Mrs. Clemm asks her to persuade George H. Colton to purchase "Ulalume" for the *American Review*: "If he will only take the poem, Eddie can have a pair of shoes. He [Colton] has it—I carried it [to him] last week, and Eddie says it is his best. You will speak to him about it, won't you?" Mrs. Gove readily consents, although she has reservations that she does not express to Mrs. Clemm: "We had already read the poem in conclave, and Heaven forgive us, we could not make head or tail to it. It might as well have been in any of the lost languages, for any meaning we could extract from its melodious numbers. I remember saying that I believed it was only a hoax that Poe was passing off for poetry, to see how far his name would go in imposing upon people" (Nichols [1863], pp. 9–11).

CA. NOVEMBER. NEW YORK. Colton accepts "Ulalume," paying for it immediately. The purchase price is sufficient for "a pair of gaiters, and twelve shillings over" (Nichols [1863], p. 11).

NOVEMBER. PHILADELPHIA. *Godey's Lady's Book* contains Poe's critique "Tale-Writing—Nathaniel Hawthorne."

NOVEMBER. EDINBURGH, SCOTLAND. *Blackwood's Magazine* contains a nineteen-page critique of Wiley and Putnam's "Library of American Books." After briefly dismissing Cornelius Mathews' *Big Abel and the Little Manhattan* as "heinous trash," the reviewer condemns the "superfluous and futile" pleas for "Americanism in Literature" voiced in William Gilmore Simms's *Views and Reviews* and Margaret Fuller's *Papers on Literature and Art*. He regards Hawthorne as a serious writer of high merit, devoting some five pages to *Mosses from an Old Manse*. Poe is accorded equal space, though the verdict on his *Tales* seems less favorable:

No one can read these tales, then close the volume, as he may with a thousand other tales, and straightway forget what manner of book he has been reading. Commonplace is the last epithet that can be applied to them. They are strange—powerful—more strange than pleasing . . . . In fine, one is not sorry to have read these tales; one has no desire to read them twice.

They are not framed according to the usual manner of stories. On each occasion, it is something quite other than the mere story that the author has in view, and which has impelled him to write. In one, he is desirous of illustrating La Place's doctrine of probabilities as applied to human events. In another he displays his acumen in unravelling or in constructing a tangled chain of circumstantial evidence. In a third ("The Black Cat") he appears at first to aim at rivalling the fantastic horrors of Hoffman, but you soon observe that the wild and horrible invention in which he deals, is strictly in the service of an abstract idea which it is there to illustrate. His analytic observation has led him, he thinks, to detect in men's minds an absolute spirit of "perversity," prompting them to do the very opposite of what reason and mankind pronounce to be right, simply because they *do* pronounce it to be right. The punishment of this sort of diabolic spirit of perversity, he brings about by a train of circumstances as hideous, incongruous, and absurd, as the sentiment itself.

There is, in the usual sense of the word, no passion in these tales, neither is there any attempt made at dramatic dialogue. . . . The style, too, has nothing peculiarly commendable; and when the embellishments of metaphor and illustration are attempted, they are awkward, strained, infelicitous. But the tales rivet the attention. There is a marvellous skill in putting together the close array of facts and of details which make up the narrative . . . . In one of his papers he describes the Mahlström, or what he chooses to imagine the Mahlström may be, and by dint of this careful and De Foe-like painting, the horrid whirlpool is so placed before the mind, that we feel as if we had seen, and been down into it.

12 NOVEMBER. NEW YORK. Writing in the office of the *Home Journal*, Nathaniel P. Willis replies to a communication from Poe: "I could not find time *possibly* to go to the concert, but why did you not send the paragraph yourself. You knew of course that it would go in." Not long ago Willis received a letter from Rosalie Poe in Richmond, inquiring about her brother's whereabouts: "supposing you had mov'd, I could not inform her. You seem as neglectful of your sister as I am of mine, but private letters are 'the last ounce that breaks the camel's back' of a literary man" (MB–G; dating demonstrated by Reece [1954], p. 82).

23 NOVEMBER. PHILLIPS, MAINE. George W. Eveleth writes Evert A. Duyckinck in New York. He praises Duyckinck's article on Poe in the *Home Journal* for 9 January:

I thank you for this kindly speaking of *my favorite one* while "pestered and annoyed by those miserable penny-a-liners."
   Where is Mr. Poe—what is he doing—and what is he likely to do?—He has promised me several times that I should have the privilege of taking a monthly magazine—"The Stylus"—conducted by himself. . . . I know he is competent so far as talent, tact, and genius are concerned—but am afraid those *irregularities* of his, as well as a want of money, will prevent.
   Does he continue to drink hard yet, or has he reformed, as Mr. Colton of Am. Review—tells me he is in hopes he has? Mr. Colton informed me in his last letter that Mr. Poe resides in the *County* of Westchester, but didn't name the town. . . .
   Mr. Colton has made me agent for the distribution of his Review—but I have been tarrying somewhat, a *little* in hopes that Mr. Poe's promise would be fulfilled, as I had rather work for his "Stylus" than for the Review.
   Do you think proper to answer this medley? I would especially like to know where Mr. Poe is, so that I can write him (Eveleth, p. 24).

CA. 25 NOVEMBER. FORDHAM. Poe sends "An Enigma" to a magazine, probably Mrs. Kirkland's *Union Magazine*. This acrostic sonnet conceals the name Sarah Anna Lewis.

27 NOVEMBER. Poe writes Mrs. Lewis in Brooklyn: "A thousand thanks for your repeated kindness, and, above all, for the comforting and cheering words of your note." He accepts her advice "as a command" which neither

his heart nor his reason could disobey. "A day or two ago I sent to one of the Magazines the sonnet enclosed. Its tone is somewhat too light; but it embodies a riddle which I wish to put you to the trouble of expounding" (*L*, 2:352–53).

DECEMBER. NEW YORK. The *American Review* contains Poe's "Ulalume: A Ballad," preceded by the dedication "To—— —— ——." The poem is unsigned, in keeping with the magazine's practice when publishing poetry.

[In his dedication Poe was almost certainly thinking of Sarah Anna Lewis or Marie Louise Shew, or of a formula which would gratify both.]

1 DECEMBER. George H. Colton, editor of the *Review*, dies at age twenty-nine. He is succeeded by James D. Whelpley.

8 DECEMBER. FORDHAM. Poe writes Willis, thanking him for his "note of three or four weeks ago" [presumably the 12 November letter]. Poe is forwarding this month's *American Review*, which contains his "Ulalume." Although he does not wish "to be known as its author just now," he would be grateful if Willis would reprint it in the *Home Journal*, "with a word of *inquiry* as to who wrote it" (*L*, 2:718).

BEFORE 12 DECEMBER. PHILLIPS, MAINE. Eveleth writes Williamson & Burns, publishers of the *Weekly Universe*. Apparently, he informs them that Poe has stopped drinking and suggests that they support the *Stylus* (12 December reply).

12 DECEMBER. NEW YORK. Under the heading "To Correspondents" the *Weekly Universe* carries this reply: "G. W. E.—*Phillips Me.* We don't know where the gentleman you inquire for, is residing; but are glad to hear from you, that he is so careful of himself. The enterprise you suggest might do, but we are too busy to undertake it" (Eveleth, pp. 19, 25).

CA. 15 DECEMBER. PHILADELPHIA. The *John-Donkey*, a satiric weekly edited by Thomas Dunn English and George G. Foster, commences publication. The first number, dated 1 January 1848, contains this oblique allusion to Poe's drinking: "A NICE JOB. We understand that Mr. E. A. POE has been employed to furnish the railing for the new railroad over Broadway. He was seen going up street a few days ago, apparently laying out the road."

17 DECEMBER. BROOKLYN. In the *Daily Eagle* Walt Whitman welcomes "the initiative number" of the *John-Donkey*, "a new quarto illustrated

journal of humor and drive-away-careism." As a sample of the magazine's humor—"the real coarse, but deep, true stuff"—Whitman reprints the fictitious report of Poe's current employment.

24 DECEMBER. NEW YORK. On Christmas Eve Poe accompanies Marie Louise Shew and "a Lady friend" to a midnight service conducted by Reverend William Augustus Muhlenberg. Mrs. Shew recalls:

He [Poe] went with us, followed the service like a "churchman", looking directly towards the chancel, and holding one side of my prayer book, sang the psalms with us, and to my astonishment struck up a tenor to our sopranos and, got along nicely during the first part of the sermon, which was on the subject of the sympathies of our Lord, to our wants. The passage being often repeated, "He was a man of sorrows and acquainted with grief." He begged me to stay quiet that he would wait for me outside, and he rushed out, *too excited to stay*. I knew he would not leave us to return home alone, (altho' my friend thought it doubtful), and so after the sermon as I began to feel anxious (as we were in a strange church) I looked back and saw his pale face, and as the congregation rose to sing the Hymn, "Jesus Saviour of my soul," he appeared at my side, and sang the Hymn, without looking at the book, in a fine clear tenor. . . . I did not dare to ask him why he left, but he mentioned after we got home, that the subject "*was marvelously handled*, and ought to have melted many hard hearts" and ever after this he never passed Doctor Muhlenbergs 20th St. Free Church without going in (letter to J. H. Ingram, ca. 15 April 1875, Miller [1977], pp. 132–33).

1847. Thomas Dunn English's 1843 temperance novel containing a hostile caricature of Poe is published as a book by William B. Smith & Co., its title altered to *Walter Woolfe; or, The Doom of the Drinker*.

1847? PARIS. The French poet Charles Baudelaire encounters several of Poe's stories in translation. Excited by his discovery, he begins to collect Poe's publications in English (P. F. Quinn, pp. 14–15, 70–72, 87).

LATE 1847? NEW YORK. "The Raven" is reprinted in the *Literary Annual* for 1848 (Heartman and Canny, p. 116).

LATE 1847? FORDHAM. Mrs. Shew is repelled by Sarah Anna Lewis:

Mr. Poe was indebted to her [Mrs. Lewis], that is, she paid Mrs. Clemm in advance, when they were needy, and poor Poe *had to notice* her writings, and praise them. He expressed to me the *great mortification it was to him*, and I child like I hated the fat gaudily dressed woman whom I often found sitting in Mrs. Clemm's little kitchen, waiting to see the man of genius, who had rushed out to escape her, to the fields and forest—or to the grounds of the Catholic school in the vicinity. I remember Mrs. C[lemm] sending me after him in great secrecy one day & I found him sitting on a favorite rock muttering his desire to die, and get rid of *Literary bores* (Shew to J. H. Ingram, 3 April 1875, Miller [1977], p. 120).

SARAH HELEN WHITMAN
(from the painting by C. Giovanni Thompson)
Providence Athenaeum

CHAPTER TEN

Eureka *and* Mrs. *Whitman*

1848

Poe begins the year 1848 with renewed energy and enthusiasm, working on his cosmological treatise *Eureka* and issuing a prospectus for the *Stylus*. He plans a promotional tour for the proposed magazine in the Southern and Western states, hoping to raise the necessary expenses by delivering an abbreviated version of *Eureka* as a public lecture. The 3 February lecture in New York, entitled "The Universe," attracts a small but appreciative audience. The poetess Sarah Helen Whitman, a widow living in Providence, Rhode Island, brings herself to Poe's attention by contributing a poem "To Edgar A. Poe" to Miss Anne C. Lynch's valentine party on 14 February. On 2 March Poe sends his 1831 verses "To Helen" to Mrs. Whitman; around 1 June he forwards the manuscript of a new poem he has specifically addressed to her. Early in July Poe visits Lowell, Massachusetts, as the guest of the local poetess Mrs. Jane Ermina Locke; there he delivers a 10 July lecture on "The Poets and Poetry of America." Around 11 July the New York publisher George P. Putnam issues *Eureka*, which receives mixed reviews and has only a limited sale. In late July Poe travels to Richmond, where he renews old friendships, indulges in intermittent drinking, and prepares to depart on a tour promoting the *Stylus*. There he receives two stanzas of poetry which Mrs. Whitman has sent him to acknowledge the manuscript poem he forwarded to her around 1 June. Poe immediately leaves for New York, determined to make her acquaintance. On 21 September he calls on her in Providence, subsequently declaring his love for her and urging her to marry him. After he returns to his home at Fordham, Mrs. Whitman writes him to decline his proposal of marriage, explaining that she is older than he and in poor health. Poe calls on her again in late October, asking her to reconsider her answer. The next few days he spends in Lowell with the family of Annie Richmond, a young married woman whom he had met during his July visit. In early November he returns to Providence, where Mrs. Whitman shows him one or more letters she has received questioning his integrity. Deeply hurt, Poe drinks to excess and becomes ill; afterwards Mrs. Whitman consents to a conditional engagement, assuming he totally abstains from alcohol. Poe is back at Fordham on 14 November, but he pays Mrs. Whitman a brief visit early in December. Her mother Anna Power strongly opposes the proposed marriage; as soon as Poe leaves, Mrs. Power obtains legal control of her family's estate, placing it out of his reach. Poe returns to Providence on 20 December, when he lectures on "The Poetic Principle" before an audience of almost two thousand people. Mrs. Whitman agrees to an immediate marriage; but when Poe begins to drink on the morning of 23 December, she realizes that he cannot free himself from his alcoholism and abruptly cancels their engagement. He leaves for New York that evening, never to see her again.

*

1848

*

JANUARY OR BEFORE. FORDHAM. Poe begins work on *Eureka*. Mrs. Clemm recalls: "He [Poe] never liked to be alone, and I used to sit up with him, often until four o'clock in the morning, he at his desk, writing, and I dozing in my chair. When he was composing 'Eureka,' we used to walk up and down the garden, his arm around me, mine around him, until I was so tired I could not walk. He would stop every few minutes and explain his ideas to me, and ask if I understood him" (quoted by Woodberry, 2:236; cf. Didier [1877], p. 104, and Stoddard [1903], pp. 157–58).

JANUARY OR BEFORE. Poe prepares a fragmentary manuscript entitled "Literary America," containing critical sketches of Richard Adams Locke, Thomas Dunn English, and Christopher Pearse Cranch (Quinn, pp. 560–61).

JANUARY. Poe has printed a prospectus announcing the *Stylus*: "In the first number of The Stylus the editor will commence the publication of a work on which he has been employed unremittingly for the last two years. It will be called 'Literary America,' and will endeavor to present, much in detail, that great desideratum, a *faithful* account of the literary productions, literary people, and literary affairs of the United States." The *Stylus* will be concerned only with literature, the fine arts, and the drama: "In regard to what is going on, within the limits assigned, throughout the civilized world, it will be a principal object of the magazine to keep its readers really *au courant*. For this end accurate arrangements have been made at London, Paris, Rome and Vienna. The most distinguished of American scholars [Charles Anthon] has agreed to superintend the department of classical letters" (copy in NN–B).

JANUARY. PHILADELPHIA. *Graham's Magazine* contains an installment of Poe's "Marginalia."

JANUARY. RICHMOND. The *Southern Literary Messenger* contains Philip Pendleton Cooke's sketch "Edgar A. Poe," described as "a sequel to Mr. Lowell's Memoir" in the February 1845 *Graham's*. Cooke discusses "The Raven," "The Facts in the Case of M. Valdemar," and other writings which have appeared since Lowell's biography. "I believe Mr. P. has been for some time ill—has recently sustained a heavy domestic bereavement—and is only now returning to his literary labors."

JANUARY. NEW YORK. In the "Editor's Table" of the *Knickerbocker Magazine*, Lewis Gaylord Clark summarizes the largely unfavorable review of Wiley and Putnam's "Library of American Books" in the November 1847 *Blackwood's*, quoting the Scottish critic's condemnations of Cornelius Mathews, William Gilmore Simms, and Margaret Fuller. "Of Mr. POE'S 'Tales' the reviewer remarks, that while they cannot be called commonplace, they evince little taste and much analytic power. [']One is not sorry to have read them—one has no desire to read them twice.' "

1 JANUARY. In the *Home Journal* Nathaniel P. Willis reprints "Ulalume: A Ballad" without identifying the author, as Poe had requested in his 8 December 1847 letter. In a prefatory query headed "Epicureanism in Language," Willis observes: "We do not know how many readers we have who will enjoy as we do, the following exquisitely piquant and skilful exercise of rarity and niceness of language. It is a poem which we find in the *American Review*, full of beauty and oddity in sentiment and versification, but a curiosity, (and a delicious one, we think,) in its philologic flavor. Who is the author?"

4 JANUARY. Poe replies to George W. Eveleth's 27 July 1847 letter: "I have been living ever since in a constant state of intention to write, and finally concluded not to write at all until I could say something definite about The Stylus and other matters. You perceive that I now send you a Prospectus." Poe's critique of Hawthorne has finally been published, in *Godey's Lady's Book* for November 1847; he encloses his "Ulalume," reprinted in the *Home Journal*. "The Rationale of Verse," which he originally submitted to George H. Colton for the *American Review*, was later sold to *Graham's Magazine*: "in Grahams hands it is still—but not to remain even there; for I mean to get it back, revise or rewrite it . . . and deliver it as a lecture when I go South & West on my Magazine expedition. . . . My health is better—best." Poe answers Eveleth's question about the "terrible evil" in his life which led to his "irregularities":

Six years ago, a wife, whom I loved as no man ever loved before, ruptured a blood-vessel in singing. Her life was despaired of. I took leave of her forever & underwent all the agonies of her death. She recovered partially and I again hoped. At the end of a year the vessel broke again—I went through precisely the same scene. Again in about a year afterward. Then again—again—again & even once again at varying intervals. Each time I felt all the agonies of her death—and at each accession of the disorder I loved her more dearly & clung to her life with more desperate pertinacity. But I am constitutionally sensitive—nervous in a very unusual degree. I became insane, with long intervals of horrible sanity. During these fits of absolute unconsciousness I drank, God only knows how often or how much (L, 2:354–57; Moldenhauer [1973], pp. 65–67; *Stylus* prospectus now in NN–B).

8 JANUARY. PHILADELPHIA. In the *John-Donkey* Thomas Dunn English comments: "MR. EDGAR A. POE. By some kind of mistake, a little squib was fired off at this very estimable young man, in our first number [issued ca. 15 December 1847]. We should not have recalled it to the memory of our readers, had not the 'Miner's Journal,' at Pottsville, [Pennsylvania,] thought proper to make it the occasion to puff Mr. POE. That writer does not deserve such cruel treatment at the hands of his friends. He has no objections to be abused, when the abuse comes from men of talent; but to be praised by the editor of the Miner's Journal, [then Eli Bowen,] is an insult not to be forgiven."

11 JANUARY. PHILLIPS, MAINE. Eveleth replies to Poe's 4 January letter: "I had become fearful that matters were going wrong with you, as I heard nothing from you, neither by letter nor *per* the newspapers which have always been so regardful of your welfare. . . . I like 'Hawthorne' generally—don't think it is the best critical article you have ever written. 'Ulalume' is the only piece of *poetry* I have read for some time—'tis a beauty—Before I had read two verses of it in the Am. Rev. I stopped, went back again, read it over, and vowed that Edgar A. Poe was its author." Eveleth quotes reports about Poe contained in four letters sent to him last year: from George H. Colton on 24 July and 15 October, from Louis A. Godey on 6 August, and from the editors of the *Weekly Universe* on 17 August. Godey's letter gave Eveleth "the first positive intimation" that Poe had a drinking problem: "I had suspected something long before—was afraid, from the wild imaginations manifested in your writings, that you were an opium-eater—had some chance for hope that this might not be the case, as the same wildness was evident in your childhood productions—supposed that you could not have acquired the habit when so young, and therefore *hoped*" (Eveleth, pp. 16–18).

11 JANUARY. BROOKLYN. In the *Daily Eagle* Walt Whitman prints "A Jig in Prose," an unsigned parody of "The Raven" (Brasher, pp. 30–31).

17 JANUARY. FORDHAM. Poe writes H. D. Chapin in New York:

Mrs. Shew intimated to me, not long ago, that you would, perhaps, lend me your aid in my endeavour to re-establish myself in the literary world . . . . When I last spoke with you, I mentioned my design of going to see Mr. [John] Neal at Portland, and there, with his influence, deliver a Lecture—the proceeds of which might enable me to take the first steps towards my proposed Magazine:—that is to say, put, perhaps, $100 in my pocket; which would give me the necessary outfit and start me on my tour. But, since our conversation, I have been thinking that a better course would be to make interest among my friends here—in N. Y. city—and deliver a Lecture, in the first instance, at the Society Library. With this object in view, may I beg of you so far to assist me as to procure for me the use of the Lecture Room? The difficulty with me is that payment for the Room is demanded *in advance* and I have no money. I believe the price is $15.

In a postscript Poe thanks Chapin for a "note of introduction" to James Watson Webb, editor of the *Morning Courier*: "As yet I have not found an opportunity of presenting it—thinking it best to do so when I speak to him about the Lecture" (*L*, 2:357–58).

17 JANUARY. Poe writes Louis A. Godey in Philadelphia: "What do you say to an article? I have one which I think may please you. Shall I send it and draw as usual?—deducting, of course, the $5 you were so kind as to loan me when in Philadelphia. . . . The article is imaginative—*not* critical—and will make rather more than 5 pp" (Ostrom [1974], pp. 532–33).

19 JANUARY. PHILADELPHIA. Godey replies to Poe (cited on Poe's letter).

AFTER 19 JANUARY? FORDHAM? Poe forwards the article, presumably his tale "Mellonta Tauta" (published in *Godey's Lady's Book* for February 1849).

22 JANUARY. PHILADELPHIA. Under the heading "Poe's Last Poem" the *Saturday Courier* reprints "Ulalume" from the *Home Journal* of 1 January, prefacing it with an unfavorable criticism:

We copy the following poem, partly, because Willis has called attention to it, but principally, because we have a word or two to say in relation to Edgar A. Poe, who is undoubtedly its author. No other American poet, in the first place, has the same command of language and power of versification: it is in no one else's vein— it is too *charnel* in its nature; while Mr. Poe is especially at home in pieces of a sepulchral character. "Ulalume" is a continuation of the same Golgothian idiosyncrasy that produced the "Conqueror Worm," the "Fall of the House of Usher," "Ligeia," "Berenice," the revivification of Monsieur Valdemar . . . . We pity the man who can write such things, and, while we wonder at the artistic talent displayed by Mr. Poe in the working up of his repulsive subjects,—a wonder which it is his sole object to create, we remember his story or poem precisely as we would recall a cancer or tumor under which we had suffered, with feelings of absolute pain, terror and horror, if not disgust. There was a time when we considered Poe a man of genius, a very pardonable because natural mistake, and one, moreover, into which the larger mass of his readers have fallen. He is a man of great talent—wonderful talent—wonderful powers of ratiocination, nothing more, and withal not at all original. In short we question if he ever produced an entirely original article: indeed, he admits, we have understood, quite as much himself.

[The *Courier*'s editor was then Andrew McMakin.]

22 JANUARY. FORDHAM. Poe writes Nathaniel P. Willis that he intends to establish a magazine "entirely out of the control of a publisher," to be called the *Stylus*: "I must get a list of, at least, five hundred subscribers to begin with:—nearly two hundred I have already. I propose, however, to go South and West, among my personal and literary friends—old college and West Point acquaintances—and see what I can do. In order to get the means of taking the first step, I propose to lecture at the Society Library, on Thursday, the 3d of February." Poe's subject will be "The Universe"; he asks Willis to announce the lecture in the *Home Journal* (L, 2:359).

23 JANUARY. NEW YORK. Anne C. Lynch writes Sarah Helen Whitman in Providence, Rhode Island: "I am going to have another Valentine party on the 14th of next month, & I should be delighted to have some contributions from you. Your last year's efforts were so happy & so much admired I do not see how you can refuse. I wish very much that you could be here" (RPB–W; cf. entries for 14, 21 FEBRUARY 1846 and 16, 31 JANUARY, 14 FEBRUARY 1847).

AFTER 23 JANUARY. PROVIDENCE. Mrs. Whitman sends Miss Lynch several valentine poems, including one addressed to Poe. She inquires about Poe (Lynch's 31 January reply).

29 JANUARY. PHILADELPHIA. In the *John-Donkey* Thomas Dunn English publishes "Sophia Maria," a weak parody of "Ulalume."

29 JANUARY. NEW YORK. The *New World* contains a favorable advance notice of Poe's 3 February lecture on "The Universe" (Pollin [1975a], p. 28).

30? JANUARY. The *Weekly Universe* announces the lecture: "Mr. Poe is not merely a man of science—not merely a poet—not merely a man of letters. He is all combined; and perhaps he is something more—but whatever he may be he is sure of giving a lecture worth hearing" (quoted in Eveleth to Poe, 9 July).

31 JANUARY. The *Morning Express* and the *Evening Express* carry a report that Poe will lecture on Thursday evening at the Society Library: "Mr. Poe's subject for the occasion is 'The Universe,'—a theme which he will doubtless invest with that spirit of quaint originality and treat with that degree of taste and ability which have already gained for him a wide reputation both at home and abroad. We take pleasure in calling the attention of our readers to this lecture of Mr. Poe's and trust that it will be attended by a fitting audience." The report is reprinted in the *Semi-Weekly Express* of 1 February.

31 JANUARY. Miss Lynch writes Mrs. Whitman in Providence: "I recieved [*sic*] your letter & the valentines enclosed, this evening & hasten to reply to it. . . . I will endeavor to answer your queries . . . . Poe I have seen nothing of for more than a year past. There was a great war in *bluestockingdom* some time ago & Poe did not behave very honorably in it—the truth is that with all his genius he has no moral sense, & he said & did a great many things that were very abominable. He has lived several miles from town since then & although I have had no particular difference [with him], I now scarcely ever see him" (RPB–W).

FEBRUARY. PHILADELPHIA. *Graham's Magazine* contains a brief installment of Poe's "Marginalia."

2–3 FEBRUARY. NEW YORK. The *Daily Tribune* carries this advertisement: "Edgar A. Poe will lecture at the Society Library on Thursday evening, the 3d inst at half-past 7. Subject, 'The Universe.' Tickets 50 cents—to be had at the door."

BEFORE 3 FEBRUARY. PHILADELPHIA. In the *John-Donkey* for 5 February English scoffs: "BAD IN EITHER CASE. Mr. POE, who used to flourish in this city, is announced to deliver a lecture on the 'Universe' at the N. Y. Society Library. Some of our friends say that they hope he will not disappoint his auditors, as he did once before. We suspect he will, whether he delivers his lecture or not."

BEFORE 3 FEBRUARY. NEW YORK. In the *Home Journal* for 5 February Willis comments:

EDGAR A. POE.—We, by accident, omitted to mention, in our last week's paper, that our friend and former editorial associate, Mr. Poe, was to deliver a Lecture, on Thursday evening, February 3d, at the "Society Library." The subject is rather a broad one—"The Universe;" but from a mind so original, no text could furnish any clue to what would probably be the sermon. There is but one thing certain about it, that it will be compact of thought, most fresh, startling, and suggestive. . . .

We understand that the purpose of Mr. Poe's Lectures is to raise the necessary capital for the establishment of a magazine, which he proposes to call "THE STYLUS." They who like literature without trammels, and criticism without gloves, should send in their names forthwith as subscribers. If there be in the world a born anatomist of thought, it is Mr. Poe. He takes genius and its imitations to pieces with a skill wholly unequalled on either side [of] the water. . . .

3 FEBRUARY. The *Daily Tribune* reports that Poe will lecture tonight, quoting Willis' advance notice in the *Home Journal*. The *Morning Express* and the *Evening Express* also carry a favorable announcement: "The novelty of his subject, 'The Universe,' and the universally acknowledged ability of the lecturer, will undoubtedly bring together a large audience."

3 FEBRUARY. William Cullen Bryant's *Evening Post* announces Poe's lecture tonight (Pollin [1975a], p. 28).

3 FEBRUARY. At 7:30 PM Poe lectures on "The Universe" at the Society Library, corner of Broadway and Leonard Street. Maunsell B. Field, a young lawyer, recalls: "It was a stormy night, and there were not more than sixty persons present in the lecture-room. I have seen no portrait of POE that does justice to his pale, delicate, intellectual face and magnificent eyes. His lecture was a rhapsody of the most intense brilliancy. He appeared inspired, and his inspiration affected the scant audience almost painfully. He wore his coat tightly buttoned across his slender chest; his eyes seemed to glow like those of his own raven, and he kept us entranced for two hours and a half" (Field, p. 224).

3 FEBRUARY. Later in the evening John Henry Hopkins, Jr., a divinity student at the General Theological Seminary, writes a long, appreciative review of Poe's lecture at the home of Marie Louise Shew, 47 Bond Street (Mrs. Shew to J. H. Ingram, 3 April 1875, Miller [1977], p. 120).

4 FEBRUARY. The *Daily Tribune* reports:

The Lecture of E. A. POE, Esq. on "The Universe," was not very largely attended, but the intelligence of his auditory compensated for its deficiency in numbers. His remarks on a subject—the contemplation of which is infinite, (a word, as Mr. Poe happily said, used in the *effort* to express the thought of a thought) were characterized by the strong analytical powers and intense capacity of imagination, which distinguish him, rather than by any shadow of probability, which might assist the soul in its graspings after the unattainable. The substance of Mr. Poe's theory of the Universe, briefly stated, is, that at some inconceivable period of past time, an exertion of the Divine essence created throughout immeasurable space, the systems and clusters of systems which have been revealed to us by Astronomy, yet whose extent we can never measure; that these clustering systems, circling round still grander systems, to an infinite degree, are influenced by a universal tendency to agglomeration, or union in one overwhelming globe; that when, at an inconceivable period in the future this shall take place, each individual soul that inhabits every sun and planet, shall return into the Deity of which it now forms a part, when all matter will disappear and the great drama of the Universe be acted over in some other region of space.

4 FEBRUARY. The *Morning Express* contains Hopkins' lengthy review of the lecture, unquestionably "the most elaborate and profound" he ever heard. "The work [lecture] has all the completeness and oneness of plot required in a poem, with all the detail and accuracy required in a scientific lecture. . . . Starting from the Deity, as a comet from the Sun, it went careering onward in its march through infinite space, approaching more and more closely the comprehension of man, until bending its course gradually homeward at length, it drew nearer and nearer, grew brighter and brighter, until it buried itself in the blaze of glory from whence it had its birth. It would be impossible to give any respectable report of this extraordinary work of Art without devoting several columns to it, and even then justice could not be done." Hopkins summarizes Poe's arguments in the order they were given. "The conclusion of this brilliant effort was greeted with warm applause by the audience, who had listened with enchained attention throughout." The unsigned review is reprinted in this afternoon's *Evening Express* and in the *Semi-Weekly Express* for 9 February (attribution in Poe's 29 February letters to G. W. Eveleth and G. E. Isbell).

[Hopkins' detailed synopsis reveals that Poe's lecture·was quite similar in content and organization to his published text, *Eureka*.]

4 FEBRUARY. Under the heading "Hyperbolic Nonsense," the *Commercial Advertiser* reprints part of Hopkins' review from the *Morning Express*. The afternoon paper comments: "Well, would not 'several columns' be space enough for such a presentation? As to that start from the Deity, and the ultimate burial in a blaze of glory—it is beyond our comprehension, but being editorial it is doubtless all right."

4 FEBRUARY. Evert A. Duyckinck writes his brother George in Paris: "Poe delivered a lecture last evening on the Universe—full of a ludicrous

dryness of scientific phrase—a mountainous piece of absurdity for a popular lecture and moreover an introduction to his projected magazine—the Stylus: for which it was to furnish funds. Why it drove people from the room, instead of calling in subscribers" (NN–D).

5 FEBRUARY. The *Albion* reports: "EDGAR A. POE'S Lecture on the Universe was attended by a select, but highly appreciative audience, that remained attentive and interested for nearly three hours, under the Lecturer's powerful, able, and profound analytical exposition of his peculiar theory, on the origin, creation, and final destiny of the Universe. . . . His delivery alone, although a minor accomplishment in a lecturer, is so pure, finished and chaste in its style—that on a popular subject he could not fail to attract audiences." The *Albion* understands that Poe's lecture "will shortly be published" and has "no doubt but that it will meet with an extensive circulation."

5 FEBRUARY. PHILADELPHIA. The *Saturday Evening Post* reviews the 29 January issue of English's *John-Donkey*: "Among the articles . . . is a capital parody on a poem recently published in the Knickerbocker [*American Review*], and supposed to have been written by E. A. Poe—at least it is decidedly Poe-ish."

6? FEBRUARY. NEW YORK. The *Weekly Universe* comments on Poe's lecture: "To those who could comprehend its scope and follow closely its train of reasoning, the lecture was profoundly interesting as delivered, and would be still better, to be read, with time to pause and reflect . . . . The fault of the lecture was its length . . . . Two hours is a long session—and that Mr. Poe fastened the attention of his audience for more than that period, to such a subject, is quite significant of the character of his discourse" (Stedman and Woodberry, 9:314; paper identified in Eveleth to Poe, 9 July).

9 FEBRUARY. The *Morning Express* publishes a 5 February letter from a pseudonymous correspondent, "Spes Credula," who reacts to this paper's report of Poe's lecture:

I have admired the collection of tales published by Mr. Poe, some time since, (the Gold Bug and other tales,) in which you may recollect, occurs a conversation with a dying man while in a state of magnetic trance. In that conversation, very much the same ideas may be found, respecting "the universe," which Mr. Poe has reproduced in this lecture. . . . One cannot fail to be extremely interested, in what is there [in "Mesmeric Revelation"] said, as well as by the manner in which it is said. But, while we admire Mr. Poe for his captivating and energetic style of expression—while we are struck with the strange audacity of speculation which characterises him as a thinker, we should be careful that so erratic a genius do[es] not lead us astray in forbidden paths.

It is with unaffected diffidence that I venture to suggest that the great staple of all these strange speculations may be found in those old systems of philosophy which taught the eternity of matter. A very striking identity of thought at least will be found in the systems of Pythagoras, Plato, Xenophanes, Epicurus, Aristotle . . . .

I know that a newspaper is not the proper place for a homily; but permit me to suggest in conclusion that whatever Science may pretend to discover, in relation to the world of matter, she can give us no idea of the origin of things. Revelation alone discloses to us a satisfactory and reliable idea of God.

The editors of the *Express*, James Brooks and William B. Townsend, explain that while they willingly printed this "well intended and learned communication," they "would notice one point in which the writer seems to have mistaken Mr. Poe's meaning . . . . Mr. Poe was so far from maintaining the *eternity of matter*, as '*Spes Credula*' supposes, that he distinctly asserted that those primary particles irradiated throughout all space, were the immediate result of the volition of the Godhead, a volition and action which continued only during a limited time. If this is not equivalent to *creation*, we do not know what is." The letter and the editorial comment on it are reprinted in this afternoon's *Evening Express* and in the *Semi-Weekly Express* for 11 February.

BEFORE 10 FEBRUARY. Under the heading "Mr. Poe upon the Universe," the *New World* for 12 February carries a review by "Decius," who complains that the lecture of "some two hours and a half" was extraordinarily long: "At the end of an hour and a half, some of us began to be quite sensible of the lapse of time . . . . Still no end was visible; the thin leaves, one after another, of the neat manuscript, were gracefully turned over; yet, oh, a plenty more were evidently left behind, abiding patiently 'their appointed time.'" The reviewer summarizes Poe's arguments at length, suggesting that he is indebted to Robert Chambers' *Vestiges of Creation* as well as to the work of Sir William Herschel and the Marquis de Laplace. Poe's lecture "contained the fruits of much thought and study . . . . Resolved, as it would seem, to bring before the public a work which he evidently felt proudly conscious to be worthy the attention of his audience for the manner, if not the materials of its execution, he unflinchingly marched onward to the close with uniform and stately steps; unmindful whether his hearers were pleased or not; perhaps sometimes unconscious of their presence, as he turned up his cold, abstracted eye, unwarmed even by the fire of invention, not upon the men and women before him, but toward those sublime celestial orbs, about whose origin and destiny he was discoursing in such lofty language" (Stedman and Woodberry, 9:314–15; see also Pollin [1975a], p. 28).

10 FEBRUARY. BINGHAMPTON, NEW YORK. George E. Isbell writes Poe, inquiring about his lecture. Isbell discusses the review in the *New World* and Chambers' *Vestiges of Creation* (Poe's 29 February reply).

11 FEBRUARY. WOODLANDS, SOUTH CAROLINA. William Gilmore Simms replies to a letter from Evert A. Duyckinck, who presumably criticized Poe's lecture: "Poe is a very remarkable man. It is great pity that he should be wasted and should waste himself, as he does. I should like to see him succeed—still more gladly see him *deserve wholly* to succeed" (Simms, 2:394–98; cf. Duyckinck's 4 FEBRUARY letter to his brother).

11 FEBRUARY. NEW YORK. James Watson Webb's *Morning Courier* favorably reviews Poe's lecture, praising him for developing Laplace's nebular hypothesis far beyond what this French astronomer envisioned and for relating both the formation and the eventual destruction of the universe to the law of gravitation. The lecture is "a nobler effort than any other Mr. Poe has yet given to the world" (Quinn, p. 539; see also Pollin [1975a], p. 27).

12 FEBRUARY. BOSTON. The *Boston Journal* quotes a portion of the review in the *Morning Courier*, commenting sarcastically: "Mr. Poe is already a great man. If he establishes this theory to the satisfaction of learned and philosophical astronomers, his greatness will be greater than ever" (Eveleth, pp. 19, 26–27).

12 FEBRUARY. NEW YORK. The *Literary World* reviews Poe's lecture, briefly summarizing his arguments. "The freedom and boldness of the speculations, together with the nervousness and vivacity of the reading, made the whole performance in the highest degree entertaining; and its publication will be anticipated with much interest by the many admirers of the author."

12 FEBRUARY. The *Home Journal* reprints the favorable review of Poe's lecture from the *Albion* of 5 February.

[This paper's failure to give its own review might be attributed to the illness of Poe's friend Willis, who was confined to bed during February and March (Reece [1954], p. 82; Taylor, pp. 118–19).]

12 FEBRUARY. PHILADELPHIA. The *Saturday Evening Post* publishes a 5 February letter from "Gothamite," its New York correspondent, who discusses several lectures given in that city during the past week:

The crack lecture . . . has been that of Edgar A. Poe, the Raven Poet. His theme was the—*Universe*—and the discourse, upon the whole, was one of the most unique and well digested, that I have ever heard. I cannot give you an abstract of it, for it occupied in its delivery only *two hours and a half*, but it was eminently Poe-ish from beginning to end, and of course exceedingly interesting. It displayed an extensive knowledge of astronomy, abounded in passages of fine philosophy, contained an abundance of analytical writing, and an occasional burst of genuine eloquence, at one time, somewhat poetical, and at another, rather amusing and witty. His subject *was* the *Universe*—but he treated it in a style that could not be called universal. With the proceeds of his Lectures it is Mr. Poe's intention to start a new Magazine, but if he succeeds in establishing a permanent affair it will indeed be a marvel.

The *Saturday Courier* contains a paragraph headed "Theory of the Universe," apparently written by the editor Andrew McMakin:

Edgar A. Poe delivered a lecture in New York, last week on the "Universe," in which, from a brief notice of his views that we have seen, we infer that he propounds a doctrine somewhat similar to one advanced a century or two ago by Spinoza, that man is a mere extension or part of Deity. Mr. Poe thinks that there is a tendency to consolidation and material unity in our great stellar system, and that, in the lapse of ages, all the suns and earths of our great system will fall into one, and man be absorbed into his Creator, as a part of him. After this, there will be another exertion of creative power, and the whole thing be done over again. Of course, this is all theory, and to the great majority of enlightened and philosophical thinkers, not very good theory at that.

12 FEBRUARY. The *Saturday Gazette* scoffs at Poe's theory (Pollin [1975a], p. 28).

12 FEBRUARY. The *John-Donkey* contains an installment of "The Adventures of Don Key Haughty," Thomas Dunn English's travesty of Cervantes' *Don Quixote*. The title character Don Key Haughty, an impractical reformer based on Horace Greeley, is imprisoned "in the Tombs," where he encounters an unnamed poet obviously meant to be Poe, "a melancholy-looking little man, in a rusty suit of black." The poet promptly delivers an unsolicited lecture: "The poem is the rhythmical creation of beauty . . . whenever it possesses an object or an end—whenever it has anything like sense—or whenever point is not entirely sacrificed to euphony, it can no longer claim the name of poem, or be regarded as a work of art." To illustrate his thesis he recites "Rosaline: A Dactylo-Spondaic Poem," an absurd composition of his own which he declares "incomparably superior to that of any writer ever known."

13 FEBRUARY OR BEFORE. FORDHAM. Poe revises his 1846 acrostic valentine addressed to Mrs. Frances S. Osgood. He submits a copy of the poem, dated "*Valentine's Eve, 1848*," to James L. DeGraw, publisher of the *Union Magazine* (facsimile in Woodberry, 2:182–83; see also Mabbott [1969],

1:387–88, and entries for 13, 14 FEBRUARY 1846, and 17, 18, 24 FEBRUARY, 10 MARCH 1849).

14 FEBRUARY OR BEFORE. Poe sends Marie Louise Shew a manuscript copy of his valentine poem addressed to her, giving it the heading "To Marie Louise" (published in the *Columbian Magazine* for March; see Mabbott [1969], 1:405–09, and Miller [1977], pp. 115, 125).

14 FEBRUARY. NEW YORK. Anne C. Lynch's valentine soiree is held at her home, 109 Clinton Place. Among the valentines read to the assembled guests is Sarah Helen Whitman's "To Edgar A. Poe," romantically addressing Poe as "The Raven" (published in the *Home Journal*, 18 March).

21 FEBRUARY. Miss Lynch writes Mrs. Whitman in Providence:

Our party last Monday evening every one said was very brilliant.—There was an immense crowd, many more than I expected . . . . Your valentines were all read[;] some of them I have sent to the Home Journal at the request of Morris & Willis . . . . The one to Poe I admired exceedingly & would like to have published with your consent with the others, but he is in such bad odour with most persons who visit me that if I were to recieve [*sic*] him, I should lose the company of many whom I value more. [Name obliterated] will not go where he visits & several others have an inveterate prejudice against him. The valentines will appear next week[;] I shall send you a copy of course (RPB–W).

[The name Mrs. Whitman scratched out was probably that of Mrs. Elizabeth F. Ellet (cf. Poe to Mrs. Whitman, 24 November).]

BEFORE 29 FEBRUARY. Poe prepares a revised prospectus for the *Stylus*, dated April. It is similar to the January prospectus, except that it omits the paragraph announcing the serialization of his "Literary America" (Heartman and Canny, pp. 118–21).

29 FEBRUARY. Poe replies to George E. Isbell's 10 February letter, writing on stationery bearing the revised *Stylus* prospectus. Poe has not seen Chambers' *Vestiges of Creation*: "The extracts of the work which have fallen in my way, abound in inaccuracies of fact:—still these may not materially affect the general argument. . . . The notice of my Lecture, which appeared in the 'New-World', was written by some one grossly incompetent to the task which he undertook. No idea of what I said can be gleaned from either that or any other of the newspaper notices—with the exception, perhaps, of the 'Express'—where the critique was written by a gentleman of much scientific acquirement—Mr E. A. [John Henry] Hopkins, of Vermont. I enclose you his Report—which, however, is inaccurate in numerous partic-

ulars." When the lecture is published, Poe will send Isbell a copy (*L*, 2:362–64).

29 FEBRUARY. Poe replies to George W. Eveleth's 11 January letter. He now intends to leave for Richmond on 10 March, Willis' "somewhat premature announcement" of the *Stylus* forcing him to begin his promotional tour sooner than he had planned.

"The Rationale of Verse" will appear in "Graham" after all:—I will stop in Phil: to see the proofs. . . . The editor of the "Weekly Universe" speaks kindly and I find no fault with his representing my habits as "shockingly irregular". . . . The fact is thus:—My *habits* are rigorously abstemious and I omit nothing of the natural regimen requisite for health:—i,e—I rise early, eat moderately, drink nothing but water, and take abundant and regular exercise in the open air. But this is my private life—my studious and literary life—and of course escapes the eye of the world. The desire for society comes upon me only when I have become excited by drink. Then *only* I go—that is, at these times only I *have been* in the practice of going among my friends: who seldom, or in fact never, having seen me unless excited, take it for granted that I am always so.

Poe encloses Hopkins' account of his lecture from the *Morning Express* (*L*, 2:360–62)

[Poe did not leave for Richmond until late July.]

AFTER FEBRUARY. Poe obtains the return of "The Rationale of Verse" from *Graham's Magazine* (published in the *Southern Literary Messenger*, October and November numbers).

MARCH. The *Columbian Magazine* contains Poe's valentine poem addressed to Marie Louise Shew, under the heading "To—— —— ——."

MARCH. The *Union Magazine* contains Poe's "Sonnet," an acrostic poem concealing the name Sarah Anna Lewis (subsequently entitled "An Enigma"; cf. Poe to Mrs. Lewis, 27 November 1847).

MARCH. PHILADELPHIA. *Graham's Magazine* contains an installment of "Marginalia": Poe discusses the credulous republication of his "Mesmeric Revelation" and "The Facts in the Case of M. Valdemar" by the London *Popular Record of Modern Science* (cf. entries for 29 NOVEMBER 1845 and 10 JANUARY 1846).

2 MARCH OR BEFORE. FORDHAM. Poe receives the manuscript of Mrs. Whitman's valentine poem "To Edgar A. Poe," forwarded to him by Miss Lynch through Mrs. Osgood. "He recognized the handwriting having two

or three years before been shown by Miss Lynch some MS. verses I had sent her for the editor of the *Democratic Review*" (Mrs. Whitman quoted by Ticknor, pp. 47–48).

2 MARCH. From a copy of *The Raven and Other Poems*, Poe removes the last page of text, containing his 1831 poem "To Helen," and forwards it anonymously to Mrs. Whitman (postmarked envelope and detached page in InU–L; cf. Poe's explanation in his 1 October letter to her).

AFTER 2 MARCH. PROVIDENCE. Mrs. Whitman receives "To Helen." A "gentleman from New York" tells her that the address on the envelope is "in Poe's handwriting" (Whitman to J. H. Ingram, 6 March 1874, Miller [1979], p. 60).

4 MARCH. NEW YORK. Under the heading "The Valentine Party" the *Home Journal* prints forty-two short poems read at Miss Lynch's soiree.

AFTER 4 MARCH? PROVIDENCE. Mrs. Whitman receives a copy of the published valentines, forwarded by Miss Lynch. She writes Miss Lynch to request the publication of her "To Edgar A. Poe," which was not included in the *Home Journal* article (implied by Lynch to Whitman, 21 February and 10 March).

9 MARCH. PHILLIPS, MAINE. Eveleth replies to Poe's 29 February letter. He identifies the New York *Weekly Universe*: "It was originally published under the title of the 'Weekly Dispatch,' but changed a few months ago to its present one. . . . I have noticed that articles which were published in it as original were copied into other papers, and credited to the Sunday Dispatch, a paper which I have never seen." He believes he has formed "a correct idea" of Poe's lecture on "The Universe" from Hopkins' account; the only other notice of it he saw appeared in the *Boston Journal*, a paper which often sneers at Poe. Quoting this paper's 12 February report, Eveleth observes: "Praises you but don't intend it for praise" (Eveleth, pp. 18–20).

10 MARCH. NEW YORK. Miss Lynch replies to a letter from Mrs. Whitman in Providence: "I really do not think it would be any advantage to you to publish the Valentine to Poe not because it is not beautiful in itself but there is a deeply rooted prejudice against him which I trust he will overcome. I wish you would not mention this & if you still wish it published [&] if you will send me another copy I will ask some one to have it done. I e[a]rnestly request you not to mention this because I have no quarrel with Poe & admire his genius as much as any one can" (RPB–W).

18 MARCH. The *Home Journal* publishes Mrs. Whitman's "To Edgar A. Poe," prefacing it with this editorial explanation: "The following Valentine, by one of America's most justly distinguished poetesses, was among the number received at the Valentine *soirée*, commemorated in our paper of the 4th instant. A *poem*, however, whose intrinsic beauty takes it quite out of the category of ordinary Valentines, seemed to demand the honor of separate publication." In the ten-stanza poem Mrs. Whitman invites Poe to share a "lofty eyrie" with her:

> Oh, thou grim and ancient Raven,
>   From the Night's Plutonian shore,
> Oft, in dreams, thy ghastly pinions
>   Wave and flutter round my door—
> Oft thy shadow dims the moonlight
>   Sleeping on my chamber floor!
>
> Romeo talks of "white doves trooping
>   Amid crows, athwart the night;"
> But to see thy dark wing swooping
>   Down the silver path of light,
> Amid swans and dovelets stooping,
>   Were, to me, a nobler sight.
>
> . . . .
>
> Midst the roaring of machinery,
>   And the dismal shriek of steam,
> While each popinjay, and parrot,
>   Makes the golden age his theme,
> Oft, methinks, I hear thee croaking,
>   "All is but an idle dream."
>
> While these warbling "guests of summer"
>   Prate of "Progress" evermore,
> And, by dint of *iron foundries*,
>   Would this golden age restore,
> Still, methinks, I hear thee croaking,
>   Hoarsely croaking, "Nevermore."

18 MARCH. PHILADELPHIA. The *John-Donkey* contains Thomas Dunn English's "Natural History of the John-donkey." He describes the "two kinds of JOHN-DONKEYS—those who *were made* Donkeys—and those who have *made Donkeys of themselves*." The latter "usually walk erect on two legs, and have all the appearance of men. . . . The ranks of the *Poe*-ts and philosophers are infested with them."

26 MARCH. NEW YORK. Mrs. Frances S. Osgood writes Mrs. Whitman in Providence: "I see by the Home Journal that your beautiful invocation has

reached the Raven in his eyrie and I suppose, ere this, he has *swooped* upon your little *dove cote* in Providence. May Providence protect you if he has!— for his croak the most eloquent imaginable. He is in truth 'A glorious devil, with large heart & brain' " (RPB–W).

28 MARCH. Miss Lynch writes Mrs. Whitman in Providence: "Your Raven was much admired in the Home Journal. Gen M. ['General' George P. Morris] met me one day in great extacies [ecstasies] over the exquisite poem or valentine he had just recd for the paper, which I had seen of course before" (RPB–W).

30 MARCH. FORDHAM. Poe writes Mrs. Shew in New York:

Dearest Louise—You see that I am not yet off to Richmond as I proposed. I have been detained by some very unexpected and very important matters which I will explain to you when I see you. What *is* the reason that you have not been out?—I believe the *only* reason is that you suspect I am really anxious to see you.

When you see Mr Hopkins I wish you would say to him that I would take it as an especial favor if he would pay me a visit at Fordham next Sunday. I have something to communicate to him *of the highest importance* and about which I need his advice. Won't you get him to come—& come with him to show him the way? (PP–G; cf. imperfect transcript given by Ingram, p. 352, and reproduced in *L*, 2:364–65).

BEFORE APRIL. Poe copies and corrects Miss Harriet B. Winslow's manuscript poem "To the Author of 'The Raven' " (Mabbott [1969], 1:492–93).

APRIL. PHILADELPHIA. *Graham's Magazine* contains a revised version of Miss Winslow's poem.

2? APRIL. FORDHAM. John Henry Hopkins, Jr., visits Poe, accompanied by Mrs. Shew (date suggested by Poe to Shew, 30 March; see also Hopkins to Poe, 15 May, and Poe to Shew, June).

[In his 9 February 1875 letter to Mrs. Shew (then Mrs. Houghton), Hopkins described his interview with Poe:

It was in regard to his brilliant lecture "Eureka," which I had heard on the occasion of its first delivery, and in which I was much interested, having made a report of it for one of the daily papers. He was thinking of printing it in book form. I did all I could to persuade him to omit the bold declaration of Pantheism at the close, which was not necessary to the completeness or beauty of the lecture. But I soon found that *that* was the dearest part of the whole to him; and we got into quite a discussion on the subject of Pantheism. For some time his tone and manner were very quiet, though slowly changing as we went on; until at last, a look of scornful pride worthy of Milton's Satan flashed over his pale, delicate face & broad brow, and a strange thrill nerved and dilated for an instant his slight figure, as he exclaimed, "My whole nature utterly *revolts* at the idea that there is any Being in the Universe superior to *myself!*" I knew then that there was no use in further argument (Miller [1977], pp. 100–01).]

15 APRIL. PHILADELPHIA. In the *John-Donkey* English comments: "POE'S NEW DUNCIAD. We hear it stated in certain quarters, that Mr. POE is about to resume his sketches of character, commenced in the Lady's Book something more than a year ago. These biographies were well received by the public albeit some authors were not altogether pleased with their showing up. Mr. POE is a close analyst, a correct poet and a perfect windfall of a critic. He is a ripe scholar, too; dead ripe; rather too ripe; perhaps gone to seed."

[English may have been referring to "Literary America," a continuation of "The Literati" which Poe had announced in the January prospectus of the *Stylus*.]

LATE APRIL? NEW YORK. The publisher George P. Putnam, formerly of Wiley and Putnam, accepts the manuscript of *Eureka*. He recalls the initial visit of the author, "a gentleman with a somewhat nervous and excited manner," to his office at 155 Broadway:

Seated at my desk, and looking at me a full minute with his "glittering eye," he at length said: "I am Mr. Poe." I was "all ear," of course, and sincerely interested. It was the author of "The Raven," and of "The Gold Bug!" "I hardly know," said the poet, after a pause, "how to begin what I have to say. It is a matter of profound importance." After another pause, the poet seeming to be in a tremor of excitement, he at length went on to say that the publication he had to propose was of momentous interest. Newton's discovery of gravitation was a mere incident compared to the discoveries revealed in this book. It would at once command such universal and intense attention that the publisher might give up all other enterprises, and make this one book the business of his lifetime. An edition of fifty thousand copies might be sufficient to begin with . . . . I was really impressed— but not overcome. Promising a decision on Monday (it was late Saturday, P.M.), the poet had to rest so long in uncertainty about the *extent* of the edition—partly reconciled, by a small loan, meanwhile. We *did* venture, not upon fifty thousand, but five hundred (Putnam, p. 471).

LATE APRIL? The *Weekly Universe* reports that Poe has prepared his lecture on "The Universe" for publication: "We think it will rank as his noblest work" (quoted in Eveleth to Poe, 9 July).

LATE APRIL? Poe dines with Rufus W. Griswold; afterwards he becomes intoxicated and sends a request for help to Mrs. Shew's home, 47 Bond

Street. She asks Hopkins and Roland S. Houghton to go to his aid. Hopkins recalls: "Dr. Houghton and I found him [Poe] crazy-drunk in the hands of the police, and took him home to Fordham (eleven miles), where we found poor Mrs. Clemm waiting for him. He had been gone three days,—went to draw pay for an article, got into a spree, spent all, and we had to leave $5, with Mrs. Clemm for immediate necessities, as there was not a penny in the house" (Hopkins to Shew, 9 February 1875, Miller [1977], pp. 100–101; see also Shew to J. H. Ingram, 16 February 1875, pp. 104–05).

EARLY MAY. At Mrs. Shew's home Poe completes the first draft of "The Bells," a manuscript of seventeen lines bearing the ascription "By Mrs. M. L. Shew." She recalls: "He came in and said, 'Marie Louise, I have to write a poem. I have no feeling, no sentiment, no inspiration—' I answered we will have supper and I will help you. So after tea had been served in a conservatory with the windows open, near a church—I playfully said, here is paper. A Bell (very jolly and sharp) rang at the corner of the street. He said I so dislike the noise of bells tonight. I cannot write. I have no subject. I am exhausted. So I took his pen and wrote 'The Bells. By E. A. Poe,['] and I mimic[k]ed his style, and wrote the Bells, the little silver Bells &c. &c. he finishing each line" (Shew to Ingram, 23 January 1875, Miller [1977], pp. 98–99; see also Mabbott [1969], 1:429–30, 434, and Moldenhauer [1973], pp. 12–13).

EARLY MAY. Dr. John W. Francis examines Poe at Mrs. Shew's home, diagnosing heart disease (Miller [1977], p. 99; cf. Poe's denial of diagnosis in 1 October letter to Mrs. Whitman).

EARLY MAY? LOWELL, MASSACHUSETTS. The poetess Mrs. Jane Ermina Locke replies to a letter from Poe. She expresses her deep interest in his welfare and indicates a desire to obtain an account of his life and his portrait. She is reluctant, however, to answer his requests for information on her own life: "They attach to the brief page of my own history an importance—an 'all' that while it surprises, grieves me. . . . Can it be that because you absolutely know 'nothing' of me—because of what seems to you my obscurity there may be something wrong that makes you secretly hesitate to call me friend" (quoted in Poe's 19 May reply).

[Poe hoped to remarry, as demonstrated by his subsequent courtships of Mrs. Whitman and Mrs. Elmira Royster Shelton; the tactful questions he directed to Mrs. Locke were designed to determine whether she was a widow (cf. Bardwell Heywood to Miss Annie Sawyer, 2 October).]

MAY. FORDHAM. Poe sends a letter of recommendation to the shipowner Charles H. Marshall. Poe believes that Dr. Freeman, a neighborhood physician, is fully qualified for the post he seeks, that of surgeon on board the passenger ship *United States*: "I have great pleasure in mentioning that he [Dr. Freeman] has attended my family for the last two years" (*L*, 2:368).

3 MAY. Poe replies to a letter from the Philadelphia poetaster Henry B. Hirst: "I am glad to hear that you are getting out 'Endymion', of which you *must* know that I think highly—very highly—if I *did* fall asleep while hearing it read." Poe is now living at Fordham, Westchester County, "14 miles" from New York by railroad: "Should you have any trouble about finding me, inquire at the office of the 'Home Journal'—or 'Union Magazine' " (*L*, 2:365).

15 MAY. NEW YORK. John Henry Hopkins, Jr., writes Poe about *Eureka*:

On glancing over your MS. the other day at Mr. Putnam's, I perceived that you had added a new developement of your ideas. After the closing[,] the magnificent and sublime thought of a new universe springing into existence at Every throb of the Divine heart, (a passage at which in my humble judgment, the work should *end*,) you go on to explain the *Divine* heart as being *our own*, and then lay down a system of complete and pure pantheism.

Now I do not intend to object to this on theological grounds at present, for that would lead me into an almost interminable discussion, besides being out of place in me. But I think that on further reflection you will see that *scientifically* it is unsound, and contradictory of other parts of your theory.

1st. You do not deny I suppose that God is *Infinite*. Yet you make the primary irradiation of matter *limited* both in time and in extent—How can infinity resolve itself, or diffuse itself or *expand* itself into *finity*? If God is infinite and the *whole* deity exists now only under the form of the Universe, the irradiation *must* have been infinite in time & extent also . . . .

2nd. But this is not all. You know well that the great body of Christians regard pantheism as a damnable heresy, if not worse. Such a brand would be a blight upon your book, which not even *your* genius could efface, and your great discovery would at once be ranked by the majority among the vain dreams of skepticism and the empty chimaeras of infidelity. If published as it now stands, I should myself be compelled to attack *that* part of it, for I could not in conscience do otherwise (MB–G).

19 MAY. FORDHAM. Poe writes Mrs. Jane Ermina Locke in Lowell, apologizing for failing to answer her "last kind and noble letter" more promptly: "But for duties that, just now, *will not* be neglected or even postponed—the proof-reading of a work of scientific detail [*Eureka*], in which a trivial error would involve me in very serious embarrassment—I would, ere this, have been in Lowell—to clasp you by the hand—and to

thank you personally for all that I owe you:—and oh, I feel that this is *very—very* much." Poe again asks Mrs. Locke for the details of her "personal history," explaining that his secluded existence at Fordham has prevented him from learning anything about her: "I feel that you cannot misunderstand me. . . . Tell me only of the ties—if any exist—that bind you to the world:—and yet I perceive that I may have done very wrong in asking you this:—now that I have asked it, it seems to me the maddest of questions, involving, possibly, the most visionary of hopes." Mrs. Locke can find biographical sketches of Poe in *Graham's Magazine* for February 1845 and in the *Southern Literary Messenger* for January 1848: "The only portrait, I believe, was in 'Graham' " (*L*, 2:366–68).

22 MAY. NEW YORK. Poe and George P. Putnam sign a printed "Memorandum of Agreement," stipulating that *Eureka* will be published on or before 15 June. After the publisher has recovered the cost of publication, he will pay the author at the rate of "ten percent upon the retail price of all copies that have been or may be sold," payments to be made in February and August of each year (PP–G; see CA. 11 JULY for actual publication).

23 MAY. Poe signs a promissory note: "Received of George P. Putnam Fourteen Dollars money loaned, to be repaid out of the proceeds of the Copyright of my work entitled 'Eureka, a Prose Poem'; and I hereby engage, in case the sales of said work do not cover the expenses, according to the account rendered by said Putnam in January 1849, to repay the said amount of Fourteen Dollars; and I also engage not to ask or apply for any other loans or advances from said Putnam in any way, and to wait until January 1849 for the statement of account as above, before making any demand whatever." The note in Poe's hand is also signed by two witnesses, Maria Clemm and Marie Louise Shew (facsimile in Nelson, p. 168).

23, 25, 27 MAY. PARIS. *La Démocratie pacifique* contains "Le Scarabée d'or," a translation of "The Gold-Bug" by Isabelle Meunier (Mabbott [1978], 3:805–06).

BEFORE 24 MAY. PROVIDENCE, RHODE ISLAND. The English authoress Anna Blackwell, who had boarded with Poe and Mrs. Clemm last autumn, comes to Providence to receive "magnetic treatment" from Professor de Bonneville. She discusses Poe with Mrs. Sarah Helen Whitman (Varner [1940], p. 289; Whitman to J. H. Ingram, 14 February 1875, Miller [1979], p. 255).

CA. 24 MAY. Miss Blackwell writes Poe, asking his advice about publishing a collection of her poetry (Poe's 14 June reply).

1848

LATE MAY. FORDHAM. The authoress Maria J. McIntosh makes Poe's acquaintance at the home of Mr. Lindsay, a relative of Mrs. Mary Osborne. Poe learns that Miss McIntosh is a friend of Mrs. Whitman and that she is about to visit Providence; he enthusiastically discusses Mrs. Whitman's writings with her (Whitman to Ingram, 6 March 1874 and 14 February 1875, Miller [1979], pp. 61, 255–56; see also *L*, 2:375–76, 528).

JUNE OR BEFORE. NEW YORK. Marie Louise Shew is persuaded that a continued association with Poe would be detrimental to her spiritual well-being: "Mr. Hopkins was a great admirer of Mr. Poe, and often met him at my house, but when the question of pantheism came up, you see he thought him either insane or a hopeless infadel [*sic*], and . . . he would tell the story of that dreadful night when they took him home to Fordham, Mr. Poe reciting, 'some unheard of jargon with glorious pathos—or deadly hate' . . . . *Of course I felt he was lost, either way*" (Shew to Ingram, 16 February 1875, Miller [1977], pp. 104–05).

JUNE OR BEFORE. Mrs. Shew writes Poe at Fordham, declining further intimacy (Poe's June reply).

[On 3 April 1875 Mrs. Shew wrote Ingram: "Mr. Poe always treated me with respect and I was to him a friend in need, and a friend indeed, but he was so excentric, and so unlike others, and I was also, that I had to define a position, I was bound to take, and it hurt his feelings, and after he was dead I deeply regret[t]ed my letter to him" (Miller [1977], p. 124).]

JUNE. FORDHAM. Poe replies to Mrs. Shew: "Can it be true Louise that you have the idea fixed in your mind to desert your unhappy and unfortunate friend and patient. . . . I have read over your letter again, and again, and can not make it possible with any degree of certainty, that you wrote it in your right mind (*I know you did not without tears of anguish and regret*) . . . . Oh Louise how many sorrows are before you, your ingenuous and sympathetic nature, will be constantly wounded in contact with the hollow heartless world, and for me alas! unless some true and tender and pure womanly love saves me, I shall hardly last a year longer, alone!" Poe sadly recalls Mrs. Shew's last visit to Fordham, when she accompanied Hopkins in early April: "I heard your voice as you passed out of my sight leaving me with the Parson, 'The man of God, The servant of the most High.' He stood smiling and bowing at the madman Poe! *But, that* I had invited him to my house, I would have rushed out into Gods light and freedom!" (*L*, 2:372–74).

JUNE. CINCINNATI. The *Gentleman's Magazine* commences publication. In the first number Poe's name appears on a list of prominent American authors said to have sent "letters and assurances" promising contributions. This monthly expires in August with its third number, nothing by Poe having been printed (Heartman and Canny, pp. 197–98; Hull, p. 701).

CA. 1 JUNE. FORDHAM. Poe sends his poem beginning "I saw thee once— once only—years ago" to Mrs. Whitman in Providence. Although the manuscript bears "no signature . . . nor any title," she recognizes the handwriting as Poe's by comparing it with that on the 2 March envelope in which he sent her his 1831 "To Helen" (Whitman to Ingram, 6 March 1874, Miller [1979], p. 60; see also *L*, 2:386, 409).

[Poe's 1848 poem commemorates the brief glimpse he had of Mrs. Whitman on "a July midnight" in 1845; subsequent editors have called it "the second 'To Helen' " to distinguish it from his 1831 verses.]

Mrs. Whitman's home on Benefit Street, Providence

1 JUNE. LOWELL, MASSACHUSETTS. Mrs. Jane Ermina Locke completes "The True Poet," a poem addressed to Poe (New York *Evening Post*, 3 August).

3 JUNE. PHILADELPHIA. The *John-Donkey* contains Thomas Dunn English's "Hints to Authors: On the Germanesque," an attack on Poe in the guise of purported instruction. Any aspirant author can learn the "Germanesque"

mode: "Indeed, judging by the works and mind of its chief and almost only follower on this side of the Atlantic, it is a pure art, almost mechanical—requiring neither genius, taste, wit, nor judgment—and accessible to every impudent and contemptible mountebank, who may choose to slander a lady [Mrs. Ellet], and then plead insanity to shelter himself from the vengeance of her relatives." By way of illustration English reprints his "Tale of a Gray Tadpole," a parody of Poe's fiction originally published in the Philadelphia *Irish Citizen* as "The Ghost of a Grey Tadpole." This story "has been attributed to Mr. POE. We are not sure that it is from the pen of that very distinguished writer; but if not his, is a palpable imitation of his style."

7 JUNE. FORDHAM. Poe writes Charles Astor Bristed in New York. Recalling Bristed's "former kindness," Poe explains that he is "desperately circumstanced" and knows of no other person who might be both able and willing to aid him: "My last hope of extricating myself from the difficulties which are pressing me to death, is in going personally to a distant connexion near Richmond, Va, and endeavoring to interest him in my behalf. With a very little help all would go well with me—but even that little I cannot obtain; the effort to overcome one trouble only serving to plunge me in another. Will you forgive me, then, if I ask you to loan me the means of getting to Richmond? . . . Mr Putnam has my book [*Eureka*] in press, but he could make me no advance, beyond $14—some weeks ago" (L, 2:368–69).

AFTER 7 JUNE? NEW YORK. Poe calls on Bristed, sending in his engraved card, bordered in black to indicate mourning for Virginia's death, and bearing this handwritten request: "Will Mr Bristed honor Mr Poe with a few minutes private conversation?" Poe probably tells Bristed that he needs to visit Richmond to promote his forthcoming magazine, the *Stylus*; possibly he identifies the distant relative who might support this project as Edward Valentine (suggested by Poe to Bristed, 7 June, and to Valentine, 20 November; facsimile of Poe's card in Quinn, p. 567).

14 JUNE. FORDHAM. Poe replies to Anna Blackwell's "letter of three weeks ago," claiming (falsely) that he failed to answer it sooner because he has been "absent from home rather more than that time" and "only this moment received it." Although Miss Blackwell's poems are "infinitely superior to many," she will have difficulty in publishing them: "The Appletons will publish them, leaving you the eventual copyright, but binding you to supply all loss resulting from the publication:—and they will allow you ten per cent on all values effected after all expences are paid—so long as they continue to publish the book. No publisher will

make better terms with you than these." Poe wonders why Miss Blackwell has gone to Providence: "Do you know Mrs Whitman? I feel deep interest in her poetry and character. I have never seen her—but once. Anne Lynch, however, told me many things about the romance of her character which singularly interested me and excited my curiosity. . . . Can you not tell me something about her—any thing—every thing you know—and *keep my secret*—that is to say let no one know that I have asked you to do so?" (*L*, 2:369–71).

15 JUNE. Poe writes Bayard Taylor, who is editing the *Union Magazine* during Mrs. Caroline M. Kirkland's absence in Europe. If Taylor finds the enclosed poem [presumably the second "To Helen"] suitable for the *Union*, Poe asks to be informed how much he can pay for it and when it could appear. Poe regrets that he has never thanked Taylor for his "picturesque and vigorous" sketches of European travel published in 1846, *Views A-Foot*: "when they reached me, and long afterwards, I was too ill to write—and latterly I have been every day hoping to have an opportunity of making your acquaintance and thanking you in person" (*L*, 2:371; for Taylor's editorship, see Derby, pp. 597–99, and Taylor, pp. 122, 127–28).

17 JUNE. NEW YORK. The *Literary World* carries an advertisement for George P. Putnam, Publisher, who announces several forthcoming books: "*Eureka* . . . By EDGAR A. POE, Esq. . . . *In June*."

17 JUNE. PHILADELPHIA. The *John-Donkey* contains "REVIEW OF NEW BOOKS: BY E. A. POE," in which English reprints verbatim the satire on Poe's literary criticism which had appeared in the New York *Town* of 17 May 1845, a mock notice of the fictitious title *Adventures, Life and Opinions of John Smith*.

17, 20, 22, 24 JUNE. PARIS. *Le Journal du Loiret* reprints Isabelle Meunier's translation of "The Gold-Bug" from *La Démocratie pacifique* of 23, 25, 27 May (Mabbott [1978], 3:806).

21 JUNE. FORDHAM. Poe writes Mrs. Sarah Anna Lewis in New York: "I have been spending a couple of hours most pleasantly, my dear Stella, in reading and re-reading your 'Child of the Sea'. When it appears in print—less enticing to the eye, perhaps, than your own graceful MS.—I shall endeavor to do it critical justice in full; but in the meantime permit me to say, briefly, that I think it well conducted as a whole—abounding in narrative passages of unusual force—but especially remarkable for the boldness and poetic fervor of its sentimental portions, where a very striking *originality* is manifested" (*L*, 2:372; Ostrom [1969], pp. 36–37).

LATE JUNE. PROVIDENCE. Maria J. McIntosh spends an evening at Sarah Helen Whitman's home, Anna Blackwell also being present. Mrs. Whitman recalls: "Miss M[cIntosh] said, 'Mrs. W[hitman], on just such a night as this one month ago I met Mr. Poe for the first time at the house of a gentleman in Fordham—a Mr. Lindsay . . . his whole talk was about you.' . . . Miss Blackwell then said that she had received a letter from Poe to much the same effect two or three weeks before, but had not thought to speak of it to me. She afterwards at my request gave me the letter, which she said she had not answered" (14 February 1875 letter to J. H. Ingram, Miller [1979], pp. 255–56; see also p. 61).

LATE? JUNE. FORDHAM. Mrs. Jane Ermina Locke travels to Fordham to meet Poe, spending the day at his cottage. She suggests that he deliver a lecture in Lowell, inviting him to stay at her home. Poe presumably discovers that his correspondent is not a widow, but a married woman older than himself, with five children (Annie Richmond to Ingram, 13 March 1877, Miller [1977], p. 166; see also Reilly [1972], p. 210, and Miller [1979], pp. 162, 346).

JULY OR BEFORE. NEW YORK STATE. Poe makes a walking tour of "one or two" of the Hudson River counties north of Fordham (implied by his sketch "Landor's Cottage").

JULY. CHARLESTON, SOUTH CAROLINA. The *Southern Quarterly Review* contains an article "Fugitive Poetry of America" by "A. S. P.," who discusses "The Raven" at length, quoting several stanzas. While this critic praises Poe "for the production of so remarkable a metrical novelty," he finds fault on other grounds:

The psychology of the poem is deformed by the same error which characterizes some of this writer's prose productions, a wild and unbridled extravagance. Scenery and incidents of themselves insignificant are made to produce a most powerful effect upon the mind of the *dramatis personae*. . . . A rap at the door and a flutter of the curtain exert as powerful an influence over a man, as they would over a child who had been frightened to the verge of idiocy by terrible ghost stories. It seems as if the author wrote under the influence of opium, or attempted to describe the fantastic terrors which afflict a sufferer from *delirium tremens*. A sound mind is incapable of such vagaries, and finds it very difficult to sympathize with them.

EARLY JULY? LOWELL, MASSACHUSETTS. Mrs. Locke makes arrangements for Poe's lecture (Miller [1977], p. 166).

7 JULY. The *Daily Journal & Courier* reports: "We are requested to state that Mr Edgar A. Poe will lecture in Wentworth's Hall, on Monday evening,

10th inst., on the Poets and Poetry of America; and give recitations from various authors. He will also read his beautiful and popular poem, 'The Raven.' " The *Journal* also carries a brief advertisement, which is repeated in the 8 and 10 July issues: "MR. EDGAR A. POE, of N. York, will deliver a Lecture to the citizens of Lowell . . . . Tickets to be had at the stores of Bixby & Co., Carleton & Hovey, Merrill & Heywood, Oliver March, James C. Ayer, and at the Hall."

8 JULY. The *Lowell Advertiser* reports: "Mr E. A. Poe, the well known poet and critic, is expected to visit Lowell this week. On Monday evening of next week, he will comply with the wishes of his many admirers in our city, by giving an entertainment in Wentworth's Hall. The entertainment will consist of a lecture on 'the poets and poetry of America' . . . . Mr Poe is too well known to need comment of ours. His friends and foes, (for all critics have foes) acknowledge his talents to be of the highest order. It will be quite a treat, and no every-day-affair."

9 JULY. PHILLIPS, MAINE. George W. Eveleth writes Poe, inquiring when his lecture on "The Universe" will be published. He quotes favorable notices of the lecture and an announcement of its forthcoming publication from the New York *Weekly Universe*. Eveleth has recently read the unsigned critique of Poe's *Tales* and other American books in *Blackwood's Magazine* for November 1847: "It appears to me that the writer here (in speaking of yours) contradicts himself in some instances—that he often finds fault, in words, where his manner and tone show that he *would* applaud—and that in many cases he takes unnecessary pains *to remove objections*, to reconcile things which would not be raised as objections by any other than the shallow-headed. . . . I have been, and am, half inclined to put down the article as written by none other than one Edgar A. Poe" (Eveleth, pp. 20–22).

10 JULY OR BEFORE. LOWELL. Poe arrives in Lowell, taking lodging at Wamesit Cottage on the Concord River, the home of Mrs. Locke and her husband, the attorney John G. Locke (Reilly [1972], p. 210).

10 JULY OR BEFORE. Mrs. Locke introduces Poe to her friend and neighbor Annie Richmond, wife of the well-to-do paper manufacturer Charles B. Richmond (Coburn, pp. 468–69).

[In "Landor's Cottage," published in the Boston *Flag of Our Union* for 9 June 1849, Poe gave a fictionalized account of his first meeting with Mrs. Richmond:

I rapped with my stick against the door [of the cottage], which stood half open. Instantly a figure advanced to the threshold—that of a young woman about twenty-eight years of age—slender, or rather slight, and somewhat above the medium height. As she approached, with a certain *modest decision* of step altogether indescribable, I said to myself, "Surely here I have found the perfection of natural, in contradistinction from artificial *grace*." The second impression which she made on me, but by far the more vivid of the two, was that of *enthusiasm*. So intense an expression of *romance*, perhaps I should call it, or of unworldliness, as that which gleamed from her deep-set eyes, had never so sunk into my heart of hearts before. . . . The eyes of Annie (I heard some one from the interior call her "Annie, darling!") were "spiritual gray;" her hair, a light chestnut.

In a 5 February 1877 letter to J. H. Ingram, Annie recalled her initial impressions of Poe: "He seemed so *unlike* any other person, I had ever known, that I could not think of him in the same way—he was incomparable—not to be measured by any ordinary standard—& all the events of his life, which he narrated to me, had a flavor of *unreality* about them, just like his stories" (Miller [1977], pp. 162–63; see also p. 166).]

10 JULY. The *Daily Journal & Courier* carries a laudatory advance notice of Poe's lecture this evening, possibly contributed by Mrs. Locke:

His subject will be, The Poets and Poetry of America, interspersed with various recitations, and, to conclude, at the *particular request* of his friends, with his own most beautiful and highly imaginative Poem of "The Raven." This, with several other Poems of scarcely less merit, have ranked him, both in this country, and in Europe, if we may judge at all by the critical and biographical notices of him in Foreign Reviews, as a *Poet* of the highest order. As a *Prose-writer* few go before him according to Griswold, Lowell, and others.—His Tales, in which are "Valdemar," "The fall of the House of Usher," which 'tis said French writers have so much admired as to *steal*, at the risk of their own reputation for plagiarism, no one can read without a thrilling admiration. . . .

This is the first time Mr Poe has ever visited our city, and we hope for its intellectual and literary reputation that he may have a crowded house.

10 JULY. Poe lectures on "The Poets and Poetry of America," paying especial attention to female poets and highly praising Mrs. Lewis, Miss Lynch, Mrs. Osgood, and Mrs. Whitman (Poe's letter to Annie Richmond, after 1 October; manuscript fragment of lecture Poe gave Mrs. Whitman, after 20 October).

[Many years later Sarah H. Heywood, Mrs. Richmond's younger sister, recalled Poe's lecture: "His manner of rendering some of the selections . . . fascinated me, although he gave no attempt at dramatic effect. Everything was rendered with pure intonation and perfect enunciation, marked attention being paid to the rhythm: he almost *sang* the more musical versifications. I recall more perfectly than anything else, the modulations of his smooth baritone voice, as he recited the opening lines of Byron's 'Bride of Abydos'—'Know ye the land where the cypress and myrtle'—measuring the dactylic movement as perfectly as if he were scanning it: the effect was very pleasing. . . . I did not hear the conversation at Mrs. Richmond's after the lecture, when a few persons came in to meet him" (Ingram, p. 389; also in Gill, pp. 209–11).]

10–11 JULY. After the lecture Poe spends "the remainder of the evening and part of the next day" at Annie Richmond's home on Ames Street, where he relates a somewhat romanticized account of his early life to her brother Bardwell Heywood (Bardwell to Miss Sawyer, 2 October).

11 JULY. The *Lowell Advertiser* reports: "MR POE'S LECTURE on the Poets and Poetry of America, last evening, was deservedly listened to with much attention. His remarks upon the system by which criticisms and puffs are ground out, were, we are inclined to believe, too true."

CA. 11 JULY. NEW YORK. George P. Putnam issues *Eureka: A Prose Poem*, a small volume priced at seventy-five cents. The text is preceded by Poe's "Preface":

To the few who love me and whom I love—to those who feel rather than to those who think—to the dreamers and those who put faith in dreams as in the only realities—I offer this Book of Truths, not in its character of Truth-Teller, but for the Beauty that abounds in its Truth; constituting it true. To these I present the composition as an Art-Product alone:—let us say as a Romance; or, if I be not urging too lofty a claim, as a Poem.

What I here propound is true:—therefore it cannot die:—or if by any means it be now trodden down so that 'it die, it will "rise again to the Life Everlasting."

Nevertheless it is as a Poem only that I wish this work to be judged after I am dead.

12 JULY. In the *Morning Express* the editor James Brooks reviews *Eureka*:

A most extraordinary essay upon the Material and Spiritual Universe,—but one to which we are at this moment unable to do anything like adequate justice,—the work itself having barely made its appearance from the press of Mr. Putnam. Those of our readers who remember a report of Mr. POE'S Lecture at the Society Library, a few months ago, which appeared in this journal at the time, may gather some idea of the work before us from the fact that that lecture has been expanded, with really consummate art . . . . We shall be greatly surprised if this work do[es] not create a most profound sensation among the literary and scientific classes all over the Union . . . . In respect of novelty, Mr. POE'S new theory of the Universe will certainly attract universal attention, inasmuch as it is demonstrated, so to speak, with a degree of logical acumen which has certainly not been equalled since the days of Sir Isaac Newton . . . . But we must bring our brief notice of this extraordinary book to a hurried close here—earnestly recommending it to every one of our readers as one that can in no event fail to shed an unfading lustre upon the American name, as a work of almost unequalled power in respect of philosoph-ical research and speculative force. Mr. POE has appropriately dedicated it, "with very profound respect," to *Alexander Von Humboldt*, whose well-known "COSMOS" he very justly ranks higher than any other work upon the same subject.

The review is reprinted in today's *Evening Express*.

12 JULY. The *Commercial Advertiser* notices *Eureka*: "We have not read this book, but intend to con it over without loss of time. We expect to find in it some brilliant thoughts, and some truths, with much eccentricity. The author calls it 'an art-product—a romance—or perchance a poem.' We should not be surprised to find it verify the description."

14 JULY. The *Journal of Commerce* favorably notices *Eureka* (Pollin [1975a], p. 29; [1980], p. 28).

14 JULY. FORDHAM. Poe writes the Georgia poet Thomas Holley Chivers, who is visiting New York: "I have just returned from an excursion to Lowell:—this is the reason why I have not been to see you. My mother [Mrs. Clemm] will leave this note at your hotel in the event of your not being in when she calls. I am *very* anxious to see you—as I propose going on to Richmond on Monday [17 July]. Can you not come out to Fordham & spend tomorrow & Sunday with me? . . . The cars for Fordham leave the dépôt at the City Hall almost every hour" (*L*, 2:375; Chivers [1957], p. 74).

15 JULY. Poe writes the Fordham authoress Mrs. Mary Osborne: "May I beg of you to make my acknowledgments as warmly as possible—or as admissible—to Miss [Maria J.] McIntosh, for the favor she has done me in sending me the book—rendered doubly valuable by her autograph? Will you request for me, also, her acceptance of a late work of my own—'Eureka'—which accompanies this note? I have ventured to send with it, too, a duplicate copy, in the hope that Mrs Osborne will honor me by receiving it as an expression of my very sincere esteem and friendship" (*L*, 2:375–76).

15 JULY. NEW YORK. The *Albion* reviews *Eureka*, quoting Poe's preface in its entirety: "Passing over the manifest tone of self-complacency that runs through this introduction, deeming it very venial in a dreamy poet, we turned over a few pages, but found to our surprise that all the poetry was in the preface. *Eureka*, in point of fact, is an 'Essay on the Material and Spiritual Universe' . . . . It is obvious, therefore, that there is a singular discrepancy between the preface and the essay. . . . the latter is deep, abstruse, and metaphysical, as far as a hasty glance enables one to judge

. . . . We doubt not that with Mr. Poe's keen research and undoubted talents, he has written what will draw upon him criticism the most thorough and acute, and we trust for his own sake that there will prove to be no *romance* at all in 'Eureka.' "

15 JULY. The *Evening Mirror* and the *Evening Post* contain brief notices of *Eureka*, neither reviewer having had time to read the book (Pollin [1975a], p. 29; [1980], p. 28).

15 JULY. PHILADELPHIA. The *Saturday Evening Post* publishes a 10 July letter from its New York correspondent, Bayard Taylor, who mentions several forthcoming books, including "Poe's prose-poem of *Eureka*, in which his new theory of the universe will be revealed. Whether the readers of the work will echo its title, on perusal, is a question to be decided; but many, I have no doubt, will answer with the Raven: 'Nevermore!' " (Laverty [1951], p. 346; cf. Taylor, p. 122).

15 JULY. PARIS. In *La Liberté de penser* Charles Baudelaire publishes "Révélation magnetique," his translation of "Mesmeric Revelation," prefacing it with a brief appreciative essay on Poe's writings (P. F. Quinn, pp. 89–93).

17 JULY OR LATER. NEW YORK. Poe leaves for Richmond "to obtain subscriptions for 'The Stylus,' intending, if successful there, to make a tour of the Southern States before returning to the North" (Mrs. Whitman to R. H. Stoddard, 30 September 1872, Stoddard [1884], 1:155; cf. Poe to Chivers, 14 July 1848).

19 JULY. PHILADELPHIA. The *Dollar Newspaper* copies the notice of *Eureka* which had appeared in the New York *Commercial Advertiser* on 12 July (Phillips, 2:1266; Pollin [1980], p. 28).

20 JULY. BOSTON. In the *Evening Transcript* Epes Sargent, the new editor, reviews *Eureka*:

Mr Poe . . . dedicates his work . . . to Alexander Von Humboldt. So ingeniously does he smatter of astronomical systems, concentric circles, centrifugal forces, planetary distances, the Nebular theory and the star Alpha Lyrae, that we should not be surprised if the great cosmogonist himself were to be dismayed by the lavish ostentation of scientific lore . . . . There is talent unquestionably in these fanciful speculations, and we are occasionally reminded of that remarkable work [Robert Chambers'] "The Vestiges of Creation" by the character and tendency of the author's scientific romancing. But the vital element of sincerity is wanting. The mocking smile of the hoaxer is seen behind his grave mask. He is more anxious to mystify and confound than to persuade, or even to instruct . . . .

Sargent hopes that Poe will "exercise his really fine talents upon something more profitable to himself and his readers."

22 JULY. The *Saturday Rambler* reports that Poe "is about publishing a prose-poem" revealing "his new theory of the universe" (Pollin [1975a], p. 28; [1980], p. 28).

22 JULY. The *Boston Museum* reports: "Edgar A. Poe has been lecturing and giving recitations of his own verse, at Lowell." This issue also contains a reprint of "The Gold-Bug."

22 JULY. NEW YORK. The *Literary World* lists *Eureka* among the books published during the past week.

29 JULY. The *Home Journal* contains a five-stanza poem by Sarah Helen Whitman, written in response to Poe's second "To Helen" and quoting the phrase *"Beauty which is Hope"* from his unpublished manuscript (Reilly [1965], pp. 188, 234, 265).

[Mrs. Whitman's poem, headed "Stanzas" in the *Journal*, was subsequently entitled "A Night in August." Poe did not see it, as he recalled in his 1 October letter to her: "of all my set of the 'Home Journal', I failed in receiving only that individual number which contained your published verses."]

29 JULY. The *Literary World* contains a long review of *Eureka*, unsigned but written by John Henry Hopkins, Jr. *Eureka* opens with "a keen burlesque on the Aristotelian and Baconian methods of ascertaining truth"; the author then "pours forth his rhapsodical ecstasies in glorification of the third mode—the noble art of *guessing*." Hopkins agrees that a guess is "as good as anything else, provided it *hits*." Poe's guesses are "apparently near the mark" when he is "accounting for the principle of the Newtonian Law of Gravity" or explaining "the formation of stars and suns, luminous and non-luminous, moons and planets with their rings, &c., . . . according to the nebular theory of La Place." While the "physical portion" of Poe's theory may be largely true, his theological speculations are "intolerable." Hopkins condemns "the system of Pantheism which is more or less inwoven into the texture of the whole book, but displays itself most broadly at the end." The author is guilty of absurd inconsistencies:

On pp. 28, 29, Mr. Poe speaks of "God" and "the Godhead" as a Christian or a deist might speak—as being One. On p. 103 he has the "hardihood" to assert that we have a right to infer that there are an infinity of universes (?) such as ours, of which "Each exists, apart and independently, in *the bosom of its proper and particular god*." This makes Mr. Poe a polytheist—a believer in an *infinite* number of *proper and particular* gods, existing *apart and independently*. On page 141 it appears that this infinity of gods is forgotten, and Mr. Poe cannot conceive "that anything exists *greater than his own soul*" . . . . All this is extraordinary nonsense, if not blasphemy; and it may very possibly be *both* (attribution in Poe to C. F. Hoffman, 20 September).

31 JULY. A copy of *Eureka* is deposited, for copyright, in the Clerk's Office of the United States District Court, Southern District of New York State (Nelson, pp. 173, 201).

31 JULY. BROOKLYN. The *Daily Eagle* favorably notices *Eureka*, which contains "new and startling" thoughts about God, man, and immortality, written in a poetic style (Pollin [1975a], p. 28; [1980], p. 28).

LATE JULY. RICHMOND. Poe calls on his early love Sarah Elmira Royster, now the well-to-do widow Mrs. Shelton. "I . . . was amazed to see him— but knew him instantly—He came up to me in the most enthusiastic manner and said: 'Oh! Elmira, is this you?' " (Mrs. Shelton's reminiscences transcribed by E. V. Valentine on 19 November 1875, ViRVal).

[Although Quinn (pp. 571, 629) doubted that Poe saw Mrs. Shelton in the summer of 1848, Mrs. Whitman stated repeatedly that he renewed the acquaintance at this time, basing her testimony upon what Poe told her in the autumn of 1848. "During this visit to Richmond, late in July, 1848, Mr. Poe had called on Mrs. Shelton . . . . Having been received by her with great kindness he was urged by one of their mutual friends to renew his addresses to her. He was tempted to follow this advice" (Mrs. Whitman to R. H. Stoddard, 30 September 1872, Stoddard [1884], 1:155). "I think he [Poe] told Mr. Pabodie that the years of their separation had greatly changed the tastes & idiosyncrasies of both" (Whitman to Mrs. Clemm, 4 April 1859, *W*, 17:424, or Quinn and Hart, p. 44).]

CA. AUGUST. PROVIDENCE. Mrs. Whitman receives a visit from Rufus W. Griswold, who obtains her permission to include several of her poems in his forthcoming anthology *The Female Poets of America*. She recalls: "He spoke of Poe's interest in my writings & said that he [Poe] had been delivering a lecture on the poetesses of America in Lowell . . . . I asked him how it was that Poe had incurred the enmity of so many of the literary men of New York. He said it certainly was not that he had done anything exceptionally wrong to *deserve* it—that he had *always* said Poe was not so much to blame in his literary embroilments as were his enemies" (letter to J. H. Ingram, 6 March 1874, Miller [1979], pp. 60–61; cf. Whitman to Griswold, 13 February 1849, PHi, which alludes to his visit "last summer").

EARLY AUGUST. Mrs. Whitman sends Poe these two stanzas transcribed from her poem to him published in the *Home Journal* for 29 July:

> A low bewildering melody
> Is murmuring in my ear—
> Tones such as in the twilight wood
> The aspen thrills to hear
> When Faunus slumbers on the hill
> And all the entranced boughs are still.
>
> The jasmine twines her snowy stars
> Into a fairer wreath—
> The lily through my lattice bars
> Exhales a sweeter breath—
> And, gazing on Night's starry cope,
> I dwell with *"Beauty which is Hope"*.

Her manuscript is "without signature . . . dated Providence R. I. August 1848." Because she addresses it to Fordham—which has no post office—it is delivered instead to the post office in nearby West Farms, where it is detained (Whitman to Mrs. Julia Deane Freeman, 20 January 1859, Varner [1940], pp. 296–97; see also *L*, 2:386).

AUGUST. NEW YORK. The *Democratic Review* contains Poe's "The Literati of New-York: S. Anna Lewis," an unsigned critique in which he praises Mrs. Lewis' forthcoming volume *The Child of the Sea and Other Poems*, "now in the press." The *Review* briefly notices *Eureka*: "Mr. Poe is too well and favorably known not only to the reading public of this country but of England to make an extended notice of his peculiar excellence at all necessary here. The work now published by Mr. Putnam will doubtless be readily sought."

AUGUST. In his *Merchants' Magazine* Freeman Hunt reviews *Eureka*: "It is well the author has, by his own admission, brought this startling work into the provinces of poetry or romance. As a work of the imagination, it teems with the highest beauty of view and glorious thought. There is, there must be, much of the *true* in the grand Utopia of the universe thus imaged forth, because the presence of the *true* is intuitively *felt*. And then, Mr. Poe has a wonderful faculty of illustrating his theories. He unites the precision of mathematical acumen with the creative energy of the wildest imagination, and uses *facts* or *fancies*, as the exigencies demand, with equal facility."

AUGUST. The *New Church Repository*, a Swedenborgian organ edited by George Bush, reviews *Eureka*:

A poet here enters upon profound speculations, shooting ahead of the Newtons, Laplaces, Herschells, and Nicholses, in the solution of the great problems of the Universe. He calls his work a poem, perhaps because, with Madame De Stael, he regards the Universe itself as more like a poem than a machine . . . . We might perhaps feel the want of a certain property termed *demonstration* as a buttress to his reasonings, but that the author has effectually estopped any such inconvenient demand in his case by the peremptory position that "in this world, at least, there is *no such thing* as demonstration" . . . . Waving, however, the application of this sweeping *negatur* to his own speculations, we refuse not to concede that the work before us does offer some hints towards solving no less a problem than that of the *cause of gravitation*, before which the grandest geniuses have shrank abashed. Of this we can scarcely make the barest *statement* in a manner which shall do full justice to the propounder's thought, but we may afford an inkling of it by saying that he assumes a created unitary and irrelative particle as the first principle or germ of the Universe, and supposes an internal force, identical with the Divine volition, to have radiated or projected all but an infinity of minimal atoms from this parent particle into the regions of space, and that the attraction of gravitation is nothing else than a *conatus* on the part of these atoms to return to the central unity.

Many of Poe's ideas were anticipated by Emanuel Swedenborg in his *Outlines on the Infinite*. Since "the worst feature" of *Eureka* is a "pantheistic tendency," the reviewer recommends that Poe read this earlier treatise, hoping that "he may feel the force of Swedenborg's reasoning in regard to the being and agency of a God distinct from nature."

AUGUST. LOWELL. Jane Ermina Locke sends Poe her "Ermina's Tale," a manuscript poem of thirty-one stanzas describing her reactions to him:

> Then forth there came to my enraptured sight,—
>   From whence I know not—how—or why it came—
> A mortal form!—*immortal*—*veiled*!—in light
>   That well nigh had consumed my heart . . . .
>
> Around his brow was twined a serpent wreath,—
>   And to his fingers swayed harpstrings of fire,
> That swelled forlornest strains, burthening the breath
>   Of air, to memories of uncrowned desire. . . .
>
> I felt as in the presence of a god!
>   My heart awe-struck, sent up a censer flame
> With fingers clasped; flower burthened was the sod,
>   And there the figure knelt as best it *me* became! . . .
>
> I felt his clasp, as lip to lip he pressed,
>   Listened, beguiled as to an angel's tone,
> To his impassioned words;—*then sank to rest,*
>   *In trance divine my heart upon his own!*

The poem, presumably forwarded to Fordham, is accompanied by Mrs. Locke's brief letter: "I hope you will *acknowledge* the *receipt* of this *immediately*, tho' more than this I shall not entreat of you, le[a]ving all to *your own* discretion and *feelings*, *mine* are written out, and you cannot mistake them; therefore you can judge of the safety of any thing you may say to me, or of the manner in which it will be received" (Reilly [1972], pp. 210–12).

AUGUST? RICHMOND. Poe makes the acquaintance of John R. Thompson, editor of the *Southern Literary Messenger*, who accepts "The Rationale of Verse" for publication (Thompson to P. P. Cooke, 17 October).

[Years later Thompson left a reminiscence which is exaggerated but not altogether untrue:

I was editing the "Messenger" . . . when one day, probably in the latter part of 1848, on going home for lunch my mother told me that a stranger had called to see me, and had left a message to the effect that for a week past a man calling himself Poe had been wandering around Rocketts (a rather disreputable suburb of Richmond) in a state of intoxication and apparent destitution, and that his friends, if he had any, ought to look after him. I immediately took a carriage and drove down to Rocketts, and spent the afternoon in a vain search . . . . Ten days, perhaps, had passed, and in the press of occupation the matter had entirely gone from my mind, when on a certain morning a person whom I had never seen before entered the office, asked if I was Mr. Thompson, and then said, "My name is Poe," without further introduction or explanation. . . . He was unmistakably a gentleman of education and refinement, with the indescribable marks of genius in his face, which was of almost marble whiteness. He was dressed with perfect neatness; but one could see signs of poverty in the well-worn clothes, though his manner betrayed no consciousness of the fact. . . .
Poe was not what is called "a regular drinker," but he was what is worse, a most irregular one, the desire for stimulants seeming to seize him like an attack of madness which he was powerless to resist. . . . After a month, perhaps, of total abstinence, he would be "off" for a week . . . . Once I found him in a saloon called "The Alhambra," frequented by gamblers and sporting men. He was mounted on a marble-top table, declaiming passages from his then unpublished [*sic*] "Eureka" to a motley crowd, to whom it was as unintelligible as so much Hebrew (quoted by Dimmock, p. 316).

The "Rocketts," a wharf district on the James River, is luridly described in Thompson's 9 November 1849 letter to E. H. N. Patterson, which places Poe at "the residence of Mr. John MacKenzie" (Quinn, pp. 569–70). If Poe did not stay with the Mackenzie family, who had adopted his sister Rosalie, perhaps he shared "bachelor lodgings" with Hugh Pleasants, editor of the *Richmond Whig* (asserted by Woodberry, 2:271, and Phillips, 2:1306, 1310–12).]

AUGUST? Poe challenges John M. Daniel, the young editor of the *Semi-Weekly Examiner*, to a duel (Poe to Mrs. Clemm, 28?–29? August 1849).

[The duel, which never took place, was probably related to Poe's problems with alcohol and money (cf. the *Examiner's* 19 January 1849 notice of his engagement to Mrs. Whitman). Several days after Poe's death Daniel wrote: "Thousands have seen him [Poe] drunk in the streets of this city. In all his visits save the last, he was in a state approaching mania. Whenever he tasted alchohol he seldom stopt drinking it so long as he was able. . . . His taste for drink was a simple disease—no source of pleasure nor of excitement" (*Examiner*, 19 October 1849).]

The "Rocketts," Richmond's wharf district
Virginia State Library

AUGUST? Mrs. Jane Clark, who had met Poe in 1835 during his *Messenger* editorship, recalls: "When in Richmond he [Poe] generally stayed with the Mackenzies at *Duncan Lodge* . . . . One day he came in with his sister [Rosalie] and two of the Mackenzies and stopped with me. There were some other people present, and he read *The Raven* for us. He shut out the daylight and read by an astral lamp" (quoted by Weiss [1907], pp. 159–64; see also *W*, 1:222–23, and Mabbott [1969], 1:564; for "Duncan Lodge," see Scott [1941], pp. 215–17).

2 AUGUST. PHILADELPHIA. The *North American* briefly notices *Eureka* (Pollin [1980], p. 28).

3 AUGUST. NEW YORK. The *Daily Tribune* reviews *Eureka*: "This is one of the most remarkable books we have read in a long time. As a poem, it has the quality of a bold and exhaustless force of imagination; as an essay on the Material and Spiritual Universe, which it would more properly be termed, it is marked with the keenest analysis and the most singular ingenuity." Poe's 3 February lecture on "The Universe" has been "wrought out into a more perfect shape, with some additional illustrations. . . . The tenacity with which he pursues the subject along the farthest brink of finite knowledge, and the daring with which he throws aside all previous systems of philosophers and theologians, constitute the chief merit of the book. . . . We do not admire, however, the attempt at humor, in his description of the contents of a bottle floating in the *Mare tenebrarum*; it degrades the high aim with which the work sets out." Recommending *Eureka* to "all who take an interest in the subject," the *Tribune* excerpts from Poe's conclusion his "wild conjecture" equating "the Heart Divine" with that of mankind itself.

3 AUGUST. The *Evening Post* contains Mrs. Locke's "The True Poet" a nine-stanza poem addressed to Poe and dated "Wamesit Cottage, June 1st" (Reilly [1972], pp. 209–10, 219).

5 AUGUST. WESTFORD, MASSACHUSETTS. Bardwell Heywood writes Miss Annie Sawyer in Lowell, alluding to Mrs. Locke's infatuation with Poe (Coburn, p. 469).

6 AUGUST. NEW YORK. Charles F. Briggs writes Rufus W. Griswold, furnishing information on his career: "Poe said, in his absurd ['Literati'] sketch of me, that 'Harry Franco' was published in the Knickerbocker, but not a line of it was ever published in that Magazine" (Griswold [1898], pp. 240–42).

12 AUGUST. The *Home Journal* reviews *Eureka*:

In the spirit of bold speculation and ideal thought, Mr. Poe has undertaken, in the little treatise before us, to expound a theory of the universe. He begins by repudiating the idea that the arcana of nature are to be completely explored by induction. He recognizes the intuitive and unconscious process as the source of discovery . . . . In a word, he believes in a kind of *scientific inspiration* . . . . Mr. Poe recognizes but two absolute principles in the universe—attraction and repulsion. He assumes a unit or particle as the germ of all subsequent creation, and imagines an innate power—which he identifies with divine volition—to have projected from this atom an infinity of other atoms into space, and that gravitation is only an attempt on the part of those to return to their central unity.

Eureka is "not a demonstrative so much as a suggestive work," which probably contains "as much phantasy as fact." The book has "brilliant rhetorical passages," but reveals "no great novelty in the scientific ideas advanced." It shares "a certain correspondence of tone" with Chambers' *Vestiges of Creation* and Swedenborg's writings on the Infinite.

12 AUGUST. PHILADELPHIA. In the *John-Donkey* Thomas Dunn English comments: "GREAT LITERARY CRASH. We learn that a row of shelves, occupying one side of the publishing house of our friend WILEY [Putnam], broke down on Saturday, with a tremendous crash, which startled the clerks from their afternoon naps, and made the worthy publisher himself look up from his ledger. . . . It appears that a new porter, not yet acquainted with the specific gravity of the various American authors, had imprudently piled the entire edition of POE'S new poem 'Eureka,' upon these shelves. It is only wonderful, considering the immense ponderosity of the burden, that not only the shelves, but the whole building did not come to the ground."

19 AUGUST. LONDON. The *Athenaeum* lists *Eureka* under "New American Books" (Pollin [1975a], p. 28; [1980], p. 27).

23, 30 AUGUST. OQUAWKA, ILLINOIS. The *Oquawka Spectator* reprints "The Fall of the House of Usher" in two installments, identifying Poe as the author (McElroy, p. 257; Mabbott [1978], 2:397).

26 AUGUST. NEW YORK. The *Gazette of the Union* favorably notices *Eureka* (Pollin [1975a], p. 29; [1980], p. 28).

LATE AUGUST. FORDHAM. Mrs. Clemm apparently sees Poe's name on a list of persons having uncollected letters at the West Farms post office. She forwards the letter, containing the stanzas Mrs. Whitman transcribed early in the month, to Richmond (Poe to Whitman, 1 October).

SUMMER. PROVIDENCE? Miss Anne C. Lynch gives Mrs. Whitman her version of the early 1846 scandal involving Poe's handling of Mrs. Elizabeth F. Ellet's love letters (Whitman to J. H. Ingram, 11 February 1874, Miller [1979], pp. 20–21).

LATE SUMMER. NEW YORK. John Sartain, the engraver, and William Sloanaker, the former business manager of *Graham's Magazine*, purchase the *Union Magazine* from its publisher James L. DeGraw for $5,000 (Sartain, pp. 218–19).

[The editor Caroline M. Kirkland wrote Charles S. Francis from London on 7 September: "My little world has been turned upside down, as I hear—the *Union* is dissolved for *Sartain*!" (Derby, p. 582). From the beginning of the new volume, in January 1849, the monthly was published in Philadelphia as *Sartain's Union Magazine*.]

BEFORE SEPTEMBER? FORDHAM. Annie Richmond visits Mrs. Clemm (Bardwell Heywood to Miss Sawyer, 2 October).

SEPTEMBER. NEW YORK. In the "Editor's Table" of the *Knickerbocker Magazine*, Lewis Gaylord Clark scoffs at a correspondent "who has been reading '*Poe on the Creation.*' "

SEPTEMBER. RICHMOND. The *Southern Literary Messenger* contains Poe's review of Mrs. Lewis' *The Child of the Sea and Other Poems*, in which he expands his favorable advance notice published in the August *Democratic Review*.

2 SEPTEMBER. ATHENS, GEORGIA. The *Southern Literary Gazette* publishes a 24 August letter from a correspondent in Lake George, New York, who discusses *Eureka*: "It is a discourse on the system of the universe on this thesis:—'In the original unity of the first thing lies the secondary cause of all things, with the germ of their inevitable annihilation.' I do not profess, at least in the present state of the thermometer, to be equal to the agitation of this subject. . . . The admirers of the author's tales, which are some of the most original publications the country has produced, should procure a copy."

BEFORE 5 SEPTEMBER. RICHMOND. Poe receives the letter Mrs. Sarah Helen Whitman mailed from Providence in early August, containing only her unsigned verses quoting the phrase "*Beauty which is Hope*" from the manuscript poem he sent her around 1 June. Although Poe had intended on this "*very day*" to leave "on a tour"—presumably to promote the *Stylus* in the South—he decides instead to return to the North and seek Mrs. Whitman's acquaintance (Poe to Whitman, 1 October).

5 SEPTEMBER. NEW YORK. Using the pseudonym "Edward S. T. Grey," Poe writes Mrs. Whitman in Providence: "Being engaged in making a collection of autographs of the most distinguished American authors, I am, of course, anxious to procure your own, and if you would so far honor me as to reply, however briefly, to this note, I would take it as a *very especial* favor" (L, 2:379).

[Mrs. Whitman later wrote this explanation on the letter: "Sent by E. A. P. under an assumed name in order to ascertain if [I was] in Providence."]

7 SEPTEMBER. AUGUSTA, MAINE. The *Maine Farmer* reprints "The Gold-Bug" (Mabbott [1978], 3:806).

12 SEPTEMBER. RICHMOND. In the *Semi-Weekly Examiner* John M. Daniel notices the September *Southern Literary Messenger*: "There is also in this number a review of Mrs. Lewis' Poems, from the pen of Edgar Poe. We are bound to say, the article is a very *poor* one; but still it is from Poe himself, and he is a great man."

12 SEPTEMBER. NEW YORK. William Cullen Bryant replies to a letter from his friend Richard Henry Dana, an admirer of Poe's poetry: "You have much to say of Mr. P., of whom I think very well in many respects, but who has some peculiarities in his character which show it, perhaps, not to be quite a healthy one. I shall be glad to be useful to him in any way; but how can you, who know me, ask me to *get* acquainted with anybody? I do not know that I ever got acquainted with anybody of set purpose in my life" (C. H. Brown, p. 320, or Godwin, 2:37–38).

13 SEPTEMBER. OQUAWKA, ILLINOIS. The *Oquawka Spectator* reprints Poe's poem "Lenore," giving it the title "Dirge" (McElroy, pp. 257–58; Mabbott [1969], 1:334).

15 SEPTEMBER. NEW YORK. Miss Maria J. McIntosh writes Mrs. Whitman in Providence: "This letter will be handed to you by Mr Edgar A Poe. He is already so well known to you that any thing more than the announcement of his name would be an impertinence from me. I feel much obliged to Mr Poe for permitting me thus to associate myself with an incident so agreeable to both of you, as I feel persuaded your first meeting will prove" (RPB–W).

BEFORE 20 SEPTEMBER. POTTSVILLE, PENNSYLVANIA. Eli Bowen, the former editor of the *Columbia Spy*, writes Poe. He is now editing the *Miner's Journal*, a weekly newspaper in Pottsville; he invites Poe to furnish its New York correspondence. Bowen's friend Dr. Samuel A. Whitaker of Phoenixville, Pennsylvania, would like to have a copy of "The Raven" in the author's hand (Bowen to Whitaker, 25 September; Poe to Bowen, 18 October).

CA. 20 SEPTEMBER. FORDHAM. Poe replies to Bowen, enclosing a copy of "The Raven" inscribed to Dr. Whitaker. Poe inquires whether Bowen could join him in issuing the *Stylus*; he apparently discusses his sketch "Landor's Cottage," which might not be suitable for the *Miner's Journal* (Poe to Bowen, 18 October; facsimile of "Raven" manuscript in Gimbel, pp. 167–68).

20 SEPTEMBER. Poe writes Charles Fenno Hoffman, editor of the *Literary World*, protesting the unsigned review of *Eureka* in the 29 July issue. The reviewer has distorted Poe's text by asserting that he endorses "*guessing*" as a means of ascertaining truth: "What I *really* say is this:—That there is no absolute *certainty* either in the Aristotelian or Baconian process—that, for this reason, neither Philosophy . . . has a right to sneer at that seemingly imaginative process called Intuition (by which the great Kepler attained his laws;) since 'Intuition,' after all, 'is but the conviction arising from those *in*ductions or *de*ductions of which the processes are so shadowy as to escape our consciousness, elude our reason or defy our capacity of expression.' " A "second misrepresentation" is the suggestion that Poe is largely indebted to Laplace: "The *ground* covered by the great French astronomer compares with that covered by my theory, as a bubble compares with the ocean on which it floats." The young "Student of Theology" who wrote the review has also misquoted and distorted Poe's references to God: "Were these 'misrepresentations' . . . made for any less serious a purpose than that of branding my book as 'impious' and myself as a 'pantheist,' . . . I would have permitted their dishonesty to pass unnoticed, through pure contempt for the boyishness—for the *turn-down-shirt-collar-ness* of their tone" (*L*, 2:379–82).

[Hoffman did not publish Poe's letter protesting Hopkins' review. Mrs. Shew later observed: "the description of 'the turn down shirt collar' was so like the artistic habit of dress of Mr. Hopkins when he was a theological student" (16 May 1875 letter to J. H. Ingram, Miller [1977], p. 141).]

21 SEPTEMBER. PROVIDENCE. Poe calls on Mrs. Whitman at her home, 76 Benefit Street, presenting Miss McIntosh's 15 September letter of introduction (Whitman to R. H. Stoddard, 30 September 1872, Stoddard [1884], p. 156).

21? SEPTEMBER? Poe gives Mrs. Whitman the Wiley and Putnam editions of *The Raven and Other Poems* and his *Tales*, bound together in one cloth volume with this inscription on the flyleaf: "To Mrs Sarah Helen Whitman—from the most devoted of her friends. Edgar A Poe" (Wakeman, item 948; cf. Miller [1979], pp. 122–23).

21? SEPTEMBER? Poe gives Mrs. Whitman a complete set of the *Broadway Journal*. In her presence he goes through the two bound volumes and initials the more important of his unsigned contributions with a penciled "P" (volumes in CSmH; Hull, p. 518; Miller [1979], p. 22).

22? SEPTEMBER. In the morning Poe and Mrs. Whitman visit the Athenaeum library. She asks him whether he ever read "Ulalume," an unsigned poem in the *American Review* for December 1847: "To my infinite surprise, he told me that he himself was the author. Turning to a bound volume of the *Review* which was in the alcove where we were sitting, he wrote his name at the bottom" (Whitman to J. H. Ingram, 10 April 1874, Miller [1979], pp. 116–17; see also p. 243).

22? SEPTEMBER. Poe and Mrs. Whitman call at Anna Blackwell's hotel, leaving an invitation for her "to join a party of friends to meet him that evening" (Whitman to Ingram, 14 February 1875, Miller [1979], p. 256; see also p. 483).

22? SEPTEMBER. In the afternoon Miss Blackwell sends a note to Mrs. Whitman: "I regret very much, my dear friend, that I did not have the pleasure of seeing you & Mr Poe this morning, especially as I am, as usual, so far from well, that I do not think it probable I can avail myself of yr kind invitation for this evening. . . . What about the 'garden of roses' & are the flowers still blooming? I begin to feel *on the wing*; my passage on board the 'Sarah Land' being engaged" (RPB–W).

[Miss Blackwell was to return to England in a few weeks. Her allusion to roses indicates that she had been permitted to read the unpublished poem Poe sent Mrs. Whitman around 1 June. The second "To Helen" depicts "an enchanted garden" of a thousand roses in which Mrs. Whitman is said to have been standing when Poe first glimpsed her.]

22? SEPTEMBER. In the evening Poe is introduced to Mrs. Whitman's friends at her home. One of the guests is probably her neighbor William J. Pabodie, an attorney who is a minor poet.

[Mrs. J. K. Barney, another friend, left a reminiscence which may refer to this occasion: "Poe and Mrs. Whitman sat across the room from each other. . . . All [present] were drawn toward Poe, whose eyes were gleaming and whose utterance was most eloquent. His eyes were fixed on Mrs. Whitman. . . . Of a sudden the company perceived that Poe and Helen were greatly agitated. Simultaneously both arose from their chairs and walked toward the center of the room. Meeting, he held her in his arms, kissed her; they stood for a moment, then he led her to her seat. There was a dead silence through all this strange proceeding" (Phillips, 2:1315–16).]

23? SEPTEMBER. Poe tells Mrs. Whitman of his early life in Richmond, discussing John Allan, Mrs. Stanard, and Elmira Royster, now Mrs. Shelton (Whitman letters to Mrs. Clemm in *W*, 17:422–30, or Quinn and Hart, pp. 41–49, and to J. H. Ingram in Miller [1979], pp. 95, 104).

23? SEPTEMBER. Poe and Mrs. Whitman visit the Swan Point Cemetery on the outskirts of Providence, overlooking the Seekonk River. Here she listens to his proposal of marriage: "he endeavored . . . to persuade me that my influence and my presence would have power to lift his life out of the torpor of despair which had weighed upon him, and give an inspiration to his genius, of which he had as yet given no token. Notwithstanding the eloquence with which he urged upon me his wishes and his hopes, I knew too well that I could not exercise over him the power which he ascribed to me. I was, moreover, wholly dependent on my mother [Mrs. Anna Power], and her life was bound up in mine" (Whitman to R. H. Stoddard, 30 September 1872, Stoddard [1884], 1:156; see also Phillips, 2:1317, and Varner [1940], pp. 301–03).

24? SEPTEMBER. Mrs. Whitman recalls: "In bidding him [Poe] farewell, I promised to write to him & explain to him many things which I could not impart to him in conversation" (23 March 1874 letter to Ingram, Miller [1979], p. 90).

[Poe seems to have parted with Mrs. Whitman on Sunday, 24 September; he did not leave Providence that evening, because the steamboat to New York did not operate on Sundays (advertisements for service, Providence *Evening Transcript*, 20 September and later).]

25 SEPTEMBER. In the morning Poe revisits the Swan Point Cemetery alone; at 6:00 PM he boards the regular mail train to Stonington, Connecticut, where he transfers to Captain Richard Peck's steamboat *Connecticut*, bound for New York (schedule in today's *Evening Transcript*).

[Poe recalled this day in his 18 October letter to Mrs. Whitman: "I cannot explain to you—since I cannot myself comprehend—the feeling which urged me not to see you again before going—not to bid you a second time *farewell*. I had a sad foreboding at heart."]

25 SEPTEMBER. POTTSVILLE, PENNSYLVANIA. Eli Bowen writes Dr. Samuel A. Whitaker in Phoenixville, Pennsylvania: "I have the pleasure of transmitting to you, a copy of *The Raven* in the handwriting of the author. I received it on Saturday [23 September], and having taken the liberty of

showing it to several of my friends, the paper has become somewhat ruffled—nevertheless you can make it out" (PP–G).

BEFORE 30 SEPTEMBER. PROVIDENCE. Mrs. Whitman writes Poe, assuring him of her affection and regard, but giving several reasons for not accepting his proposal of marriage: "You will, perhaps, attempt to convince me that my person is agreeable to you—that my countenance interests you:— but in this respect I am so variable that I should inevitably disappoint you if you hoped to find in me to-morrow the same aspect which won you to-day. And, again, although my reverence for your intellect and my admiration of your genius make me feel like a *child* in your presence, you are not, perhaps, aware that I am many years [six years] older than yourself. I *fear* you do not know it, and that if you *had* known it you would not have felt for me as you do." Mrs. Whitman's health makes it unwise for her to marry: she has a weak heart and a nervous temperament. "I find that I cannot now tell you all that I promised. I can only say to you that had I youth and health and beauty, I would live for you and die with you. *Now*, were I to allow myself to love you, I could only enjoy a bright, brief hour of rapture and die" (quoted in Poe's 1 October reply).

30 SEPTEMBER. FORDHAM. On Saturday evening Poe receives Mrs. Whitman's letter (stated in Poe's second letter to her, 18 October).

1 OCTOBER. On "Sunday Night" Poe replies to Mrs. Whitman, repeating the passionate declaration of love he made during their "walk in the cemetery." He recounts the history of his growing awareness of her, beginning with the "few casual words" about her spoken by Anne C. Lynch in early 1845, and ending with his receipt of her verses in Richmond last month. Poe assures Mrs. Whitman (an ardent believer in predestination and spiritualism) that he gradually came to realize that their destinies were "interwoven" by "Fate," asking her to reflect upon the almost miraculous "coincidences" apparent in their several exchanges of unsigned poems. He recalls their first meeting on 21 September: "As you entered the room, pale, timid, hesitating, and evidently oppressed at heart; as your eyes rested appealingly, for one brief moment, upon mine, I felt, for the first time in my life, and tremblingly acknowledged, the existence of spiritual influences altogether out of the reach of the reason. I saw that you were *Helen—my* Helen—the Helen of a thousand dreams." Quoting Mrs. Whitman's objections that she is older than he and not in good health, Poe asserts: "I am older than you; and if illness and sorrow have made you seem older than you are—is not all this the best of reasons for my loving you the more? . . . Long-continued nervous disorder . . . will give rise to *all* the symptoms of heart-disease and so deceive the most skillful

physicians—as even in my own case they were deceived. . . . My love—my faith—should instil into your bosom a praeternatural calm. You would rest from care—from all worldly agitation. You would get better, and finally well" (L, 2:382–91).

AFTER 1? OCTOBER. Poe writes Annie Richmond in Lowell: "This note will be handed you by Mrs Stella Anna Lewis, of whose poetic genius you will remember I spoke so much at length in my late lecture at Lowell. . . . I feel assured that you have but to know her personally to be as proud of her friendship as, unquestionably, she must and will be of your own" (L, 2:398–99).

AFTER 1? OCTOBER. Poe gives Mrs. Lewis a letter of introduction addressed to Jane Ermina Locke in Lowell. He requests Mrs. Locke to show Mrs. Lewis "every attention" (L, 2:398).

AFTER 1 OCTOBER? NEW YORK. The *Weekly Universe* publishes a letter by Poe protesting Hopkins' attack on *Eureka* in the 29 July *Literary World* (Eveleth to Poe, 3 July 1849; cf. Poe to Hoffman, 20 September 1848).

2 OCTOBER. WESTFORD, MASSACHUSETTS. Bardwell Heywood writes Miss Annie Sawyer in Lowell: "Since writing you before [on 5 August] I have seen Mrs. Locke and laid myself under solemn and everlasting obligation not to divulge what I know of herself and Edgar A. Poe. . . . I will tell you this much. You are aware that Mr. Poe is a widower. In a singular way (I wish I could tell you how) he got the impression that Mrs. L. was a widow. A correspondence was commenced and kept up which was 'touching certainly,' neither party ever having seen the other. At length he came to Lowell called upon Mrs. L. at Wamesit Cottage.—'Nuf said! She has a husband and three or four [five] children!!" Poe's 10 July lecture in Lowell was "a brilliant affair." Afterwards Bardwell's sister Annie Richmond entertained him at her home: " 'Twas then that I learned something of his history. . . . He spoke of his wife in a most eloquent and touching manner, the tears running down his cheeks in torrents. Spoke of her as beautiful beyond description, as lovely beyond conception, and my sister, who has since visited his mother [Mrs. Clemm] in N. Y., says she (Virginia) is represented as being almost an angel on earth" (Coburn, pp. 470–71).

3 OCTOBER. FORDHAM. On "Tuesday Morning" Poe adds this postscript to his 1 October letter to Mrs. Whitman: "I beg you to believe, dear Helen, that I replied to your letter *immediately* upon its receipt; but a most unusual storm, up to this moment, precludes all access to the City." He

encloses a lock of his hair in the letter, which he apparently mails later in the day (*L*, 2:390; see also Miller [1979], p. 156).

7 OCTOBER. NEW YORK. The *Literary World* carries a valedictory by Charles Fenno Hoffman, whose editorship ended with the 30 September issue. The weekly is now owned and edited by Evert A. Duyckinck and his younger brother George L. Duyckinck.

AFTER 10 OCTOBER. PROVIDENCE. Mrs. Whitman replies to Poe. While she admits that she could sense the love embodied in his letter, she gives additional reasons for declining marriage, citing her financial dependence on her mother and apparently her responsibilities toward her mother and her unmarried younger sister, Susan Anna Power. She inquires why so many persons have formed unfavorable opinions of Poe's character: "How often I have heard men and even women say of you—'He has great intellectual power, but *no* principle—*no* moral sense' " (quoted in Poe's 18 October reply; cf. Miss Lynch's letters to Whitman, 31 January, 21 February, and 10 March).

BEFORE 14 OCTOBER. RICHMOND. The *Southern Literary Messenger* for October contains the first half of "The Rationale of Verse."

14 OCTOBER. NEW YORK. The *Home Journal* reviews the *Messenger*: "The original prose articles are, first—'The Rationale of Verse,' by Edgar A. Poe, who justly remarks that there is a prevailing ignorance upon this subject, and he treats it in this article with much analytical acumen. A reference to the carefully finished, free and original style of the 'Raven,' will furnish a practical illustration of his theory. The admirable variety, pause and cadence of the versification of that poem, could only have emanated from a mind well acquainted with the art."

17 OCTOBER. RICHMOND. John R. Thompson, the *Messenger*'s editor, replies to a letter from Philip Pendleton Cooke:

Poe is not in Richmond. He remained here about 3 weeks, horribly drunk and discoursing "Eureka" every night to the audiences of the Bar Rooms. His friends tried to get him sober and set him to work but to no effect and were compelled at last to reship him to New York. I was very anxious for him to write something for me, while he remained here, but his lucid intervals were so brief and infrequent that it was quite impossible. "The Rationale of Verse" I took—more as an act of charity than anything else, for though exhibiting great acquaintance with the subject, it is altogether too bizarre and too technical for the general reader. Poe is a singular fellow indeed (Quinn, p. 568).

18 OCTOBER. FORDHAM. Poe replies to Mrs. Whitman's second letter. He fears that she does not love him, because she imposed on him "the torture of eight days' silence—of eight days' terrible suspense." Quoting her inquiry about his reputation, Poe declares: "I swear to you that my soul is incapable of dishonor—that, with the exception of occasional follies and excesses which I bitterly lament, but to which I have been driven by intolerable sorrow, and which are hourly committed by others without attracting any notice whatever—I can call to mind no act of my life which would bring a blush to my cheek—or to yours." His enemies have slandered him because he has been an "unscrupulously honest" critic who condemns "the pretensions of ignorance, arrogance, or imbecility," both in literature and in life: "Ah, Helen, I have a hundred friends for every individual enemy—but has it never occurred to you that you do not live *among* my friends? Miss Lynch, Miss Fuller, Miss Blackwell, Mrs Ellet— neither these nor any within their influence, are my friends." Poe had dreaded that Mrs. Whitman might be "in worldly circumstances" superior to his own: "the horror with which . . . I have seen affection made a subject of barter . . . inspired me with the resolution that, under *no* circumstances, would I marry where 'interest,' as the world terms it, could be suspected as, on my part, the object of the marriage." He was actually relieved to learn that Mrs. Whitman is dependent on her mother (*L*, 2:391–98).

18 OCTOBER. Poe replies to a letter from T. L. Dunnell of Providence, who has invited him to deliver a lecture before that city's Franklin Lyceum on 13 December. Poe gladly accepts this "very flattering invitation"; he will arrive in Providence on the appointed day (*L*, 2:391).

18 OCTOBER. Poe writes Eli Bowen, editor of the Pottsville, Pennsylvania, *Miner's Journal*: "About three weeks ago [ca. 20 September] I wrote you quite a long letter, enclosing a MS copy of 'The Raven' and making you a proposition in regard to the establishment of a Magazine—but have received no reply. . . . I have now to say that I am willing to accept your offer about the Correspondence, and will commence whenever you think proper—*provided* you decline the *tour* &c as I suggested" (Ostrom [1974], pp. 533–34).

[The "*tour*" seems to have been Poe's sketch "Landor's Cottage," which describes "a pedestrian tour last summer, through one or two of the river counties of New York."]

AFTER 20 OCTOBER. PROVIDENCE. Before Mrs. Whitman has had time to reply to Poe's 18 October letter, she receives a visit from him. Poe explains that he is on his way to Lowell, having been invited by some friends there to repeat his lecture on "The Poets and Poetry of America." He urges her to reconsider his proposal of marriage, suggesting that she defer her decision for a week and that she send him an answer at Lowell. She promises to write him there (Whitman to R. H. Stoddard, 30 September 1872, Stoddard [1884], 1:156; and Whitman to J. H. Ingram, 25 October 1875, Miller [1979], p. 346).

Poe shows Mrs. Whitman the manuscript of his lecture, giving her two pages of it which contain a favorable evaluation of her poetry as well as that of Miss Lynch and Mrs. Osgood (Whitman to Mrs. Clemm, 3 February [1850 or later], Quinn and Hart, pp. 39–40; see also Miller [1979], pp. 36, 155, 243, 466).

[Poe did not repeat his lecture in Lowell. According to Mrs. Whitman, the excitement attending the 1848 Presidential election made its delivery impractical (Stoddard [1884], 1:156–57; Miller [1979], p. 463).]

AFTER 20 OCTOBER. LOWELL. Upon his arrival in Lowell Poe takes lodging in "Wamesit Cottage," the home of Jane Ermina Locke and her husband John G. Locke; he soon moves to Annie Richmond's house on Ames Street, thereby permanently alienating Mrs. Locke (Miller [1979], pp. 311–12, 346).

[On 18 February 1849 Poe wrote Mrs. Richmond: "I quarrelled with the Lockes *solely* on your account & Mr R[ichmond]'s—It was obviously my interest to keep in with them, & moreover they had rendered me some services which entitled them to my gratitude . . . . It was only when I heard them declare that through their patronage alone, you were admitted into society—that your husband was everything despicable—that it would ruin my mother [Mrs. Clemm] even to enter your doors—it was only when such insults were offered *to you*, whom I sincerely & most purely loved, & to Mr R. whom I had every reason to like & respect, that I arose & left their house & incurred the unrelenting vengeance of that worst of all fiends, 'a woman scorned.' "]

25 OCTOBER. NEW YORK. George P. Putnam publishes *A Fable for Critics*, a verse satire on American authors containing this estimate of Poe:

> There comes Poe, with his raven, like Barnaby Rudge,
> Three-fifths of him genius and two-fifths sheer fudge,
> Who talks like a book of iambs and pentameters,
> In a way to make people of common sense damn metres,
> Who has written some things quite the best of their kind,
> But the heart somehow seems all squeezed out by the mind.

[Although issued anonymously, the poem was widely known to be by James Russell Lowell. The title page carried the date of 31 October; but according to Scudder, 1:249–50, Putnam released the book on 25 October. It was advertised for sale in the *Literary World* of 28 October.]

LATE OCTOBER. WESTFORD, MASSACHUSETTS. Poe visits the farm of Annie Richmond's parents, the Heywoods. He discusses *Eureka* with John B. Willard, a Unitarian minister, and other members of the Westford Reading Circle. Bardwell Heywood recalls: "In October he [Poe] spent three days with us, during which time the reading circle met at our house. I then had the pleasure of hearing Mr. Poe and Mr. Willard converse. It was a treat, I assure you. Mr. W. sustained himself admirably and showed himself deeply read, though he had such an antagonist as he does not often meet. . . . Mr. Poe recited some of his best poems before the circle, among which were 'The Raven,' 'Eulalamme,' etc. . . . I said he promised to read 'Eureka' aloud at Westford. So he did, but what with riding, walking and climbing rugged hills, we found no time to sit down and read" (24 December letter to Miss Sawyer).

Sarah H. Heywood recalls:

During the day he [Poe] strolled off by himself, "to look at the hills," he said. I remember standing in the low porch with my sister [Annie Richmond], as we saw him returning, and as soon as he stepped from the dusty street on to the green sward which sloped from our door, he removed his hat, and came to us with uncovered head, his eyes seeming larger and more luminous than ever with the exhilaration of his walk. . . .

My memory photographs him again, sitting before an open wood fire, in the early autumn evening, gazing intently into the glowing coal, holding the hand of a dear friend—"Annie"—while for a long time no one spoke, and the only sound was the ticking of the tall old clock in the corner of the room. . . .

The next morning I was to go to school, and before I returned he would be gone. I went to say "Good-bye" to him, when, with that ample gracious courtesy of his which included even the rustic school-girl, he said, "I will walk with you" (Ingram, pp. 390–91; also in Gill, pp. 211–13).

LATE OCTOBER OR EARLY NOVEMBER? LOWELL. Poe writes Mrs. Clemm at Fordham: "God bless you my own dear mother. I do not think it would be advisable for you to write, unless there is some *very* great necessity—for I might not get your letter" (manuscript fragment printed in Ostrom [1974], pp. 534–35).

NOVEMBER. NEW YORK. The *Union Magazine* publishes Poe's second "To Helen" under the heading "To—— —— ——," chosen by him to represent "Sarah Helen Whitman."

NOVEMBER. BOSTON. The *Pictorial National Library* reprints Poe's tale "The Black Cat" (Heartman and Canny, pp. 239–40; Mabbott [1978], 3:849).

CA. NOVEMBER. RICHMOND. John R. Thompson writes Poe at Fordham, soliciting a contribution for the January 1849 number of the *Southern Literary Messenger* (Poe's 7 December reply).

1 NOVEMBER. PHILADELPHIA. The *Dollar Newspaper* reprints "The Raven" (Heartman and Canny, p. 181).

CA. 2 NOVEMBER. PROVIDENCE. Mrs. Whitman sends Poe an indecisive reply to his proposal of marriage. She recalls: "I delayed writing from day to day, unwilling to say the word which might separate us forever, & unable to give him the answer which he besought me to accord him. At last I wrote a brief note, which I felt afterwards must have perplexed & agitated him. He wrote by return mail to say that he should be at Providence on the following evening" (Whitman to J. H. Ingram, 25 October 1875, Miller [1979], pp. 346–47; cf. Stoddard [1884], 1:156).

3 NOVEMBER. LOWELL. On Friday Poe replies briefly to Mrs. Whitman, promising to call on her Saturday evening (Poe to Whitman, 7 November).

3–4 NOVEMBER. Annie Richmond comforts Poe, who is deeply depressed. She advises him to marry Mrs. Whitman, telling him what to say when he sees the older woman. Poe extracts a promise from Annie that she will come to him if he should be near death (Poe to Annie, 16 November).

4 NOVEMBER. PROVIDENCE. The *Daily Journal* reports: "The spirited young men of the Franklin Lyceum, announce a brilliant course of lectures for the coming year." The speakers will include Daniel Webster, Oliver Wendell Holmes, Edgar A. Poe, and "others of high reputation."

4 NOVEMBER. Poe arrives in Providence but does not call on Mrs. Whitman. He spends "a long, long, hideous night of despair" in a hotel room (Poe to Annie, 16 November).

[Quinn, p. 592, observed that Poe "loved 'Annie' as a man loves a woman, while he loved Helen Whitman as a poet loves a poetess . . . . Many a perfectly normal man has approached his engagement or his wedding with one woman, whom he loves well enough to marry, clouded by his knowledge that if another woman were free, he would be trying to win her instead."]

"Ultima Thule" daguerreotype of Poe, 9 November 1848
Richard Gimbel Collection, Philadelphia Free Library

"Ultima Thule": Enlarged
(from the copy formerly owned by Sarah Helen Whitman)
American Antiquarian Society

"Whitman" Daguerreotype of Poe, 13 November 1848
(daguerreotype in case photographed by John Miller Documents)
Special Collections, Brown University Library

"Whitman": Enlarged and reversed
(restoration by Preservation Photography, Savannah, Georgia)

"Stella" daguerreotype of Poe
University of Virginia Library

"Annie" daguerreotype of Poe
J. Paul Getty Museum

"Pratt" daguerreotype of Poe, late September 1849
(from the copy formerly owned by John R. Thompson)
Woodberry's *Life of Poe*

"Pratt": Detail from the Thompson copy
(restoration by Preservation Photography, Savannah, Georgia)
Columbia University Library

5 NOVEMBER. BOSTON. In his 16 November letter to Annie, Poe describes this day:

I arose [in Providence] & endeavored to quiet my mind by a rapid walk in the cold, keen air—but all *would* not do—the demon tormented me still. Finally I procured two ounces of laud[a]num & without returning to my Hotel, took the cars back to Boston. When I arrived, I wrote you a letter, in which I opened my whole heart to you—to *you*—my Annie, whom I so madly, so distractedly love—I told you how my struggles were more than I could bear—how my soul revolted from saying the words which were to be said [to Mrs. Whitman]—and that not even for your dear sake, could I bring myself to say them. I then reminded you of that holy promise, which was the last I exacted from you in parting—the promise that, under all circumstances, you would come to me on my bed of death—I implored you to come *then*—mentioning the place where I should be found in Boston—Having written this letter, I swallowed about half the laud[a]num & hurried to the Post-Office—intending not to take the rest until I saw you—for, I did not doubt for one moment, that *my own* Annie would keep her sacred promise—But I had not calculated on the strength of the laudanum, for, before I reached the Post Office my reason was entirely gone, & the letter was never put in. . . . A friend was at hand, who aided & (if it can be called saving) saved me.

7 NOVEMBER. PROVIDENCE. Early on Tuesday morning Poe visits Mrs. Whitman's home. She recalls: "I felt quite unable to see him, having passed a restless & troubled night on account of his failure to be in Providence on Saturday evening, as he had purposed. I sent word to him by a servant that I would see him at noon. He replied [to the servant] that he had an engagement & must see me at once" (Whitman to Ingram, 25 October 1875, Miller [1979], p. 347).

Poe sends Mrs. Whitman a note: "I have *no* engagements, but am *very* ill—so much so that I must go home, if possible—but if you say 'stay', I will try & do so. If you cannot see me—write me *one word* to say that you *do* love me and that, *under all circumstances*, you will be mine. Remember that these coveted words you have never yet spoken . . . . It was not in my power to be here on Saturday as I proposed, or I would undoubtedly have kept my promise" (*L*, 2:399–400).

Mrs. Whitman sends Poe a message that she "would meet him in half an hour at the Athen[a]eum" (her annotation on his note; see *L*, 2:531).

Mrs. Whitman recalls her interview with Poe: "He . . . told me that, agitated by my note [of ca. 2 November], he had taken the cars for Providence via Boston, but had on arriving in Providence taken something at a druggists which bewildered him instead of composing him, that he entered the next train for Boston, & remained there ill & depressed until Monday." Poe reproaches Mrs. Whitman "for so long delaying to send the promised letter, & then sending one so vague & illusive [elusive]"; he urges her "to marry him *at once*, and return with him to New York" (Whitman to Ingram, 25 October 1875, Miller [1979], p. 347).

8 NOVEMBER. In the afternoon Mrs. Whitman has a second interview with Poe: "As an additional reason for *delaying* a marriage which, under any circumstances, seemed to all my friends full of evil portents, I read to him some passages from a letter which I had recently received from one of his New York associates. He seemed deeply pained at the result of our interview" (Whitman to G. W. Eveleth, 17 January 1866, Miller [1977], pp. 219–21).

In the evening Poe begins drinking in the barroom of his hotel; he sends Mrs. Whitman "a note of renunciation & farewell." She recalls: "The handwriting showed that it was written in a state of great excitement. . . . I supposed that he had taken the evening train for New York via Stonington . . . [I] passed a night of unspeakable anxiety in thinking what might befall him travelling alone in such a state of mental perturbation" (Whitman to Ingram, 25 October 1875, Miller [1979], p. 348).

9 NOVEMBER. Mrs. Whitman recalls:

A Mr. MacFarlane, who had been very kind to Poe during the night & who had become deeply interested in him, persuaded him in the morning to go with him to the office of Masury & Hartshorn to sit for a daguerreotype. Soon after he left the office, he came alone to my mother's house in a state of wild & delirious excitement, calling upon me to save him from some terrible impending doom.

The tones of his voice were appalling & rang through the house. Never have I heard anything so awful, even to sublimity.

It was long before I could nerve myself to see him. My mother was with him more than two hours before I entered the room. He hailed me as an angel sent to save him from perdition. When my mother requested me to have a cup of strong coffee prepared for him, he clung to me so frantically as to tear away a piece of the muslin dress I wore.

In the afternoon he grew more composed, & my mother sent for Dr. A. H. Okie, who, finding symptoms of cerebral congestion, advised his being taken to the house of his friend Wm. J. Pabodie, where he was kindly cared for (Whitman to Ingram, 25 October 1875, Miller [1979], p. 348; for "Ultima Thule" daguerreotype, see pp. 22, 38, 72, 319–21).

BEFORE 11 NOVEMBER. RICHMOND. The *Southern Literary Messenger* for November contains the second half of "The Rationale of Verse."

11 NOVEMBER. NEW YORK. The *Home Journal* reviews the *Messenger*, noticing "a continuation" of Poe's essay among the "leading prose papers."

11 NOVEMBER. ATHENS, GEORGIA. The *Southern Literary Gazette* reviews the *Messenger*: "Mr. Poe continues the 'Rationale of Verse,' and is out against English *hexameters* without mercy. He thinks [Longfellow's]

'Evangeline' 'very respectable prose,' and nothing else. 'Tis easy to find fault, we know. Can you do better, Mr. Poe?"

BEFORE 13 NOVEMBER. PROVIDENCE. With many misgivings Mrs. Whitman agrees to a "conditional engagement" with Poe. If he completely refrains from drinking, she will try to obtain the consent of her mother, Mrs. Power, "before the end of December." She recalls: "My mother was inflexibly opposed to our union, and being in a pecuniary point of view entirely dependent upon her, I *could* not, if I would, have acted without her concurrence. Many painful scenes occurred during his several visits to Providence in consequence of this opposition" (Whitman to Mrs. Mary E. Hewitt, 27–28 September 1850, Williams, pp. 761–62; see also Stoddard [1884], 1:157–58).

[On 20 March 1874 Mrs. Whitman wrote John Henry Ingram:

I hope you will not think . . . that my family were harsh or ungracious to him [Poe]. They were, *at times*, even ready to place implicit trust in his power to retrieve his destiny. *No* person could be long near him in his healthier moods, without loving him & putting faith in the sweetness & goodness of his nature & feeling that he had a reserved power of self-control that needed only favoring circumstances to bring his fine qualities of heart & mind into perfect equipoise. But after seeing the morbid sensitiveness of his nature & finding how slight a wound could disturb his serenity, how trivial a disappointment could unbalance his whole being, no one could feel assured of his perseverance in the thorny paths of self-denial & endurance. My mother did say more than once in his presence that my death would not be regarded by her so great an evil as my marriage under circumstances of such ominous import (Miller [1979], p. 88).

Mrs. Whitman had been disturbed by Poe's behavior on 9 November, but believed that she might be able to influence him. In her 21 July 1874 letter to Ingram, she stated frankly: "If I had never seen Poe intoxicated, I should never have consented to marry him; had he kept his promise never again to taste wine, I should never have broken the engagement" (Miller [1979], p. 193).]

13 NOVEMBER. Poe has his daguerreotype taken for Mrs. Whitman at the office of Masury & Hartshorn. At 6:00 PM he leaves Providence on the train to Stonington, Connecticut, where he boards the steamer *Massachusetts*, bound for New York. Mrs. Whitman recalls: "An hour or two after he had left the city certain representations were made to my family in relation to the imprudence of the conditional engagement subsisting between us which augmented almost to phrenzy my mother's opposition to the relation. During the painful scenes which followed, I chanced to look toward the western horizon & saw there *Arcturus* shining resplendently

through a rift in the clouds . . . . To my excited imagination everything at that time seemed a portent or an omen. . . . That night, an hour after midnight, I wrote under a strange accession of prophetic exaltation the lines 'To Arcturus' " (16 March 1874 letter to Ingram, Miller [1979], pp. 76–79; train schedules in *Evening Transcript*).

[When Poe was taking leave of Mrs. Whitman, he had spoken "of Arcturus as a star with which he had associated some romantic fancies" (Whitman to Mrs. Hewitt, 27–28 September 1850, Williams, pp. 765–66). Her "To Arcturus," collected in her *Hours of Life, and Other Poems* (1853), reads in part:

> Hast thou not stooped from heaven, fair star! to be
> So near me in this hour of agony?—
> So near—so bright—so glorious, that I seem
> To lie entranced as in some wondrous dream—
> All earthly joys forgot—all earthly fear
> Purged in the light of thy resplendent sphere:
> Gazing upon thee, till thy flaming eye
> Dilates and kindles through the stormy sky;
> While, in its depths withdrawn—far, far away—
> I see the dawn of a diviner day
> (Reilly [1965], pp. 189–90, 233–36).]

14 NOVEMBER. NEW YORK. Poe writes Mrs. Whitman: "My own dearest Helen, *so* kind so true, so generous—so unmoved by all that would have moved one who had been less than angel . . . . I am calm & tranquil & but for a strange shadow of coming evil which haunts me I should be happy. That I am not supremely happy, even when I feel your dear love at my heart, terrifies me. What can this mean? . . . It is 5 o'clock [AM] & the boat is just being made fast to the wharf. I shall start in the train that leaves New York at 7 for Fordham. I write this to show you that I have not *dared* to break my promise to you." In a postscript Poe expresses his gratitude for William J. Pabodie's kindness to him during his illness in Providence (*L*, 2:400, 719–20; Ticknor, p. 95).

16 NOVEMBER. FORDHAM. Poe writes Annie Richmond in Lowell: "So long as I think that you *know* I love you, as no man ever loved woman—so long as I think you comprehend in some measure, the fervor with which I adore you, *so* long, no worldly trouble can ever render me absolutely wretched. But oh, *my darling*, *my* Annie, my own sweet *sister* Annie, my *pure* beautiful angel—*wife* of my soul—to be mine hereafter & *forever in the Heavens*—how shall I explain to you the *bitter*, *bitter* anguish which has tortured me since I left you?" Poe recalls the first two days after he left Lowell, describing his anguished night in a Providence hotel on 4 Novem-

ber and his consumption of laudanum in Boston on 5 November. After he recovered from the laudanum, he returned to Providence:

Here I saw *her* [Mrs. Whitman], & spoke, for *your* sake, the words which you urged me to speak—Ah Annie Annie! *my* Annie!—*is* your heart *so* strong?—is there *no* hope!—is there *none?*—I feel that I *must* die if I persist, & yet, how can I now retract with honor? . . . Think—oh *think* for me—before the words—the vows are spoken, which put yet another terrible *bar* between us . . . . I am at home now with my dear muddie [Mrs. Clemm] who is endeavoring to comfort me—but the sole words which soothe me, are those in which she speaks of "*my Annie*"—she tells me that she has written you, begging you to come on to Fordham—ah beloved Annie, IS IT NOT POSSIBLE? I am so *ill*—so terribly, hopelessly ILL in body and mind, that I feel I CANNOT live, unless I can feel your sweet, gentle, loving hand pressed upon my forehead (*L*, 2:400–04).

16 NOVEMBER. Mrs. Clemm writes Annie:

God has heard my prayers and once more returned my poor, darling Eddy to me. But *how changed*! I scarcely knew him. I was nearly distracted at not hearing from him. . . . I have read his letter to you, and have told him I think it very selfish, to wish you to come; for I know, my darling child, it would be inconvenient. . . . He raved all night about you, but is now more composed. I too am very sick, but will do all I can to cheer and comfort him. . . . Have you heard anything of Mrs. L[ocke] since her tragic performance? I never liked her, and said so from the first (Ingram, p. 394; also in *W*, 17:391–92).

17 NOVEMBER. PROVIDENCE. Mrs. Whitman replies briefly to Poe's 14 November letter. She expresses concern over his health, promising that he will receive a long letter from her on Tuesday, 21 November (Poe to Whitman, 22 November).

18? NOVEMBER. NEW YORK. The *Home Journal* publishes an unsigned poem addressed to Poe (Poe to Mrs. Whitman, 26 November; Mrs. Clemm to Annie Richmond, 28 November or later 1848 and 11 January 1849).

20 NOVEMBER. Poe writes Edward Valentine, the brother of his foster mother Frances Allan, in Richmond: "I call to mind . . . that, during my childhood, you were very kind to me, and, I believe, very fond of me. . . . I venture to throw myself upon your generosity & ask you to lend me $200. With this sum I should be able to take the first steps in an enterprise where there could be no doubt of my success, and which, if successful, would, in one or two years ensure me fortune and very great influence. I refer to the establishment of a Magazine [the *Stylus*] for which I have already a good list of subscribers" (*L*, 2:404).

20 NOVEMBER. Poe writes Valentine's niece, the young Richmond poetess Susan Archer Talley: "If Miss Talley will, upon reading the enclosed letter [to Valentine], seal it and forward it to its address with a word from herself in behalf of the writer, she will confer the greatest of favors upon one who most profoundly respects and admires her genius, tho he cannot as yet boast of her personal acquaintance" (Weiss [1904], p. 1013).

CA. 20 NOVEMBER. PROVIDENCE. Mrs. Whitman writes Poe, enclosing her poem "To Arcturus" and requesting his comments on it. She has arranged for the republication of his "Ulalume" in a Providence newspaper. Although she has been "tortured" by unfavorable reports about Poe's character, these have since been explained to her satisfaction. Their proposed marriage depends entirely on the firmness of his resolve (Poe's 24 November reply).

22 NOVEMBER. The *Daily Journal* reprints "Ulalume," prefacing it with Nathaniel P. Willis' query about its authorship from the New York *Home Journal* of 1 January. The *Daily Journal* observes that a "Southern paper," when reprinting the ballad, wrongly attributed it to Willis: "by way of rendering unto Caesar the things that are Caesar's, we now correct the mistake—which would have been natural enough but for the wide difference of *style* between 'Ulalume' and anything written by Willis. 'Ulalume,' although published anonymously in 'The American Review,' is known to be the composition of EDGAR A. POE."

[At Mrs. Whitman's suggestion, Poe omitted the poem's last stanza in this republication (Miller [1979], p. 98).]

22 NOVEMBER. FORDHAM. Poe writes Mrs. Whitman: "Last Monday [20 November] I received your note, dated Friday [17 November], and promising that on Tuesday [21 November] I should get a long letter from you. It has not yet reached me, but I presume will be at the P.O. [in New York] when I send this in. In the meantime, I write these few words to thank you, from the depths of my heart, for the dear expressions of your note . . . . The terrible excitement under which I suffered, has subsided, and I am as calm as I well could be, remembering what has past. . . . My mother [Mrs. Clemm] was delighted with your wish to be remembered" (L, 2:405).

23 NOVEMBER. Poe writes Sarah H. Heywood in Westford, Massachusetts: "If there is any pity in your heart reply immediately to this letter, & let me know *why* it is, I do not hear from Annie . . . . I wrote her a long letter eight days ago, enclosing one from my mother who wrote again on the 19th[.] Not one word has reached us in reply[;] oh Sarah, if I did not

love your sister, with the *purest* & most unexacting love, I would not dare confide in you—but you do know, how truly—how *purely* I love her . . . . In my wildest dreams, I have never fancied any being so totally lovely—so *good*—so *true*—so *noble* so *pure*—so *virtuous*—her silence fills my whole soul with terror" (*L*, 2:405–06).

BEFORE 24 NOVEMBER. NEW YORK. The *Home Journal* for 25 November contains a letter discussing several American poetesses from "C. M." This correspondent praises Mrs. Sarah J. Hale's "Three Hours," the longest poem in her latest collection, *Three Hours, or the Vigil of Love*. "The idea in one line—in the second part—'The sound, it died in the arms of night,'—has been boldly plagiarized by an American male poet—in a recent production."

["C. M." was probably Caroline May, whose anthology *The American Female Poets* had appeared a few weeks earlier. In Poe's second "To Helen," published in the November *Union Magazine*, "the very roses' odors" are said to have "Died in the arms of the adoring airs."]

24 NOVEMBER. FORDHAM. Poe replies to Mrs. Whitman's letter of ca. 20 November: "all does *not* depend, dear Helen, upon my firmness—all depends upon the sincerity of your love." Quoting her statement that she has been "tortured" by unfounded reports about him, he warns her to beware of Mrs. Elizabeth F. Ellet: "No sooner will Mrs E. hear of my proposals to yourself, than she will set in operation every conceivable chicanery to frustrate me . . . . You will be sure to receive anonymous letters so skillfully contrived as to deceive the most sagacious." Poe describes the controversy in early 1846 involving his handling of Mrs. Ellet's letters to him: "Forgive me that I let these wrongs prey upon me—I did not so bitterly feel them until they threatened to deprive me of you. I confess, too, that the intolerable insults of your mother & sister still rankle at my heart—but for your dear sake I will endeavor to be calm." Mrs. Whitman's "To Arcturus" is "truly beautiful"; Poe suggests several revisions. "When 'Ulalume' appears, cut it out & enclose it:—newspapers seldom reach me." He is forwarding the letter from "C. M." published in this week's *Home Journal*: "The accusation will enable you to see how groundless such accusations *may* be, even when seemingly best founded. Mrs H[ale]'s book was published 3 months ago. You had my poem about the first of June" (*L*, 2:406–09).

BEFORE 25 NOVEMBER. PROVIDENCE. T. L. Dunnell writes Poe, asking him to deliver his lecture before the Franklin Lyceum on 6 December instead of the date originally scheduled, 13 December (Poe to Whitman, 26 November, and to Dunnell, 27 November).

BEFORE 26 NOVEMBER. HARTFORD, CONNECTICUT. Rufus White Griswold reprints "The Raven" in the *New England Weekly Gazette* (Bayless [1934], pp. 69–72).

[This obscure editor is a different individual from Poe's first biographer, the anthologer Rufus Wilmot Griswold. When used elsewhere the name refers to the latter figure.]

26 NOVEMBER. FORDHAM. Poe writes Mrs. Whitman, returning her poem "To Arcturus." He protests her proposed deletion of the two lines depicting "the dawn of a diviner day"; he asks, "is that dawn no longer perceptible?" Poe encloses an unsigned poem addressed to him, requesting her aid in identifying the author: "It is from last Saturday's 'Home Journal.' Somebody sent it to me in M.S." Yesterday he received a letter from T. L. Dunnell: "He says that they have 'lost' their lecturer for the 6th prox. & offers me that night . . . . I cannot be in Providence before the 13th." Rufus White Griswold has recently reprinted "The Raven" in his Hartford newspaper: "I enclose his editorial comments—so that you have quite a budget of enclosures." In a postscript Poe asks Mrs. Whitman to mail him "*as soon as possible*" three articles of his which she will find "among the *critical papers*" he gave her: "The Philosophy of Composition," his critique of Hawthorne in the November 1847 *Godey's*, and "a review of 'Longfellow's Poems.' " He needs to refer to these in writing his lecture (*L*, 2:409–11).

27 NOVEMBER. Poe replies to Dunnell: "I fully perceive the force of what you say—that the chance of a good audience is better for the earlier day, and thank you for your suggestion—while I regret that other arrangements will not permit me to avail myself of it. I believe that I must adhere to the 13th, and hope that my decision will put you to no inconvenience" (*L*, 2:720–21).

27 NOVEMBER. LOUISVILLE, KENTUCKY? Frederick William Thomas writes Poe, enclosing a prospectus of his forthcoming *Chronicle of Western Literature* (Poe's 14 February 1849 reply; review of Thomas' periodical in New York *Home Journal*, 20 January 1849).

CA. 27? NOVEMBER. PROVIDENCE. Mrs. Whitman promptly returns the three articles Poe requested in his 26 November letter. She believes that "Grace Greenwood" [pseudonym of Sara Jane Lippincott] wrote the poem addressed to him in the *Home Journal*. She asks Poe to send a brief note signed with his full signature to William J. Pabodie, who wishes to obtain his autograph (Mrs. Clemm to Annie Richmond, 28 November or later, and Poe to Pabodie, 4 December; see also Miller [1979], p. 98).

BEFORE 28 NOVEMBER? LOWELL. Annie Richmond replies to Poe's 16 November letter, asking him to make a promise (implied by Mrs. Clemm to Annie, 28 November or later).

28 NOVEMBER OR BEFORE? FORDHAM. Poe writes Annie, making a promise.

[Annie recalled that Mrs. Clemm borrowed "the letter containing this promise" and never returned it (Miller [1977], p. 25).]

28 NOVEMBER OR LATER. Mrs. Clemm writes Annie, discussing Poe's engagement with Mrs. Whitman: "I so much fear *she* is not calculated to make him happy. I fear I will not love her. I *know* I shall never love her as I do *you*, my own darling. . . . Thank you a thousand times, *dearest*, for inducing Eddy to make that promise to you, and which I feel so sure he will *never* violate. . . . Did you see the lines addressed to *our* Eddy in the 'Home Journal' week before last? . . . Mrs. W. says they were written by Grace Greenwood! They were sent to Eddy in *manuscript*, and Mrs. W. says she *knows* it to be Grace Greenwood's" (Miller [1977], pp. 24–26).

29 NOVEMBER. RICHMOND. Susan Archer Talley replies to Poe's 20 November letter: "Miss Talley will take pleasure in complying with Mr. Poe's request so far as she is herself concerned & cannot but feel gratified at the trust reposed in her by one whose genius she has ever regarded with so profound an admiration. Mr. Valentine will be in Richmond in the course of a week or two, & Miss Talley prefers waiting till then, to forwarding Mr. Poe's letter immediately . . . . She has little doubt of the success of his application, & need not assure Mr. Poe that his communication will be made known to Mr. Valentine only" (*W*, 17:324).

LATE NOVEMBER? NEW YORK. Miss Anne C. Lynch writes William J. Pabodie in Providence: "I hear that Mrs Whitman has concluded, contrary to the lady in the song, to become 'Mrs Poe.' I should like to know if this is really so" (InU–L).

[Miss Lynch was alluding to the song of *"Gaffer Poe,"* preserved in Anne E. C. Clarke's reminiscence. It contained the refrain *"I'll never marry you and be called Mrs. Poe"* (Sartain, p. 216).]

LATE NOVEMBER? PROVIDENCE. Mrs. Whitman recalls: "soon after Mrs. [Frances S.] Osgood learned from some of Poe's friends in New York that we were engaged, she came to Providence on purpose to see me . . . . She threw herself at my feet & covered my hands with tears & kisses; she told me all the enthusiasm that she had felt for him & her unchanged & unchanging interest in him & his best welfare. In answer to her questions,

I told her of the poem which he had sent me[,] of his visit[s] to Providence, of his letters, & of all that she wished to know. When I spoke of the letters of ten or twelve pages, she seemed almost incredulous. She said his letters to her were all very brief" (Whitman to J. H. Ingram, 11 May 1874, Miller [1979], p. 154–55; see also Miller [1977], p. 218, [1979], p. 382, and Williams, p. 769).

CA. DECEMBER. PHILADELPHIA. John Sartain pays $15 for an eighteen-line poem entitled "The Bells.—A Song," the first of three versions of "The Bells" that Poe will submit to *Sartain's Union Magazine* (editorial in December 1849 number; Sartain, p. 220).

DECEMBER. NEW YORK. *Holden's Dollar Magazine* contains an installment of John Tomlin's pseudonymous serial, "The Autobiography of a Monomaniac" edited by "Joe Bottom," which incorporates the texts of many letters he received from literary celebrities. Tomlin prints Poe's 5 October 1842 letter to him; in a footnote he comments humorously on the *Tales of the Grotesque and Arabesque.*

DECEMBER. In his *Merchants' Magazine* Freeman Hunt reviews Lowell's *A Fable for Critics*: "Our friends Bryant, Halleck, Willis, Whittier, Poe, and, last but not least, Harry Franco, (Briggs,) are, in our judgment, as genuine life pictures as were ever sketched with pen or pencil, in prose or verse. The severity, if any, is lost in the general fidelity of the delineations."

EARLY DECEMBER? Poe agrees to contribute literary criticism to the forthcoming *American Metropolitan Magazine*, to be edited by William Landon and published by Israel Post (prospectus in first number, dated January 1849; Mrs. Whitman's statements to J. H. Ingram, Miller [1979], pp. 35, 104).

EARLY DECEMBER? In the office of the *Metropolitan*, 259 Broadway, Poe reads Mrs. Frances S. Osgood's "Lines from an Unpublished Drama," which will appear in the first number. "He . . . believed them [the verses] to be addressed to himself. With his impressible & impulsive temperament . . . they must have deeply affected him" (Mrs. Whitman to Mary E. Hewitt, 4 October 1850, Williams, pp. 767–68).

EARLY DECEMBER? PROVIDENCE. T. L. Dunnell presumably replies to Poe's 27 November letter, changing the date of his lecture from 13 December to 20 December (implied by delivery of lecture on latter date).

4 DECEMBER. FORDHAM. Complying with Mrs. Whitman's request, Poe sends William J. Pabodie a brief letter signed with his full signature: "On the principle of [']better late than never' I seize the first opportunity afforded me, in the midst of cares and vexations of all kinds, to write you a few words of cordial thanks for your considerate and gentlemanly attentions to me while in Providence. . . . Please say to Mrs. W., when you next see her, that I thank her for the 'papers' and for her promptitude. . . . Edgar Allan Poe" (L, 2:411–12; facsimile in Stoddard [1884], 1:158–59; cf. Whitman to Poe, ca. 27? November).

7 DECEMBER. Poe writes John R. Thompson in Richmond: "I have been out of town for some weeks, and your letter, in consequence, did not reach me as soon as it should.—*Now*, of course, it will be out of my power to send you anything in time for your January number [of the *Southern Literary Messenger*]—but as soon as I find time to write an article such as I think will suit you, you shall hear from me. . . . Can you spare me the number of the Messenger containing Miss Talley's beautiful lines entitled 'Genius'? If I am not very much mistaken 'Susan' will ere long, stand at the head of American poetesses" (L, 2:721–22).

AFTER 7 DECEMBER. PROVIDENCE. Poe visits Mrs. Whitman.

[Quinn, p. 582, argued that Poe did not return to Providence until his 20 December lecture; but Mrs. Whitman clearly referred to an early December visit in her 30 September 1872 letter to Stoddard and in her 4 January 1876 letter to Ingram (Stoddard [1884], 1:158; Miller [1979], p. 382). See also 12 DECEMBER.]

11 DECEMBER. MILLERS TAVERN, ESSEX COUNTY, VIRGINIA. Elmira Shelton writes her cousin Philip A. Fitzhugh in Richmond: "My heart is with you all—tho' I think it very doubtful whether I shall return untill the 1st Jan'y" (TxU–HRCL).

[Quinn, p. 629, wrongfully inferred that this letter proved that Elmira "had not met Poe at that time." In fact, it does not mention Poe, or even allude to him.]

12 DECEMBER. PROVIDENCE. Poe reads Mrs. Whitman's "Hours of Life."

[On 12 December 1849 she wrote Rufus W. Griswold: "It is just a year ago to-day since Mr Poe read with me the greater part of this poem and his remarks, indicative of surprise & pleasure, were the more gratifying to me because I had feared that as the poem was not conformed to his own poetical creed, either in scope or structure[,] he would have been disposed to criticise rather than admire. He urged me at the time to fill up the unfinished portions of it & prepare it for immediate publication" (PHi; printed by Vincent, pp. 162–67).]

12 DECEMBER OR LATER. Poe leaves Providence and returns to Fordham (indicated by Poe to Whitman, 16 December).

BEFORE 15 DECEMBER. Mrs. Anna Power realizes that her daughter Mrs. Whitman intends to persist in her engagement to Poe. Mrs. Power therefore decides to obtain sole control of the estate left her family by her sister Ruth Marsh, thus placing it beyond the reach of her prospective son-in-law (15 December documents).

15 DECEMBER. The *Daily Journal* and the *Evening Transcript* carry this advertisement:

FRANKLIN LYCEUM LECTURES. The Fifth Lecture of the course will be delivered in Howard's Hall, on WEDNESDAY EVENING, Dec. 20th, by EDGAR A. POE, Esq.

Tickets to be had at Gladding & Proud's Bookstore, and at Leland's Music store, next door below the entrance to the Hall.

Doors open at 6½—Lecture at 7½ o'clock.

The notice is repeated daily in both papers.

15 DECEMBER. Mrs. Power signs a document of transfer in the presence of two witnesses, Henry Martin and William J. Pabodie. "To Charles F. Tillinghast Administrator . . . of the estate of Ruth Marsh . . . . You are hereby required in conformity to the provisions of the Will of the above named Ruth Marsh to pay to me the Subscriber [Anna Power] the Whole of the Estate . . . consisting of Bank Stocks and Notes." The document itemizes sixty-six shares of stock issued by six banks, as well as notes totalling $5,318.00 signed by private individuals and "secured by Mortgage of Real Estate."

Mrs. Power's daughters sign a supporting document: "We Sarah Helen Whitman and Susan Anna Power legatees named in the will of the within named Ruth Marsh . . . hereby unite in the preceding request of Anna Power that the whole of the Estate . . . be transferred to her" (Harrison and Dailey, p. 446; also in Harrison [1909], pp. 47–48).

15? DECEMBER. Mrs. Whitman sends a letter to Poe and one to Mrs. Clemm. She apparently informs them of her mother's action regarding her aunt's estate (Poe's reply).

16 DECEMBER. The *Republican Herald* reports that Poe will lecture at Howard's Hall on Wednesday evening, 20 December.

16 DECEMBER. NEW YORK. Poe writes Mrs. Whitman: "My *own dearest* Helen—Your letters—to my mother & myself—have just been received, & I hasten to reply, in season for this afternoons [mail]. . . . I cannot be in Providence until Wednesday morning; and, as I must try and get some sleep after I arrive, it is more than probable that I shall not see you until about 2, P.M. Keep up heart—*for all will go well.* My mother sends her dearest love and says she will return good for evil & treat you *much* better than *your* mother has treated me" (*L*, 2:412, 533; facsimile in Ticknor, after p. 162).

[In this letter Poe probably commented unfavorably on Mrs. Power's action. The manuscript was cut in two after the word "afternoons" and a portion of the text excised and destroyed, presumably by Mrs. Whitman.]

BEFORE 18 DECEMBER. PHILADELPHIA. Carey & Hart publish Rufus W. Griswold's anthology *The Female Poets of America* (Griswold [1898], pp. 245–46; Bayless, p. 150).

[Heartman and Canny, p. 127, wrongly attributed Griswold's sketch of Sarah Anna Lewis to Poe. In it Griswold sarcastically suggested that Mrs. Lewis' "The Forsaken," which had been warmly praised by "the acute critic Mr. Edgar A. Poe," was plagiarized from "a very fine poem by [William] Motherwell." See also Poe to Griswold, 28 June 1849.]

18 DECEMBER. OQUAWKA, ILLINOIS. Edward H. N. Patterson, the junior editor of the *Oquawka Spectator*, sends Poe a letter in care of the publisher George P. Putnam. Patterson invites Poe to join him in establishing a national magazine, possibly explaining that he will come into sufficient financial means on his twenty-first birthday, 27 January 1849 (Poe's reply, late April 1849; McElroy, p. 256).

18 DECEMBER. PROVIDENCE. The *Manufacturers and Farmers Journal* contains an advertisement for Poe's lecture on 20 December.

19 DECEMBER. NEW YORK. Poe calls on the poetess Mary E. Hewitt, to whom he expresses a doubt that he and Mrs. Whitman will actually be married.

[Griswold gave a distorted version of this interview in his 1850 "Memoir," pp. xxix–xxx, making it appear that Poe maliciously intended to break his engagement. Mrs. Hewitt wrote Mrs. Whitman on 2 October 1850, giving an accurate account:

As Mr Poe arose to leave he said "I am going to Providence this afternoon[.]" "I hear you are about to be married" I replied. He stood with the knob of the parlour door in his hand, and as I said this drew himself up with a look of great reserve and replied "that marriage will never take place[.]" "But" I persisted, "it is said you are already published[.]" Still standing like a statue with a most rigid face, he repeated "It will never take place." These were his words and *this was all*. He bade me good morning on the instant and I never saw him more. Mr Griswold came in the afternoon and in reply to my "Mr Poe was here this morning" said "He has gone to be married I think[.]" In answer to which I repeated what Mr Poe had said (transcript in Mrs. Whitman's hand, MB–G).]

20 DECEMBER. PROVIDENCE. Poe arrives early in the morning, taking lodging in the Earl House, a large hotel operated by Robert Earl at 67 North Main Street (Phillips, 2:1393; Mabbott [1978], 3:1361, 1367).

20 DECEMBER. The *Daily Journal* comments:

THE LECTURE BEFORE THE FRANKLIN LYCEUM, this evening, will be delivered by EDGAR A. POE, one of the most remarkable literary men of this country. To an imagination of singular strength and brilliancy, he adds a wonderful power of analysis. He will not fail to make an interesting lecture, and the subject which we understand he has selected, *"The Poetic Principle,"* is one well calculated for his peculiar abilities.

The *Evening Transcript* also reports that Poe, "the celebrated Poetical writer," will speak tonight: "This lecture will be attended with a great deal of interest, our readers being so familiar with his numerous productions."

20 DECEMBER. At 7:30 PM Poe lectures on "The Poetic Principle" in Howard's Hall, before an audience of "1800 people" (Poe to Annie Richmond, 28 December).

[William J. Pabodie estimated the attendance at "some two thousand persons" (11 June 1852 letter to R. W. Griswold, *W*, 17:413). Stephen H. Arnold left this reminiscence: "Poe . . . had read 'The Raven,' 'The Bells,' and other selections, in his best manner. Mrs. Whitman was seated just in front of him and my mother, my sister Rebecca and I were a little way off at the side—on his right—where we could observe both him and Mrs. Whitman and get every change of expression. This had been very interesting but became intensely so when in closing he read Edward C. Pinkney's lines—'I fill this cup to one made up of loveliness alone'—all the while looking down into her eyes" (Harrison and Dailey, p. 447; cf. *W*, 14:280–81).]

21 OR 22 DECEMBER. Presumably impressed by the success of Poe's lecture, Mrs. Whitman agrees to an "immediate marriage." Mrs. Power grudgingly consents to the union, insisting that Poe first sign a document acknowledging her control of her family's estate (Williams, pp. 761–62).

22 DECEMBER. With William J. Pabodie as a witness, Poe endorses copies of the two documents Mrs. Power and her daughters sent to Charles F. Tillinghast, administrator of the estate, on 15 December. He then signs a statement appended to these copies: "Whereas a Marriage is intended between the above named Sarah H. Whitman and the Subscriber Edgar A. Poe,—I hereby approve of and assent to the transfer of the property in the manner proposed" (Harrison and Dailey, p. 446, or Harrison [1909], p. 49).

22 DECEMBER. In the evening Poe attends a social gathering at Mrs. Whitman's home. Although he has been drinking, he is "very quiet." He promises Mrs. Whitman and her friends that he will abstain from alcohol (Pabodie to Griswold, 11 June 1852, W, 17:413; see also Williams, p. 762).

23 DECEMBER. Early in the morning Poe drinks a single glass of wine at the Earl House. He then calls on Mrs. Whitman: "Mr. Poe manifested and expressed the most profound contrition and regret [for the preceding evening], and was profuse in his promises of amendment. He was still urgently anxious that the marriage should take place before he left the City" (Pabodie to Griswold, W, 17:413; see also Stoddard [1884], 1:158).

23 DECEMBER. With Mrs. Whitman's consent, Poe writes a brief note to Reverend Nathan Bourne Crocker, minister of St. John's Episcopal Church: "Will Dr. Crocker have the kindness to publish the banns of matrimony between Mrs. Sarah Helen Whitman and myself, on Sunday [24 December] and on Monday. When we have decided on the day of the marriage we will inform you, and will thank you to perform the ceremony" (L, 2:413; Chivers [1957], p. 155).

[Poe handed the note to Pabodie, asking him to deliver it in person. "I delayed complying with his request, in the hope that the union might yet be prevented" (Pabodie to Griswold, W, 17:414).]

23 DECEMBER. Poe writes Mrs. Clemm: "We shall be married on Monday [25 December], and will be at Fordham on Tuesday" (L, 2:412).

23 DECEMBER. Mrs. Whitman recalls her last day in Poe's company:

We rode out together in the morning & passed the greater part of the day in making preparations for my sudden change of abode. In the afternoon, while we were together at one of the circulating libraries of the city, a communication was handed me cautioning me against this imprudent marriage & informing me of many things in Mr. Poe's recent career with which I was previously unacquainted. I was at the same time informed that he had *already* violated the solemn promises that he had made to me & to my friends on the preceding evening. . . . I felt utterly helpless of being able to exercise any permanent influence over his life. On our return home I announced to him what I had heard &, in his presence, countermanded the order, which he had previously given, for the delivery of the note he had addressed to Dr. Crocker. He earnestly endeavoured to persuade me that I had been misinformed, especially in relation to his having that very morning called for wine at the bar of the hotel where he boarded. . . . My mother on being informed of what had transpired had a brief interview with Mr. Poe which resulted in his determination to return immediately to New York. In her presence & in that of his friend, Mr. Pabodie, I bade him farewell, with feelings of profound commiseration for his fate . . . . While he was endeavouring to win from me an assurance that our parting should not be a final one, my mother saved me from a response by insisting upon the immediate termination of the interview. Mr. Poe then started up and left the house with an expression of bitter resentment at what he termed, the "intolerable insults" of my family. I never saw him more (27–28 September 1850 letter to Mrs. Hewitt, Williams, pp. 762–63; cf. Miller [1979], p. 145).

23 DECEMBER. At 6:00 PM Poe leaves Providence "in the Stonington express train, accompanied to the cars by Mr. Pabodie"; at Stonington, Connecticut, he boards Captain Joel Stone's steamer *Massachusetts*, which arrives in New York early the next day (Whitman to R. H. Stoddard, 30 September 1872, Stoddard [1884], 1:158; schedules in Providence *Evening Transcript*).

24 DECEMBER. WESTFORD, MASSACHUSETTS. Bardwell Heywood writes Miss Annie Sawyer in Lowell, describing Poe's late October visit to his parents' farm in Westford (Coburn, pp. 472–74).

24 DECEMBER. NEW LONDON, CONNECTICUT. The *Daily Star* reports: "Edgar A. Poe, Esq., the celebrated poet and critic, is about to lead to the Hymenial altar, Mrs. Sarah H. Whitman, of Providence, a well known and popular authoress."

26 DECEMBER. NEW YORK. The *Morning Express* copies the *Star*'s report.

28 DECEMBER. LOWELL. The *Daily Journal & Courier* copies the *Star*'s report.

28 DECEMBER. FORDHAM. Mrs. Clemm writes Annie Richmond in Low-

ell: "I feel so happy in *all* my troubles. Eddy is not going to marry Mrs. W. . . . All the papers say he is going to lead to the altar the *talented*, *rich*, and *beautiful* Mrs. W" (fragment printed by Ingram, p. 395).

28 DECEMBER. Poe sends Annie a note accompanying Mrs. Clemm's letter: "My own dear Mother will explain to you how it is that I cannot write to you in full—but I *must* write only a few words to let you *see* that I am well, lest you suspect me to be ill. . . . I *hope* that I distinguished myself at the Lecture [in Providence]—I *tried* to do so, for your sake. There were 1800 people present, and such applause! I did so much better than I did at Lowell" (*L*, 2:413).

BEFORE 29 DECEMBER. NEW YORK. The first number of the *American Metropolitan Magazine*, dated January 1849, contains Mrs. Frances S. Osgood's "Lines from an Unpublished Drama," possibly addressed to Poe. A prospectus on the back cover lists Poe among the writers who have agreed to contribute (Hull, p. 694; Reece [1954], p. 165).

29 DECEMBER. The *Daily Tribune* notices the *Metropolitan*.

30 DECEMBER. PHILADELPHIA. The *Quaker City*, a weekly newspaper edited by George Lippard, commences publication. In this issue Lippard prints the first installment of his "Literary and Political Police," satires featuring Poe as a magistrate ("Justice Poe") meting out punishments to various literary "criminals," including Rufus W. Griswold and Joel T. Headley. Subsequent installments appear intermittently during the winter and spring of 1849.

LATE 1848. HARTFORD, CONNECTICUT. Henry S. Parsons publishes Mrs. Elizabeth Oakes Smith's anthology *The Lover's Gift*, which contains Poe's 1831 poem "To Helen" and his stanza "To F[rance]s S. O[sgoo]d," both apparently reprinted from *The Raven and Other Poems* (Heartman and Canny, p. 276; Mabbott [1969], 1:165, 234, 584).

LATE 1848? FORDHAM? Poe returns the manuscript of Mrs. Sarah Anna Lewis' "The Prisoner of Perotè" to her, penciling a note on the last page: "Upon the whole I think this the most spirited poem you have written. . . . You will observe that I have taken the liberty of making some *suggestions* in the body of the poem—the force of which, I think, would be *much* increased by the introduction of an occasional *short* line" (*L*, 2:413–14, 534; Mabbott [1969], 1:493–96).

1848 AND 1849. Poe keeps a notebook in which he lists likely subscribers and contributors to his proposed magazine, the *Stylus* (Rose and Savoye).

ANNIE RICHMOND
University of Lowell Library

CHAPTER ELEVEN

"For Annie" and the Final Journey

1849

In the early months of 1849 Poe expresses his aspirations in his letters to Annie Richmond of Lowell, Massachusetts, a young woman whom he met, and fell in love with, during his two visits to this city last year. As Annie is happily married, Poe realizes that his love for her must remain platonic. Her husband Charles B. Richmond, a wealthy paper manufacturer, is tolerant of her innocent affection for the famous poet. In February Poe begins to contribute to the *Flag of Our Union*, a widely circulated, cheaply printed Boston weekly which pays him well. Since he is privately contemptuous of this ephemeral newspaper, he arranges for a poem dedicated to Mrs. Richmond to be reprinted in a more prestigious journal: "For Annie," published on 21 April in the *Flag* dated 28 April, appears several days later in the 28 April issue of the New York *Home Journal*, much to the annoyance of the *Flag*'s proprietor. At the end of April Poe's dreams of his own magazine are rekindled when he receives a letter from Edward H. N. Patterson of Oquawka, Illinois. Though only twenty-one Patterson has considerable funds and the control of a printing office; he wishes to establish a national literary journal of which Poe would be sole editor and half owner. On 29 June Poe departs from New York on a trip to Richmond, intending to promote the proposed magazine by delivering lectures in this city and elsewhere in the South. When he stops in Philadelphia, however, he drinks to excess and suffers the agonizing hallucinations characteristic of "*mania-à-potu*" (delirium tremens). John Sartain, publisher of *Sartain's Union Magazine*, cares for him until he recovers. To Sartain Poe sells his revised poem "The Bells" and his newest one, "Annabel Lee." After he arrives in Richmond on 14 July, he proposes marriage to his early love Sarah Elmira Royster, now the well-to-do widow Mrs. Shelton. On 17 August he delivers his lecture on "The Poetic Principle" to a large audience at the Exchange Hotel; he repeats it in Norfolk, Virginia, on 14 September, and in Richmond on 24 September. Sometime during August Poe apparently has one or more drinking bouts, which leave him fearful of the possible effects of another indulgence. On 27 August he joins a Richmond chapter of the Sons of Temperance, whose members pledge themselves to abstain from alcohol. By late August most of Poe's Richmond acquaintances believe that he is engaged to Mrs. Shelton; in fact, she hesitates to accept his proposal because the provisions of her late husband's will make it financially disadvantageous for her to remarry. By 22 September she finally consents and writes a cordial letter to Mrs. Clemm. On 27 September Poe leaves Richmond for New York, intending to return in a few days with Mrs. Clemm; but when he stops in Baltimore, he begins drinking heavily. On 3 October, an election day, he is discovered in a comatose condition at the polling place for Baltimore's Fourth Ward. He dies of delirium tremens at the Washington College Hospital on 7 October.

*

1849

*

JANUARY OR BEFORE. NEW YORK. Poe submits his sketch "Landor's Cottage" to the *American Metropolitan Magazine* (Poe to Annie Richmond, ca. 21 January and 23 March; Mrs. Clemm to Annie, 11 January).

JANUARY. *Holden's Dollar Magazine*, now edited by Charles F. Briggs, contains "A Mirror for Authors" by "Motley Manners, Esq." These pseudonymous verses by Augustine J. H. Duganne satirize the leading American poets, who are also caricatured in accompanying illustrations by Felix O. C. Darley. Duganne devotes twenty-two lines to Poe, whom Darley represents as an Indian holding a tomahawk and a scalping knife:

> With tomahawk upraised for deadly blow,
> Behold our literary Mohawk, Poe!
> Sworn tyrant he o'er all who sin in verse—
> His own the standard, damns he all that's worse;
> And surely not for this shall he be blamed—
> For worse than his deserves that it be damned!
>
> Who can so well detect the plagiary's flaw?
> "Set thief to catch thief" is an ancient saw:
> Who can so scourge a fool to shreds and slivers?
> Promoted slaves oft make the best slave drivers!
> Iambic Poe! of tyro bards the terror—
> *Ego* is he—the world his pocket-mirror!
> (Reilly [1973], pp. 9–12).

JANUARY. The *Church Review and Ecclesiastical Register* discusses Poe's *Eureka*, attacking his advocacy of pantheism (Laverty [1951], p. 346).

JANUARY AND LATER. PROVIDENCE, RHODE ISLAND. Mrs. Sarah Helen Whitman writes Mrs. Frances S. Osgood in New York, "many times . . . during the winter & spring," to request information on Poe's "health &

welfare." She receives no reply (Whitman to R. W. Griswold, 12 December 1849, PHi).

BEFORE 5 JANUARY. NEW YORK. George P. Putnam publishes Mrs. Osgood's poem *A Letter About the Lions*, which provides humorous gossip about many American authors, mostly New Yorkers. Only four lines are devoted to Poe:

> But where's the Raven, who could sing,
> To thrill the rudest soul once,
> Who higher soared, on wounded wing,
> Than others, with their *whole* ones?

5 JANUARY. The *Daily Tribune* briefly reviews Mrs. Osgood's "neat, naive and tasteful pamphlet."

11 JANUARY. FORDHAM. Mrs. Clemm writes Annie Richmond in Lowell:

The match is entirely broken off between Eddy and Mrs. Whitman. He has been at home *three weeks* and has not written to her once. . . . Dear Eddy is writing most industriously, and I have every hope that we will, in a short time, surmount most of our difficulties. He writes from ten till four every day. . . . We have found out who wrote those verses that we attributed to Grace Greenwood: they were written by Mrs. Welby, of Kentucky. . . . Eddy wrote a tale ["Landor's Cottage"] and sent it to the publisher, and in it was a description of *you* with the name of the lady, "Darling Annie." . . . Did you see the lines to Eddy in a new magazine just come out, called the *Metropolitan?* They are by Mrs. Osgood, and very beautiful. . . . Have you seen Lowell's satire [*A Fable for Critics*], and Mrs. Osgood's letter about the lions? Something about Eddy in both (Ingram, pp. 399–400).

11 JANUARY. Poe sends Annie a letter enclosed in Mrs. Clemm's: "Oh, Annie, in spite of so many worldly sorrows—in spite of all the trouble and *misrepresentation* (so hard to bear) that Poverty has entailed on me for so long a time—in spite of *all* this I am *so*—*so* happy to think that you *really* love me. . . . there is *nothing* in this world worth living for except love— love *not* such as I once thought I felt for Mrs. [Whitman] but such as burns in my very soul for *you*—so pure—so unworldly—a love which would make *all* sacrifices for your sake." Poe asks to be remembered to Annie's sister Sarah, her brother Bardwell, her young daughter Caddy, her parents, and her husband Charles B. Richmond (*L*, 2:414–15; see also Ingram, pp. 400–01).

13 JANUARY OR BEFORE. PHILADELPHIA. *Godey's Lady's Book* for February contains Poe's tale "Mellonta Tauta."

13 JANUARY. NEW YORK. The *Daily Tribune* carries an advertisement for the February *Godey's*, "this day published."

13 JANUARY. Poe writes John R. Thompson in Richmond, thanking him for forwarding the *Southern Literary Messenger* containing Susan Archer Talley's poem "Genius." Poe is enclosing his initial installment of "Marginalia," excerpted from the *Democratic Review* for November 1844: "I send it that, by glancing it over—especially the prefatory remarks—you may perceive the general *design*—which I think well adapted to the purposes of such a Magazine as yours . . . . My object in writing you now, is to propose that I continue the papers in 'The Messenger'—running them through the year, at the rate of 5 pages each month . . . . You might afford me, as before, I presume, $2 per page. . . . If you think well of my proposal, I will send you the two first numbers (10 pp.) immediately on receipt of a letter from you" (L, 2:415–17).

19 JANUARY. RICHMOND. In the *Semi-Weekly Examiner* John M. Daniel comments:

> Mr. EDGAR A. POE, a gentleman with whom the citizens of Richmond have some acquaintance, and whom the public also know as an erratic, moon struck, and very disorderly poet—much given to "Ravens," "Dreamland" and bar-rooms, is about to be married to Mrs. Sarah H. Whitman, of Providence, Rhode Island. Mrs. Whitman is a widow, and also a poetess. Her deceased husband was a poet too, and an extensive one. Mrs. Whitman was a Miss Sarah H. Powers [Power] before she married Mr. John Whitman, and has written many clever effusions. The paper from which we get the news, hopes that if Mr. Poe and Mrs. Whitman get married, they will be very happy, and have a house-full of very fat babies. We hope so too. We also hope he will leave off getting drunk in restoratives, and keep his money in his pockets, except when he takes it out to pay his bills.

20 JANUARY. FORDHAM. Poe writes John Priestley of the *American Review* in New York, forwarding "About Critics and Criticism." He asks Priestley to submit his article to the monthly's editor, James D. Whelpley: "see if he can give me $10 for it" (L, 2:417).

BEFORE 21 JANUARY. LOWELL. Annie Richmond writes Poe. Her family and friends have heard that Mrs. Whitman has spoken harshly of Poe's conduct during their recent engagement: "I will not repeat *all* her vile & slanderous words—you have doubtless heard them—but one thing she says that I cannot *deny* though I do not believe it—viz—that you had been *published to her once*, & that on the Sat. preceding the Sabbath on which you were to have been published for the *second time*, she went herself to the Rev Mr Crocker's, & *after stating her reasons for so doing*, requested him to stop all further proceedings." Annie hopes that Poe can refute these assertions (fragment quoted in Poe to Mrs. Whitman, ca. 21 January).

[The banns of matrimony were, of course, never published. Mrs. Whitman did not call on Reverend Crocker; she simply stopped the delivery of Poe's note to him requesting the announcement of the marriage (see 23 DECEMBER 1848). Annie wrote Poe to satisfy her husband and his relatives, as she explained in her 14 January 1877 letter to J. H. Ingram: "Mr. Richmond's family were at that time living in Providence & were continually sending him the gossip in circulation there, about this unhappy affair—In answer to their inquiries as to what 'Mr. Poe said about it,' I replied, that Mrs. W's statement was a false one, but nothing would do—they must have something more definite—of course I had no other alternative, but to tell him [Poe] as briefly as I could, my reasons for troubling him, & ask some explanation" (Miller [1977], p. 159). Mrs. Whitman herself never criticized Poe, as she explained in her 12 December 1849 letter to R. W. Griswold: "Many of the circumstances attending my seperation [sic] from Mr Poe were (greatly to my regret) matters of public notoriety at the time, but no one has ever heard me allude to them or to Mr Poe's reputed errors but in terms of extenuation & kindness" (PHi).]

CA. 21 JANUARY. FORDHAM. Poe writes Mrs. Whitman in Providence, quoting the accusation contained in Annie's letter to him: "That *you* Mrs W[hitman] have uttered, promulgated or in any way countenanced this pitiable falsehood, I do not & cannot believe—some person equally your enemy & mine has been its author—but what I beg of you is, to write me at once a few lines in explanation . . . . Your simple disavowal is all that I wish . . . . Heaven knows that I would shrink from wounding or grieving you! I blame no one but your Mother . . . . I bitterly lament my own weaknesses, & nothing is farther from my heart than to blame you for yours . . . . It has been my intention to say simply, that our marriage was postponed on account of your ill health" (L, 2:420–42).

CA. 21 JANUARY. Poe writes Annie in Lowell: "I felt *deeply* wounded by the cruel statements of your letter—and yet I had anticipated nearly all. . . . In fact, Annie, I am beginning to grow wiser, and do not care so much as I did for the opinions of a world in which I see, with my own eyes, that to act generously is to be considered as designing, and that to be poor is to be a villain. I must get rich—rich. . . . I deeply regret that Mr. R[ichmond] should think ill of me." Poe encloses his letter to Mrs. Whitman, which he has dated 25 January, several days in advance: "Read it—show it only to those in whom you have faith, and then *seal* it with wax and mail it from Boston. . . . When her answer comes I will send it to you: that will convince you of the truth." Yesterday Poe sent his "About Critics and Criticism" to the *American Review*; not long ago he gave the *American Metropolitan Magazine* his "Landor's Cottage," which "has something about Annie in it." The *Southern Literary Messenger* will publish fifty pages of his "Marginalia," five pages to appear in each monthly issue. "I have also made permanent engagements with every magazine in America (except *Peterson's National*), including a Cincinnati magazine called *The Gentlemen's*. So you see that I have only to keep up my spirits to get out of all my pecuniary troubles" (*L*, 2:417–20).

21 JANUARY. WASHINGTON. Horace Greeley writes Rufus W. Griswold in New York: "Do you know Sarah Helen Whitman? Of course, you have heard it rumored that she is to marry Poe. Well, she has seemed to me a good girl, and—you know what Poe is. Now I know a widow of doubtful age will marry almost any sort of a white man, but this seems to me a terrible conjunction. Has Mrs. Whitman no friend within your knowledge that can faithfully *explain* Poe to her?" (MB–G).

22 JANUARY. BOSTON. Frederick Gleason, publisher of the *Flag of Our Union*, writes Poe, inviting him to contribute regularly to this weekly newspaper. Park Benjamin, Mrs. Osgood, and Mrs. Lydia H. Sigourney are already engaged as contributors; Gleason can pay Poe "about 5$ a 'Graham page' " (Poe to Gleason, 5 February, and to Annie, 8 February).

CA. 23? JANUARY. LOWELL. Annie Richmond receives Poe's letter of ca. 21 January. She makes her own copy of the letter to Mrs. Whitman Poe enclosed (Annie's transcript in ViU–I).

24 JANUARY. OQUAWKA, ILLINOIS. The *Oquawka Spectator* reports Poe's engagement to Mrs. Whitman (McElroy, p. 264).

CA. 25? JANUARY. BOSTON. Annie (or someone appointed by her) mails Poe's letter to Mrs. Whitman, as he requested (Boston postmark mentioned in Whitman to R. W. Griswold, 12 December 1849, PHi).

BEFORE 31 JANUARY. RICHMOND. John R. Thompson replies to Poe's 13 January letter. He agrees to publish the new series of "Marginalia" in the *Messenger* (implied by Poe's letters to him, 13 and 31 January).

31 JANUARY. NEW YORK. Poe writes Thompson: "Accompanying this letter, by mail, are eleven pages of 'Marginalia', done up in *a roll*. Would it not be advisable to preface the series with the prefatory remarks I made use of originally—in the 'Democratic Review'? They would serve to ex-

plain the character of the papers. You *have* the original preface in the printed pages I enclosed you. . . . Should there be any of these gossiping affairs which, for *any* reason, you disapprove, just cut them out (whole) & preserve them for me. Publish only those which suit you entirely. The *order* in which they appear is immaterial" (facsimile in Moldenhauer [1973], pp. 70–71).

FEBRUARY OR BEFORE. Poe writes Bayard Taylor, a contributing editor of *Graham's Magazine* resident in New York. He encloses a favorable review of Mrs. Sarah Anna Lewis' *The Child of the Sea and Other Poems*, asking that it be published anonymously (Stoddard [1889], p. 113, and [1903], pp. 159–60; Mott, pp. 551–52; review printed in April *Graham's*).

FEBRUARY? The *American Review* returns Poe's "About Critics and Criticism": this magazine can no longer pay for contributions (Poe to Priestley, 20 January, and to Annie, after 5? May; article published in *Graham's*, January 1850).

FEBRUARY. The *Columbian Magazine* ceases publication (cf. Poe to Annie, after 5? May).

FEBRUARY. BUFFALO, NEW YORK. The *Western Literary Messenger* reviews the *Southern Literary Messenger* for January: "The ablest pens at the South are enlisted in its service, aside from the aid rendered by such northern writers as Poe, Tuckerman, etc."

FEBRUARY. AMHERST, MASSACHUSETTS. The *Indicator*, published at Amherst College, contains a long, hostile critique of Poe's *Eureka* (Nelson, p. 180; Pollin [1980], p. 28).

FEBRUARY. BOSTON. The *Boston Museum* contains Mrs. Jane Ermina Locke's "The Broken Charm," a poem commemorating the end of her infatuation with Poe (Reilly [1976], pp. [10–11]).

FEBRUARY. RICHMOND. The *Southern Literary Messenger* contains a favorable review of Rufus W. Griswold's *The Female Poets of America*.

[For his 1850 "Memoir" of Poe, p. vi, Griswold fabricated a "Poe letter" which acknowledged this unsigned review. James A. Harrison reprinted Griswold's forgery in his 1902 edition (*W*, 17:326–27); subsequent scholars have used it as a basis for attributing the review to Poe (cf. Heartman and Canny, p. 261, and Hull, p. 194). Other evidence to establish Poe's authorship seems lacking. While the *Messenger*'s reviewer praised Susan Archer Talley (whom Poe admired), he also placed Mrs. Elizabeth F. Ellet (whom Poe detested) at the head of his list of the "most accomplished" poetesses. The review might have been written by the editor John R. Thompson, a friend of Griswold as well as an admirer of Miss Talley (cf. Thompson to Griswold, 31 August and 20 September 1848, PHi).]

EARLY FEBRUARY. PROVIDENCE. Mrs. Whitman returns home, "having passed the last four or five weeks in New Bedford & in Boston" (Whitman to Griswold, 13 February 1849, PHi).

She receives Poe's letter to her, written ca. 21 January and mailed from Boston several days later: "I would not have hesitated for a moment to have complied with his request had I not have feared that by so doing we might both be involved in a recurrence of the unhappy scenes which had preceded & attended our seperation [sic] . . . . With a heavy heart, & after the most dispassionate reflection, I resolved, for his sake rather than my own, not to reply" (Whitman to Griswold, 12 December 1849, PHi).

EARLY FEBRUARY. Mrs. Whitman receives a letter from Israel Post, publisher of the *American Metropolitan Magazine*, who reminds her of her promise to contribute to the February number. She recalls: "I found in a hurried search among my MSS. and papers a copy of unpublished stanzas, written several years before as an accompaniment to an Italian air for the guitar. Here was an intimation of what Macbeth calls 'fate and metaphysical aid.' I felt that Poe would interpret the last verse as a response to the entreaty made to me in his letter—the letter which I had not dared to answer. The verses . . . were published in the February number of the magazine, which, I think, did not appear before the middle of March" (Whitman to R. H. Stoddard, 30 September 1872, Stoddard [1884], 1:159; cf. her 20 February 1874 letter to J. H. Ingram in Miller [1979], pp. 35–36).

[Mrs. Whitman's "Stanzas for Music," published under her name in the *Metropolitan*, bore the title "Our Island of Dreams" in the 1853 and 1879 collections of her poetry. The verses portray the plight of two lovers who "parted in anger, to meet never more." Mrs. Whitman composed this fourth and final stanza only after receiving the letters from Poe and Post:

> When the clouds that now veil from us Heaven's fair light
> Their soft, silver lining turn forth on the night,
> When time shall the vapors of falsehood dispel,
> He shall know if I loved him, but never how well
> (Reilly [1965], pp. 191–92; Mabbott [1969], 1:472).]

3 FEBRUARY. NEW YORK. Poe signs a promissory note for $67, payable at the end of sixty days to Isaac Cooper (NNPM).

5? FEBRUARY. Poe gives "A Valentine," a revision of his 1846 acrostic concealing Mrs. Osgood's name, to Mr. French, the New York agent of the *Flag of Our Union*. He apparently receives five dollars for this brief poem (Poe to Annie, 8 February).

5 FEBRUARY. Poe replies to the 22 January letter from Frederick Gleason, publisher of this Boston weekly: "I shall be happy to contribute, as often as possible, to 'The Flag'. In the course of next week, I will send you a tale or sketch; and in the meantime I leave with Mr. French a short poem which I hope will please you" (*L*, 2:724).

6 FEBRUARY. FORDHAM. Poe completes a second, greatly expanded version of "The Bells" (Poe to Annie, 8 February).

7 FEBRUARY. Poe completes his tale "Hop-Frog" (Poe to Annie).

8 FEBRUARY. Poe writes Annie Richmond in Lowell:

Our darling mother [Mrs. Clemm] is just going to town, where, I hope, she will find a sweet letter from you, or from Sarah [Heywood], but, as it is so long since I have written, I *must* send a few words . . . . I have been *so* busy, dear Annie, ever since I returned from Providence—six weeks ago. I have not suffered a day to pass without writing from a page to three pages. Yesterday, I wrote five, and the day before a poem considerably longer than "The Raven." I call it "The Bells." . . . The 5 prose pages I finished yesterday are called—what do you think?—I am sure you will never guess—"*Hop-Frog!*" Only think of *your* Eddy writing a story with *such* a name . . . . It will be published in a weekly paper, of Boston, called "The Flag of Our Union"—not a *very* respectable journal, perhaps, in a literary point of view, but one that pays as high prices as most of the Magazines. The proprietor wrote to me, offering about 5$ a "Graham page" and as I was anxious to get out of my pecuniary difficulties, I accepted the offer. He gives $5 for a Sonnet, also. Mrs Osgood, Park Benjamin, & Mrs Sigourney are engaged (*L*, 2:425–26).

9 FEBRUARY. LOWELL. The *Daily Journal & Courier* reprints Mrs. Jane Ermina Locke's "The True Poet," a poem addressed to Poe which originally appeared in the New York *Evening Post* of 3 August 1848 (Reilly [1972], pp. 209–10, 219).

CA. 12? FEBRUARY. FORDHAM. Poe forwards a review of James Russell Lowell's *A Fable for Critics* to John R. Thompson in Richmond (Poe to Thomas, 14 February).

14 FEBRUARY. Poe replies to the letter Frederick William Thomas sent him on 27 November 1848: it has finally reached him, "after having taken, at its leisure, a very considerable tour among the P. Offices." Poe is glad to learn that his friend is returning to "the field of Letters" by starting a new periodical, the *Chronicle of Western Literature*:

Depend upon it, after all, Thomas, Literature is the most noble of professions. In fact, it is about the only one fit for a man. For my own part, there is no seducing me from the path. I shall be a *littérateur*, at least, all my life; nor would I abandon the hopes which still lead me on for all the gold in California. . . . I have read the Prospectus of the "Chronicle" and like it much especially the part where you talk about "letting go the finger" of that conceited booby, the East . . . . I wish you would come down on the Frogpondians. They are getting worse and worse, and pretend not to be aware that there *are* any literary people out of Boston.

Just "a day or two ago" Poe sent a review of Lowell's *Fable* to the *Southern Literary Messenger*: "I only hope Thompson will print it. Lowell is a ranting abolitionist and *deserves* a good using up." Although Poe has never met Thomas' co-editor on the *Chronicle*, he knows him by reputation: "Eames, I think, was talking to me about him in Washington once, and spoke very highly of him in many respects." Poe appends a brief notice of Sarah Anna Lewis, asking Thomas to publish it "editorially" in the *Chronicle*: "The lady spoken of is a most particular friend of mine, and deserves *all* I have said of her" (*L*, 2:426–29; notice of Mrs. Lewis in *W*, 13:225–26).

["Eames" was almost certainly Charles Eames, the editor who reprinted "Ligeia" and other Poe compositions in the New York *New World* early in 1845; he subsequently settled in Washington, where he became acquainted with Thomas. The discussion mentioned probably occurred when Poe visited the capital around late July, 1847.]

16 FEBRUARY. Poe writes Evert A. Duyckinck, editor of the *Literary World*: "Perhaps, in the conversation I had with you, in your office, about 'Ulalume', I did not make you comprehend precisely what *was* the request I made." By way of further explanation Poe encloses the editorial prefacing the poem's republication in the Providence *Daily Journal* of 22 November 1848, which explains that he, not Nathaniel P. Willis, is the author. If Duyckinck will simply reprint this paper's remarks along with the poem, "it will make every thing straight" (*L*, 2:429; *Literary World* of 3 March).

17 FEBRUARY. BRUNSWICK, MAINE. George W. Eveleth writes Poe. He has just finished "a somewhat hasty perusal" of *Eureka*: "I was gratified at coming upon the idea with regard to the origin of the rotation of the heavenly bodies, because it coincided with the one which I had given upon the same point. I gave it on my own authority, never having seen, to my

recollection, any thing of the like elsewhere. Nevertheless, it may have been advanced hundreds of times . . . . Do I understand you to give this idea as only your own way of accounting for the rotation or is it that also of Laplace?" Eveleth encloses his essay "The Nucleus of our Planet in a State of Igneous Liquefaction," written "two or three months ago," which outlines much the same theory that Poe advocates in *Eureka*. He submitted this article to Silliman's *American Journal of Science* in New Haven, Connecticut, which has yet to print it; and he also sent a copy to Professor John W. Draper of New York University, requesting his opinion of it. Draper recently replied, enclosing two essays of his own. In response to Eveleth's questions, Draper stated that he never met Poe and knew nothing of Poe's proposed magazine, the *Stylus*, whose prospects for success he doubted. Eveleth still retains his faith in Poe's plan: "If you get the Stylus upon its route before the end of the next three months, send me a specimen of it hither to Brunswick . . . . I am attending the Medical Lectures [at the Maine Medical School]. I may thereby have a chance to introduce a copy or two of the Maga. to the good people of this place— perhaps to the students or Professors of the College" (Eveleth, pp. 22–23).

17 FEBRUARY. BOSTON. The *Flag of Our Union* for 24 February contains this editorial announcement: " 'A Valentine,' a very peculiar article, from our regular contributor, EDGAR A. POE. To appear in our next."

BEFORE 18 FEBRUARY. PHILADELPHIA. *Sartain's Union Magazine* for March contains Poe's "A Valentine," preceded by the dedication "To—— —— ——." In the "Editorial" section at the back of the issue, John Sartain calls attention to the poem: "The Valentine by EDGAR A. POE, will, we venture to predict, make as many guessers as readers of his most provoking riddle."

[Early in 1848 Poe submitted "A Valentine" to James L. DeGraw, who published the *Union Magazine* in New York. The poem did not appear at that time; since DeGraw subsequently disposed of the magazine and left for California—without returning the manuscript—Poe felt free to offer a second copy to Frederick Gleason, proprietor of the *Flag of Our Union*. The publication in *Sartain's* occurred at least a week before that in the *Flag* (see Poe to Annie, 1? March, and Gleason's explanation to his readers, 10 March).]

18 FEBRUARY. LOWELL. Annie Richmond writes Poe, quoting from "A Valentine," which she has seen in *Sartain's* (Poe's reply, 1? March).

18 FEBRUARY. FORDHAM. With "a heavy heart" Poe writes Annie: "I must abandon my proposed visit to Lowell & God only knows when I shall see &

clasp you by the hand. I have come to this determination to-day, after looking over some of your letters to me & my mother [Mrs. Clemm], written since I left you. You have not *said* it to me, but I have been enabled to glean from what you *have* said, that Mr Richmond has permitted himself (perhaps without knowing it) to be influenced against me, by the malignant misrepresentations of Mr & Mrs Locke." Poe explains that he quarreled with the Lockes during his second visit to Lowell, in late October 1848, only because they made insulting remarks about Annie and her husband. Considering the offense Poe offered to Mrs. Locke's "insane vanity & self-esteem," he is not surprised that she has been "ransacking the world for scandal" to use against him; but he "certainly did not anticipate that any man *in his senses*, would ever *listen* to accusations, from so suspicious a source." Poe has regretfully come to the conclusion that Mr. Richmond must have some other reason for objecting to him:

I much fear that he has mistaken the nature—the purity of that affection which I feel for you, & have not scrupled to avow . . . . God knows dear *dear* Annie, with what horror I would have shrunk from insulting a nature so *divine* as yours, with any impure or earthly love—But since it is clear that Mr R. cannot enter into my feelings on this topic, & that he even suspects *what is not*, it only remains for me beloved Annie to consult *your* happiness . . . . Not only must I *not* visit you [at] Lowell, but I must discontinue my letters & you yours—I cannot & *will* not have it on my conscience that I have interfered with the domestic happiness of the only being in the whole world, whom I have loved, at the same time with truth & with *purity* (L, 2:429–32).

AFTER 18 FEBRUARY. LOWELL. Annie receives Poe's letter and shows it to her husband. Mr. Richmond writes the Lockes, "denouncing them in the *strongest terms*." He asks Annie "to *urge* Mrs. Clemm and Mr. Poe to come on" (Annie to J. H. Ingram, after 13 March 1877, Miller [1977], p. 168).

24 FEBRUARY. BOSTON. The *Flag of Our Union* for 3 March contains Poe's "A Valentine," preceded by this introduction: "At a 'Valentine Soiree,' in New York, the following enigmatical lines were received, among others, and read aloud to the company. The verses were enclosed in an envelope, addressed '*To her whose name is written within.*' As no lady present could so read the riddle as to find her name written in it, the Valentine remained, and still remains, unclaimed. Can any of the readers of the FLAG discover for whom it is intended?"

LATE FEBRUARY? FORDHAM. Poe forwards the second version of "The Bells" to *Sartain's Union Magazine*, which previously purchased the original eighteen-line version for $15. He apparently receives an additional $25 for the expanded poem (dating implied by Poe to Annie, 8 February and 1? March; Mabbott [1969], 1:431).

CA. MARCH. PROVIDENCE. Sarah Helen Whitman submits a five-stanza poem, dated *"Isle of Rhodes, March* 1849" and entitled simply "Lines," to the *Southern Literary Messenger*. The verses seem to convey a reconciliatory message, presumably intended for Poe:

> I bade thee stay. Too well I know
>> The fault was mine, mine only;
> I dared not think upon the past
>> All desolate and lonely.
>
> I know not if my soul could bear
>> In absence to regret thee,
> To strive alone with its despair,
>> Still seeking to forget thee
>> (published in June *Messenger*).

MARCH. RICHMOND. The *Messenger* contains Poe's unsigned review of *A Fable for Critics*: "Mr. Lowell has committed an irrevocable *faux pas* and lowered himself at least fifty per cent in the literary public opinion."

1? MARCH. FORDHAM. Poe writes Annie Richmond in Lowell: "Your letter (one of them) was dated the 18th:—how, then, *did* you ever see, or know anything about the Valentine from which you quote, when it was not published until the 3d March—that is, it was issued in the 'Flag' dated 3d March, but which was issued the Saturday previous—Feb 24. How *did* you see it so early as Feb. 18.?" The *Flag of Our Union* now has two unpublished tales by Poe, "Hop-Frog" and "X-ing a Paragrab." *Sartain's Union Magazine* will publish "The Bells" (*L*, 2:725).

1 MARCH. Poe writes Annie's sister Sarah H. Heywood: "My dear sweet sister—why have you not kept your promise & written me. Do not *you* be influenced against me by *anybody*—at least in my absence when I have it not in my power either to deny or to explain." The brief note is apparently enclosed in Poe's letter to Annie (*L*, 2:432).

AFTER 1 MARCH. BOSTON. Frederick Gleason, proprietor of the *Flag of Our Union*, writes Poe, asking him to explain the appearance of "A Valentine" in *Sartain's* for March (Gleason's explanation to his readers, 10 March).

AFTER 1 MARCH. FORDHAM. Poe replies to Gleason, stating that last year he submitted the poem to James L. DeGraw, former publisher of the *Union Magazine*. Without Poe's knowledge or consent, DeGraw gave the manuscript to John Sartain, the new publisher (Gleason's explanation, 10 March).

3 MARCH. BOSTON. The *Flag of Our Union* for 10 March contains the solution of Poe's acrostic: "To translate the address of the Valentine which appeared in our last paper from the pen of Edgar A. Poe, read the first letter of the first line in connection with the second letter of the second line, the third letter of the third line, the fourth of the fourth, and so on to the end. The name of our contributor, Frances Sargent Osgood, will thus appear." Next week the *Flag* will publish "Hop-Frog," a new "prose sketch" by Poe, its "regular contributor."

3 MARCH. NEW YORK. The *Literary World* reprints "Ulalume: A Ballad," preceded by Evert A. Duyckinck's explanation: "The following fascinating poem, which is from the pen of EDGAR A. POE, has been drifting about in the Newspapers under anonymous or mistaken imputation of authorship,—having been attributed to N. P. WILLIS. We now restore it to its proper owner. It originally appeared without name in the American Review. In peculiarity of versification, and a certain cold moonlight witchery, it has much of the power of the author's 'Raven.' " This printing restores the final stanza, omitted in the 22 November 1848 republication in the Providence *Daily Journal*.

8 MARCH. FORDHAM. Poe writes Duyckinck in New York. He left "Von Kempelen and his Discovery" with Duyckinck's brother George. This tale is a hoax written "in the plausible or verisimilar style," which announces that a European scientist has discovered a way to turn lead into gold: "I thought that such a style, applied to the gold-excitement, could not fail of effect. My sincere opinion is that nine persons out of ten (even among the best-informed) will *believe* the quiz (provided the design does not leak out before publication) and that thus, acting as a sudden, although of course a very temporary, *check* to the gold-fever, it will create a *stir* to some purpose." Although the tale was prepared for the *Flag of Our Union*, Poe fears that "it will be quite thrown away" if published there: "The proprietor will give me $15 for it on presentation to his agent here; and my object in referring the article to you is simply to see if you could not venture to take it for the 'World'. If so, I am willing to take for it $10—or, in fact, whatever you think you can afford." Poe thanks Duyckinck for reprinting "Ulalume" (*L*, 2:433–34).

10 MARCH. BOSTON. The *Flag* for 17 March contains Poe's "Hop-Frog: Or, The Eight Chained Ourang-Outangs." The publisher Frederick Gleason comments:

> That Valentine, by Poe.
>
> Having received a poem from our regular contributor, Edgar A. Poe, Esq., and having paid for the same as *original*, we were not a little surprised to see the poem

appear in Sartain's Union Magazine for March, uncredited, and as original, though in the table of contents, on the cover, it is omitted. We at once addressed Mr. Poe, for an explanation, lest it should appear that we had taken the Valentine from the Magazine without credit. His answer to us is full and satisfactory. The said poem was written and handed to Mr. De Graw, a gentleman who proposed to start a Magazine in New York, but who gave up the project, and started himself for California. Mr. Poe, learning of this, thought, of course, his composition was his own again, and sent it to us as one of his regular contributions for the Flag; and was himself as much surprised as we could be, to see it, not long afterwards, in the Magazine, though the publisher does not say there that it was written for his pages. It was doubtless handed by Mr. De Graw to Sartain, and published thus without any intent to wrong any one. We make this statement, as in duty bound to Mr. Poe, and ourselves.

CA. 15 MARCH. NEW YORK. The *American Metropolitan Magazine* ceases publication. The second and final number, dated February, contains Mrs. Whitman's "Stanzas for Music," intended as a discreet reply to Poe. She recalls: "I was much blamed at the time for allowing them [these verses] to be published. They were supposed to be addressed to Mr. Poe and were copied into many of the papers" (Whitman to Mrs. Mary E. Hewitt, 10 October 1850, Williams, p. 769; cf. Stoddard [1884], 1:159, and Miller [1979], p. 35).

AFTER 15? MARCH. The *Metropolitan* returns to Poe his unpublished sketch "Landor's Cottage" (Poe to Annie, 23 March).

17 MARCH. BOSTON. The *Flag of Our Union* for 24 March contains this announcement: " 'A Dream within a Dream,' a poem, by our regular contributor, EDGAR A. POE, filed for next week."

20 MARCH. NEW YORK. The *Evening Mirror* reprints Poe's "A Valentine" under the heading "A Riddle for Somebody to Unriddle" (Heartman and Canny, p. 235).

23 MARCH. Poe writes Annie Richmond in Lowell: "I am so happy in being able to afford Mr. R. [Charles B. Richmond] proof of something in which he seems to doubt me. You remember that Mr. and Mrs. Locke strenuously denied having spoken ill of you to me." Poe received several letters from Jane Ermina Locke which were "filled with abuse" of Annie and her husband; but since he returned them to the Lowell poetess, he could not produce them as evidence of her ill will toward the Richmonds. He looked over the letters Mrs. Locke sent Mrs. Clemm, but unfortunately found nothing in them that would corroborate his account of her slanders: "Well! what *do* you think? Mrs. Locke has again written my mother, and I enclose her letter. Read it! You will find it thoroughly

corroborative of all I said. . . . You will see that she admits having cautioned me against you, as I said, and in fact admits all that I accused her of." Poe is also enclosing "For Annie"; he solicits Annie's opinion of this new poem, which he has sold to the *Flag of Our Union*: "By the way, did you get 'Hop-Frog'? I sent it to you by mail, not knowing whether you ever see the paper . . . . I am sorry to say that the *Metropolitan* has stopped, and 'Landor's Cottage' is returned upon my hands unprinted. I think the lines 'For Annie' (those I now send) much the *best* I have ever written—but an author can seldom depend on his own estimate of his own works . . . . Do not let these verses go *out of your possession* until you see them in print" (*L*, 2:434–36; Ingram, pp. 406–08).

24 MARCH. BOSTON. The *Flag of Our Union* for 31 March contains Poe's "A Dream Within a Dream."

APRIL? NEW YORK. Poe gives "Landor's Cottage" to Mr. French, agent for the *Flag* (Poe to Annie, after 5? May).

APRIL? [1849?] Poe accompanies the poet William Ross Wallace to Mathew B. Brady's "Daguerreian Gallery" at 205 Broadway, corner of Fulton Street. Brady makes a daguerreotype of Poe free of charge (Gimbel, pp. 169, 187; Horan, p. 10, plate 46; Meredith, pp. 30–31, plate 20).

APRIL. PHILADELPHIA. *Graham's Magazine* contains Poe's unsigned review of Sarah Anna Lewis' *The Child of the Sea and Other Poems* (attribution in Stoddard [1889], p. 113, and [1903], pp. 159–60).

APRIL. CINCINNATI. The *Western Quarterly Review* contains an unsigned review of Mrs. Lewis' volume by Poe, longer than that in the April *Graham's*. This notice is a partial recast of his signed criticism in the *Southern Literary Messenger* for September 1848 (attribution also implied in Poe to Mrs. Clemm, 28?–29? August).

APRIL. RICHMOND. The *Southern Literary Messenger* publishes the first of five installments of "Marginalia." The editor John R. Thompson furnishes this explanatory note: "Some years since Mr. Poe wrote for several of the Northern magazines a series of critical brevities under the title of 'Marginalia.' They attracted great attention at that time and since, as characteristic of the author, and we are sure that our readers will be gratified at his resuming them in the Messenger. By way of introduction, we republish the original preface from the Democratic Review."

1 APRIL. FORDHAM. Poe writes Anson Gleason Chester, a young Presbyterian minister in Saratoga Springs, New York: "In reply to your very flattering request for an autograph poem, I have the honor of copying for you the subjoined lines just written ['For Annie']. As they will be sold to one of our periodicals, may I beg of you not to let them pass out of your possession until published?" (InU–L).

7 APRIL. BOSTON. The *Flag of Our Union* for 14 April contains Poe's tale "Von Kempelen and his Discovery." His poem "Eldorado" is announced: "in our next number."

10 APRIL. WASHINGTON. Frederick William Thomas receives Poe's 14 February letter, originally addressed to him in Louisville, Kentucky. It has been redirected several times (L, 2:537).

14 APRIL. ATHENS, GEORGIA. The *Southern Literary Gazette* notices this month's *Southern Literary Messenger*. From "Marginalia" the *Gazette* quotes the paragraph of "bitterest sarcasm" in which Poe recommends this quotation from Laurence Sterne's *Tristram Shandy* (Book VI, Chapter 1) as a motto for the *North American Review*: "As we rode along the valley we saw a herd of asses on the top of one of the mountains—how they viewed and *reviewed* us!" Poe's genius must be acknowledged, even by "those who most dislike his wild extravagancies and psychological transcendentalisms."

14 APRIL. BOSTON. The *Flag of Our Union* for 21 April contains Poe's "Eldorado." The next issue will feature his "For Annie," a poem "peculiar and characteristic."

20 APRIL. FORDHAM. Poe forwards a manuscript copy of "For Annie" to Nathaniel P. Willis, co-editor of the New York *Home Journal*: "The poem . . . has been just published in a paper for which sheer necessity compels me to write, now and then. It pays well as times go—but unquestionably it ought to pay ten prices; for whatever I send it I feel I am consigning to the tomb of the Capulets." Poe asks Willis to reprint "For Annie" in the *Home Journal*. The poem's source could be cited as "a late Boston paper"; there is no need to mention the *Flag of Our Union* by name. "I have not forgotten how a 'good word in season' from you made 'The Raven,' and made 'Ulalume,' (which, by-the-way, people have done me the honor of attributing to you)—therefore I *would* ask you (if I dared,) to say something of these lines—if they please you" (L, 2:436–37).

20 APRIL OR LATER. NEW YORK. Willis sends "For Annie" to the printer, writing a note on Poe's manuscript: "Will Mr. Babcock please put this on

the second page *this* week, & leave me twenty lines room for an introduction" (Mabbott [1969], 1:455).

21 APRIL. BOSTON. The *Flag* for 28 April contains "For Annie," printed under the caption "Written for The Flag of Our Union." The issue also contains "The Voices of the Night—A POE-UM" by "Professor Shortfellow," a parody of "The Raven" reprinted from the *Boston Courier*.

AFTER 21 APRIL. NEW YORK. The *Home Journal* for 28 April contains "For Annie" without any acknowledgment of its prior publication. In a preface headed "ODD POEM," Willis comments:

> The following exquisite specimen of the *private property in words* has been sent us by a friend . . . . POE certainly has that gift of nature, which an abstract man should be most proud of—a type of mind different from all others without being less truthful in its perceptions for that difference; and though (to use two long words) this kind of *idiosyncracy* is necessarily *idiopathic*, and, from want of sympathy, cannot be largely popular, it is as valuable as rarity in any thing else, and to be admired by connoisseurs proportionately. Money (to tell a useless truth) could not be better laid out for the honor of this period of American literature—neither by the government, by a society, nor by an individual—than in giving EDGAR POE a competent annuity, on condition that he should never write except upon impulse, never dilute his thoughts for the magazines, and never publish any thing till it had been written a year. And this *because* the threatening dropsy of our country's literature is its copying the GREGARIOUSNESS which prevails in every thing else, while Mr. POE is not only peculiar in himself, but unsusceptible of imitation. We have Bulwers by hundreds, Mrs. Hemanses by thousands, Byrons common as shirt-collars, every kind of writer "by the lot," and less of *individualesque genius* than any other country in the world.

28 APRIL. BOSTON. The *Flag* for 5 May announces that "X-ing a Paragrab," a "capital prose sketch" by Poe, will appear in the next issue.

LATE APRIL. NEW YORK. Poe replies to an 18 December 1848 letter from Edward H. N. Patterson of Oquawka, Illinois, which he has "only this moment" received. He explains that he collects his mail at the post office in New York: "When, by accident or misapprehension, letters are especially directed to me at Fordham, the clerks—some of them who do not know my arrangements—forward them to West-Farms, the nearest Post-Office town, and one which I rarely visit. Thus it happened with *your* letter—on account of the request which you made Mr. [George P.] Putnam, I presume, 'to forward it to my residence'." Poe expresses his readiness to join Patterson in establishing a national magazine: "I do not think . . . that a Magazine could succeed, to any great extent, under the precise form, title, and general plan which (no doubt hurriedly) you have suggested; but your idea of the duplicate publication, East & West, strikes me forcibly." He outlines his own concepts: "We must aim high—address the intellect—the higher classes—of the country (with reference, also, to a certain amount of foreign circulation) and put the work at $5 . . . . Such a Mag. would begin to pay after 1000 subscribers; and with 5000 would be a fortune worth talking about . . . . My plan, in getting up such a work as I propose, would be to take a tour through the principal States—especially West & South—visiting the small towns more particularly than the large ones—lecturing as I went, to pay expenses." If Patterson's own views are in accord with these, Poe will endeavor to visit him at Oquawka or to meet him at any place he suggests (L, 2:439–41).

LATE APRIL? BOSTON. The *Flag of Our Union* apparently sends a printed circular to Poe and other contributors, stating that it can no longer pay for articles (implied by Poe to Annie, after 5? May).

CA. MAY. NEW YORK. Rufus W. Griswold invites Poe to contribute several new poems to the forthcoming tenth edition of his anthology *The Poets and Poetry of America* (Poe's reply).

CA. MAY. FORDHAM. Poe writes Griswold: "I enclose perfect copies of the lines 'For Annie' and 'Annabel Lee'—in hope that you may make room for them." He copies his revised last stanza of "Lenore," a poem Griswold has promised to insert. "Willis . . . has done me the honor to speak very pointedly in praise of 'The Raven'—I enclose what he said—& if you could contrive to introduce it, you would render me an essential favor" (L, 2:445–46).

MAY. PHILADELPHIA. *Graham's Magazine* contains the first half of Poe's "Fifty Suggestions," brief observations in the style of "Marginalia."

MAY. RICHMOND. The *Southern Literary Messenger* contains a second installment of "Marginalia."

EARLY MAY? FORDHAM. Mrs. Clemm writes Annie Richmond at Lowell, stating that Poe is very ill (Poe to Annie, after 5? May).

EARLY MAY? LOWELL. Mrs. Jane Ermina Locke writes Poe, apparently assuring him of her continued affection and regard. She plans to publish a detailed account of her relations with him, thinly disguising it as a work of fiction (Poe to Annie, after 5? May).

EARLY MAY? Annie Richmond writes Poe, expressing concern over his health. She has seen "For Annie" in the *Home Journal* for 28 April; she asks if Poe can identify the "friend," mentioned in Willis' preface, who sent the poem to this paper (Poe to Annie, after 5? May).

5 MAY. BOSTON. The *Flag of Our Union* for 12 May contains Poe's humorous sketch "X-ing a Paragrab." The issue also carries this protest, written by the publisher Frederick Gleason or his editor Maturin M. Ballou:

CREDIT.—The Home Journal, after paying a deservedly high compliment to our regular contributor, Edgar A. Poe, copies a long poem written by him for the Flag, without a word of credit. This is a point on which we have learned to be somewhat sensitive, scrupulously giving credit in all instances, and as earnestly exacting the same.

AFTER 5? MAY. FORDHAM. Poe replies to Annie Richmond: "You will see by this note that I am nearly, if not quite, well—so be no longer uneasy on my account. I was not so ill as my mother [Mrs. Clemm] supposed, and she is so anxious about me that she takes alarm often without cause. It is not so much *ill* that I have been as depressed in spirits . . . . I have met one disappointment after another. The *Columbian Magazine*, in the first place, failed—then [Israel] Post's *Union* (taking with it my principal dependence); then the *Whig Review* was forced to stop paying for contributions—then the *Democratic*." Poe was "obliged to quarrel" with a publisher [possibly Louis A. Godey]; and a journal with which he "had made a regular engagement for $10 a week" [presumably the *Flag of Our Union*] has sent "a circular to correspondents, pleading poverty and declining to receive any more articles." The *Southern Literary Messenger*, which owes him "a good deal," has not been able to pay; he is thus dependent on *Sartain's* and *Graham's*, neither a reliable source of income. He describes a letter he recently received from Mrs. Locke: "She says she is about to publish a detailed account of *all* that occurred between us, under guise of romance, with fictitious names, &c.,—that she will make me appear noble, generous, &c. &c.—nothing bad—that she will 'do justice to my motives,' &c. &c." Poe himself sent "For Annie" to the *Home Journal*, because the *Flag of Our Union* "so misprinted" the poem: "I was resolved to have a true copy. The *Flag* has two of my articles yet—'A Sonnet to my Mother,' and 'Landor's Cottage.' . . . I have written a ballad called 'Annabel Lee,' which I will send you soon" (L, 2:437–39).

AFTER 5? MAY. Mrs. Clemm appends a message to Poe's letter: "Thank you a thousand times for your letter, my dear 'Annie.' Do not believe Eddy; he has been very ill, but is now better. I thought he would *die* several times" (Ingram, pp. 410–11).

7 MAY. OQUAWKA, ILLINOIS. Edward H. N. Patterson replies to Poe's letter written in late April:

Your opinions, strengthened as they have been by experience, have had their weight in convincing me that it would probably be better to establish at the onset a high priced, and correspondingly hightoned periodical . . . . When I wrote you before, I had not given the subject that consideration which it deserved,—my principal object, at that time, being to enlist your sympathies and interests in a periodical, the literary contents of which should be *exclusively* under your control, believing that such an enterprize would prove successful, not doubting that even a cheap Magazine, under *your* editorial control, could be made to pay well, and at the same time exert a beneficial influence upon American Literature.

Patterson would publish their proposed magazine "in monthly numbers, at Oquawka, Illinois, containing, in every number, 96 pages . . . at the rate of $5 per annum." To Poe, the editor, would fall "the task of selecting an appropriate name" for the journal: "Make out a list of contributors and write a prospectus, and forward to me as soon as you can so that I may at once commence operations." They will divide the profits equally: "the books to be faithfully kept, in the publication office at Oquawka, and one half of all receipts from subscriptions, and private and agency sales, to be forwarded to you monthly." If Poe agrees to these proposals, Patterson will visit him in New York "during the latter part of July or 1st of August" to complete their arrangements: "We ought to get out the first number early in January next" (draft of letter in InU–L; printed in *W*, 17:352–55, with canceled words italicized and placed in parentheses).

16 MAY. The *Oquawka Spectator* reprints "For Annie" from the *Home Journal* of 28 April. Patterson, the junior editor, provides this preface:

A Remarkable Poem

We give below a most singularly conceived and oddly expressed poem. It is from the pen of the celebrated EDGAR A. POE—the only man who could have written it. There is no author who has a finer perception of the power of words than POE; and in addition to this delicate critical perception, he possesses a peculiarity of style which is Originality itself, and one which no one has yet been able successfully to imitate (McElroy, p. 259).

BEFORE 17 MAY. BROOKLYN? Mrs. Sarah Anna Lewis asks Poe for a manuscript copy of "For Annie." Apparently, she also requests two other favors of him: that he try to induce her publisher George P. Putnam to issue a second edition of her poetry, and that he write a favorable sketch of her and then persuade Rufus W. Griswold to insert it in the subsequent editions of *The Female Poets of America* (Poe to Mrs. Lewis, 17 May, to Putnam, 18 May, and to Griswold, 28 June).

CA. 17? MAY. LOWELL. Sarah Helen Whitman visits Jane Ermina Locke at her home, Wamesit Cottage. She recalls: "In the spring of 1849 I recieved [*sic*] many letters from Mrs L. urging me to visit her at Lowell. She was at that time a stranger to me and I of course declined the invitation. She, however, would take no denial & renewed her entreaties so pressingly & with such earnest assurances of having important information to impart which could not be entrusted to a letter, that I at length consented to pass a week with her. . . . Her object in seeking my acquaintance was unquestionably to prevent any renewal of my correspondence with Mr Poe, by whom she concieved [*sic*] herself to have been deeply wronged" (Whitman to Mrs. Clemm, 24 November [1852], *W*, 17:419–21; facsimile in Quinn and Hart, pp. 36–39).

17 MAY. FORDHAM. Poe writes Mrs. Lewis in Brooklyn: "I have not been well enough, lately, to copy the lines 'For Annie' but will copy them today. In regard to the other matter, depend upon me—as in *all* respects you may, with implicit confidence. Please make a memorandum as explicit as possible—so that I may know precisely what you wish" (*L*, 2:442; Moldenhauer [1973], p. 72).

18 MAY. Poe writes George P. Putnam in New York. Several of Mrs. Lewis' friends have suggested that she issue a second edition of *The Child of the Sea and Other Poems*, expanded to include the poetry she has recently written: "My object, in this note, is to submit the idea to your consideration.—Mrs Lewis has an unusually large circle of personal friends, has been highly praised by the critics, is very popular as an authoress and daily growing more so . . . . If the volume suggested were prepared in season for the next Holidays, I think you will agree with me that it could not fail of success" (*L*, 2:442–43; Moldenhauer [1973], pp. 72–73).

20 MAY. NEW YORK. Putnam replies to Poe, presumably declining to issue a second edition (cited on Poe's letter).

23 MAY. Poe writes Edward H. N. Patterson in Oquawka, Illinois. Although Patterson's 7 May letter arrived "in due course of mail," Poe has delayed his answer for a week in order that he might thoroughly consider the proposed magazine: "I shrink from making any attempt which *may* fail. . . . I confess that some serious difficulties present themselves. . . . Your residence at Okquawka [*sic*] is certainly one of the most serious of these difficulties; and I submit to you whether it be not possible to put on our title-page 'Published simultaneously at New-York & *St Louis*'—or something equivalent." Upon the whole Poe agrees to Patterson's plan; he

is enclosing a title page which he designed for his own proposed journal, the *Stylus*, "about a year ago." As Poe's project has already been announced, this name should be retained. "We will find the 7 months between now and January brief enough for our preparations. . . . To-day I am going *to* Boston & Lowell, to remain a week; and immediately afterwards I will start for Richmond, where I will await your answer to this letter. Please direct to me *there*, under cover, or to the care of John R. Thompson, Edr of the 'South. Lit. Messenger.' On receipt of your letter (should you still be in the mind you now are) I will proceed to St Louis & there meet you. . . . I must ask you to advance half of the sum I need to begin with—about $100. Please, therefore, enclose $50 in your reply, which I will get at Richmond" (*L*, 2:443–44).

24? MAY. LOWELL. Mrs. Whitman ends her brief visit with Mrs. Locke; she leaves the city on the same day that Poe arrives.

[On 25 October 1875 Mrs. Whitman wrote J. H. Ingram: "I began to suspect that she [Mrs. Locke] had hoped to pique the Raven [Poe] by exhibiting me as her guest . . . . At all events, she told me as an inducement for me to prolong my stay a day or two after the time fixed for my departure, that she had taken care he should hear of my visit, & she had reason to think he would be in Lowell during the time fixed for my stay. My heart thrilled at the thought of seeing him again, but I could not accede to her request. We crossed each other on the road! I did not *know* it until a letter from Mrs. L[ocke] informed me of the fact; but if you were not such a sceptic as to spiritual or magnetic phenomena, I could tell you of a strange experience which happened to me as the two trains rushed past each other between Boston & Lowell" (Miller [1979], p. 349).]

26 MAY. BOSTON. The *Flag of Our Union* for 2 June announces that Poe's "Landor's Cottage" will appear in the next issue.

26 MAY. The *Boston Museum* reprints Poe's tale "A Descent into the Maelström" from *Graham's Magazine* of May 1841 (Mabbott [1978], 2:577).

LATE MAY. NEW YORK. Stringer & Townsend, 222 Broadway, publish John E. Tuel's *The Moral for Authors*, a verse satire aimed at British and American literati. In "Part II," devoted to native writers, Tuel's narrator recalls that he sought fame in literary endeavor but found instead a "dismal row / Of *croaking* authors dire, led on by POE, / All pecking at my lean and hungry book." This introduction is followed by a long parody entitled "Plutonian Shore" and dated "*Raven Creek, In the Year of Poetry*":

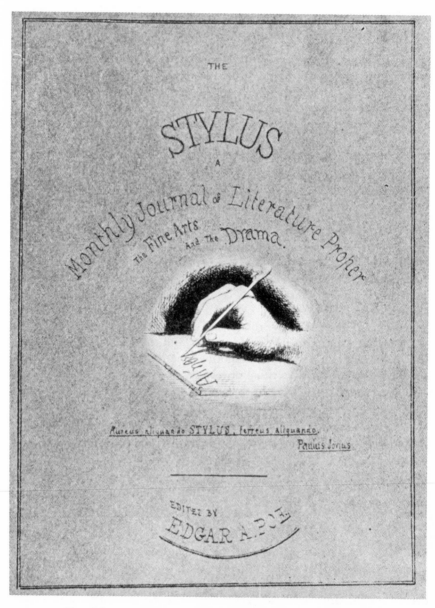

The title page Poe sent Edward H. N. Patterson on 23 May

Once upon a midnight dreary, as I ponder'd weak and weary
Over many a weary volume of recent published lore—
While I nodded o'er *"The Sleeper,"* suddenly I heard a creeper,
As of some one peering deeper—deeper in my chamber door;
'Tis some author new, I mutter'd, or some other midnight bore;
Only this, and nothing more!

The nocturnal visitor proves to be a "young aspiring Author" delivering an unsolicited manuscript, which the narrator reluctantly reads:

"Author!" said I, "Imp of Evil—Author great, or God or Devil,
Whether PUTNAM sent or HARPER toss'd thee here ashore,
Dull and stupid yet undaunted—on this sheet romantic wasted—
On this floor by volumes haunted—tell me plainly, I implore,
Is there—*is* there sense in this? tell me, tell me, I implore."
Quoth the Author, "Read it o'er!"

LATE MAY TO EARLY JUNE. LOWELL. Poe spends "something more than a week" with Annie Richmond and her family. He visits the Franklin Grammar School, of which her brother Bardwell Heywood has recently been elected principal; here he is attracted to a young teacher of twenty-one, Miss Eliza Jane Butterfield (Bardwell to Miss Sawyer, 16 June; Freeman [1967], pp. 389–91, and [1971], pp. 115–17).

Reverend Warren H. Cudworth, friend and pastor to the Richmond family, prepares a cryptogram to test Poe's ability as a cryptographer. "Mr Poe solved this cipher, in one-fifth of the time it took me to write it" (Cudworth in Lowell *Weekly Journal*, 19 April 1850; clipping in ViU–I).

Poe gives Annie a manuscript copy of the third version of "The Bells," containing his final revisions in ink and pencil (Annie's letters to J. H. Ingram in Miller [1977], pp. 153–55, 160–61, 166, 182–84; partial facsimile of "Bells" manuscript in Gill, after p. 206; original in NNPM).

LATE MAY OR EARLY JUNE? At Annie's request Poe sits for a Lowell daguerreotypist, possibly George C. Gilchrest, 82 Merrimack Street, or Samuel P. Howes, 112 Merrimack (information supplied by Michael J. Deas, from his forthcoming book on Poe portraiture; Uchida, pp. 1–4, 13).

[At least two plates were taken at this sitting. The most attractive has been called the "Stella" daguerreotype, from a copy that Sarah Anna Lewis gave John Henry Ingram and which came to the University of Virginia with the Ingram Collection. The other plate has been known variously as the "Annie" daguerreotype, from Mrs. Richmond's own copy, or as the "Painter" daguerreotype, from a copy that Mrs. Clemm gave William Painter of Baltimore in 1868. The "Annie" is now at the J. Paul Getty

Museum; the "Painter," at the Maryland Historical Society. In her 3 October 1876 letter to Ingram, Annie Richmond criticized this likeness: "Mr. Poe's [picture] does not do him justice . . . his face was thin, & . . . he looks very stout, & his features heavy" (Miller [1977], pp. 152–54).]

JUNE. PHILADELPHIA. *Graham's Magazine* contains the conclusion of Poe's "Fifty Suggestions."

JUNE. RICHMOND. The *Southern Literary Messenger* contains a second installment of "Marginalia" as well as Mrs. Whitman's "Lines" dated "*March* 1849*,*" a brief poem apparently intended as a reconciliatory message for Poe.

EARLY JUNE. FORDHAM. Having returned from Lowell, Poe writes Annie, apparently telling her that he will leave for Richmond on 11 June (Poe to Annie, 16 June).

EARLY JUNE. Poe writes Samuel D. Patterson, who became the publisher of *Graham's Magazine* in 1848. He explains that he mailed several articles to *Graham's*, but that his draft on the magazine, written in Lowell, was returned unpaid (Poe to Annie, 16 June).

EARLY JUNE. PHILADELPHIA. Samuel D. Patterson replies to Poe, stating that the articles were never received (Poe to Annie, 16 June).

SUMMER. PROVIDENCE. Mrs. Whitman receives "many letters" from Mrs. Locke, containing "frequent allusions to the subject [Poe] that so deeply engrossed her feelings." She recalls: "I saw however that she [Mrs. Locke] was too much under the influence of wounded pride to exercise a calm judgement in the matter, and said but little in reply to her representations" (Whitman to Mrs. Clemm, 24 November [1852], *W*, 17:419–21; facsimile in Quinn and Hart, pp. 36–39).

CA. 1? JUNE. OQUAWKA, ILLINOIS. Edward H. N. Patterson promptly replies to Poe's 23 May letter. As requested, he forwards $50 to Poe at Richmond, in care of John R. Thompson (Poe to Patterson, 19 July and 7 August).

2 JUNE. BOSTON. The *Flag of Our Union* for 9 June contains Poe's "Landor's Cottage," described in the subheading as "A Pendant to 'The Domain of Arnheim.'"

2 JUNE. NEW YORK. The *Literary World* reviews John E. Tuel's *The Moral for Authors*, mentioning Poe as one of the American writers satirized "in characteristic verses modelled on their own style."

7 JUNE. OQUAWKA, ILLINOIS. Edward H. N. Patterson sends Poe another letter addressed to Richmond. In it he apparently proposes that they publish a three-dollar magazine instead of a five-dollar one (Poe to Patterson, 19 July and 7 August).

9 JUNE. NEW YORK. Poe writes John R. Thompson in Richmond: "It was my design to be in Richmond about the first of this month—but now it will be the 18th or 20th before I can leave New-York. . . . Please send me $10 if you can possibly spare it. . . . Most probably you will have received, ere this, a letter for me, addressed to your care at Richmond. In such case, may I ask you to forward it here under cover with your reply?— but if it has not reached you when this letter does, please retain it (when it arrives) until you see me in Richmond" (*L*, 2:446).

BEFORE 10 JUNE. LOWELL. Annie replies to the letter Poe sent her after his return to Fordham. She asks him to write her before he leaves for Richmond; she has sent his "love" to Miss Butterfield, the young teacher at the Franklin Grammar School (Poe to Annie, 16 June).

AFTER 10 JUNE. RICHMOND. Thompson receives Poe's 9 June letter as well as the two letters Edward H. N. Patterson sent Poe in his care. Thompson decides not to forward Patterson's letters to New York, since he expects to see Poe in several days (implied by Poe to Patterson, 19 July).

16 JUNE. LOWELL? Bardwell Heywood writes Miss Annie Sawyer:

Mr. Poe has just spent something more than a week with us, and so anxious was I lest I should lose the benefit of his original thoughts, which were continually dripping from his lips, that I spent almost every moment out of school in his presence. . . . Would to God Mr. Poe could give me the thousandth part of his gigantic intellect. . . .

Some men, I now think, are great in spite of themselves. They can no more help being distinguished than I can help being otherwise. Mr. Poe seems to be of that class. He seems to be entirely unconscious of his extraordinary mental power, and yet cannot fail to discover it to everyone with whom he converses, if but for a moment.

He honored my school with two visits while in the city, though I suppose I should have seen him there but once had he not fallen in love with one of the assistants [Miss Eliza Jane Butterfield]. He confessed that he called on purpose to see her. So I took him into her room the moment he entered, and left them alone.

Whether he proposed or not I have not ascertained. I only noticed an uncommon flush upon her cheek when they came out (Coburn, pp. 474–75).

16 JUNE. FORDHAM. Poe replies to the letter Annie Richmond sent him before 10 June: "You must have been thinking all kinds of hard thoughts of your Eddie for the last week—for you asked me to write before I started for Richmond and I was to have started last Monday (the 11th) . . . . I have been *on the point* of starting every day since I wrote—and so put off writing . . . . *When* I can go now, is uncertain." He has discovered the reason for the return of his draft on *Graham's Magazine*, which caused him "such annoyance and mortification" during his visit to Lowell. The articles he mailed to *Graham's* never arrived: "I enclose the publishers' reply to my letter of enquiry. The Postmaster here is investigating the matter & in all probability the articles will be found & the draft paid by the time you get this." Poe is also enclosing a letter Mrs. Locke recently sent Mrs. Clemm as well as the "long MS. poem" that she sent him last August, "Ermina's Tale." He asks whether Annie has seen Tuel's new satire *The Moral for Authors*: "who, in the name of Heaven[,] *is* J. E. Tuel? The book is miserably stupid. He has a long parody of the Raven." Poe regrets that he was forced to part "so coldly" from Annie's sister Sarah H. Heywood; he asks to be remembered to her parents and husband, to her young daughter Caddy and her brother Bardwell Heywood. "How *dared* you send my love to Miss B[utterfield].? Look over my letter and see if I even so much as mentioned her name. *Dear* Annie, my heart reproached me (after I parted with you) for having, even in jest, requested Bardwell to 'remember me to Miss B.' I thought it might have *pained* you in some measure" (*L*, 2:446–48; Moldenhauer [1973], pp. 73–74).

23 JUNE. BOSTON. The *Flag of Our Union* for 30 June announces that Poe's "Sonnet—To my Mother" will appear in the next issue.

26 JUNE. NEW YORK. Poe writes George W. Eveleth in Brunswick, Maine: "On the principle of 'better late than never', I avail myself of a few moments' leisure to say a word or two in reply to your last letter [of 17 February] . . . . The essay you enclose, on the igneous liquidity of the Earth, embodies some truth, and evinces much sagacity—but no doubt ere this you have perceived that you have been groping in the dark as regards the general subject. Before theorizing ourselves on such topics, it is always wisest to make ourselves acquainted with the actually ascertained facts & established doctrines. . . . Let me know frankly how 'Eureka' impresses you." Professor John W. Draper belongs to the school of "Hogites," those strict empirical thinkers satirized in *Eureka*: "A merely perceptive man with no intrinsic force—no power of generalization—in short a pompous nobody." Poe encloses "For Annie," taken from the *Home Journal*

for 28 April: "How do you like it?—you know I put much faith in your poetical judgments. . . . Do you ever see 'The Literary World'?" Poe has simply been "awaiting the *best opportunity*" before beginning his own journal, the *Stylus*: "I am now going to Richmond to 'see about it'—& *possibly* I may get out the first number on next January" (*L*, 2:449–50).

28 JUNE. NEW YORK. Poe replies to a letter from H. S. Root, who wishes to locate a copy of Dr. Pliny Earle's *Marathon, and Other Poems*: "I fancy the edition—(one only was published)—is out of print. The Doctor himself, when I last heard of him, was Superintendent of the Asylum for the Insane, at Bloomingdale, near this city" (*L*, 2:451–52).

28 JUNE. Poe writes Rufus W. Griswold: "Since I have more critically examined your 'Female Poets' it occurs to me that you have not *quite* done justice to our common friend, Mrs. Lewis; and if you could oblige me so far as to substitute, for your no doubt hurried notice, a somewhat longer one prepared by myself (subject, of course, to your emendations) I would reciprocate the favor when, where, and *as* you please." Poe will leave his sketch of Sarah Anna Lewis in a sealed package at her home in Brooklyn, but she is "unaware" of his intentions. "I would rather she should consider herself as indebted to *you* for the favor, at all points. By calling on Mrs. L., and asking for a package to your address, you can at any moment get it. I would not, of course, put you to any *expense* in this matter:—all cost shall be promptly defrayed" (*L*, 2:450–51).

[It is unlikely that Mrs. Lewis was unaware of Poe's action: in his 17 May letter to her, he seems to be requesting a biographical "memorandum" to use in preparing this sketch. Sylvanus D. Lewis, her husband, was to defray the cost of having it set in type (cf. Lewis to Griswold, 3 September). Although Griswold never inserted the sketch in *The Female Poets of America*, he did include it in his edition of Poe's works (rpt. *W*, 13:215–25).]

BEFORE 29 JUNE. Poe gives a manuscript copy of "Annabel Lee" to John W. Moore, a bookkeeper who has aided him in the past (Phillips, 2:1414; Mabbott [1969], 1:475).

BEFORE 29 JUNE. FORDHAM. Poe informs Mrs. Clemm that, in the event of his death, he would like Rufus W. Griswold to "act as his Literary Executor, and superintend the publication of his works," and Nathaniel P. Willis to write "observations upon his life and character . . . in vindication of his memory" (Mrs. Clemm's "Preface" to Griswold's edition, rpt. *W*, 1:347–48).

[Mrs. Clemm claimed that Poe left written requests naming an executor and a biographer. These documents have never been located and may never have existed; but it is not unlikely that Poe expressed his wishes to Mrs. Clemm, even if only orally.]

29 JUNE. BROOKLYN. On Friday afternoon Poe and Mrs. Clemm dine with Mrs. Lewis and her husband at their home, 125 Dean Street. At 5:00 PM Poe leaves for Richmond. Sylvanus D. Lewis recalls: "When he [Poe] finally departed on his last trip south, the kissing and handshaking were at my front-door. He was hopeful; we were sad: and tears gushed in torrents as he kissed his 'dear Muddie' and my wife, 'good-bye' " (letter to S. S. Rice, 11 October 1875, Rice, pp. 86–87; see also Mrs. Lewis to G. W. Eveleth, 11 February and 6 November 1854, Miller [1977], pp. 198–200).

30 JUNE. NEW YORK. After spending the night with Mrs. Lewis, Mrs. Clemm returns to Fordham. At the post office in New York she receives a letter from Annie, with another letter for Poe enclosed (Clemm to Annie, 9 July and 4 August).

30 JUNE. BOSTON. The *Flag of Our Union* for 7 July contains Poe's "Sonnet—To my Mother," expressing his love for Mrs. Clemm.

30 JUNE. PHILADELPHIA. Poe arrives in Philadelphia, where he begins drinking. His valise, containing two lectures he intends to deliver in Richmond, is misplaced at the railway station (Poe to Mrs. Clemm, 7 and 14 July).

JULY. RICHMOND. The *Southern Literary Messenger* contains a fourth installment of Poe's "Marginalia."

1? JULY. PHILADELPHIA. Poe is taken to prison "for getting drunk" (Poe to Mrs. Clemm, 7 July).

[John Sartain stated that Poe was detained "for a few hours only" in Moyamensing, the Philadelphia County prison at Tenth and Reed Streets: "I learned later that when his turn came in the motley group before Mayor Gilpin, some one said, 'Why, this is Poe, the poet,' and he was dismissed without the customary fine" (Sartain, p. 210). Reports in the *Pennsylvanian* and other newspapers issued in early July establish that persons arrested for intoxication were indeed brought before the Mayor and fined; but Joel Jones held that office in 1849, Charles Gilpin not being elected until 1850.]

2? JULY. On "Monday afternoon" Poe calls on John Sartain in his engraving studio, located in the first floor of his house at 28 Sansom Street (later numbered 728). Poe is "pale and haggard, with a wild and frightened expression in his eyes"; he asks Sartain for "a refuge and protection," explaining that "some men" are trying to kill him. Sartain recalls: "I assured him that he was welcome, that in my house he would be perfectly safe, and he could stay as long as he liked . . . . From such fear of assassination his mind gradually veered round to an idea of self-destruction, and his words clearly indicated this tendency. After a long silence he said suddenly, 'If this mustache of mine were removed I should not be so readily recognized; will you lend me a razor, that I may shave it off?' I told him that as I never shaved I had no razor, but if he wanted it removed I could readily do it for him with scissors. Accordingly I took him to the bathroom and performed the operation successfully" (Sartain, pp. 206–07).

In the evening Sartain accompanies Poe to the Fairmount Waterworks, overlooking the Schuylkill River: "He [Poe] complained that his feet hurt him, being chafed by his shoes, which were worn down on the outer side of the heel. So for ease and comfort he wore my slippers . . . . After getting the omnibus we rode to its stopping-place, a little short of Fairmount . . . . I kept on his left side, [between him and the river,] and on approaching the foot of the bridge [over the river] guided him off to the right by a gentle pressure, until we reached the lofty flight of steep wooden steps which ascended almost to the top of the reservoir." After they climb these stairs Poe describes the "weird and fantastic" visions which he experienced during his confinement in Moyamensing, including an hallucination in which he saw Mrs. Clemm being dismembered. Sartain recalls: "The horror of the imagined scene [involving Mrs. Clemm] threw him into a sort of convulsion. . . . It came into my mind that Poe might possibly in a sudden fit of frenzy leap freely forth with me in his arms into the black depth below . . . . I suggested at last that as it appeared we were not to have the moon we might as well go down again. He agreed, and we descended the steep stairway slowly and cautiously, holding well to the hand-rails. . . . I got him safe home, and gave him a bed on a sofa in the dining-room, while I slept alongside him on three chairs, without undressing" (Sartain, pp. 207–12; cf. George Lippard's description of Poe's shoes, 12 July, and Poe to Mrs. Clemm, 19 July).

3 JULY. PHILLIPS, MAINE. George W. Eveleth writes Poe at New York, replying to his 26 June letter:

Really, I was glad to hear from you, *though* thus "late"—I had begun to think that you might have decided it to be *trifling* to notice your humble friend *away back in Maine.* . . .

Frankly, "Eureka" impresses me as *every poem*, rightly so called, impresses me—as a consistency, and therefore, as a truth. I am a full believer in *dreams* such as this. . . . there are points nevertheless which are not settled entirely to my satisfaction. For one example, "the stars of those times, from being fewer, will be larger, etc"—These bodies, these *monstrous masses*, you are going to have rush into an embrace to form a homogeneous mass—*one particle*—merely by the force of gravitation. Now, *I* can hardly conceive of such a union's taking place without the aid of chemistry and cohesion—in order for the action of which, those masses must first be separated into atoms. . . .

I *like* your poem—"For Annie"—can't tell what makes me like it—it is simple, almost childish; but it is beautiful in its simplicity. I saw it before you sent it to me, in the Flag of Our Union, published as original. How happens it that Willis gives it as *sent by a friend?*—I have seen also your other articles, prose and verse, in the "Flag"—Why do you write for that *cheap-literature* broad-sheet?—does the publisher pay you well?

Eveleth does not often see the *Literary World*; but he read the hostile review of *Eureka* in the 29 July 1848 issue, as well as Poe's reply to it published in the New York *Weekly Universe*: "I can't help thinking that both notice and reply were intended *to pull wool over the eyes*" (ViU).

4? JULY. PHILADELPHIA. On the "second morning" Poe appears to be "so much like his old self" that John Sartain allows him to leave the house alone. After "an hour or two" Poe returns, convinced that his fears of persecution and unworldly visions were all hallucinations "created by his own excited imagination" (Sartain, p. 212).

7 JULY. Poe writes Mrs. Clemm: "I have been *so* ill—have had the cholera, or spasms quite as bad, and can now hardly hold the pen . . . . The very instant you get this, *come* to me. The joy of seeing you will almost compensate for our sorrows. We can but die together. It is no use to reason with me *now*; I must die. I have no desire to live since I have done 'Eureka.' . . . You have been all in all to me, darling, ever beloved mother, and dearest, truest friend. . . . I have been taken to prison once since I came here for getting drunk; but *then* I was not" (L, 2:452).

7 JULY. Poe writes Sarah Anna Lewis in Brooklyn, enclosing his letter to Mrs. Clemm: "Give the enclosed *speedily* to my darling mother. It might get into wrong hands" (L, 2:452–53; Moldenhauer [1973], pp. 74–75).

CA. 8? JULY. BROOKLYN. Mrs. Lewis receives Poe's note, but she does not forward the enclosed letter to Mrs. Clemm (Clemm to Annie, 4 August).

9 JULY. FORDHAM. Mrs. Clemm writes Annie Richmond in Lowell:

Eddy has been gone ten days, and I have not heard one word from him. Do you wonder that I *am distracted*? I fear everything. . . . Eddy was obliged to go through Philadelphia, and how much I fear he has got into some trouble there; he promised me *so* sincerely to write thence. I ought to have heard last Monday, and now it is Monday again and not one word. . . . The day after he left New York, I left Mrs. Lewis and started for home. I called on a rich friend who had made many

JOHN SARTAIN
National Portrait Gallery, Smithsonian Institution, Washington, D. C.

promises, but never knew our situation. I frankly told her. . . . If Eddy gets to Richmond safely and can succeed in what he intends doing, we will be relieved of part of our difficulties; but if he comes home in trouble and sick, I know not what is to become of us (Ingram, pp. 416–17; also in *W*, 17:393–94).

CA. 10 JULY. PHILADELPHIA. Poe completely recovers from the "attack of *mania-à-potu*" which has disabled him for "more than ten days." He finds his missing valise at the train depot (Poe to Mrs. Clemm, 14 and 19 July).

AFTER 10 JULY? Poe sells his new poem "Annabel Lee" and his final text of "The Bells" to *Sartain's Union Magazine*. John Sartain apparently gives him another five dollars for this third version of "The Bells," having previously paid fifteen for the first and twenty-five for the second. On the manuscript of "Annabel Lee," John S. Hart, the literary editor of *Sartain's*, writes "$5 . . . paid when it was accepted," presumably to indicate a partial payment, the balance either having been paid in advance or to be paid after publication (editorials in *Sartain's*, December 1849 and January 1850; Sartain, p. 220; Mabbott [1969], 1:431, 476).

AFTER 10? JULY. Henry Graham Ashmead, a boy of eleven, encounters Poe in the office of *Sartain's*, northwest corner of Walnut and Third Streets. Ashmead is examining one of the "fine, imported steel prints" which are sometimes reproduced in the magazine:

. . . a gentleman of distinguished bearing but somewhat seedily attired, who had been talking with Prof. John S. Hart, approached me and noticing the print I held in my hand delightfully explained its story. I thanked him and told him I must be going. He asked me where I lived; when I told him, he replied, "I am going that way and will walk with you, my lad." . . . I was charmed by the stranger's delightful conversation and flattered, as a child would be, by his considerate attention. . . . That afternoon a lady, calling on my mother, chanced to remark she had seen me talking with a person evidently in needy circumstances from his attire. Mother inquired who I had been with; I could give no information, but that I had met him in the magazine office . . . . That very evening Mr. Sartain called and Mother asked him who the stranger was, and she was told that he was no less a personage than Edgar Allan Poe (quoted by Phillips, 2:1296–97).

AFTER 10? JULY. Poe gives a manuscript copy of "Annabel Lee" to his friend Henry B. Hirst (Mabbott [1969], 1:475–76).

AFTER 10? JULY. Poe contributes his "Sonnet—To my Mother," slightly revised, to the forthcoming *Leaflets of Memory* for 1850, edited by the physician Reynell Coates and published by E. H. Butler & Co. (annual reviewed in December *Sartain's*; Heartman and Canny, p. 128; Mabbott [1969], 1:466).

12 JULY OR BEFORE. Hoping to borrow money for his trip to Richmond, Poe calls on several well-to-do Philadelphians whose writings he had previously praised: "these eminent persons" allow him "to wait in anterooms and offices" but decline to help him (George Lippard's reminiscence in the *Sunday Mercury*, before 3 October 1853, rpt. Eaves, pp. 46–49).

12 JULY. Poe, "poorly clad, and with but one shoe," climbs "up four stairways" to the printing office of the *Quaker City*, a weekly newspaper edited by his young admirer George Lippard. Poe tells Lippard that he has "no bread to eat—no place to sleep." Since Lippard has "just paid his last quarter's rent," he cannot give Poe any money; but he tries to locate someone who can: "he [Lippard] went from door to door, but everybody was out of town. It was a wretched day; cholera bulletins upon every newspaper door, and a hot sun pouring down over half deserted streets" (Lippard's 1853 reminiscence, Eaves, pp. 46–47).

13 JULY. Early in the morning Lippard returns to his office and finds Poe there, "sitting at the table in one corner, his head between his hands." Lippard again goes out; "after some searching" he locates the magazine publishers Louis A. Godey and Samuel D. Patterson, each of whom gives him five dollars for Poe. John Sartain contributes a smaller sum; his clerk William F. Miskey gives "all he had—a dollar." Lippard's friend Charles Chauncey Burr, an editor and clergyman, persuades Poe to come to his home on Seventh Street, south of Poplar. Lippard and Burr stay with Poe throughout the day; in the evening they accompany him to the depot at Eleventh and Market Streets, where he boards the 10:00 PM train to Baltimore (Lippard's 1853 reminiscence, Eaves, pp. 47–48; see also Poe to Mrs. Clemm, 19 July).

[On 22 November 1849 Lippard wrote Rufus W. Griswold: "C. C. Burr, John Sartain, L. A. Godey, S. D. Patterson, were the only persons in this city, whom (last summer), I could induce to give one cent to save Poe from Starvation. These gentlemen (and Mr. Miskey clerk of Sartain's I may add) acted in the most honorable manner" (MB–G). Burr paid Poe's fare to Baltimore; a ticket cost three dollars, "2nd class $2.50" (train schedules in *Germantown Telegraph*, 4 July). In the *Quaker City* for 20 October, Lippard recalled: "When we parted from him [Poe] in the cars, he held our [Lippard's] hand for a long time, and seemed loth to leave us—there was in his voice, look and manner, something of a Presentiment that his strange and stormy life was near its close."]

CA. 14? JULY. BROOKLYN. Mrs. Clemm, worried by her failure to hear from Poe, goes to Sarah Anna Lewis' home; here she is given the 7 July letter that he sent her in care of Mrs. Lewis. As Mrs. Clemm has no money, she cannot comply with Poe's request that she come to Philadelphia; instead she writes "several gentlemen" there, urgently inquiring about him (Clemm to Annie, 30 July and 4 August).

14 JULY. RICHMOND. Poe arrives in Richmond and takes a room in the new American Hotel, southwest corner of Eleventh and Main Streets. He later moves to less expensive quarters in the Swan Tavern, a frame lodging house built in the 1780's, located on the north side of Broad Street between Eighth and Ninth (Weiss [1878], p. 708; see also *W*, 1:311–12, 315, 321, and Scott [1950], pp. 93, 97, 139).

14 JULY. Before retiring for the night Poe writes Mrs. Clemm at Fordham: "I am *so* ill while I write—but I resolved that come what would, I would not sleep again without easing your dear heart . . . . My valise was lost for ten days. At last I found it at the depot in Philadelphia, but (you will scarcely credit it) they had opened it and stolen *both lectures*. Oh, Mother, think of the blow to me this evening, when on examining the valise, these lectures were gone. All my object here is over unless I can recover them or re-write one of them. . . . I got here with two dollars over—of which I inclose you one. Oh God, my Mother, shall we ever again meet? If possible, oh COME! My clothes are *so horrible* . . . . Write instantly" (*L*, 2:453–55).

CA. 16? JULY. A "day or two" after his arrival Poe and his sister Rosalie call on Susan Archer Talley, a poetess of twenty-seven, at her family's residence "Talavera," a farmhouse in the city's western suburbs (later 2315 West Grace Street). Miss Talley recalls:

As I entered the parlor, Poe was seated near an open window, quietly conversing. His attitude was easy and graceful, with one arm lightly resting upon the back of his chair. His dark curling hair was thrown back from his broad forehead—a style in which he habitually wore it. At sight of him, the impression produced upon me was of a refined, high-bred, and chivalrous gentleman. . . . He rose on my entrance, and, other visitors being present, stood with one hand resting on the back of his chair, awaiting my greeting. So dignified was his manner, so reserved his expression, that I experienced an involuntary recoil, until I turned to him and saw his eyes suddenly brighten as I offered my hand; a barrier seemed to melt between us, and I felt that we were no longer strangers (Weiss [1878], p. 708; for "Talavera," see Scott [1940], pp. 191–92, and [1950], p. 157).

CA. 17 JULY. NEW YORK OR FORDHAM. Mrs. Clemm answers Poe's 14 July letter, complying with his request to write "instantly" (Poe's reply; Clemm to Annie, 4 August).

19 JULY. RICHMOND. Poe writes Mrs. Clemm:

Oh, if you only knew how your dear letter comforted me! It acted like magic. Most of my suffering arose from that terrible idea which I could not get rid of— the idea that you were dead. For more than ten days I was totally deranged, although I was not drinking one drop; and during this interval I imagined the most horrible calamities. . . .

All was hallucination, arising from an attack which I had never before experienced—an attack of *mania-à-potu*. May Heaven grant that it prove a warning to me for the rest of my days. . . .

To L[ippard] and to C[hauncey] B[urr] (and in some measure, also, to Mr. S[artain]) I am indebted for more than life. They remained with me (L[ippard] and B[urr]) all day on Friday last, comforted me and aided me in coming to my senses. L[ippard] saw G[odey], who said everything kind of me, and sent me five dollars; and [Samuel D.] P[atterson] sent another five. B[urr] procured me a ticket as far as Baltimore, and the passage from there to Richmond was seven dollars. I have not drank anything since Friday morning, and then only a little Port wine.

Poe apparently informs Mrs. Clemm that he will leave Richmond in a few days to visit a friend in the nearby countryside (partial text in Burr, pp. 30–31, rpt. *L*, 2:455–56; see also Clemm to Annie, 30 July).

19 JULY. Poe writes George Lippard in Philadelphia. Upon his arrival in Richmond he discovered that the two lectures he planned to deliver here were missing from his valise. He believes that the manuscripts were lost or stolen during his stay in Philadelphia; he asks Lippard to try to locate them (Lippard to R. W. Griswold, 22 November 1849, MB-G; cf. Poe to Mrs. Clemm, 14 July).

[In his letter to Griswold, Lippard recalled: "Myself and C. C. Burr did our best to find them, at that time, but in vain." The two lectures were probably "The Poets and Poetry of America" and "The Poetic Principle," both of which Poe had successfully delivered in the past year (see 10 JULY and 20 DECEMBER 1848). He either found, or reconstructed, "The Poetic Principle," because he was able to announce a lecture by the end of the month (see 31 JULY).]

19 JULY. Poe writes Edward H. N. Patterson in Oquawka, Illinois: "I have just arrived in Richmond and your letter is only this moment received—or rather your two letters with the enclosures ($50. etc.) I have not yet read them and write now merely to let you know that they are safe" (*L*, 2:456–57).

BEFORE 21 JULY. Poe sees John R. Thompson, editor of the *Southern Literary Messenger*. He gives his opinions on three poems that Thompson intends to contribute to the forthcoming tenth edition of Rufus W. Griswold's *The Poets and Poetry of America* (implied by Thompson to Griswold, 21 July).

21 JULY. Thompson writes Griswold in New York, submitting his three poems for the anthology: "Mr. Edgar Poe says 'La Morgue' is by far the best performance of the three and is worth republishing" (PHi).

BEFORE 23? JULY. Mrs. W. A. R. Nye, whose husband is a printer for the *Richmond Whig*, writes Mrs. Clemm in Fordham. She will invite Poe to stay at her home while he is in Richmond (Clemm to Annie, 30 July).

23 JULY. NEW YORK? Mrs. Clemm receives Poe's 19 July letter (Clemm to Annie, 30 July).

24 JULY. RICHMOND. Under the heading "Edgar A. Poe," the *Richmond Whig* reports that "this gentleman, who is a native of this city," has acquired literary recognition in France. The *Whig* quotes a recent number of the London *Literary Gazette*, in which a "Paris correspondent" discusses the growing interest in American authors among the French: "Perhaps . . . the clever writer [E. D. Forgues] who signs himself 'Old Nick,' deserves a word of gratitude from the Americans, as he has both written about and translated from them. He it was who made the name of Edgar Poe familiar here."

30 JULY. FORDHAM. Mrs. Clemm replies to a 27 July letter from Annie Richmond in Lowell: "This day week received a letter from my own sweet Eddy. He writes he is better in health and rather better in spirits. He assures me he never did anything while he was so deranged that was in the *least disgraceful*. He fancied he was pursued by the police but it was not so. I have gained all the particulars from several gentlemen to whom I wrote when I found I could not go to him. . . . Dear Eddy wrote me in his last that he was going from Richmond in a few days, to stay with a friend in the country for a short time." In the past week Mrs. Clemm has also received a letter from a "dear friend in Richmond, Mrs. Nye," who plans to have Poe "stay at her house, and says she will take every care of him" (excerpts in Ingram, p. 417, and Miller [1977], p. 27).

31 JULY. RICHMOND. The *Daily Republican* reports:

We are gratified to state that EDGAR A. POE, Esq., who is now in Richmond, the place of his nativity, on a visit, is about to afford to our citizens an intellectual feast, in the way of a lecture; and such as all, who are familiar with the genius of the man, can readily imagine will be of a high order.

The Lecture which Mr. Poe proposes to deliver in Richmond, is that which he gave with such *éclat* a winter or two ago, ["The Poetic Principle,"] before the Lyceum Association of Providence, Rhode Island.

To introduce Poe to those readers who "may not already be familiar with his literary productions," the *Republican* reprints "For Annie" (a "little gem of a poem") and Nathaniel P. Willis' preface to it from the New York *Home Journal* for 28 April.

LATE JULY? Poe proposes marriage to his early love Sarah Elmira Royster, now the widow Mrs. Shelton, whose acquaintance he had renewed when he visited Richmond a year ago. Mrs. Shelton recalls their conversations at her home on East Grace Street, between Twenty-Fourth and Twenty-Fifth, in the "Church Hill" section of the city:

That very morning I told him [Poe] I was going to church[,] that I never let any thing interfere with that, that he must call again[;] and when he did call again he renewed his addresses. I laughed at it, he looked very serious and said he was in earnest and had been thinking about it [marriage] for a long time. Then I found out that he was very serious and I became serious. I told him if he would not take a positive denial he must give me time to consider of it—and he said a love that hesitated was not a love for him. But he sat there a long time and was very pleasant and cheerful. He conceded to visit me frequently (Mrs. Shelton's reminiscences transcribed by E. V. Valentine on 19 November 1875, ViRVal; for her house in "Church Hill," see Weiss [1907], pp. 194, 196, and Scott [1950], p. 40).

END OF JULY OR EARLY AUGUST. NEAR RICHMOND. While visiting a friend in the countryside, Poe writes Mrs. Clemm at Fordham: "The weather is awfully hot, and, besides all this, I am so homesick I don't know what to do. I never wanted to see any one half so bad as I want to see my own darling mother. . . . When I am with you I can bear anything, but when I am away from you I am too miserable to live" (fragment in Burr, p. 29, rpt. *L*, 2:453; dating suggested by Clemm to Annie, 30 July and 4 August).

CA. AUGUST. BROOKLYN. Mrs. Sarah Anna Lewis writes Poe at Richmond (cited as "first letter" in Poe to Lewis, 18 September).

AUGUST. RICHMOND. The *Southern Literary Messenger* contains Poe's laudatory notice of Mrs. Frances S. Osgood's literary career and her poetry.

AUGUST? Young Oscar P. Fitzgerald, later a bishop, sees Poe:

A compact, well-set man about five feet six [eight] inches high, straight as an arrow, easy-gaited, with white linen coat and trousers, black velvet vest and broad Panama hat, features sad yet finely cut, shapely head, and eyes that were strangely magnetic as you looked into them—this is the image of Edgar Allan Poe most vivid to my mind as I saw him one warm day in Richmond in 1849. There was a fascination about him that everybody felt. Meeting him in the midst of thousands a stranger would stop to get a second look, and to ask, "Who is he?" He was *distingué* in a peculiar sense—a man bearing the stamp of genius and the charm of a melancholy that drew one toward him with a strange sympathy.

Young Basil L. Gildersleeve, later a professor of Greek, sees Poe: "He was lodging at some poor place in Broad street [the Swan Tavern] . . . . I saw him repeatedly in that thoroughfare—a poetical figure, if there ever was one, clad in black as was the fashion then—slender—erect—the subtle lines of his face fixed in meditation. I thought him wonderfully handsome, the mouth being the only weak point. I was too shy to seek an introduction to the poet, but John R. Thompson procured for me Poe's autograph, a possession of which I was naturally very proud" (reminiscences in Harrison [1900], pp. 2259–61; rpt. W, 1:315–20).

The future sculptor Edward V. Valentine, then a boy of eleven, sees Poe: "I remember . . . that he passed our house one day. 'There goes Edgar Poe,' cried my brother [William Winston Valentine], and I rushed out into the street, passed him and stood near the sidewalk as he went by. I then stared at him with all the eyes I had, for his name was so often mentioned by members of our family" (Valentine's "Address at Opening of the Poe Shrine," typescript in ViRVal).

AUGUST? Poe is again indisposed by drinking. The poetess Susan Archer Talley recalls:

All that I knew of the matter was when a friend informed me that "Mr. Poe was too unwell to see us that evening." A day or two after this he sent a message by his sister [Rosalie Poe] requesting some flowers, in return for which came a dainty note of thanks, written in a tremulous hand. He again wrote, inclosing a little anonymous poem which he had found in some newspaper and admired; and on the day following he made his appearance among us, but so pale, tremulous and apparently subdued as to convince me that he had been seriously ill. On this occasion he had been at his rooms at the "Old Swan" where he was carefully tended by Mrs. Mackenzie's family, but on a second and more serious relapse he was taken by Dr. Mackenzie and Dr. Gibbon Carter to Duncan's Lodge [home of the Mackenzie family], where during some days his life was in imminent danger. Assiduous attention saved him, but it was the opinion of the physicians that another such attack would prove fatal. This they told him, warning him seriously of the danger. His reply was that if people would not tempt him, he would not fall. Dr. Carter relates how, on this occasion, he had a long conversation with him, in which Poe expressed the most earnest desire to break from the thralldom of his besetting sin, and told of his many unavailing struggles to do so. He was moved even to tears, and finally declared, in the most solemn manner, that this time he *would* restrain himself,—*would* withstand any temptation. He kept his word as long as he remained in Richmond (Weiss [1878], p. 712; see also reminiscences of

Dr. George W. Rawlings, *W*, 1:311–12, and Whitty [1911], p. lxxiii, and entries for 27 and 31 AUGUST).

4 AUGUST. FORDHAM. Mrs. Clemm writes Annie Richmond in Lowell:

It is nearly two weeks since I have heard from my poor Eddy. I fancy every thing in the world. . . . Yesterday was five weeks since he left, and the misery I have endured since I cannot tell you. When I parted with him aboard of the steam boat, he was so dejected but still tried to cheer me. . . . The day after he left I received yours with one to him enclosed. Oh! if it had only come one day sooner. He had waited a week in hopes to hear from you. . . . Mrs. Lewis promised him to see me often and see that I did not suffer. For a whole fortnight I heard nothing from her, at last I went there, and would you believe it? She had a letter from Eddy to me begging her for Gods sake to send it to me without a moment's delay. It was enclosed in a one to her, of two lines . . . . I wrote to dear Eddy [at Richmond] and have told him that I have wanted for nothing, have told him that Mrs. L. has been *very kind* to me and did not breathe about the detention of the letter. It takes all I can get to take me in and out of New York. . . . I enclose to you the last letter [of 19 July] I got from *our* dear Eddy, take care of it for if I should lose *him* I would never forgive myself for parting with it for an instant. . . . If you write him, do not say that I told you the *cause* of his illness [in Philadelphia]. But oh Annie tell him your fears and intreat him for all our sakes to refrain altogether (Miller [1977], pp. 27–31).

7 AUGUST. RICHMOND. Poe writes Edward H. N. Patterson in Oquawka, Illinois: "The date of your last letter was June 7 . . . I am only just now sitting down to reply. The fault, Heaven knows, has not been mine. I have suffered worse than death—not so much from the Cholera as from its long-continued consequences in debility and congestion of the brain." Poe cannot agree to Patterson's proposal that they issue a less expensive journal: "a $3 Magazine (however well it might succeed (temporarily) under the guidance of another) would inevitably fail under mine. . . . So far as regards all *my* friends and supporters—so far as concerns all that class to whom *I* should look for sympathy and nearly all of whom I proposed to see personally—the mere idea of a '$3 Magazine' would suggest namby-pamby-ism & frivolity. Moreover, even with a far more diminished circulation than you suggest, the *profits* of a $5 work would exceed those of a $3 one." It is probably too late for them to publish their first number in January: "But a Mag. might be issued *in July* very well—and if you think it *possible* that your views might be changed, I will still visit you at St L[ouis]" (*L*, 2:457–58).

8 AUGUST. OQUAWKA, ILLINOIS. The *Oquawka Spectator* reprints Poe's "Sonnet—To my Mother," with this preface by Patterson:

BEAUTIFUL SONNET.—We copy below a sonnet which recently appeared in the

THE SWAN TAVERN

Flag of Our Union. For beauty of versification, and touching simplicity of expression, we have rarely seen its equal. It most admirably combines beauty and appropriateness of language, originality of thought and expression, and delicately worded Eulogy. If any sonnet has ever appeared, which, taken as a whole, can surpass this in all that constitutes *true poetry*, we have yet to see it (McElroy, pp. 259–60).

10 AUGUST. RICHMOND. The *Richmond Whig* notices the *Southern Literary Messenger* for August, praising the "well written review of Mrs. Osgood's poems, by Edgar A. Poe, Esq."

CA. 13 AUGUST. NEW YORK OR FORDHAM. Mrs. Clemm receives a letter from Poe enclosed in one from Mrs. W. A. R. Nye. Apparently, Mrs. Nye suggests that Mrs. Clemm come to Richmond (Clemm to Annie, 3 September).

CA. 13? AUGUST. BROOKLYN. Rufus W. Griswold calls at Mrs. Lewis' home and receives the package Poe left there for him: it contains the laudatory sketch of this poetess Poe wrote to replace the unfavorable one Griswold put in the first edition of his *Female Poets of America* (Bayless, pp. 159, 282; cf. Poe to Griswold, 28 June, and Mrs. Clemm to Griswold, 4 September).

14 AUGUST. RICHMOND. In the *Semi-Weekly Examiner* John M. Daniel notices this month's *Messenger*: "Edgar A. Poe contributes a Review of Mrs. Frances S. Osgood—one of the insect authoresses who are Sapphos and Hemans combined, and of whom this soil is most surprisingly fertile. Mrs. Osgood is better than most of them. She has written some very pretty copies of verses. The best of them is that entitled 'Caprice,'—which seems to have escaped Mr. Poe's notice."

15 AUGUST. Under the heading "Novel Lecture," the *Daily Republican* comments: "Our readers will perceive, by a notice in another column, that EDGAR A. POE, Esq., is to deliver a Lecture . . . . The originality and beauty of Mr. Poe's compositions, both in prose and poetry, warrant us in saying that the Lecture will be instructive and full of interest." The accompanying advertisement is repeated on 16 August:

EDGAR A. POE will lecture on the Poetic Principle, (with various recitations,) at the Exchange Concert Room, on Friday evening next, the 17th, at eight o'clock. Tickets 25 cents—for sale at the various bookstores.

17 AUGUST. In the *Examiner* Daniel briefly announces Poe's lecture this evening. The *Republican* reminds its readers: "Those who desire to enjoy a rich treat, should hear this effort of Mr. Poe's." The *Richmond Whig* contains the same advertisement which had appeared in the *Republican* as well as a long editorial notice:

With the object of giving some idea of the nature and character of the entertainment offered our citizens, this evening, at the Exchange Hall, we would mention that, this Lecture, on the Poetic principle, is one of a course delivered before the Providence Lyceum last Fall—the other lecturers being Rufus Choate, Theodore Parker, Alonzo Potter, (Bishop of Pennsylvania,) Louis Agassiz, the French Savant, and Daniel Webster. Daniel Webster opened the course. Mr. Poe had the largest audience of the season—more than 1600 persons.

Observing that Poe will recite "The Raven" at the lecture's conclusion, the *Whig* quotes the praises accorded this poem by Nathaniel P. Willis in the New York *Evening Mirror* of 29 January 1845 and by Elizabeth Barrett Barrett, "now Mrs Browning," in her April 1846 letter to Poe.

17 AUGUST. Poe apparently writes Willis in New York (unverified item cited in *L*, 2:629, and Ostrom [1981], p. 247).

17 AUGUST. At 8:00 PM Poe lectures on "The Poetic Principle" in the Concert Room of the Exchange Hotel, corner of Franklin and Fourteenth Streets. The novelist John Esten Cooke recalls: "The lecturer stood in a graceful attitude, leaning one hand on a small table beside him, and his wonderfully clear and musical voice speedily brought the audience under

its spell. Those who heard this strange voice once, never afterwards forgot it. It was certainly unlike any other that I have ever listened to: and the exquisite, if objectionable 'sing-song,' as he repeated 'The Raven,' Hood's 'Fair Inez' and other verse, resembled music. . . . The lecture ended in the midst of applause" (Cooke, pp. 2–3; for the Exchange Hotel, see Scott [1950], pp. 127, 129–30).

18 AUGUST. BOSTON. The *Boston Museum* reprints Poe's tale "The Facts in the Case of M. Valdemar" (Heartman and Canny, p. 159; Mabbott [1978], 3:1232).

20 AUGUST. RICHMOND. The *Daily Republican* reports:

Edgar A. Poe's Lecture.

The lecture of this talented gentleman, at the Exchange Concert Room on Friday evening, was one of the richest intellectual treats we have ever had the good fortune to hear, and it affords us pleasure to state, that, notwithstanding the absence of many of our citizens in the country and elsewhere, and the oppressive warmth of the weather on the occasion, Mr. Poe was honored with the presence of a large, respectable, and intelligent audience. After some interesting and gracefully spoken remarks on the "Poetic principle," he entertained his audience with the recitation of several of the choicest poetic gems of standard authors. The clearness and melody of his voice, and the harmonious accentuation of his words, were soul inspiring, and invested with additional beauty the poems he recited. The effect on the audience was perceptible: at one time, the rehearsal of some pleasing composition would cause an enlivening sensation; and again, he would produce a sympathetic feeling of sadness, resembling sorrow, "as the mist resembles rain," by the representation of a pathetic poem. His tribute to Woman was of the most exalted and glowing character. Mr. Poe, in conclusion, favored the audience with his own beautiful production, "The Raven."

All present must have highly appreciated the entertainment, and we trust that Mr. Poe will give us another illustration of his fine literary acquirements.

21 AUGUST. The *Richmond Whig* comments: "We attended the Lecture of Mr. Poe, on Friday night, with the expectation of hearing nothing more than the common dissertation upon the poetic faculty—a sort of second edition of the *ars poetica* of Horace . . . . We must say that we were never more delighted in our lives . . . . The lecture of Mr. Poe was full of strong, manly sense—manifesting an acquaintance with poets and their styles perfectly *unique*, we think, in this community. . . . We venture to ask Mr. Poe to make one more representation before us."

In the *Semi-Weekly Examiner* John M. Daniel reviews Poe's lecture at length:

We were glad to hear the lecturer explode what he very properly pronounced to be, the poetic "heresy of modern times," to wit: that poetry should have a purpose, an end to accomplish beyond that of ministering to our sense of the beautiful.—We have in these days poets of humanity and poets of universal suffrage, poets whose mission it is to break down corn laws and poets to build up workhouses. . . .

The various pieces of criticism upon the popular poets of this country were, for the most part, just, and were all entertaining. But we were disappointed in Mr. Poe's recitations. We had heard a great deal of his manner; but it does not answer our wants. His voice is soft and distinct, but neither clear nor sonorous. He does not make rhyme effective; he reads all verse like blank verse; and yet he gives it a sing song of his own more monotonous than any versification. . . . He did not make his own "Raven" an effective piece of reading. . . .

A large audience was in attendance. Indeed, the concert room was completely filled. Mr. Poe commenced his career in this city; and those who had not seen him since the days of [his] obscurity, of course felt no little curiosity to behold so famous a townsman. Mr. Poe is a small thin man, slightly formed, keen visaged, with dark complexion, dark hair, and we believe dark eyes. His face is not an ordinary one. The forehead is well developed, and the nose somewhat more prominent than usual. Mr. Poe is a man of very decided genius. Indeed we know of no other writer in the United States, who has half the chance to be remembered in the history of literature. But his reputation will rest on a very small minority of his compositions. Among all his poems there are only two pieces which are not execrably bad—"The Raven" and "Dreamland." The majority of his prose compositions are the children of want and dyspepsia, of the printer's devils and the blue devils. Had he possessed the power of *applying* his creative faculty—as have the Miltons, the Shakspeares, and all the other *demiurgi*,—he would have been a very great man. But there is not one trace of that power in any of his compositions that we have read; and if rumor is to be credited, his career has been that of the Marlowes, the Jonsons, the Dekkers and the Websters, the old dramatists and translunary rowdies of the Elizabethan age. Had Mr. Poe possessed talent in the place of genius, he might have been a popular and money making author. He would have written a great many more good things than he has; but his title to immortality would not and could not be surer than it is.—For the few things that this author has written which are at all tolerable, are coins stamped with the unmistakeable die. They are of themselves—*sui generis*—unlike any diagrams in Time's Kaleidoscope, either past, present or to come—and gleam with the diamond hues of eternity.

The review is reprinted in the *Weekly Examiner* of 24 August.

21 AUGUST. OQUAWKA, ILLINOIS. Edward H. N. Patterson replies to Poe's 7 August letter: "In publishing a $5 magazine, of 96 pp., monthly,—page same size as *Graham's* . . . it would be necessary for me to make an outlay of at least $1,100 (this amount including a supply of paper for three months for 2,000 copies). Now, if you are sure that, as you before thought, 1,000 subscribers can be obtained who will pay upon receipt of the first number, then you may consider me pledged to be with you in the

undertaking." If Poe agrees to this proposition, he should plan to meet Patterson on 15 October in Saint Louis, where they can "settle on arrangements" for their magazine: "You may associate my name with your own in the matter, the same as if I had met you in person. . . . The first number can be issued in July" (W, 17:365–66).

22 AUGUST. RICHMOND. John Esten Cooke writes his brother Philip Pendleton Cooke:

I have left so little space as to be unable to speak of Poe's lecture on the "Poetic Principle" at the Exchange. It was fine particularly the recitations. He repeated Pinckneys "Her health!" [Edward Coote Pinkney's "A Health"] with electric affect [effect] and among others (Hoods Fair Inez "which always had a peculiar charm for him" and his "Take her up tenderly") he gave us *my* gem of gems, my essence of the essence of poetry [Tennyson's] "The Days that are no more" from the "Princess." I never saw a person yet who read it without being maddened almost with its beauty.

I'll tell you how Poe looks[,] what his lecture was like and all about him so you'll only write at once (PP–G).

24 AUGUST OR LATER? Poe attends a lecture by "Mr. Taverner, Principal Shaksperian Lecturer," in the Concert Room of the Exchange Hotel (Poe to Mrs. Clemm, 28?–29? August; advertisements for Taverner's lectures in the *Daily Republican*, 24, 25, 27 August).

BEFORE 25? AUGUST. Reports that Poe will marry Mrs. Elmira Shelton begin to circulate in Richmond. Learning of the rumored engagement, the Mackenzie family, who had adopted Poe's sister Rosalie, frequently entertain him at "Duncan Lodge," their large home in the western suburbs (Poe to Mrs. Clemm, 28?–29? August; for "Duncan Lodge," see Scott [1941], pp. 215–17).

[Five days after Poe's death, John M. Daniel recalled: "It was universally reported that he [Poe] was engaged to be married. The lady was a widow, of wealth and beauty, who was an old flame of his, and whom he declared to be the ideal and original of his Lenore" (*Semi-Weekly Examiner*, 12 October).]

26? AUGUST. In the evening Poe visits the home of John H. Strobia, who had been a friend of his foster mother Frances Allan (Poe to Mrs. Clemm, 28?–29? August; Whitty [1911], pp. xxiv, lxxxi; Scott [1950], pp. 75, 276).

BEFORE 27? AUGUST. John Loud, a piano manufacturer from Philadelphia, offers Poe $100 to edit a volume of poems by his wife, Mrs. Marguerite St.

Leon Loud (Poe to Mrs. Clemm, 28?–29? August and 18 September, and to Mrs. Loud, 18 September).

BEFORE 27? AUGUST. OAKY GROVE, GEORGIA? Thomas Holley Chivers writes Poe at Richmond (cited in Poe to Mrs. Clemm, 28?–29? August).

27 AUGUST. FORDHAM. Mrs. Clemm writes Rufus W. Griswold in New York:

Mr. Poe has been absent from home for some weeks; he is now in Richmond and has been very ill, and unable to send me any money since he left . . . . I have been without the necessaries of life for many days, and would not apply to any one, in hopes that I would soon receive some aid from my poor Eddy. . . . I confide in you, dear sir, and beg you to loan me a small sum until I can receive some from him. I have not the means to go to the city, but a note addressed to Mrs. Maria Clemm, care of E. A. Poe, New York, will reach me. A gentleman in the neighborhood asks every day for me at the post-office (Woodberry, 2:323–24; also in *W*, 17:394–95).

27 AUGUST. RICHMOND. On Monday evening Poe is initiated into the Shockoe Hill Division, No. 54, of the Sons of Temperance, at the chapter's meeting place on the south side of Broad Street "nearly opposite Brook Av[enue]." The presiding officer William J. Glenn, a young tailor, recalls: "Mr Poe . . . during his stay here made his home at the old Swann Tavern . . . there Mr Poe made the acquaintance of some member of the organization . . . was proposed for membership elected and ini[ti]ated . . . . I presided at the meeting and administered the obligation [oath] to the candidate. . . . There had been to us no intimation that Mr Poe had violated his pledge [to abstain from alcohol] before leaving Richmond" (Glenn to E. V. Valentine, 29 June 1899, ViRVal; see also *W*, 1:320–22, and 31 AUGUST).

27? AUGUST. In the evening Poe calls on the family of Michael B. Poitiaux at their home on North Ninth˙Street, in the "French Garden" section. Miss Catherine Elizabeth Poitiaux, an unmarried daughter who had been Poe's playmate in childhood, recalls his visit: "His unfortunate propensity [for drinking] had made us refuse to see him on a former occasion, but this time he unexpectedly entered the room in which I was sitting, saying as I rose to meet him: 'Old friend, you see I would not be denied.' He only stayed a few minutes, but in that short time left an impression on my memory which has never since been effaced. He was to be married in a few weeks to a lady of our city [Mrs. Shelton], and as he stood upon the steps bidding me farewell, I asked, alluding to his marriage, when I should see him again. It was no fancy, but a strange reality, that a gray shadow such as I had never seen before, save on the face of the dying, passed across his" (1852 reminiscence quoted in Whitty [1911], pp. lxxxi–lxxxii; Scott [1950], pp. 261–67).

28?–29? AUGUST. Over the course of several days Poe writes a long letter to Mrs. Clemm at Fordham:

Every body says that if I lecture again & put the tickets at 50 cts, I will clear $100. I *never* was received with so much enthusiasm. The papers have done nothing but praise me before the lecture & since. I enclose one of the notices—the only one in which the slightest word of disparagement appears. It is written by [John M.] Daniel—the man whom I challenged when I was here last year. I have been invited out a great deal—but could seldom go, on account of not having a dress coat. To-night Rose [Rosalie Poe] & I are to spend the evening at Elmira's [Mrs. Shelton's]. Last night I was at [Michael B.] Poitiaux's—the night before at [John H.] Strobia's, where I saw my dear friend Eliza Lambert ʃ . . . Since the report of my intended marriage, the McKenzies have overwhelmed me with attentions. Their house is so crowded that they *could* not ask me to stay. . . . Mr [John] Loud, the husband of Mrs. St Leon Loud, the poetess of Philadelphia, called on me the other day and offered me $100 to edit his wife's poems. Of course, I accepted the offer.

Poe inquires whether Mrs. Sarah Anna Lewis ever received the April number of the *Western Quarterly Review*, which contained his notice of her poetry. He suggests that Mrs. Clemm come to Richmond: "You know we could easily pay off what we owe at Fordham . . . but I want to live *near* Annie. . . . Do not tell me anything about Annie—I cannot bear to hear it now—unless you can tell me that Mr. R. [Annie's husband] is dead.—I have got the wedding ring [for Mrs. Shelton].—and shall have no difficulty, I think, in getting a dress-coat" (L, 2:458–60).

28? AUGUST. Poe and his sister Rosalie spend the evening at Mrs. Shelton's home (implied by Poe's letter to Mrs. Clemm).

31 AUGUST. The *Banner of Temperance* reports:

Edgar A. Poe, Esq.

This gentleman who has been in our city for some weeks past, and who has been ministering to the delight of our citizens in several highly interesting lectures, was initiated as a Son of Temperance in [the] Shockoe Hill Division, No. 54, on last Monday night. We mention the fact, conceiving that it will be gratifying to the friends of temperance to know that a gentleman of Mr. Poe's fine talents and rare attainments has been enlisted in the cause. We trust his pen will sometimes be employed in its behalf. A vast amount of good might be accomplished by so pungent and forcible a writer.

SEPTEMBER. PROVIDENCE, RHODE ISLAND. Mrs. Sarah Helen Whitman completes a six-stanza poem commemorating Poe's marriage proposal to her, made a year ago in the Swan Point Cemetery overlooking the Seekonk River:

> Dost thou remember that September day
> When by the Seekonk's lonely wave we stood,
> And marked the langour of repose that lay,
> Softer than sleep, on valley, wave, and wood?
>
> . . . .
>
> I dared not listen to thy words, nor turn
> To meet the pleading language of thine eyes,
> I only *felt* their power, and in the urn
> Of memory, treasured their sweet rhapsodies.

She submits the poem, headed "Lines," to *Graham's Magazine* (published in November number; subsequently entitled "The Last Flowers"; see Reilly [1965], pp. 193–94, 234, 266).

SEPTEMBER. RICHMOND. The *Southern Literary Messenger* contains a fifth and final installment of Poe's "Marginalia."

EARLY SEPTEMBER? Poe moves from the Swan Tavern to the Madison House at Tenth and Bank Streets, an inexpensive lodging establishment occupying two buildings which were originally used for other purposes (Poe to Mrs. Clemm, 18 September; Little, p. 104).

1 SEPTEMBER. The *Daily Republican* reprints the announcement of Poe's initiation into the Sons of Temperance from the 31 August *Banner of Temperance*.

CA. 1 SEPTEMBER? Poe mails his letter of 28?–29? August to Mrs. Clemm (suggested by Clemm to Annie, 3 September, and to R. W. Griswold, 4 September).

3 SEPTEMBER. FORDHAM. Mrs. Clemm writes Annie Richmond in Lowell: "I have heard nothing from our poor dear Eddie since I last wrote you. It is three weeks since I have had one line from him—the letter I received from Mrs. Nye was the last I heard from him. I think perhaps she told him she had written for me, and he is constantly expecting me, this I think is the most likely reason. Or else he is entirely bereft of *his senses*. . . . I have written to Mr. R. [Annie's husband] to ask him to loan me enough to go to him, if he *does* I will go the moment I get it" (Miller [1977], pp. 31–32).

3 SEPTEMBER. BROOKLYN. The attorney Sylvanus D. Lewis writes Rufus W. Griswold in New York: "You said to me, when I saw you last, that you intended to rewrite the Sketch of Mrs. Lewis, for your new Edition of the 'Female Poets.' . . . It will incur, I think you said, an expense of about $2.60 per page. If you prepare the sketch, and do the proof-reading I think it no more than fair that I should be at the expense of the new Stereotyping. You will please, therefore, let me know, as soon as you can ascertain, the number of pages, and I will send you my check for the amount" (Griswold [1898], p. 252).

[Lewis and his wife almost certainly knew that Poe had already written a new sketch and that Griswold had received it, though they preferred to profess ignorance of the matter (cf. Mrs. Lewis to Griswold, 20 September [1850], W, 17:415–16). Griswold never altered his original notice.]

4 SEPTEMBER. FORDHAM. Mrs. Clemm writes Griswold: "I understand from Mrs. Lewis you received the package Mr. Poe left at her house for you. I wish you to publish it [Poe's sketch of Mrs. Lewis] exactly as he has written it. If you will do so I will promise you a favorable review of your books as they appear. You know the influence I have with Mr. Poe . . . . I have just heard from him, he writes in fine spirits and says his prospects are excellent" (W, 17:395; cf. Poe to Griswold, 28 June).

5 SEPTEMBER. OQUAWKA, ILLINOIS. In the *Oquawka Spectator* Edward H. N. Patterson comments: "Edgar A. Poe, the celebrated poet, is now lecturing in his native city, Richmond, Virginia. His great erudition, added to his giant intellect and a most felicitous command of language[,] cannot fail to render his lectures very popular" (McElroy, p. 263).

7 SEPTEMBER. RALEIGH, NORTH CAROLINA. The *Raleigh Times* reports that Poe has joined the Sons of Temperance, quoting the Richmond *Banner of Temperance* of 31 August (Moore, p. 360).

9 SEPTEMBER OR BEFORE. NORFOLK, VIRGINIA. Poe travels to Norfolk, where he intends to deliver his lecture on "The Poetic Principle." He spends several days at Old Point Comfort, a nearby ocean resort, apparently as the guest of his friends, Mr. and Mrs. French (Phillips, 2:1469–72).

9 SEPTEMBER. OLD POINT COMFORT, VIRGINIA. On "Sunday evening" Poe is the cynosure of a "little group" gathered on the veranda of the Hygeia Hotel. Miss Susan V. C. Ingram recalls:

There were several of us girls, all friends, and all of us knew Mr. Poe. I can see just how we looked sitting about there in our white dresses. There was a young collegian, too, who was my particular [boy] friend. . . .

Mr. Poe sat there in that quiet way of his which made you feel his presence. After a while my aunt [Mrs. French], who was nearer his age, said:—"This seems to be just the time and place for poetry, Mr. Poe."

And it was. We all felt it. The old Hygeia stood some distance from the water, but with nothing between it and the ocean. It was moonlight and the light shone over everything with that undimmed light that it has in the South. There were many persons on the long verandas that surrounded the hotel, but they seemed remote and far away. Our little party was absolutely cut off from everything except that lovely view of the water shining in the moonlight and its gentle music borne to us on the soft breeze. Poe felt the influence. How could a poet help it? And when we seconded the request that he recite for us he agreed readily.

I do not remember all of the poems that he recited. There was "The Raven" and "Annabel Lee," and last of all he gave us "Ulalume," including the last stanza, of which he remarked that he feared that it might not be intelligible to us . . . .

I was not old enough or experienced enough to understand what the words [of "Ulalume"] really meant . . . . I did, however, feel their beauty, and I said to him when he had finished, "It is quite clear to me, and I admire the poem very much" (reminiscence in *New York Herald*, 19 February 1905, Third Section, p. 4; cf. Phillips, 2:1467–74; for the Hygeia Hotel, see T. J. Wertenbaker, p. 324).

10 SEPTEMBER. Complying with Miss Ingram's request, Poe transcribes "Ulalume" for her. In the evening he places the copy under her door at the Hygeia Hotel, accompanied by a brief note: "I fear that you will find the verses scarcely more intelligible to day in my manuscript than last night in my recitation. I would endeavor to explain to you what I really meant—or what I really fancied I meant by the poem, if it were not that I remember Dr Johnson's bitter and rather just remarks about the folly of explaining what, if worth explanation, should explain itself" (*L*, 2:460).

[Miss Ingram recalled that Poe's manuscript "made quite a scroll and must have taken him a long time to write out. The ten stanzas were written on five large sheets of paper pasted together in the neatest possible way, end to end. He wrote such a beautiful, fair hand it was a joy to look upon it" (*New York Herald*, 19 February 1905).]

BEFORE 11 SEPTEMBER. CINCINNATI. The *Daily Atlas* reports: "Edgar A. Poe is lecturing on Poets and Poetry, at Richmond, Va."

BEFORE 11 SEPTEMBER. PHILADELPHIA. The *Evening Bulletin* reports: "Edgar A. Poe has joined the Sons of Temperance at Shockoe Hill, Virginia."

11 SEPTEMBER. RICHMOND. The *Richmond Whig* reprints the reports from the Cincinnati *Atlas* and Philadelphia *Bulletin*. The *Whig* comments: "Mr.

Poe has only given our citizens the treat of one lecture; but as he is still among us, we trust he may be induced to repeat." The report in the *Bulletin* "is correct; '*at* Shockoe Hill' though is *in* Richmond."

12 SEPTEMBER. OQUAWKA, ILLINOIS. The *Oquawka Spectator* reprints "The Raven." In an editorial on the second page Edward H. N. Patterson comments: "We publish on our first page, this week, one of the most remarkable poems ever written. Mr. Poe has long held the rank of one of our very best poets, and The Raven is in his best style. We bespeak for it a careful perusal. There will be found running through it, clothed in a robe of euphonious rhymes and remarkably appropriate language, an Idea well worthy of the pen of its author—the never-dying existence of the memory" (McElroy, p. 260).

CA. 12? SEPTEMBER. NORFOLK. Poe is entertained by Mrs. Susan Maxwell at her fashionable home on Bermuda Street. Herbert M. Nash, a medical student who frequently visits Mrs. Maxwell's sixteen-year-old daughter Helen, recalls: "I met . . . the distinguished visitor and had the privilege of listening to his interesting conversation and of hearing him recite some of his favorite poems, among them 'The Raven,' 'The Bells,' and 'Annabel Lee' " (Dr. Nash's 1909 reminiscence in Kent and Patton, pp. 26–31; see also Phillips, 2:1467, 1472).

CA. 12? SEPTEMBER. Poe visits Miss Susan V. C. Ingram at her family's home on the outskirts of Norfolk. She recalls: "Although I was only a slip of a girl and he what seemed to me then quite an old man, and a great literary one at that, we got on together beautifully. . . . I was fond of orris root and always had the odor of it about my clothes. . . . 'I like it, too,' he said. 'Do you know what it makes me think of? My adopted mother [Frances Allan]. Whenever the bureau drawers in her room were opened there came from them a whiff of orris root, and ever since when I smell it I go back to the time when I was a little boy' " (*New York Herald*, 19 February 1905).

CA. 12? SEPTEMBER. Poe writes Mrs. Clemm at Fordham, informing her that he has joined the Sons of Temperance and enclosing a copy of his pledge to abstain from alcohol (Clemm to Annie, 15 September).

13 SEPTEMBER. The *American Beacon* and the *Daily Southern Argus* carry this advertisement:

EDGAR A. POE will lecture on "THE POETIC PRINCIPLE" (with various recitations) on Friday night, (the 14th) at 8 o'clock, in the Lecture Room of the Academy.— Tickets 50 cents, to be had at the door.

The editors of the *Beacon* call attention to the lecture, reprinting the report of Poe's growing reputation in France from the *Richmond Whig* of 24 July. The *Argus* identifies Poe as "a gentleman of fine literary taste and one of the most successful authors in the country," predicting that his lecture will be "a rare intellectual treat." This paper reprints his poem "Lenore."

14 SEPTEMBER. The advertisement is repeated in both the *Beacon* and the *Argus*. The editors of the *Beacon* comment: "This is the evening for Mr. Poe's lecture at the Academy. The subject selected for the occasion, 'The Poetic Principle,' is one affording a large field for the display of the genius, and fine literary acquirements for which this gentleman is so distinguished . . . . Mr. Poe delivered the same lecture a short time since in Richmond with marked success." To give some idea of the lecture the *Beacon* reprints the laudatory account of it carried by the *Richmond Whig* on 17 August. The *Argus* also reminds its readers of Poe's lecture tonight: "Norfolk has frequently been taunted for her want of literary taste—but we hope our citizens will, upon the present occasion, vindicate themselves against such an imputation." In another column the *Argus* prints a letter from an unnamed subscriber: "As [Poe is] one who claims Virginia for his alma mater, his literary attainments are entitled to respect from us . . . . As a critic in the department of poetry, he has long held the first position . . . . To say nothing of the esteem in which he is held at the North, it is gratifying to know that he has been favorably received in Richmond, where the high character of his entertainments has been appreciated by large and fashionable audiences."

14 SEPTEMBER. At 8:00 PM Poe lectures before a small but enthusiastic audience at the Norfolk Academy (17 September reviews; illustration of Academy in Phillips, 2:1475).

15 SEPTEMBER. FORDHAM. Mrs. Clemm writes Annie Richmond in Lowell:

I have had a severe attack of nervous fever, and am now only able to be up long enough to write this—this will account to you for my not answering Mr. R[ich-mond]'s kind letter and enclosure of 5 dollars—it found me ill, and if he had sent me sufficient to have gone to Eddy, I could not have done so until now. The anxiety I felt about him brought on my sickness. But my Annie the dark dark clouds I think are beginning to break. I send you his letter [written 28?–29? August], the only one I received for nearly four weeks. I yesterday received a very short one [written ca. 12? September] with the slip of paper I enclose. God of his great mercy grant he may keep this pledge. . . . Gen. [George P.] Morris—& Mr. [Evert A.] Duyckinck both say he only wanted that—I mean to be temperate—to be the *greatest man living*!! (Miller [1977], pp. 32–33).

15 SEPTEMBER. BOSTON. The *Boston Museum* reports: "Edgar A. Poe, the poet and critic, has joined the Sons of Temperance."

17 SEPTEMBER. NORFOLK. The *American Beacon* reports:

Mr. Poe delivered a lecture on "The Poetic Principle," with various recitations, at the Lecture Room of the Academy, on Friday evening. The main proposition of the lecture, which was discussed with great ingenuity, was that there could not be a long poem . . . . Milton's Paradise Lost and the Iliad, were cited in illustration, which he said were but a succession of brilliant poetic scintillations—a collection of short poems. . . . In elucidation of his opinions, Mr. Poe recited with fine effect, extracts from the poetic effusions of Longfellow, Bryant, Willis, and Edward Pinkney, who he said was born too far South to be appreciated by the North American Quarterly Review—and from the works of Shell[e]y, Byron, Moore, Hood and others. . . . These recitations were received with rounds of applause from the intelligent audience.

Mr. Poe concluded the lecture by reciting by request, his brilliant fantasy, "The Raven."

The *Daily Southern Argus* also praises Poe's lecture: "Chaste and classic in its style of composition—smooth and graceful in its delivery, it had the happiest effect upon the fashionable audience, who manifested their appreciation by the profoundest attention. His recitations were exquisite, and elicited the warmest admiration. For about an hour, every one present seemed charmed and delighted with the rich intellectual entertainment afforded them by Mr. Poe's disquisition on 'The Poetic Principle'; and our only regret arose from the fact that there were so few to partake of it."

17 SEPTEMBER. RICHMOND. Arriving from Norfolk in the evening, Poe finds two letters from Mrs. Clemm awaiting him. Enclosed in one of them is a letter to him from Mrs. Sarah Anna Lewis (Poe to Clemm, 18 September).

18 SEPTEMBER. In the *Semi-Weekly Examiner* John M. Daniel reports: "Edgar Poe has been delivering his lecture with éclat in Norfolk." The *Richmond Whig* reprints Poe's poem "Lenore."

18 SEPTEMBER. Poe replies to the two letters from Mrs. Clemm at Fordham: "I cannot tell you the joy they gave me . . . . Elmira [Shelton] has just got home from the country. I spent last evening with her. I think she loves me more devotedly than any one I ever knew & I cannot help loving her in return. Nothing is yet definitely settled and it will not do to hurry matters. I [lec]tured at Norfolk on Monday [Friday] & cleared enough to settle my bill here at the Madison House with $2 over. I had a highly fashionable audience, but Norfolk is a small place & there were 2

JOHN M. DANIEL
Virginia Historical Society

exhibitions the same night. Next Monday I lecture again here & expect to have a large audience." On next Tuesday Poe hopes to leave for Philadelphia, where he will fulfill his commission to edit a volume of Mrs. Marguerite St. Leon Loud's poetry: "*If possible* I will get married before I start . . . . My poor poor Muddy I am still unable to send you even one dollar—but keep up heart—I hope that our troubles are nearly over" (*L*, 2:461–62; facsimile in Quinn and Hart, pp. 24–25).

18 SEPTEMBER. Poe writes a brief note to Mrs. Lewis, acknowledging the letter from her he received last night. "If I have not written you in reply to your first cherished letter [received some time before], think anything of my silence except that I am ungrateful or unmindful of you . . . . I hope very soon to see you and clasp your dear hand." He apparently encloses the note in his letter to Mrs. Clemm (*L*, 2:462; Moldenhauer [1973], p. 75).

18 SEPTEMBER. Poe writes Mrs. Loud in Philadelphia: "Not being quite sure whether a letter addressed simply to 'Mr John Loud' would reach your husband—that is to say, not remembering whether he had a middle name or not—I have taken the liberty of writing directly to yourself . . . . I find it impossible to leave Richmond before Tuesday next—the 25 th. On the 26 th I hope to have the pleasure of calling on you . . . . There will be quite time enough to have your book issued as proposed" (*L*, 2:727–28).

18 SEPTEMBER OR LATER? William A. Pratt takes Poe's daguerreotype at his "Daguerreian Gallery," 145 Main Street, south side, near Eleventh. Pratt recalls: "I knew him [Poe] well, and he had often promised me to sit for a picture . . . . I was standing at my street door when he came along and spoke to me. I reminded him of his unfulfilled promise . . . . He replied, 'Why, I am not dressed for it.' 'Never mind that,' said I; 'I'll gladly take you just as you are.' . . . Three weeks later he was dead in Baltimore" (quoted by Dimmock, p. 315).

19 SEPTEMBER. PHILADELPHIA. The *Dollar Newspaper* reports that Poe has joined the Sons of Temperance (Phillips, 2:1432).

21 SEPTEMBER. RICHMOND. The *Daily Republican* and the *Richmond Whig* carry this advertisement: "EDGAR A. POE will repeat his late Lecture on 'THE POETIC PRINCIPLE' on Monday night, Sept. 24th, at 8 o'clock. TICK-ETS 50 cents—to be had at the door."

CA. 22? SEPTEMBER. Elmira Shelton finally accepts Poe's proposal of marriage (Poe to Mrs. Clemm, ca. 22? September; Mrs. Shelton to her, 22 September).

[Mrs. Shelton's reasons for hesitating seem to have been primarily financial, because by marrying Poe she would move from affluence to insecurity. Her husband Alexander B. Shelton had died on 12 July 1844 at the age of thirty-seven. His will, probated on 5 August 1844, required a bond of "one hundred thousand dollars," indicating a very substantial estate. In the will Shelton appointed his wife the sole executor of his estate and granted her all "the profits and income" from it, "so long as she lives and remains my widow." Upon her death the estate was to be "equally divided" between their "three children Ann Elizabeth Shelton, Southall Bohannan Shelton and Alexander Barret Shelton." The will contained two clauses which Shelton no doubt hoped would keep his fortune intact for his children and discourage impecunious suitors from pursuing his widow: "In the event of my wife's marrying again, I then give her one fourth of the nett proceeds [of the estate] during her life. . . . If my wife shall marry again then immediately upon the happening of that event I do hereby revoke and annul the appointment aforesaid of her as my executrix and request that the Court will revoke her powers as such, and require her to deliver up my estate from her possession and management" (Will Book Eleven, pp. 493–95, Circuit Court of Henrico County). Two of Shelton's children, Ann Elizabeth and Southall, were alive and living with their mother in 1849; they reputedly opposed Poe's courtship of her (Dietz, pp. 38–47).]

CA. 22? SEPTEMBER. Poe writes Mrs. Clemm in Fordham, informing her that he and Mrs. Shelton are to be married. He describes the modest financial arrangements necessitated by the clauses in Alexander B. Shelton's will. He plans to leave for New York in a few days; Mrs. Clemm is to return with him to Richmond.

[In April 1859 Mrs. Clemm loaned the last two letters she received from Poe to Sarah Helen Whitman, who was then preparing her *Edgar Poe and his Critics* and wished to learn whether Poe had actually been engaged to Mrs. Shelton (Whitman-Clemm correspondence in Harrison and Dailey, p. 448, and Quinn and Hart, pp. 43–47). One of these was probably Poe's relatively brief 18 September letter; the other has almost certainly been lost, but Mrs. Whitman left a memorandum which indicates its contents:

In these [last two] letters he spoke as if the marriage [to Mrs. Shelton] would soon take place—spoke of the lady's property as having been secured to her and her son [Southall], a boy of ten years of age, so that she could only use the income. Assured her [Mrs. Clemm] that she would at least always have with them a comfortable home secure from the anxiety and cares she had so long endured. It had been arranged that he was to undertake the boy's education which would add to *their* resources and give him occupation. Sent a parting message to Mrs. Charles Richmond who had been so kind to himself and his mother during the preceding winter (Harrison and Dailey, p. 451).

Mrs. Whitman also mentioned the lost letter she saw to J. H. Ingram, strongly asserting "that Mrs. Shelton had *accepted* him [Poe], & that the affair was irrevocably fixed" (Whitman-Ingram correspondence in Miller [1979], pp. 42, 305, 339, 377, 383, 388). On 11 October 1849 Mrs. Shelton wrote Mrs. Clemm: "The pleasure I anticipated on his [Poe's] return with you, dear friend! to Richmond, was too great, ever to have been realized, and should teach me the folly of expecting bliss on earth" (Chivers [1957], pp. 178–80).]

22 SEPTEMBER. Mrs. Shelton writes Mrs. Clemm at Fordham:

You will no doubt be much surprised to receive a letter from one whom you have never seen. . . . Mr Poe has been very solicitous that I should write to you, and I do assure you, it is with emotions of pleasure that I now do so—I am fully prepared to *love* you, and I do sincerely hope that our spirits may be congenial . . . . I have just spent a very happy evening with your dear Edgar, and I know it will be gratifying to you, to know, that he is all that you could desire him to be, sober, temperate, moral, & much beloved—He shewed me a letter of yours, in which you spoke affectionately of me, and for which I feel very much gratified & complimented . . . . Edgar speaks frequently & very affectionately of your daughter & his Virginia, for which I love him but the more . . . . I remember seeing Edgar, & his lovely wife, very soon after they were married—I met them—I never shall forget my feelings at the time—They were indescribable, almost agonizing—"However in an instant," I remembered that I was a married woman, and banished them from me, as I would a poisonous reptile (Quinn, pp. 634–35; Quinn and Hart, pp. 26–27).

22 SEPTEMBER. BOSTON. The *Flag of Our Union* for 29 September reports: "Edgar A. Poe the poet and lecturer has lately joined the temperance society."

24 SEPTEMBER. RICHMOND. The *Daily Republican* comments: "We would remind our readers that Mr. Poe will repeat his lecture on the 'Poetic Principle' to-night, at the Exchange Concert Room. Although it is a repetition, we are sure that few, if any, who attended his first lecture, would be unwilling to hear it over again, and those who were not present on that occasion, will deprive themselves of a delightful entertainment by failing to attend to-night."

24 SEPTEMBER. At 8:00 PM Poe lectures in the Concert Room of the Exchange Hotel. Miss Susan Archer Talley recalls:

I was present at this lecture, with my mother and sister and Rose [Rosalie] Poe
. . . . I noticed that Poe had no manuscript, and that, though he stood like a
statue, he held his audience as motionless as himself—fascinated by his voice and
expression. Rose pointed out to me Mrs. Shelton, seated conspicuously in front of
the platform, facing the lecturer. This position gave me a good view of her, with
her large, deep-set, light-blue eyes and sunken cheeks, her straight features, high
forehead and cold expression of countenance. Doubtless she had been handsome in
her youth, but the impression which she produced upon me was that of a sensible,
practical woman, the reverse of a poet's ideal (Weiss [1907], pp. 199–200).

[On 28 September 1874 Edward V. Valentine wrote J. H. Ingram, giving
the reminiscences of his elder brother William Winston Valentine:

My brother who heard Poe lecture on the "Poetic Principle" . . . remembers his
personal appearance—He speaks of the pallor which overspread his face contrasted
with the dark hair which fell on the summit of his forehead with an inclination to
curl. His brow was fine and expressive—his eyes dark and restless—in the mouth
firmness mingled with an element of scorn and discontent. Firm and erect gait,
but nervous and emphatic manner. Man of fine address and cordial in his intercourse with his friends, but looked as though he rarely smiled from joy, to which
Poe seemed to be a stranger, and which might be partly attributable to the great
struggle for self control in which he seemed to be constantly engaged. There was
little variation and much sadness in the intonations of his voice—yet this very
sadness was so completely in harmony with his history as to excite on the part of
this community a deep interest in him both as a lecturer and reader (ViU–I).]

25 SEPTEMBER. The *Semi-Weekly Examiner* reprints "The Raven." The editor
John M. Daniel explains:

MR. EDGAR A. POE lectured again last night on the "Poetic Principle," and
concluded his lecture, as before, with his now celebrated poem of the Raven. As
the attention of many in this city is now directed to this singular performance,
and as Mr. Poe's poems, from which only is it to be obtained in the book stores,
have been long out of print, we furnish our readers, to-day, with the only correct
copy ever published—which we are enabled to do by the courtesy of Mr. Poe
himself.

The "Raven" has taken rank over the whole world of literature, as the very first
poem as yet produced on the American continent. . . . But while this poem
maintains a rank so high among all persons of catholic and generally cultivated
taste, we can conceive the wrath of many who will read it for the first time in the
columns of this newspaper. Those who have formed their taste in the Pope and
Dryden school, whose earliest poetical acquaintance is Milton, and whose latest
Hammond and Cowper—with a small sprinkling of Moore and Byron—will not
be apt to relish on first sight a poem tinged so deeply with the dyes of the
nineteenth century. The poem will make an impression on them which they will
not be able to explain—but that will irritate them. . . . Such will angrily pronounce the Raven flat nonsense. Another class will be disgusted therewith, because
they can see no purpose, no allegory, no "meaning," as they express it, in the

poem. . . . The worth of the "Raven" is not in any "moral," nor is its charm in the construction of its story. Its great and wonderful merits consist in the strange, beautiful and fantastic imagery and colors with which the simple subject is clothed—the grave and supernatural tone with which it rolls on the ear—the extraordinary vividness of the word painting,—and the powerful but altogether indefinable appeal which is made throughout to the organs of ideality and marvellousness. Added to these is a versification indescribably sweet and wonderfully difficult—winding and convoluted about like the mazes of some complicated overture by Beethoven. . . . It is stamped with the image of true genius—and genius in its happiest hour. It is one of those things an author never does but once.

25? SEPTEMBER. Poe visits "Talavera," home of the Talley family, in the "evening of the day previous to that appointed for his departure from Richmond." Miss Talley recalls: "He spoke of his future, seeming to anticipate it with an eager delight, like that of youth. He declared that the last few weeks in the society of his old and new friends had been the happiest that he had known for many years, and that when he again left New York he should there leave behind all the trouble and vexation of his past life" (Weiss [1878], pp. 713–14).

26 SEPTEMBER. The *Daily Republican* reports that Poe's lecture on Monday was "less numerously attended" than expected: "there was, nevertheless, a large, attentive and appreciative audience present, whom Mr. Poe entertained during the evening by the recitation of several poetic *morceaux*." The *Daily Times* also praises the lecture: "We have seldom heard a voice of such melodious modulations as Mr. Poe's."

26? SEPTEMBER. Poe has his sister Rosalie deliver a manuscript copy of "For Annie" and an accompanying note to Miss Talley, who had expressed a desire to see this poem (Weiss [1878], p. 714).

26? SEPTEMBER. Poe calls on John M. Daniel at the office of the *Semi-Weekly Examiner*, north side of Main Street between Eleventh and Twelfth (*Examiner*, 2 and 9 October).

26 SEPTEMBER. Poe calls on John R. Thompson at the office of the *Southern Literary Messenger*, northeast corner of Capitol Square and Franklin Street. He explains that he is leaving for New York tomorrow morning and that he plans to stop in Philadelphia, where he will edit a volume of Mrs. Loud's poetry. He borrows five dollars from Thompson to help with his travel expenses, giving him in return a manuscript of "Annabel Lee." Thompson gives Poe a letter to deliver to Rufus W. Griswold in Philadelphia (Thompson to Griswold, 10 October; Thompson's reminiscences quoted by Gill, p. 231).

[Poe had previously sold "Annabel Lee" to *Sartain's Union Magazine*. He almost certainly gave the manuscript to Thompson as a keepsake, not as a contribution; but Thompson published the poem in the November *Messenger*, claiming that it was "designed for this magazine." On 11 November he wrote Griswold that he had paid Poe "a high price" for the right to publish the poem: "I lost nearly as much by his death as yourself, as I had paid him for a prose article *to be written*, and he owed me something at that time" (PHi). Thompson's statements about Poe, like those of Mrs. Weiss, are open to question when they are not corroborated by other documents.]

26 SEPTEMBER. Mrs. Shelton recalls: "He [Poe] came up to my house on the evening of the 26*th* Sept. to take leave of me—He was very sad, and complained of being quite sick; I felt his pulse, and found he had considerable fever, and did not think it probable that he would be able to start the next morning, (Thursday) as he anticipated—I felt so wretched about him all of that night, that I went up early the next morning to enquire after him, when, much to my regret, he had left in the boat for Baltimore" (letter to Mrs. Clemm, 11 October, Chivers [1957], pp. 178–80).

26 SEPTEMBER. Later in the evening, "about half-past nine," Poe visits the office of young John F. Carter, M.D., at Broad and Seventeenth Streets, possibly in search of medication for his fever. Afterwards he has a late supper at Sadler's Restaurant, south side of Main Street between Fifteenth and Sixteenth. Dr. Carter recalls: "Saddler [*sic*] . . . informed me that Poe had left his house at exactly twelve that night, starting for the Baltimore boat in company with several companions . . . the boat was to leave at four o'clock" (Carter, pp. 565–66; cf. Weiss [1878], p. 714, [1907], pp. 203–04, and Whitty [1911], p. lxxxiii).

27 SEPTEMBER. Poe leaves Richmond on a steamer bound for Baltimore, possibly the *Pocahontas* under Captain Parrish (schedules in Quinn, pp. 755–56).

28 SEPTEMBER. BALTIMORE. The *Pocahontas* arrives from Richmond (reports of ship arrivals in the *American* and the *Sun*, 29 September).

OCTOBER. ATHENS, GEORGIA. *Wheler's Southern Monthly Magazine* reports: "Edgar A. Poe, the poet, has joined the Sons of Temperance."

2 OCTOBER. RICHMOND. In the *Semi-Weekly Examiner* Daniel reports: "Mr. Edgar Poe has left Richmond for New York. It is understood, however, that he will return, and perhaps settle here."

BEFORE 3 OCTOBER. BALTIMORE. Poe begins drinking heavily, apparently after being persuaded to take a single glass of alcohol by old friends (Dr. J. J. Moran's statements to W. T. D. Clemm on 7 October; J. P. Kennedy's diary entry on 10 October).

[On 1 November 1849 Neilson Poe wrote Rufus W. Griswold: "The history of the last few days of his [Poe's] life is known to no one so well as to myself, and is of touching & melancholy interest, as well [as] of the most admonitory import. I think I can demonstrate that he passed, by *a single indulgence*, from a condition of perfect sobriety to one bordering upon the madness usually occasioned only by long continued intoxication, and that he is entitled to a far more favourable judgment upon his last hours than he has received" (NN–B).]

3 OCTOBER. WEDNESDAY. The *Sun* reports: "An election takes place throughout the State to-day for members of Congress and for members of the [Maryland] House of Delegates." The paper lists the polling places in Baltimore, asking every qualified voter to exercise "the right of franchise."

3 OCTOBER. Joseph W. Walker, a printer, encounters Poe at "Gunner's Hall," a tavern operated by Cornelius Ryan at 44 East Lombard Street, being used today as the polling place for the Fourth Ward. Walker sends this urgent message to Poe's old friend Joseph Evans Snodgrass: "There is a gentleman, rather the worse for wear, at Ryan's 4th ward polls, who goes under the cognomen of Edgar A. Poe, and who appears in great distress, & he says he is acquainted with you, and I assure you, he is in need of immediate assistance" (Miller [1977], pp. 85–86; cf. polls list in the *Sun* and Baltimore Directory for 1849).

[Walker had been employed as a typesetter for Snodgrass' defunct weekly, the *Saturday Visiter*, and knew of this editor's admiration for Poe (Snodgrass [1867], p. 283). William Hand Browne observed: "At that time the polls were usually held at public houses, and the candidates saw that every voter had all the whiskey he wanted" (letter to J. H. Ingram, 13 January 1909, ViU–I).]

3 OCTOBER. In the afternoon Snodgrass goes to the polling place. He recalls:

When I entered the bar-room of the house, I instantly recognized the face of one whom I had often seen and knew well, although it wore an aspect of vacant stupidity which made me shudder. The intellectual flash of his eye had vanished, or rather had been quenched in the bowl; but the broad, capacious forehead of the author of "The Raven," . . . was still there, with a width, in the region of ideality, such as few men have ever possessed. But perhaps I would not have so readily recognized him had I not been notified of his apparel. His hat—or rather the hat of somebody else, for he had evidently been robbed of his clothing, or cheated in an exchange—was a cheap palm-leaf one, without a band, and soiled; his coat, of commonest alpaca, and evidently "second hand"; and his pants of gray-mixed cassimere, dingy and badly fitting. He wore neither vest nor neckcloth, if I remember aright, while his shirt was sadly crumpled and soiled. He was so utterly stupefied with liquor that I thought it best not to seek recognition or conversation, especially as he was surrounded by a crowd of drinking men, actuated by idle curiosity rather than sympathy. I immediately ordered a room for him, where he could be comfortable until I got word to his relatives—for there were several in Baltimore. Just at that moment, one or two of the persons referred to, getting information of the case, arrived at the spot. They declined to take private care of him, assigning as a reason, that he had been very abusive and ungrateful on former occasions, when drunk, and advised that he be sent to a hospital. . . . So insensible was he, that we had to carry him to the carriage as if a corpse. The muscles of articulation seemed paralyzed to speechlessness, and mere incoherent mutterings were all that were heard (Snodgrass [1856], p. 24).

[In his 1867 account, p. 284, Snodgrass identified the person who suggested a hospital as "Mr. H——, a relative of Mr. Poe's by marriage": this would have been Henry Herring, who had married Poe's aunt Eliza in 1814.]

3 OCTOBER. Poe is admitted to the Washington College Hospital, corner of Broadway and Hampstead Street.

[On 15 November 1849 Dr. John J. Moran, the resident physician, replied to Mrs. Clemm's letter of inquiry:

Presuming you are already aware of the malady of which Mr. Poe died [delirium tremens] I need only state concisely the particulars of his circumstances from his entrance until his decease—

When brought to the Hospital he was unconscious of his condition—who brought him or with whom he had been associating. He remained in this condition from 5. *Ock* in the afternoon—the hour of his admission—until 3 next morning. . . .

To this state succeeded tremor of of [*sic*] the limbs, and at first a busy, but not violent or active delirium—constant talking—and vacant converse with spectral and imaginary objects on the walls. His face was pale and his whole person drenched in perspiration—We were unable to induce tranquillity before the second day [5 October] after his admission (facsimile in Quinn and Hart, pp. 31–34).]

4 OCTOBER. Neilson Poe learns that his second cousin Edgar is at the Washington College Hospital: "As soon as I heard that he was at the college, I went over, but his physicians did not think it advisable that I should see him, as he was very excitable—The next day [5 October] I

called & sent him changes of linen &c. And was gratified to learn that he was much better" (letter to Mrs. Clemm, 11 October 1849, Quinn and Hart, pp. 29–31).

5–7 OCTOBER. On Friday, 5 October, Dr. John J. Moran questions Poe:

Having left orders with the nurses to that effect, I was summoned to his bedside so soon as conscious[ness] supervened, and questioned him in reference to his family—place of residence—relatives &c. But his answers were incoherent & unsatisfactory. He told me, however, he had a wife in Richmond (which, I have since learned was not the fact) that he did not know when he left that city or what had become of his trunk of clothing. Wishing to rally and sustain his now fast sinking hopes I told him I hoped, that in a few days he would be able to enjoy the society of his friends here, and I would be most happy to contribute in every possible way to his ease & comfort. At this he broke out with much energy, and said the best thing his best friend could do would be to blow out his brains with a pistol—that when he beheld his degradation he was ready to ["]sink in the earth &c[.]" Shortly after giving expression to these words Mr. Poe seemed to dose & I left him for a short time. When I returned I found him in a violent delirium, resisting the efforts of two nurses to keep him in bed. This state continued until Saturday evening (he was admitted on Wednesday) when he commenced calling for one "Reynolds", which he did through the night up to *three* on Sunday morning. At this time a very decided change began to affect him. Having become enfeebled from exertion he became quiet and seemed to rest for a short time, then gently moving his head he said *"Lord help my poor Soul"* and expired! (Moran to Mrs. Clemm, 15 November, Quinn and Hart, pp. 31–34).

7 OCTOBER. SUNDAY. Neilson Poe learns of his cousin's death: "He [Poe] died on Sunday morning, about 5 o'clock . . . . I was never so much shocked, in my life, as when, on Sunday morning, notice was sent to me that he was dead. Mr [Henry] Herring & myself immediately took the necessary steps for his funeral, which took place on Monday afternoon at four o clock" (Neilson to Mrs. Clemm, 11 October, Quinn and Hart, pp. 29–31).

7 OCTOBER. Dr. Moran calls on Reverend William T. D. Clemm, a cousin of Poe's wife Virginia, at the parsonage of the Caroline Street Methodist Episcopal Church. Moran asks Clemm to perform the services at Poe's funeral tomorrow, explaining the circumstances of his death:

"Mr. Poe," said the Doctor, "came to Baltimore on his way to Philadelphia . . . . Upon landing on the wharf from the Norfolk steamer, Mr. Poe was greeted by some of his old and former associates, who insisted that they should take a sociable glass of ardent spirits together for old acquaintance sake. To these persuasions the unfortunate poet yielded. This was the first drink he had taken for several months. Sad enough for Poe; it revived his latent appetite for drink, and

The Washington College Hospital

the result was a terrible debauch which ended with his death. He lost all his wardrobe; was clad in tattered garments, and had on, when found, an old straw hat which no one would have picked up in the street. His appearance and condition were pitiable in the extreme, and in that drunken and stupefied state he was brought to my hospital. Everything that medical skill and faithful nursing could suggest was done for him, but all to no purpose. He was unconscious or delirious during the entire time—some sixteen [eighty-four] hours—with but one short interval" (Moran's statements reconstructed in Reverend Clemm's 20 February 1889 letter to E. R. Reynolds, ViU–I; cf. Snodgrass' description of Poe's hat in 3 October entry).

7–8 OCTOBER. Poe's remains are "visited by some of the first individuals of the city, many of them anxious to have a lock of his hair" (Moran to Mrs. Clemm, 15 November, Quinn and Hart, pp. 31–34).

8 OCTOBER. On Monday morning the *Sun* carries this report:

DEATH OF EDGAR A. POE.—We regret to learn that Edgar A. Poe, Esq., the distinguished American poet, scholar and critic, died in this city yesterday morning, after an illness of four or five days.—This announcement, coming so sudden and unexpected, will cause poignant regret among all who admire genius, and have sympathy for the frailties too often attending it. Mr. Poe, we believe, was a native of this State, though reared by a foster-father at Richmond, Va., where he lately spent some time on a visit. He was in the 38th year of his age.

8 OCTOBER. At 4:00 PM Poe's funeral procession leaves from the Washington College Hospital. Charles William Hubner, later a poet and editor, recalls:

While on my way to art school, when about fourteen years old, I passed a hospital, a plain coffin was being taken to a hearse standing at the curb, two gentlemen stood, with bared heads, while the attendants placed the casket into the hearse. With boyish curiosity I asked of one of the men:
"Please sir, who are they going to bury?"
He replied: "My son, that is the body of a great poet, Edgar Allan Poe, you will learn all about him some day."
The two men entered the only carriage which followed the hearse. I watched them as long as they were in sight (G. P. Clark, p. 1).

[Reverend William T. D. Clemm stated: "The funeral was . . . utterly without ostentation. But one hack was employed, and four persons occupied it." The carriage actually seems to have carried five persons: Clemm himself, Neilson Poe, Joseph Evans Snodgrass, Henry Herring, and Z. Collins Lee, a Baltimore lawyer who had been Poe's classmate at the University of Virginia (Reverend Clemm to E. R. Reynolds, 20 February 1889, ViU–I; see also Neilson to Mrs. Clemm, 11 October 1849, Quinn and Hart, pp. 29–31).]

Poe is buried in the small Presbyterian cemetery at the southeast corner of Fayette and Greene Streets. J. Alden Weston, a young onlooker, recalls: "On arrival there [of the funeral procession] five or six gentlemen, including the officiating minister [Reverend Clemm], descended from the carriages [sic] and followed the coffin to the grave . . . . The burial ceremony, which did not occupy more than three minutes, was so cold-blooded and unchristianlike as to provoke on my part a sense of anger difficult to suppress. . . . In justice to the people of Baltimore I must say that if the funeral had been postponed for a single day, until the death was generally known, a far more imposing escort to the tomb and one more worthy of the many admirers of the poet in the city would have taken place" (G. P. Clark, pp. 1–2).

[Henry Herring recalled: "He [Poe] was buried in his grandfather's (David Poe) lot near the centre of the graveyard, wherein were buried his grandmother and several others of the family. I furnished a neat mahogany coffin, and Mr. Ne[i]lson Poe the hack and hearse" (Woodberry, 2:448). Besides the occupants of the hack, at least five other persons attended the burial service: the church sexton George W. Spence, the undertaker Charles Suter, Poe's early schoolmaster Joseph H. Clarke, and Poe's first cousin, the former Elizabeth Rebecca Herring, and her husband Edmund Morton Smith (Mabbott [1969], 1:569; Phillips, 2:1510–11; Rice, pp. 44–45).]

8 OCTOBER. NEW YORK. In the afternoon Horace Greeley, editor of the *Daily Tribune*, learns of Poe's death "by telegraph." Greeley asks his friend and protégé Rufus W. Griswold "to prepare some account of the deceased for the next morning's paper" (Greeley's reminiscence quoted by Woodberry, 2:450).

8 OCTOBER. In the evening Griswold makes an entry in his diary: "Wrote, hastily, two or three colum[n]s about Poe, for the Tribune" (Griswold [1898], p. 252).

9 OCTOBER. The *Daily Tribune* contains Griswold's long obituary of Poe, signed with the pseudonym "Ludwig." The announcement of Poe's death "will startle many, *but few will be grieved by it.* The poet was well known personally or by reputation, in all this country; he had readers in England, and in several of the states of Continental Europe; *but he had few or no friends*; and the regrets for his death will be suggested principally by the consideration that in him literary art lost one of its most brilliant, but erratic stars." After giving a chronological account of Poe's career, Griswold assesses his personal character, depicting him as an unbalanced misanthrope who dwelt "in ideal realms—in heaven or hell." Griswold prints "Annabel Lee," the poet's last poem: "Mr. Poe presented it in MS. to the writer of these paragraphs, just before he left New York." The obituary is reprinted in the *Weekly Tribune* for 20 October, the *Richmond Enquirer* for 13 October, and the Philadelphia *Saturday Evening Post* for 20 October (full text in *W*, 1:348–59).

9 OCTOBER. The *Journal of Commerce* comments on Poe's death: "For some years past he has been more or less ill, and the announcement of his death is not unexpected, though none the less melancholy on that account." Poe had few equals: "He stands in a position among our poets and prose writers which has made him the envy of many and the admiration of all." Although he was "better known as a *severe* critic than otherwise," he had "a warm and noble heart, as those who best knew him can testify" (Quinn, p. 645).

9 OCTOBER. The *New York Herald* prints a dispatch from its Baltimore correspondent, dated 8 October:

Our city was yesterday shocked with the announcement of the death of Edgar A. Poe, Esq., who arrived in this city about a week since, after a successful tour through Virginia, where he delivered a series of able lectures. On last Wednesday, election day, he was found near the Fourth ward polls laboring under an attack of *mania à potu*, and in a most shocking condition. Being recognized by some of our citizens, he was placed in a carriage and conveyed to the Washington Hospital, where every attention has been bestowed on him. He lingered, however, until yesterday morning, when death put a period to his existence. He was a most eccentric genius, with many friends and many foes, but all, I feel satisfied, will view with regret the sad fate of the poet and critic. His last days were spent in the same institution where Dr. Lopland [John Lofland] the Milford Bard, spent so many of his latter years, laboring under the effects of the same sad disease.

[Whoever the *Herald's* correspondent may have been, he provided authentic information not found in the other obituaries: the day and place Poe was discovered, the name of the hospital where he was taken, and the cause of his death.]

9 OCTOBER. Mrs. Clemm writes Neilson Poe in Baltimore: "I have heard this moment of the death of my dear son Edgar—I cannot believe it, and have written to you, to try and ascertain the fact and particulars—he has been at the South for the last three months, and was on his way home—the paper states he died in Baltimore yesterday—If it is true God have mercy on me, for he was the last I had to cling to and love, will you write the *instant* you receive this and relieve this dreadful uncertainty—My mind is prepared to *hear all*—conceal nothing from me" (facsimile in Quinn and Hart, facing p. 28).

9 OCTOBER. Mrs. Clemm writes Nathaniel P. Willis, co-editor of the *Home Journal*: "I have this morning heard of the death of my darling Eddie. . . . Can you give me any circumstances or particulars. . . . I need not ask you to notice his death and to speak well of him. I know you will. But say what an affectionate son he was to me, his poor desolate mother" (quoted in Willis' defense of Poe, *Journal* for 20 October).

9 OCTOBER. Mrs. Clemm writes Annie Richmond in Lowell: "Annie my Eddy is dead he died in Baltimore yesterday—Annie my Annie pray for me your desolate friend. My senses *will leave me*—I will write the moment I hear the particulars, I have written to Baltimore—write and advise me what to do" (Robbins [1960], p. 45).

9 OCTOBER. WASHINGTON. Under the heading "Telegraphic Reports" the *Daily National Intelligencer* prints an 8 October dispatch from Baltimore: "Edgar A. Poe, distinguished as a writer, . . . died in this city yesterday morning" (Bandy [1981], p. 32).

9 OCTOBER. PHILADELPHIA. The *Pennsylvanian* and the *Public Ledger* reprint Poe's obituary from yesterday's Baltimore *Sun*. In the *Spirit of the Times* the editor John S. Du Solle briefly announces the death of his friend Poe.

9 OCTOBER. RICHMOND. The *Daily Republican* and the *Richmond Whig* reprint the obituary from yesterday's Baltimore *Sun*. The *Whig* comments: "The news of the death of Mr. Poe will fall with a heavy and crushing weight upon one in this city who is related to him by the tender tie of sister [Rosalie Poe]; and who can hardly have had any previous knowledge of his illness; whilst it will be read with profound regret by all who appreciate generous qualities, or admired genius." The *Semi-Weekly Examiner* contains John M. Daniel's reaction: "We were inexpressibly shocked by the receipt of a Baltimore paper, just as we were going to press, containing an editorial announcement of EDGAR A. POE'S death. . . . It seems but a few hours since he left the writer's office in high spirits, full of hope and in better health than he had been for years. . . . We still hope the news is not true."

9 OCTOBER. BOSTON. The *Evening Transcript* comments on Poe's death: "He had talents, with which he might have done great things, had he united to them stable principles, earnest purposes and self-denying habits. Some of his poems are marked with flashes of genius and originality. . . . As a critic he was intolerably conceited, undiscriminating and prejudiced" (Pollin [1972c], pp. 129–30).

9 OCTOBER. LOWELL, MASSACHUSETTS. The *Daily Journal & Courier* reports that Poe died "in Baltimore on Sunday."

9 OCTOBER. BALTIMORE. The *Baltimore Clipper* reports that Poe died on "the 8th [7th] instant of congestion of the brain . . . . Mr. Poe was well known as a writer of great ability."

9? OCTOBER. The *Evening Patriot* contains a long obituary:

We sincerely regret to hear of the melancholy death of EDGAR A. POE, who expired in this city on Sunday morning about five o'clock, at the early age of 38 years, after an illness of about a week. His disease was congestion of the brain.

Mr. Poe was equally remarkable for his genius and his acquirements. . . . He was acquainted, in a greater or less[er] degree, with the ancient languages, and with French, Spanish, Italian and German, and had an accurate knowledge of most branches of science and art. . . . Mr. Poe's writings, both in prose and poetry, have for several years past had an established reputation. They were peculiar, and far from being without striking faults; but there is scarcely one of them that can be read by a person of judgment, without leading him to the conclusion that the author was a man of genius truly original; of a taste refined by diligent study and comparison; and of information, varied, comprehensive and minute. . . .

Mr. Poe is said to have been a man of polished manners, fine colloquial powers, warm and amiable impulses, and of a high and sometimes haughty spirit. It is deeply to be deplored that his great powers, which might have enabled him to soar so high and to have acquired for himself so much of fame and prosperity, were obscured and crippled by the frailties and weaknesses which have too often attended eminent genius in all ages.

The *Patriot* reprints "The Raven" as a memorial to Poe (obituary and poem reprinted in the *Richmond Whig*, 12 October).

10 OCTOBER. Poe's early benefactor John P. Kennedy writes in his diary:

On Sunday last Edgar A. Poe died in town here at the hospital from the effects of a debauch. He had been to Richmond, was returning to New York, where he lived, and, I understand, was soon to be married to a lady in Richmond of quite good fortune [Mrs. Shelton]. He fell in with some companion here who seduced him to the bottle, which it was said he had renounced some time ago. The consequence was fever, delirium, and madness, and in a few days a termination of his sad career in the hospital. Poor Poe! He was an original and exquisite poet, and one of the best prose writers in this country. His works are amongst the very best of their kind. His taste was replete with classical flavor, and he wrote in the spirit of an old Greek philosopher (MdBJ–P; Woodberry, 2:349–50).

10 OCTOBER. PHILADELPHIA. The *Dollar Newspaper* and the *Germantown Telegraph* briefly report Poe's death. In the *Spirit of the Times* John S. Du Solle reprints the Baltimore dispatch found in yesterday's *New York Herald*, which attributed Poe's death to delirium tremens. Du Solle comments: "poor Poe . . . with all his faults, we loved him for his transcendent genius."

10 OCTOBER. NEW YORK. In the supplement to the *Daily Tribune*, Horace Greeley reprints Poe's second "To Helen," observing: "It was addressed to a woman of kindred genius, [Mrs. Whitman,] to whom, it is not a secret that sometime since the death of his first wife, he was for a short time engaged to be married. We know the scene, in a neighboring city; and we know that the incident of his seeing the person under such circumstances is literally true" (Bayless, p. 165).

10 OCTOBER. NORFOLK, VIRGINIA. The *American Beacon* reprints Poe's obituary from the Baltimore *Sun* "of Monday." The *Daily Southern Argus* cites the report in the *Sun*, praising Poe as "a distinguished poet, scholar and critic. Only a few weeks ago he delivered a literary lecture in this city, which was greatly applauded."

ELMIRA SHELTON
(from a daguerreotype formerly owned by her daughter Ann Elizabeth)

10 OCTOBER. RICHMOND. John R. Thompson writes Rufus W. Griswold: "When poor Poe left here, some three weeks since, I gave him a letter which he promised me to deliver into your hands; but as the papers state that he had been seven days in the hospital at Baltimore before his unhappy death, I make sure that he did not reach Philadelphia and by consequence that you did not receive the letter." This undelivered letter contained Thompson's biographical "memoranda," which Griswold solicited in the letter he wrote from Philadelphia "about a month ago." Thompson now repeats this information, to be published along with several of his poems in the next edition of Griswold's *Poets and Poetry of America*. "Poor Poe! I cannot think of his fate without deep commiseration. The evening before his departure from Richmond he was with me and spoke in the highest spirits of his resolves and prospects for the future. He had become a Son of Temperance and was soon to be married to a lady here [Mrs. Shelton]. But his lack of stability, of fixed principles of character, frustrated all his plans and extinguished them in a dishonored grave" (PHi).

10 OCTOBER. LOWELL, MASSACHUSETTS. The *Daily Journal & Courier* contains a second notice of Poe's death, quoting Griswold's "Ludwig" obituary from yesterday's New York *Daily Tribune*.

10 OCTOBER. Annie Richmond writes Mrs. Clemm at Fordham:

Oh my mother, my darling darling mother oh what shall I say to you—how *can* I comfort you . . . . oh if I could only have laid down *my* life for his, that he might have been spared to you—but mother it is the will of God, and we must submit, and Heaven grant us strength, to bear it . . . . your letter [of yesterday] has this moment reached me, but I had seen a notice of his death, a few moments previous in the paper—oh mother, when I read it, I said, no, no it is *not* true *my* Eddie *can't be dead*, no it is *not* so I *could not* believe it, until I got your letter . . . . my own heart is breaking, and I cannot offer you consolation that I would, *now*, but mother, I *will* pray for you, and for myself, that I may be able to comfort you—Mr R. [Annie's husband] begs that you will come on here, soon as you can, and stay with us long as you please—Do dear mother, gather up *all his papers and books*, and take them and come to your own Annie (Quinn and Hart, pp. 53–54).

List of Sources

Allan	Carlisle Allan. "Cadet Edgar Allan Poe, U.S.A." *American Mercury* 29 (August 1933):446–55.
Allen	Hervey Allen. *Israfel: The Life and Times of Edgar Allan Poe.* 2d ed., rev. New York: Farrar & Rinehart, 1934.
Allen and Mabbott	Hervey Allen and Thomas Ollive Mabbott. *Poe's Brother: The Poems of William Henry Leonard Poe.* New York: George H. Doran, 1926.
R. T. P. Allen	Robert T. P. Allen. "Edgar Allan Poe." *Scribner's Monthly* 11 (November 1875):142–43.
Alterton	Margaret Alterton. *The Origins of Poe's Critical Theory.* Iowa City: University of Iowa, 1925.
Ames	William E. Ames. *A History of the "National Intelligencer."* Chapel Hill: University of North Carolina Press, 1972.
Bandy (1964)	William T. Bandy. "Poe's Secret Translator: Amédée Pichot." *Modern Language Notes* 79 (May 1964):277–80.
Bandy (1981)	———. "Two Notes on Poe's Death." *Poe Studies* 14 (December 1981):32.
Bandy (1982)	———. "Poe, Duane and Duffee." *University of Mississippi Studies in English* ns 3 (1982):81–95.
E. W. Barnes	Eric Wollencott Barnes. *The Lady of "Fashion": The Life and the Theatre of Anna Cora Mowatt.* New York: Scribner's, 1954.
H. F. Barnes	Homer F. Barnes. *Charles Fenno Hoffman.* New York: Columbia University Press, 1930.
Bayless	Joy Bayless. *Rufus Wilmot Griswold: Poe's Literary Executor.* Nashville, Tenn.: Vanderbilt University Press, 1943.
Bayless (1934)	———. "Another Rufus W. Griswold as a Critic of Poe." *American Literature* 6 (March 1934):69–72.
Benton	Joel Benton. "Poe's Opinion of 'The Raven.' " *Forum* 22 (February 1897):731–33.

Birss John H. Birss. "Poe in Fordham: A Reminiscence." *Notes and Queries* 173 (18 December 1937):440.

Bohner Charles H. Bohner. *John Pendleton Kennedy: Gentleman from Baltimore*. Baltimore: Johns Hopkins Press, 1961.

Bohner (1958) ————. "The Poe-Kennedy Friendship." *Pennsylvania Magazine of History and Biography* 82 (April 1958):220–22.

Bondurant Agnes M. Bondurant. *Poe's Richmond*. Richmond: Garrett & Massie, 1942.

Brasher Thomas L. Brasher. "A Whitman Parody of 'The Raven'?" *Poe Studies* 1 (October 1968):30–31.

Briggs Charles F. Briggs. "The Personality of Poe." *Independent* 29 (13 December 1877):1–2.

Brigham Clarence S. Brigham, ed. *Edgar Allan Poe's Contributions to "Alexander's Weekly Messenger."* Worcester, Mass.: American Antiquarian Society, 1943.

Brown Alexander Brown. *The Cabells and Their Kin*. Boston: Houghton Mifflin, 1895.

C. H. Brown Charles H. Brown. *William Cullen Bryant*. New York: Scribner's, 1971.

Browning (1898) Frederic G. Kenyon, ed. *The Letters of Elizabeth Barrett Browning*. 2 vols. New York: Macmillan, 1898.

Browning (1969) Elvan Kintner, ed. *The Letters of Robert Browning and Elizabeth Barrett Barrett, 1845–1846*. 2 vols. Cambridge, Mass.: Harvard University Press, 1969.

Buckingham Joseph T. Buckingham. *Personal Memoirs and Recollections of Editorial Life*. 2 vols. Boston: Ticknor, Reed & Fields, 1852.

Burr Charles Chauncey Burr. "Character of Edgar A. Poe." *Nineteenth Century* (Philadelphia) 5 (February 1852):19–33.

A. R. Burr Anna Robeson Burr. *Weir Mitchell: His Life and Letters*. New York: Duffield & Co., 1929.

Burwell William M. Burwell. "Edgar A. Poe and His College Contemporaries." *University of Virginia Alumni Bulletin*, 3d Series, 16 (April 1923):168–80. Reprinted from the *New Orleans Times-Democrat*, 18 May 1884.

Cambiaire Célestin Pierre Cambiaire. *The Influence of Edgar Allan Poe in France*. New York: G. E. Stechert & Co., 1927.

Cameron (1973) Kenneth Walter Cameron. "Young Poe and the Army—Victorian Editing." *American Transcendental*

Quarterly no. 20 (Fall 1973):Supplement, Part Four, 154–82.

Cameron (1974)

———. "Notes on Young Poe's Reading." *American Transcendental Quarterly* no. 24 (Fall 1974):Supplement, 33–34.

Campbell (1912)

Killis Campbell. "Some Unpublished Documents Relating to Poe's Early Years." *Sewanee Review* 20 (April 1912):201–12.

Campbell (1916)

———. "New Notes on Poe's Early Years." *Dial* 60 (17 February 1916):143–46.

Campbell (1917)

———, ed. *The Poems of Edgar Allan Poe.* Boston: Ginn & Co., 1917.

Campbell (1917a)

Killis Campbell. "The Kennedy Papers." *Sewanee Review* 25 (January, April, and July 1917):1–19, 193–208, 348–60.

Campbell (1933)

———. *The Mind of Poe and Other Studies.* Cambridge, Mass.: Harvard University Press, 1933.

Campbell (1936)

———. [A review of David K. Jackson's *Poe and "The Southern Literary Messenger"*] *Modern Language Notes* 51 (November 1936):487–88.

Carlson

Eric W. Carlson, ed. *The Recognition of Edgar Allan Poe: Selected Criticism Since 1829.* Ann Arbor: University of Michigan Press, 1966.

Carter

John F. Carter, M.D. "Edgar Poe's Last Night in Richmond." *Lippincott's Magazine* 70 (November 1902):562–66.

Cauthen

Irby B. Cauthen, Jr. "Lowell on Poe: An Unpublished Comment, 1879." *American Literature* 24 (May 1952):230–33.

Chase

Lewis Chase. "Poe's Playmates in Kilmarnock." *Dial* 61 (19 October 1916):303.

Chivers (1952)

Richard Beale Davis, ed. *Chivers' Life of Poe.* New York: E. P. Dutton & Co., 1952.

Chivers (1957)

Emma Lester Chase and Lois Ferry Parks, eds. *The Complete Works of Thomas Holley Chivers, Volume I: The Correspondence.* Providence, R. I.: Brown University Press, 1957.

Church

Randolph W. Church. "*Al Aaraaf* and the Unknown Critic." *Virginia Cavalcade* (Virginia State Library in Richmond) 5 (Summer 1955):4–7.

Clark

Leslie W. Dunlap, ed. *The Letters of Willis Gaylord Clark and Lewis Gaylord Clark.* New York: New York Public Library, 1940.

G. P. Clark	George P. Clark. "Two Unnoticed Recollections of Poe's Funeral." *Poe Studies* 3 (June 1970):1–2.
Coburn	Frederick W. Coburn. "Poe as Seen by the Brother of 'Annie.' " *New England Quarterly* 16 (September 1943):468–76.
Cohen	B. Bernard Cohen and Lucian A. Cohen. "Poe and Griswold Once More." *American Literature* 34 (March 1962):97–101.
Colton	Cullen B. Colton. "George Hooker Colton and the Publication of 'The Raven.' " *American Literature* 10 (November 1938):319–30.
Cooke	John Esten Cooke. *Poe as a Literary Critic.* Ed. N. Bryllion Fagin. Baltimore: Johns Hopkins Press, 1946.
Cottom	Peter Cottom, comp. *The American Star: Being a Choice Collection of the Most Approved Patriotic & Other Songs.* 2d ed. Richmond: Peter Cottom, 1817.
Crane	Mukhtar Ali Isani. "Reminiscences of Poe by an Employee of the *Broadway Journal.*" *Poe Studies* 6 (December 1973):33–34. Reminiscences of Alexander T. Crane reprinted from the Omaha, Nebraska, *Sunday World-Herald*, 13 July 1902.
Crocker	*Catalogue of the Library of Charles Templeton Crocker.* Hillsborough, Cal., 1918.
CSmH	Henry E. Huntington Library, San Marino, California.
Curtis	Caroline Ticknor, ed. "Some Early Letters of George William Curtis." *Atlantic Monthly* 114 (September 1914):363–76.
Dameron	J. Lasley Dameron. "Thomas Ollive Mabbott on the Canon of Poe's Reviews." *Poe Studies* 5 (December 1972):56–57.
Dameron and Cauthen	J. Lasley Dameron and Irby B. Cauthen, Jr. *Edgar Allan Poe: A Bibliography of Criticism, 1827–1967.* Charlottesville: University Press of Virginia, 1974.
Damon	S. Foster Damon. *Thomas Holley Chivers, Friend of Poe.* New York: Harper & Brothers, 1930.
Davis	Richard Beale Davis. *Francis Walker Gilmer: Life and Learning in Jefferson's Virginia.* Richmond: Dietz Press, 1939.
H. C. Davis	Henry Campbell Davis. "Poe's Stormy Voyage in 1827 is Described." Charleston, S. C., *News and Courier* 5 January 1941, Section II, p. 3.
Deas	Michael J. Deas. *The Portraits and Daguerreotypes of Ed-*

gar Allan Poe. Forthcoming from the University Press of Virginia.

Derby   J[ames] C. Derby. *Fifty Years Among Authors, Books and Publishers*. New York: G. W. Carleton & Co., 1884.

Dedmond   Francis P. Dedmond. "Willis and Morris Add a Partner—and Poe." *Notes and Queries* 198 (June 1953):253–54.

Dickens   Madeline House, Graham Storey, and Kathleen Tillotson, eds. *The Letters of Charles Dickens, Volume Three: 1842–1843*. Oxford, England: Clarendon Press of Oxford University, 1974.

Didier   Eugene L. Didier. *The Life and Poems of Edgar Allan Poe*.
(1877)   New York: W. J. Widdleton, 1877.

Didier   _____ . *The Poe Cult and Other Poe Papers*. New York:
(1909)   Broadway Publishing Co., 1909.

Dietz   F[rieda] Meredith Dietz. "Poe's First and Final Love." *Southern Literary Messenger* (revived) 5 (March 1943):38–47.

Dimmock   Thomas Dimmock. "Notes on Poe." *Century Magazine* ns 28 (June 1895):315–16.

DLC–EA   Library of Congress, Washington, D.C. Ellis-Allan Papers.

DLC–RB   Rare Book Room.

Eaves   T. C. Duncan Eaves. "Poe's Last Visit to Philadelphia." *American Literature* 26 (March 1954):44–51.

Ehrlich   Heyward Ehrlich. "The *Broadway Journal*: Briggs's Dilemma and Poe's Strategy." *Bulletin of the New York Public Library* 73 (February 1969):74–93.

Ellis   Thomas H. Ellis. "Edgar Allan Poe." *Richmond Standard* 7 May 1881, p. 2.

English   Thomas Dunn English. "Reminiscences of Poe." *Independent* 48 (15, 22, 29 October, 5 November 1896):1381–82, 1415–16, 1448, 1480–81.

Evans   May Garrettson Evans. "Poe in Amity Street." *Maryland Historical Magazine* 36 (December 1941):363–80.

Eveleth   Thomas Ollive Mabbott, ed. *The Letters from George W. Eveleth to Edgar Allan Poe*. New York: New York Public Library, 1922.

Exman   Eugene Exman. *The Brothers Harper: A Unique Publishing Partnership and Its Impact upon the Cultural Life of America from 1817 to 1853*. New York: Harper & Row, 1965.

Field	Maunsell B. Field. *Memories of Many Men*. New York: Harper & Brothers, 1874.
Fisher	Benjamin Franklin Fisher, IV, ed. *Poe at Work: Seven Textual Studies*. Baltimore: Edgar Allan Poe Society, 1978.
G. D. Fisher	George D. Fisher. *History and Reminiscences of the Monumental Church, Richmond, Va., from 1814 to 1878*. Richmond: Whittet & Shepperson, 1880.
Freeman (1967)	Fred B. Freeman, Jr. "The Identity of Poe's 'Miss B.' " *American Literature* 39 (November 1967):389–91.
Freeman (1971)	————— . "A Note on Poe's 'Miss B.' " *American Literature* 43 (March 1971):115–17.
French	John C. French. "Poe and the *Baltimore Saturday Visiter*." *Modern Language Notes* 33 (May 1918):257–67.
Gerber	Gerald E. Gerber. "E. P. Whipple Attacks Poe: A New Review." *American Literature* 53 (March 1981):110–13.
Gibson	T[homas] W[are] Gibson. "Poe at West Point." *Harper's Monthly* 35 (November 1867):754–56.
Gill	William F. Gill. *The Life of Edgar Allan Poe*. New York: C. T. Dillingham, 1877.
Gimbel	Richard Gimbel. " 'Quoth the Raven': A Catalogue of the Exhibition." *Yale University Library Gazette* 33 (April 1959):139–89.
Godwin	Parke Godwin. *A Biography of William Cullen Bryant*. 2 vols. New York: D. Appleton & Co., 1883.
Golden	Alan Golden. "Edgar Allan Poe at the *Broadway Journal*." *Poe Messenger* (Poe Museum in Richmond) 12 (Summer 1982):1–6.
Goodwin	William A. R. Goodwin, D.D. *History of the Theological Seminary in Virginia*. 2 vols. New York: Edwin S. Gorham, 1923.
Graham	George R. Graham. "The Late Edgar Allan Poe." *Graham's Magazine* 36 (March 1850):224–26.
Gravely	William Henry Gravely, Jr. "The Early Political and Literary Career of Thomas Dunn English." Ph.D. diss., University of Virginia, 1953.
Graves	Charles Marshall Graves. "Landmarks of Poe in Richmond, Including Some Hitherto Unpublished Portraits of His Friends." *Century Magazine* ns 45 (April 1904):909–20.
Greeley	Horace Greeley. *Recollections of a Busy Life*. New York: J. B. Ford & Co., 1868.

Griswold (1850) — Rufus Wilmot Griswold. "Memoir of the Author." In *The Literati . . . By Edgar A. Poe* (New York: J. S. Redfield, 1850), pp. v–xxxix. *The Literati*, third in Griswold's four-volume edition of Poe, appeared in September 1850; his "Memoir" was moved to the first volume (*Tales*) in subsequent printings.

Griswold (1898) — _____. *Passages from the Correspondence and Other Papers of Rufus W. Griswold*. Ed. W[illiam] M. Griswold. Cambridge, Mass.: W. M. Griswold, 1898.

Guilds — John C. Guilds, Jr. "A Note on Poe's Unhappy Home Life." *Library Notes* (Duke University) no. 22 (July 1949):5–7.

Hammond — Alexander Hammond. "Edgar Allan Poe's *Tales of the Folio Club*: The Evolution of a Lost Book." *Library Chronicle* (University of Pennsylvania) 41 (1976):13–43. Reprinted in Fisher's *Poe at Work* (1978), pp. 13–43.

Harris — A[manda] B[artlett] Harris. "Edgar A. Poe." *Hearth and Home* 8 (9 January 1875):24.

Harrison (1900) — James A. Harrison. "New Glimpses of Poe." *Independent* 52 (6, 13, 20 September 1900):2158–61, 2201–02, 2259–61.

Harrison (1906) — _____. "A Poe Miscellany." *Independent* 61 (1 November 1906):1044–51.

Harrison (1909) — _____, ed. *The Last Letters of Edgar Allan Poe to Sarah Helen Whitman*. New York: G. P. Putnam's Sons, 1909.

Harrison and Dailey — James A. Harrison and Charlotte F. Dailey. "Poe and Mrs. Whitman: New Light on a Romantic Episode." *Century Magazine* ns 55 (January 1909):439–52.

Haskell — John D. Haskell. "Poe, Literary *Soirées*, and Coffee." *Poe Studies* 8 (December 1975):47.

Hatvary — George E. Hatvary. "Poe's Possible Authorship of 'An Opinion on Dreams.' " *Poe Studies* 14 (December 1981):21–22.

Heartman and Canny — Charles F. Heartman and James R. Canny, comps. *A Bibliography of First Printings of the Writings of Edgar Allan Poe*. 2d ed., rev. Hattiesburg, Miss.: Book Farm, 1943.

Herndon — G. Melvin Herndon. "From Scotch Orphan to Virginia Planter: William Galt, Jr., 1801–1851." *Virginia Magazine of History and Biography* 87 (July

1979):326–43.

Hewitt
(1877)

John Hill Hewitt. *Shadows on the Wall or Glimpses of the Past: A Retrospect of the Past Fifty Years*. Baltimore: Turnbull Brothers, 1877.

Hewitt
(1949)

———— . *Recollections of Poe*. Ed. Richard Barksdale Harwell. Atlanta: Emory University Library, 1949.

Higginson

Thomas Wentworth Higginson. "Short Studies of American Authors, II: Poe." *Literary World* (Boston) 10 (15 March 1879):89–90.

Hoole

William Stanley Hoole. "Poe in Charleston, S. C." *American Literature* 6 (March 1934):78–80.

Horan

James D. Horan. *Mathew Brady: Historian with a Camera*. 1955; rpt. New York: Bonanza Books, n.d.

Hubbell

Jay B. Hubbell. *The South in American Literature, 1607–1900*. Durham, N.C.: Duke University Press, 1954.

Hubbell
(1941)

———— . "Poe's Mother, with a Note on John Allan." *William and Mary Quarterly* 21 (July 1941):250–54.

Hubbell
(1954)

———— . "Charles Chauncey Burr: Friend of Poe." *PMLA* 69 (September 1954):833–40.

Hull

William Doyle Hull, II. "A Canon of the Critical Works of Edgar Allan Poe." Ph.D. diss., University of Virginia, 1941.

Hunter

William Elijah Hunter. "Poe and His English Schoolmaster." *Athenaeum* no. 2660 (19 October 1878): 496–97.

Hyneman

Esther F. Hyneman. *Edgar Allan Poe: An Annotated Bibliography of Books and Articles in English, 1827–1973*. Boston: G. K. Hall & Co., 1974.

Ingram

John Henry Ingram. *Edgar Allan Poe: His Life, Letters, and Opinions*. 1886; rpt. New York: AMS Press, 1965.

Ingram List

John Carl Miller, comp. *John Henry Ingram's Poe Collection at the University of Virginia*. Charlottesville: University Press of Virginia, 1960.

InU–L

Lilly Library, Indiana University, Bloomington.

Irving

Washington Irving. *Letters, Volume III: 1839–1845*. Ed. Ralph M. Aderman, Herbert L. Kleinfield, and Jenifer S. Banks. Boston: Twayne Publishers, 1982.

Jackson
(1933)

David K. Jackson. "Poe Notes: 'Pinakidia' and 'Some Ancient Greek Authors.' " *American Literature* 5 (November 1933):258–67.

Jackson
(1934)
———— . *Poe and "The Southern Literary Messenger."* Richmond: Dietz Press, 1934. Reprinted New York: Haskell House, 1970.

Jackson
(1934a)
———— . " 'Some Ancient Greek Authors': A Work of Edgar A. Poe." *Notes and Queries* 166 (26 May 1934):368.

Jackson
(1935)
———— . "Four of Poe's Critiques in the Baltimore Newspapers." *Modern Language Notes* 50 (April 1935):251–56.

Jackson
(1936)
———— . "Some Unpublished Letters of T. W. White to Lucian Minor." *Tyler's Quarterly Historical and Genealogical Magazine* 17 (April 1936): 224–43, and 18 (July 1936):32–49.

Jackson
(1974)
———— . "A Poe Hoax Comes Before the U. S. Senate." *Poe Studies* 7 (December 1974):47–48.

Jackson
(1976a)
———— . "Two Notes: A Joseph H. Clarke Manuscript and Something about a Mr. Persico." *Poe Studies* 9 (June 1976):22.

Jackson
(1976b)
———— . "A Poe Bibliographical Note." *Library Notes* (Duke University) no. 46 (September 1976):29–31.

Jackson
(1977)
———— . "A Man Named Bool: A Shadow on the Wall." *Poe Studies* 10 (December 1977):44.

Jackson
(1979)
———— . "The Identity of Maria Clemm's Friend, the Judge." *Poe Studies* 12 (June 1979):20.

Jackson
(1981)
———— . "Another Reprint of Poe's 'The Oblong Box.' " *University of Mississippi Studies in English* ns 2 (1981):109–10.

Jackson
(1982)
———— . "An Uncollected Letter of James Kirke Paulding." *Poe Studies* 15 (December 1982):41.

Jackson
(1983)
———— . "William Wilson: Another Possible Source for the Name." *Poe Studies* 16 (June 1983):13.

Jacobs
Robert D. Jacobs. *Poe: Journalist & Critic.* Baton Rouge: Louisiana State University Press, 1969.

Johnson
Rue Corbett Johnson. "The Theatrical Career of William E. Burton." Ph.D. diss., Indiana University, 1967.

Kent
Charles W[illiam] Kent, comp. *The Unveiling of the Bust of Edgar Allan Poe in the Library of the University of Virginia, October the Seventh, Eighteen Hundred and Ninety-Nine.* Lynchburg, Va.: J. P. Bell Co., 1901.

Kent
(1901)
———— ."An Episode in the Early Life of Poe." *Century Magazine* ns 40 (October 1901):955–56.

Kent
(1917)

————— ."Poe's Student Days at the University of Virginia." *Bookman* (New York) 44 (January 1917):517–25. Originally published in vol. 13 (July 1901):430–40.

Kent and
Patton

————— and John S. Patton, eds. *The Book of the Poe Centenary*. Charlottesville: University of Virginia, 1909.

Kettell

Samuel Kettell, comp. *Specimens of American Poetry*. 3 vols. Boston: S. G. Goodrich, 1829.

L

John Ward Ostrom, ed. *The Letters of Edgar Allan Poe*. 2 vols. 1948; rpt. with a supplement, New York: Gordian Press, 1966.

Laverty
(1948)

Carroll D. Laverty. "Poe in 1847." *American Literature* 20 (May 1948):163–68.

Laverty
(1951)

————— . "Science and Pseudo-Science in the Writings of Edgar Allan Poe." Ph.D. diss., Duke University, 1951.

Leary

Lewis Leary. "Miss Octavia's Autograph Album and Edgar Allan Poe." *Columbia Library Columns* (Columbia University) 17 (February 1968):9–15.

Lease

Benjamin Lease. *That Wild Fellow John Neal and the American Literary Revolution*. Chicago: University of Chicago Press, 1972.

Leslie

Tom Taylor, ed. *Autobiographical Recollections, By the Late Charles Robert Leslie, R.A.* Boston: Ticknor and Fields, 1860.

Lincoln

Roy P. Basler, ed. *The Collected Works of Abraham Lincoln*. 8 vols. New Brunswick, N. J.: Rutgers University Press, 1953–1955.

Little

John P. Little. *History of Richmond*. 1851; rpt. Richmond: Dietz Printing Co., 1933.

Longfellow
(1886)

Samuel Longfellow, ed. *Life of Henry Wadsworth Longfellow*. 2 vols. Boston: Ticknor and Co., 1886.

Longfellow
(1966)

Andrew Hilen, ed. *The Letters of Henry Wadsworth Longfellow, Volume II: 1837–1843*. Cambridge, Mass.: Harvard University Press, 1966.

Longfellow
(1972)

————— , ed. *Letters, Volume III: 1844–1856*. 1972.

Mrs. Longfellow

Edward Wagenknecht, ed. *Mrs. Longfellow: Selected Letters and Journals of Fanny Appleton Longfellow*. New York: Longmans, Green and Co., 1956.

Lord

W[illiam] W[ilberforce] Lord. *The Complete Poetical Works of W. W. Lord*. Ed. Thomas Ollive Mabbott. New York: Random House, 1938.

Lowell	Charles Eliot Norton, ed. *Letters of James Russell Lowell.* 2 vols. New York: Harper & Brothers, 1894.
McElroy	M. D. McElroy. "Poe's Last Partner: E. H. N. Patterson of Oquawka, Illinois." *Papers on Language & Literature* 7 (Summer 1971):252–71.
Mabbott (1919)	Thomas Ollive Mabbott. "Some Classical Allusions in Poe." *Classical Weekly* 12 (20 January 1919):94.
Mabbott (1920)	———. "A Few Notes on Poe." *Modern Language Notes* 35 (June 1920):373–74.
Mabbott (1932)	———. "Newly-Identified Reviews by Edgar Poe." *Notes and Queries* 163 (17 December 1932):441.
Mabbott (1933)	———. "Greeley's Estimate of Poe." *Autograph Album* 1 (December 1933):14–16, 61.
Mabbott (1937)	———. "Letters from Mary E. Hewitt to Poe." In *A Christmas Book from the Department of English, Hunter College,* ed. Blanche Colton Williams (Brooklyn, N. Y.: Comet Press, 1937), pp. 116–21.
Mabbott (1941)	———, ed. *Tamerlane and Other Poems, By Edgar Allan Poe.* Facsimile of 1827 edition. New York: Facsimile Text Society, 1941.
Mabbott (1942)	———, ed. *The Raven and Other Poems, By Edgar Allan Poe.* Facsimile of 1845 edition: J. Lorimer Graham copy with the author's handwritten corrections. New York: Facsimile Text Society, 1942.
Mabbott (1943)	———. "Poe's 'Original Conundrums.' " *Notes and Queries* 184 (5 June 1943):328–29.
Mabbott (1949)	———. "An Unfavourable Reaction to Poe, in 1842." *Notes and Queries* 194 (19 March 1949):122–23.
Mabbott (1969)	———, ed. *Collected Works of Edgar Allan Poe, Volume I: Poems.* Cambridge, Mass.: Harvard University Press, 1969.
Mabbott (1978)	Thomas Ollive Mabbott with the assistance of Eleanor D. Kewer and Maureen C. Mabbott, eds. *Collected Works of Edgar Allan Poe: Tales and Sketches.* Volume II: 1831–1842. Volume III: 1843–1849. Cambridge, Mass.: Harvard University Press, 1978.
MB–G	Rufus W. Griswold Collection, Department of Rare Books and Manuscripts, Boston Public Library.
MdBJ–P	George Peabody Library of Johns Hopkins University, Baltimore.
Meagher	Margaret Meagher. *History of Education in Richmond.* Richmond: Virginia Division of Works Progress Administration, 1939.

Meredith	Roy Meredith. *Mr. Lincoln's Camera Man: Mathew B. Brady*. 2d ed., rev. New York: Dover Publications, 1974.
MH–H	Houghton Library, Harvard University, Cambridge, Massachusetts.
MiDAAA–P	William Page Papers, Archives of American Art, Detroit, Michigan.
Miller (1976)	John Carl Miller. "Did Edgar Allan Poe Really Sell a Slave?" *Poe Studies* 9 (December 1976):52–53.
Miller (1977)	_____ . *Building Poe Biography*. Baton Rouge: Louisiana State University Press, 1977.
Miller (1979)	_____ . *Poe's Helen Remembers*. Charlottesville: University Press‹of Virginia, 1979.
Minor	Benjamin Blake Minor. *The Southern Literary Messenger, 1834–1864*. New York: Neale Publishing Co., 1905.
Mitchell	Donald G[rant] Mitchell. *American Lands and Letters*. 2 vols. New York: Scribner's, 1898–1899.
Moldenhauer (1971)	Joseph J. Moldenhauer. "Beyond the Tamarind Tree: A New Poe Letter." *American Literature* 42 (January 1971):468–77.
Moldenhauer (1973)	_____ , comp. *A Descriptive Catalog of Edgar Allan Poe Manuscripts in the Humanities Research Center Library*. Austin: University of Texas at Austin, 1973.
Moldenhauer (1977)	_____ . "Poe's 'The Spectacles': A New Text from Manuscript." In *Studies in the American Renaissance: 1977*, ed. Joel Myerson (Boston: Twayne Publishers, 1978), pp. 179–234.
Moore	Rayburn S. Moore. "A Note on Poe and the Sons of Temperance." *American Literature* 30 (November 1958):359–61.
Mordecai	Samuel Mordecai. *Virginia, Especially Richmond, in By-Gone Days*. 2d ed., rev. 1860; rpt. Richmond: Dietz Press, 1946.
Moss (1963)	Sidney P. Moss. *Poe's Literary Battles: The Critic in the Context of His Literary Milieu*. Durham, N. C.: Duke University Press, 1963.
Moss (1968)	_____ . "Poe and the Saint Louis *Daily Reveille*." *Poe Studies* 1 (October 1968):18–21.
Moss (1970)	_____ . *Poe's Major Crisis: His Libel Suit and New York's Literary World*. Durham, N. C.: Duke University Press, 1970.
Moss (1978)	_____ . "Poe's 'Two Long Interviews' with Dickens." *Poe Studies* 11 (June 1978):10–12.

Mott	Frank Luther Mott. *A History of American Magazines, 1741–1850*. Cambridge, Mass.: Harvard University Press, 1930.
Moyne	Ernest John Moyne. "Did Edgar Allan Poe Lecture at Newark Academy?" *Delaware Notes* (University of Delaware) 26th series (1953):1–19.
National Archives	National Archives, Washington, D. C.
NcD–G	William R. Perkins Library, Duke University, Durham, North Carolina. William Galt, Jr., Papers.
NcD–M	Jacob Mordecai Papers.
NcD–ME	Munford-Ellis Family Papers.
Neal	John Neal. *John Neal to Edgar A. Poe*. Ysleta, Tex.: Edwin B. Hill, 1942.
Nelson	Roland W. Nelson. "Apparatus for a Definitive Edition of Poe's *Eureka*." In *Studies in the American Renaissance: 1978*, ed. Joel Myerson (Boston: Twayne Publishers, 1978), pp. 161–205.
NHi	New York Historical Society, New York City.
Nichols (1855)	Mary Gove Nichols. *Mary Lyndon; or, Revelations of a Life*. New York, 1855.
Nichols (1863)	_____ . *Reminiscences of Edgar Allan Poe*. 1863; rpt. New York: Union Square Book Shop, 1931.
NN–B	New York Public Library, New York City. Henry W. and Albert A. Berg Collection.
NN–D	Evert A. Duyckinck Papers.
NN–Mss	Manuscripts Division.
NNC	Butler Library, Columbia University, New York City.
NNPM	Pierpont Morgan Library, New York City.
Nolan	J. Bennett Nolan. *Israfel in Berkshire: Edgar Allan Poe's Visit to Reading*. Reading, Pa.: Pennsylvania Optical Co., 1948.
Odell	George C. D. Odell. *Annals of the New York Stage, Volume II: 1798–1821*. New York: Columbia University Press, 1927.
Oelke	Karl E. Oelke. "Poe at West Point—A Revaluation." *Poe Studies* 6 (June 1973):1–6.
Osborne	William S. Osborne. "Kennedy on Poe: An Unpublished Letter." *Modern Language Notes* 75 (January 1960):17–18.
Ostrom (1942)	John Ward Ostrom. "Two Unpublished Poe Letters." *Americana* 36 (January 1942):67–71.
Ostrom (1969)	_____ . "Poe's MS. Letter to Stella Lewis—Recently Located." *Poe Studies* 2 (April 1969):36–37.

Ostrom (1974)	———— . "Fourth Supplement to *The Letters of Poe*." *American Literature* 45 (January 1974):513–36.
Ostrom (1981)	———— . "Revised Check List of the Correspondence of Edgar Allan Poe." In *Studies in the American Renaissance: 1981*, ed. Joel Myerson (Boston: Twayne Publishers, 1981), pp. 169–255.
Paulding	Ralph M. Aderman, ed. *The Letters of James Kirke Paulding*. Madison: University of Wisconsin Press, 1962.
PHi	Historical Society of Pennsylvania, Philadelphia.
Phillips	Mary E. Phillips. *Edgar Allan Poe, The Man*. 2 vols. Chicago: John C. Winston, 1926.
Pollin (1968)	Burton R. Pollin. *Dictionary of Names and Titles in Poe's Collected Works*. New York: Da Capo Press, 1968.
Pollin (1969)	———— . "Poe in the *Boston Notion*." *New England Quarterly* 42 (December 1969):585–89.
Pollin (1970)	———— . *Discoveries in Poe*. Notre Dame, Ind.: University of Notre Dame Press, 1970.
Pollin (1970a)	———— . "Poe's Dr. Ollapod." *American Literature* 42 (March 1970):80–82.
Pollin (1970b)	———— . "Poe and the *Boston Notion*." *English Language Notes* 8 (September 1970):23–28.
Pollin (1972a)	———— . "Poe's 'Mystification': Its Source in Fay's *Norman Leslie*." *Mississippi Quarterly* 25 (Spring 1972):111–30.
Pollin (1972b)	———— . "An 1839 Review of Poe's *Tales* in Willis' *The Corsair*." *Poe Studies* 5 (December 1972):56.
Pollin (1972c)	———— . "The Temperance Movement and Its Friends Look at Poe." *COSTERUS* (Amsterdam) 2 (1972):119–44.
Pollin (1974)	———— . "Poe's *Narrative of Arthur Gordon Pym* and the Contemporary Reviewers." *Studies in American Fiction* 2 (Spring 1974):37–56.
Pollin (1975a)	———— . "Contemporary Reviews of *Eureka*: A Checklist." *American Transcendental Quarterly* no. 26 (Spring 1975): part one, pp. 26–30. Also printed in *Poe as Literary Cosmologer: Studies on "Eureka,"* ed. Richard P. Benton (Hartford, Conn.: Transcendental Books, 1975), pp. 26–30.
Pollin (1975b)	———— . "Three More Early Notices of *Pym* and the Snowden Connection." *Poe Studies* 8 (December 1975):32–35.

Pollin
(1977)

—————. "Poe's 'Murders in the Rue Morgue': The Ingenious Web Unravelled." In *Studies in the American Renaissance: 1977*, ed. Joel Myerson (Boston: Twayne Publishers, 1978), pp. 235–59.

Pollin
(1978a)

—————. "Hans Pfaall: A False Variant and the Phallic Fallacy." *Mississippi Quarterly* 31 (Fall 1978):519–27.

Pollin
(1978b)

—————. "Pym's *Narrative* in the American Newspapers: More Uncollected Notices." *Poe Studies* 11 (June 1978):8–10.

Pollin
(1980)

—————. "Poe 'Viewed and *Reviewed*': An Annotated Checklist of Contemporaneous Notices." *Poe Studies* 13 (December 1980):17–28.

Pollin
(1981)

Edgar Allan Poe. *The Imaginary Voyages: The Narrative of Arthur Gordon Pym, The Unparalleled Adventure of one Hans Pfaall, The Journal of Julius Rodman*. Ed. Burton R. Pollin. Boston: Twayne Publishers, 1981.

Pollin
(1985)

—————. *The Brevities: Pinakidia, Marginalia, Fifty Suggestions, and Other Works*. Ed. Burton R. Pollin. New York: Gordian Press, 1985.

Pollin
(1985a)

Burton R. Pollin. "The Richmond *Compiler* and Poe in 1845: Two Hostile Notices." *Poe Studies* 18 (June 1985):6–7.

PP–G

Richard Gimbel Collection, Rare Book Department, Philadelphia Free Library.

Putnam

George P. Putnam. "Leaves from a Publisher's Letter-book." *Putnam's Magazine* ns 4 (October 1869):467–74.

Quinn

Arthur Hobson Quinn. *Edgar Allan Poe: A Critical Biography*. 1941; rpt. New York: Cooper Square Publishers, 1969.

Quinn and Hart

Arthur Hobson Quinn and Richard H. Hart, eds. *Edgar Allan Poe: Letters and Documents in the Enoch Pratt Free Library*. New York: Scholars' Facsimiles & Reprints, 1941.

P. F. Quinn

Patrick F. Quinn. *The French Face of Edgar Poe*. Carbondale: Southern Illinois University Press, 1957.

Rede

Kenneth Rede. "Poe Notes: From an Investigator's Notebook." *American Literature* 5 (March 1933):49–54.

Reece
(1954)

James B. Reece. "Poe and the New York Literati." Ph.D. diss., Duke University, 1954.

Reece

—————. "A Reexamination of a Poe Date: Mrs. El-

(1970) let's Letters." *American Literature* 42 (May 1970):157–64.

Reid Mayne Reid. "A Dead Man Defended: Being Some Reminiscences of the Poet Poe." *Onward* (New York) 1 (April 1869):305–08.

Reilly John Edward Reilly. "Poe in Imaginative Literature: A (1965) Study of American Drama, Fiction, and Poetry Devoted to Edgar Allan Poe or His Works." Ph.D. diss., University of Virginia, 1965.

Reilly ———. "Ermina's Gales: The Poems Jane Locke De-(1972) voted to Poe." In *Papers on Poe: Essays in Honor of John Ward Ostrom*, ed. Richard P. Veler (Springfield, O.: Chantry Music Press, 1972), pp. 206–20.

Reilly ———. "Poe in Pillory: An Early Version of a Satire (1973) by A. J. H. Duganne." *Poe Studies* 6 (June 1973):9–12.

Reilly ———. *The Image of Poe in American Poetry*. Balti-(1976) more: Enoch Pratt Free Library, Edgar Allan Poe Society, and the Library of the University of Baltimore, 1976.

Rice Sara Sigourney Rice, ed. *Edgar Allan Poe: A Memorial Volume*. Baltimore: Turnbull Brothers, 1877.

Robbins J. Albert Robbins. "The History of *Graham's Maga-*(1947) *zine*." Ph.D. diss., University of Pennsylvania, 1947.

Robbins ———. "Edgar Poe and His Friends: A Sampler of (1960) Letters Written to Sarah Helen Whitman." *Indiana University Bookman* no. 4 (March 1960):5–45.

Robbins ———. "Edgar Poe and the Philadelphians: A Remi-(1972) niscence by a Contemporary." *Poe Studies* 5 (December 1972):45–48.

Robertson John W. Robertson, M.D. *Bibliography of the Writings of Edgar A. Poe*. 2 vols. San Francisco: Russian Hill Private Press, 1934.

Rose and Alexander G. Rose, III, and Jeffrey Alan Savoye. *Such*
Savoye *Friends As These: Edgar Allan Poe's List of Subscribers and Contributors to his Dream Magazine*. Baltimore: Enoch Pratt Free Library, Edgar Allan Poe Society, and Library of the University of Baltimore, 1986.

Rosenbach Hyman Polock Rosenbach. "Reminiscences of Edgar A. Poe" [given by Horace Wemyss Smith]. *American* (Philadelphia) 13 (26 February 1887):296.

Rosenthal Bernard Rosenthal. "Poe, Slavery, and the *Southern Literary Messenger*: A Reexamination." *Poe Studies* 7 (December 1974):29–38.

RPB–W	Sarah Helen Whitman Papers, John Hay Library, Brown University, Providence, Rhode Island.
Rudd	Alice Böhmer Rudd. *Shockoe Hill Cemetery, Richmond, Virginia: Register of Interments, April 10, 1822–December 31, 1950.* 2 vols. Washington, 1960.
Russell	J. Thomas Russell. *Edgar Allan Poe: The Army Years.* USMA Library Bulletin, No. 10. West Point, N. Y.: United States Military Academy, 1972.
Sartain	John Sartain. *The Reminiscences of a Very Old Man, 1808–1897.* 1899; rpt. New York and London: Benjamin Blom, 1969.
Scharf	J. Thomas Scharf. *The Chronicles of Baltimore.* Baltimore: Turnbull Brothers, 1874.
Schulte	Amanda Pogue Schulte. *Facts About Poe: Portraits & Daguerreotypes of Edgar Allan Poe.* Charlottesville: University of Virginia, 1926.
Scott (1941)	Mary Wingfield Scott. *Houses of Old Richmond.* 1941; rpt. New York: Bonanza Books, n.d.
Scott (1950)	———. *Old Richmond Neighborhoods.* 1950; rpt. Richmond: Valentine Museum, 1975.
Scudder	Horace Elisha Scudder. *James Russell Lowell: A Biography.* 2 vols. Boston: Houghton Mifflin, 1901.
Semmes	John E. Semmes. *John H. B. Latrobe and His Times, 1803–1891.* Baltimore: Norman, Remington Co., 1917.
Seylaz	Louis Seylaz. *Edgar Poe et les premiers symbolistes français.* 1923; rpt. Gèneve: Slatkine Reprints, 1979.
Sherley	Douglass Sherley. "Old Oddity Papers, IV: Edgar Allan Poe While a Student at the University of Virginia." *Virginia University Magazine* 19 (March and April 1880):376–81, 426–45.
Shockley	Martin Staples Shockley. *The Richmond Stage, 1784–1812.* Charlottesville: University Press of Virginia, 1977.
Shockley (1941)	———. *"Timour the Tartar* and Poe's *Tamerlane."* *PMLA* 56 (December 1941):1103–06.
Shuman	R. Baird Shuman. "Longfellow, Poe, and *The Waif."* *PMLA* 76 (March 1961):155–56.
Simms	Mary C. Simms Oliphant, Alfred Taylor Odell, and T. C. Duncan Eaves, eds. *The Letters of William Gilmore Simms.* 5 vols. Columbia: University of South Carolina Press, 1952–1956.
Smith	Mary Alice Wyman, ed. *Selections from the Autobiography of Elizabeth Oakes Smith.* Lewiston, Me.: Lewiston

Journal Co., 1924.

Smyth — Albert H. Smyth. *The Philadelphia Magazines and Their Contributors, 1741–1850.* 1892; rpt. Freeport, N. Y.: Books for Libraries Press, 1970.

Snodgrass (1856) — Joseph Evans Snodgrass. "Death and Burial of Edgar A. Poe." *Life Illustrated* (New York) ns 2 (17 May 1856):24. Reprinted from the *Woman's Temperance Paper.*

Snodgrass (1867) — _____ . "The Facts of Poe's Death and Burial." *Beadle's Monthly* 3 (March 1867):283–87.

Spannuth and Mabbott — Jacob E. Spannuth and Thomas Ollive Mabbott, eds. *Doings of Gotham: Poe's Contributions to "The Columbia Spy."* Pottsville, Pa.: Jacob E. Spannuth, 1929.

Stanard — Mary Newton Stanard, ed. *Edgar Allan Poe Letters Till Now Unpublished, in the Valentine Museum, Richmond, Virginia.* Philadelphia: J. B. Lippincott Co., 1925.

Stearns — Theodore Pease Stearns. "A Prohibitionist Shakes Dice with Poe." *Outlook* 126 (1 September 1920):25–26.

Stedman and Woodberry — Edmund Clarence Stedman and George Edward Woodberry, eds. *The Works of Edgar Allan Poe.* 10 vols. Chicago: Stone & Kimball, 1894–1896.

Stoddard (1872) — Richard Henry Stoddard. "Edgar Allan Poe." *Harper's Monthly* 45 (September 1872):557–68.

Stoddard (1884) — _____ , ed. *The Works of Edgar Allan Poe.* 6 vols. New York: A. C. Armstrong & Son, 1884. Stoddard's "Life of Poe" appears in Volume I, pp. 1–200.

Stoddard (1889) — _____ . "Edgar Allan Poe." *Lippincott's Magazine* 43 (January 1889):107–15.

Stoddard (1903) — _____ . *Recollections, Personal and Literary.* New York: A. S. Barnes and Co., 1903.

Stovall (1965) — Floyd Stovall, ed. *The Poems of Edgar Allan Poe.* Charlottesville: University Press of Virginia, 1965.

Stovall (1967) — _____ . "Edgar Poe and the University of Virginia." *Virginia Quarterly Review* 43 (Spring 1967):297–317.

Stovall (1969) — _____ . *Edgar Poe the Poet: Essays New and Old on the Man and His Work.* Charlottesville: University Press of Virginia, 1969.

Tanselle (1962) — G. Thomas Tanselle. "Unrecorded Early Reprintings of Two Poe Tales." *Papers of the Bibliographical Society of America* 56 (2d Quarter 1962):252.

Tanselle (1963) — _____ . "Two More Appearances of 'The Raven.' " *Papers of the Bibliographical Society of America* 57 (2d Quarter 1963):229–30.

Taylor	Marie Hansen-Taylor and Horace E. Scudder, eds. *Life and Letters of Bayard Taylor*. Boston: Houghton Mifflin, 1884.
Thomas (1975)	Dwight Thomas. "James F. Otis and 'Autography': A New Poe Correspondent." *Poe Studies* 8 (June 1975):12–15.
Thomas (1978)	———— . "Poe in Philadelphia, 1838–1844: A Documentary Record." Ph.D. diss., University of Pennsylvania, 1978.
Thomas (1979)	———— . "Poe, English, and *The Doom of the Drinker*: A Mystery Resolved." *Princeton University Library Chronicle* 40 (Spring 1979):257–68.
Thomas (1982)	———— . "William E. Burton and His Premium Scheme: New Light on Poe Biography." *University of Mississippi Studies in English* ns 3 (1982):68–80.
Ticknor	Caroline Ticknor. *Poe's Helen*. New York: Scribner's, 1916.
Tuckerman	Henry T. Tuckerman. "A Memoir of the Author." In *Old New York . . . By John W. Francis, M.D., LL.D.* New York: W. J. Widdleton, 1866.
TxU–HRCL	Humanities Research Center Library, University of Texas at Austin.
Uchida	Ichigoro Uchida. "The Daguerreotypes of Edgar Allan Poe Taken in New England in 1848." Offprint from *Collected Essays, No. 25* (Tokyo, Japan: Kyoritsu Women's Junior College, 1982).
USMA	United States Military Academy, West Point, New York.
Van Cleef	Augustus Van Cleef. "Poe's Mary." *Harper's Monthly* 78 (March 1889):634–40.
Vann	J. Don Vann. "Three More Contemporary Reviews of *Pym*." *Poe Studies* 9 (December 1976):43–44.
Varner (1933)	John Grier Varner. *Edgar Allan Poe and the Philadelphia "Saturday Courier."* Charlottesville: University of Virginia, 1933.
Varner (1940)	———— . "Sarah Helen Whitman: Seeress of Providence." Ph.D. diss., University of Virginia, 1940.
ViHi	Virginia Historical Society, Richmond.
Vincent	H. P. Vincent. "A Sarah Helen Whitman Letter about Edgar Allan Poe." *American Literature* 13 (May 1941):162–67.
ViRPM	Poe Museum, Richmond.
ViRVal	Valentine Museum, Richmond.

ViRVal–THE   Thomas H. Ellis memorandum: "A paper prepared for Mrs Margaret K. Ellis, in the 85th year of her age; from old letters in the possession of her son, T. H. E[llis]—1875."

ViU   Alderman Library, University of Virginia, Charlottesville.

ViU–I   John Henry Ingram's Poe Collection.

Vi–W–TC   Tucker-Coleman Papers, Earl G. Swem Library, College of William and Mary, Williamsburg, Virginia.

VtMiM   Abernethy Library of American Literature, Middlebury College, Middlebury, Vermont.

W   James A. Harrison, ed. *The Complete Works of Edgar Allan Poe*. 17 vols. 1902; rpt. New York: AMS Press, 1965.

Wakeman   *The Stephen H. Wakeman Collection of Books of Nineteenth Century American Writers*. New York: American Art Association, 1924. Itemized catalog, with the prices paid at the auction held 28–29 April 1924.

Walsh   John Walsh. *Poe the Detective: The Curious Circumstances Behind "The Mystery of Marie Roget."* New Brunswick, N. J.: Rutgers University Press, 1968.

Watts   Charles H. Watts, II. "Poe, Irving, and *The Southern Literary Messenger*." *American Literature* 27 (May 1955):249–51.

Wegelin   Oscar Wegelin. "The Printer of Poe's *Tamerlane*." *New York Historical Society Quarterly Bulletin* 24 (January 1940):23–25.

Weidman (1968)   Bette Statsky Weidman. "Charles Frederick Briggs: A Critical Biography." Ph.D. diss., Columbia University, 1968.

Weidman (1979)   ———. "The Pinto Letters of Charles Frederick Briggs." In *Studies in the American Renaissance: 1979*, ed. Joel Myerson (Boston: Twayne Publishers, 1979), pp. 93–157.

Weiss (1878)   Susan Archer Weiss. "Last Days of Edgar A. Poe." *Scribner's Monthly* 15 (March 1878):707–16.

Weiss (1883)   ———. "The Sister of Edgar A. Poe." *Continent* 3 (27 June 1883):816–19.

Weiss (1904)   ———. "Reminiscences of Edgar A. Poe." *Independent* 56 (5 May 1904):1010–14, and 57 (25 August 1904):443–48.

Weiss (1907)   ———. *The Home Life of Poe*. New York: Broadway Publishing Co., 1907.

Wells   Ross Wells. "College 'Lit' First to Recognize Poe." *Richmond Times-Dispatch* 6 October 1935, Section V, p. 3.

Wertenbaker (1868)   William Wertenbaker. "Edgar A. Poe." *Virginia University Magazine* 7 (November–December 1868):114–17. Reprinted in vol. 49 (January 1887):226–29.

Wertenbaker (1879)   Douglass Sherley. "Mr. William Wertenbaker—His Golden Wedding." *Virginia University Magazine* 19 (October 1879):42–47.

T. J. Wertenbaker   Thomas J. Wertenbaker. *Norfolk: Historic Southern Port.* Durham, N. C.: Duke University Press, 1931.

Whitman   Sarah Helen Whitman. *Edgar Poe and his Critics.* New York: Rudd & Carleton, 1860.

Walt Whitman   Floyd Stovall, ed. *Walt Whitman: Prose Works 1892.* 2 vols. New York: New York University Press, 1963–1964.

Whitty   J[ames] H[oward] Whitty, ed. *The Complete Poems of Edgar Allan Poe.* Boston: Houghton Mifflin, 1911. Whitty's "Memoir" of Poe appears on pp. xix–lxxxvi.

Whitty (1935)   ———. "A Parrot." *Colophon* ns 1 (Autumn 1935):188–90.

Widener   A[braham] S. W[olf] Rosenbach, comp. *A Catalogue of the Books and Manuscripts of Harry Elkins Widener.* 2 vols. Philadelphia, 1918.

Williams   Stanley T. Williams. "New Letters about Poe." *Yale Review* ns 14 (July 1925):755–73.

Wilmer (1859)   Lambert A. Wilmer. *Our Press Gang; or, A Complete Exposition of the Corruptions and Crimes of the American Newspapers.* Philadelphia: J. T. Lloyd, 1859.

Wilmer (1941)   ———. *Merlin, Baltimore, 1827: Together with "Recollections of Edgar A. Poe."* Ed. Thomas Ollive Mabbott. New York: Scholars' Facsimiles & Reprints, 1941.

M. E. Wilmer   Margaret E. Wilmer. "Another View of Edgar A. Poe." *Beadle's Monthly* 3 (April 1867):385–86.

Wilson (1923)   James Southall Wilson. "Poe at the University of Virginia: Unpublished Letters from the Ingram Collection." *University of Virginia Alumni Bulletin,* 3d series, 16 (April 1923):163–67.

Wilson (1924)   ———. "Unpublished Letters of Edgar Allan Poe." *Century Magazine* ns 85 (March 1924):652–56.

J. G. Wilson (1869)   James Grant Wilson. *The Life and Letters of Fitz-Greene Halleck.* New York: D. Appleton and Co., 1869.

J. G. Wilson
(1893)

————— . *The Memorial History of the City of New York from Its First Settlement to the Year 1892*. New York: New-York History Co., 1893.

Woodberry

George E[dward] Woodberry. *The Life of Edgar Allan Poe, Personal and Literary*. 2 vols. 1909; rpt. New York: Biblo and Tannen, 1965.

Yannella

Donald Yannella and Kathleen Malone Yannella. "Evert A. Duyckinck's 'Diary: May 29–November 8, 1847.'" In *Studies in the American Renaissance: 1978*, ed. Joel Myerson (Boston: Twayne Publishers, 1978), pp. 207–58.

Index

Nothing is indexed under Edgar Allan Poe. All his stories and poems, as well as his more noteworthy essays and miscellanies, are indexed under their titles. Works by others are generally listed under the authors' names. This index is intended to be comprehensive, but not exhaustive. It does not include all the names and titles in the text, only those likely to be of significance to researchers; and these are often indexed selectively, excluding references which seem tangential or redundant. Individuals mentioned only once—briefly and casually—may be omitted if they appear to have had no demonstrable bearing upon Poe's life or intellectual development. All magazines and newspapers mentioned in the text are included, and the listings for those to which Poe contributed have subheadings for his contributions. There has been no attempt, however, to give the titles of all the fillers and other minor pieces which Poe wrote for periodicals. His book reviews are entered under the names of the authors considered; but books which would seem of slight interest to most researchers—e.g., treatises on gardening or medicine—are not cited, either by author or title. Information on Poe is also indexed under pertinent locations (England, France, and the American cities he lived in or visited), the educational institutions he attended (University of Virginia and West Point), his proposed journals (*Penn Magazine* and the *Stylus*), and the following topic headings: alcoholism, athletic ability, ballooning, cats, childhood illnesses, cholera, coffee, copyright, cryptography, daguerreotypes, Episcopal High School, financial difficulties, foreign languages, Germanism, Greece, honorary memberships, income, insanity, Junior Debating Society, Junior Volunteers, lectures and readings, literary criticism, mesmerism, opium, painting, Philadelphia Custom House, phrenology, physical appearance, plagiarism, portraits, power of analysis, religious concepts, Rutgers Female Institute, schools, slavery and abolitionism, street pavements, tailors' bills, teaching, Thespian Society, Transcendentalism, and U. S. Army.

INDEX

INDEX

Browning, Mrs. Robert: see Elizabeth Barrett Barrett

Bryan, Daniel, xviii, 365, 371–76

Bryant, William Cullen, xvii-xviii, 241, 244, 294–95, 330, 397, 432, 446–47, 499, 509–10, 512, 587, 608, 631, 720, 754, 774, 836

Buchanan, Reverend John, 15, 43

Buckingham, Edwin, 129

Buckingham, Joseph T., xviii, 8, 129, 579

Bulfinch, Stephen Greenleaf, 190, 205, 210

Bulwer-Lytton, Edward, 150; Poe's review of *Rienzi*, 189, 191, 193, 202–04; 227, 239, 295, 321, 344, 365; *Zanoni* review not by Poe, 368–70; 439; Poe's review of *Poems*, 501, 505; 800

Burke, Christiana, xviii

Burke, Edmund, 590

Burke, William, xviii, 52, 54–60, 64, 137, 211, 221

Burling, Ebenezer, xviii, 46, 65, 78, 127

Burling, Martha, xviii, 43

Burns, Robert, 569

Burr, Aaron, 334, 394

Burr, Charles Chauncey, xviii, 130, 817, 819

Burton, William E., xviii-xix; begins *Burton's Gentleman's Magazine*, 245; condemns Poe's *Pym*, 254; sole proprietor of *Burton's*, 258; Poe seeks employment from, 261–62; Burton introduces Poe to Philadelphia literati, 263; absent in New York, 265–66; Poe "taxed with the twaddle of," 272; "Mr B. pays for nothing," 276; Burton announces premium contest, 277–78, 280; his engagement in Charleston, 280; Poe objects to contest, 283; 287; Burton extends contest, 292, then cancels it, 293–94; his engagement in Baltimore, 294; his National Theatre, 294, 297–98; orders three dollars withheld from Poe's salary, 295–96, and advertises magazine for sale, 296–98, 303–04; fires Poe, 297–99; Poe denounces Burton's "infamous" contest, 302–03; Burton alludes to Poe's drinking, 307; sells magazine, 309; 312, 317; fails to return J. R. Lowell poem entered in contest, 320–21; Poe denies Burton's "slanders" about his drinking, 322

Burton's Gentleman's Magazine (Philadelphia), xv, xix, xxvi, 245, 254, 258; Poe becomes assistant editor, 261–63; Poe's association praised, 265–66, 269; Poe's dissatisfaction with, 272; contributors no longer paid, 276; advertisement for 1840 volumes, 277–78; offered for sale, 296–98, 303–04, and sold,

309; circulation, 309, 345; Poe's contributions, (June 1839) 262–63, (July) 264–65, (August) 266, (September) 267, (October) 272–73, (November) 274, (December) 278, (January 1840) 285, (February) 288, (March) 292, (April) 293, (May) 294, (June) 302, (July) 304, (August) 305. See also William E. Burton and "income"

Burwell, William McCreery, xix, 75–76

Bush, George, xix, 485–86, 587, 636, 641, 747

Butler, Mrs. Frances Anne (Fanny Kemble), 155, 157

Butterfield, Eliza Jane, xix, 807, 809–10

Byron, George Gordon, 94, 149, 155, 284, 632, 679, 741, 800, 836, 841

"Byron and Miss Chaworth," 478

Cabell, Julia Mayo, xix, 60

Cabell, Robert Gamble, 56–57, 59–60

Cabell, Dr. Robert Henry, xix, 60

Caldwell, William W., Jr., 580

Calvert, George H., 157

Camden Journal (South Carolina), 174, 226

Campbell, Major John, 91, 93

Campbell, Thomas, 108, 339

Carey, Edward L., xix, 189, 280, 319, 463

Carey, Henry Charles, xix, 135–36, 142–43, 149, 152, 168, 170, 175, 181–82, 191

Carey, John L., 281

Carey, Mathew, xix, 207, 220, 231

Carey & Hart, xix, 181–82, 189, 261, 280, 319, 339, 363–64, 463, 470, 487, 658, 678, 694, 699, 777

Carey & Lea (later Carey, Lea & Carey), xix, xxxi; Poe submits "Al Aaraaf," 94–97; firm considers his "Tales of the Folio Club," 135–36, 142–43, 149, 168, 170, 175; Poe corresponds with firm, 181–82, 191. See also Lea & Blanchard

Carlyle, Thomas, 431, 438, 602, 615, 632, 668

Carpenter, W. H., et al, 243

Carter, Dr. Gibbon, 822

Carter, Dr. John F., 843

Carter, Mrs. Mary Gibbon, xxvi

Carter, Robert, xix, 397–98, 403, 406, 411, 416, 437, 439, 521–22, 524–25, 645

Cary, Henry, 647

Casket (Philadelphia), xxvi, xxxvi, 107, 120; purchased by G. R. Graham, 260; merged with *Burton's*, 309, 345; 476

Cass, Lewis, 214

INDEX

Osborn, Laughton, xxxiv–xxxv; Poe's review of *Confessions of a Poet*, 151–55; his condemnation of *The Vision of Rubeta*, 517, and Osborn's reaction, 561–63; 573, 589, 641

Osborne, Mrs. Mary, 735, 743

Osgood, Mrs. Frances S., xxxv; Poe praises her in New York lecture, 509–10, and is introduced to her, 511–13, 518; her pseudonyms, 522; she addresses Poe in "So Let It Be," 523–24; 525; Poe's "Impromptu" addressed to her, 528; 534, 539–40; he follows her to Providence, 544–46; 547, 553; her "Ida Grey," 556; 565; she addresses him in "Echo-Song," 569–70; 573, 585, 593; her salutation to him as "Israfel," 597; Poe lauds her *Poems* in *Broadway Journal*, 603; 604–06, 616, 620; Mrs. Ellet intervenes in her correspondence with Poe, 622–24; Poe composes "A Valentine" (February 1846 acrostic) for Mrs. Osgood, 624–26; he praises her poetry in *Godey's*, 627; 634, 637, 639–40; Mrs. Osgood protests rumors spread by Mrs. Ellet, 647, 651–52; included in Poe's "Literati," 662; 670, 673–74, 687; E. J. Thomas writes her about Poe's libel suit, 696; 700, 725, 727, 729–30, 741, 762; Mrs. Osgood visits Mrs. Whitman, 773–74; possibly addresses "Lines" to Poe in *Metropolitan*, 774, 781; neglects to answer Mrs. Whitman's inquiries about him, 784–85; mentions him in *A Letter About the Lions*, 785; 788, 791, 796; Poe notices Mrs. Osgood in *Messenger*, 821, 824–25

Osgood, Samuel S., xxxv, 545, 608, 687

O'Sullivan, John L., xxxv, 260, 375, 379, 495, 587

Otis, James Frederick, xxxv, 191, 203, 208, 210–11

"Our Amateur Poets," 398, 401, 431–32, 434–35

"Our Contributors" series (*Graham's Magazine*), 430, 436, 446, 454, 456, 462, 490, 533

"Our Magazine Literature" (not by Poe), xvii

"Outis" (pseudonym): his letter to *Evening Mirror*, 510–11, and Poe's "Reply," 514, 516–18, 520, 522–23

Oxford Examiner (North Carolina), 217

Pabodie, William J., xxxv, 746, 756, 766, 768, 772–73, 775–76, 778–80

Page, William, xvii–xviii, 411, 500, 521–22, 524, 554–55, 645

painting, Poe's aptitude for, xxvi, 69, 75, 500

"Palaestine," 191, 203

Palladium (Boston): see *New-England Palladium*

"Parnassus": see "American Parnassus"

Patriot (Providence, Rhode Island), 323

Patterson, Edward H. N., xxxv–xxxvi, 777, 783, 800–01, 803–06, 808–09, 819, 823–24, 827–28, 832, 834

Patterson, Henry S., 416

Patterson, Louisa Gabriella: see Louisa Allan

Patterson, Samuel D., xxvii, xxxvi, 402–03, 433–35, 808, 817, 819

Paulding, James Kirke, xxxvi; encourages T. W. White, 140; praises Poe's "Lion-izing," 159, 162; 164, 169, 171, 175; finds Poe "the best of all our going writers," 184; submits Poe's tales to Harpers and writes White, 192–93, and Poe, 195; 200, 208–10, 212–14, 229, 231, 239, 244; Poe seeks clerkship from, 248; 330, 401, 431, 570

Paul Ulric: see Morris Mattson

Pease, Peter Pindar, 71–72, 79, 115–16

Pedder, Anna and Bessie, xxxvi, 248, 279

Pedder, James, xxxvi, 245, 248, 279, 282, 294

Penn Magazine (Poe's proposed journal): early plans for quality magazine, 166, 272, 287; Poe prepares prospectus, 297, and sends it to newspapers, 298–303; his "want of capital," 303; he solicits aid from Georgia relatives and others, 304–07; receives subscriptions from South and West, 307–10, 316; forced to postpone, 311–13; seeks contributors of "*caste*," 316–18; first number cancelled because of financial crisis, 318–19, 320, 322–23; Poe hopes G. R. Graham will fund project, 329–32, 340–42, 345; J. E. Dow and F. W. Thomas express support, 346–48; Poe seeks Robert Tyler's aid, 359–60, 365–66; makes "earnest although *secret* exertions" to resume project, 373–75; *Penn* announced in *New-York Mirror* and other papers, 376–77; 380–81; Custom House appointment to give Poe "a certain resource," 382–83; name changed to *Stylus*, 398–99. See also *Stylus*

Pennsylvania Inquirer (Philadelphia), xxxiv, 250, 265, 279, 298, 345, 395, 399, 402, 414, 417, 421, 423, 426, 430, 441, 444, 447–48, 503

Pennsylvanian (Philadelphia), xxxiv, 186, 218, 250, 267–69, 275, 279–80, 283, 321, 384, 399, 402, 427, 431, 434, 440, 448, 812, 851

Pennsylvania Sentinel (Philadelphia), 233